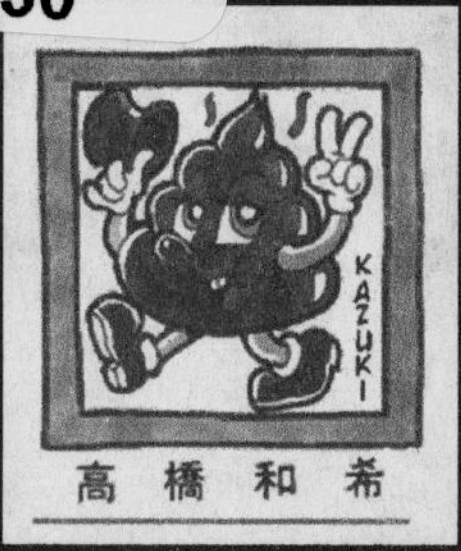
KAZUKI
高橋和希

THIS HAPPENED TO ME IN 7TH GRADE. MR. "W," MY HOMEROOM TEACHER, NEVER LIKED ME. ONCE HE SAID THIS IN FRONT OF THE WHOLE CLASS:

"TAKAHASHI! ALL YOU DO IS EAT, SLEEP AND POOP. YOU'RE A POOP-MAKING MACHINE!"

THE WHOLE CLASS ERUPTED IN LAUGHTER. I LAUGHED TOO, BUT I CLENCHED MY FIST AND THOUGHT TO MYSELF, "I COULD JUST PUNCH YOU RIGHT NOW!"

I WAS MAD. BUT I THOUGHT, A POOP-MAKING MACHINE CAN'T WRITE MANGA! THAT'S WHEN I DECIDED TO BECOME A MANGA ARTIST.

-KAZUKI TAKAHASHI, 2001

Artist/author Kazuki Takahashi first tried to break into the manga business in 1982, but success eluded him until **Yu-Gi-Oh!** debuted in the Japanese **Weekly Shonen Jump** magazine in 1996. **Yu-Gi-Oh!**'s themes of friendship and fighting, together with Takahashi's weird and wonderful art, soon became enormously successful, spawning a real-world card game, video games, and two anime series. A lifelong gamer, Takahashi enjoys Shogi (Japanese chess), Mahjong, card games, and tabletop RPGs, among other games.

Yu-Gi-Oh!
3-in-1 Edition
Volume 10

handwritten: Y MANGA YUG V. 28-29-30

SHONEN JUMP Manga Omnibus Edition
A compilation of the graphic novel volumes 28-29-30

STORY AND ART BY Kazuki Takahashi

Translation & English Adaptation/Joe Yamazaki
Touch-up Art & Lettering/Eric Erbes
Design/Andrea Rice (Manga Edition)
Design/Sam Elzway (Omnibus Edition)
Editor/Jason Thompson (Manga Edition)
Editor/Erica Yee (Omnibus Edition)

Printed in the U.S.A.

Published by VIZ Media, LLC
P.O. Box 77010
San Francisco, CA 94107

10 9 8 7 6 5 4 3 2 1
Omnibus edition first printing, May 2017

SHONEN JUMP MANGA

Vol. 28
DUEL THE LIGHTNING!
STORY AND ART BY
KAZUKI TAKAHASHI

THE STORY SO FAR...

YUGI MUTOU/
YU-GI-OH

When 10th grader Yugi solved the Millennium Puzzle, another spirit took up residence in his body...Yu-Gi-Oh, the King of Games, a dark avenger who challenges evildoers to "Shadow Games" of life and death!

YUGI FACES DEADLY ENEMIES!

Using his gaming skills, Yugi fights ruthless adversaries like Maximillion Pegasus, multimillionaire creator of the collectible card game "Duel Monsters," and Ryo Bakura, whose friendly personality turns evil when he is possessed by the spirit of the Millennium Ring. But Yugi's greatest rival is Seto Kaiba, the world's second-greatest gamer—and the ruthless teenage president of Kaiba Corporation. At first, Kaiba and Yugi are bitter enemies, but after fighting against a common adversary—Pegasus—they come to respect one another. But for all his powers, there is one thing Yu-Gi-Oh cannot do: remember who he is and where he came from.

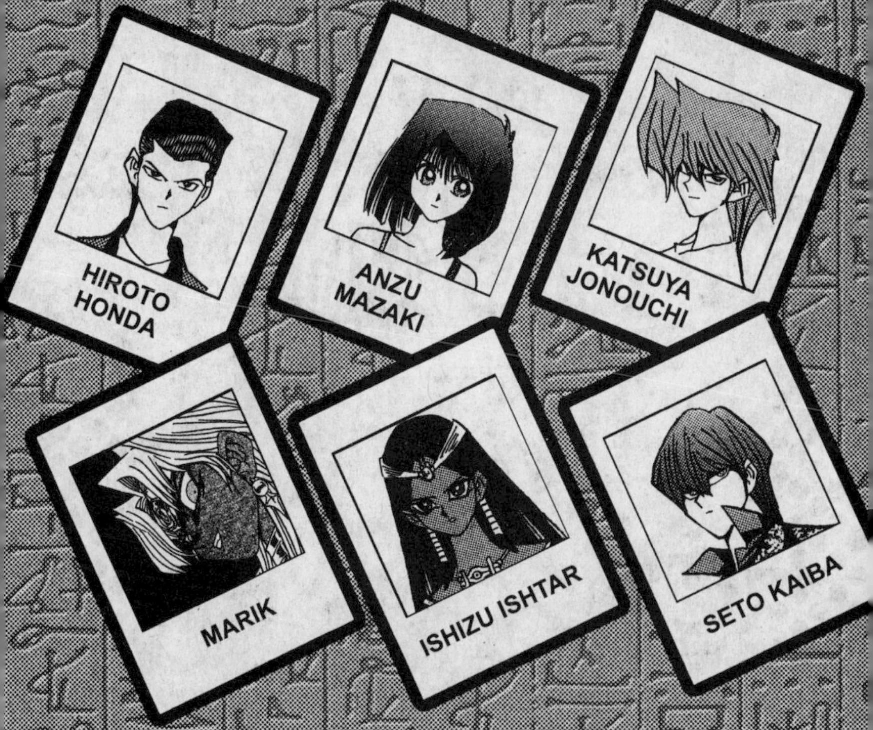
HIROTO HONDA
ANZU MAZAKI
KATSUYA JONOUCHI
MARIK
ISHIZU ISHTAR
SETO KAIBA

THE TABLET OF THE PHARAOH'S MEMORIES

Then one day, when an Egyptian museum exhibit comes to Japan, Yugi sees an ancient carving of himself as an Egyptian pharaoh! The curator of the exhibit, Ishizu Ishtar, explains that there are seven Millennium Items, which were made to fit into a stone tablet in a hidden shrine in Egypt. According to the legend, when the seven Items are brought together, the pharaoh will regain his memories of his past life.

THE EGYPTIAN GOD CARDS

But there is another piece of the puzzle—the three Egyptian God Cards, the rarest cards on Earth. To collect the God Cards, Kaiba announces "Battle City," an enormous "Duel Monsters" tournament. As the tournament rages, Yugi, Kaiba and Marik—Ishizu's evil brother—struggle for possession of the three God Cards. On the eve of the Battle City finals, Ishizu reveals the dark past of the Ishtar family, which has turned Marik into a revenge-crazed madman determined to kill the pharaoh and rule the world. Now, four semi-finalists remain: Yugi, Kaiba, Jonouchi and Marik. Everyone except Jonouchi has a God Card. In an arena on the mysterious Alcatraz Island, they fight a preliminary four-way battle to determine the order of the duels...

YU-GI-OH! DUELIST

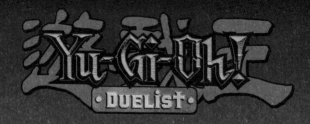

Vol. 28

CONTENTS

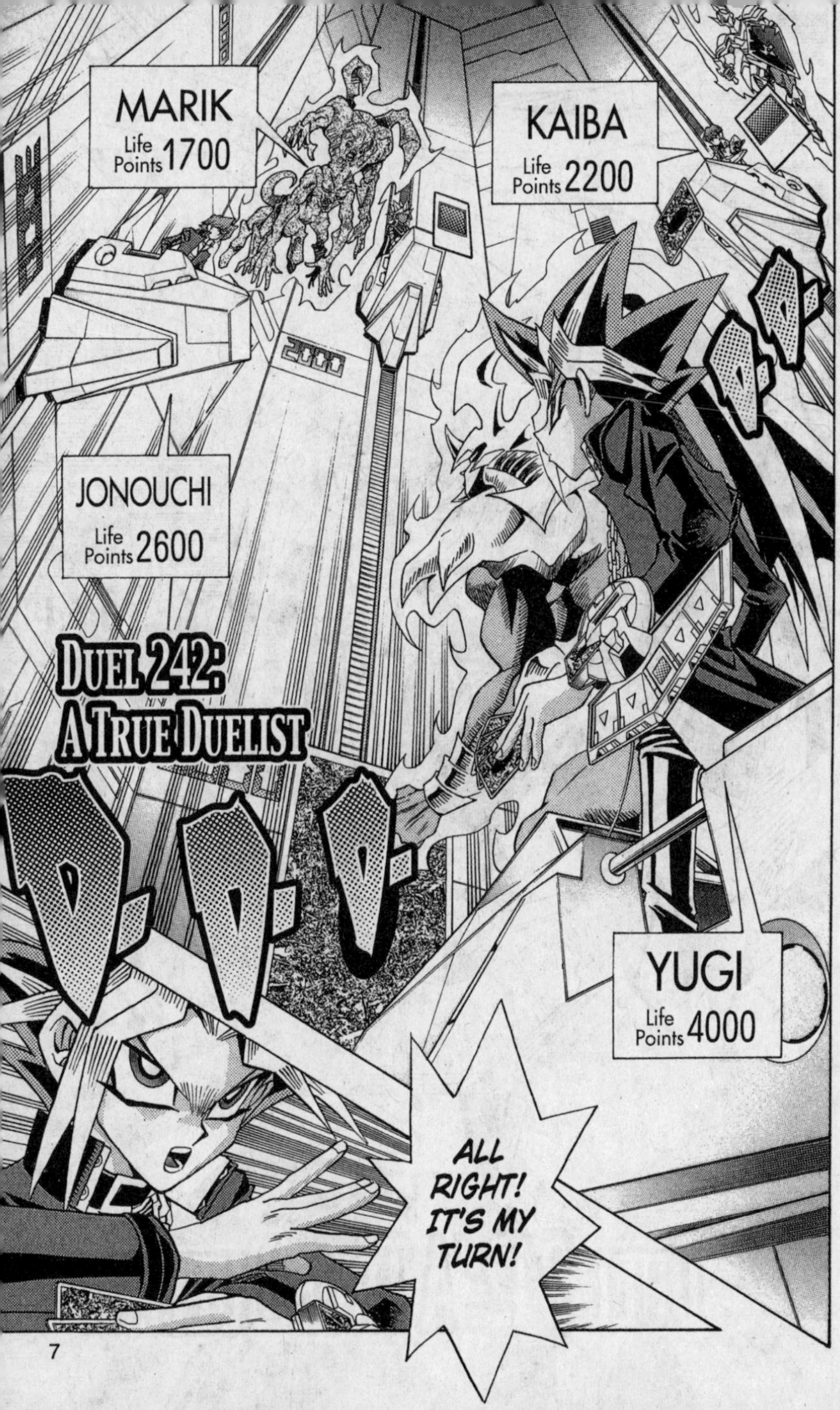
KAIBA Life Points 2200
MARIK Life Points 1700
JONOUCHI Life Points 2600
DUEL 242: A TRUE DUELIST
YUGI Life Points 4000
ALL RIGHT! IT'S MY TURN!

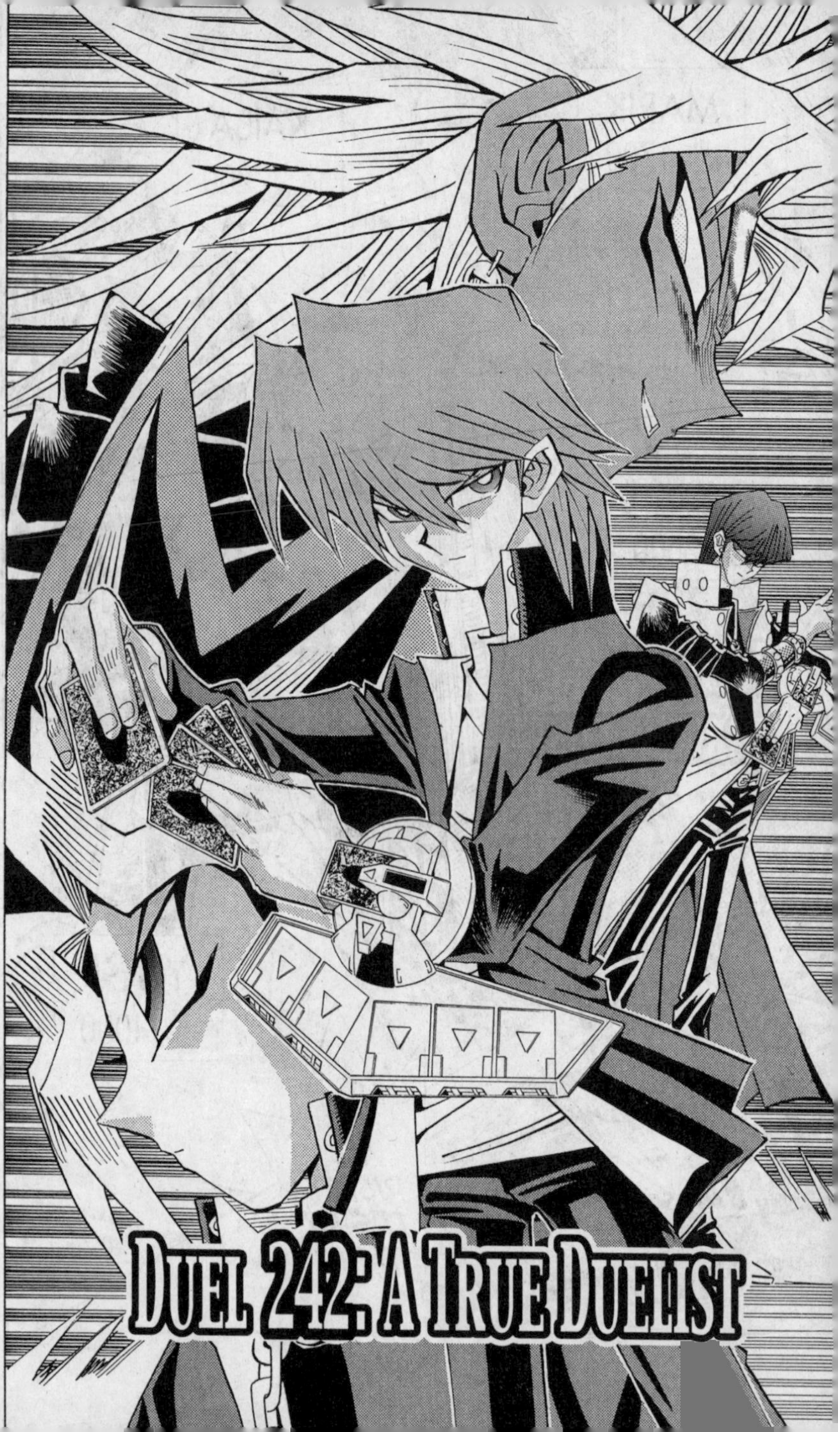
DUEL 242: A TRUE DUELIST

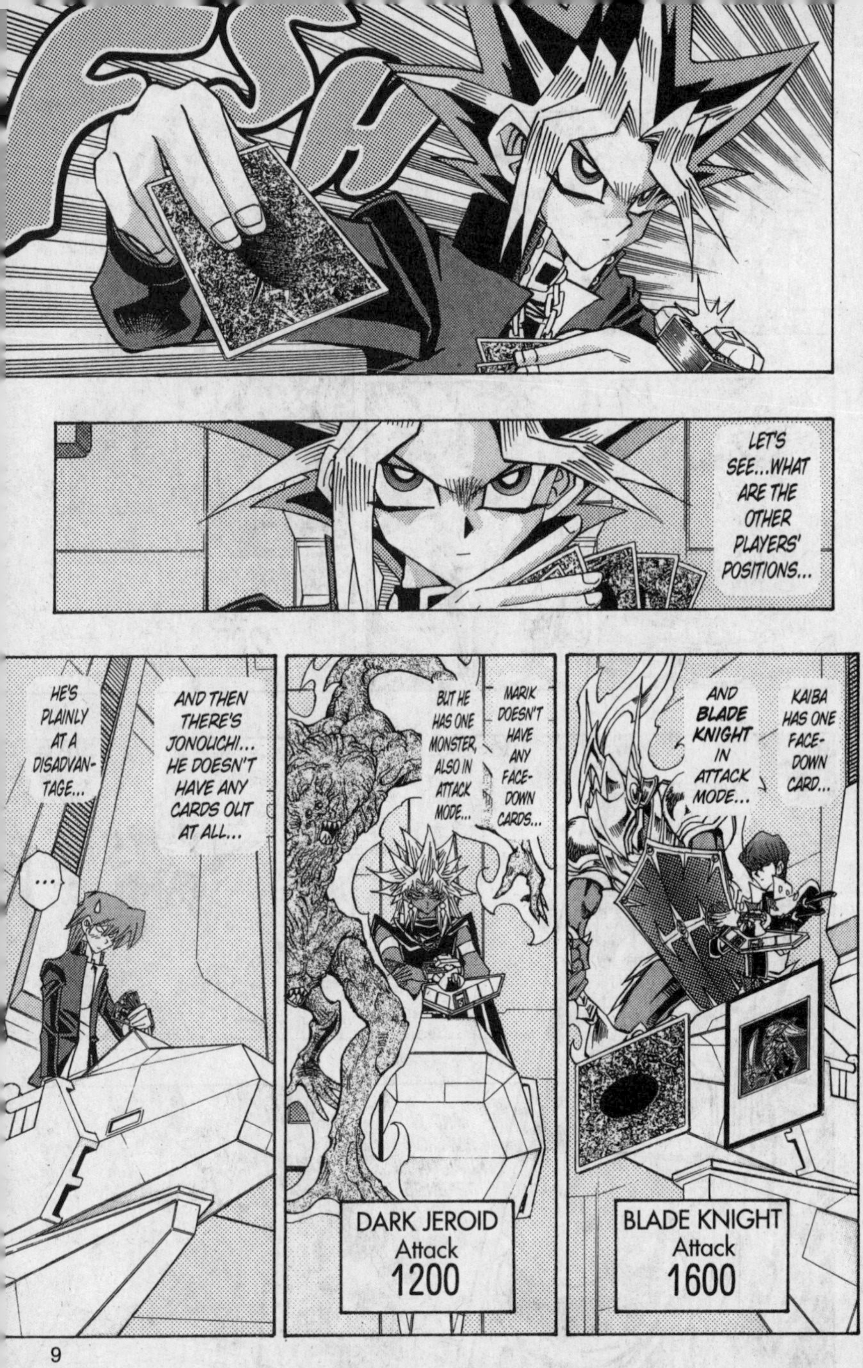
LET'S SEE...WHAT ARE THE OTHER PLAYERS' POSITIONS...
KAIBA HAS ONE FACE-DOWN CARD...
AND BLADE KNIGHT IN ATTACK MODE...
BLADE KNIGHT Attack 1600
MARIK DOESN'T HAVE ANY FACE-DOWN CARDS...
BUT HE HAS ONE MONSTER, ALSO IN ATTACK MODE...
DARK JEROID Attack 1200
AND THEN THERE'S JONOUCHI... HE DOESN'T HAVE ANY CARDS OUT AT ALL...
HE'S PLAINLY AT A DISADVANTAGE...
...

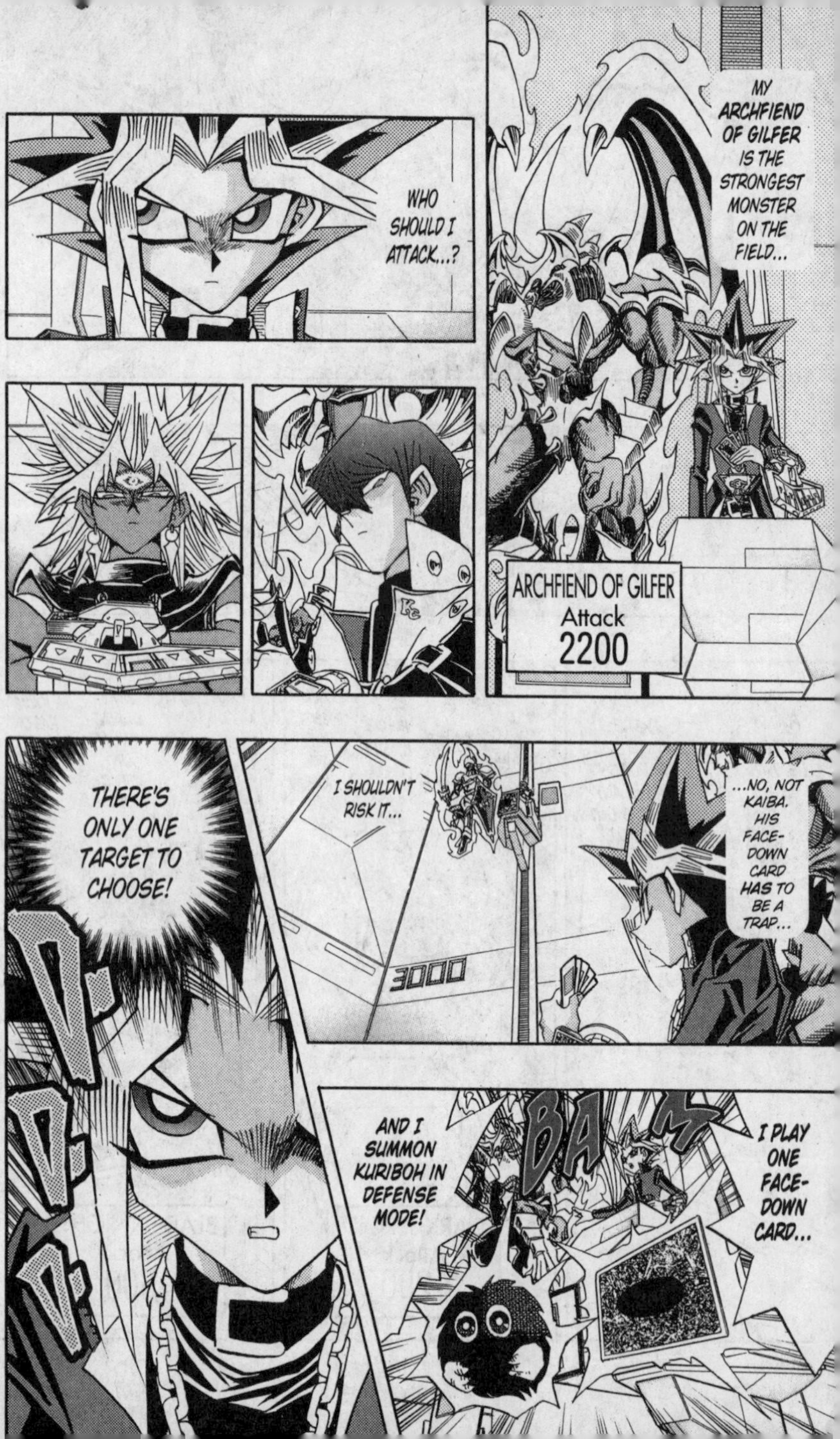
MY ARCHFIEND OF GILFER IS THE STRONGEST MONSTER ON THE FIELD...
ARCHFIEND OF GILFER
Attack
2200
WHO SHOULD I ATTACK...?
...NO, NOT KAIBA. HIS FACE-DOWN CARD HAS TO BE A TRAP...
I SHOULDN'T RISK IT...
3000
I PLAY ONE FACE-DOWN CARD...
BAM
AND I SUMMON KURIBOH IN DEFENSE MODE!
THERE'S ONLY ONE TARGET TO CHOOSE!

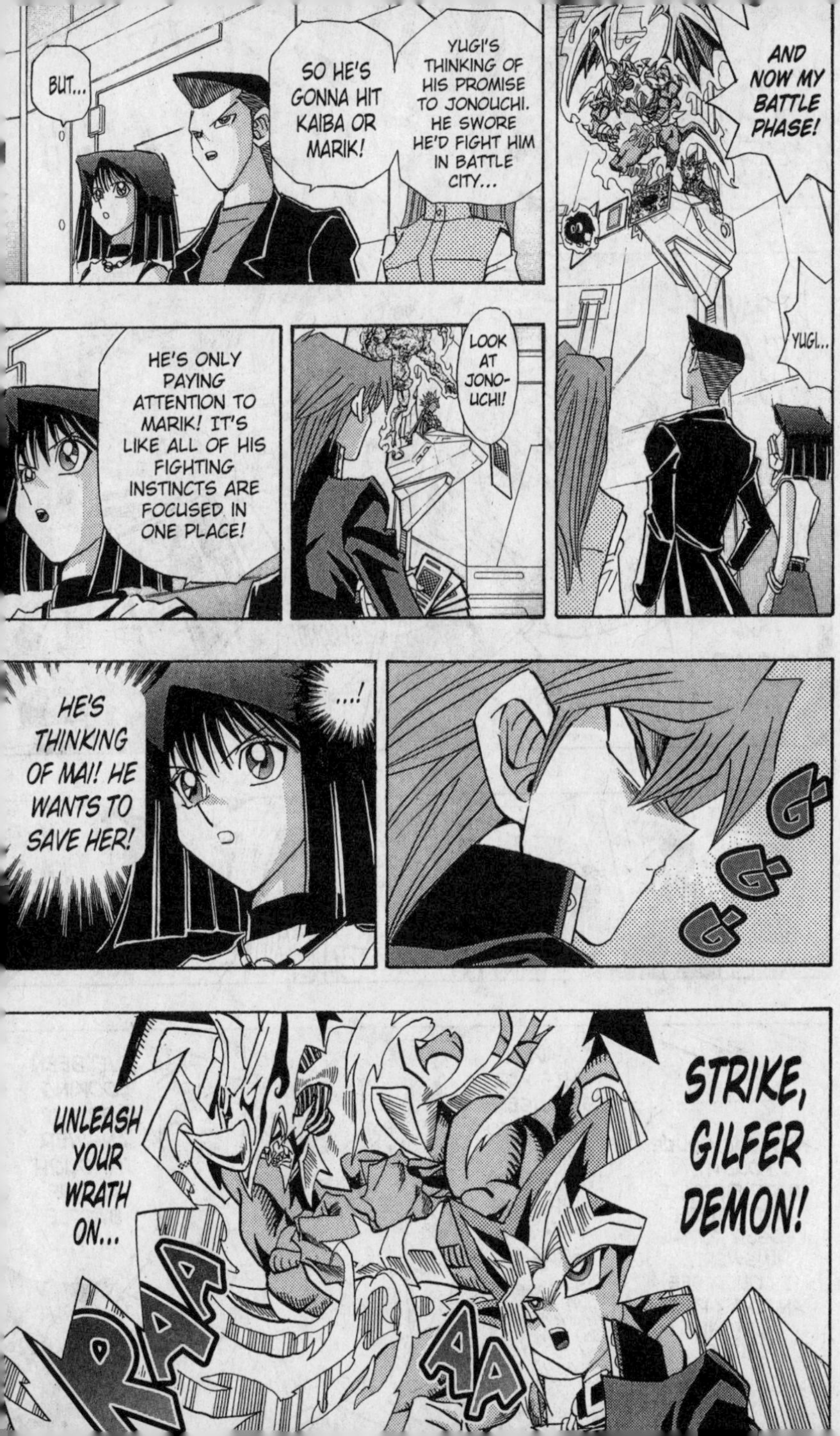
AND NOW MY BATTLE PHASE!
YUGI'S THINKING OF HIS PROMISE TO JONOUCHI. HE SWORE HE'D FIGHT HIM IN BATTLE CITY...
SO HE'S GONNA HIT KAIBA OR MARIK!
BUT...
YUGI...
LOOK AT JONOUCHI!
HE'S ONLY PAYING ATTENTION TO MARIK! IT'S LIKE ALL OF HIS FIGHTING INSTINCTS ARE FOCUSED IN ONE PLACE!
G G G
...!
HE'S THINKING OF MAI! HE WANTS TO SAVE HER!
STRIKE, GILFER DEMON!
UNLEASH YOUR WRATH ON...
RAAAA

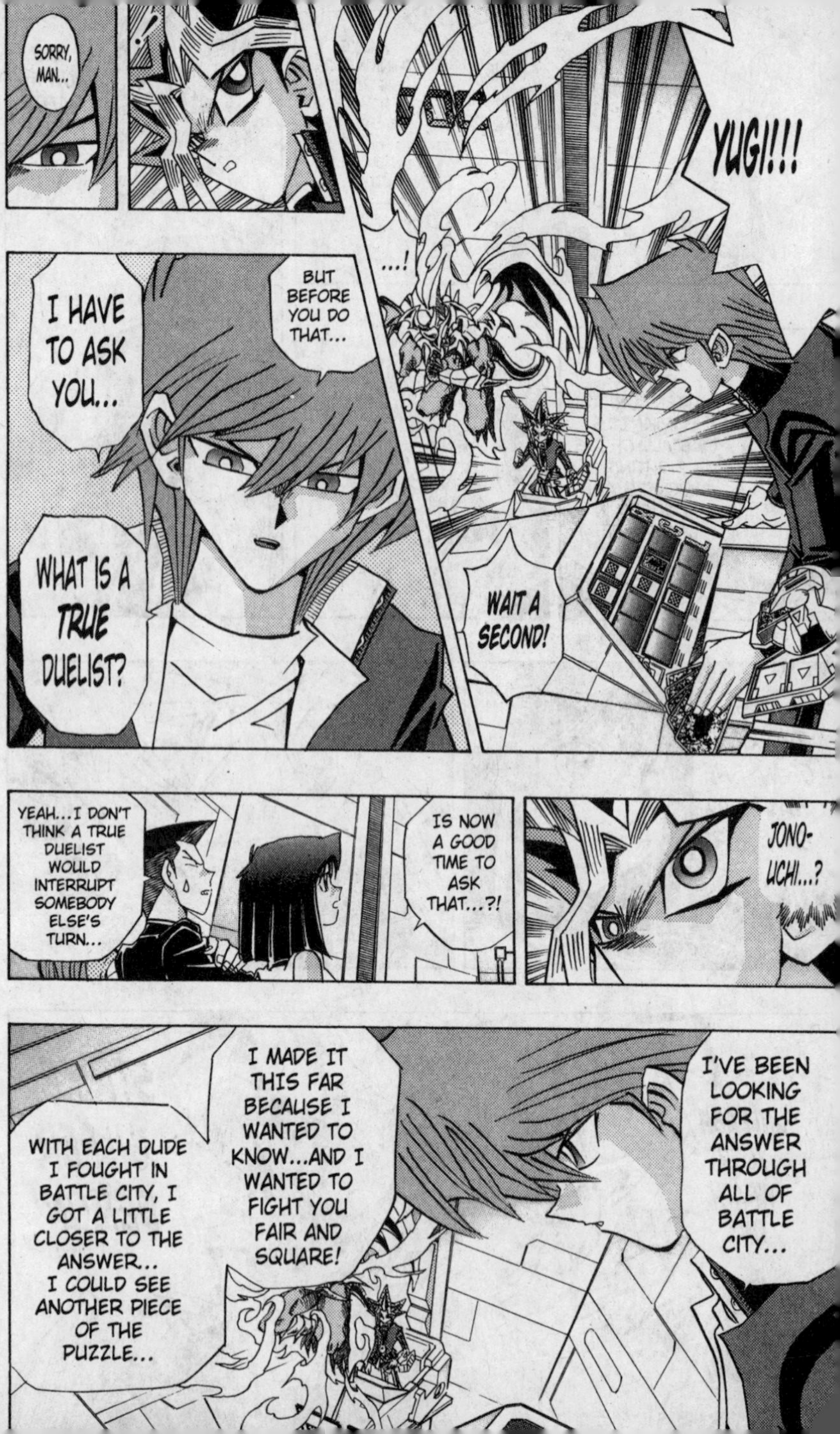
YUGI!!!
...!
WAIT A SECOND!
SORRY, MAN...
BUT BEFORE YOU DO THAT...
I HAVE TO ASK YOU...
WHAT IS A TRUE DUELIST?
JONO-UCHI...?
IS NOW A GOOD TIME TO ASK THAT...?!
YEAH...I DON'T THINK A TRUE DUELIST WOULD INTERRUPT SOMEBODY ELSE'S TURN...
I'VE BEEN LOOKING FOR THE ANSWER THROUGH ALL OF BATTLE CITY...
I MADE IT THIS FAR BECAUSE I WANTED TO KNOW...AND I WANTED TO FIGHT YOU FAIR AND SQUARE!
WITH EACH DUDE I FOUGHT IN BATTLE CITY, I GOT A LITTLE CLOSER TO THE ANSWER... I COULD SEE ANOTHER PIECE OF THE PUZZLE...

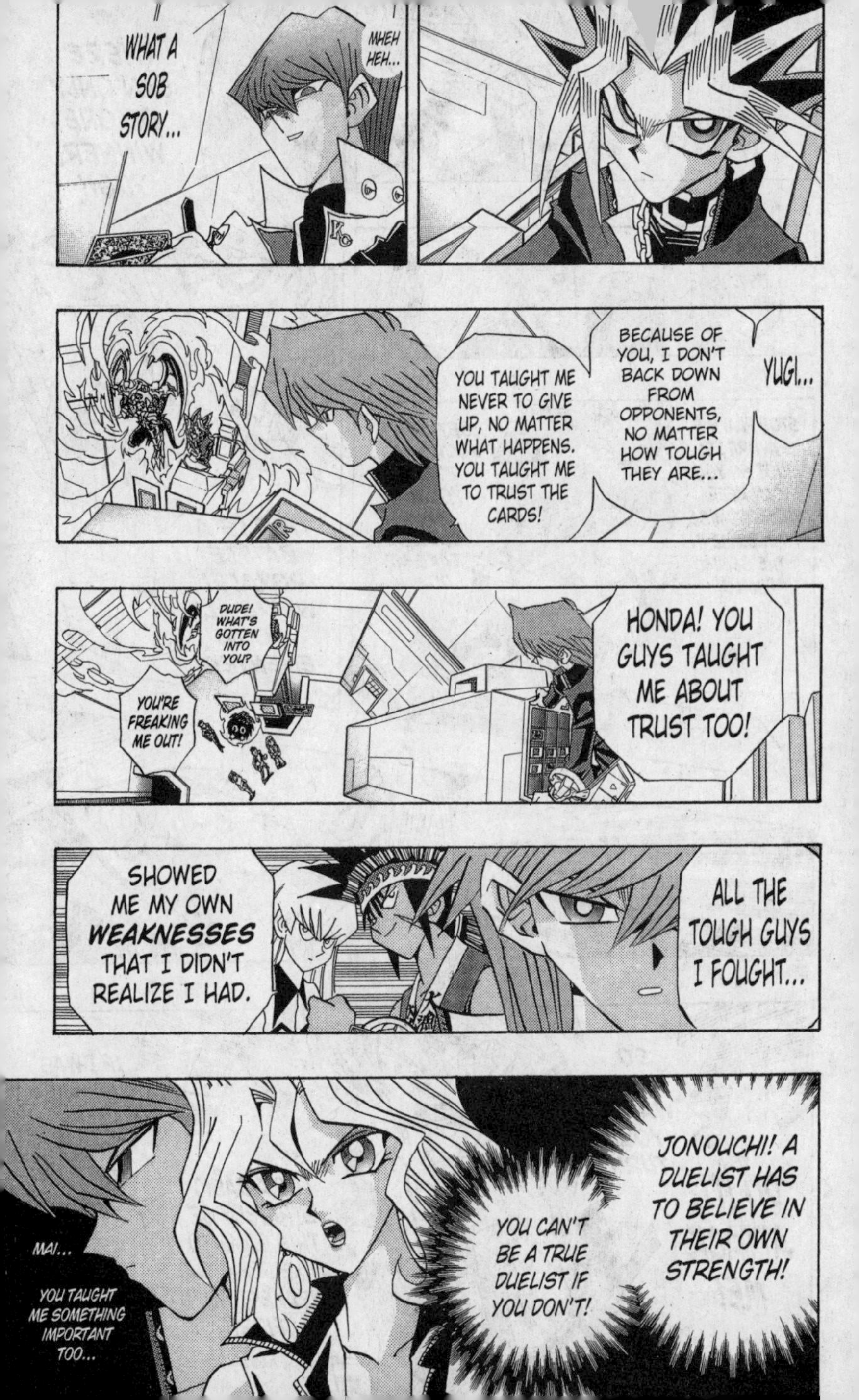
MHEH HEH...
WHAT A SOB STORY...
YUGI...
BECAUSE OF YOU, I DON'T BACK DOWN FROM OPPONENTS, NO MATTER HOW TOUGH THEY ARE...
YOU TAUGHT ME NEVER TO GIVE UP, NO MATTER WHAT HAPPENS. YOU TAUGHT ME TO TRUST THE CARDS!
HONDA! YOU GUYS TAUGHT ME ABOUT TRUST TOO!
DUDE! WHAT'S GOTTEN INTO YOU?
YOU'RE FREAKING ME OUT!
ALL THE TOUGH GUYS I FOUGHT...
SHOWED ME MY OWN ***WEAKNESSES*** THAT I DIDN'T REALIZE I HAD.
JONOUCHI! A DUELIST HAS TO BELIEVE IN THEIR OWN STRENGTH!
YOU CAN'T BE A TRUE DUELIST IF YOU DON'T!
MAI...
YOU TAUGHT ME SOMETHING IMPORTANT TOO...

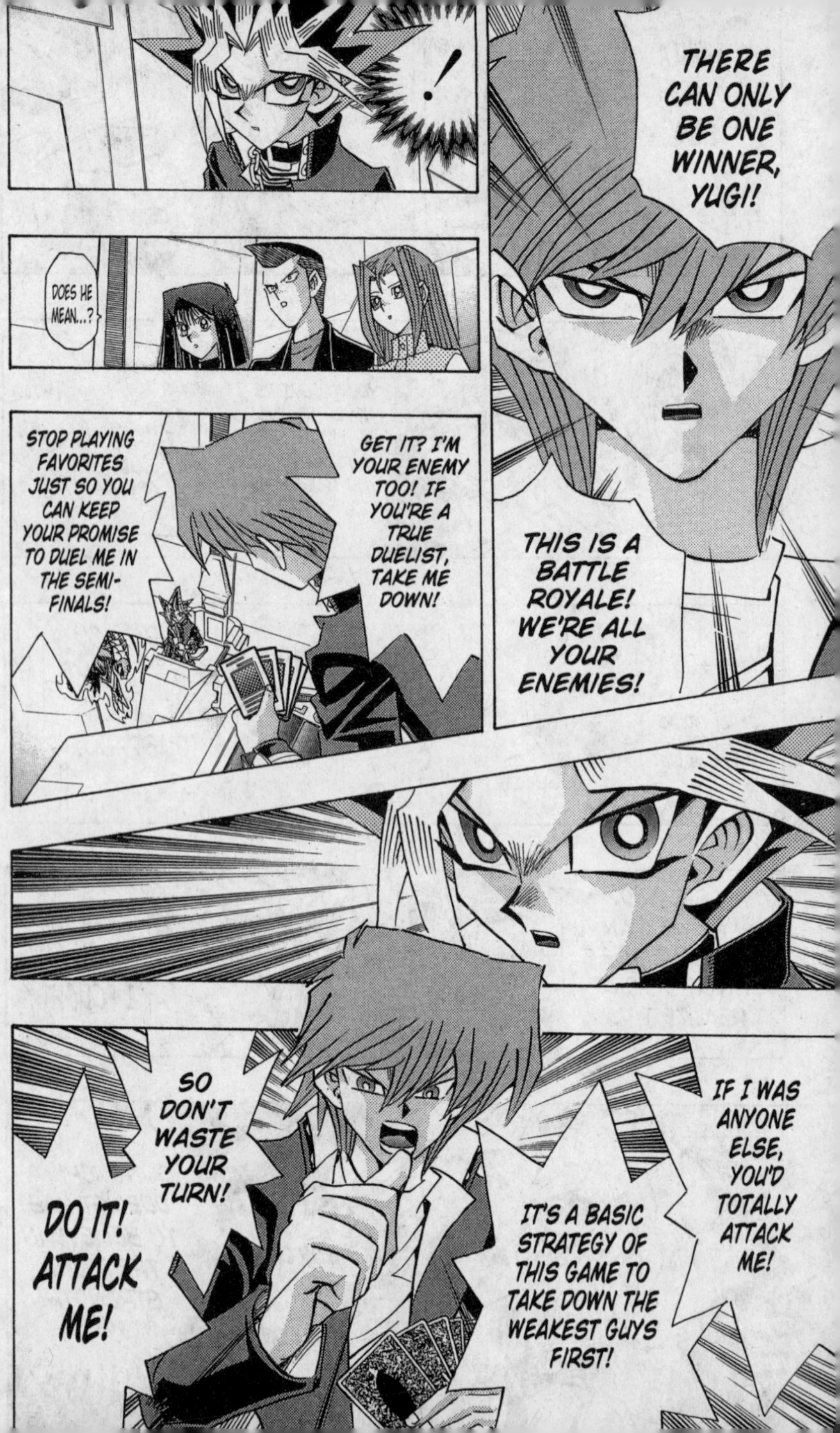
THERE CAN ONLY BE ONE WINNER, YUGI!
THIS IS A BATTLE ROYALE! WE'RE ALL YOUR ENEMIES!
!
DOES HE MEAN...?
GET IT? I'M YOUR ENEMY TOO! IF YOU'RE A TRUE DUELIST, TAKE ME DOWN!
STOP PLAYING FAVORITES JUST SO YOU CAN KEEP YOUR PROMISE TO DUEL ME IN THE SEMI-FINALS!
IF I WAS ANYONE ELSE, YOU'D TOTALLY ATTACK ME!
IT'S A BASIC STRATEGY OF THIS GAME TO TAKE DOWN THE WEAKEST GUYS FIRST!
SO DON'T WASTE YOUR TURN!
DO IT! ATTACK ME!

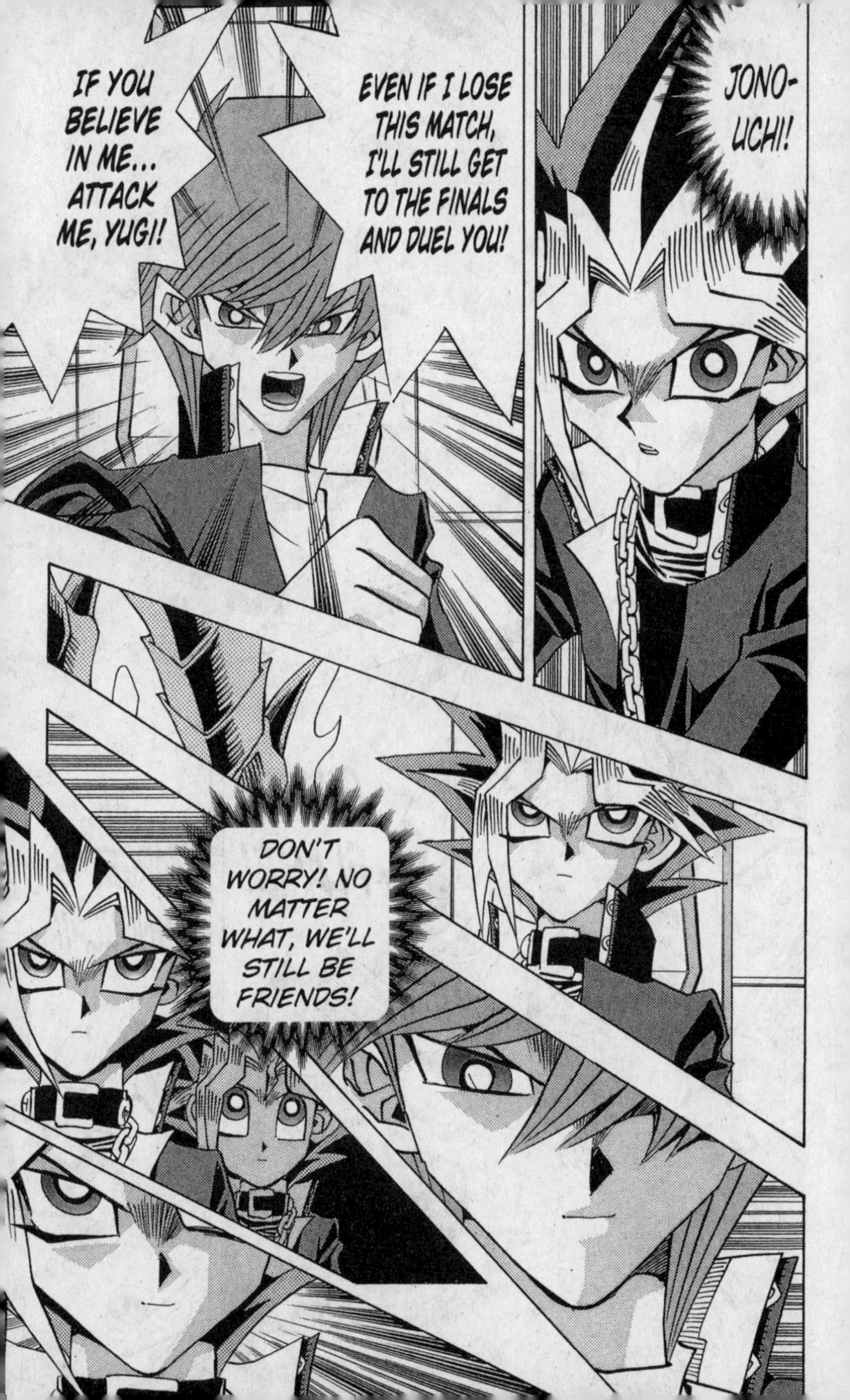
JONO-UCHI!
EVEN IF I LOSE THIS MATCH, I'LL STILL GET TO THE FINALS AND DUEL YOU!
IF YOU BELIEVE IN ME... ATTACK ME, YUGI!
DON'T WORRY! NO MATTER WHAT, WE'LL STILL BE FRIENDS!

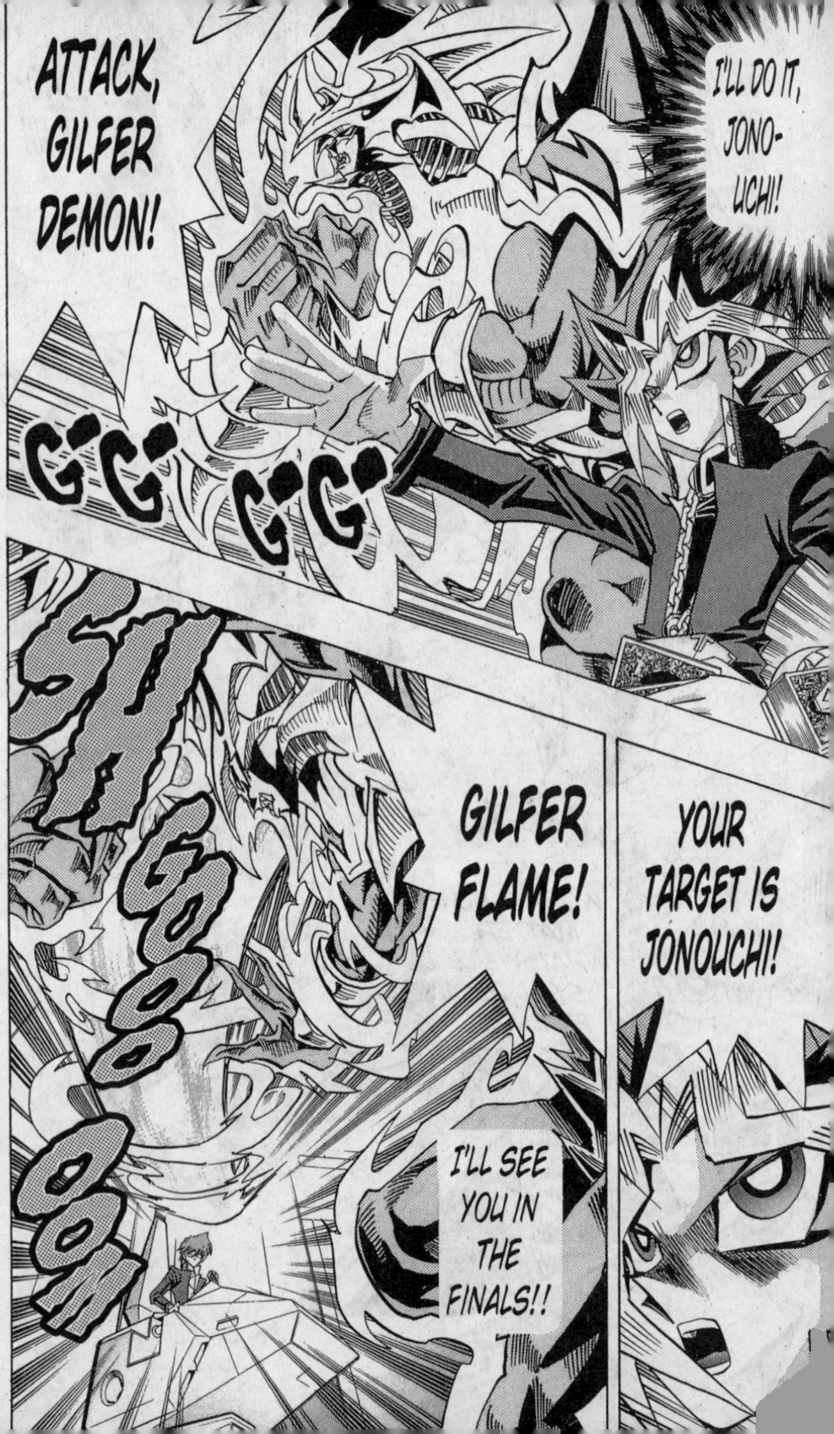
I'LL DO IT, JONOUCHI!
ATTACK, GILFER DEMON!
G-G-G-G
YOUR TARGET IS JONOUCHI!
GILFER FLAME!
I'LL SEE YOU IN THE FINALS!!

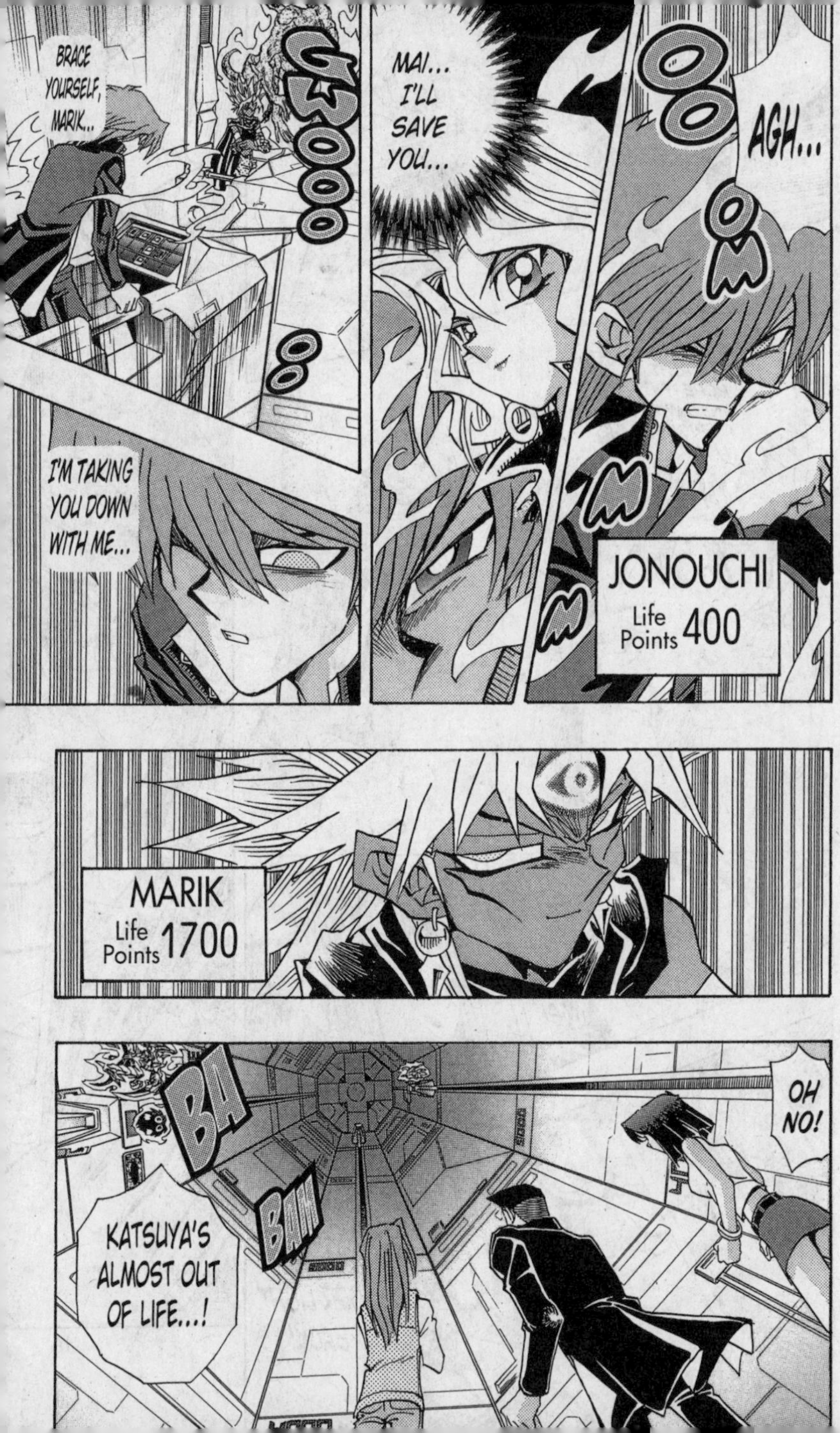
OOOOMMMM
AGH...
JONOUCHI
Life Points 400
MAI... I'LL SAVE YOU...
BRACE YOURSELF, MARIK...
GWOOOOO
OO
I'M TAKING YOU DOWN WITH ME...
MARIK
Life Points 1700
OH NO!
BA
BAM
KATSUYA'S ALMOST OUT OF LIFE...!

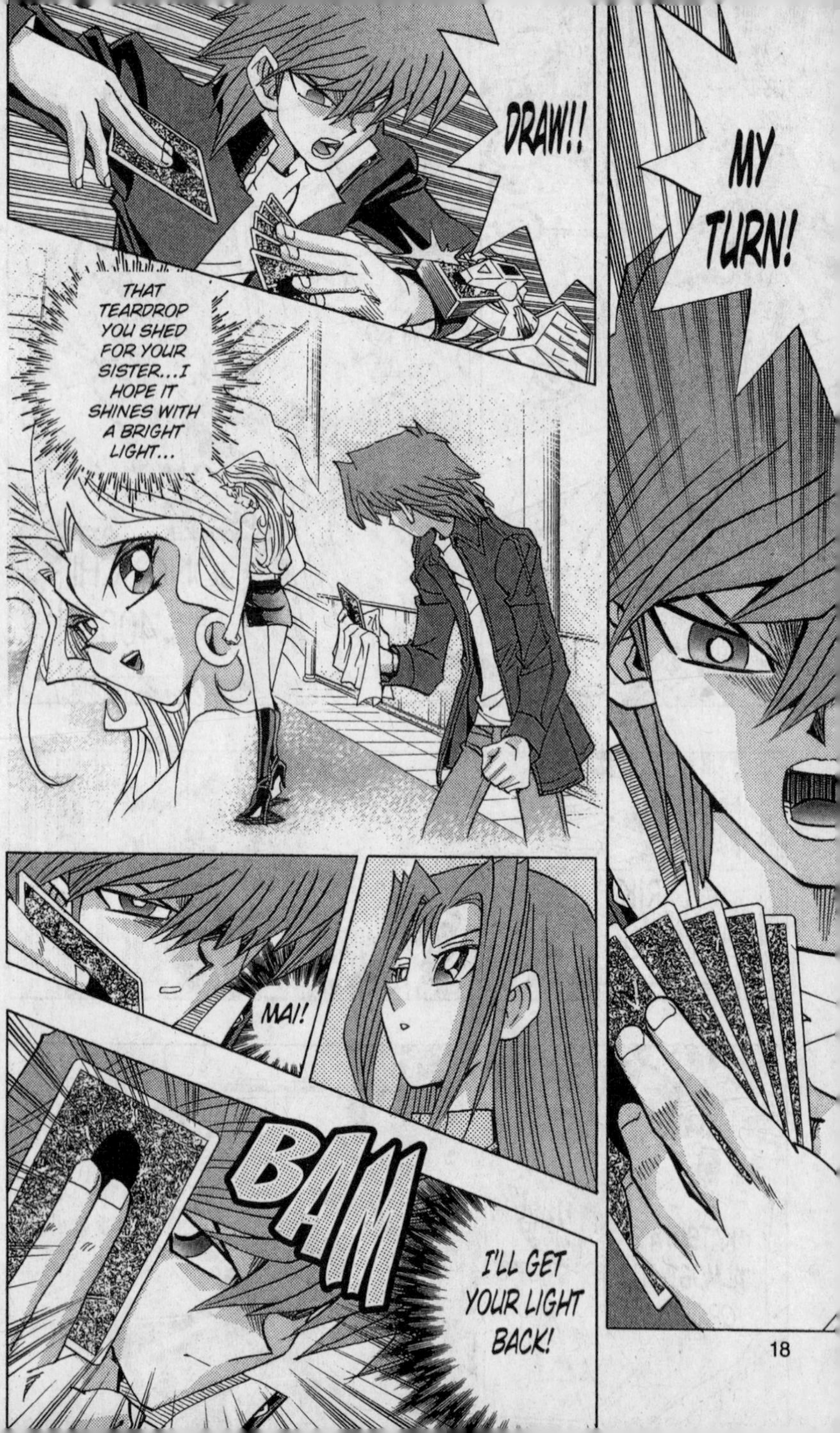
MY TURN!
DRAW!!
THAT TEARDROP YOU SHED FOR YOUR SISTER...I HOPE IT SHINES WITH A BRIGHT LIGHT...
MAI!
BAM
I'LL GET YOUR LIGHT BACK!

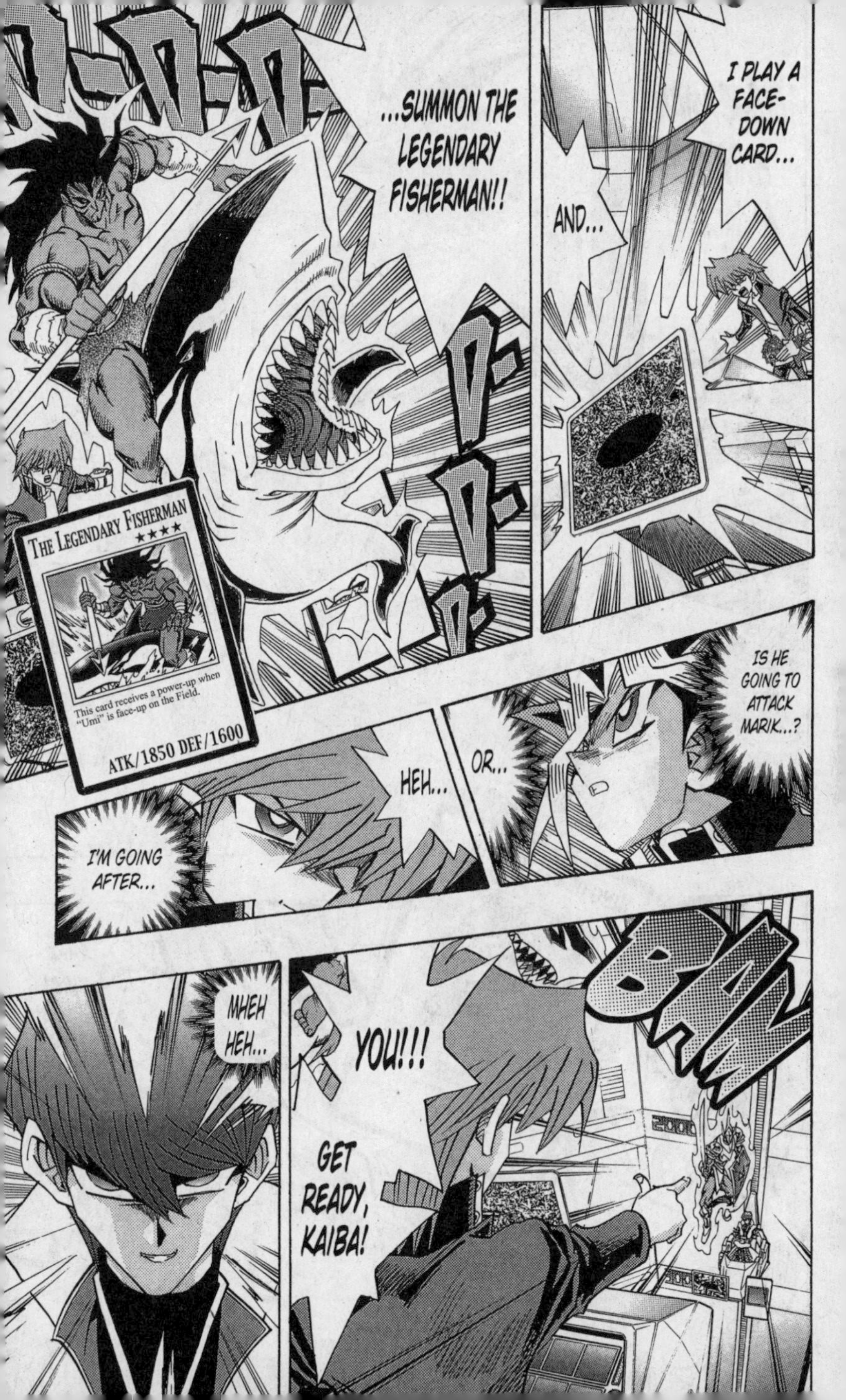
I PLAY A FACE-DOWN CARD...
AND...
...SUMMON THE LEGENDARY FISHERMAN!!
THE LEGENDARY FISHERMAN ★★★★
This card receives a power-up when "Umi" is face-up on the Field.
ATK/1850 DEF/1600
IS HE GOING TO ATTACK MARIK...?
OR...
HEH...
I'M GOING AFTER...
BAM
YOU!!!
GET READY, KAIBA!
MHEH HEH...

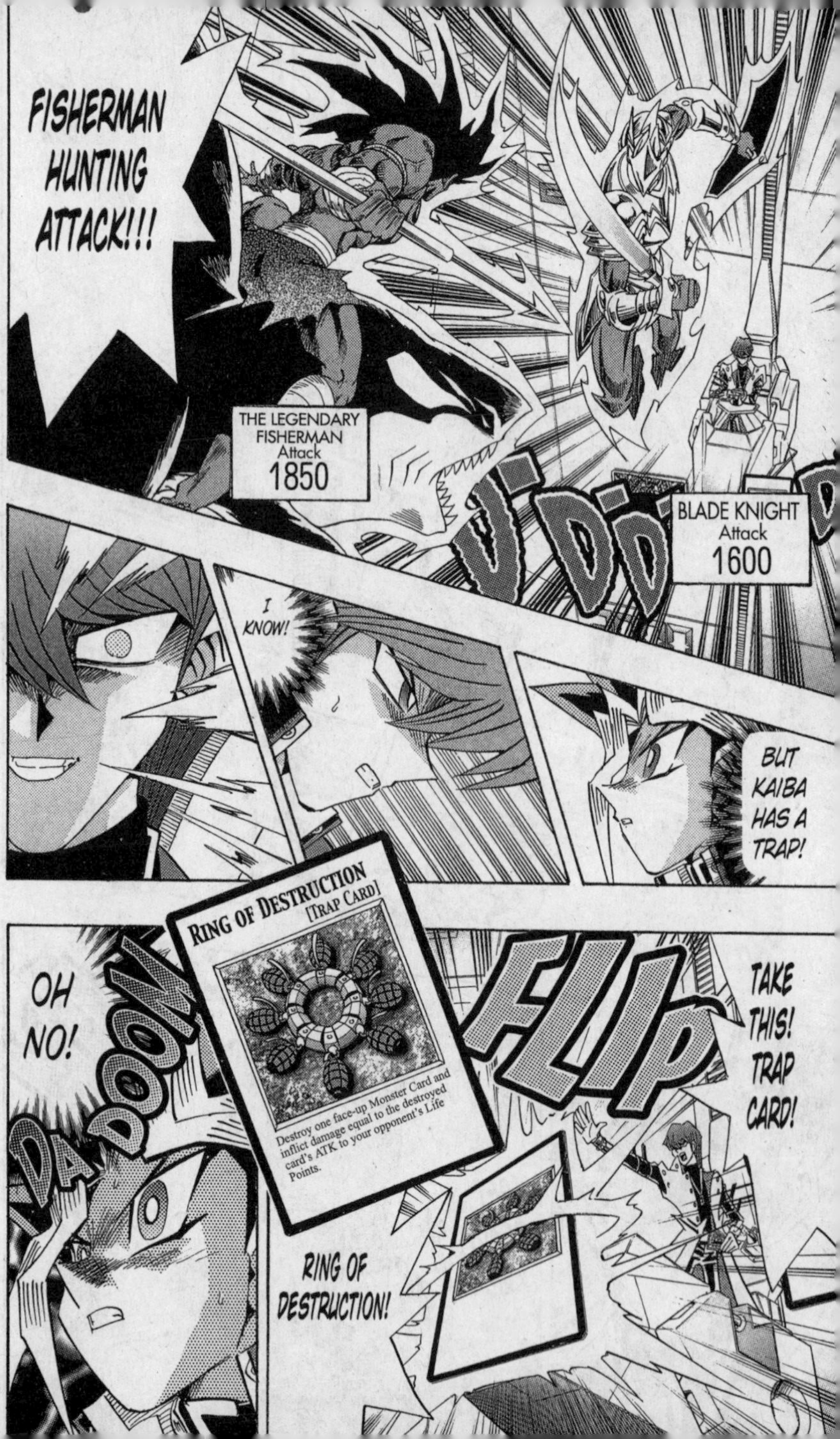
FISHERMAN HUNTING ATTACK!!!
THE LEGENDARY FISHERMAN Attack 1850
BLADE KNIGHT Attack 1600
BUT KAIBA HAS A TRAP!
I KNOW!
TAKE THIS! TRAP CARD!
FLIP
RING OF DESTRUCTION [TRAP CARD]
Destroy one face-up Monster Card and inflict damage equal to the destroyed card's ATK to your opponent's Life Points.
RING OF DESTRUCTION!
OH NO!
DA DOOM

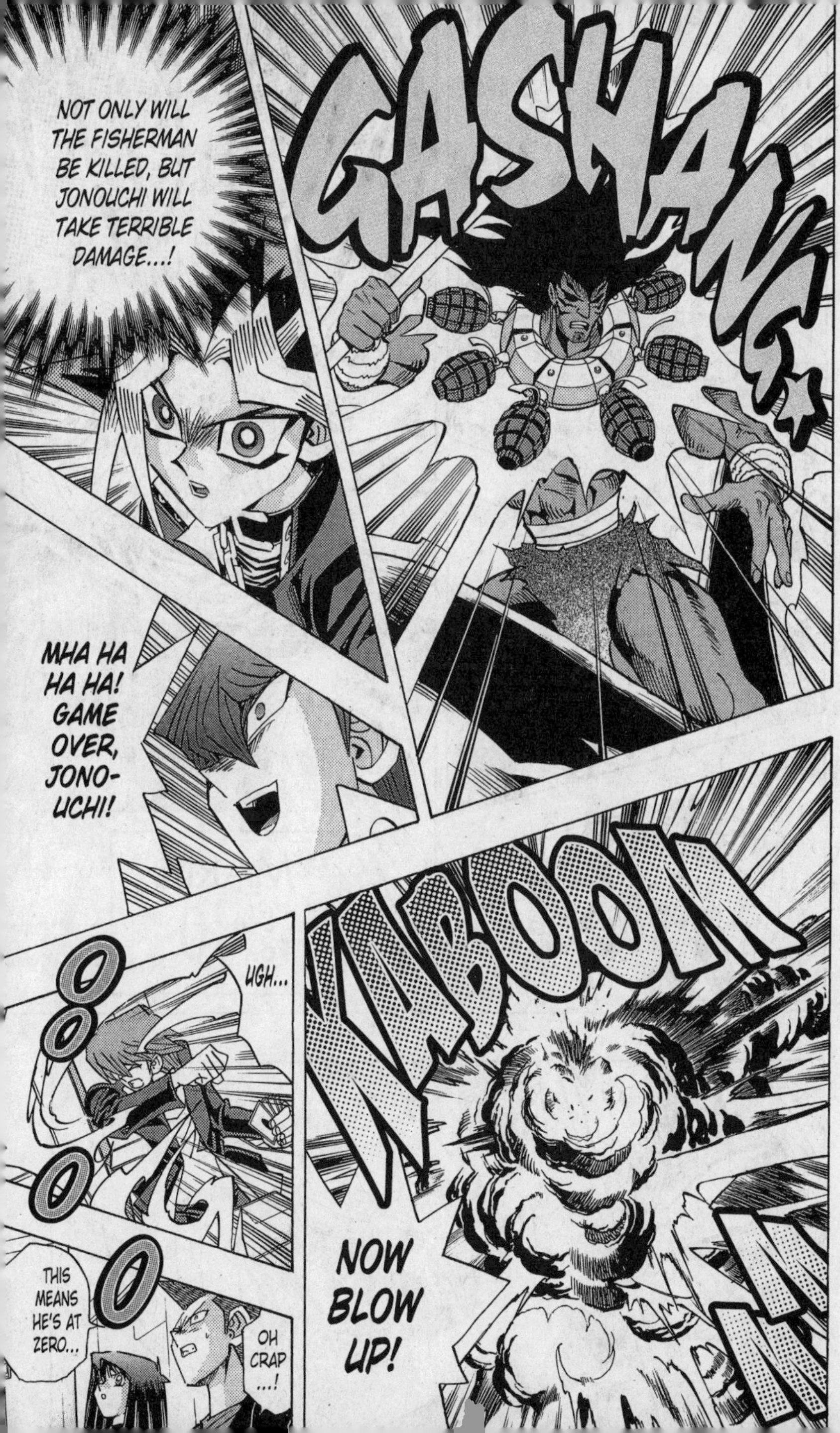
GASHAN!
NOT ONLY WILL THE FISHERMAN BE KILLED, BUT JONOUCHI WILL TAKE TERRIBLE DAMAGE...!
MHA HA HA HA! GAME OVER, JONO-UCHI!
KABOOM
NOW BLOW UP!
UGH...
THIS MEANS HE'S AT ZERO...
OH CRAP...!

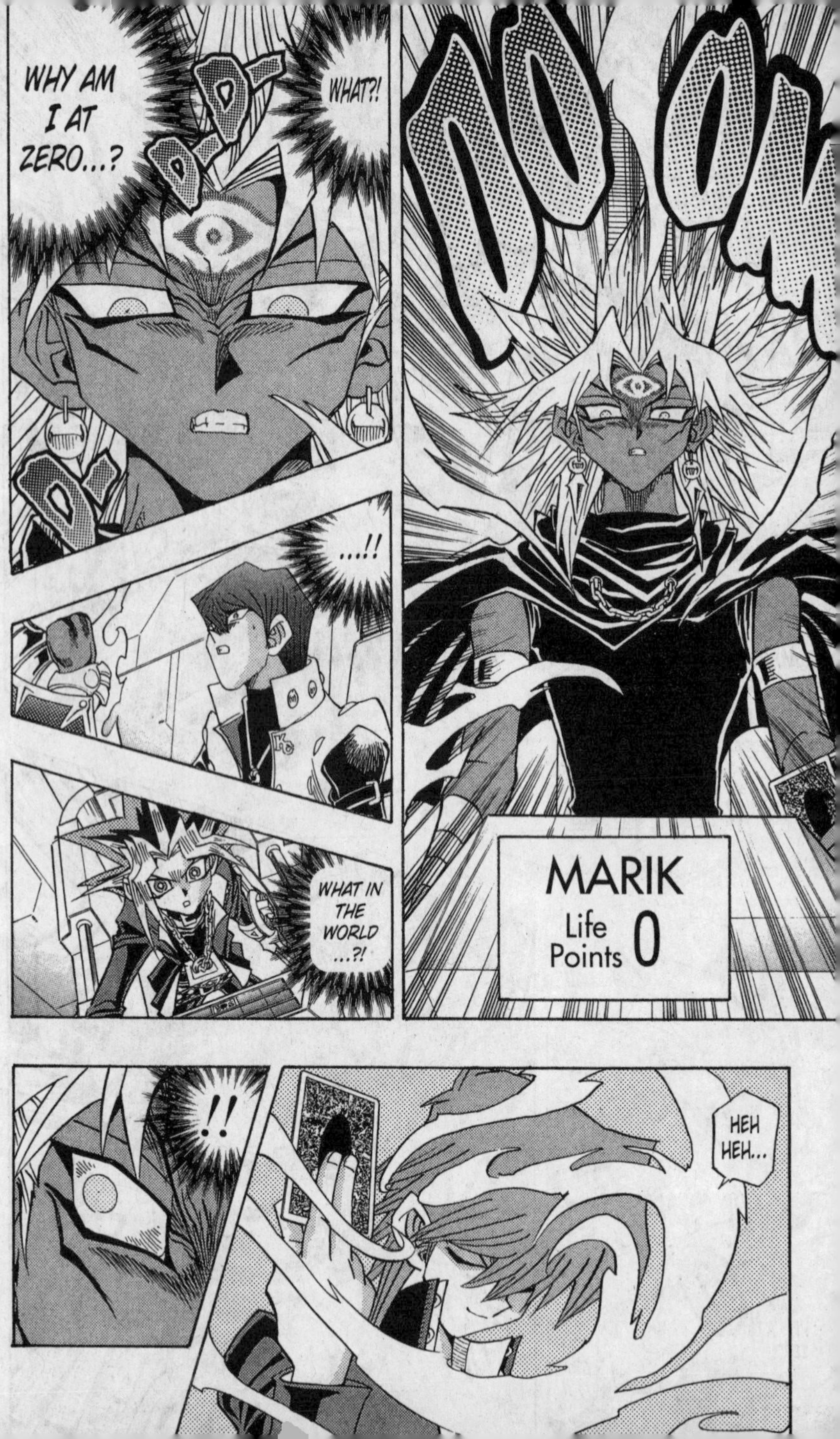
DO OM
MARIK
Life Points 0
WHAT?!
WHY AM I AT ZERO...?
D D D
...!!
WHAT IN THE WORLD ...?!
HEH HEH...
!!

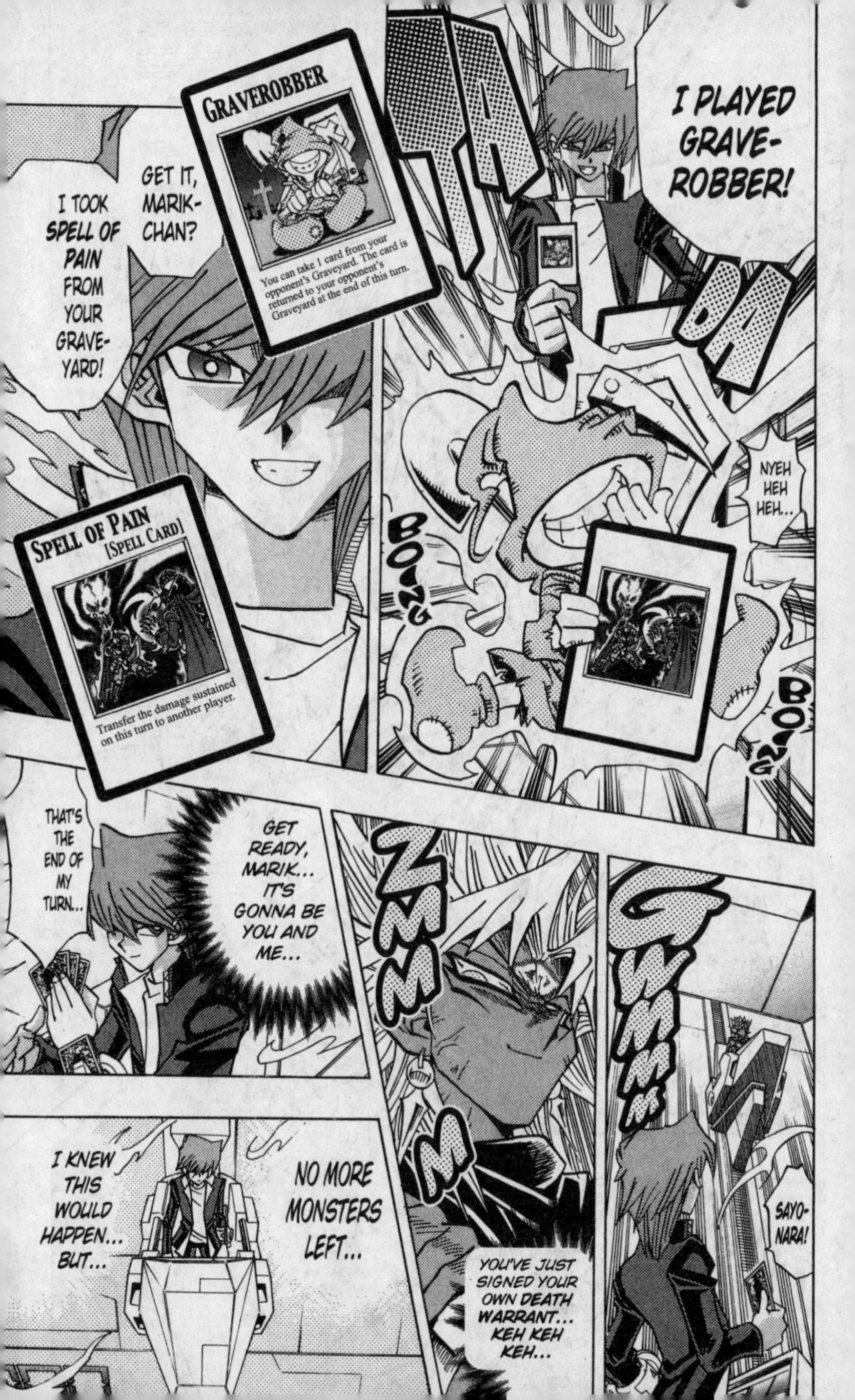
TA
I PLAYED GRAVE-ROBBER!
DA
NYEH HEH HEH...
BOING
BOING
GET IT, MARIK-CHAN?
I TOOK SPELL OF PAIN FROM YOUR GRAVE-YARD!
GRAVEROBBER
You can take 1 card from your opponent's Graveyard. The card is returned to your opponent's Graveyard at the end of this turn.
SPELL OF PAIN
[SPELL CARD]
Transfer the damage sustained on this turn to another player.
GMMMM
SAYO-NARA!
ZMMM
YOU'VE JUST SIGNED YOUR OWN DEATH WARRANT... KEH KEH KEH...
THAT'S THE END OF MY TURN...
GET READY, MARIK... IT'S GONNA BE YOU AND ME...
NO MORE MONSTERS LEFT...
I KNEW THIS WOULD HAPPEN... BUT...

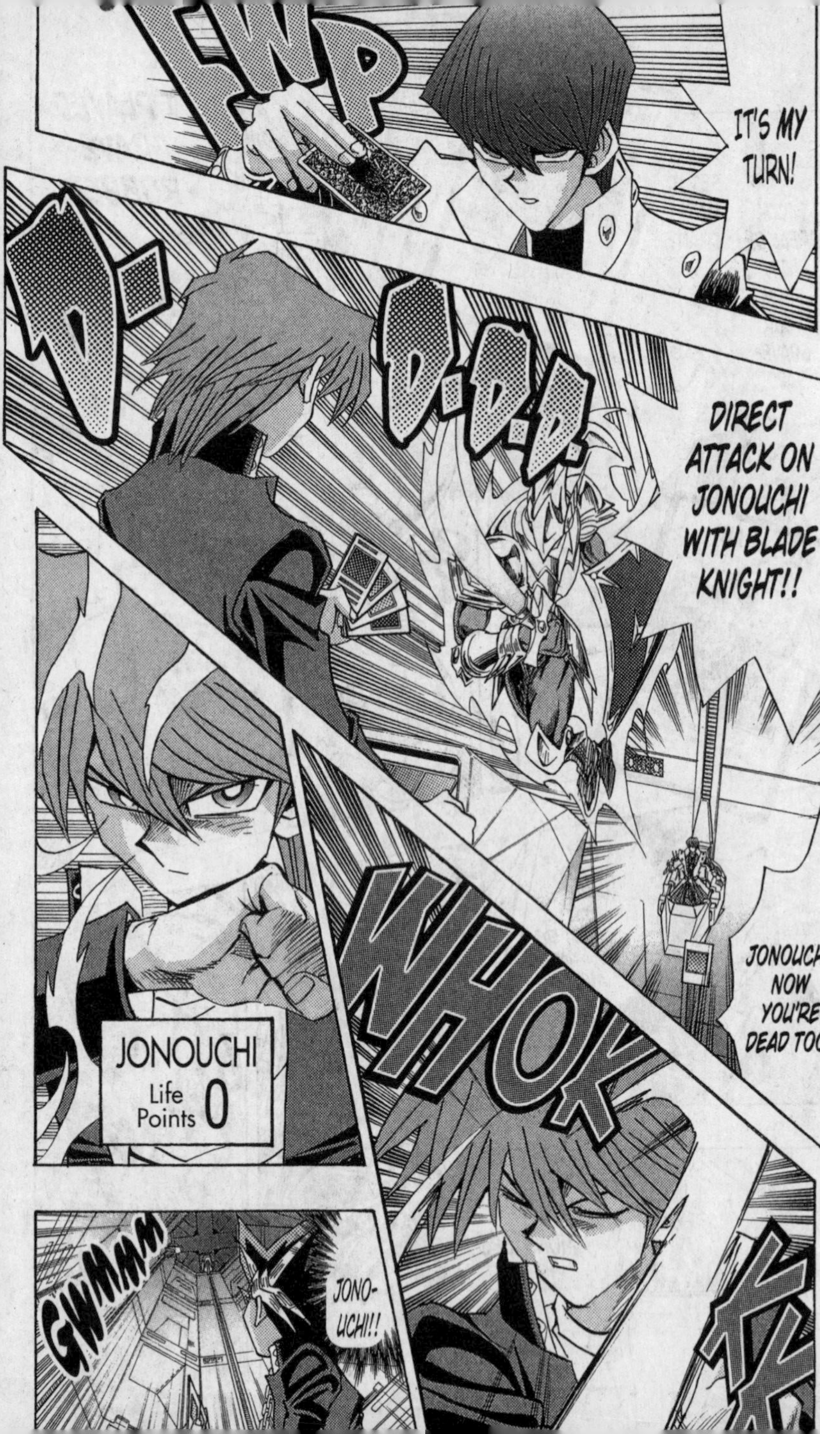
FWP
IT'S MY TURN!
DIRECT ATTACK ON JONOUCHI WITH BLADE KNIGHT!!
JONOUCHI, NOW YOU'RE DEAD TOO!
JONOUCHI
Life Points 0
JONO-UCHI!!

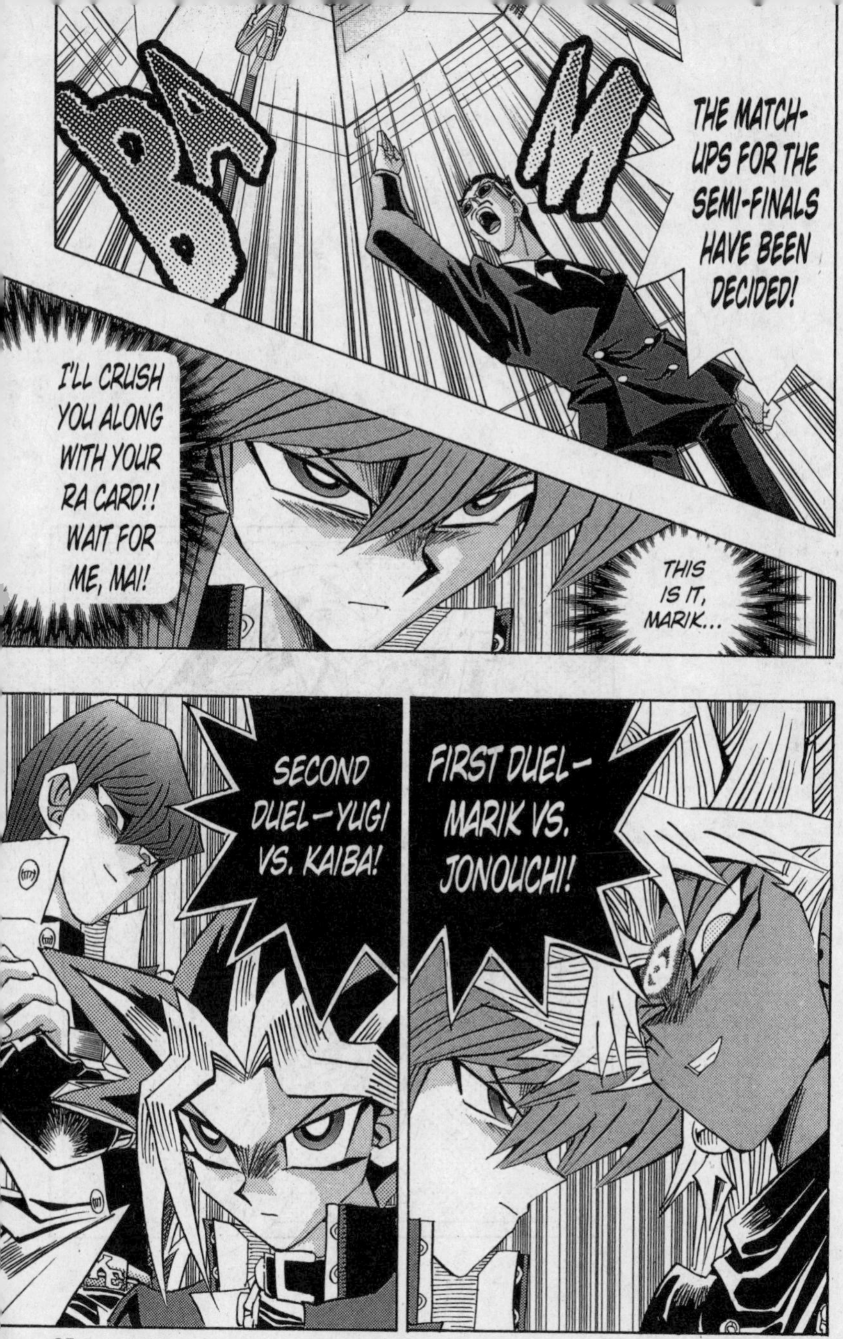
THE MATCH-UPS FOR THE SEMI-FINALS HAVE BEEN DECIDED!
THIS IS IT, MARIK...
I'LL CRUSH YOU ALONG WITH YOUR RA CARD!! WAIT FOR ME, MAI!
FIRST DUEL—MARIK VS. JONOUCHI!
SECOND DUEL—YUGI VS. KAIBA!

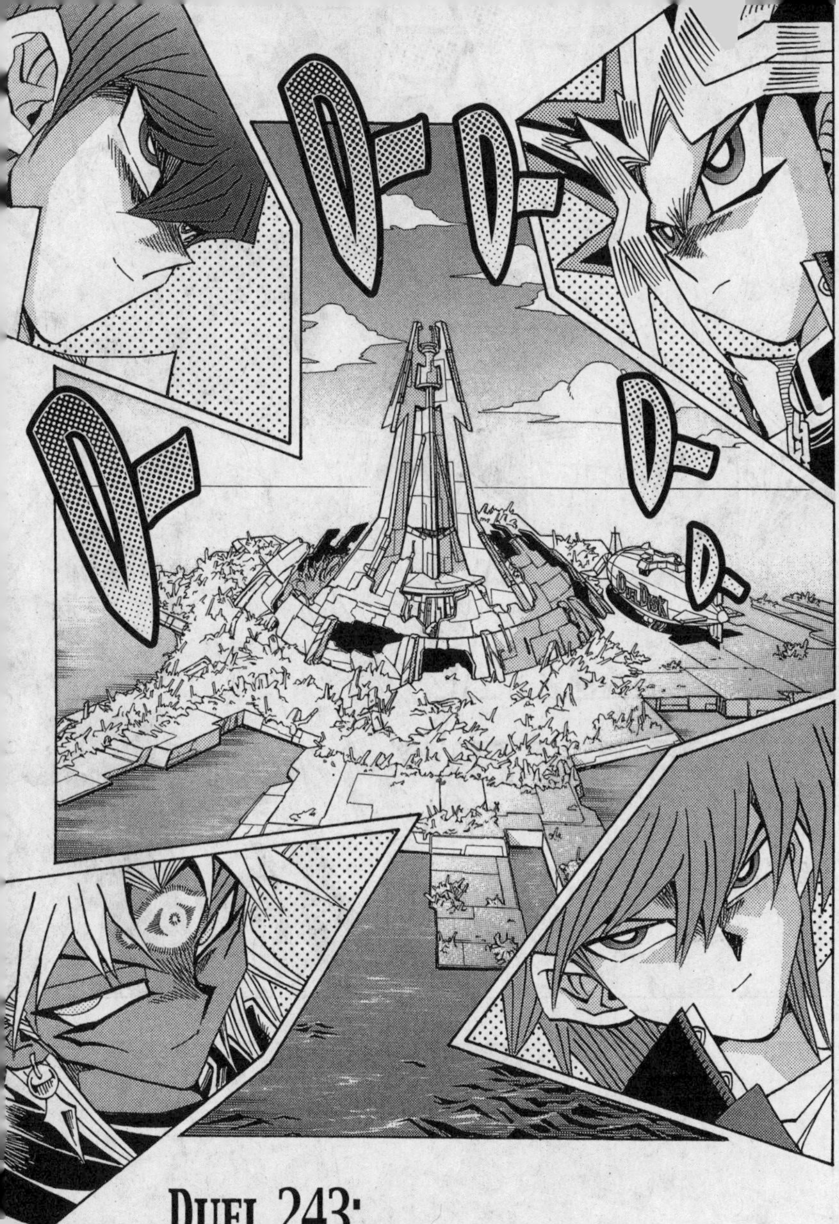
D-D-
D-D-
D-

DUEL 243:
THE FINAL STAGE!

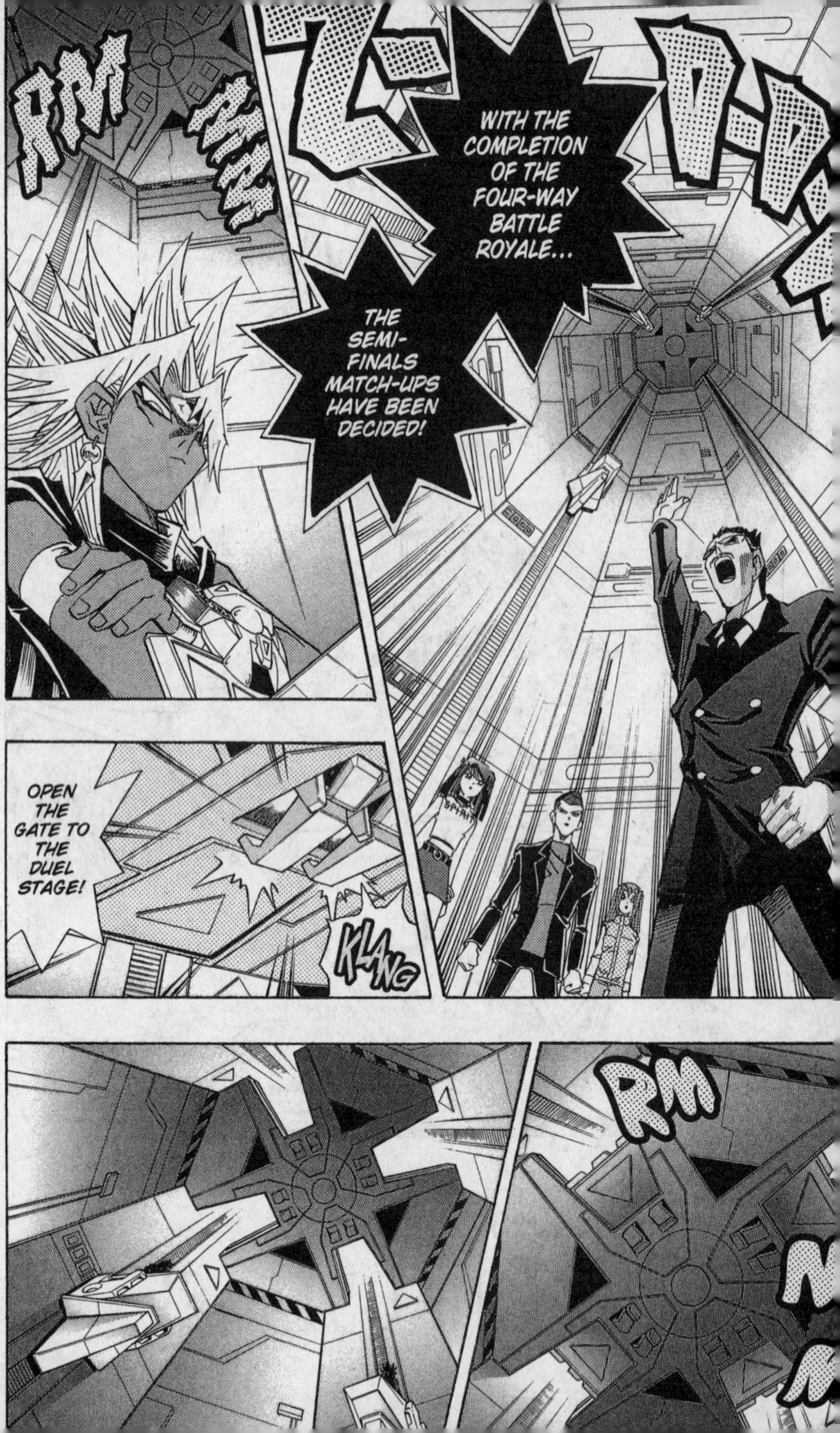

WITH THE COMPLETION OF THE FOUR-WAY BATTLE ROYALE...
THE SEMI-FINALS MATCH-UPS HAVE BEEN DECIDED!
RM
OPEN THE GATE TO THE DUEL STAGE!
KLANG
RM

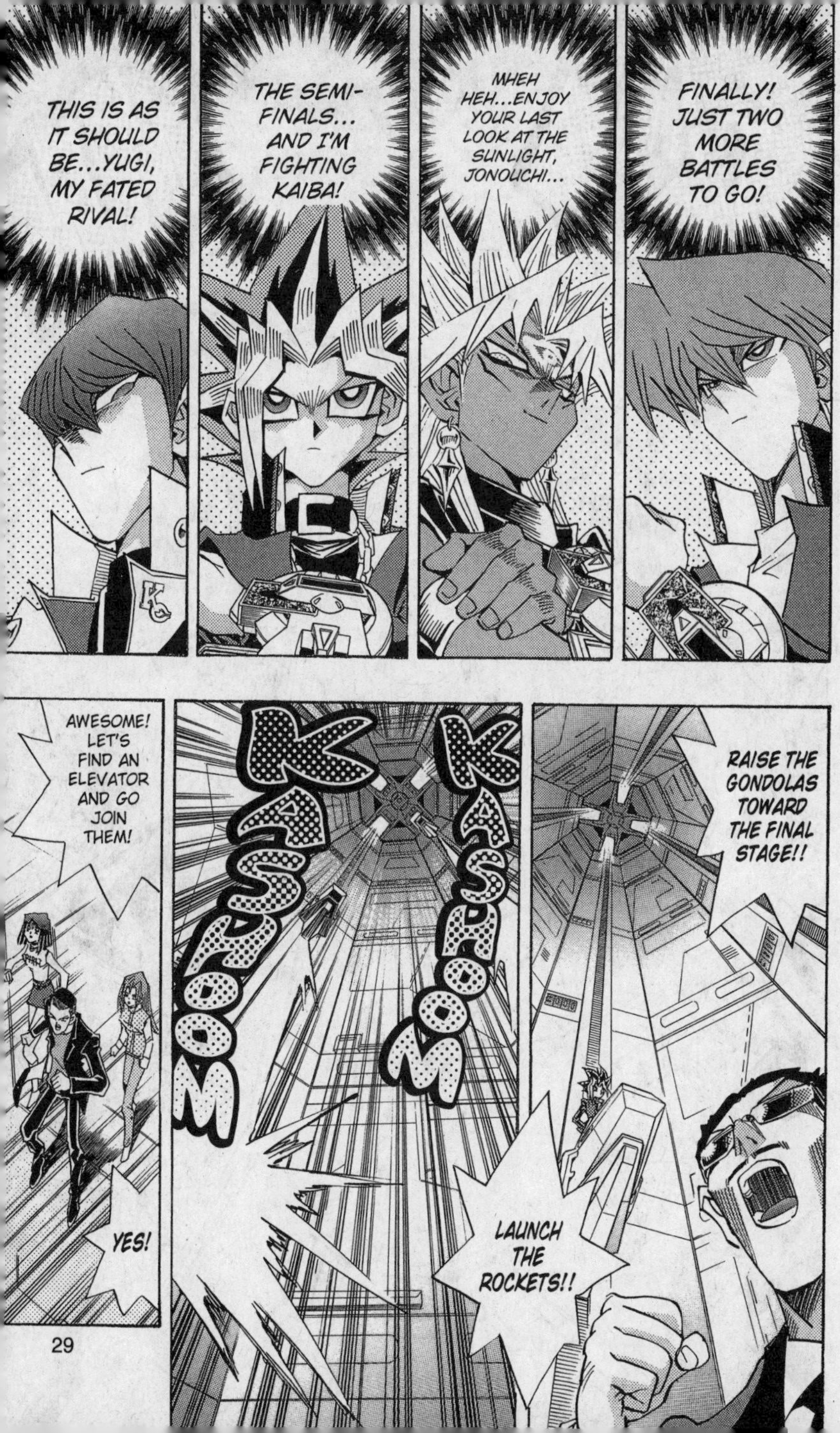
FINALLY! JUST TWO MORE BATTLES TO GO!
MHEH HEH...ENJOY YOUR LAST LOOK AT THE SUNLIGHT, JONOUCHI...
THE SEMI-FINALS... AND I'M FIGHTING KAIBA!
THIS IS AS IT SHOULD BE...YUGI, MY FATED RIVAL!
RAISE THE GONDOLAS TOWARD THE FINAL STAGE!!
LAUNCH THE ROCKETS!!
KASHOOM
KASHOOM
AWESOME! LET'S FIND AN ELEVATOR AND GO JOIN THEM!
YES!

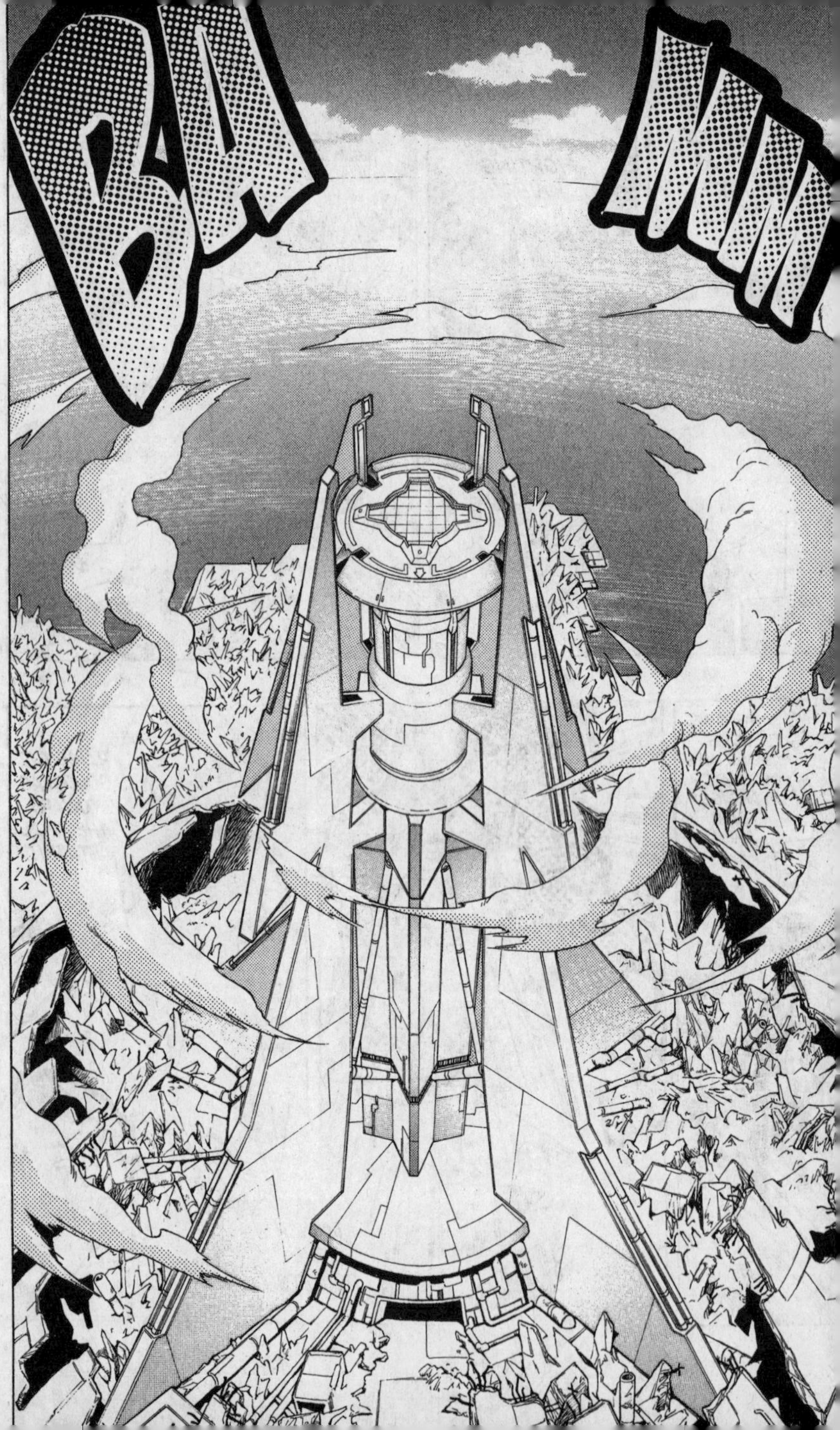
BA
MM

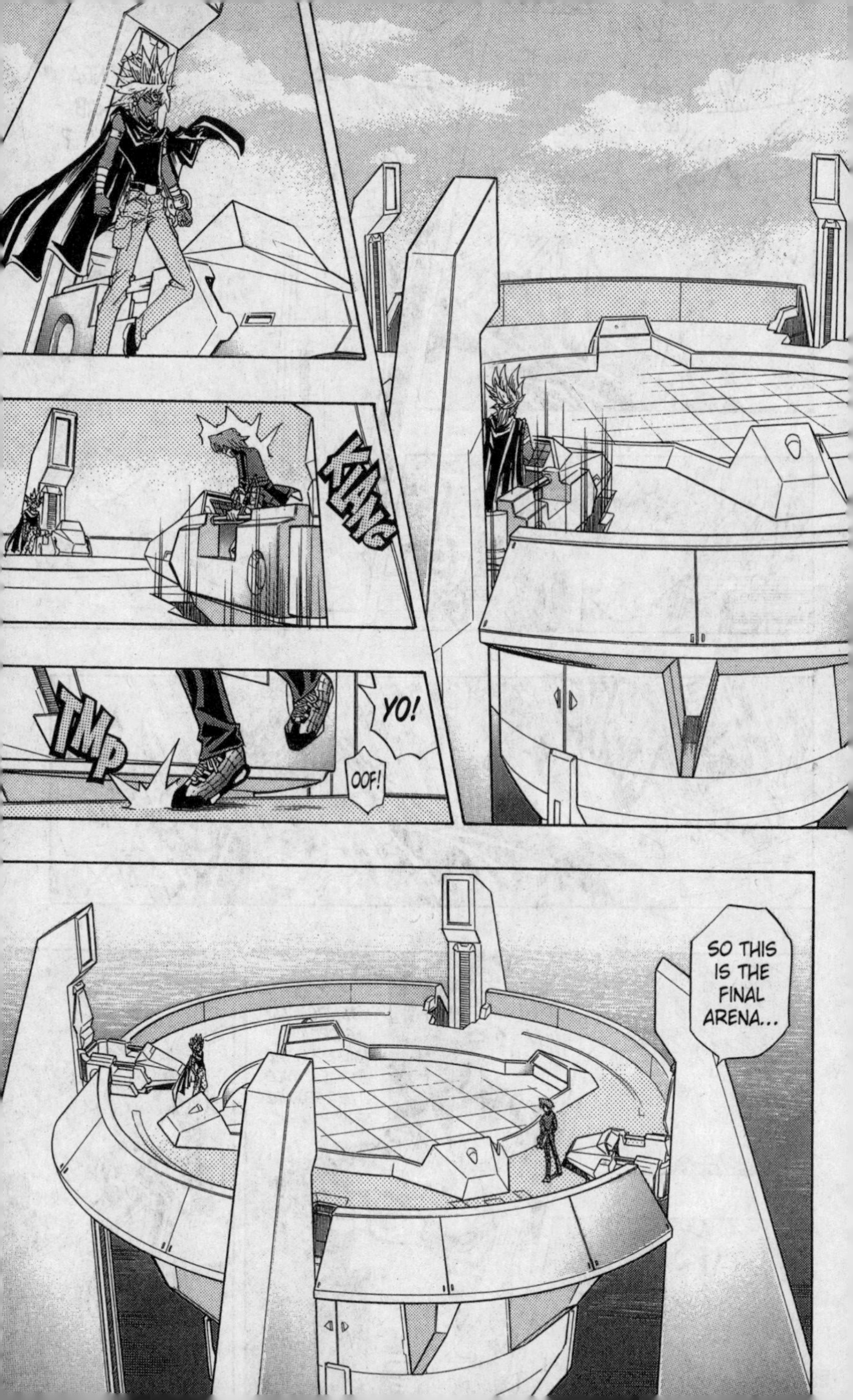
KLANG
YO!
TMP
OOF!
SO THIS IS THE FINAL ARENA...

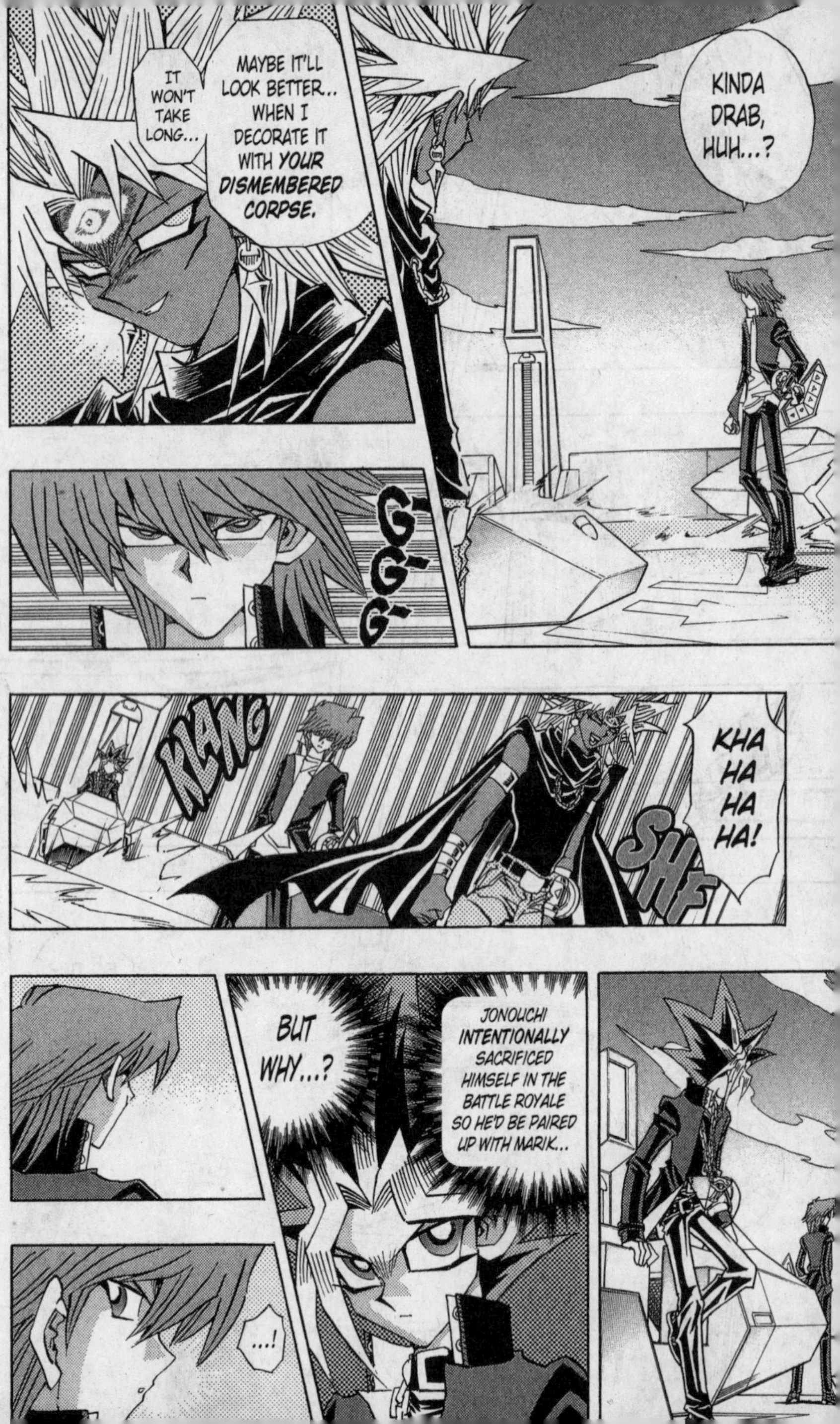
KINDA DRAB, HUH...?
MAYBE IT'LL LOOK BETTER... WHEN I DECORATE IT WITH YOUR DISMEMBERED CORPSE.
IT WON'T TAKE LONG...
G-G-G-
KHA HA HA HA!
SHF
KLANG
JONOUCHI INTENTIONALLY SACRIFICED HIMSELF IN THE BATTLE ROYALE SO HE'D BE PAIRED UP WITH MARIK...
BUT WHY...?
...!

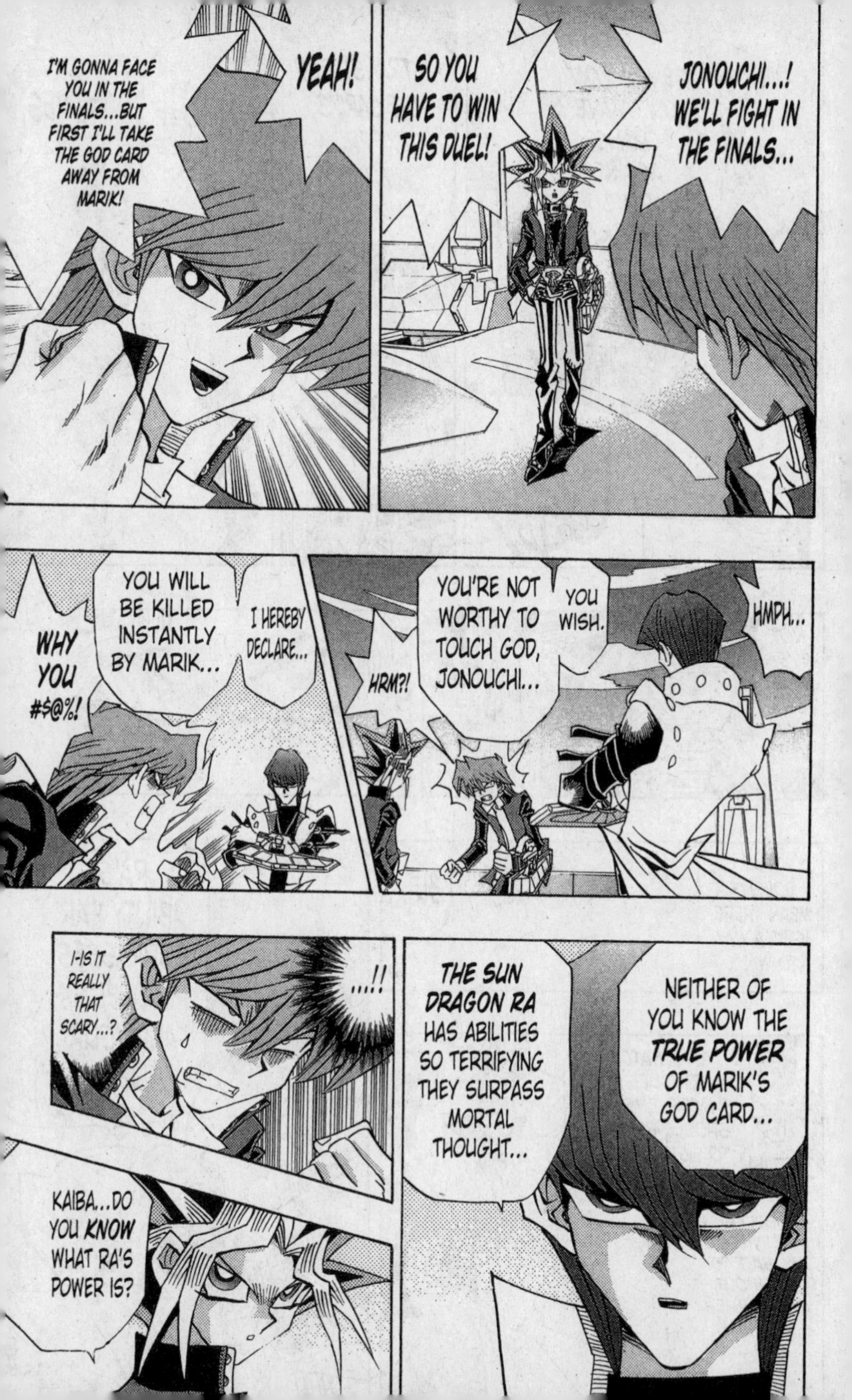
JONOUCHI...! WE'LL FIGHT IN THE FINALS...
SO YOU HAVE TO WIN THIS DUEL!
YEAH!
I'M GONNA FACE YOU IN THE FINALS...BUT FIRST I'LL TAKE THE GOD CARD AWAY FROM MARIK!
HMPH...
YOU WISH.
YOU'RE NOT WORTHY TO TOUCH GOD, JONOUCHI...
HRM?!
I HEREBY DECLARE...
YOU WILL BE KILLED INSTANTLY BY MARIK...
WHY YOU #$@%!
NEITHER OF YOU KNOW THE TRUE POWER OF MARIK'S GOD CARD...
THE SUN DRAGON RA HAS ABILITIES SO TERRIFYING THEY SURPASS MORTAL THOUGHT...
...!!
I-IS IT REALLY THAT SCARY...?
KAIBA...DO YOU KNOW WHAT RA'S POWER IS?

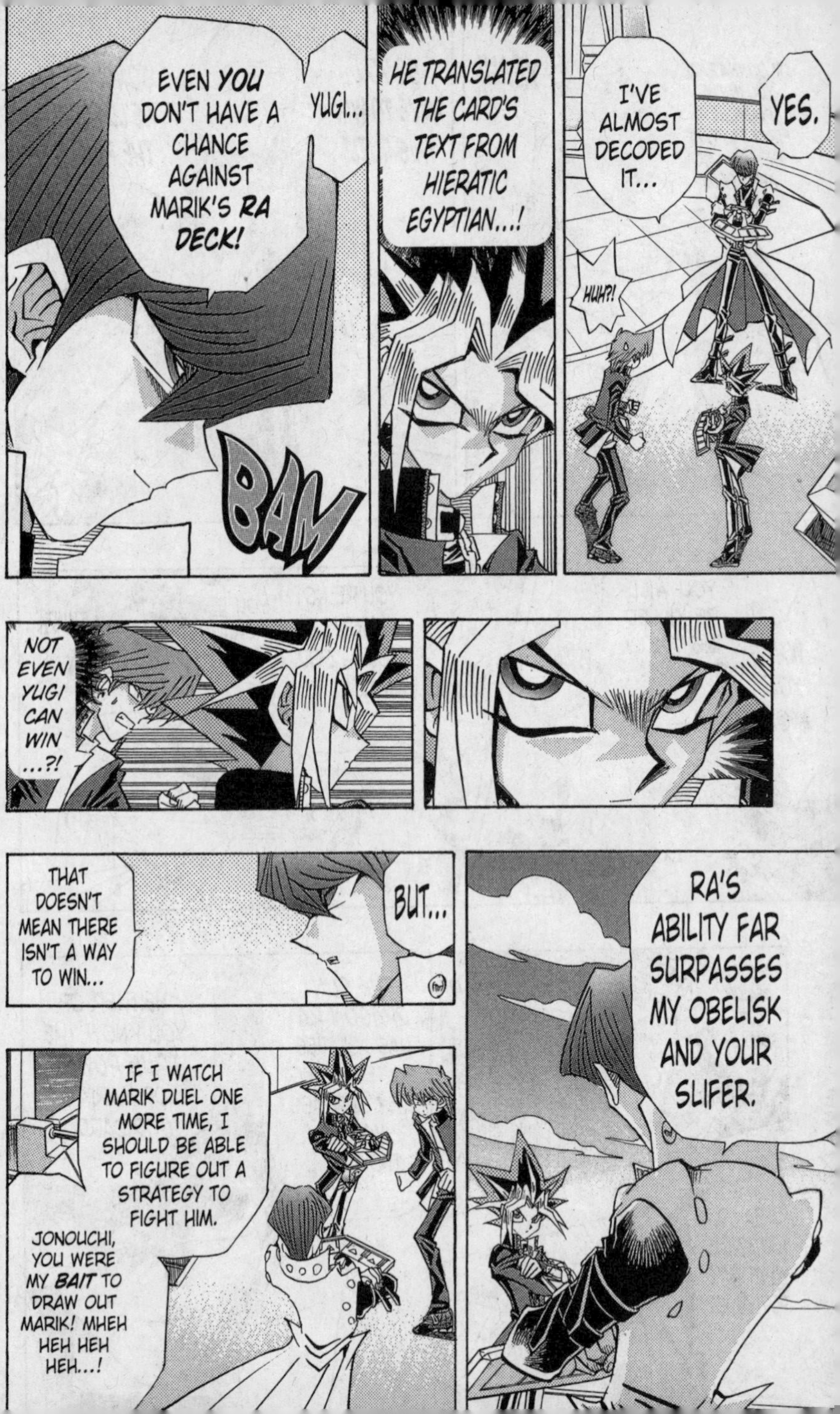
YES.
I'VE ALMOST DECODED IT...
HUH?!
HE TRANSLATED THE CARD'S TEXT FROM HIERATIC EGYPTIAN...!
YUGI...
EVEN YOU DON'T HAVE A CHANCE AGAINST MARIK'S RA DECK!
BAM
NOT EVEN YUGI CAN WIN ...?!
RA'S ABILITY FAR SURPASSES MY OBELISK AND YOUR SLIFER.
BUT...
THAT DOESN'T MEAN THERE ISN'T A WAY TO WIN...
IF I WATCH MARIK DUEL ONE MORE TIME, I SHOULD BE ABLE TO FIGURE OUT A STRATEGY TO FIGHT HIM.
JONOUCHI, YOU WERE MY BAIT TO DRAW OUT MARIK! MHEH HEH HEH HEH...!

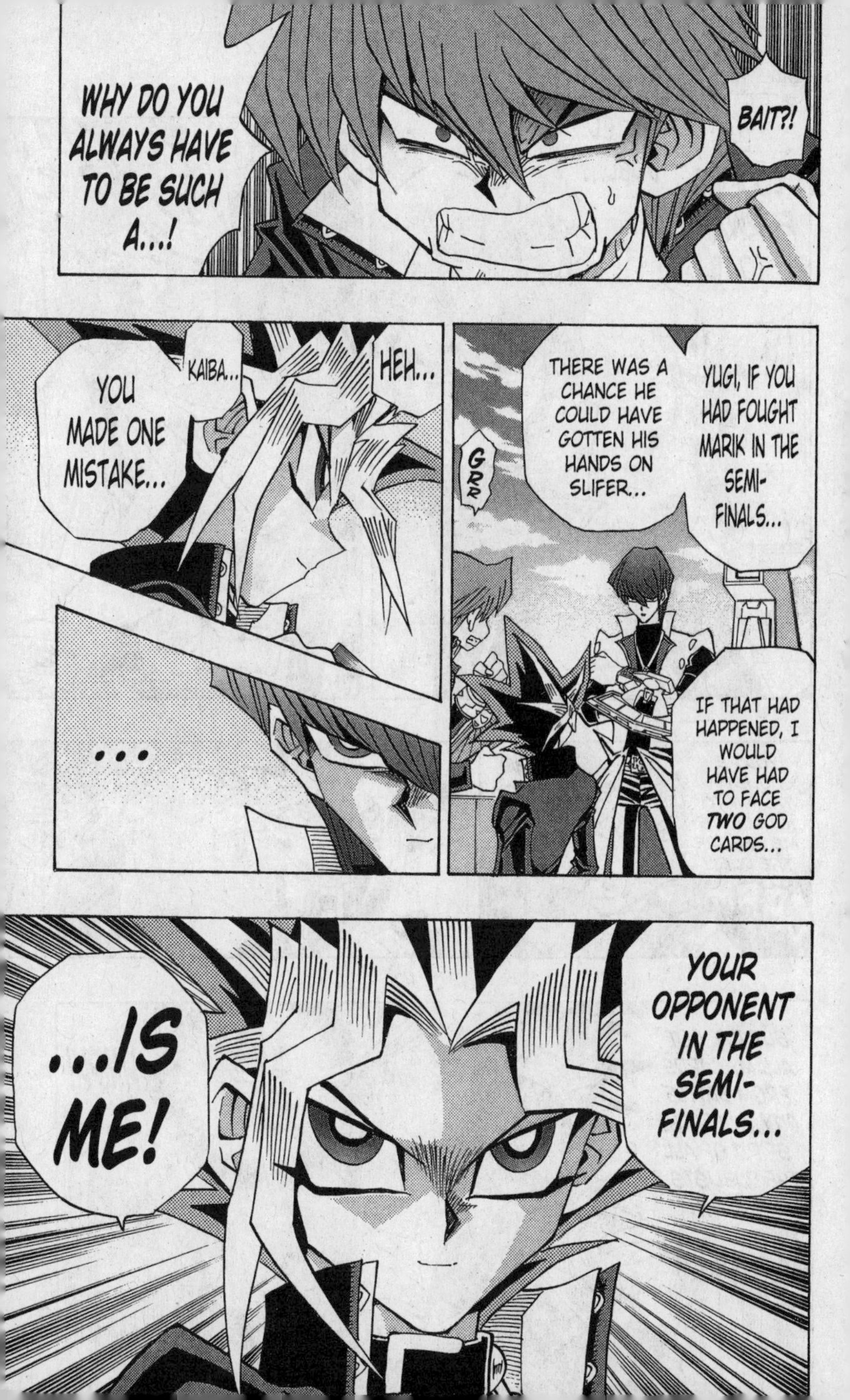
BAIT?!
WHY DO YOU ALWAYS HAVE TO BE SUCH A...!
YUGI, IF YOU HAD FOUGHT MARIK IN THE SEMI-FINALS...
THERE WAS A CHANCE HE COULD HAVE GOTTEN HIS HANDS ON SLIFER...
GRR
IF THAT HAD HAPPENED, I WOULD HAVE HAD TO FACE *TWO* GOD CARDS...
HEH...
KAIBA...
YOU MADE ONE MISTAKE...
...
YOUR OPPONENT IN THE SEMI-FINALS...
...IS ME!

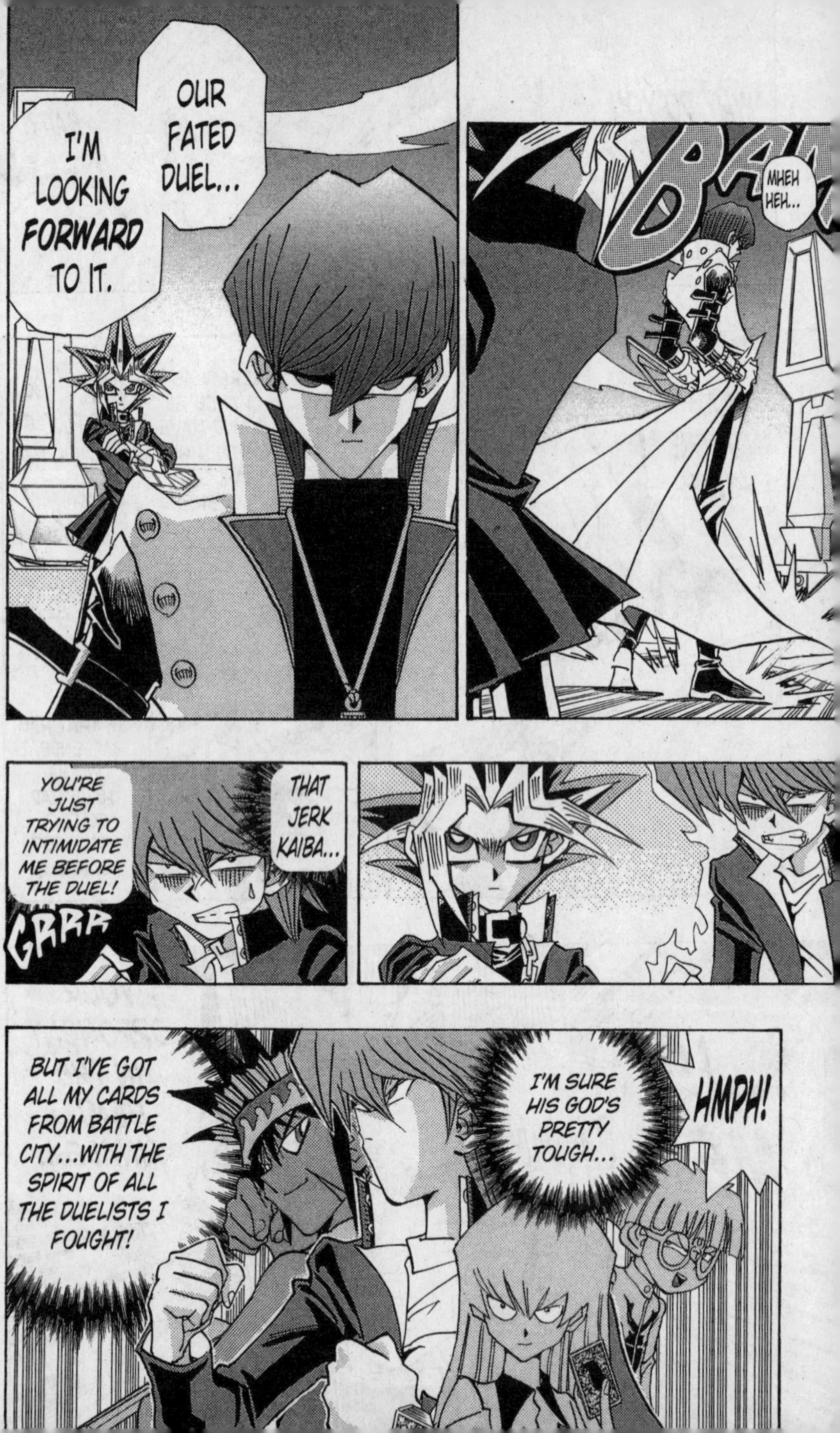
BA
MHEH HEH...
OUR FATED DUEL...
I'M LOOKING **FORWARD** TO IT.
THAT JERK KAIBA...
YOU'RE JUST TRYING TO INTIMIDATE ME BEFORE THE DUEL!
GRRR
HMPH!
I'M SURE HIS GOD'S PRETTY TOUGH...
BUT I'VE GOT ALL MY CARDS FROM BATTLE CITY...WITH THE SPIRIT OF ALL THE DUELISTS I FOUGHT!

READ THIS WAY

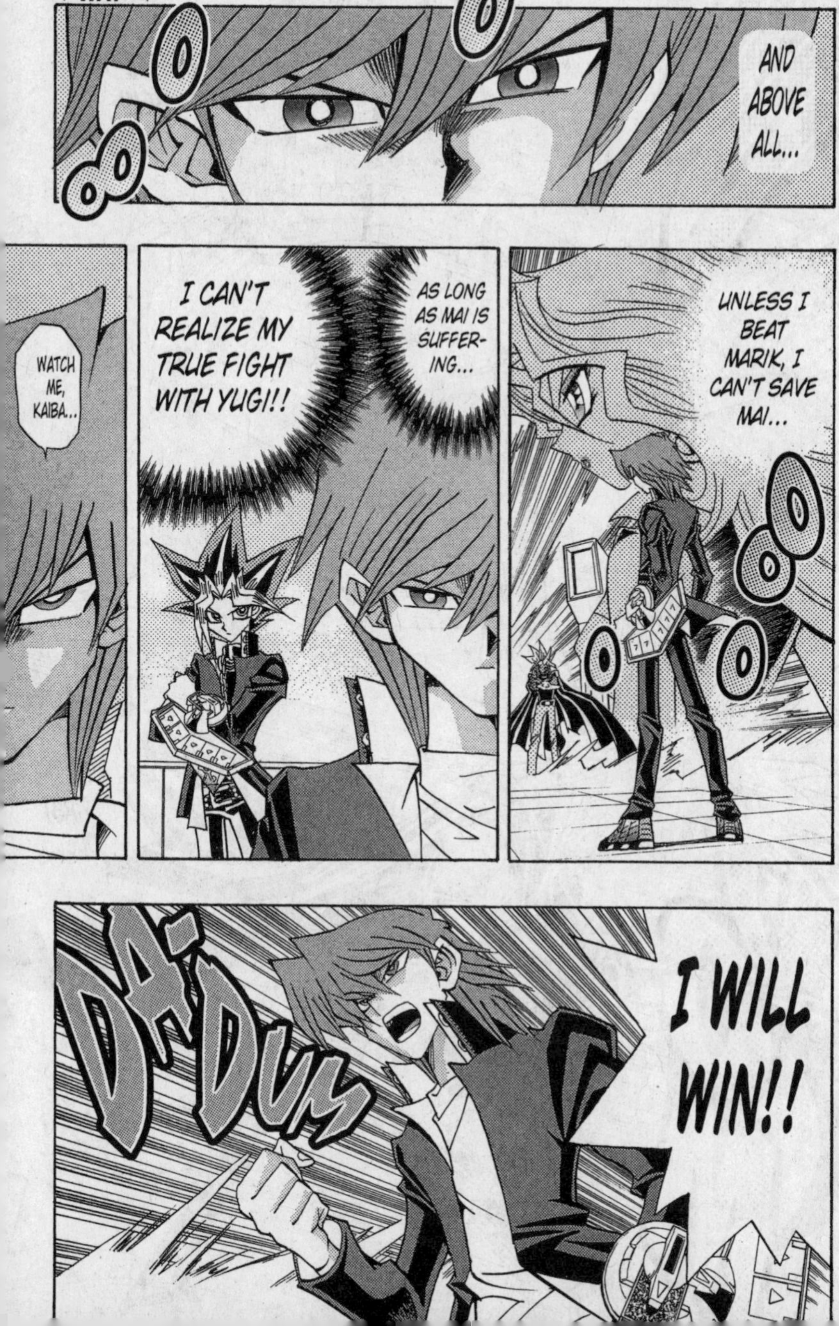
AND ABOVE ALL...
UNLESS I BEAT MARIK, I CAN'T SAVE MAI...
AS LONG AS MAI IS SUFFER-ING...
I CAN'T REALIZE MY TRUE FIGHT WITH YUGI!!
WATCH ME, KAIBA...
I WILL WIN!!
DA-DUM

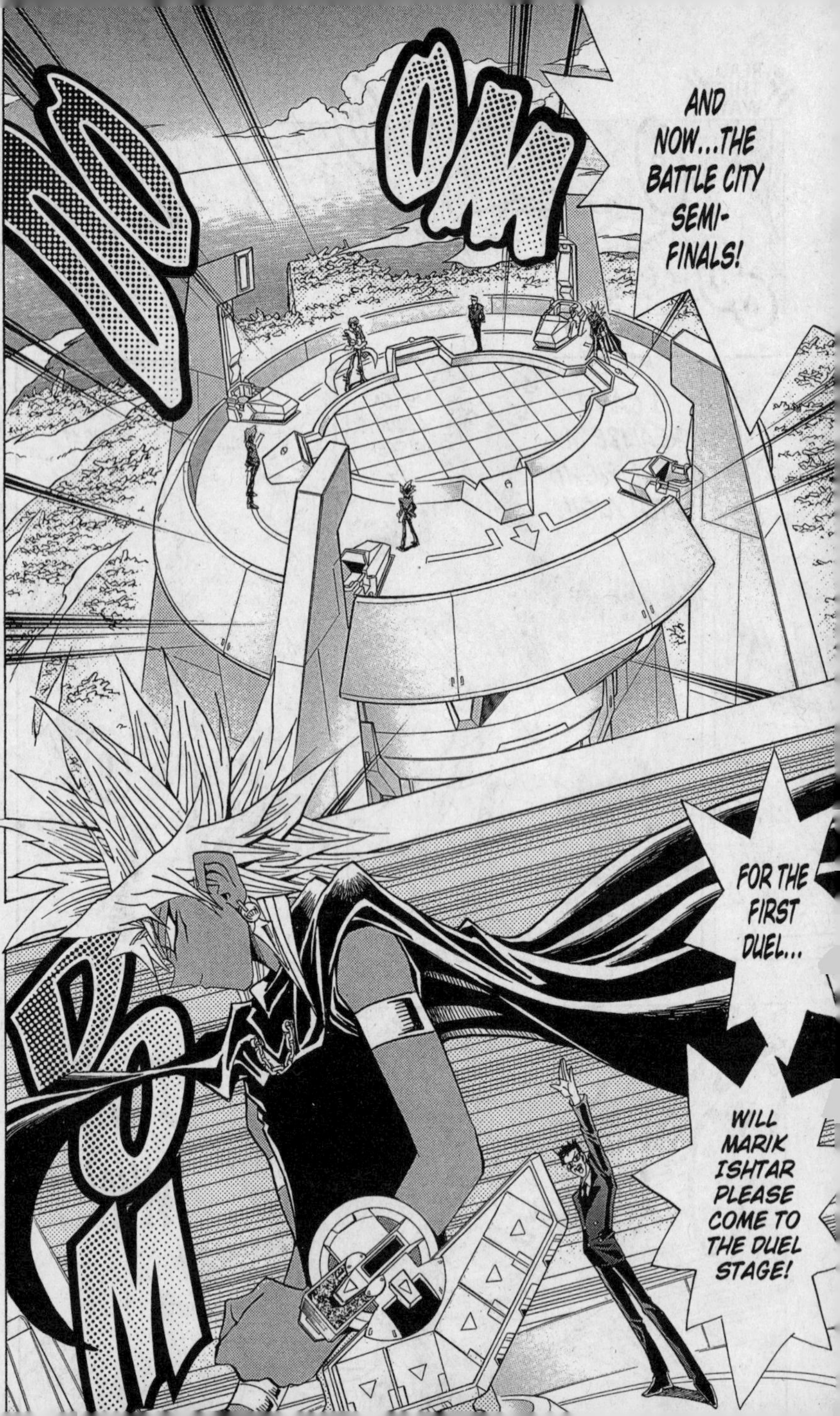
AND NOW...THE BATTLE CITY SEMI-FINALS!
FOR THE FIRST DUEL...
WILL MARIK ISHTAR PLEASE COME TO THE DUEL STAGE!

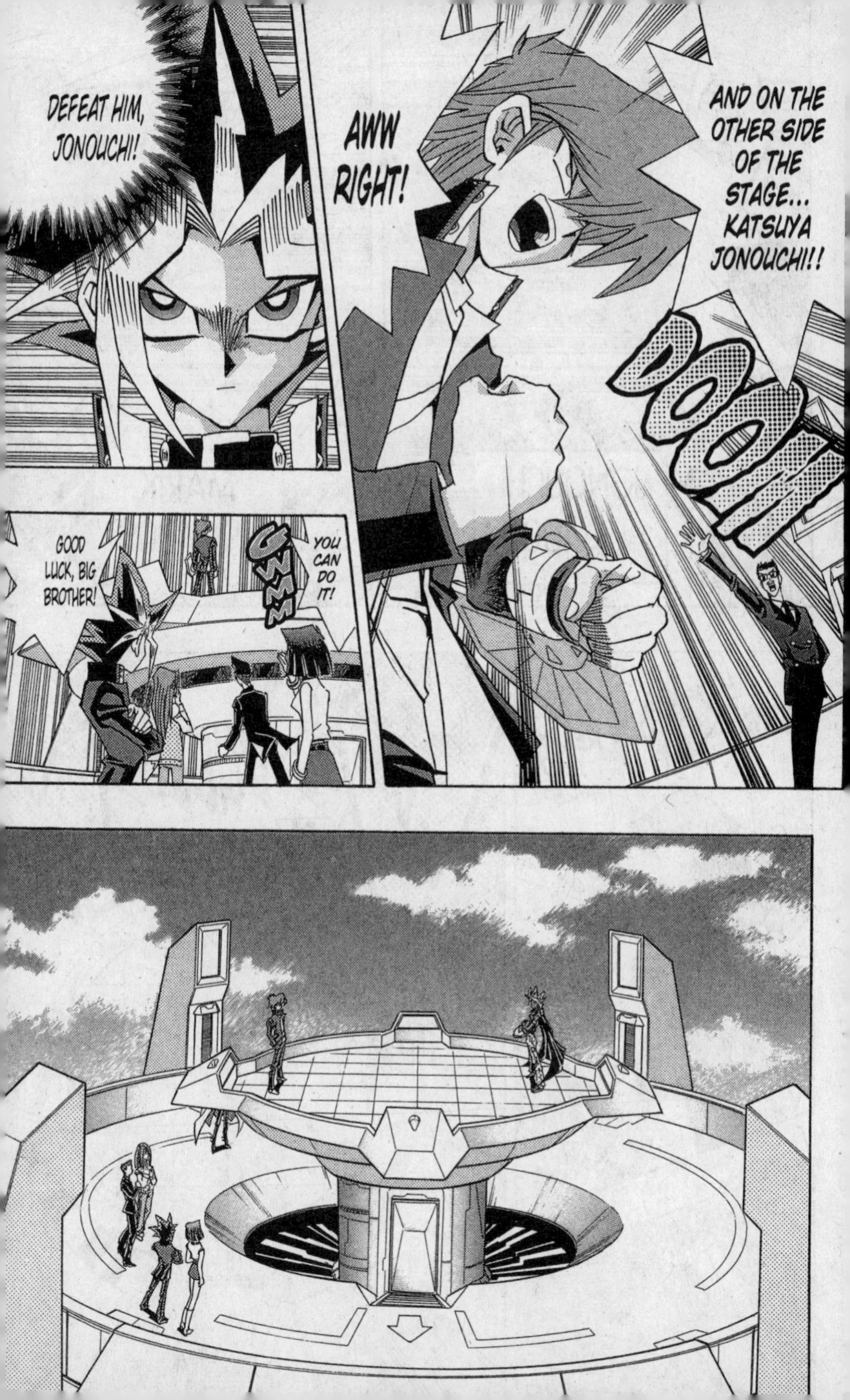
AND ON THE OTHER SIDE OF THE STAGE... KATSUYA JONOUCHI!!
AWW RIGHT!
DOOM
DEFEAT HIM, JONOUCHI!
YOU CAN DO IT!
GOOD LUCK, BIG BROTHER!

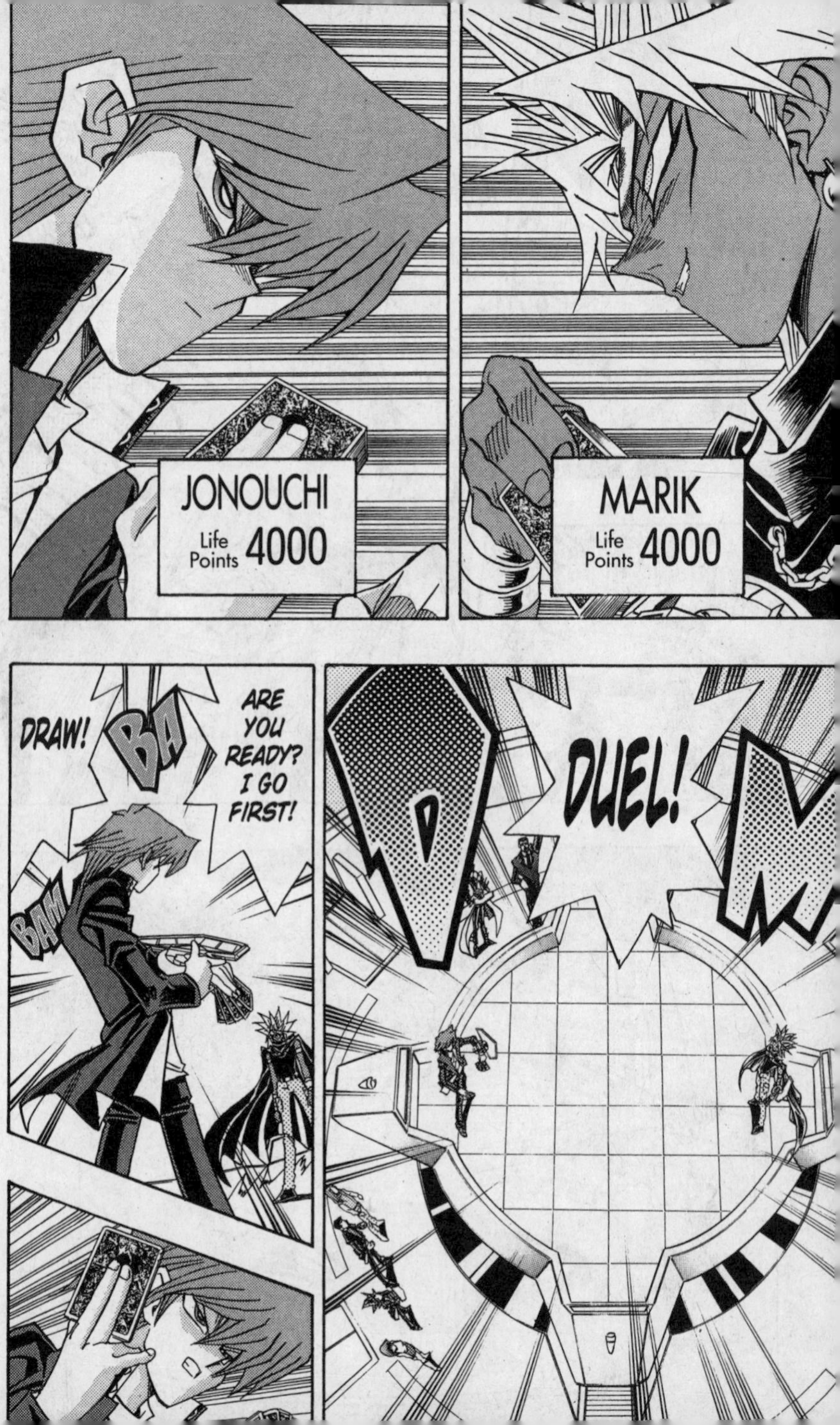
MARIK
Life Points 4000
JONOUCHI
Life Points 4000
M
DUEL!
D
ARE YOU READY? I GO FIRST!
BA
DRAW!
BAM

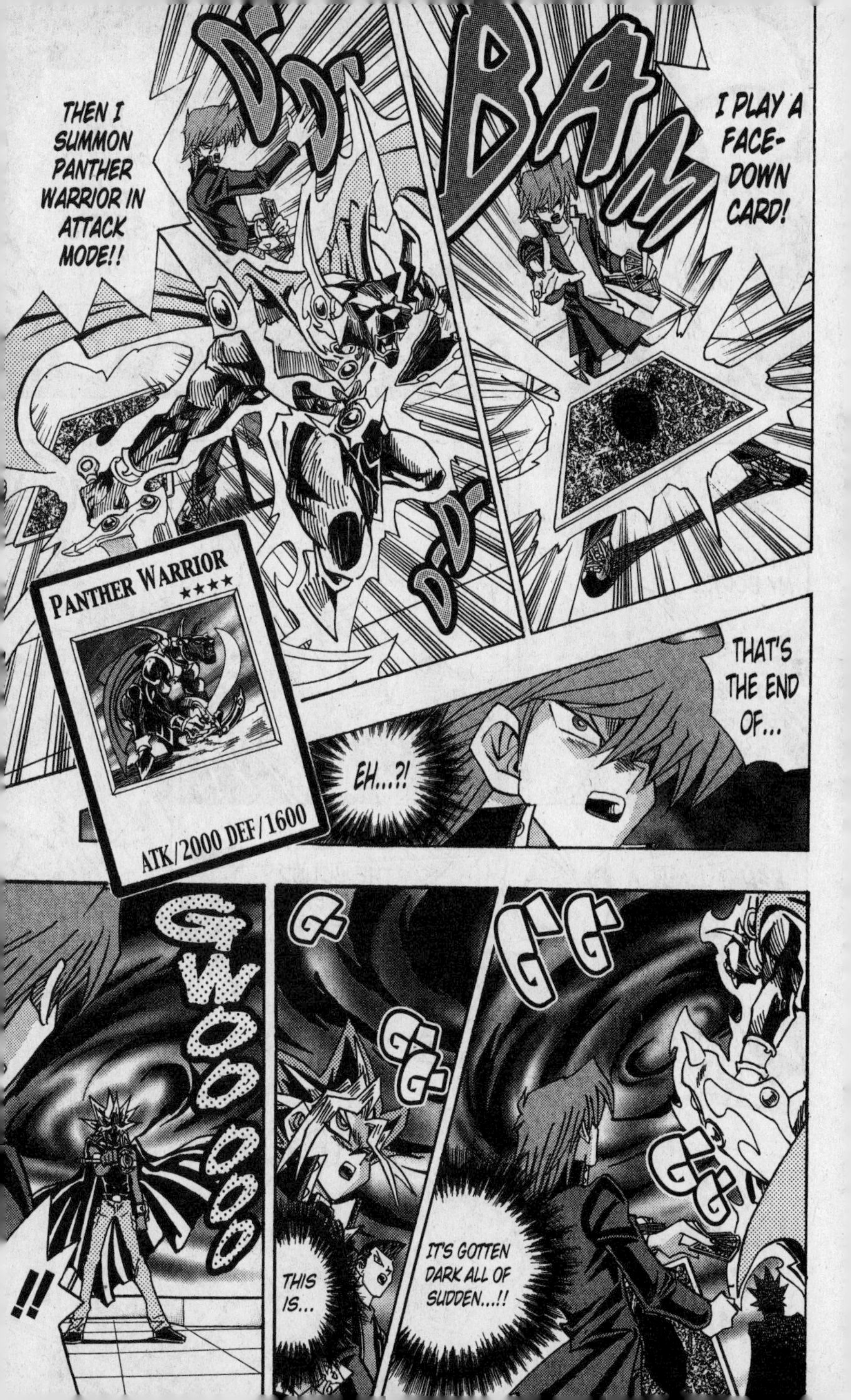
BAM
I PLAY A FACE-DOWN CARD!
THEN I SUMMON PANTHER WARRIOR IN ATTACK MODE!!
PANTHER WARRIOR ★★★★
ATK/2000 DEF/1600
THAT'S THE END OF...
EH...?!
IT'S GOTTEN DARK ALL OF SUDDEN...!!
THIS IS...
GWOOOOOO!!

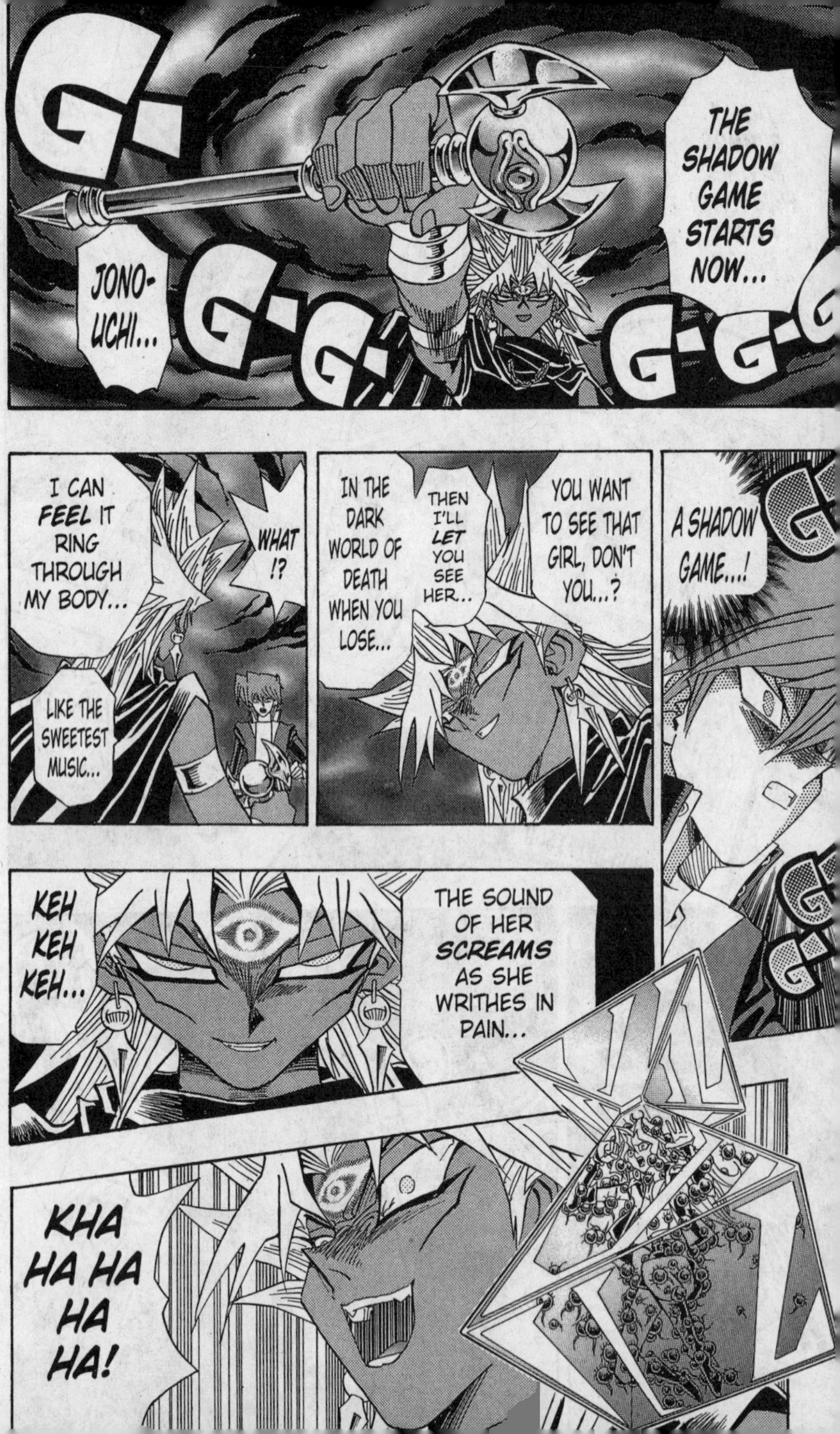
THE SHADOW GAME STARTS NOW...
G-G-G
JONO-UCHI...
G-G-
G-
A SHADOW GAME...!
G-
G-G-
YOU WANT TO SEE THAT GIRL, DON'T YOU...?
THEN I'LL *LET* YOU SEE HER...
IN THE DARK WORLD OF DEATH WHEN YOU LOSE...
WHAT!?
I CAN *FEEL* IT RING THROUGH MY BODY...
LIKE THE SWEETEST MUSIC...
THE SOUND OF HER *SCREAMS* AS SHE WRITHES IN PAIN...
KEH KEH KEH...
KHA HA HA HA HA!

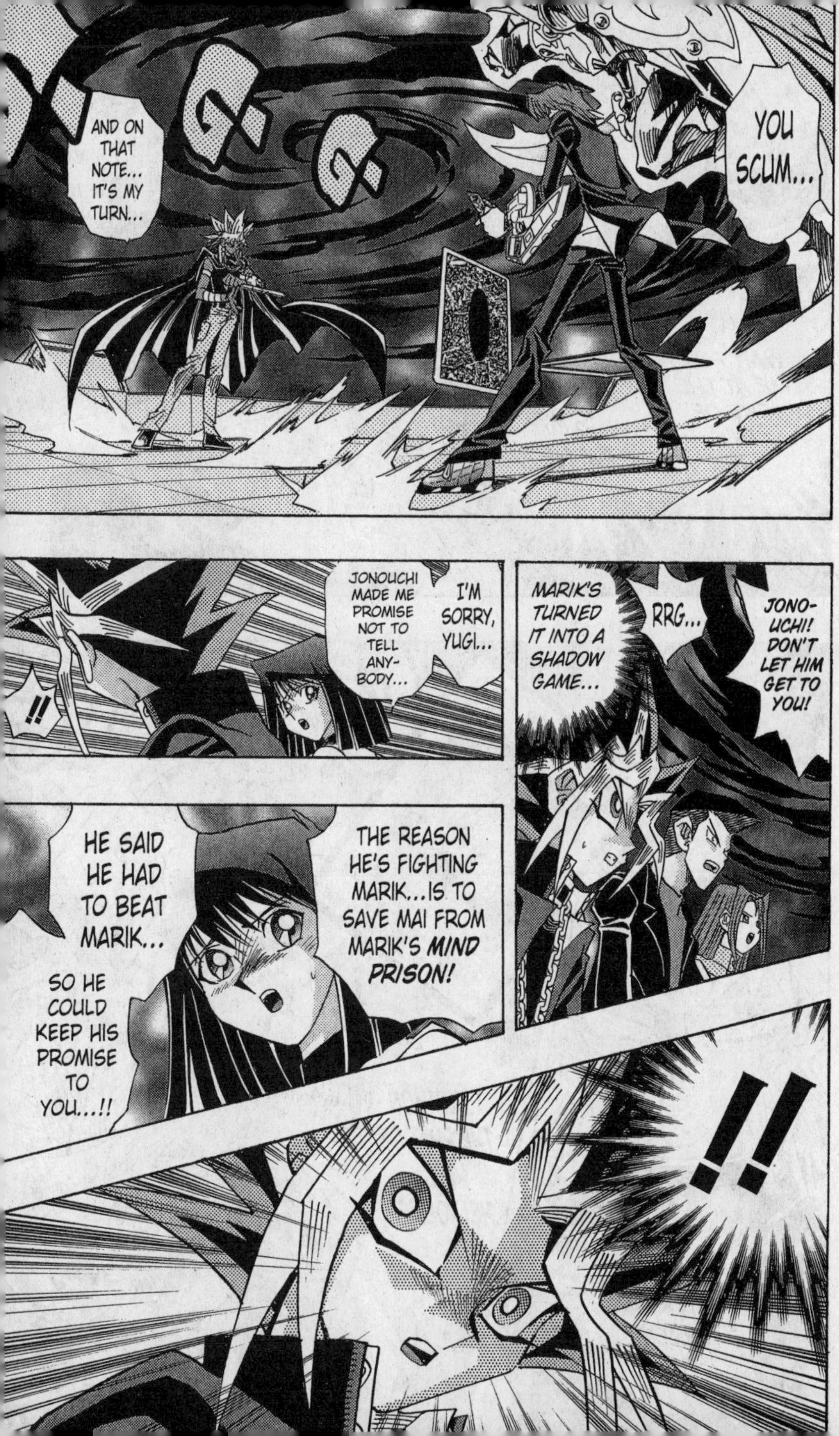
YOU SCUM...
AND ON THAT NOTE... IT'S MY TURN...
JONOUCHI! DON'T LET HIM GET TO YOU!
RRG...
MARIK'S TURNED IT INTO A SHADOW GAME...
I'M SORRY, YUGI...
JONOUCHI MADE ME PROMISE NOT TO TELL ANYBODY...
!!
THE REASON HE'S FIGHTING MARIK...IS TO SAVE MAI FROM MARIK'S *MIND PRISON!*
HE SAID HE HAD TO BEAT MARIK...
SO HE COULD KEEP HIS PROMISE TO YOU...!!
!!

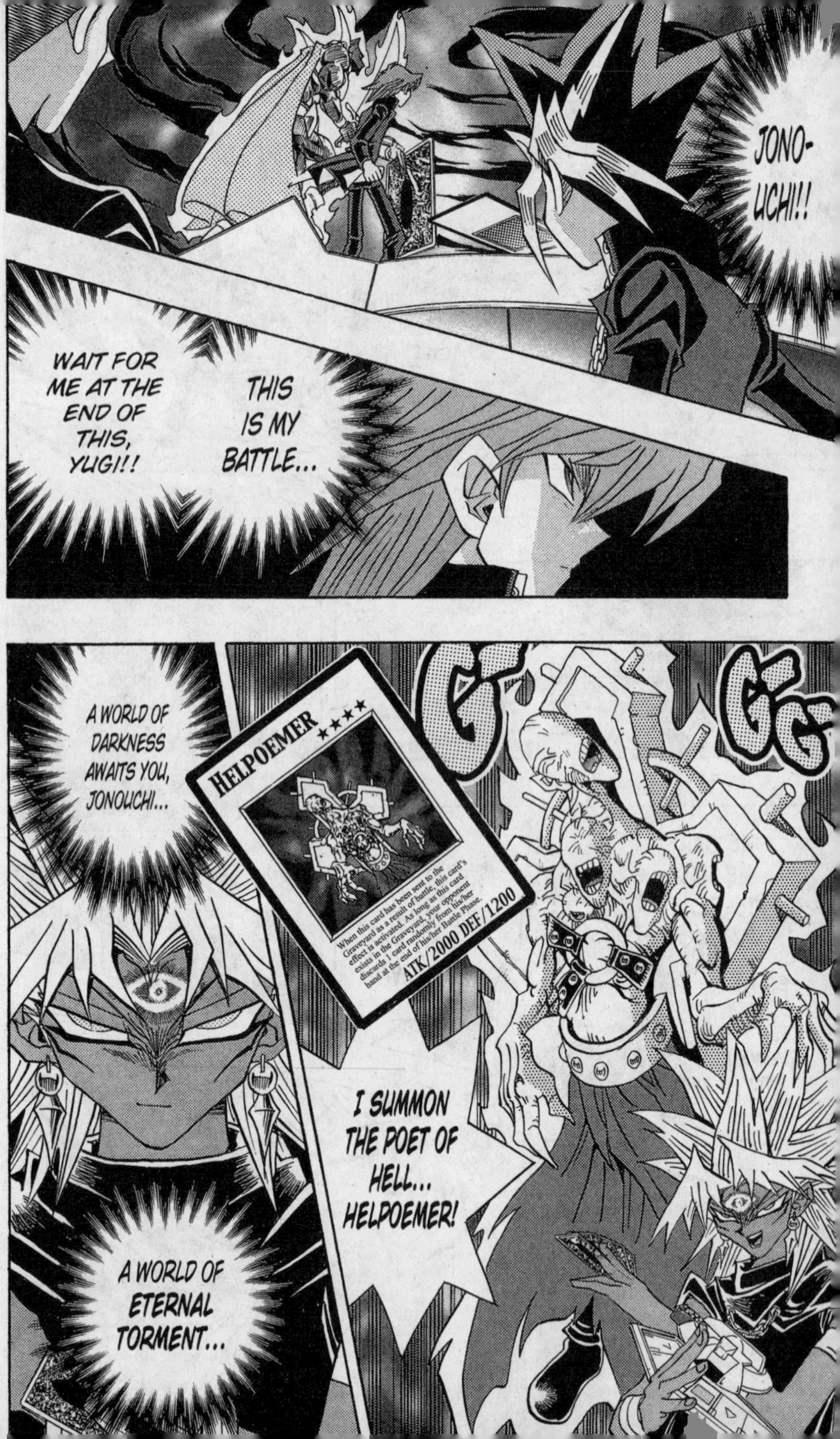
JONO-UCHI!!
THIS IS MY BATTLE...
WAIT FOR ME AT THE END OF THIS, YUGI!!
GG
G
HELPOEMER ★★★★
When this card has been sent to the Graveyard as a result of battle, this card's effect is activated. As long as this card exists in the Graveyard, your opponent discards 1 card randomly from his/her hand at the end of his/her Battle Phase.
ATK/2000 DEF/1200
I SUMMON THE POET OF HELL... HELPOEMER!
A WORLD OF DARKNESS AWAITS YOU, JONOUCHI...
A WORLD OF ETERNAL TORMENT...

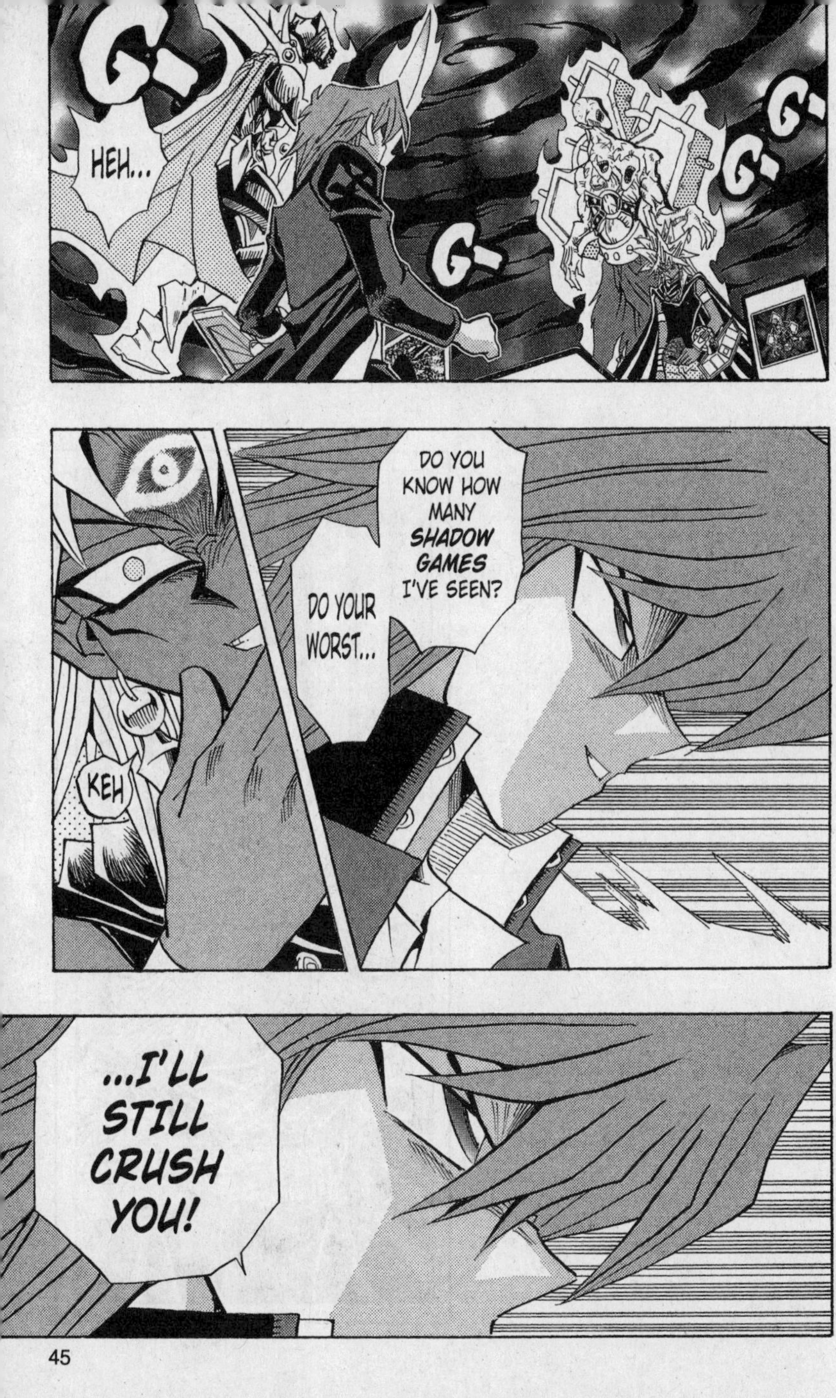
G- G- G-
G-
HEH...
G-
DO YOU KNOW HOW MANY SHADOW GAMES I'VE SEEN?
DO YOUR WORST...
KEH
...I'LL STILL CRUSH YOU!

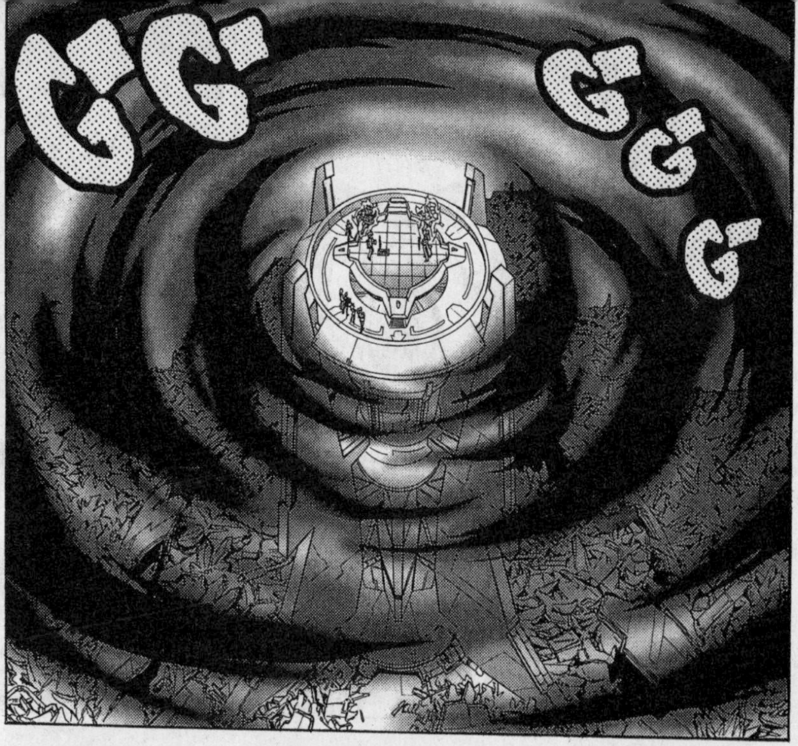
G-G-G-
G-G-

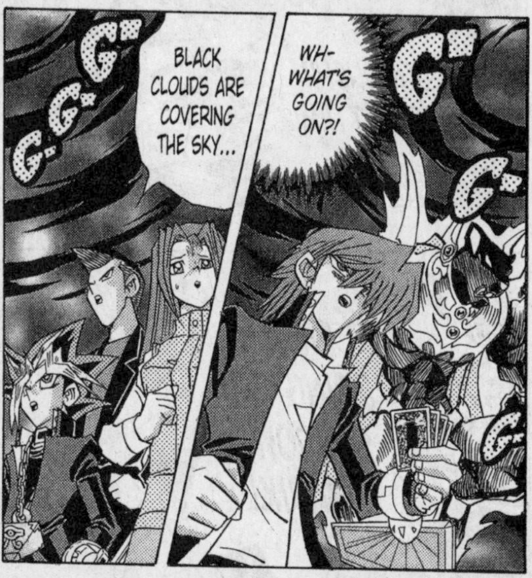
G-
WH- WHAT'S GOING ON?!
G-
G-
BLACK CLOUDS ARE COVERING THE SKY...
G-G-G-

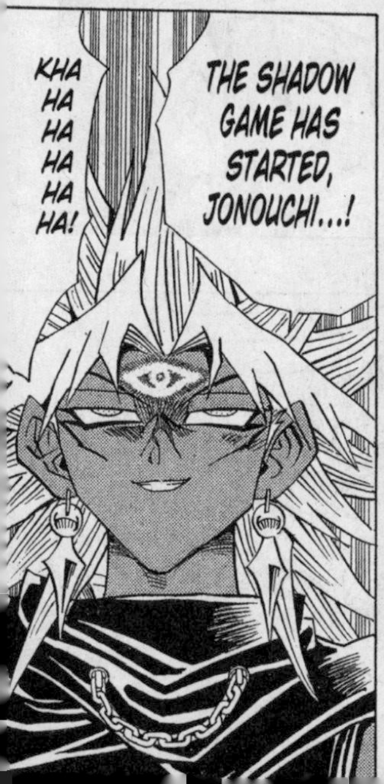
THE SHADOW GAME HAS STARTED, JONOUCHI...!
KHA HA HA HA HA HA!

Duel 244: The Hymn of Hell

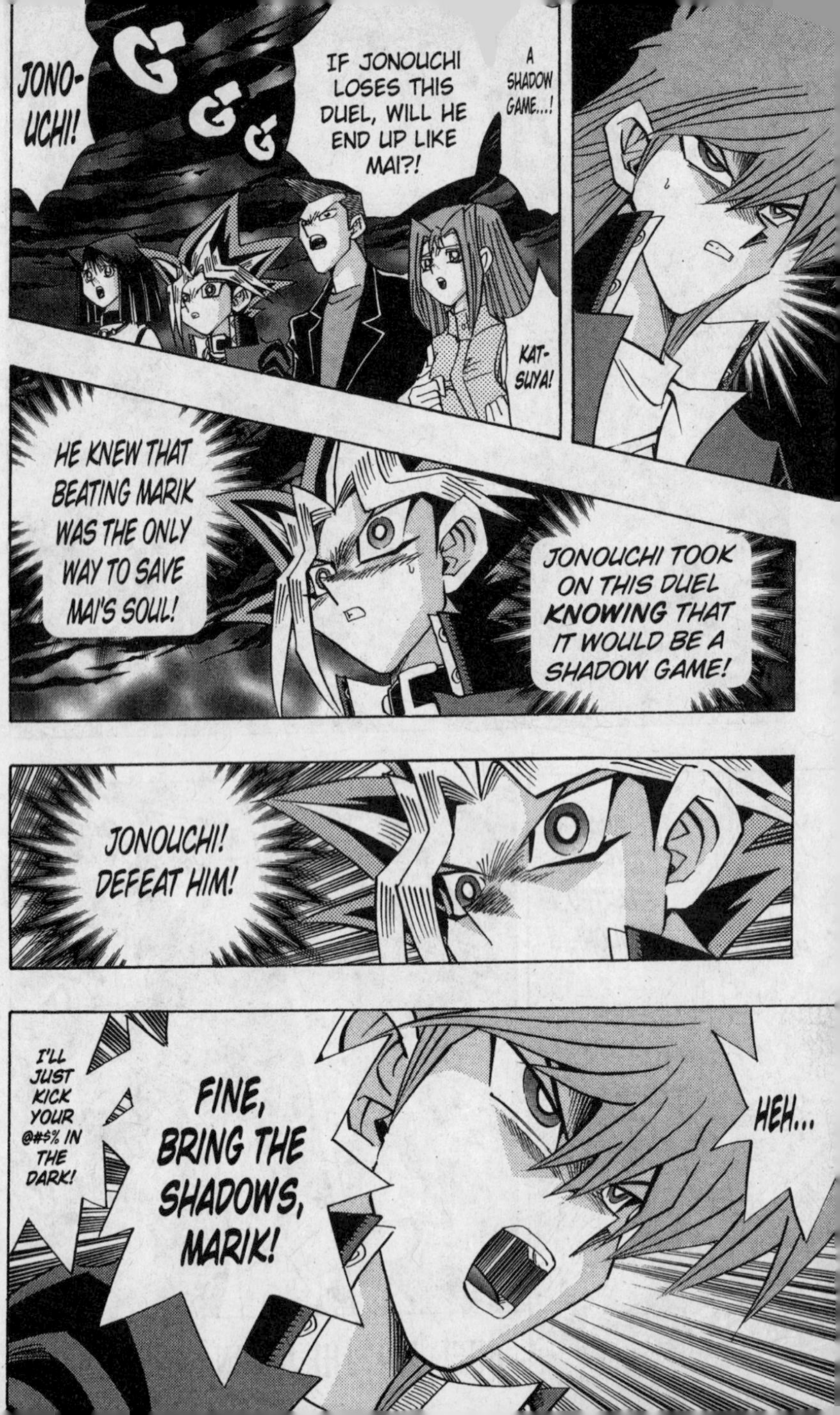
A SHADOW GAME...!
IF JONOUCHI LOSES THIS DUEL, WILL HE END UP LIKE MAI?!
G G G
JONO-UCHI!
KAT-SUYA!
JONOUCHI TOOK ON THIS DUEL KNOWING THAT IT WOULD BE A SHADOW GAME!
HE KNEW THAT BEATING MARIK WAS THE ONLY WAY TO SAVE MAI'S SOUL!
JONOUCHI! DEFEAT HIM!
HEH...
FINE, BRING THE SHADOWS, MARIK!
I'LL JUST KICK YOUR @#$% IN THE DARK!

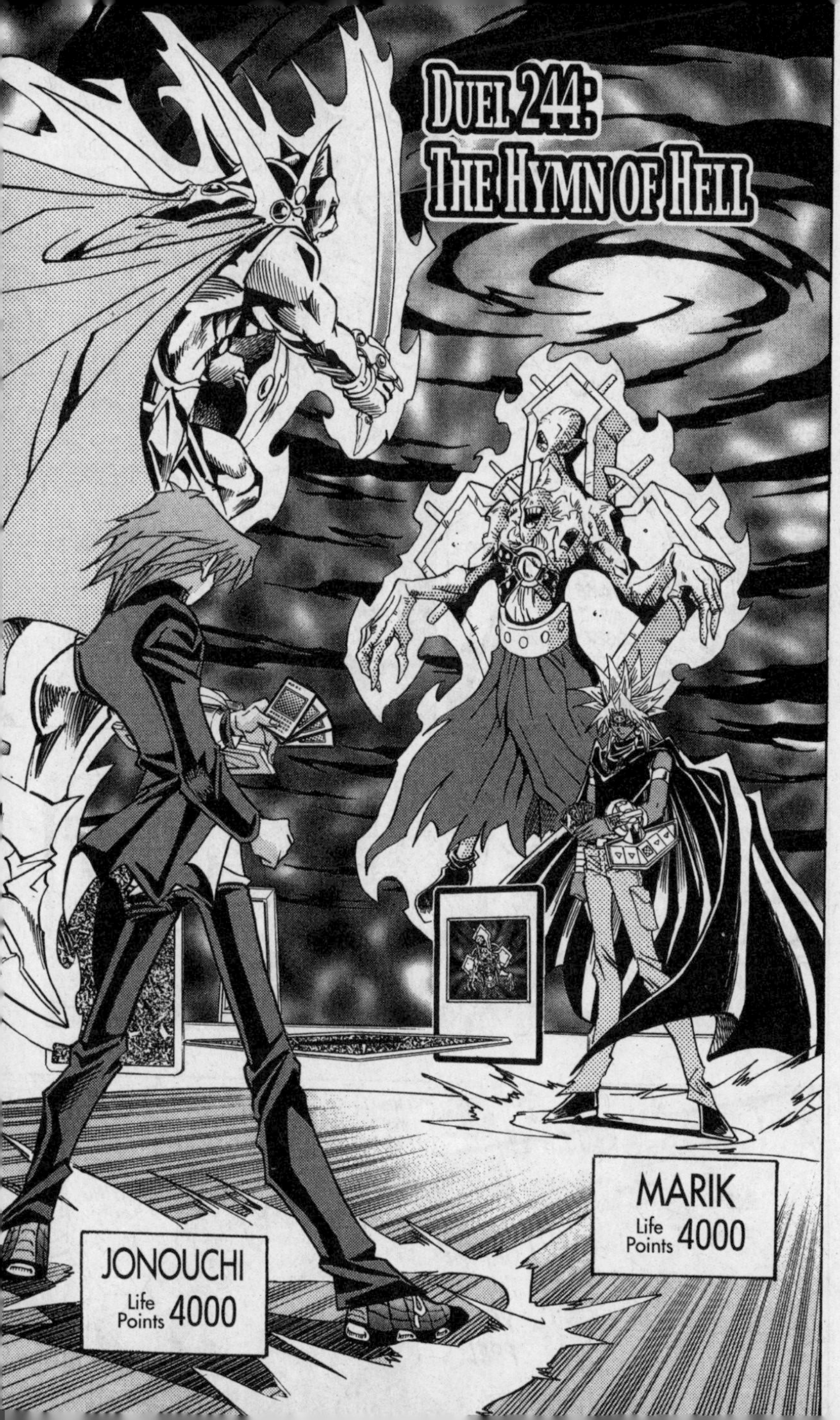
DUEL 244:
THE HYMN OF HELL
MARIK
Life Points 4000
JONOUCHI
Life Points 4000

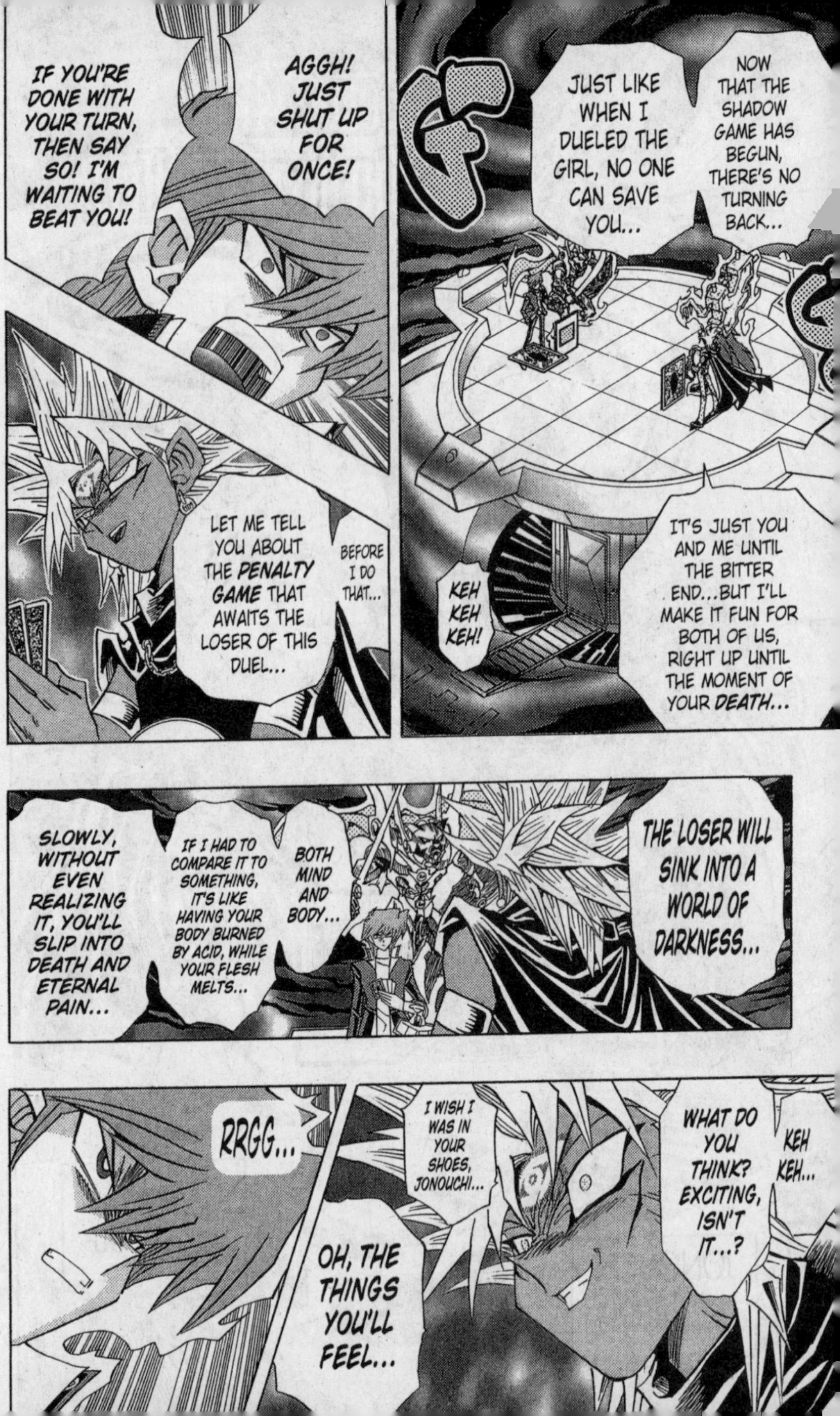
NOW THAT THE SHADOW GAME HAS BEGUN, THERE'S NO TURNING BACK...
JUST LIKE WHEN I DUELED THE GIRL, NO ONE CAN SAVE YOU...
IT'S JUST YOU AND ME UNTIL THE BITTER END...BUT I'LL MAKE IT FUN FOR BOTH OF US, RIGHT UP UNTIL THE MOMENT OF YOUR DEATH...
KEH KEH KEH!
AGGH! JUST SHUT UP FOR ONCE!
IF YOU'RE DONE WITH YOUR TURN, THEN SAY SO! I'M WAITING TO BEAT YOU!
BEFORE I DO THAT...
LET ME TELL YOU ABOUT THE PENALTY GAME THAT AWAITS THE LOSER OF THIS DUEL...
THE LOSER WILL SINK INTO A WORLD OF DARKNESS...
BOTH MIND AND BODY...
IF I HAD TO COMPARE IT TO SOMETHING, IT'S LIKE HAVING YOUR BODY BURNED BY ACID, WHILE YOUR FLESH MELTS...
SLOWLY, WITHOUT EVEN REALIZING IT, YOU'LL SLIP INTO DEATH AND ETERNAL PAIN...
KEH KEH...
WHAT DO YOU THINK? EXCITING, ISN'T IT...?
I WISH I WAS IN YOUR SHOES, JONOUCHI...
OH, THE THINGS YOU'LL FEEL...
RRGG...

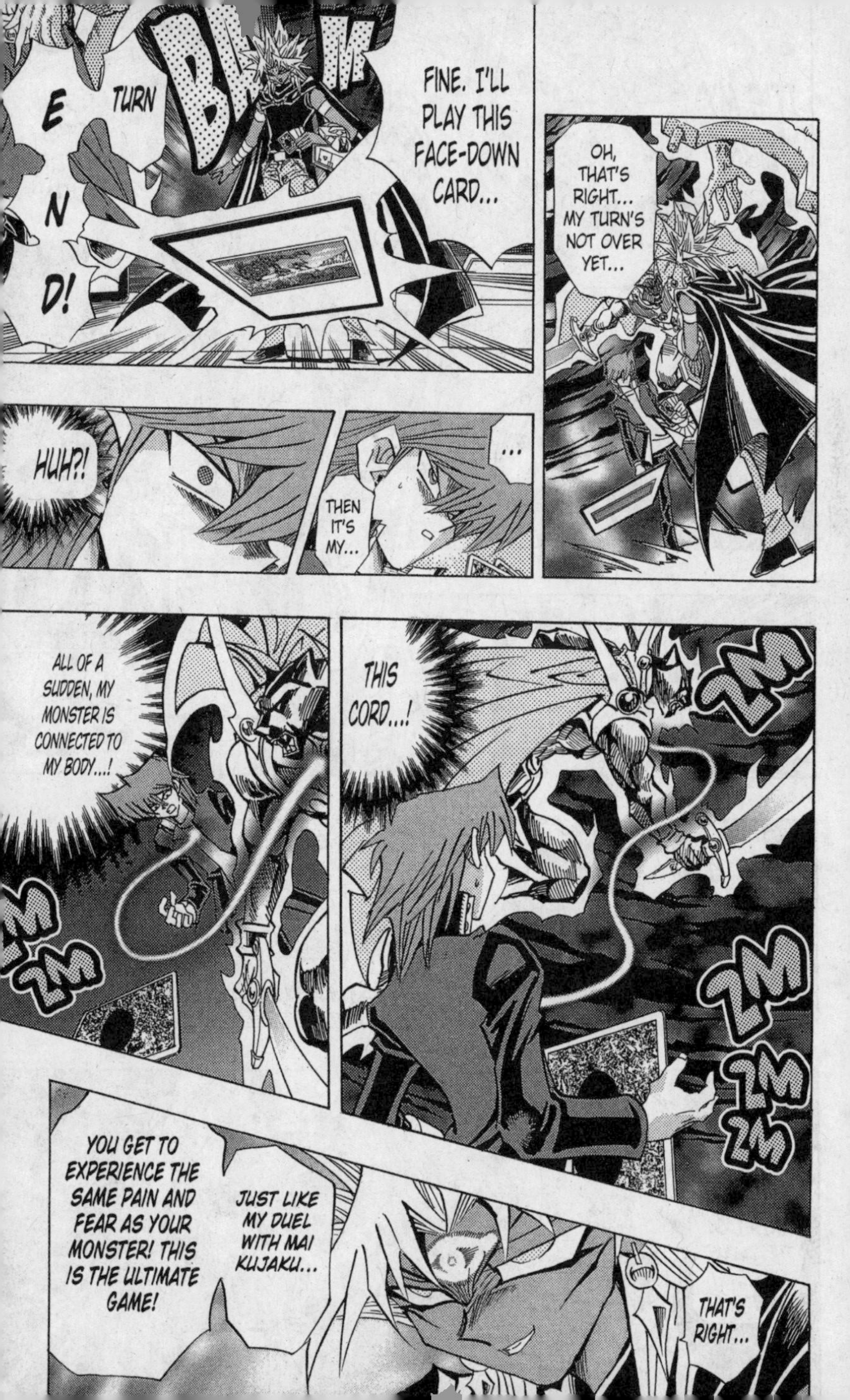
OH, THAT'S RIGHT... MY TURN'S NOT OVER YET...
FINE. I'LL PLAY THIS FACE-DOWN CARD...
BAM
TURN END!
...
THEN IT'S MY...
HUH?!
ZM ZM ZM ZM
THIS CORD...!
ALL OF A SUDDEN, MY MONSTER IS CONNECTED TO MY BODY...!
ZM ZM
THAT'S RIGHT...
JUST LIKE MY DUEL WITH MAI KUJAKU...
YOU GET TO EXPERIENCE THE SAME PAIN AND FEAR AS YOUR MONSTER! THIS IS THE ULTIMATE GAME!

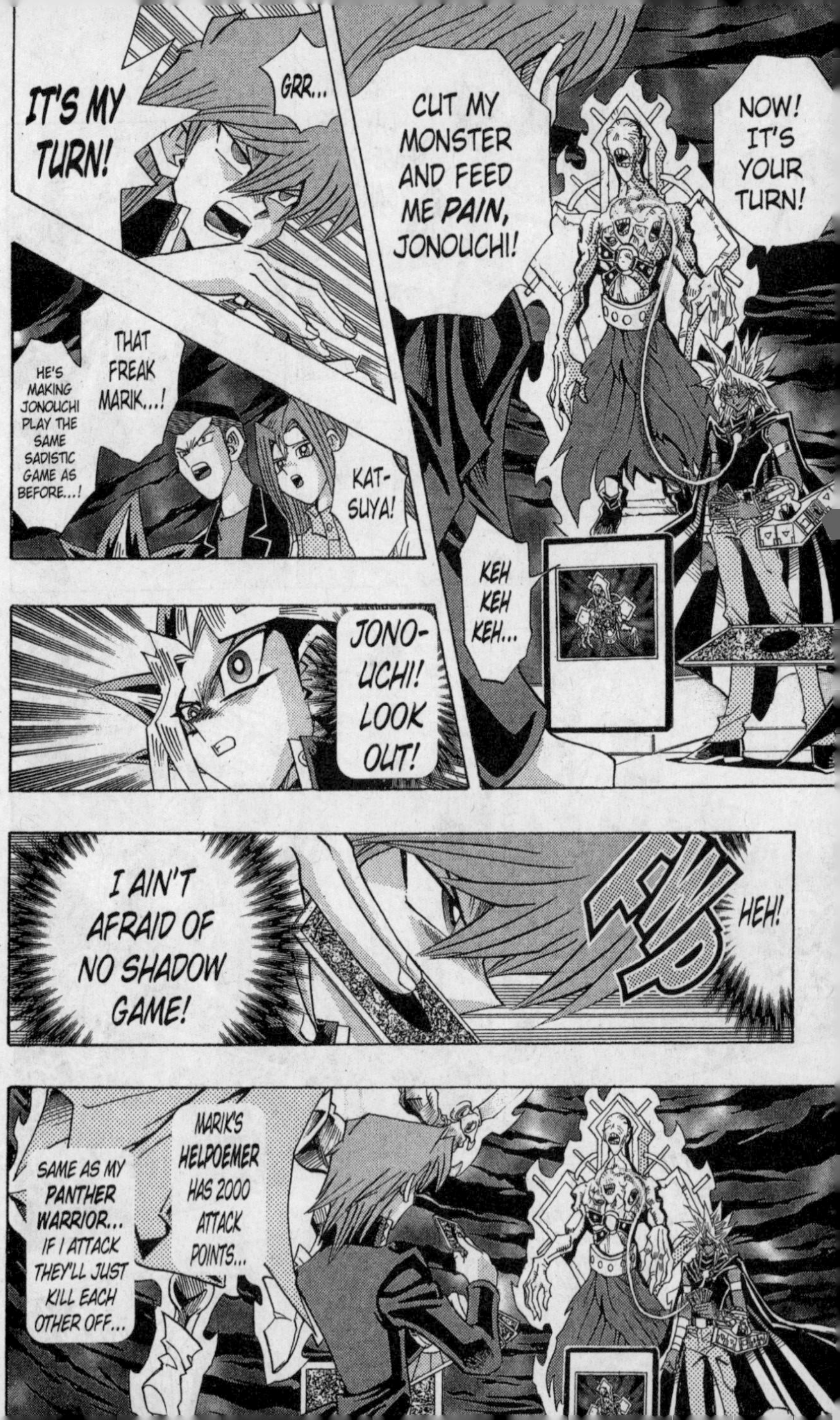
NOW! IT'S YOUR TURN!
CUT MY MONSTER AND FEED ME PAIN, JONOUCHI!
KEH KEH KEH...
GRR...
IT'S MY TURN!
KAT-SUYA!
THAT FREAK MARIK...!
HE'S MAKING JONOUCHI PLAY THE SAME SADISTIC GAME AS BEFORE...!
JONO-UCHI! LOOK OUT!
HEH!
I AIN'T AFRAID OF NO SHADOW GAME!
MARIK'S HELPOEMER HAS 2000 ATTACK POINTS...
SAME AS MY PANTHER WARRIOR... IF I ATTACK THEY'LL JUST KILL EACH OTHER OFF...

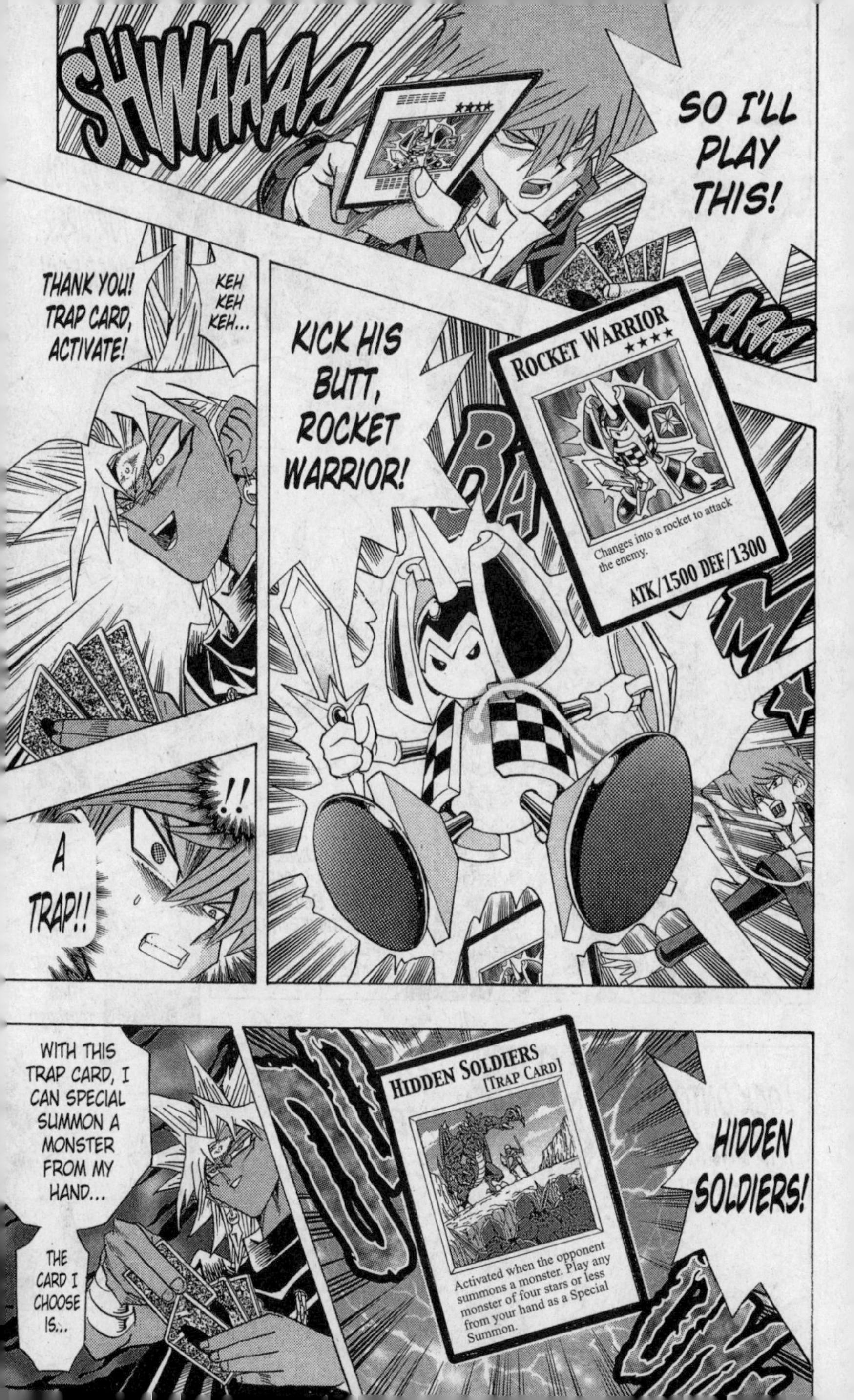
SHWAAAA
SO I'LL PLAY THIS!
KICK HIS BUTT, ROCKET WARRIOR!
ROCKET WARRIOR
Changes into a rocket to attack the enemy.
ATK/1500 DEF/1300
KEH KEH KEH...
THANK YOU! TRAP CARD, ACTIVATE!
!!
A TRAP!!
HIDDEN SOLDIERS!
HIDDEN SOLDIERS
[TRAP CARD]
Activated when the opponent summons a monster. Play any monster of four stars or less from your hand as a Special Summon.
WITH THIS TRAP CARD, I CAN SPECIAL SUMMON A MONSTER FROM MY HAND...
THE CARD I CHOOSE IS...

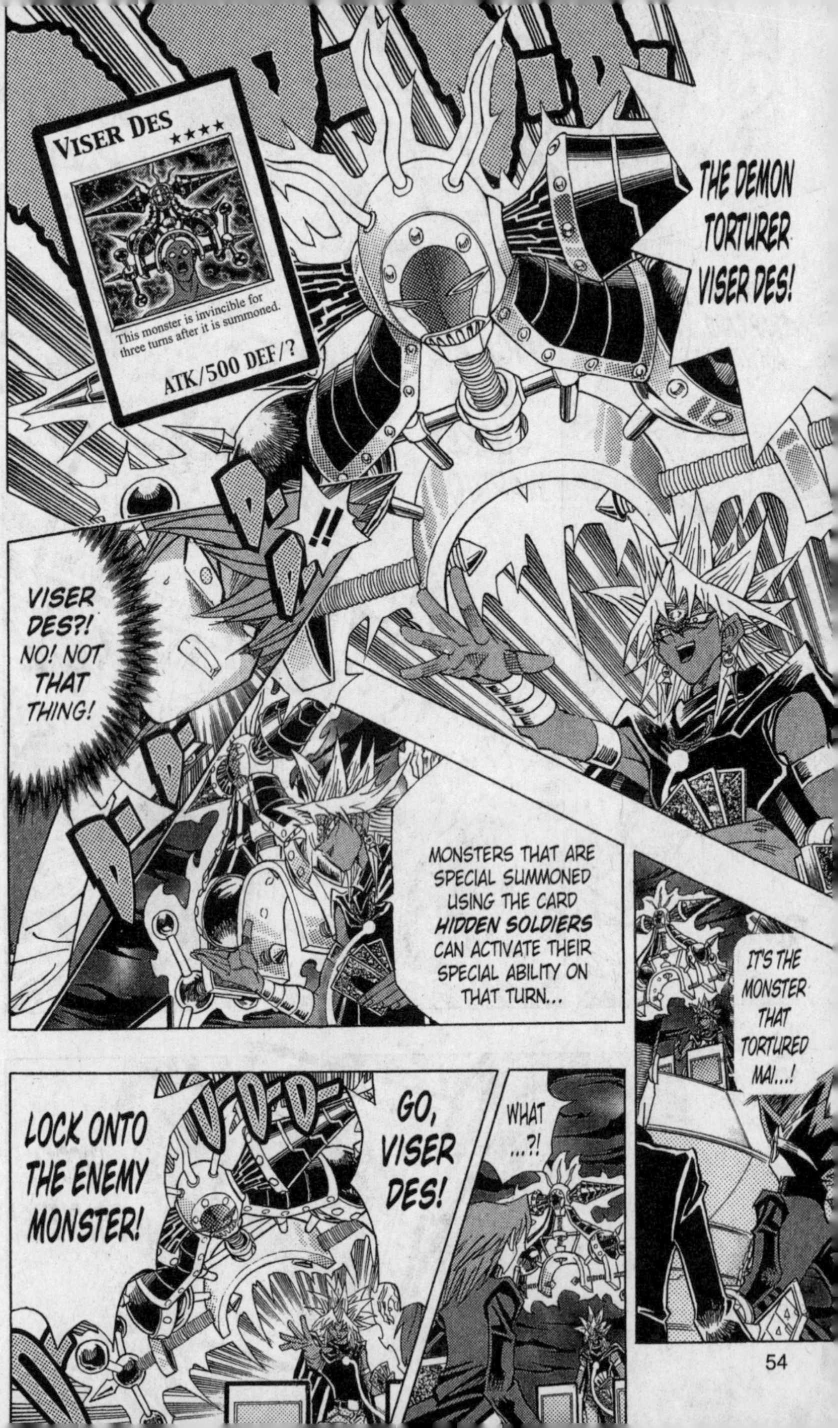

VISER DES ★★★★
This monster is invincible for three turns after it is summoned.
ATK/500 DEF/?
THE DEMON TORTURER VISER DES!
!!
VISER DES?! NO! NOT THAT THING!
IT'S THE MONSTER THAT TORTURED MAI...!
MONSTERS THAT ARE SPECIAL SUMMONED USING THE CARD HIDDEN SOLDIERS CAN ACTIVATE THEIR SPECIAL ABILITY ON THAT TURN...
WHAT ...?!
GO, VISER DES!
LOCK ONTO THE ENEMY MONSTER!

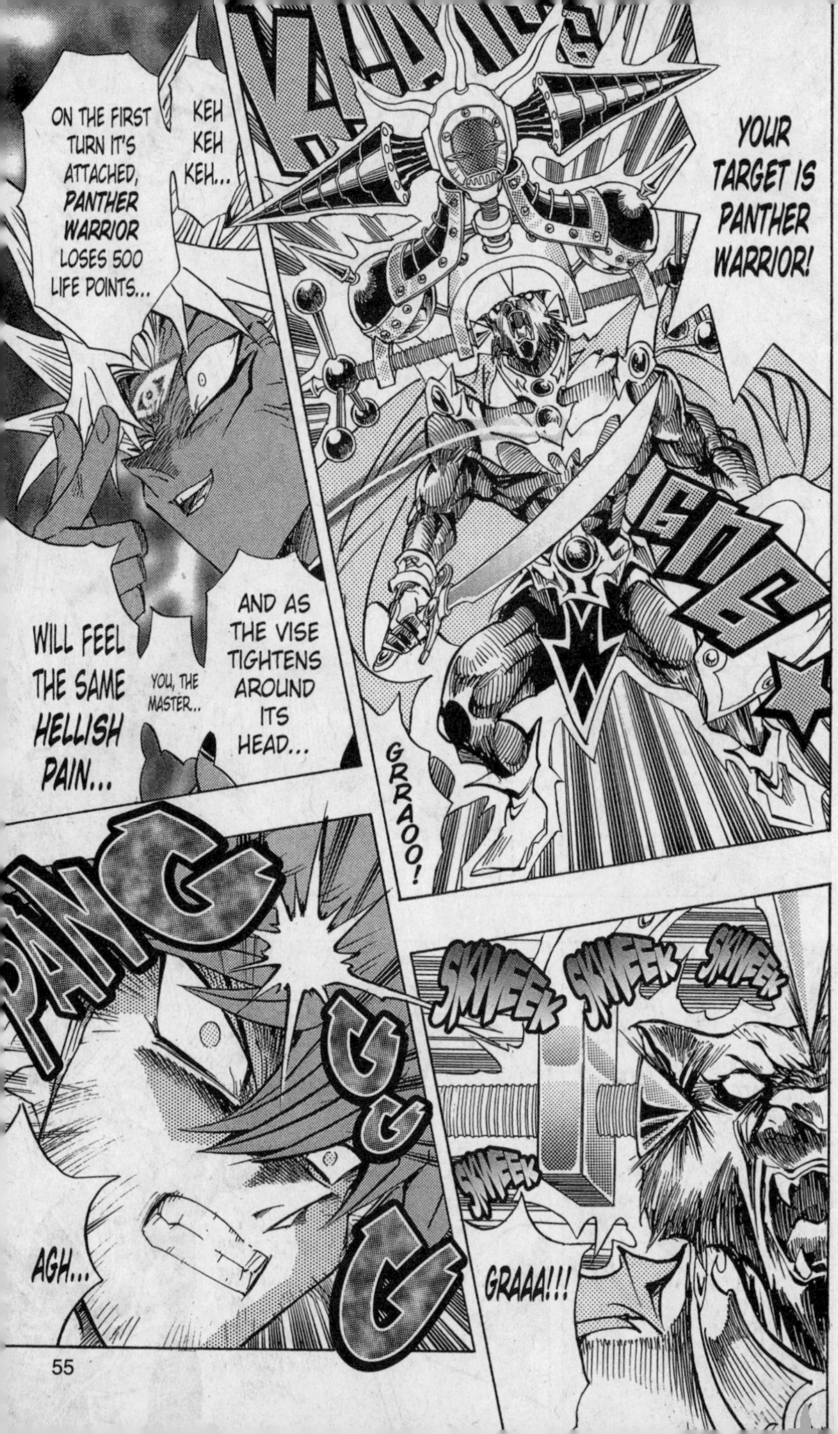
YOUR TARGET IS PANTHER WARRIOR!
GRRAOO!
KEH KEH KEH...
ON THE FIRST TURN IT'S ATTACHED, PANTHER WARRIOR LOSES 500 LIFE POINTS...
AND AS THE VISE TIGHTENS AROUND ITS HEAD...
YOU, THE MASTER...
WILL FEEL THE SAME HELLISH PAIN...
SKWEEK
SKWEEK
SKWEEK
SKWEEK
GRAAA!!!
PANG
G
G
G
AGH...

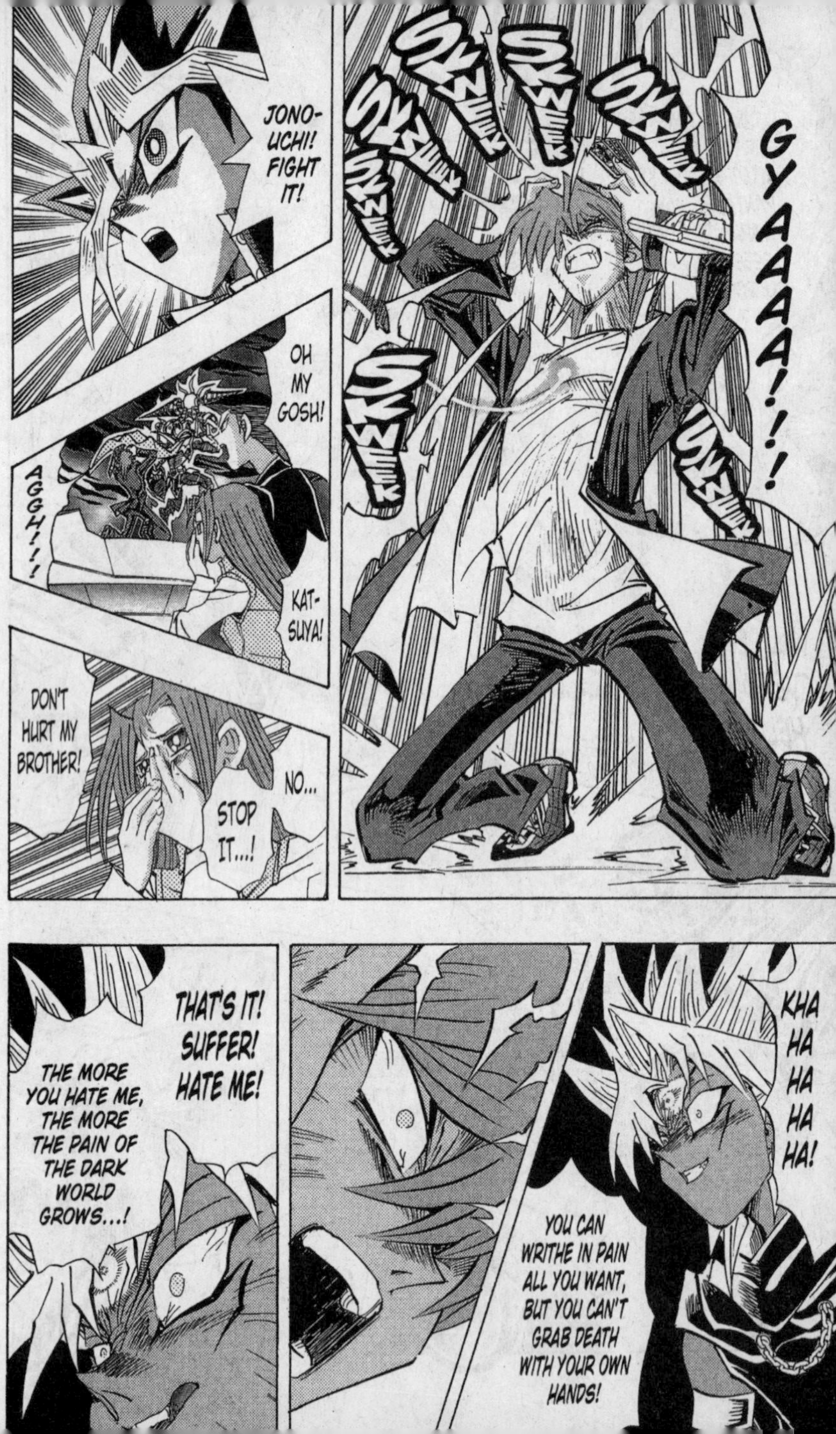
GYAAAAA!!!
SWEEK
SWEEK
SWEEK
SWEEK
SWEEK
SWEEK
JONO-UCHI! FIGHT IT!
OH MY GOSH!
AGGH!!!
KATSUYA!
NO...
STOP IT...!
DON'T HURT MY BROTHER!
KHA HA HA HA HA!
YOU CAN WRITHE IN PAIN ALL YOU WANT, BUT YOU CAN'T GRAB DEATH WITH YOUR OWN HANDS!
THAT'S IT! SUFFER! HATE ME!
THE MORE YOU HATE ME, THE MORE THE PAIN OF THE DARK WORLD GROWS...!

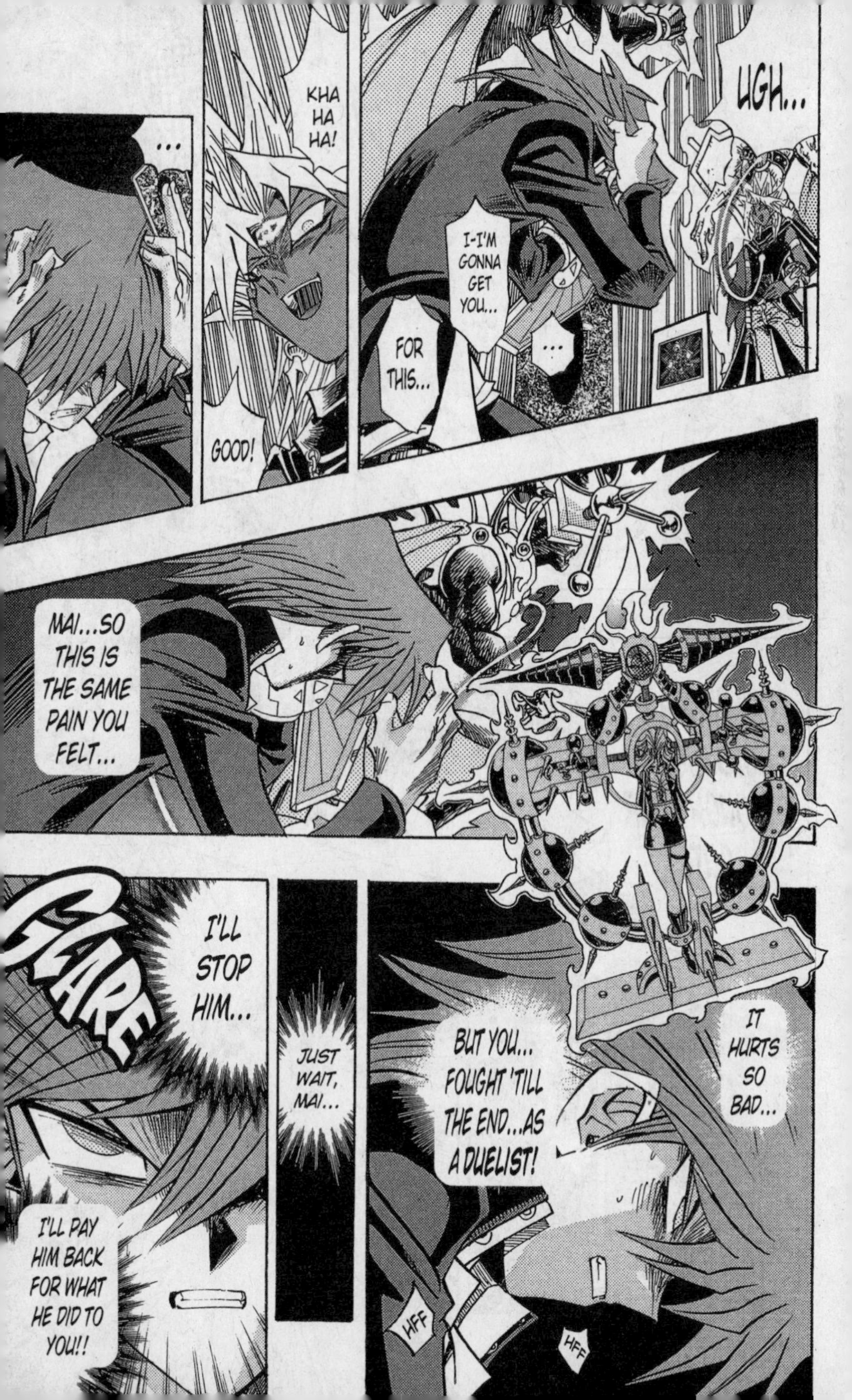
UGH...
I-I'M GONNA GET YOU...
FOR THIS...
...
KHA HA HA!
GOOD!
...
MAI...SO THIS IS THE SAME PAIN YOU FELT...
IT HURTS SO BAD...
BUT YOU... FOUGHT 'TILL THE END...AS A DUELIST!
HFF
HFF
JUST WAIT, MAI...
GLARE
I'LL STOP HIM...
I'LL PAY HIM BACK FOR WHAT HE DID TO YOU!!

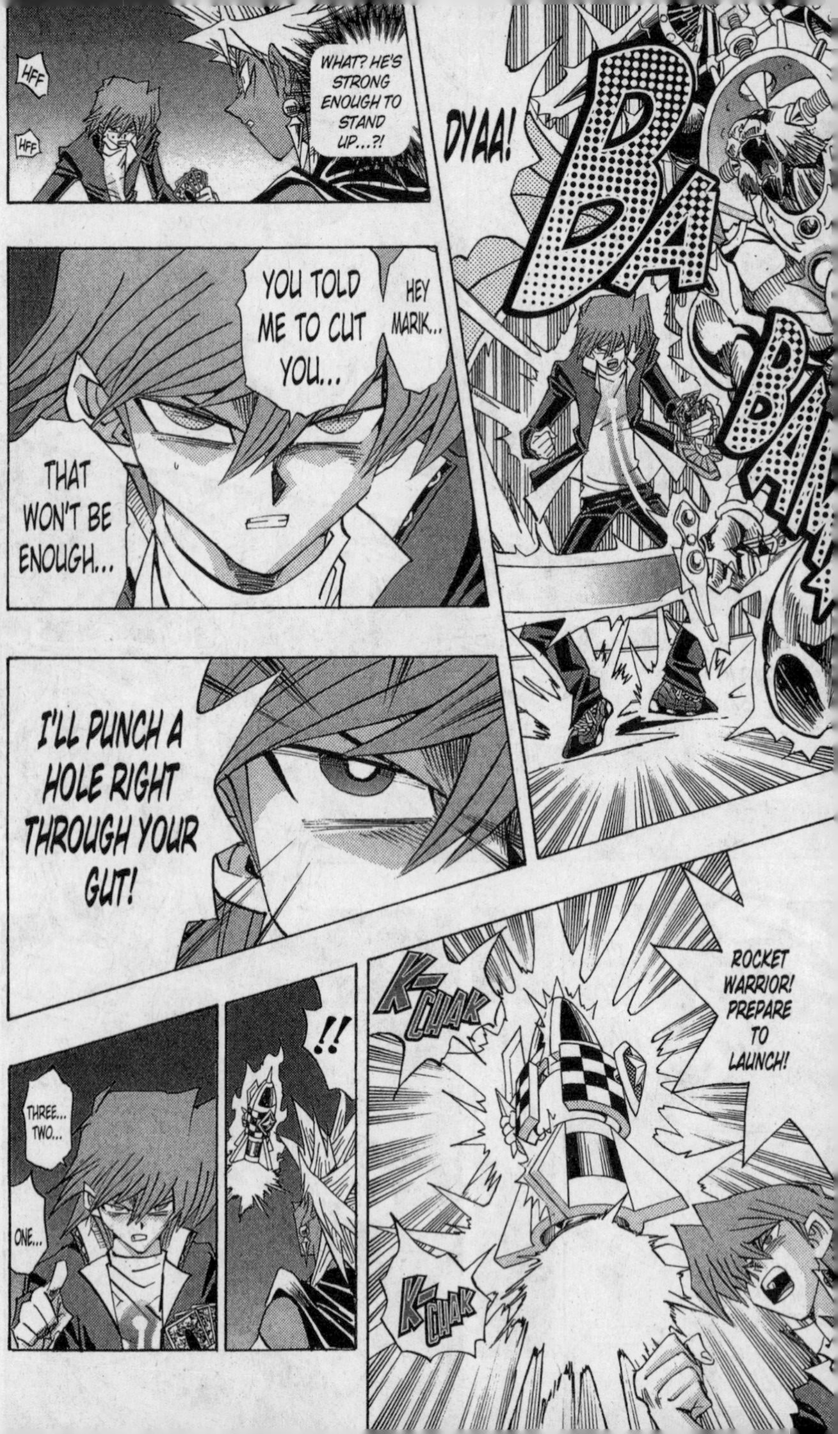
DYAA!
BADA
BADAM
HFF
HFF
WHAT? HE'S STRONG ENOUGH TO STAND UP...?!
HEY MARIK...
YOU TOLD ME TO CUT YOU...
THAT WON'T BE ENOUGH...
I'LL PUNCH A HOLE RIGHT THROUGH YOUR GUT!
ROCKET WARRIOR! PREPARE TO LAUNCH!
K-CHAK
K-CHAK
!!
THREE... TWO...
ONE...

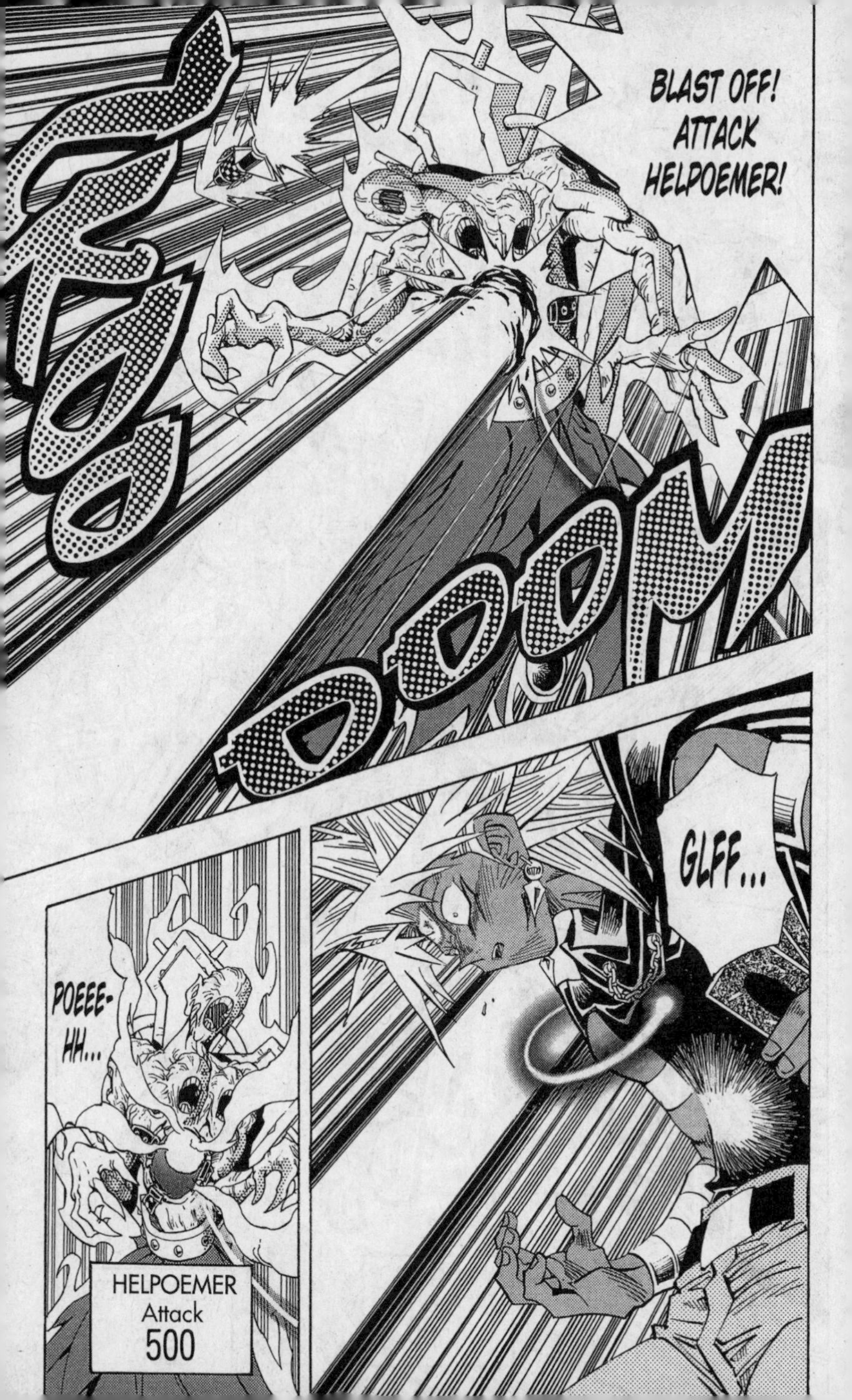
BLAST OFF! ATTACK HELPOEMER!
GLFF...
POEEE-HH...
HELPOEMER
Attack
500

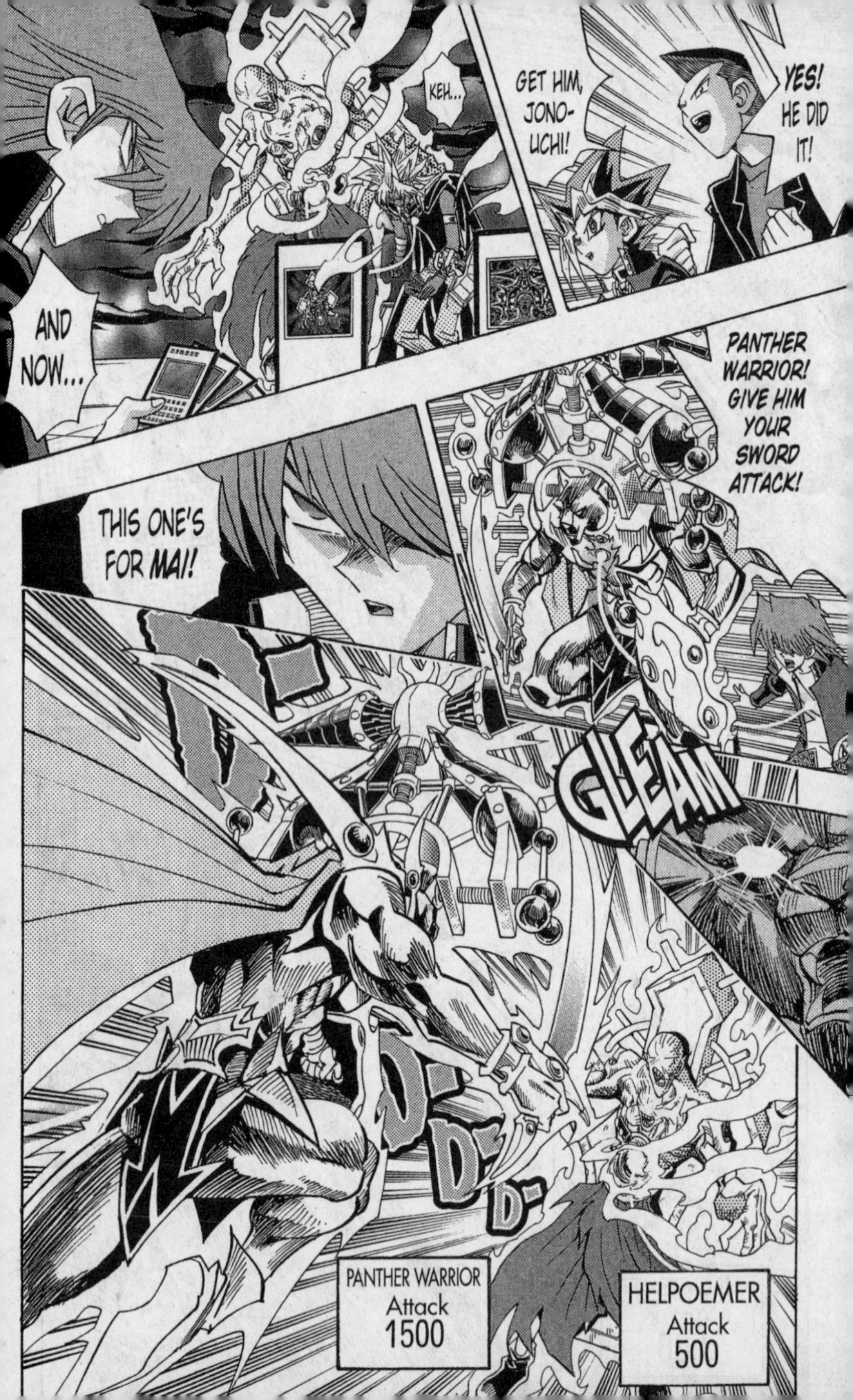
YES! HE DID IT!
GET HIM, JONO-UCHI!
KEH...
AND NOW...
PANTHER WARRIOR! GIVE HIM YOUR SWORD ATTACK!
THIS ONE'S FOR MAI!
GLEAM
D-D-D-
HELPOEMER Attack 500
PANTHER WARRIOR Attack 1500

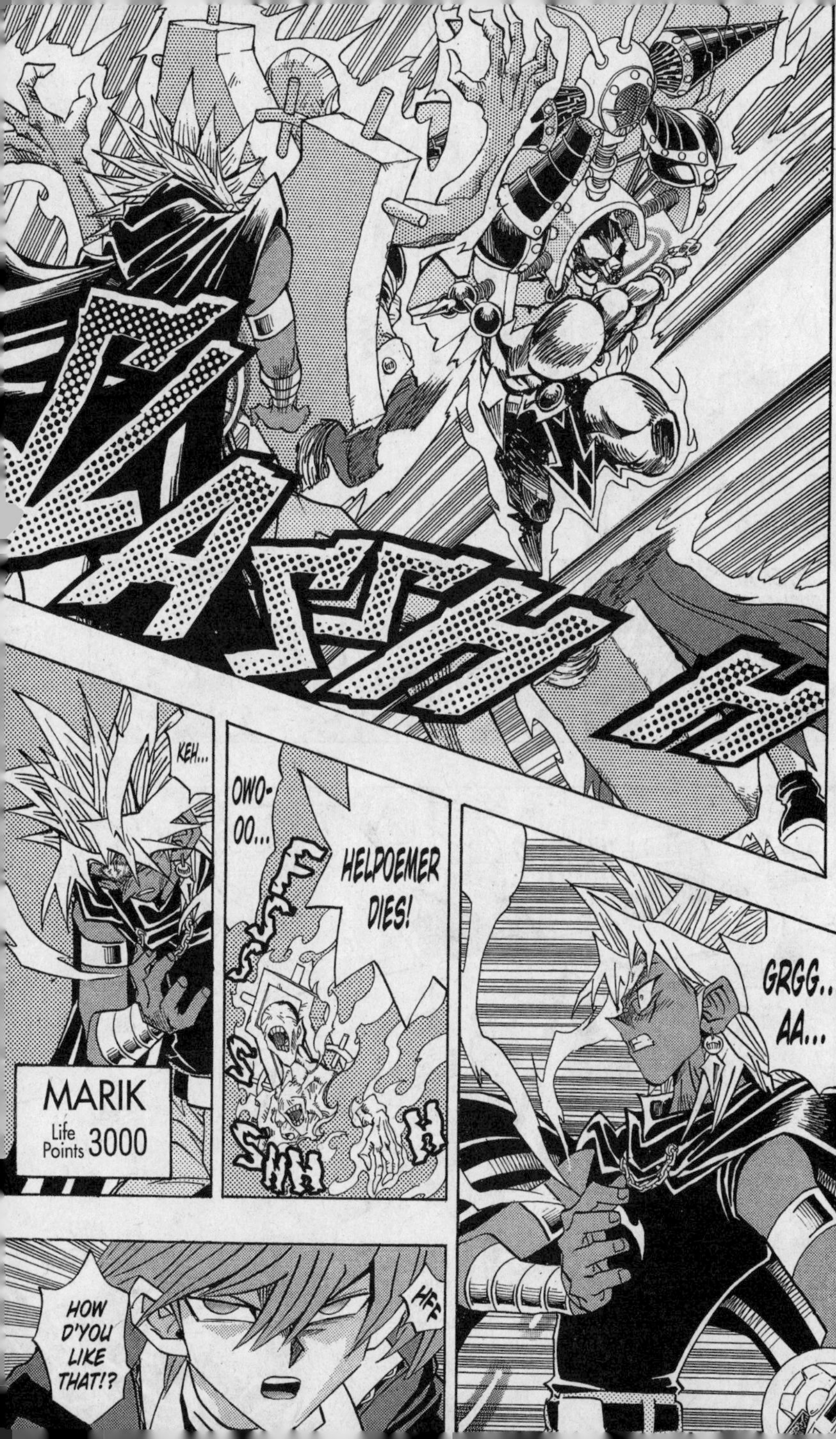
GRGG... AA...
OWOO-OO...
HELPOEMER DIES!
KEH...
MARIK
Life Points 3000
HFF
HOW D'YOU LIKE THAT!?

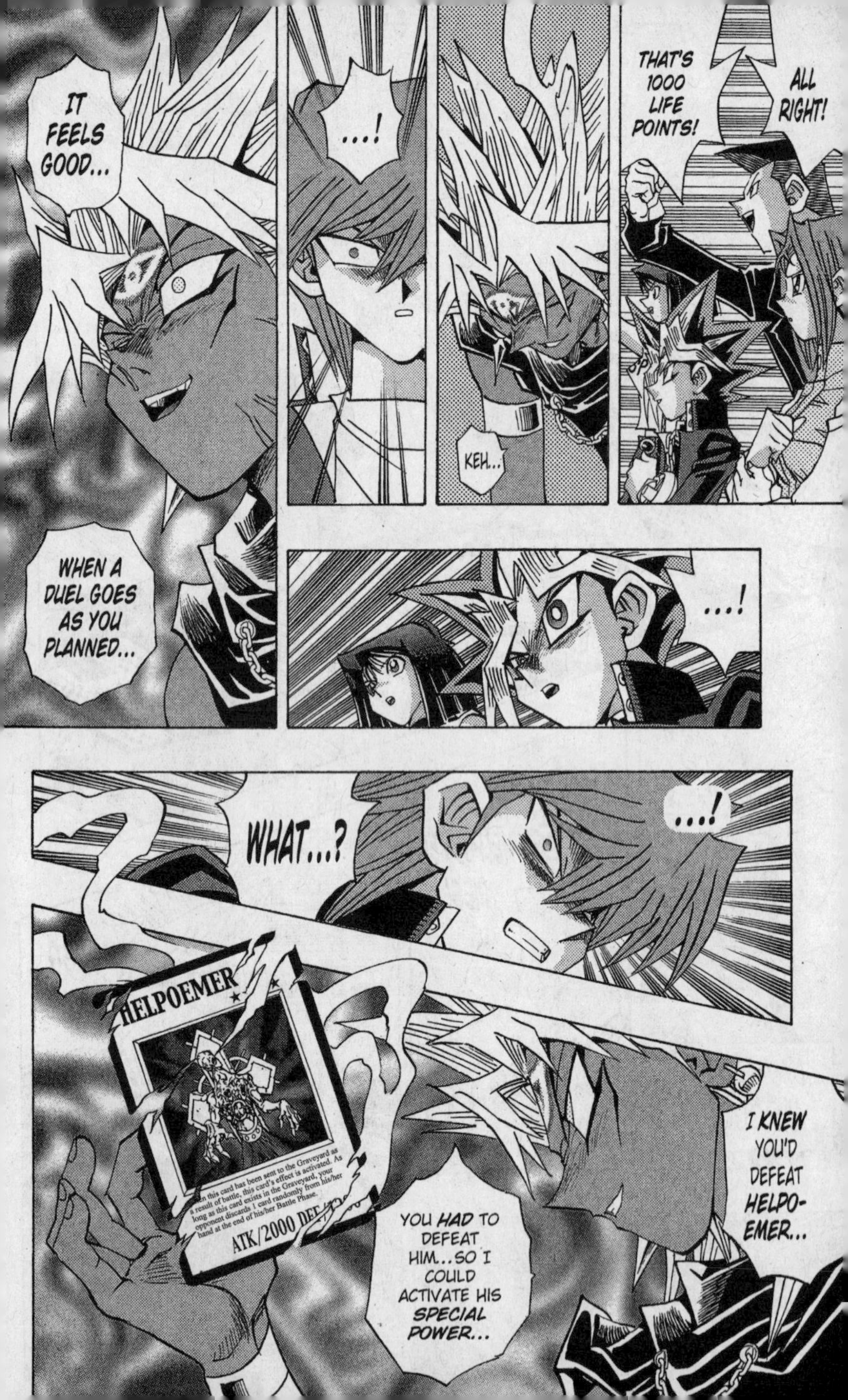
ALL RIGHT!
THAT'S 1000 LIFE POINTS!
KEH...
...!
...!
IT FEELS GOOD...
WHEN A DUEL GOES AS YOU PLANNED...
...!
WHAT...?
HELPOEMER
this card has been sent to the Graveyard as a result of battle, this card's effect is activated. As long as this card exists in the Graveyard, your opponent discards 1 card randomly from his/her hand at the end of his/her Battle Phase.
ATK/2000 DEF
I KNEW YOU'D DEFEAT HELPOEMER...
YOU *HAD* TO DEFEAT HIM...SO I COULD ACTIVATE HIS *SPECIAL POWER*...

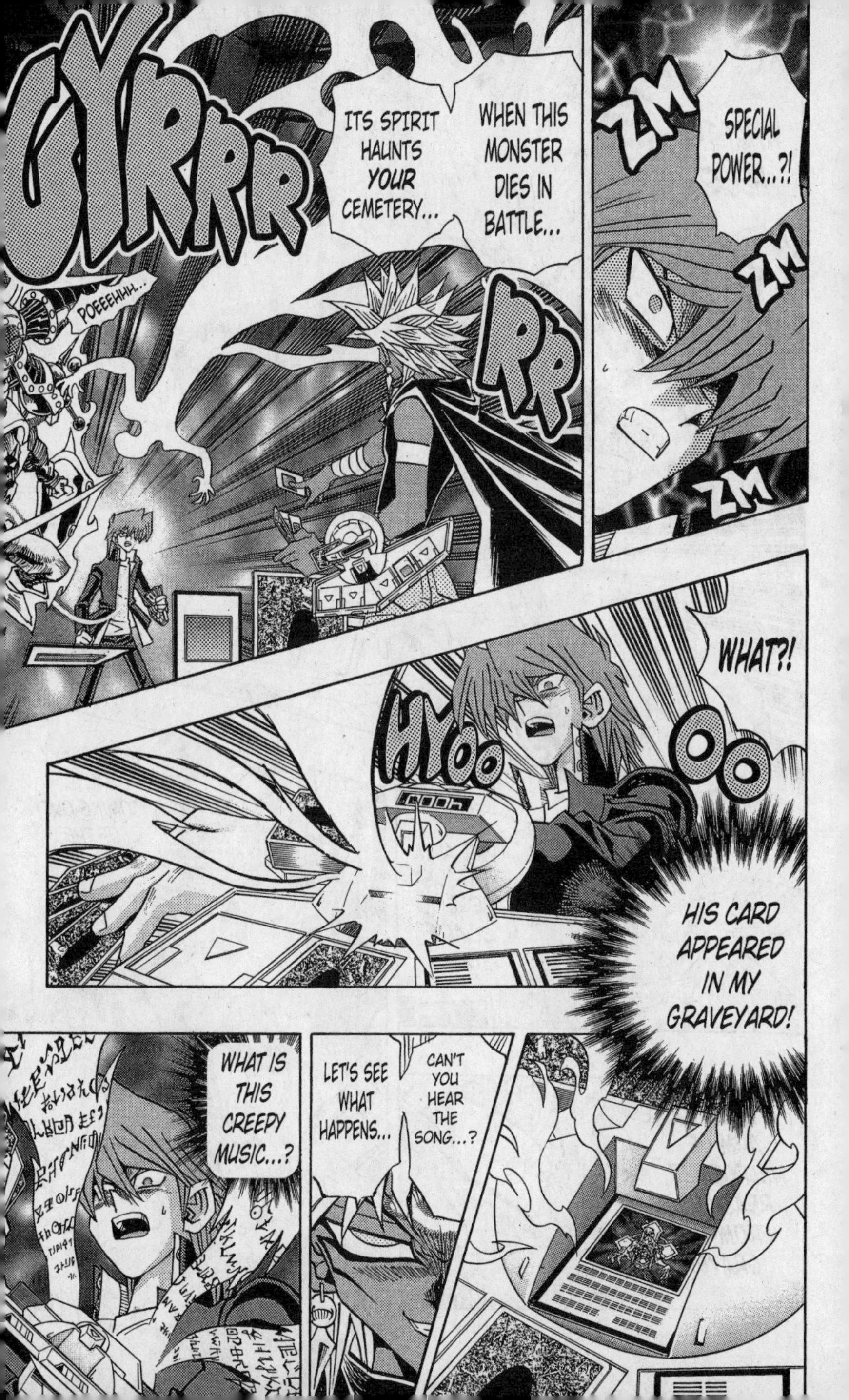
ZM
SPECIAL POWER...?!
ZM
ZM
GYRRRR
WHEN THIS MONSTER DIES IN BATTLE...
ITS SPIRIT HAUNTS YOUR CEMETERY...
POEEEHHH...
RR
WHAT?!
HYOO
OO
HIS CARD APPEARED IN MY GRAVEYARD!
CAN'T YOU HEAR THE SONG...?
LET'S SEE WHAT HAPPENS...
WHAT IS THIS CREEPY MUSIC...?

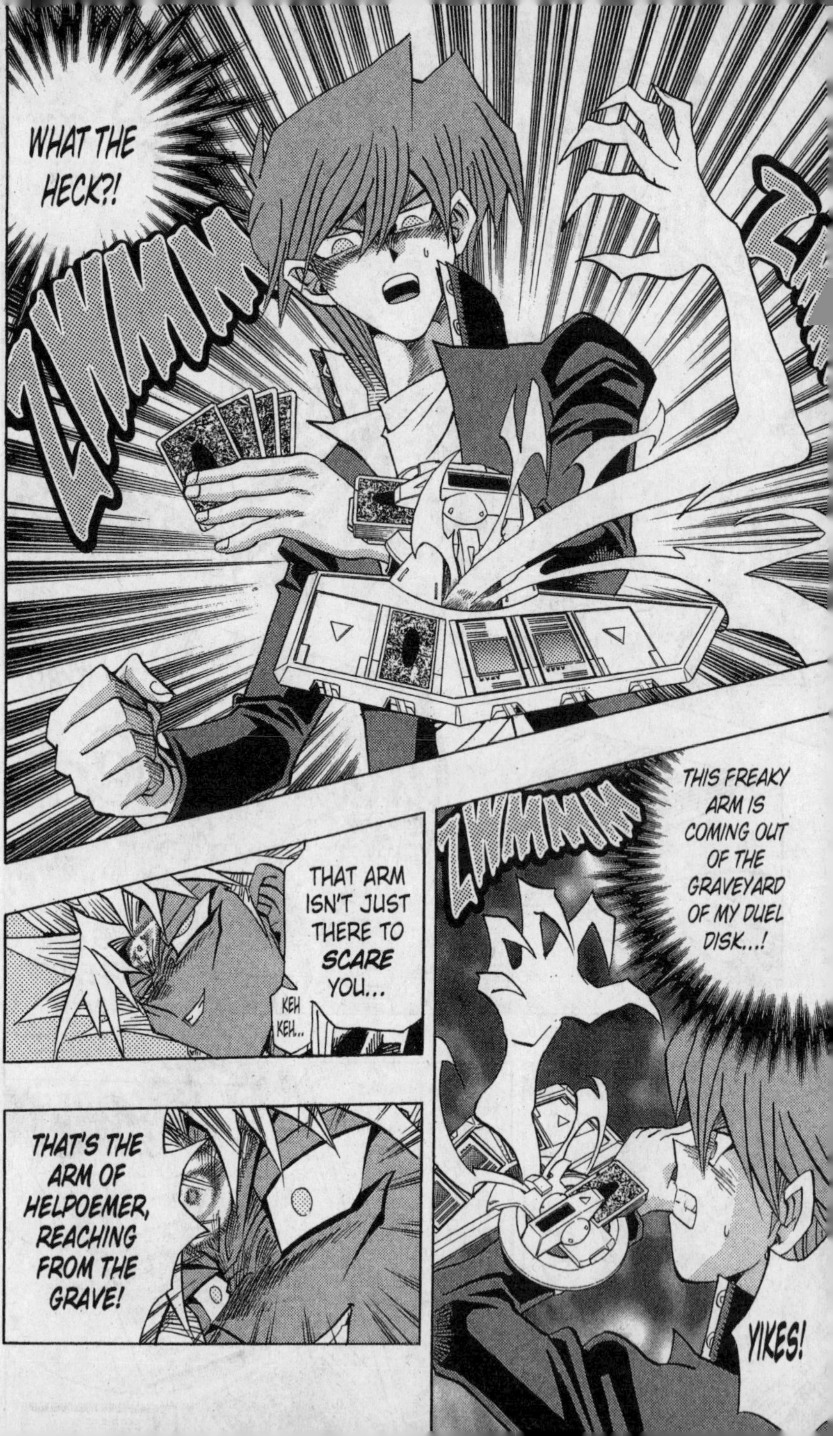

WHAT THE HECK?!
ZWMMM
ZWMMM
THIS FREAKY ARM IS COMING OUT OF THE GRAVEYARD OF MY DUEL DISK...!
YIKES!
THAT ARM ISN'T JUST THERE TO **SCARE** YOU...
KEH KEH...
THAT'S THE ARM OF HELPOEMER, REACHING FROM THE GRAVE!

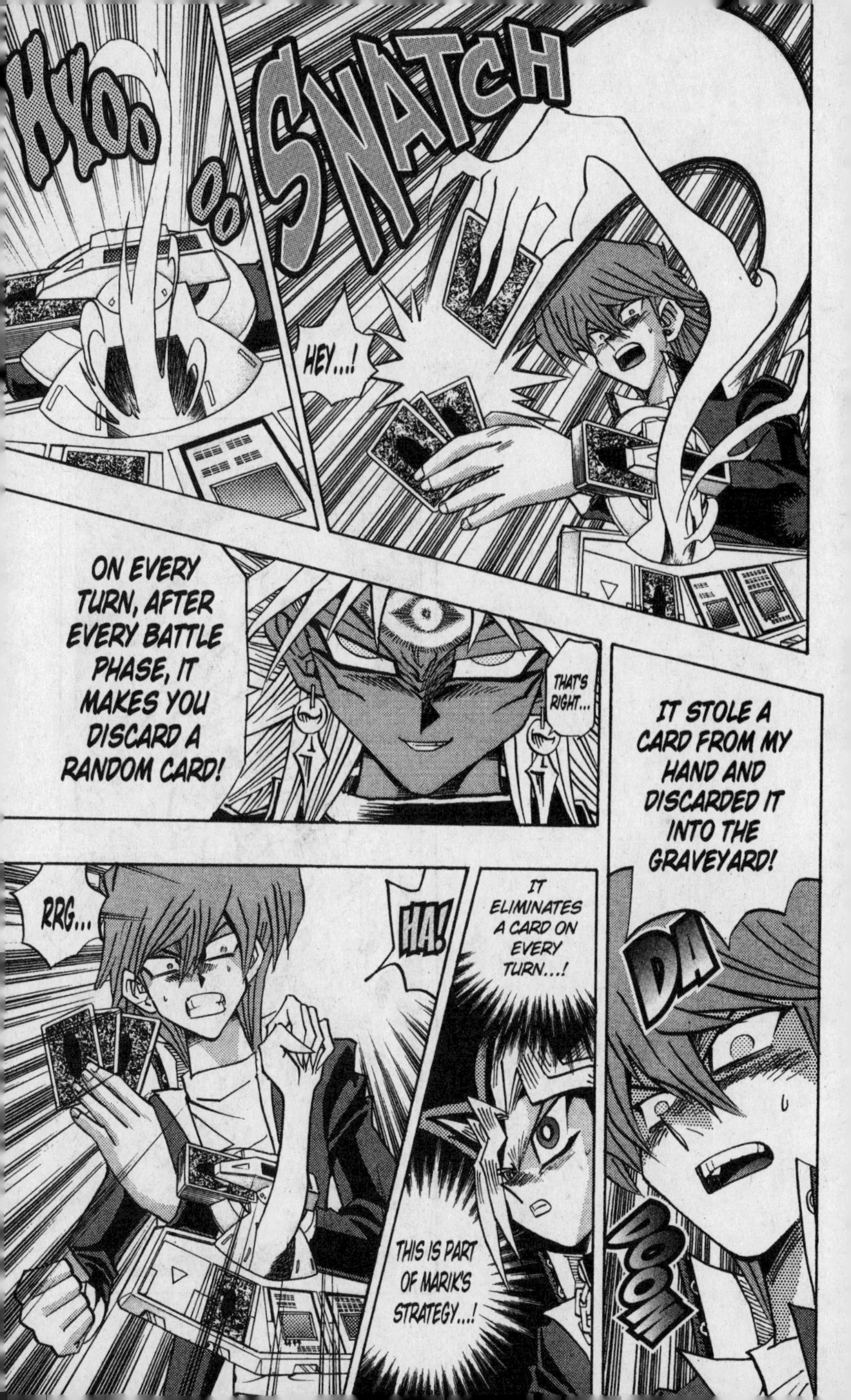
SNATCH
HEY...!
HYOO...
IT STOLE A CARD FROM MY HAND AND DISCARDED IT INTO THE GRAVEYARD!
DA
DOOM
ON EVERY TURN, AFTER EVERY BATTLE PHASE, IT MAKES YOU DISCARD A RANDOM CARD!
THAT'S RIGHT...
IT ELIMINATES A CARD ON EVERY TURN...!
HA!
THIS IS PART OF MARIK'S STRATEGY...!
RRG...

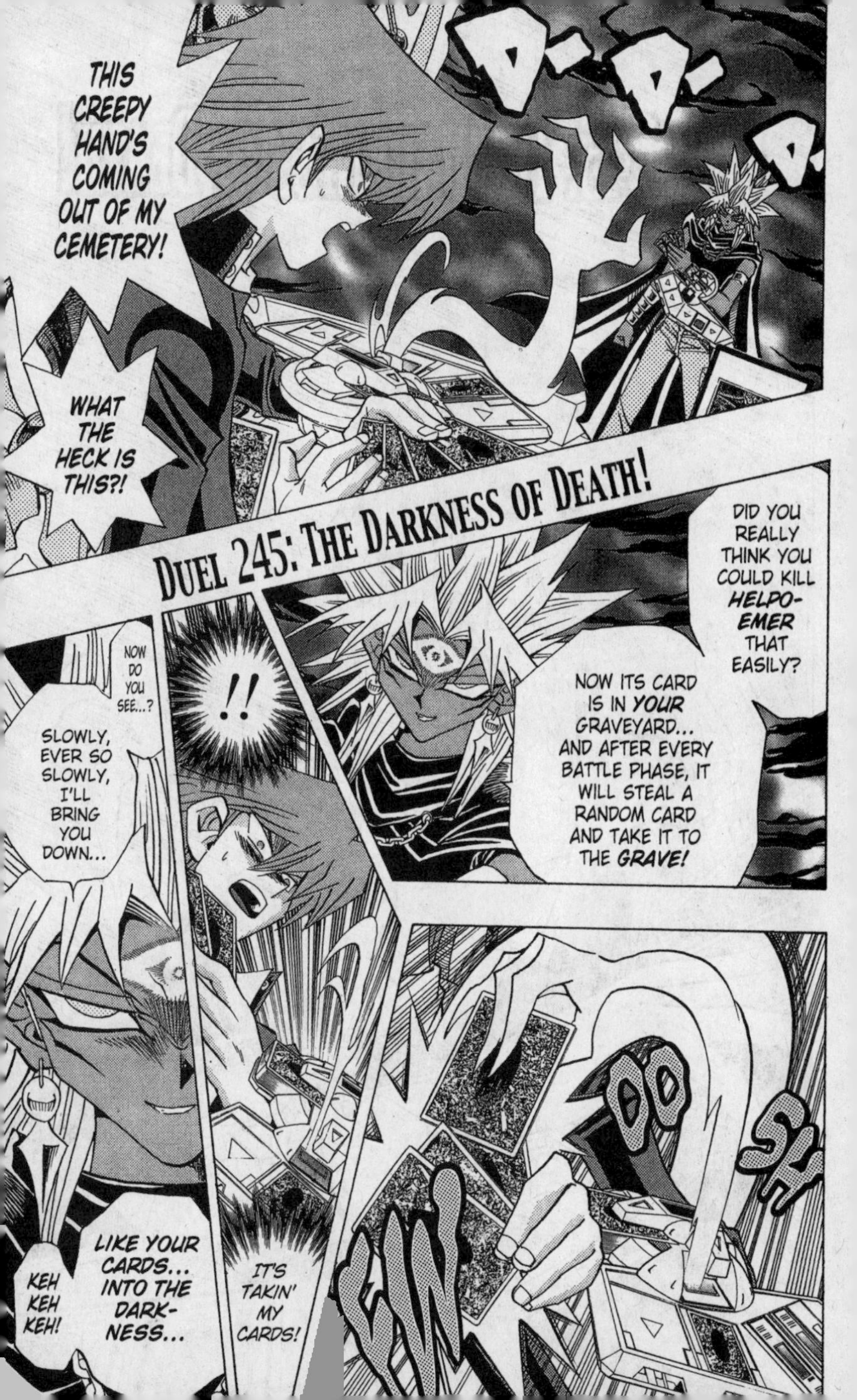
D- D- D-
THIS CREEPY HAND'S COMING OUT OF MY CEMETERY!
WHAT THE HECK IS THIS?!
Duel 245: The Darkness of Death!
DID YOU REALLY THINK YOU COULD KILL HELPOEMER THAT EASILY?
NOW ITS CARD IS IN YOUR GRAVEYARD... AND AFTER EVERY BATTLE PHASE, IT WILL STEAL A RANDOM CARD AND TAKE IT TO THE GRAVE!
!!
IT'S TAKIN' MY CARDS!
NOW DO YOU SEE...?
SLOWLY, EVER SO SLOWLY, I'LL BRING YOU DOWN...
LIKE YOUR CARDS... INTO THE DARKNESS...
KEH KEH KEH!

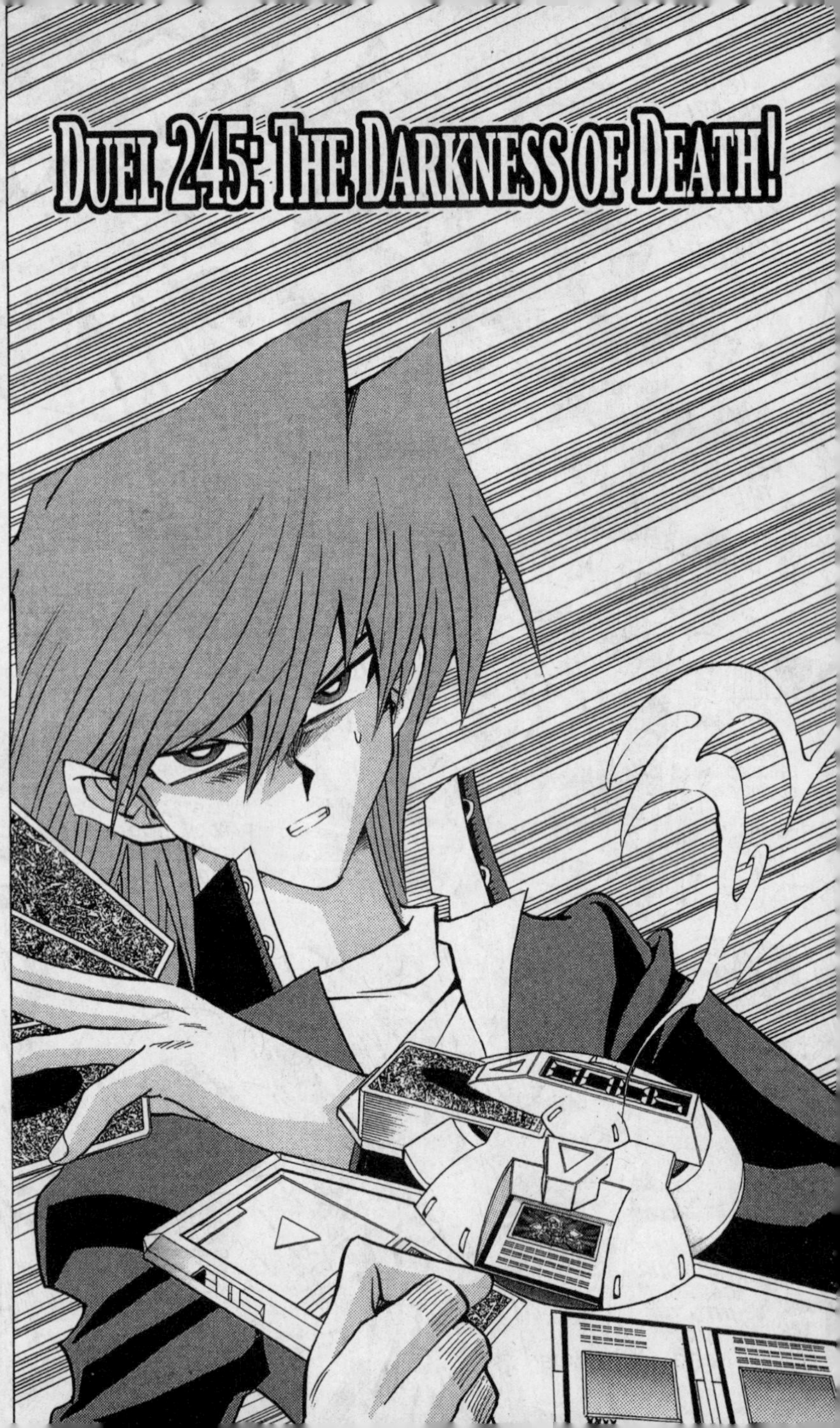
DUEL 245: THE DARKNESS OF DEATH!

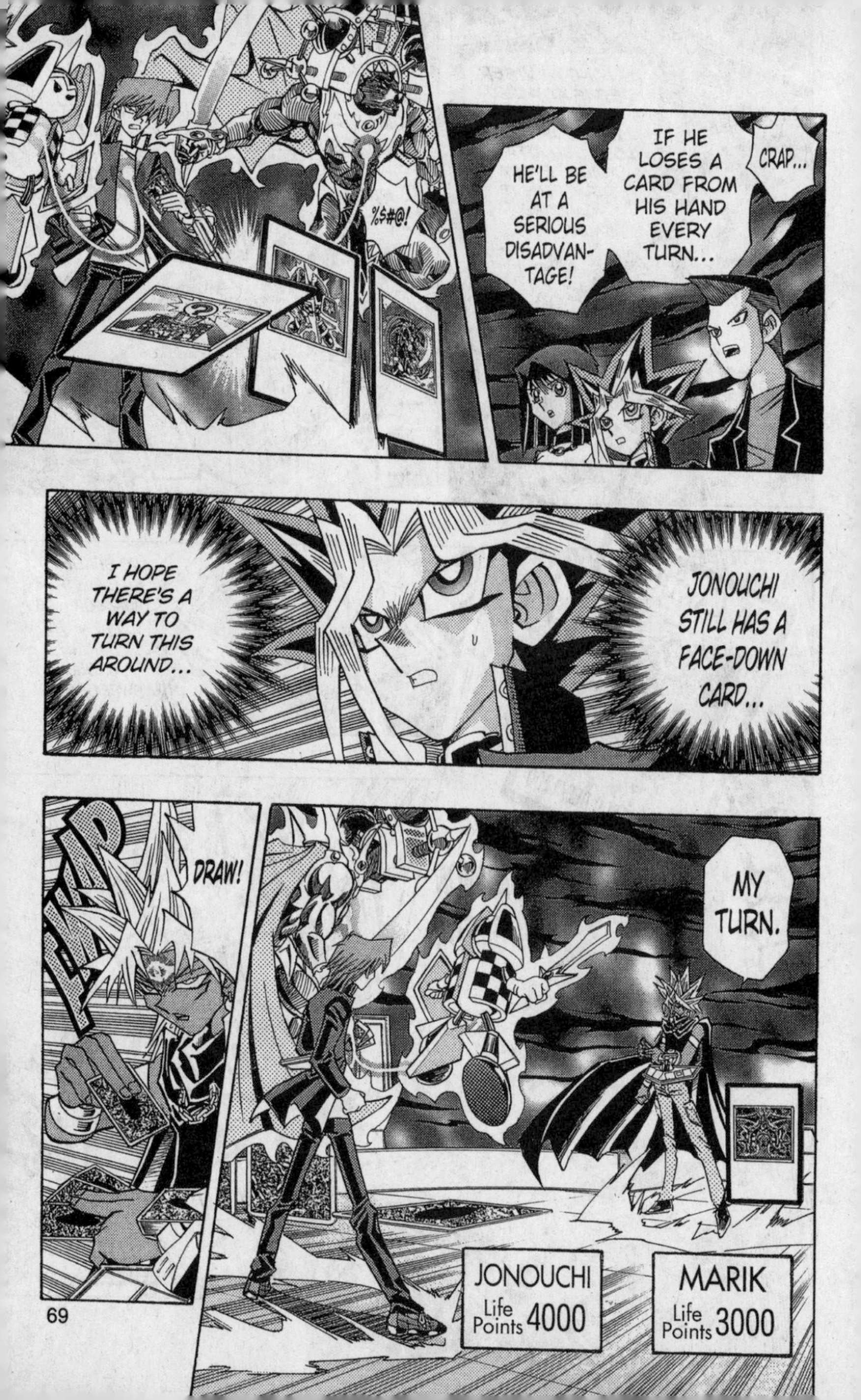
CRAP...
IF HE LOSES A CARD FROM HIS HAND EVERY TURN...
HE'LL BE AT A SERIOUS DISADVAN-TAGE!
%$#@!
JONOUCHI STILL HAS A FACE-DOWN CARD...
I HOPE THERE'S A WAY TO TURN THIS AROUND...
MY TURN.
JONOUCHI Life Points 4000
MARIK Life Points 3000
DRAW!

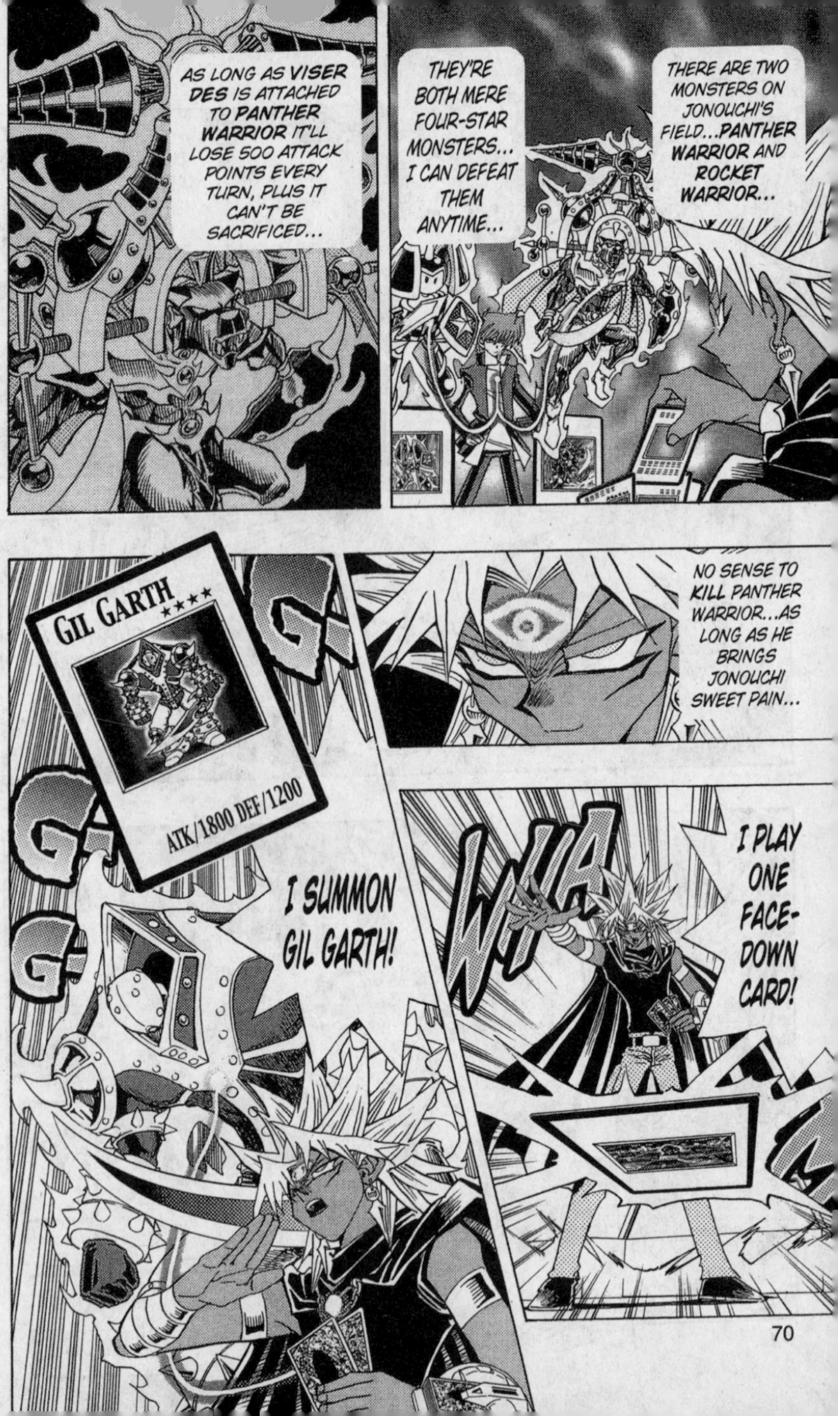
THERE ARE TWO MONSTERS ON JONOUCHI'S FIELD...PANTHER WARRIOR AND ROCKET WARRIOR...
THEY'RE BOTH MERE FOUR-STAR MONSTERS... I CAN DEFEAT THEM ANYTIME...
AS LONG AS VISER DES IS ATTACHED TO PANTHER WARRIOR IT'LL LOSE 500 ATTACK POINTS EVERY TURN, PLUS IT CAN'T BE SACRIFICED...
NO SENSE TO KILL PANTHER WARRIOR...AS LONG AS HE BRINGS JONOUCHI SWEET PAIN...
WHA
I PLAY ONE FACE-DOWN CARD!
G-
G-
G-
GIL GARTH
ATK/1800 DEF/1200
I SUMMON GIL GARTH!

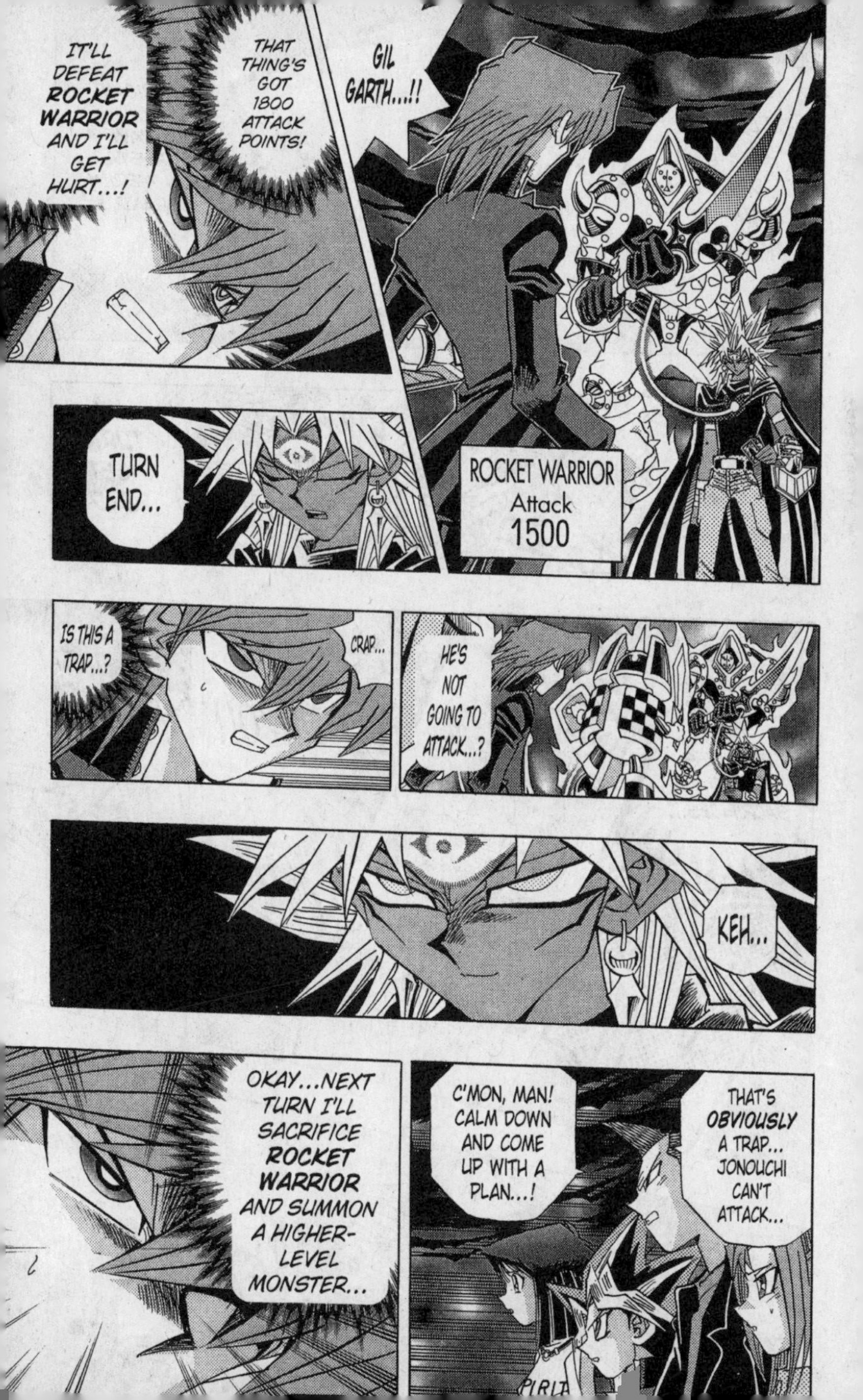
GIL GARTH...!!
ROCKET WARRIOR Attack 1500
THAT THING'S GOT 1800 ATTACK POINTS!
IT'LL DEFEAT ROCKET WARRIOR AND I'LL GET HURT...!
TURN END...
HE'S NOT GOING TO ATTACK...?
CRAP...
IS THIS A TRAP...?
KEH...
THAT'S OBVIOUSLY A TRAP... JONOUCHI CAN'T ATTACK...
C'MON, MAN! CALM DOWN AND COME UP WITH A PLAN...!
PIRI
OKAY...NEXT TURN I'LL SACRIFICE ROCKET WARRIOR AND SUMMON A HIGHER-LEVEL MONSTER...

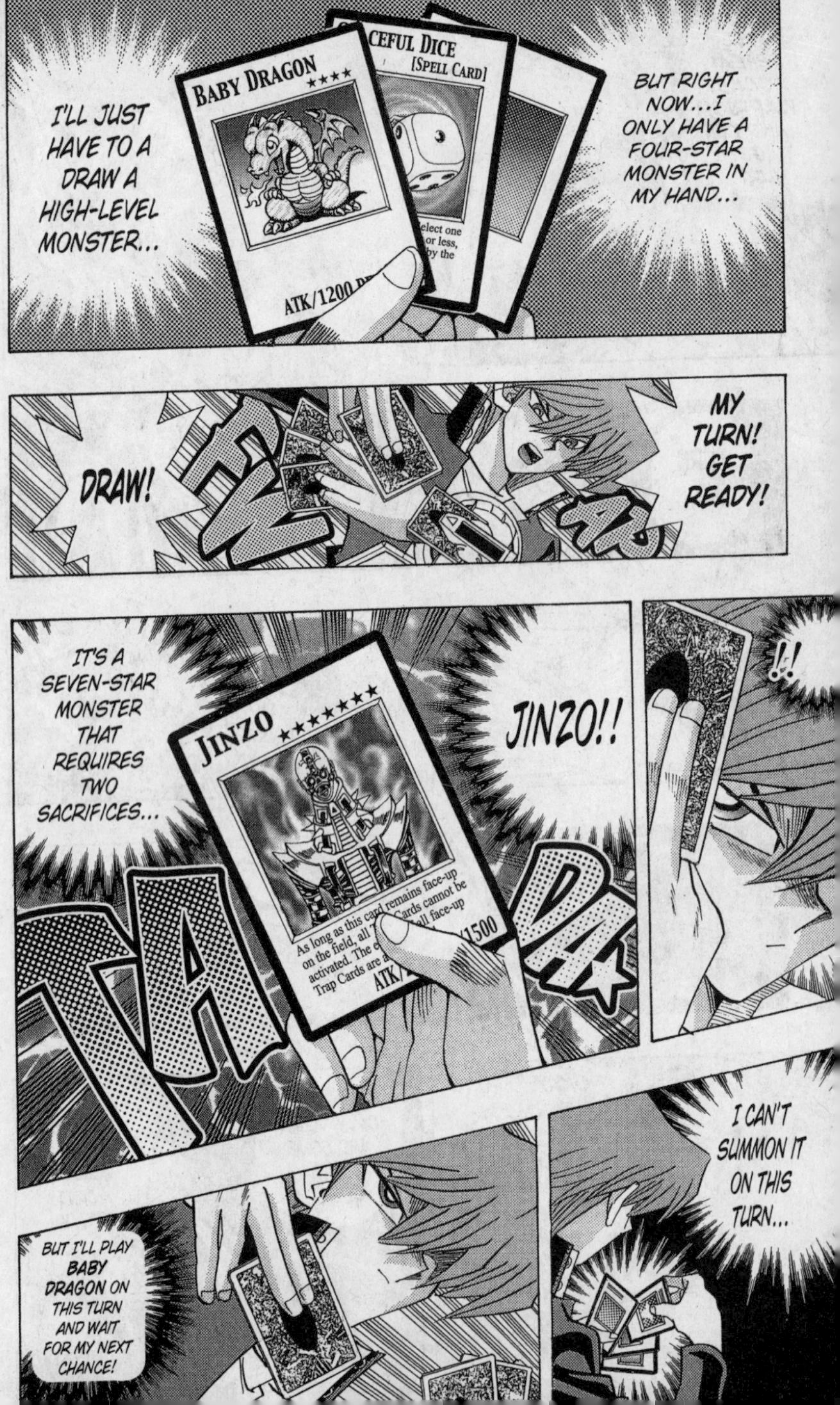

BUT RIGHT NOW...I ONLY HAVE A FOUR-STAR MONSTER IN MY HAND...
BABY DRAGON
[SPELL CARD]
ATK/1200
I'LL JUST HAVE TO A DRAW A HIGH-LEVEL MONSTER...
MY TURN! GET READY!
DRAW!
!!
JINZO!!
JINZO
IT'S A SEVEN-STAR MONSTER THAT REQUIRES TWO SACRIFICES...
I CAN'T SUMMON IT ON THIS TURN...
BUT I'LL PLAY BABY DRAGON ON THIS TURN AND WAIT FOR MY NEXT CHANCE!

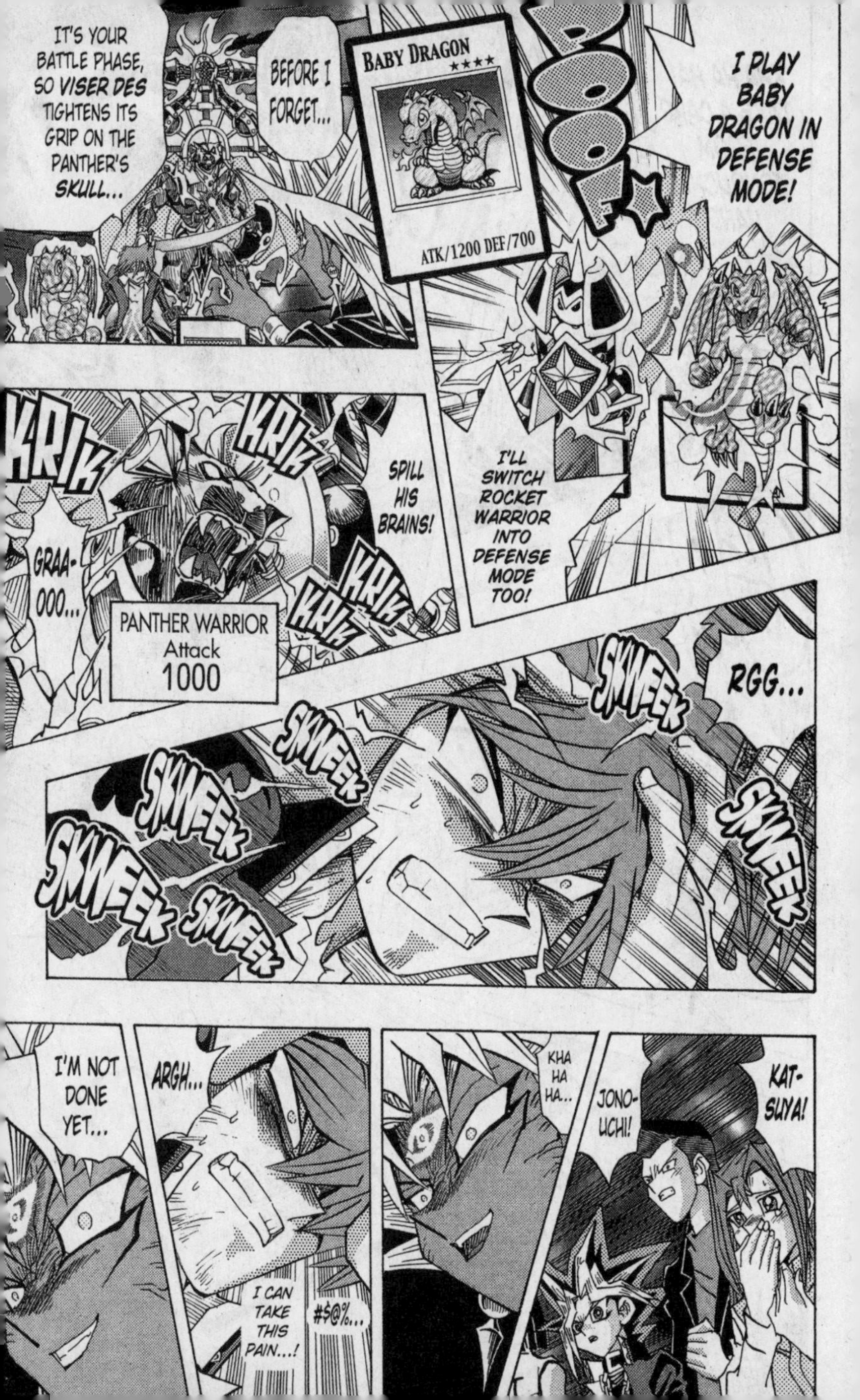
I PLAY BABY DRAGON IN DEFENSE MODE!
BOOF
BABY DRAGON ★★★★
ATK/1200 DEF/700
I'LL SWITCH ROCKET WARRIOR INTO DEFENSE MODE TOO!
BEFORE I FORGET...
IT'S YOUR BATTLE PHASE, SO VISER DES TIGHTENS ITS GRIP ON THE PANTHER'S SKULL...
SPILL HIS BRAINS!
KRIK
KRIK
KRIK
KRIK
GRAA-OOO...
PANTHER WARRIOR
Attack
1000
RGG...
SKWEEK
SKWEEK
SKWEEK
SKWEEK
SKWEEK
SKWEEK
KAT-SUYA!
JONO-UCHI!
KHA HA HA...
ARGH...
#$@%...
I CAN TAKE THIS PAIN...!
I'M NOT DONE YET...

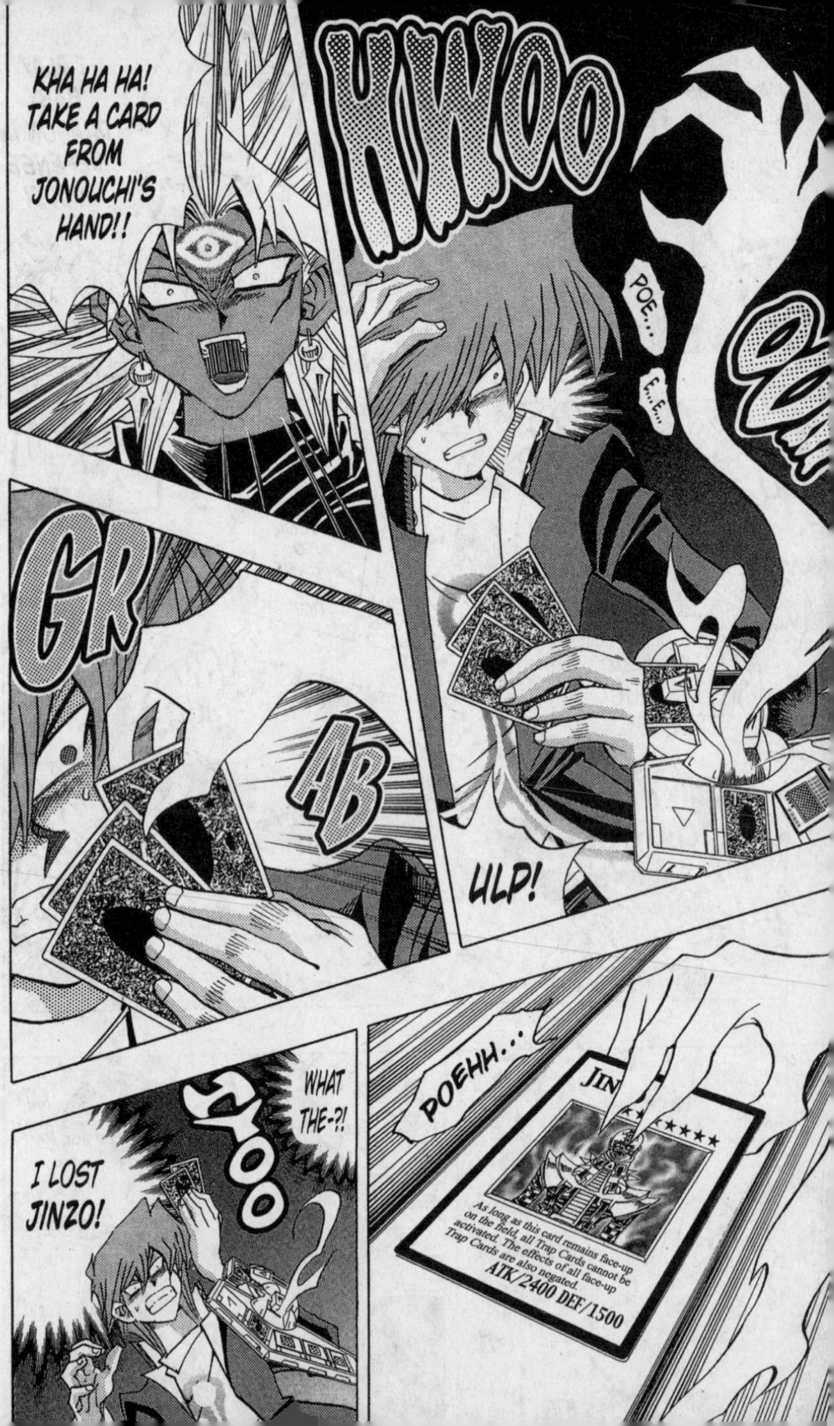
HIWOO
POE...
E...E...
ULP!
KHA HA HA!
TAKE A CARD
FROM
JONOUCHI'S
HAND!!
GR
AB
POEHH...
As long as this card remains face-up on the field, all Trap Cards cannot be activated. The effects of all face-up Trap Cards are also negated.
ATK/2400 DEF/1500
WHAT THE-?!
I LOST JINZO!

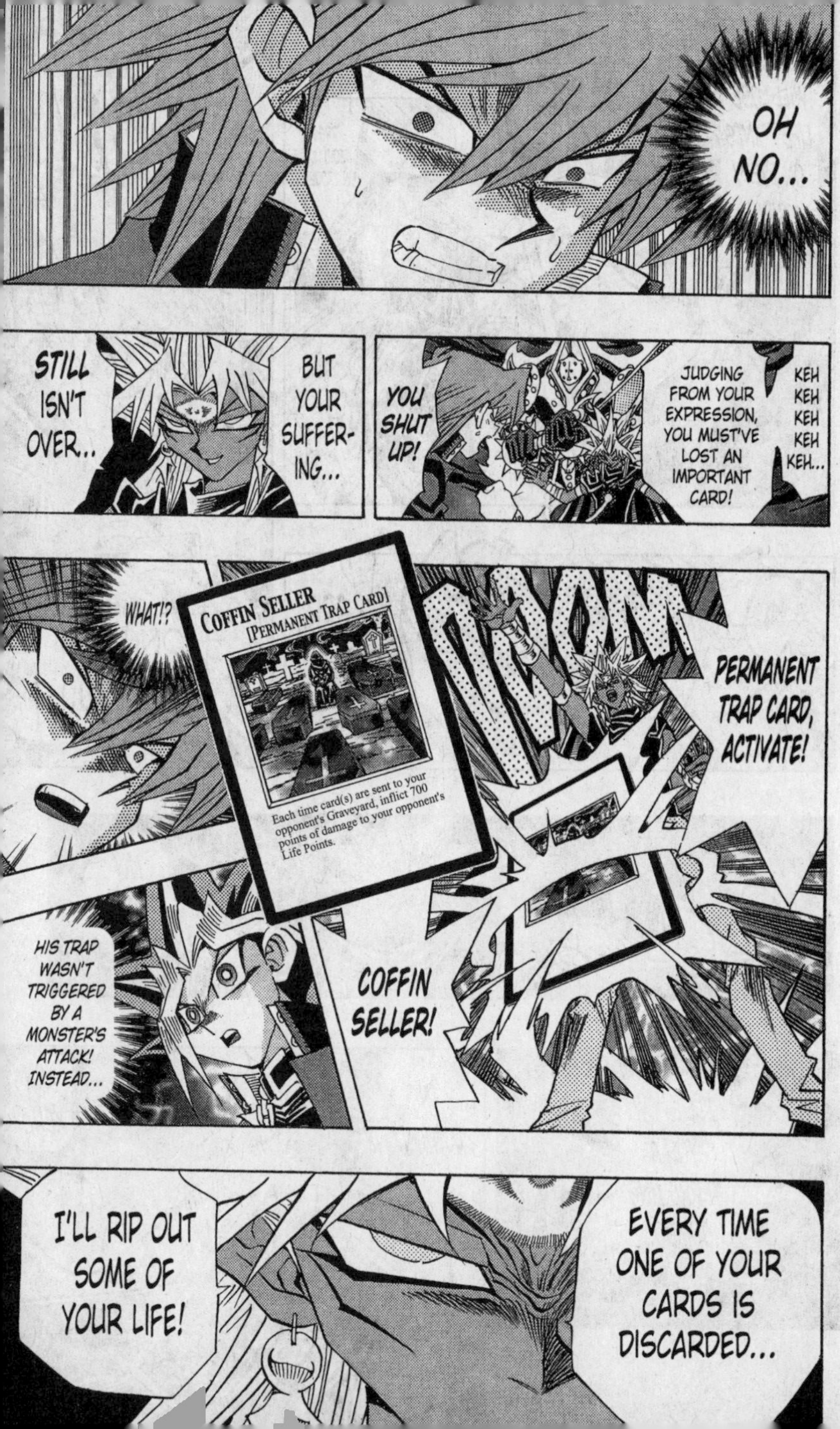
OH NO...
KEH KEH KEH KEH KEH...
JUDGING FROM YOUR EXPRESSION, YOU MUST'VE LOST AN IMPORTANT CARD!
YOU SHUT UP!
BUT YOUR SUFFER-ING...
STILL ISN'T OVER...
DOOM
PERMANENT TRAP CARD, ACTIVATE!
COFFIN SELLER!
WHAT!?
COFFIN SELLER
[PERMANENT TRAP CARD]
Each time card(s) are sent to your opponent's Graveyard, inflict 700 points of damage to your opponent's Life Points.
HIS TRAP WASN'T TRIGGERED BY A MONSTER'S ATTACK! INSTEAD...
EVERY TIME ONE OF YOUR CARDS IS DISCARDED...
I'LL RIP OUT SOME OF YOUR LIFE!

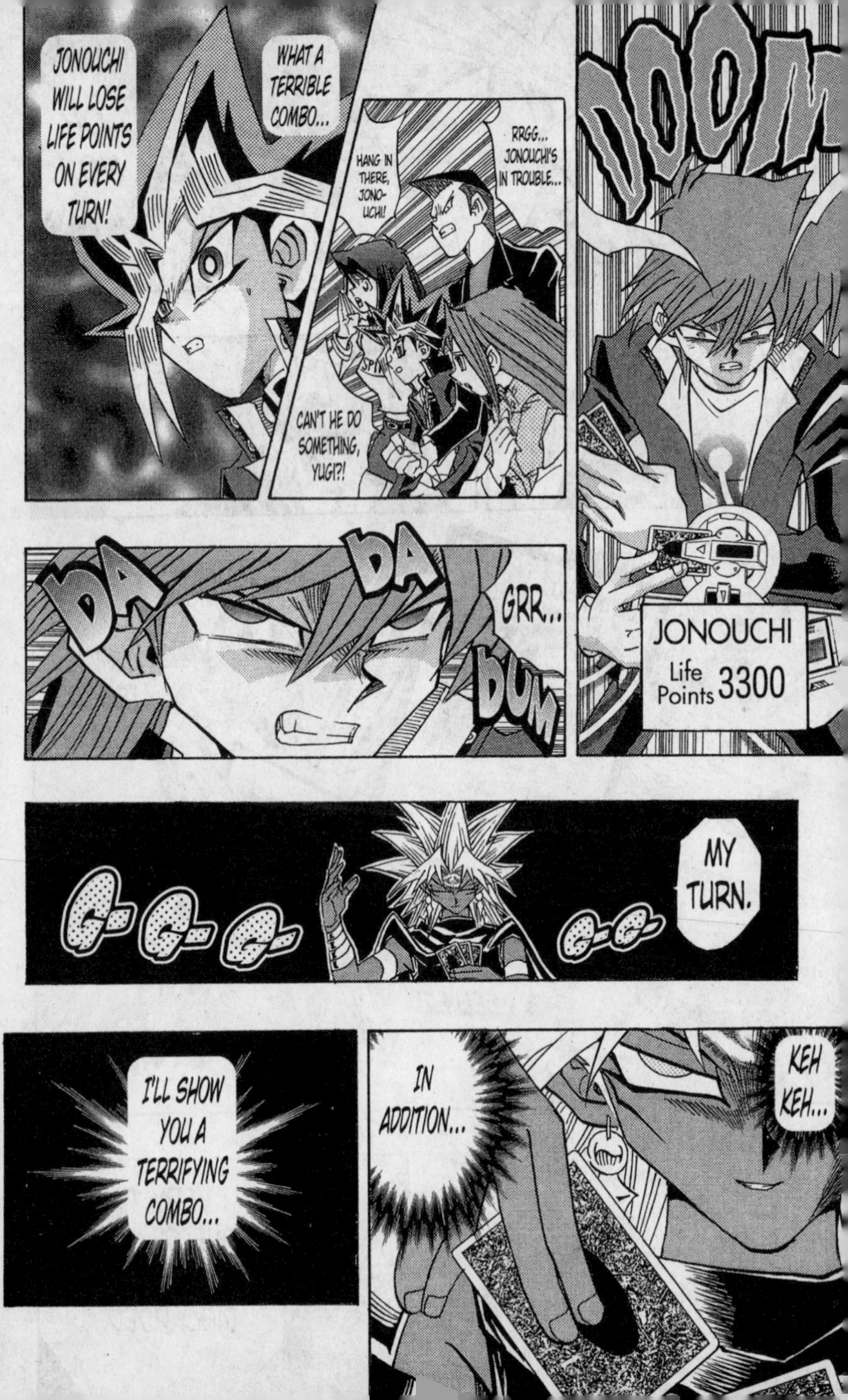
DOOM
JONOUCHI
Life Points 3300
RRGG... JONOUCHI'S IN TROUBLE...
HANG IN THERE, JONO-UCHI!
CAN'T HE DO SOMETHING, YUGI?!
WHAT A TERRIBLE COMBO...
JONOUCHI WILL LOSE LIFE POINTS ON EVERY TURN!
GRR...
DA
DA
DUM
MY TURN.
G-G-
G-G-G-
KEH KEH...
IN ADDITION...
I'LL SHOW YOU A TERRIFYING COMBO...

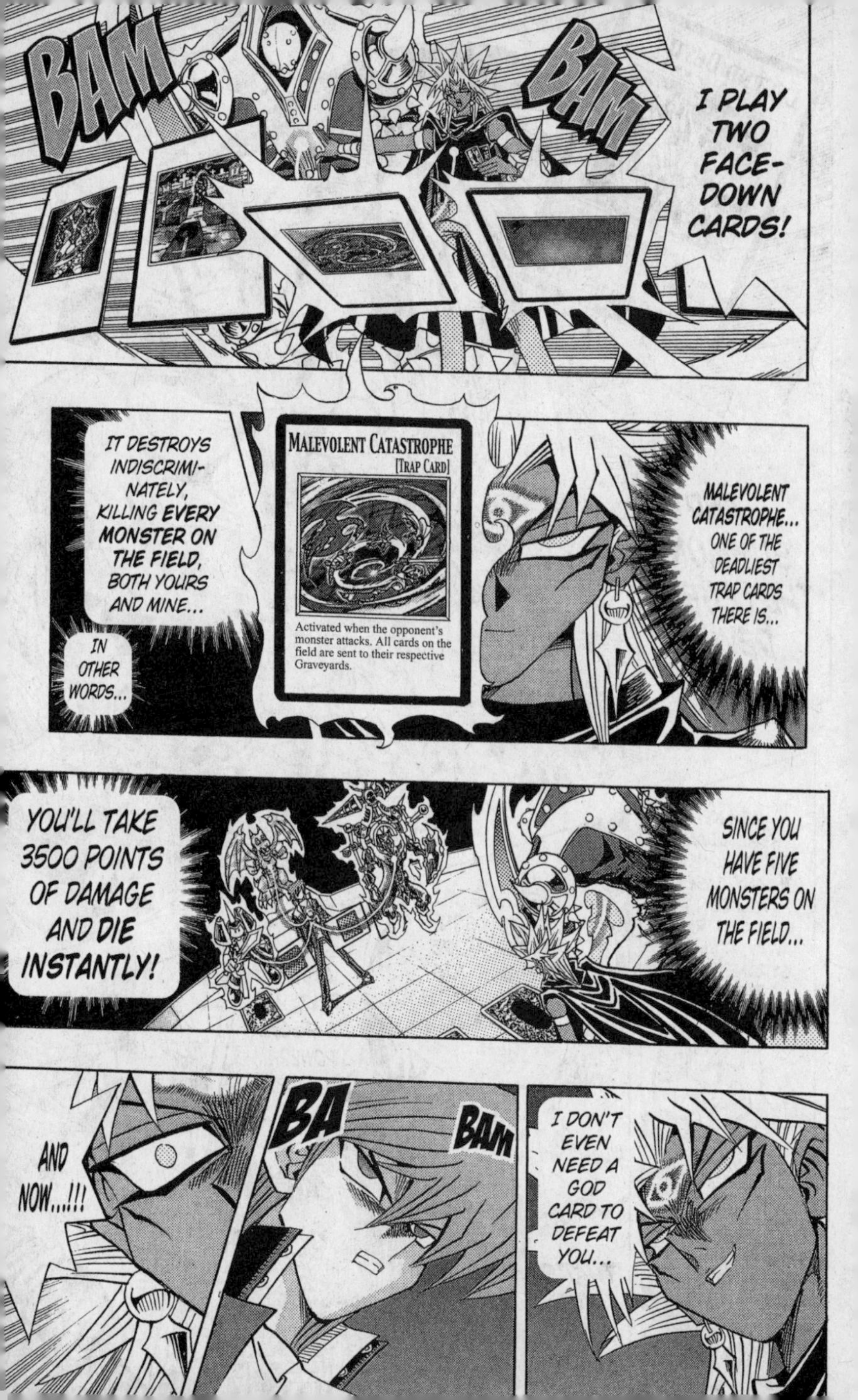
BAM
BAM
I PLAY TWO FACE-DOWN CARDS!
MALEVOLENT CATASTROPHE... ONE OF THE DEADLIEST TRAP CARDS THERE IS...
MALEVOLENT CATASTROPHE
[TRAP CARD]
Activated when the opponent's monster attacks. All cards on the field are sent to their respective Graveyards.
IT DESTROYS INDISCRIMINATELY, KILLING EVERY MONSTER ON THE FIELD, BOTH YOURS AND MINE...
IN OTHER WORDS...
SINCE YOU HAVE FIVE MONSTERS ON THE FIELD...
YOU'LL TAKE 3500 POINTS OF DAMAGE AND DIE INSTANTLY!
I DON'T EVEN NEED A GOD CARD TO DEFEAT YOU...
BA
BAM
AND NOW...!!!

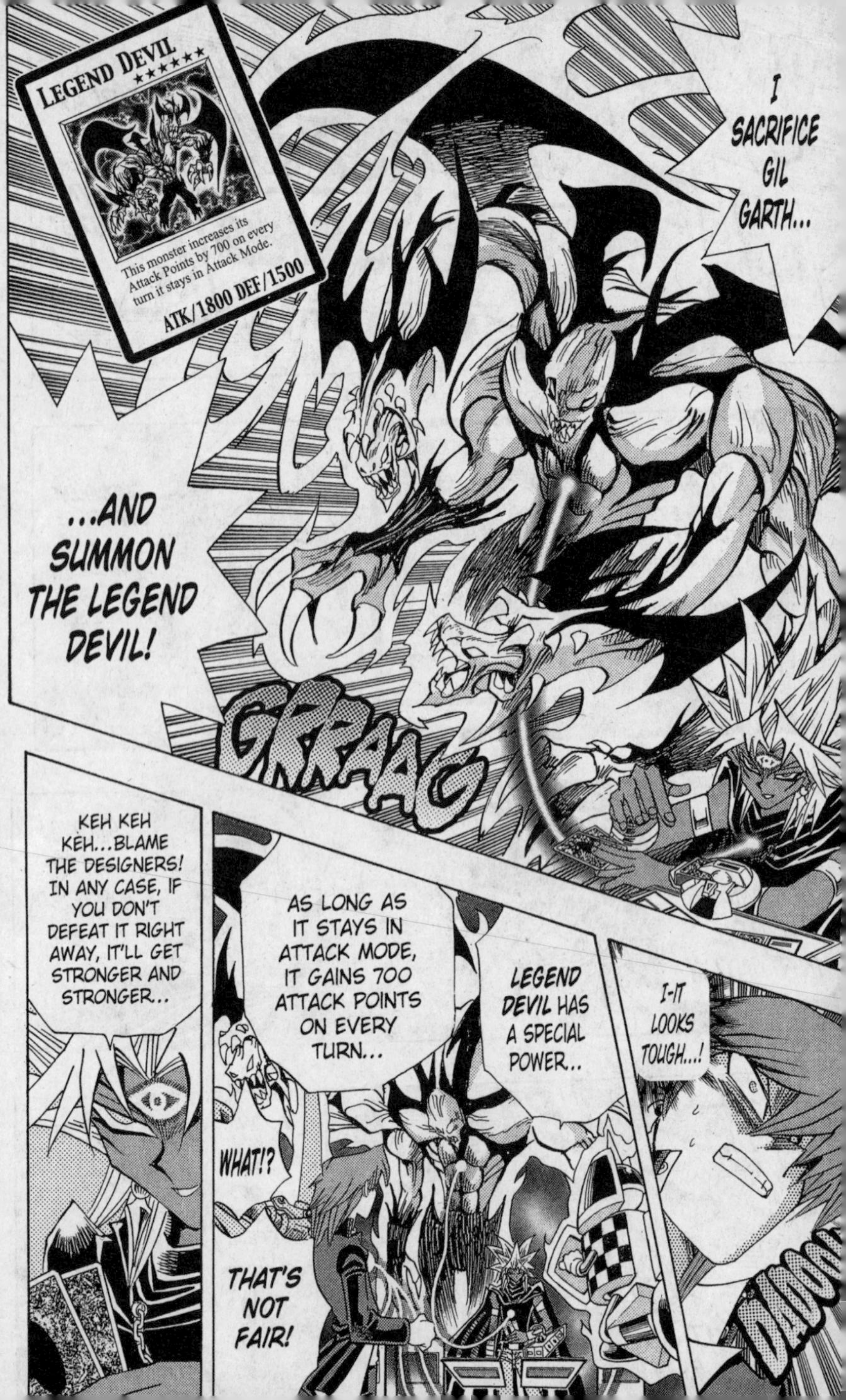
I SACRIFICE GIL GARTH...
LEGEND DEVIL
This monster increases its Attack Points by 700 on every turn it stays in Attack Mode.
ATK/1800 DEF/1500
...AND SUMMON THE LEGEND DEVIL!
GRRAAG
I-IT LOOKS TOUGH...!
LEGEND DEVIL HAS A SPECIAL POWER...
AS LONG AS IT STAYS IN ATTACK MODE, IT GAINS 700 ATTACK POINTS ON EVERY TURN...
WHAT!?
THAT'S NOT FAIR!
KEH KEH KEH...BLAME THE DESIGNERS! IN ANY CASE, IF YOU DON'T DEFEAT IT RIGHT AWAY, IT'LL GET STRONGER AND STRONGER...

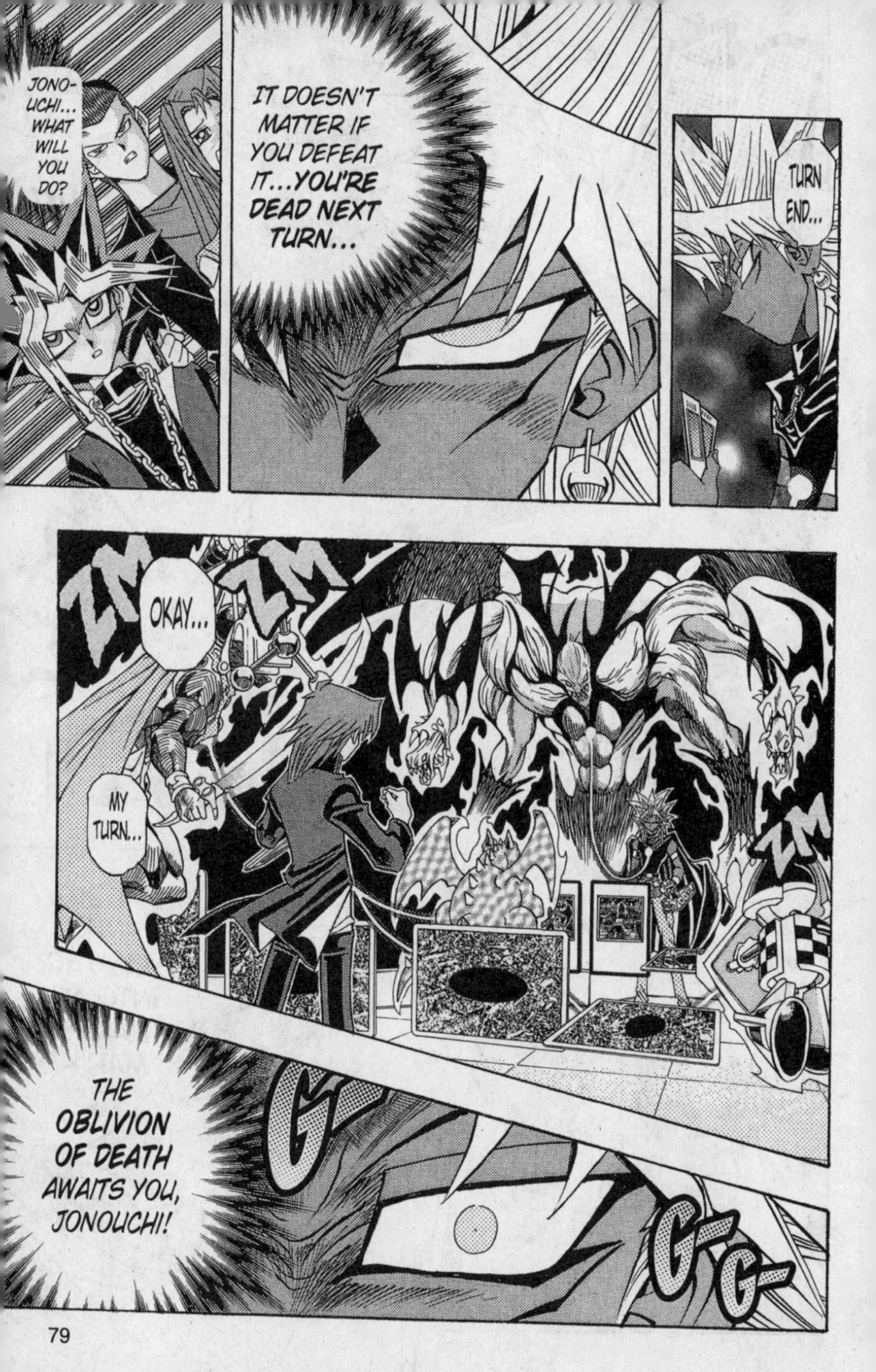
TURN END...
IT DOESN'T MATTER IF YOU DEFEAT IT...YOU'RE DEAD NEXT TURN...
JONOUCHI... WHAT WILL YOU DO?
ZM ZM
OKAY...
ZM
MY TURN...
G-G-
THE OBLIVION OF DEATH AWAITS YOU, JONOUCHI!

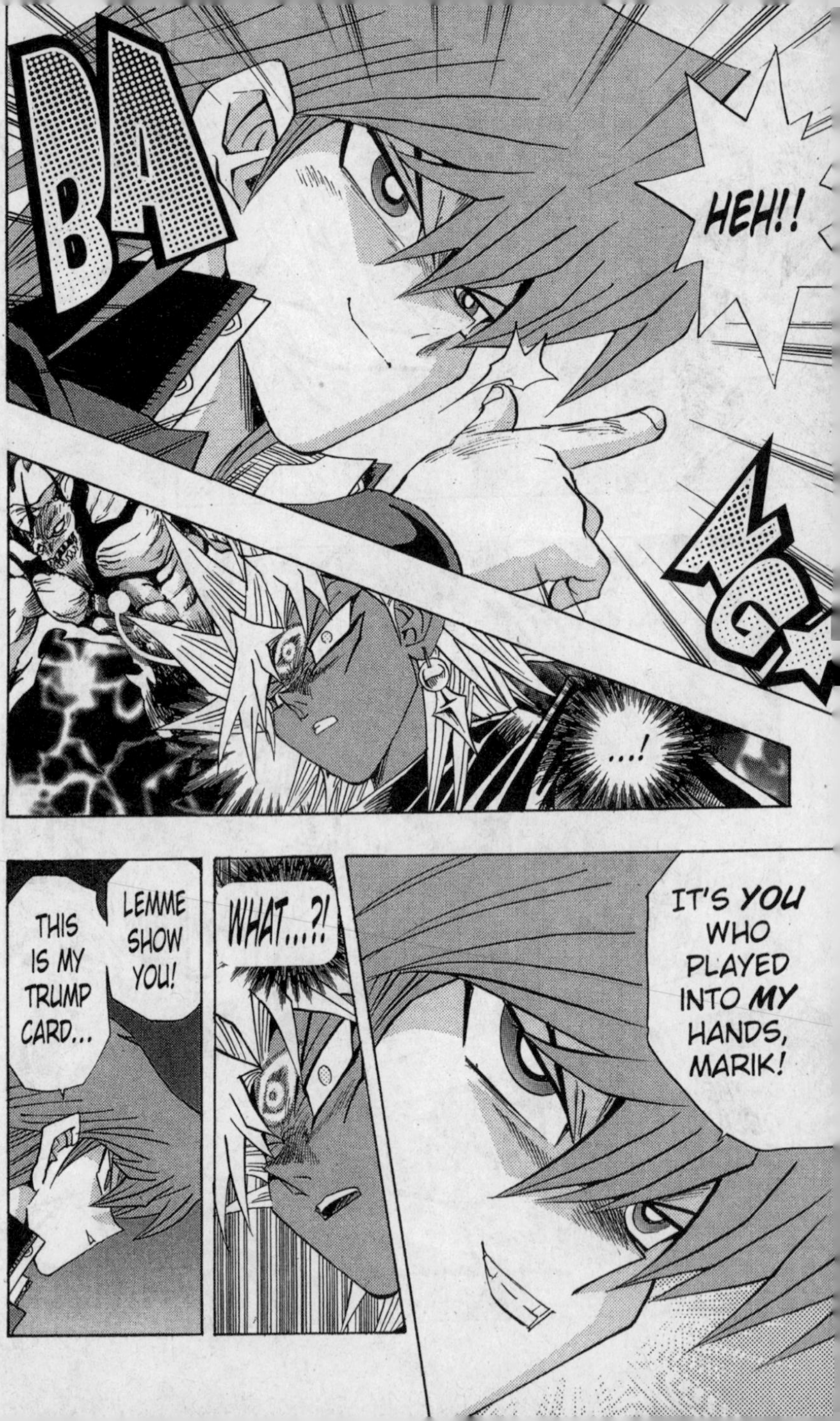
HEH!!
BA
WG
...!
IT'S *YOU* WHO PLAYED INTO *MY* HANDS, MARIK!
WHAT...?!
LEMME SHOW YOU!
THIS IS MY TRUMP CARD...

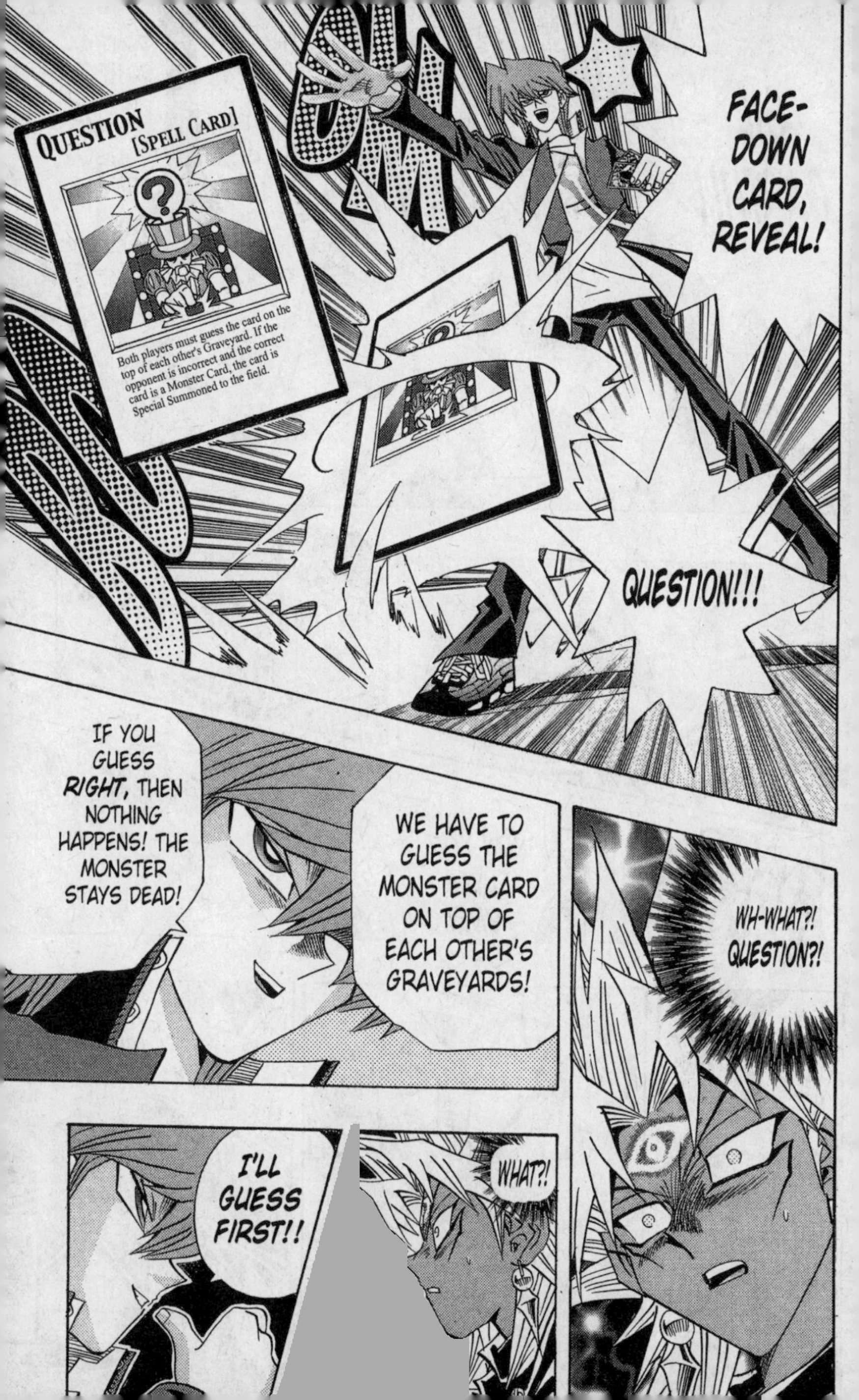
FACE-DOWN CARD, REVEAL!
QUESTION [SPELL CARD]
Both players must guess the card on the top of each other's Graveyard. If the opponent is incorrect and the correct card is a Monster Card, the card is Special Summoned to the field.
QUESTION!!!
WH-WHAT?! QUESTION?!
WE HAVE TO GUESS THE MONSTER CARD ON TOP OF EACH OTHER'S GRAVEYARDS!
IF YOU GUESS RIGHT, THEN NOTHING HAPPENS! THE MONSTER STAYS DEAD!
WHAT?!
I'LL GUESS FIRST!!

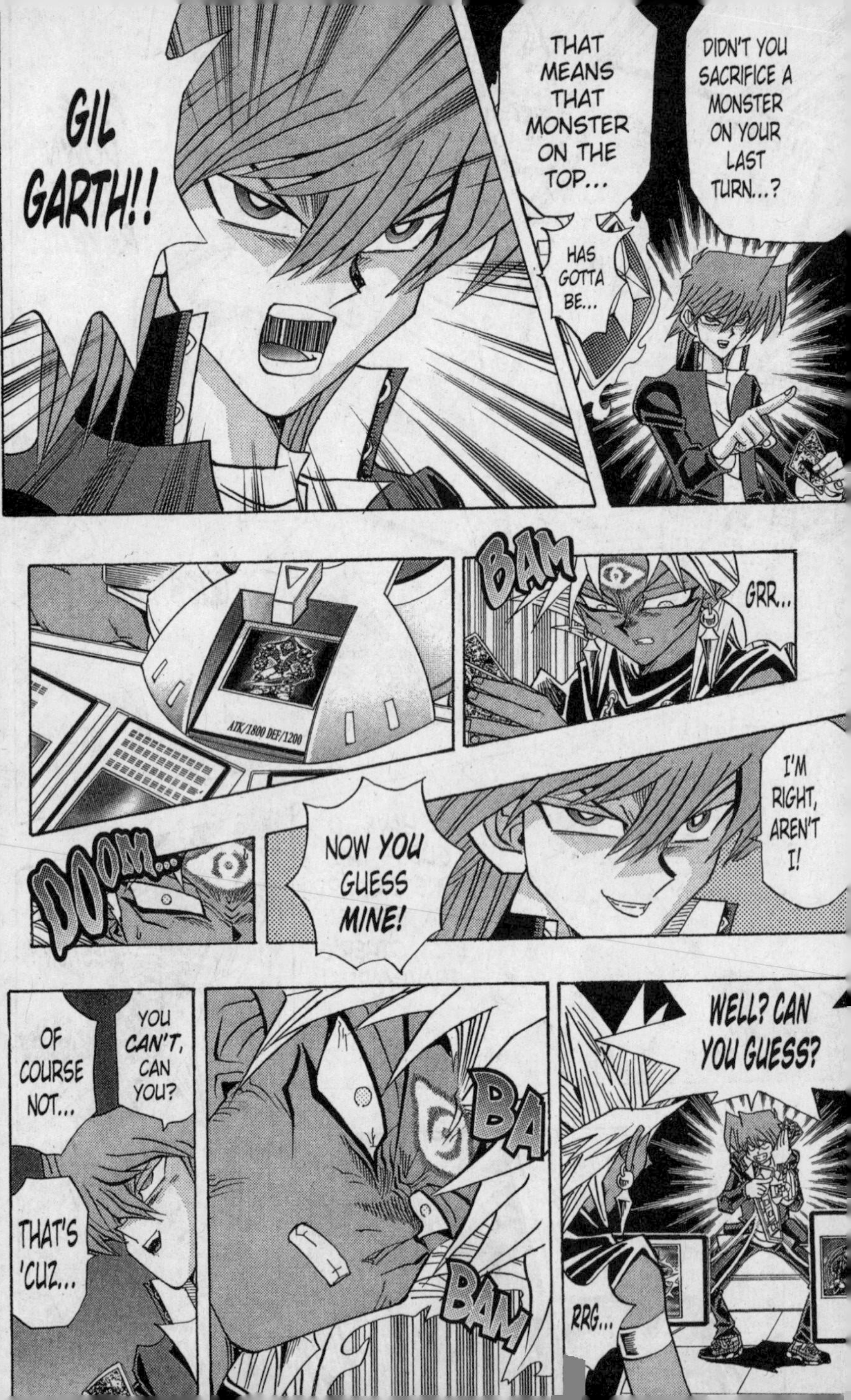
DIDN'T YOU SACRIFICE A MONSTER ON YOUR LAST TURN...?
THAT MEANS THAT MONSTER ON THE TOP...
HAS GOTTA BE...
GIL GARTH!!
BAM
GRR...
ATK/1800 DEF/1200
I'M RIGHT, AREN'T I!
NOW YOU GUESS MINE!
DOOM...
WELL? CAN YOU GUESS?
RRG...
BA
BAM
YOU CAN'T, CAN YOU?
OF COURSE NOT...
THAT'S 'CUZ...

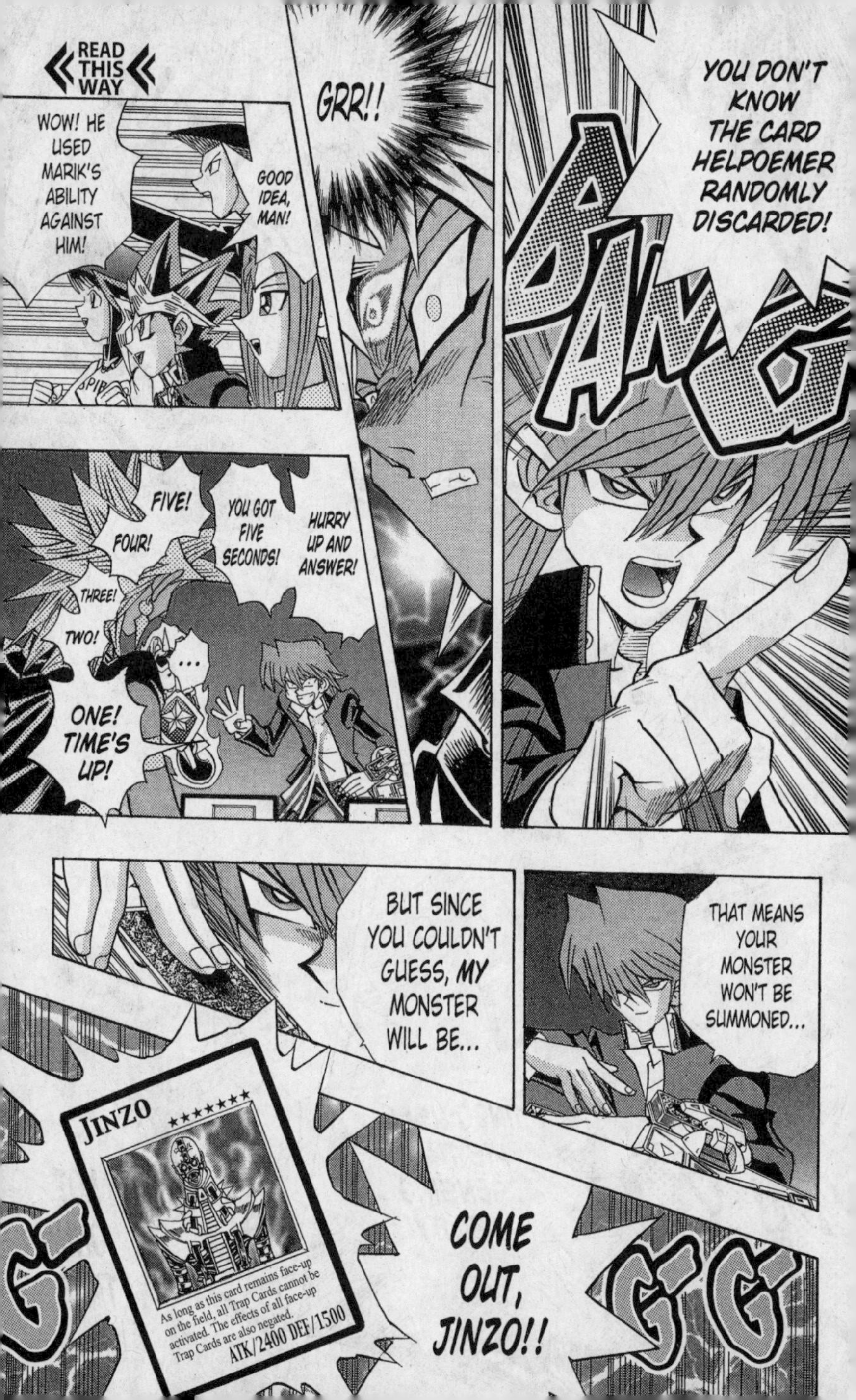
READ THIS WAY
YOU DON'T KNOW THE CARD HELPOEMER RANDOMLY DISCARDED!
GRR!!
WOW! HE USED MARIK'S ABILITY AGAINST HIM!
GOOD IDEA, MAN!
HURRY UP AND ANSWER!
YOU GOT FIVE SECONDS!
FIVE!
FOUR!
THREE!
TWO!
...
ONE! TIME'S UP!
THAT MEANS YOUR MONSTER WON'T BE SUMMONED...
BUT SINCE YOU COULDN'T GUESS, MY MONSTER WILL BE...
COME OUT, JINZO!!
JINZO
As long as this card remains face-up on the field, all Trap Cards cannot be activated. The effects of all face-up Trap Cards are also negated.
ATK/2400 DEF/1500

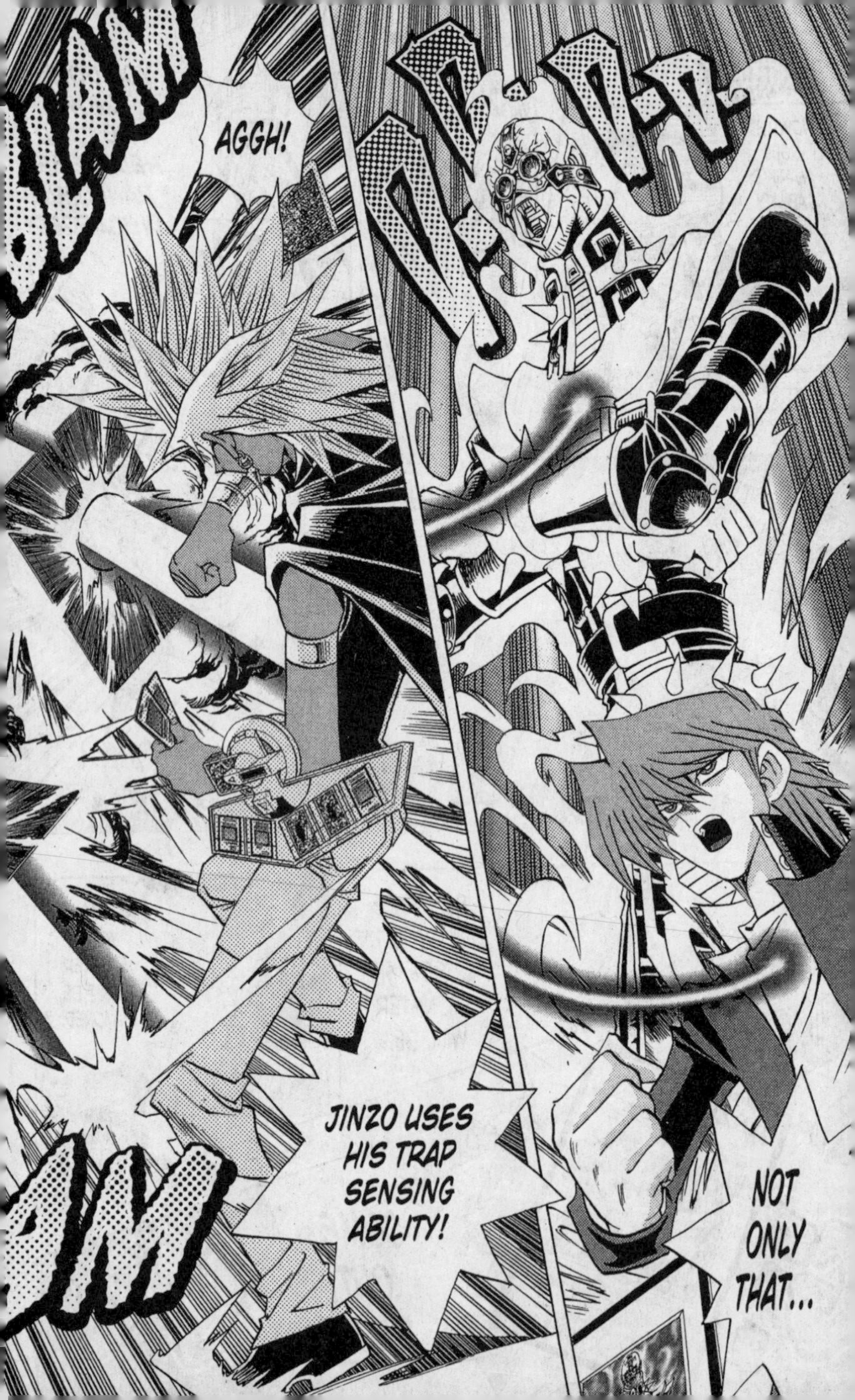
SLAM
AGGH!
JINZO USES HIS TRAP SENSING ABILITY!
NOT ONLY THAT...

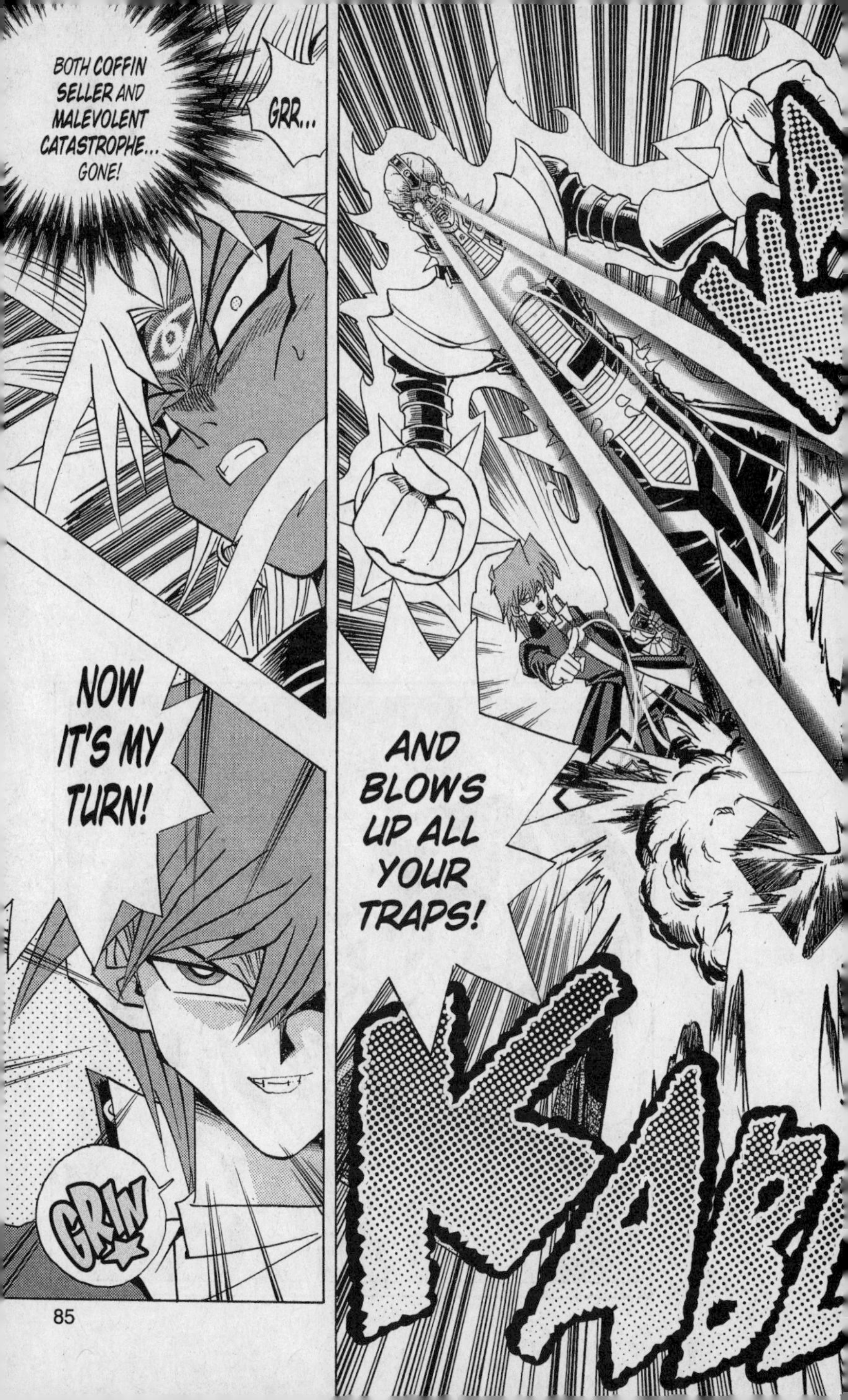
AND BLOWS UP ALL YOUR TRAPS!
BOTH COFFIN SELLER AND MALEVOLENT CATASTROPHE... GONE!
GRR...
NOW IT'S MY TURN!
GRIN

Duel 246: Cage of Fire!

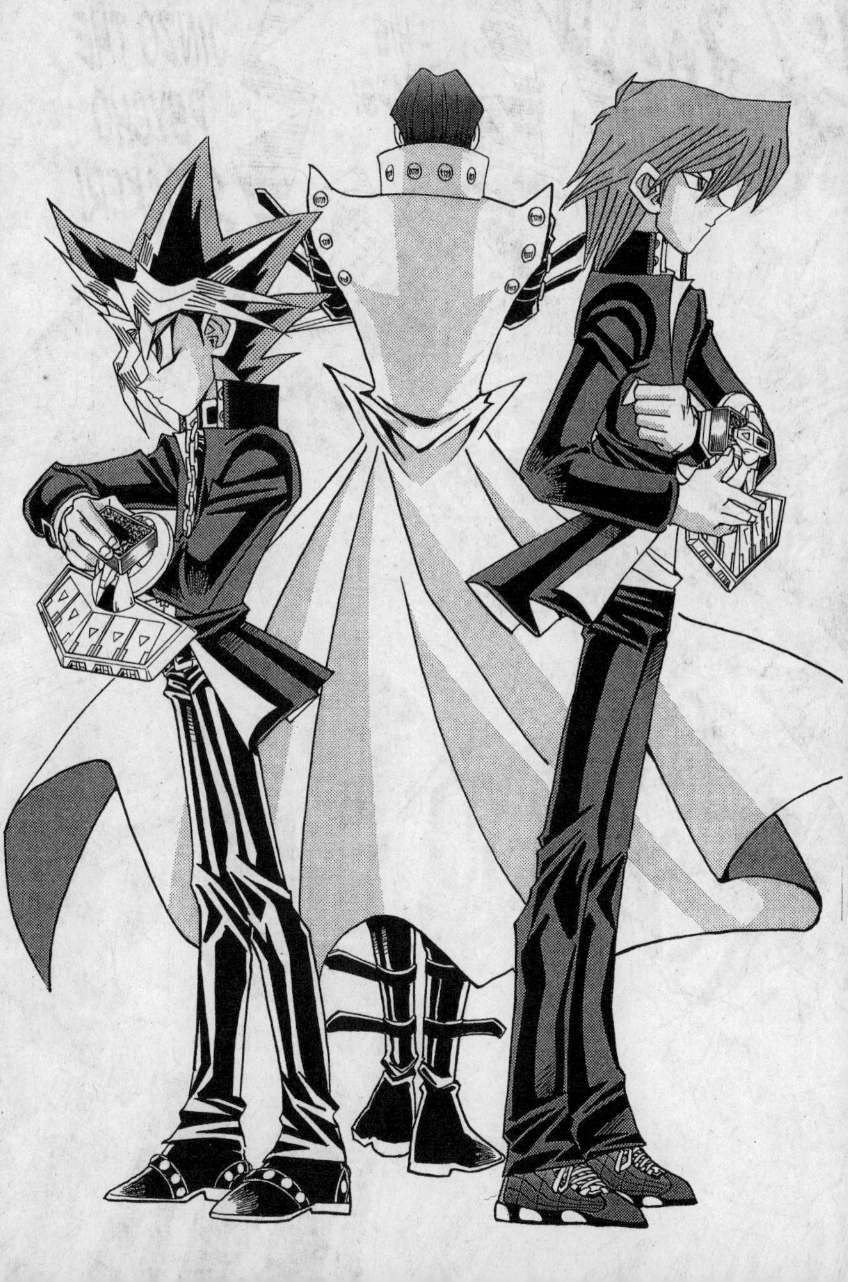

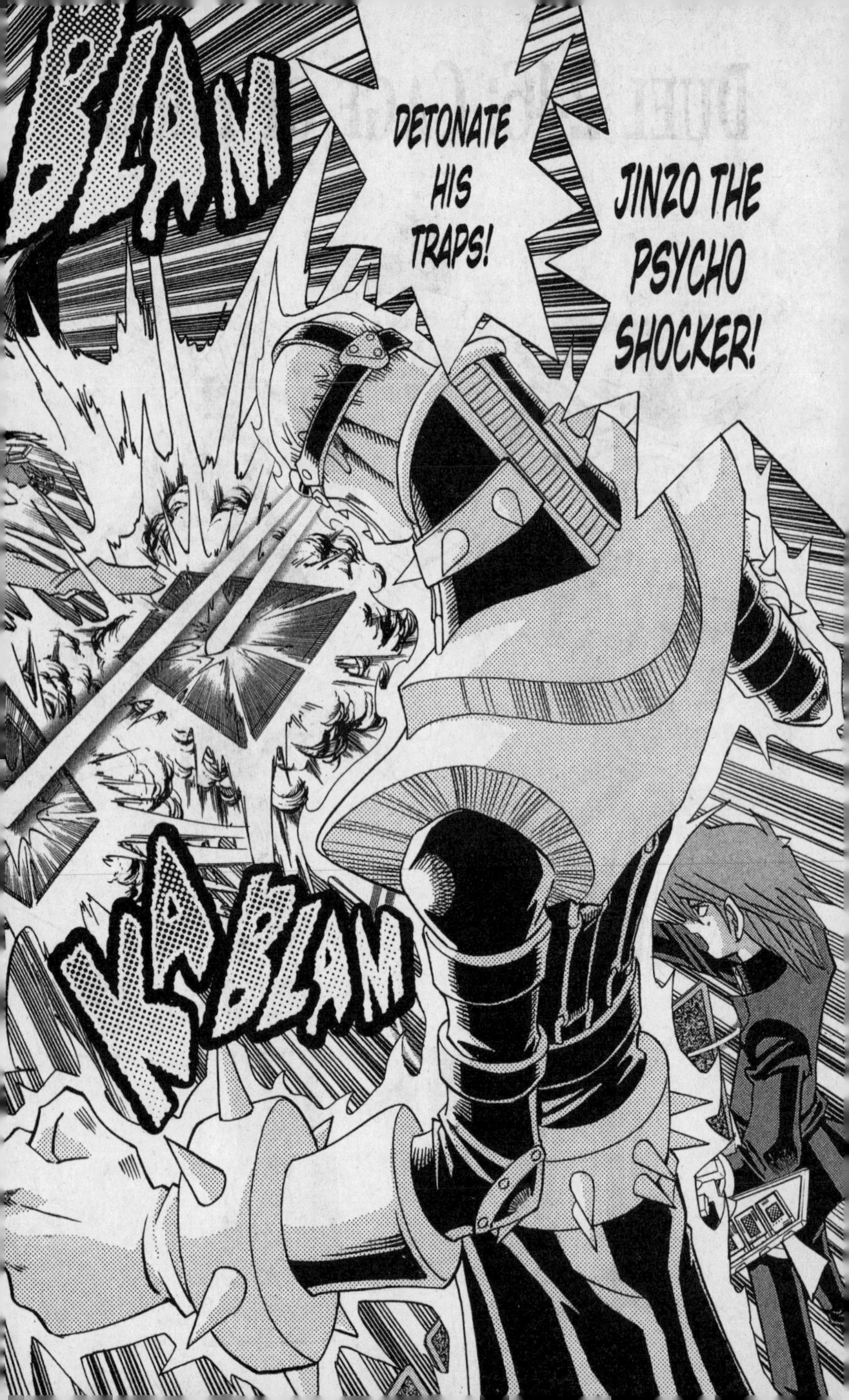
JINZO THE PSYCHO SHOCKER!
DETONATE HIS TRAPS!
BLAM
KABLAM

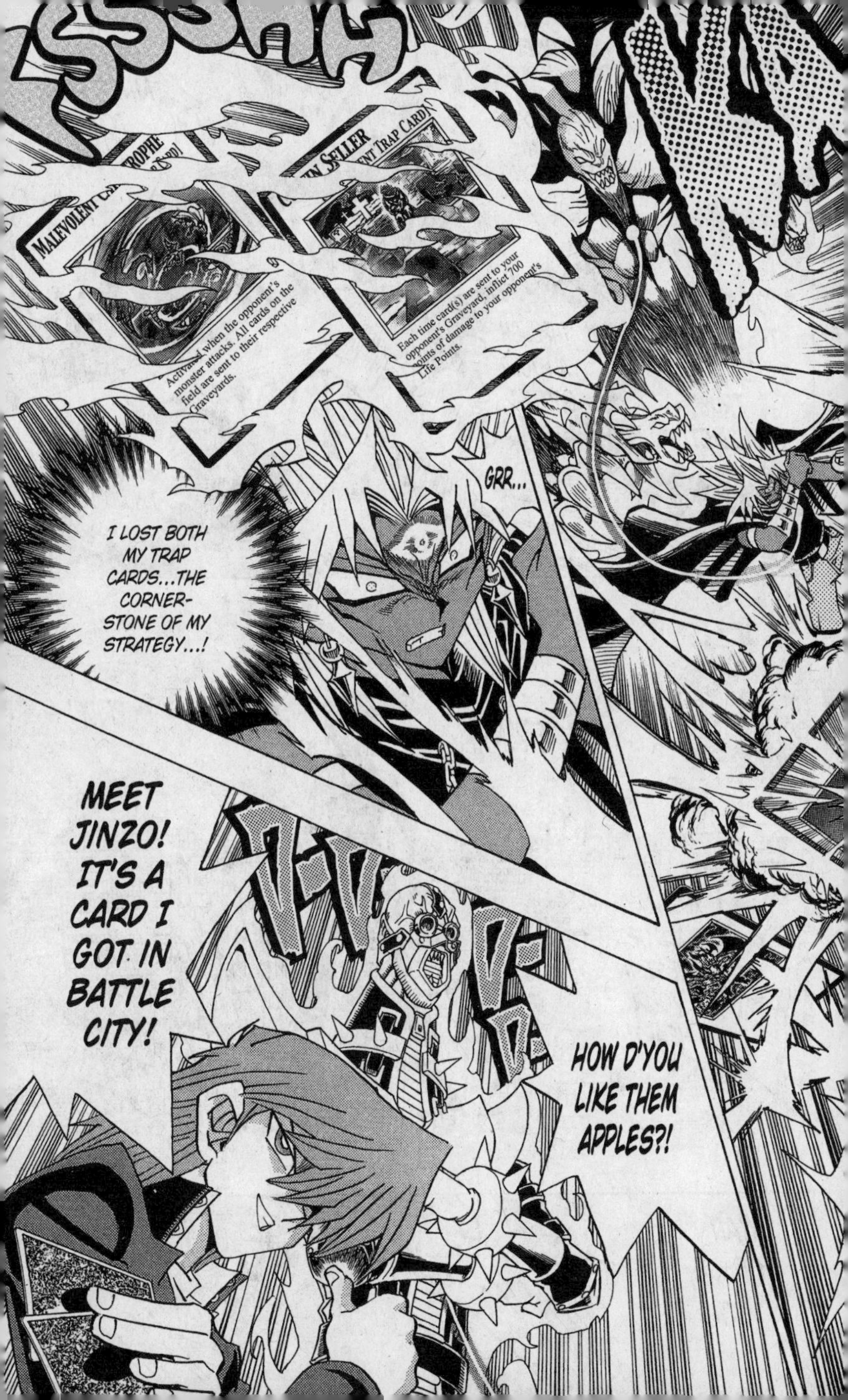

Activated when the opponent's monster attacks. All cards on the field are sent to their respective Graveyards.
Each time card(s) are sent to your opponent's Graveyard, inflict 700 points of damage to your opponent's Life Points.
GRR...
I LOST BOTH MY TRAP CARDS...THE CORNER-STONE OF MY STRATEGY...!
MEET JINZO! IT'S A CARD I GOT IN BATTLE CITY!
HOW D'YOU LIKE THEM APPLES?!

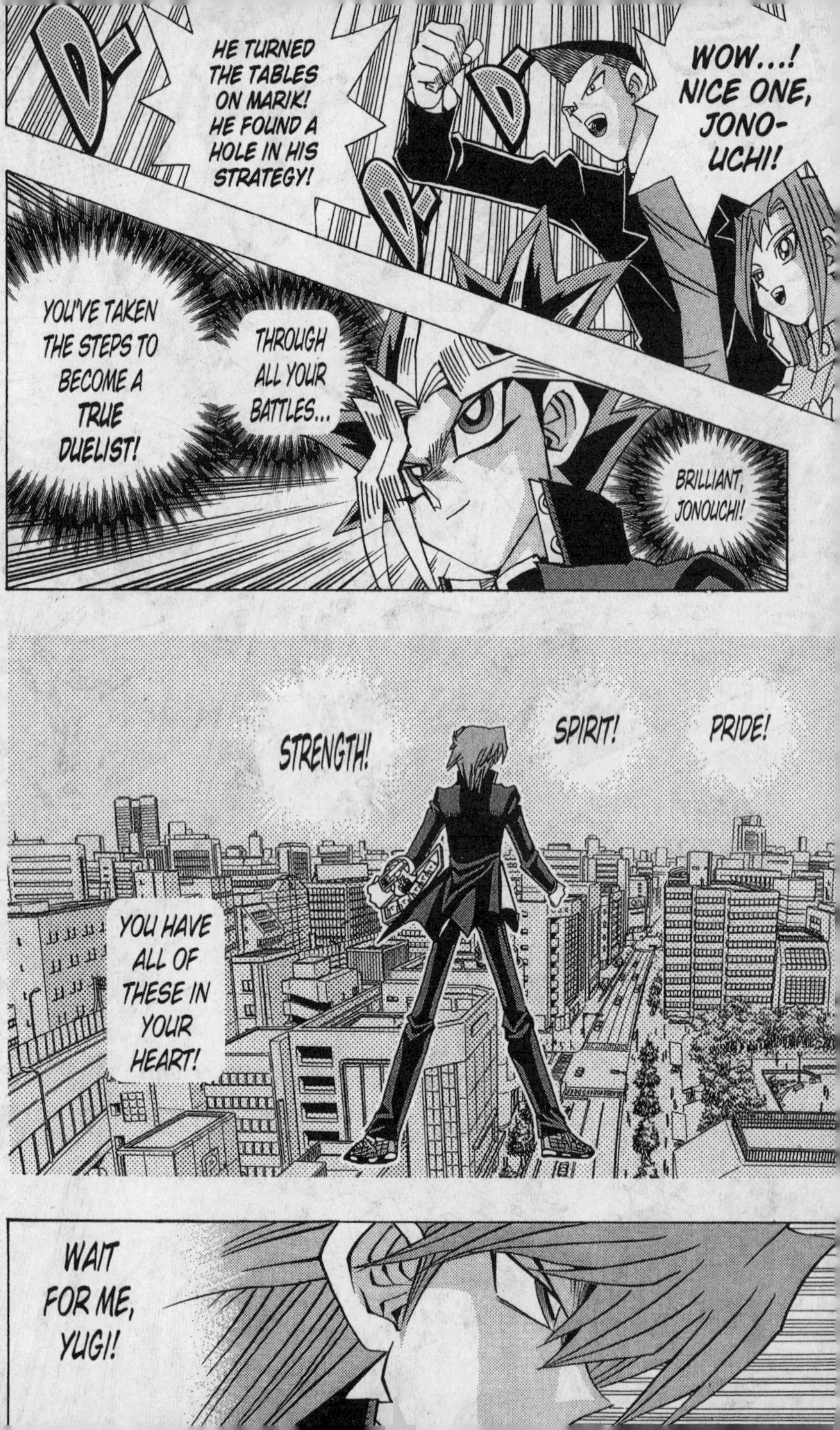
WOW...! NICE ONE, JONOUCHI!
HE TURNED THE TABLES ON MARIK! HE FOUND A HOLE IN HIS STRATEGY!
BRILLIANT, JONOUCHI!
THROUGH ALL YOUR BATTLES...
YOU'VE TAKEN THE STEPS TO BECOME A TRUE DUELIST!
PRIDE!
SPIRIT!
STRENGTH!
YOU HAVE ALL OF THESE IN YOUR HEART!
WAIT FOR ME, YUGI!

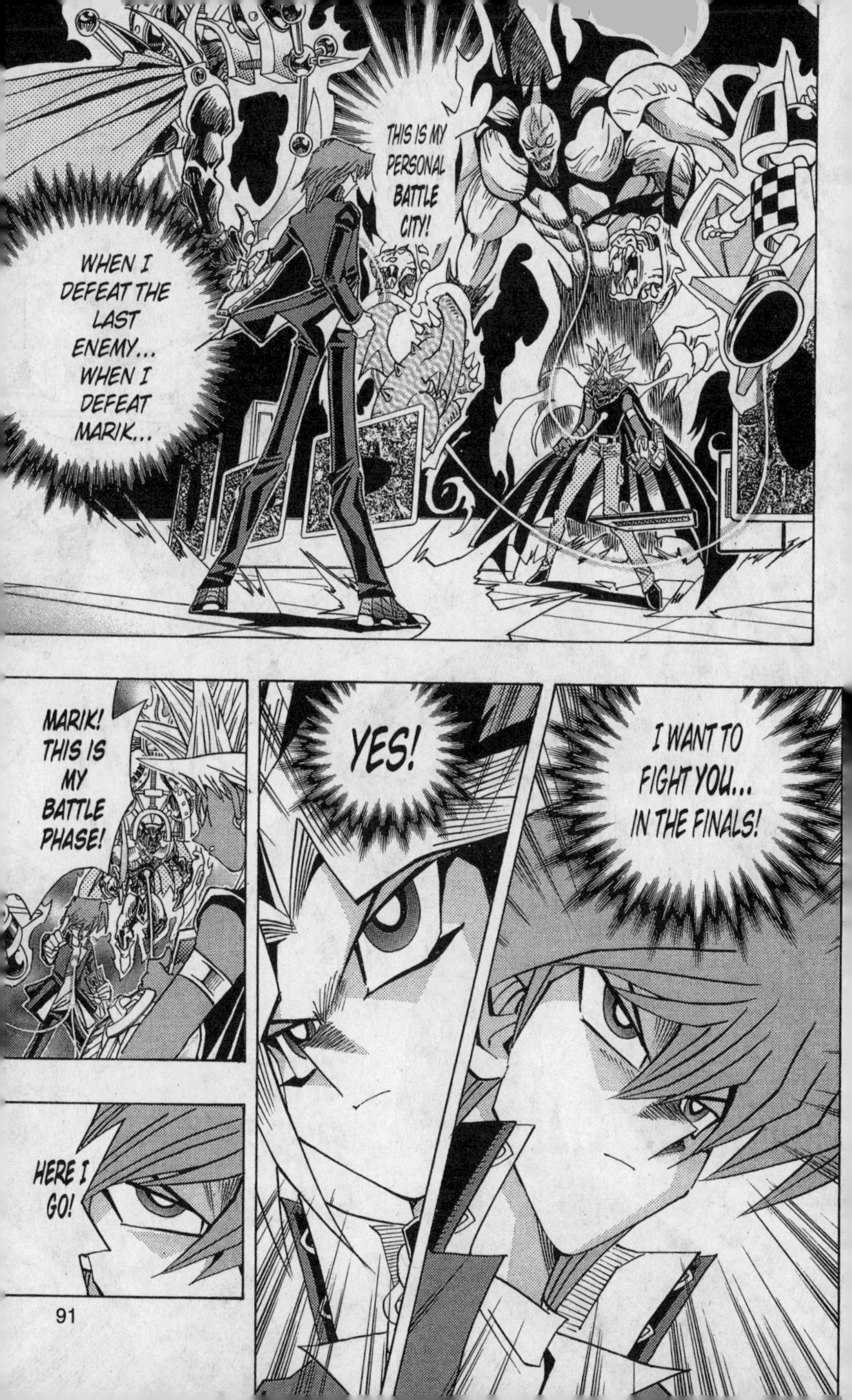
THIS IS MY PERSONAL BATTLE CITY!
WHEN I DEFEAT THE LAST ENEMY... WHEN I DEFEAT MARIK...
I WANT TO FIGHT YOU... IN THE FINALS!
YES!
MARIK! THIS IS MY BATTLE PHASE!
HERE I GO!

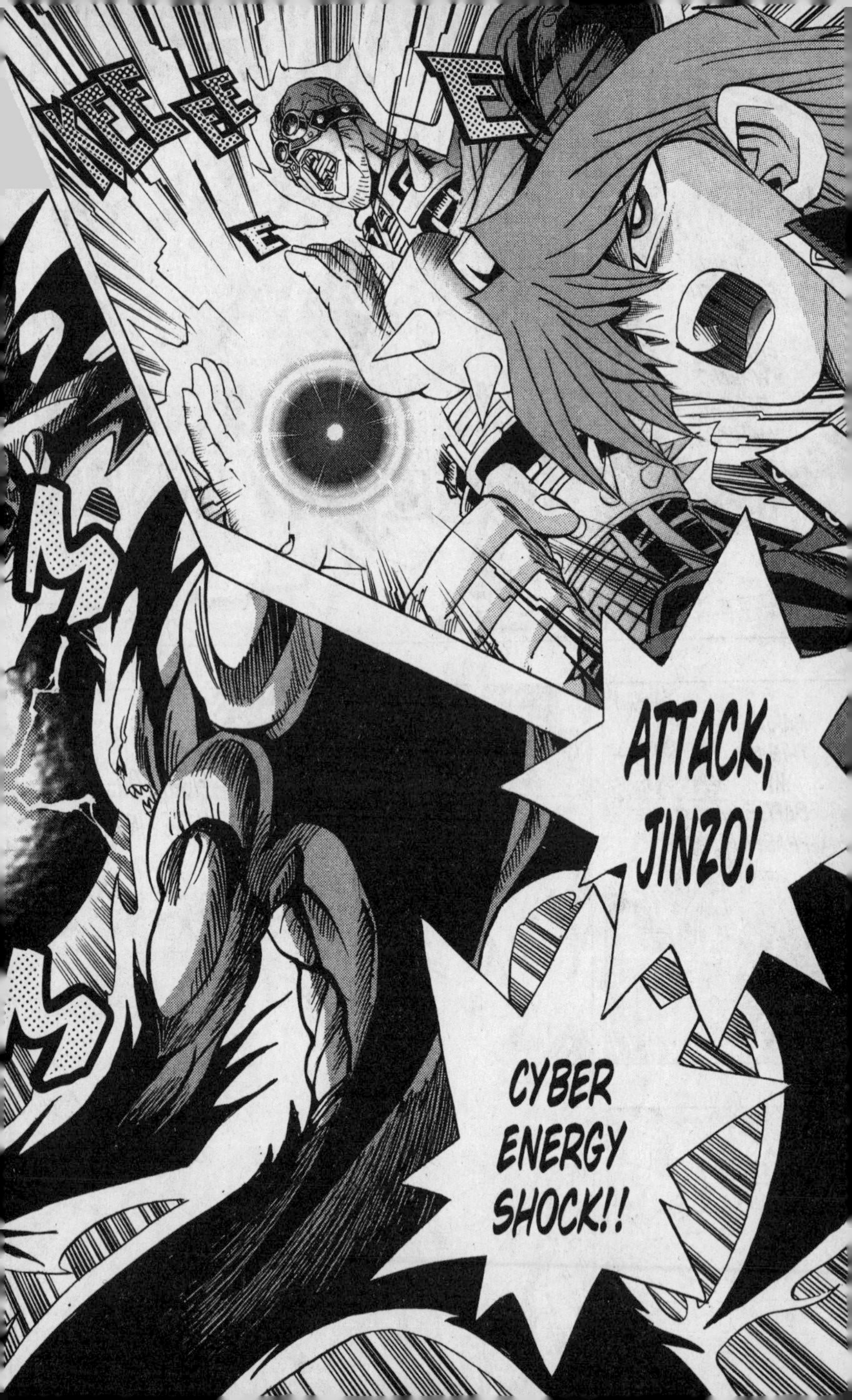
KEEEE
E
E
ATTACK, JINZO!
CYBER ENERGY SHOCK!!

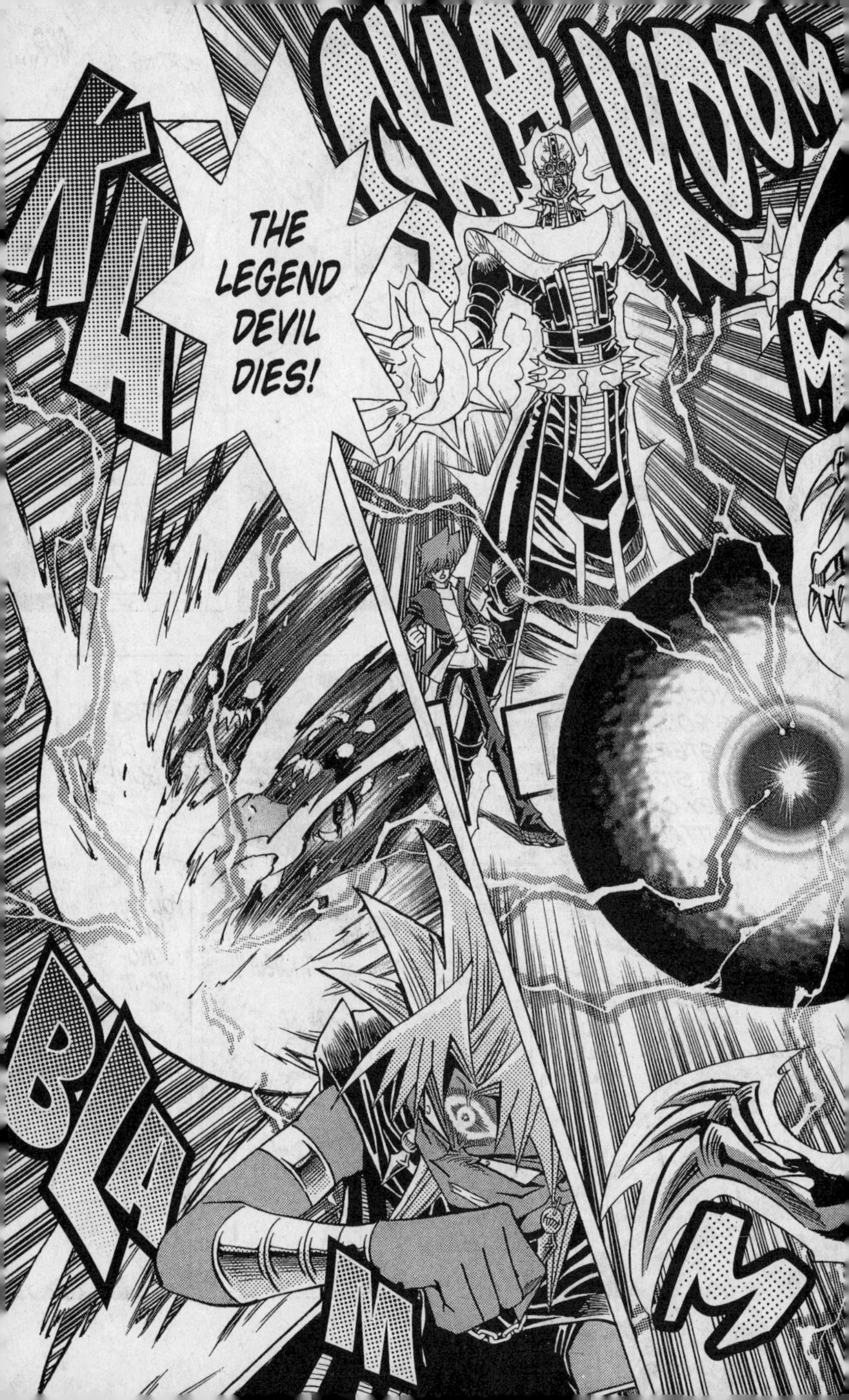
THE LEGEND DEVIL DIES!
BLAM

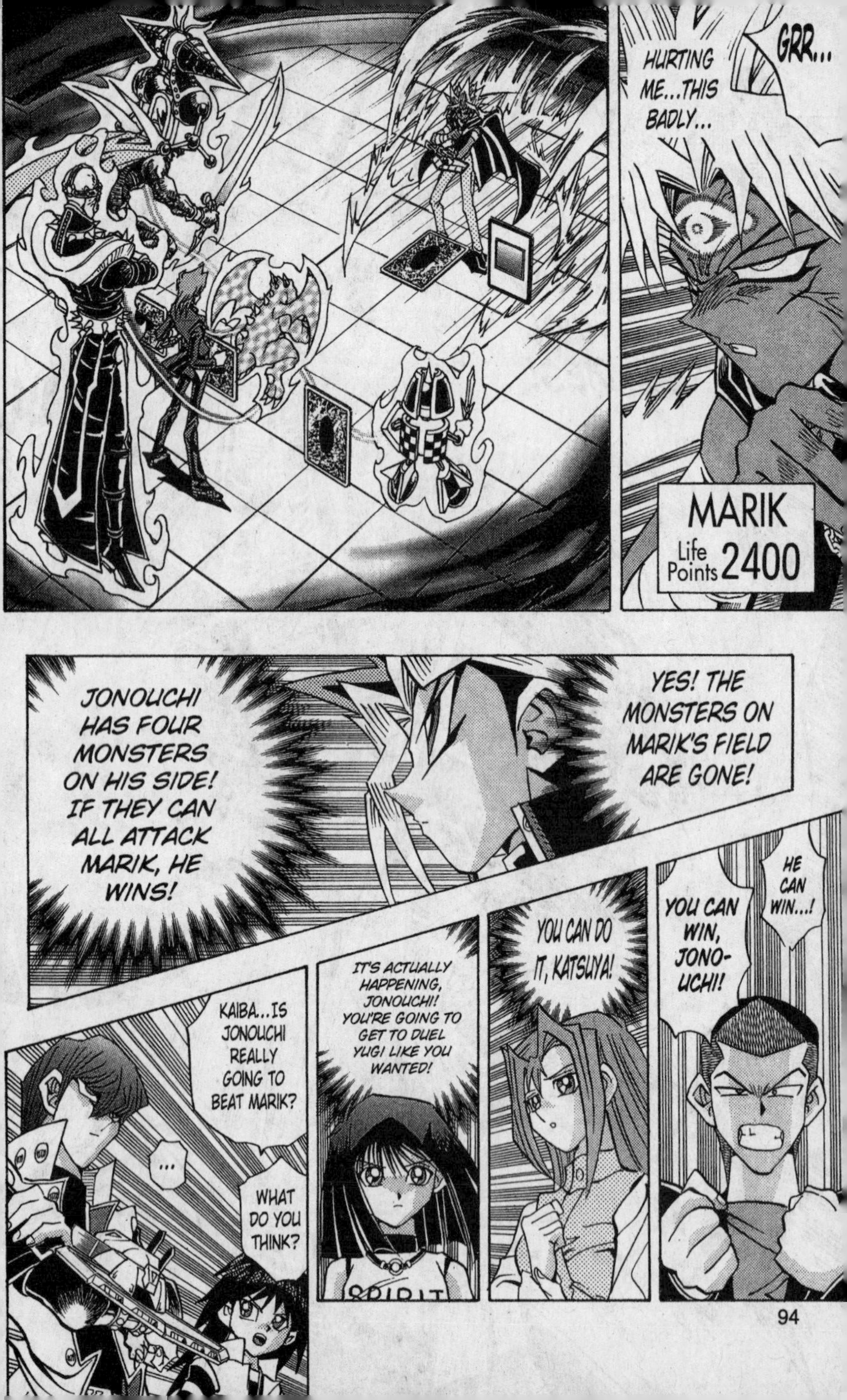
GRR...
HURTING ME...THIS BADLY...
MARIK
Life Points 2400
YES! THE MONSTERS ON MARIK'S FIELD ARE GONE!
JONOUCHI HAS FOUR MONSTERS ON HIS SIDE! IF THEY CAN ALL ATTACK MARIK, HE WINS!
HE CAN WIN...!
YOU CAN WIN, JONO-UCHI!
YOU CAN DO IT, KATSUYA!
IT'S ACTUALLY HAPPENING, JONOUCHI! YOU'RE GOING TO GET TO DUEL YUGI LIKE YOU WANTED!
KAIBA...IS JONOUCHI REALLY GOING TO BEAT MARIK?
...
WHAT DO YOU THINK?

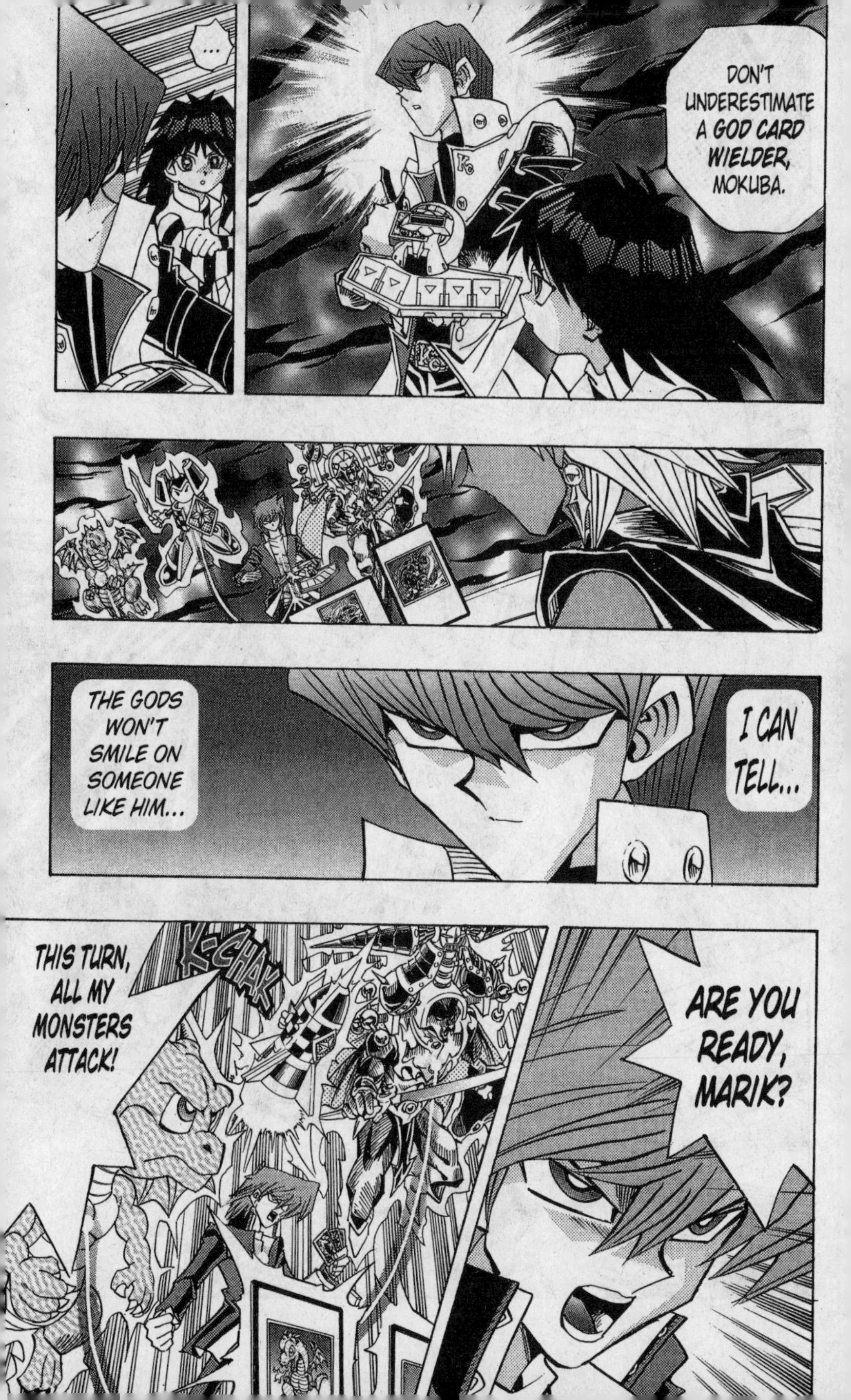
DON'T UNDERESTIMATE A GOD CARD WIELDER, MOKUBA.
...
I CAN TELL...
THE GODS WON'T SMILE ON SOMEONE LIKE HIM...
ARE YOU READY, MARIK?
THIS TURN, ALL MY MONSTERS ATTACK!
K-CHAK

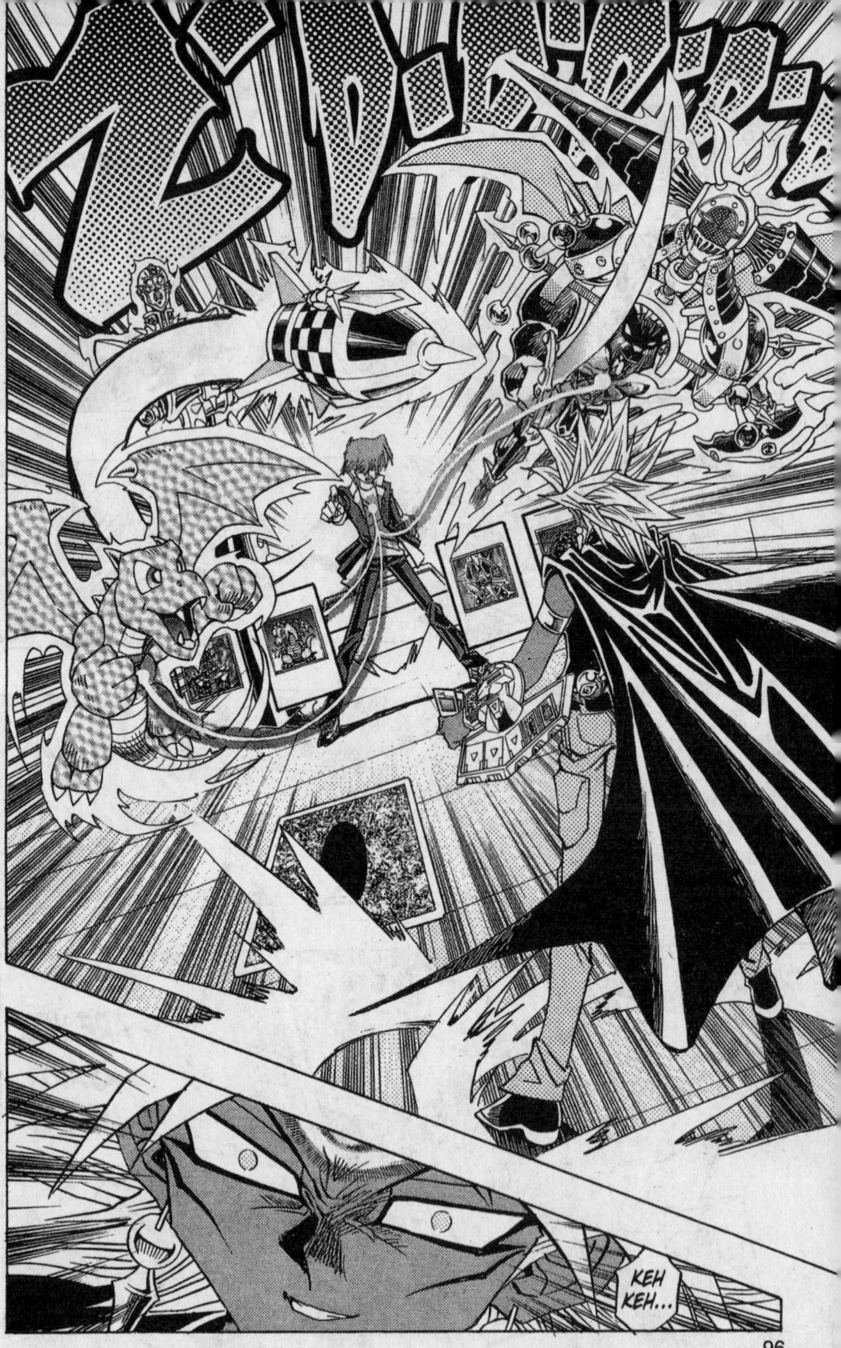
KEH KEH...

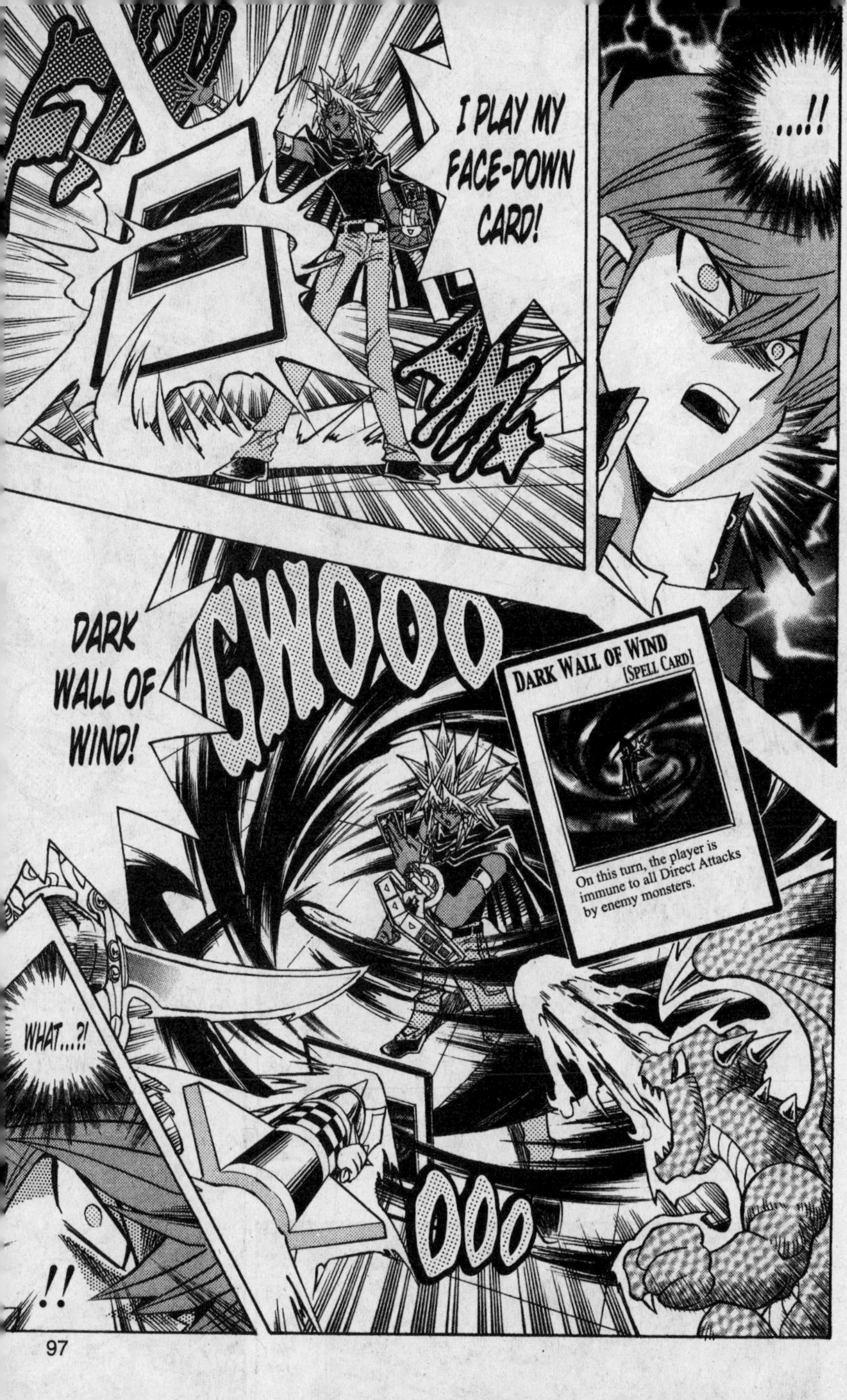
...!!
I PLAY MY FACE-DOWN CARD!
DARK WALL OF WIND!
GWOOO
DARK WALL OF WIND
[SPELL CARD]
On this turn, the player is immune to all Direct Attacks by enemy monsters.
OOO
WHAT...?!
!!

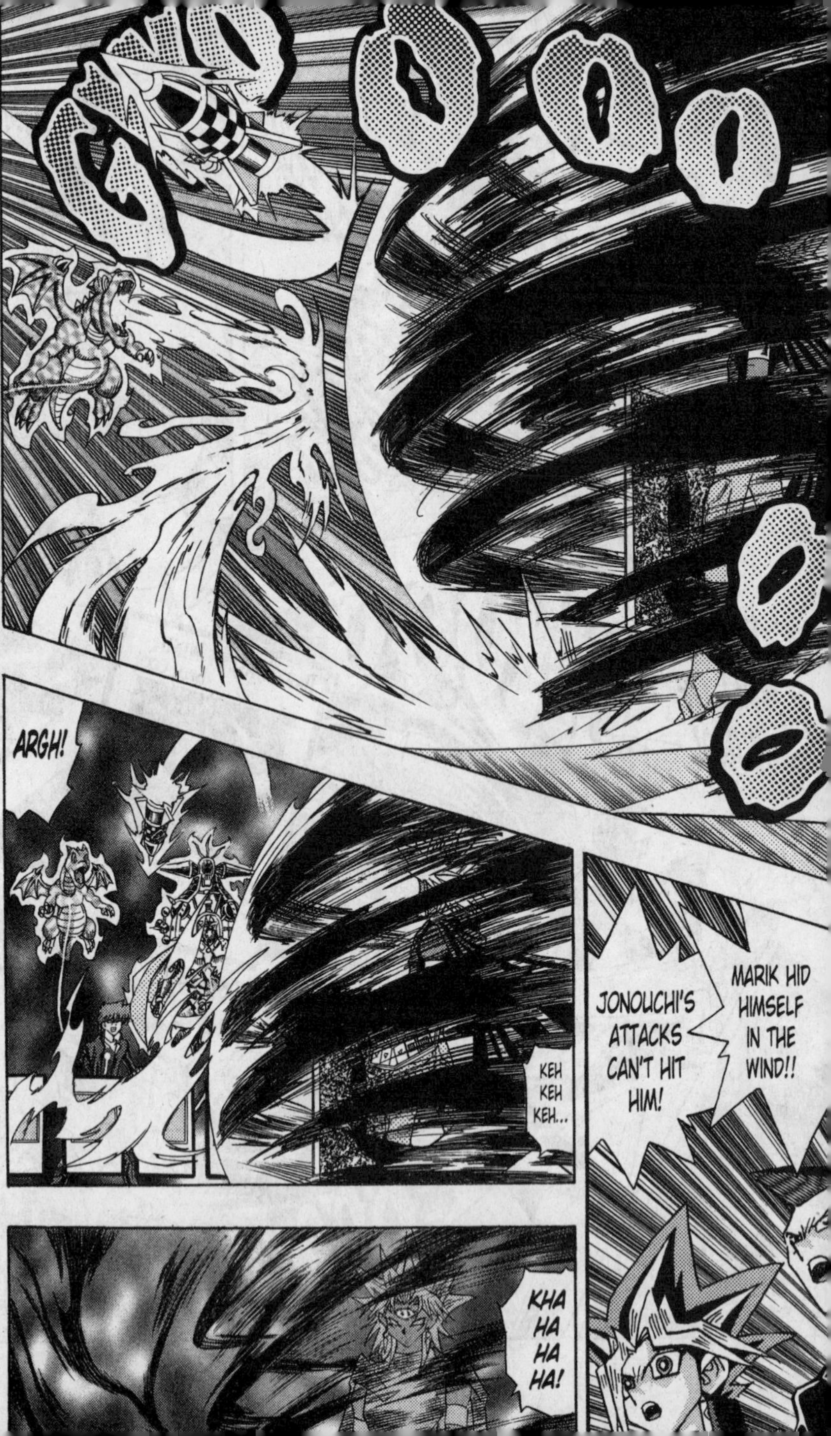
GWOOOOOO
MARIK HID HIMSELF IN THE WIND!!
JONOUCHI'S ATTACKS CAN'T HIT HIM!
ARGH!
KEH KEH KEH...
KHA HA HA HA!

READ THIS WAY

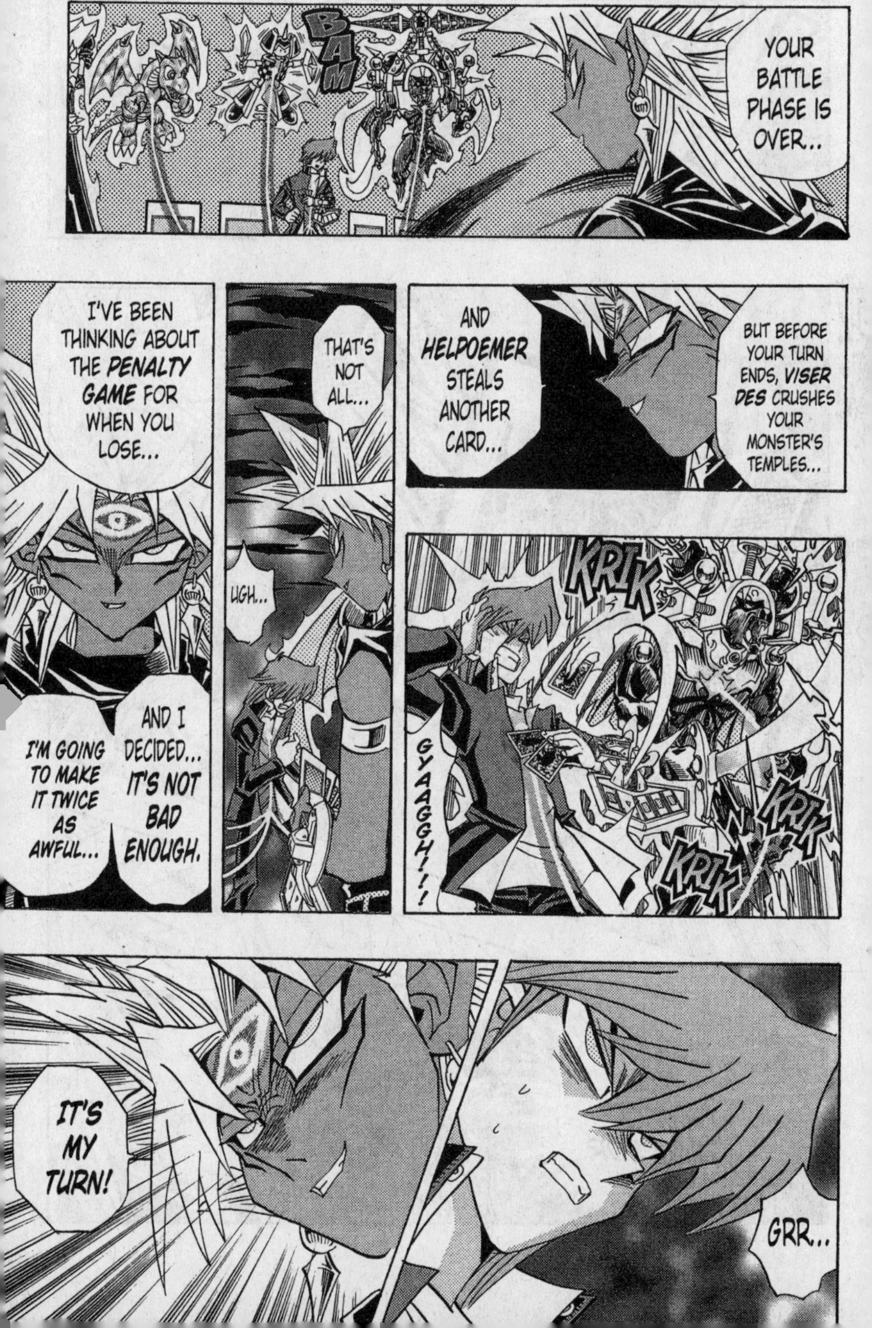
YOUR BATTLE PHASE IS OVER...
BAM
BUT BEFORE YOUR TURN ENDS, VISER DES CRUSHES YOUR MONSTER'S TEMPLES...
AND HELPOEMER STEALS ANOTHER CARD...
KRIK
GYAAAGGH!!!
KRIK
KRIK
THAT'S NOT ALL...
UGH...
I'VE BEEN THINKING ABOUT THE PENALTY GAME FOR WHEN YOU LOSE...
AND I DECIDED... IT'S NOT BAD ENOUGH.
I'M GOING TO MAKE IT TWICE AS AWFUL...
GRR...
IT'S MY TURN!

DRAW!

LAVA GOLEM

This card can only be Special Summoned by Tributing 2 monsters on your opponent's side of the field, and is summoned to your opponent's side. This card inflicts 700 points of damage to this card's controller during each Standby Phases.

ATK/2500

HERE'S A NEW PENALTY GAME FOR YOU...

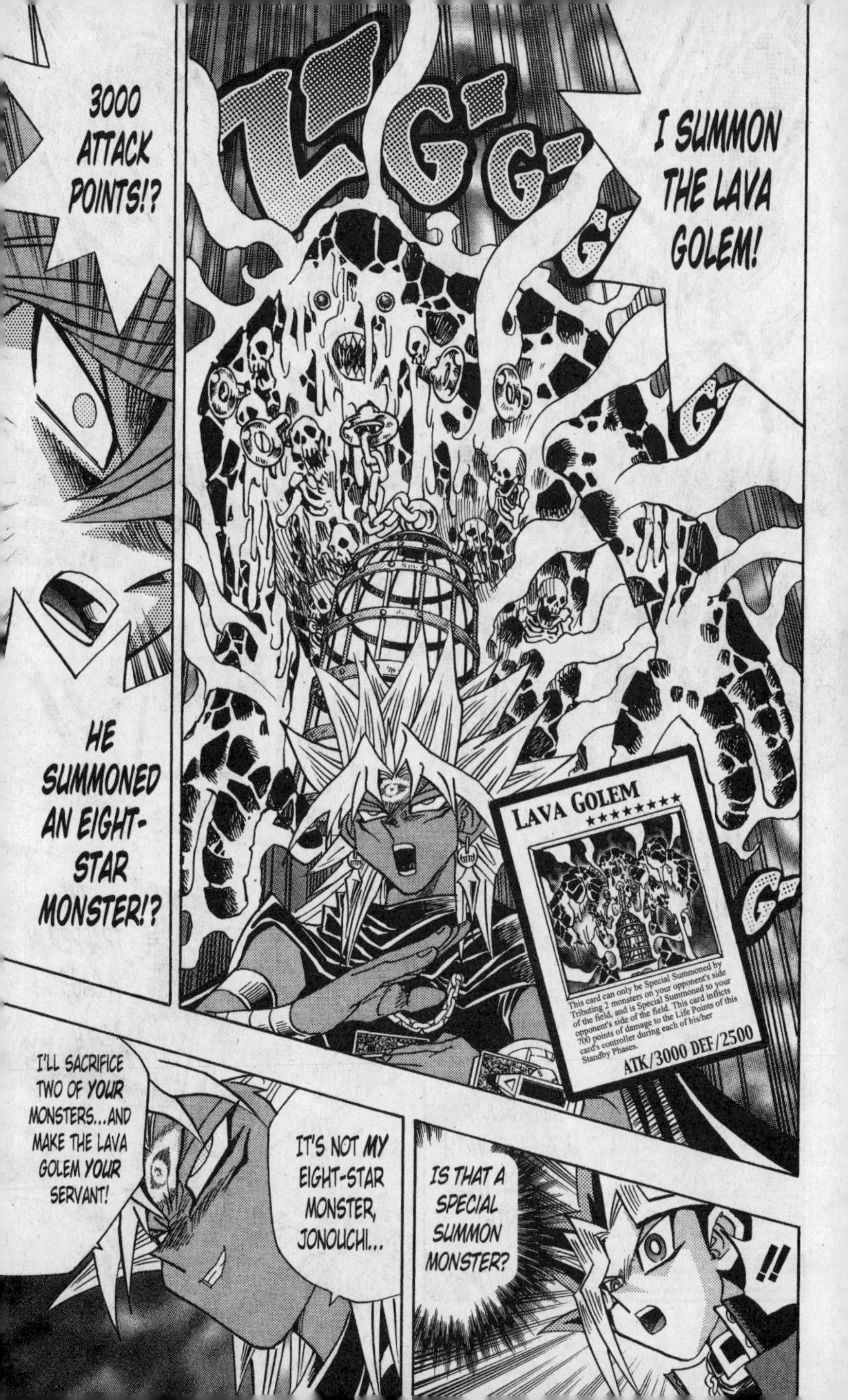
I SUMMON THE LAVA GOLEM!
LAVA GOLEM
★★★★★★★★
This card can only be Special Summoned by Tributing 2 monsters on your opponent's side of the field, and is Special Summoned to your opponent's side of the field. This card inflicts 700 points of damage to the Life Points of this card's controller during each of his/her Standby Phases.
ATK/3000 DEF/2500
3000 ATTACK POINTS!?
HE SUMMONED AN EIGHT-STAR MONSTER!?
IS THAT A SPECIAL SUMMON MONSTER?
!!
IT'S NOT MY EIGHT-STAR MONSTER, JONOUCHI...
I'LL SACRIFICE TWO OF YOUR MONSTERS...AND MAKE THE LAVA GOLEM YOUR SERVANT!

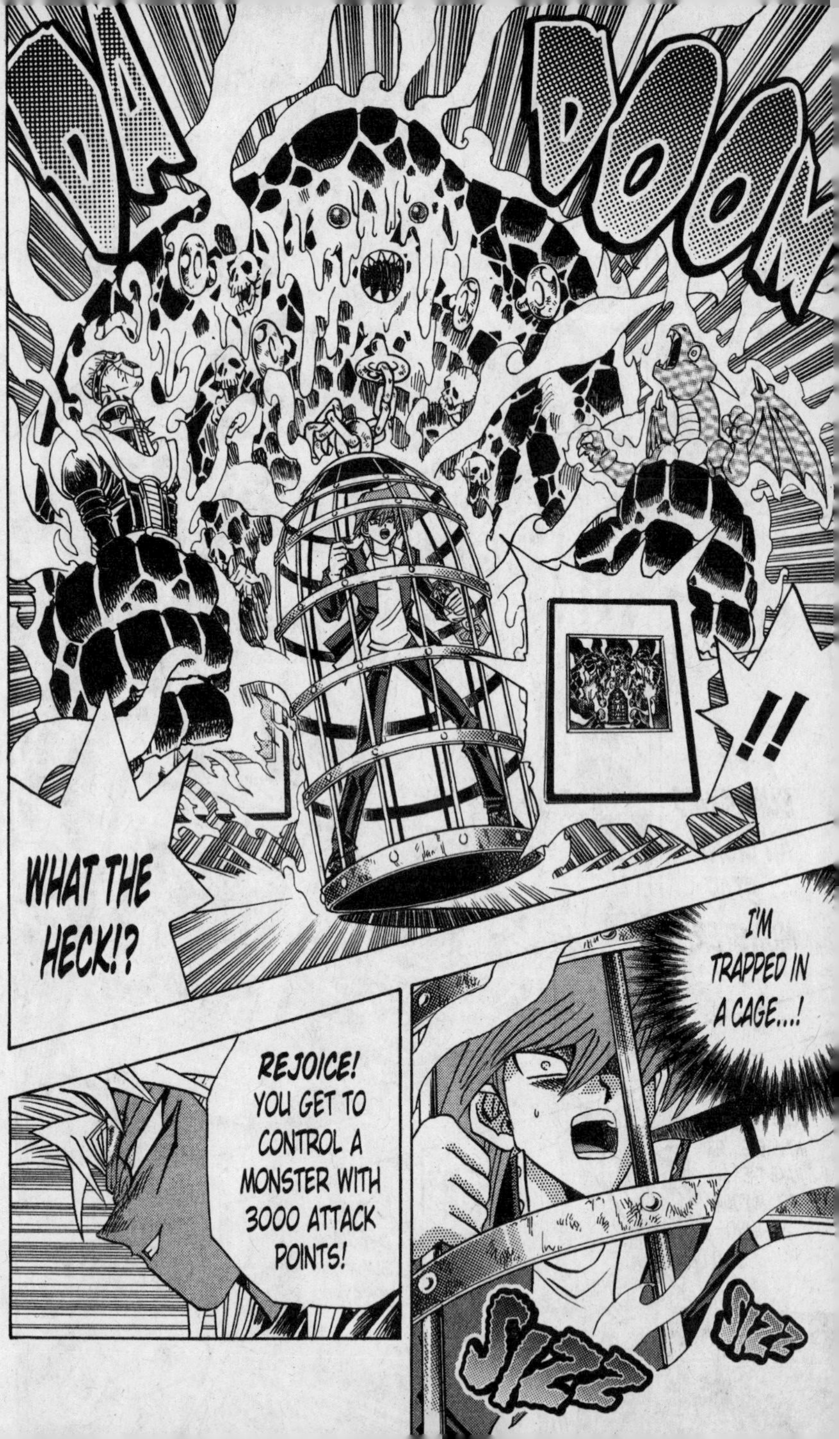
!!
WHAT THE HECK!?
I'M TRAPPED IN A CAGE...!
REJOICE! YOU GET TO CONTROL A MONSTER WITH 3000 ATTACK POINTS!

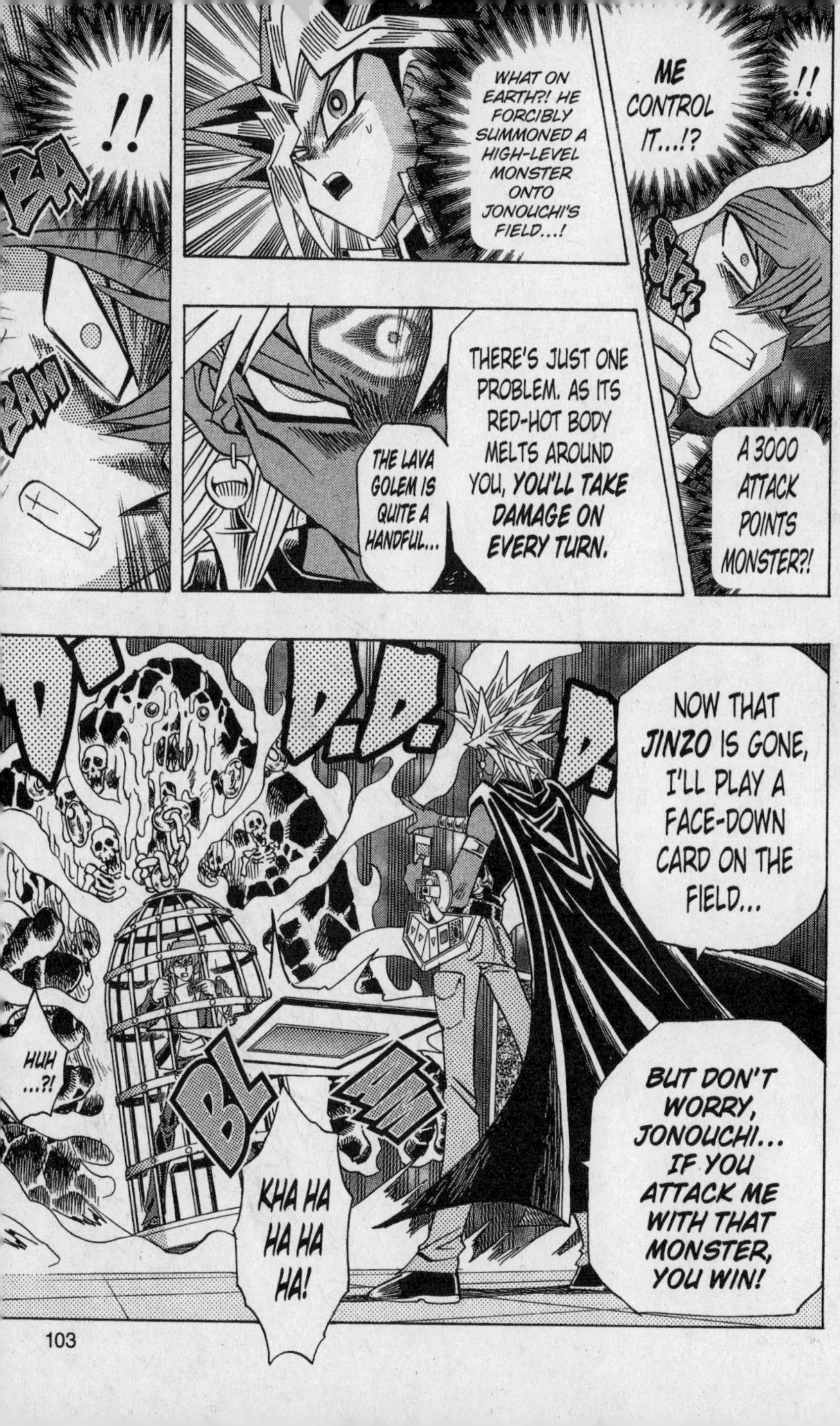
!!
ME CONTROL IT...!?
A 3000 ATTACK POINTS MONSTER?!
WHAT ON EARTH?! HE FORCIBLY SUMMONED A HIGH-LEVEL MONSTER ONTO JONOUCHI'S FIELD...!
THERE'S JUST ONE PROBLEM. AS ITS RED-HOT BODY MELTS AROUND YOU, YOU'LL TAKE DAMAGE ON EVERY TURN.
THE LAVA GOLEM IS QUITE A HANDFUL...
!!
NOW THAT JINZO IS GONE, I'LL PLAY A FACE-DOWN CARD ON THE FIELD...
BUT DON'T WORRY, JONOUCHI... IF YOU ATTACK ME WITH THAT MONSTER, YOU WIN!
KHA HA HA HA HA!
HUH ...?!

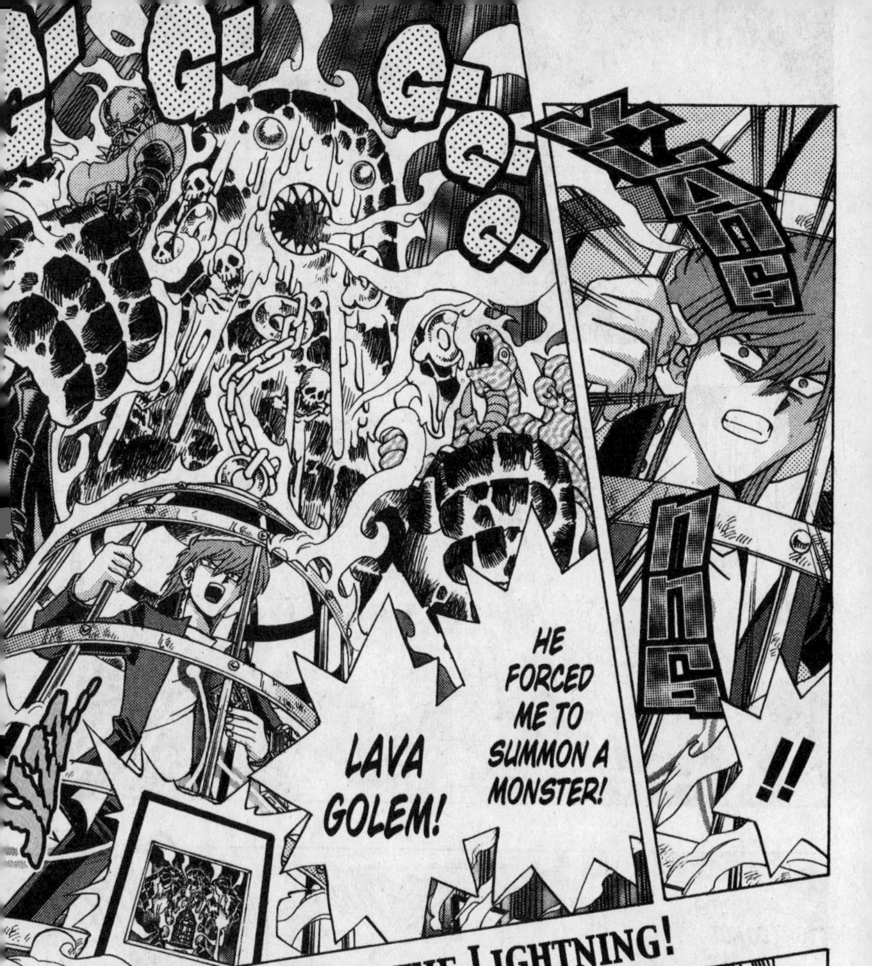
!!
HE FORCED ME TO SUMMON A MONSTER!
LAVA GOLEM!

Duel 247: Duel the Lightning!

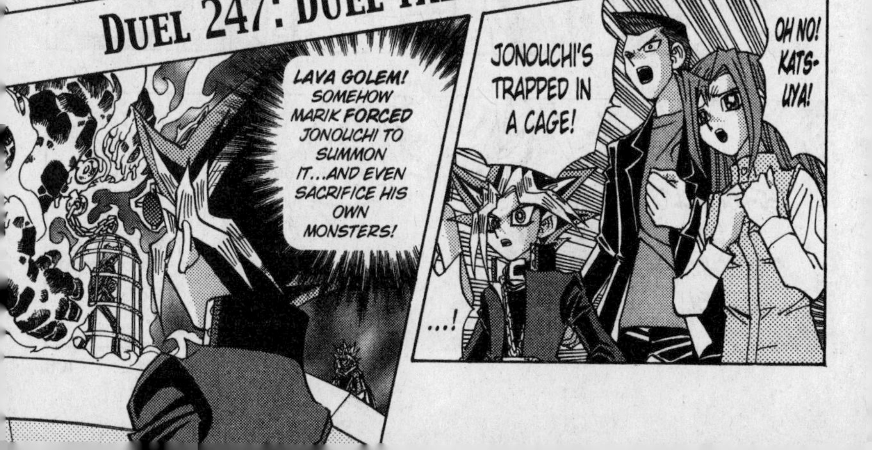
OH NO! KATS-UYA!
JONOUCHI'S TRAPPED IN A CAGE!
...!
LAVA GOLEM! SOMEHOW MARIK FORCED JONOUCHI TO SUMMON IT...AND EVEN SACRIFICE HIS OWN MONSTERS!

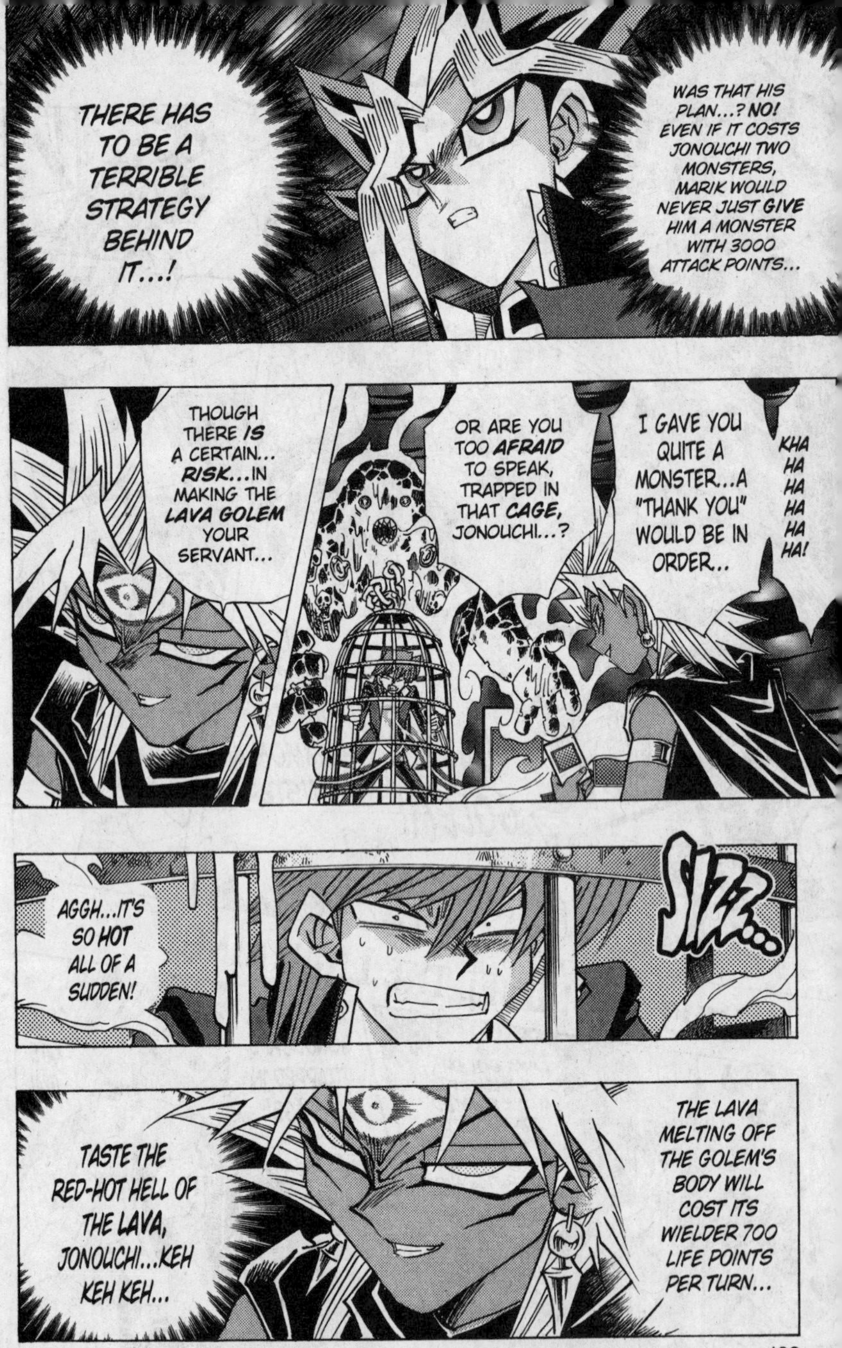
WAS THAT HIS PLAN...? NO! EVEN IF IT COSTS JONOUCHI TWO MONSTERS, MARIK WOULD NEVER JUST GIVE HIM A MONSTER WITH 3000 ATTACK POINTS...
THERE HAS TO BE A TERRIBLE STRATEGY BEHIND IT...!
I GAVE YOU QUITE A MONSTER...A "THANK YOU" WOULD BE IN ORDER...
KHA HA HA HA HA HA!
OR ARE YOU TOO AFRAID TO SPEAK, TRAPPED IN THAT CAGE, JONOUCHI...?
THOUGH THERE IS A CERTAIN... RISK...IN MAKING THE LAVA GOLEM YOUR SERVANT...
SIZZ...
AGGH...IT'S SO HOT ALL OF A SUDDEN!
THE LAVA MELTING OFF THE GOLEM'S BODY WILL COST ITS WIELDER 700 LIFE POINTS PER TURN...
TASTE THE RED-HOT HELL OF THE LAVA, JONOUCHI...KEH KEH KEH...

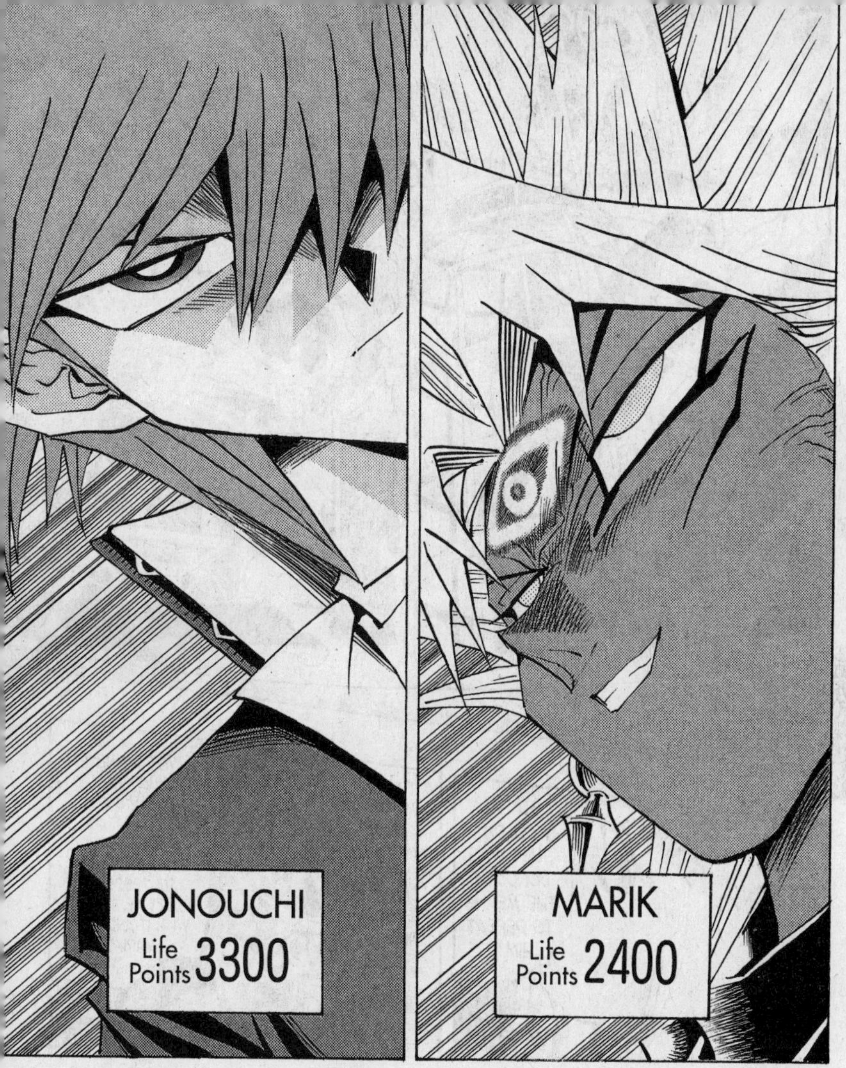
MARIK
Life Points 2400
JONOUCHI
Life Points 3300

DUEL 247: DUEL THE LIGHTNING!

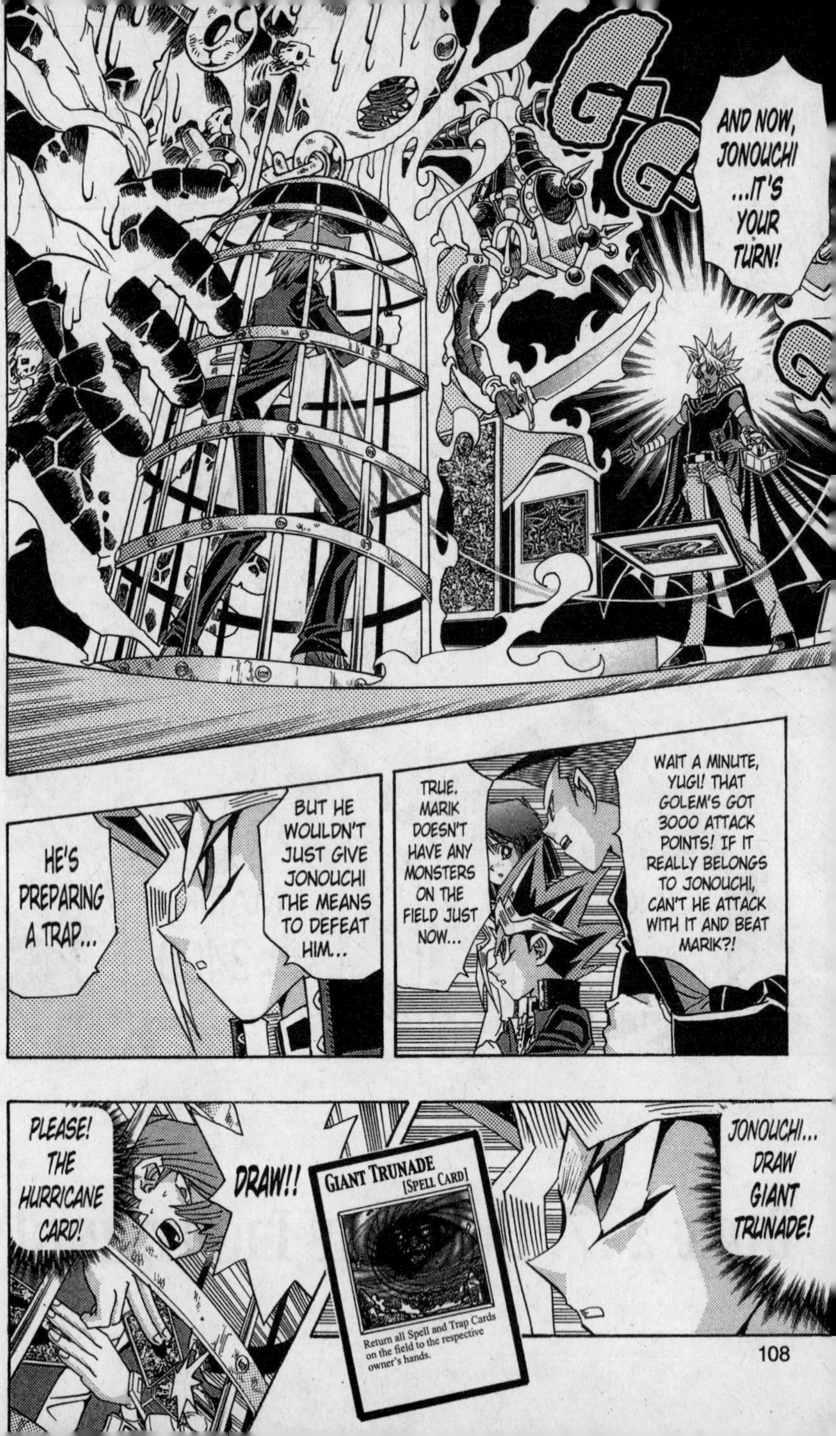
AND NOW, JONOUCHI ...IT'S YOUR TURN!
WAIT A MINUTE, YUGI! THAT GOLEM'S GOT 3000 ATTACK POINTS! IF IT REALLY BELONGS TO JONOUCHI, CAN'T HE ATTACK WITH IT AND BEAT MARIK?!
TRUE. MARIK DOESN'T HAVE ANY MONSTERS ON THE FIELD JUST NOW...
BUT HE WOULDN'T JUST GIVE JONOUCHI THE MEANS TO DEFEAT HIM...
HE'S PREPARING A TRAP...
JONOUCHI... DRAW GIANT TRUNADE!
DRAW!!
GIANT TRUNADE
[SPELL CARD]
Return all Spell and Trap Cards on the field to the respective owner's hands.
PLEASE! THE HURRICANE CARD!

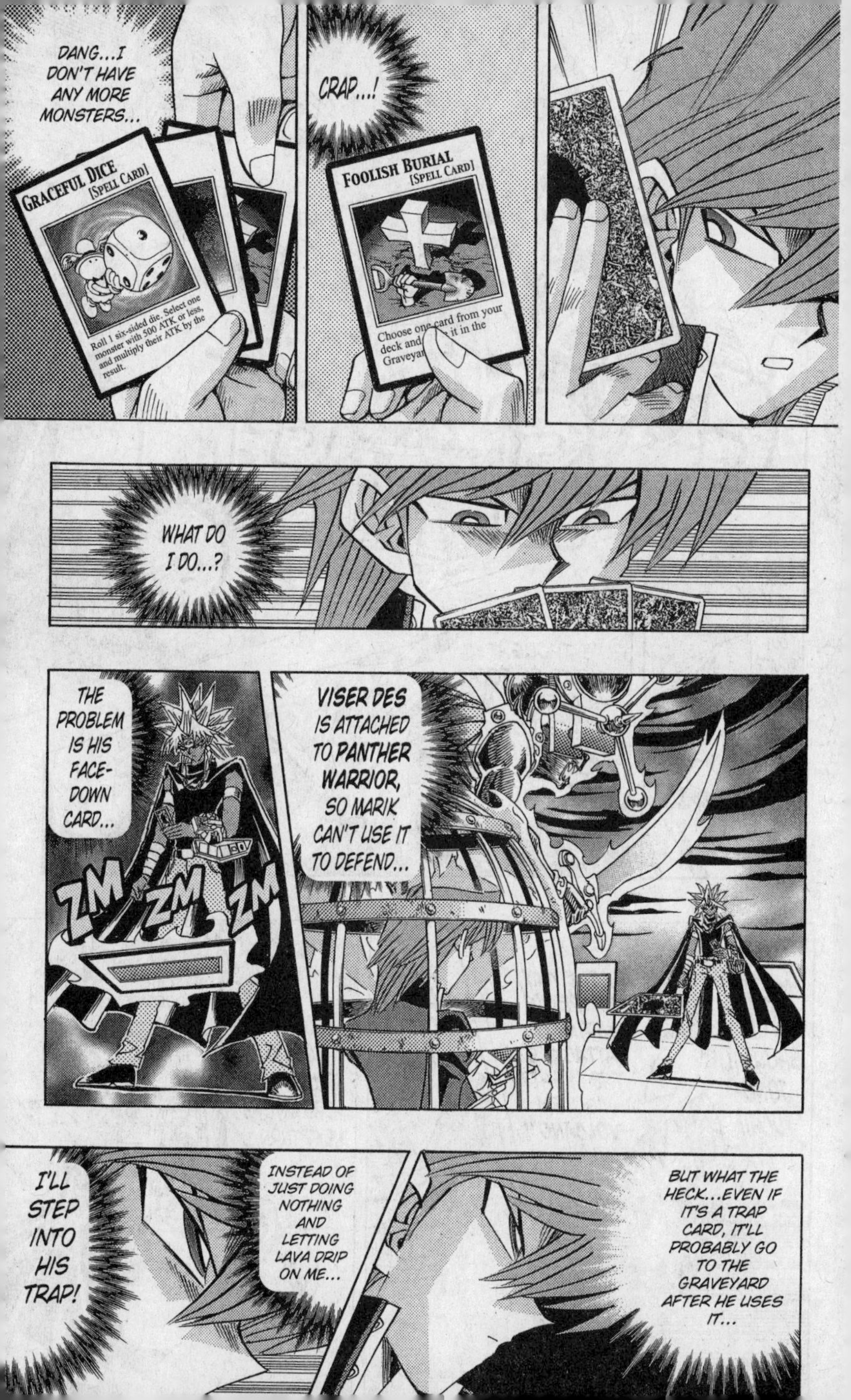
CRAP...!
FOOLISH BURIAL
[SPELL CARD]
Choose one card from your deck and it in the Graveyard
DANG...I DON'T HAVE ANY MORE MONSTERS...
GRACEFUL DICE
[SPELL CARD]
Roll 1 six-sided die. Select one monster with 500 ATK or less, and multiply their ATK by the result.
WHAT DO I DO...?
VISER DES IS ATTACHED TO PANTHER WARRIOR, SO MARIK CAN'T USE IT TO DEFEND...
THE PROBLEM IS HIS FACE-DOWN CARD...
ZM ZM ZM
BUT WHAT THE HECK...EVEN IF IT'S A TRAP CARD, IT'LL PROBABLY GO TO THE GRAVEYARD AFTER HE USES IT...
INSTEAD OF JUST DOING NOTHING AND LETTING LAVA DRIP ON ME...
I'LL STEP INTO HIS TRAP!

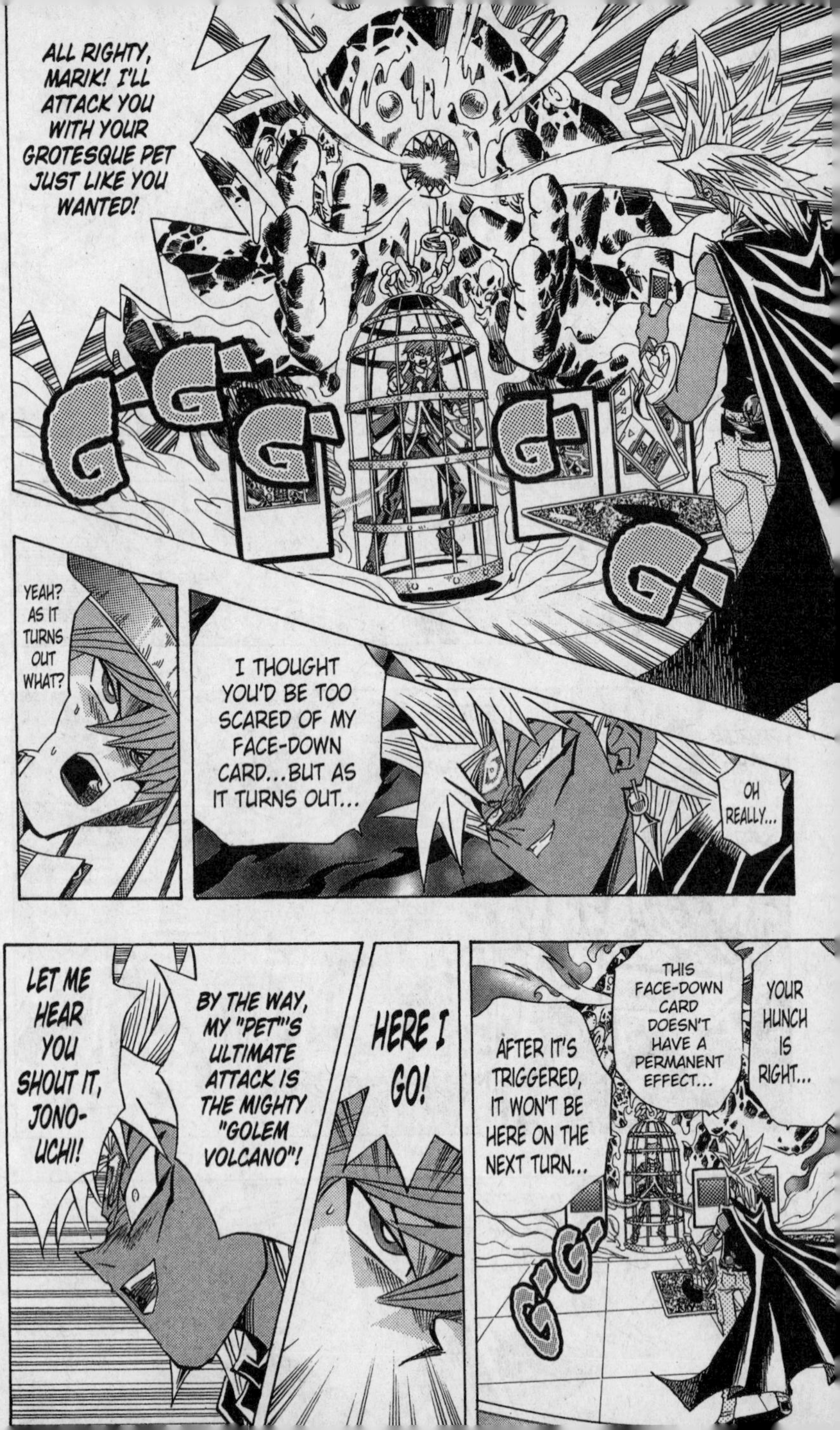
ALL RIGHTY, MARIK! I'LL ATTACK YOU WITH YOUR GROTESQUE PET JUST LIKE YOU WANTED!
G G G G G
I THOUGHT YOU'D BE TOO SCARED OF MY FACE-DOWN CARD...BUT AS IT TURNS OUT...
OH REALLY...
YEAH? AS IT TURNS OUT WHAT?
YOUR HUNCH IS RIGHT...
THIS FACE-DOWN CARD DOESN'T HAVE A PERMANENT EFFECT...
AFTER IT'S TRIGGERED, IT WON'T BE HERE ON THE NEXT TURN...
G G
HERE I GO!
BY THE WAY, MY "PET"'S ULTIMATE ATTACK IS THE MIGHTY "GOLEM VOLCANO"!
LET ME HEAR YOU SHOUT IT, JONO-UCHI!

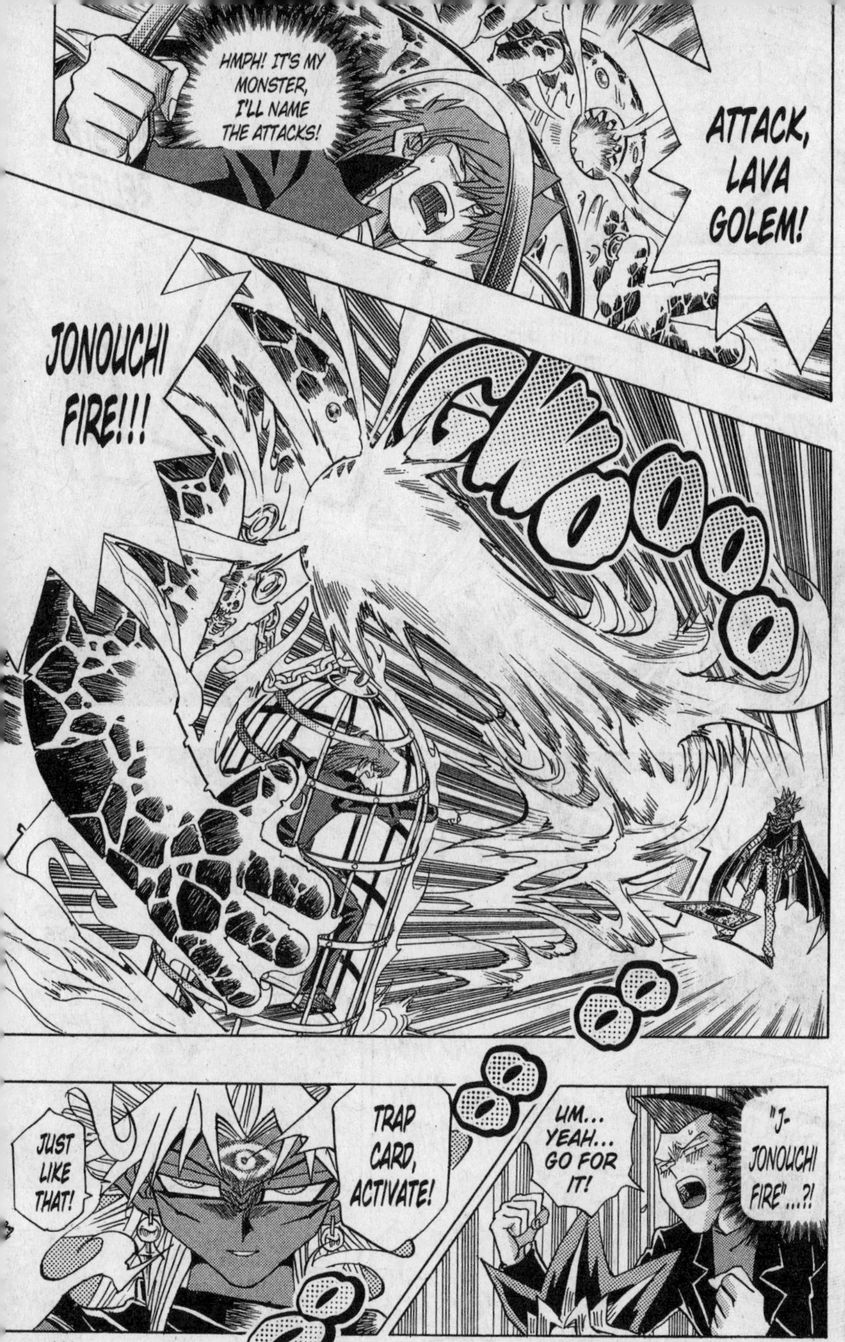
ATTACK, LAVA GOLEM!
HMPH! IT'S MY MONSTER, I'LL NAME THE ATTACKS!
JONOUCHI FIRE!!!
"J-JONOUCHI FIRE"...?!
UM... YEAH... GO FOR IT!
TRAP CARD, ACTIVATE!
JUST LIKE THAT!

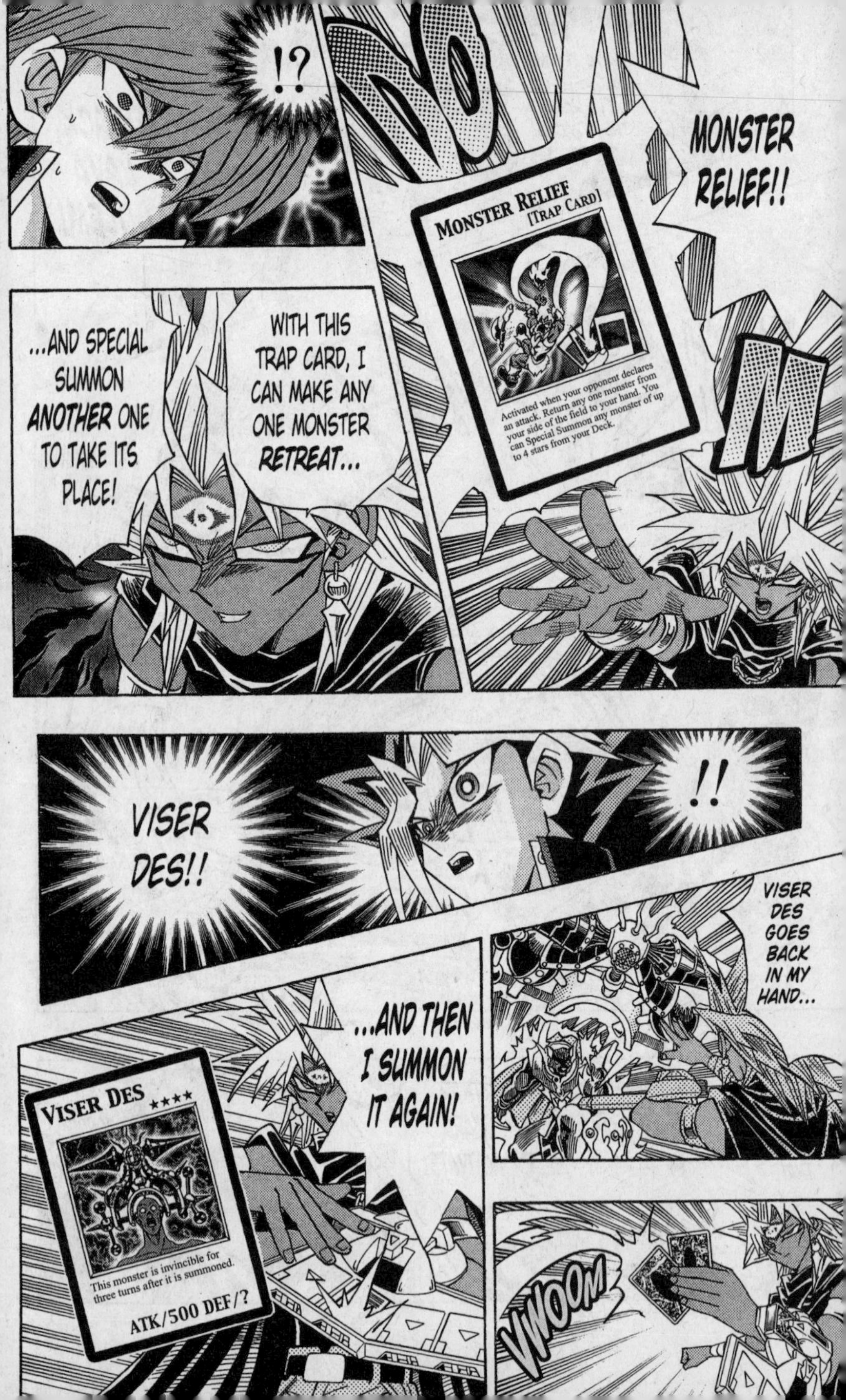

MONSTER RELIEF!!
MONSTER RELIEF [TRAP CARD]
Activated when your opponent declares an attack. Return any one monster from your side of the field to your hand. You can Special Summon any monster of up to 4 stars from your Deck.
!?
WITH THIS TRAP CARD, I CAN MAKE ANY ONE MONSTER RETREAT...
...AND SPECIAL SUMMON ANOTHER ONE TO TAKE ITS PLACE!
!!
VISER DES!!
VISER DES GOES BACK IN MY HAND...
VWOOM
...AND THEN I SUMMON IT AGAIN!
VISER DES ★★★★
This monster is invincible for three turns after it is summoned.
ATK/500 DEF/?

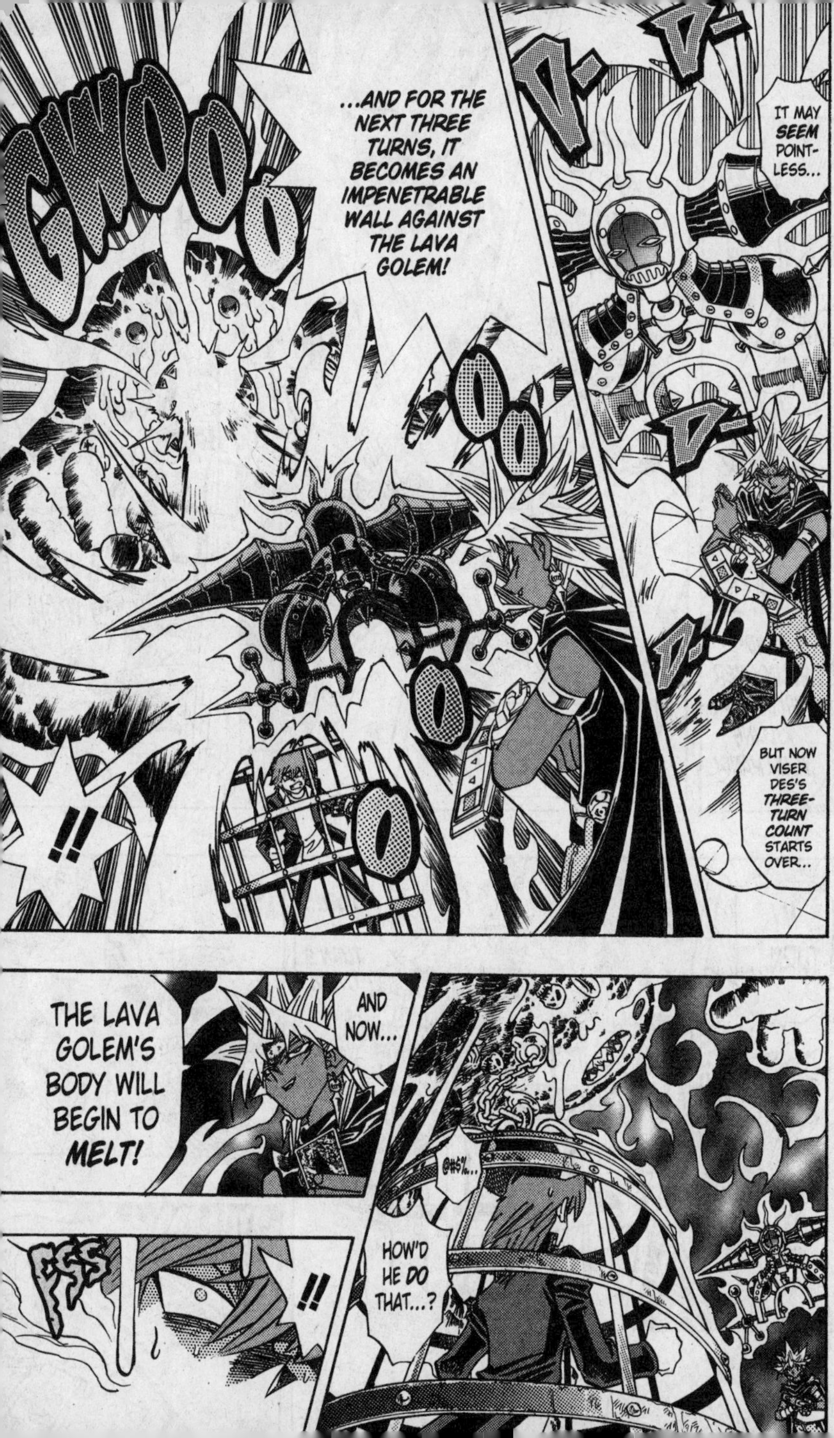
D- D-
IT MAY SEEM POINTLESS...
D-
D-
BUT NOW VISER DES'S THREE-TURN COUNT STARTS OVER...
GWOOO
OOOO
...AND FOR THE NEXT THREE TURNS, IT BECOMES AN IMPENETRABLE WALL AGAINST THE LAVA GOLEM!
!!
@#$%...
HOW'D HE DO THAT...?
AND NOW...
THE LAVA GOLEM'S BODY WILL BEGIN TO MELT!
!!
FSS

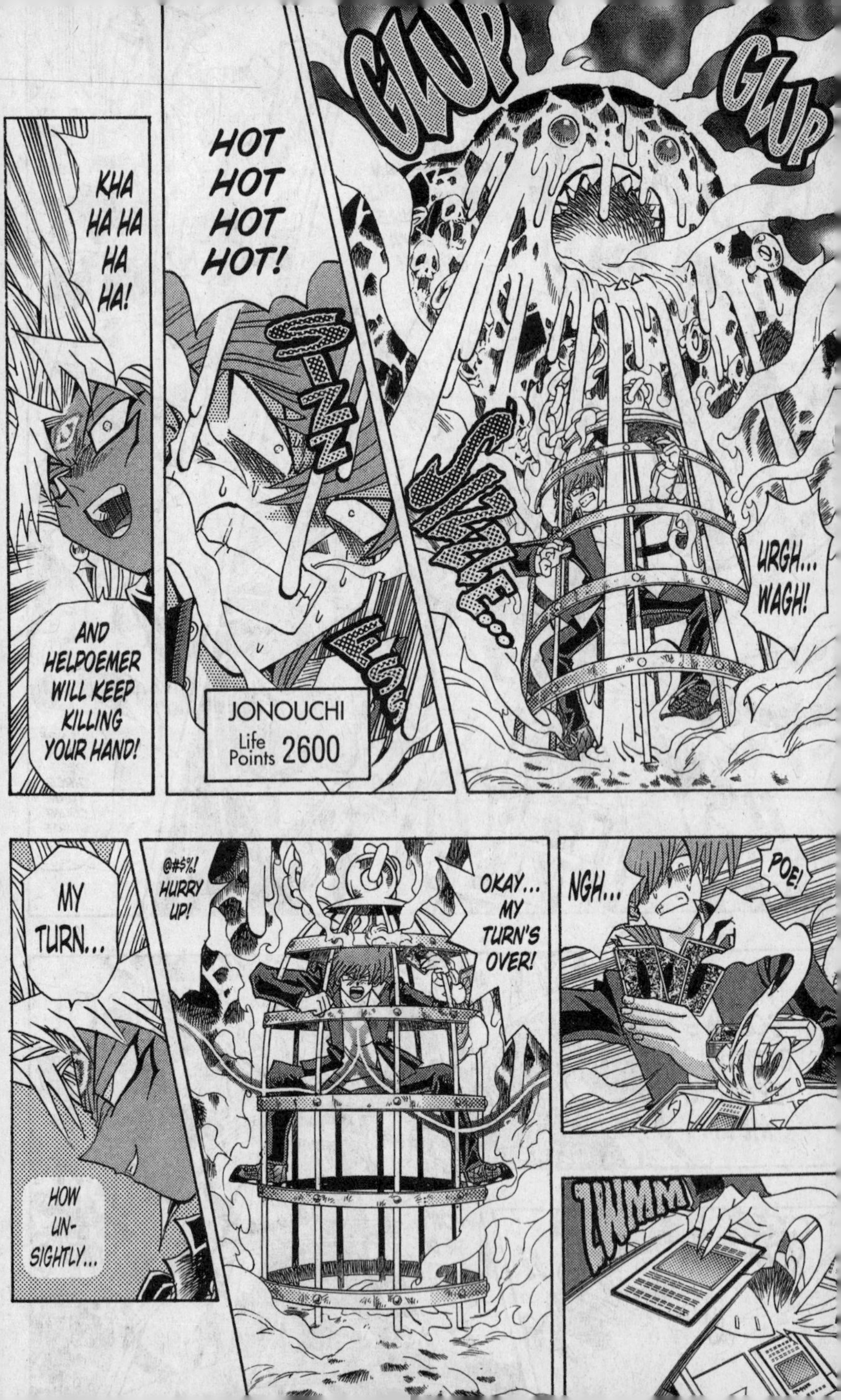
GLUP
GLUP
URGH... WAGH!
HOT HOT HOT HOT!
JONOUCHI Life Points 2600
KHA HA HA HA HA!
AND HELPOEMER WILL KEEP KILLING YOUR HAND!
POE!
NGH...
OKAY... MY TURN'S OVER!
@#$%! HURRY UP!
MY TURN...
HOW UN-SIGHTLY...

READ THIS WAY

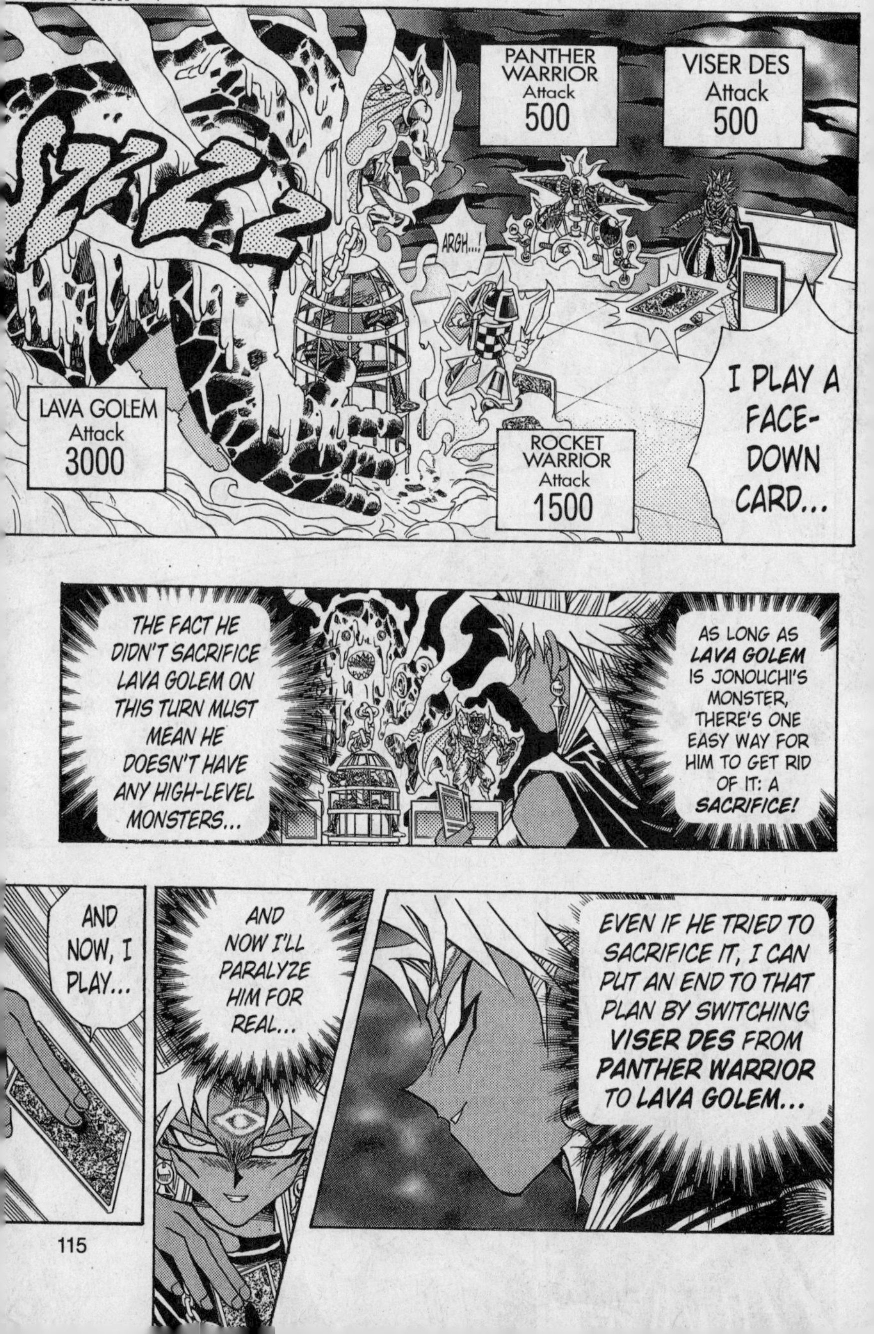

I PLAY A FACE-DOWN CARD...
VISER DES Attack 500
PANTHER WARRIOR Attack 500
ARGH...!
ROCKET WARRIOR Attack 1500
LAVA GOLEM Attack 3000
AS LONG AS LAVA GOLEM IS JONOUCHI'S MONSTER, THERE'S ONE EASY WAY FOR HIM TO GET RID OF IT: A SACRIFICE!
THE FACT HE DIDN'T SACRIFICE LAVA GOLEM ON THIS TURN MUST MEAN HE DOESN'T HAVE ANY HIGH-LEVEL MONSTERS...
EVEN IF HE TRIED TO SACRIFICE IT, I CAN PUT AN END TO THAT PLAN BY SWITCHING VISER DES FROM PANTHER WARRIOR TO LAVA GOLEM...
AND NOW I'LL PARALYZE HIM FOR REAL...
AND NOW, I PLAY...

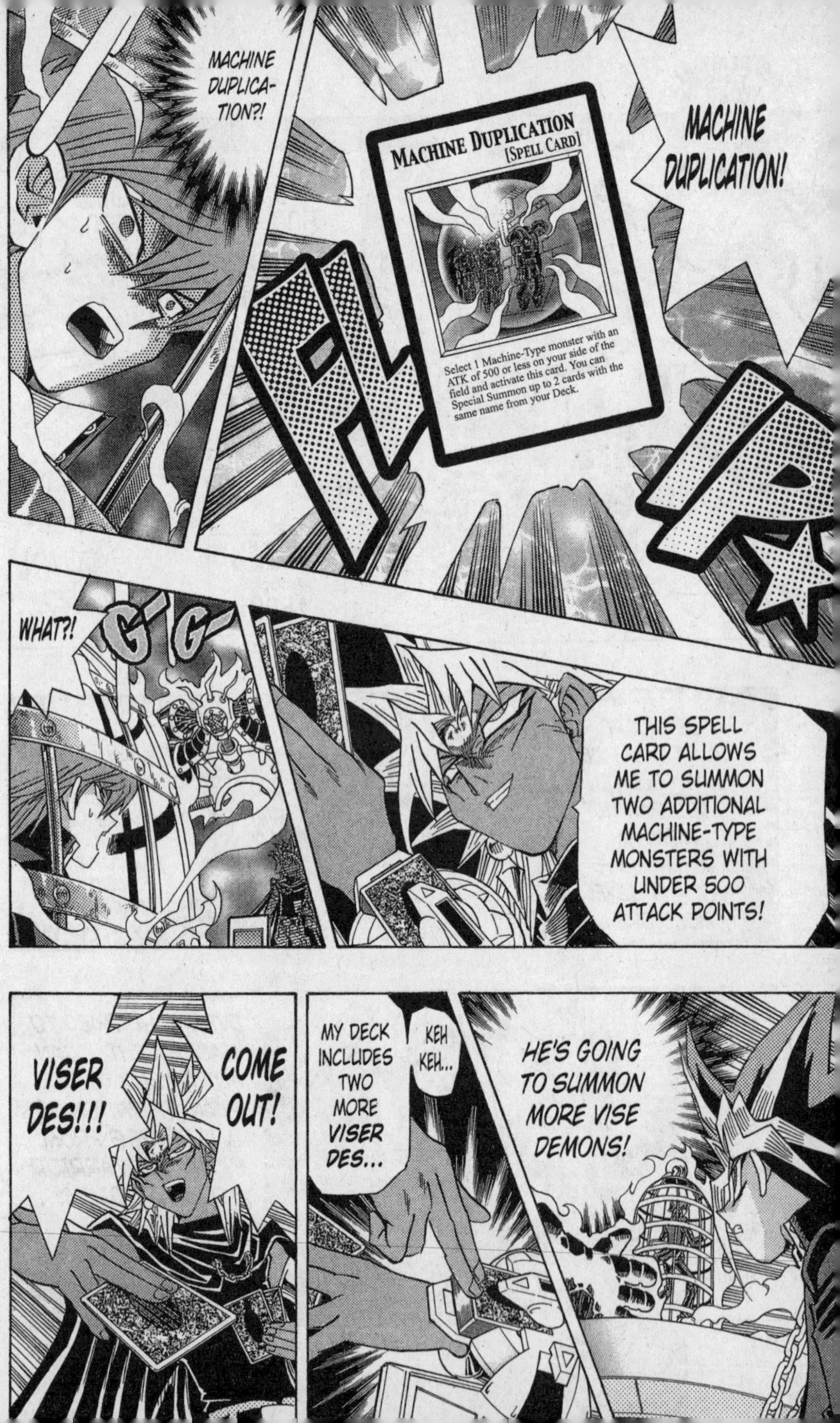
MACHINE DUPLICATION!
MACHINE DUPLICATION
[SPELL CARD]
Select 1 Machine-Type monster with an ATK of 500 or less on your side of the field and activate this card. You can Special Summon up to 2 cards with the same name from your Deck.
MACHINE DUPLICATION?!
THIS SPELL CARD ALLOWS ME TO SUMMON TWO ADDITIONAL MACHINE-TYPE MONSTERS WITH UNDER 500 ATTACK POINTS!
WHAT?!
G- G-
HE'S GOING TO SUMMON MORE VISE DEMONS!
KEH KEH...
MY DECK INCLUDES TWO MORE VISER DES...
COME OUT!
VISER DES!!!

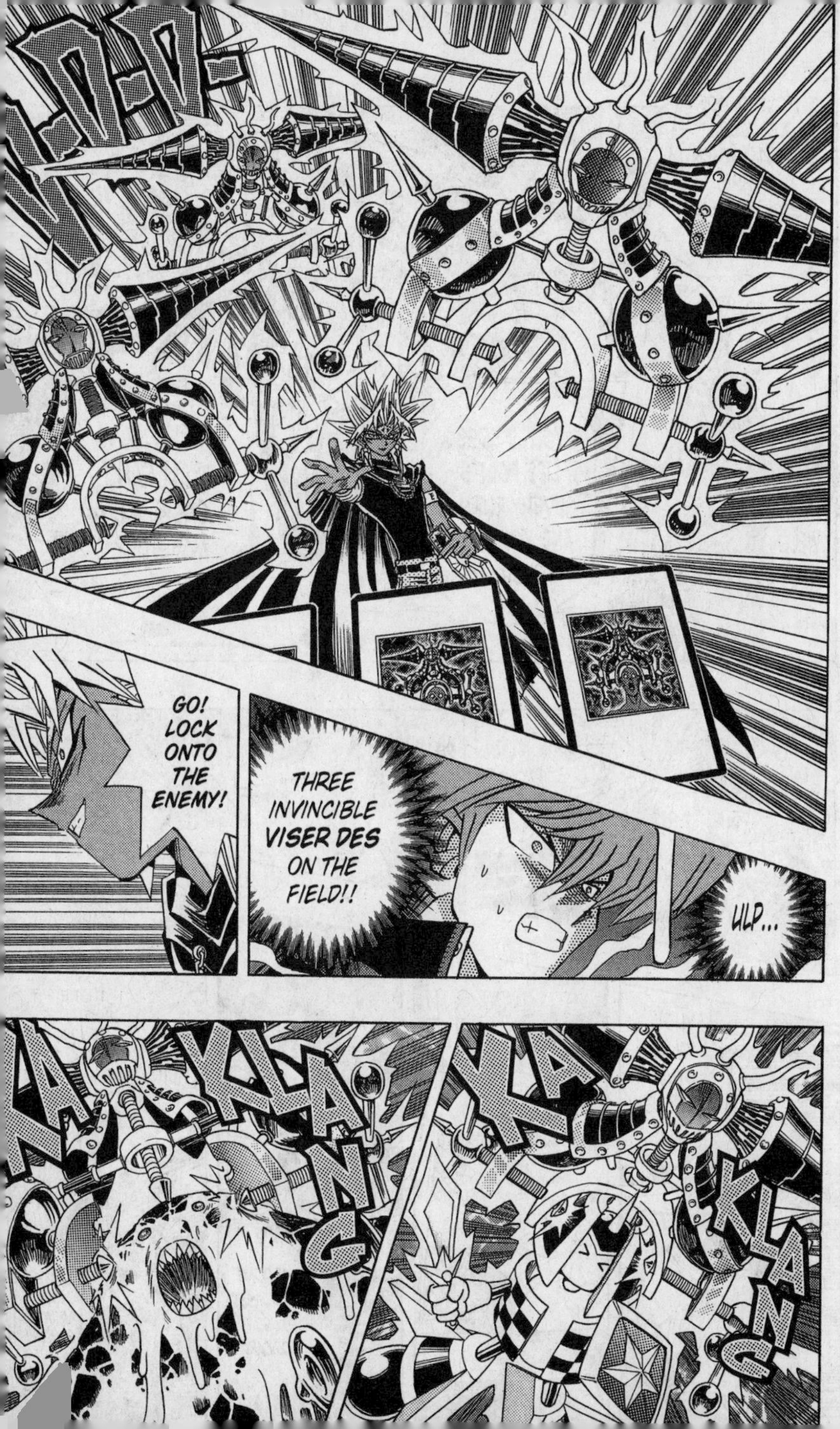
THREE INVINCIBLE VISER DES ON THE FIELD!!
ULP...
GO! LOCK ONTO THE ENEMY!
KLANG
KLANG

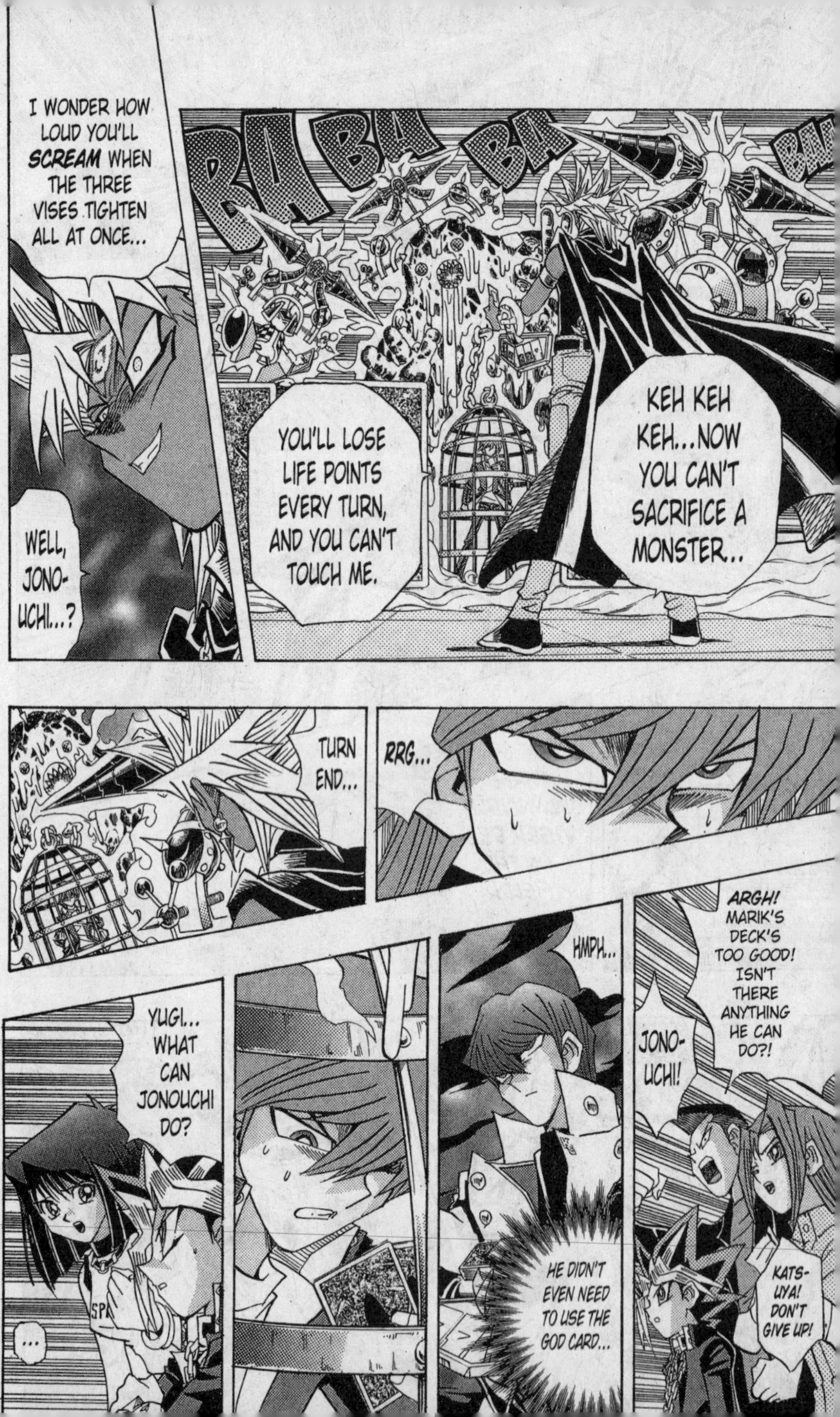
RA BA BA BA
KEH KEH KEH...NOW YOU CAN'T SACRIFICE A MONSTER...
YOU'LL LOSE LIFE POINTS EVERY TURN, AND YOU CAN'T TOUCH ME.
I WONDER HOW LOUD YOU'LL *SCREAM* WHEN THE THREE VISES TIGHTEN ALL AT ONCE...
WELL, JONO-UCHI...?
RRG...
TURN END...
ARGH! MARIK'S DECK'S TOO GOOD! ISN'T THERE ANYTHING HE CAN DO?!
JONO-UCHI!
KATS-UYA! DON'T GIVE UP!
HMPH...
HE DIDN'T EVEN NEED TO USE THE GOD CARD...
YUGI... WHAT CAN JONOUCHI DO?
...

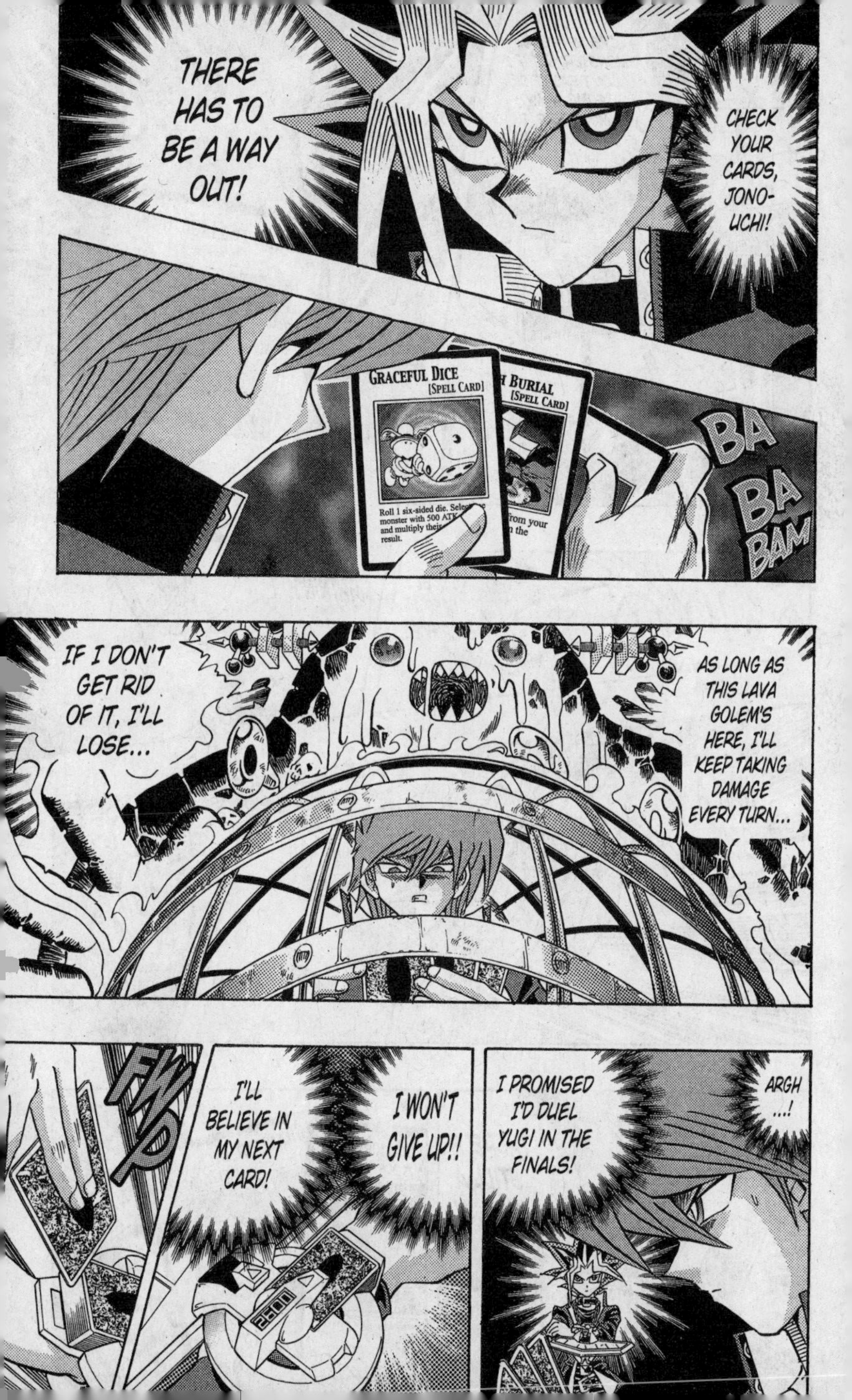

CHECK YOUR CARDS, JONO-UCHI!
THERE HAS TO BE A WAY OUT!
BA BA BAM
BURIAL
[SPELL CARD]
GRACEFUL DICE
[SPELL CARD]
AS LONG AS THIS LAVA GOLEM'S HERE, I'LL KEEP TAKING DAMAGE EVERY TURN...
IF I DON'T GET RID OF IT, I'LL LOSE...
ARGH ...!
I PROMISED I'D DUEL YUGI IN THE FINALS!
I WON'T GIVE UP!!
I'LL BELIEVE IN MY NEXT CARD!
FWIP

IT'S AN 8-STAR MONSTER, BUT IF I CAN'T SACRIFICE SOME OF MY MONSTERS, I CAN'T SUMMON IT...

GILFORD THE LIGHTNING
★★★★★★★★

If you Sacrifice Summon this card by Sacrificing 3 monsters, destroy all monsters on your opponent's side of the field.
ATK/2800 /1400

GILFORD THE LIGHTNING!

...!!

I JUST NEED A SACRIFICE...

WAIT A SEC...

THERE'S STILL A WAY...!!

GILFORD THE LIGHTNING
★★★★★★★★

GRACEFUL DICE
[SPELL CARD]

...ISH BURIAL
[SPELL CARD]

...Sacrifice Summon this card ...rificing 3 monsters, destroy ...sters on your opponent's ...the field.
ATK/2800

...sided die. Select one ...th 500 ATK or less, ...their ATK ...the

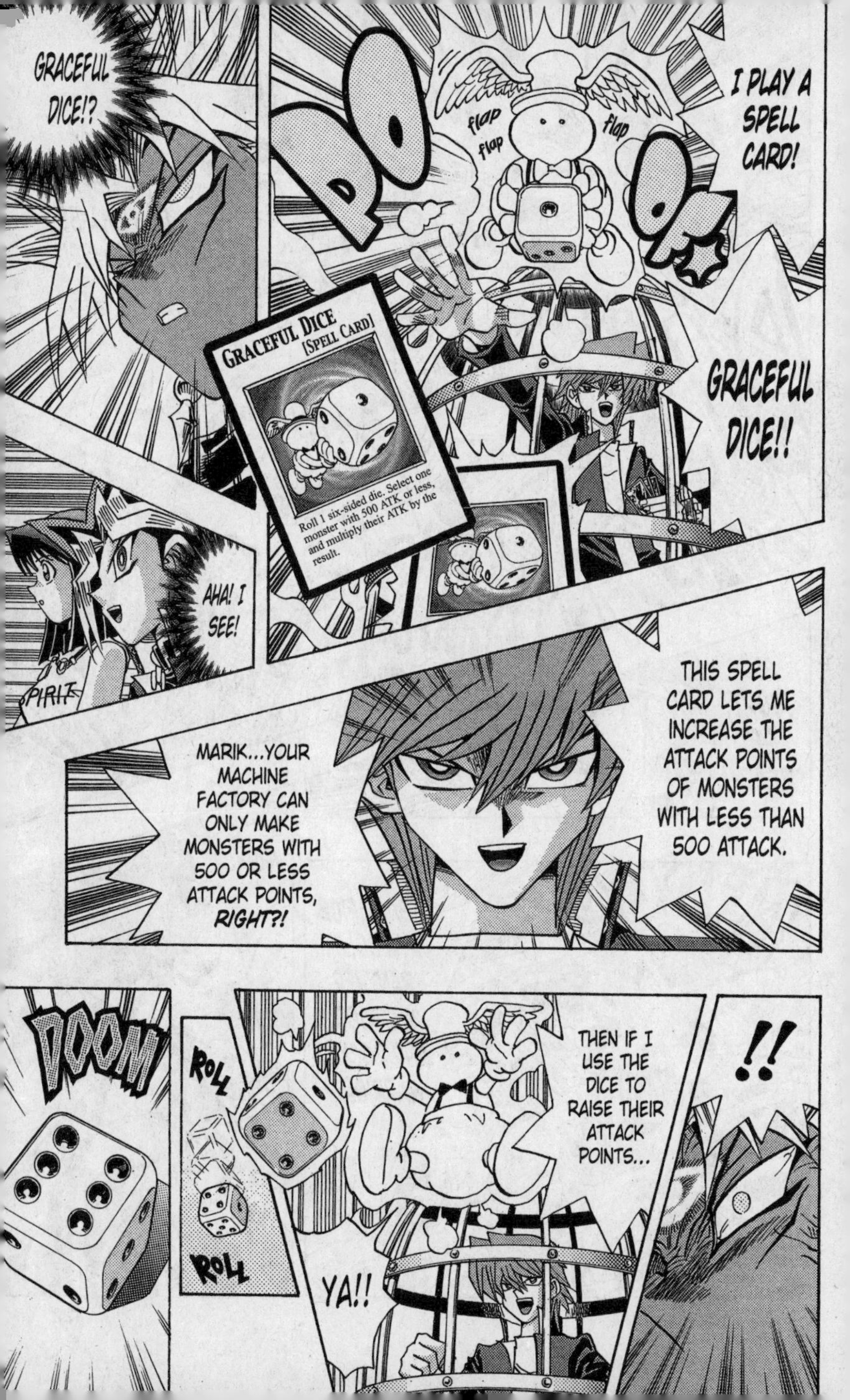
I PLAY A SPELL CARD!
POOF
flap
flap
flap
GRACEFUL DICE!!
GRACEFUL DICE
[SPELL CARD]
Roll 1 six-sided die. Select one monster with 500 ATK or less, and multiply their ATK by the result.
GRACEFUL DICE!?
AHA! I SEE!
PIRIT
THIS SPELL CARD LETS ME INCREASE THE ATTACK POINTS OF MONSTERS WITH LESS THAN 500 ATTACK.
MARIK...YOUR MACHINE FACTORY CAN ONLY MAKE MONSTERS WITH 500 OR LESS ATTACK POINTS, RIGHT?!
!!
THEN IF I USE THE DICE TO RAISE THEIR ATTACK POINTS...
YA!!
ROLL
ROLL
DOOM

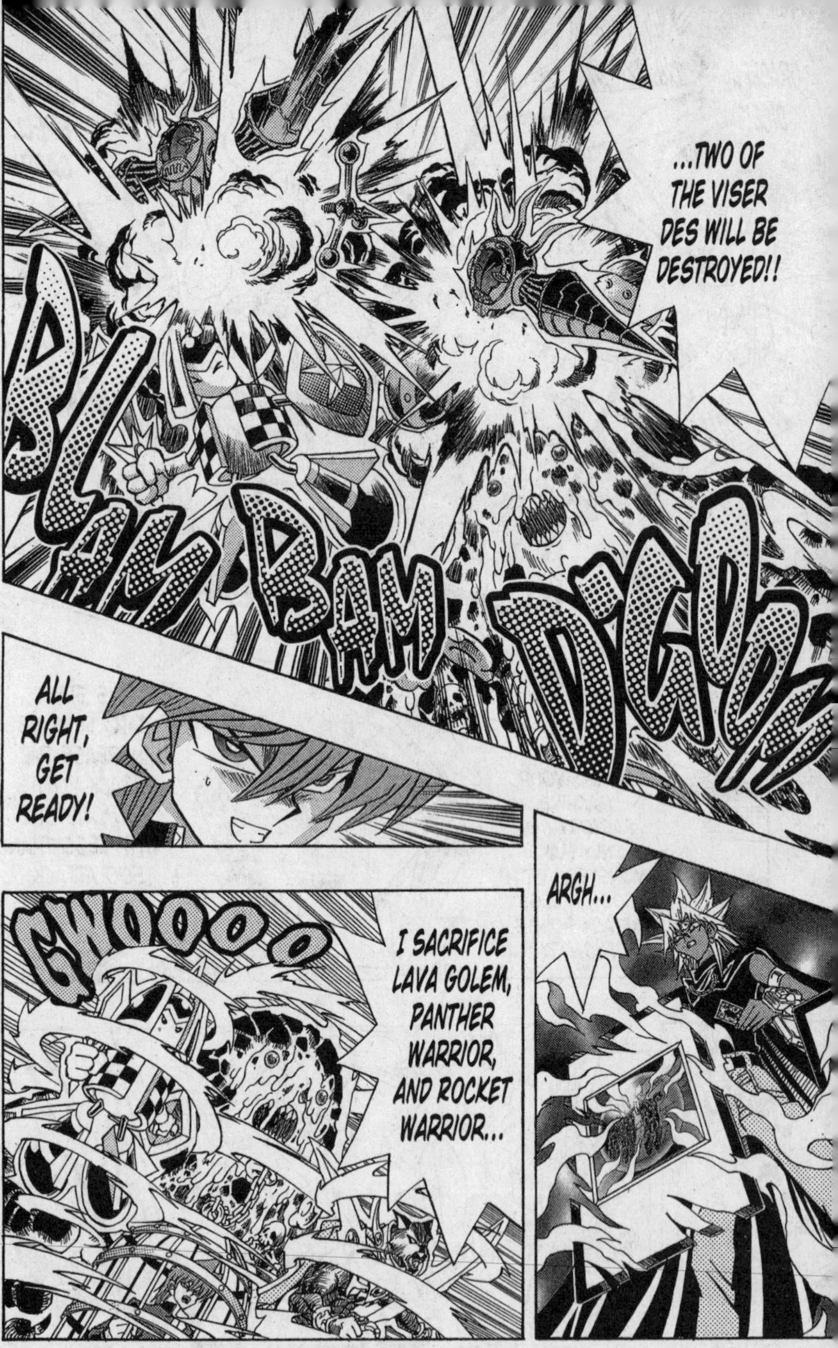
...TWO OF THE VISER DES WILL BE DESTROYED!!
BLAM
BAM
ARGH...
ALL RIGHT, GET READY!
GWOOOO
I SACRIFICE LAVA GOLEM, PANTHER WARRIOR, AND ROCKET WARRIOR...

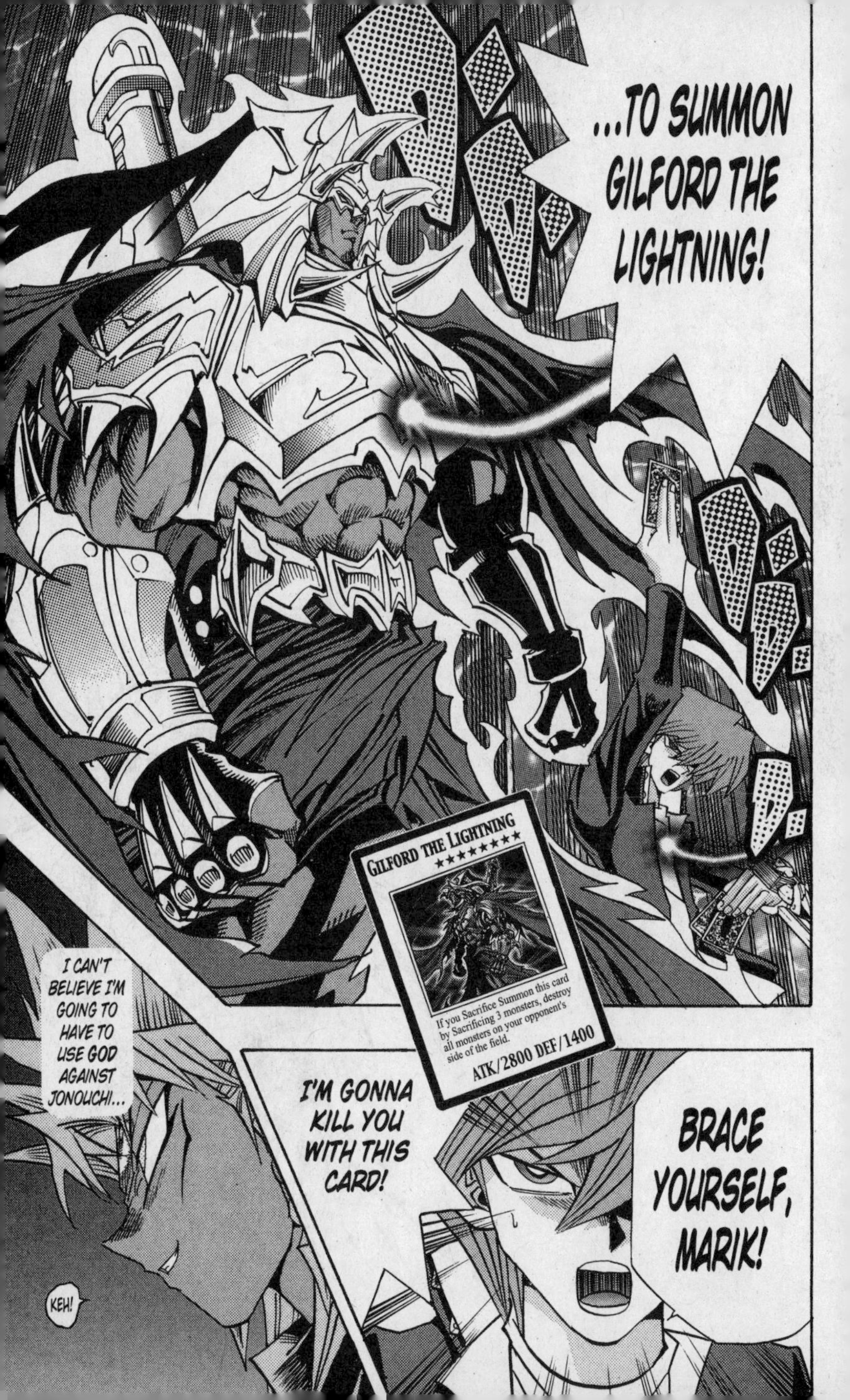
...TO SUMMON GILFORD THE LIGHTNING!
GILFORD THE LIGHTNING
If you Sacrifice Summon this card by Sacrificing 3 monsters, destroy all monsters on your opponent's side of the field.
ATK/2800 DEF/1400
BRACE YOURSELF, MARIK!
I'M GONNA KILL YOU WITH THIS CARD!
I CAN'T BELIEVE I'M GOING TO HAVE TO USE GOD AGAINST JONOUCHI...
KEH!

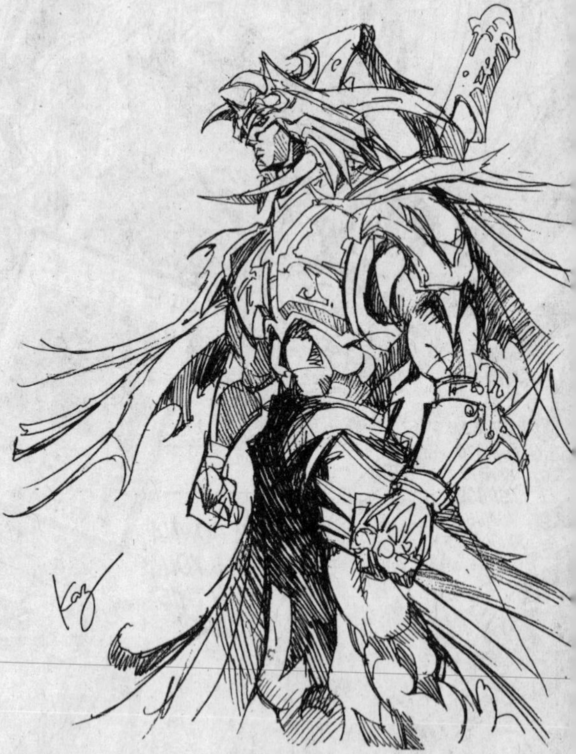
Kaz

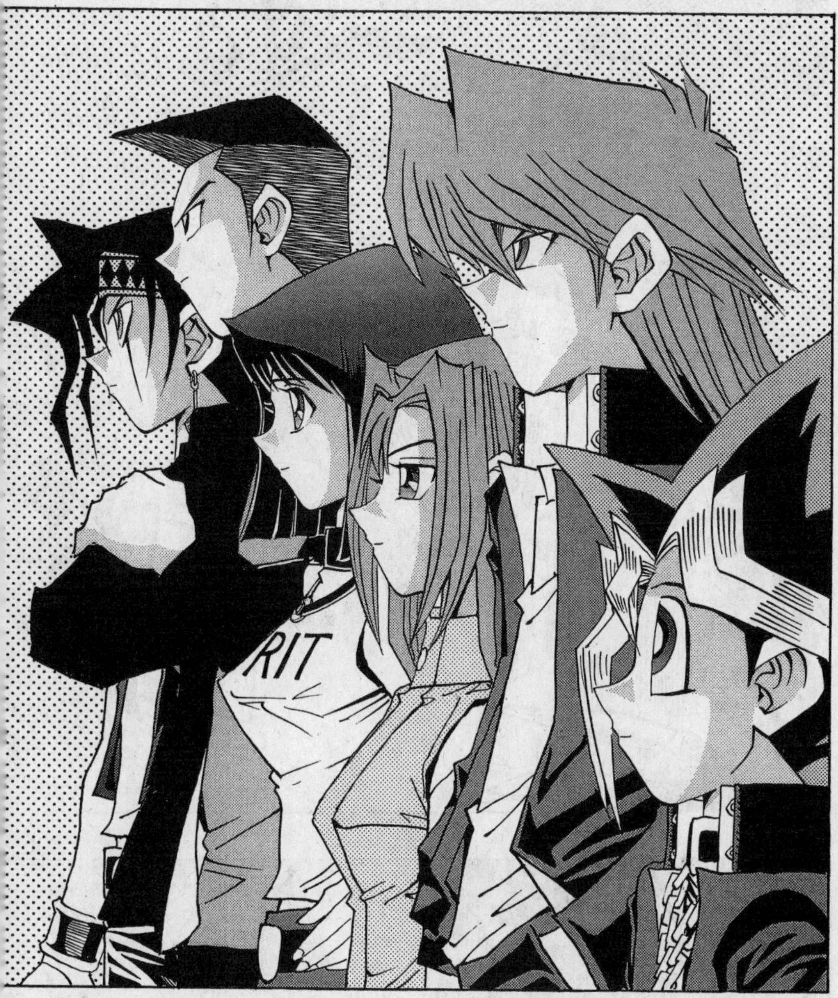
RIT

Duel 248: God's Third Power!

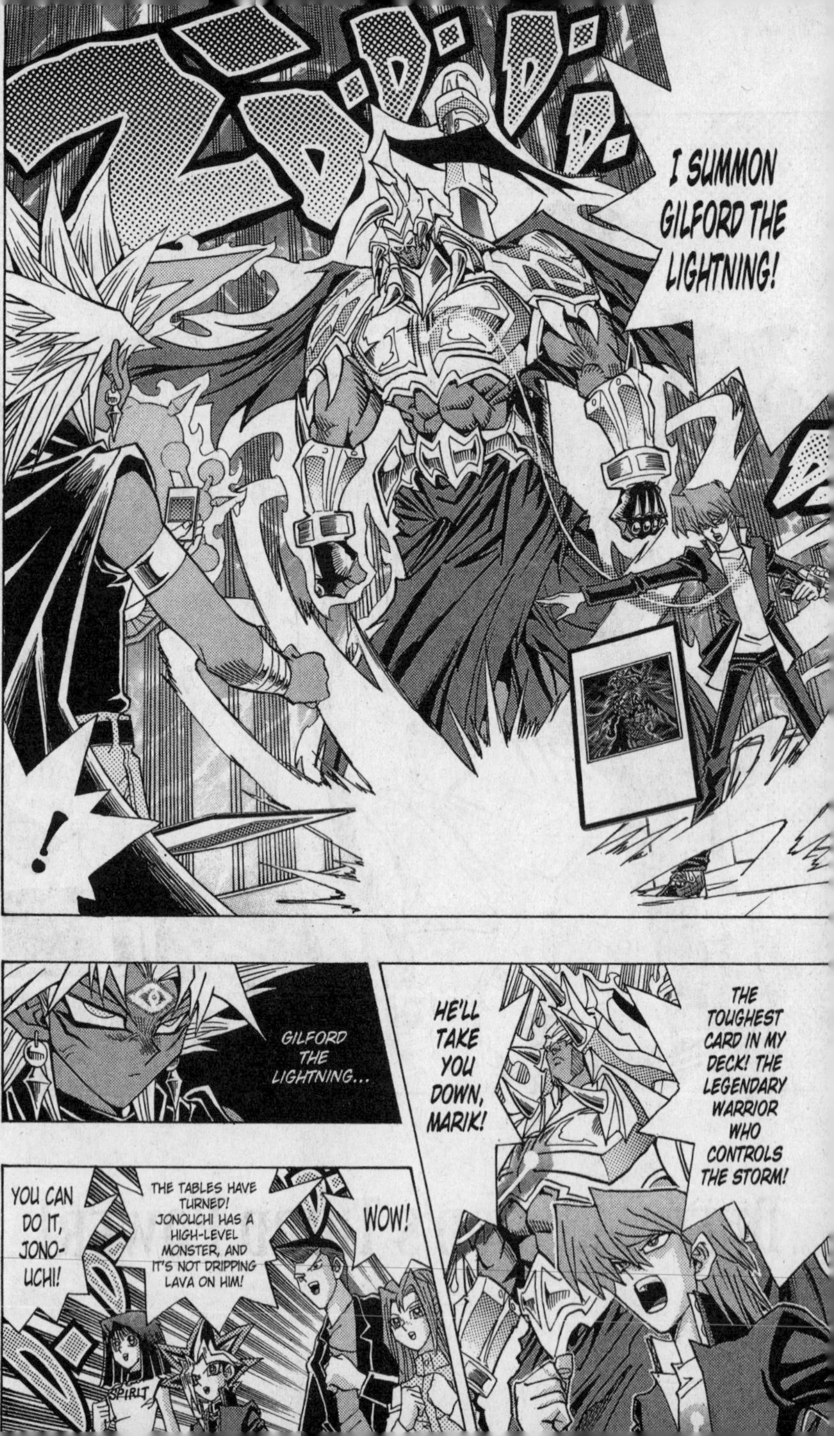
I SUMMON GILFORD THE LIGHTNING!
!
THE TOUGHEST CARD IN MY DECK! THE LEGENDARY WARRIOR WHO CONTROLS THE STORM!
HE'LL TAKE YOU DOWN, MARIK!
GILFORD THE LIGHTNING...
WOW!
THE TABLES HAVE TURNED! JONOUCHI HAS A HIGH-LEVEL MONSTER, AND IT'S NOT DRIPPING LAVA ON HIM!
YOU CAN DO IT, JONO-UCHI!
SPIRIT

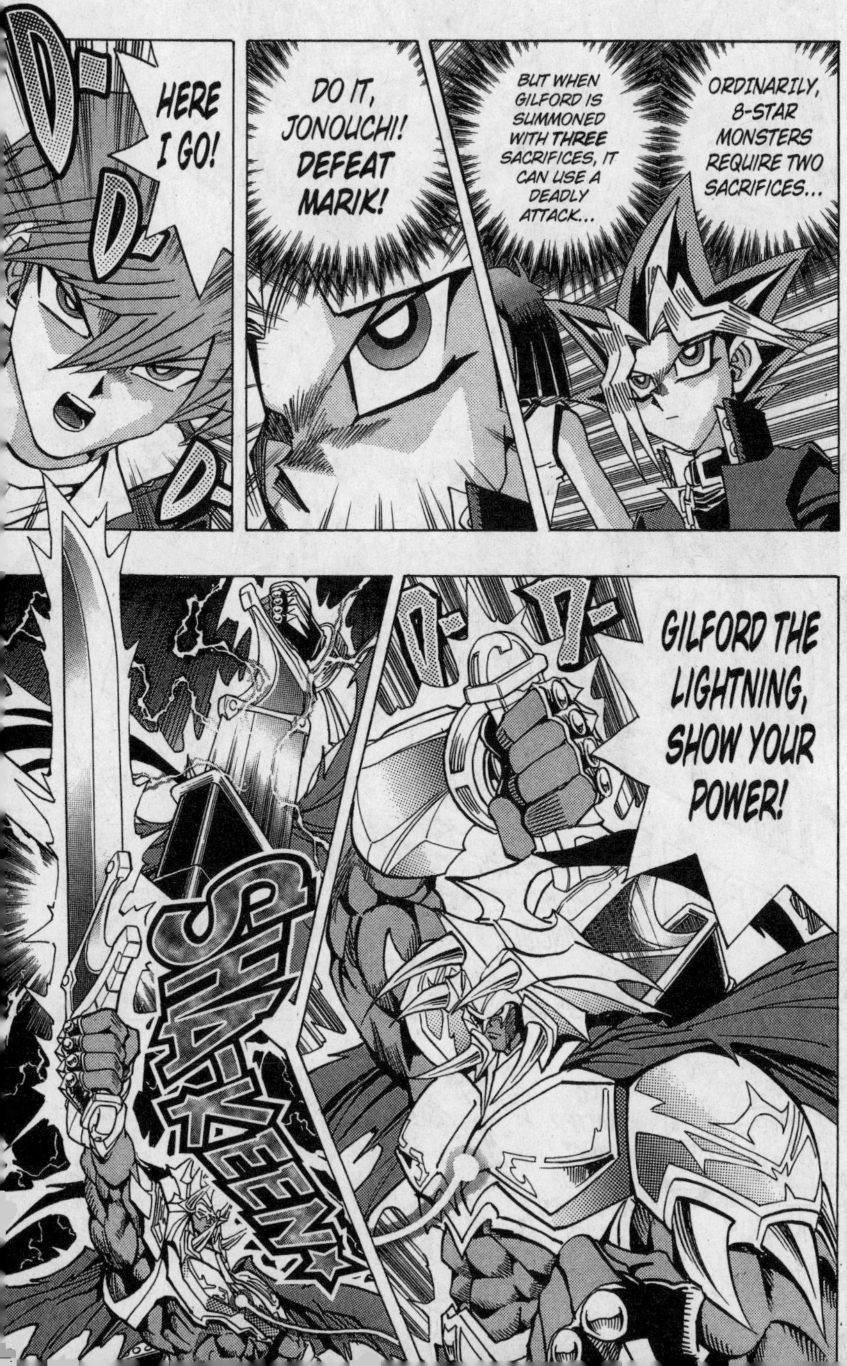
ORDINARILY, 8-STAR MONSTERS REQUIRE TWO SACRIFICES...
BUT WHEN GILFORD IS SUMMONED WITH THREE SACRIFICES, IT CAN USE A DEADLY ATTACK...
DO IT, JONOUCHI! DEFEAT MARIK!
HERE I GO!
GILFORD THE LIGHTNING, SHOW YOUR POWER!
SHAKEEN

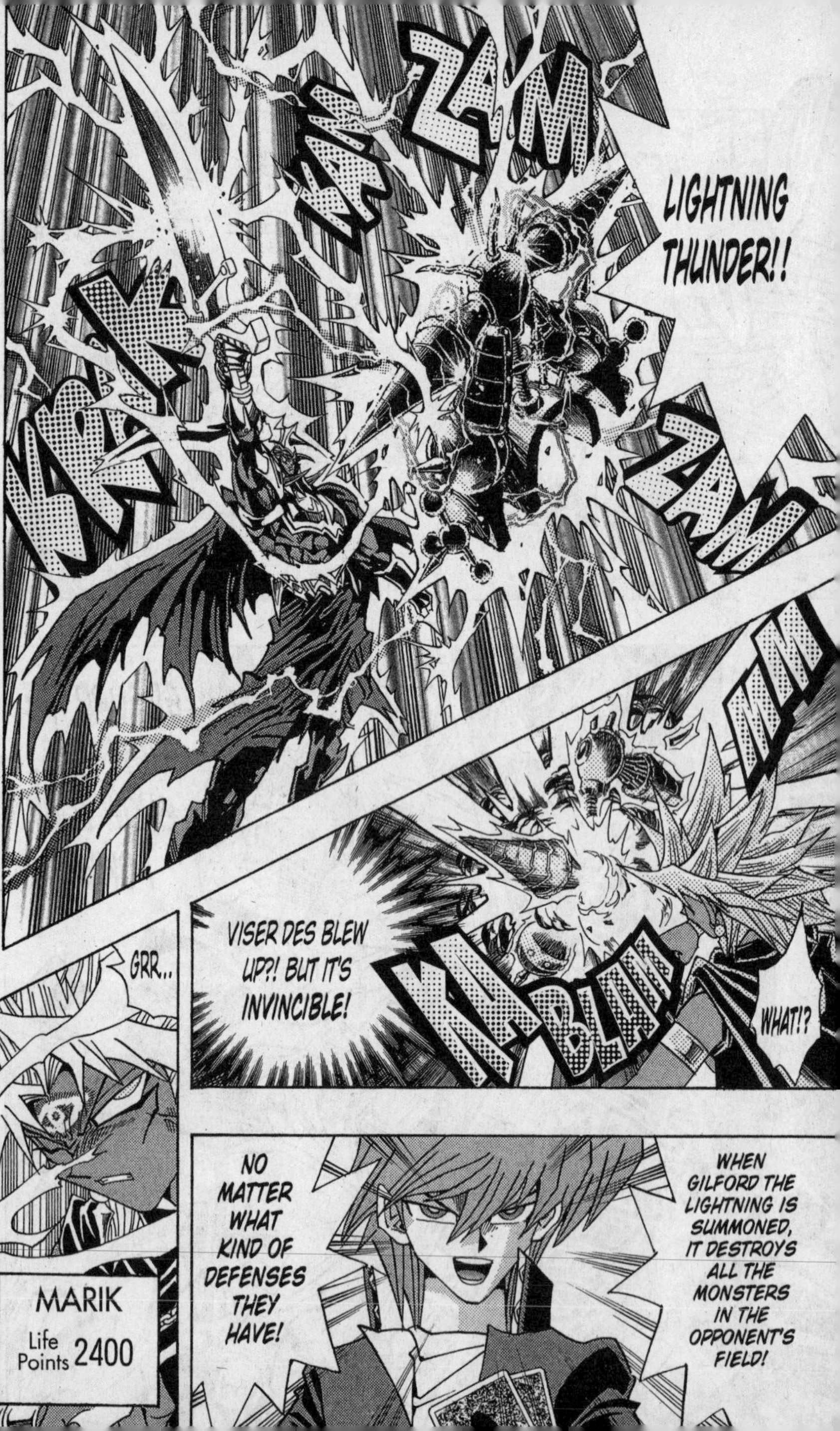
LIGHTNING THUNDER!!
ZAM
ZAM
KRAK
WHAT!?
KA-BLAM
VISER DES BLEW UP?! BUT IT'S INVINCIBLE!
WHEN GILFORD THE LIGHTNING IS SUMMONED, IT DESTROYS ALL THE MONSTERS IN THE OPPONENT'S FIELD!
NO MATTER WHAT KIND OF DEFENSES THEY HAVE!
GRR...
MARIK
Life Points 2400

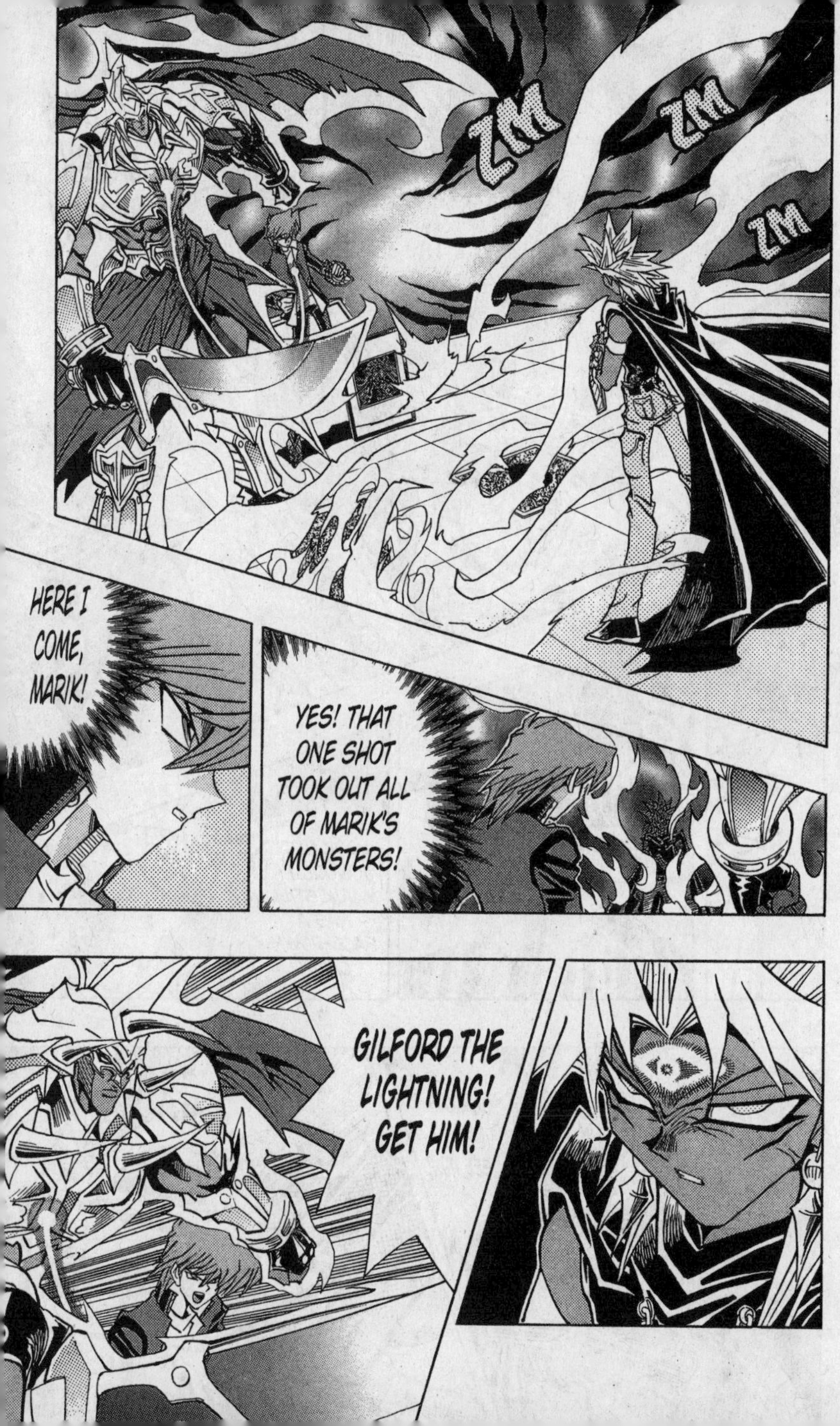
ZM
ZM
ZM
YES! THAT ONE SHOT TOOK OUT ALL OF MARIK'S MONSTERS!
HERE I COME, MARIK!
GILFORD THE LIGHTNING! GET HIM!

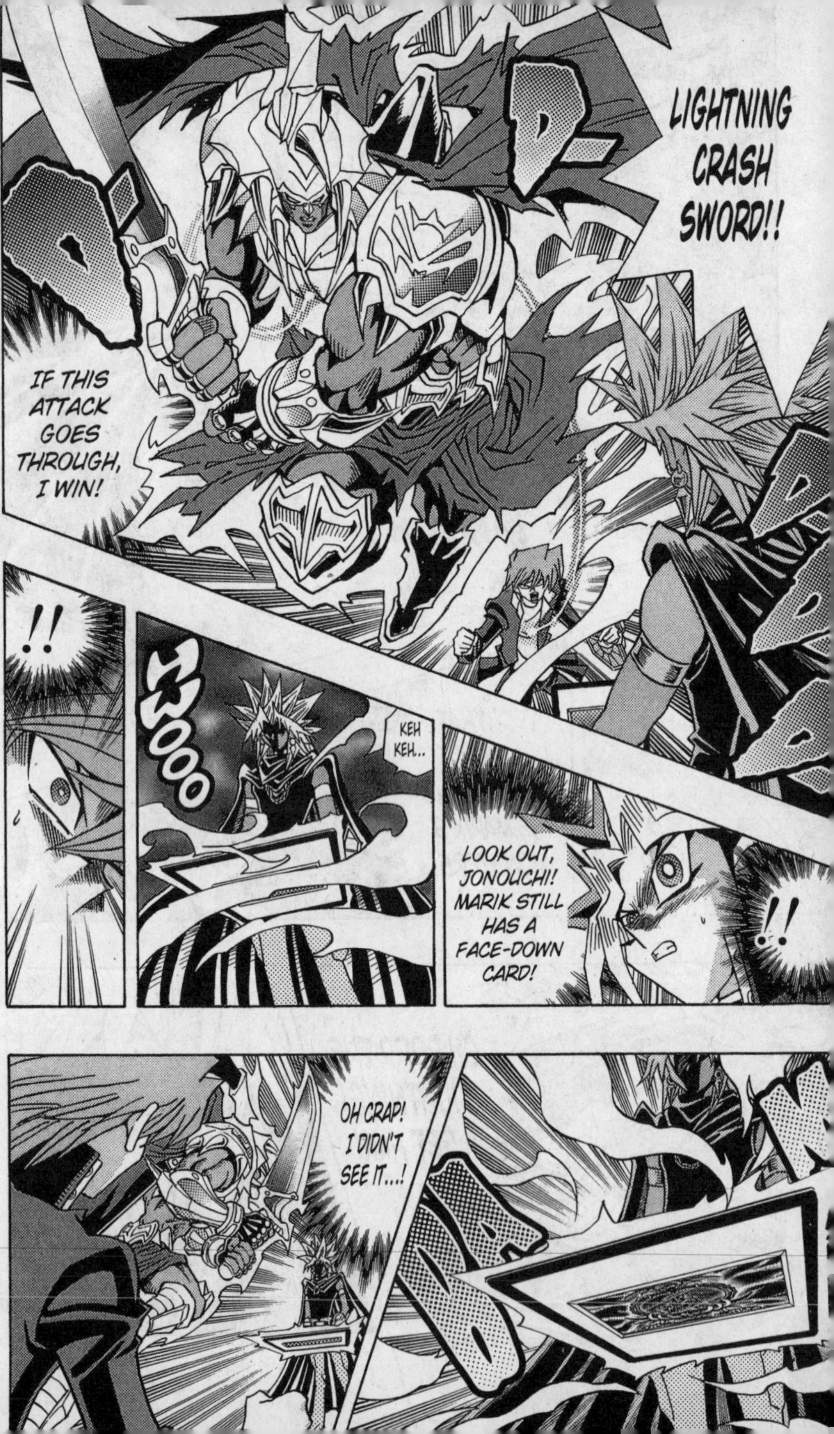
LIGHTNING CRASH SWORD!!
IF THIS ATTACK GOES THROUGH, I WIN!
LOOK OUT, JONOUCHI! MARIK STILL HAS A FACE-DOWN CARD!
!!
KEH KEH...
!!
OH CRAP! I DIDN'T SEE IT...!

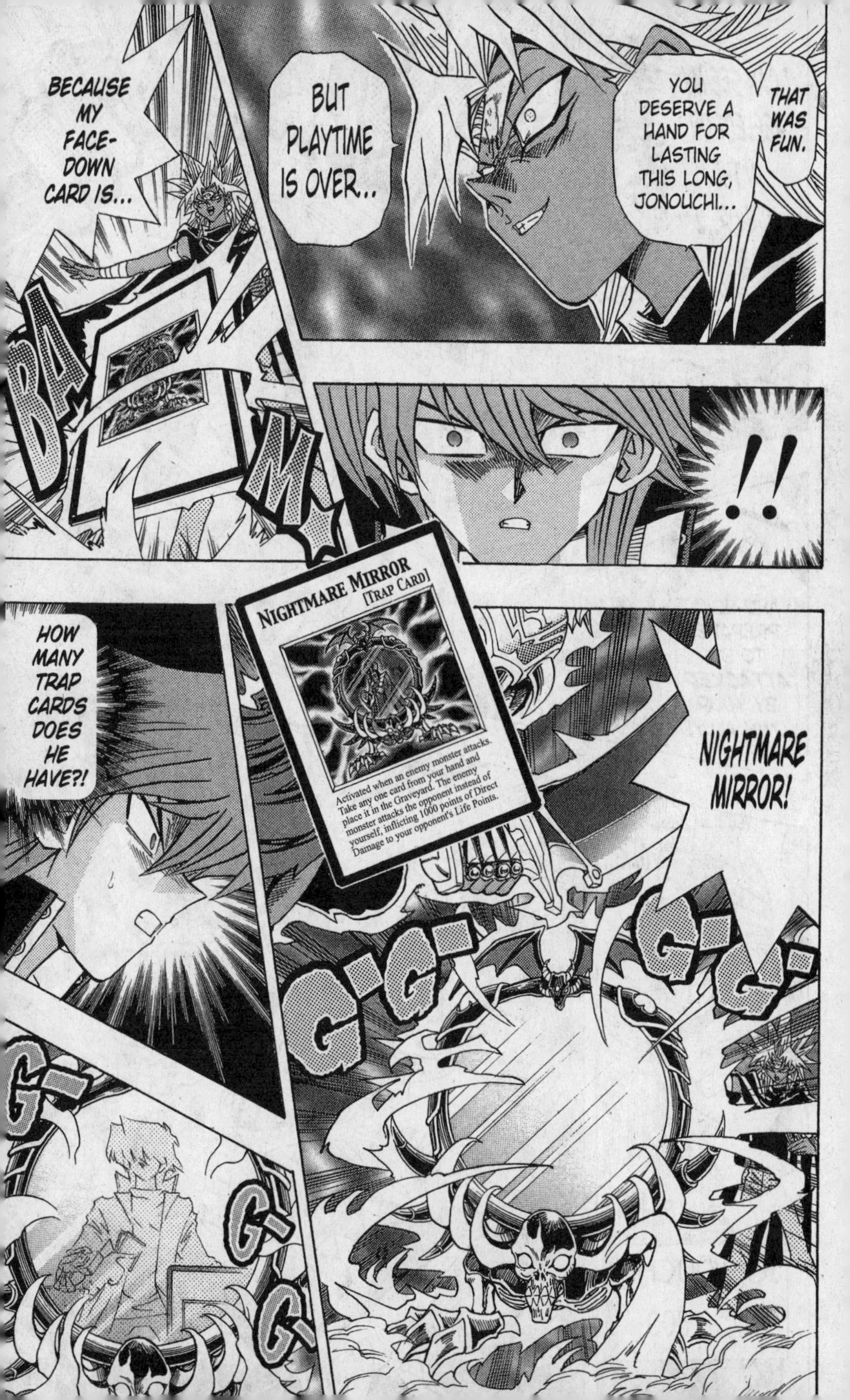
THAT WAS FUN.
YOU DESERVE A HAND FOR LASTING THIS LONG, JONOUCHI...
BUT PLAYTIME IS OVER...
BECAUSE MY FACE-DOWN CARD IS...
BAM
!!
NIGHTMARE MIRROR!
NIGHTMARE MIRROR [TRAP CARD]
Activated when an enemy monster attacks. Take any one card from your hand and place it in the Graveyard. The enemy monster attacks the opponent instead of yourself, inflicting 1000 points of Direct Damage to your opponent's Life Points.
HOW MANY TRAP CARDS DOES HE HAVE?!
G-G-G-
G-G-G-

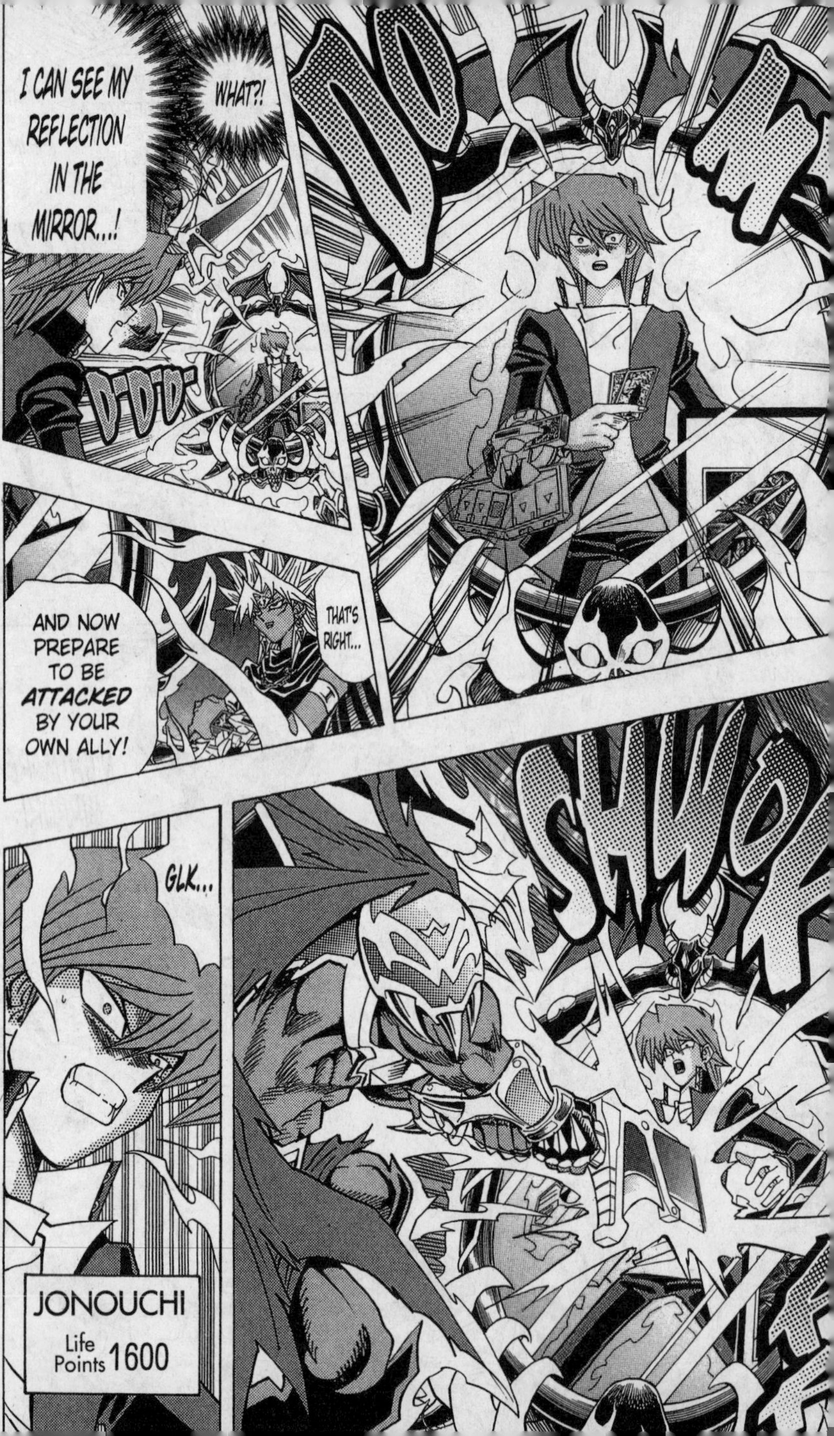
WHAT?!
I CAN SEE MY REFLECTION IN THE MIRROR...!
D-D-D-
THAT'S RIGHT...
AND NOW PREPARE TO BE ***ATTACKED*** BY YOUR OWN ALLY!
GLK...
JONOUCHI
Life Points 1600

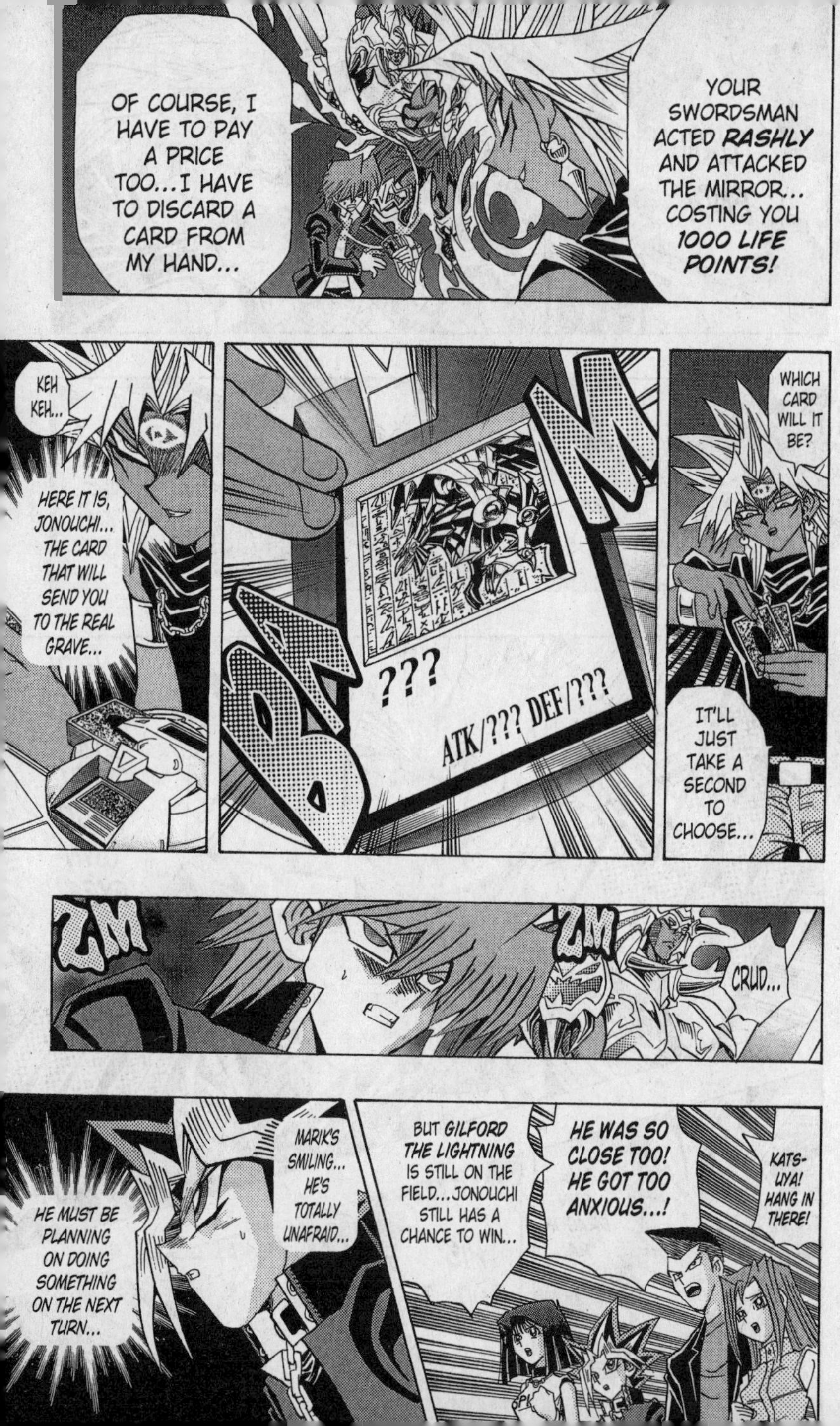
YOUR SWORDSMAN ACTED RASHLY AND ATTACKED THE MIRROR... COSTING YOU 1000 LIFE POINTS!
OF COURSE, I HAVE TO PAY A PRICE TOO...I HAVE TO DISCARD A CARD FROM MY HAND...
WHICH CARD WILL IT BE?
IT'LL JUST TAKE A SECOND TO CHOOSE...
BAM
???
ATK/??? DEF/???
KEH KEH...
HERE IT IS, JONOUCHI... THE CARD THAT WILL SEND YOU TO THE REAL GRAVE...
CRUD...
ZM
ZM
KATS-UYA! HANG IN THERE!
HE WAS SO CLOSE TOO! HE GOT TOO ANXIOUS...!
BUT GILFORD THE LIGHTNING IS STILL ON THE FIELD...JONOUCHI STILL HAS A CHANCE TO WIN...
MARIK'S SMILING... HE'S TOTALLY UNAFRAID...
HE MUST BE PLANNING ON DOING SOMETHING ON THE NEXT TURN...

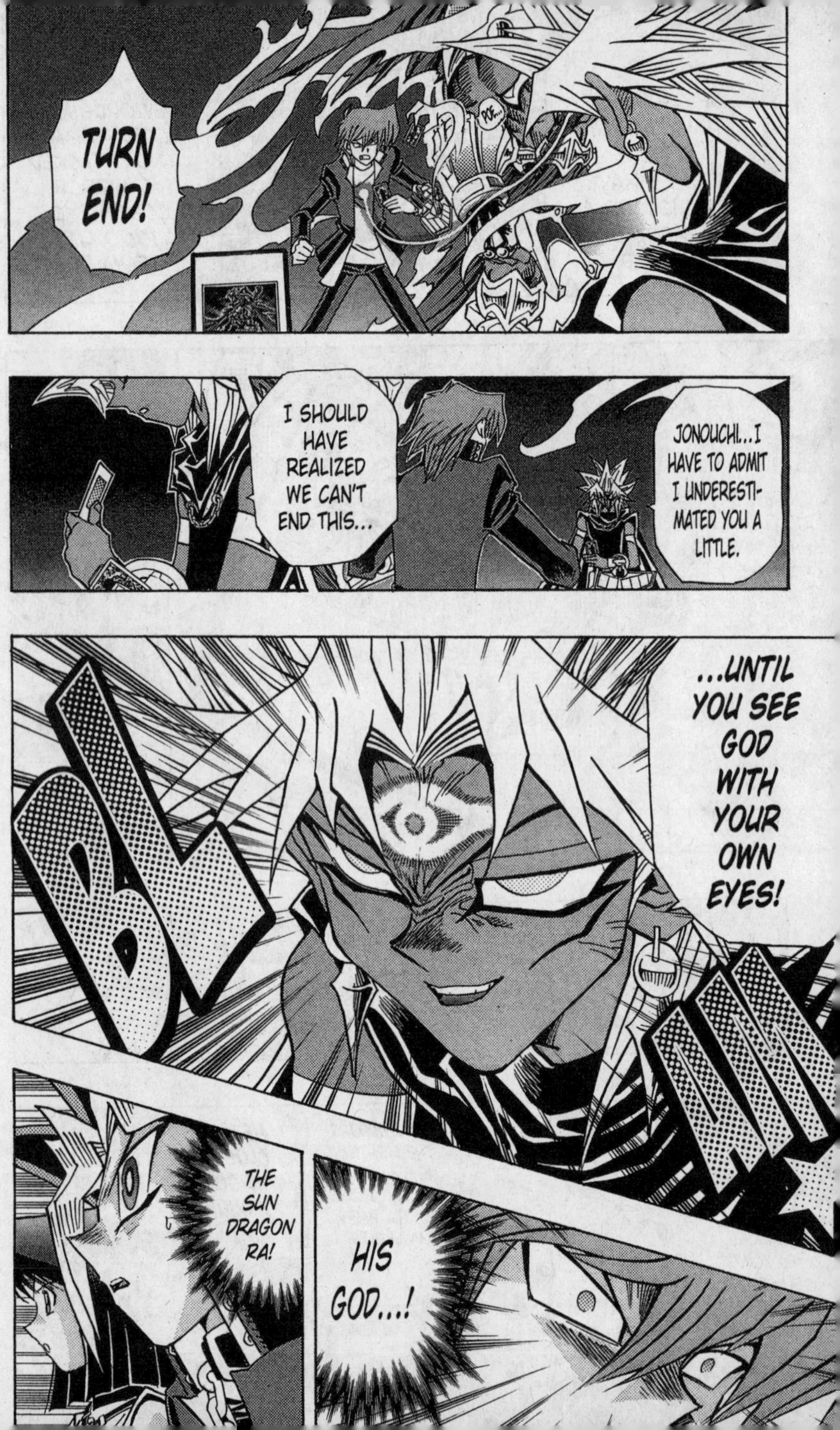
TURN END!
JONOUCHI...I HAVE TO ADMIT I UNDERESTI-MATED YOU A LITTLE.
I SHOULD HAVE REALIZED WE CAN'T END THIS...
...UNTIL YOU SEE GOD WITH YOUR OWN EYES!
HIS GOD...!
THE SUN DRAGON RA!

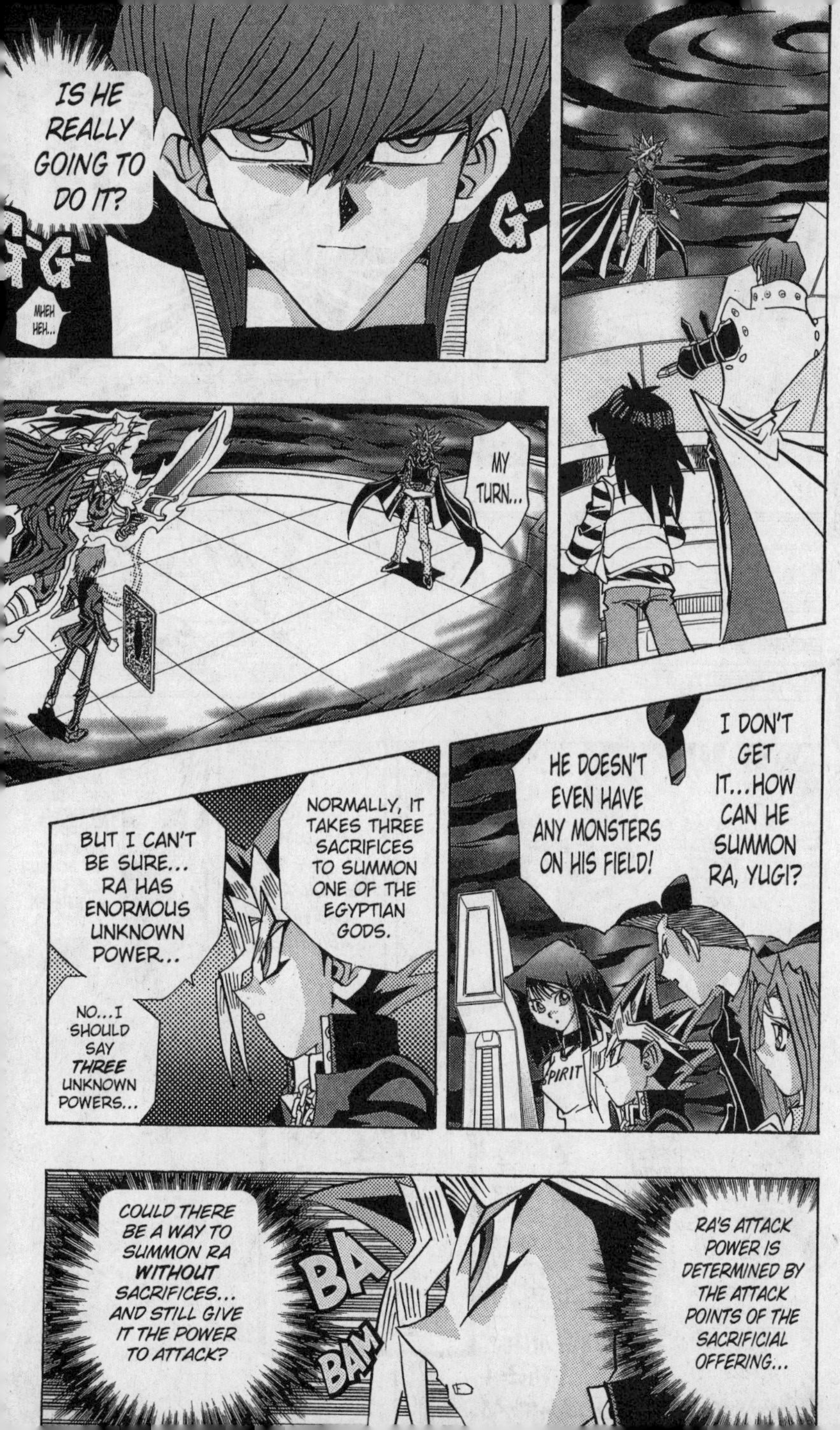
IS HE REALLY GOING TO DO IT?
G-
G-G-
MHEH HEH...
MY TURN...
I DON'T GET IT...HOW CAN HE SUMMON RA, YUGI?
HE DOESN'T EVEN HAVE ANY MONSTERS ON HIS FIELD!
NORMALLY, IT TAKES THREE SACRIFICES TO SUMMON ONE OF THE EGYPTIAN GODS.
BUT I CAN'T BE SURE... RA HAS ENORMOUS UNKNOWN POWER...
NO...I SHOULD SAY *THREE* UNKNOWN POWERS...
RA'S ATTACK POWER IS DETERMINED BY THE ATTACK POINTS OF THE SACRIFICIAL OFFERING...
BA
BAM
COULD THERE BE A WAY TO SUMMON RA **WITHOUT** SACRIFICES... AND STILL GIVE IT THE POWER TO ATTACK?

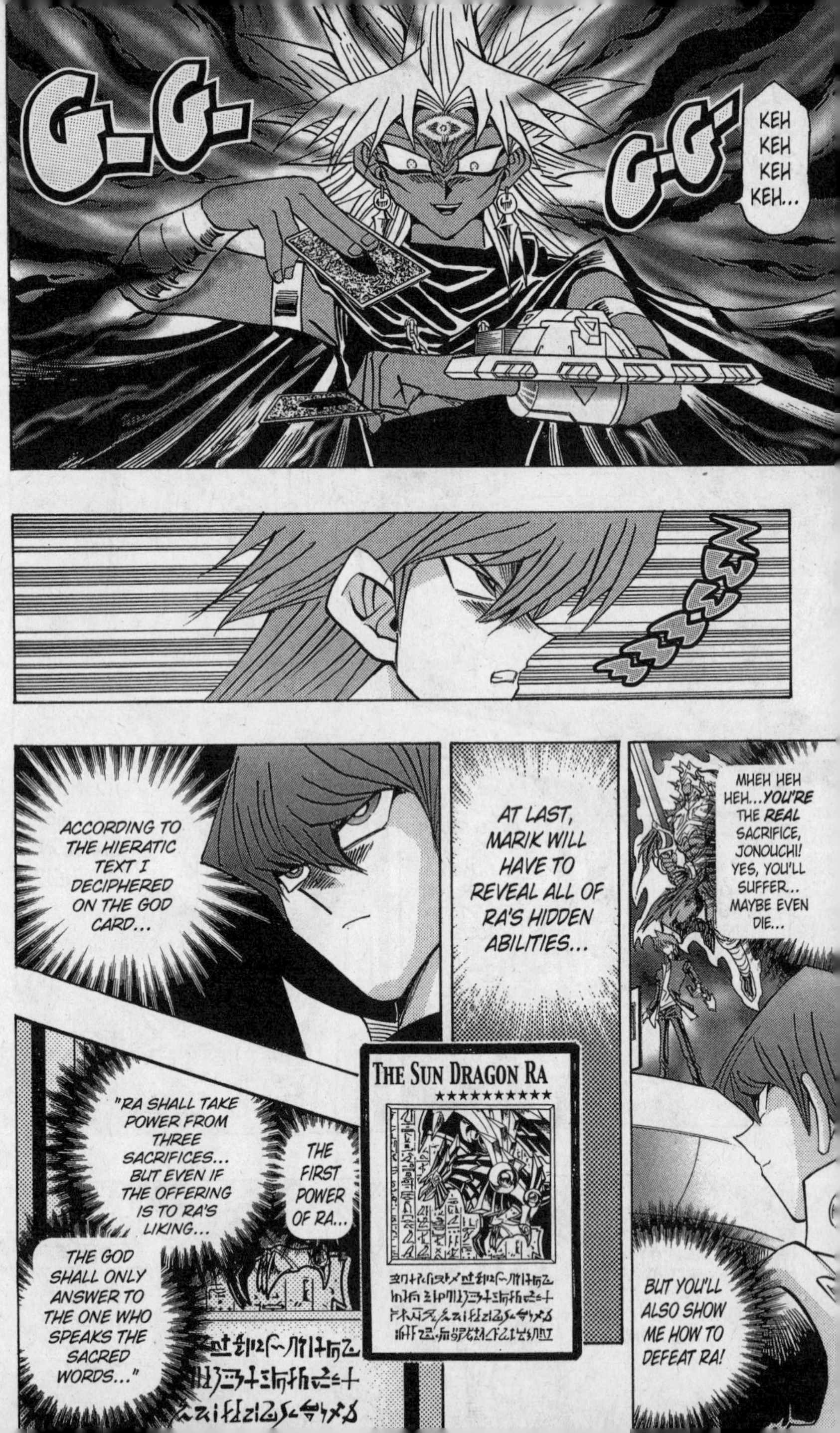
G-G-
KEH KEH KEH KEH...
G-G-
MHEH HEH HEH...YOU'RE THE REAL SACRIFICE, JONOUCHI! YES, YOU'LL SUFFER... MAYBE EVEN DIE...
BUT YOU'LL ALSO SHOW ME HOW TO DEFEAT RA!
AT LAST, MARIK WILL HAVE TO REVEAL ALL OF RA'S HIDDEN ABILITIES...
ACCORDING TO THE HIERATIC TEXT I DECIPHERED ON THE GOD CARD...
THE SUN DRAGON RA
THE FIRST POWER OF RA...
"RA SHALL TAKE POWER FROM THREE SACRIFICES... BUT EVEN IF THE OFFERING IS TO RA'S LIKING...
THE GOD SHALL ONLY ANSWER TO THE ONE WHO SPEAKS THE SACRED WORDS..."

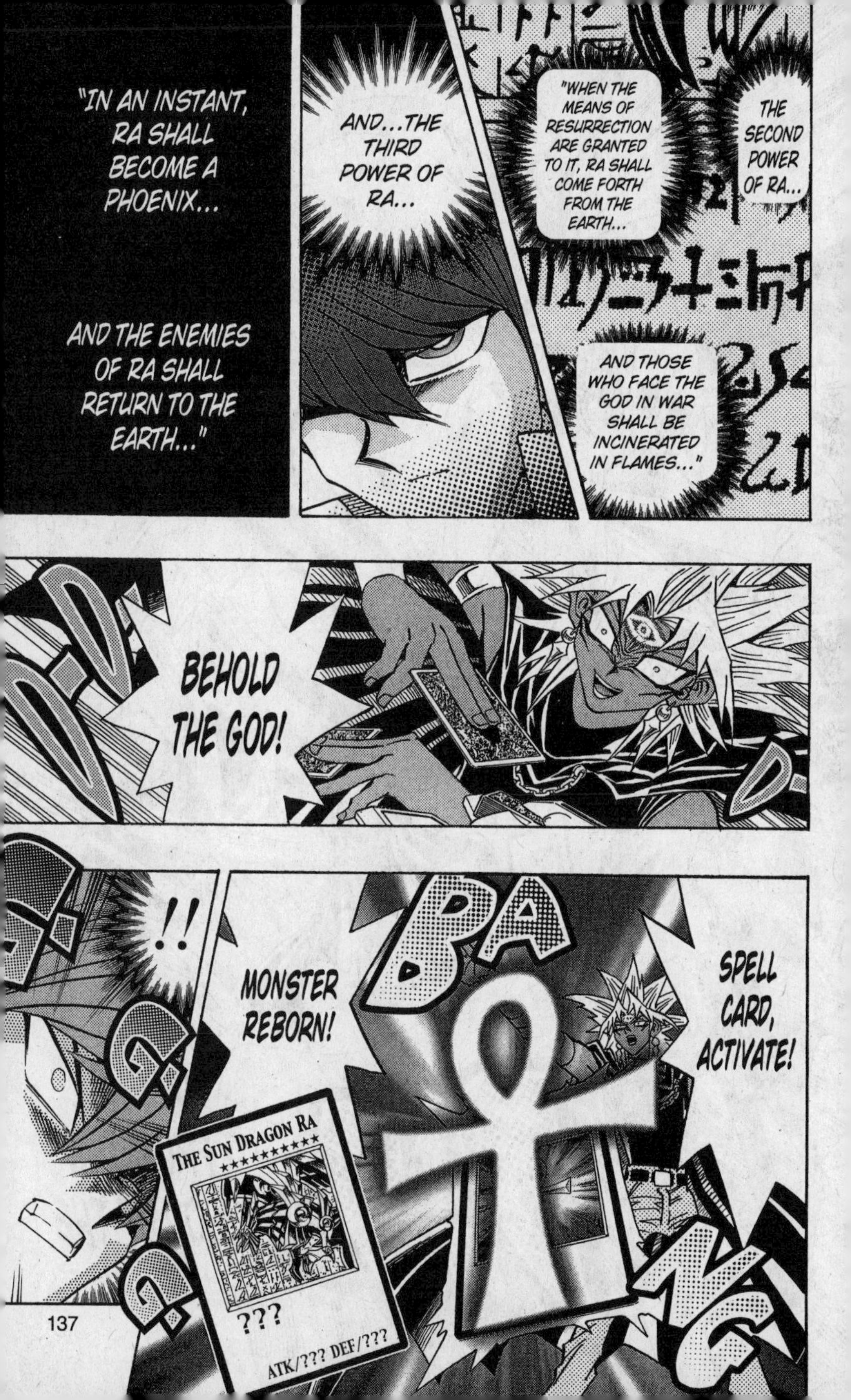
THE SECOND POWER OF RA...
"WHEN THE MEANS OF RESURRECTION ARE GRANTED TO IT, RA SHALL COME FORTH FROM THE EARTH...
AND THOSE WHO FACE THE GOD IN WAR SHALL BE INCINERATED IN FLAMES..."
AND...THE THIRD POWER OF RA...
"IN AN INSTANT, RA SHALL BECOME A PHOENIX...
AND THE ENEMIES OF RA SHALL RETURN TO THE EARTH..."
BEHOLD THE GOD!
SPELL CARD, ACTIVATE!
BA
MONSTER REBORN!
THE SUN DRAGON RA
???
ATK/??? DEF/???
!!

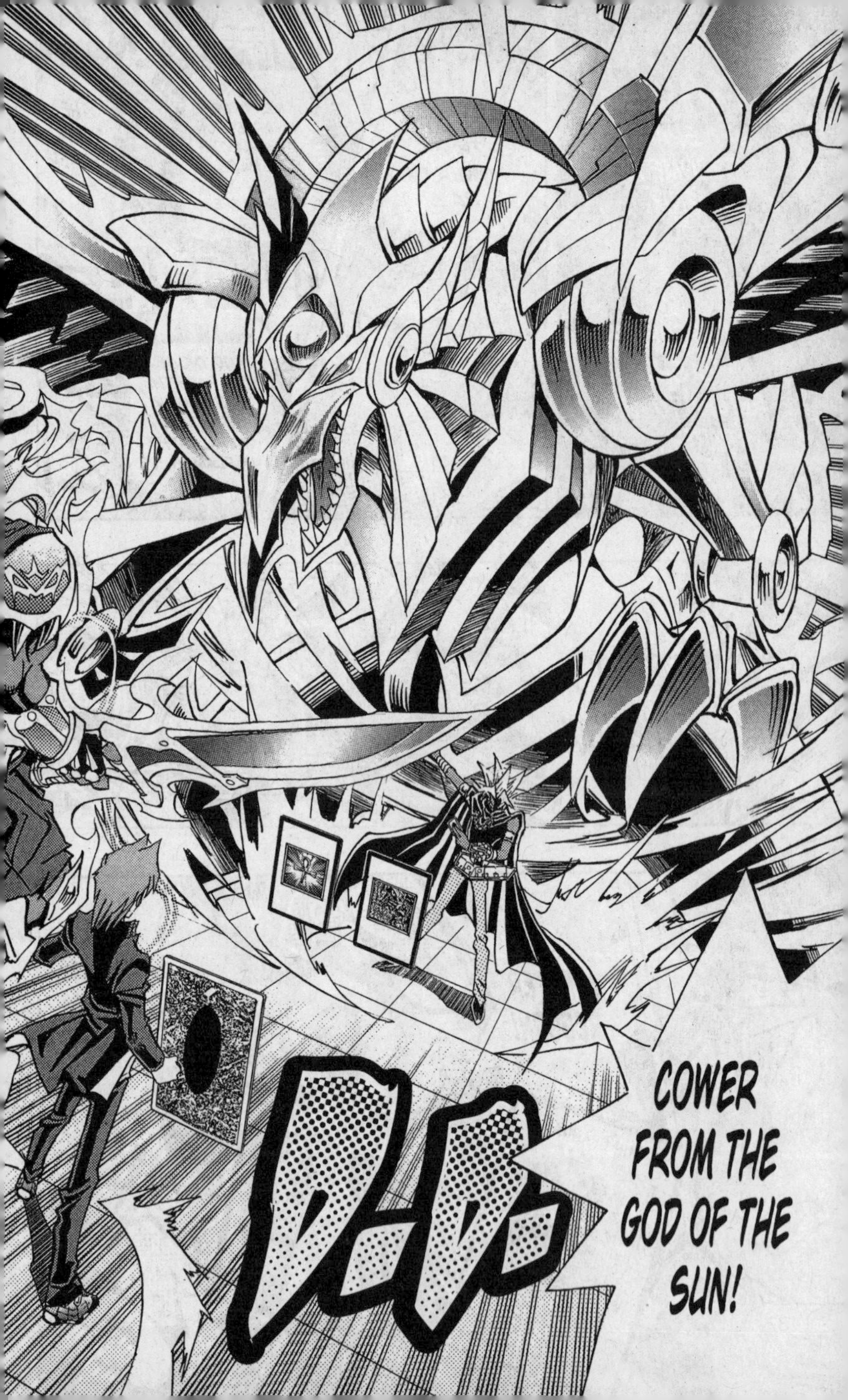
COWER FROM THE GOD OF THE SUN!

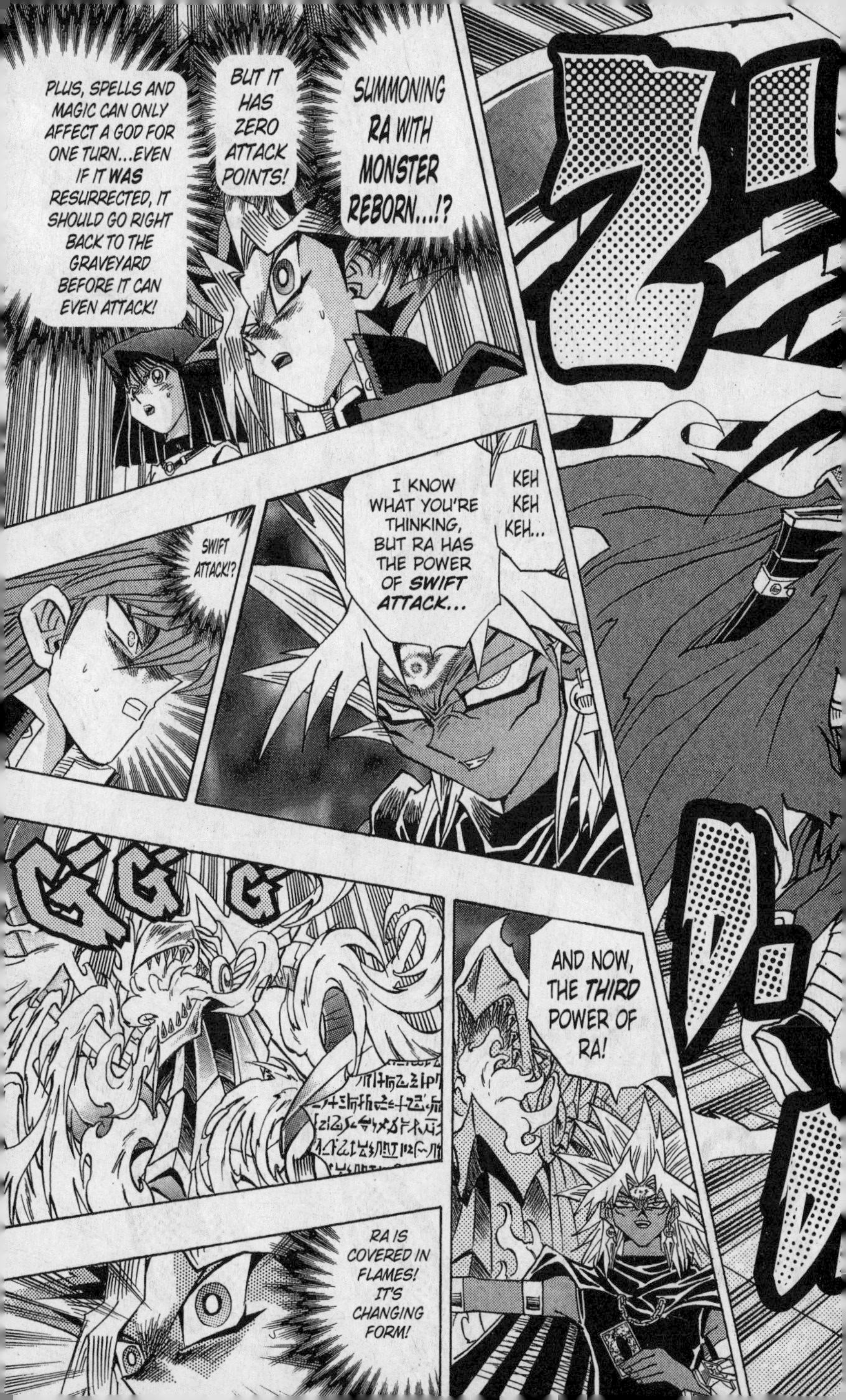
SUMMONING RA WITH MONSTER REBORN...!?
BUT IT HAS ZERO ATTACK POINTS!
PLUS, SPELLS AND MAGIC CAN ONLY AFFECT A GOD FOR ONE TURN...EVEN IF IT WAS RESURRECTED, IT SHOULD GO RIGHT BACK TO THE GRAVEYARD BEFORE IT CAN EVEN ATTACK!
KEH KEH KEH...
I KNOW WHAT YOU'RE THINKING, BUT RA HAS THE POWER OF ***SWIFT ATTACK...***
SWIFT ATTACK!?
AND NOW, THE *THIRD* POWER OF RA!
G G G
RA IS COVERED IN FLAMES! IT'S CHANGING FORM!

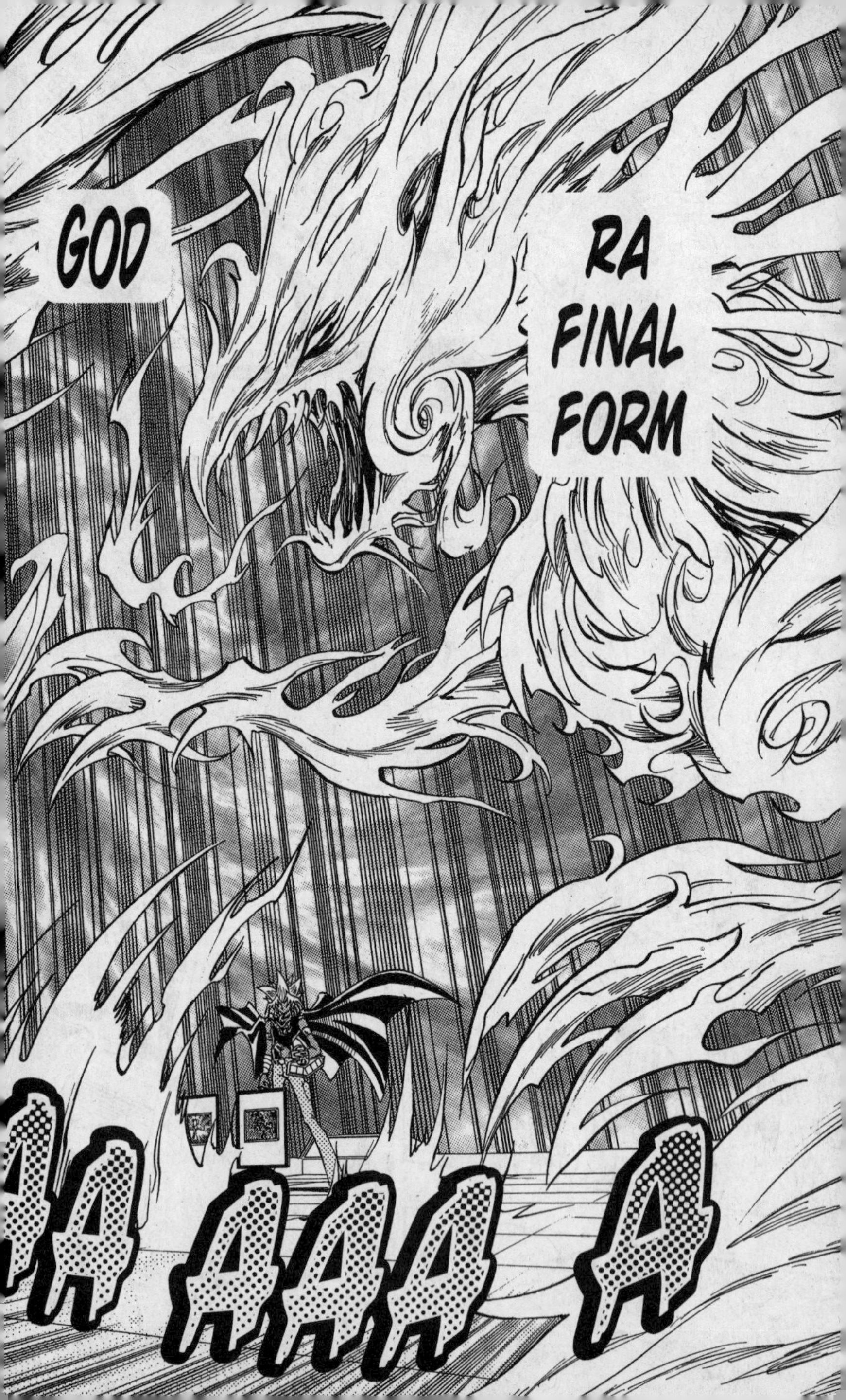
RA FINAL FORM
GOD
AA AAAA A

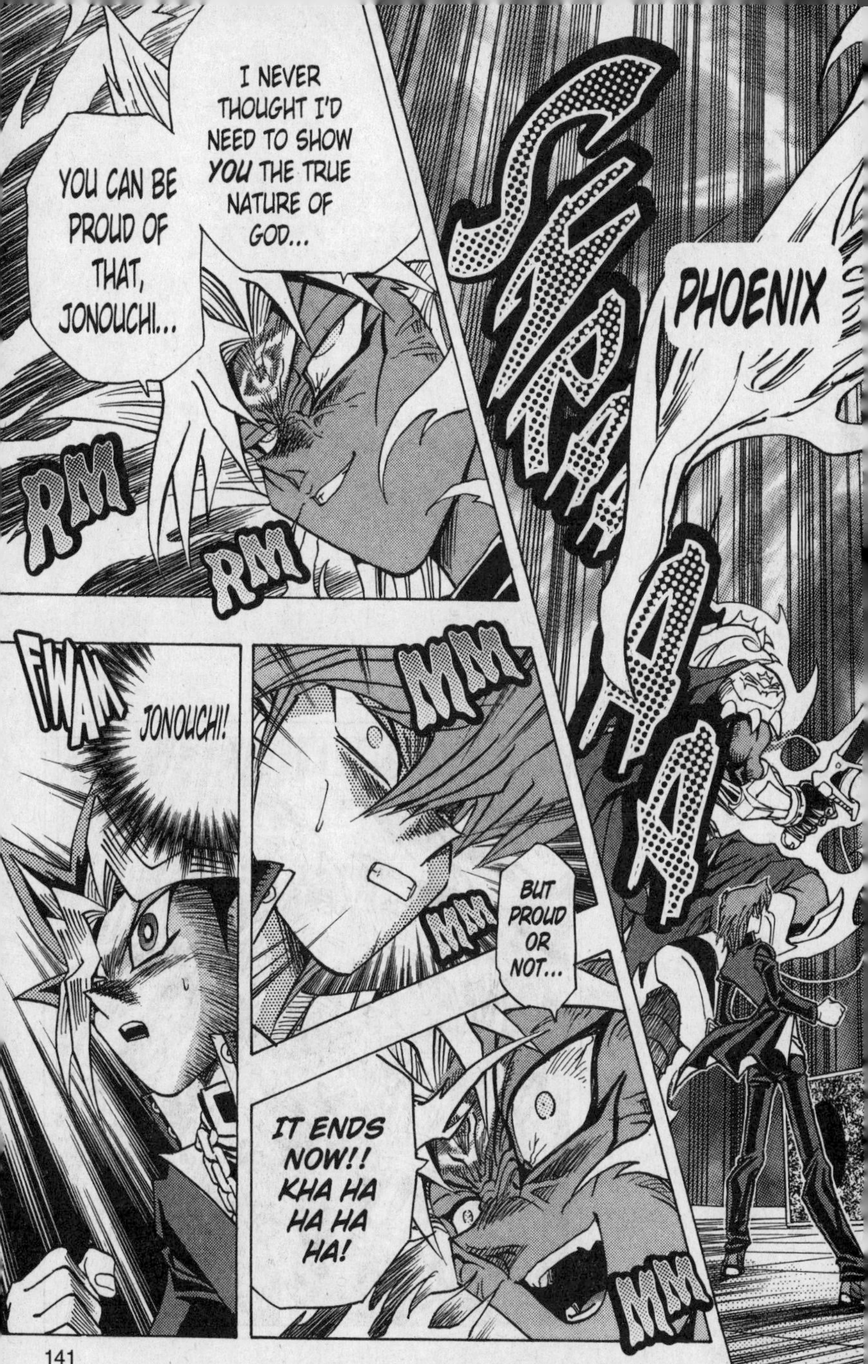
SHRAAAA
PHOENIX
I NEVER THOUGHT I'D NEED TO SHOW *YOU* THE TRUE NATURE OF GOD...
YOU CAN BE PROUD OF THAT, JONOUCHI...
RM
RM
MM
MM
BUT PROUD OR NOT...
IT ENDS NOW!! KHA HA HA HA HA!
MM
FWAM
JONOUCHI!

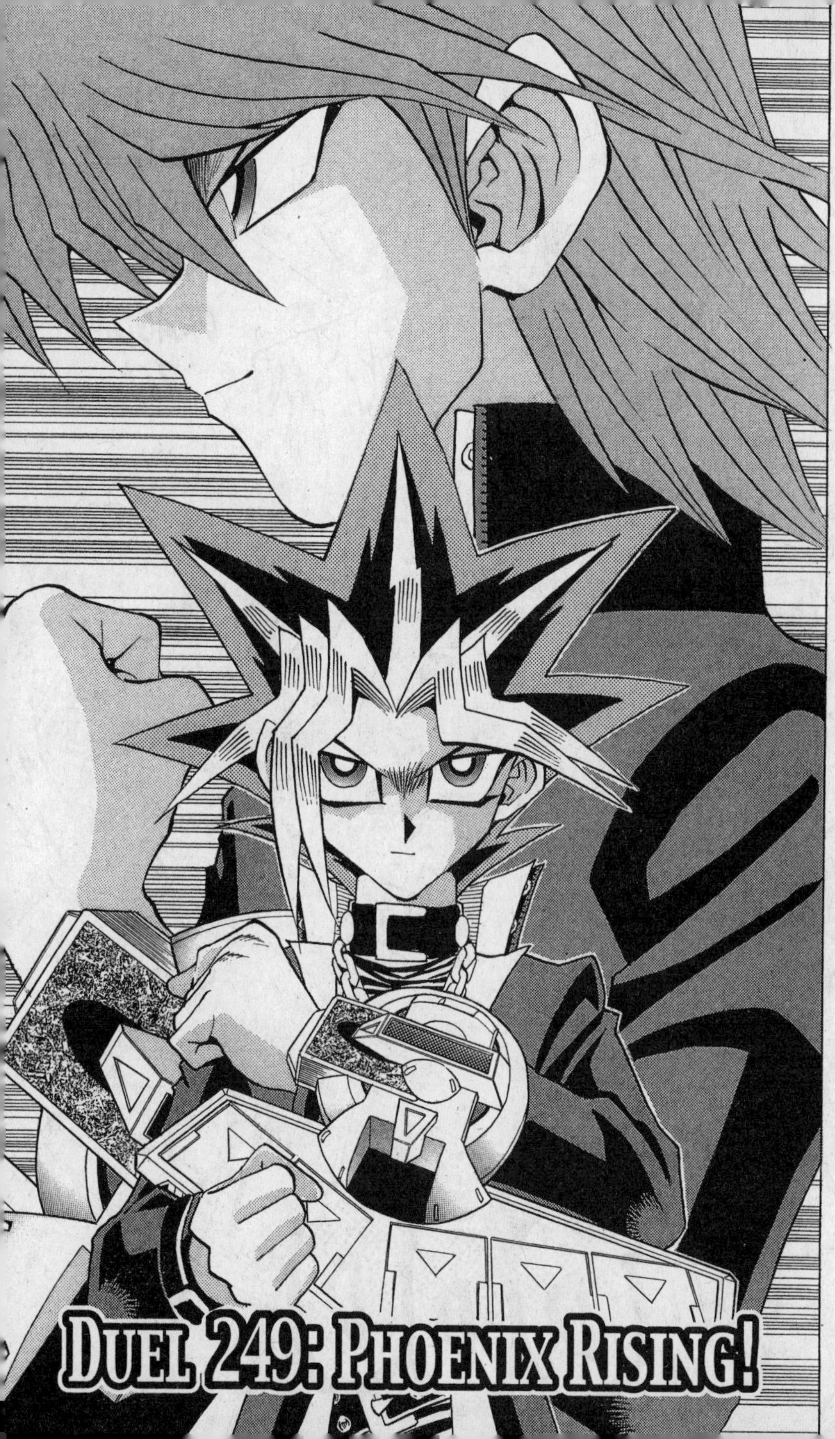
DUEL 249: PHOENIX RISING!

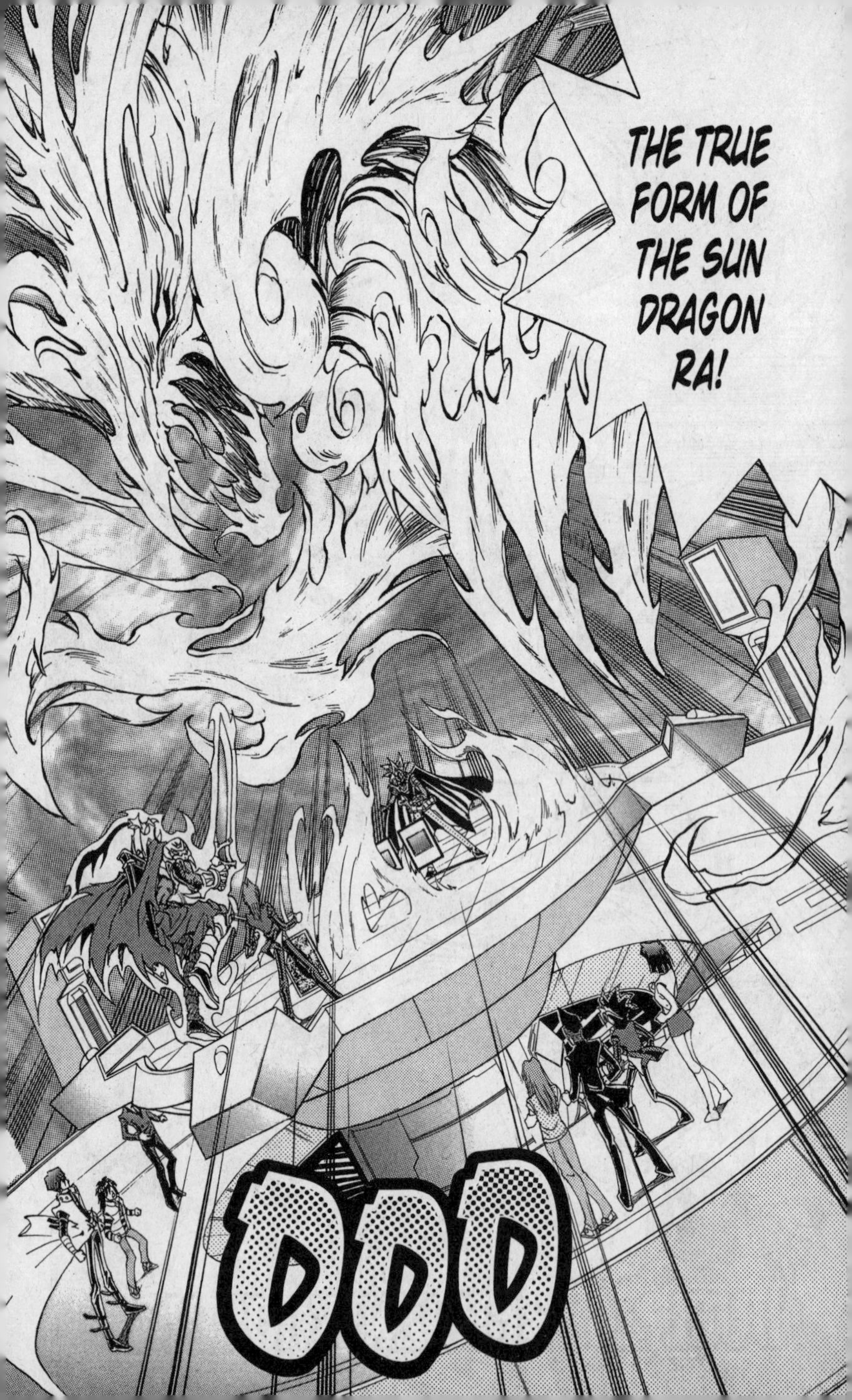
THE TRUE FORM OF THE SUN DRAGON RA!
DDD

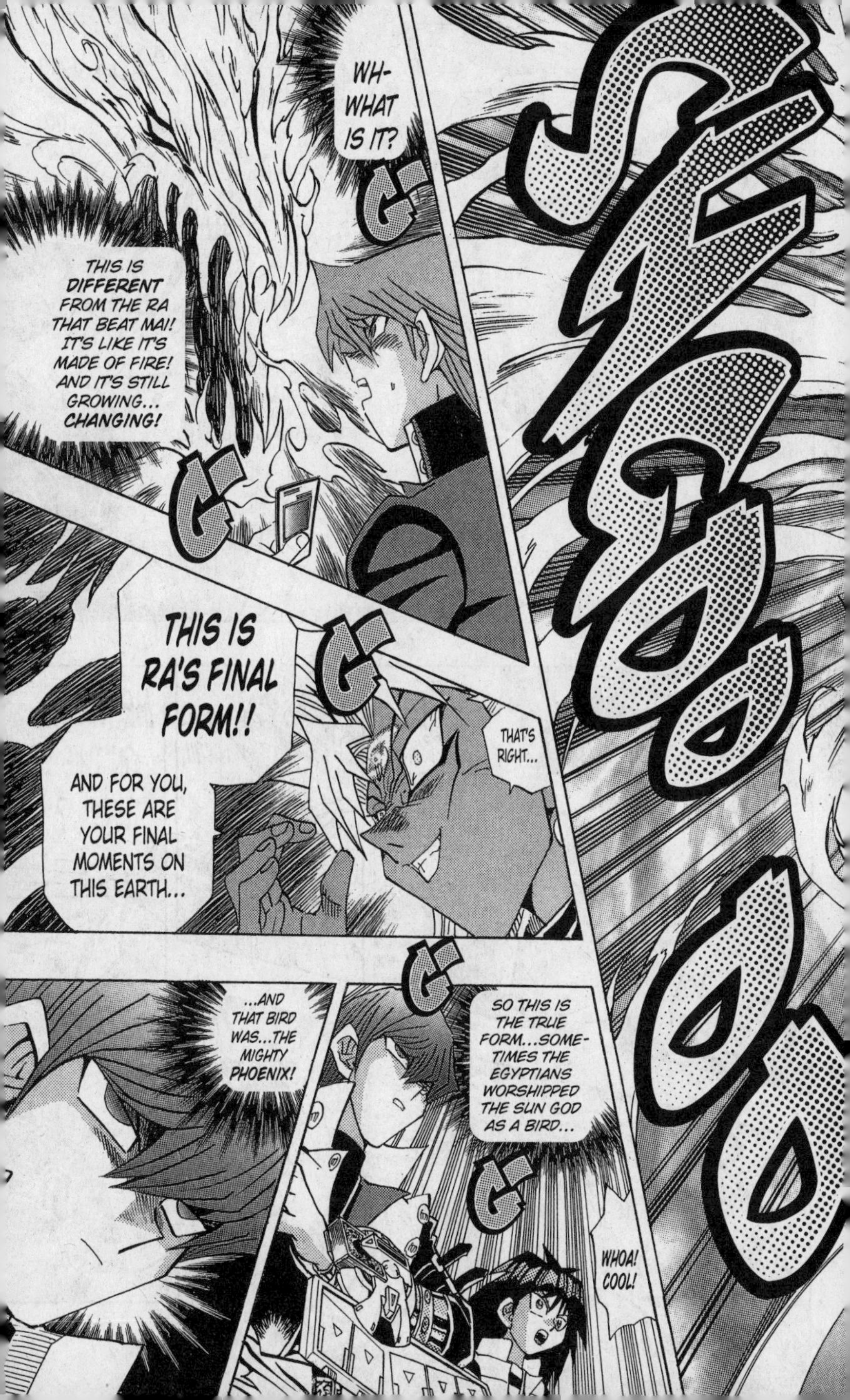
WH- WHAT IS IT?
THIS IS DIFFERENT FROM THE RA THAT BEAT MAI! IT'S LIKE IT'S MADE OF FIRE! AND IT'S STILL GROWING... CHANGING!
THAT'S RIGHT...
THIS IS RA'S FINAL FORM!!
AND FOR YOU, THESE ARE YOUR FINAL MOMENTS ON THIS EARTH...
SO THIS IS THE TRUE FORM...SOME-TIMES THE EGYPTIANS WORSHIPPED THE SUN GOD AS A BIRD...
...AND THAT BIRD WAS...THE MIGHTY PHOENIX!
WHOA! COOL!

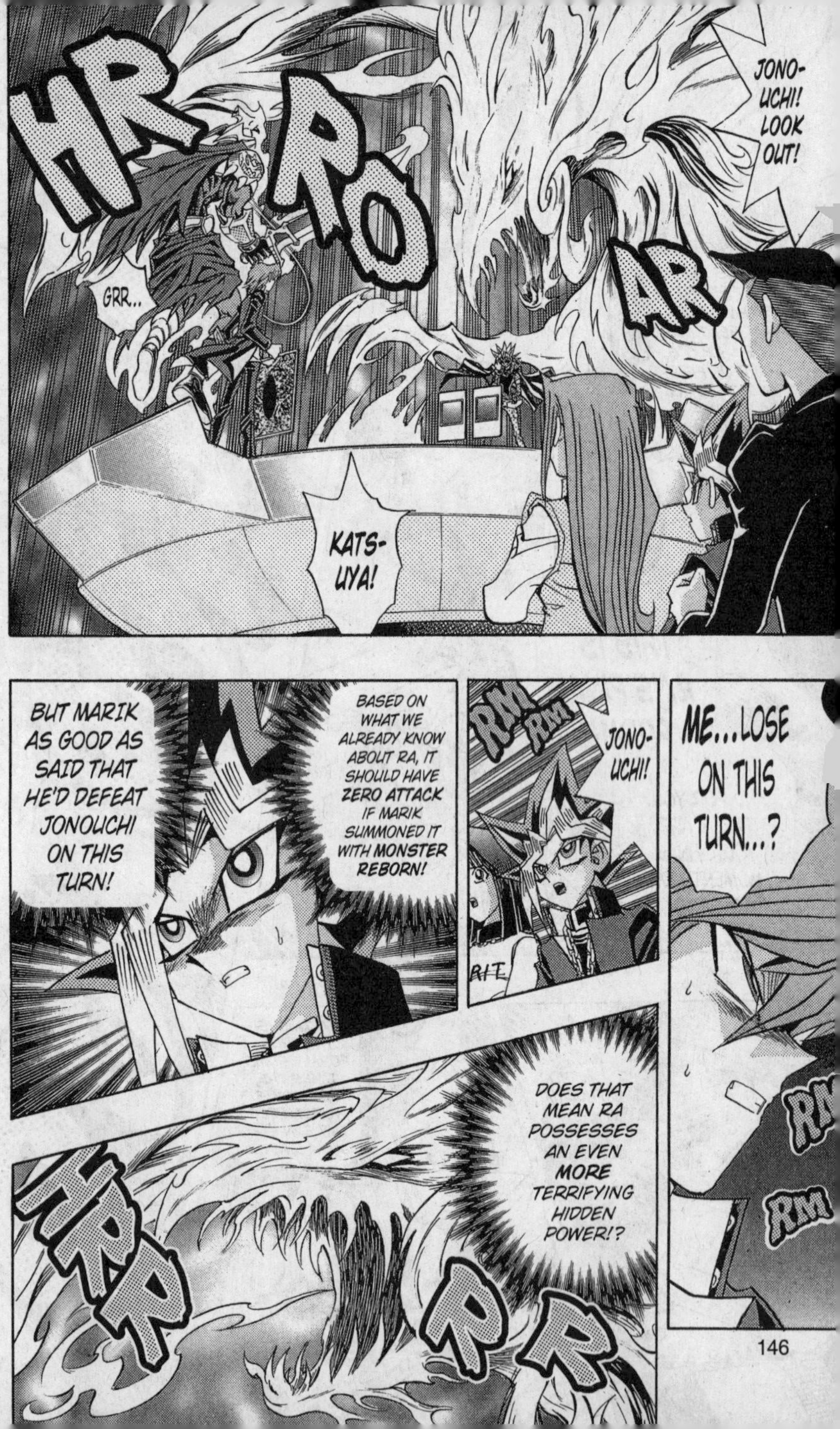
JONO-UCHI! LOOK OUT!
HR RO AR
GRR...
KATS-UYA!
ME...LOSE ON THIS TURN...?
RM RM
JONO-UCHI!
RM RM
BASED ON WHAT WE ALREADY KNOW ABOUT RA, IT SHOULD HAVE ZERO ATTACK IF MARIK SUMMONED IT WITH MONSTER REBORN!
BUT MARIK AS GOOD AS SAID THAT HE'D DEFEAT JONOUCHI ON THIS TURN!
DOES THAT MEAN RA POSSESSES AN EVEN MORE TERRIFYING HIDDEN POWER!?
HRRRR

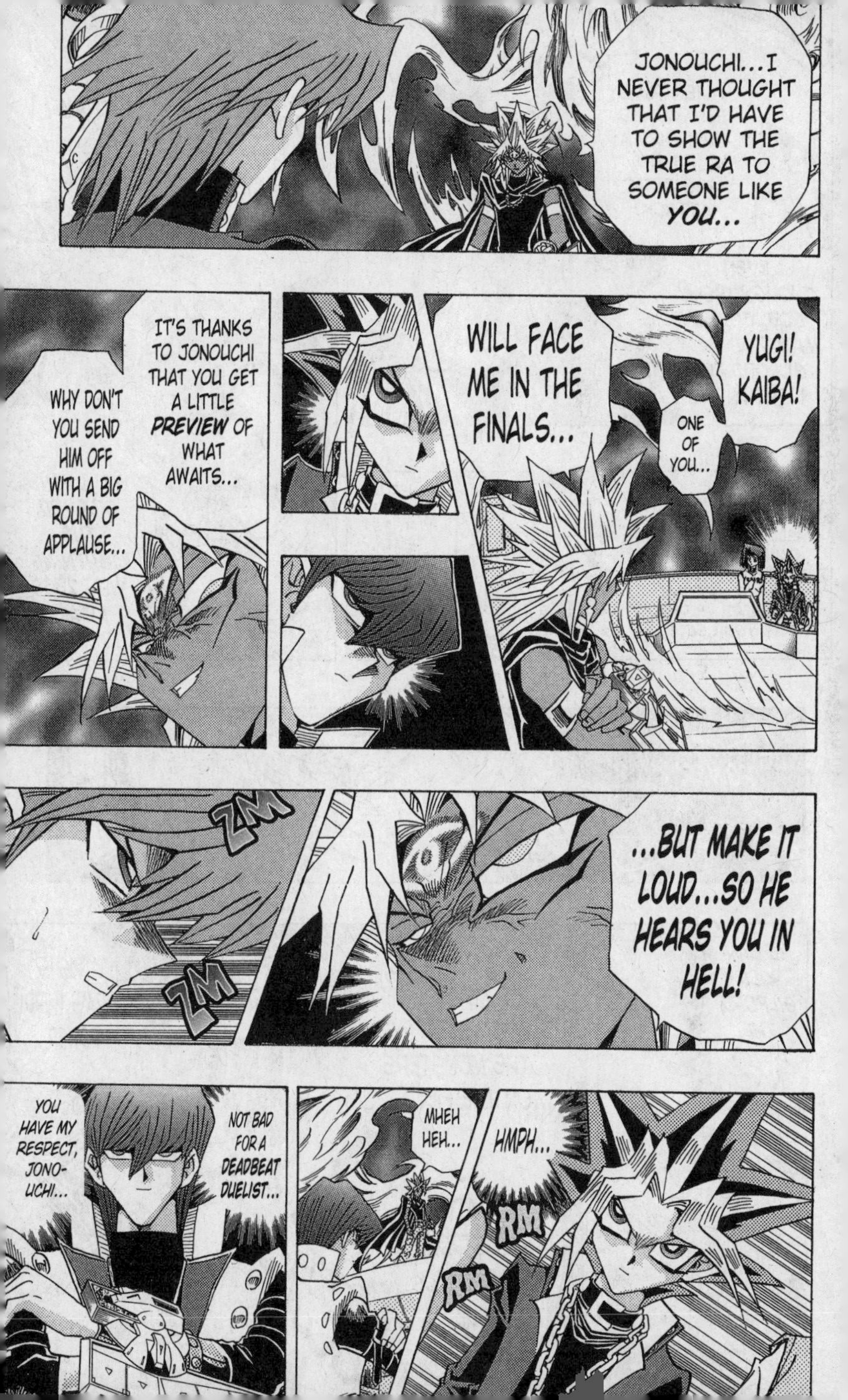
JONOUCHI...I NEVER THOUGHT THAT I'D HAVE TO SHOW THE TRUE RA TO SOMEONE LIKE *YOU*...
YUGI! KAIBA!
ONE OF YOU...
WILL FACE ME IN THE FINALS...
IT'S THANKS TO JONOUCHI THAT YOU GET A LITTLE *PREVIEW* OF WHAT AWAITS...
WHY DON'T YOU SEND HIM OFF WITH A BIG ROUND OF APPLAUSE...
...BUT MAKE IT LOUD...SO HE HEARS YOU IN HELL!
ZM
ZM
HMPH...
RM
RM
MHEH HEH...
NOT BAD FOR A DEADBEAT DUELIST...
YOU HAVE MY RESPECT, JONO-UCHI...

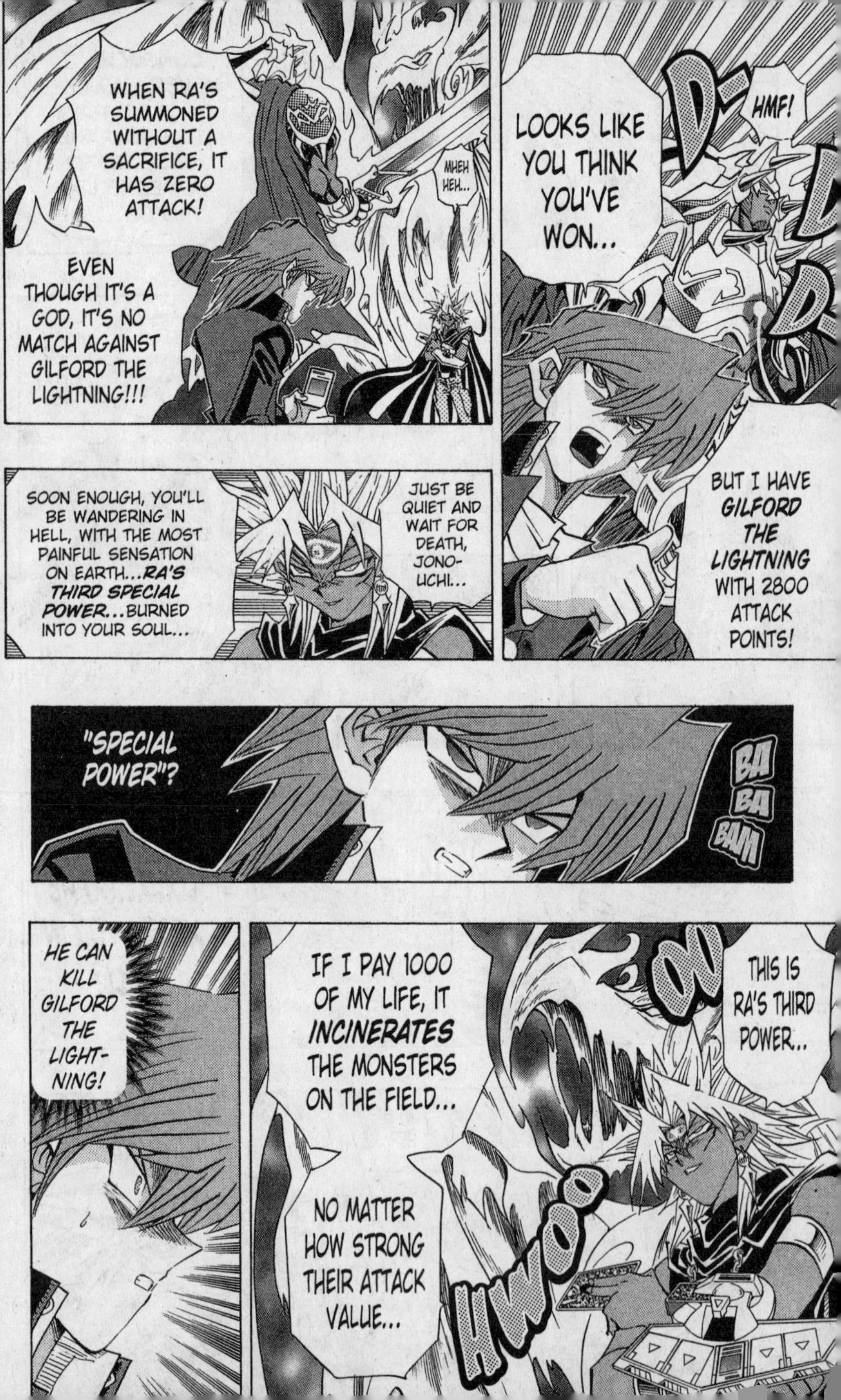
D-D-D-
HMF!
LOOKS LIKE YOU THINK YOU'VE WON...
BUT I HAVE GILFORD THE LIGHTNING WITH 2800 ATTACK POINTS!
MHEH HEH...
WHEN RA'S SUMMONED WITHOUT A SACRIFICE, IT HAS ZERO ATTACK!
EVEN THOUGH IT'S A GOD, IT'S NO MATCH AGAINST GILFORD THE LIGHTNING!!!
JUST BE QUIET AND WAIT FOR DEATH, JONO-UCHI...
SOON ENOUGH, YOU'LL BE WANDERING IN HELL, WITH THE MOST PAINFUL SENSATION ON EARTH...RA'S THIRD SPECIAL POWER...BURNED INTO YOUR SOUL...
BA BA BAM
"SPECIAL POWER"?
THIS IS RA'S THIRD POWER...
WOO
IF I PAY 1000 OF MY LIFE, IT INCINERATES THE MONSTERS ON THE FIELD...
NO MATTER HOW STRONG THEIR ATTACK VALUE...
HWOOO
HE CAN KILL GILFORD THE LIGHT-NING!

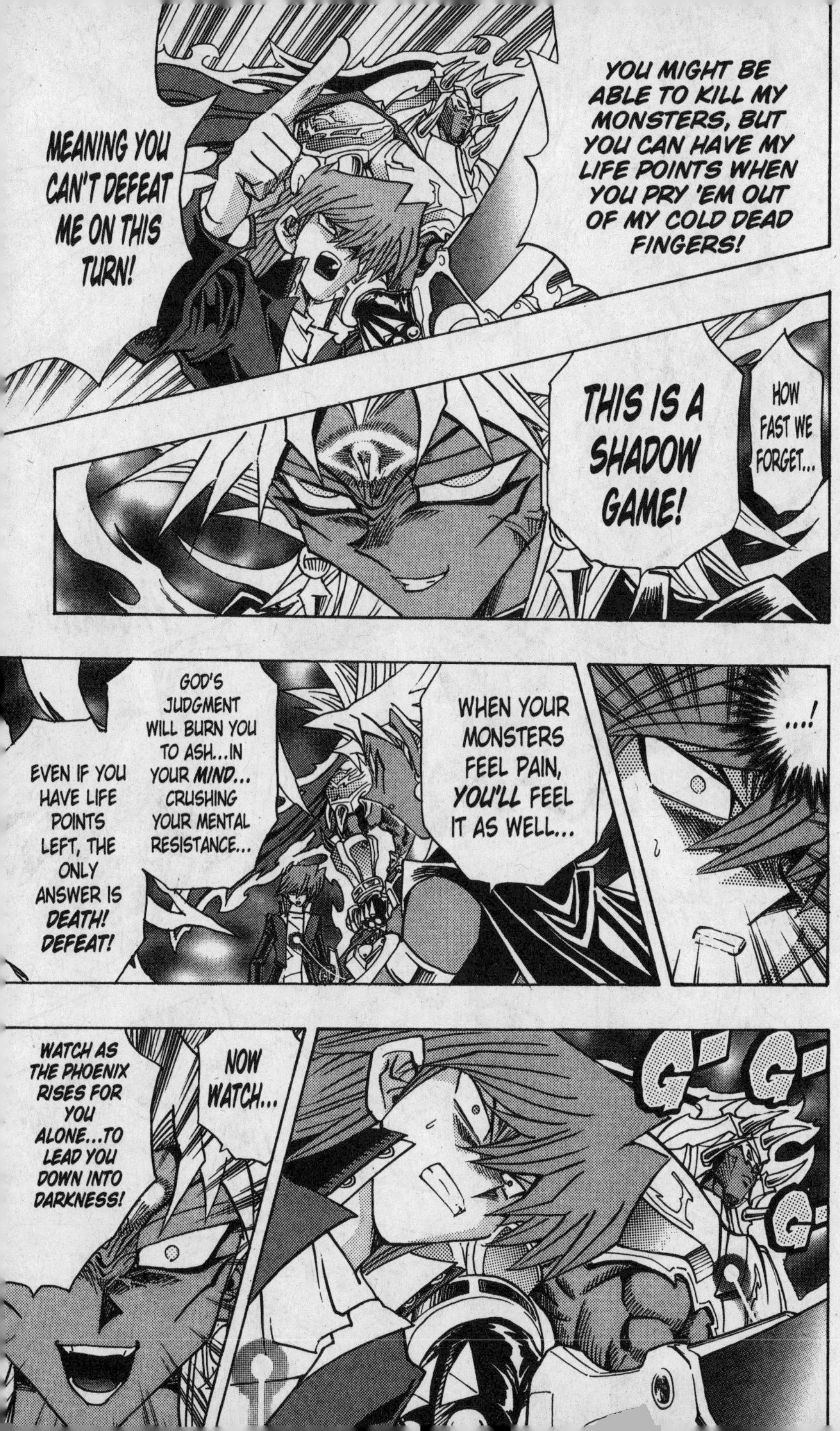
YOU MIGHT BE ABLE TO KILL MY MONSTERS, BUT YOU CAN HAVE MY LIFE POINTS WHEN YOU PRY 'EM OUT OF MY COLD DEAD FINGERS!
MEANING YOU CAN'T DEFEAT ME ON THIS TURN!
HOW FAST WE FORGET...
THIS IS A SHADOW GAME!
...!
WHEN YOUR MONSTERS FEEL PAIN, *YOU'LL* FEEL IT AS WELL...
GOD'S JUDGMENT WILL BURN YOU TO ASH...IN YOUR *MIND*... CRUSHING YOUR MENTAL RESISTANCE...
EVEN IF YOU HAVE LIFE POINTS LEFT, THE ONLY ANSWER IS *DEATH! DEFEAT!*
G' G- G- G-
NOW WATCH...
WATCH AS THE PHOENIX RISES FOR YOU ALONE...TO LEAD YOU DOWN INTO DARKNESS!

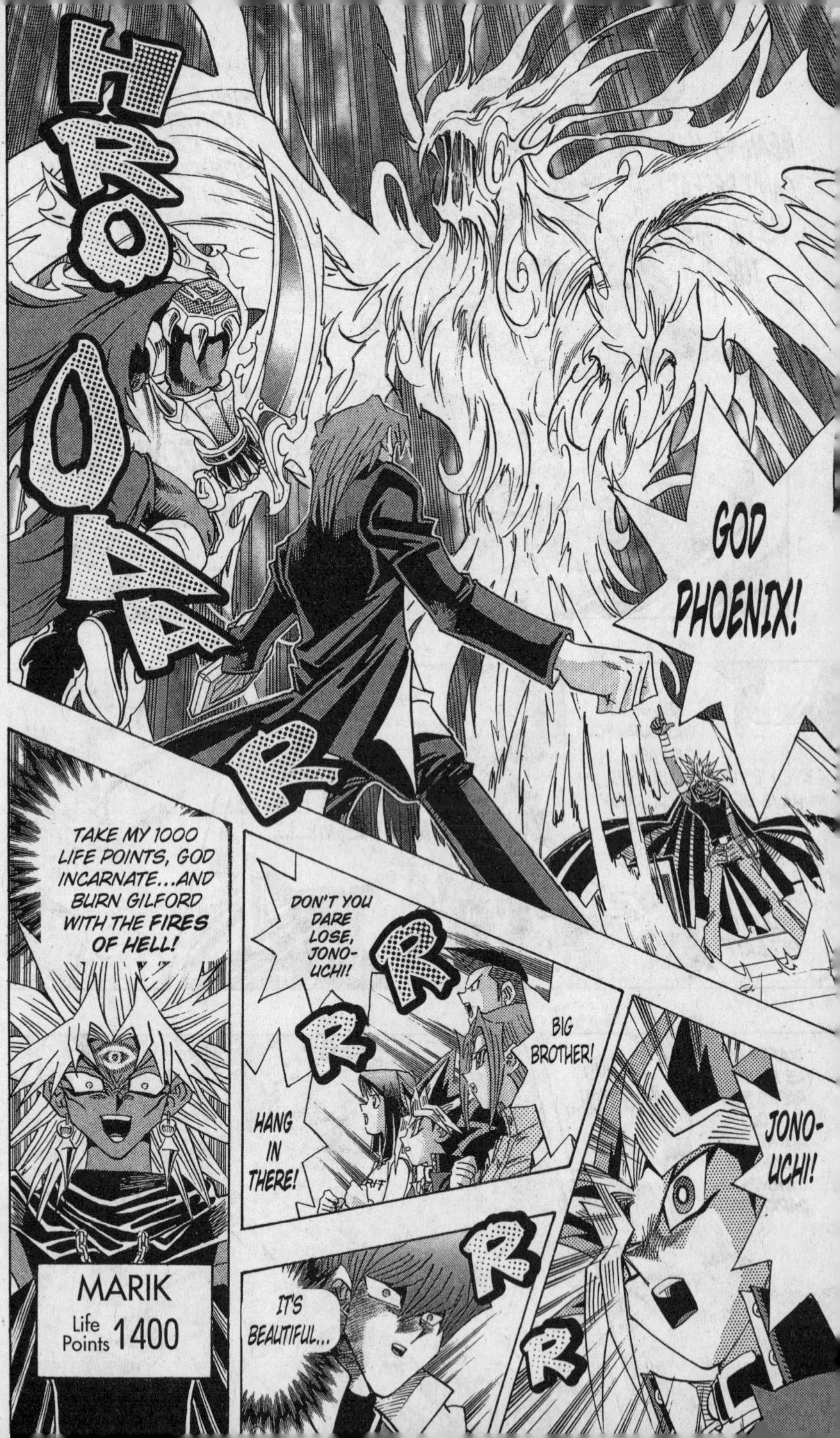
HROOAARR
GOD PHOENIX!
DON'T YOU DARE LOSE, JONO-UCHI!
RRR
BIG BROTHER!
HANG IN THERE!
JONO-UCHI!
RRR
IT'S BEAUTIFUL...
TAKE MY 1000 LIFE POINTS, GOD INCARNATE...AND BURN GILFORD WITH THE FIRES OF HELL!
MARIK
Life Points 1400

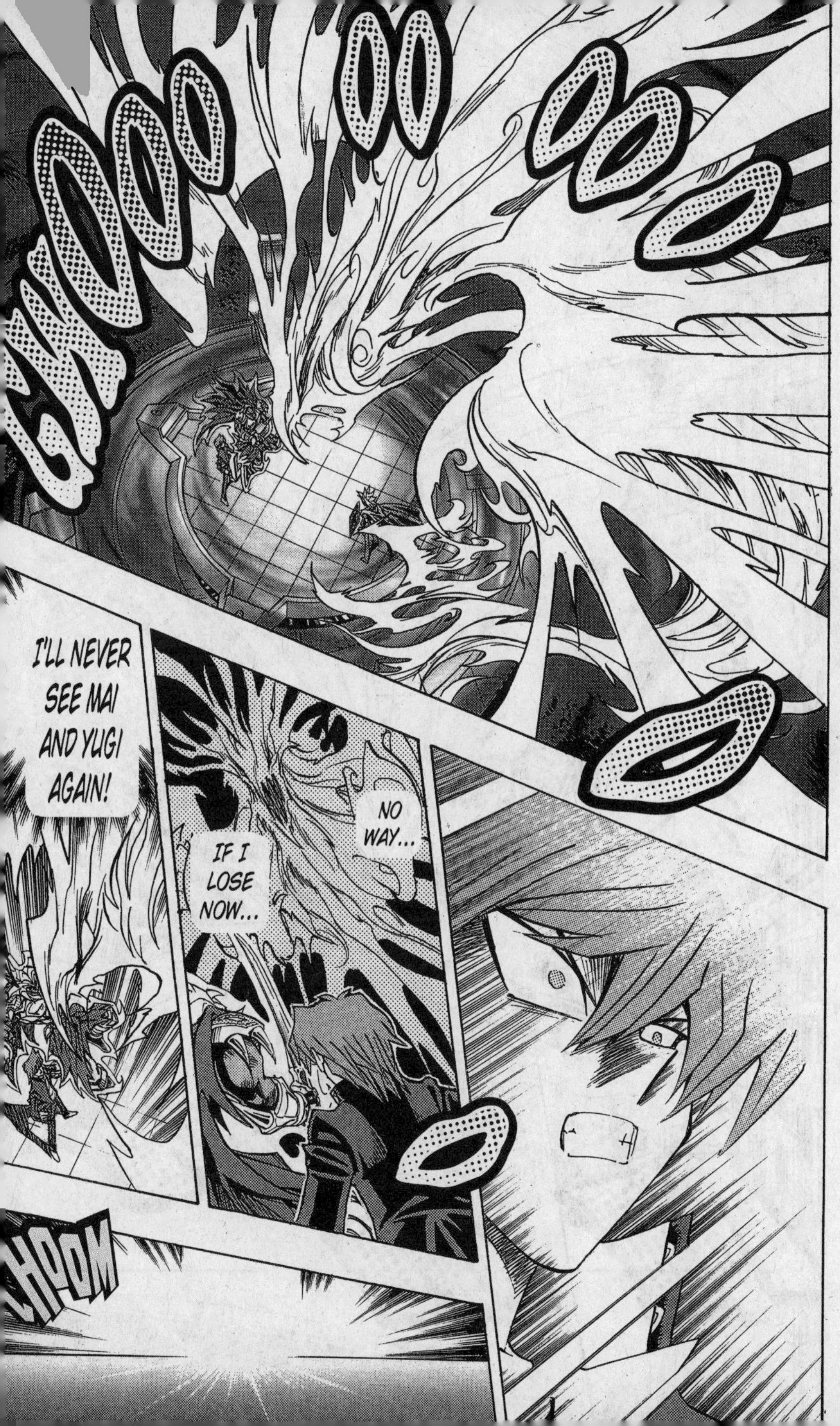
NO WAY...
IF I LOSE NOW...
I'LL NEVER SEE MAI AND YUGI AGAIN!
HOOM

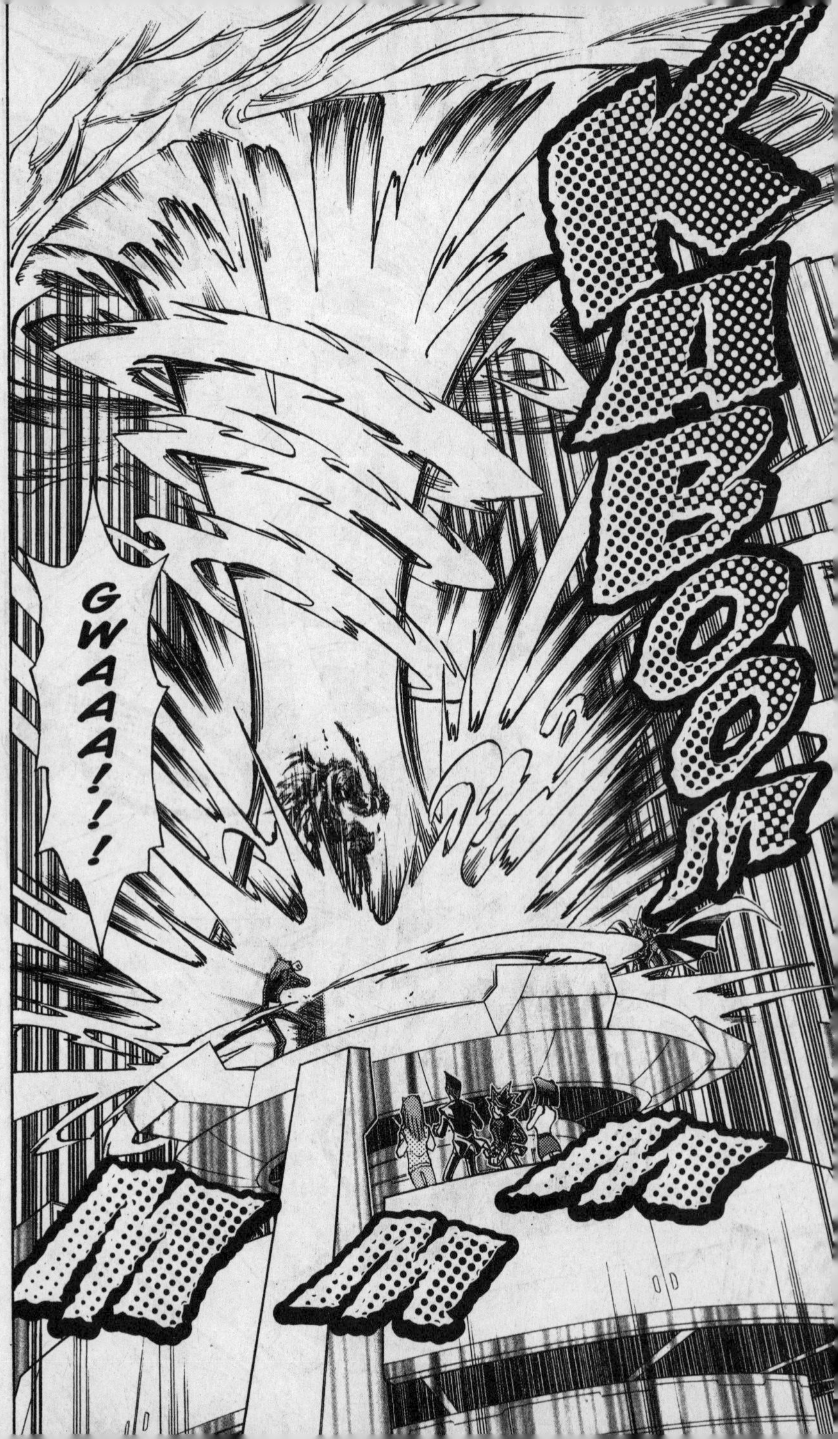
KABOOM
GWAAAA!!!

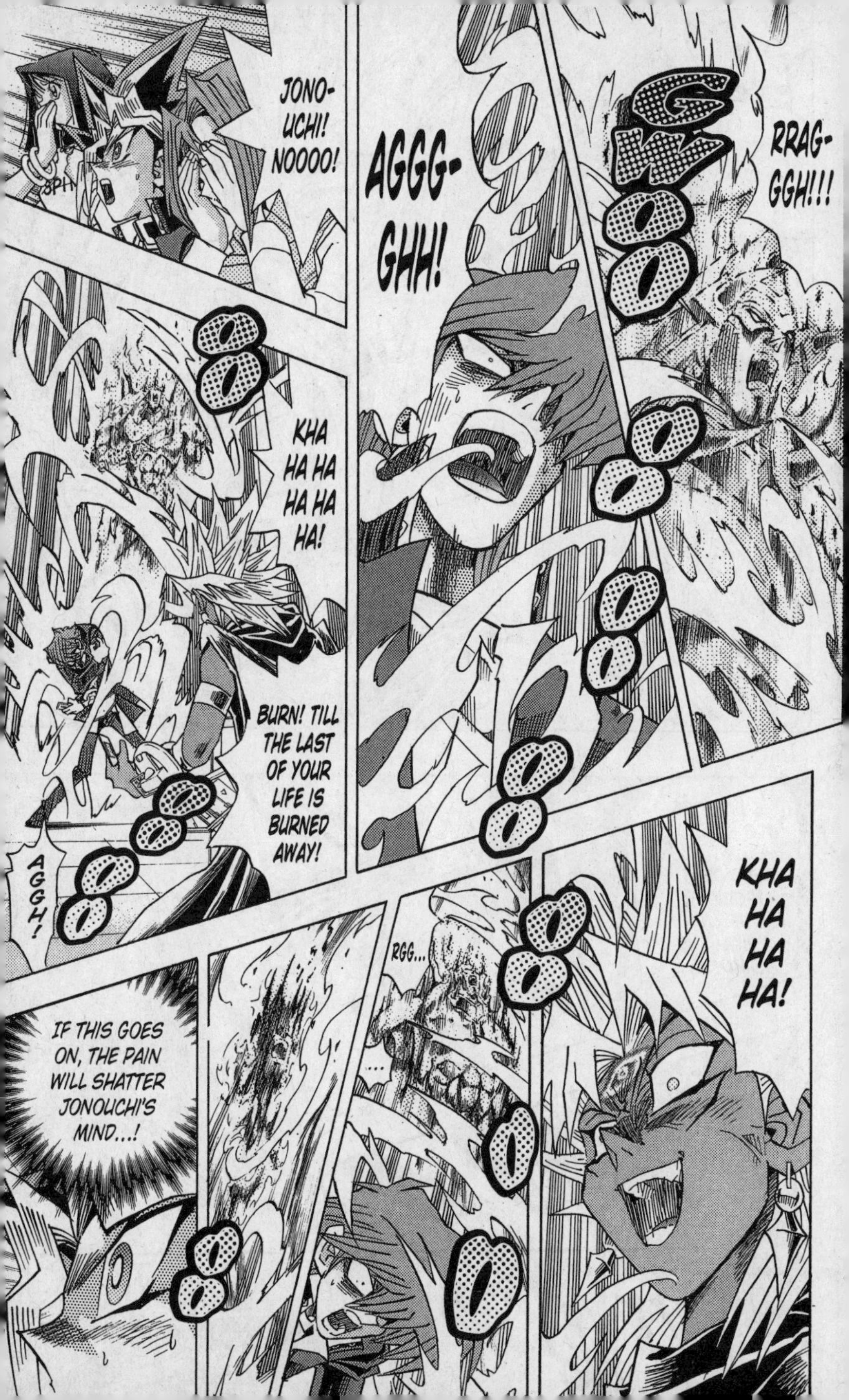
RRAG-GGH!!!
AGGG-GHH!
JONO-UCHI! NOOOO!
KHA HA HA HA HA HA!
BURN! TILL THE LAST OF YOUR LIFE IS BURNED AWAY!
AGGH!
KHA HA HA HA HA!
RGG...
...
IF THIS GOES ON, THE PAIN WILL SHATTER JONOUCHI'S MIND...!

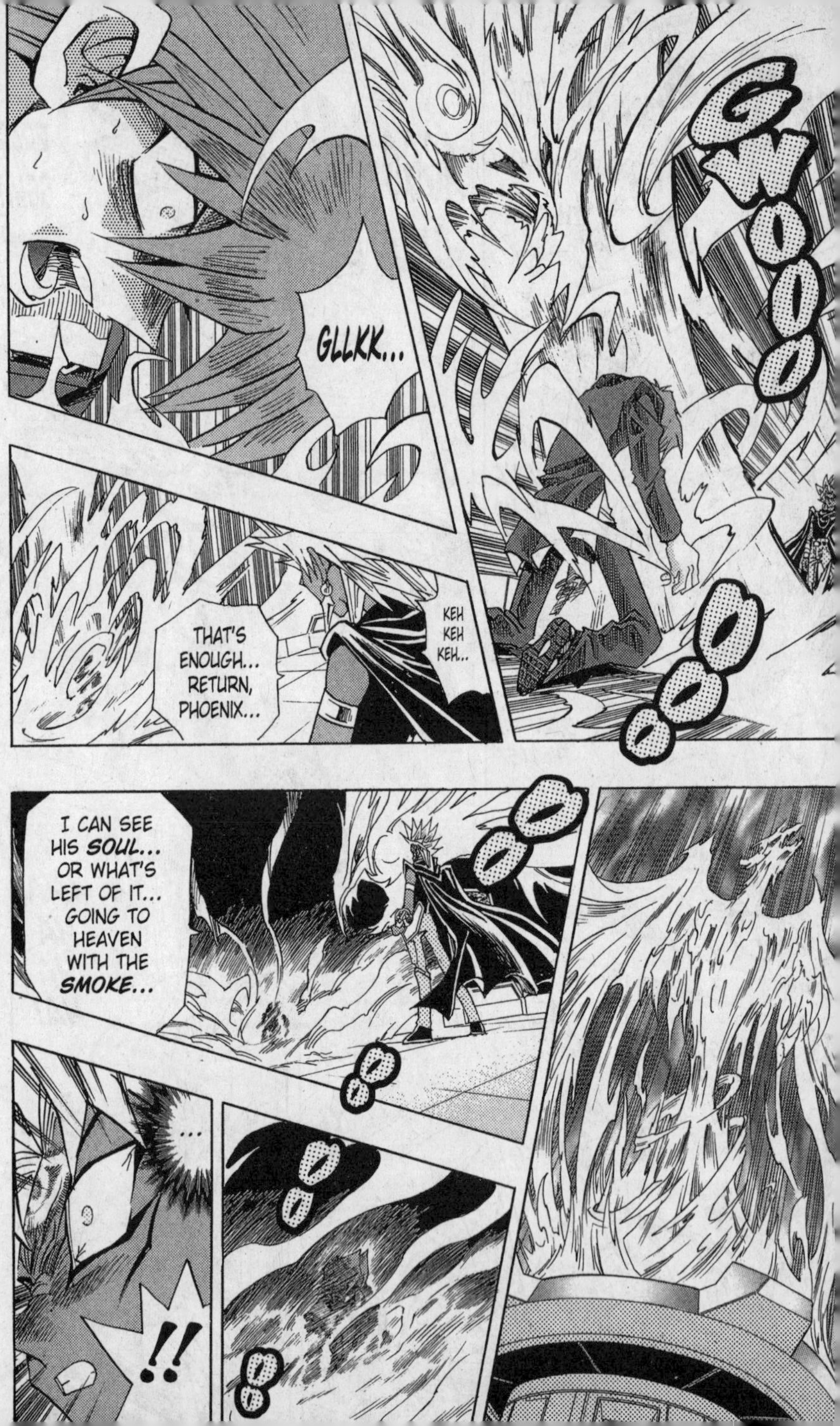
GWOOOO
GLLKK...
KEH KEH KEH...
THAT'S ENOUGH... RETURN, PHOENIX...
I CAN SEE HIS ***SOUL...*** OR WHAT'S LEFT OF IT... GOING TO HEAVEN WITH THE ***SMOKE...***
...
!!

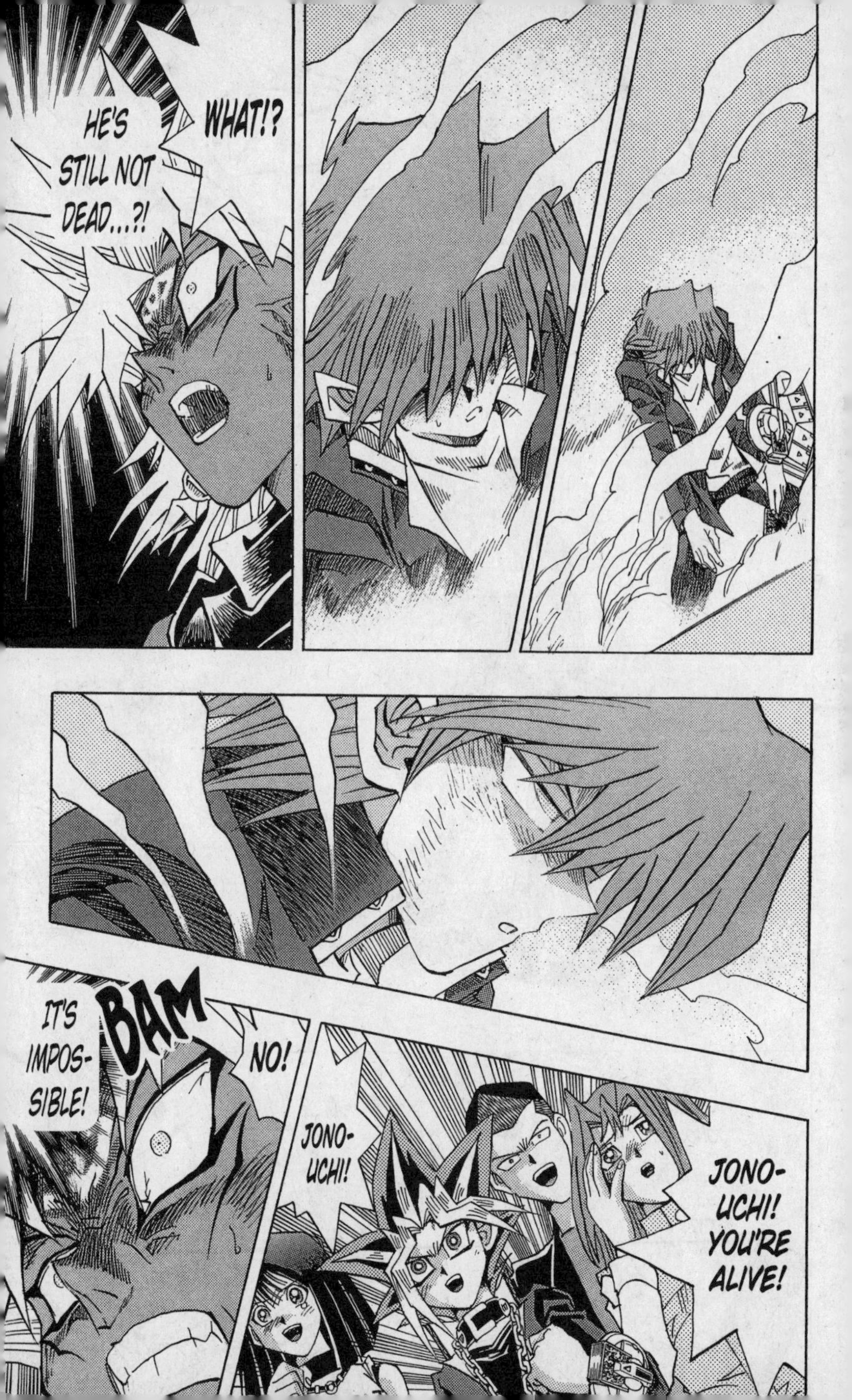
WHAT!?
HE'S STILL NOT DEAD...?!
JONO-UCHI! YOU'RE ALIVE!
JONO-UCHI!
NO!
BAM
IT'S IMPOS-SIBLE!

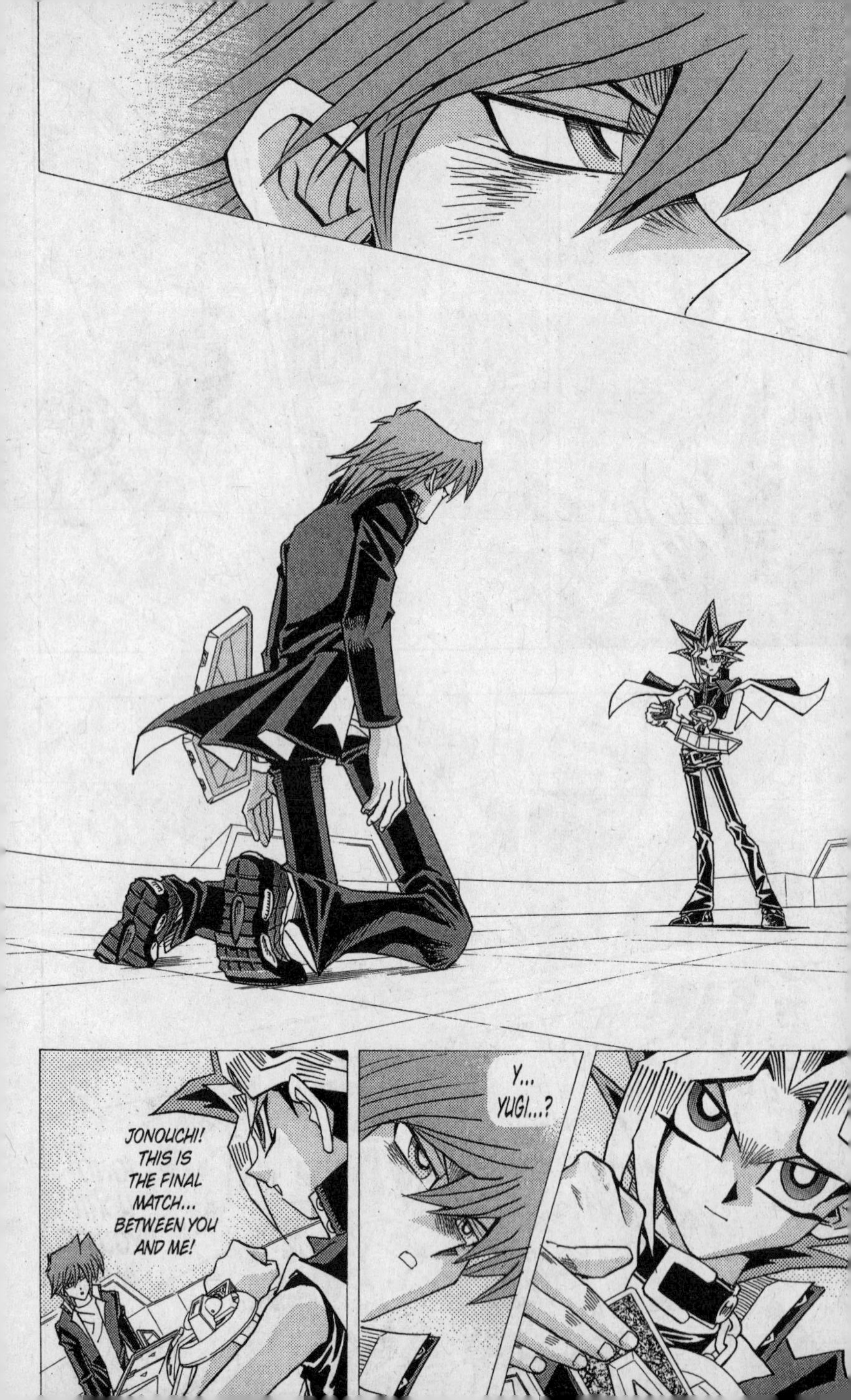
Y... YUGI...?
JONOUCHI! THIS IS THE FINAL MATCH... BETWEEN YOU AND ME!

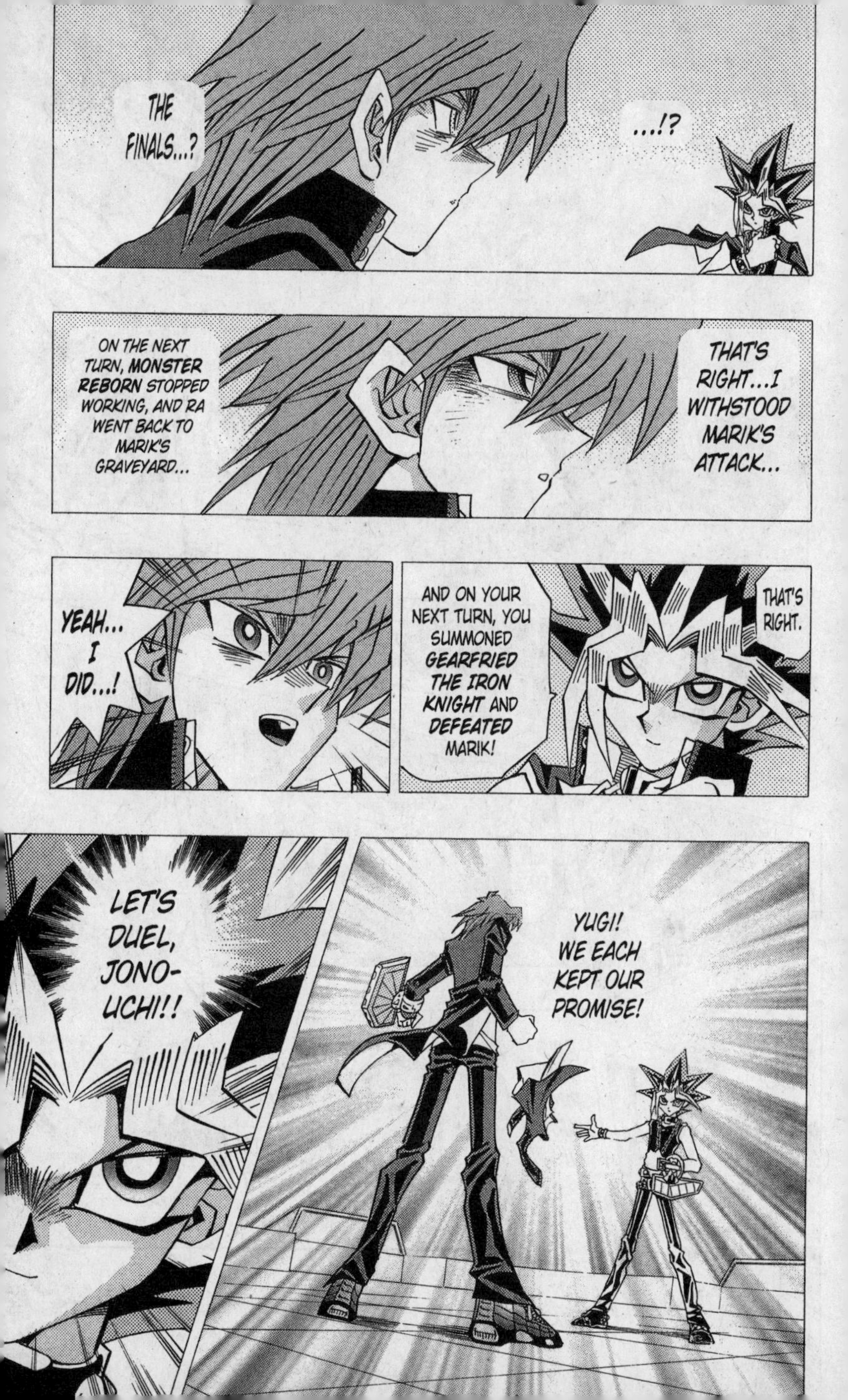
...!?
THE FINALS...?
THAT'S RIGHT...I WITHSTOOD MARIK'S ATTACK...
ON THE NEXT TURN, **MONSTER REBORN** STOPPED WORKING, AND RA WENT BACK TO MARIK'S GRAVEYARD...
THAT'S RIGHT.
AND ON YOUR NEXT TURN, YOU SUMMONED **GEARFRIED THE IRON KNIGHT** AND **DEFEATED** MARIK!
YEAH... I DID...!
YUGI! WE EACH KEPT OUR PROMISE!
LET'S DUEL, JONO-UCHI!!

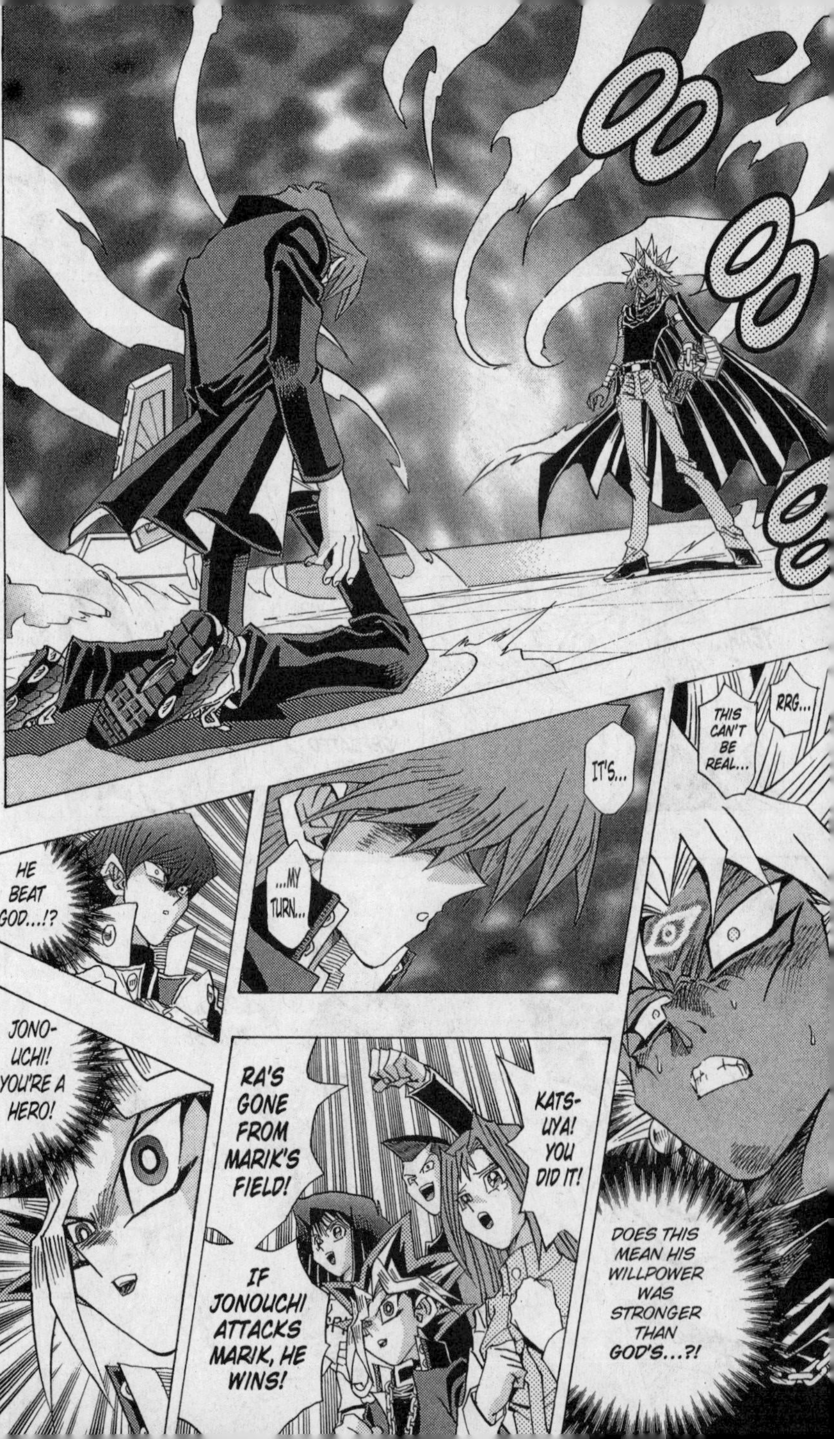
RRG...
THIS CAN'T BE REAL...
DOES THIS MEAN HIS WILLPOWER WAS STRONGER THAN GOD'S...?!
IT'S...
...MY TURN...
HE BEAT GOD...!?
KATSUYA! YOU DID IT!
RA'S GONE FROM MARIK'S FIELD!
IF JONOUCHI ATTACKS MARIK, HE WINS!
JONOUCHI! YOU'RE A HERO!

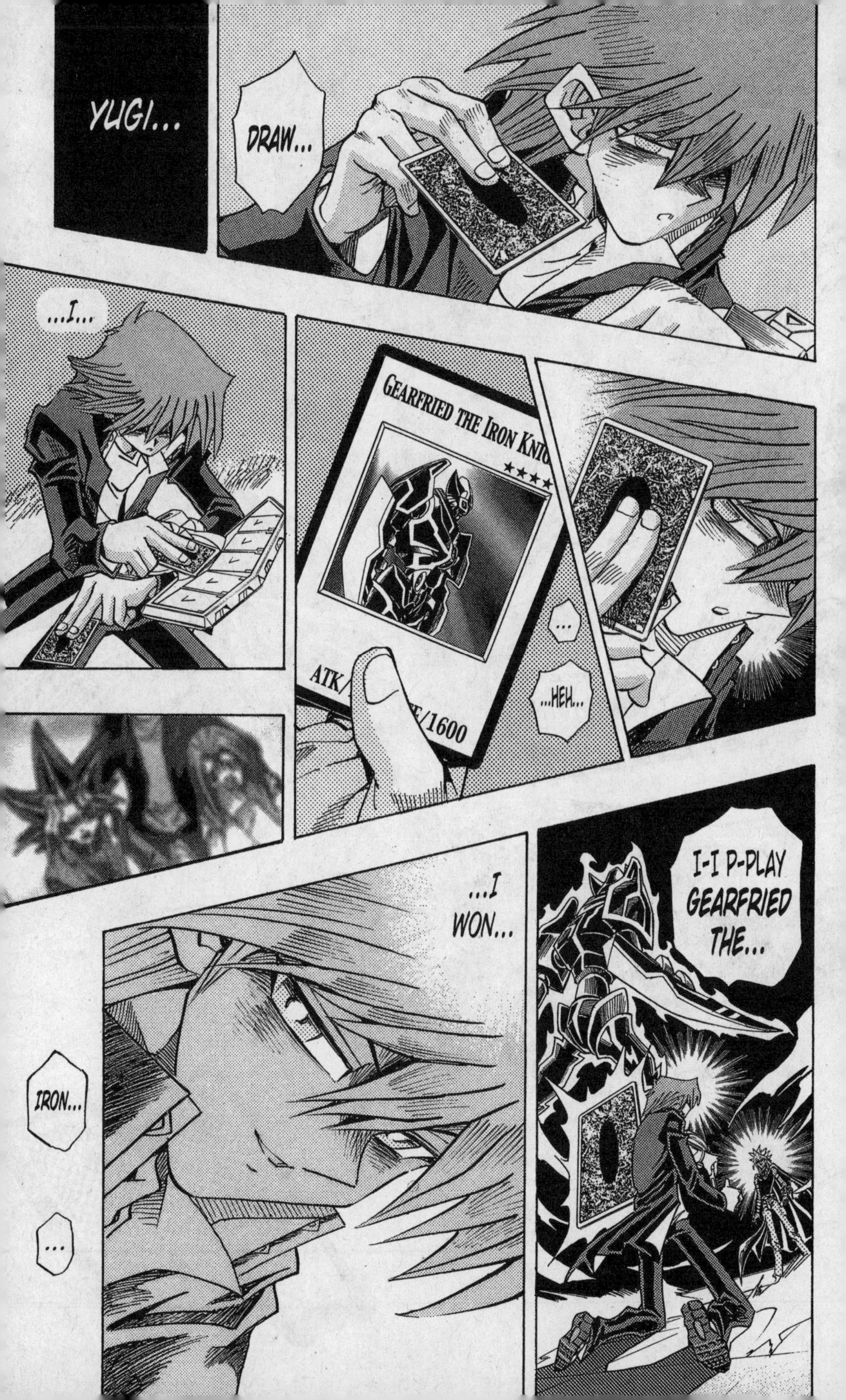
DRAW...
YUGI...
...
...HEH...
GEARFRIED THE IRON KNIG
...I...
I-I P-PLAY GEARFRIED THE...
...I WON...
IRON...
...

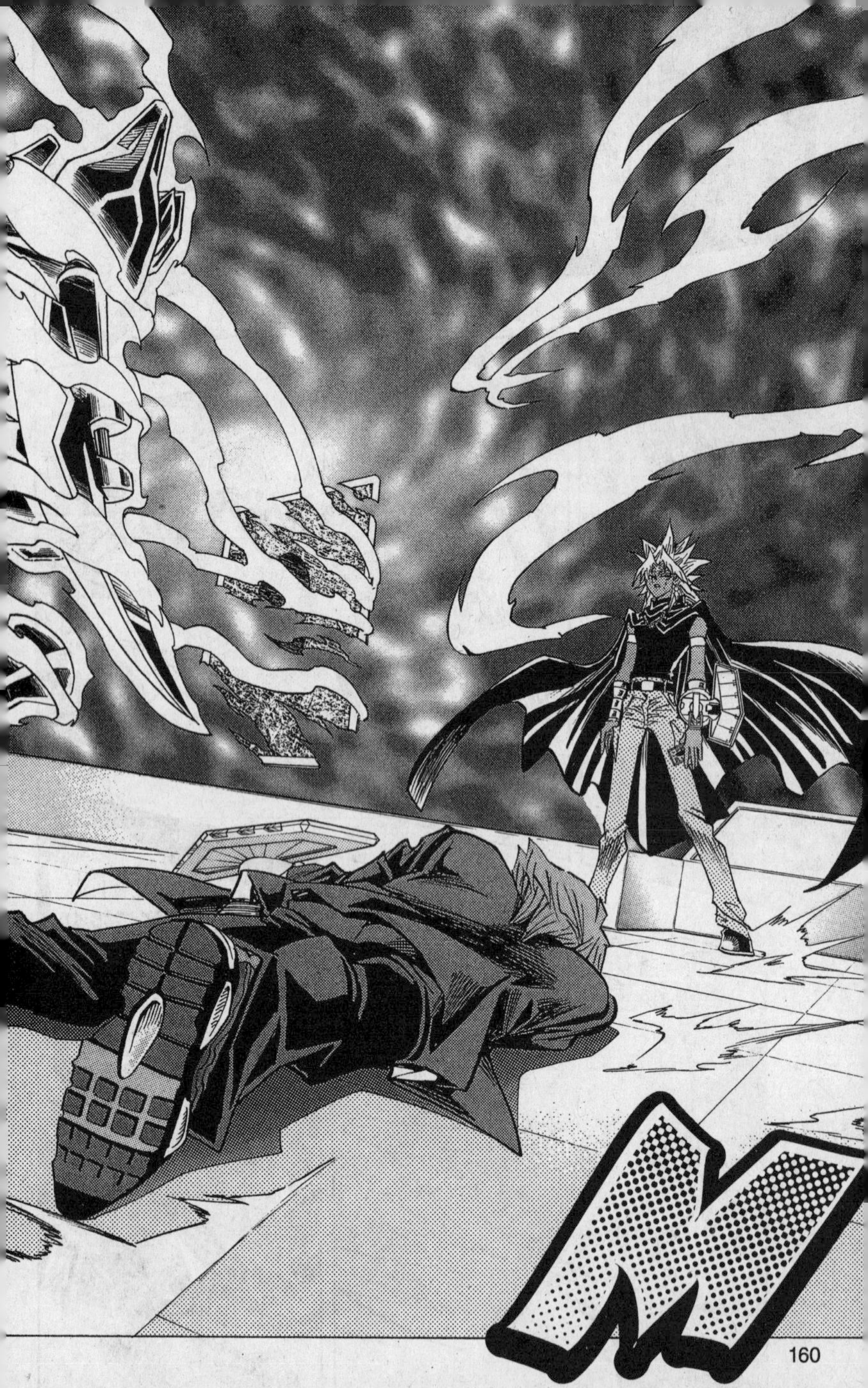
M

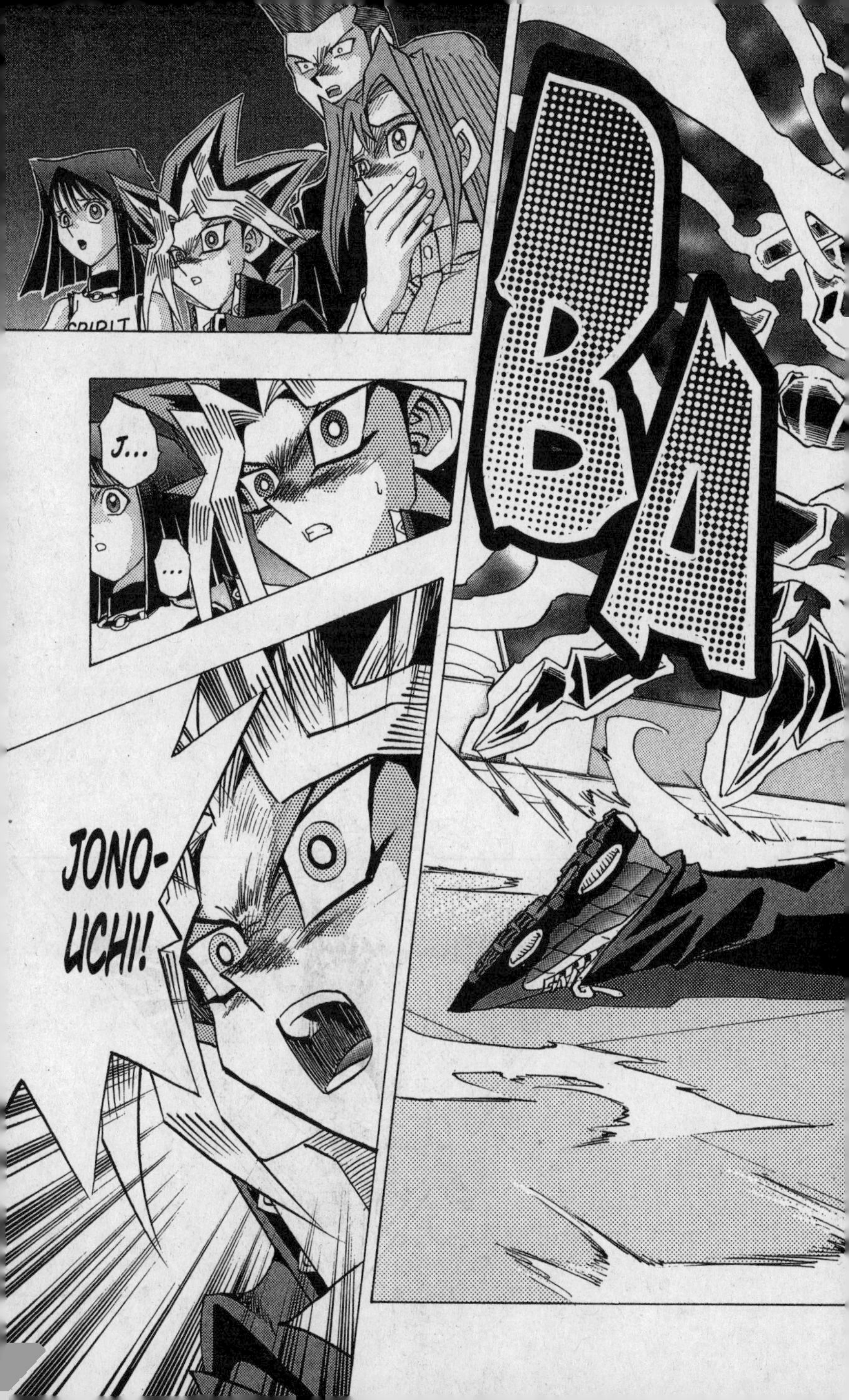
BA
J...
...
JONO-UCHI!

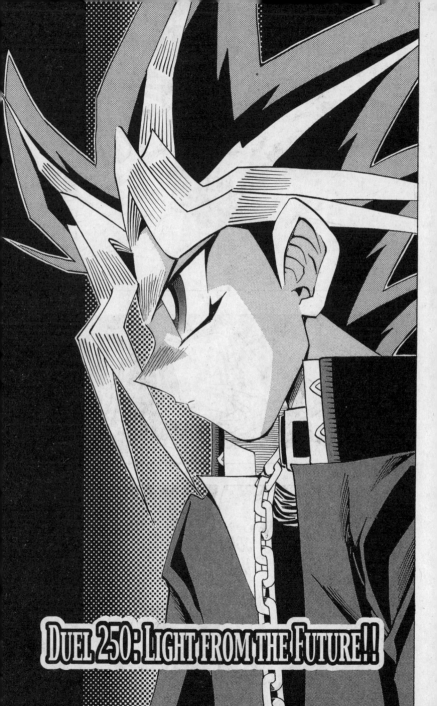

DUEL 250: LIGHT FROM THE FUTURE!!

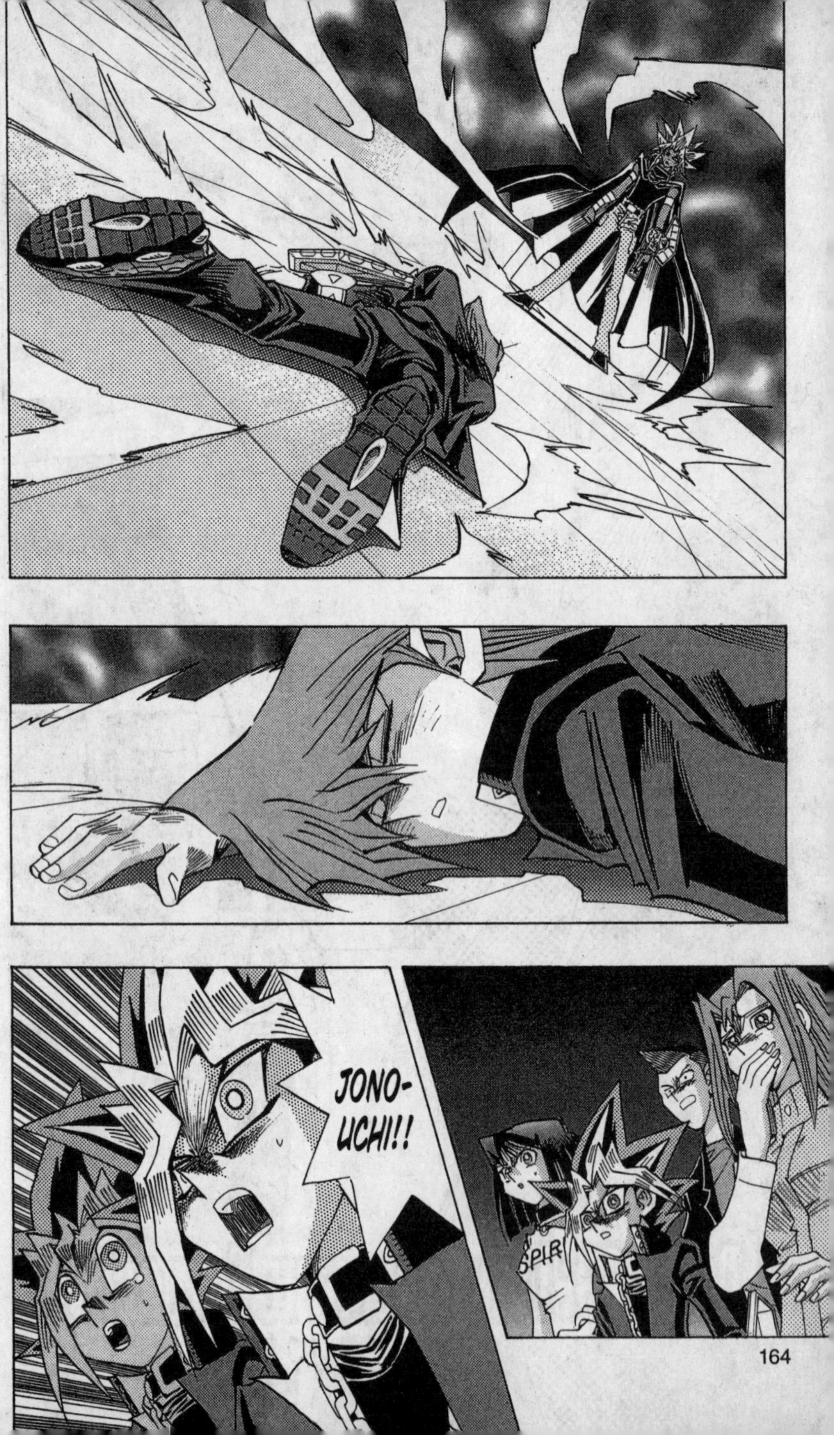
JONO-
UCHI!!

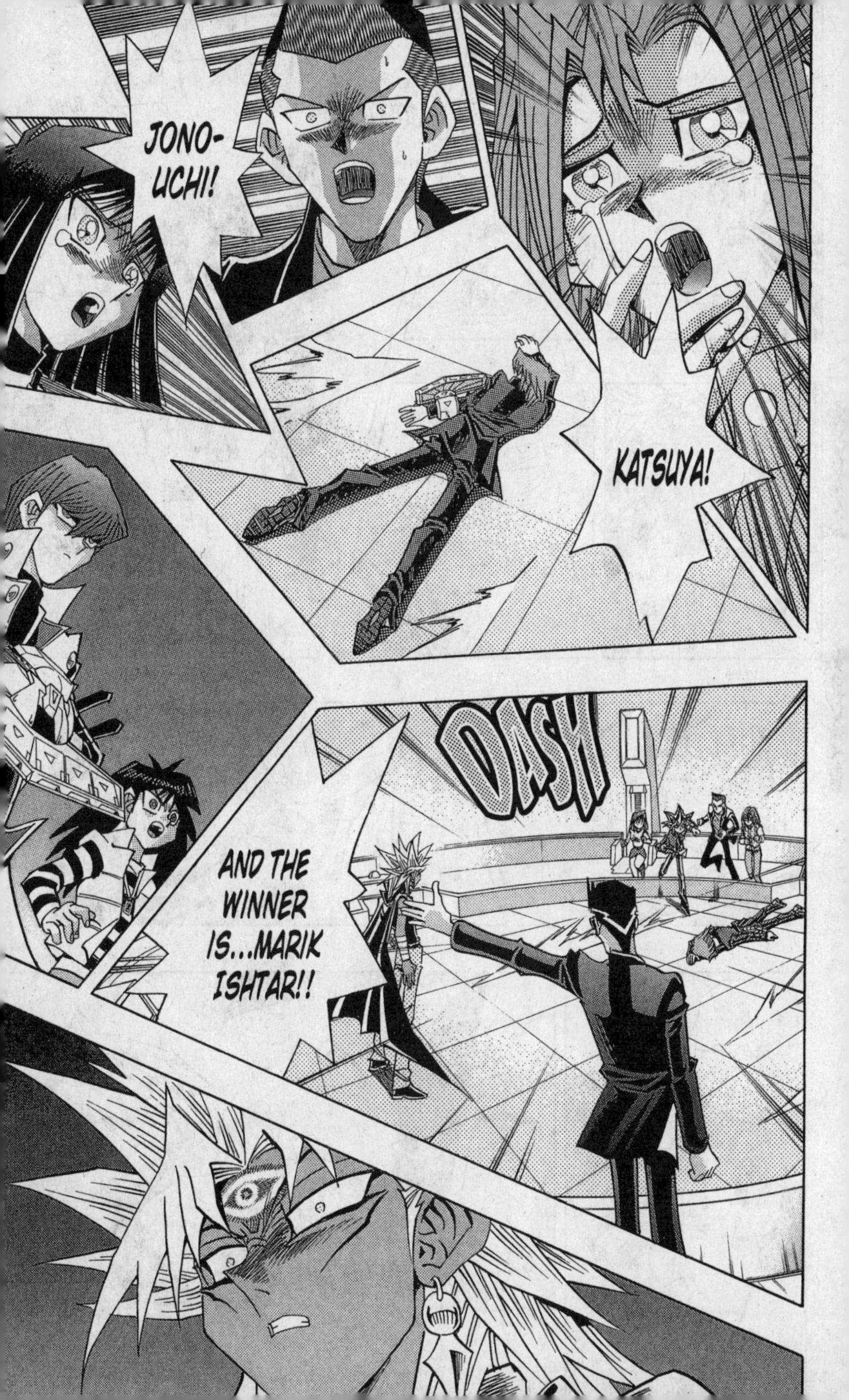
JONO-UCHI!
KATSUYA!
DASH
AND THE WINNER IS...MARIK ISHTAR!!

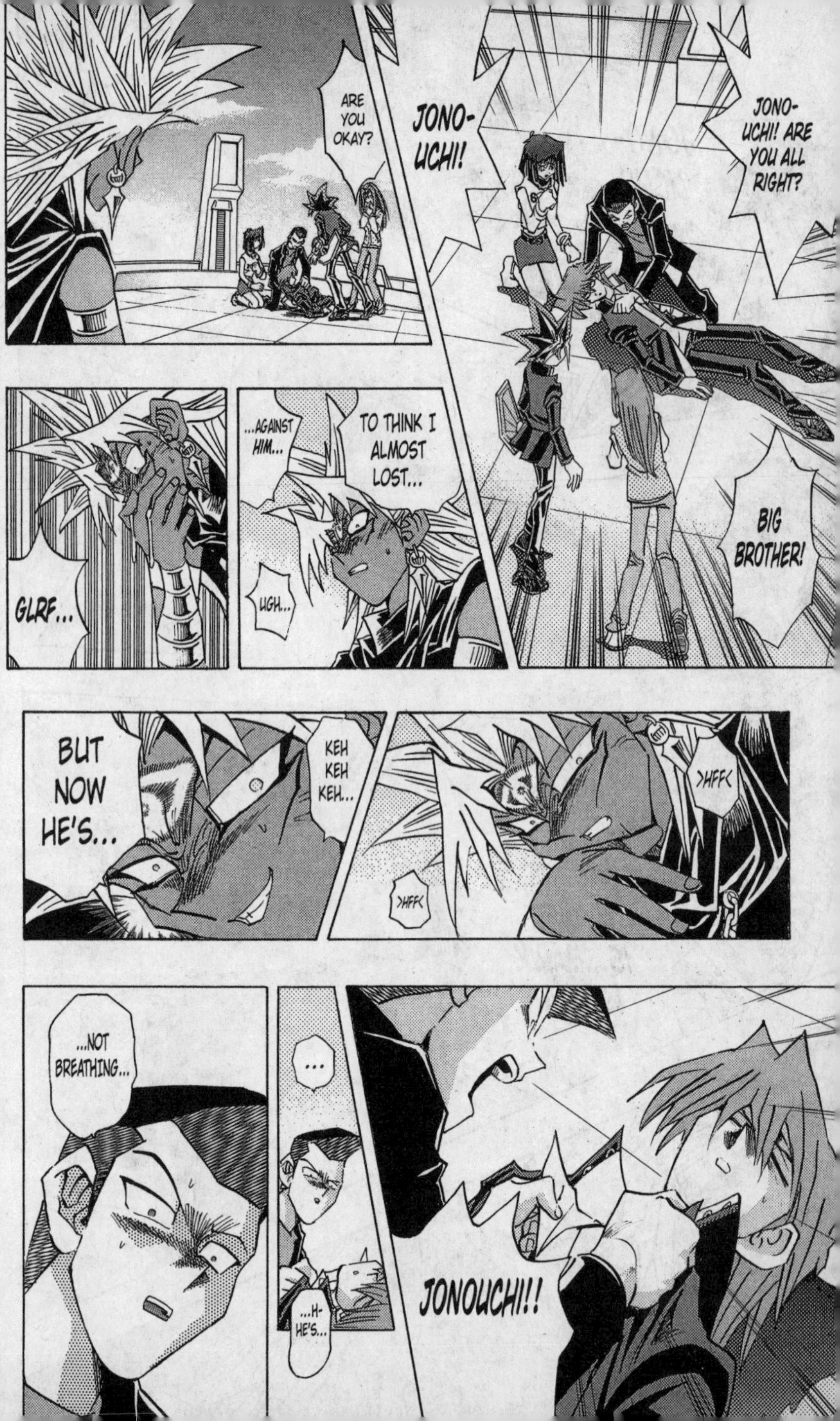

JONO-UCHI! ARE YOU ALL RIGHT?
JONO-UCHI!
BIG BROTHER!
ARE YOU OKAY?
TO THINK I ALMOST LOST...
...AGAINST HIM...
UGH...
GLRF...
>HFF<
>HFF<
KEH KEH KEH...
BUT NOW HE'S...
JONOUCHI!!
...
...H-HE'S...
...NOT BREATHING...

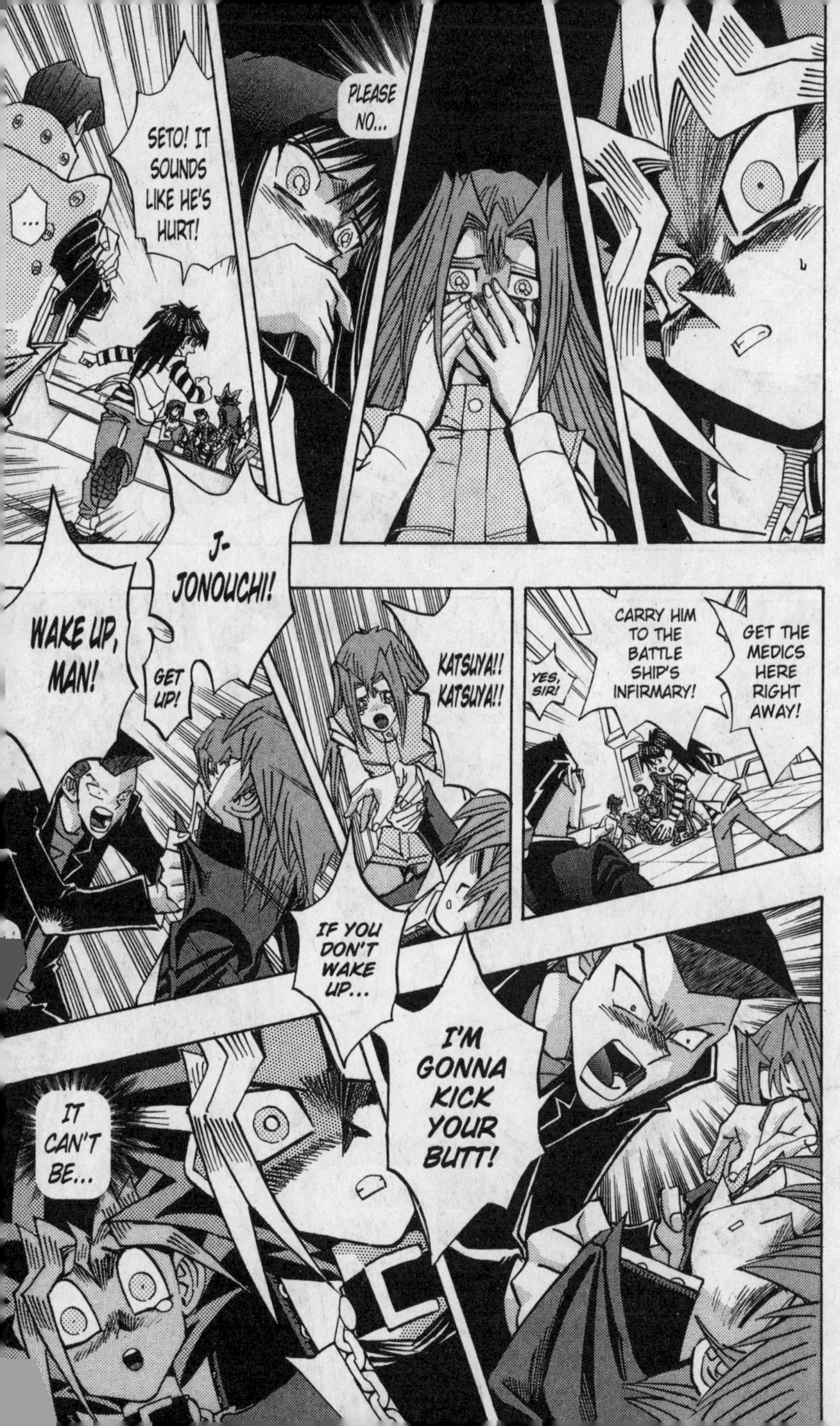
PLEASE NO...
SETO! IT SOUNDS LIKE HE'S HURT!
...
GET THE MEDICS HERE RIGHT AWAY!
CARRY HIM TO THE BATTLE SHIP'S INFIRMARY!
YES, SIR!
J-JONOUCHI!
KATSUYA!! KATSUYA!!
GET UP!
WAKE UP, MAN!
IF YOU DON'T WAKE UP...
I'M GONNA KICK YOUR BUTT!
IT CAN'T BE...

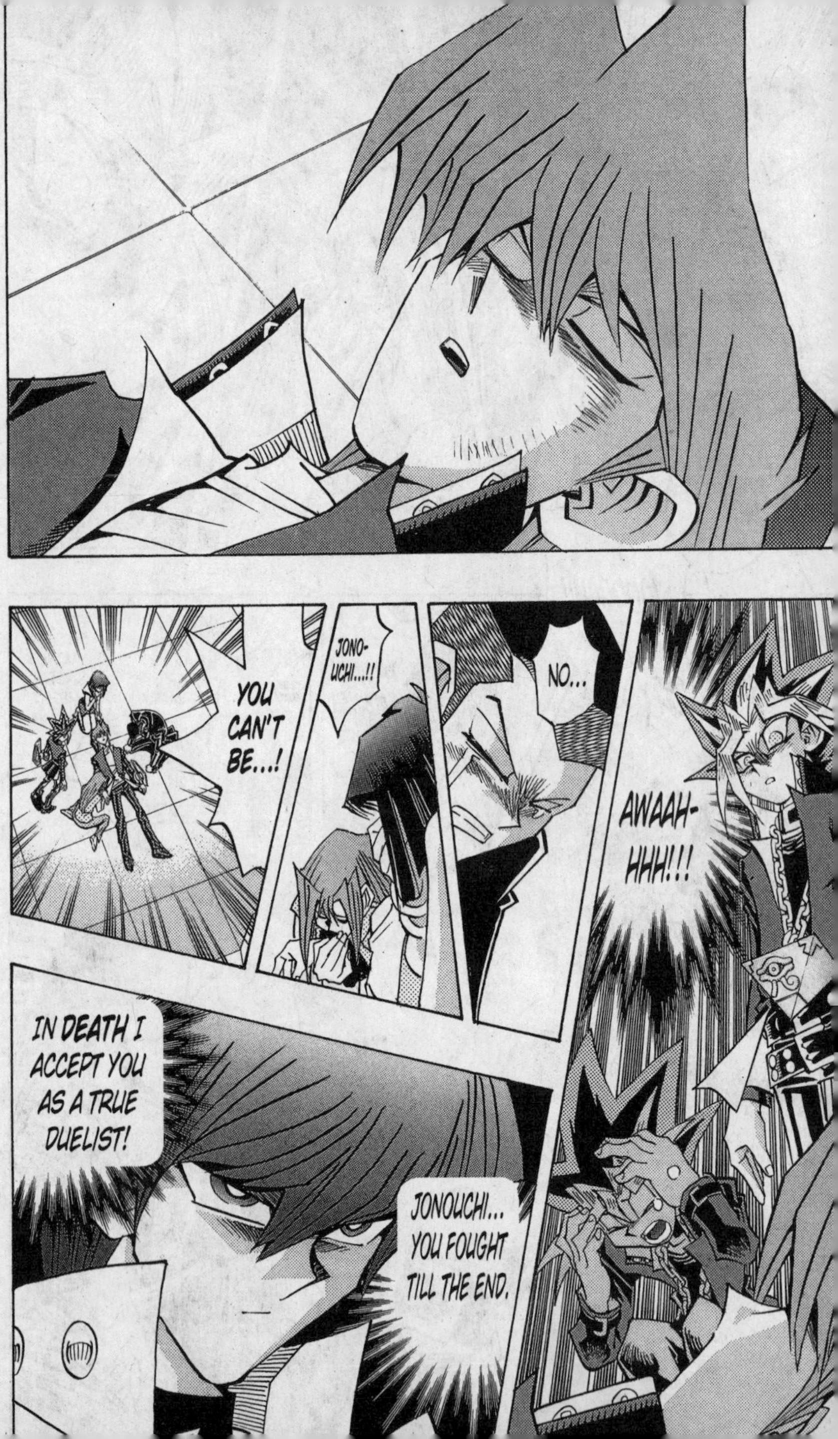
AWAAH-HHH!!!
NO...
JONOUCHI...!!
YOU CAN'T BE...!
JONOUCHI... YOU FOUGHT TILL THE END.
IN DEATH I ACCEPT YOU AS A TRUE DUELIST!

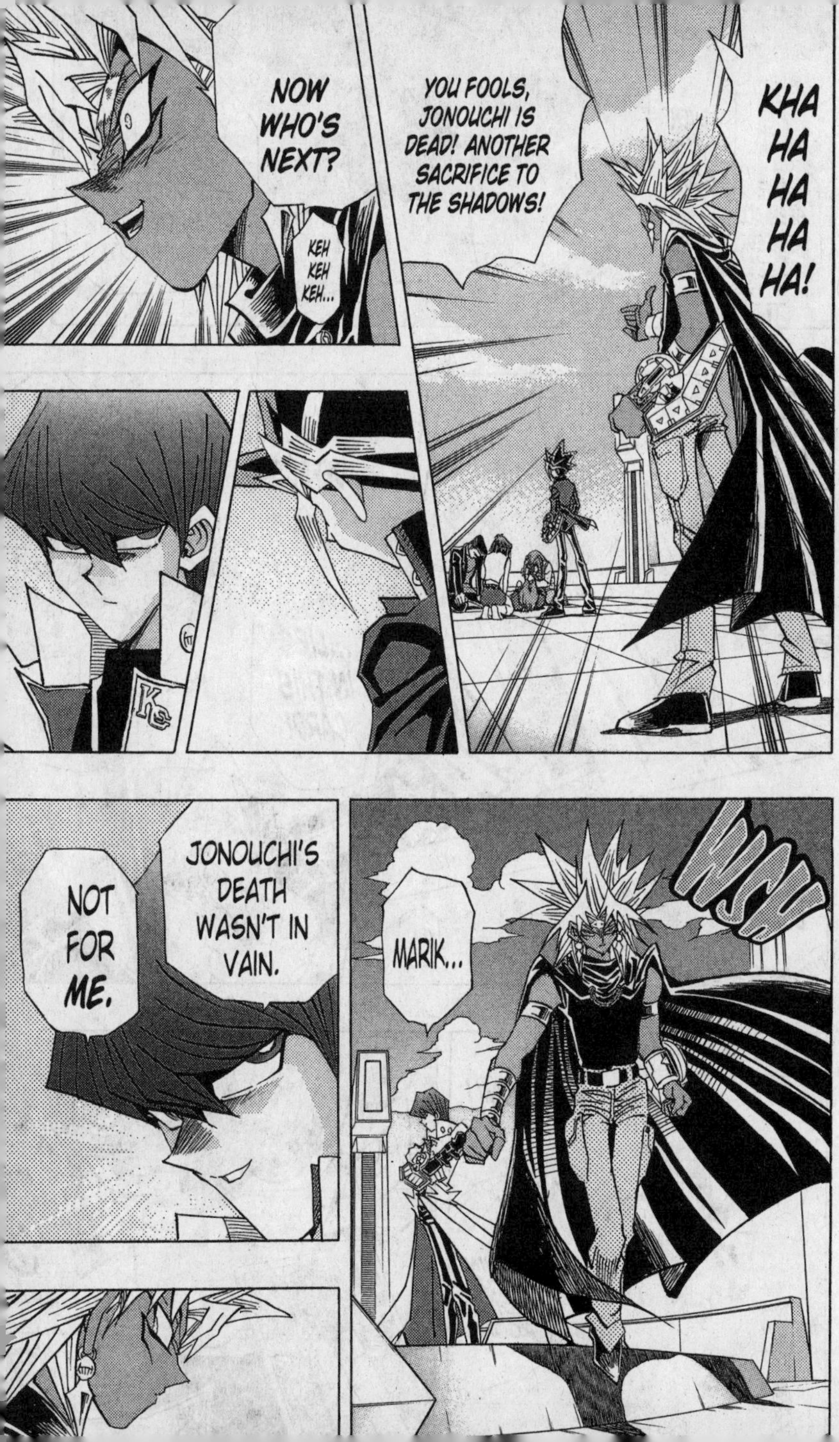
KHA HA HA HA HA!
YOU FOOLS, JONOUCHI IS DEAD! ANOTHER SACRIFICE TO THE SHADOWS!
NOW WHO'S NEXT?
KEH KEH KEH...
MARIK...
JONOUCHI'S DEATH WASN'T IN VAIN.
NOT FOR ME.
WSH

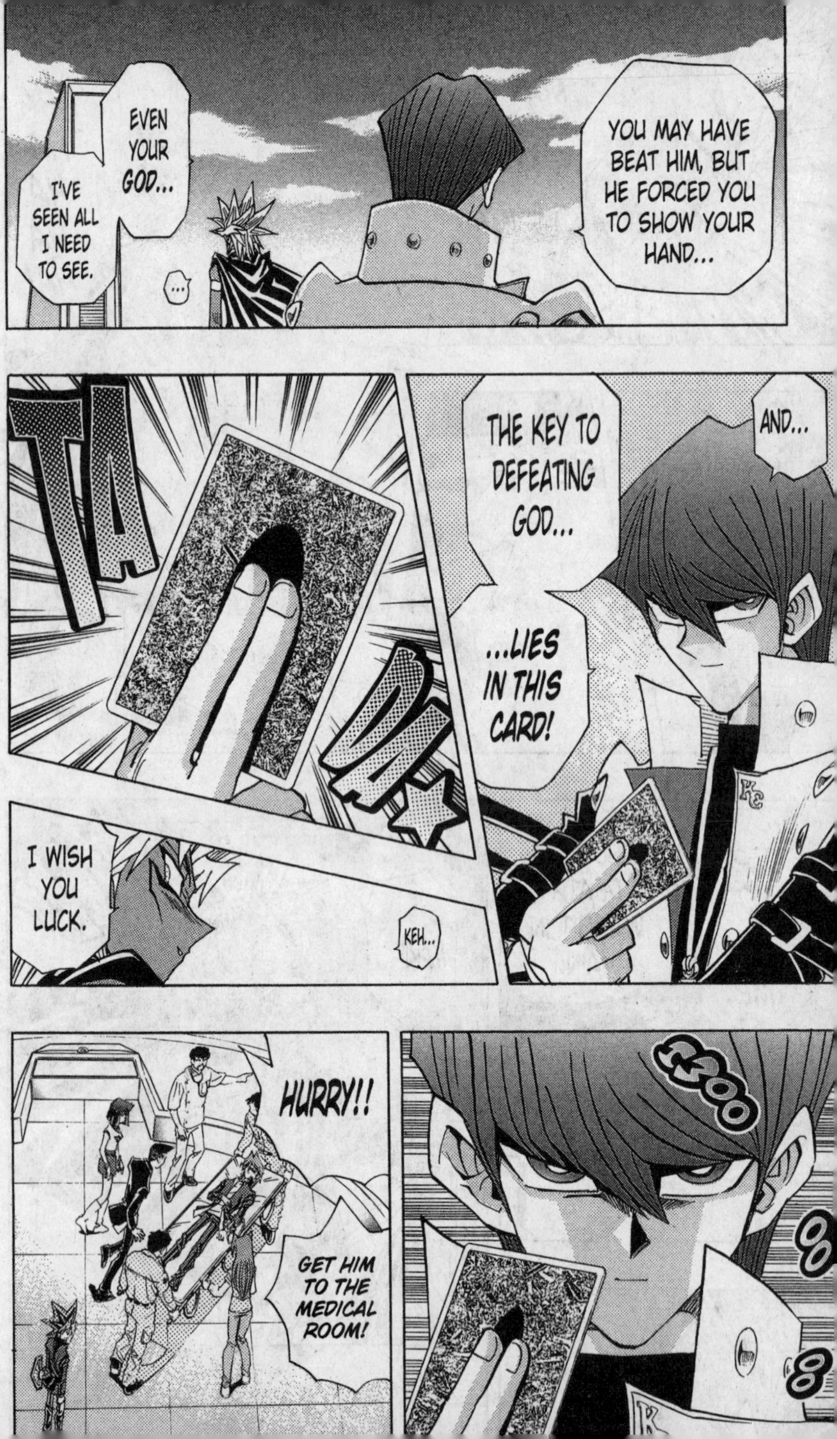
YOU MAY HAVE BEAT HIM, BUT HE FORCED YOU TO SHOW YOUR HAND...
EVEN YOUR GOD...
I'VE SEEN ALL I NEED TO SEE.
...
AND...
THE KEY TO DEFEATING GOD...
...LIES IN THIS CARD!
TA
DA
KEH...
I WISH YOU LUCK.
HURRY!!
GET HIM TO THE MEDICAL ROOM!

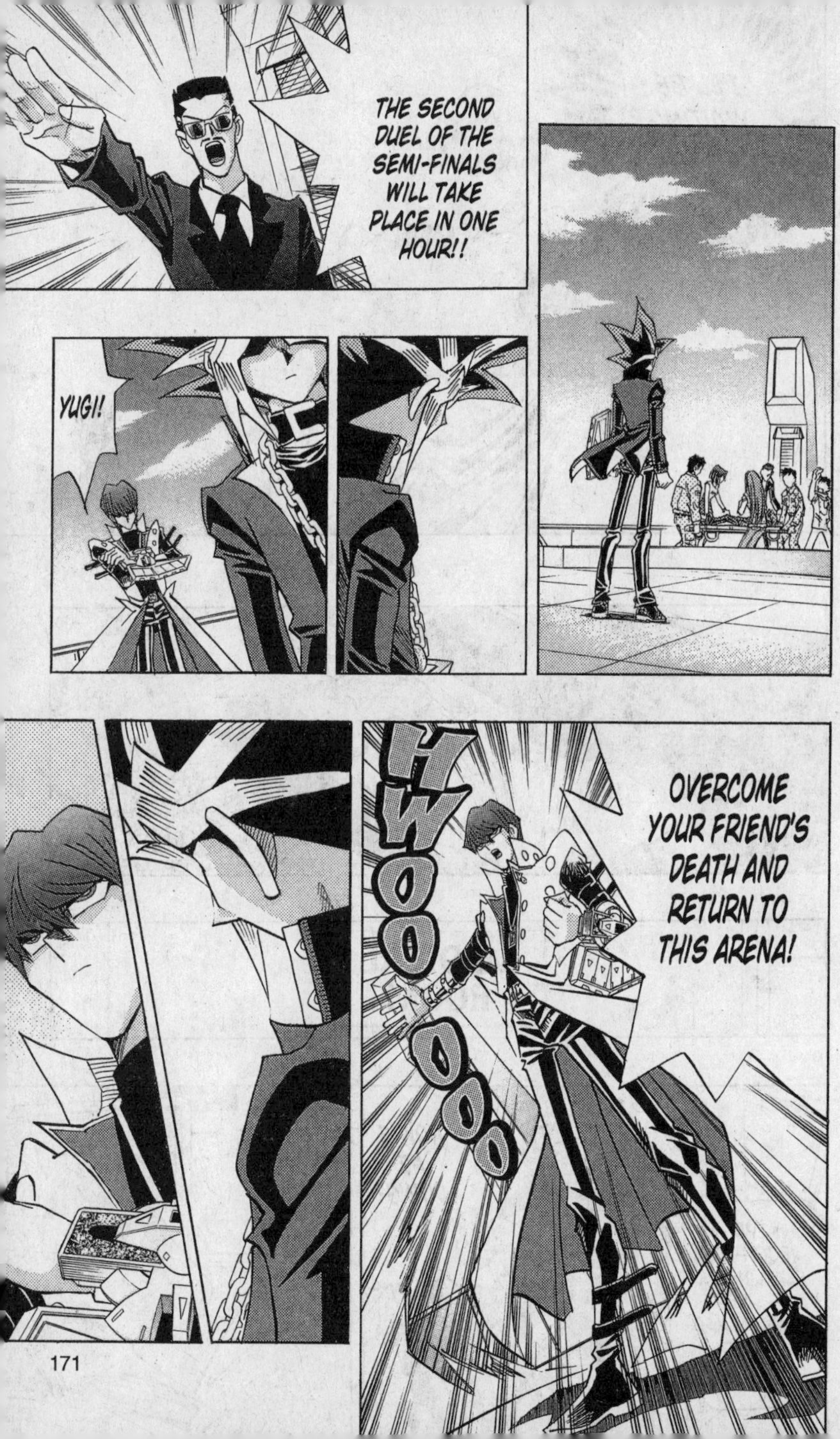
THE SECOND DUEL OF THE SEMI-FINALS WILL TAKE PLACE IN ONE HOUR!!
YUGI!
OVERCOME YOUR FRIEND'S DEATH AND RETURN TO THIS ARENA!
HWOOOOO

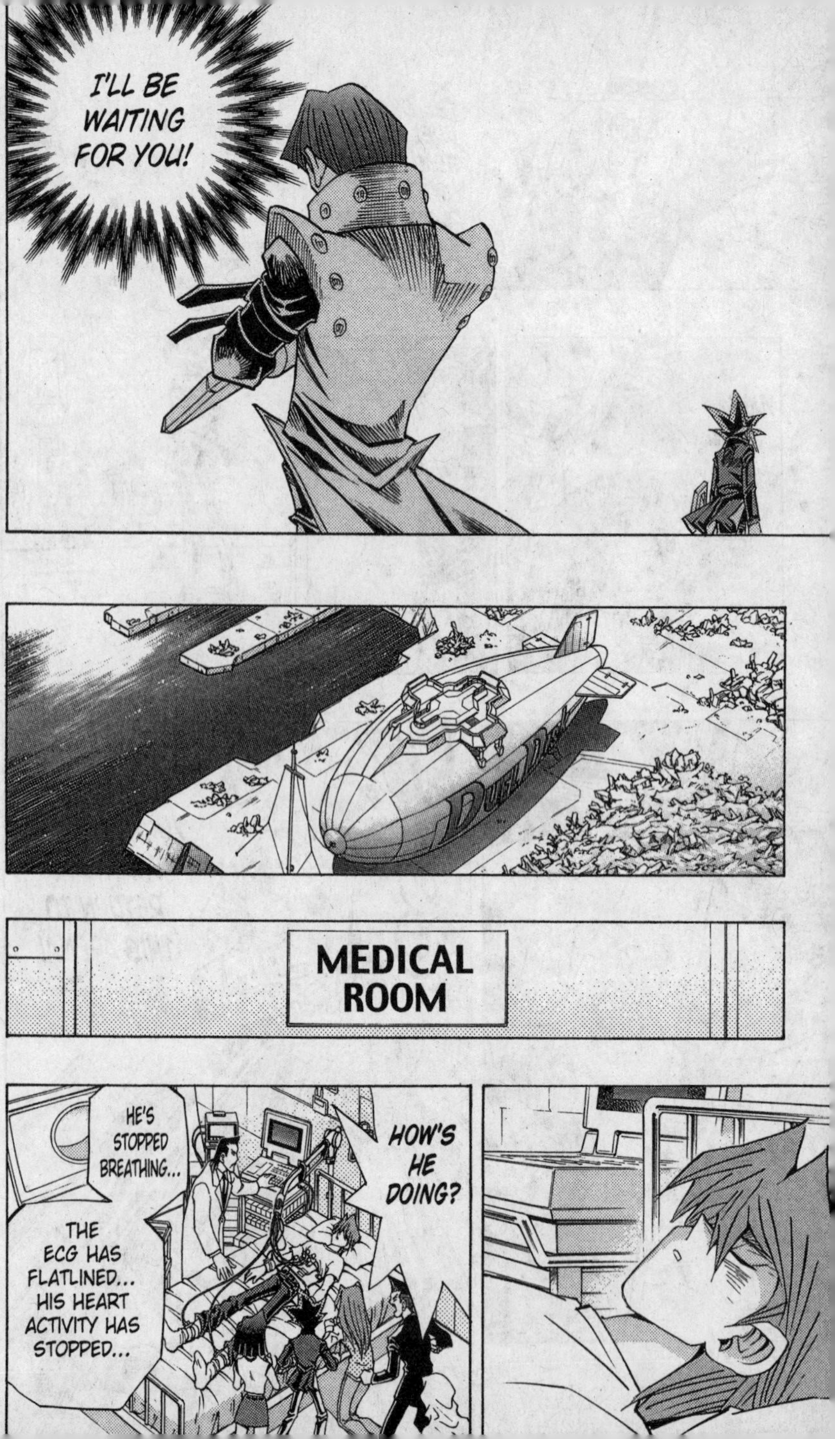
I'LL BE WAITING FOR YOU!
MEDICAL ROOM
HOW'S HE DOING?
HE'S STOPPED BREATHING...
THE ECG HAS FLATLINED... HIS HEART ACTIVITY HAS STOPPED...

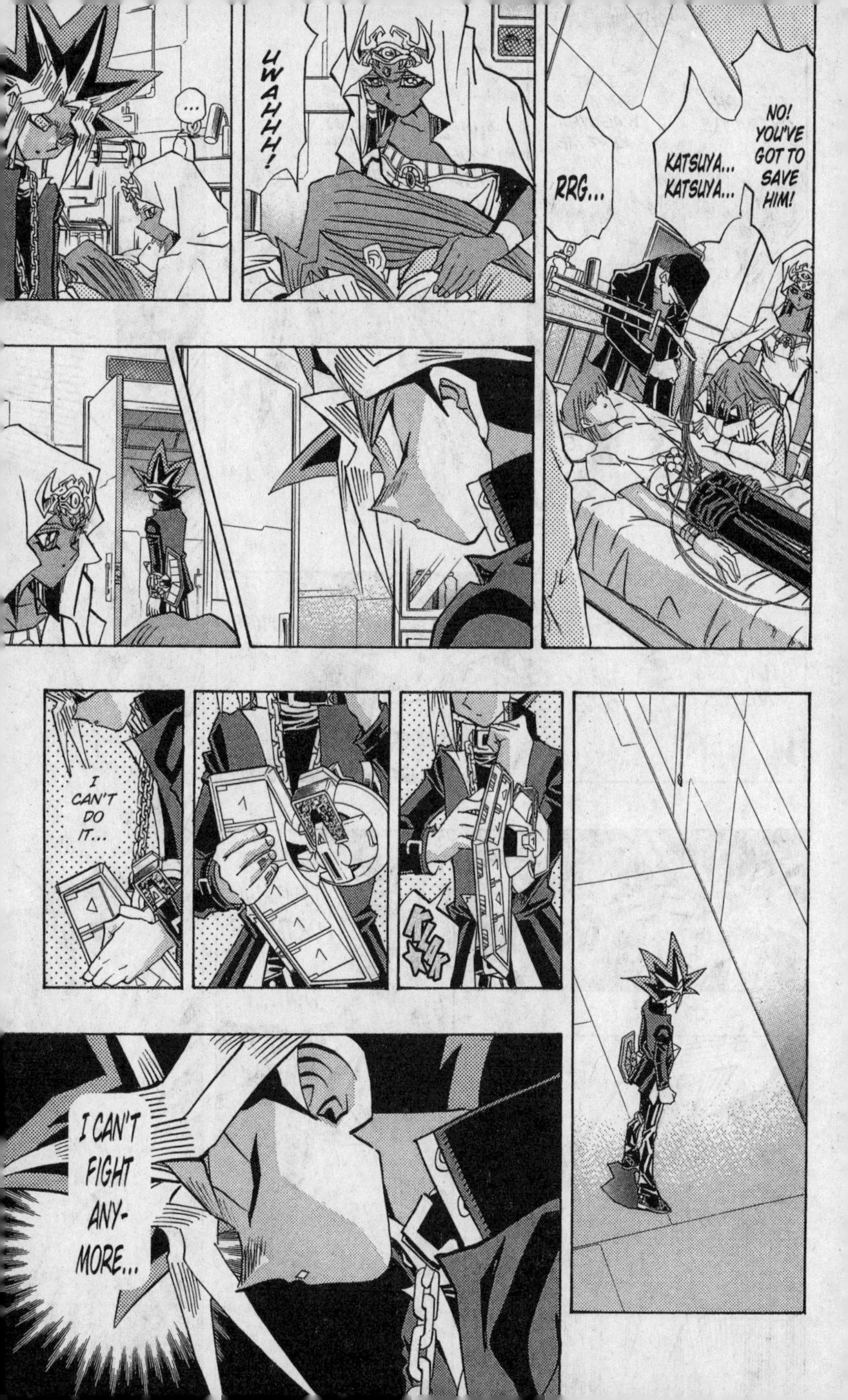
NO! YOU'VE GOT TO SAVE HIM!
KATSUYA... KATSUYA...
RRG...
UWAHHHH!
...
KLAK
I CAN'T DO IT...
I CAN'T FIGHT ANY-MORE...

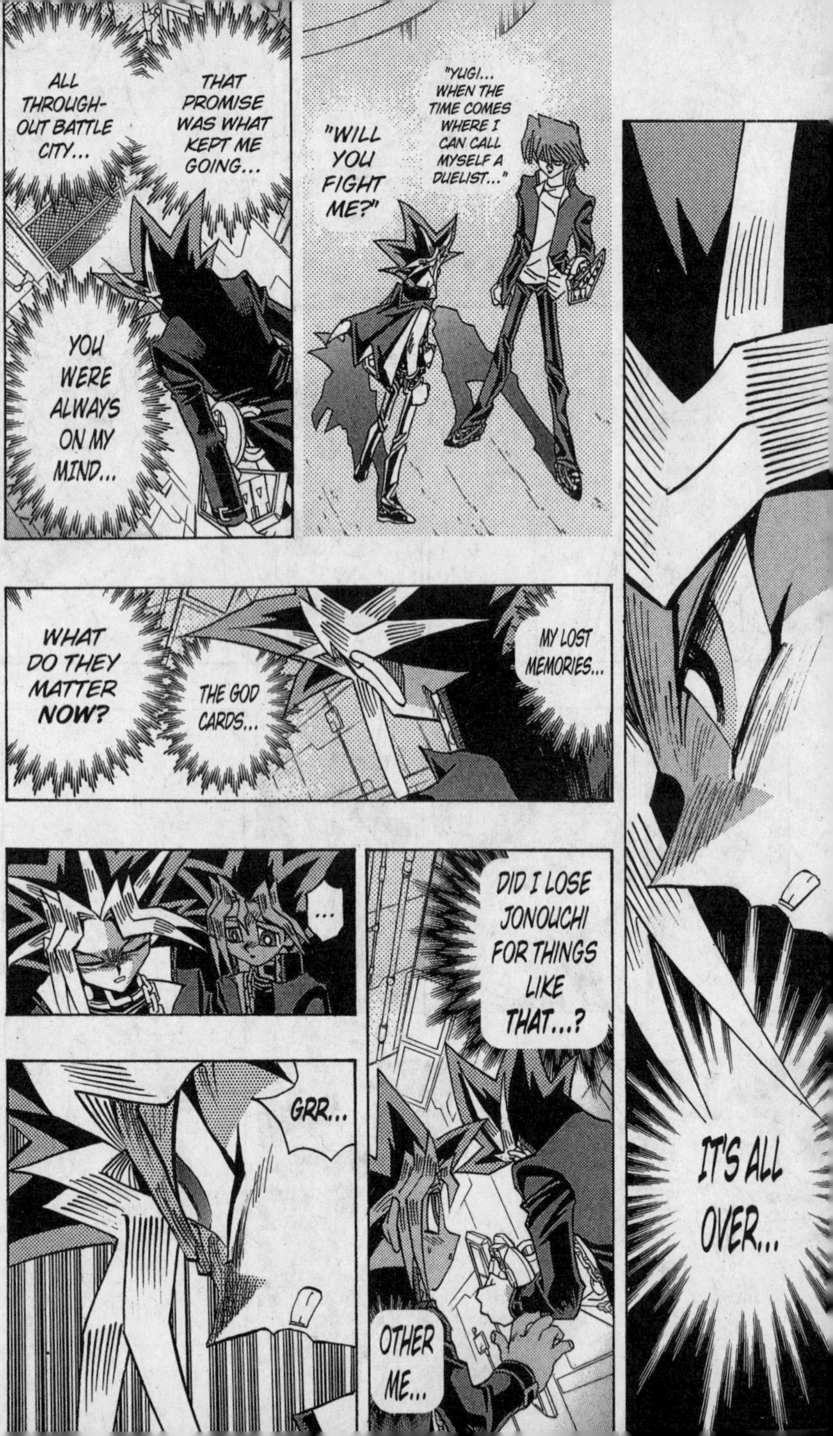
"YUGI... WHEN THE TIME COMES WHERE I CAN CALL MYSELF A DUELIST..."
"WILL YOU FIGHT ME?"
THAT PROMISE WAS WHAT KEPT ME GOING...
ALL THROUGH-OUT BATTLE CITY...
YOU WERE ALWAYS ON MY MIND...
MY LOST MEMORIES...
THE GOD CARDS...
WHAT DO THEY MATTER NOW?
DID I LOSE JONOUCHI FOR THINGS LIKE THAT...?
...
OTHER ME...
GRR...
IT'S ALL OVER...

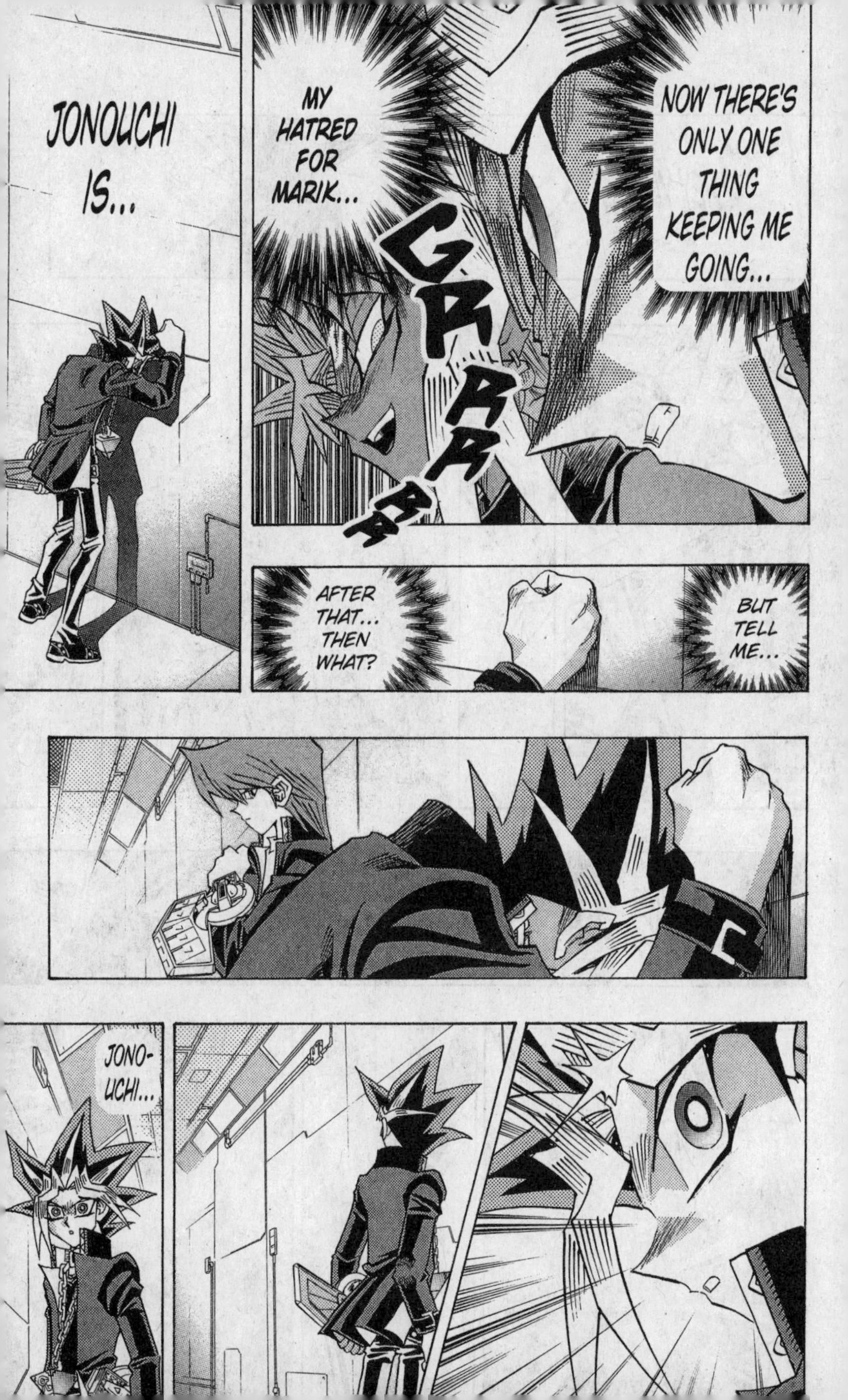
NOW THERE'S ONLY ONE THING KEEPING ME GOING...
MY HATRED FOR MARIK...
GRRRRR
BUT TELL ME...
AFTER THAT... THEN WHAT?
JONOUCHI IS...
JONO-UCHI...

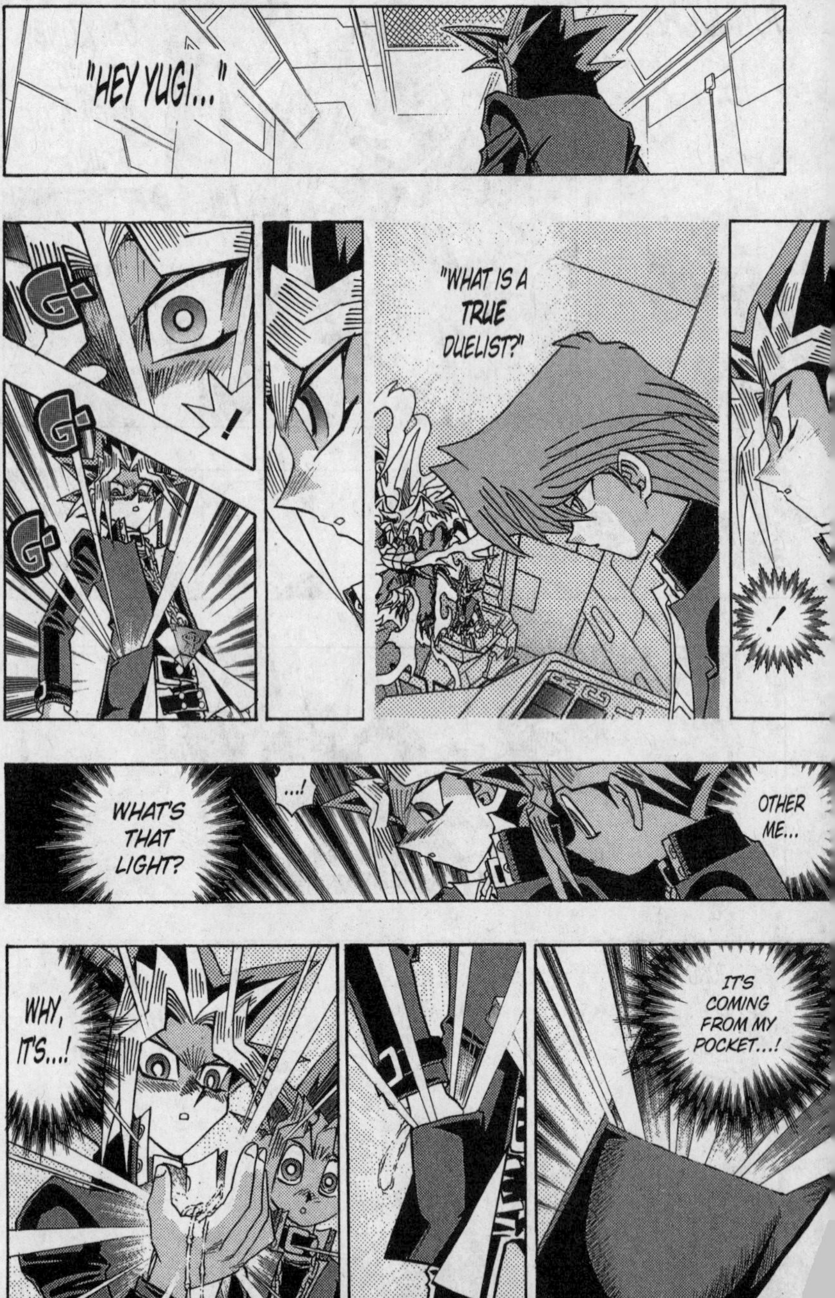
"HEY YUGI..."
!
"WHAT IS A TRUE DUELIST?"
G
!
G
G
OTHER ME...
...!
WHAT'S THAT LIGHT?
IT'S COMING FROM MY POCKET...!
WHY, IT'S...!

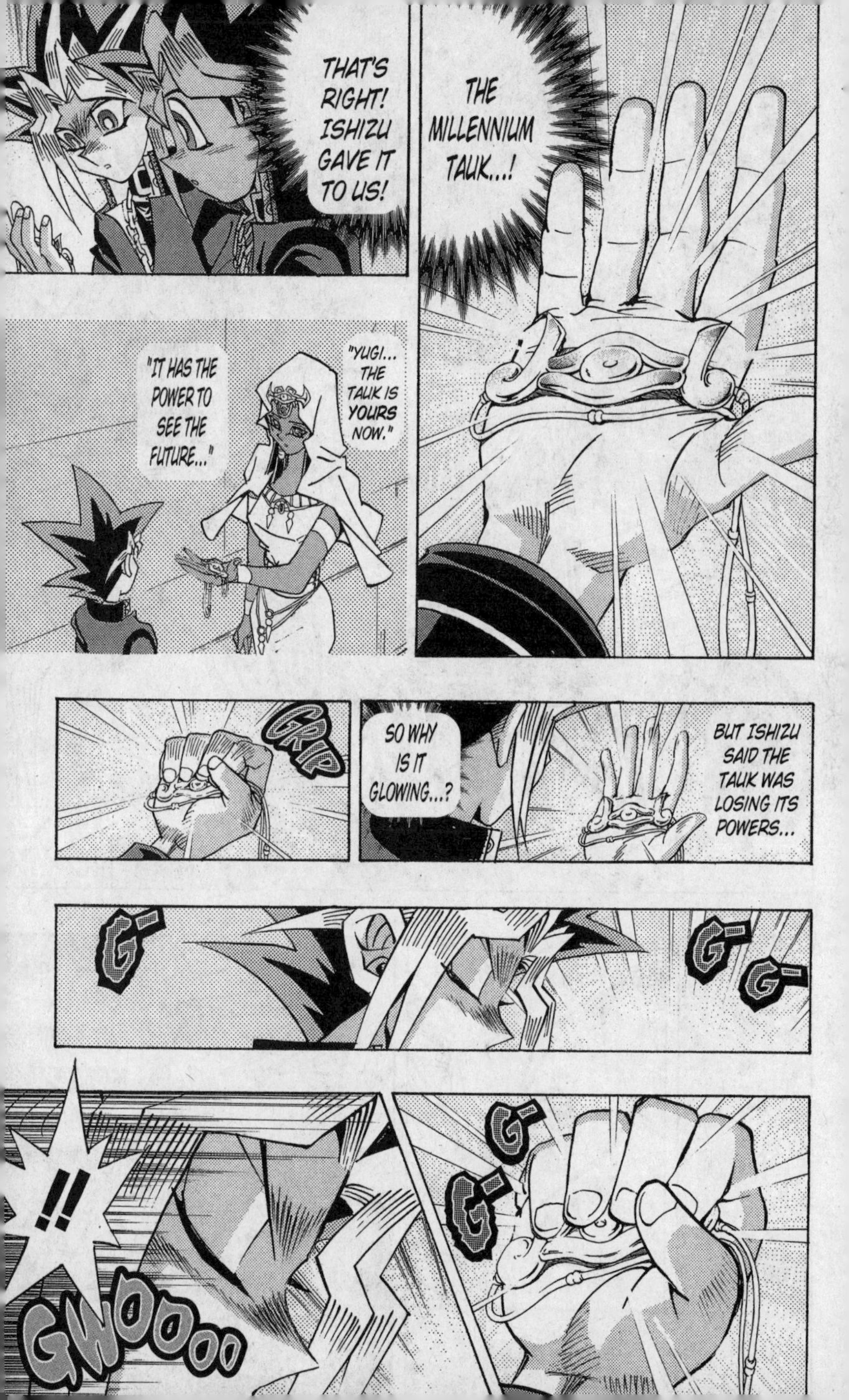
THE MILLENNIUM TAUK...!
THAT'S RIGHT! ISHIZU GAVE IT TO US!
"YUGI... THE TAUK IS YOURS NOW."
"IT HAS THE POWER TO SEE THE FUTURE..."
BUT ISHIZU SAID THE TAUK WAS LOSING ITS POWERS...
SO WHY IS IT GLOWING...?
GRIP
G-
G-
G-
G-
G-
!!
GWOOOO

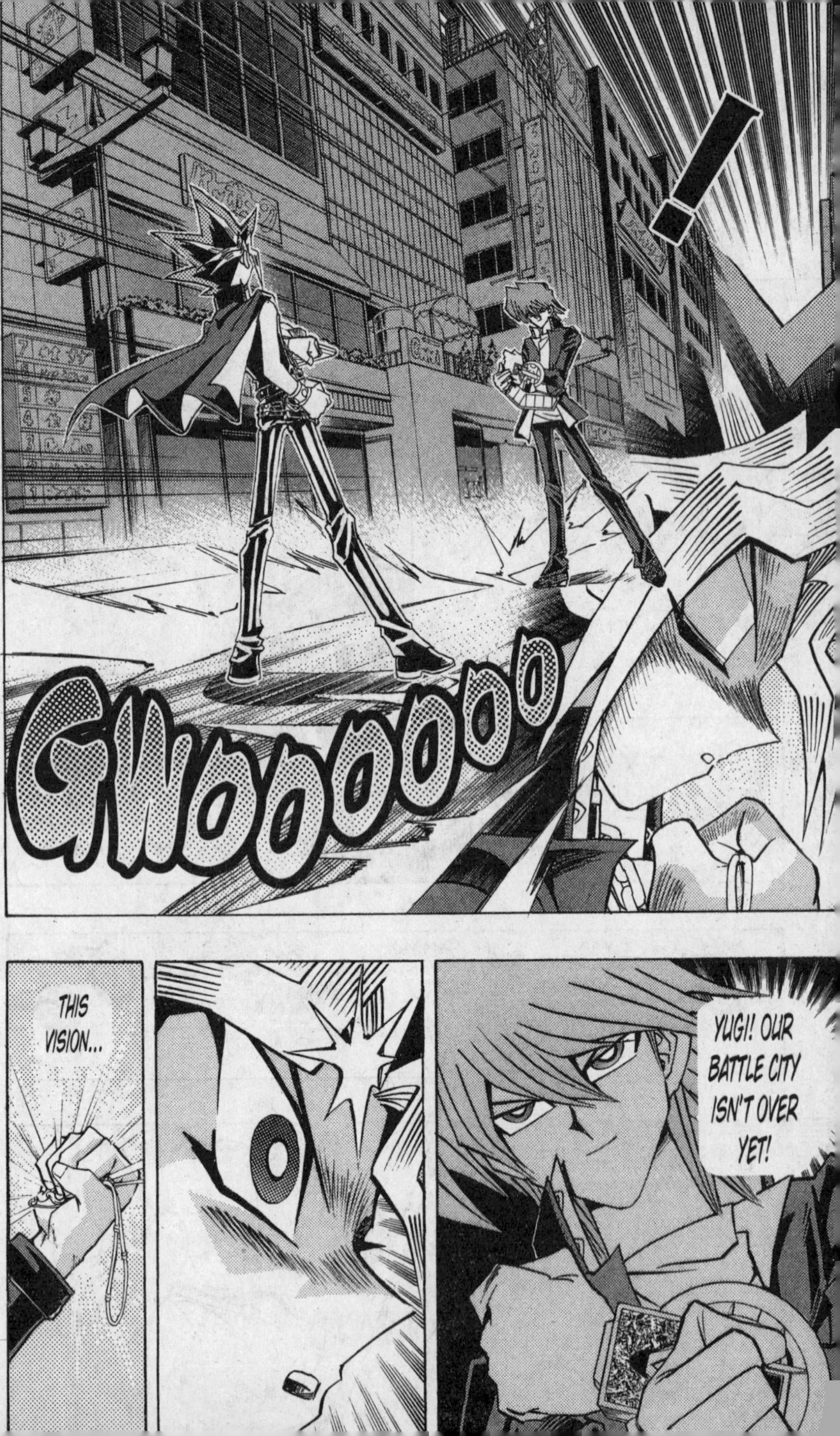
!
GWOOOOOOO
YUGI! OUR BATTLE CITY ISN'T OVER YET!
THIS VISION...

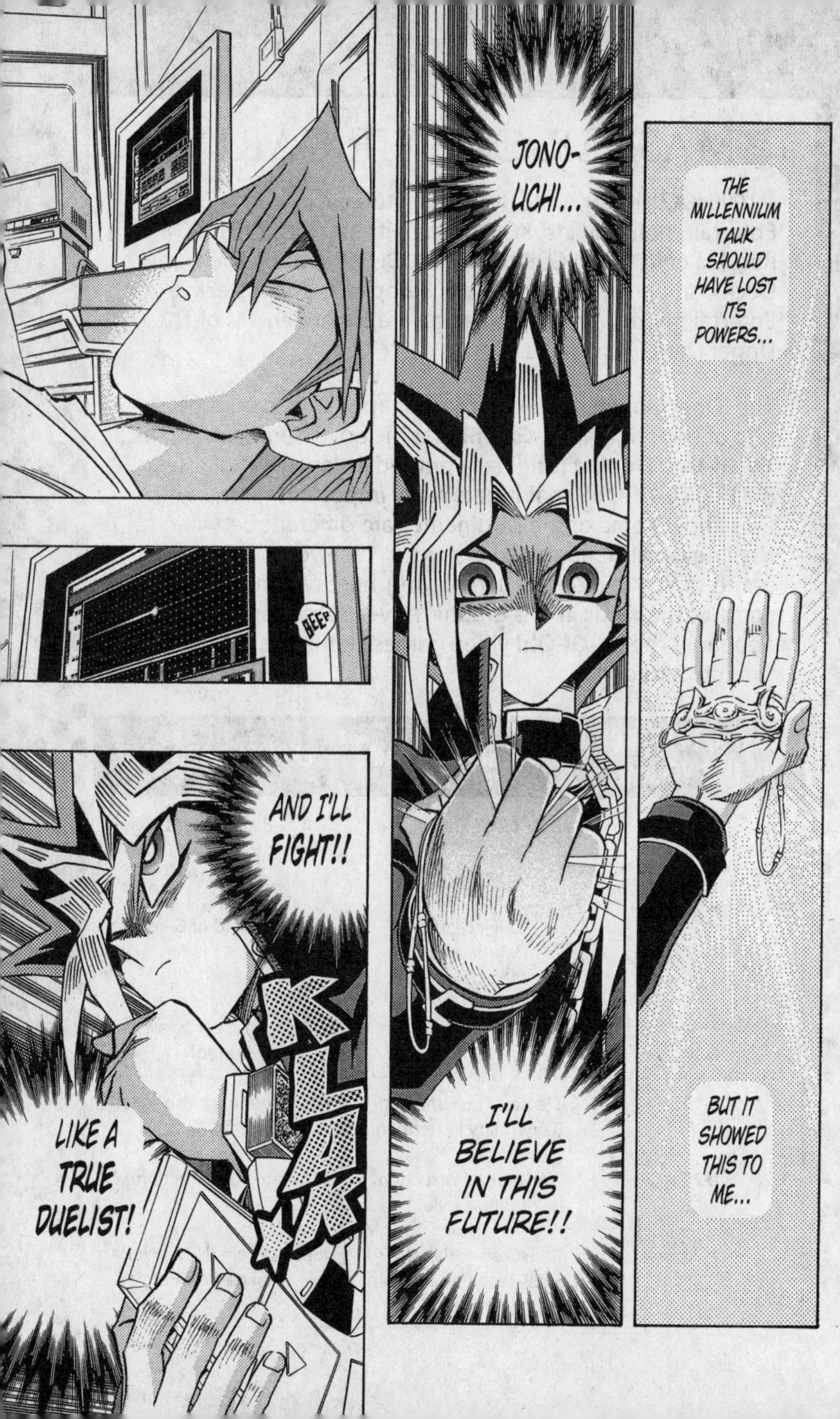
THE MILLENNIUM TAUK SHOULD HAVE LOST ITS POWERS...
BUT IT SHOWED THIS TO ME...
JONO-UCHI...
I'LL BELIEVE IN THIS FUTURE!!
BEEP
AND I'LL FIGHT!!
LIKE A TRUE DUELIST!
KLAK

MASTER OF THE CARDS

The "Duel Monsters" card game first appeared in volume two of the original **Yu-Gi-Oh!** graphic novel series, but it's in **Yu-Gi-Oh!: Duelist** (originally printed in Japan as volumes 8-31 of **Yu-Gi-Oh!**) that it gets really important. As many fans know, some of the card names are different between the English and Japanese versions. In case you play the game, or you're interested in playing, here's a rundown of some of the cards in this graphic novel. Some cards only appear in the **Yu-Gi-Oh!** video games, not in the actual trading card game.

FIRST APPEARANCE IN THIS VOLUME	JAPANESE CARD NAME	ENGLISH CARD NAME
p.7	*Blade Knight*	Blade Knight
p.7	*Dark Jeroid*	Dark Jeroid
p.7	*Gilfer Demon* (Darkness/Black Magic/Demon Clan Gilfer Demon)	Archfiend of Gilfer
p.10	*Kuribo*	Kuriboh
p.19	*Densetsu no Fisherman* (Legendary Fisherman)	The Legendary Fisherman
p.20	*Hakairin* (Destruction Ring/Circle)	Ring of Destruction
p.23	*Tsûkon no Jujutsu* (Spell/Technique of Pain)	Spell of Pain (NOTE: Not a real game card)

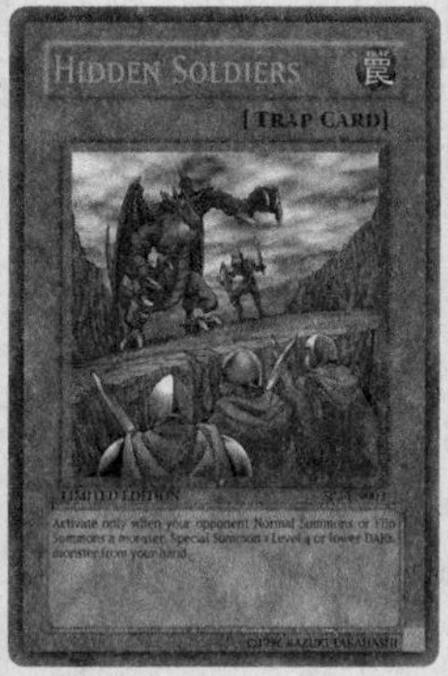
HIDDEN SOLDIERS
[TRAP CARD]
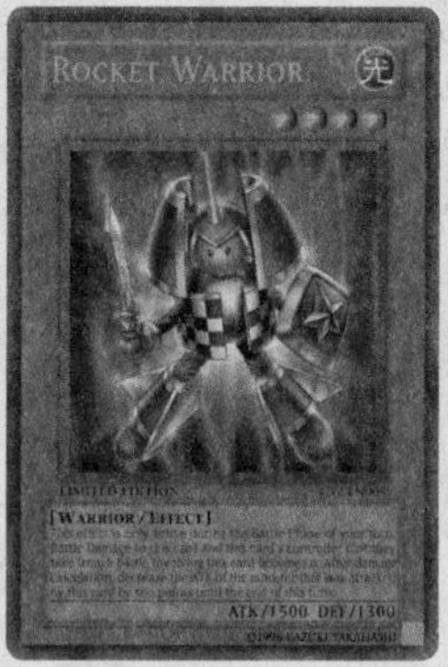
ROCKET WARRIOR
[WARRIOR / EFFECT]
ATK/1500 DEF/1300
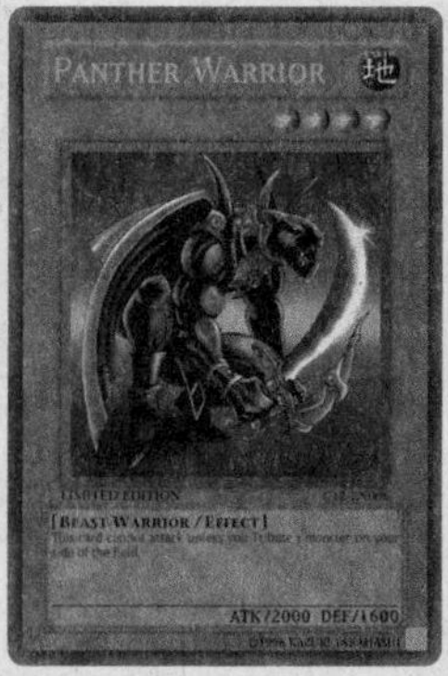
PANTHER WARRIOR
[BEAST-WARRIOR / EFFECT]
ATK/2000 DEF/1600

FIRST APPEARANCE IN THIS VOLUME	JAPANESE CARD NAME	ENGLISH CARD NAME
p.23	*Haka Arashi* (Graverobber)	Graverobber
p.41	*Shikkoku no Hyôsenshi Panther Warrior* (Jet Black Panther Warrior)	Panther Warrior
p.44	*Jigoku Shijin Helpoemer* (Hell Poet Helpoemer)	Helpoemer
p.51	*Kakure Hei* (Hidden Soldier/Army)	Hidden Soldiers
p.53	*Rocket Senshi* (Rocket Warrior)	Rocket Warrior
p.54	*Manrikimajin Viser Death* (Vise Devil/Demon God/ Genie Viser Death)	Viser Des (NOTE: Not a real game card)
p.69	*Quiz*	Question
p.70	*Gil Garth*	Gil Garth (NOTE: Not a real game card)
p.72	*Tenshi no Saikoro* (Angel Dice)	Graceful Dice

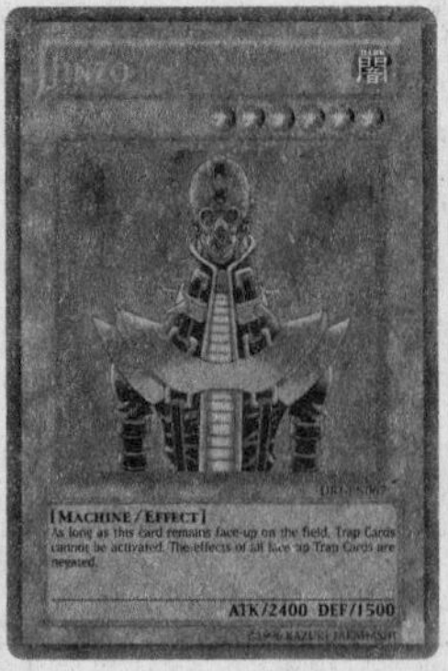
Jinzo
[Machine / Effect]
ATK/2400 DEF/1500
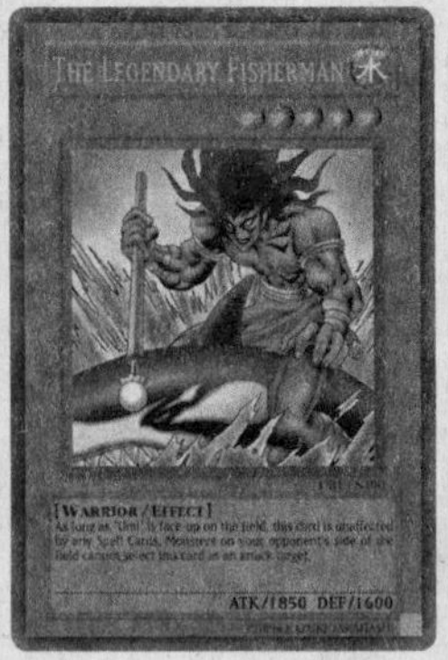
The Legendary Fisherman
[Warrior / Effect]
ATK/1850 DEF/1600
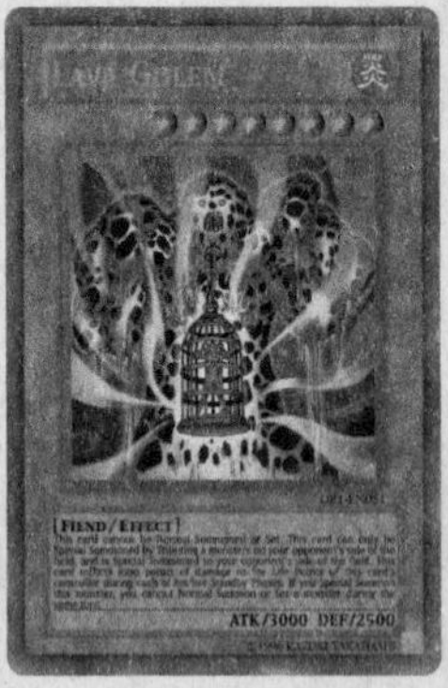
Lava Golem
[Fiend / Effect]
ATK/3000 DEF/2500

FIRST APPEARANCE IN THIS VOLUME	JAPANESE CARD NAME	ENGLISH CARD NAME
p.72	*Jinzô Ningen Psycho Shocker* (Android/Cyborg Psycho Shocker)	Jinzo
p.72	*Baby Dragon*	Baby Dragon
p.75	*Kan'okeuri* (Coffin Seller)	Coffin Seller
p.77	*Jashin no Daisaigai* (Demon/Devil/Evil God's Great Catastrophe)	Malevolent Catastrophe (NOTE: Not a real game card)
p.78	*Legend Devil*	Legend Devil (NOTE: Called "Legendary Fiend" in the anime and video games.)
p.97	*Yami no Gofûheki* (Protective Wind Wall of Darkness)	Dark Wall of Wind (NOTE: Not a real game card)
p.100	*Yôgan Majin Lava Golem* (Lava Demon Lava Golem)	Lava Golem
p.108	*Hurricane*	Giant Trunade
p.109	*Orokana Maisô* (Foolish Burial)	Foolish Burial

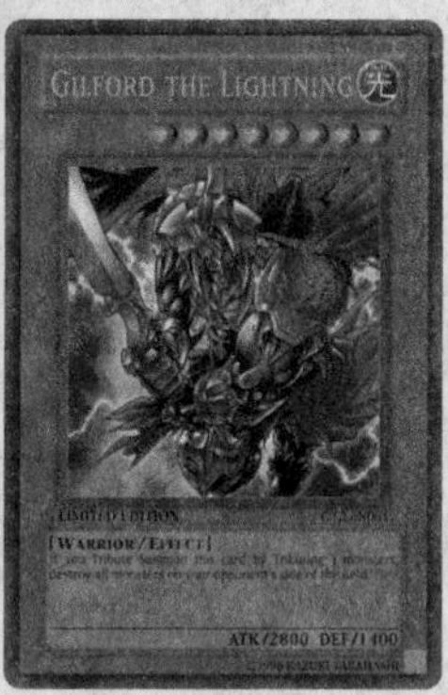
GILFORD THE LIGHTNING
[WARRIOR/EFFECT]
ATK/2800 DEF/1400

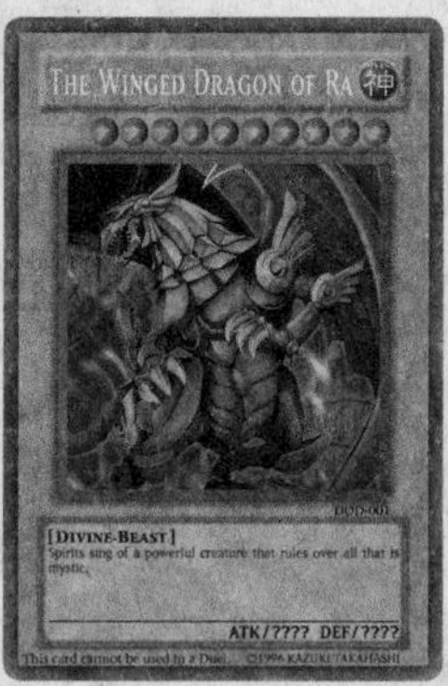
THE WINGED DRAGON OF RA
[DIVINE-BEAST]
Spirits sing of a powerful creature that rules over all that is mystic.
ATK/???? DEF/????
This card cannot be used in a Duel.
©1996 KAZUKI TAKAHASHI

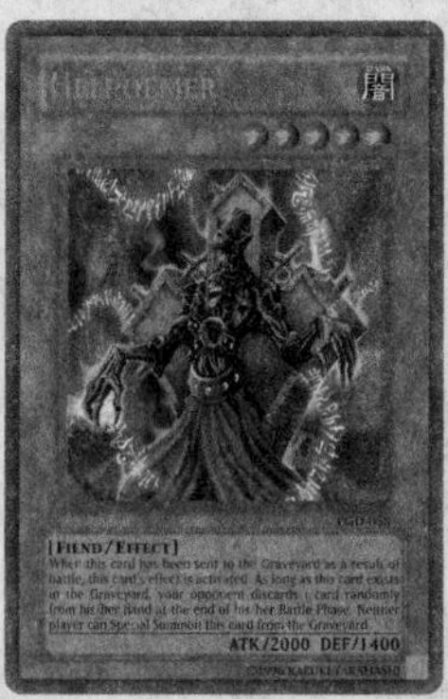
[FIEND/EFFECT]
ATK/2000 DEF/1400

FIRST APPEARANCE IN THIS VOLUME	JAPANESE CARD NAME	ENGLISH CARD NAME
p.112	*Monster Relief*	Monster Relief
p.116	*Kikai Fukuseijutsu* (Machine Proliferation Technique)	Machine Duplication
p.120	*Gilford the Lightning*	Gilford the Lightning
p.131	*Akumu no Makyô* (Demon Mirror of Nightmare)	Nightmare Mirror (NOTE: Not a real game card)
p.133	*Ra no Yokushinryû* (Ra the Winged God Dragon) (NOTE: The kanji for "sun god" is written beside the kanji for "Ra.")	The Sun Dragon Ra (NOTE: Called "The Winged Dragon of Ra" in the English anime and card game.)
p.137	*Shisha Sosei* (Resurrection of the Dead)	Monster Reborn
p.159	*Tetsu no Kishi Gear Fried* (Iron Knight Gear Fried)	Gearfried the Iron Knight

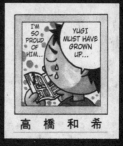

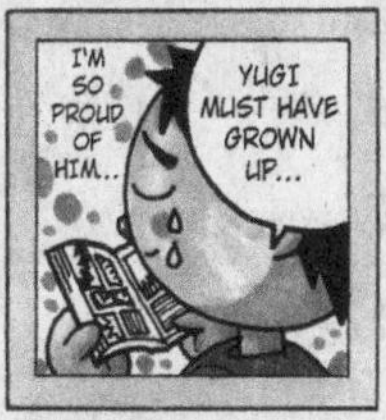
I'M SO PROUD OF HIM...
YUGI MUST HAVE GROWN UP...
高 橋 和 希

WHEN I WAS IN ELEMENTARY SCHOOL, THERE WAS A BOOK RENTAL STORE IN MY NEIGHBORHOOD. I WOULD BORROW MANGA EVERY DAY AND READ IT BEFORE GOING TO BED. SOMETIMES I WOULD READ TEN VOLUMES IN ONE NIGHT. ONE DAY I THOUGHT TO MYSELF, "WHAT'S WRONG WITH THIS MANGA? THE MAIN CHARACTER'S FACE SLOWLY CHANGES FROM THE FIRST VOLUME!"

TIME PASSED...

NOW, WHEN I LOOK AT *YU-GI-OH!* VOLUME 1, IT'S UNBELIEVABLE! THE MAIN CHARACTER'S FACE IS SLIGHTLY DIFFERENT FROM NOW. AND THAT'S HOW MY CHILDHOOD QUESTION WAS ANSWERED.

-KAZUKI TAKAHASHI, 2002

SHONEN JUMP MANGA

Vol. 29
SLIFER VS. OBELISK!
STORY AND ART BY
KAZUKI TAKAHASHI

THE STORY SO FAR...

YUGI MUTOU/ YU-GI-OH

When 10th grader Yugi solved the Millennium Puzzle, another spirit took up residence in his body…Yu-Gi-Oh, the King of Games, a dark avenger who challenges evildoers to "Shadow Games" of life and death!

YUGI FACES DEADLY ENEMIES!

Using his gaming skills, Yugi fights ruthless adversaries like Maximillion Pegasus, multimillionaire creator of the collectible card game "Duel Monsters," and Ryo Bakura, whose friendly personality turns evil when he is possessed by the spirit of the Millennium Ring. But Yugi's greatest rival is Seto Kaiba, the world's second-greatest gamer—and the ruthless teenage president of Kaiba Corporation. At first, Kaiba and Yugi are bitter enemies, but after fighting against a common adversary—Pegasus—they come to respect one another. But for all his powers, there is one thing Yu-Gi-Oh cannot do: remember who he is and where he came from.

HIROTO HONDA

ANZU MAZAKI

KATSUYA JONOUCHI

MARIK

ISHIZU ISHTAR

SETO KAIBA

 THE TABLET OF THE PHARAOH'S MEMORIES

Then one day, when an Egyptian museum exhibit comes to Japan, Yugi sees an ancient carving of himself as an Egyptian pharaoh! The curator of the exhibit, Ishizu Ishtar, explains that there are seven Millennium Items, which were made to fit into a stone tablet in a hidden shrine in Egypt. According to the legend, when the seven Items are brought together, the pharaoh will regain his memories of his past life.

 THE EGYPTIAN GOD CARDS

But there is another piece of the puzzle—the three Egyptian God Cards, the rarest cards on Earth. To collect the God Cards, Kaiba announces "Battle City," an enormous "Duel Monsters" tournament. Attracted by the scent of blood, the most powerful God Card wielder comes to Tokyo: Ishizu's insane brother Marik, who wants to murder the pharaoh to satisfy a grudge. Using his sadistic torture deck, Marik climbs to the tournament semi-finals, where he defeats Yugi's friend Jonouchi, leaving him in a deathlike state. Now, only one semi-finals match remains. Yugi and Kaiba must fight their final duel…and the winner will face Marik in the ultimate battle of the gods!

Yu-Gi-Oh! Duelist

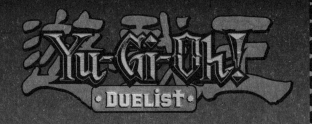

Vol. 29

CONTENTS

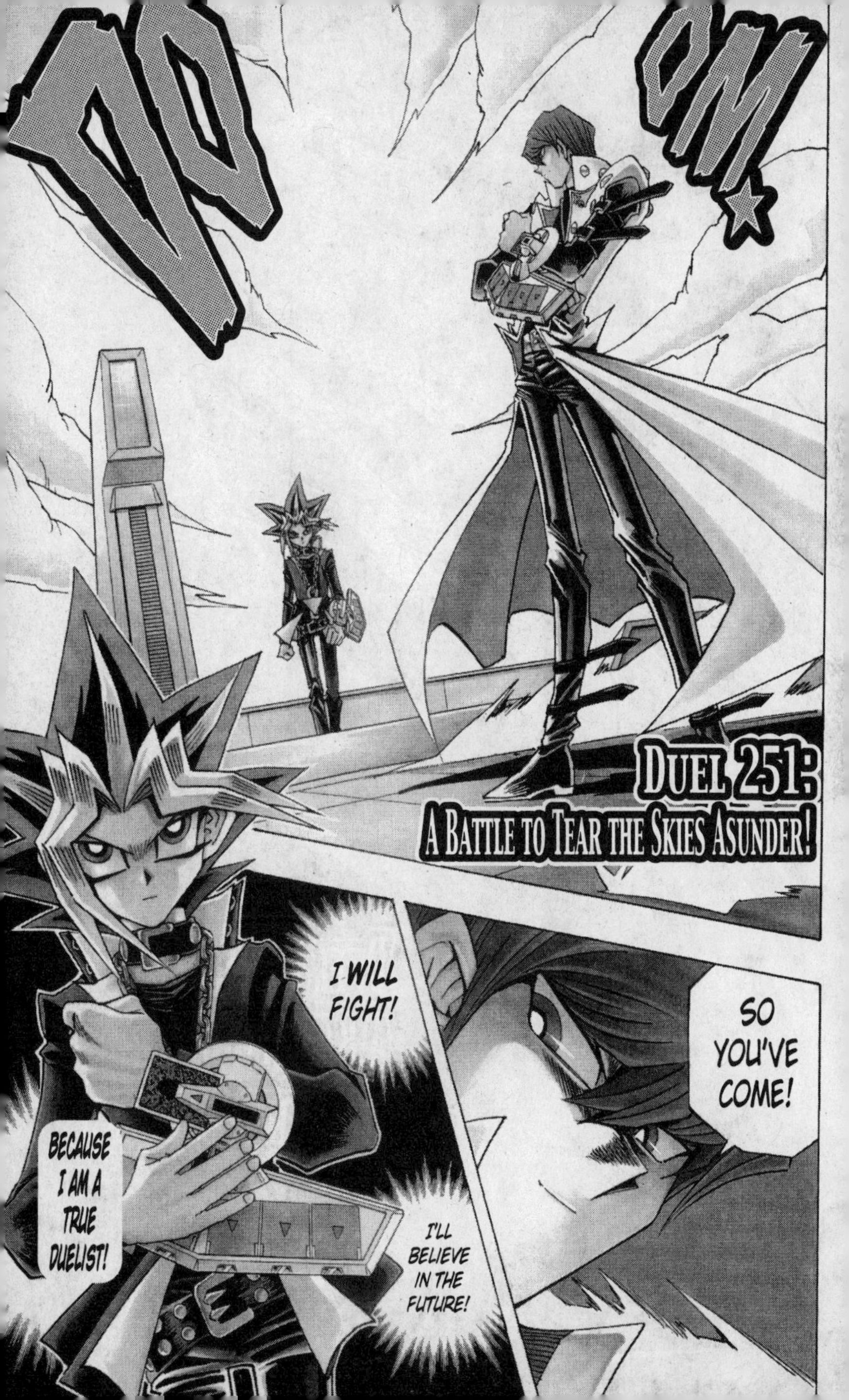
DOOM
DUEL 251:
A BATTLE TO TEAR THE SKIES ASUNDER!
SO YOU'VE COME!
I WILL FIGHT!
I'LL BELIEVE IN THE FUTURE!
BECAUSE I AM A TRUE DUELIST!

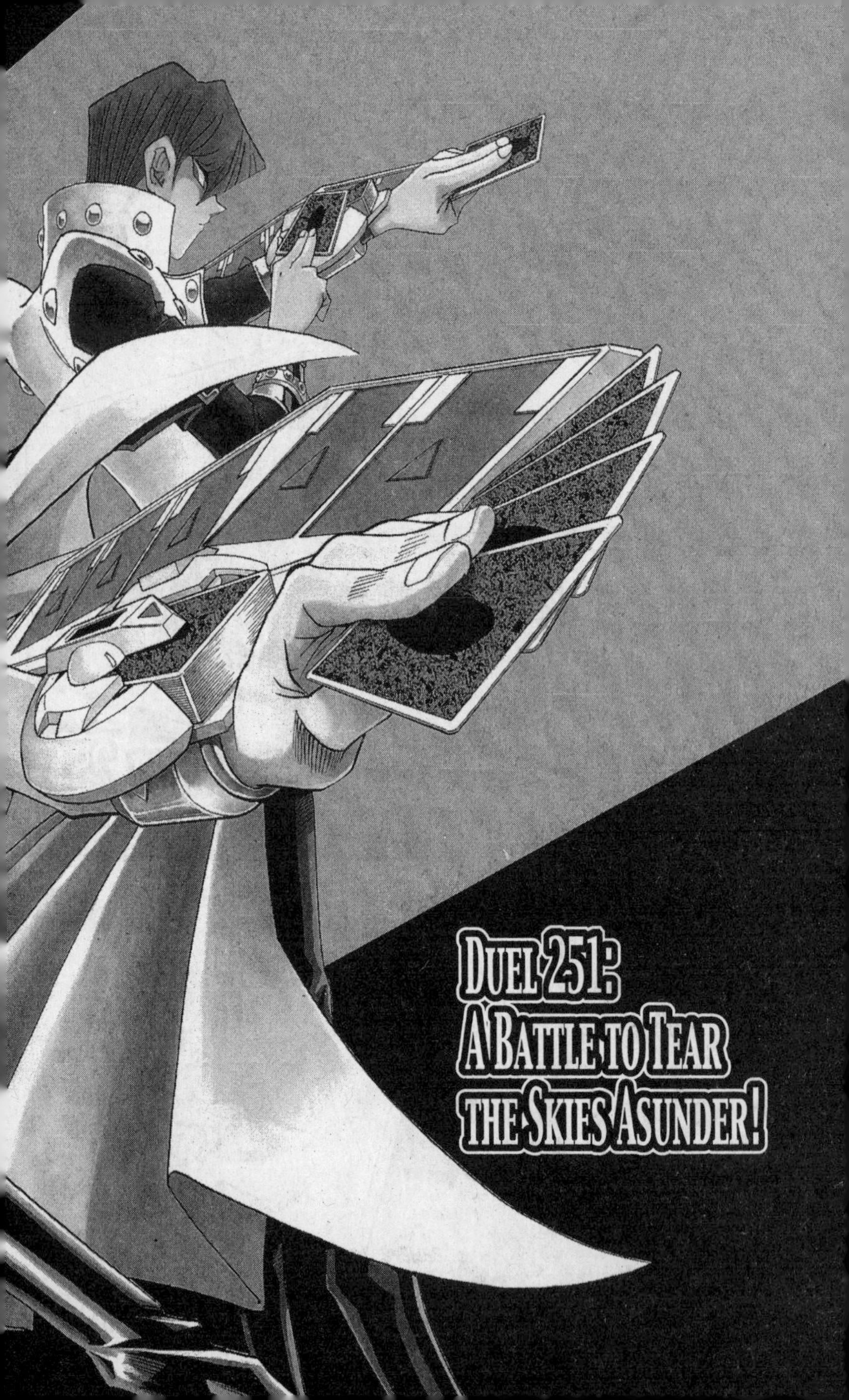

Duel 251: A Battle to Tear the Skies Asunder!

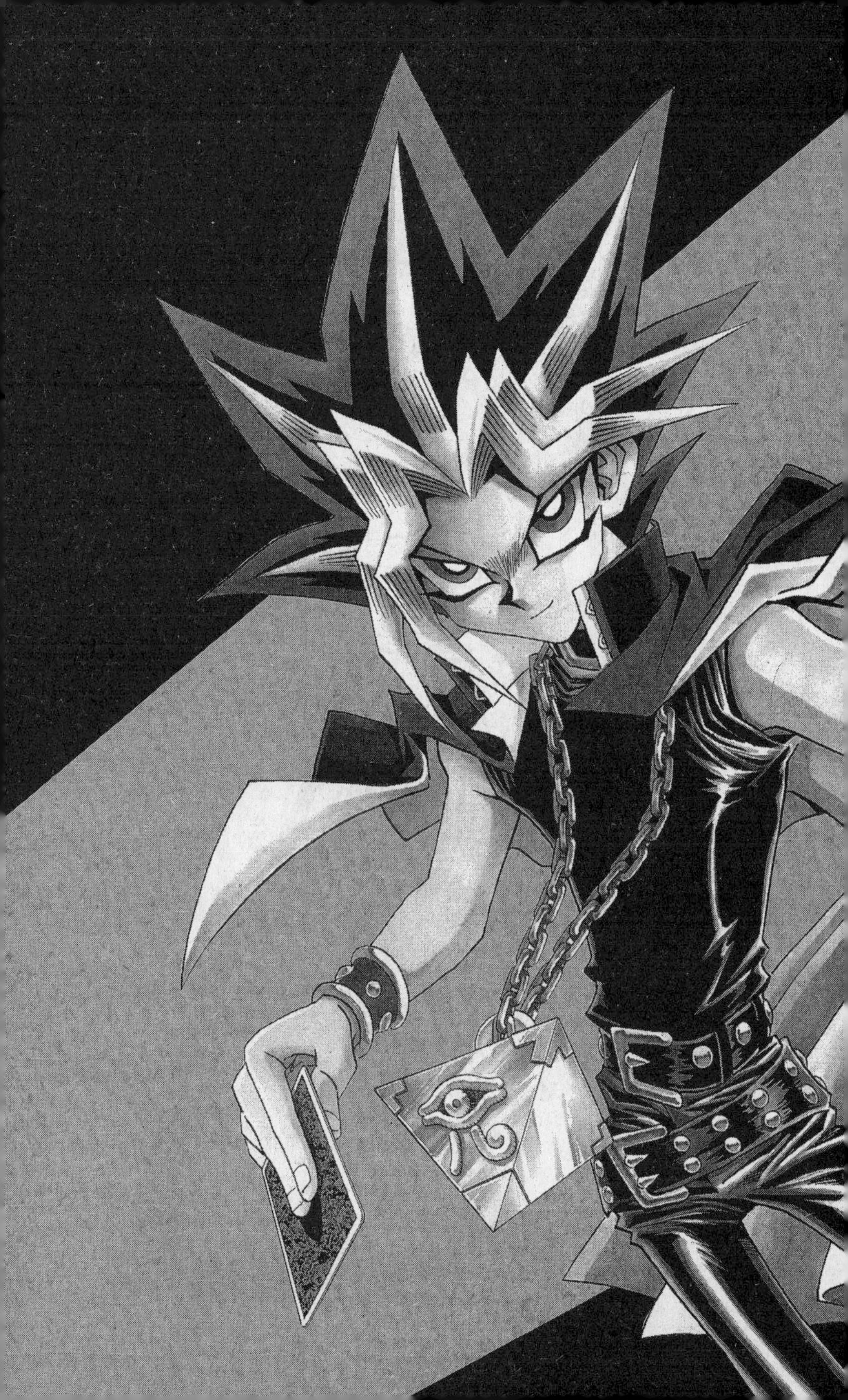

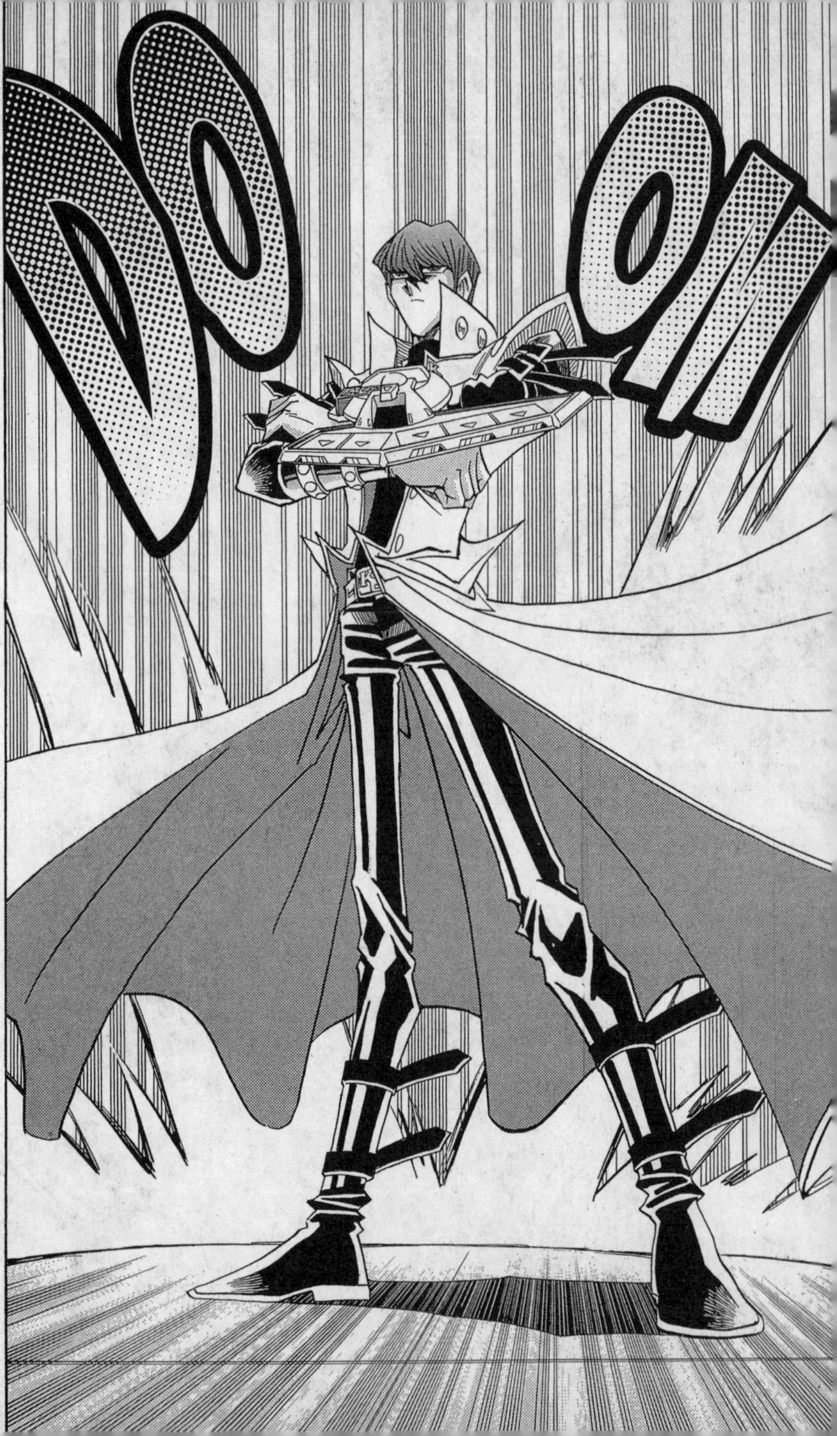
DO
OM

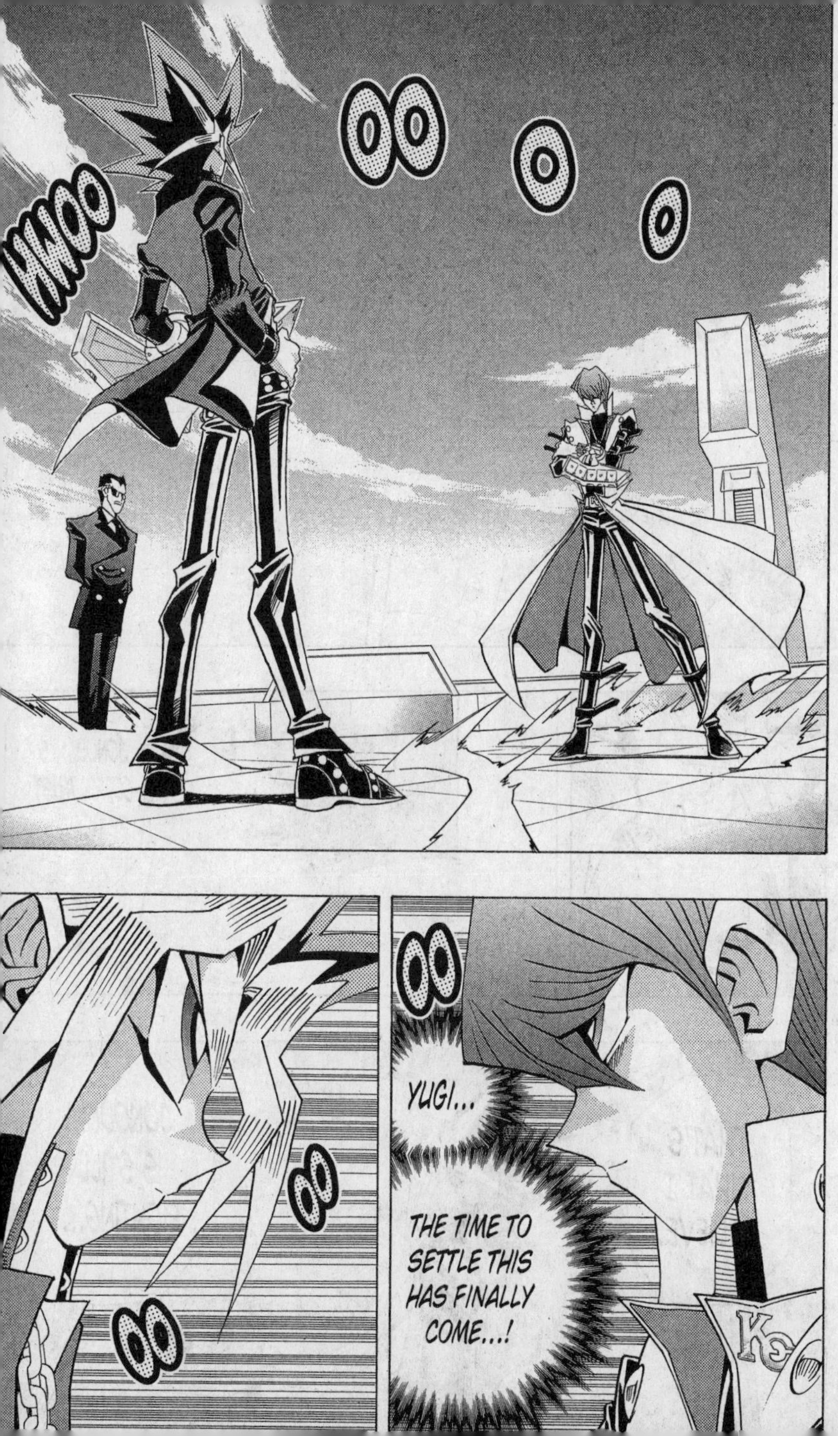
WHOO
YUGI...
THE TIME TO SETTLE THIS HAS FINALLY COME...!

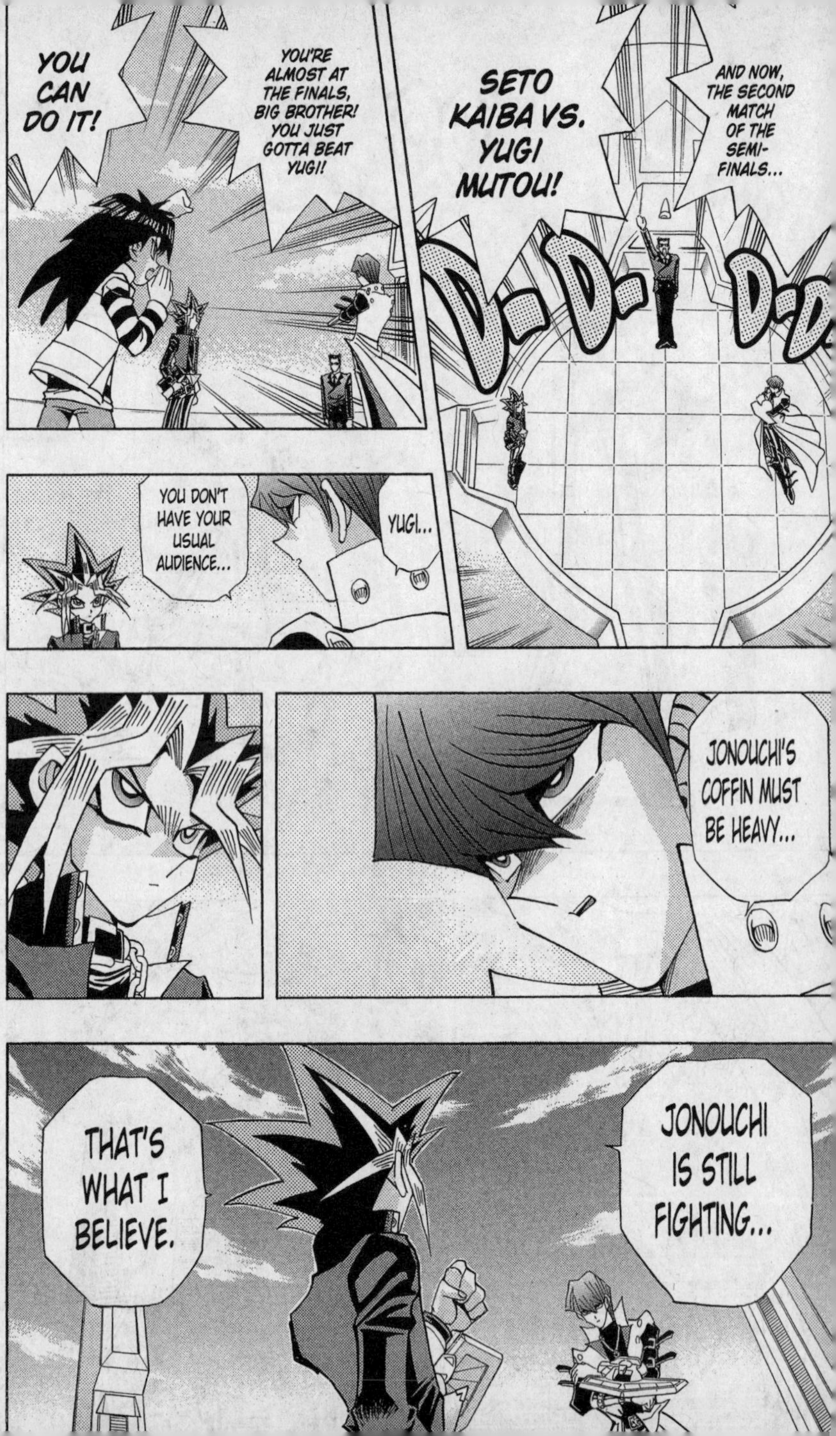
AND NOW, THE SECOND MATCH OF THE SEMI-FINALS...
SETO KAIBA VS. YUGI MUTOU!
D-D-D-D
YOU'RE ALMOST AT THE FINALS, BIG BROTHER! YOU JUST GOTTA BEAT YUGI!
YOU CAN DO IT!
YUGI...
YOU DON'T HAVE YOUR USUAL AUDIENCE...
JONOUCHI'S COFFIN MUST BE HEAVY...
JONOUCHI IS STILL FIGHTING...
THAT'S WHAT I BELIEVE.

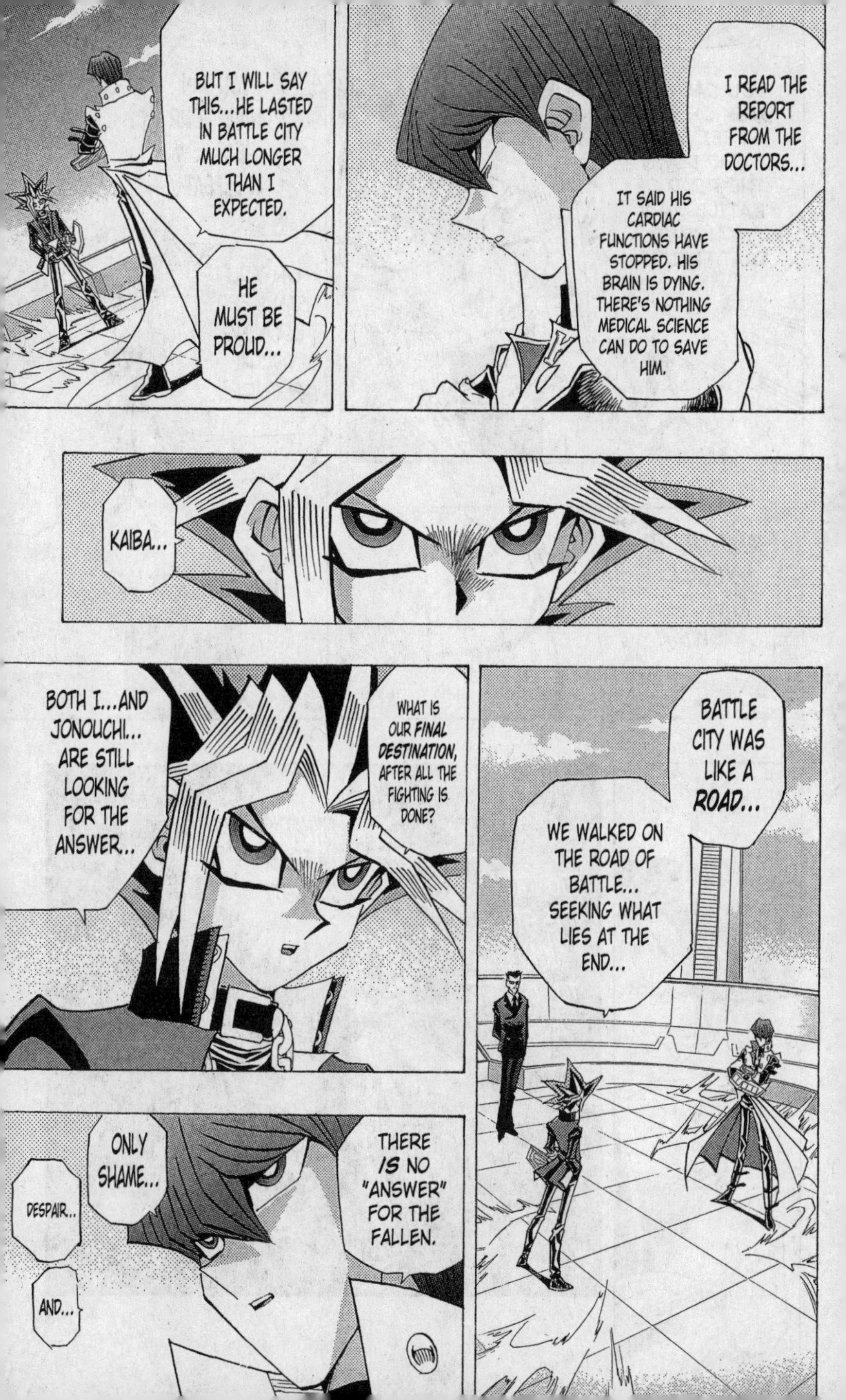
I READ THE REPORT FROM THE DOCTORS...
IT SAID HIS CARDIAC FUNCTIONS HAVE STOPPED. HIS BRAIN IS DYING. THERE'S NOTHING MEDICAL SCIENCE CAN DO TO SAVE HIM.
BUT I WILL SAY THIS...HE LASTED IN BATTLE CITY MUCH LONGER THAN I EXPECTED.
HE MUST BE PROUD...
KAIBA...
BATTLE CITY WAS LIKE A ROAD...
WE WALKED ON THE ROAD OF BATTLE... SEEKING WHAT LIES AT THE END...
WHAT IS OUR FINAL DESTINATION, AFTER ALL THE FIGHTING IS DONE?
BOTH I...AND JONOUCHI... ARE STILL LOOKING FOR THE ANSWER...
THERE IS NO "ANSWER" FOR THE FALLEN.
ONLY SHAME...
DESPAIR...
AND...

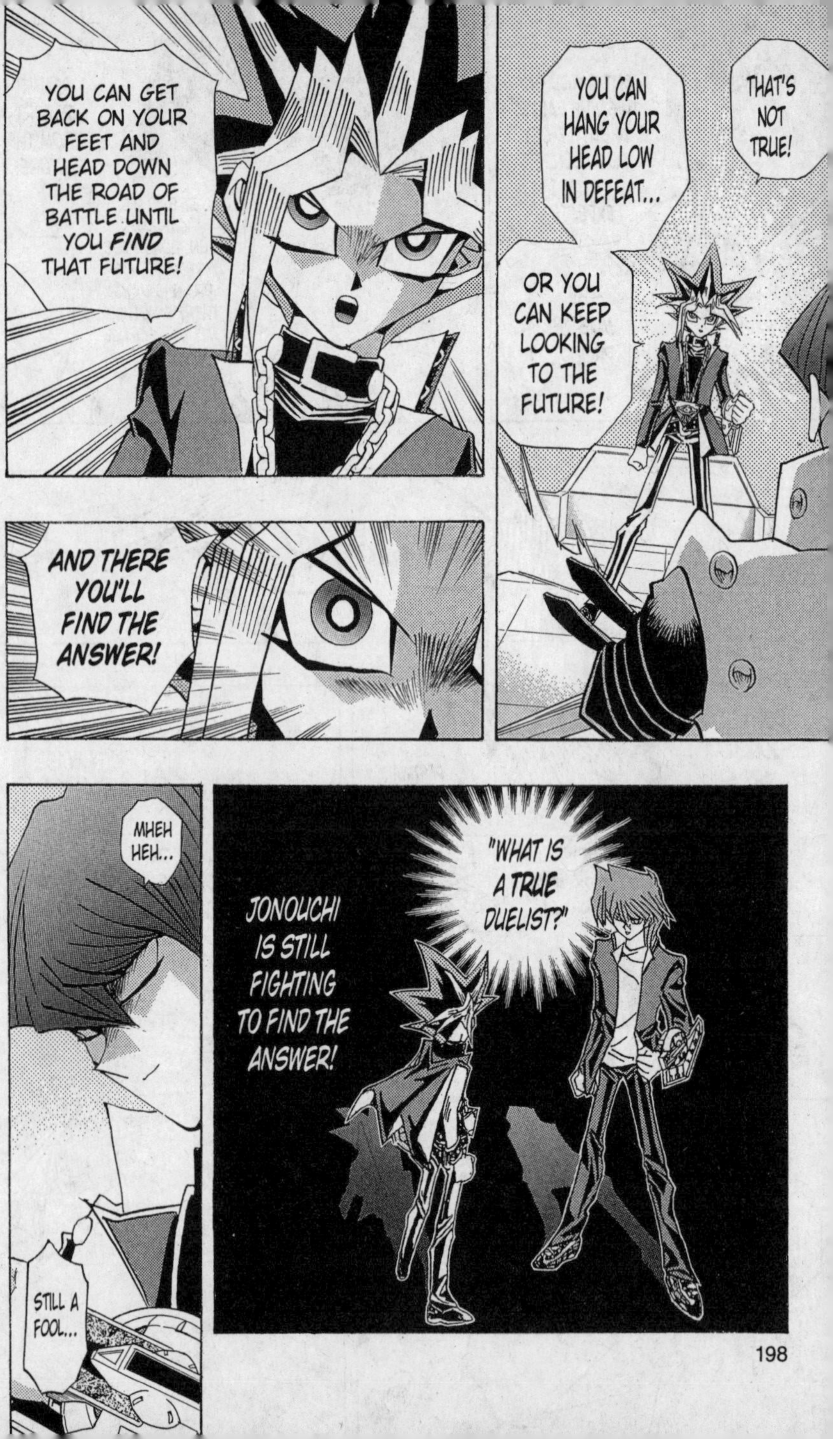
THAT'S NOT TRUE!
YOU CAN HANG YOUR HEAD LOW IN DEFEAT...
OR YOU CAN KEEP LOOKING TO THE FUTURE!
YOU CAN GET BACK ON YOUR FEET AND HEAD DOWN THE ROAD OF BATTLE UNTIL YOU *FIND* THAT FUTURE!
AND THERE YOU'LL FIND THE ANSWER!
"WHAT IS A TRUE DUELIST?"
JONOUCHI IS STILL FIGHTING TO FIND THE ANSWER!
MHEH HEH...
STILL A FOOL...

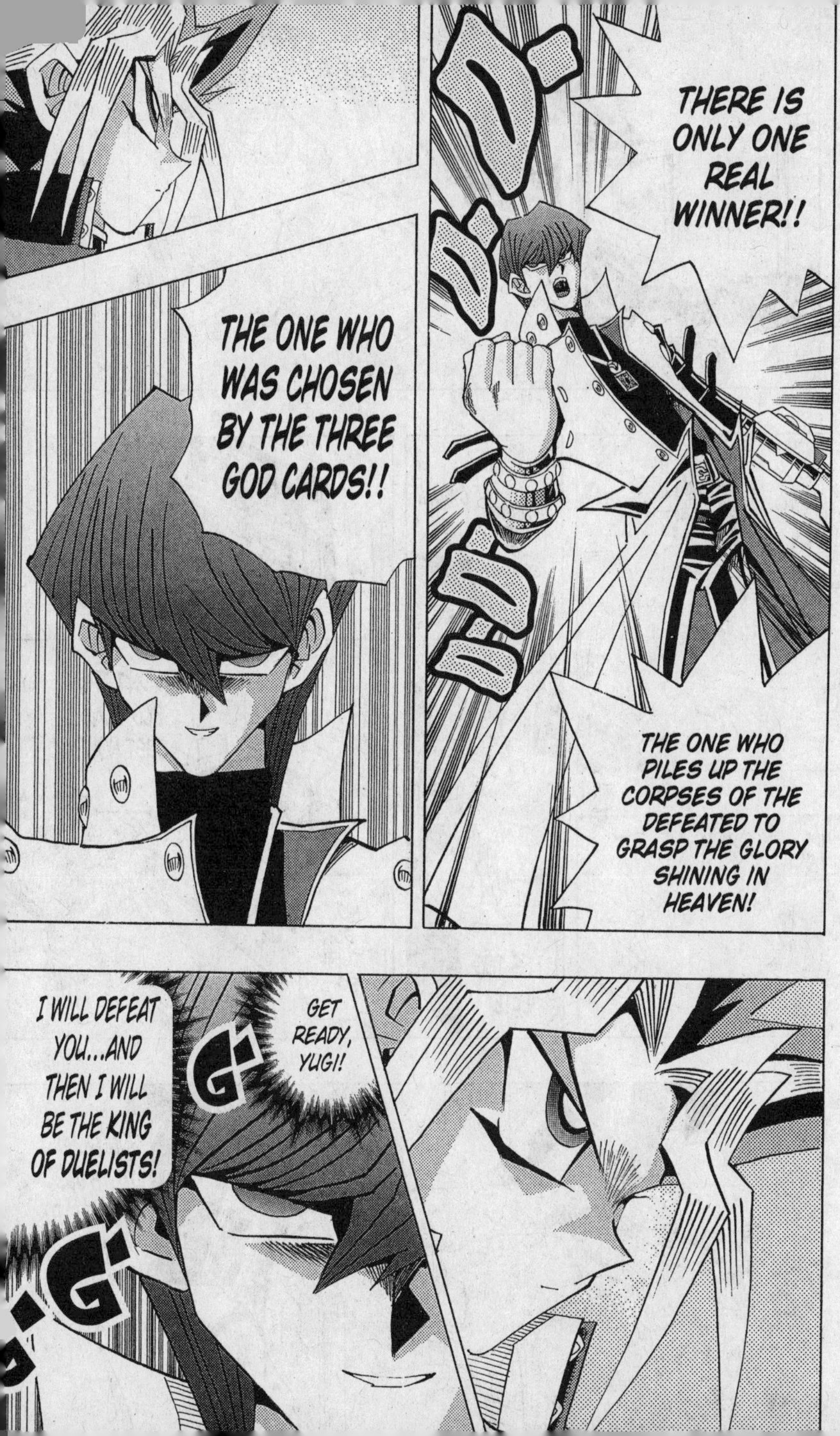
THERE IS ONLY ONE REAL WINNER!!
THE ONE WHO PILES UP THE CORPSES OF THE DEFEATED TO GRASP THE GLORY SHINING IN HEAVEN!
THE ONE WHO WAS CHOSEN BY THE THREE GOD CARDS!!
GET READY, YUGI!
I WILL DEFEAT YOU...AND THEN I WILL BE THE KING OF DUELISTS!

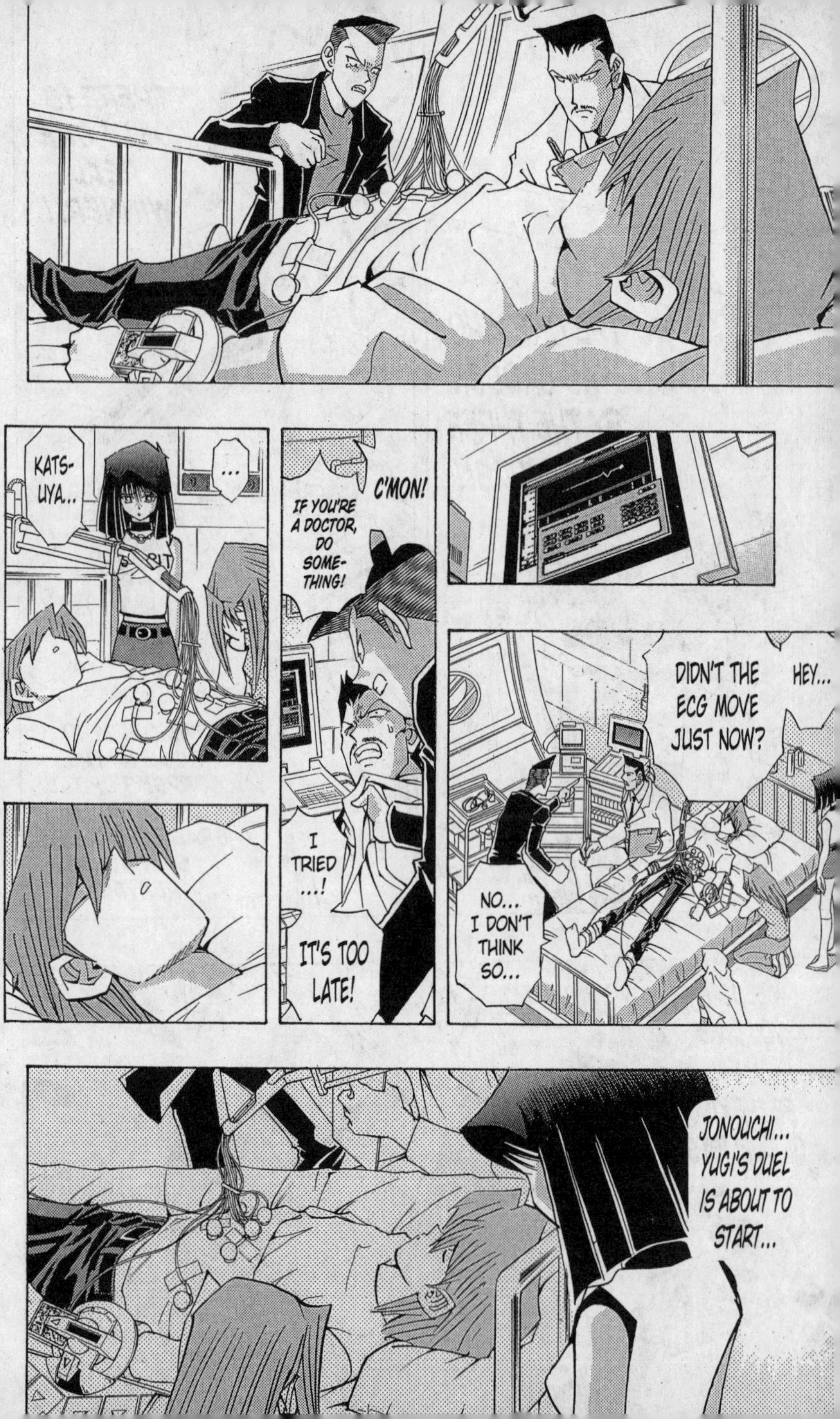
HEY...
DIDN'T THE ECG MOVE JUST NOW?
NO... I DON'T THINK SO...
C'MON!
IF YOU'RE A DOCTOR, DO SOME-THING!
I TRIED...!
IT'S TOO LATE!
...
KATS-UYA...
JONOUCHI... YUGI'S DUEL IS ABOUT TO START...

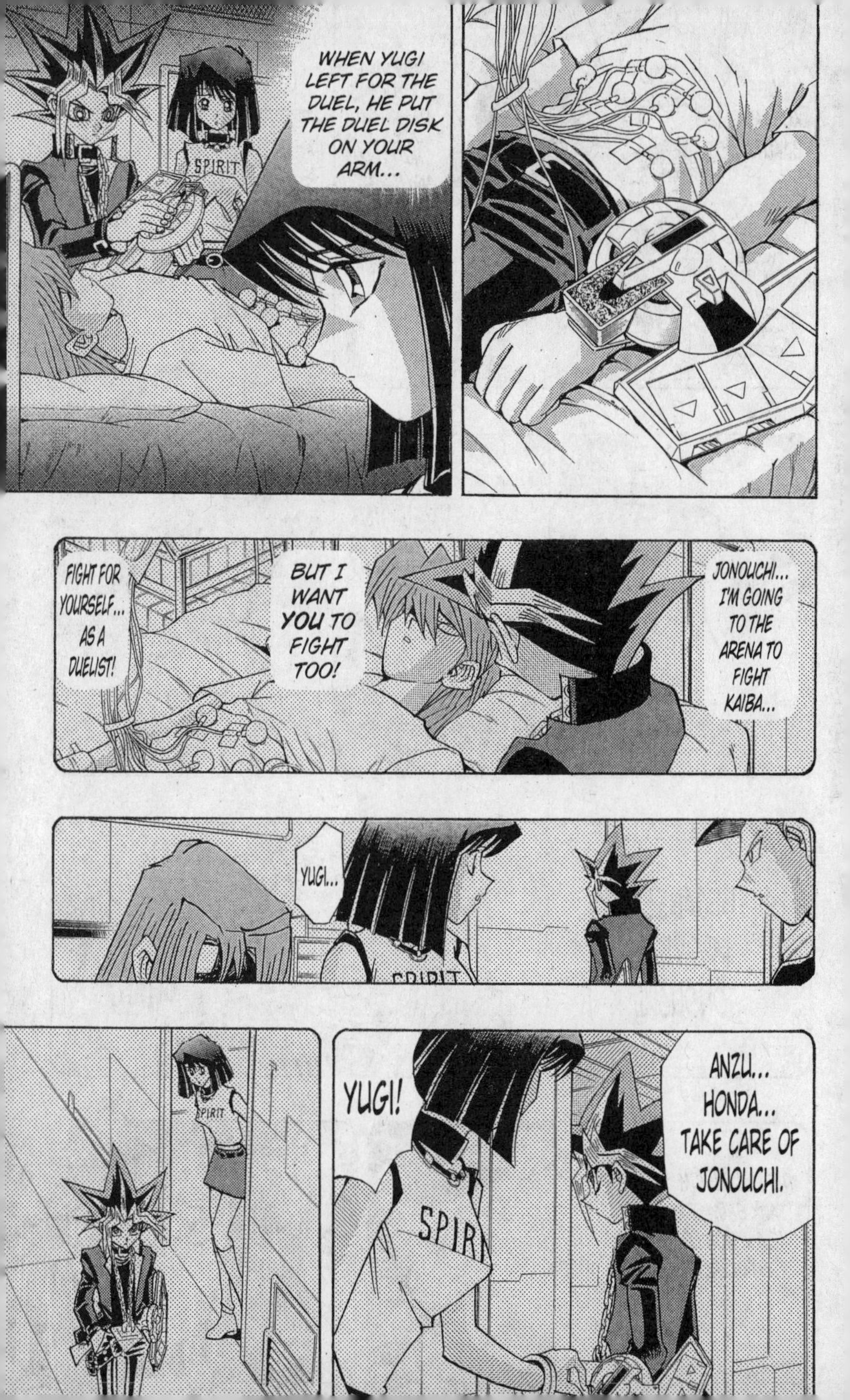
WHEN YUGI LEFT FOR THE DUEL, HE PUT THE DUEL DISK ON YOUR ARM...
JONOUCHI... I'M GOING TO THE ARENA TO FIGHT KAIBA...
BUT I WANT YOU TO FIGHT TOO!
FIGHT FOR YOURSELF... AS A DUELIST!
YUGI...
ANZU... HONDA... TAKE CARE OF JONOUCHI.
YUGI!

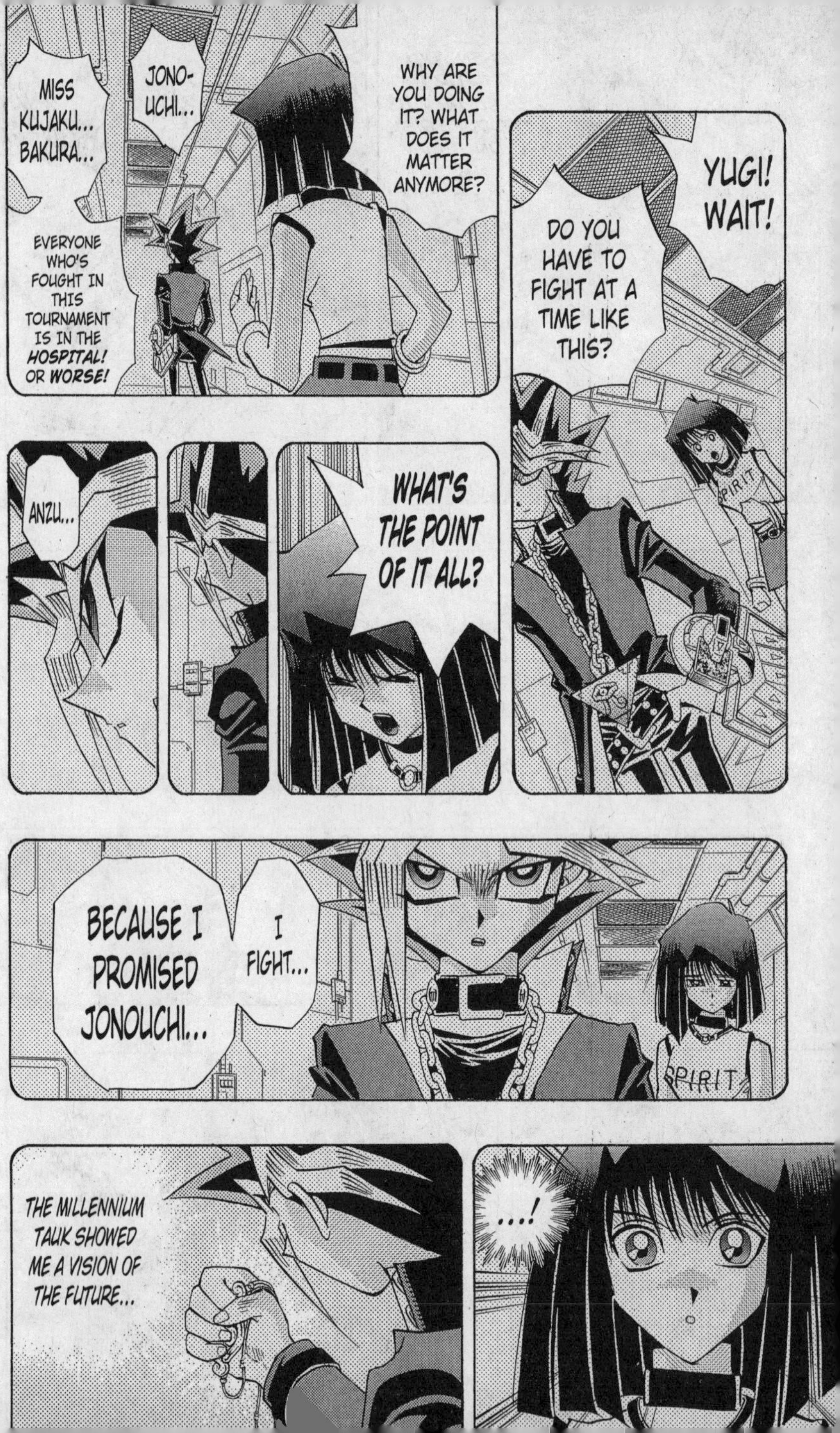
YUGI! WAIT!
DO YOU HAVE TO FIGHT AT A TIME LIKE THIS?
WHY ARE YOU DOING IT? WHAT DOES IT MATTER ANYMORE?
JONO-UCHI...
MISS KUJAKU... BAKURA...
EVERYONE WHO'S FOUGHT IN THIS TOURNAMENT IS IN THE *HOSPITAL!* OR *WORSE!*
WHAT'S THE POINT OF IT ALL?
ANZU...
I FIGHT...
BECAUSE I PROMISED JONOUCHI...
...!
THE MILLENNIUM TAUK SHOWED ME A VISION OF THE FUTURE...

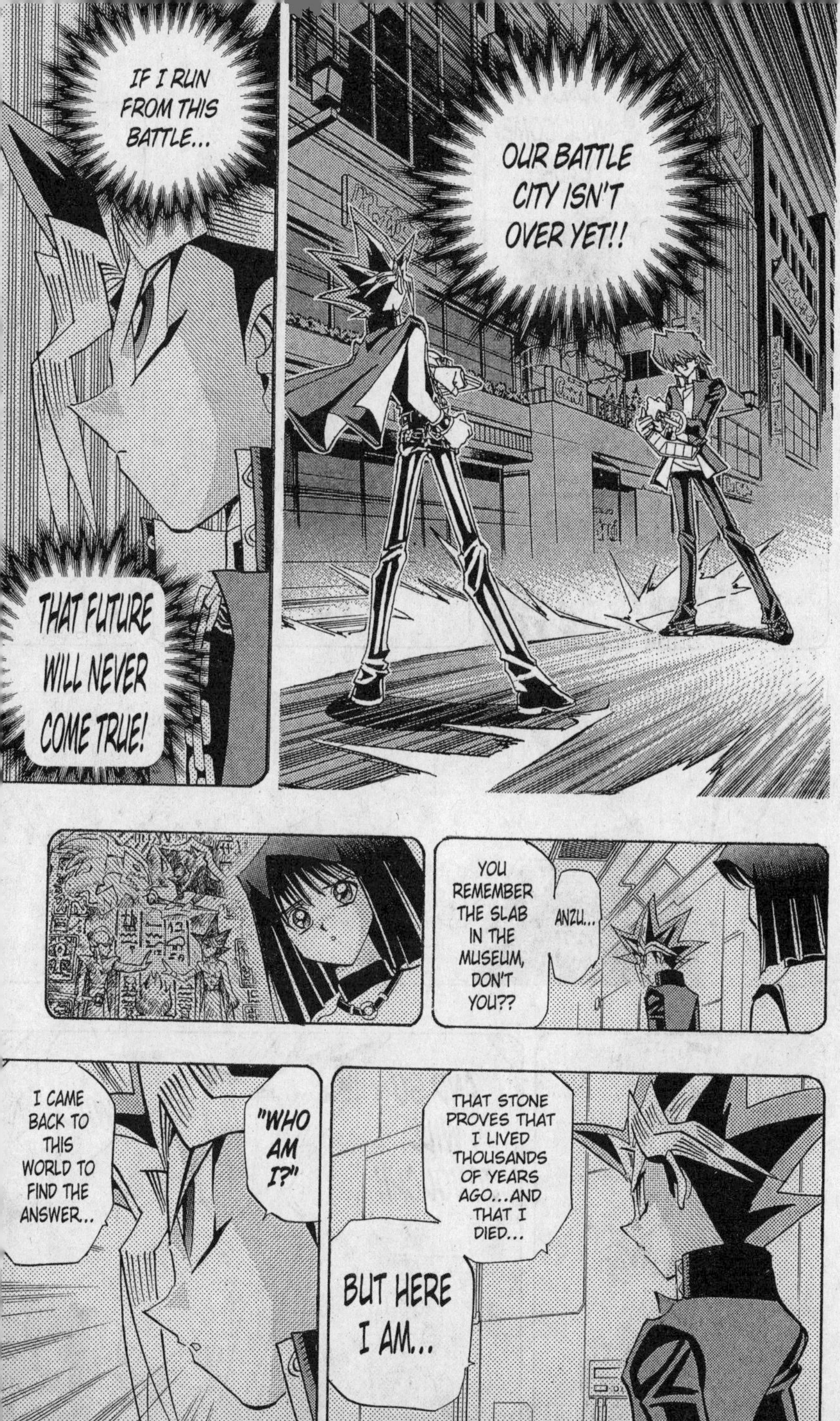
OUR BATTLE CITY ISN'T OVER YET!!
IF I RUN FROM THIS BATTLE...
THAT FUTURE WILL NEVER COME TRUE!
ANZU...
YOU REMEMBER THE SLAB IN THE MUSEUM, DON'T YOU??
THAT STONE PROVES THAT I LIVED THOUSANDS OF YEARS AGO...AND THAT I DIED...
BUT HERE I AM...
"WHO AM I?"
I CAME BACK TO THIS WORLD TO FIND THE ANSWER...

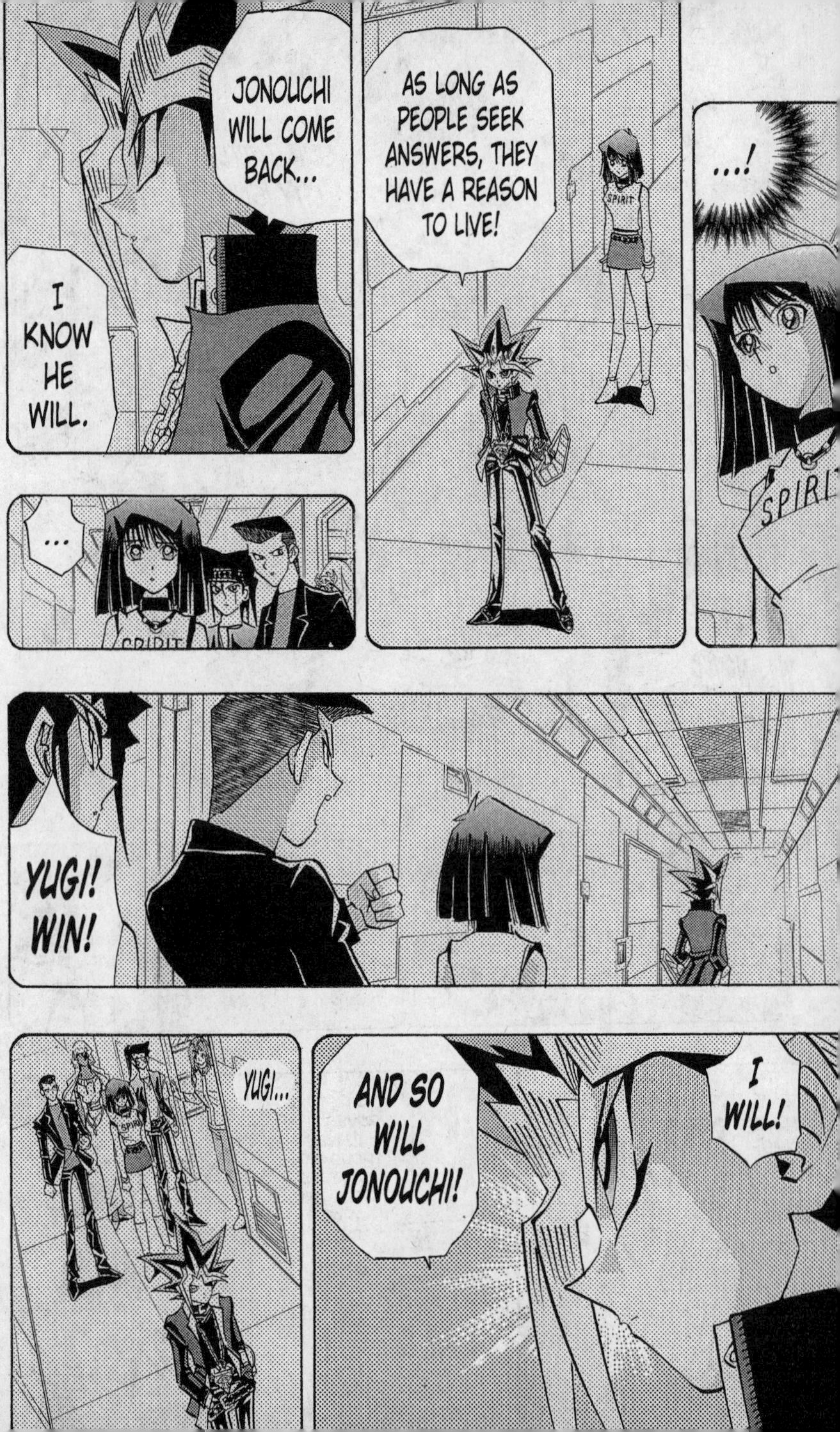
...!
AS LONG AS PEOPLE SEEK ANSWERS, THEY HAVE A REASON TO LIVE!
SPIRIT
JONOUCHI WILL COME BACK...
I KNOW HE WILL.
...
YUGI! WIN!
I WILL!
AND SO WILL JONOUCHI!
YUGI...

I SWORE...

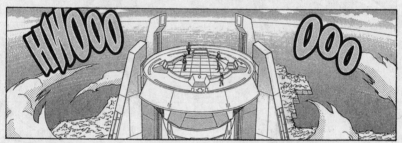

...I'D BECOME A TRUE DUELIST...

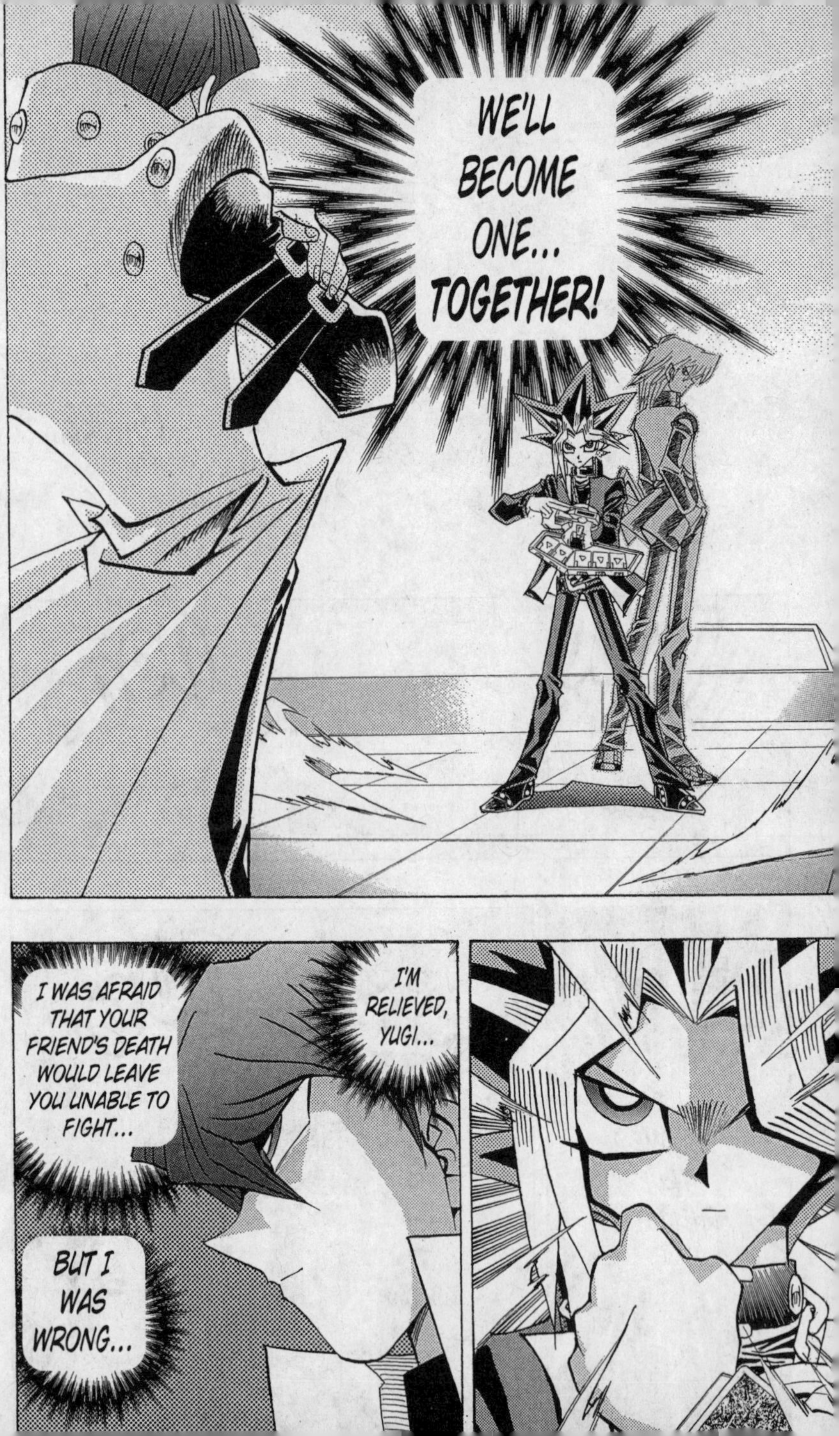
WE'LL BECOME ONE... TOGETHER!
I'M RELIEVED, YUGI...
I WAS AFRAID THAT YOUR FRIEND'S DEATH WOULD LEAVE YOU UNABLE TO FIGHT...
BUT I WAS WRONG...

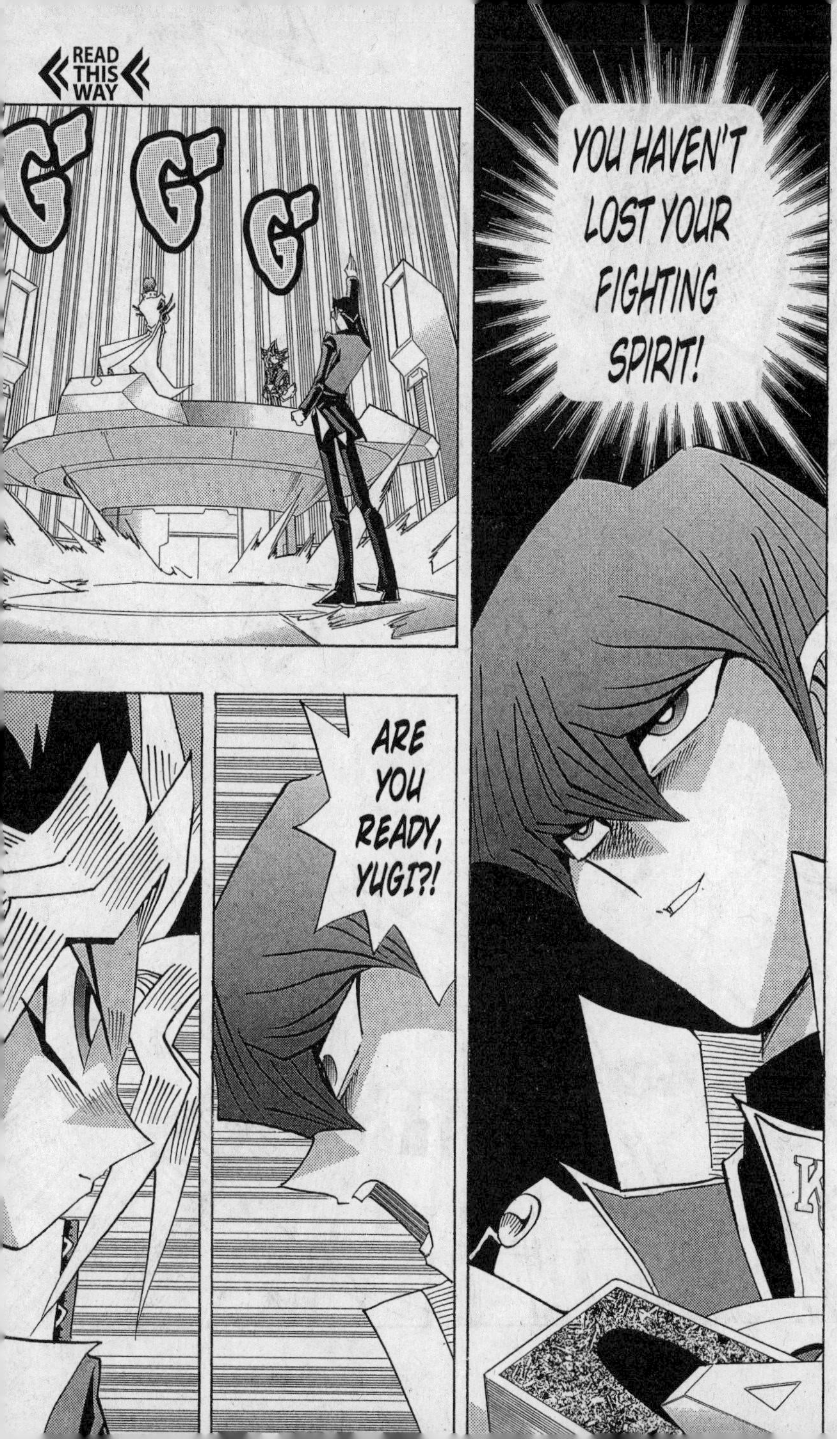
READ THIS WAY
YOU HAVEN'T LOST YOUR FIGHTING SPIRIT!
G G G
ARE YOU READY, YUGI?!

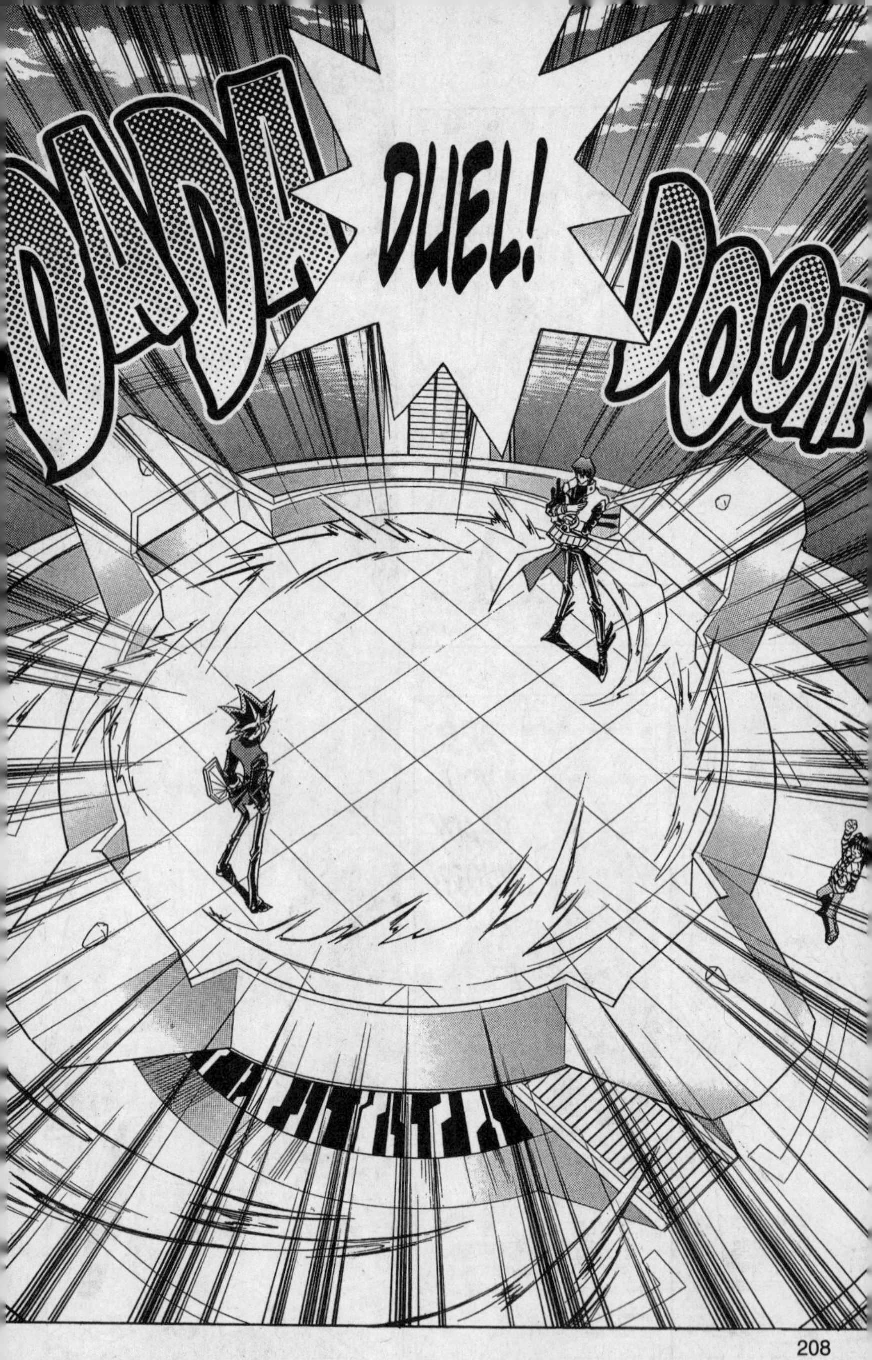
DADA
DUEL!
DOOM

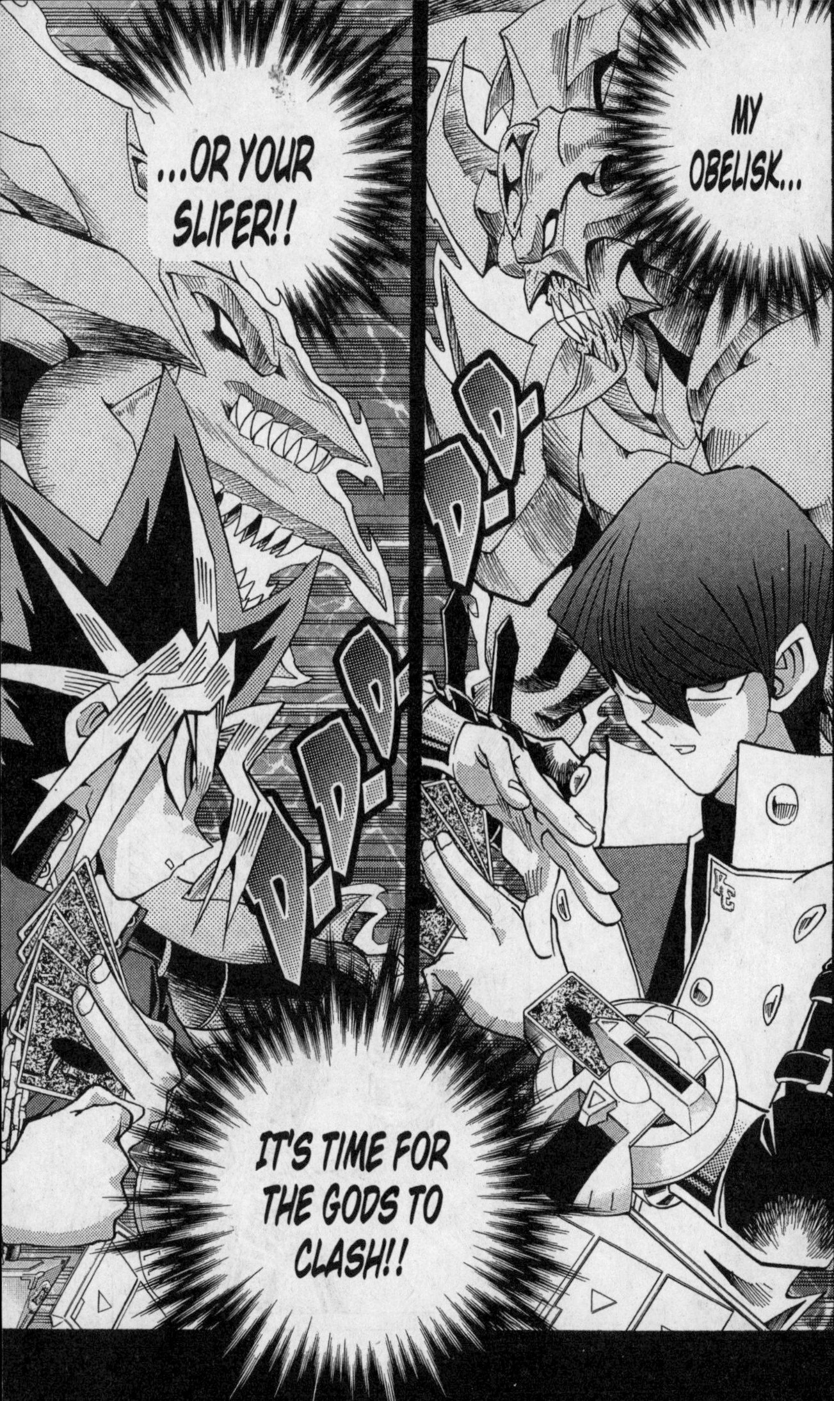
MY OBELISK...
...OR YOUR SLIFER!!
IT'S TIME FOR THE GODS TO CLASH!!

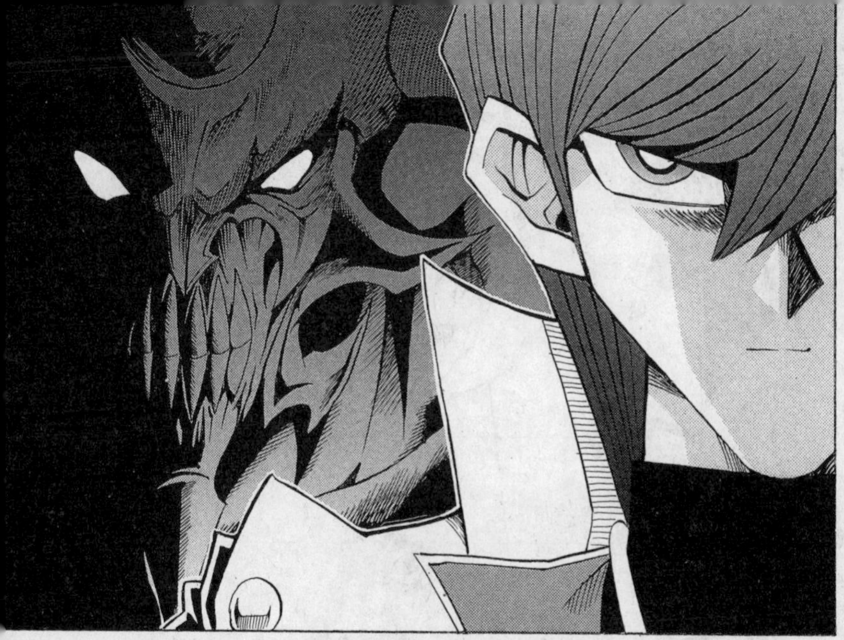

Duel 252: Sky Duel Coliseum!

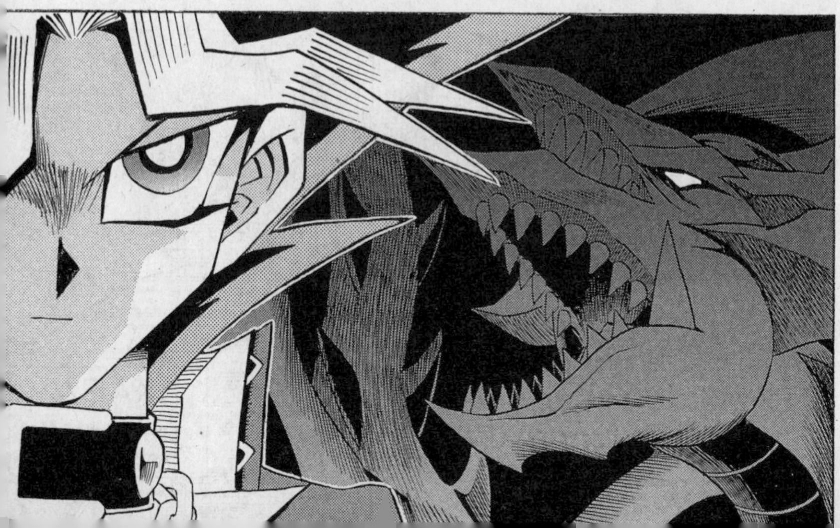

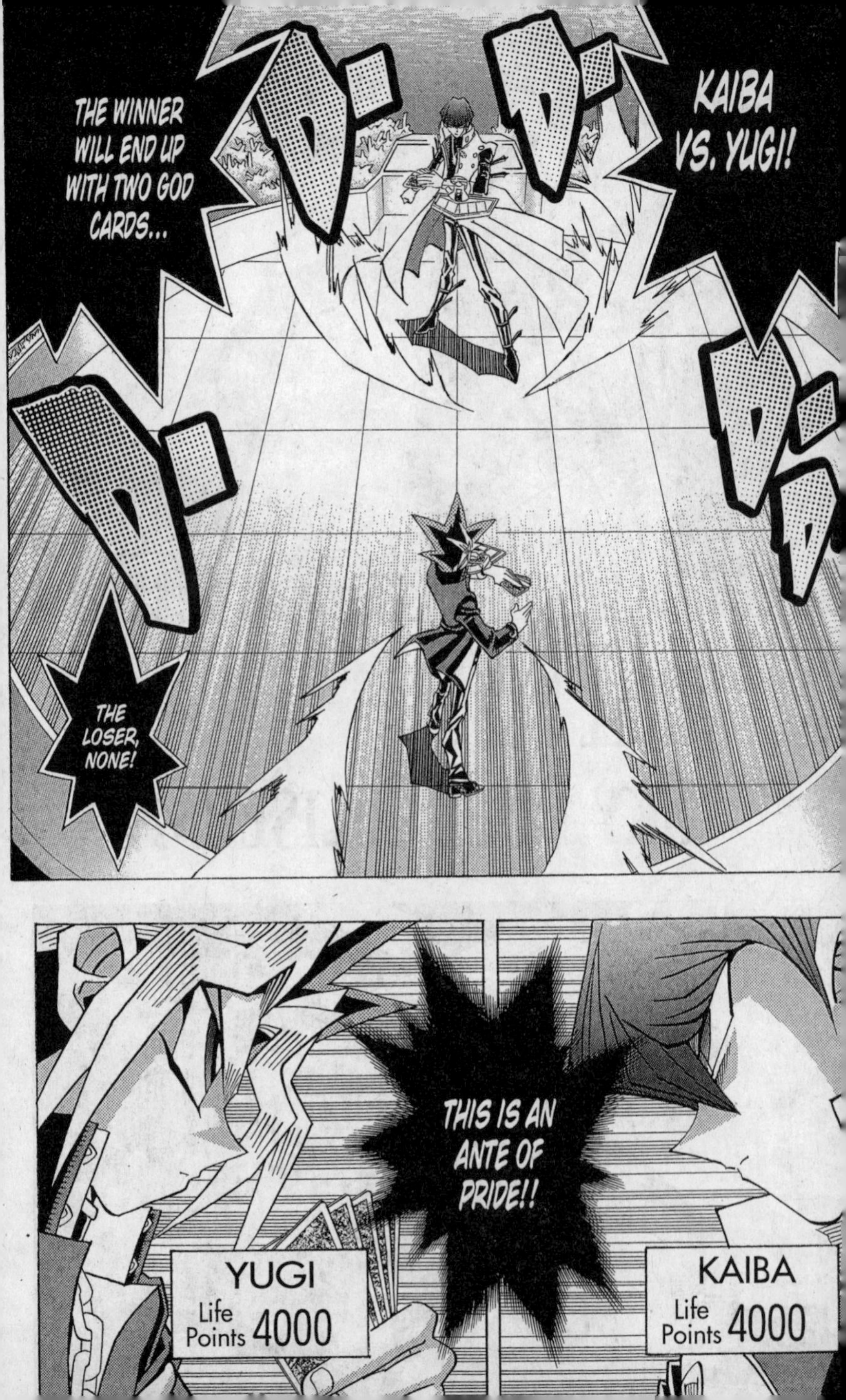
KAIBA VS. YUGI!
THE WINNER WILL END UP WITH TWO GOD CARDS...
THE LOSER, NONE!
THIS IS AN ANTE OF PRIDE!!
KAIBA Life Points 4000
YUGI Life Points 4000

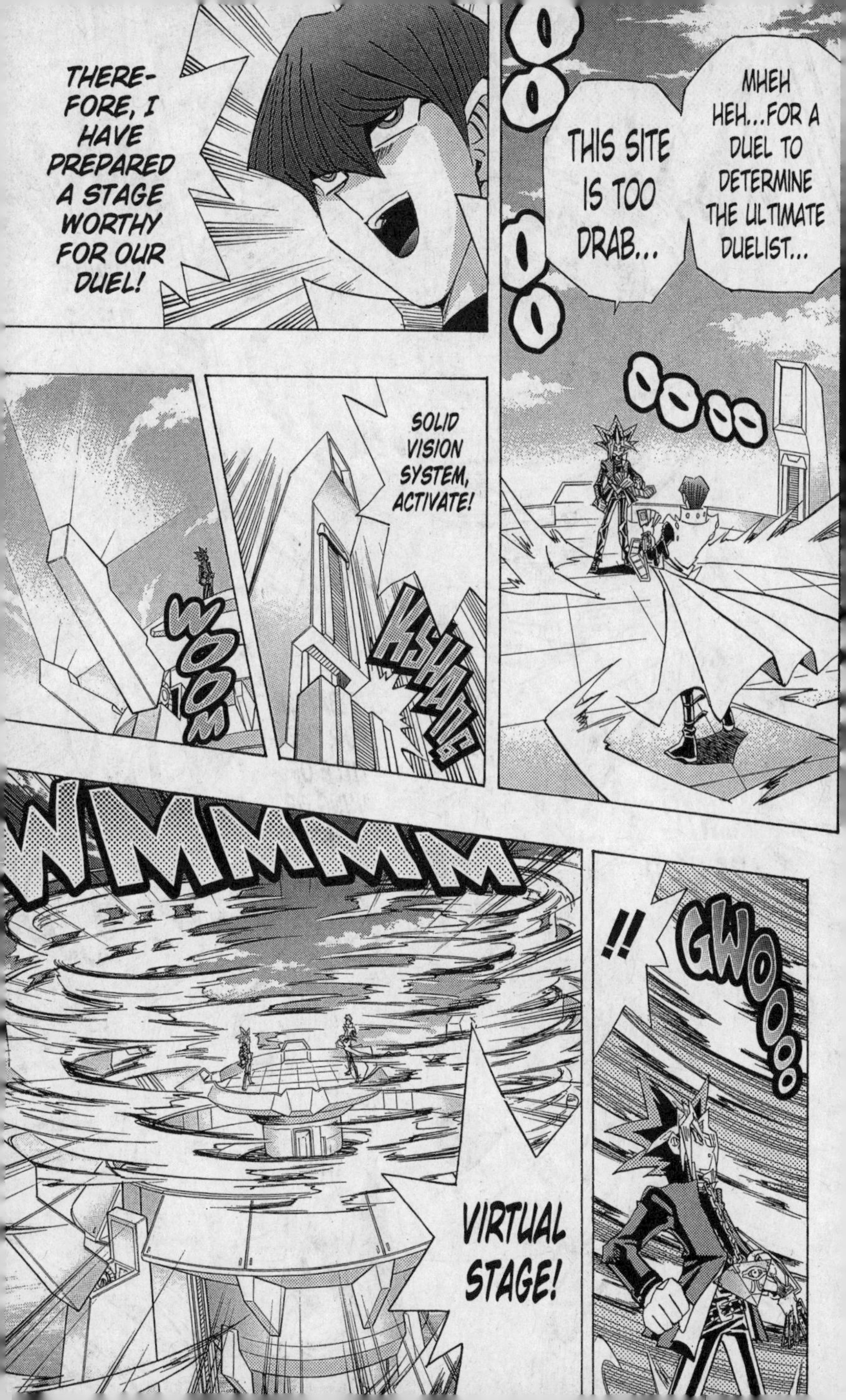
MHEH HEH...FOR A DUEL TO DETERMINE THE ULTIMATE DUELIST...
THIS SITE IS TOO DRAB...
THEREFORE, I HAVE PREPARED A STAGE WORTHY FOR OUR DUEL!
SOLID VISION SYSTEM, ACTIVATE!
KSHANG
WOOOM
!!
GWOOOOO
WMMMMM
VIRTUAL STAGE!

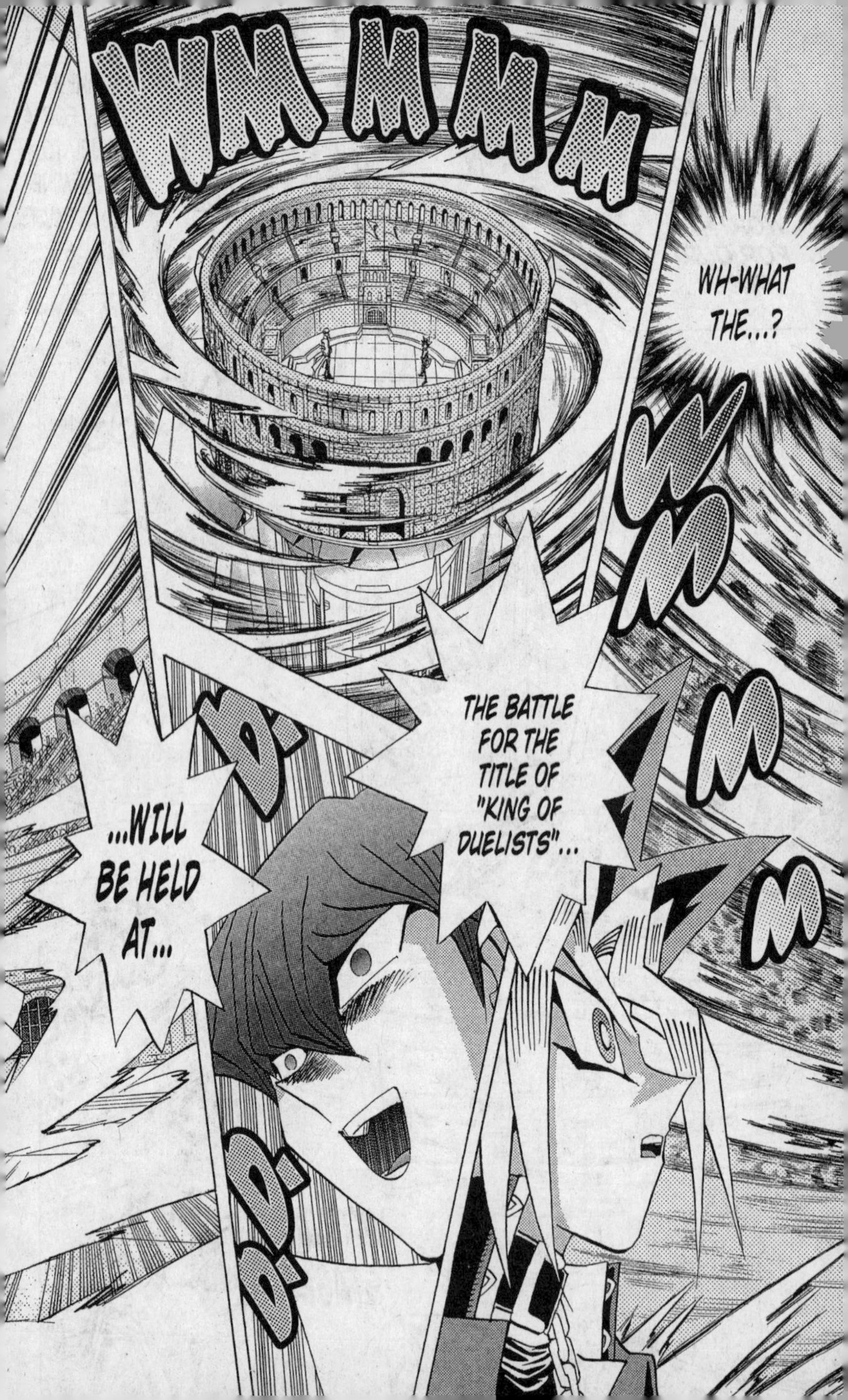
WMMMMM
WH-WHAT THE...?
WMMMM
THE BATTLE FOR THE TITLE OF "KING OF DUELISTS"...
...WILL BE HELD AT...

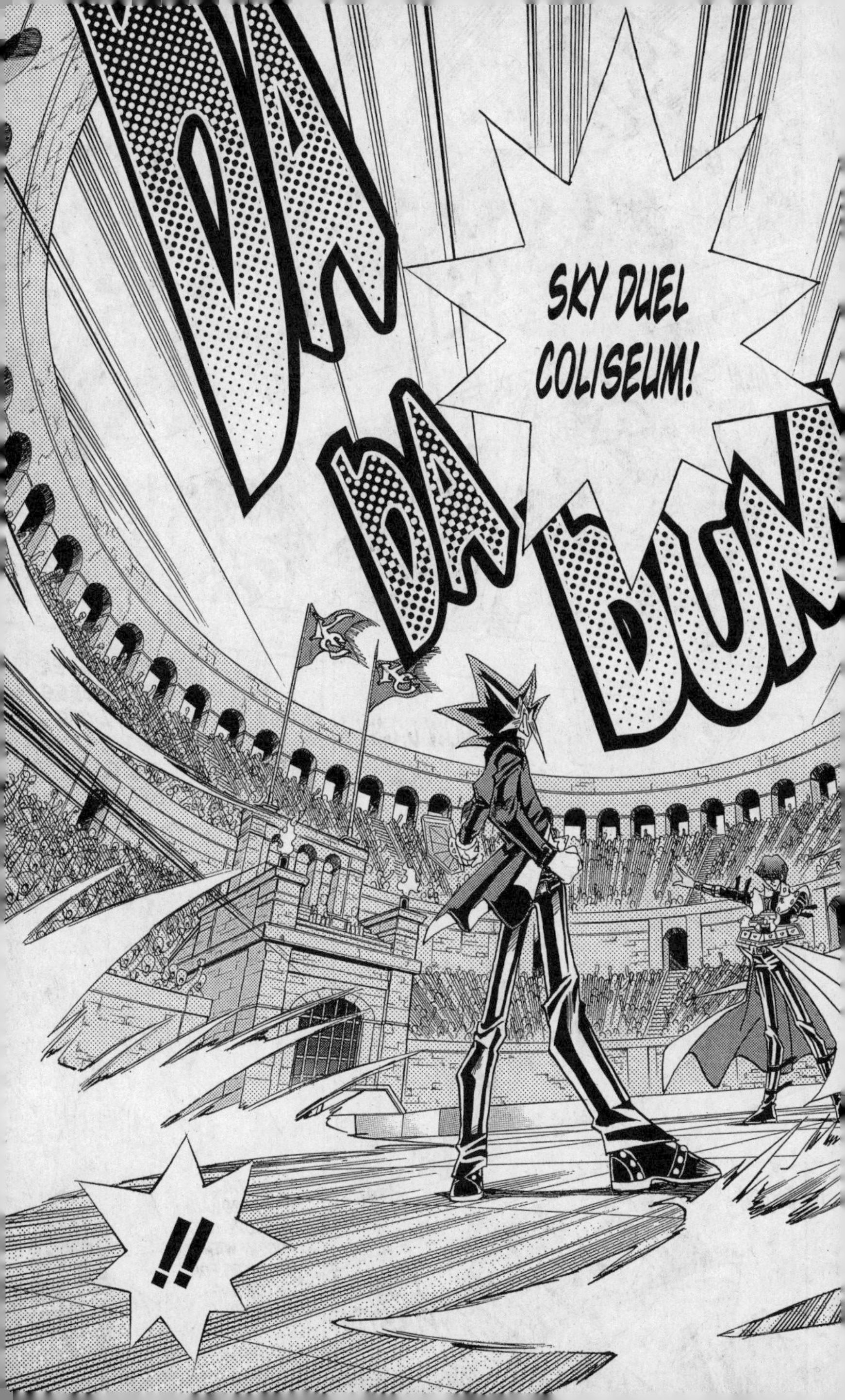
SKY DUEL COLISEUM!
DA DA- DUM
!!

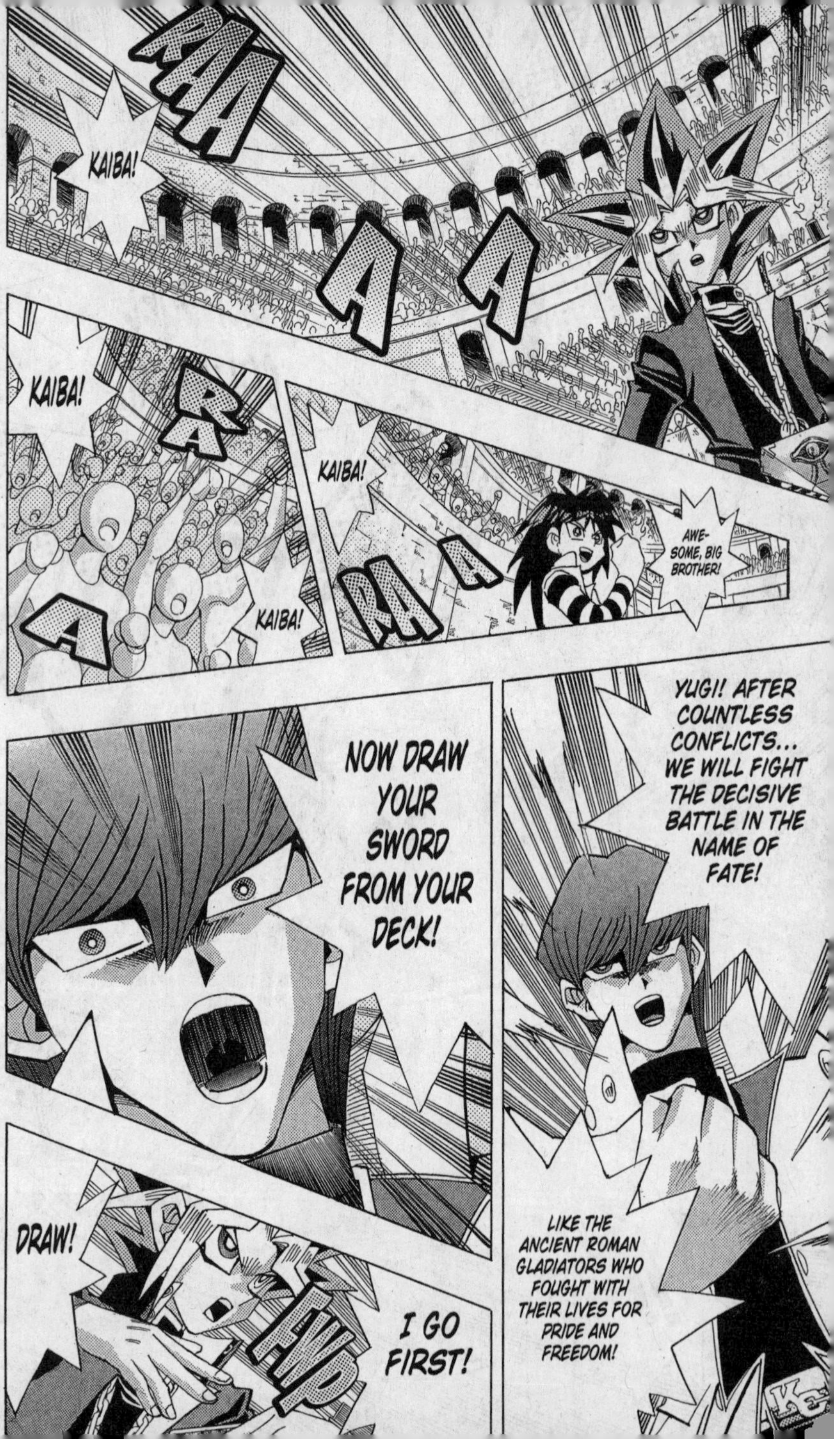
RAA
KAIBA!
A
A
KAIBA!
RAA
AWE-SOME, BIG BROTHER!
KAIBA!
RA
A
KAIBA!
A
YUGI! AFTER COUNTLESS CONFLICTS... WE WILL FIGHT THE DECISIVE BATTLE IN THE NAME OF FATE!
LIKE THE ANCIENT ROMAN GLADIATORS WHO FOUGHT WITH THEIR LIVES FOR PRIDE AND FREEDOM!
NOW DRAW YOUR SWORD FROM YOUR DECK!
DRAW!
I GO FIRST!
FWIP

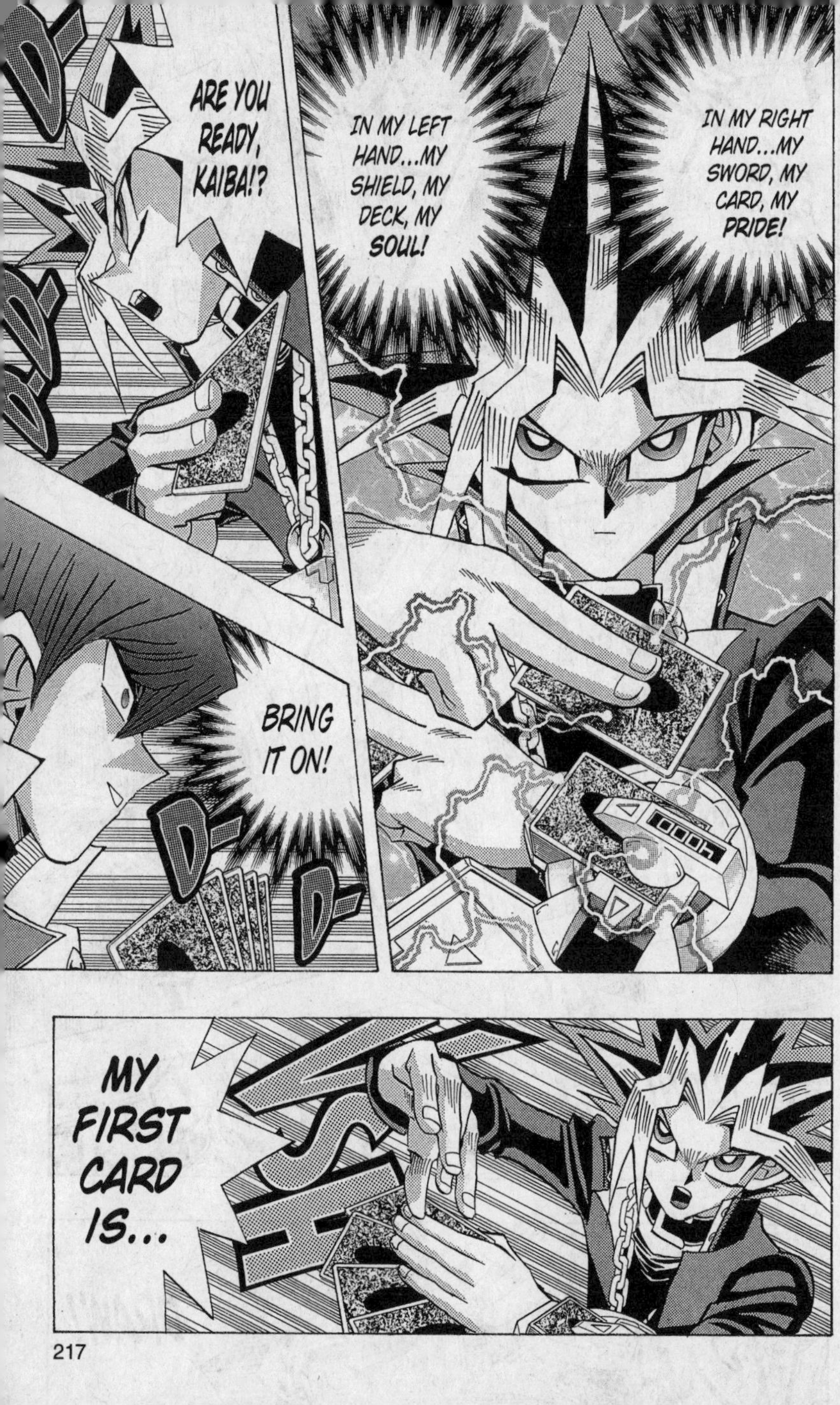

IN MY RIGHT HAND...MY SWORD, MY CARD, MY PRIDE!
IN MY LEFT HAND...MY SHIELD, MY DECK, MY SOUL!
ARE YOU READY, KAIBA!?
BRING IT ON!
D-
D-
MY FIRST CARD IS...

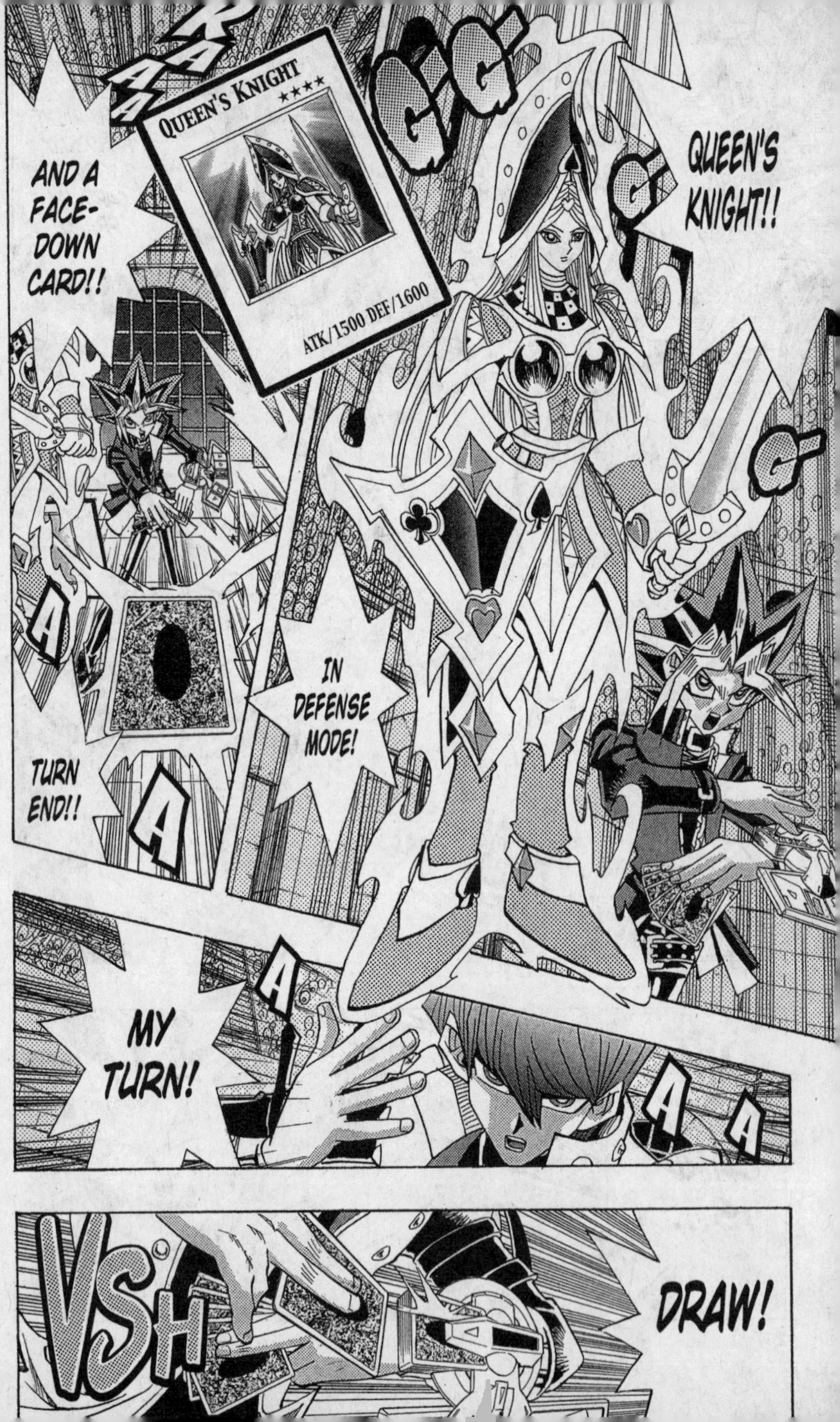

QUEEN'S KNIGHT!!
QUEEN'S KNIGHT
ATK/1500 DEF/1600
IN DEFENSE MODE!
KRAAA
AND A FACE-DOWN CARD!!
TURN END!!
MY TURN!
DRAW!
VSH

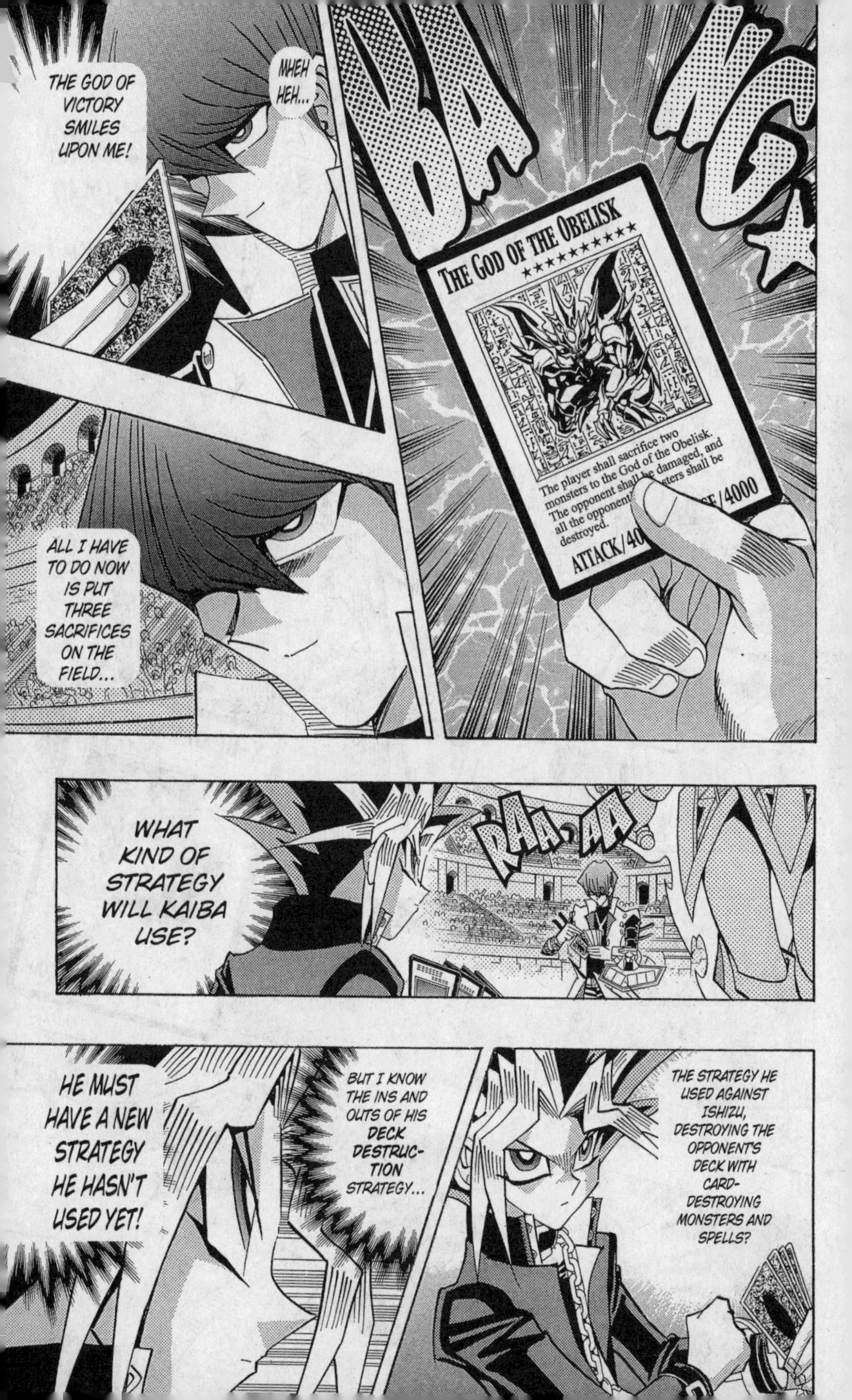
THE GOD OF THE OBELISK
The player shall sacrifice two monsters to the God of the Obelisk. The opponent shall be damaged, and all the opponent
destroyed.
ATTACK/40
/4000
MHEH HEH...
THE GOD OF VICTORY SMILES UPON ME!
ALL I HAVE TO DO NOW IS PUT THREE SACRIFICES ON THE FIELD...
RAA-AA
WHAT KIND OF STRATEGY WILL KAIBA USE?
THE STRATEGY HE USED AGAINST ISHIZU, DESTROYING THE OPPONENT'S DECK WITH CARD-DESTROYING MONSTERS AND SPELLS?
BUT I KNOW THE INS AND OUTS OF HIS DECK DESTRUCTION STRATEGY...
HE MUST HAVE A NEW STRATEGY HE HASN'T USED YET!

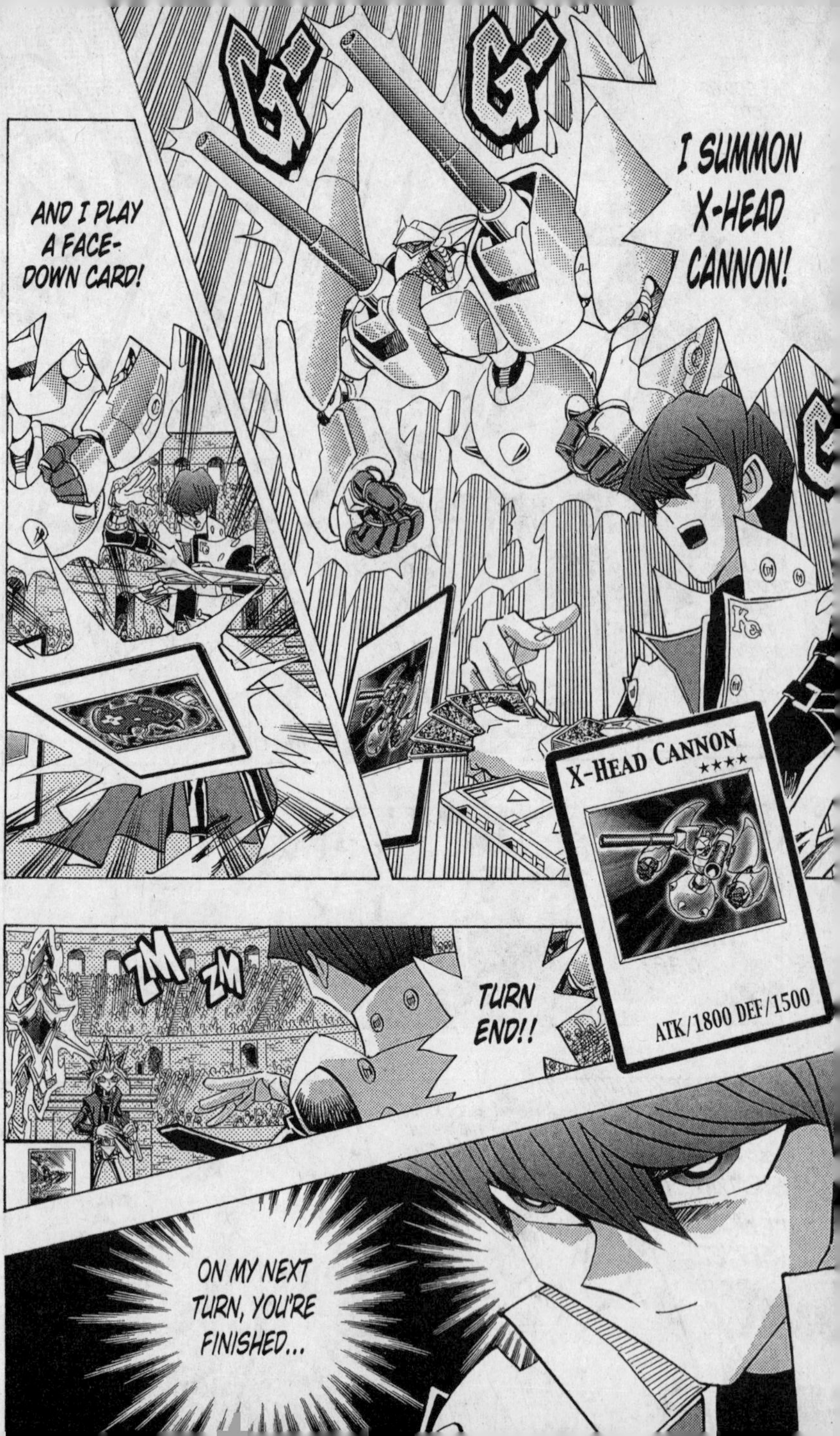
G G
I SUMMON X-HEAD CANNON!
G
AND I PLAY A FACE-DOWN CARD!
X-HEAD CANNON
★★★★
ATK/1800 DEF/1500
TURN END!!
ZM ZM
ON MY NEXT TURN, YOU'RE FINISHED...

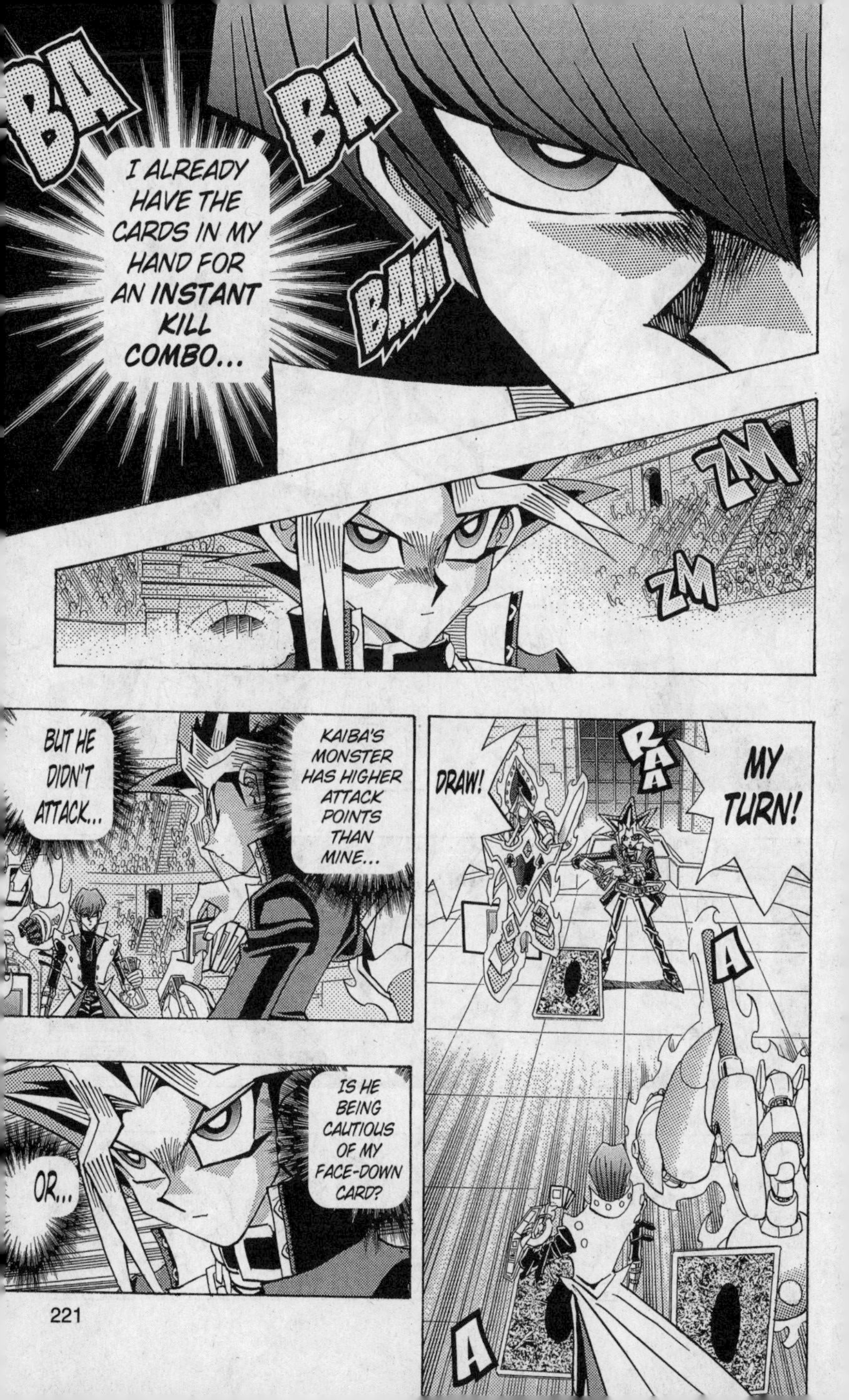
BA
BA
I ALREADY HAVE THE CARDS IN MY HAND FOR AN INSTANT KILL COMBO...
BAM
ZM
ZM
MY TURN!
RAA
DRAW!
A
A
KAIBA'S MONSTER HAS HIGHER ATTACK POINTS THAN MINE...
BUT HE DIDN'T ATTACK...
IS HE BEING CAUTIOUS OF MY FACE-DOWN CARD?
OR...

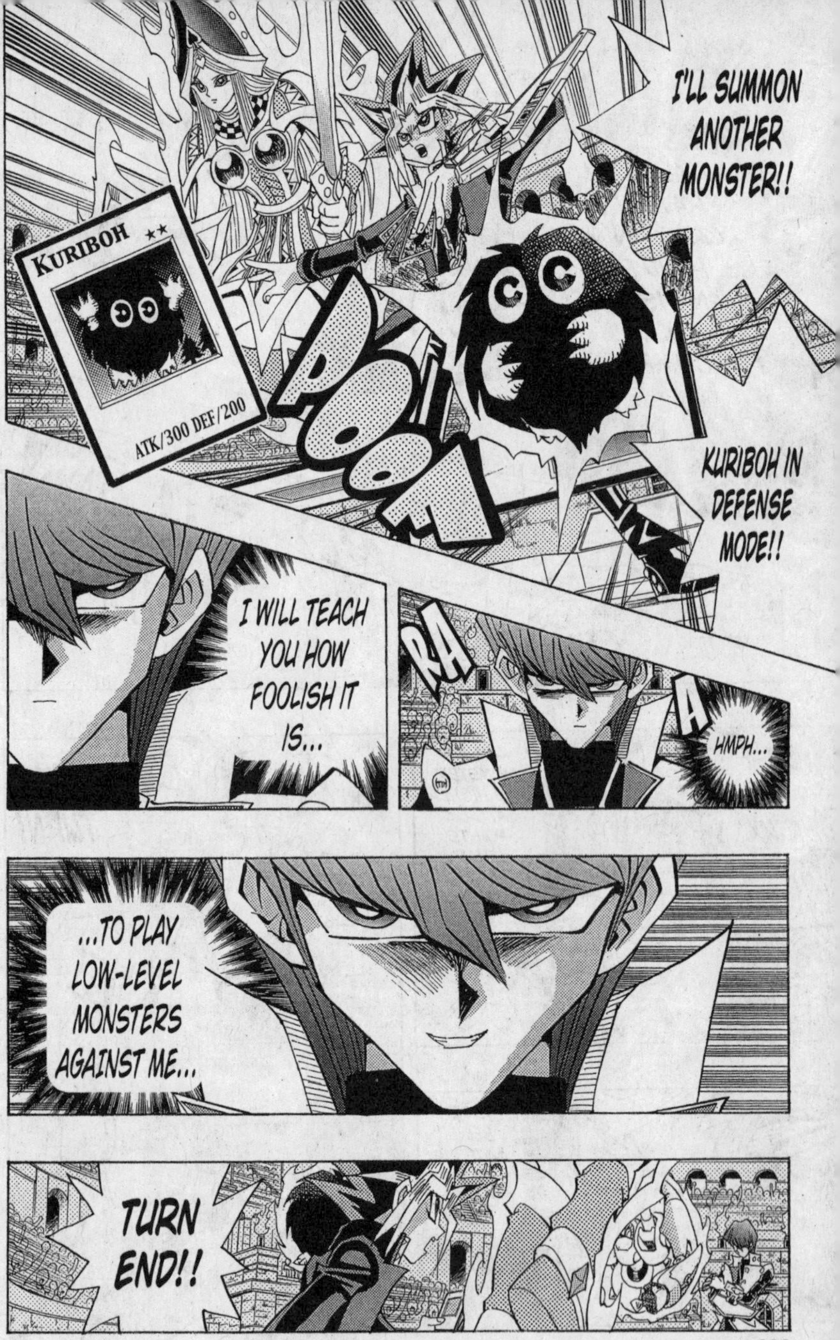
I'LL SUMMON ANOTHER MONSTER!!
KURIBOH ★★
ATK/300 DEF/200
POOF
KURIBOH IN DEFENSE MODE!!
RA
A
HMPH...
I WILL TEACH YOU HOW FOOLISH IT IS...
...TO PLAY LOW-LEVEL MONSTERS AGAINST ME...
TURN END!!

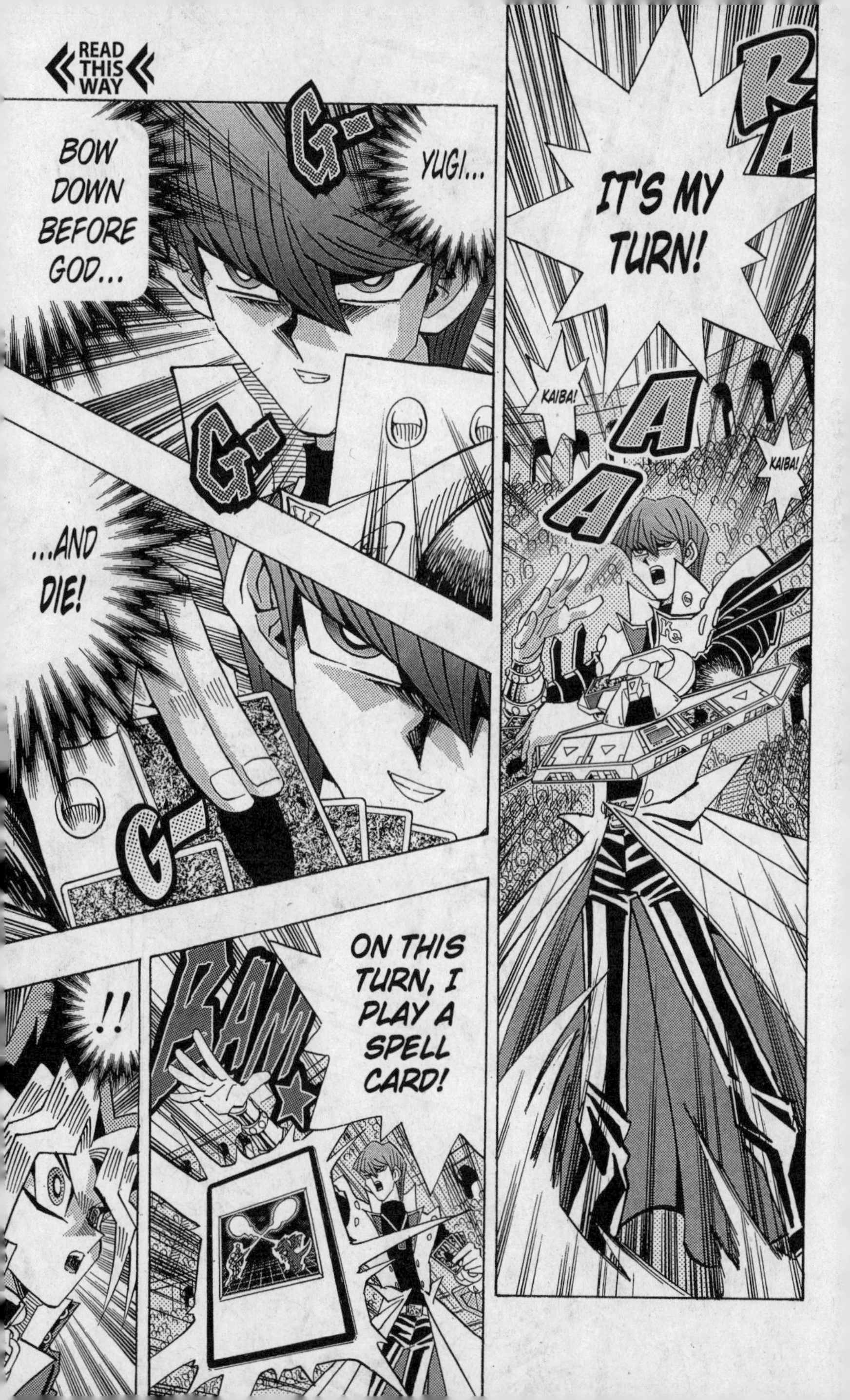
READ THIS WAY
RA
IT'S MY TURN!
KAIBA!
A
A
KAIBA!
YUGI...
G-
BOW DOWN BEFORE GOD...
G-
...AND DIE!
G-
ON THIS TURN, I PLAY A SPELL CARD!
BAM
!!

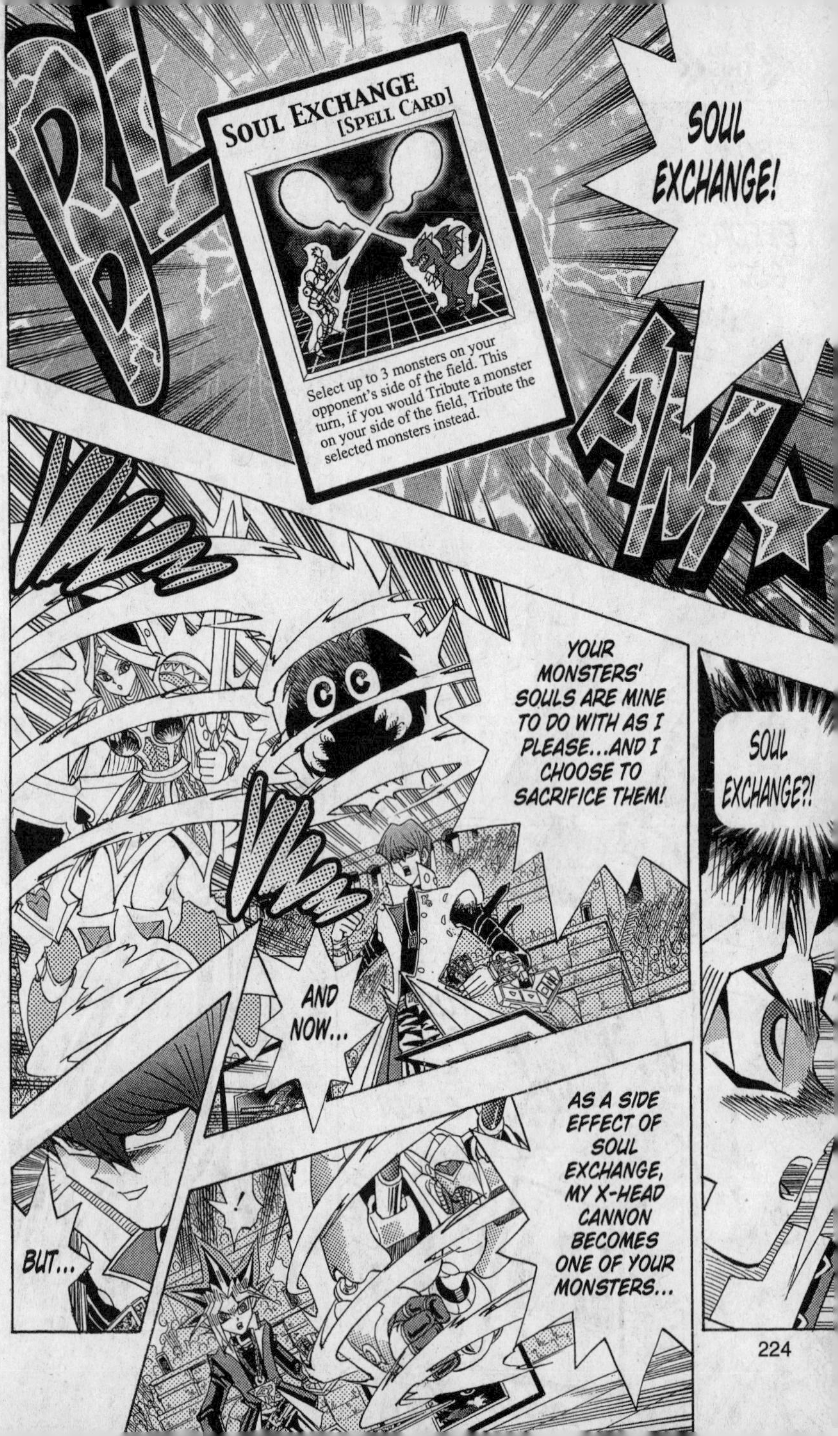
SOUL EXCHANGE!
SOUL EXCHANGE
[SPELL CARD]
Select up to 3 monsters on your opponent's side of the field. This turn, if you would Tribute a monster on your side of the field, Tribute the selected monsters instead.
SOUL EXCHANGE?!
YOUR MONSTERS' SOULS ARE MINE TO DO WITH AS I PLEASE...AND I CHOOSE TO SACRIFICE THEM!
AND NOW...
AS A SIDE EFFECT OF SOUL EXCHANGE, MY X-HEAD CANNON BECOMES ONE OF YOUR MONSTERS...
!
BUT...

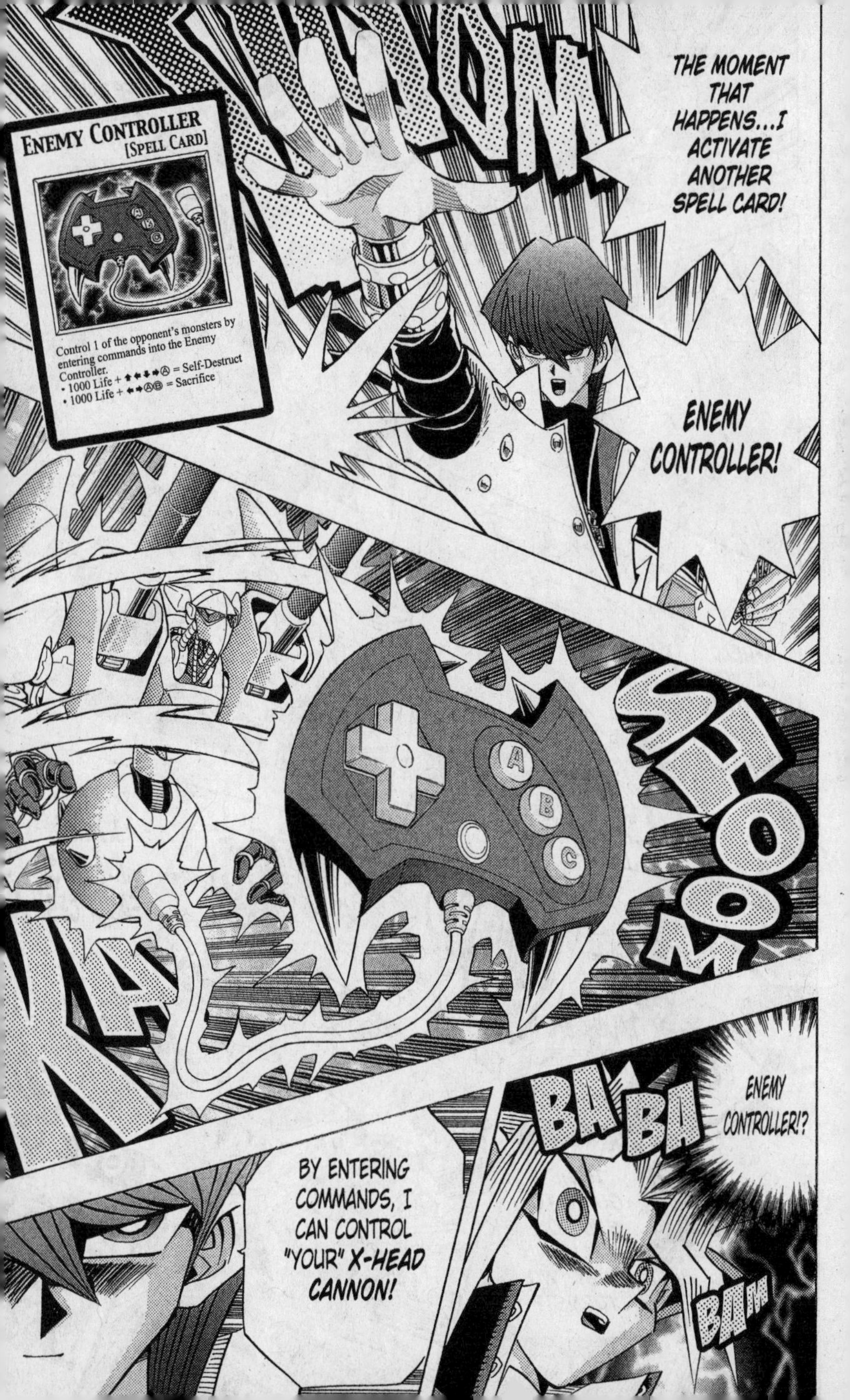
THE MOMENT THAT HAPPENS...I ACTIVATE ANOTHER SPELL CARD!
ENEMY CONTROLLER!
ENEMY CONTROLLER
[SPELL CARD]
Control 1 of the opponent's monsters by entering commands into the Enemy Controller.
• 1000 Life + ⬆⬅⬇➡Ⓐ = Self-Destruct
• 1000 Life + ⬅➡ⒶⒷ = Sacrifice
SHOOOM
A
B
C
ENEMY CONTROLLER!?
BA BA
BY ENTERING COMMANDS, I CAN CONTROL "YOUR" X-HEAD CANNON!
BAM

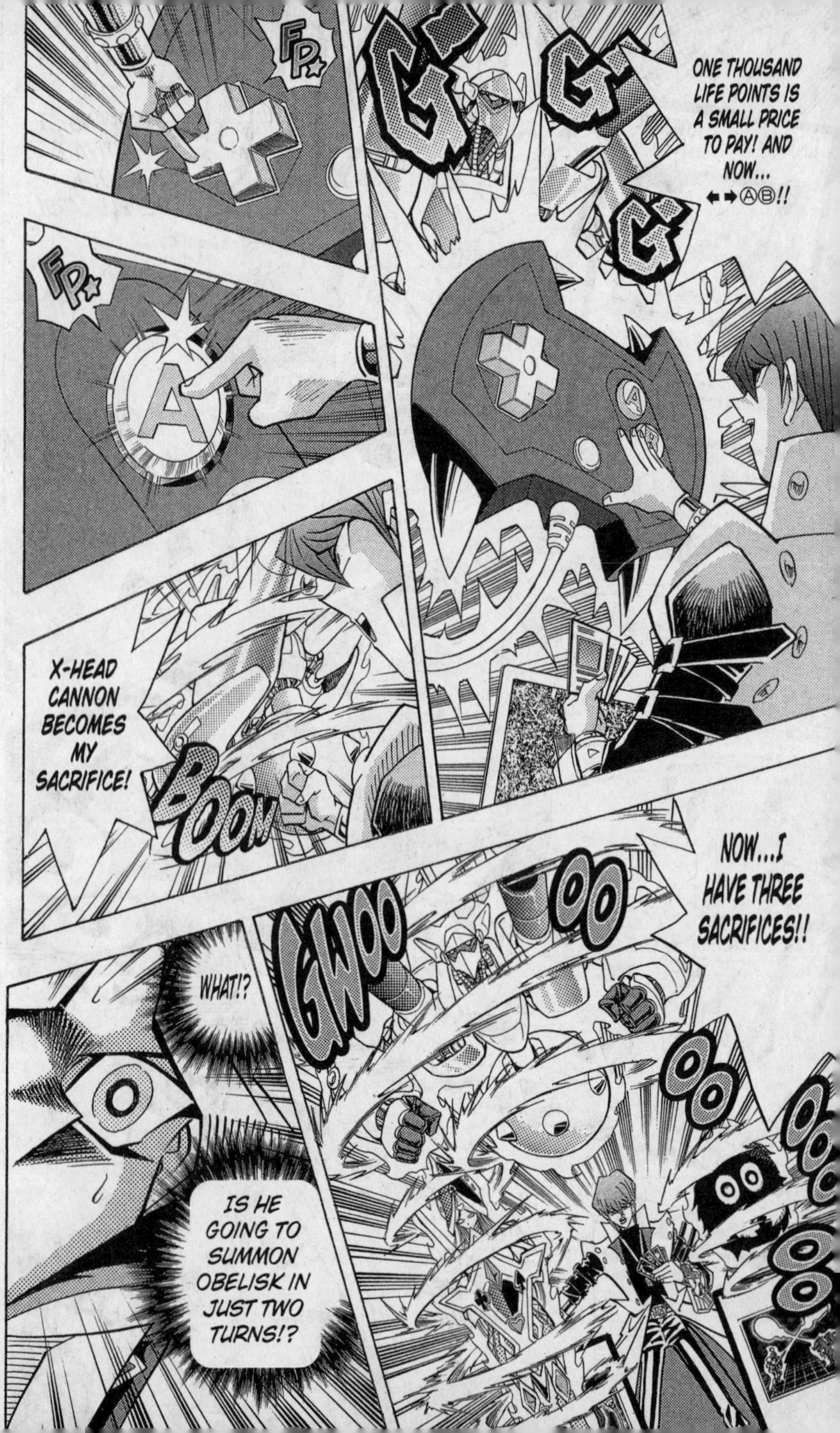

GGG
ONE THOUSAND LIFE POINTS IS A SMALL PRICE TO PAY! AND NOW... ←→ⒶⒷ!!
FP
FP
X-HEAD CANNON BECOMES MY SACRIFICE!
BOOM
NOW...I HAVE THREE SACRIFICES!!
GWOOOOOOOOO
WHAT!?
IS HE GOING TO SUMMON OBELISK IN JUST TWO TURNS!?

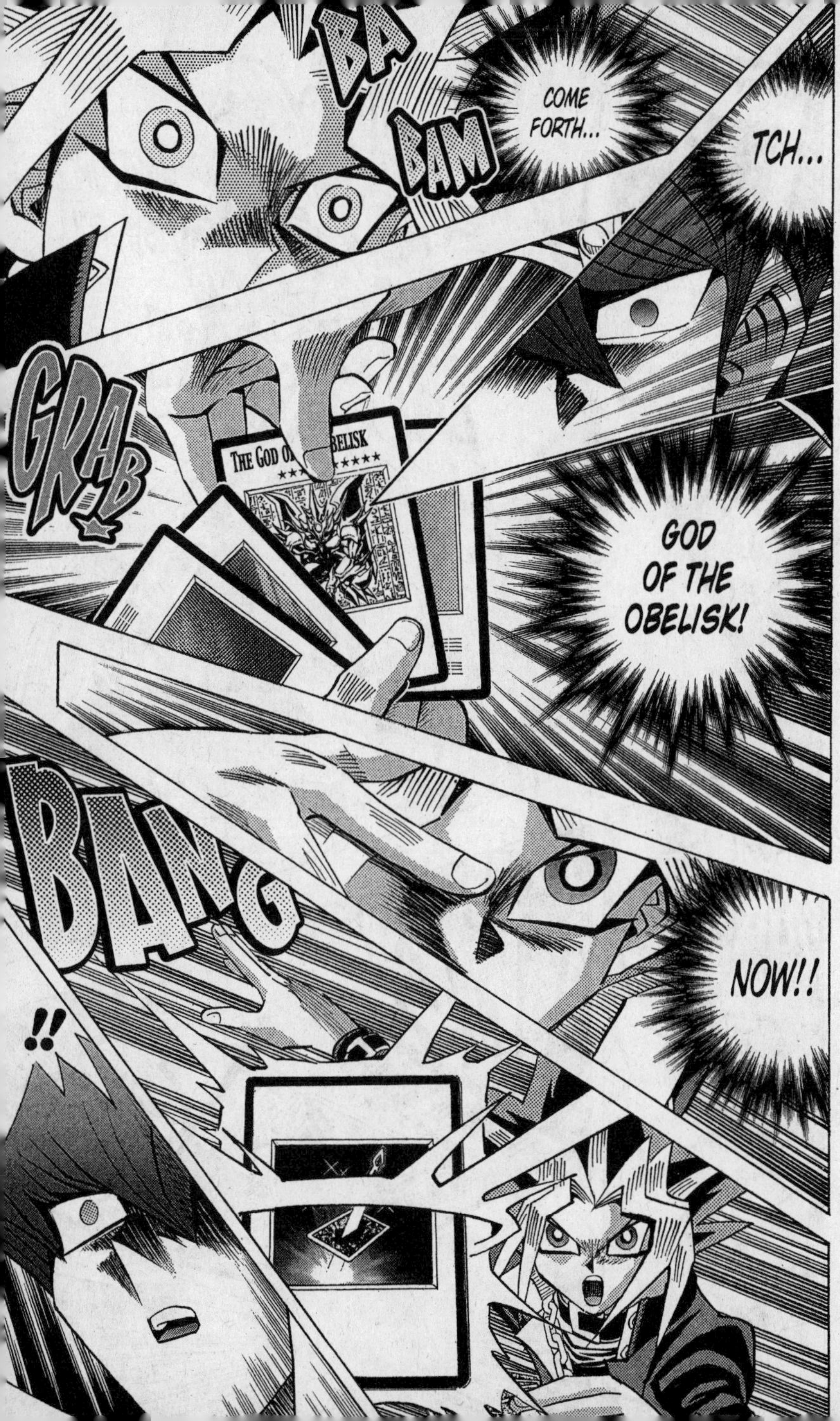
BA
BAM
COME FORTH...
TCH...
GRAB!
GOD OF THE OBELISK!
BANG
NOW!!
!!

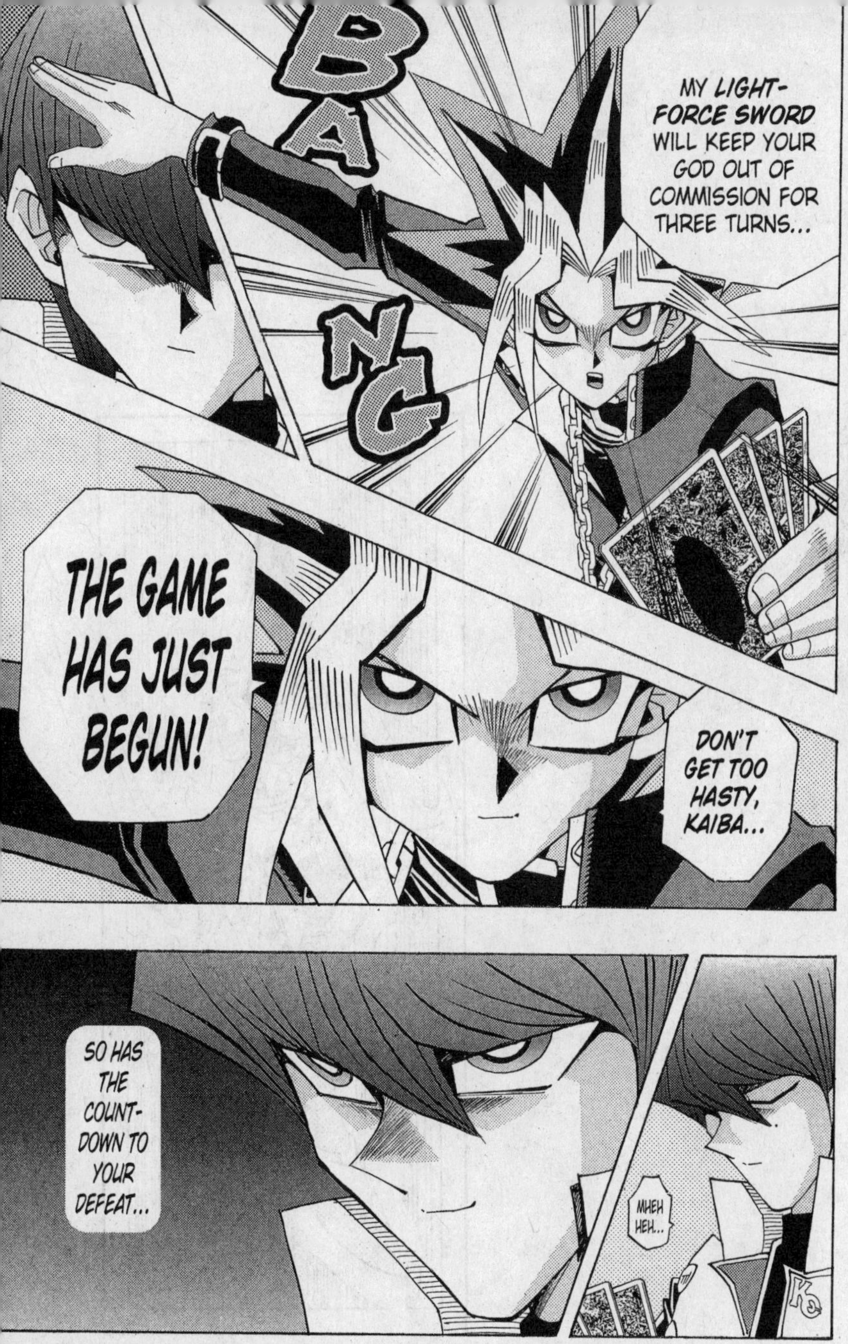
MY LIGHT-FORCE SWORD WILL KEEP YOUR GOD OUT OF COMMISSION FOR THREE TURNS...
BANG
DON'T GET TOO HASTY, KAIBA...
THE GAME HAS JUST BEGUN!
MHEH HEH...
SO HAS THE COUNT-DOWN TO YOUR DEFEAT...

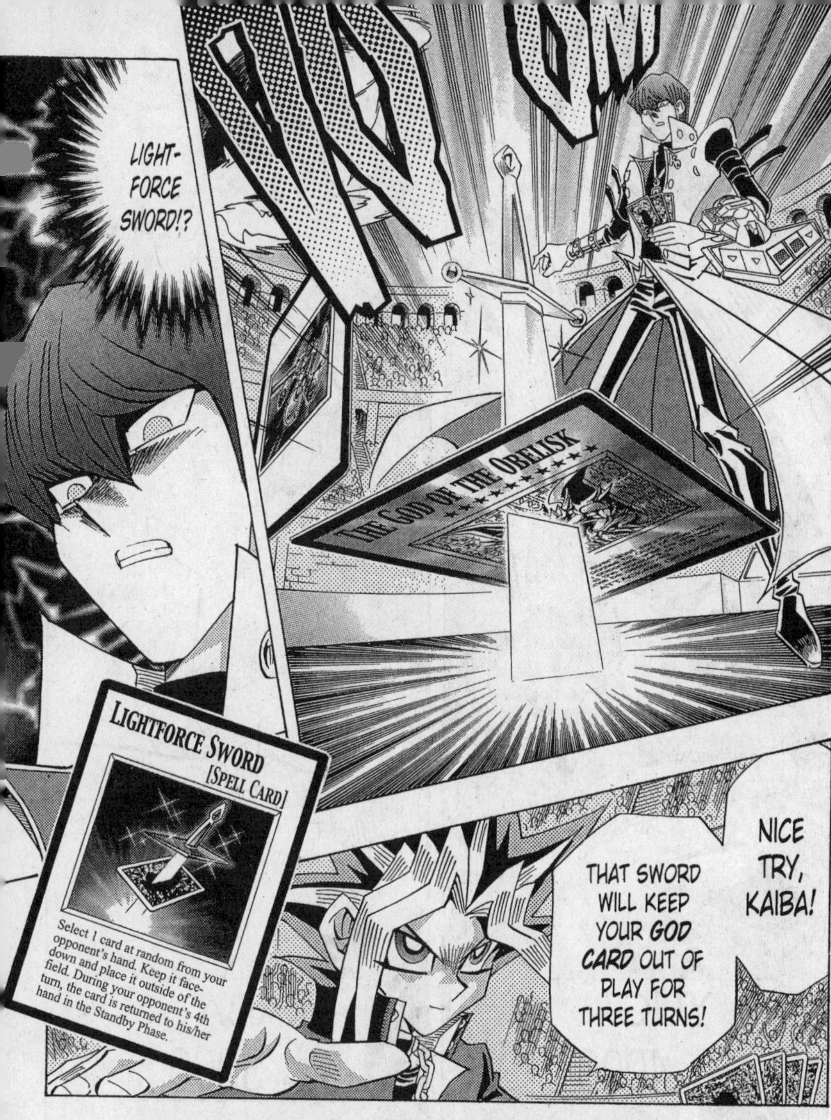
THE GOD OF THE OBELISK
LIGHT-FORCE SWORD!?
LIGHTFORCE SWORD
[SPELL CARD]
Select 1 card at random from your opponent's hand. Keep it face-down and place it outside of the field. During your opponent's 4th turn, the card is returned to his/her hand in the Standby Phase.
NICE TRY, KAIBA!
THAT SWORD WILL KEEP YOUR GOD CARD OUT OF PLAY FOR THREE TURNS!

DUEL 253: GOD IN HAND!!

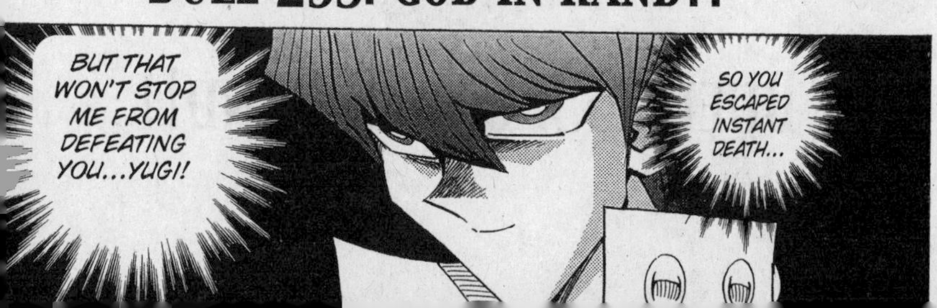
SO YOU ESCAPED INSTANT DEATH...
BUT THAT WON'T STOP ME FROM DEFEATING YOU...YUGI!

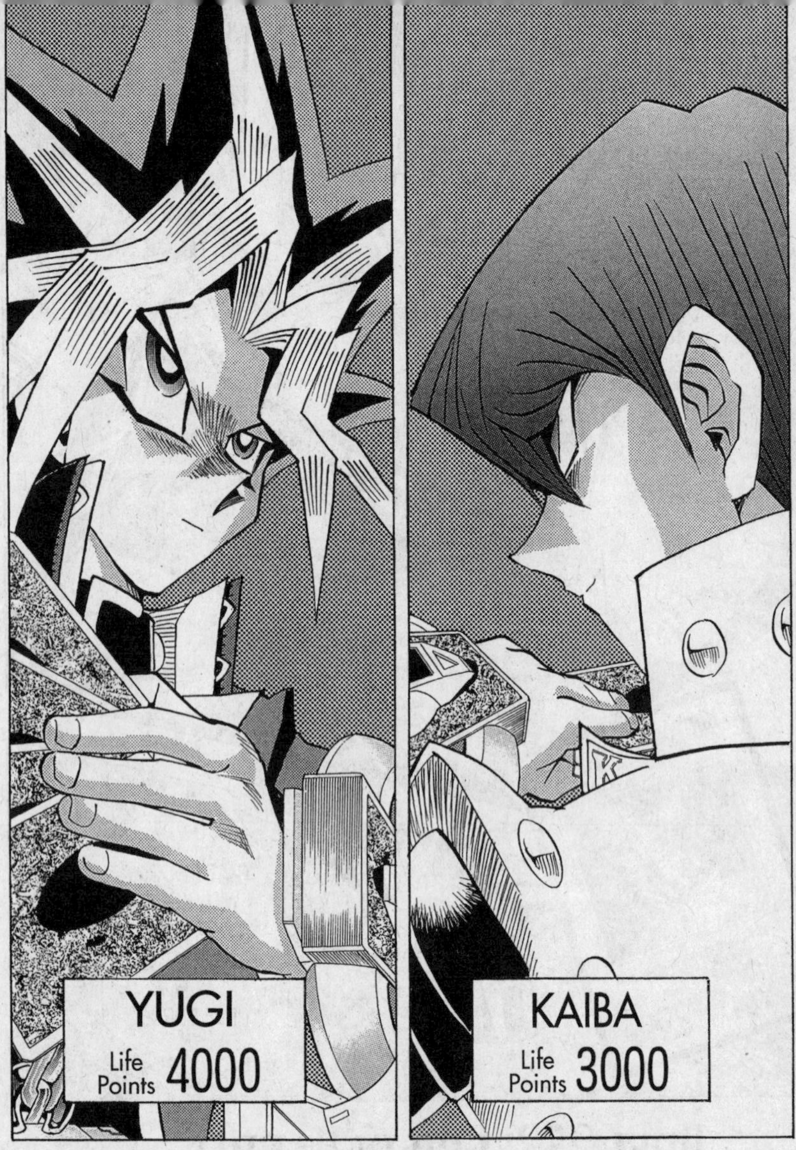
KAIBA
Life Points 3000
YUGI
Life Points 4000

Duel 253: God in Hand!!

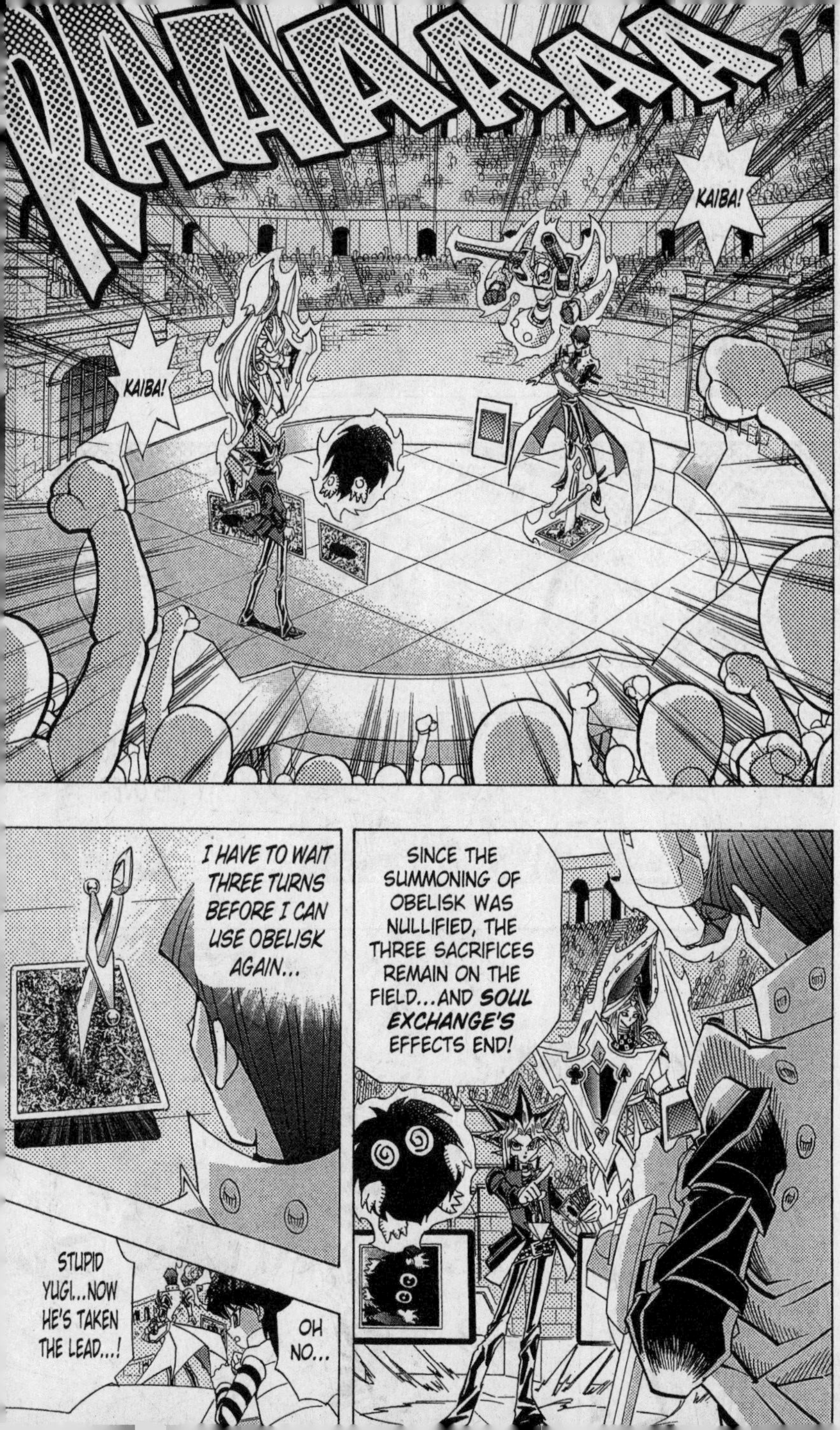
KAAAAA
KAIBA!
KAIBA!
SINCE THE SUMMONING OF OBELISK WAS NULLIFIED, THE THREE SACRIFICES REMAIN ON THE FIELD...AND SOUL EXCHANGE'S EFFECTS END!
I HAVE TO WAIT THREE TURNS BEFORE I CAN USE OBELISK AGAIN...
OH NO...
STUPID YUGI...NOW HE'S TAKEN THE LEAD...!

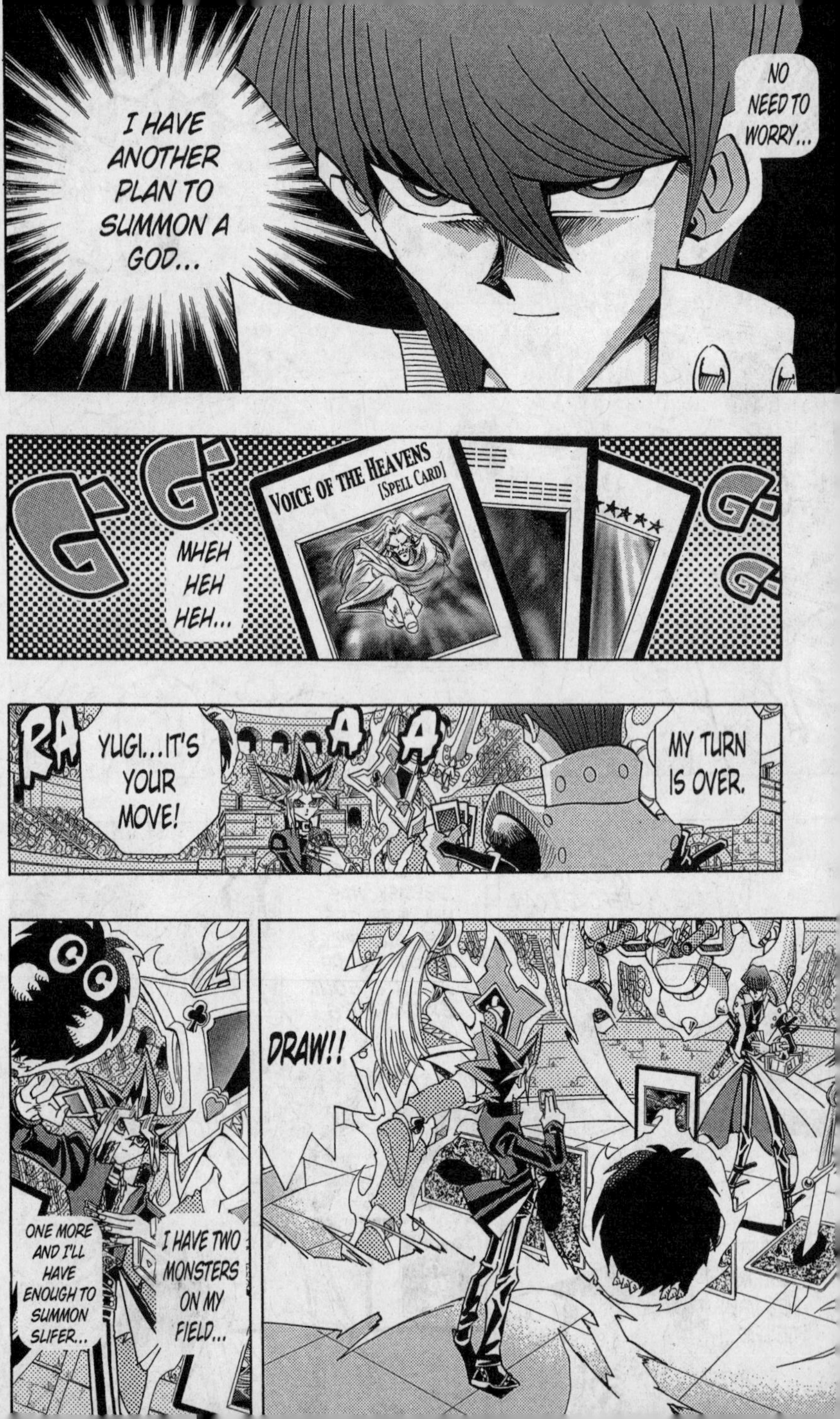
NO NEED TO WORRY...
I HAVE ANOTHER PLAN TO SUMMON A GOD...
G-
G-
VOICE OF THE HEAVENS
[SPELL CARD]
MHEH HEH HEH...
G-
G-
MY TURN IS OVER.
A
A
YUGI...IT'S YOUR MOVE!
RA
DRAW!!
I HAVE TWO MONSTERS ON MY FIELD...
ONE MORE AND I'LL HAVE ENOUGH TO SUMMON SLIFER...

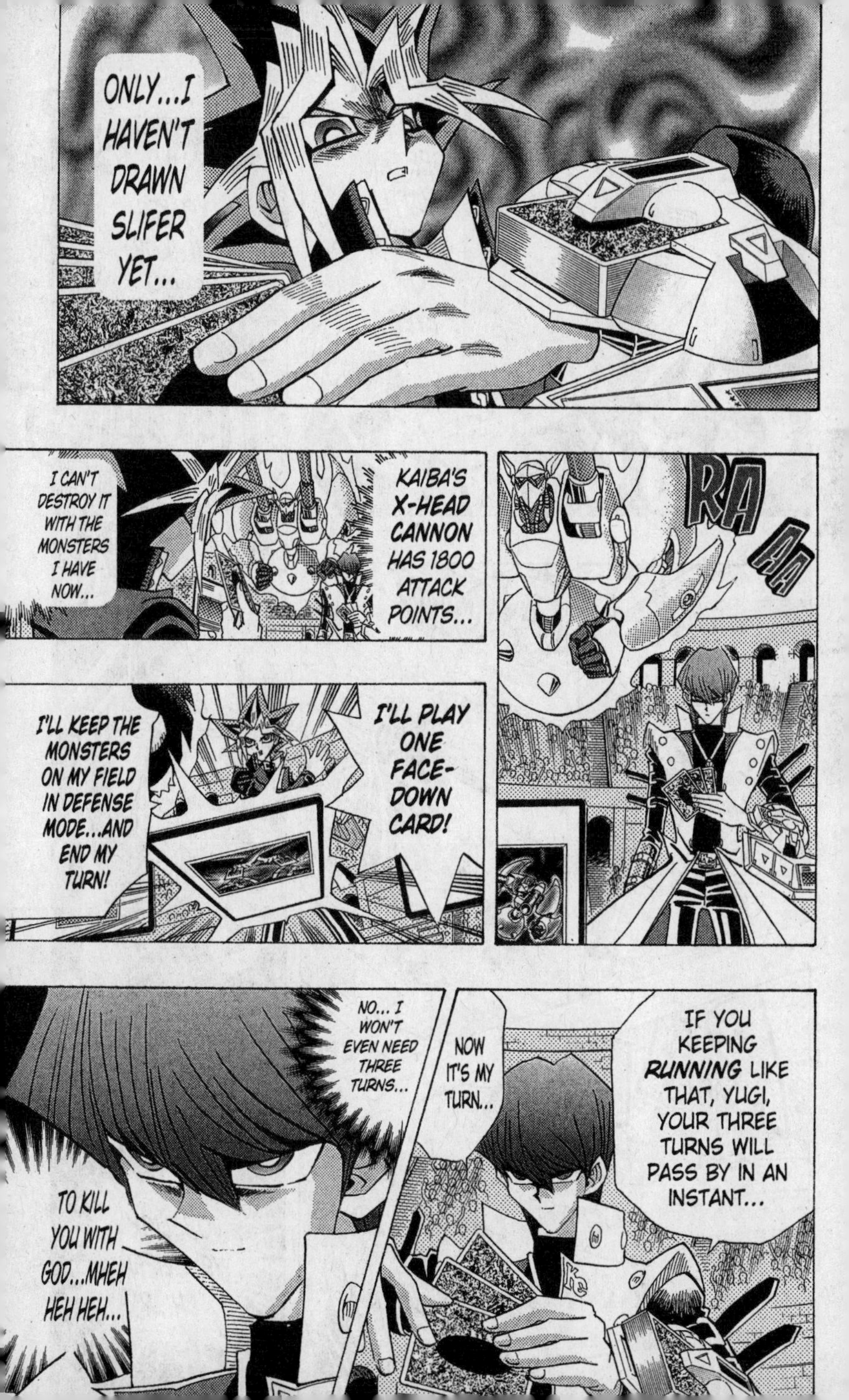

ONLY...I HAVEN'T DRAWN SLIFER YET...
RA AA
KAIBA'S X-HEAD CANNON HAS 1800 ATTACK POINTS...
I CAN'T DESTROY IT WITH THE MONSTERS I HAVE NOW...
I'LL PLAY ONE FACE-DOWN CARD!
I'LL KEEP THE MONSTERS ON MY FIELD IN DEFENSE MODE...AND END MY TURN!
IF YOU KEEPING RUNNING LIKE THAT, YUGI, YOUR THREE TURNS WILL PASS BY IN AN INSTANT...
NOW IT'S MY TURN...
NO... I WON'T EVEN NEED THREE TURNS...
TO KILL YOU WITH GOD...MHEH HEH HEH...

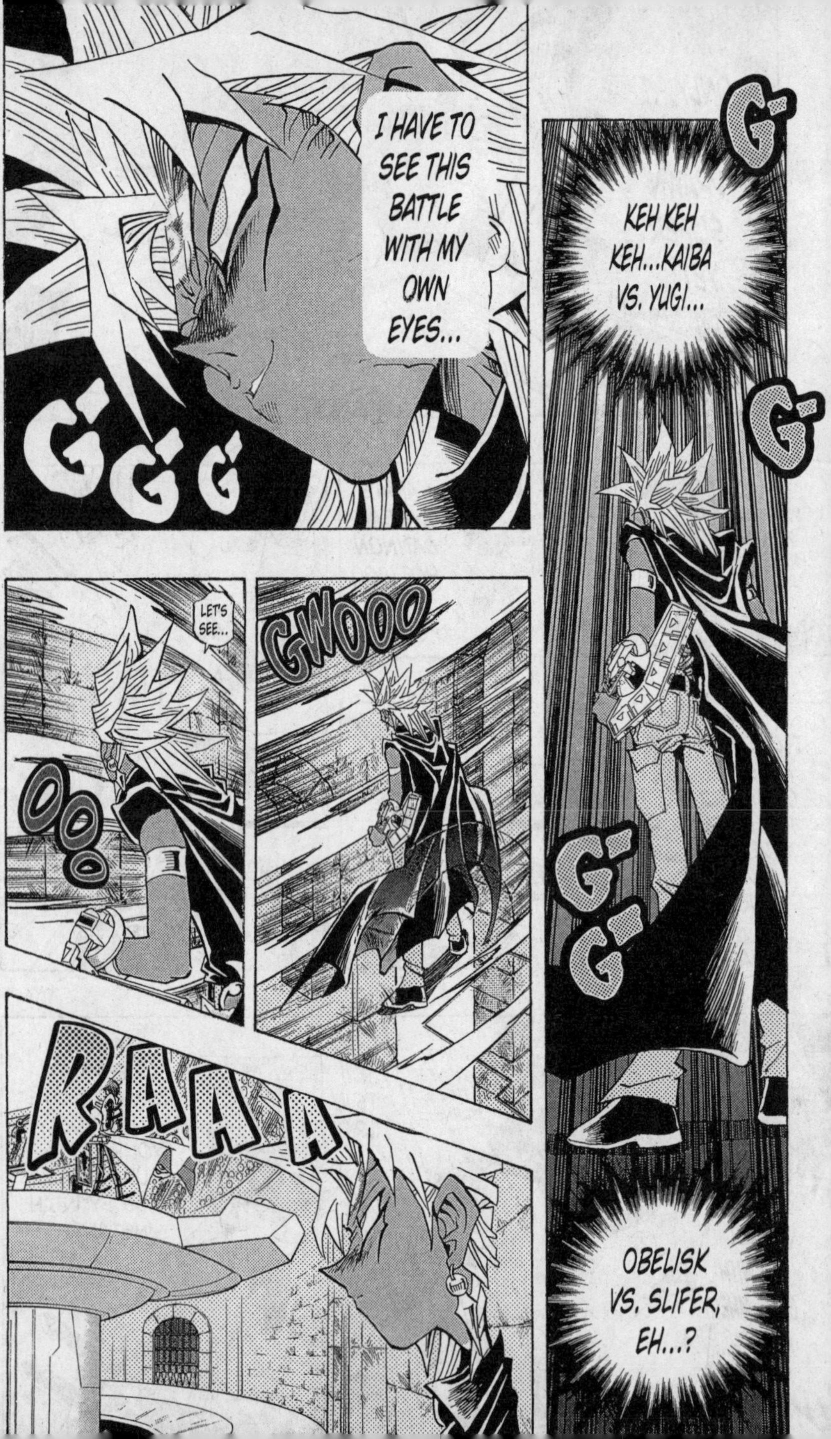
G
KEH KEH KEH...KAIBA VS. YUGI...
G
G G
OBELISK VS. SLIFER, EH...?
I HAVE TO SEE THIS BATTLE WITH MY OWN EYES...
GGG
GWOOO
LET'S SEE...
OOO
RAAA

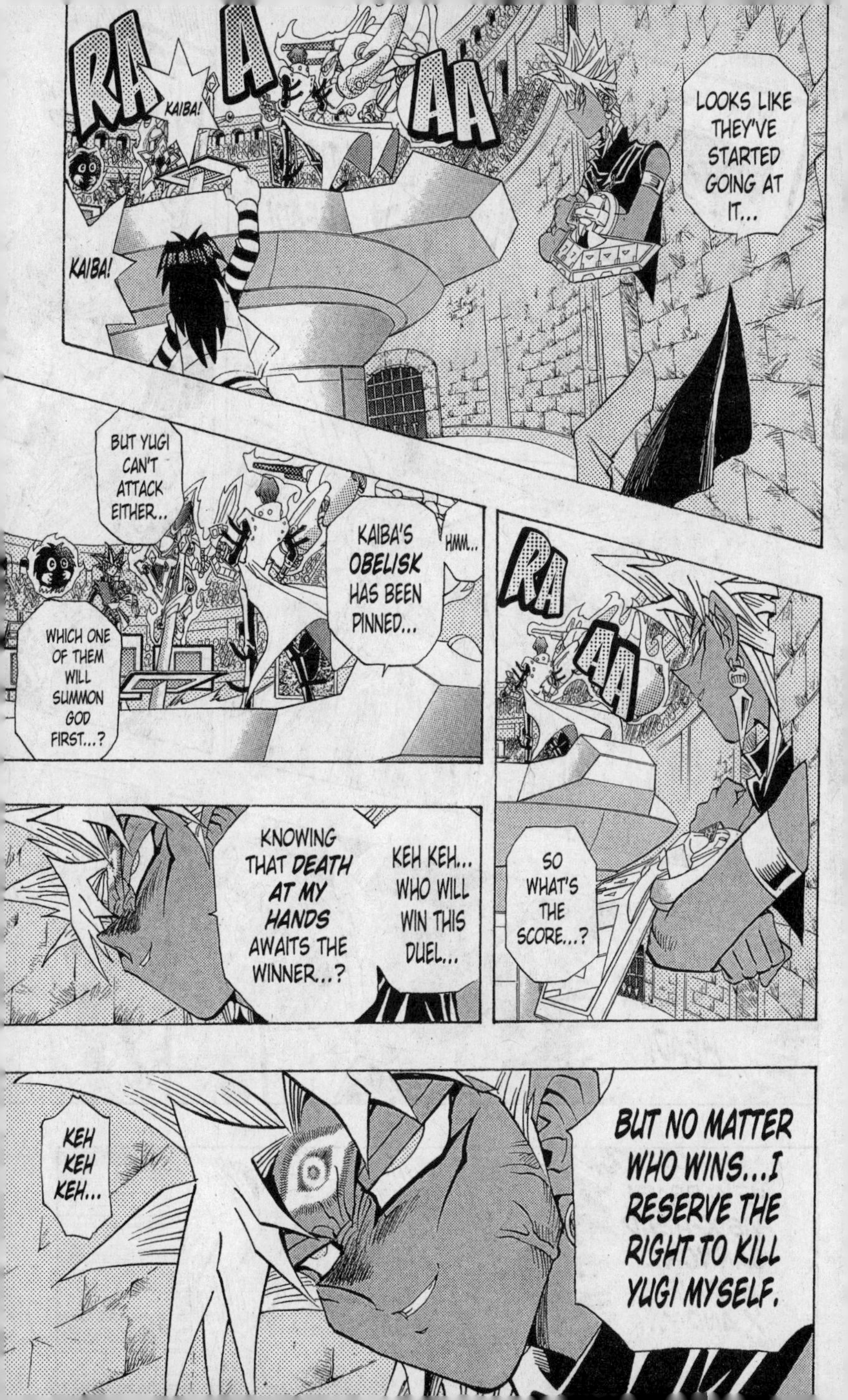
LOOKS LIKE THEY'VE STARTED GOING AT IT...
RA A AA
KAIBA!
KAIBA!
RA AA
SO WHAT'S THE SCORE...?
HMM...
KAIBA'S OBELISK HAS BEEN PINNED...
BUT YUGI CAN'T ATTACK EITHER...
WHICH ONE OF THEM WILL SUMMON GOD FIRST...?
KEH KEH... WHO WILL WIN THIS DUEL...
KNOWING THAT DEATH AT MY HANDS AWAITS THE WINNER...?
BUT NO MATTER WHO WINS...I RESERVE THE RIGHT TO KILL YUGI MYSELF.
KEH KEH KEH...

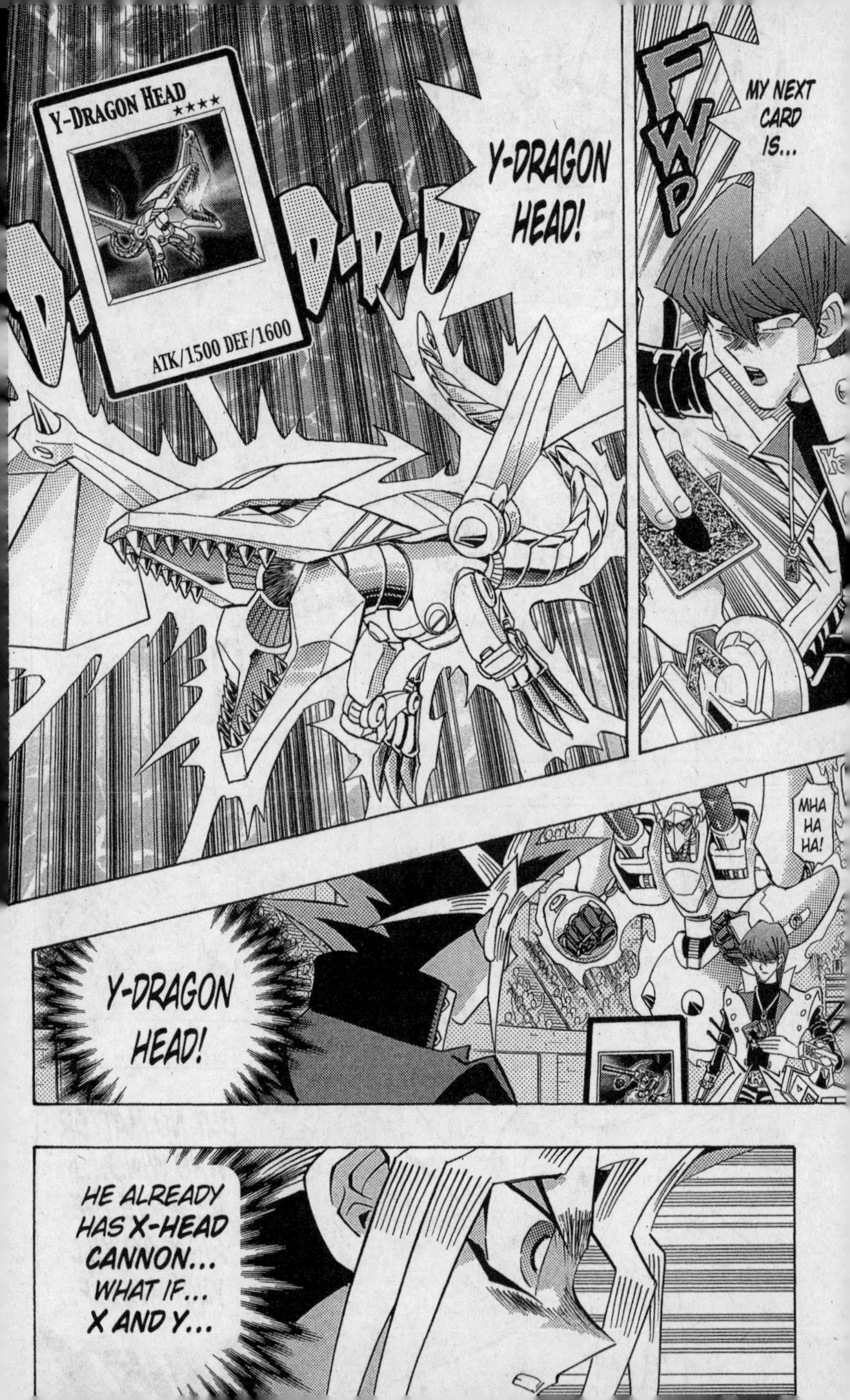
FWP
MY NEXT CARD IS...
Y-DRAGON HEAD!
Y-DRAGON HEAD ★★★★
ATK/1500 DEF/1600
D-D-D
MHA HA HA!
Y-DRAGON HEAD!
HE ALREADY HAS X-HEAD CANNON... WHAT IF... X AND Y...

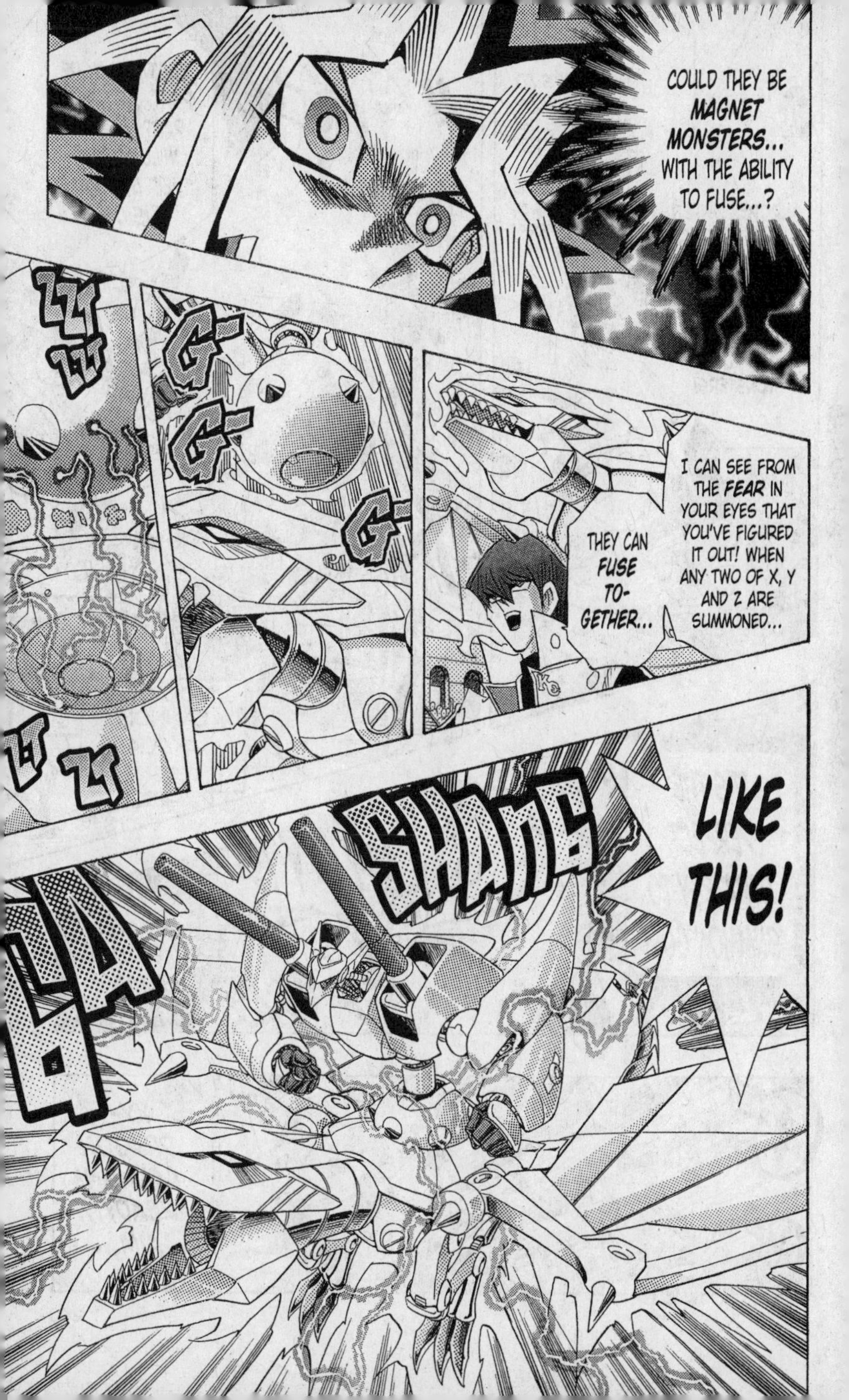
COULD THEY BE MAGNET MONSTERS... WITH THE ABILITY TO FUSE...?
I CAN SEE FROM THE FEAR IN YOUR EYES THAT YOU'VE FIGURED IT OUT! WHEN ANY TWO OF X, Y AND Z ARE SUMMONED...
THEY CAN FUSE TO-GETHER...
G- G- G-
LIKE THIS!
SHANG

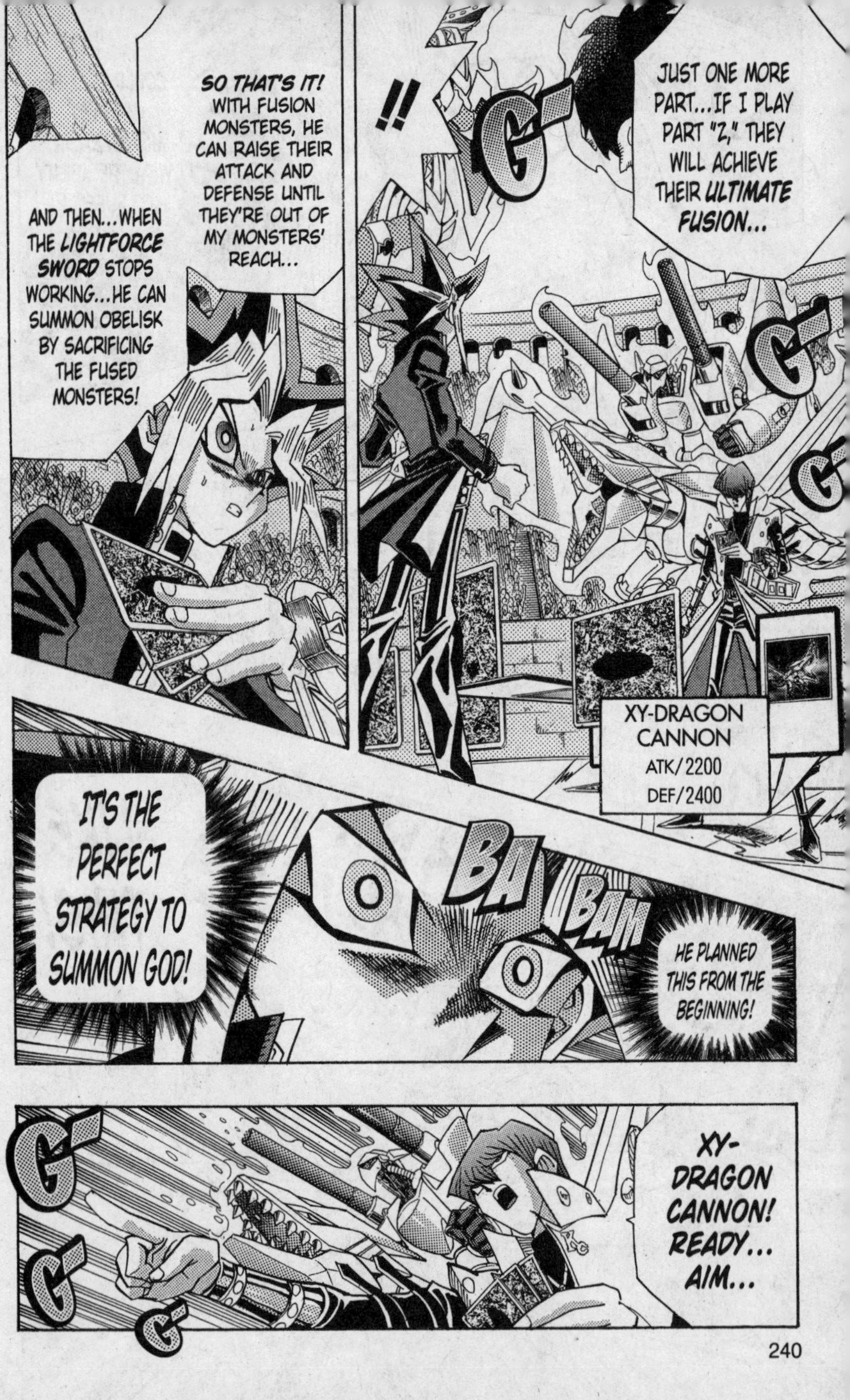
JUST ONE MORE PART...IF I PLAY PART "Z," THEY WILL ACHIEVE THEIR ULTIMATE FUSION...
!!
G
G
G
XY-DRAGON CANNON ATK/2200 DEF/2400
SO THAT'S IT! WITH FUSION MONSTERS, HE CAN RAISE THEIR ATTACK AND DEFENSE UNTIL THEY'RE OUT OF MY MONSTERS' REACH...
AND THEN...WHEN THE LIGHTFORCE SWORD STOPS WORKING...HE CAN SUMMON OBELISK BY SACRIFICING THE FUSED MONSTERS!
HE PLANNED THIS FROM THE BEGINNING!
BA BAM
IT'S THE PERFECT STRATEGY TO SUMMON GOD!
XY-DRAGON CANNON! READY... AIM...
G
G
G

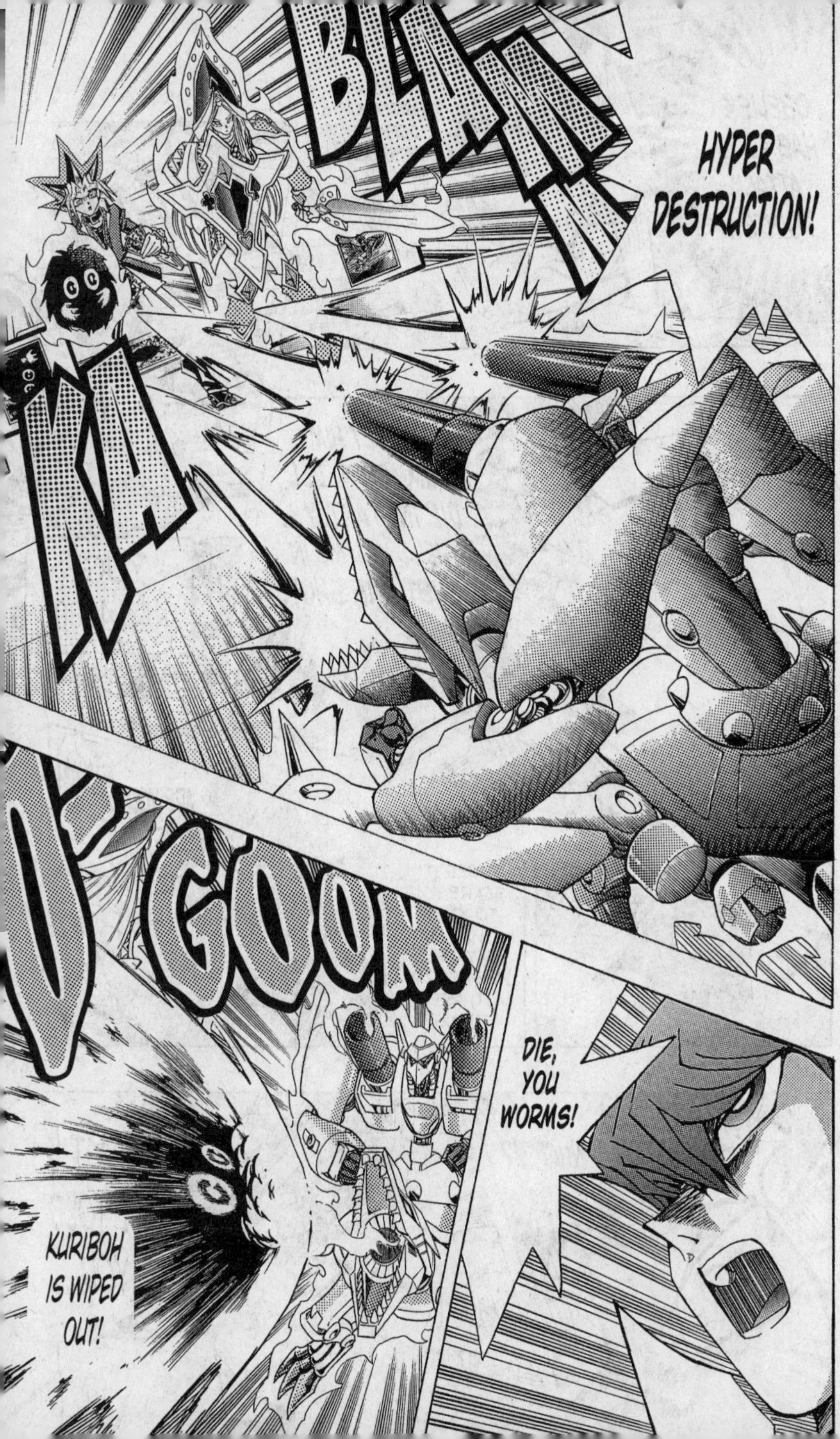
HYPER DESTRUCTION!
BLAM
KA
DIE, YOU WORMS!
GOOM
KURIBOH IS WIPED OUT!

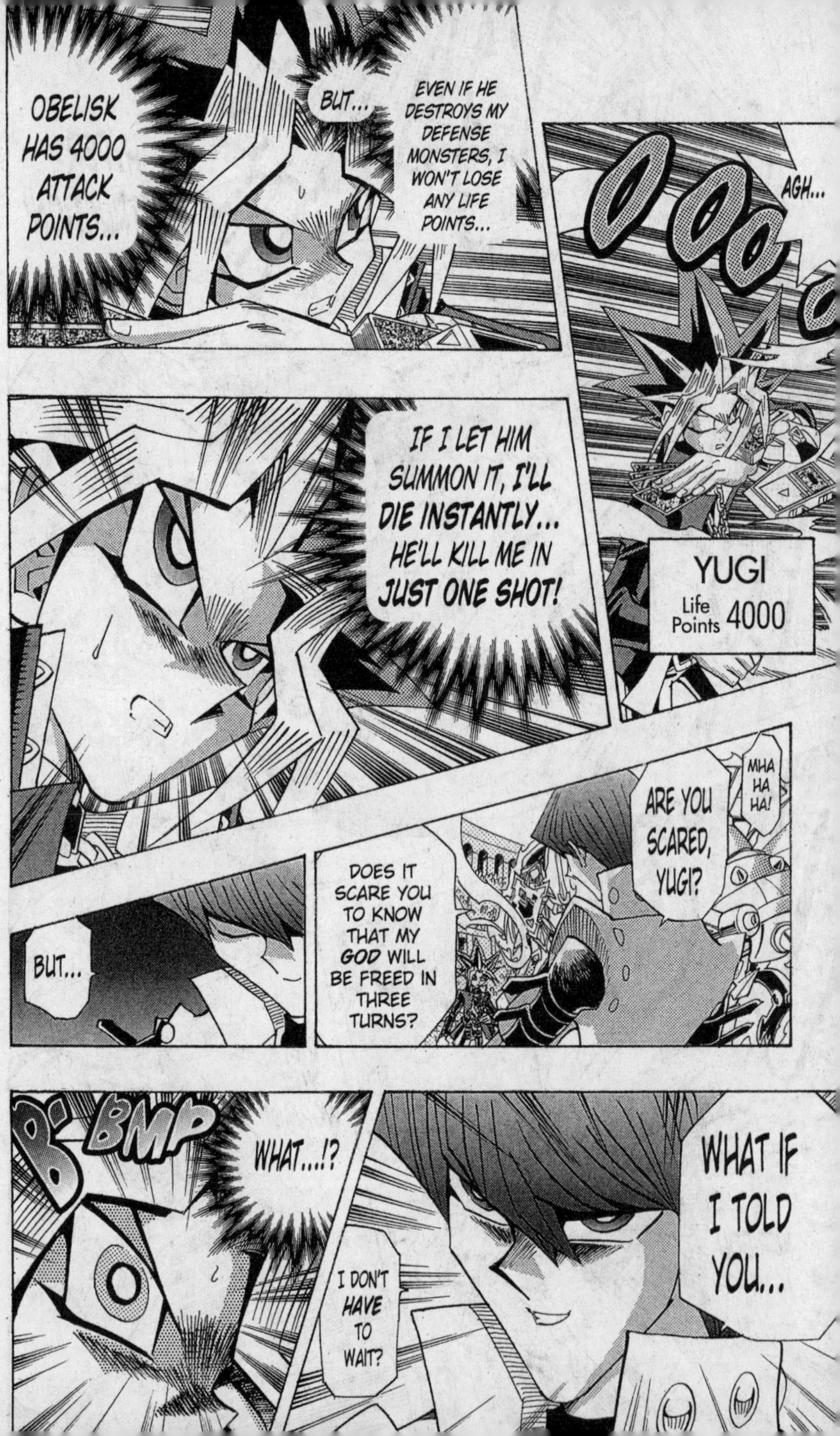
OOO
AGH...
YUGI Life Points 4000
EVEN IF HE DESTROYS MY DEFENSE MONSTERS, I WON'T LOSE ANY LIFE POINTS...
BUT...
OBELISK HAS 4000 ATTACK POINTS...
IF I LET HIM SUMMON IT, I'LL DIE INSTANTLY... HE'LL KILL ME IN JUST ONE SHOT!
MHA HA HA!
ARE YOU SCARED, YUGI?
DOES IT SCARE YOU TO KNOW THAT MY GOD WILL BE FREED IN THREE TURNS?
BUT...
WHAT IF I TOLD YOU...
I DON'T HAVE TO WAIT?
B BMP
WHAT...!?

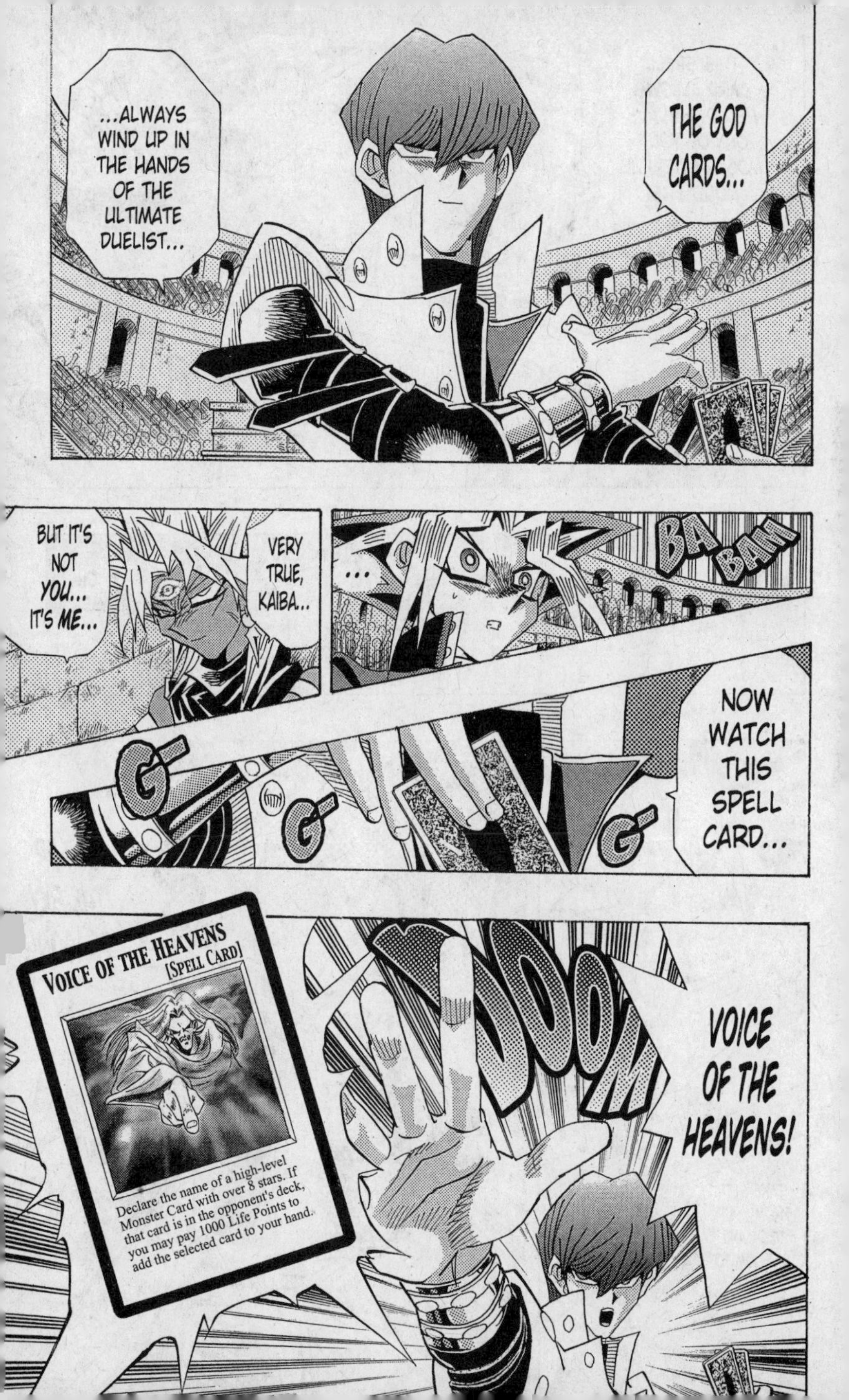
THE GOD CARDS...
...ALWAYS WIND UP IN THE HANDS OF THE ULTIMATE DUELIST...
BA BAM
...
VERY TRUE, KAIBA...
BUT IT'S NOT YOU... IT'S ME...
NOW WATCH THIS SPELL CARD...
G
G
G
VOICE OF THE HEAVENS!
DOOM
VOICE OF THE HEAVENS
[SPELL CARD]
Declare the name of a high-level Monster Card with over 8 stars. If that card is in the opponent's deck, you may pay 1000 Life Points to add the selected card to your hand.

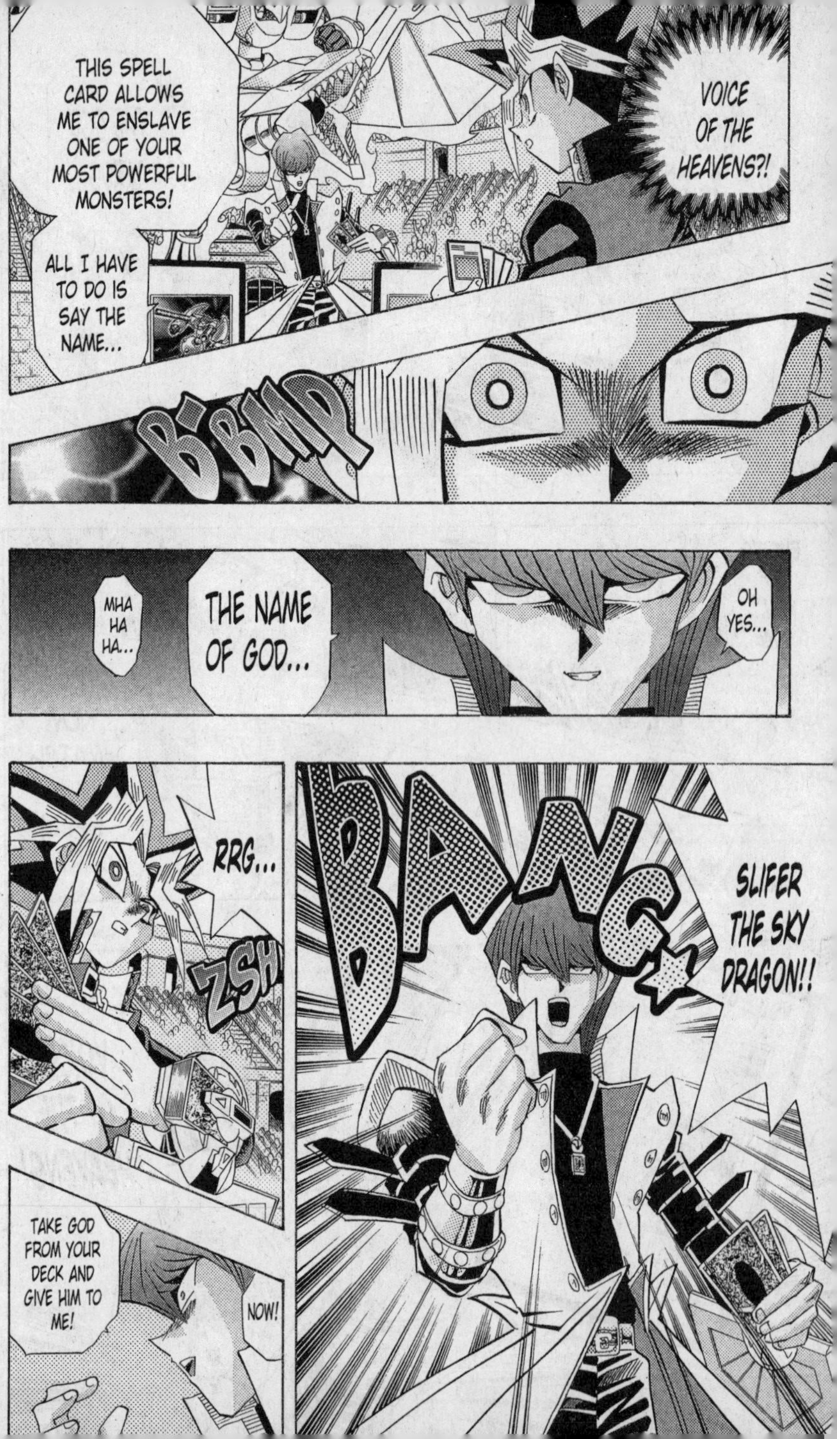
VOICE OF THE HEAVENS?!
THIS SPELL CARD ALLOWS ME TO ENSLAVE ONE OF YOUR MOST POWERFUL MONSTERS!
ALL I HAVE TO DO IS SAY THE NAME...
B'BMP
OH YES...
THE NAME OF GOD...
MHA HA HA...
BAWG
SLIFER THE SKY DRAGON!!
RRG...
ZSH
TAKE GOD FROM YOUR DECK AND GIVE HIM TO ME!
NOW!

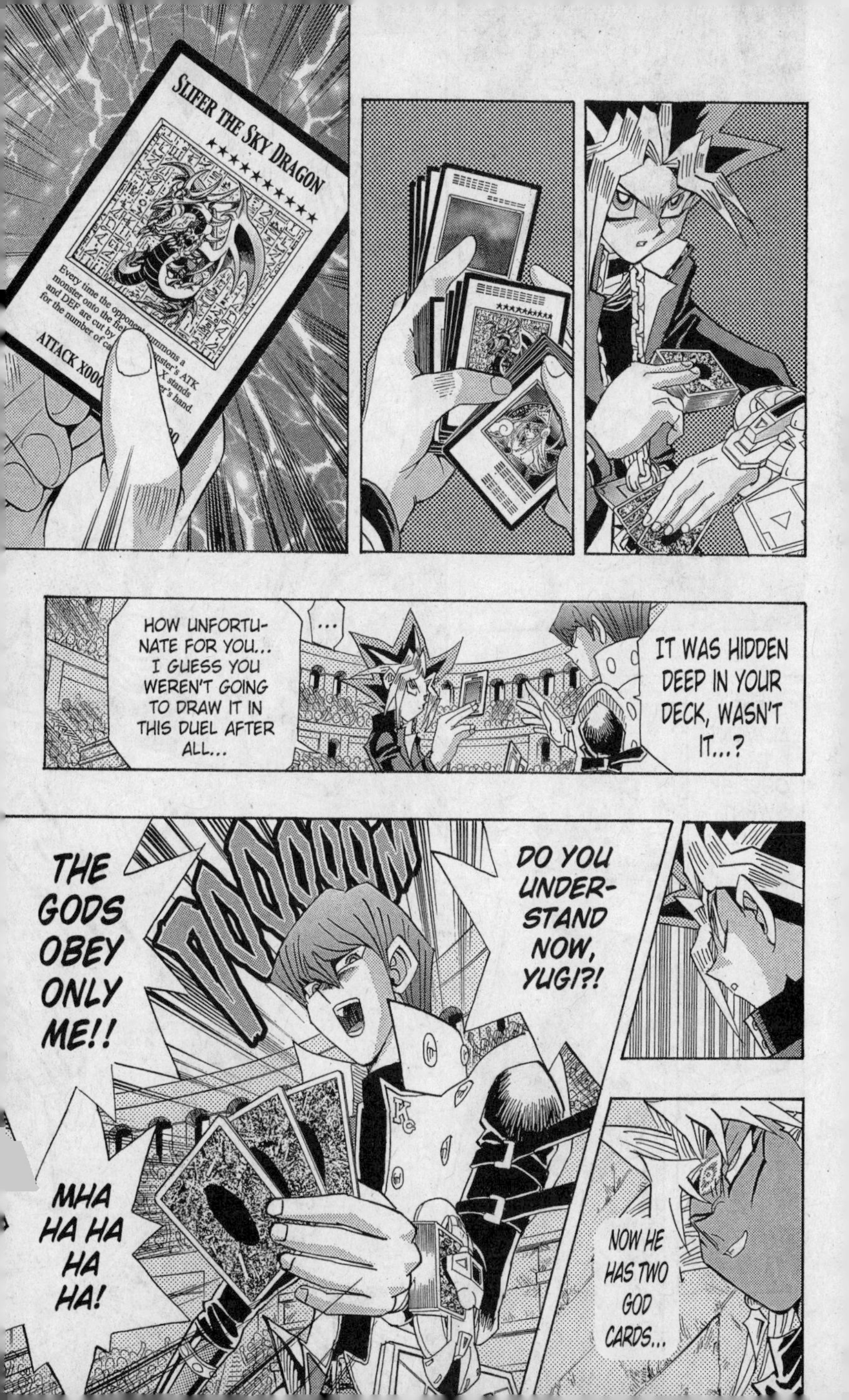
SLIFER THE SKY DRAGON
IT WAS HIDDEN DEEP IN YOUR DECK, WASN'T IT...?
...
HOW UNFORTUNATE FOR YOU... I GUESS YOU WEREN'T GOING TO DRAW IT IN THIS DUEL AFTER ALL...
NOW HE HAS TWO GOD CARDS...
DO YOU UNDERSTAND NOW, YUGI?!
DOOOOOOM
THE GODS OBEY ONLY ME!!
MHA HA HA HA HA!

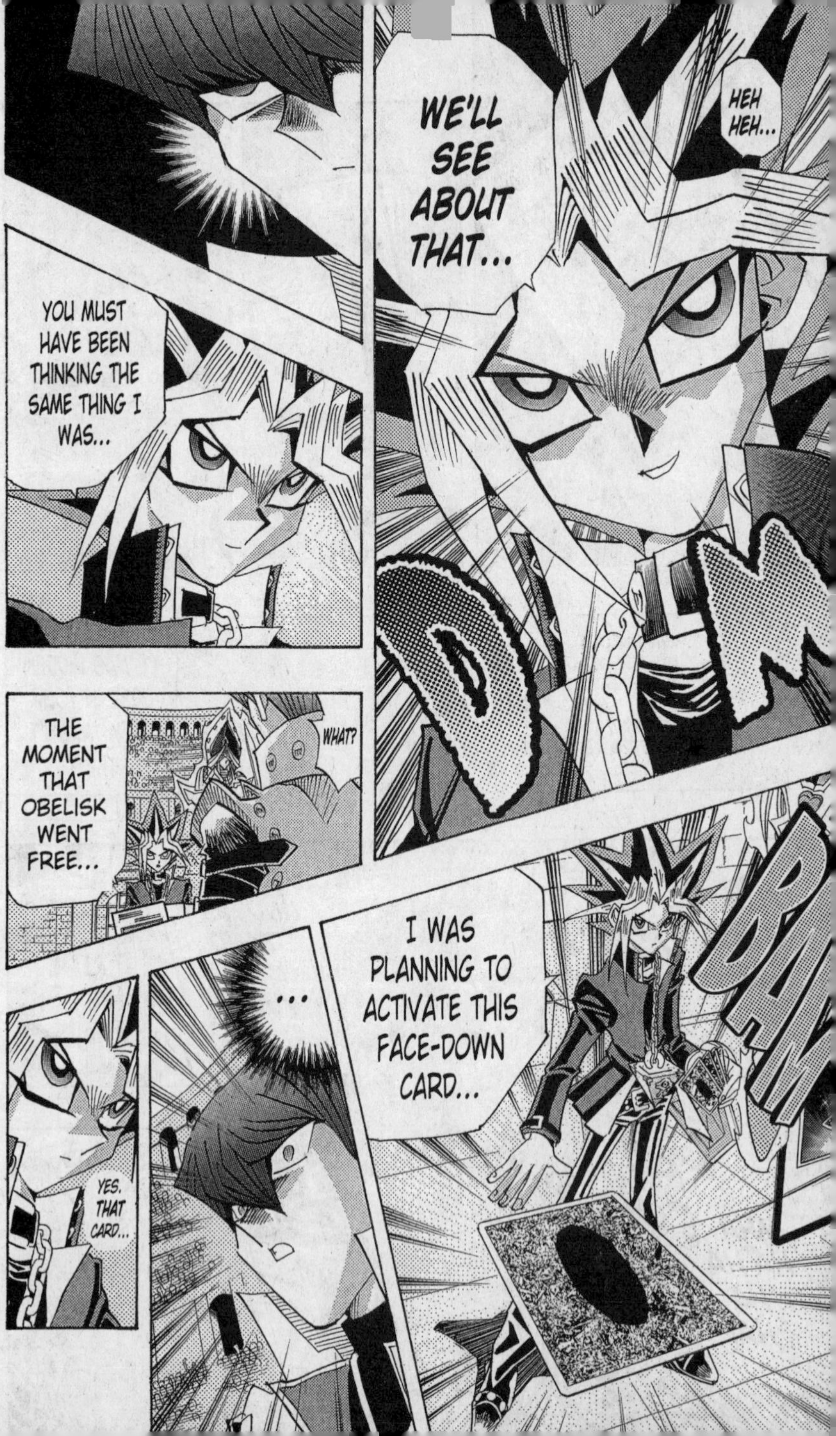
HEH HEH...
WE'LL SEE ABOUT THAT...
YOU MUST HAVE BEEN THINKING THE SAME THING I WAS...
WHAT?
THE MOMENT THAT OBELISK WENT FREE...
I WAS PLANNING TO ACTIVATE THIS FACE-DOWN CARD...
...
YES. THAT CARD...

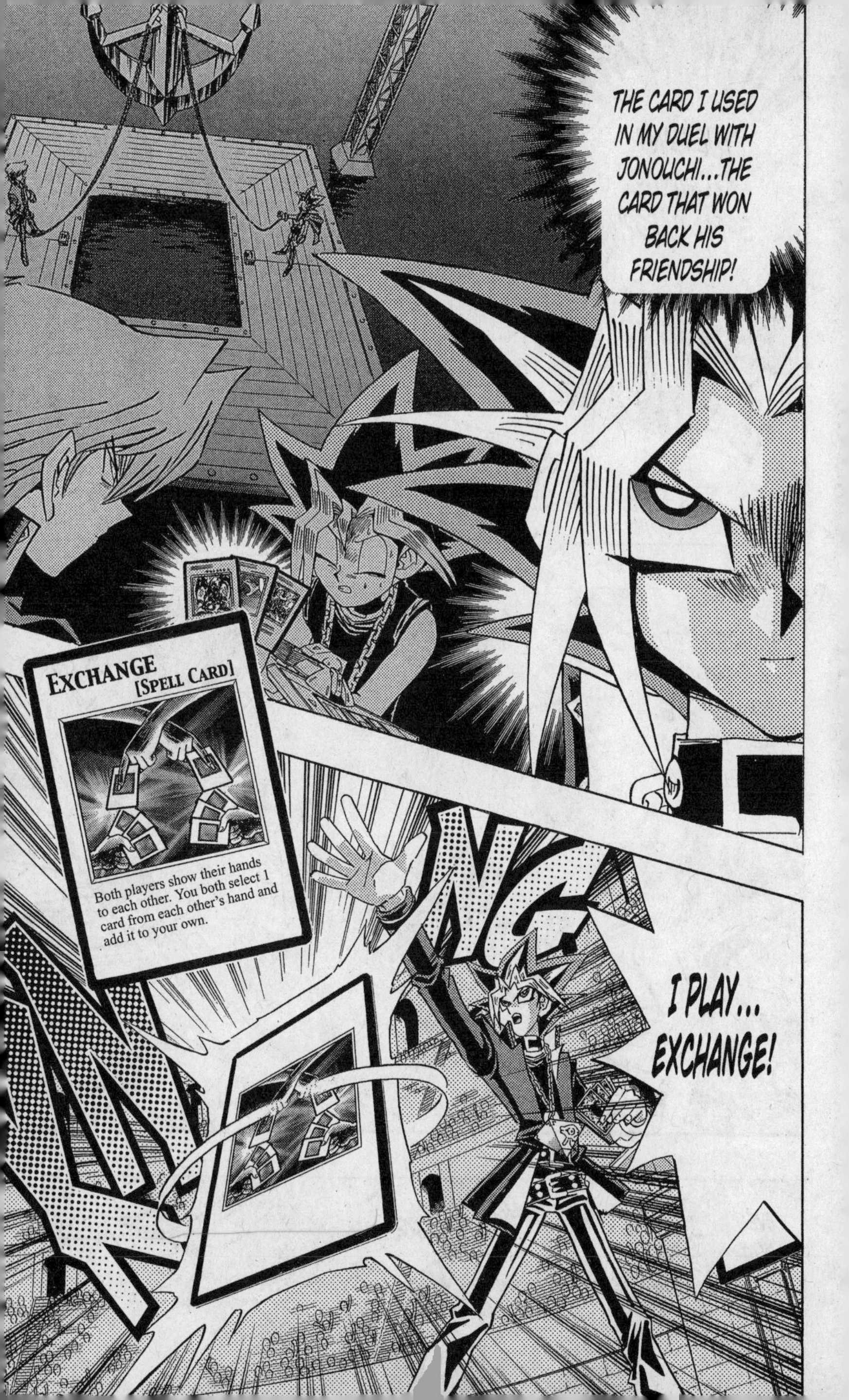
THE CARD I USED IN MY DUEL WITH JONOUCHI...THE CARD THAT WON BACK HIS FRIENDSHIP!
I PLAY... EXCHANGE!
EXCHANGE [SPELL CARD]
Both players show their hands to each other. You both select 1 card from each other's hand and add it to your own.

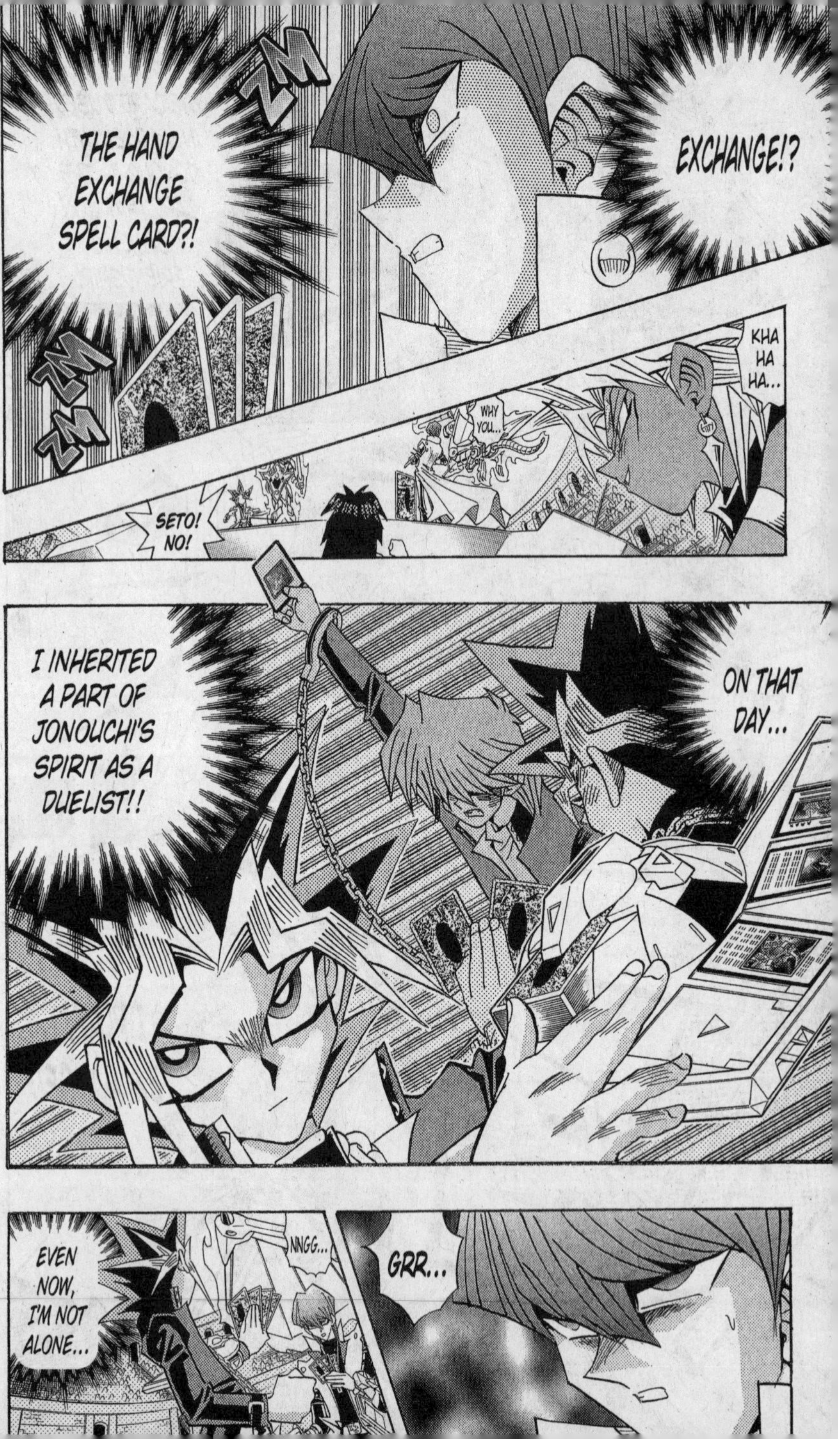
EXCHANGE!?
ZM
THE HAND EXCHANGE SPELL CARD?!
ZM ZM
KHA HA HA...
WHY YOU...
SETO! NO!
ON THAT DAY...
I INHERITED A PART OF JONOUCHI'S SPIRIT AS A DUELIST!!
GRR...
NNGG...
EVEN NOW, I'M NOT ALONE...

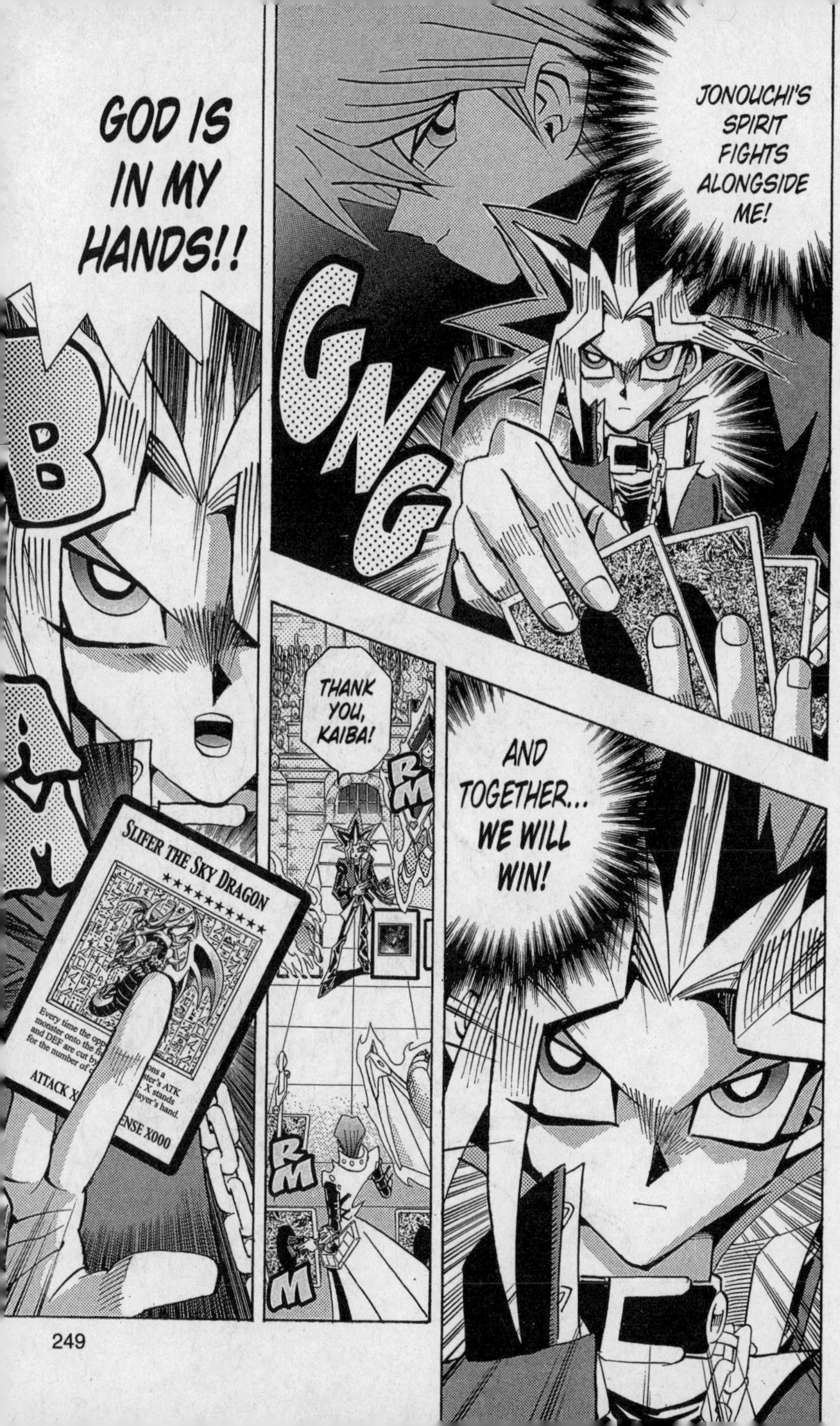
JONOUCHI'S SPIRIT FIGHTS ALONGSIDE ME!
GNG
AND TOGETHER... WE WILL WIN!
THANK YOU, KAIBA!
RM
RM
M
GOD IS IN MY HANDS!!
SLIFER THE SKY DRAGON

Kaz

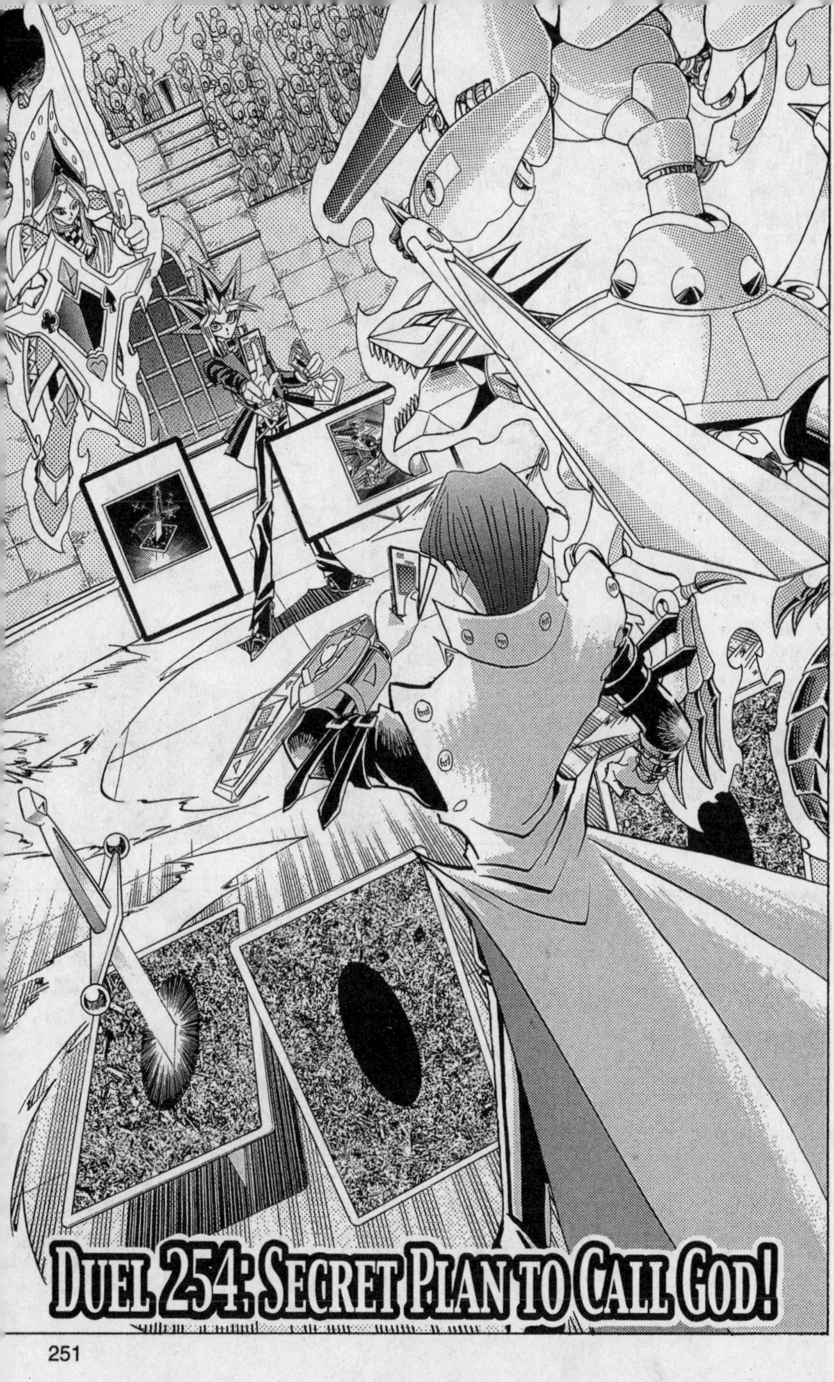
Duel 254: Secret Plan to Call God!

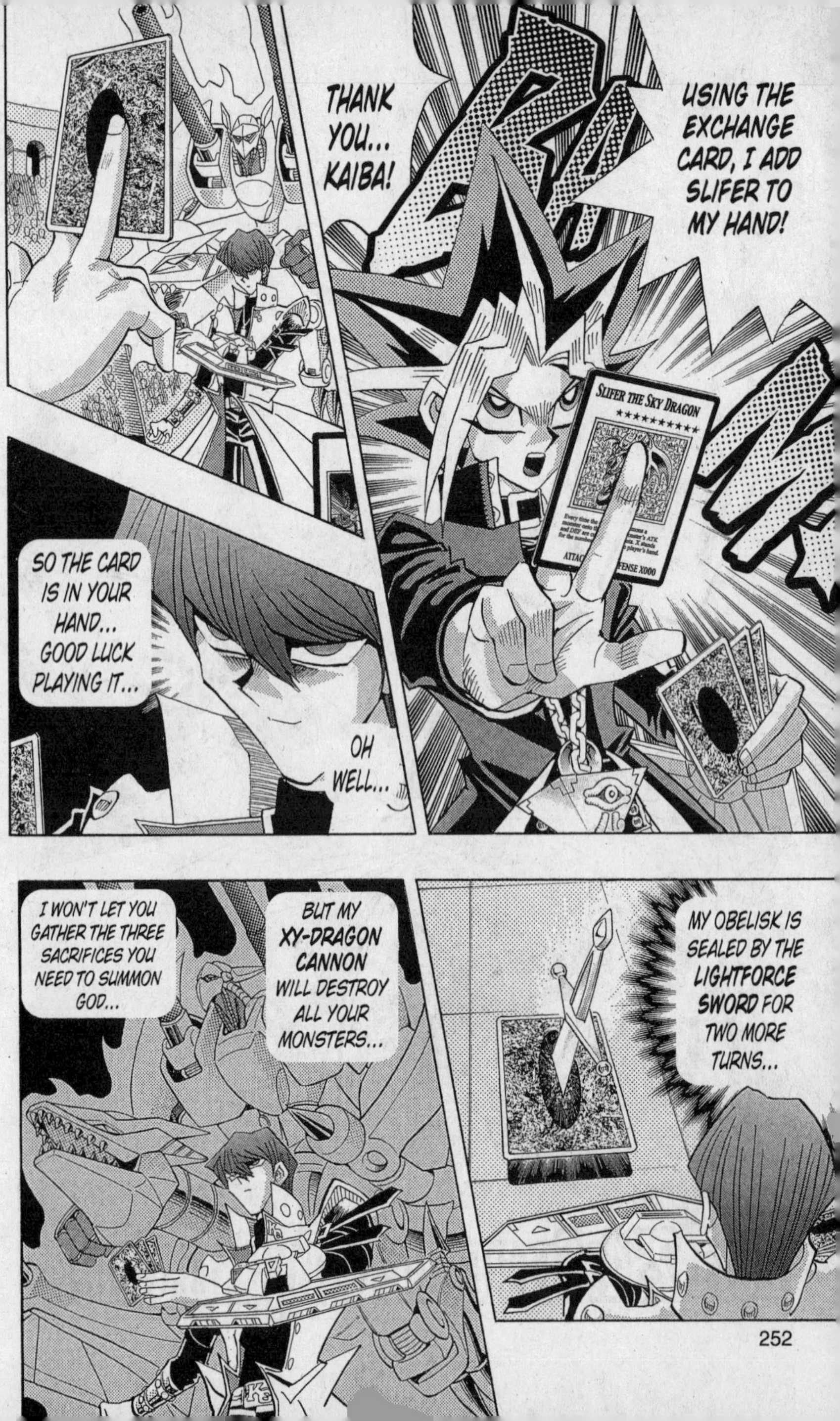
USING THE EXCHANGE CARD, I ADD SLIFER TO MY HAND!
THANK YOU... KAIBA!
SLIFER THE SKY DRAGON
SO THE CARD IS IN YOUR HAND... GOOD LUCK PLAYING IT...
OH WELL...
MY OBELISK IS SEALED BY THE LIGHTFORCE SWORD FOR TWO MORE TURNS...
BUT MY XY-DRAGON CANNON WILL DESTROY ALL YOUR MONSTERS...
I WON'T LET YOU GATHER THE THREE SACRIFICES YOU NEED TO SUMMON GOD...

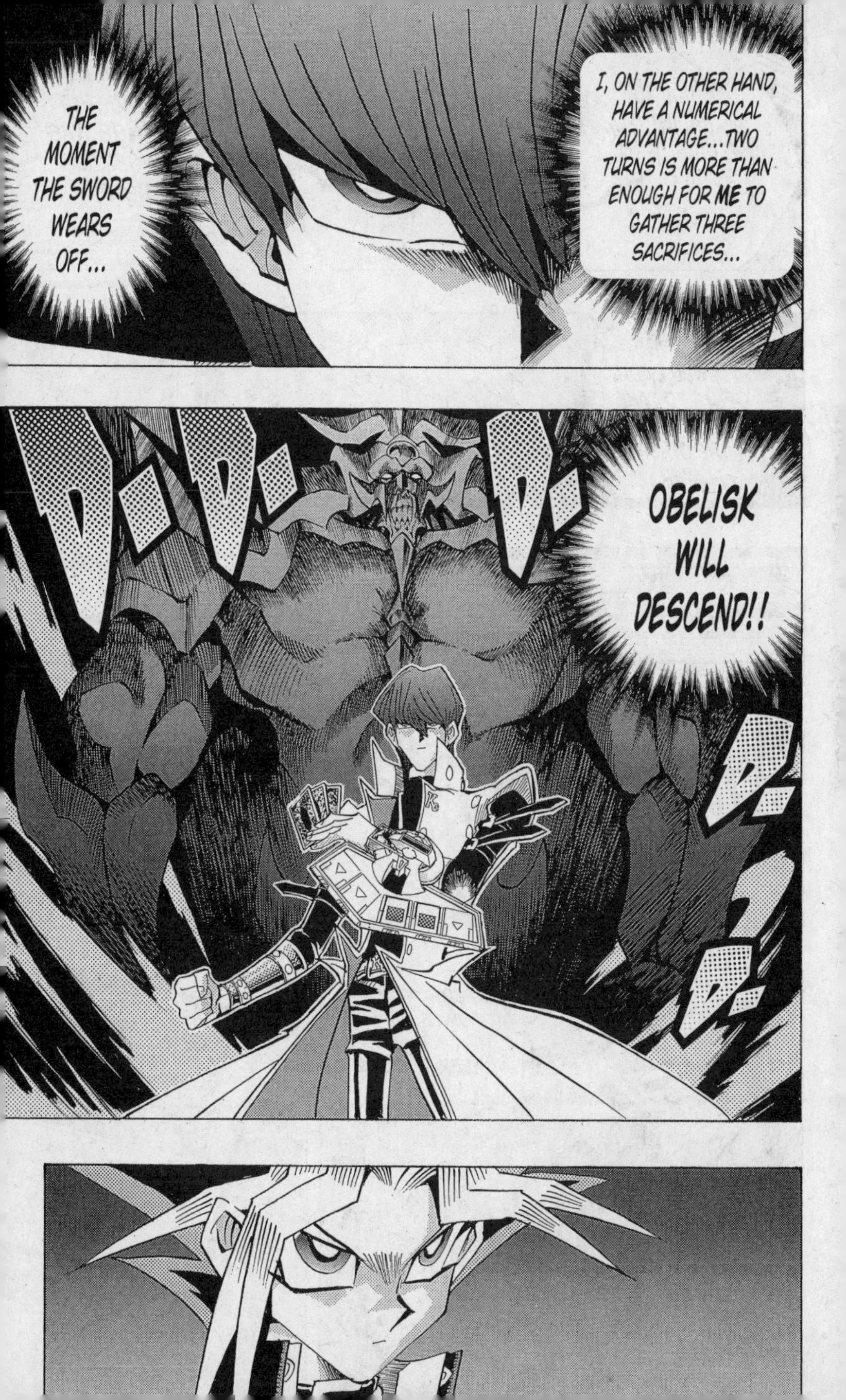

I, ON THE OTHER HAND, HAVE A NUMERICAL ADVANTAGE...TWO TURNS IS MORE THAN ENOUGH FOR ME TO GATHER THREE SACRIFICES...
THE MOMENT THE SWORD WEARS OFF...
OBELISK WILL DESCEND!!

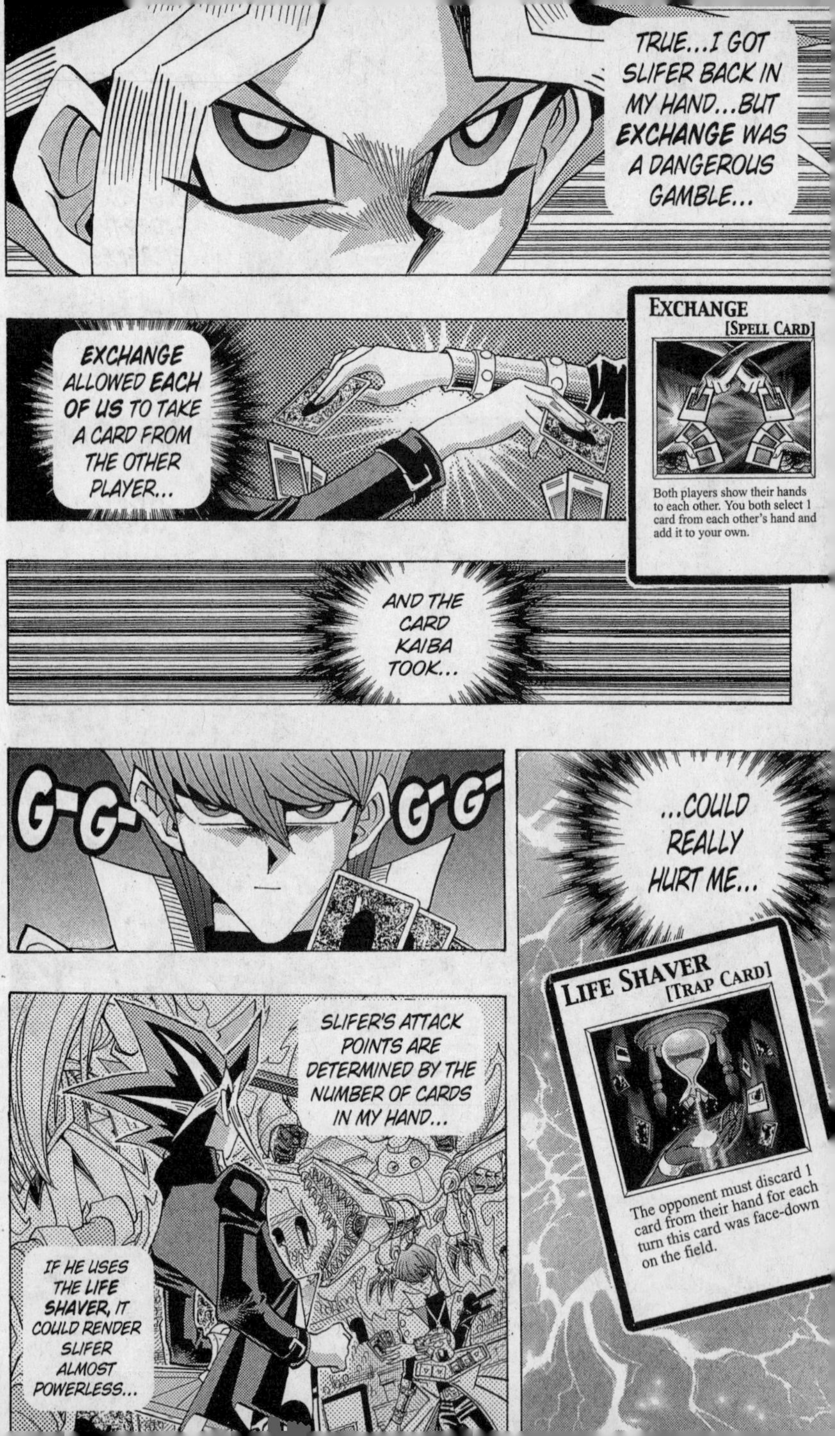
TRUE...I GOT SLIFER BACK IN MY HAND...BUT EXCHANGE WAS A DANGEROUS GAMBLE...
EXCHANGE
[SPELL CARD]
Both players show their hands to each other. You both select 1 card from each other's hand and add it to your own.
EXCHANGE ALLOWED EACH OF US TO TAKE A CARD FROM THE OTHER PLAYER...
AND THE CARD KAIBA TOOK...
...COULD REALLY HURT ME...
LIFE SHAVER
[TRAP CARD]
The opponent must discard 1 card from their hand for each turn this card was face-down on the field.
G-G-
G-G-
SLIFER'S ATTACK POINTS ARE DETERMINED BY THE NUMBER OF CARDS IN MY HAND...
IF HE USES THE LIFE SHAVER, IT COULD RENDER SLIFER ALMOST POWERLESS...

READ THIS WAY

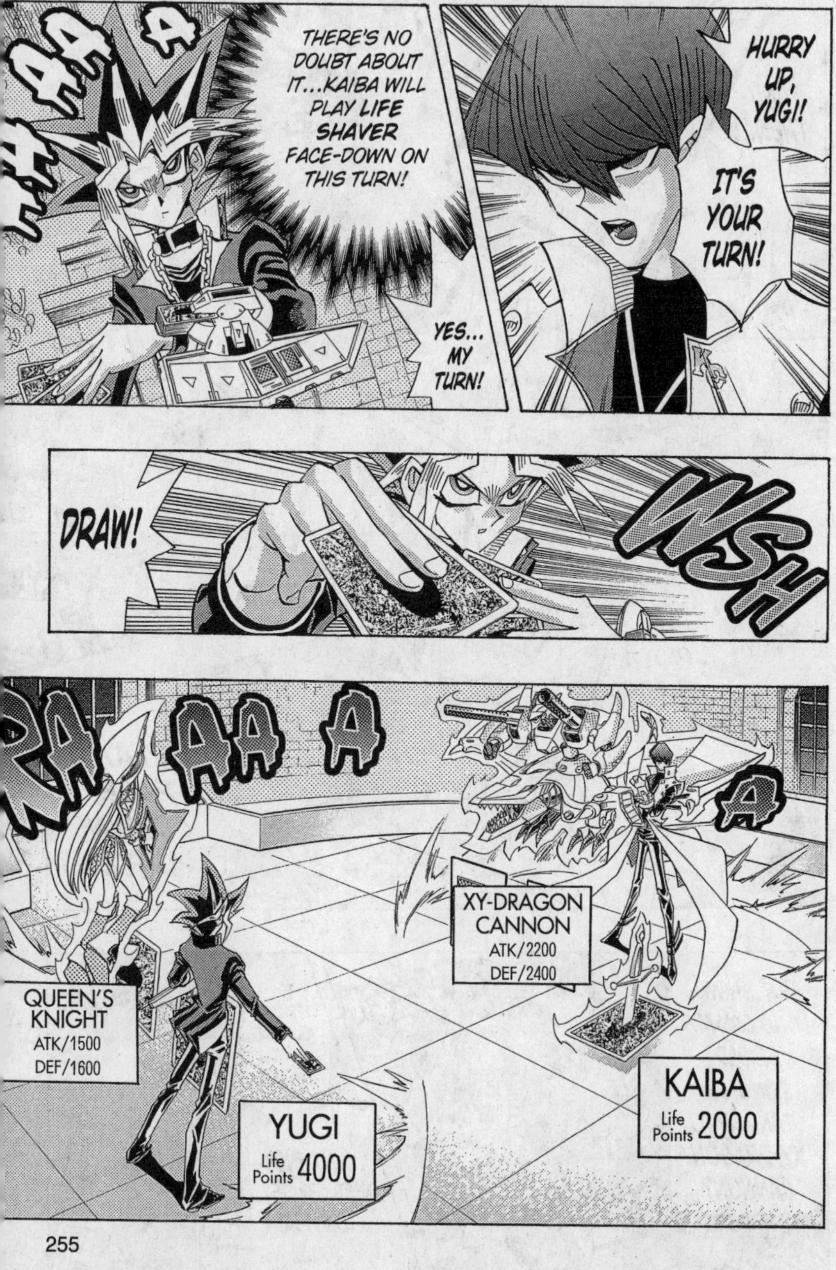

HURRY UP, YUGI!
IT'S YOUR TURN!
AA A
THERE'S NO DOUBT ABOUT IT...KAIBA WILL PLAY LIFE SHAVER FACE-DOWN ON THIS TURN!
YES... MY TURN!
VNSH
DRAW!
A
AA AA A
XY-DRAGON CANNON
ATK/2200
DEF/2400
KAIBA
Life Points 2000
QUEEN'S KNIGHT
ATK/1500
DEF/1600
YUGI
Life Points 4000

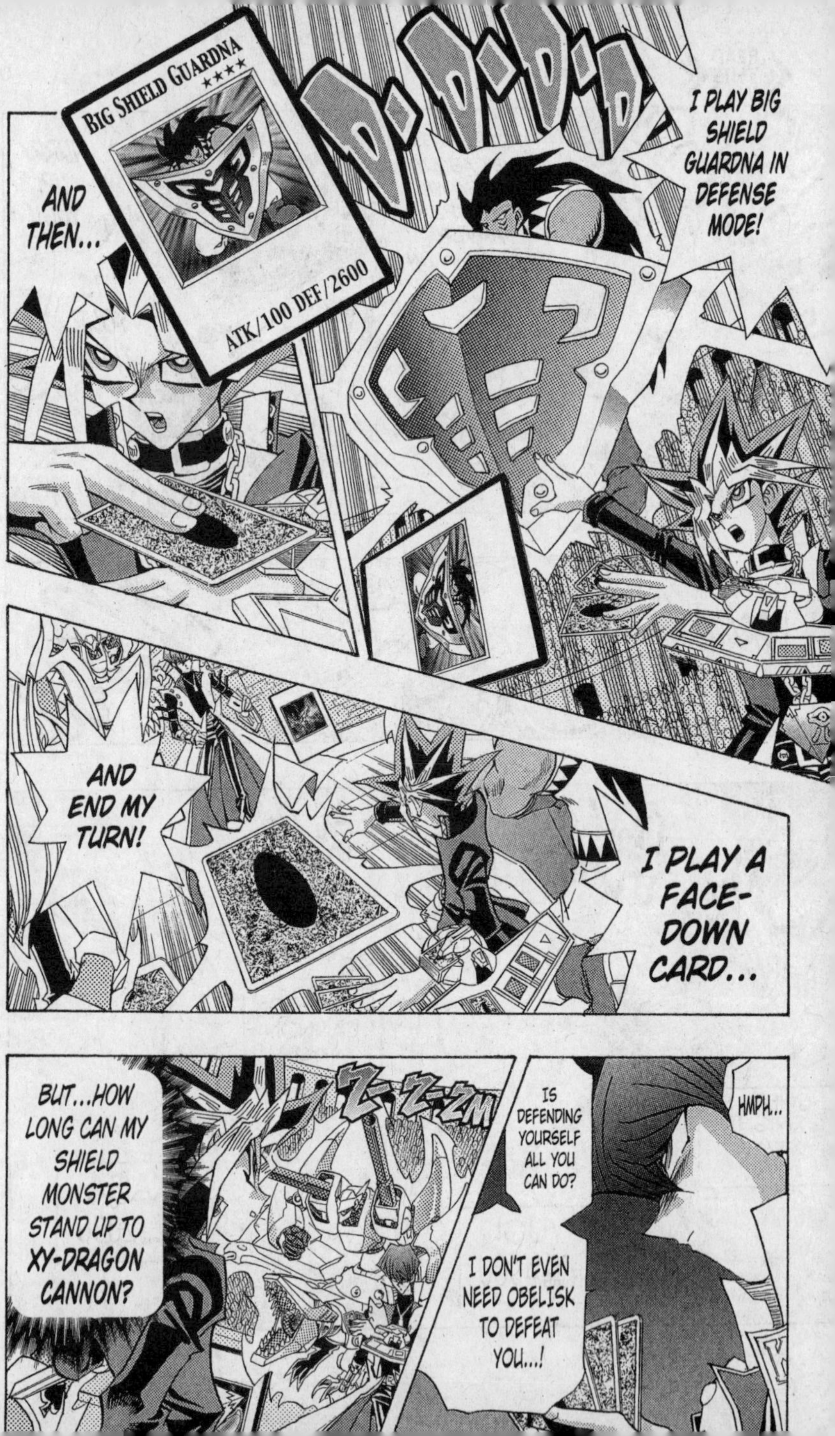

D-D-D-D
I PLAY BIG SHIELD GUARDNA IN DEFENSE MODE!
BIG SHIELD GUARDNA ★★★★
ATK/100 DEF/2600
AND THEN...
I PLAY A FACE-DOWN CARD...
AND END MY TURN!
HMPH...
IS DEFENDING YOURSELF ALL YOU CAN DO?
I DON'T EVEN NEED OBELISK TO DEFEAT YOU...!
Z-Z-ZM
BUT...HOW LONG CAN MY SHIELD MONSTER STAND UP TO XY-DRAGON CANNON?

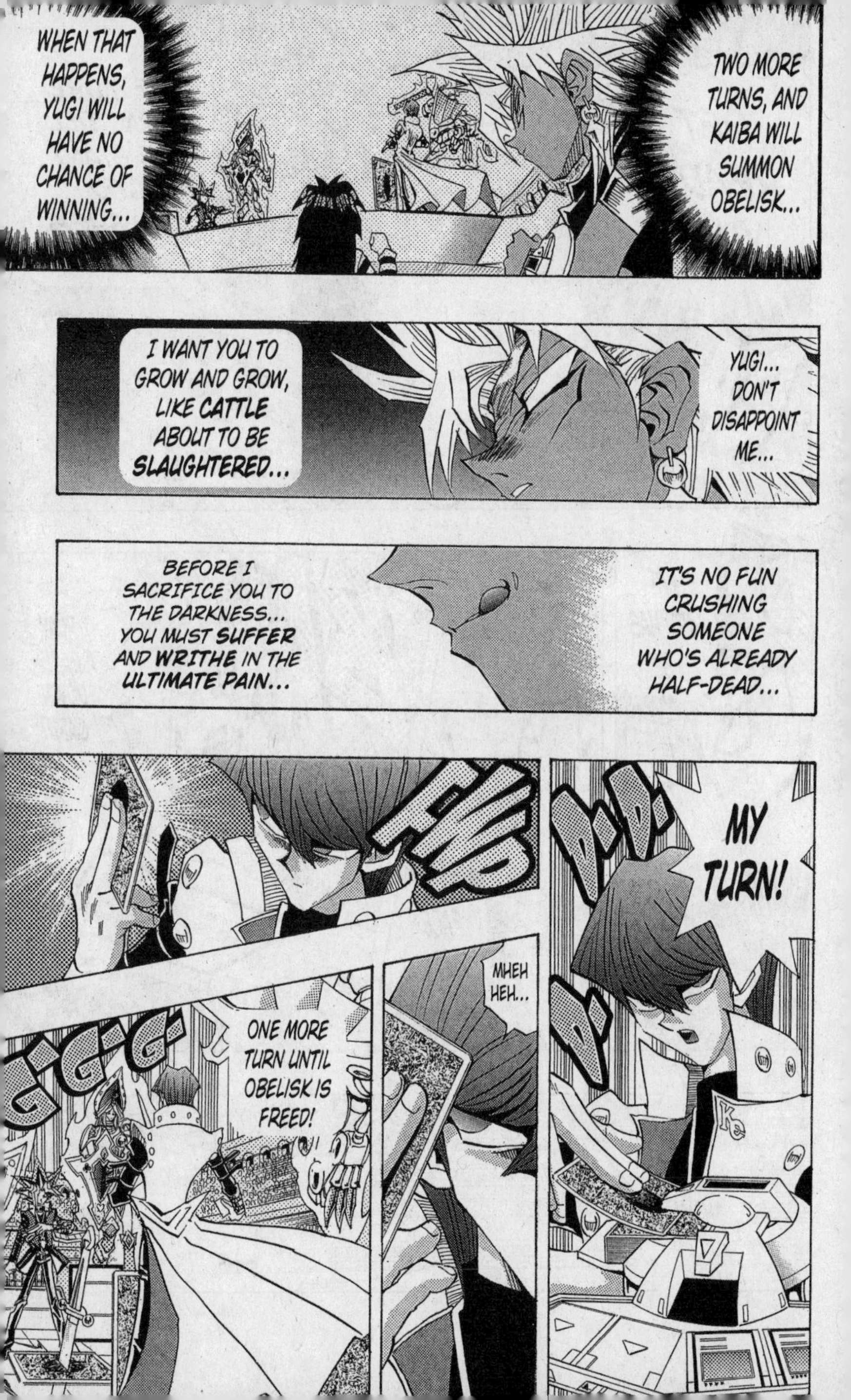
TWO MORE TURNS, AND KAIBA WILL SUMMON OBELISK...
WHEN THAT HAPPENS, YUGI WILL HAVE NO CHANCE OF WINNING...
YUGI... DON'T DISAPPOINT ME...
I WANT YOU TO GROW AND GROW, LIKE CATTLE ABOUT TO BE SLAUGHTERED...
IT'S NO FUN CRUSHING SOMEONE WHO'S ALREADY HALF-DEAD...
BEFORE I SACRIFICE YOU TO THE DARKNESS... YOU MUST SUFFER AND WRITHE IN THE ULTIMATE PAIN...
MY TURN!
MHEH HEH...
ONE MORE TURN UNTIL OBELISK IS FREED!

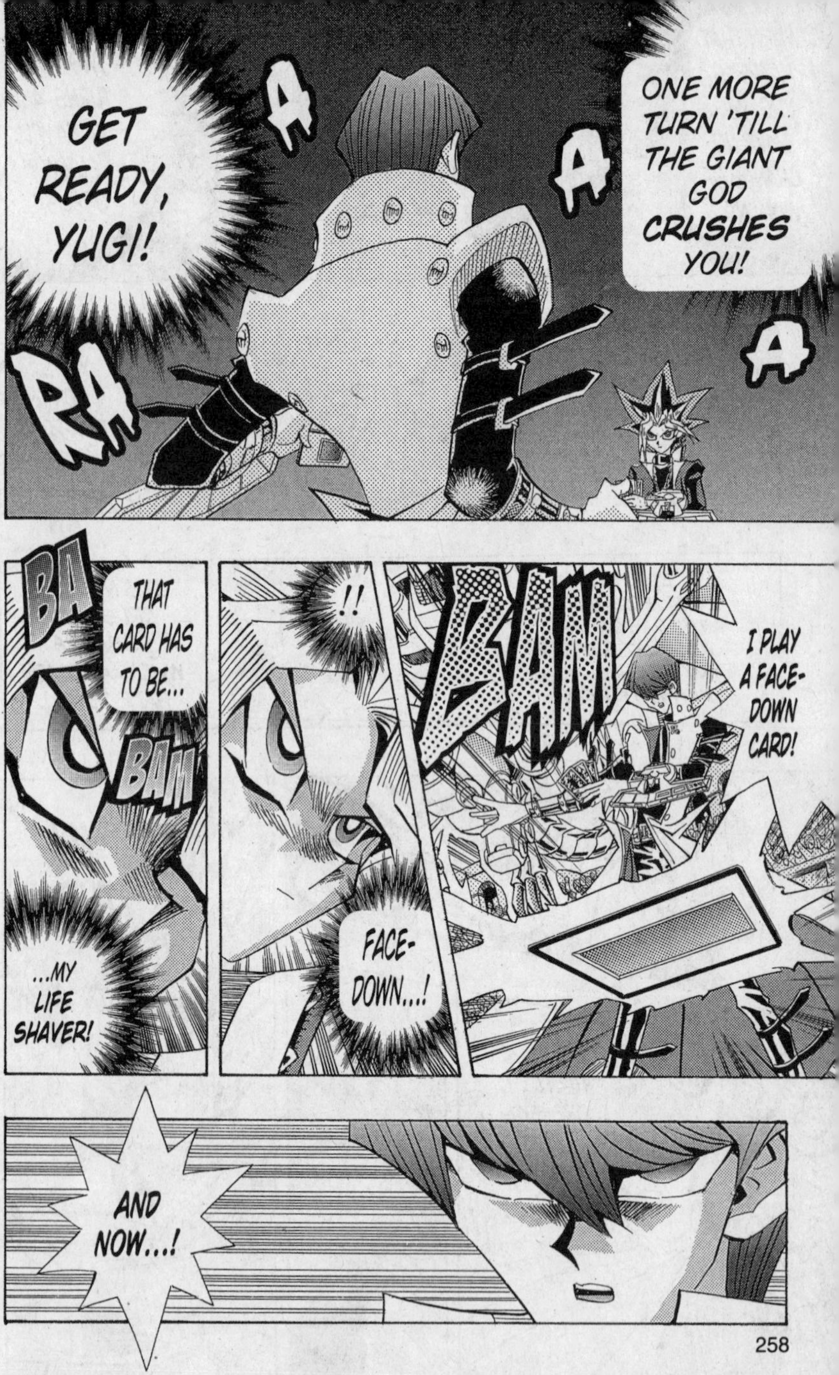
ONE MORE TURN 'TILL THE GIANT GOD CRUSHES YOU!
A
A
A
GET READY, YUGI!
RA
BAM
I PLAY A FACE-DOWN CARD!
!!
FACE-DOWN...!
BA
THAT CARD HAS TO BE...
BAM
...MY LIFE SHAVER!
AND NOW...!

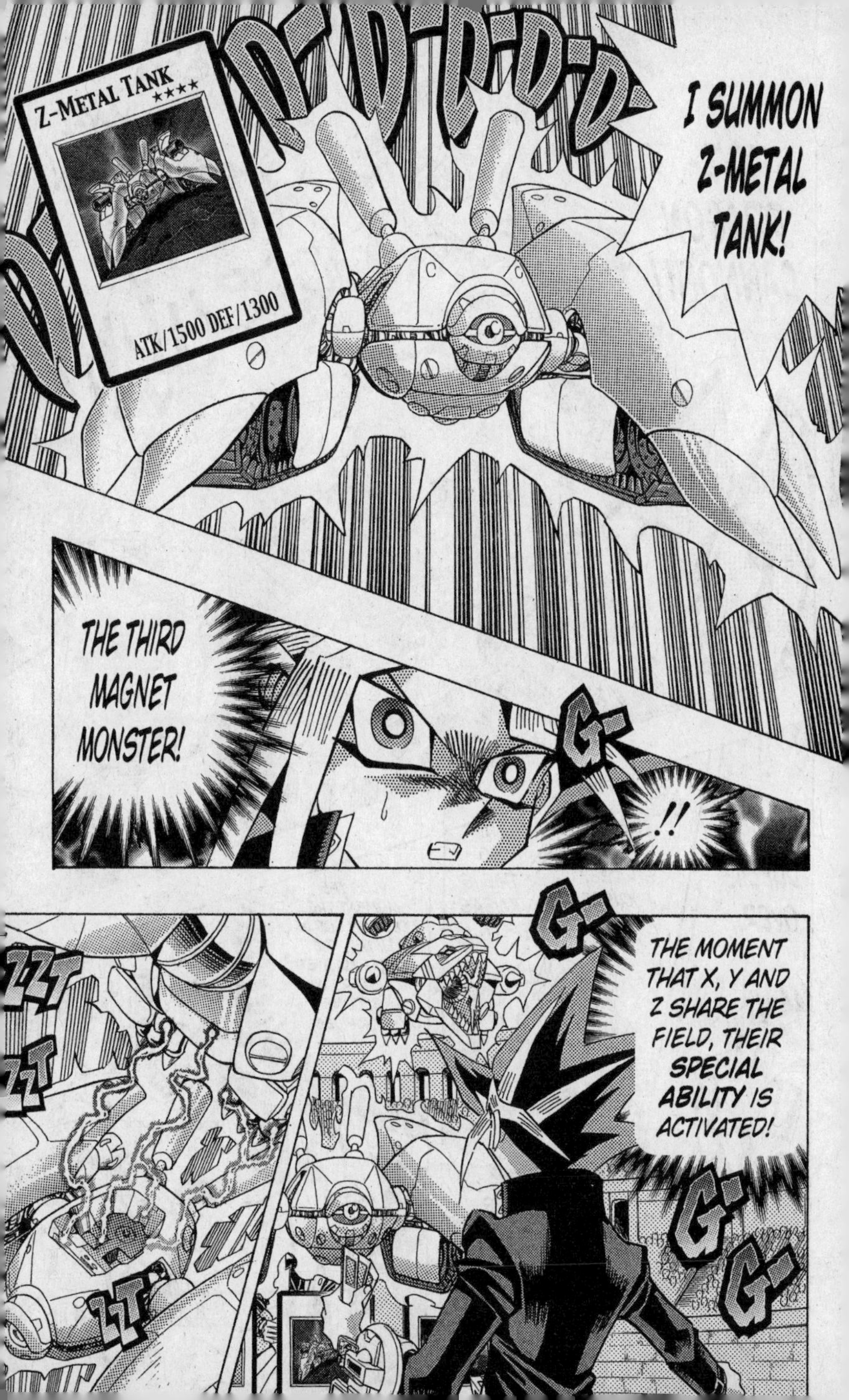
D-D-D-D-D-D-D
I SUMMON Z-METAL TANK!
Z-METAL TANK ★★★★
ATK/1500 DEF/1300
G-
!!
THE THIRD MAGNET MONSTER!
G-
THE MOMENT THAT X, Y AND Z SHARE THE FIELD, THEIR SPECIAL ABILITY IS ACTIVATED!
G-
G-
ZZT
ZZT
ZZT

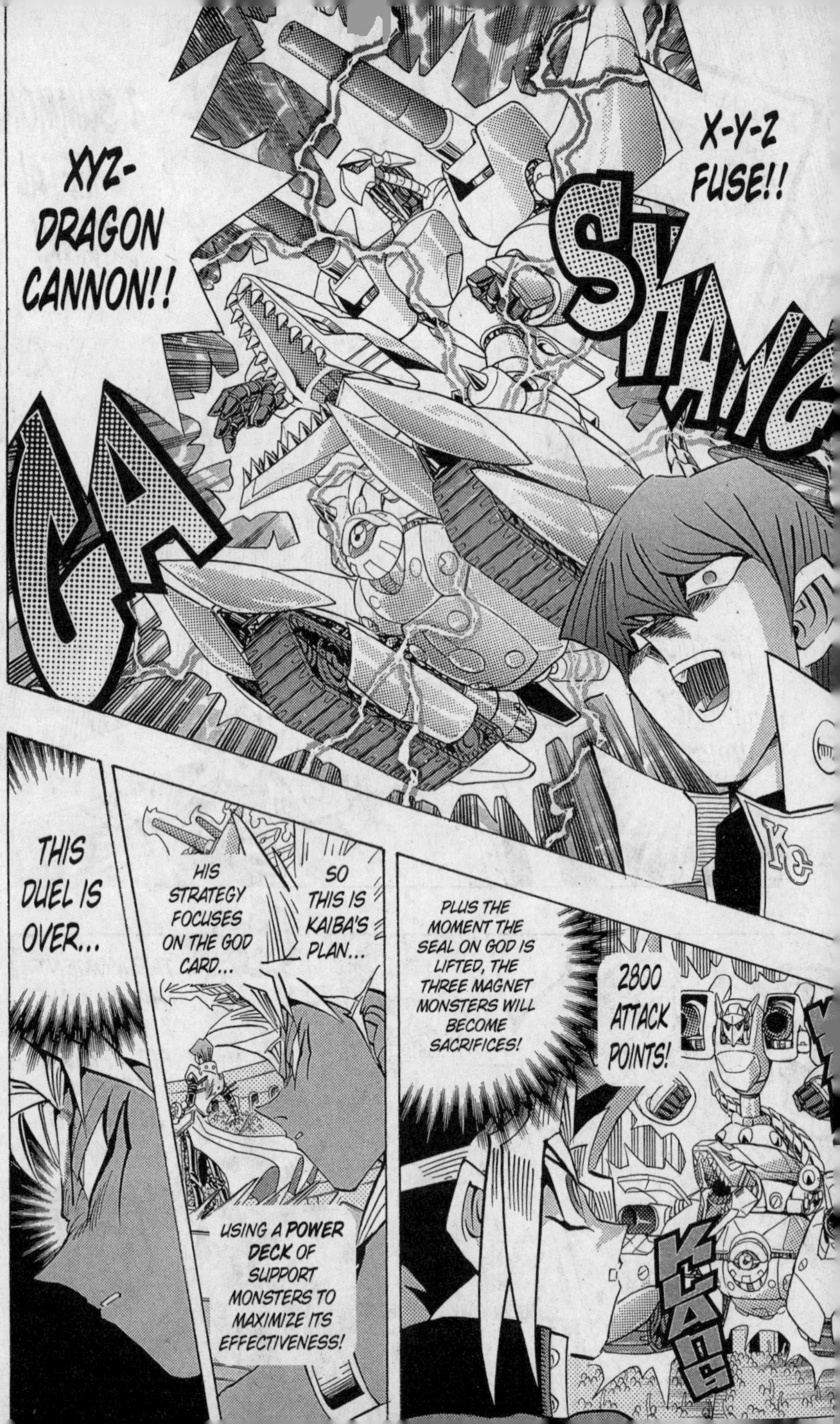
X-Y-Z FUSE!!
XYZ-DRAGON CANNON!!
2800 ATTACK POINTS!
PLUS THE MOMENT THE SEAL ON GOD IS LIFTED, THE THREE MAGNET MONSTERS WILL BECOME SACRIFICES!
KLANG
SO THIS IS KAIBA'S PLAN...
HIS STRATEGY FOCUSES ON THE GOD CARD...
USING A POWER DECK OF SUPPORT MONSTERS TO MAXIMIZE ITS EFFECTIVENESS!
THIS DUEL IS OVER...

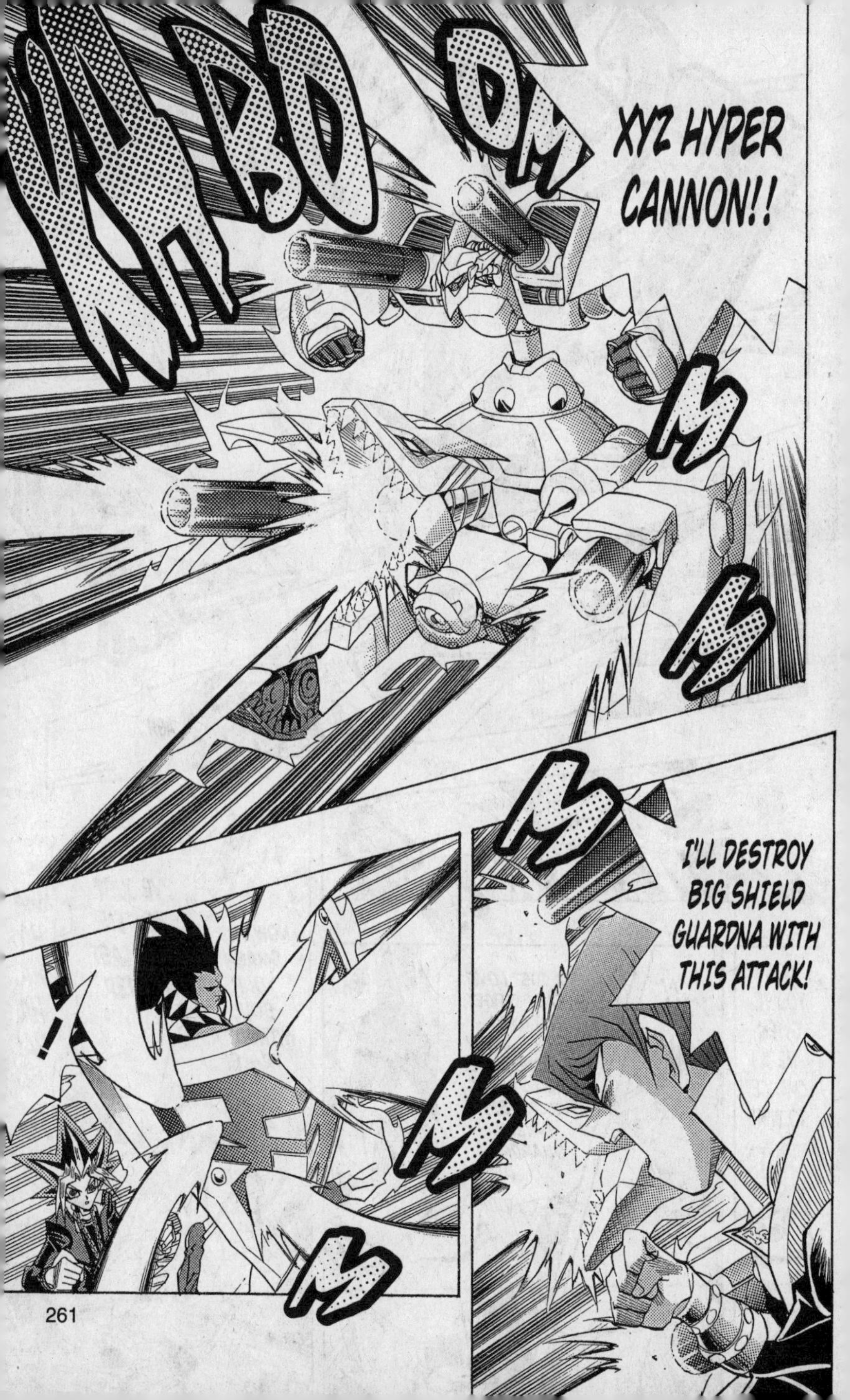
XYZ HYPER CANNON!!
I'LL DESTROY BIG SHIELD GUARDNA WITH THIS ATTACK!
!

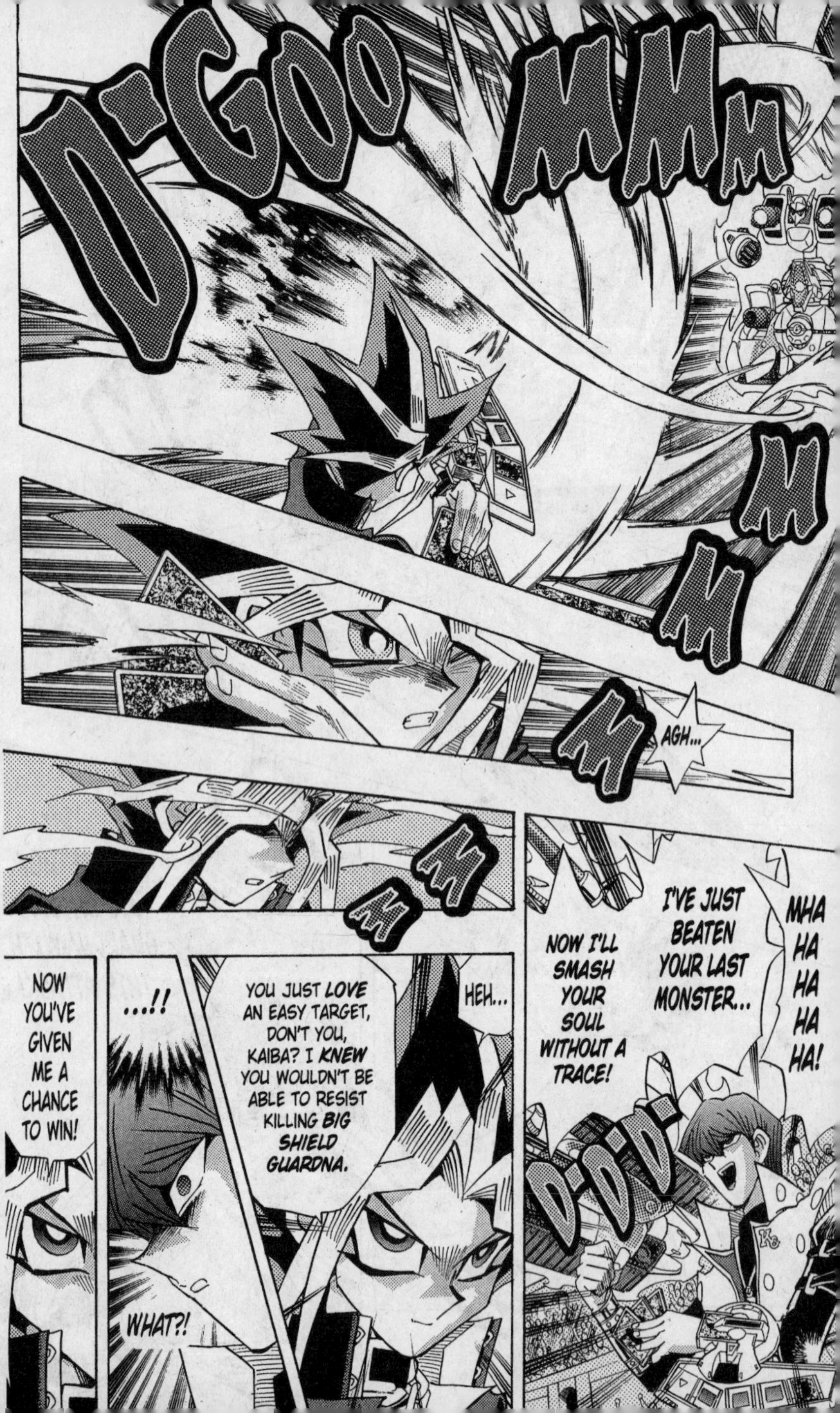

D-GOO MMM
M
M
M
M
AGH...
M
M
MHA HA HA HA HA!
I'VE JUST BEATEN YOUR LAST MONSTER...
NOW I'LL SMASH YOUR SOUL WITHOUT A TRACE!
D-D-D
HEH...
YOU JUST LOVE AN EASY TARGET, DON'T YOU, KAIBA? I KNEW YOU WOULDN'T BE ABLE TO RESIST KILLING BIG SHIELD GUARDNA.
...!!
WHAT?!
NOW YOU'VE GIVEN ME A CHANCE TO WIN!

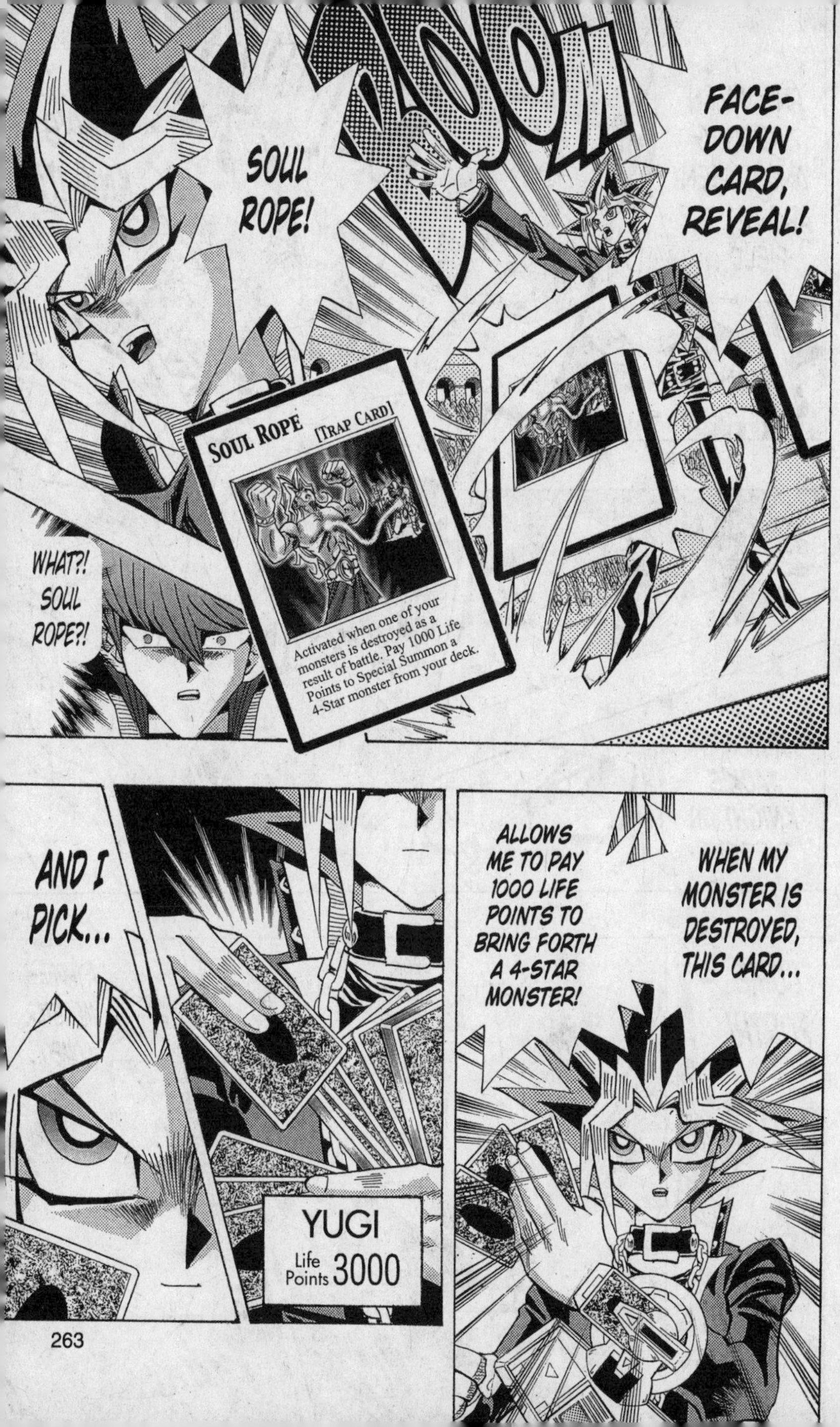
FACE-DOWN CARD, REVEAL!
ZOOM
SOUL ROPE!
SOUL ROPE [TRAP CARD]
Activated when one of your monsters is destroyed as a result of battle. Pay 1000 Life Points to Special Summon a 4-Star monster from your deck.
WHAT?! SOUL ROPE?!
WHEN MY MONSTER IS DESTROYED, THIS CARD...
ALLOWS ME TO PAY 1000 LIFE POINTS TO BRING FORTH A 4-STAR MONSTER!
AND I PICK...
YUGI
Life Points 3000

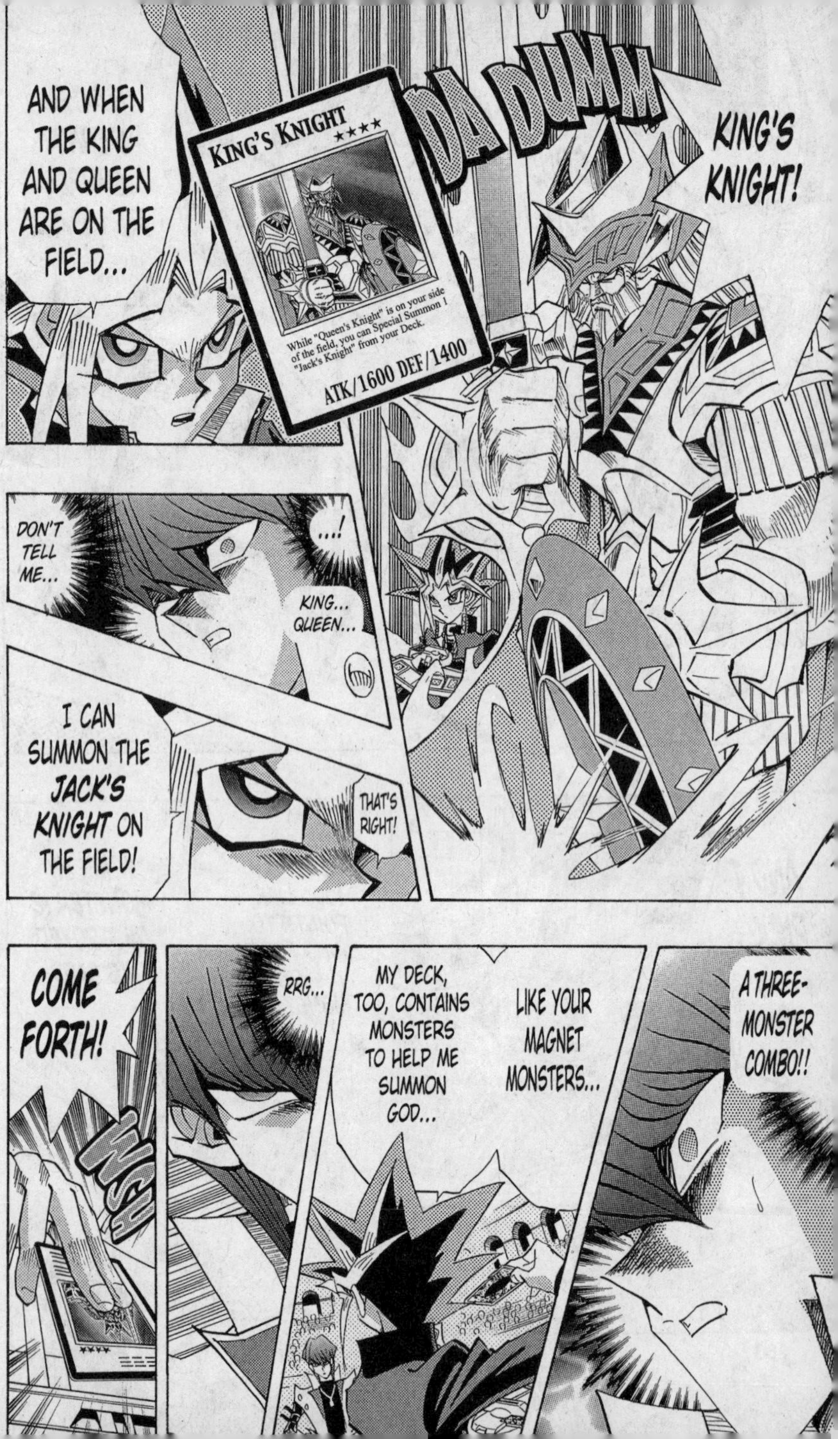
DA DUMM
KING'S KNIGHT!
AND WHEN THE KING AND QUEEN ARE ON THE FIELD...
KING'S KNIGHT ★★★★
While "Queen's Knight" is on your side of the field, you can Special Summon 1 "Jack's Knight" from your Deck.
ATK/1600 DEF/1400
...!
DON'T TELL ME...
KING... QUEEN...
THAT'S RIGHT!
I CAN SUMMON THE JACK'S KNIGHT ON THE FIELD!
A THREE-MONSTER COMBO!!
LIKE YOUR MAGNET MONSTERS...
MY DECK, TOO, CONTAINS MONSTERS TO HELP ME SUMMON GOD...
RRG...
COME FORTH!

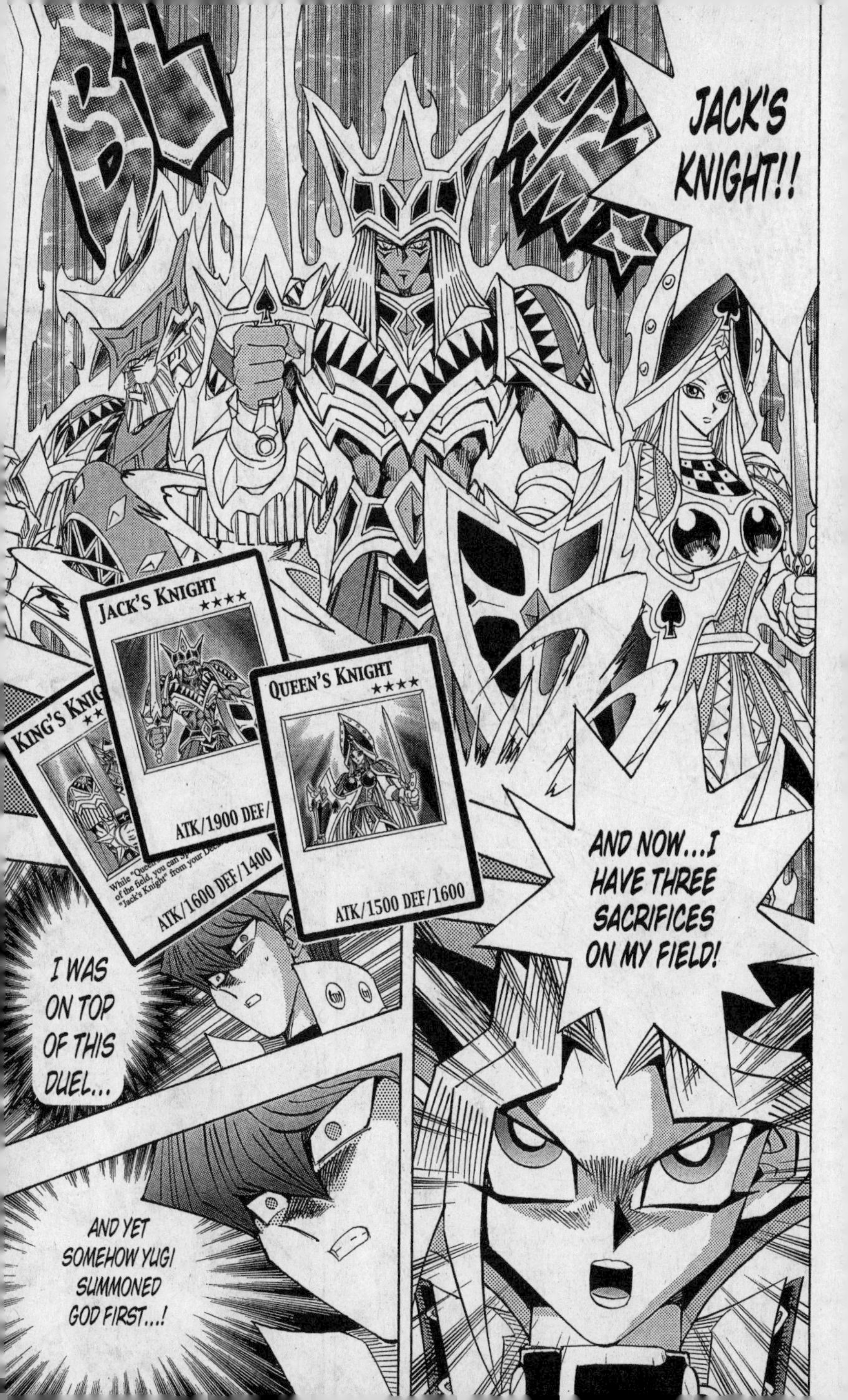
JACK'S KNIGHT!!
JACK'S KNIGHT ★★★★
ATK/1900 DEF/
QUEEN'S KNIGHT ★★★★
ATK/1500 DEF/1600
ATK/1600 DEF/1400
AND NOW...I HAVE THREE SACRIFICES ON MY FIELD!
I WAS ON TOP OF THIS DUEL...
AND YET SOMEHOW YUGI SUMMONED GOD FIRST...!

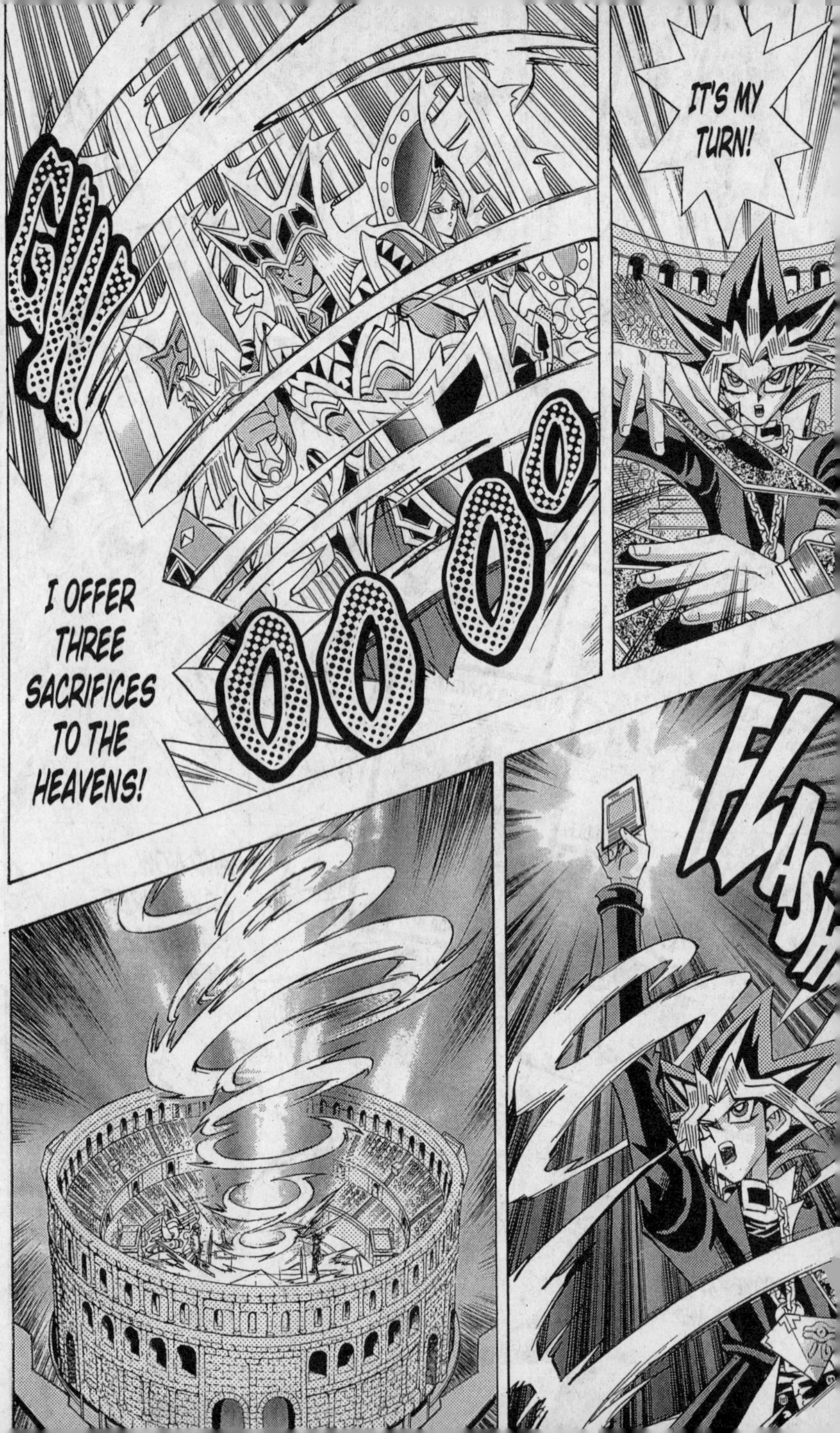
IT'S MY TURN!
GYUOOOO
I OFFER THREE SACRIFICES TO THE HEAVENS!
FLASH

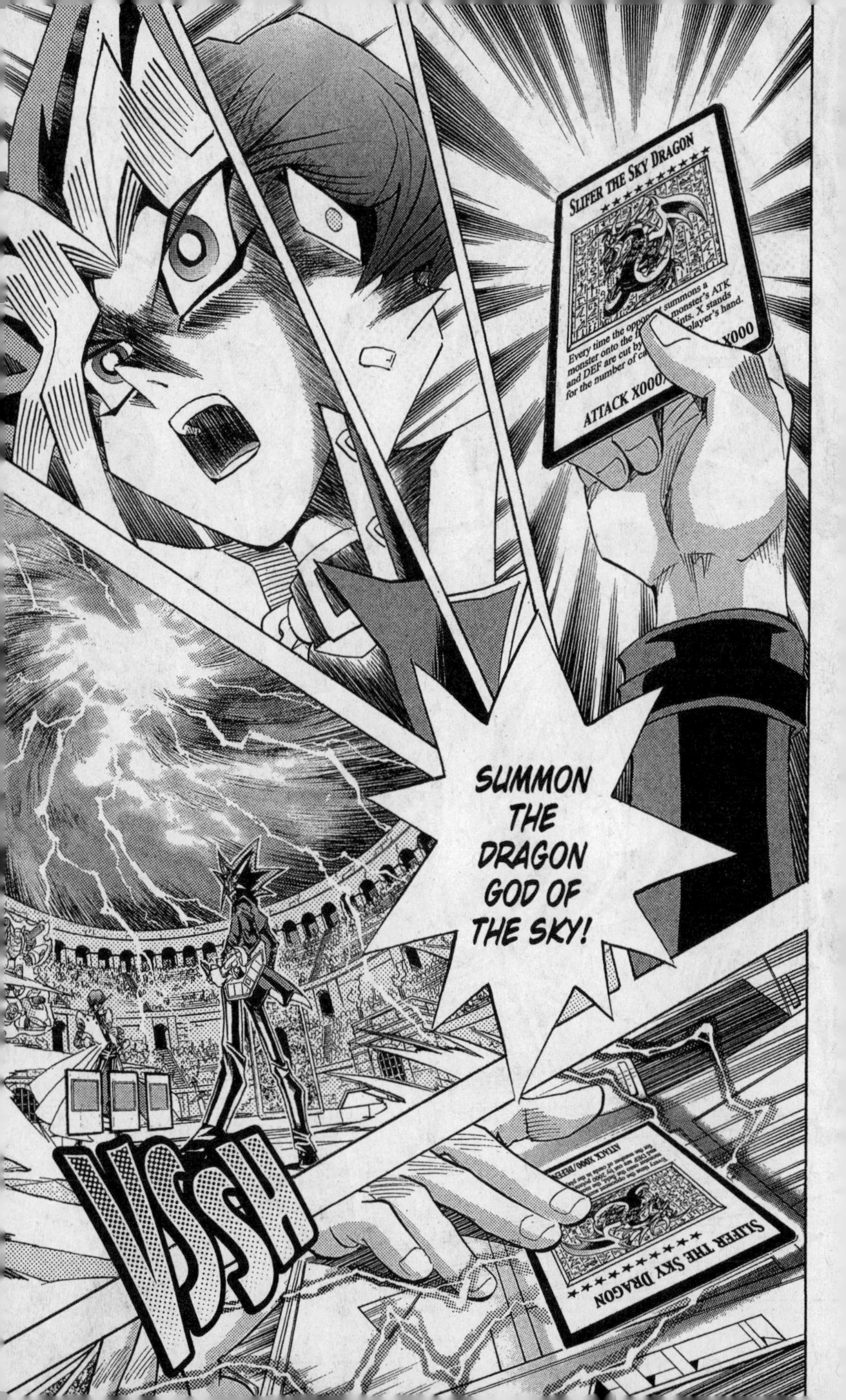
SLIFER THE SKY DRAGON
SUMMON THE DRAGON GOD OF THE SKY!
VSSH
SLIFER THE SKY DRAGON

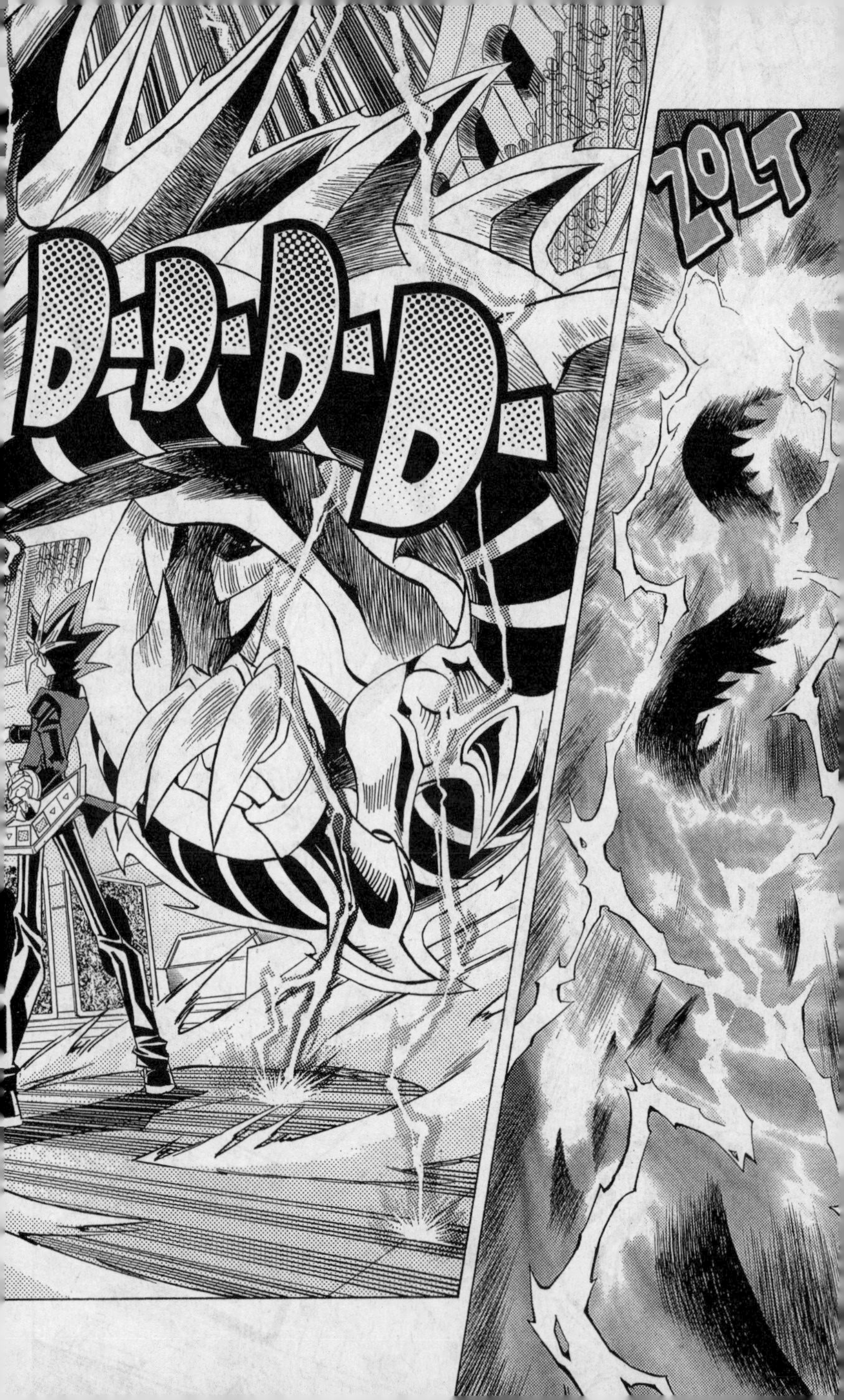
ZOLT
D-D-D-D-

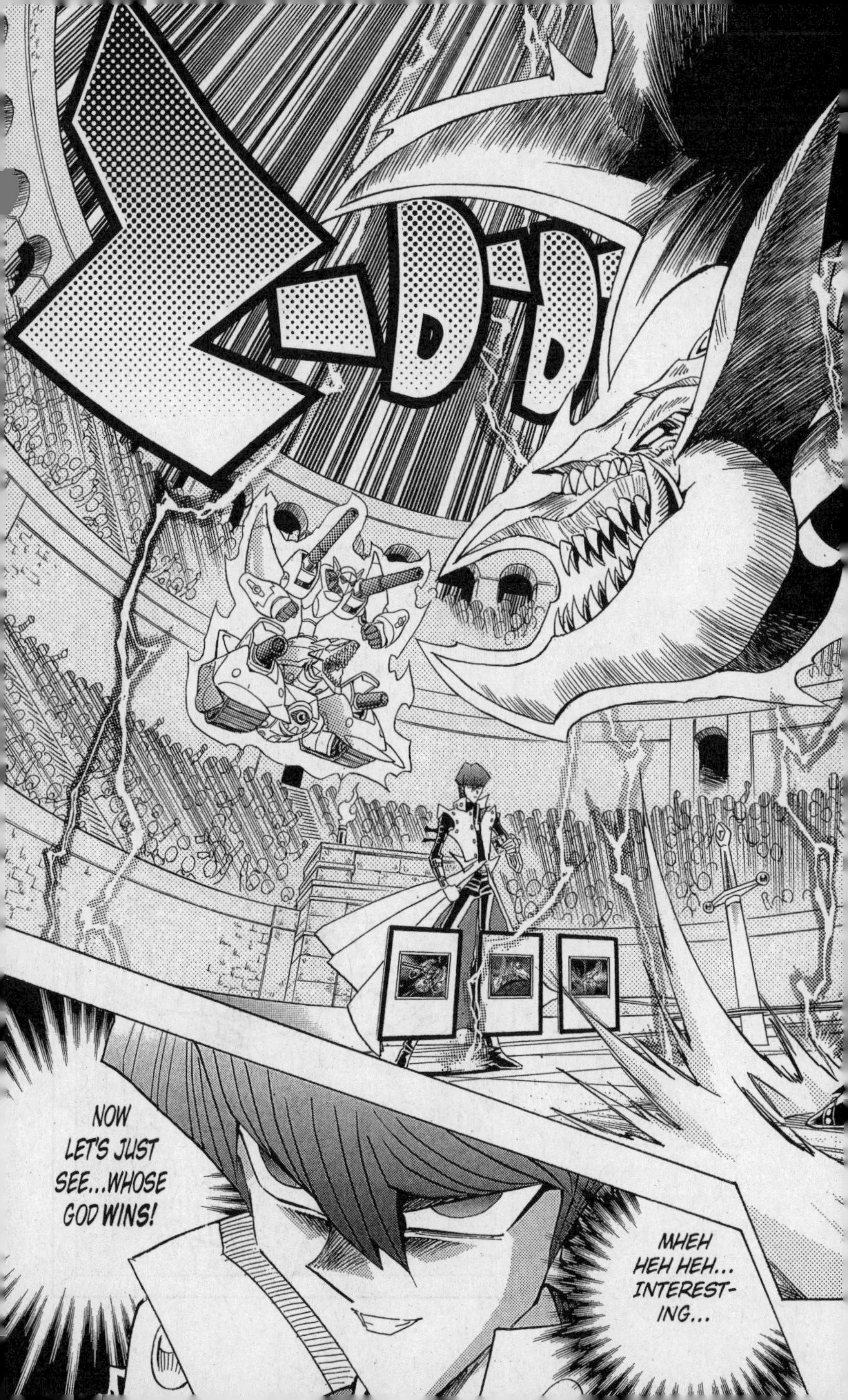

D-D-D
MHEH HEH HEH... INTEREST-ING...
NOW LET'S JUST SEE...WHOSE GOD WINS!

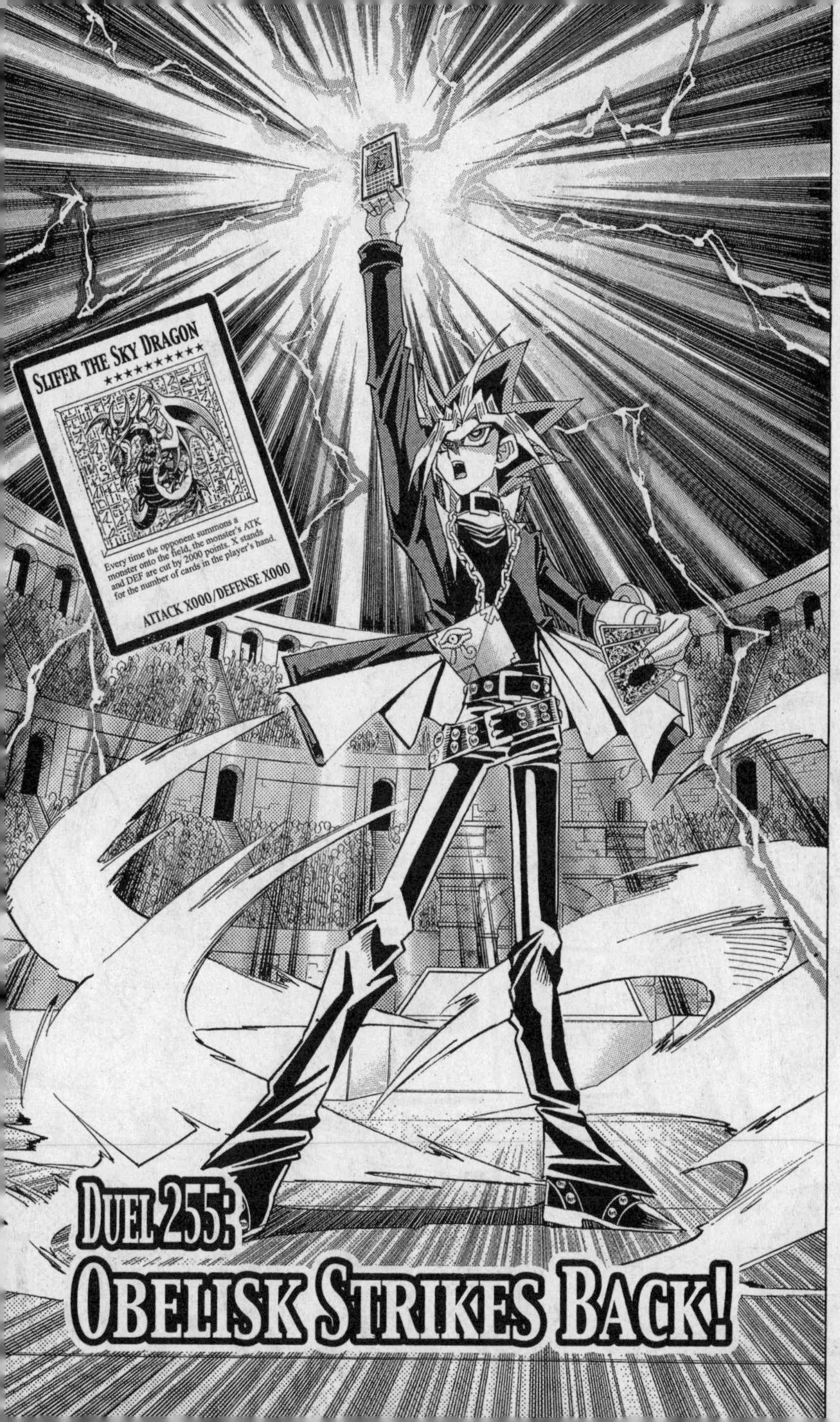
SLIFER THE SKY DRAGON
★★★★★★★★★★
Every time the opponent summons a monster onto the field, the monster's ATK and DEF are cut by 2000 points. X stands for the number of cards in the player's hand.
ATTACK X000/DEFENSE X000
DUEL 255:
OBELISK STRIKES BACK!

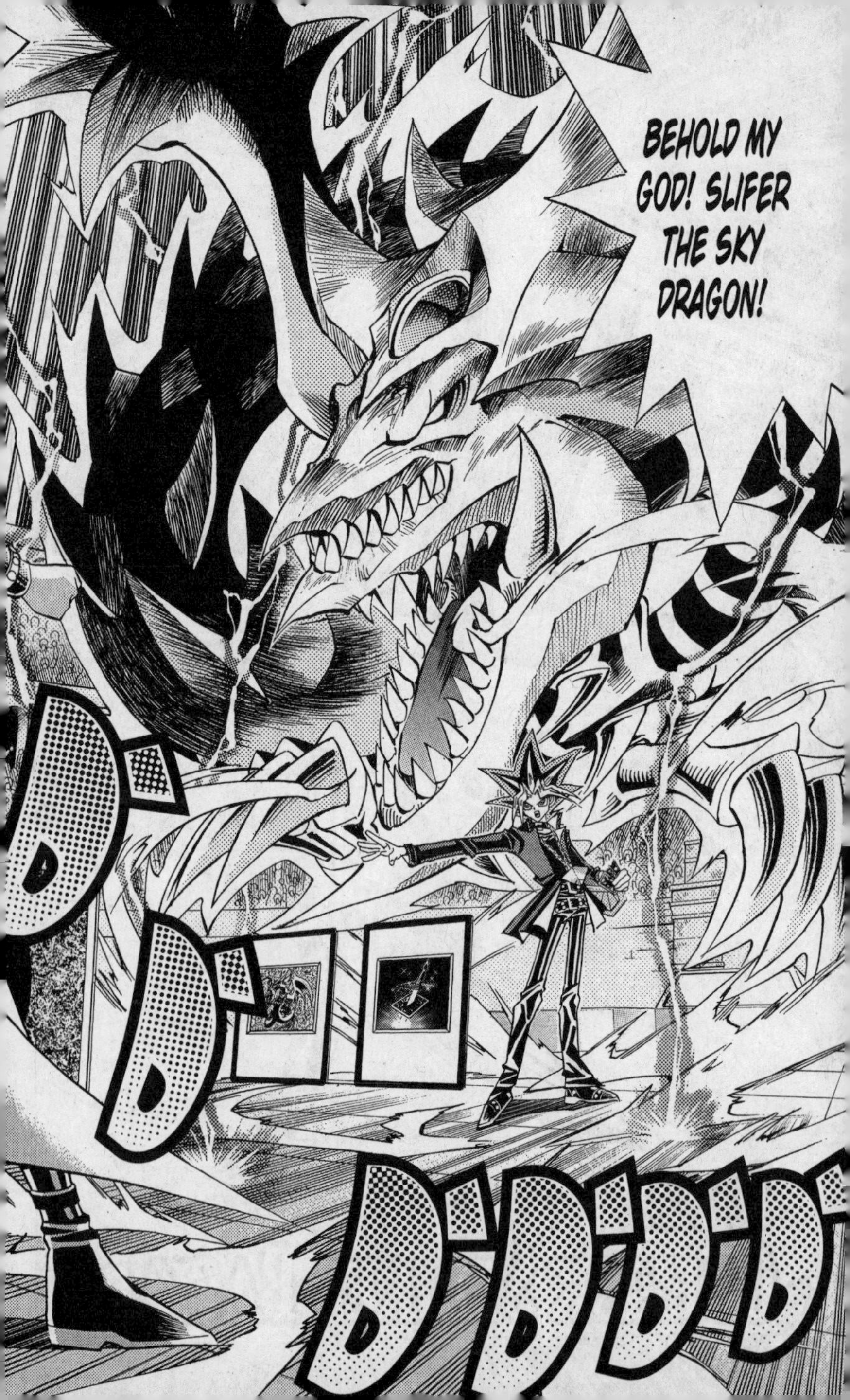
BEHOLD MY GOD! SLIFER THE SKY DRAGON!

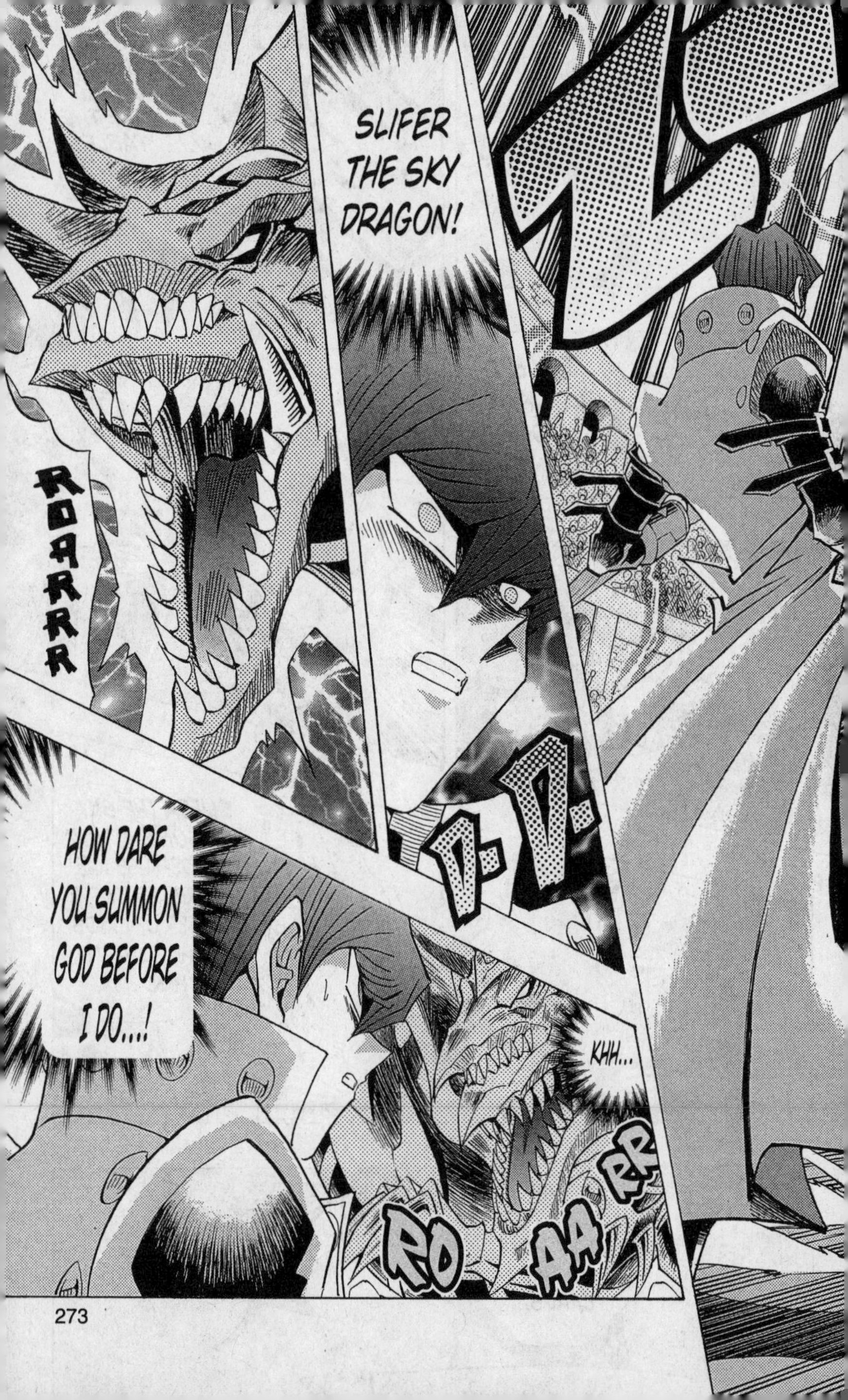
D-D-
SLIFER THE SKY DRAGON!
ROARRRR
KHH...
HOW DARE YOU SUMMON GOD BEFORE I DO...!
ROAARR

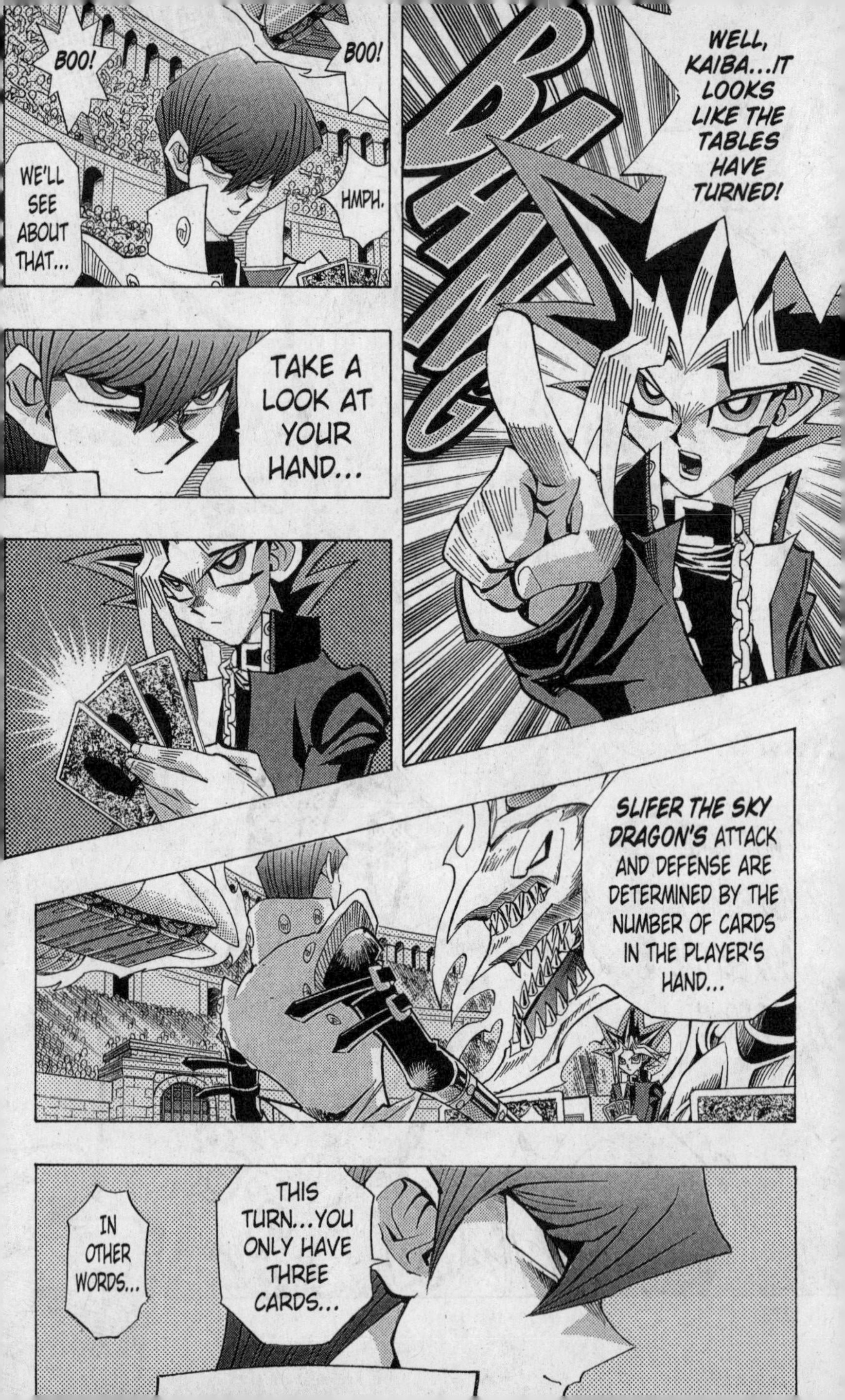
BANG
WELL, KAIBA...IT LOOKS LIKE THE TABLES HAVE TURNED!
BOO!
BOO!
HMPH.
WE'LL SEE ABOUT THAT...
TAKE A LOOK AT YOUR HAND...
SLIFER THE SKY DRAGON'S ATTACK AND DEFENSE ARE DETERMINED BY THE NUMBER OF CARDS IN THE PLAYER'S HAND...
THIS TURN...YOU ONLY HAVE THREE CARDS...
IN OTHER WORDS...

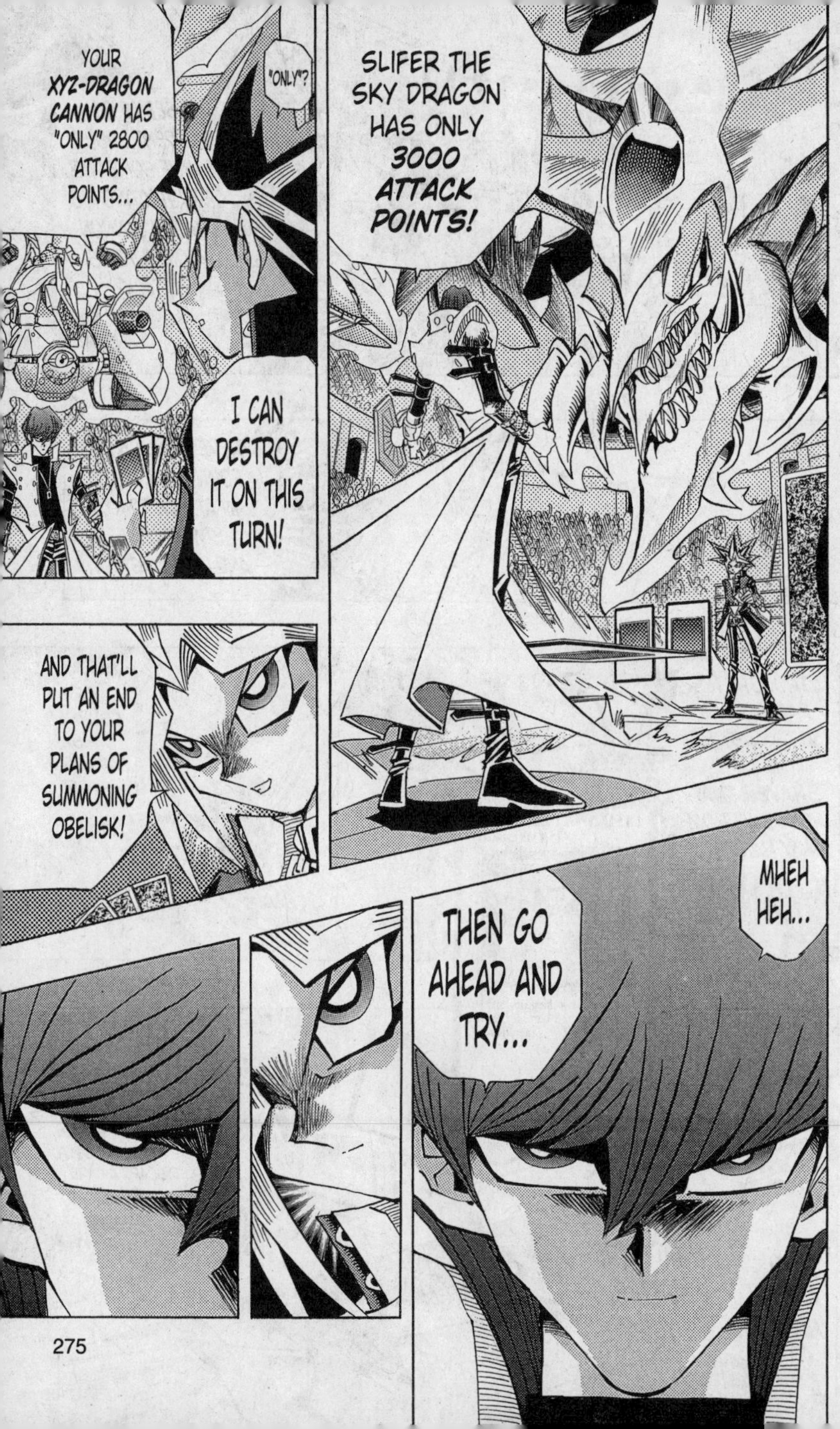
SLIFER THE SKY DRAGON HAS ONLY 3000 ATTACK POINTS!
"ONLY"?
YOUR XYZ-DRAGON CANNON HAS "ONLY" 2800 ATTACK POINTS...
I CAN DESTROY IT ON THIS TURN!
AND THAT'LL PUT AN END TO YOUR PLANS OF SUMMONING OBELISK!
MHEH HEH...
THEN GO AHEAD AND TRY...

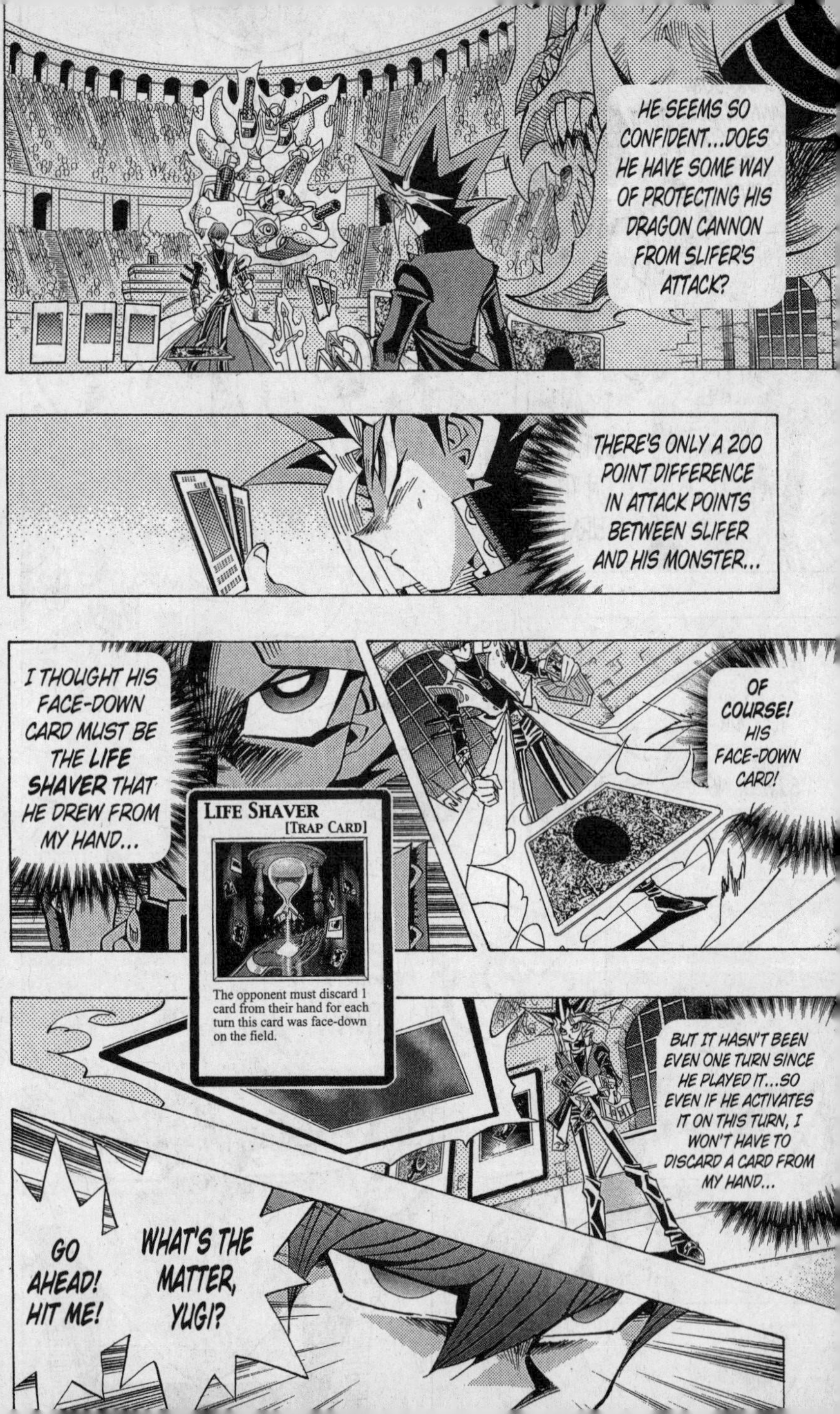
HE SEEMS SO CONFIDENT...DOES HE HAVE SOME WAY OF PROTECTING HIS DRAGON CANNON FROM SLIFER'S ATTACK?
THERE'S ONLY A 200 POINT DIFFERENCE IN ATTACK POINTS BETWEEN SLIFER AND HIS MONSTER...
OF COURSE! HIS FACE-DOWN CARD!
I THOUGHT HIS FACE-DOWN CARD MUST BE THE LIFE SHAVER THAT HE DREW FROM MY HAND...
LIFE SHAVER
[TRAP CARD]
The opponent must discard 1 card from their hand for each turn this card was face-down on the field.
BUT IT HASN'T BEEN EVEN ONE TURN SINCE HE PLAYED IT...SO EVEN IF HE ACTIVATES IT ON THIS TURN, I WON'T HAVE TO DISCARD A CARD FROM MY HAND...
WHAT'S THE MATTER, YUGI?
GO AHEAD! HIT ME!

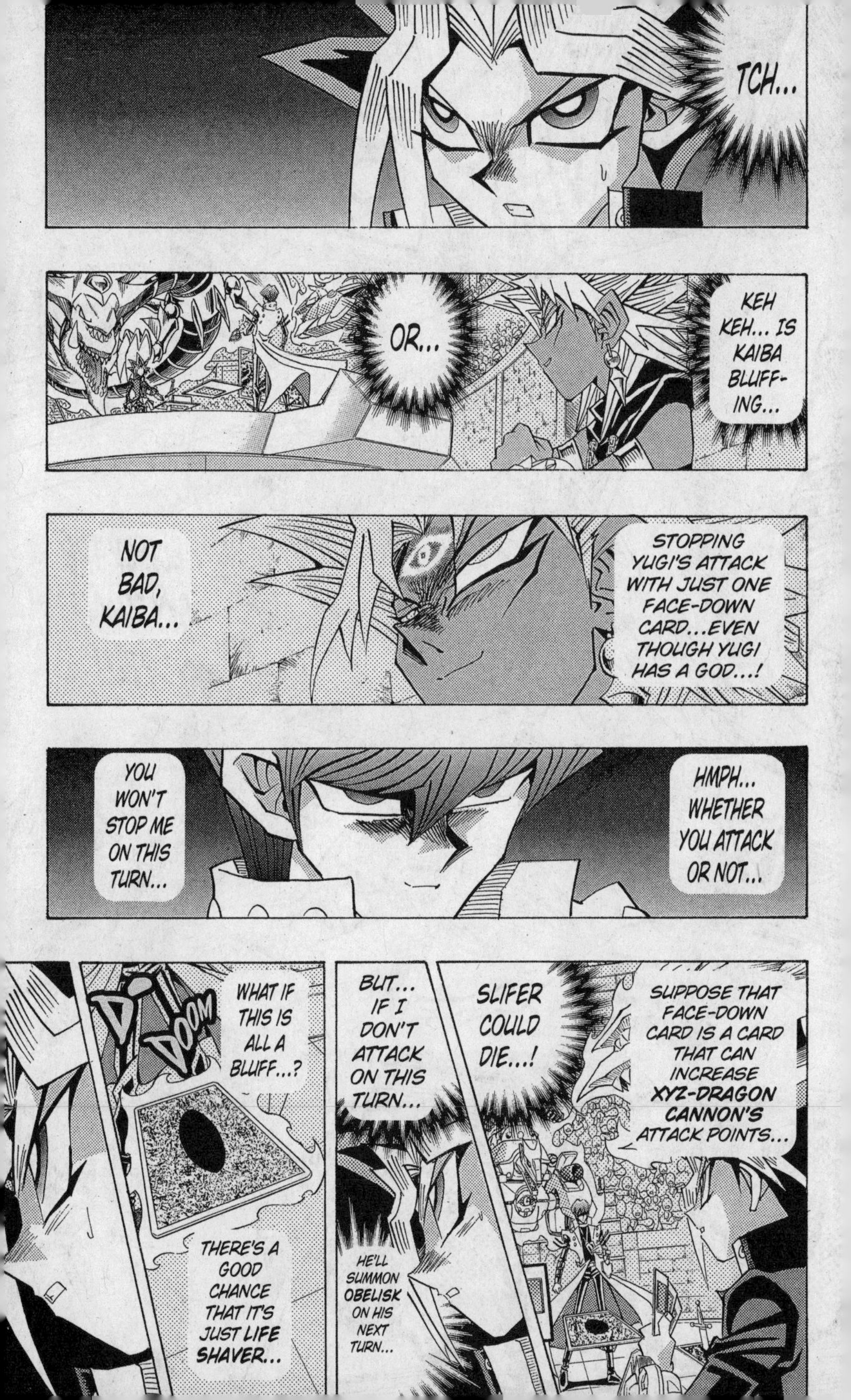

TCH...
KEH KEH... IS KAIBA BLUFFING...
OR...
STOPPING YUGI'S ATTACK WITH JUST ONE FACE-DOWN CARD...EVEN THOUGH YUGI HAS A GOD...!
NOT BAD, KAIBA...
HMPH... WHETHER YOU ATTACK OR NOT...
YOU WON'T STOP ME ON THIS TURN...
SUPPOSE THAT FACE-DOWN CARD IS A CARD THAT CAN INCREASE XYZ-DRAGON CANNON'S ATTACK POINTS...
SLIFER COULD DIE...!
BUT... IF I DON'T ATTACK ON THIS TURN...
HE'LL SUMMON OBELISK ON HIS NEXT TURN...
WHAT IF THIS IS ALL A BLUFF...?
DOOM
THERE'S A GOOD CHANCE THAT IT'S JUST LIFE SHAVER...

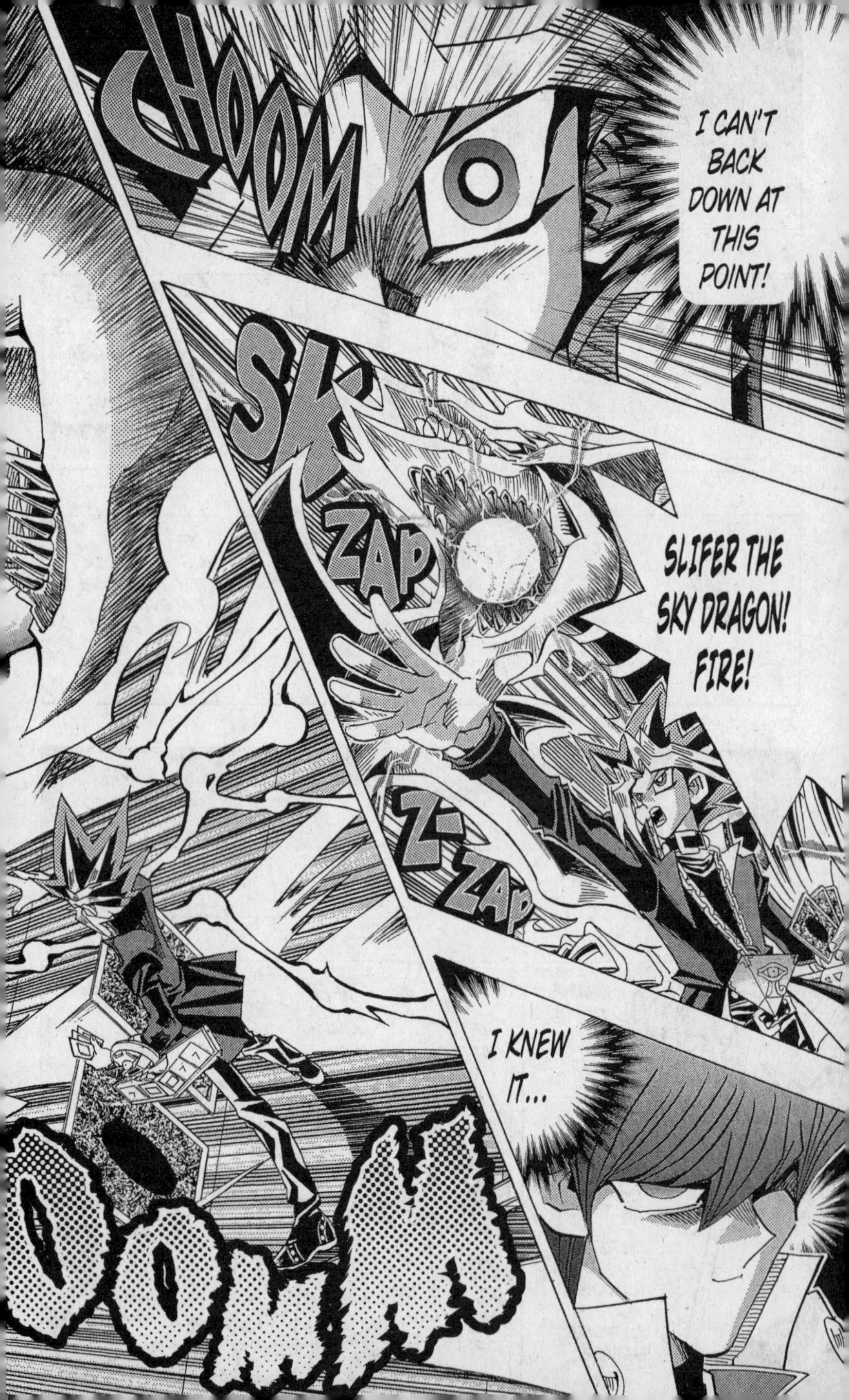
CHOOM
I CAN'T BACK DOWN AT THIS POINT!
SK
ZAP
SLIFER THE SKY DRAGON! FIRE!
Z-ZAP
I KNEW IT...
DOOM

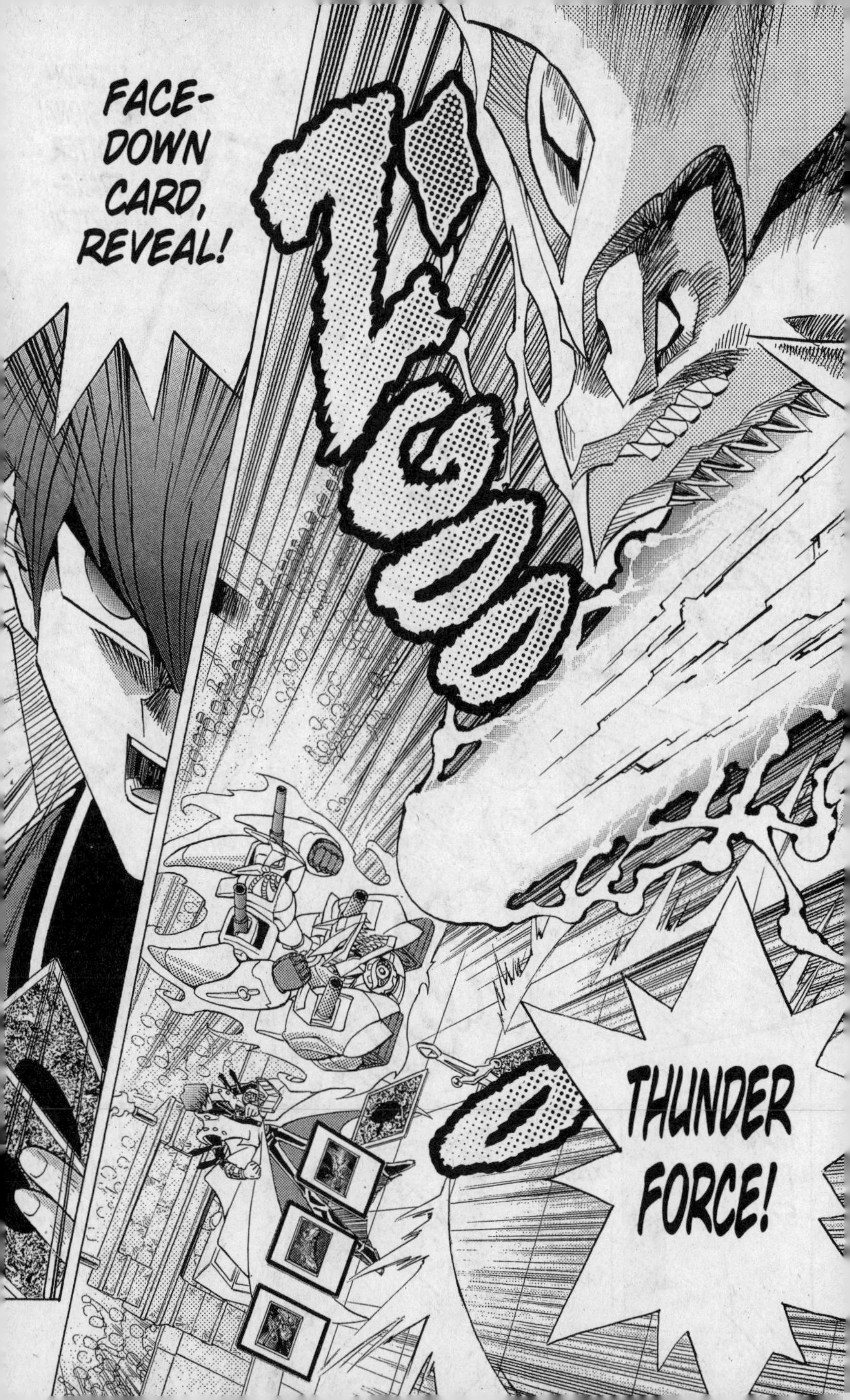
FACE-DOWN CARD, REVEAL!
THUNDER FORCE!

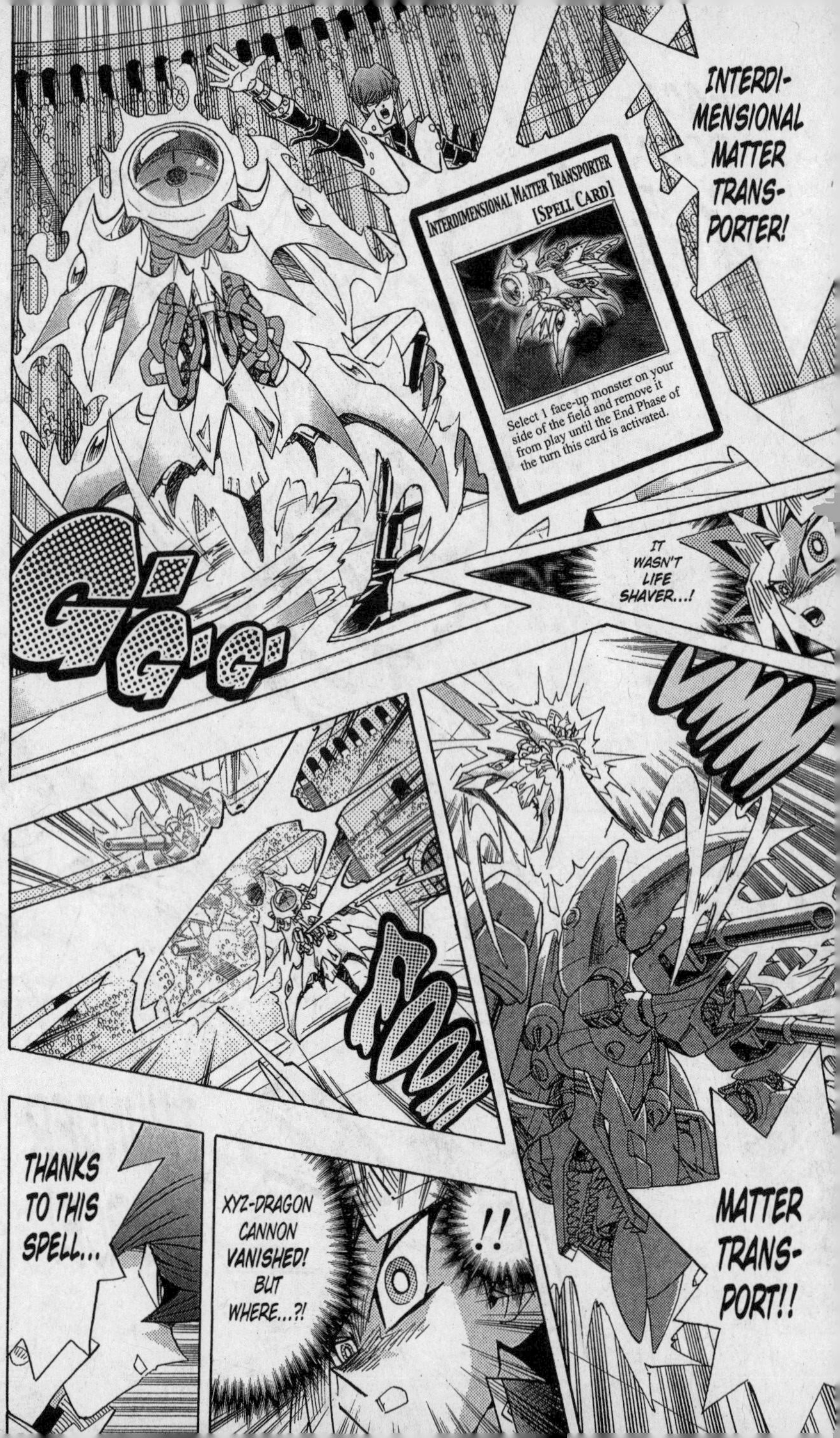
INTERDIMENSIONAL MATTER TRANSPORTER!
INTERDIMENSIONAL MATTER TRANSPORTER
[SPELL CARD]
Select 1 face-up monster on your side of the field and remove it from play until the End Phase of the turn this card is activated.
IT WASN'T LIFE SHAVER...!
MATTER TRANSPORT!!
XYZ-DRAGON CANNON VANISHED! BUT WHERE...?!
!!
THANKS TO THIS SPELL...

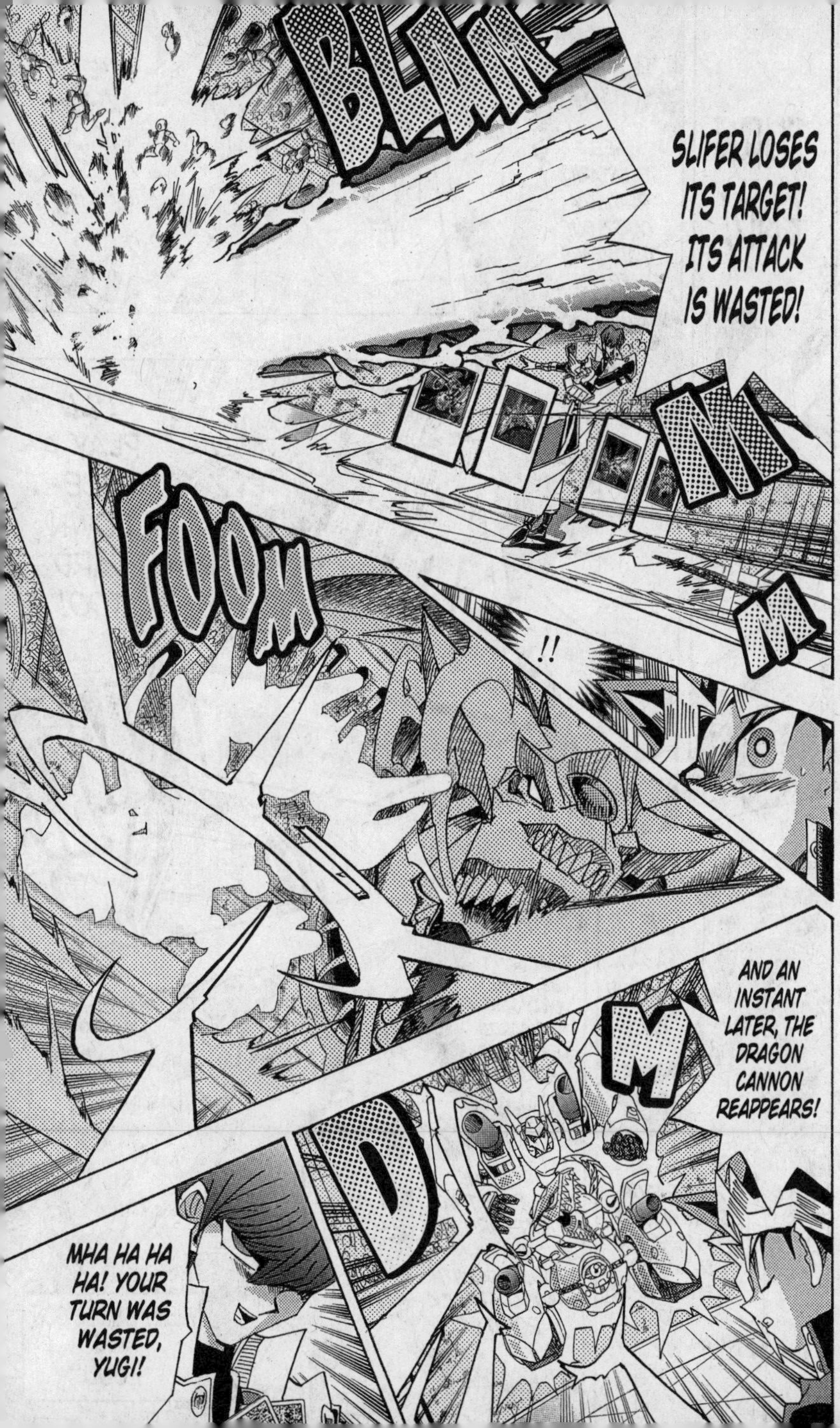
BLAM
SLIFER LOSES ITS TARGET! ITS ATTACK IS WASTED!
!!
FOOM
AND AN INSTANT LATER, THE DRAGON CANNON REAPPEARS!
MHA HA HA HA! YOUR TURN WAS WASTED, YUGI!

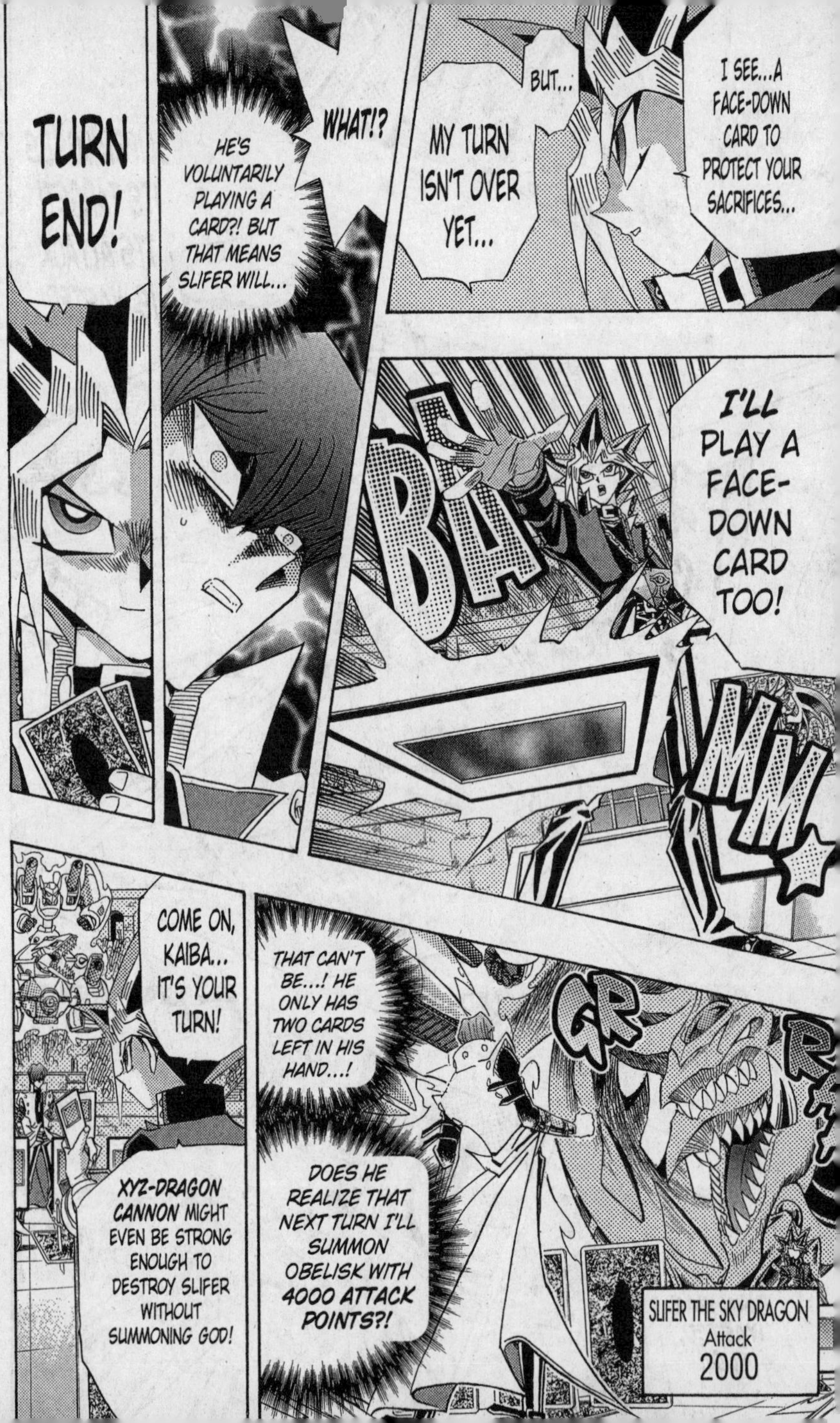
I SEE...A FACE-DOWN CARD TO PROTECT YOUR SACRIFICES...
BUT...
MY TURN ISN'T OVER YET...
I'LL PLAY A FACE-DOWN CARD TOO!
BA
MMM
WHAT!?
HE'S VOLUNTARILY PLAYING A CARD?! BUT THAT MEANS SLIFER WILL...
TURN END!
GR
R
THAT CAN'T BE...! HE ONLY HAS TWO CARDS LEFT IN HIS HAND...!
DOES HE REALIZE THAT NEXT TURN I'LL SUMMON OBELISK WITH 4000 ATTACK POINTS?!
SLIFER THE SKY DRAGON
Attack
2000
COME ON, KAIBA... IT'S YOUR TURN!
XYZ-DRAGON CANNON MIGHT EVEN BE STRONG ENOUGH TO DESTROY SLIFER WITHOUT SUMMONING GOD!

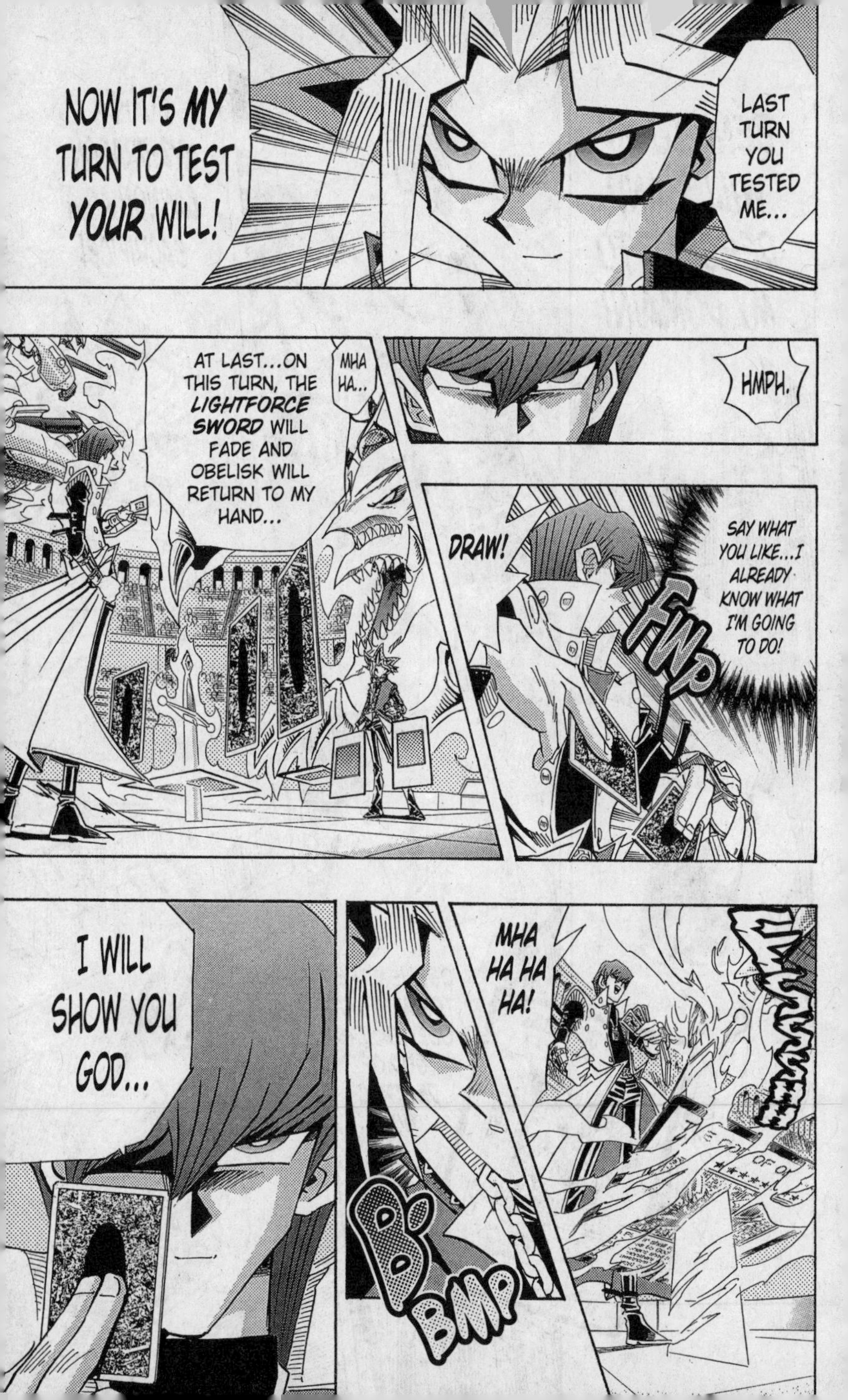
LAST TURN YOU TESTED ME...
NOW IT'S *MY* TURN TO TEST *YOUR* WILL!
HMPH.
SAY WHAT YOU LIKE...I ALREADY KNOW WHAT I'M GOING TO DO!
FWP
DRAW!
MHA HA...
AT LAST...ON THIS TURN, THE ***LIGHTFORCE SWORD*** WILL FADE AND OBELISK WILL RETURN TO MY HAND...
MHA HA HA HA!
BMP
I WILL SHOW YOU GOD...

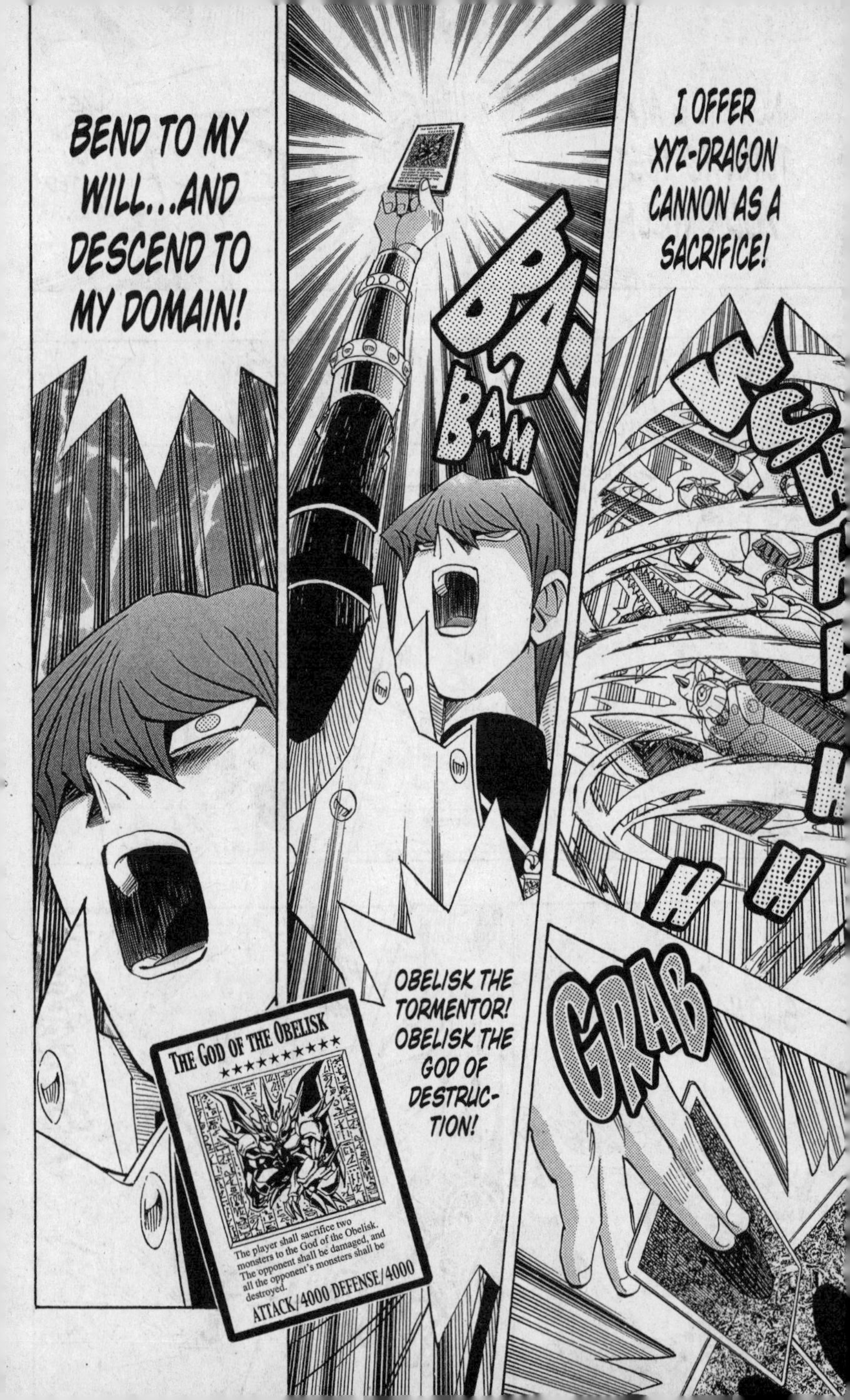
I OFFER XYZ-DRAGON CANNON AS A SACRIFICE!
WSHHHHHH
GRAB
BA-BAM
OBELISK THE TORMENTOR! OBELISK THE GOD OF DESTRUC-TION!
THE GOD OF THE OBELISK
★★★★★★★★★★
The player shall sacrifice two monsters to the God of the Obelisk. The opponent shall be damaged, and all the opponent's monsters shall be destroyed.
ATTACK/4000 DEFENSE/4000
BEND TO MY WILL...AND DESCEND TO MY DOMAIN!

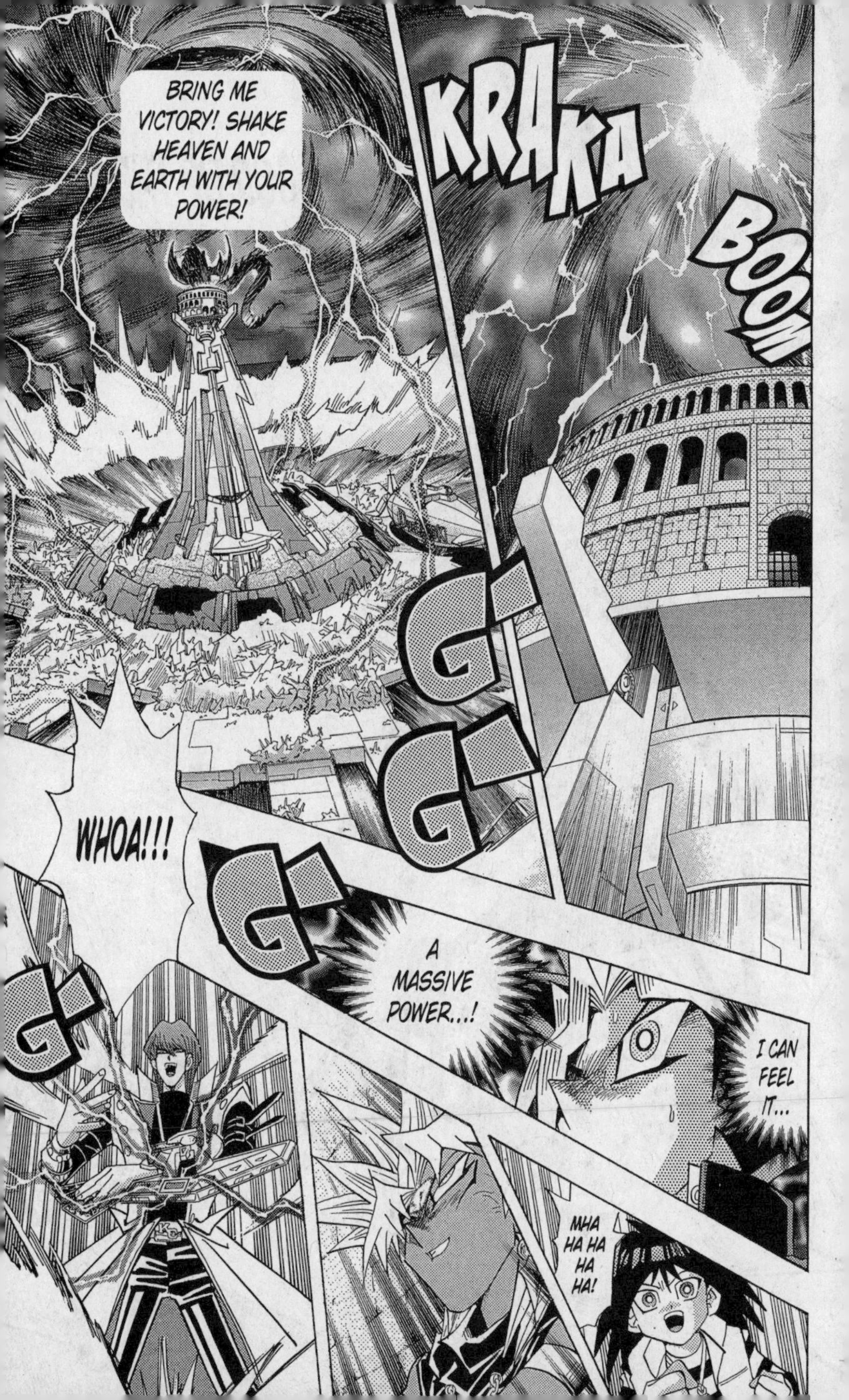
KRAKA
BOOM
G G
BRING ME VICTORY! SHAKE HEAVEN AND EARTH WITH YOUR POWER!
G G
A MASSIVE POWER...!
I CAN FEEL IT...
WHOA!!!
G
MHA HA HA HA HA!

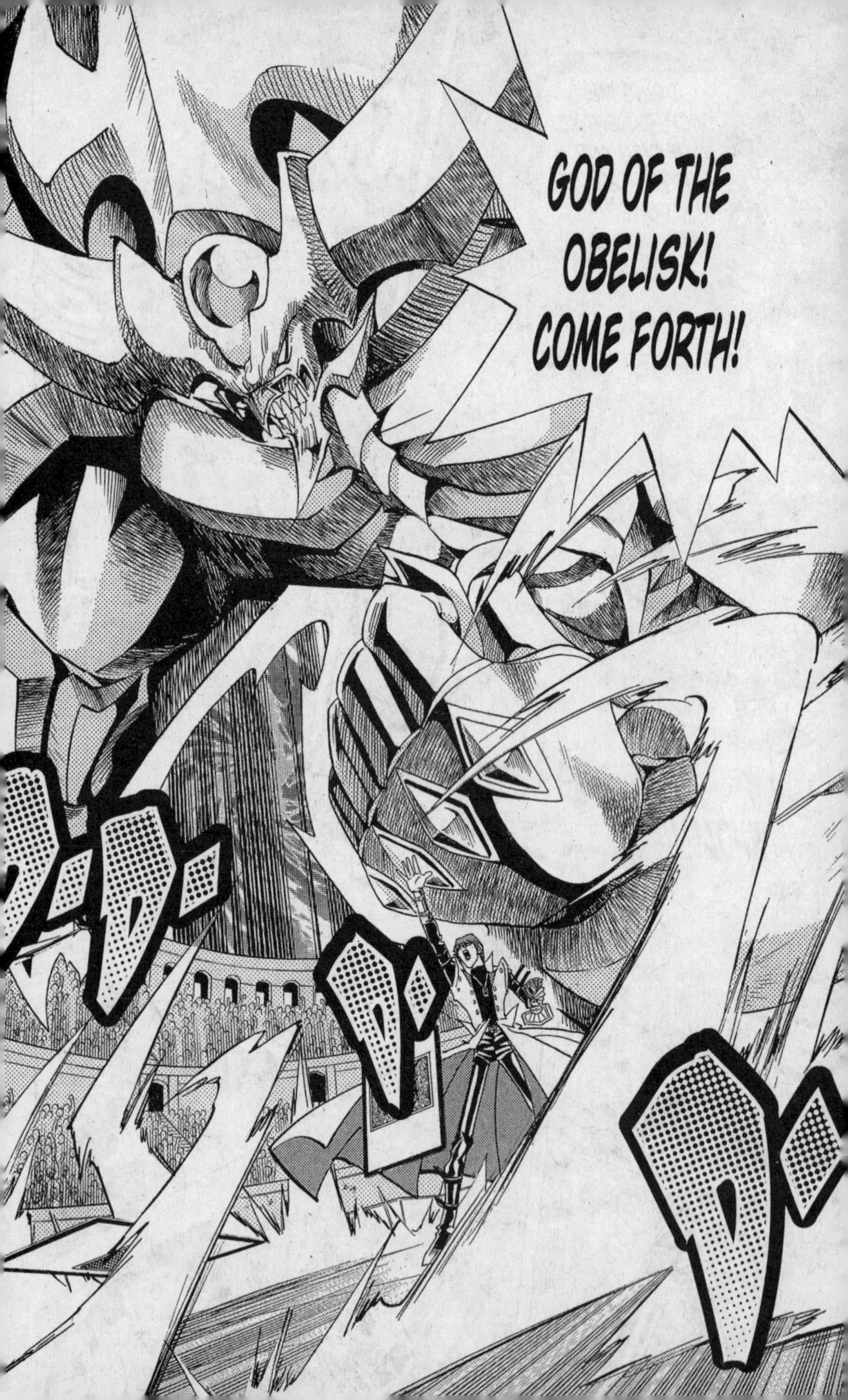
GOD OF THE OBELISK! COME FORTH!

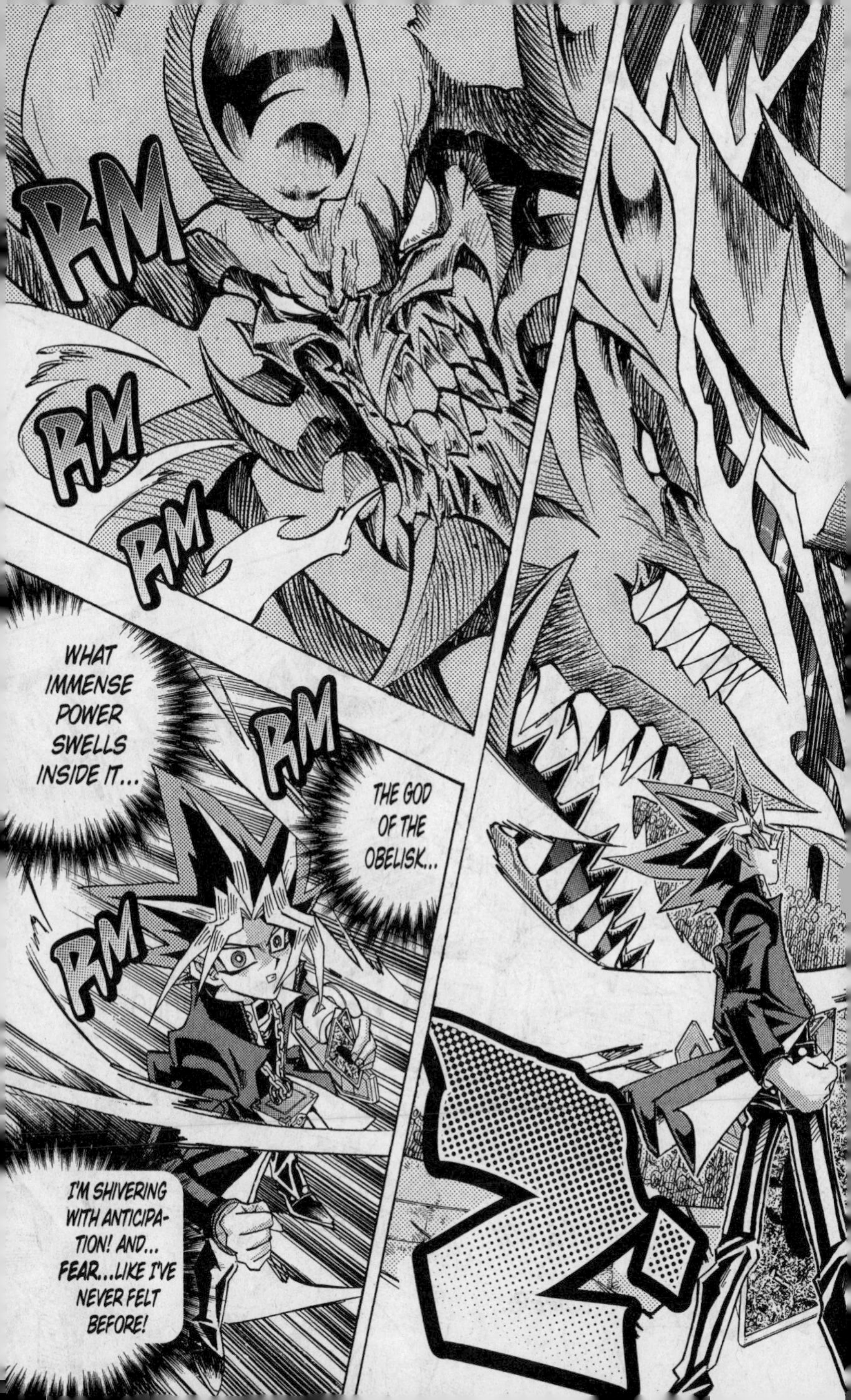
RM
RM
RM
WHAT IMMENSE POWER SWELLS INSIDE IT...
RM
THE GOD OF THE OBELISK...
RM
I'M SHIVERING WITH ANTICIPATION! AND... FEAR...LIKE I'VE NEVER FELT BEFORE!

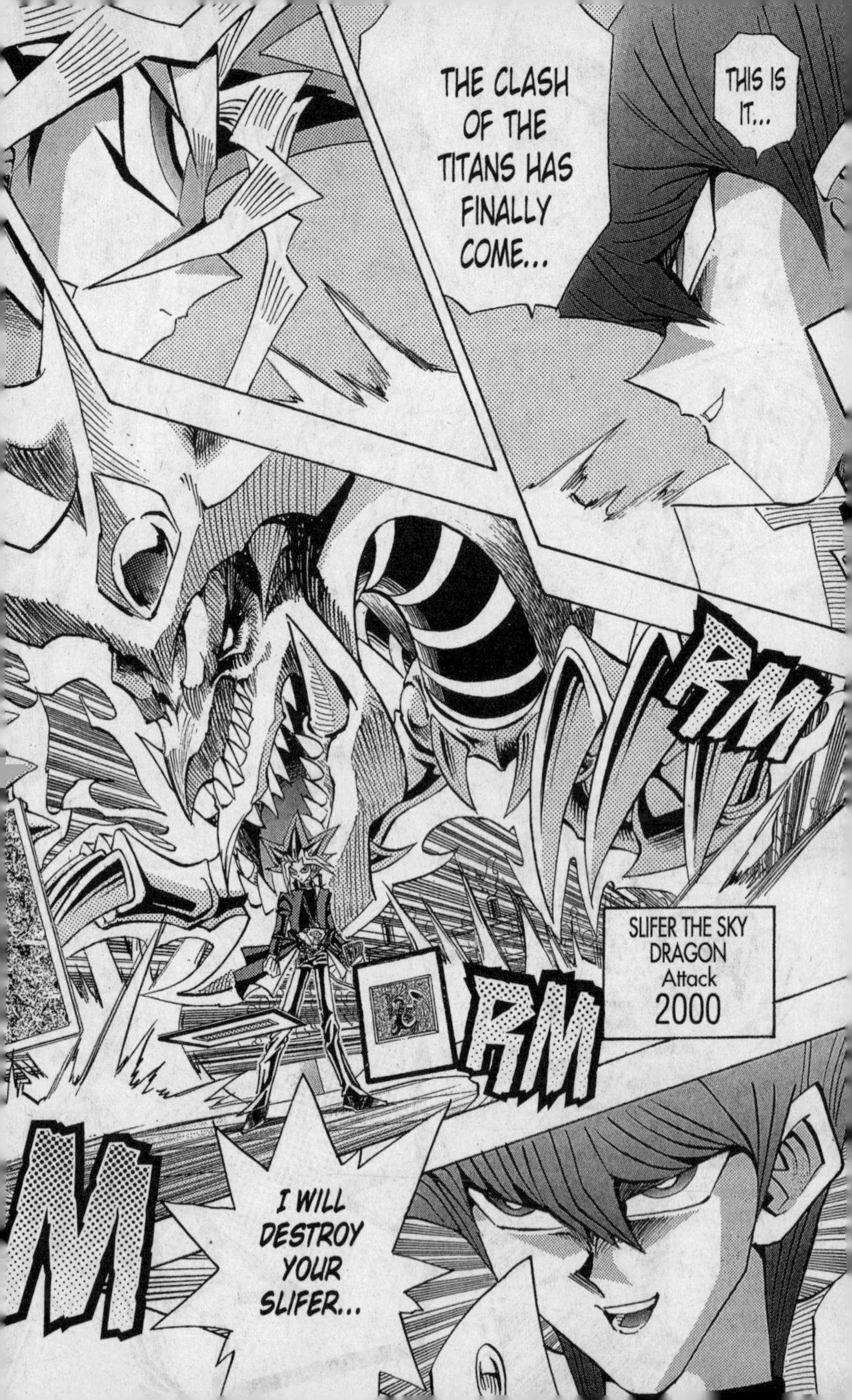
THIS IS IT...
THE CLASH OF THE TITANS HAS FINALLY COME...
RM
SLIFER THE SKY DRAGON Attack 2000
RM
M
I WILL DESTROY YOUR SLIFER...

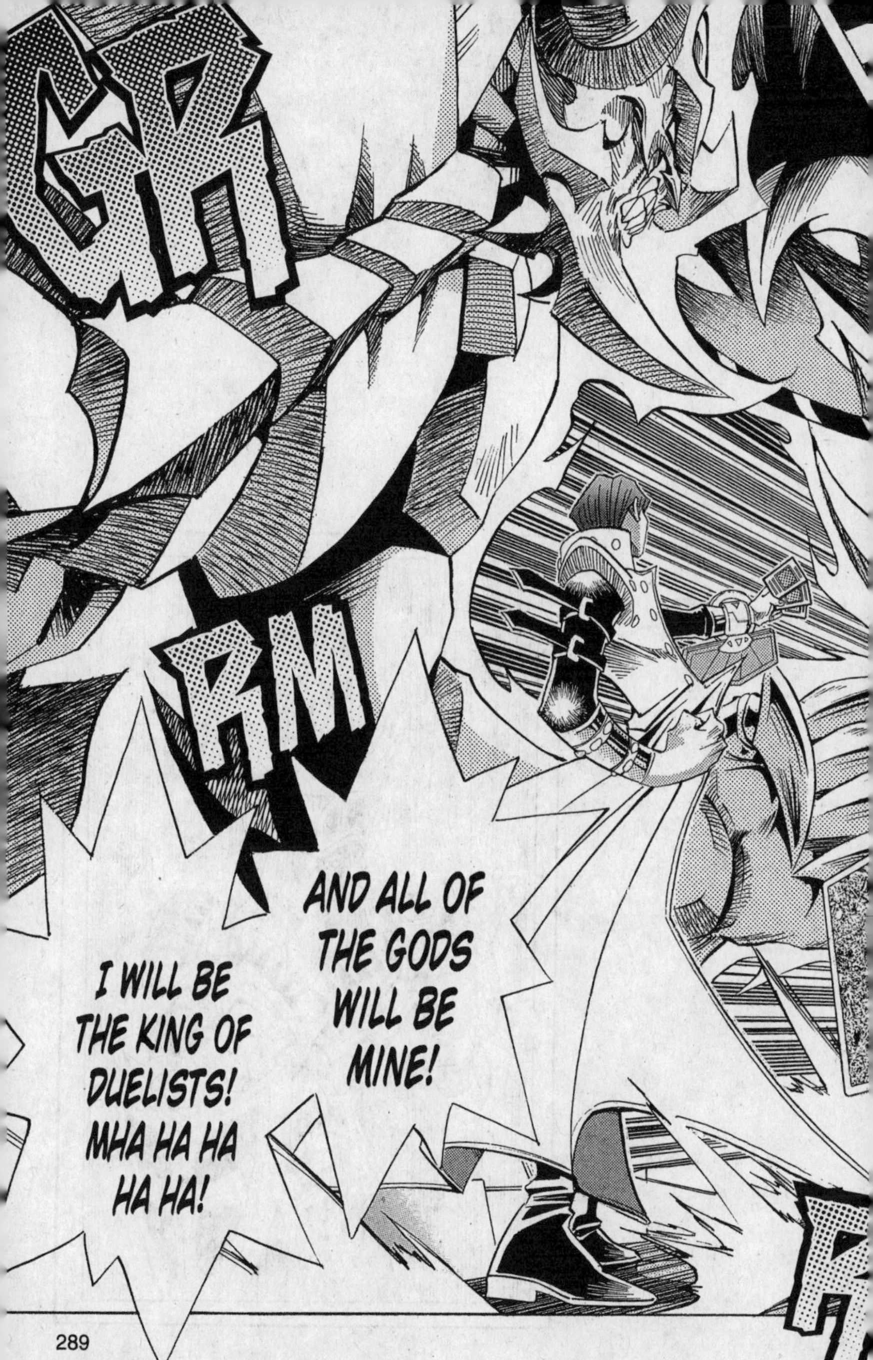
GR
RM
AND ALL OF THE GODS WILL BE MINE!
I WILL BE THE KING OF DUELISTS! MHA HA HA HA HA!

Duel 256: God vs. God!

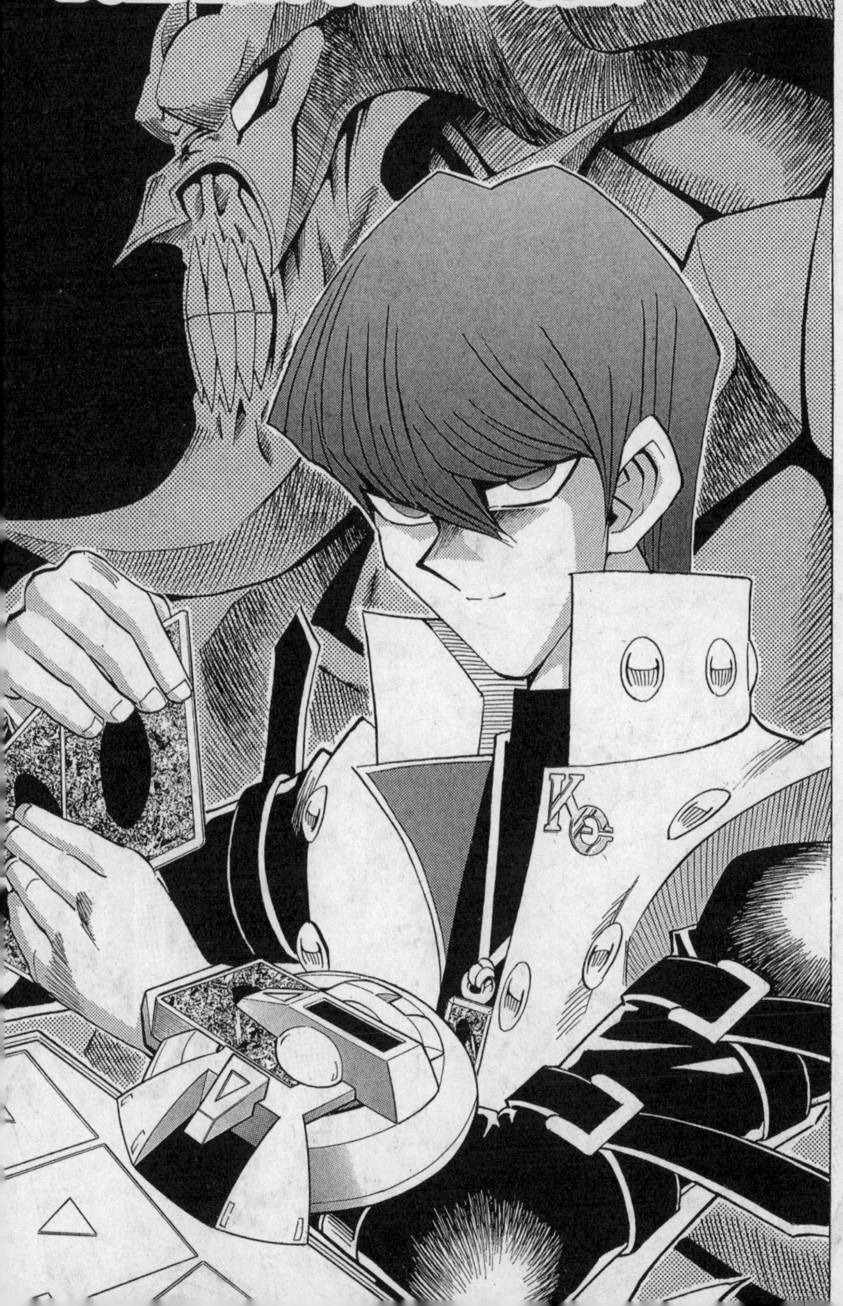
KC

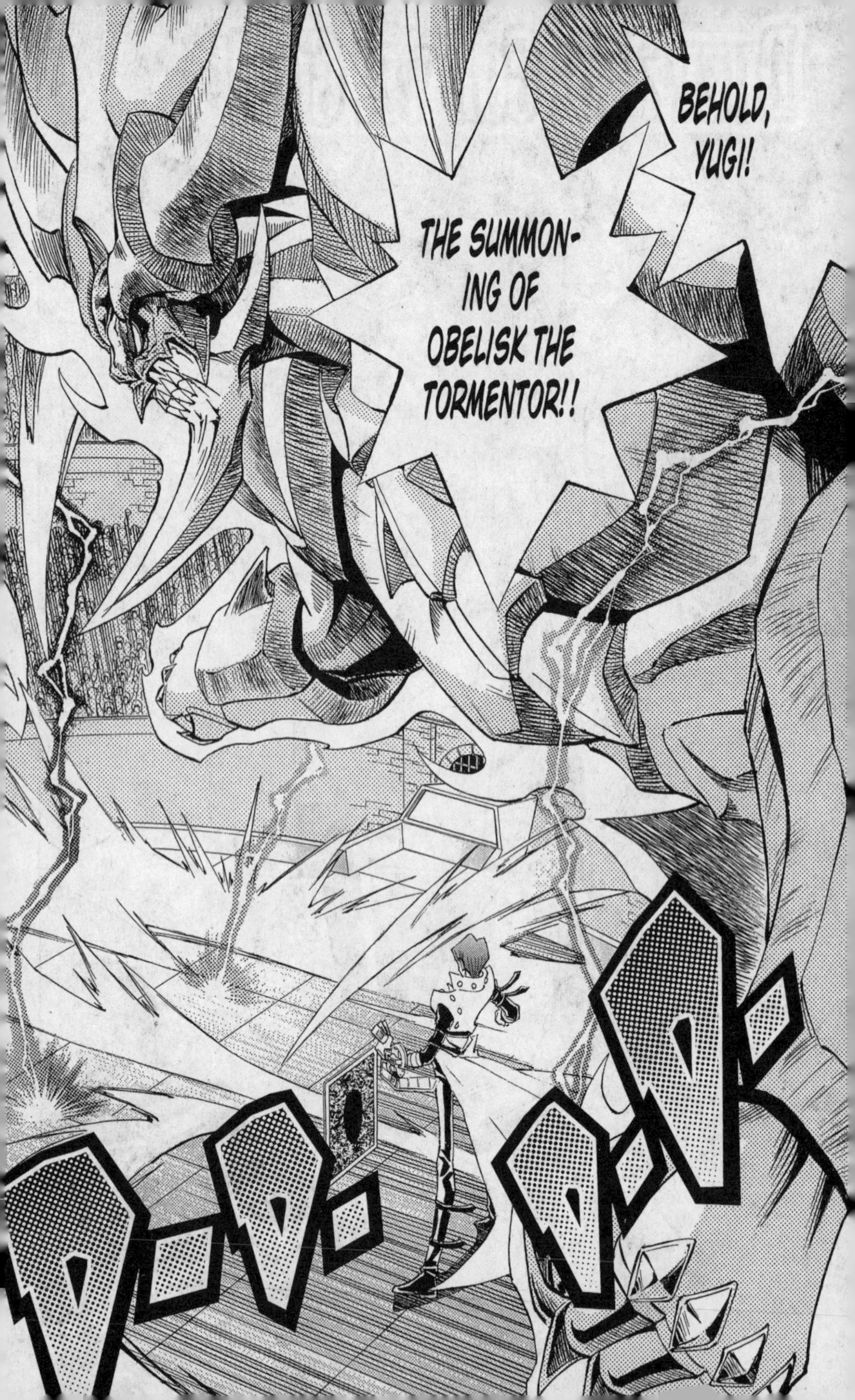
BEHOLD, YUGI!
THE SUMMONING OF OBELISK THE TORMENTOR!!

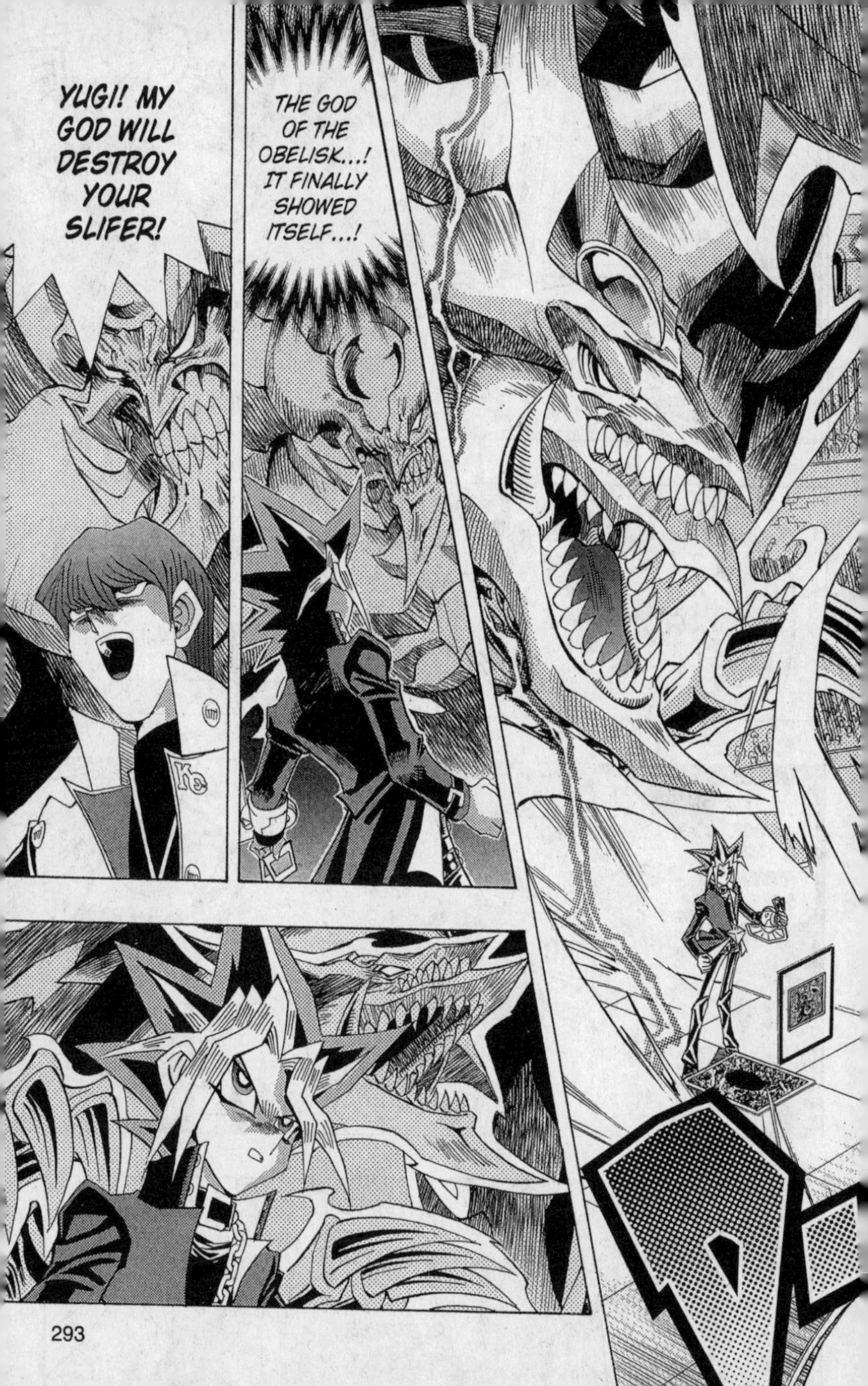
THE GOD OF THE OBELISK...! IT FINALLY SHOWED ITSELF...!
YUGI! MY GOD WILL DESTROY YOUR SLIFER!

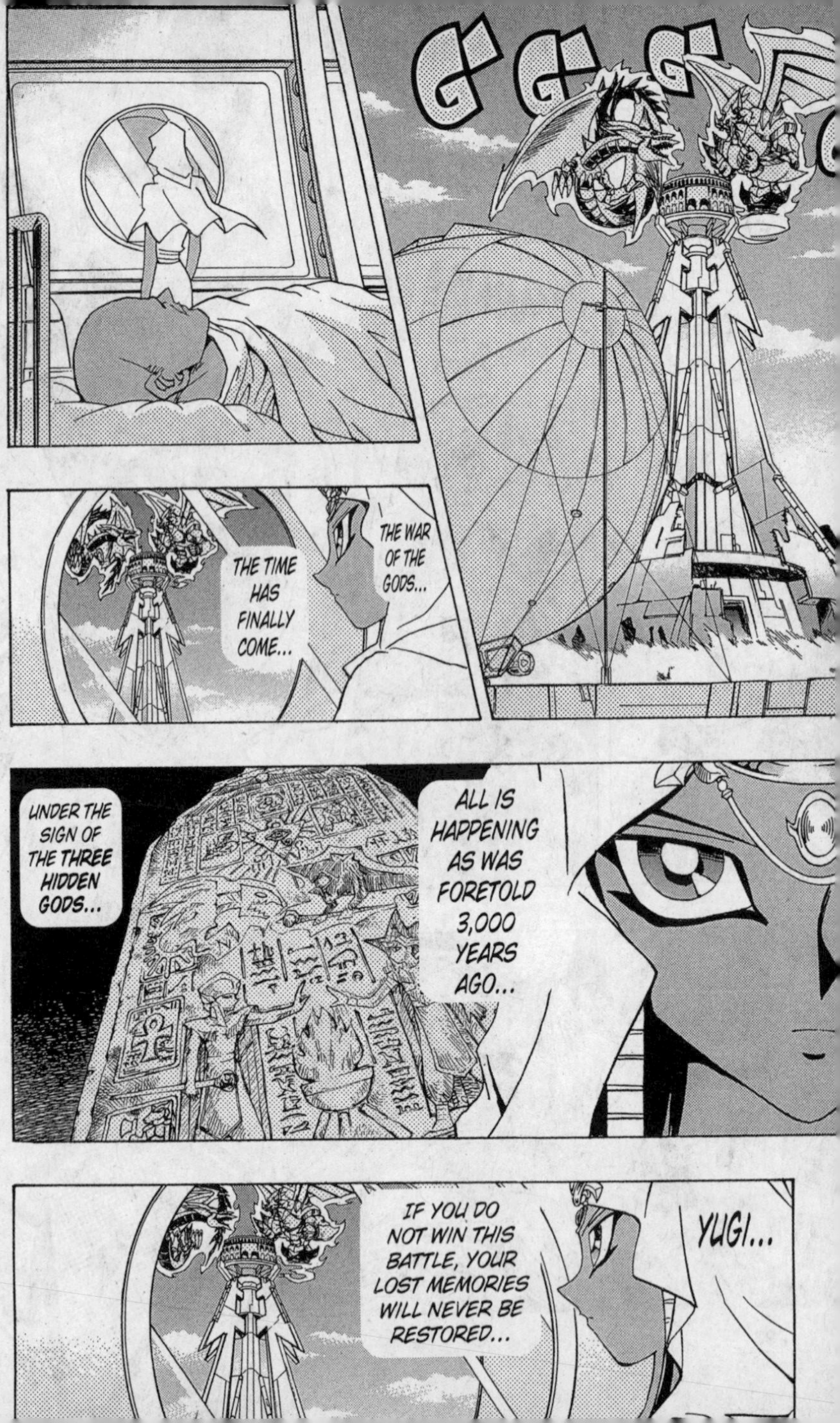
GGG
THE WAR OF THE GODS...
THE TIME HAS FINALLY COME...
ALL IS HAPPENING AS WAS FORETOLD 3,000 YEARS AGO...
UNDER THE SIGN OF THE THREE HIDDEN GODS...
YUGI...
IF YOU DO NOT WIN THIS BATTLE, YOUR LOST MEMORIES WILL NEVER BE RESTORED...

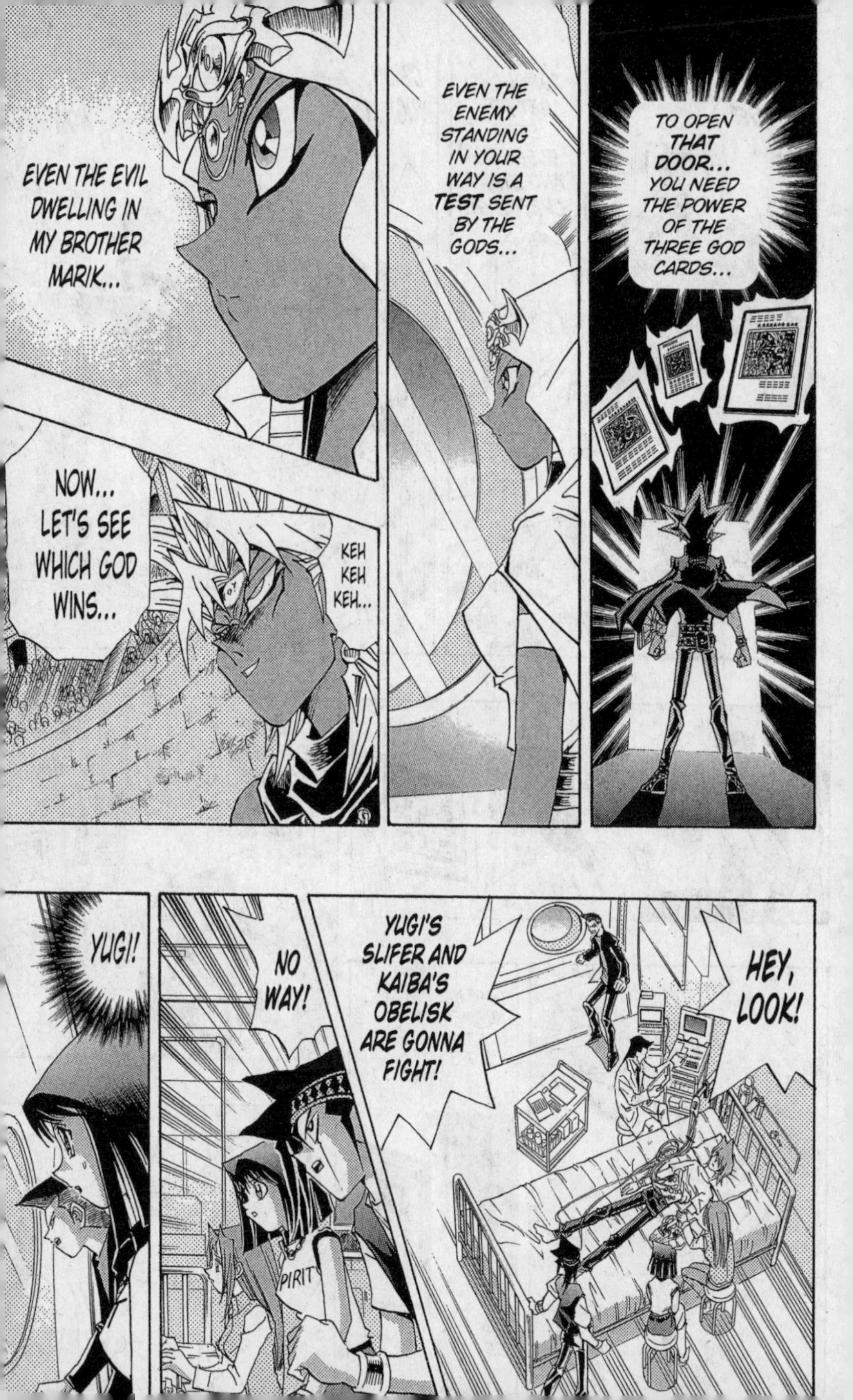
TO OPEN THAT DOOR... YOU NEED THE POWER OF THE THREE GOD CARDS...
EVEN THE ENEMY STANDING IN YOUR WAY IS A TEST SENT BY THE GODS...
EVEN THE EVIL DWELLING IN MY BROTHER MARIK...
KEH KEH KEH...
NOW... LET'S SEE WHICH GOD WINS...
HEY, LOOK!
YUGI'S SLIFER AND KAIBA'S OBELISK ARE GONNA FIGHT!
NO WAY!
PIRIT
YUGI!

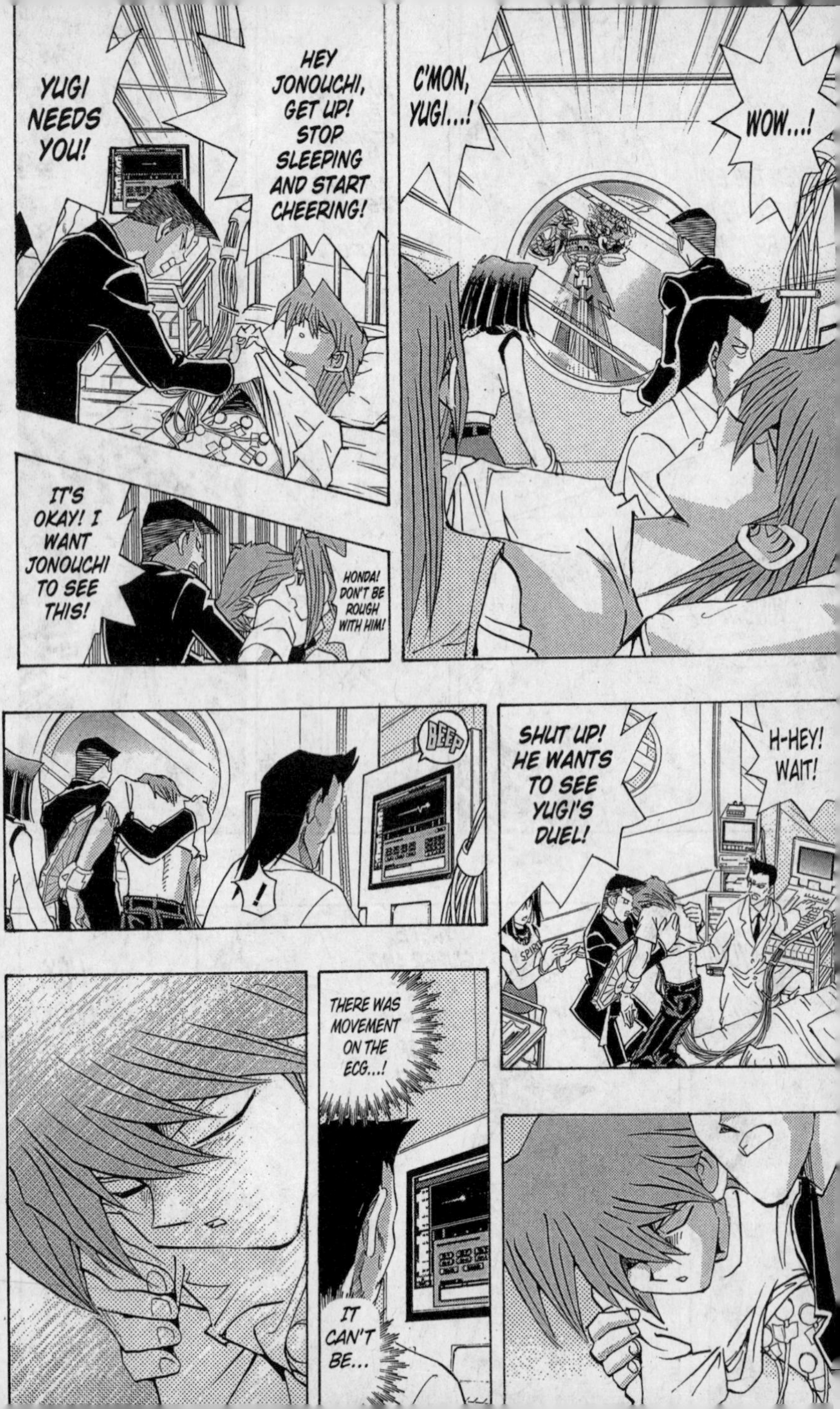
WOW...!
C'MON, YUGI...!
HEY JONOUCHI, GET UP! STOP SLEEPING AND START CHEERING!
YUGI NEEDS YOU!
HONDA! DON'T BE ROUGH WITH HIM!
IT'S OKAY! I WANT JONOUCHI TO SEE THIS!
H-HEY! WAIT!
SHUT UP! HE WANTS TO SEE YUGI'S DUEL!
BEEP
!
THERE WAS MOVEMENT ON THE ECG...!
IT CAN'T BE...

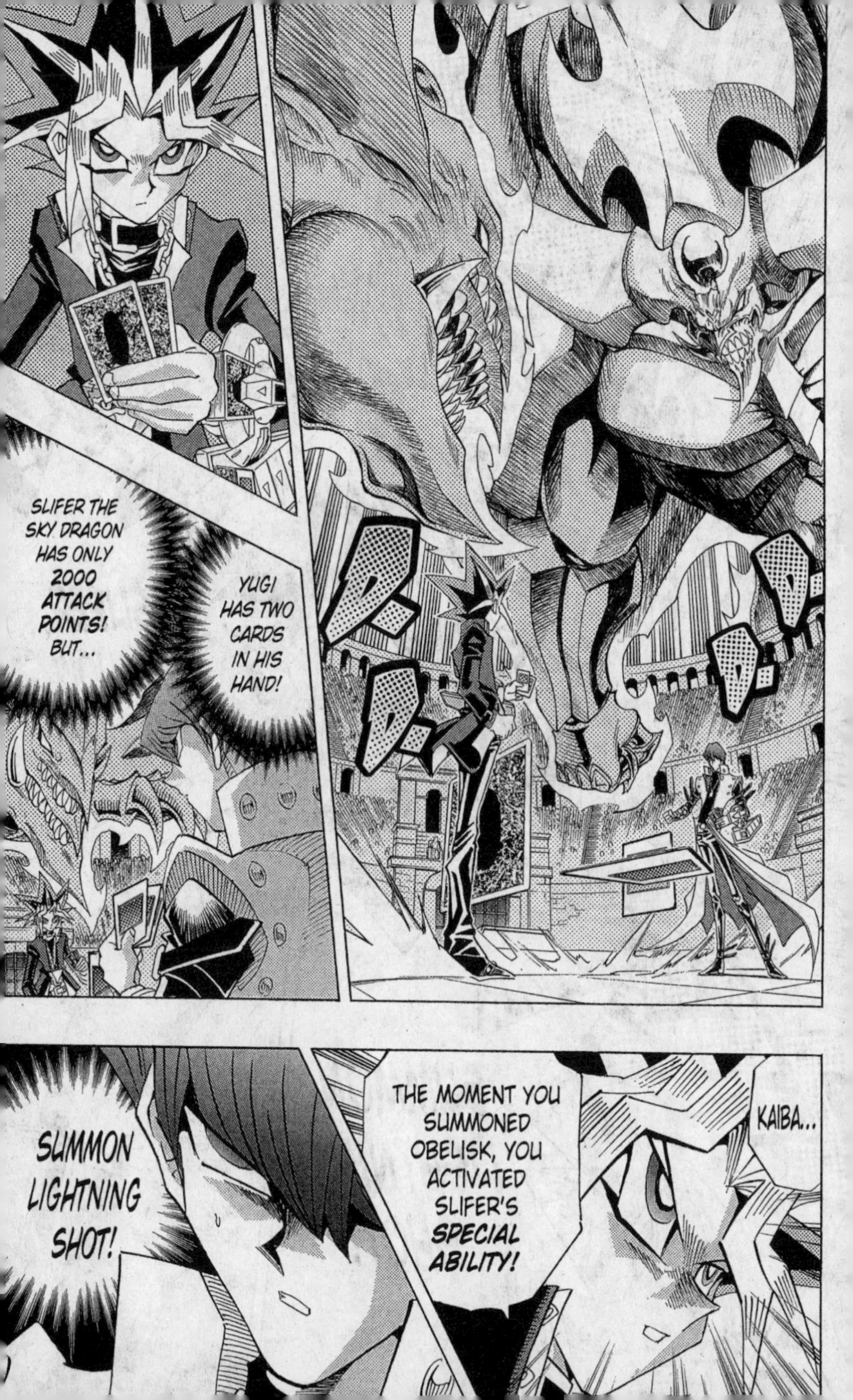
SLIFER THE SKY DRAGON HAS ONLY 2000 ATTACK POINTS! BUT...
YUGI HAS TWO CARDS IN HIS HAND!
KAIBA...
THE MOMENT YOU SUMMONED OBELISK, YOU ACTIVATED SLIFER'S SPECIAL ABILITY!
SUMMON LIGHTNING SHOT!

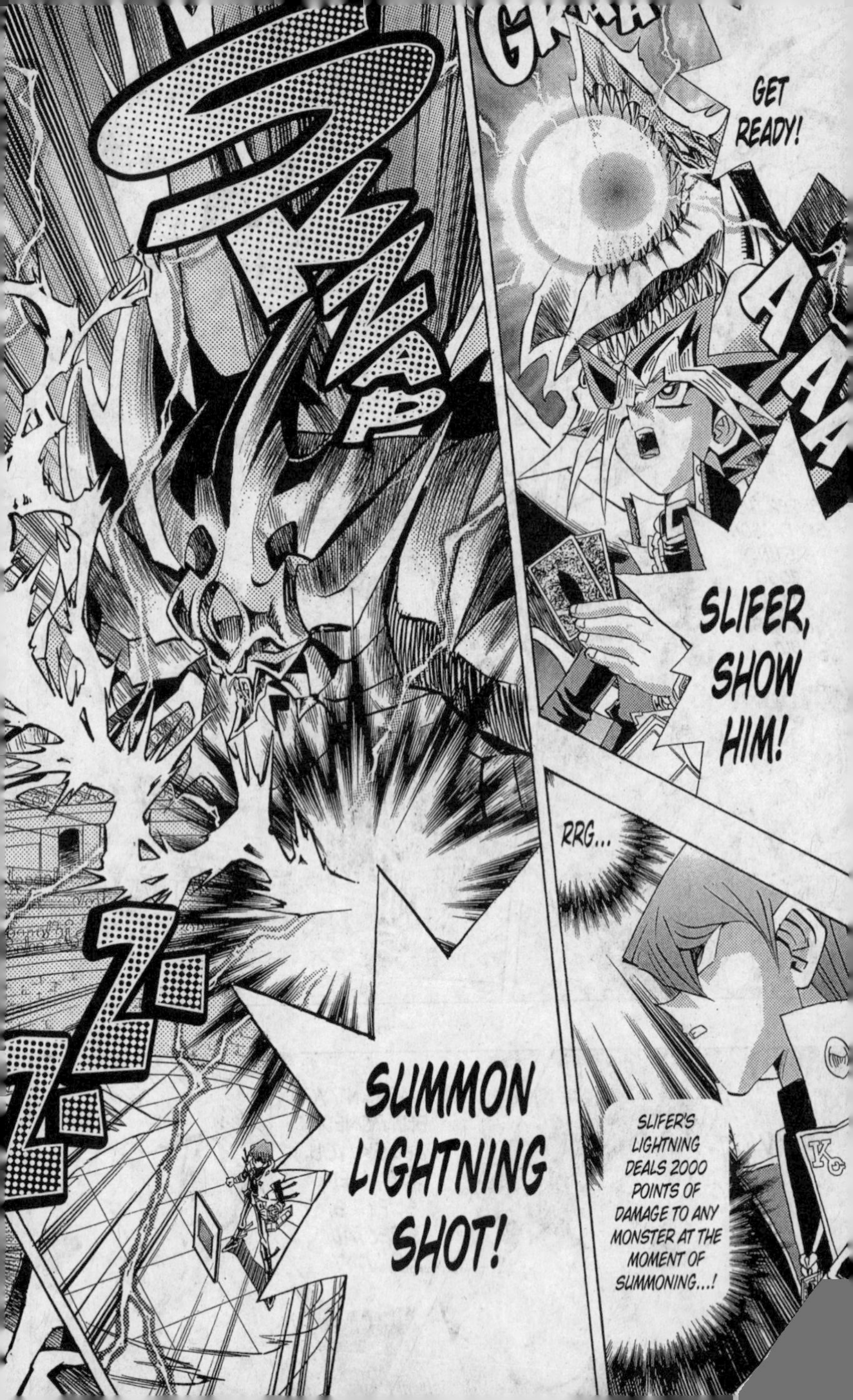
GET READY!
SLIFER, SHOW HIM!
RRG...
SLIFER'S LIGHTNING DEALS 2000 POINTS OF DAMAGE TO ANY MONSTER AT THE MOMENT OF SUMMONING...!
SUMMON LIGHTNING SHOT!

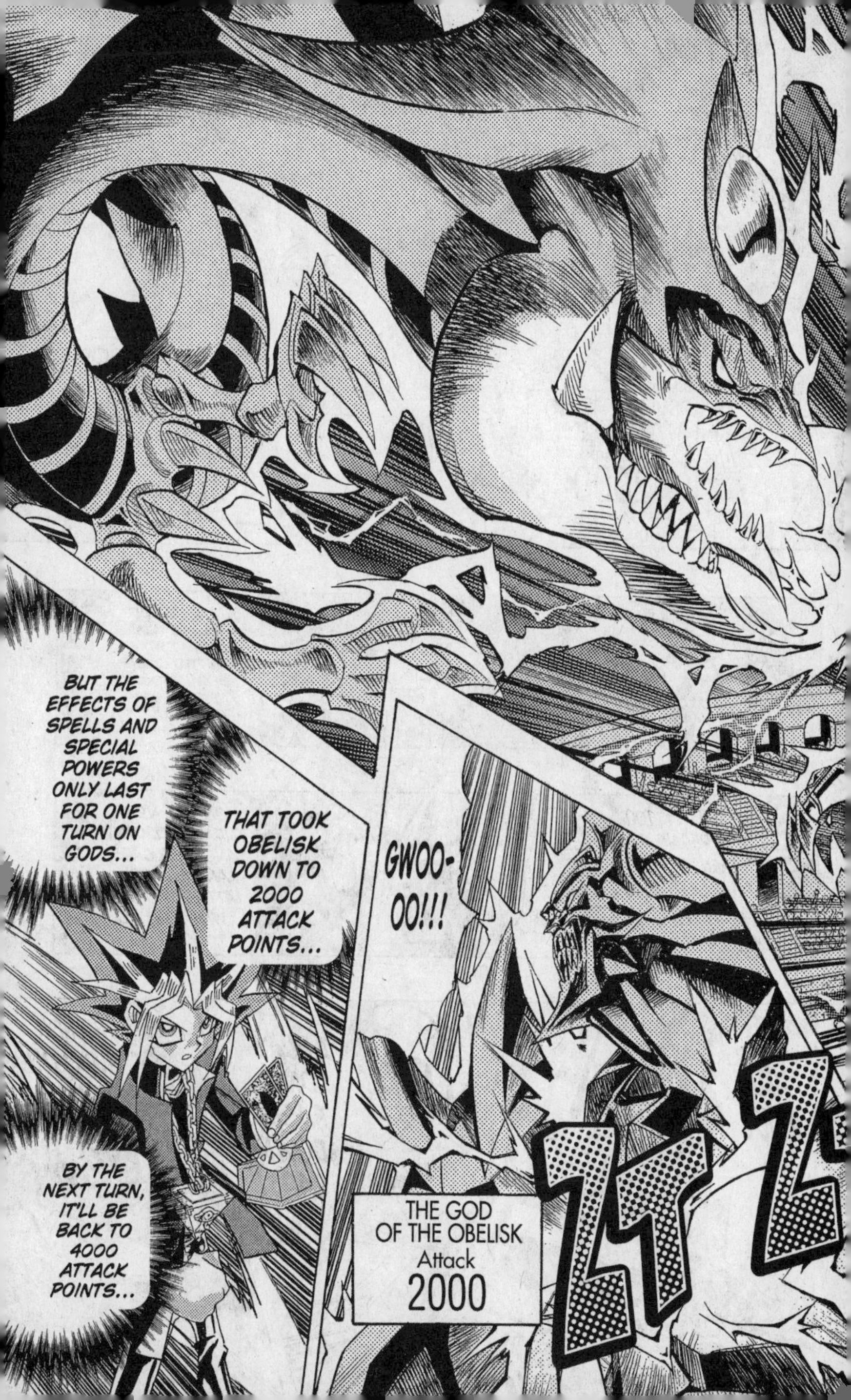
GWOO-OO!!!
THE GOD OF THE OBELISK Attack 2000
THAT TOOK OBELISK DOWN TO 2000 ATTACK POINTS...
BUT THE EFFECTS OF SPELLS AND SPECIAL POWERS ONLY LAST FOR ONE TURN ON GODS...
BY THE NEXT TURN, IT'LL BE BACK TO 4000 ATTACK POINTS...

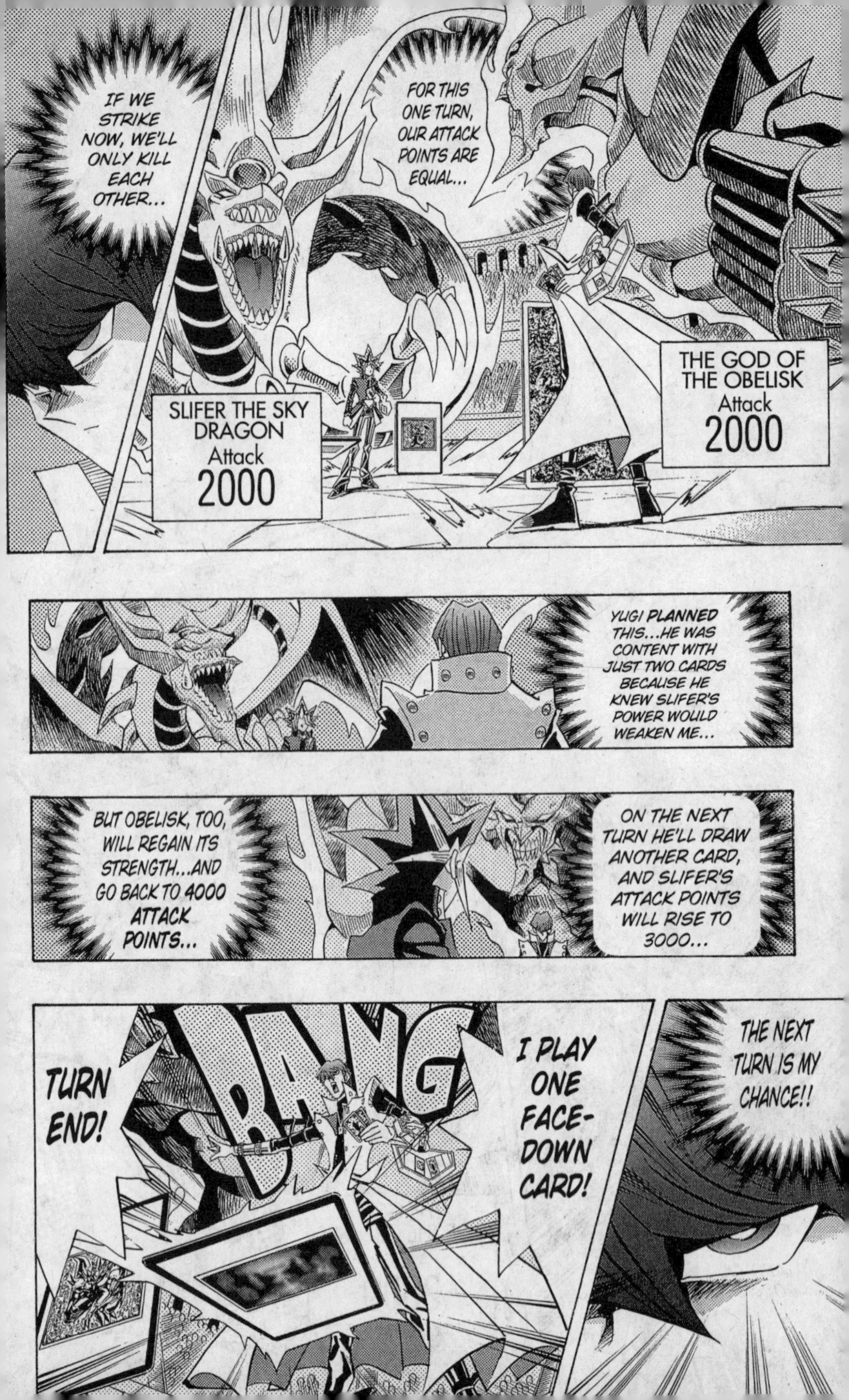
FOR THIS ONE TURN, OUR ATTACK POINTS ARE EQUAL...
THE GOD OF THE OBELISK Attack 2000
SLIFER THE SKY DRAGON Attack 2000
IF WE STRIKE NOW, WE'LL ONLY KILL EACH OTHER...
YUGI PLANNED THIS...HE WAS CONTENT WITH JUST TWO CARDS BECAUSE HE KNEW SLIFER'S POWER WOULD WEAKEN ME...
ON THE NEXT TURN HE'LL DRAW ANOTHER CARD, AND SLIFER'S ATTACK POINTS WILL RISE TO 3000...
BUT OBELISK, TOO, WILL REGAIN ITS STRENGTH...AND GO BACK TO 4000 ATTACK POINTS...
THE NEXT TURN IS MY CHANCE!!
I PLAY ONE FACE-DOWN CARD!
BANG
TURN END!

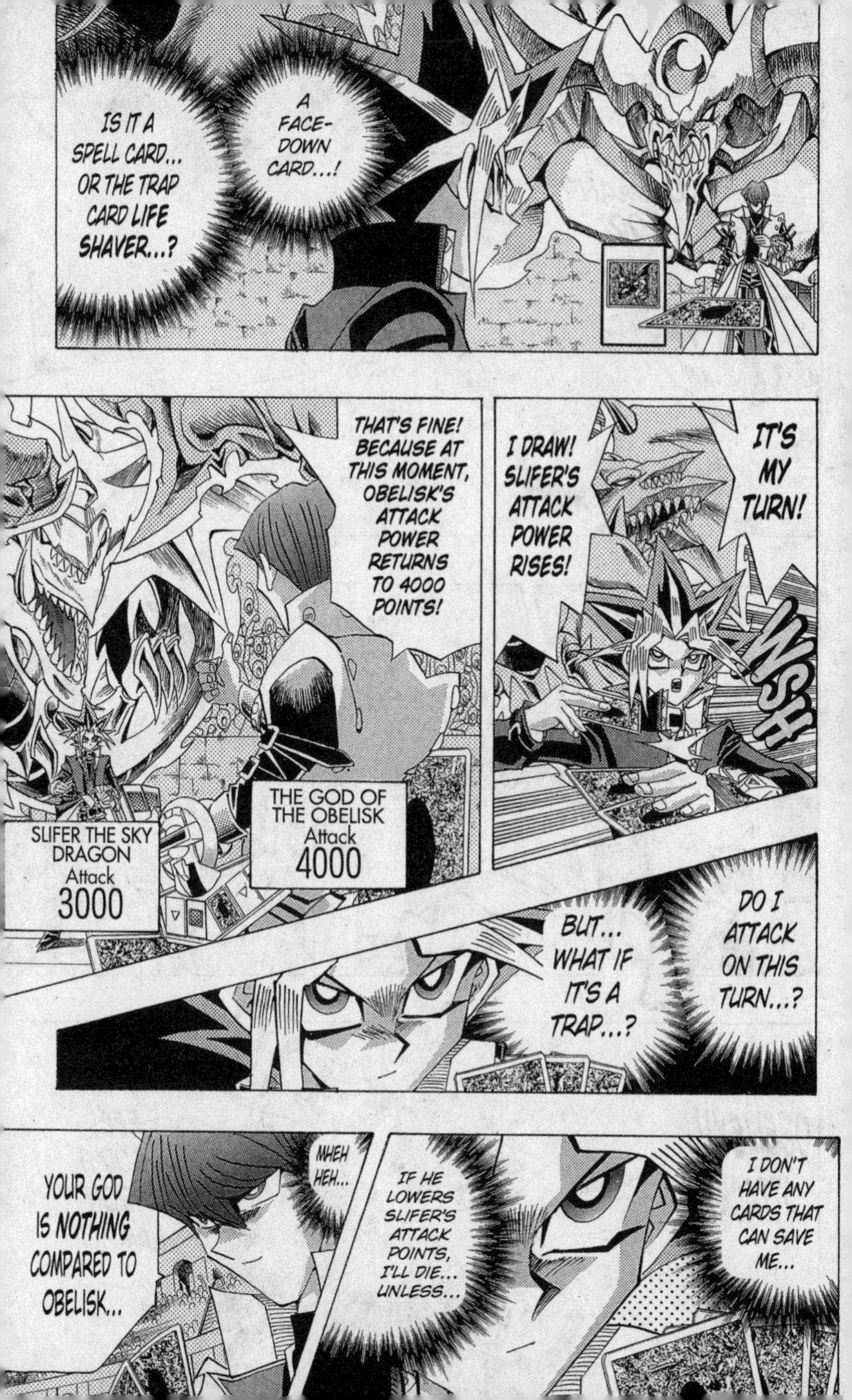

A FACE-DOWN CARD...!
IS IT A SPELL CARD... OR THE TRAP CARD LIFE SHAVER...?
IT'S MY TURN!
I DRAW! SLIFER'S ATTACK POWER RISES!
WSH
THAT'S FINE! BECAUSE AT THIS MOMENT, OBELISK'S ATTACK POWER RETURNS TO 4000 POINTS!
THE GOD OF THE OBELISK Attack 4000
SLIFER THE SKY DRAGON Attack 3000
DO I ATTACK ON THIS TURN...?
BUT... WHAT IF IT'S A TRAP...?
I DON'T HAVE ANY CARDS THAT CAN SAVE ME...
IF HE LOWERS SLIFER'S ATTACK POINTS, I'LL DIE... UNLESS...
MHEH HEH...
YOUR GOD IS NOTHING COMPARED TO OBELISK...

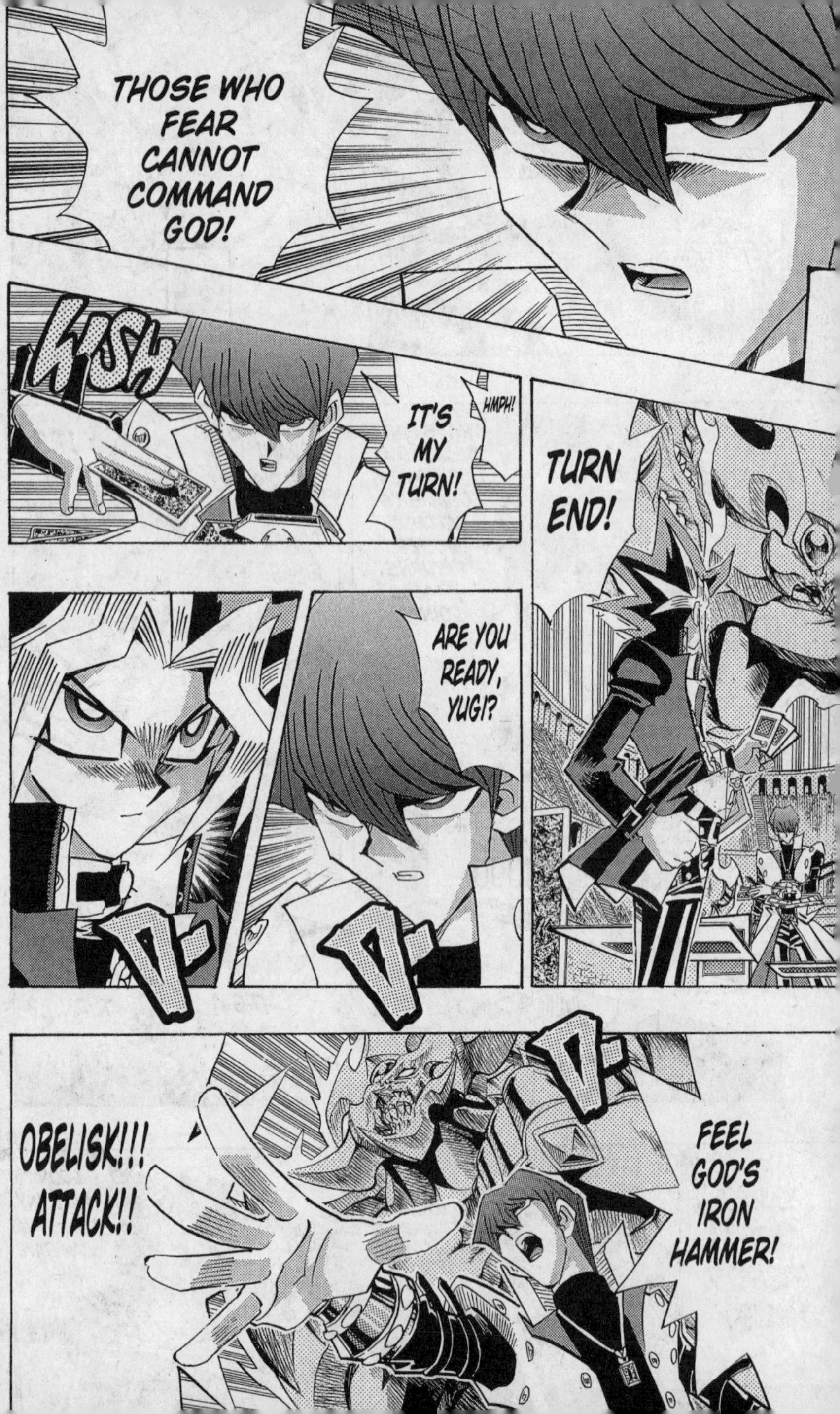
THOSE WHO FEAR CANNOT COMMAND GOD!
TURN END!
HMPH!
IT'S MY TURN!
WSH
ARE YOU READY, YUGI?
D-
D-
FEEL GOD'S IRON HAMMER!
D-
OBELISK!!! ATTACK!!

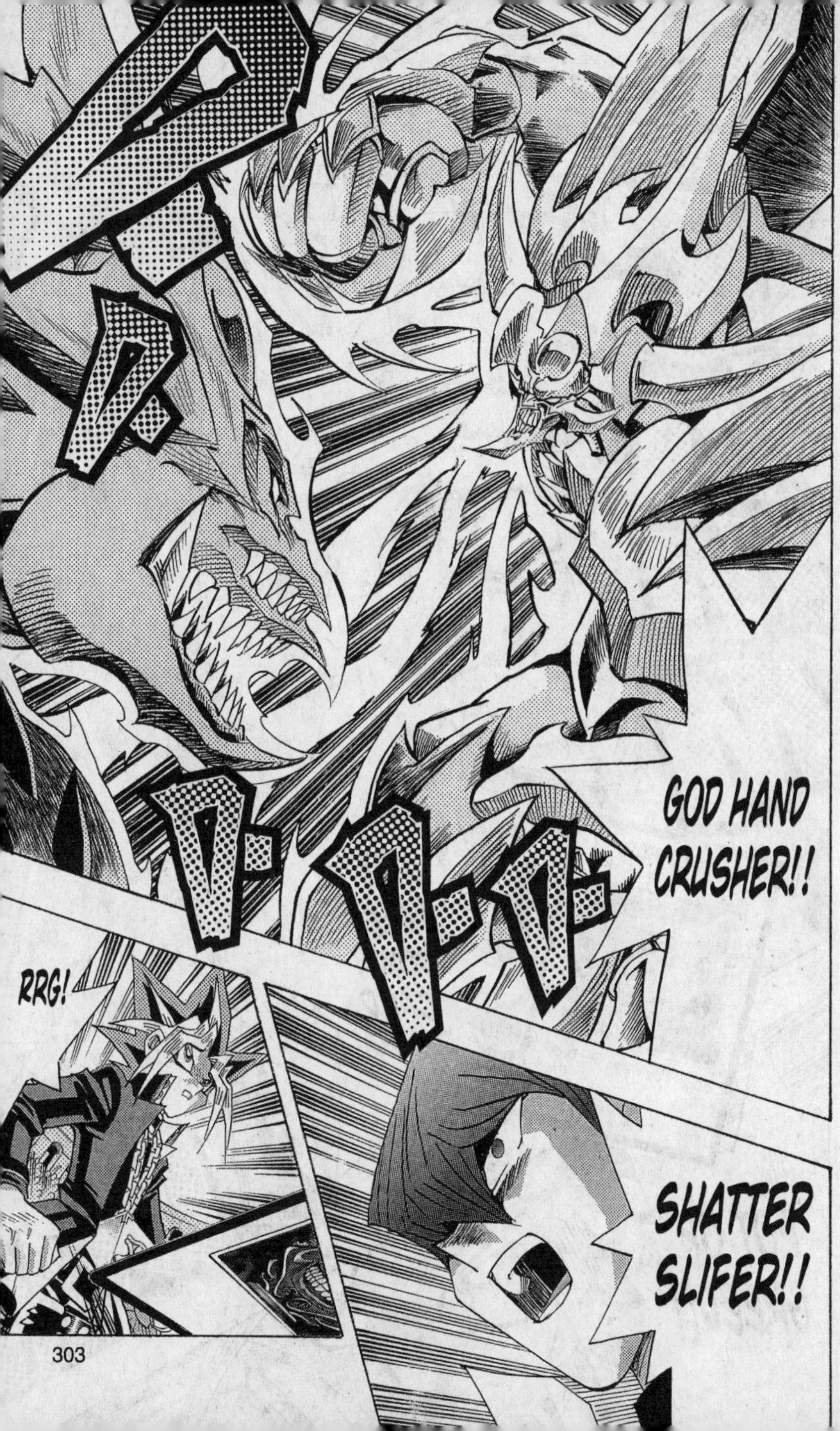
GOD HAND CRUSHER!!
SHATTER SLIFER!!
RRG!

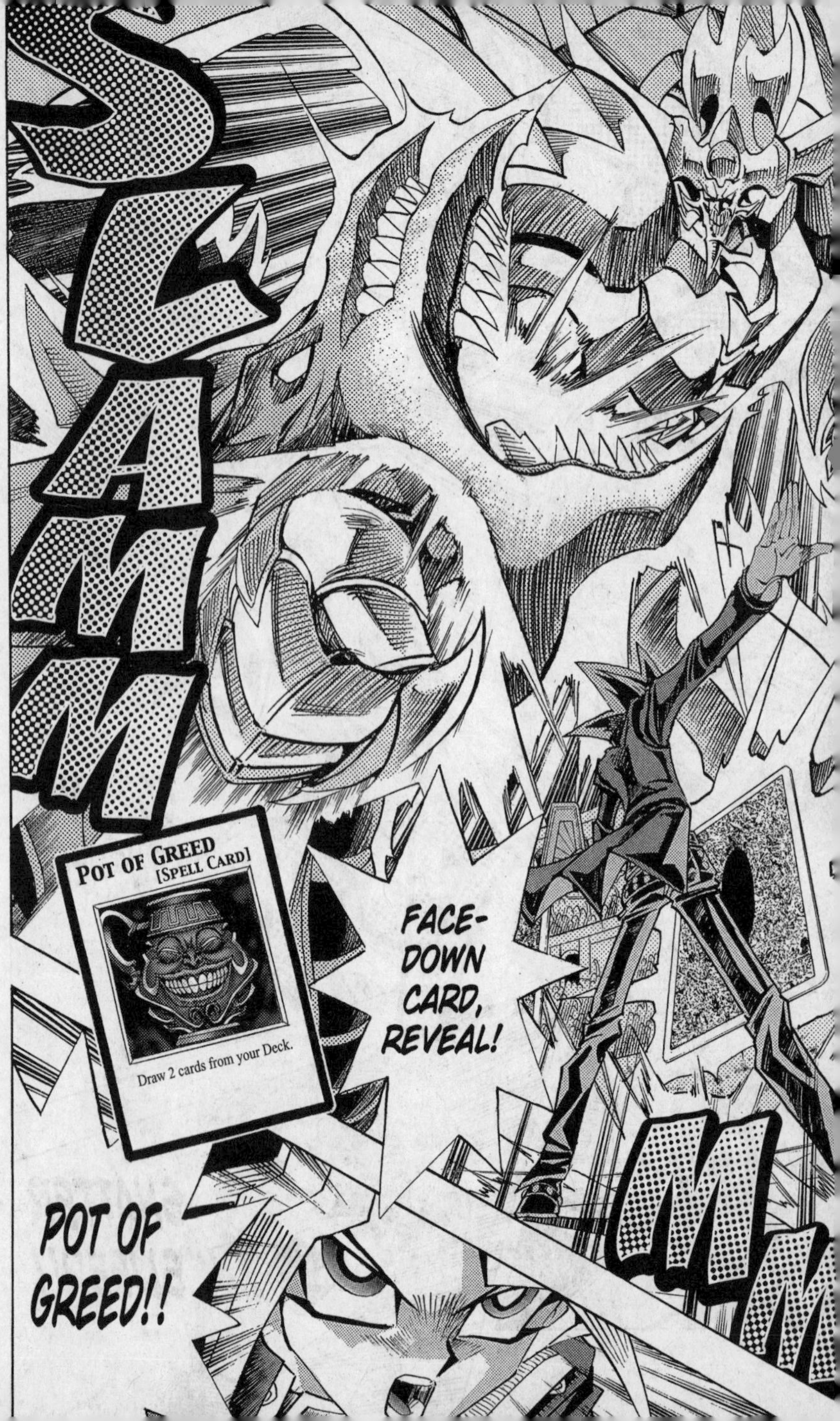
SLAMM
FACE-DOWN CARD, REVEAL!
POT OF GREED
[SPELL CARD]
Draw 2 cards from your Deck.
POT OF GREED!!
MM

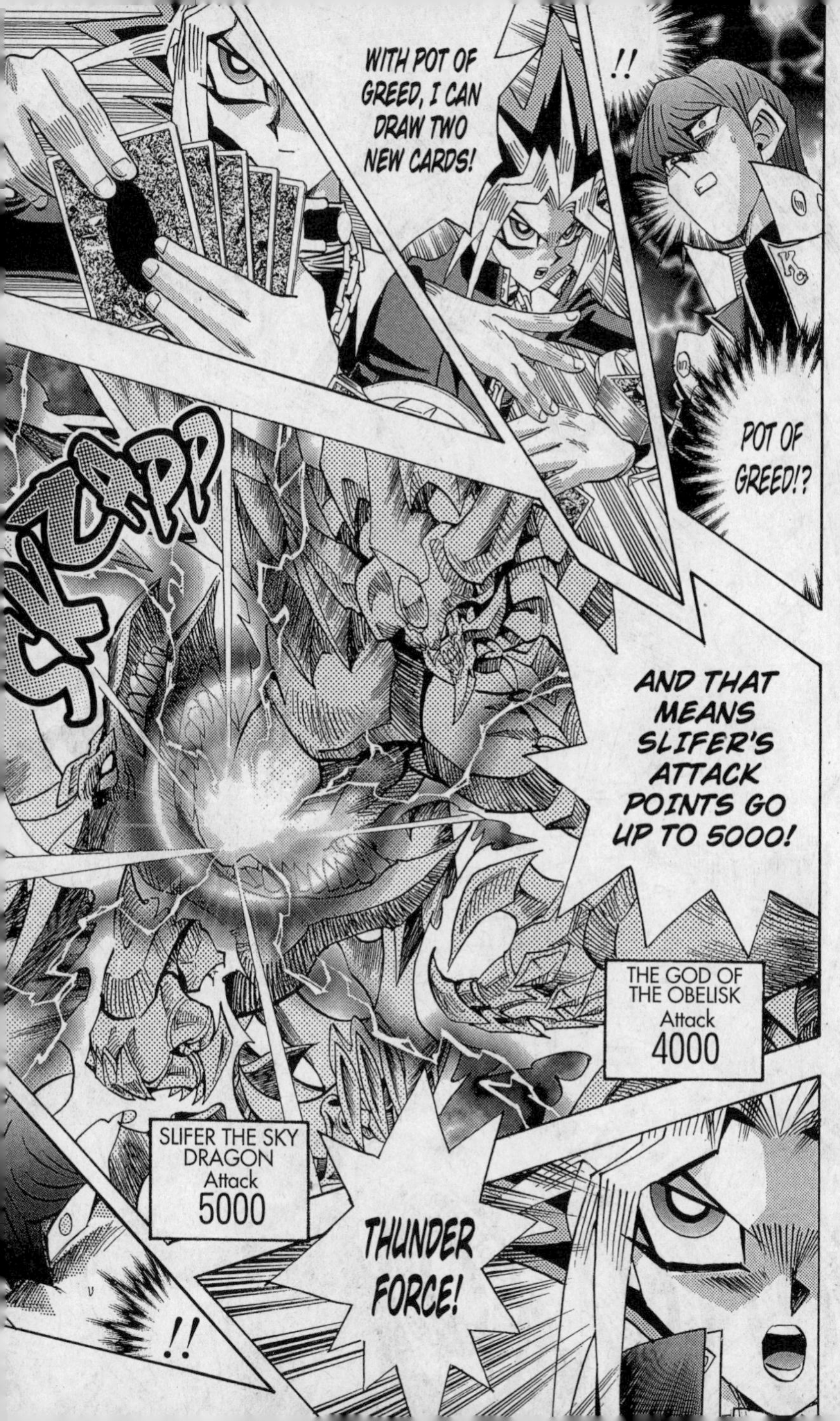
!!
POT OF GREED!?
WITH POT OF GREED, I CAN DRAW TWO NEW CARDS!
AND THAT MEANS SLIFER'S ATTACK POINTS GO UP TO 5000!
THE GOD OF THE OBELISK Attack 4000
SLIFER THE SKY DRAGON Attack 5000
THUNDER FORCE!
!!

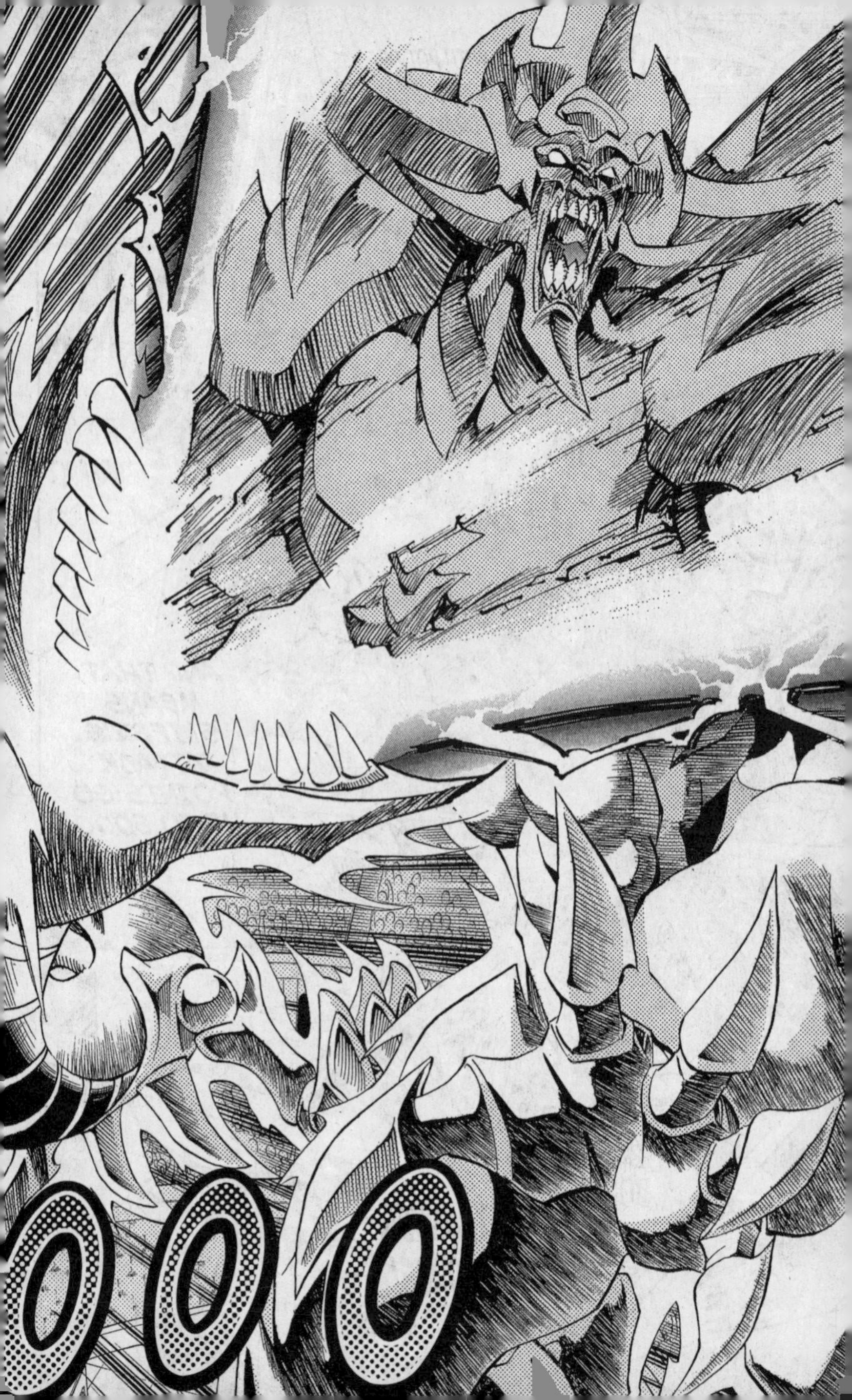
OOOO

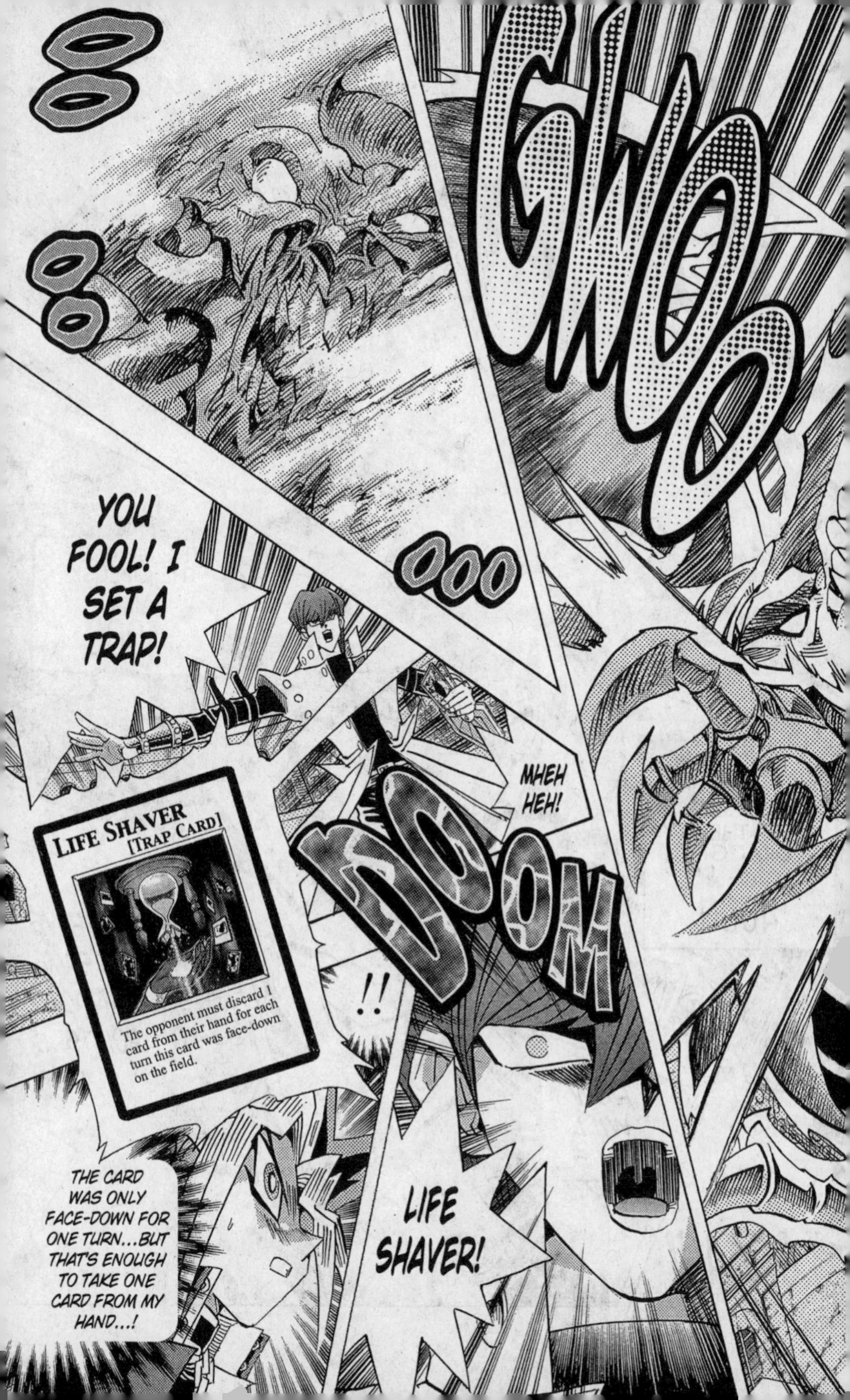

GWOO
OO
OO
OOO
YOU FOOL! I SET A TRAP!
MHEH HEH!
DOOM
LIFE SHAVER
[TRAP CARD]
The opponent must discard 1 card from their hand for each turn this card was face-down on the field.
!!
LIFE SHAVER!
THE CARD WAS ONLY FACE-DOWN FOR ONE TURN...BUT THAT'S ENOUGH TO TAKE ONE CARD FROM MY HAND...!

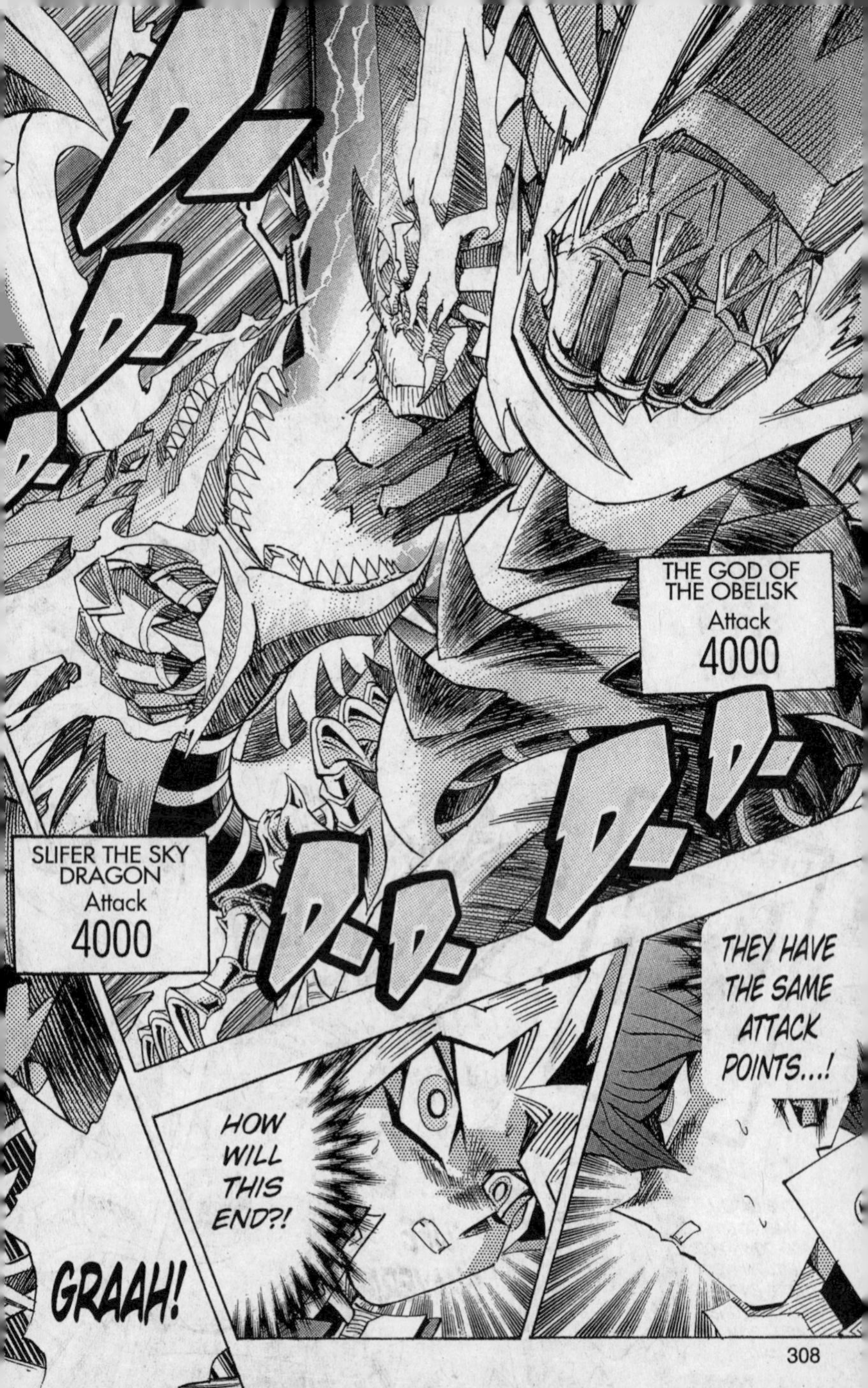
D- D- D-
THE GOD OF THE OBELISK Attack 4000
D- D- D- D-
SLIFER THE SKY DRAGON Attack 4000
THEY HAVE THE SAME ATTACK POINTS...!
HOW WILL THIS END?!
GRAAH!

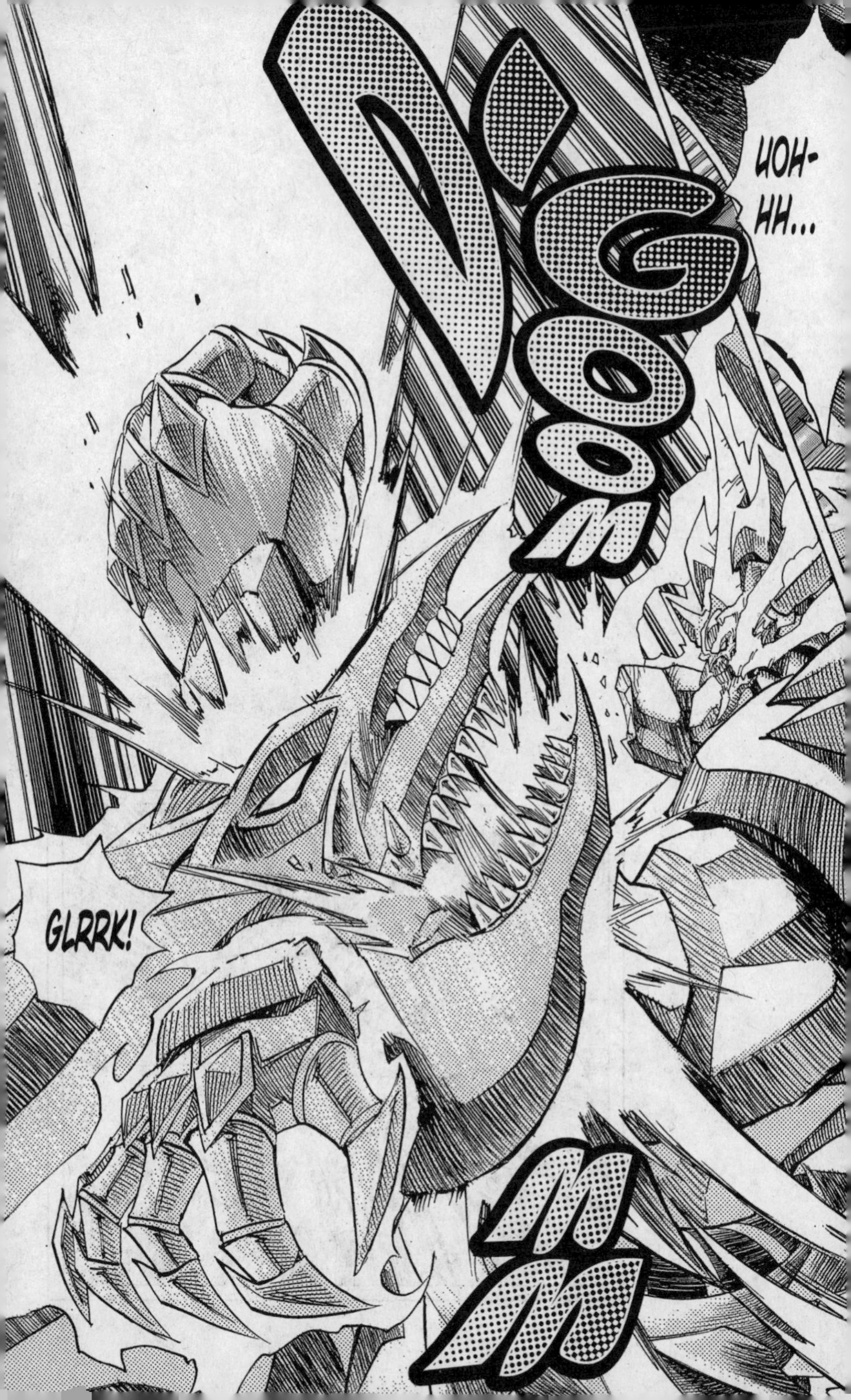
UOH-HH...
DGOOM
GLRRK!
MMM

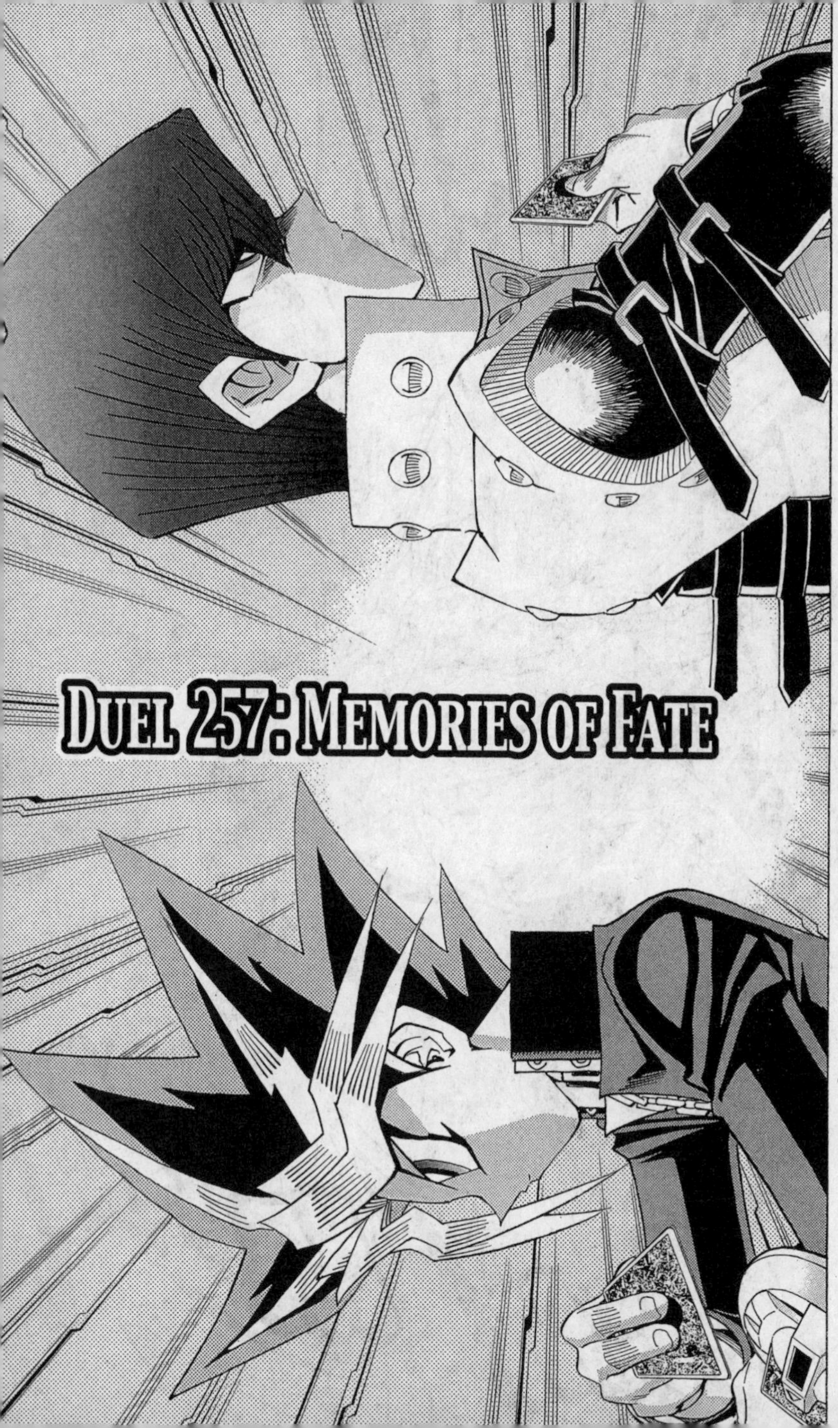
DUEL 257: MEMORIES OF FATE

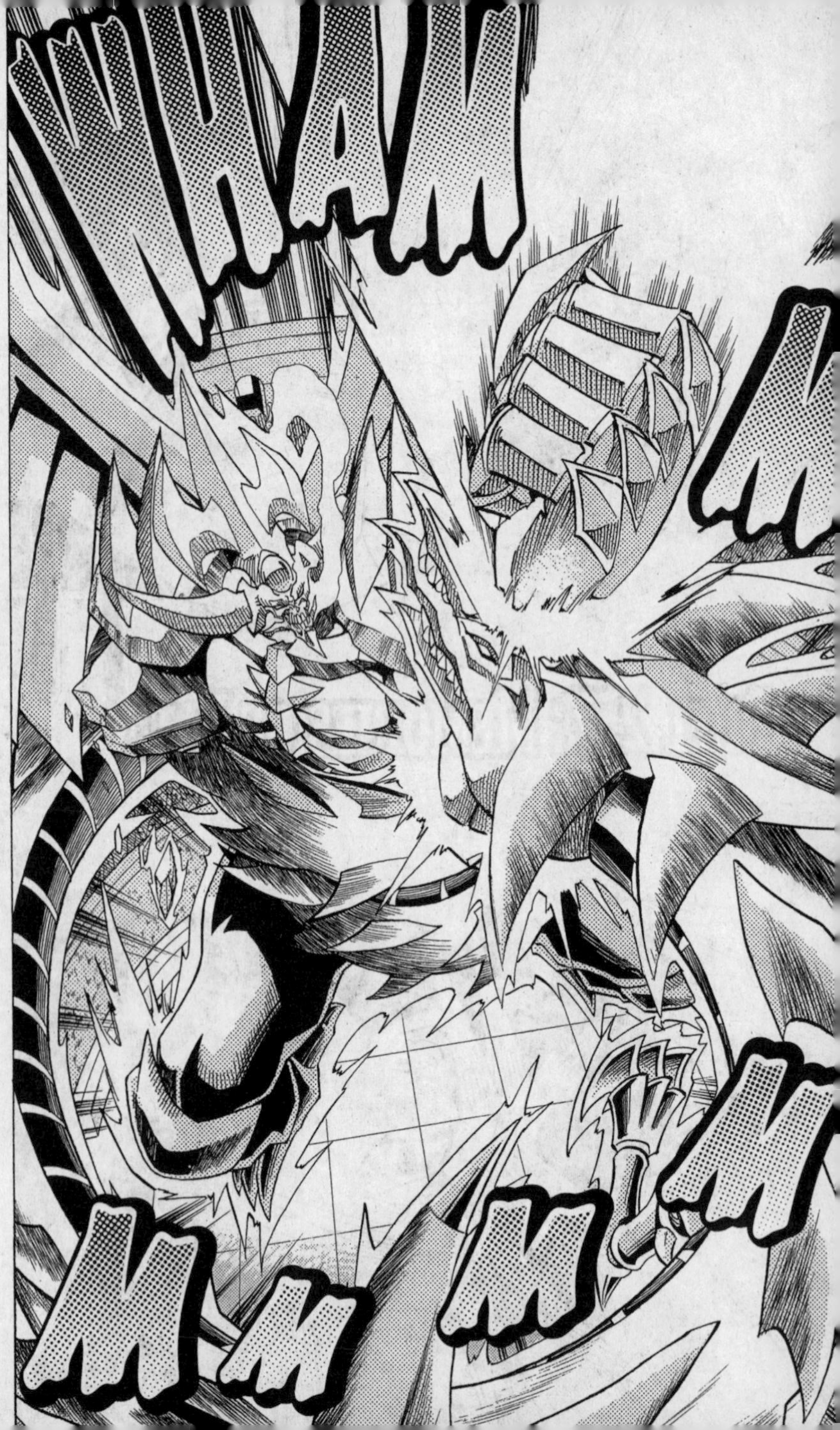
WHAM
MMMMMM

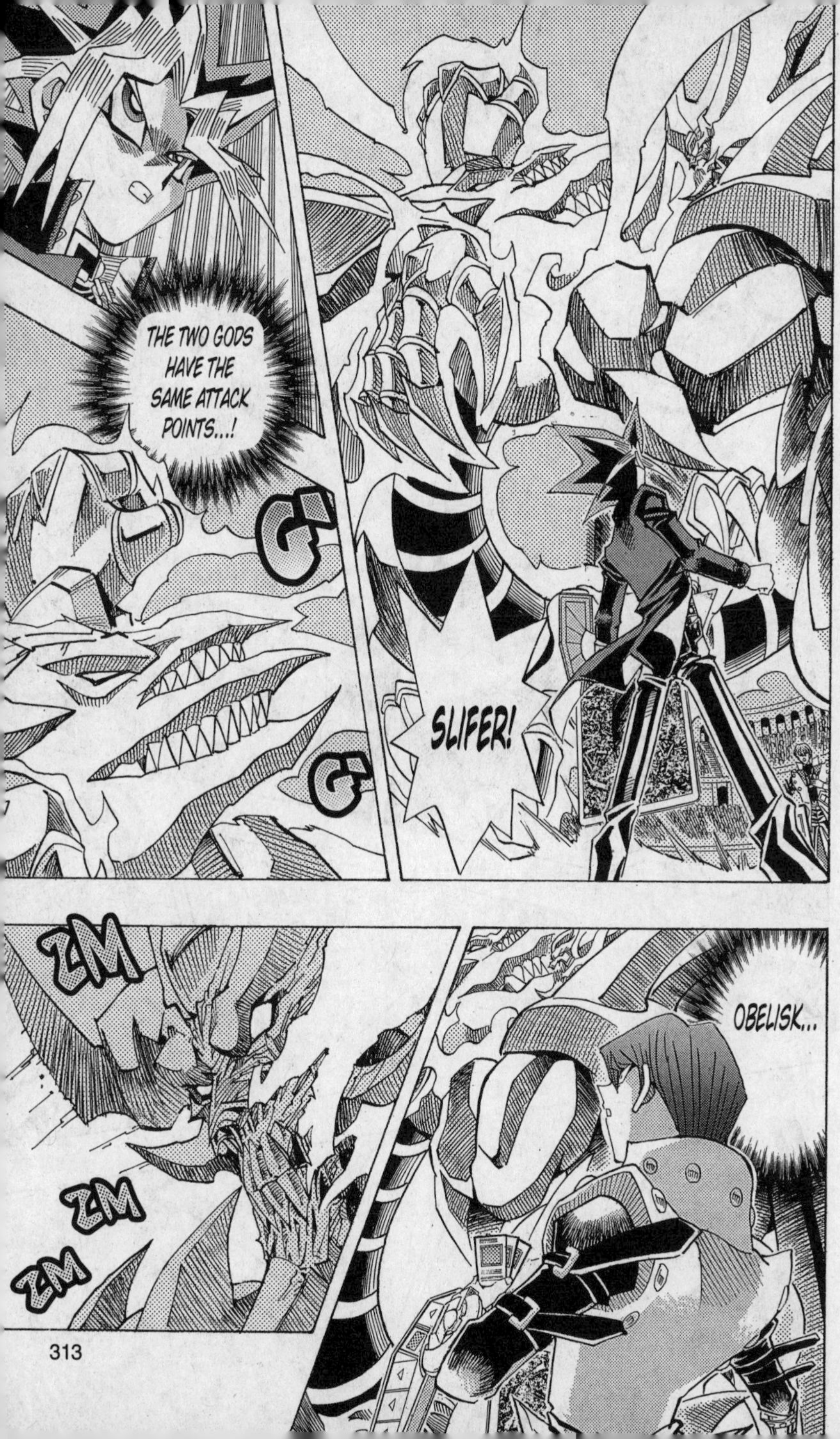
SLIFER!
THE TWO GODS HAVE THE SAME ATTACK POINTS...!
G
G
OBELISK...
ZM
ZM
ZM

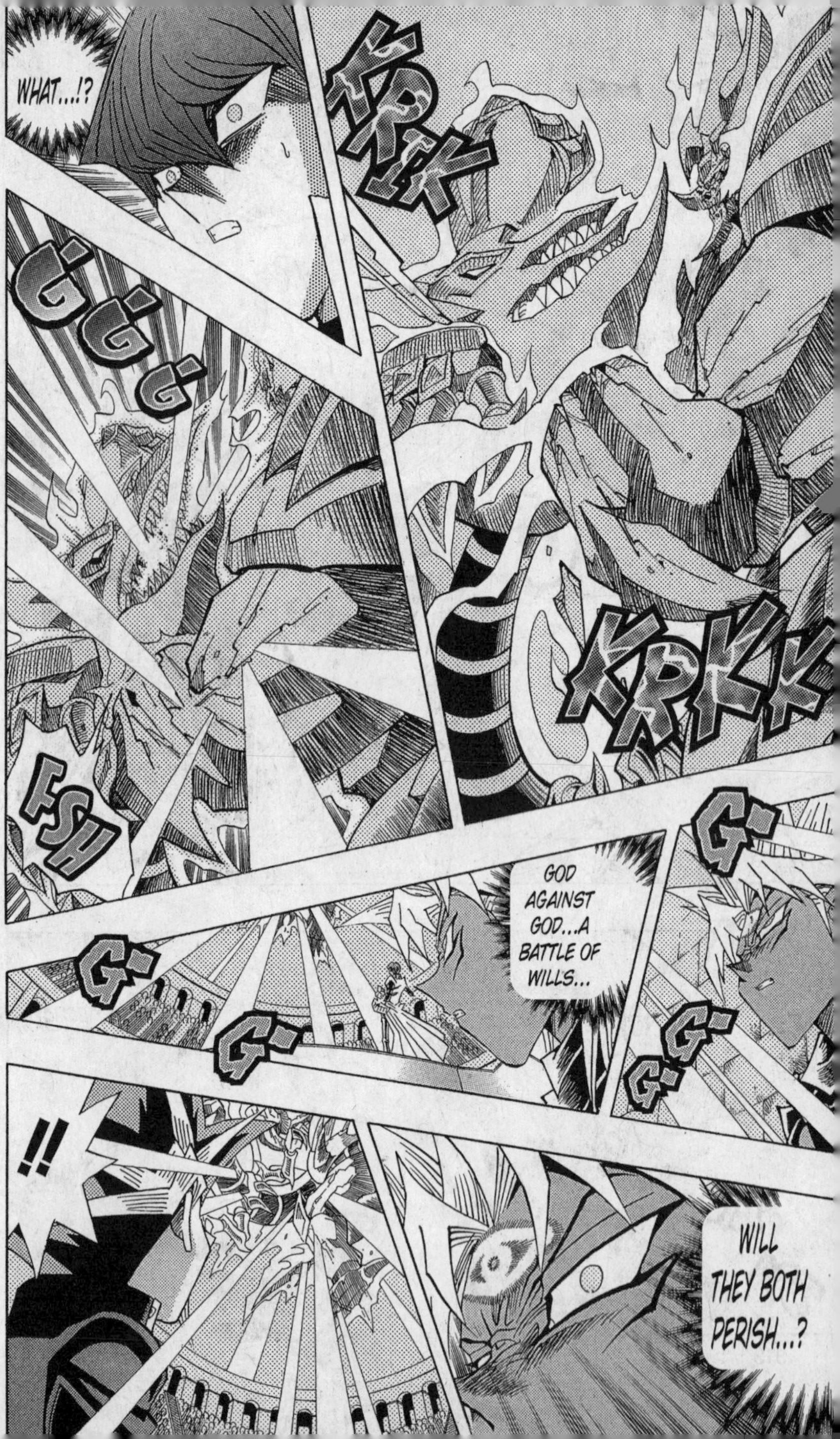
KRKK
WHAT...!?
KRKK
GGG
FSH
G
GOD AGAINST GOD...A BATTLE OF WILLS...
GG
G
G
!!
WILL THEY BOTH PERISH...?

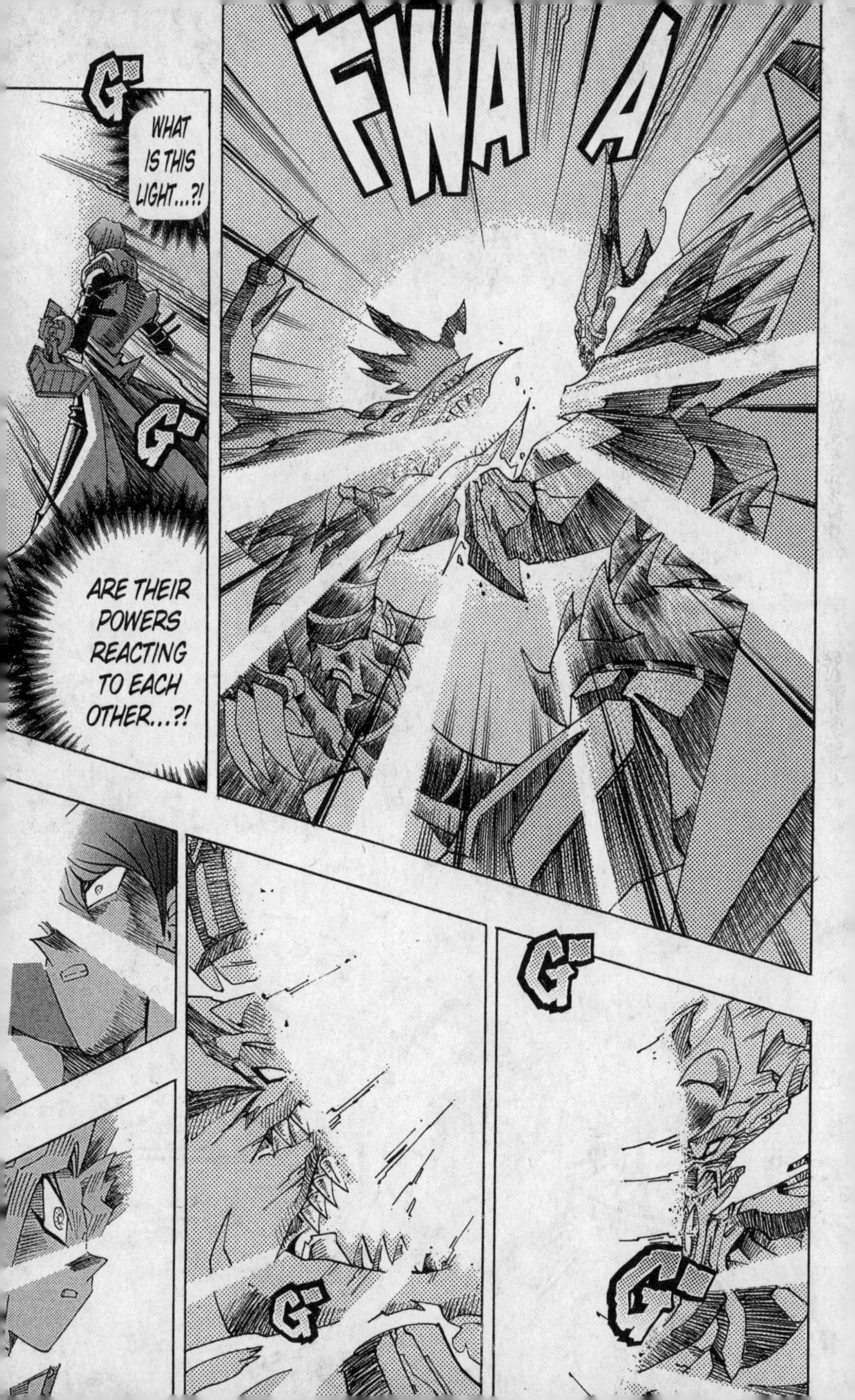
FWA A
G
WHAT IS THIS LIGHT...?!
G
ARE THEIR POWERS REACTING TO EACH OTHER...?!
G
G
G

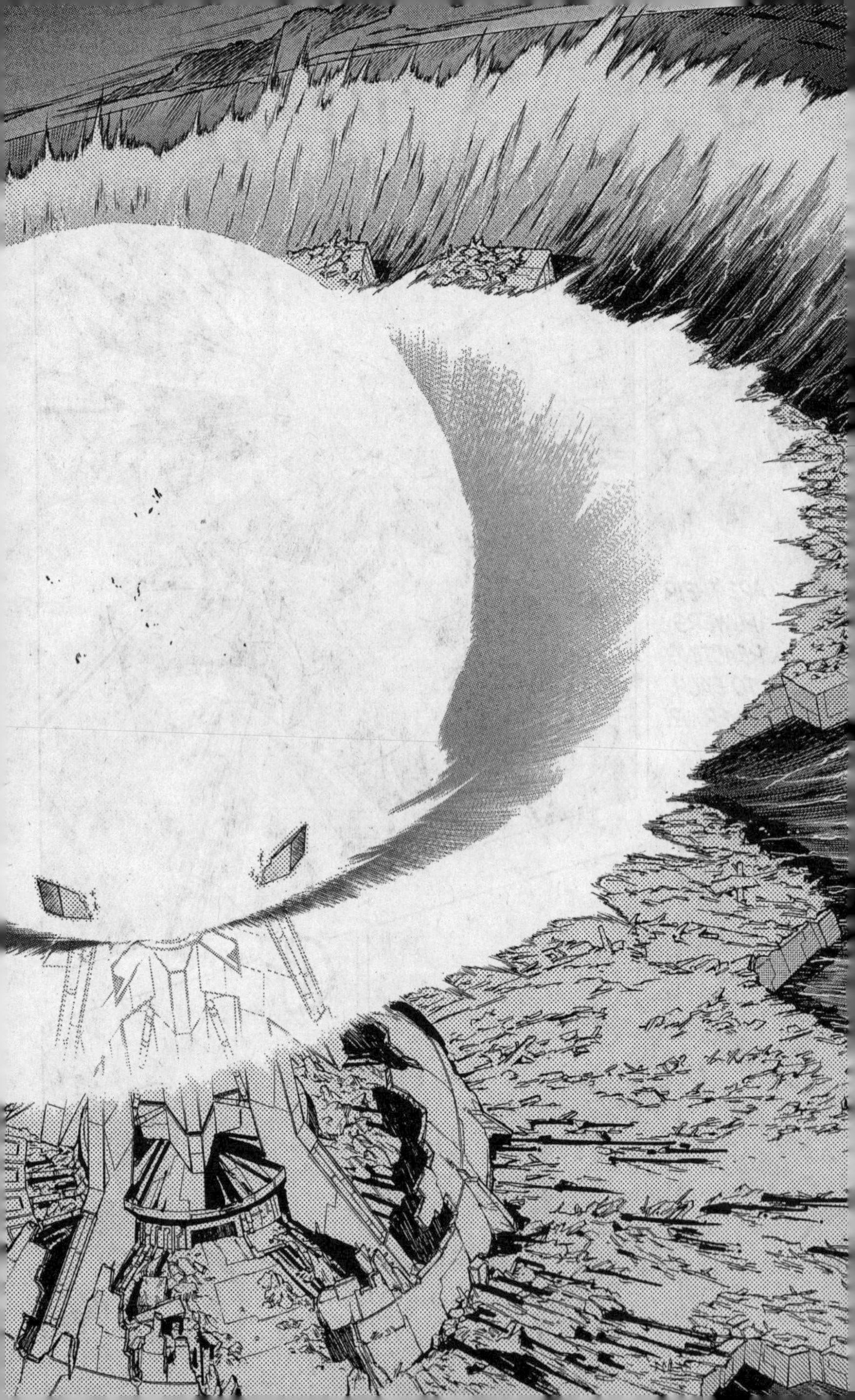

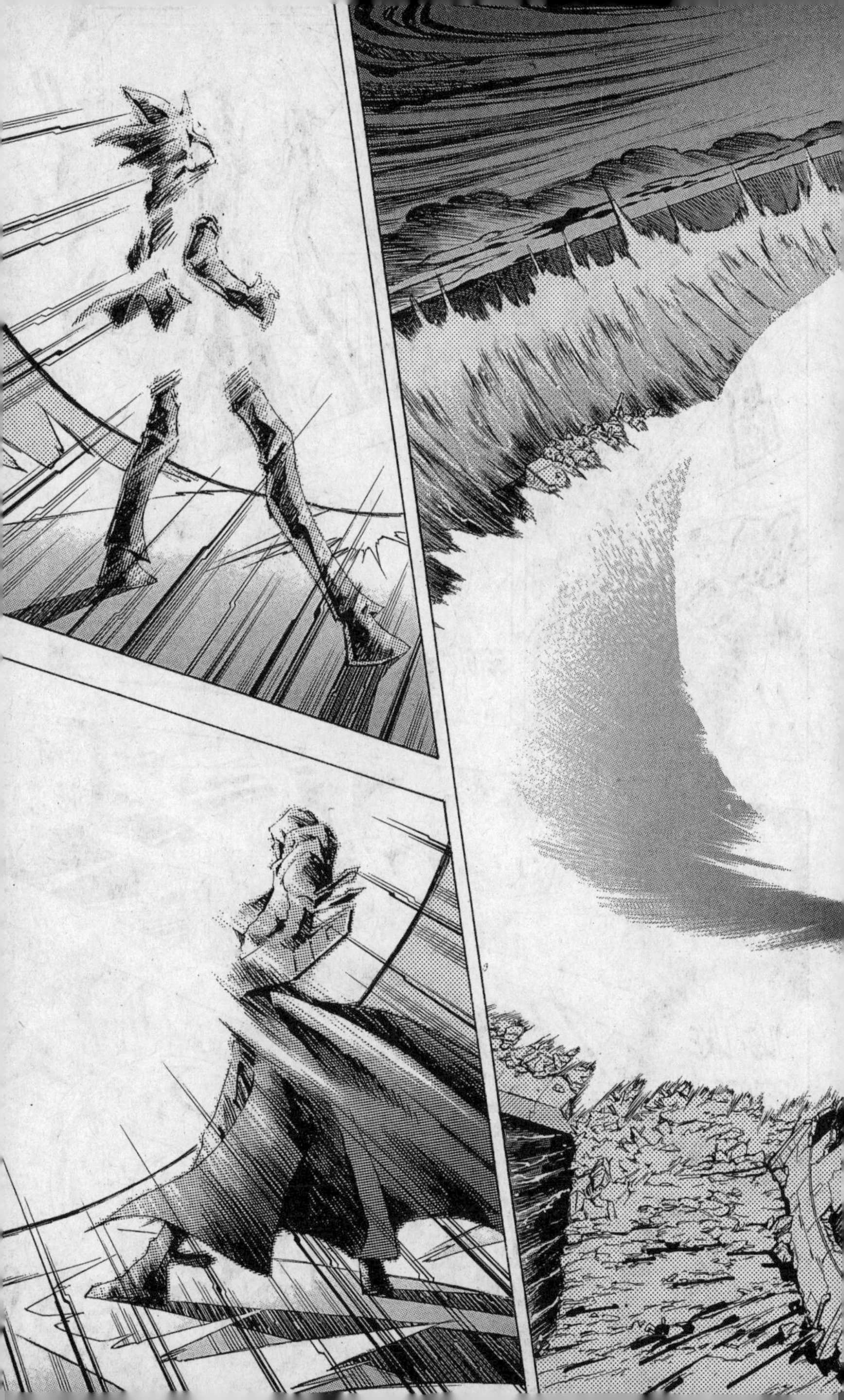

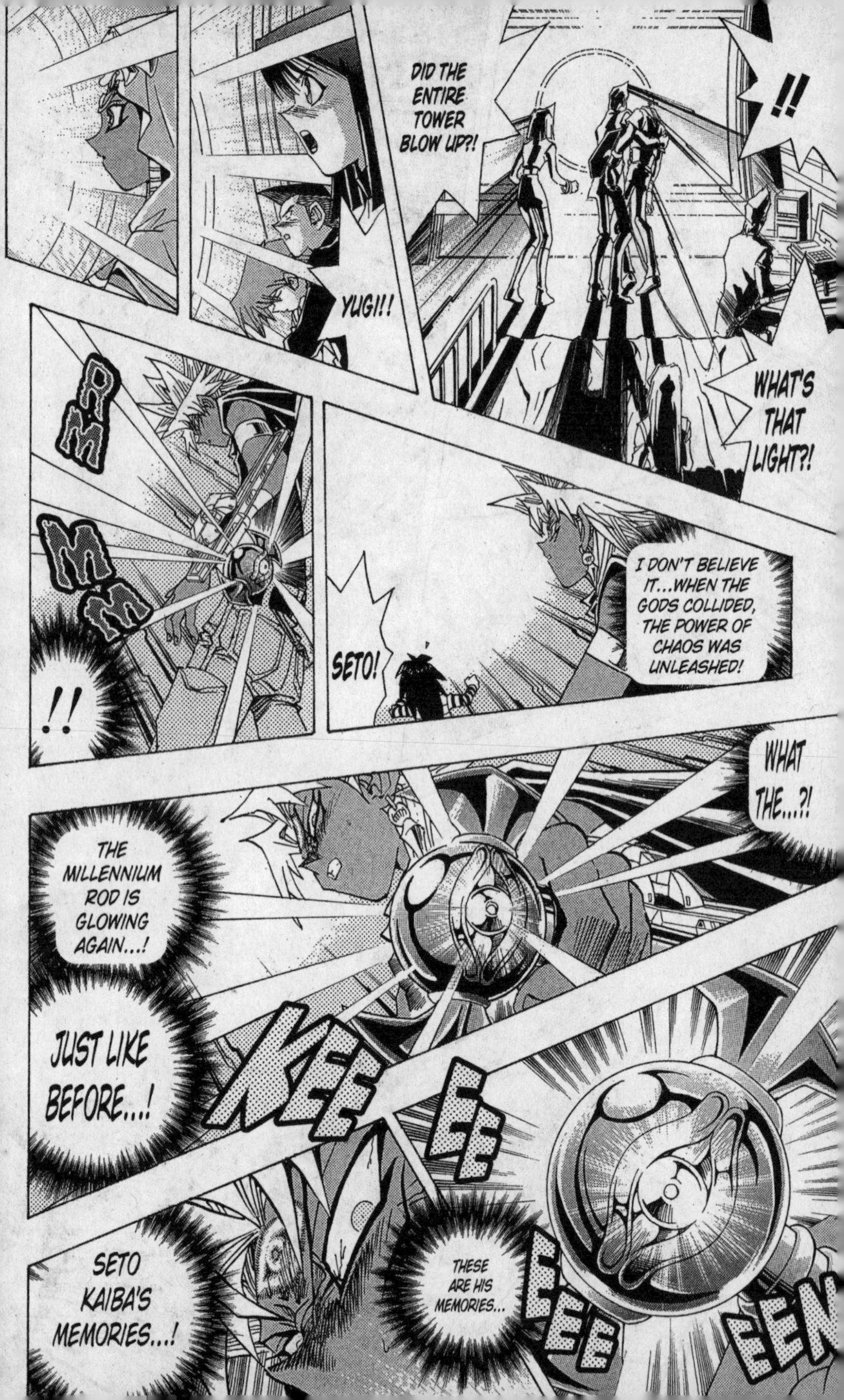
!!
DID THE ENTIRE TOWER BLOW UP?!
WHAT'S THAT LIGHT?!
YUGI!!
I DON'T BELIEVE IT...WHEN THE GODS COLLIDED, THE POWER OF CHAOS WAS UNLEASHED!
SETO!
RM
MM
!!
WHAT THE...?!
THE MILLENNIUM ROD IS GLOWING AGAIN...!
JUST LIKE BEFORE...!
KEE
EE
EEEN
EEE
THESE ARE HIS MEMORIES...
SETO KAIBA'S MEMORIES...!

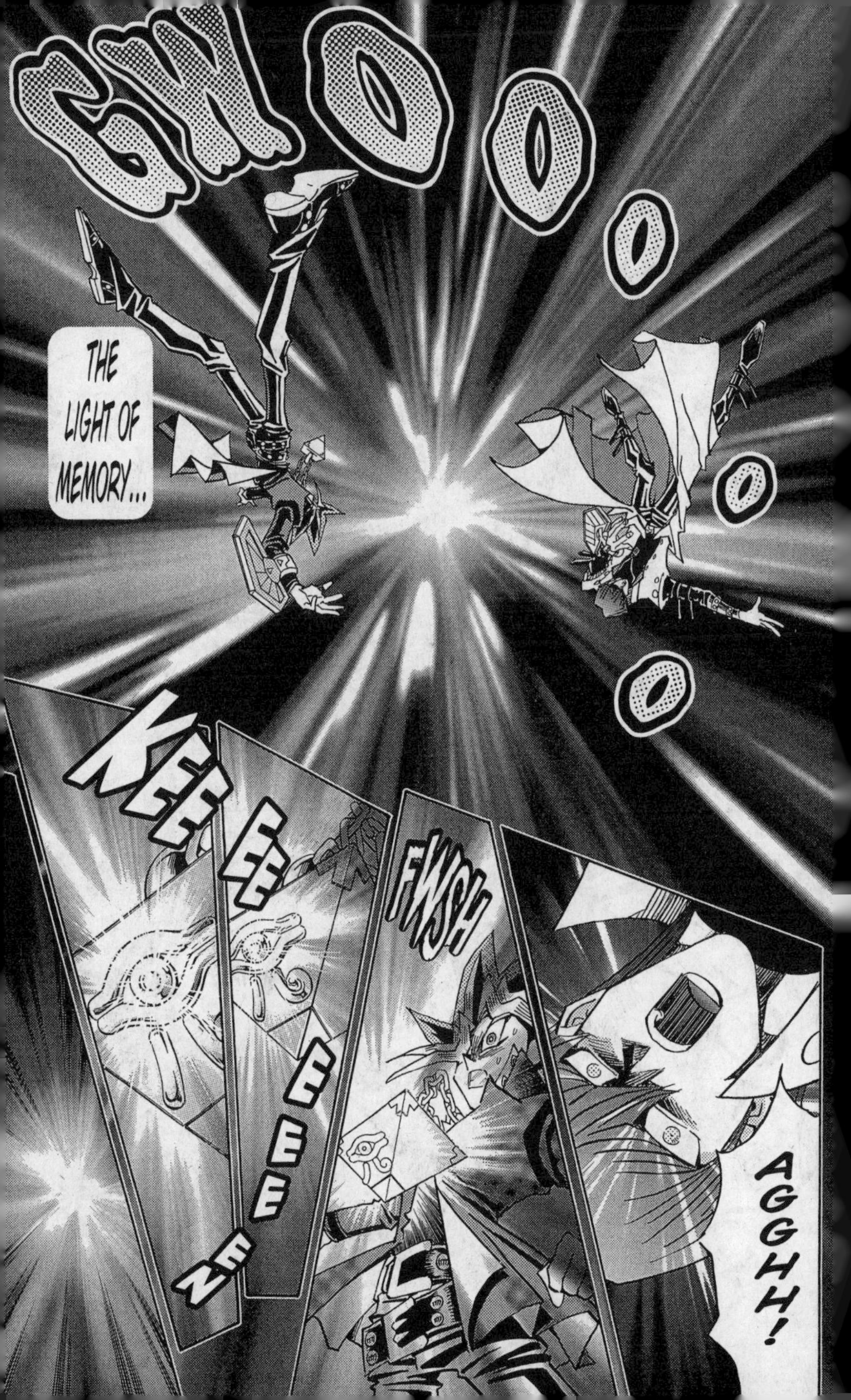

GWOOOOO
THE LIGHT OF MEMORY...
AGGHH!
FWSH
KEEEEEEEEN

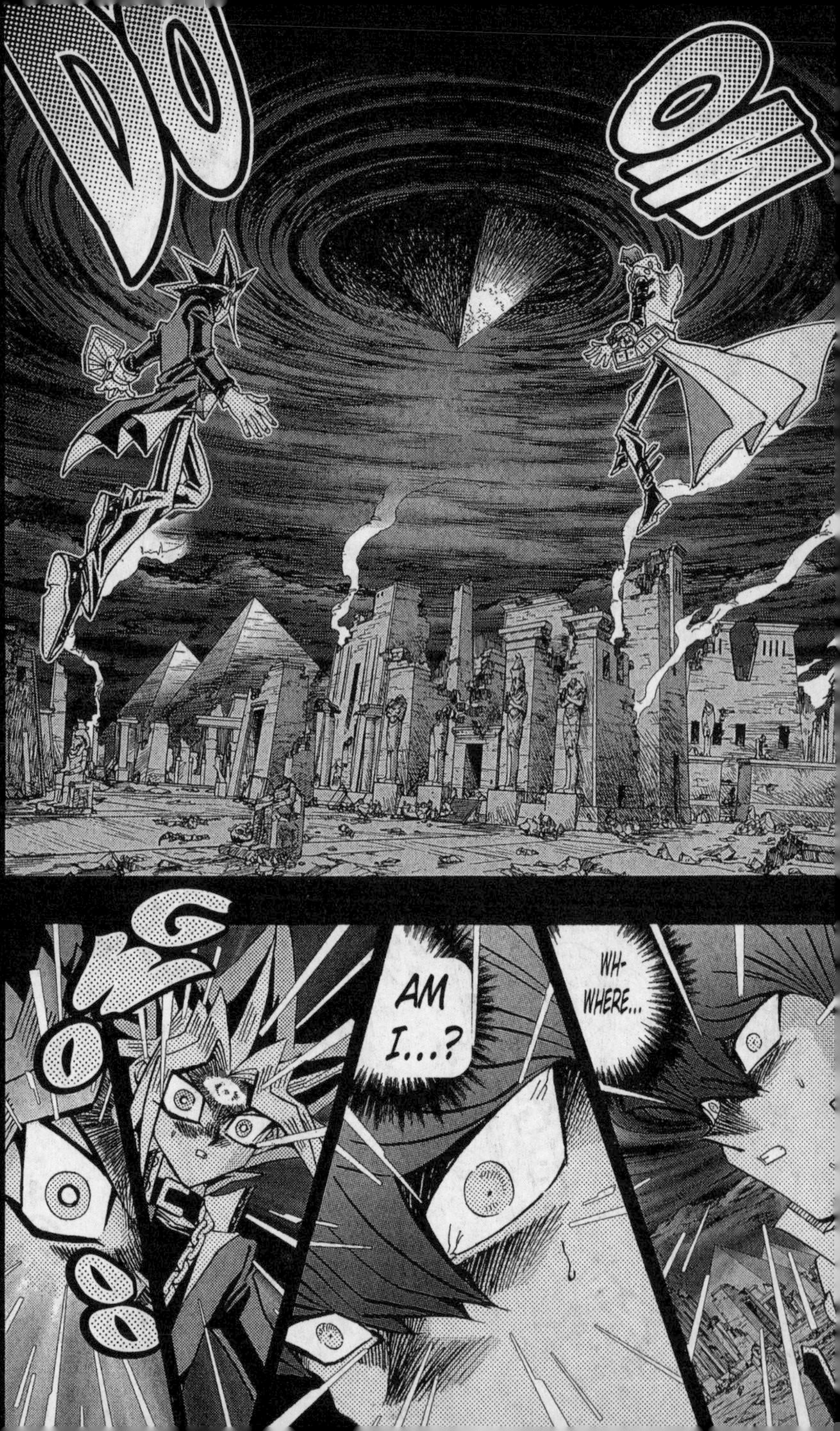
DO
OO
WH- WHERE...
AM I...?
GWOOOO

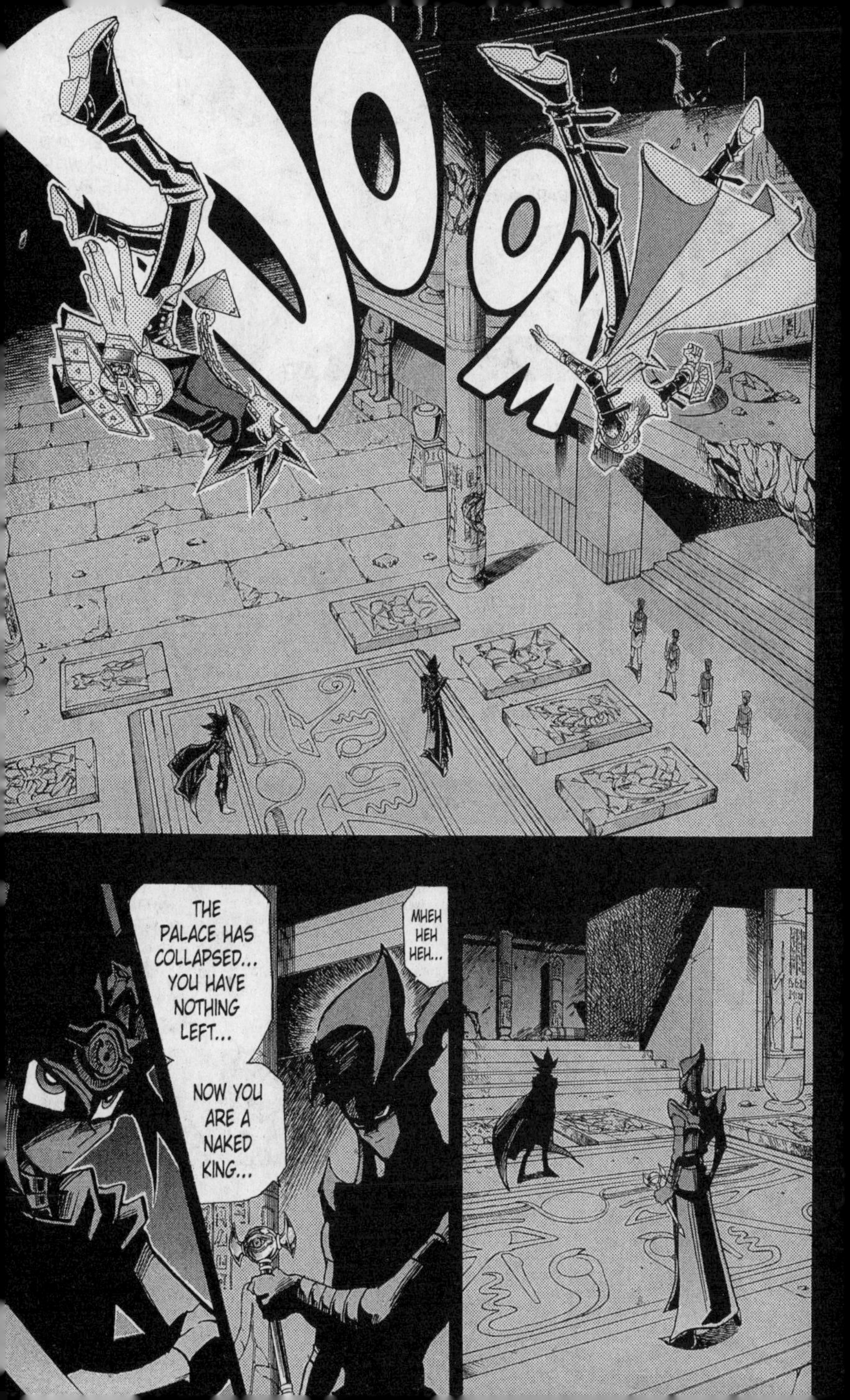
DOOM
MHEH HEH HEH...
THE PALACE HAS COLLAPSED... YOU HAVE NOTHING LEFT...
NOW YOU ARE A NAKED KING...

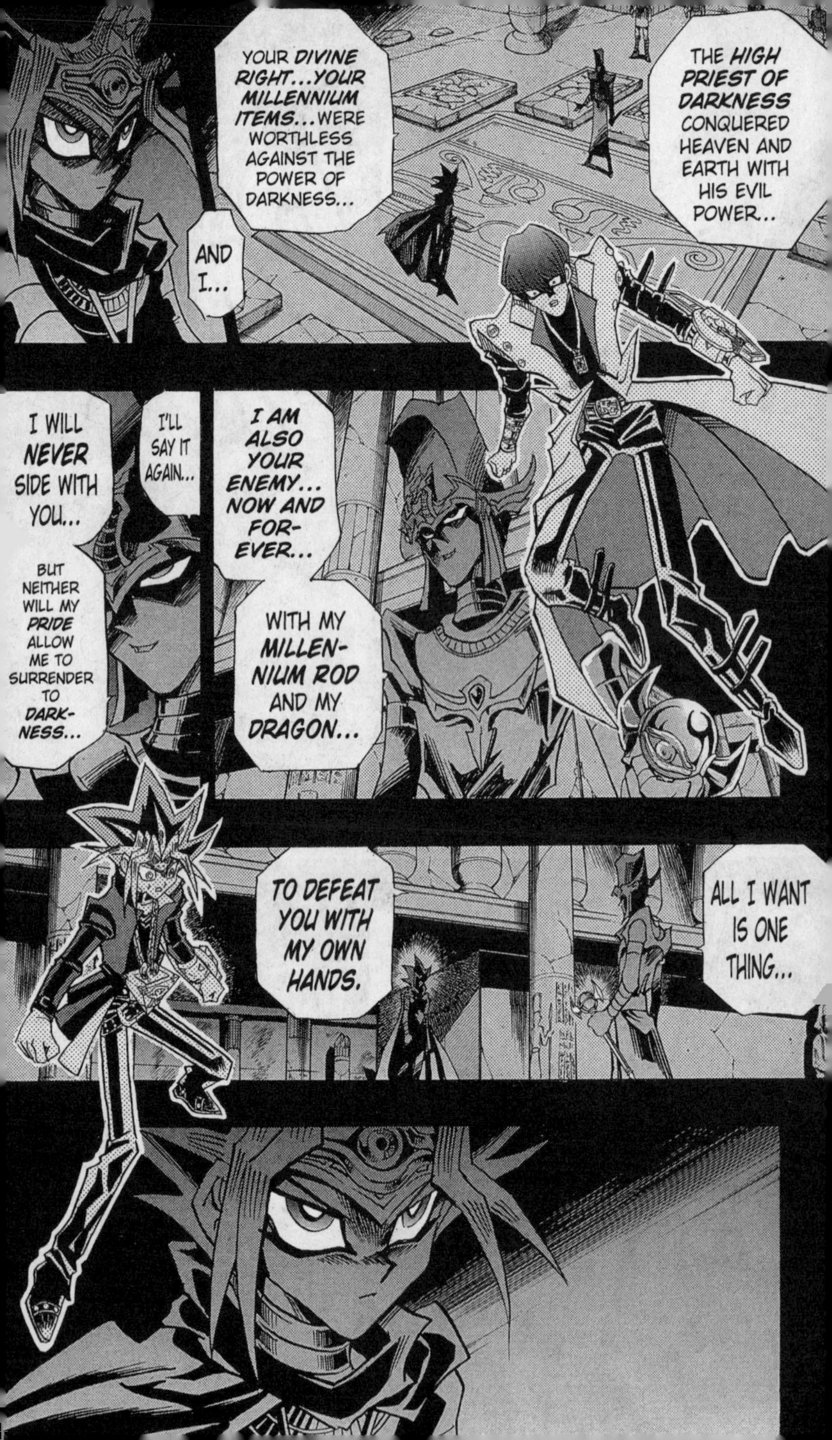
THE HIGH PRIEST OF DARKNESS CONQUERED HEAVEN AND EARTH WITH HIS EVIL POWER...
YOUR DIVINE RIGHT...YOUR MILLENNIUM ITEMS...WERE WORTHLESS AGAINST THE POWER OF DARKNESS...
AND I...
I AM ALSO YOUR ENEMY... NOW AND FOR-EVER...
WITH MY MILLEN-NIUM ROD AND MY DRAGON...
I'LL SAY IT AGAIN...
I WILL NEVER SIDE WITH YOU...
BUT NEITHER WILL MY PRIDE ALLOW ME TO SURRENDER TO DARK-NESS...
ALL I WANT IS ONE THING...
TO DEFEAT YOU WITH MY OWN HANDS.

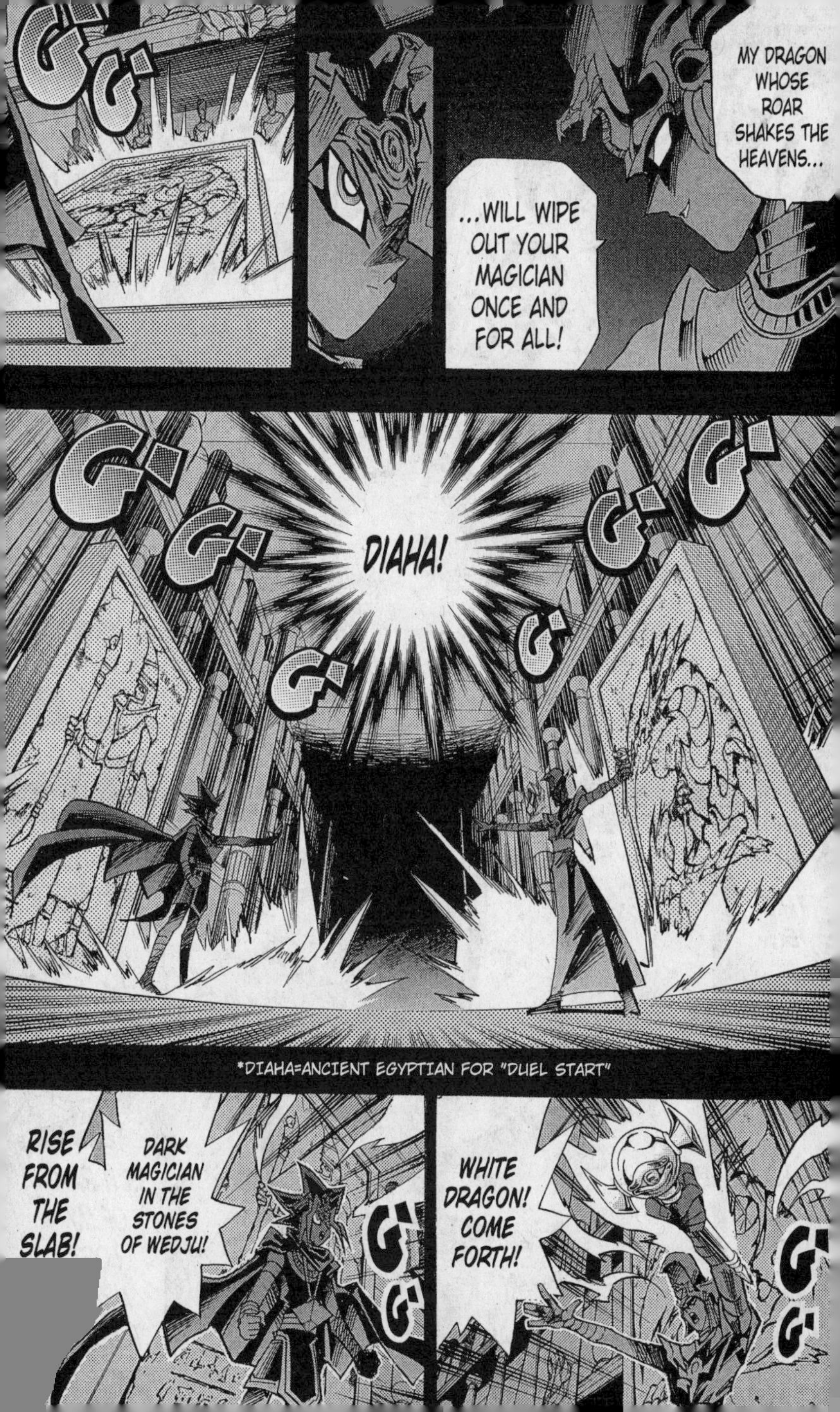

MY DRAGON WHOSE ROAR SHAKES THE HEAVENS...
...WILL WIPE OUT YOUR MAGICIAN ONCE AND FOR ALL!
G G
G G G G
DIAHA!
G G G G
*DIAHA=ANCIENT EGYPTIAN FOR "DUEL START"
WHITE DRAGON! COME FORTH!
G G
DARK MAGICIAN IN THE STONES OF WEDJU!
RISE FROM THE SLAB!
G G

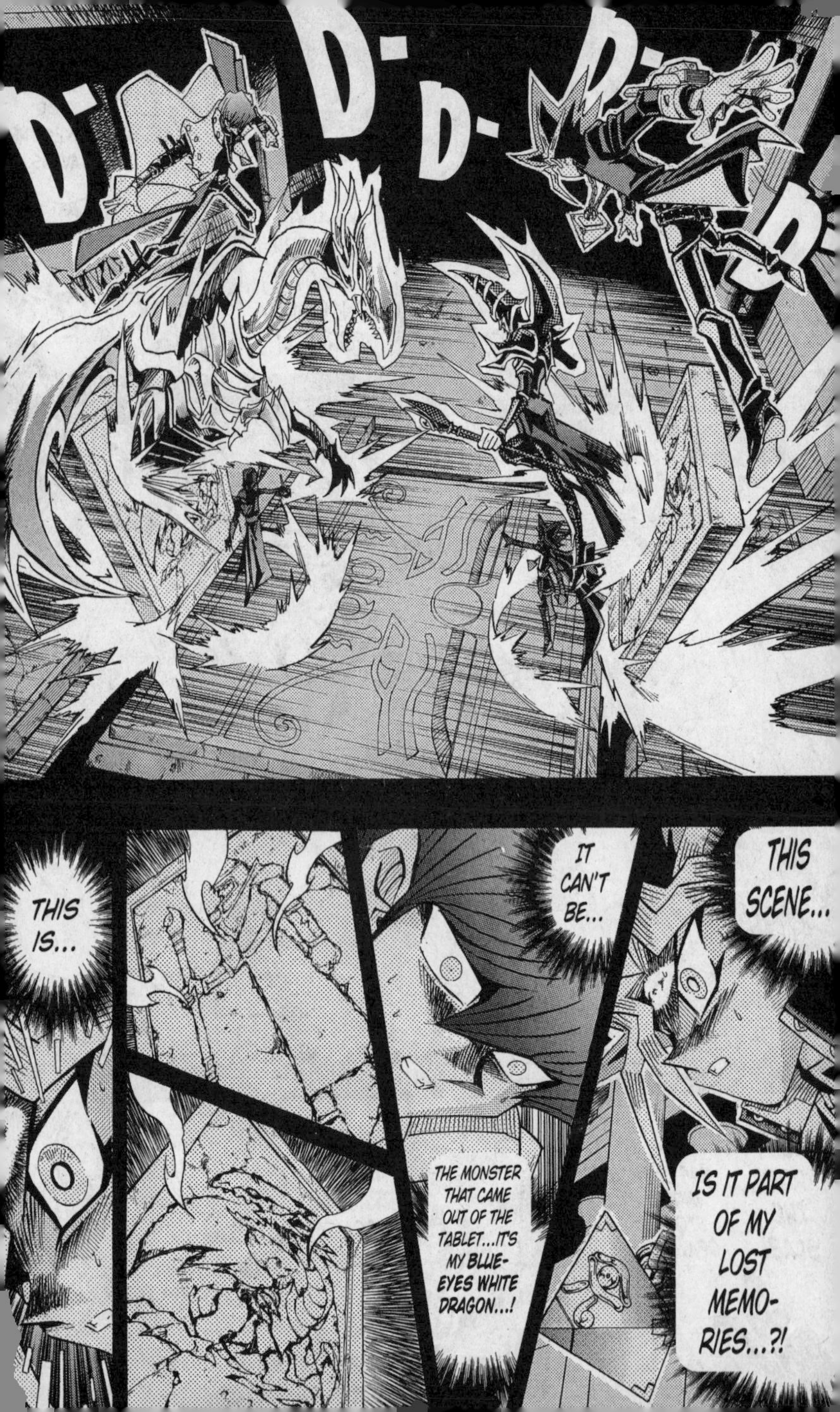
D- D- D- D- D- D-
THIS SCENE...
IS IT PART OF MY LOST MEMO-RIES...?!
IT CAN'T BE...
THE MONSTER THAT CAME OUT OF THE TABLET...IT'S MY BLUE-EYES WHITE DRAGON...!
THIS IS...

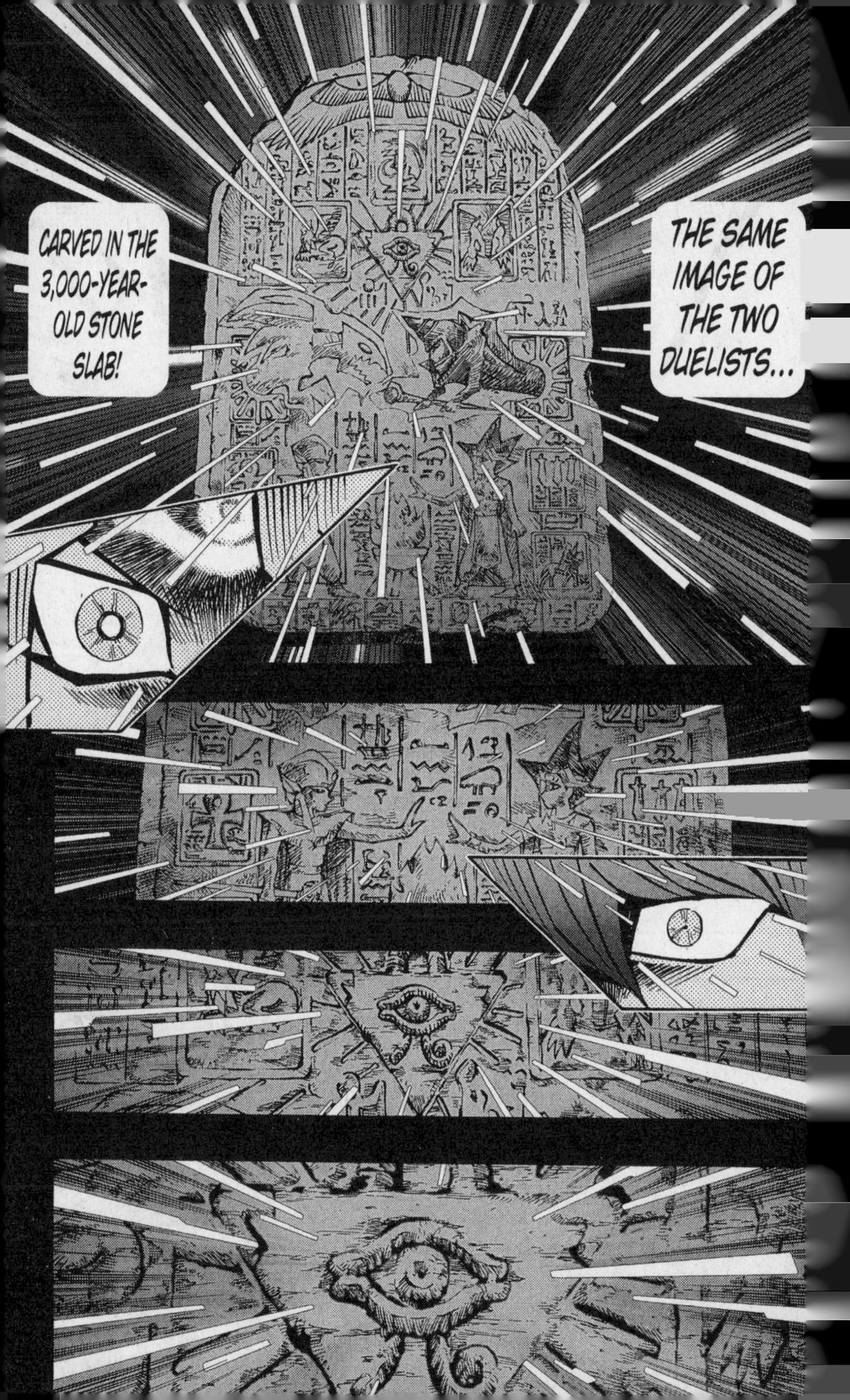
THE SAME IMAGE OF THE TWO DUELISTS...
CARVED IN THE 3,000-YEAR-OLD STONE SLAB!

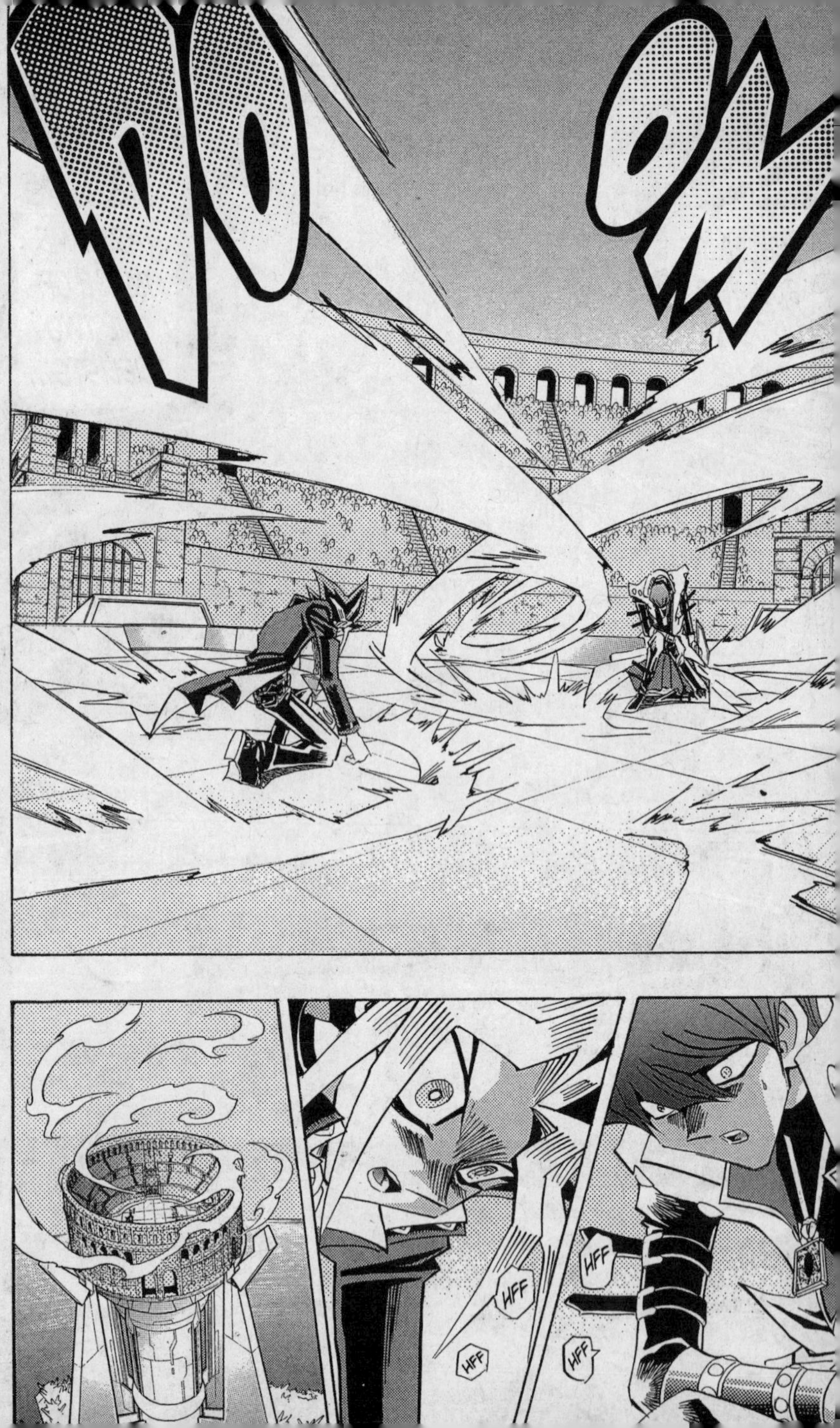
HFF
HFF
HFF
HFF

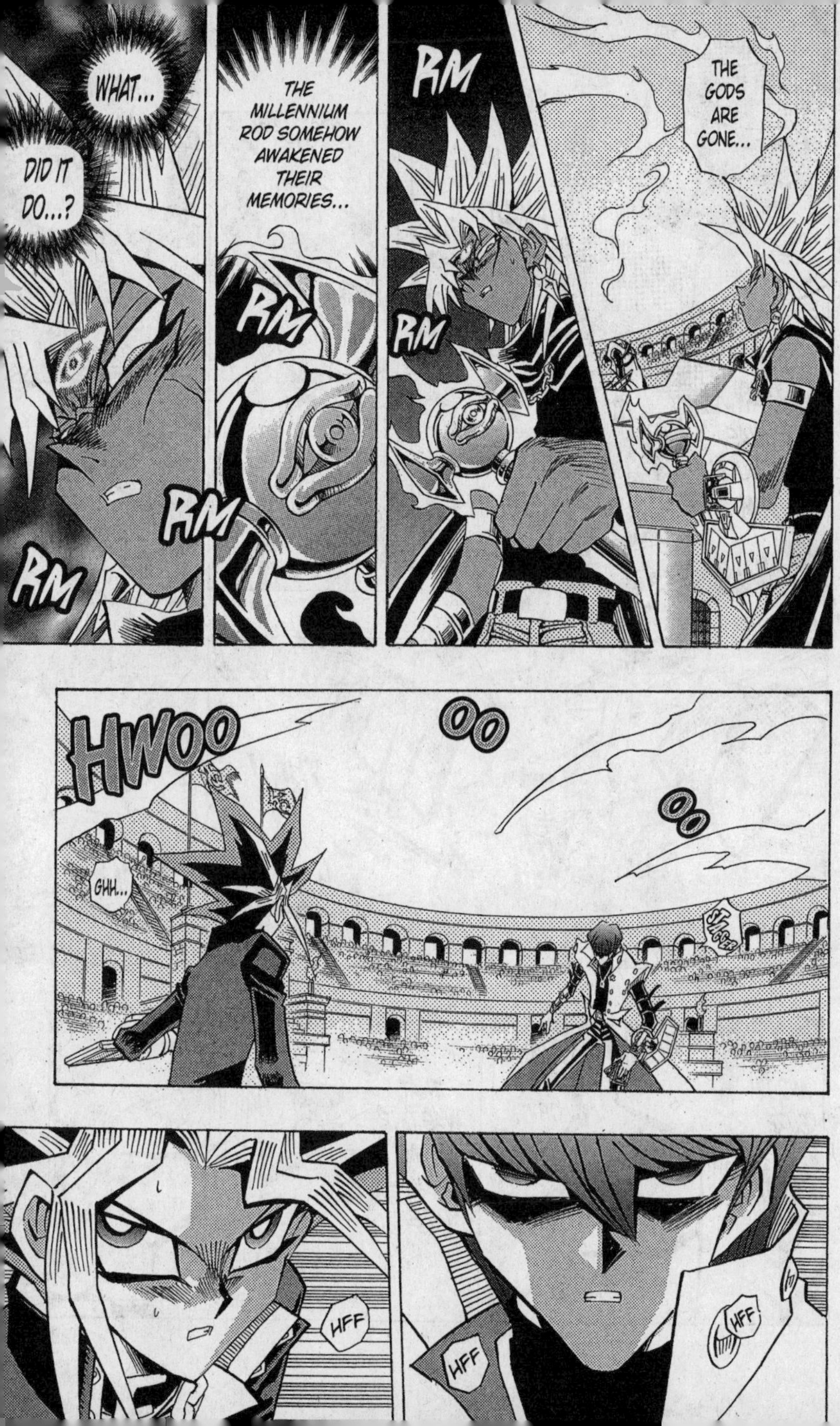
THE GODS ARE GONE...
RM
RM
THE MILLENNIUM ROD SOMEHOW AWAKENED THEIR MEMORIES...
RM
RM
WHAT...
DID IT DO...?
RM
RM
HWOO
OO
OO
GHH...
HFF
HFF
HFF

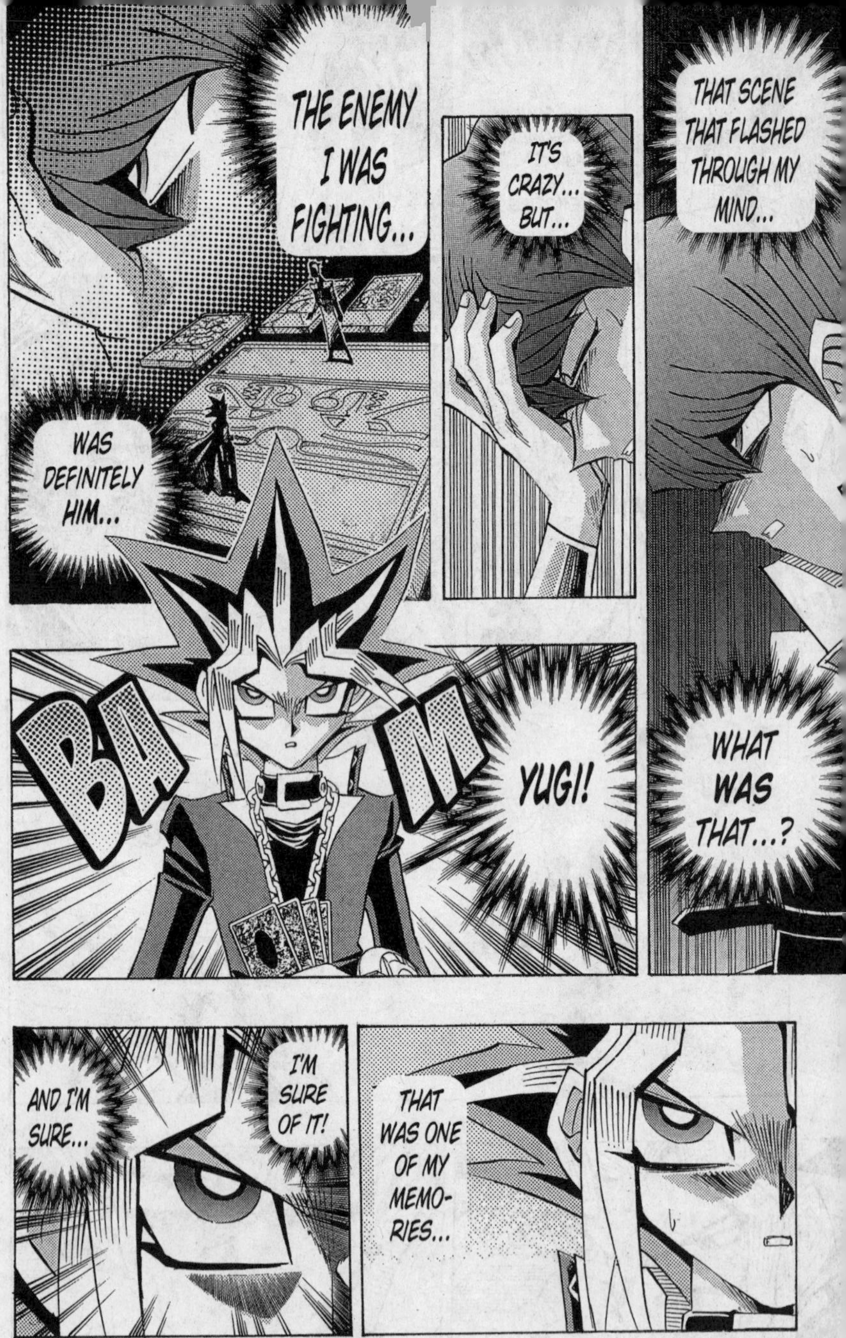
THAT SCENE THAT FLASHED THROUGH MY MIND...
WHAT WAS THAT...?
IT'S CRAZY... BUT...
THE ENEMY I WAS FIGHTING...
WAS DEFINITELY HIM...
BAM
YUGI!
THAT WAS ONE OF MY MEMO-RIES...
I'M SURE OF IT!
AND I'M SURE...

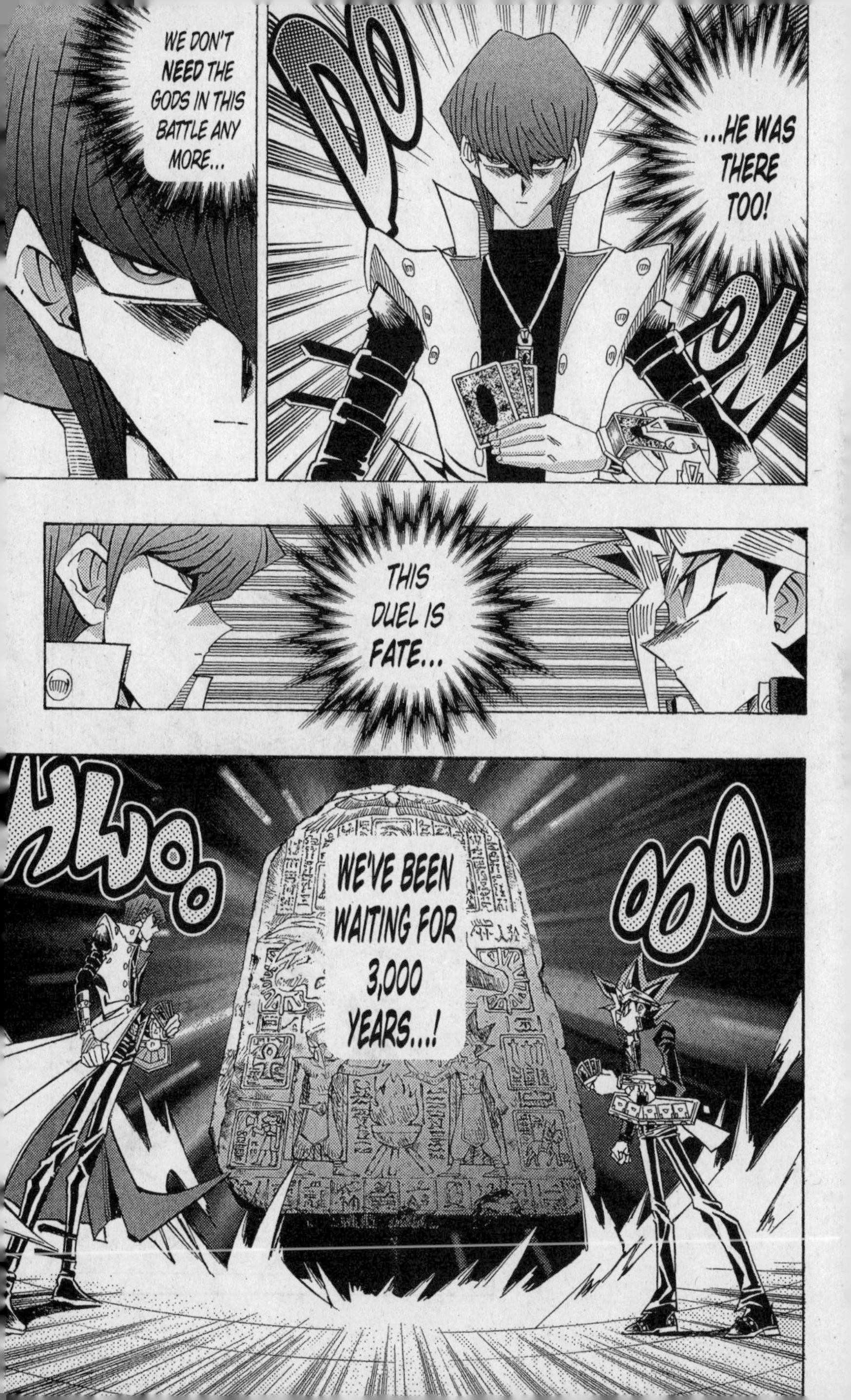
DO
...HE WAS THERE TOO!
OM
WE DON'T NEED THE GODS IN THIS BATTLE ANY MORE...
THIS DUEL IS FATE...
WE'VE BEEN WAITING FOR 3,000 YEARS...!
WHOO
OOO

READ THIS WAY

Duel 258: The Servants Surpass God

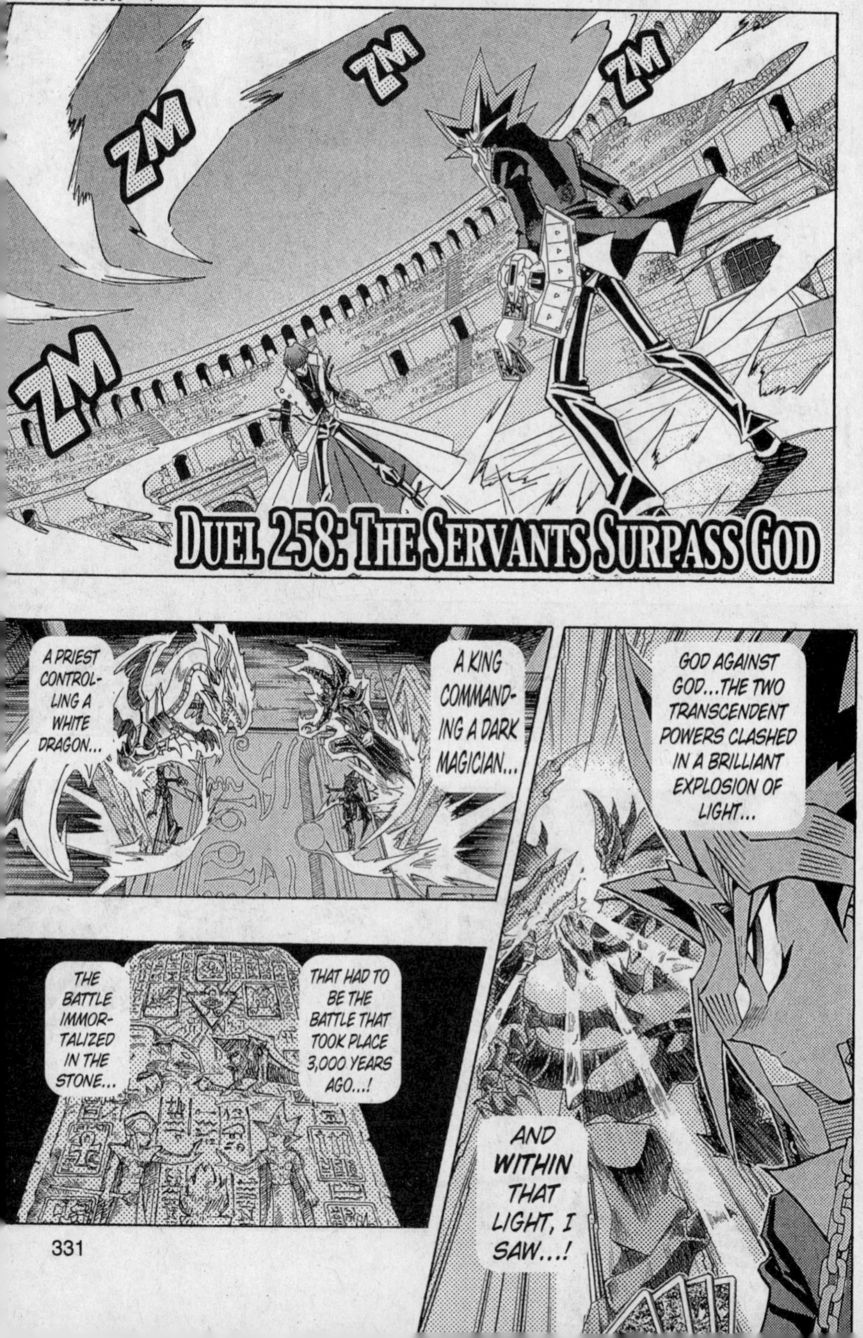
ZM
ZM
ZM
ZM
GOD AGAINST GOD...THE TWO TRANSCENDENT POWERS CLASHED IN A BRILLIANT EXPLOSION OF LIGHT...
AND WITHIN THAT LIGHT, I SAW...!
A KING COMMANDING A DARK MAGICIAN...
A PRIEST CONTROLLING A WHITE DRAGON...
THAT HAD TO BE THE BATTLE THAT TOOK PLACE 3,000 YEARS AGO...!
THE BATTLE IMMORTALIZED IN THE STONE...

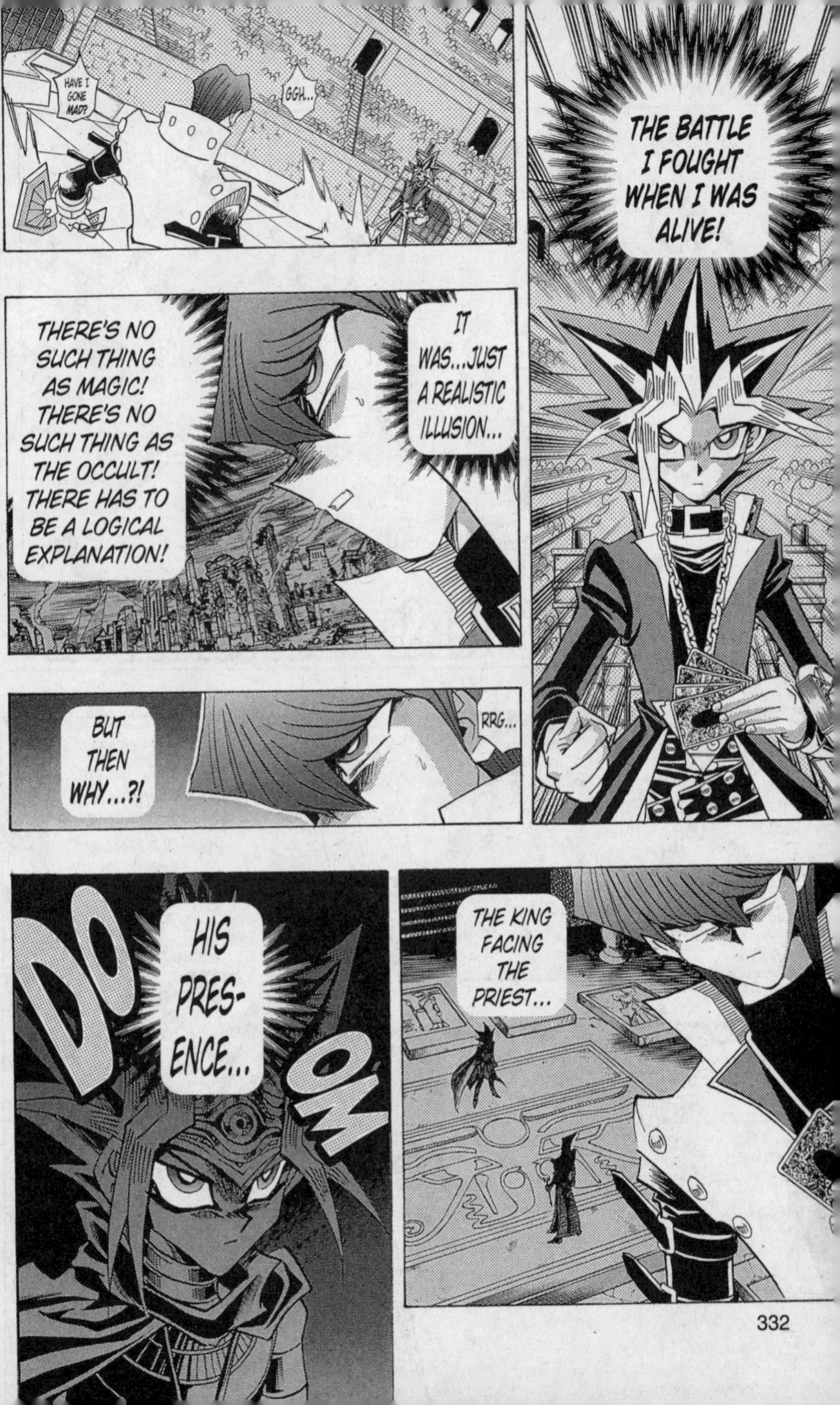

THE BATTLE I FOUGHT WHEN I WAS ALIVE!
GGH...
HAVE I GONE MAD?
IT WAS...JUST A REALISTIC ILLUSION...
THERE'S NO SUCH THING AS MAGIC! THERE'S NO SUCH THING AS THE OCCULT! THERE HAS TO BE A LOGICAL EXPLANATION!
RRG...
BUT THEN WHY...?!
THE KING FACING THE PRIEST...
HIS PRES-ENCE...
DOOM

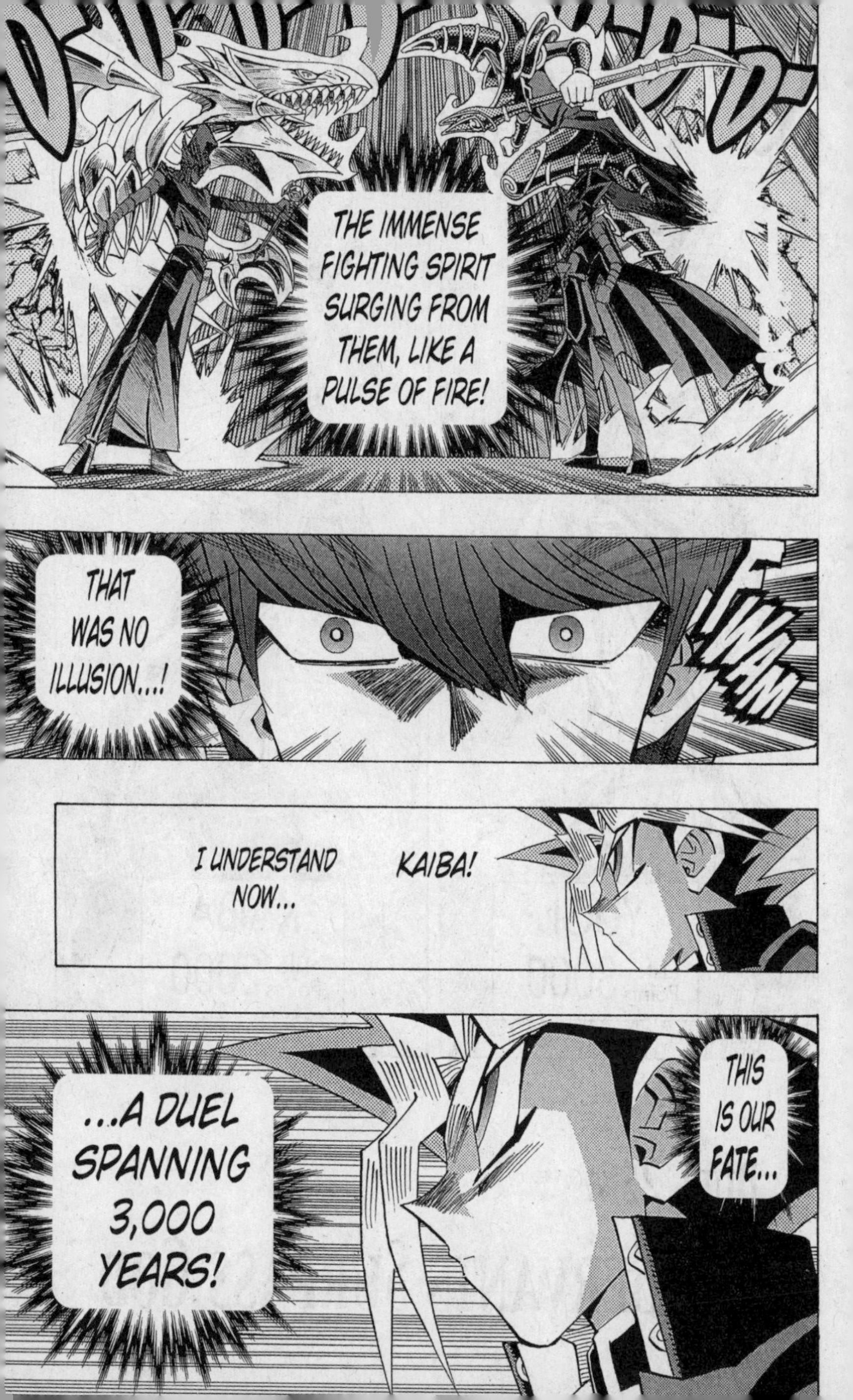
THE IMMENSE FIGHTING SPIRIT SURGING FROM THEM, LIKE A PULSE OF FIRE!
THAT WAS NO ILLUSION...!
I UNDERSTAND NOW...
KAIBA!
THIS IS OUR FATE...
...A DUEL SPANNING 3,000 YEARS!

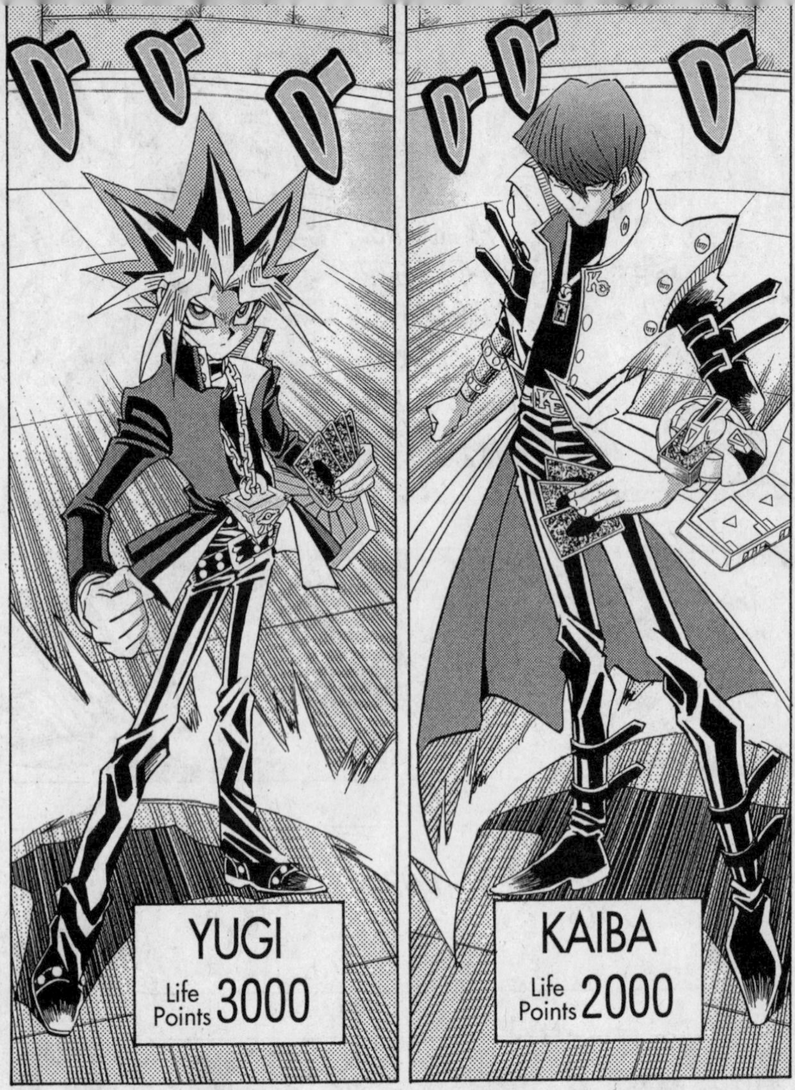
D- D- D-
KAIBA
Life Points 2000
D- D- D-
YUGI
Life Points 3000

Duel 258:

The Servants Surpass God

READ THIS WAY

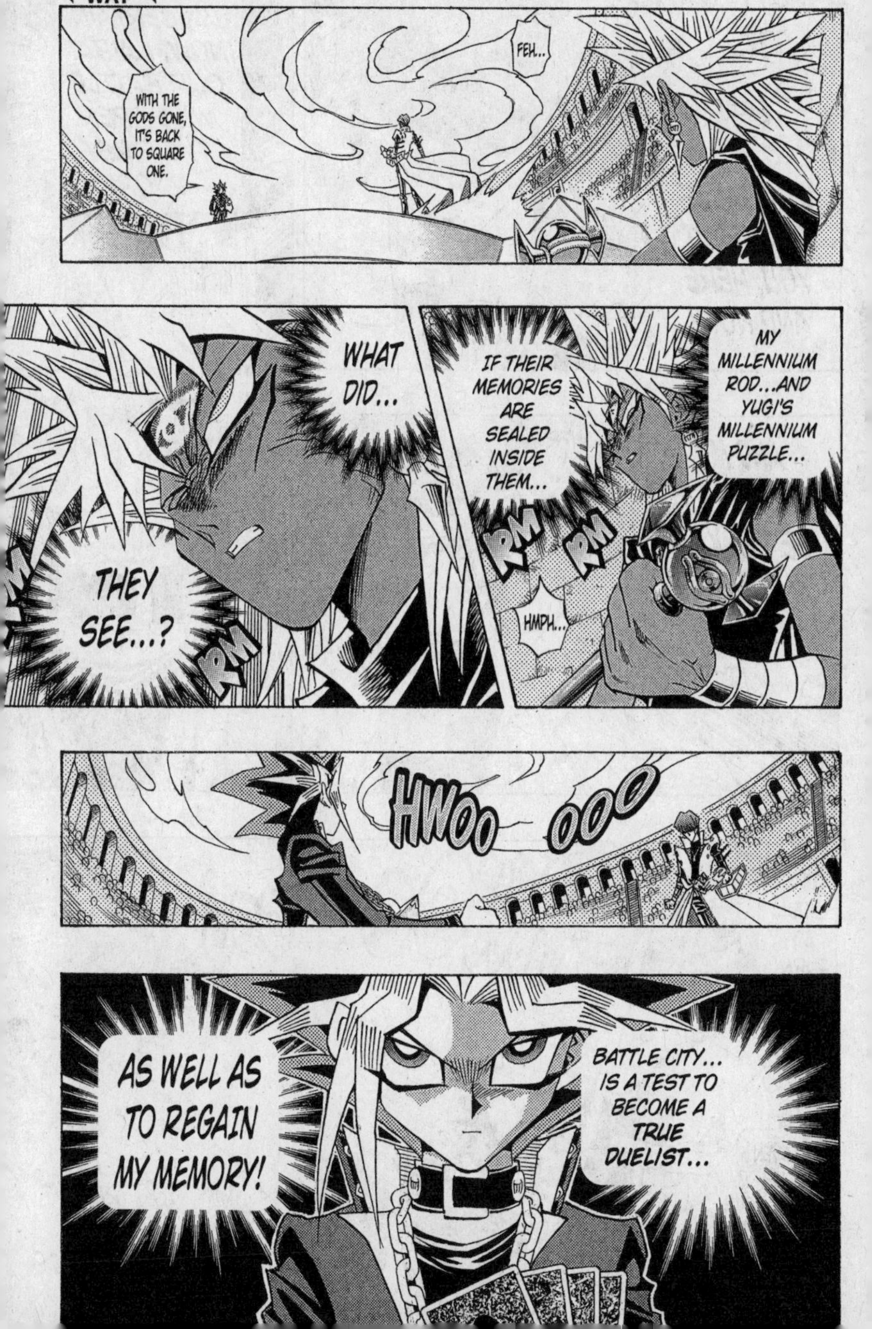
FEH...
WITH THE GODS GONE, IT'S BACK TO SQUARE ONE.
MY MILLENNIUM ROD...AND YUGI'S MILLENNIUM PUZZLE...
IF THEIR MEMORIES ARE SEALED INSIDE THEM...
RM
RM
HMPH...
WHAT DID...
THEY SEE...?
RM
HWOO OOO
BATTLE CITY... IS A TEST TO BECOME A TRUE DUELIST...
AS WELL AS TO REGAIN MY MEMORY!

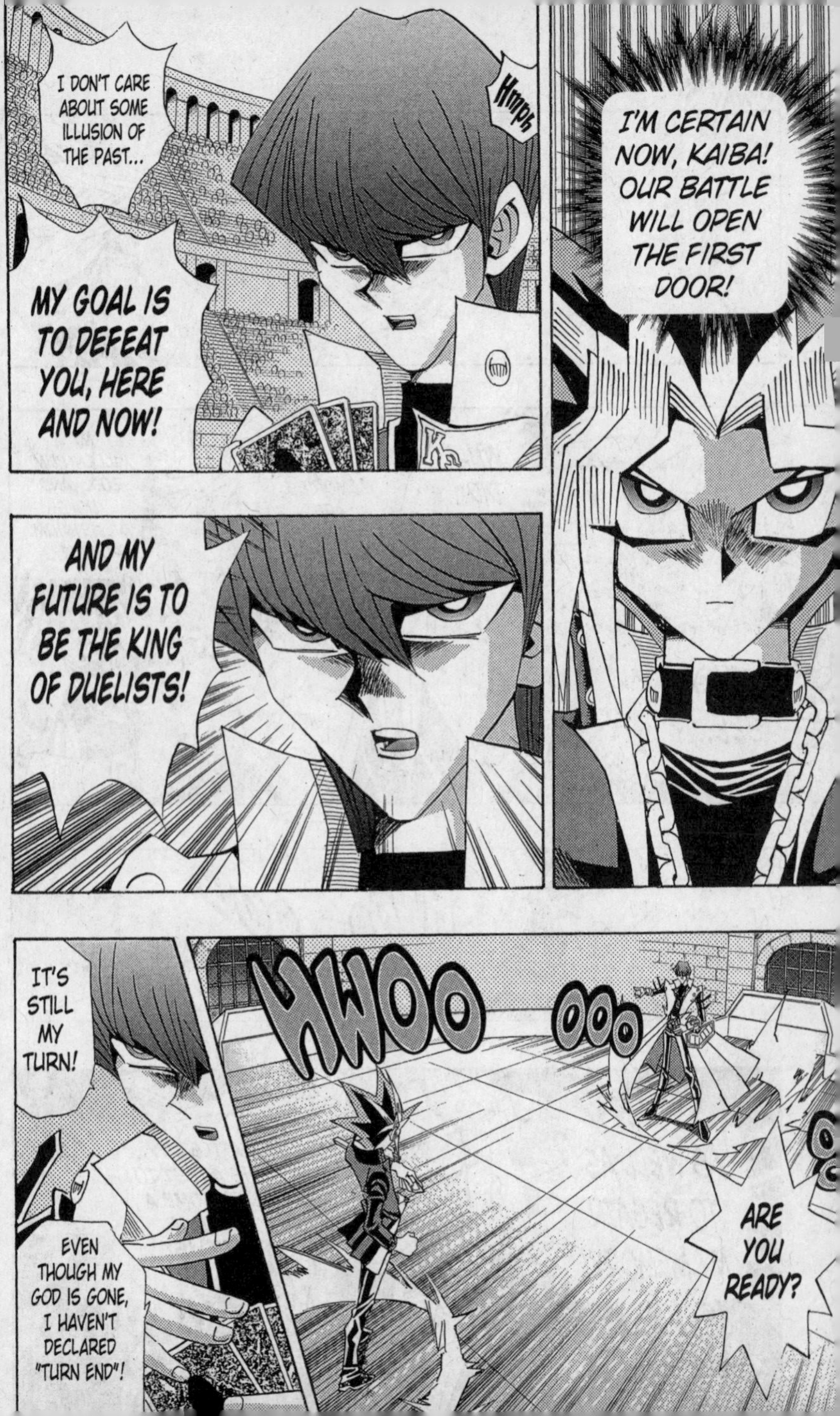
I'M CERTAIN NOW, KAIBA! OUR BATTLE WILL OPEN THE FIRST DOOR!
Hmph
I DON'T CARE ABOUT SOME ILLUSION OF THE PAST...
MY GOAL IS TO DEFEAT YOU, HERE AND NOW!
AND MY FUTURE IS TO BE THE KING OF DUELISTS!
HWOOOOO
ARE YOU READY?
IT'S STILL MY TURN!
EVEN THOUGH MY GOD IS GONE, I HAVEN'T DECLARED "TURN END"!

READ THIS WAY

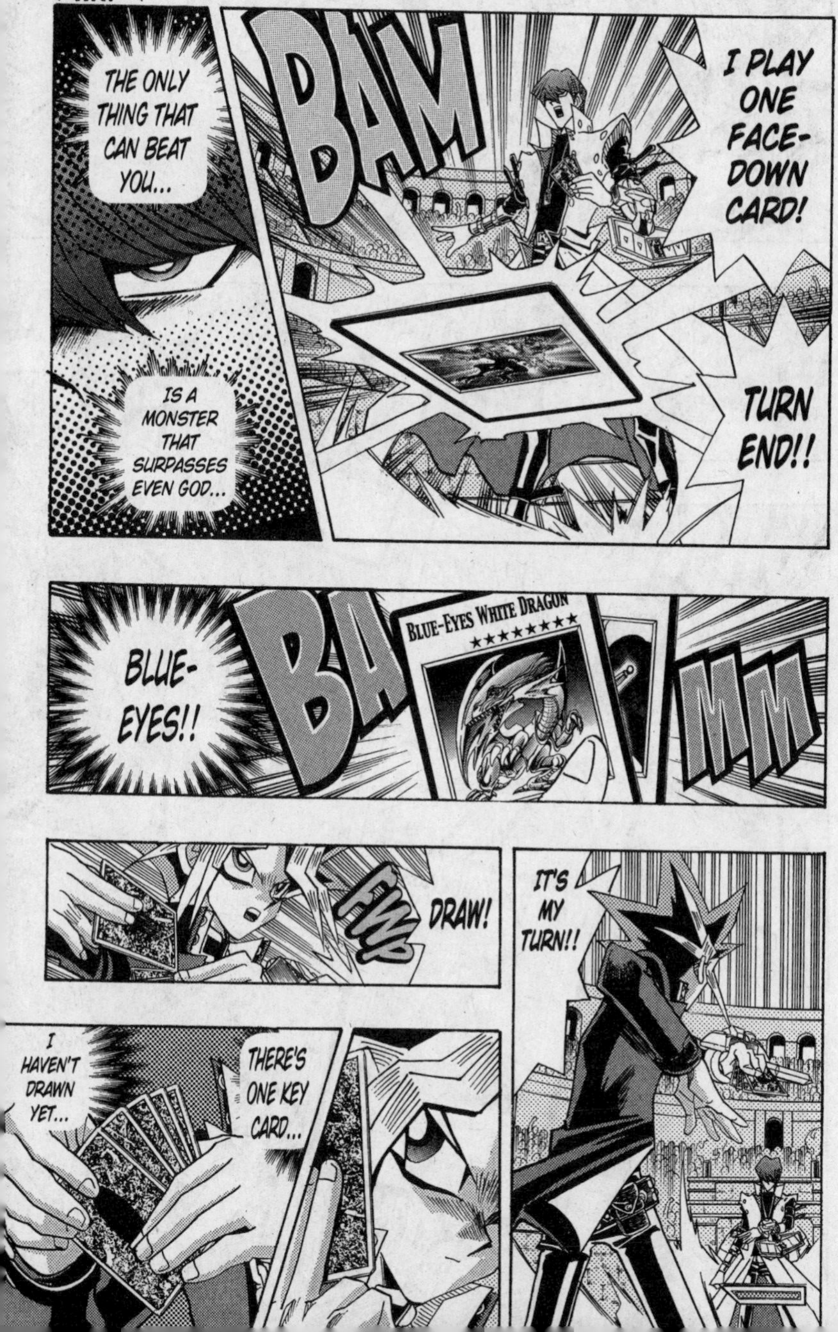
BAM
I PLAY ONE FACE-DOWN CARD!
TURN END!!
THE ONLY THING THAT CAN BEAT YOU...
IS A MONSTER THAT SURPASSES EVEN GOD...
MM
BLUE-EYES WHITE DRAGON
BA
BLUE-EYES!!
IT'S MY TURN!!
DRAW!
FWP
THERE'S ONE KEY CARD...
I HAVEN'T DRAWN YET...

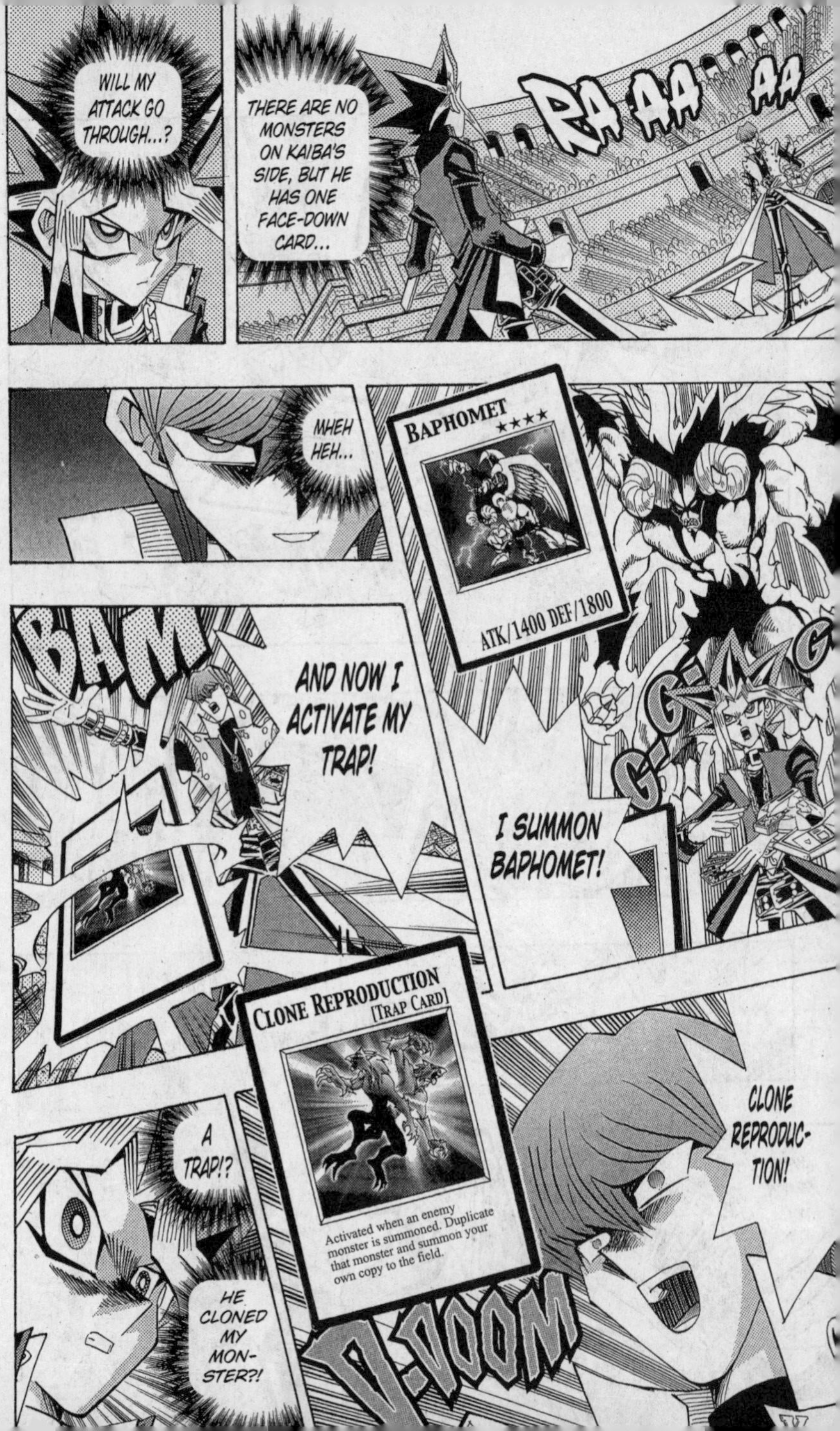
RAAAA AA
THERE ARE NO MONSTERS ON KAIBA'S SIDE, BUT HE HAS ONE FACE-DOWN CARD...
WILL MY ATTACK GO THROUGH...?
BAPHOMET ★★★★
ATK/1400 DEF/1800
G-G-G
I SUMMON BAPHOMET!
MHEH HEH...
BAM
AND NOW I ACTIVATE MY TRAP!
CLONE REPRODUCTION
[TRAP CARD]
Activated when an enemy monster is summoned. Duplicate that monster and summon your own copy to the field.
CLONE REPRODUCTION!
D-DOOM
A TRAP!?
HE CLONED MY MONSTER?!

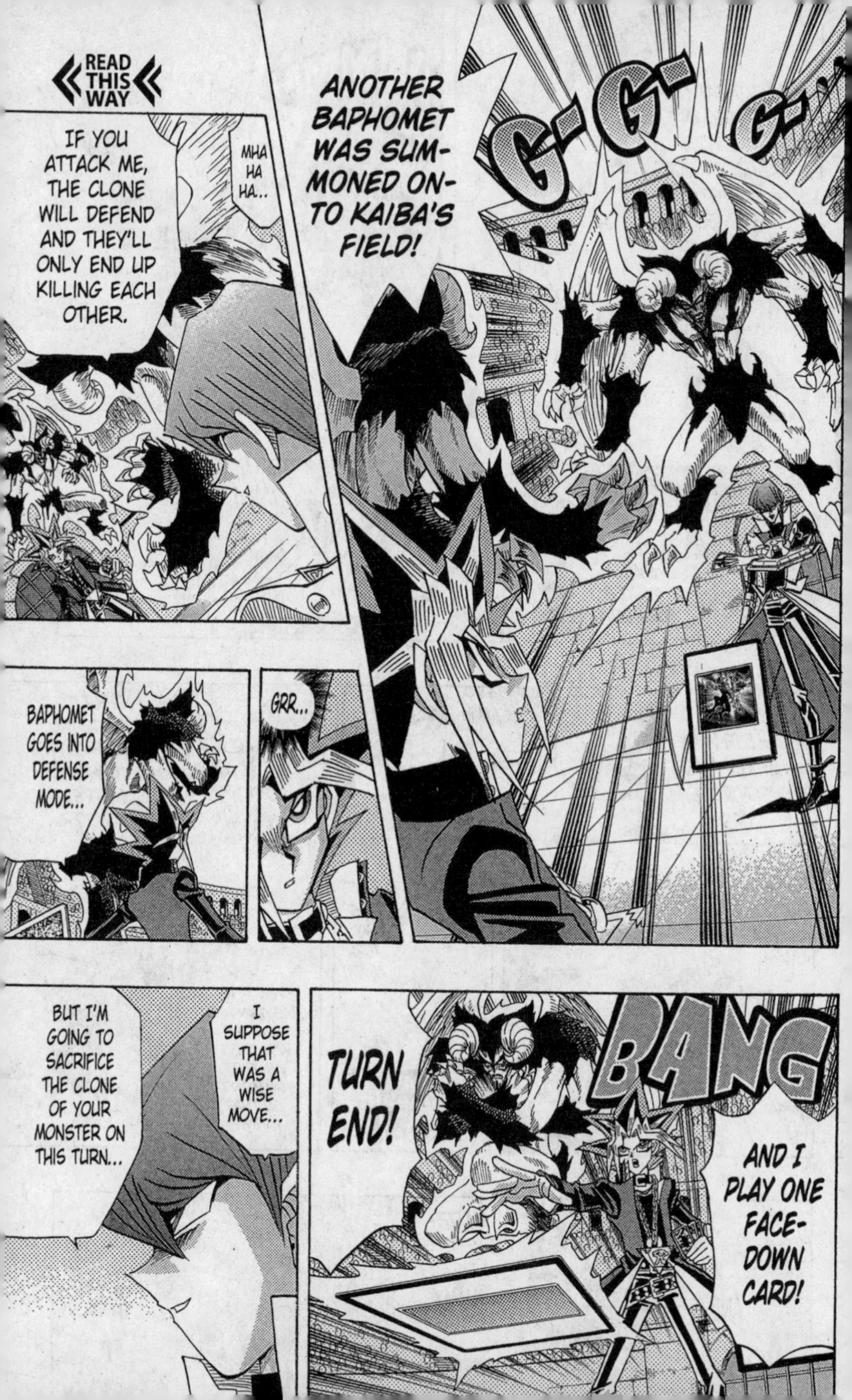
READ THIS WAY
ANOTHER BAPHOMET WAS SUMMONED ONTO KAIBA'S FIELD!
G-G-G-
MHA HA HA...
IF YOU ATTACK ME, THE CLONE WILL DEFEND AND THEY'LL ONLY END UP KILLING EACH OTHER.
GRR...
BAPHOMET GOES INTO DEFENSE MODE...
BANG
AND I PLAY ONE FACE-DOWN CARD!
TURN END!
I SUPPOSE THAT WAS A WISE MOVE...
BUT I'M GOING TO SACRIFICE THE CLONE OF YOUR MONSTER ON THIS TURN...

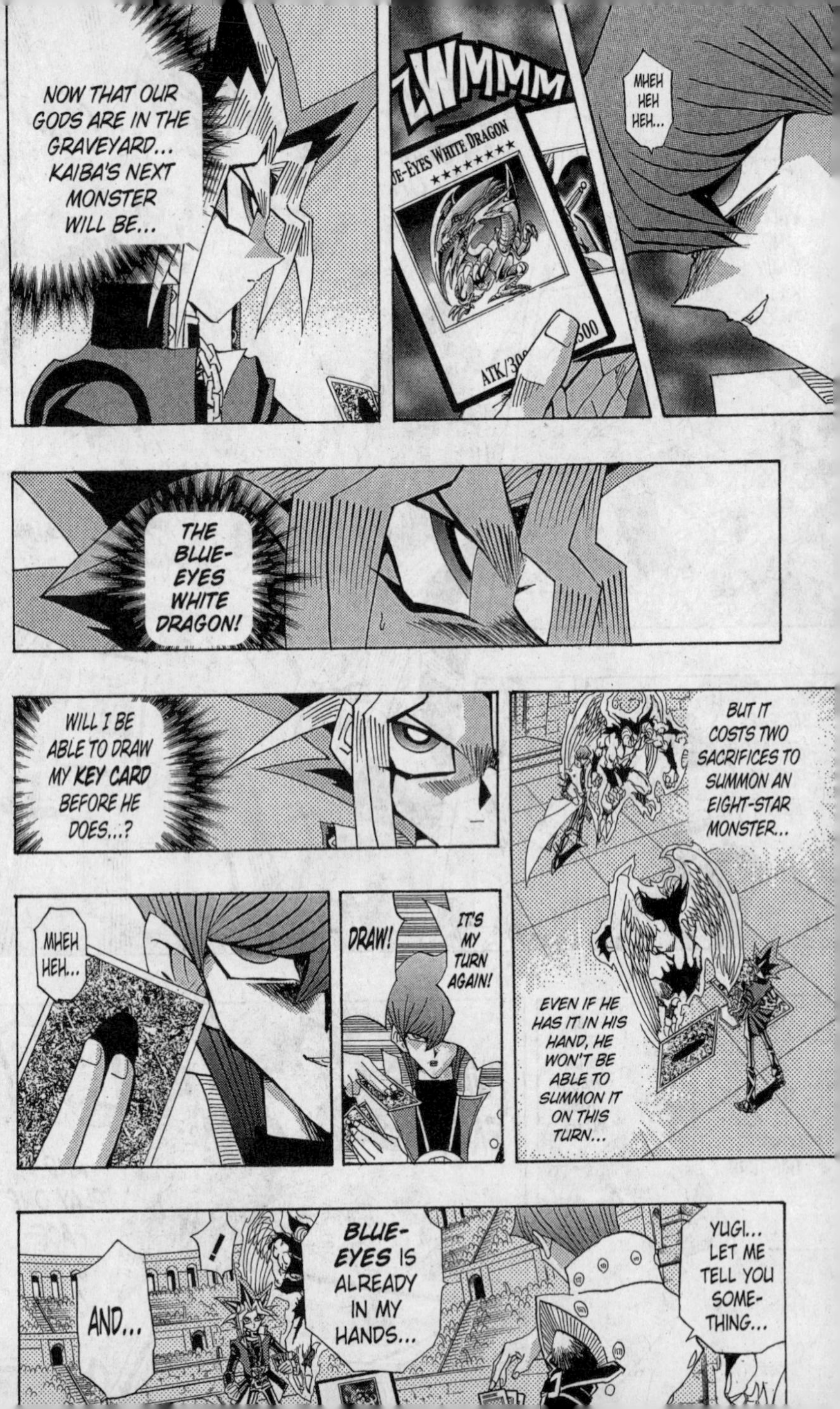
MHEH HEH HEH...
ZWMMM
NOW THAT OUR GODS ARE IN THE GRAVEYARD... KAIBA'S NEXT MONSTER WILL BE...
THE BLUE-EYES WHITE DRAGON!
BUT IT COSTS TWO SACRIFICES TO SUMMON AN EIGHT-STAR MONSTER...
EVEN IF HE HAS IT IN HIS HAND, HE WON'T BE ABLE TO SUMMON IT ON THIS TURN...
WILL I BE ABLE TO DRAW MY KEY CARD BEFORE HE DOES...?
IT'S MY TURN AGAIN!
DRAW!
MHEH HEH...
YUGI... LET ME TELL YOU SOMETHING...
BLUE-EYES IS ALREADY IN MY HANDS...
!
AND...

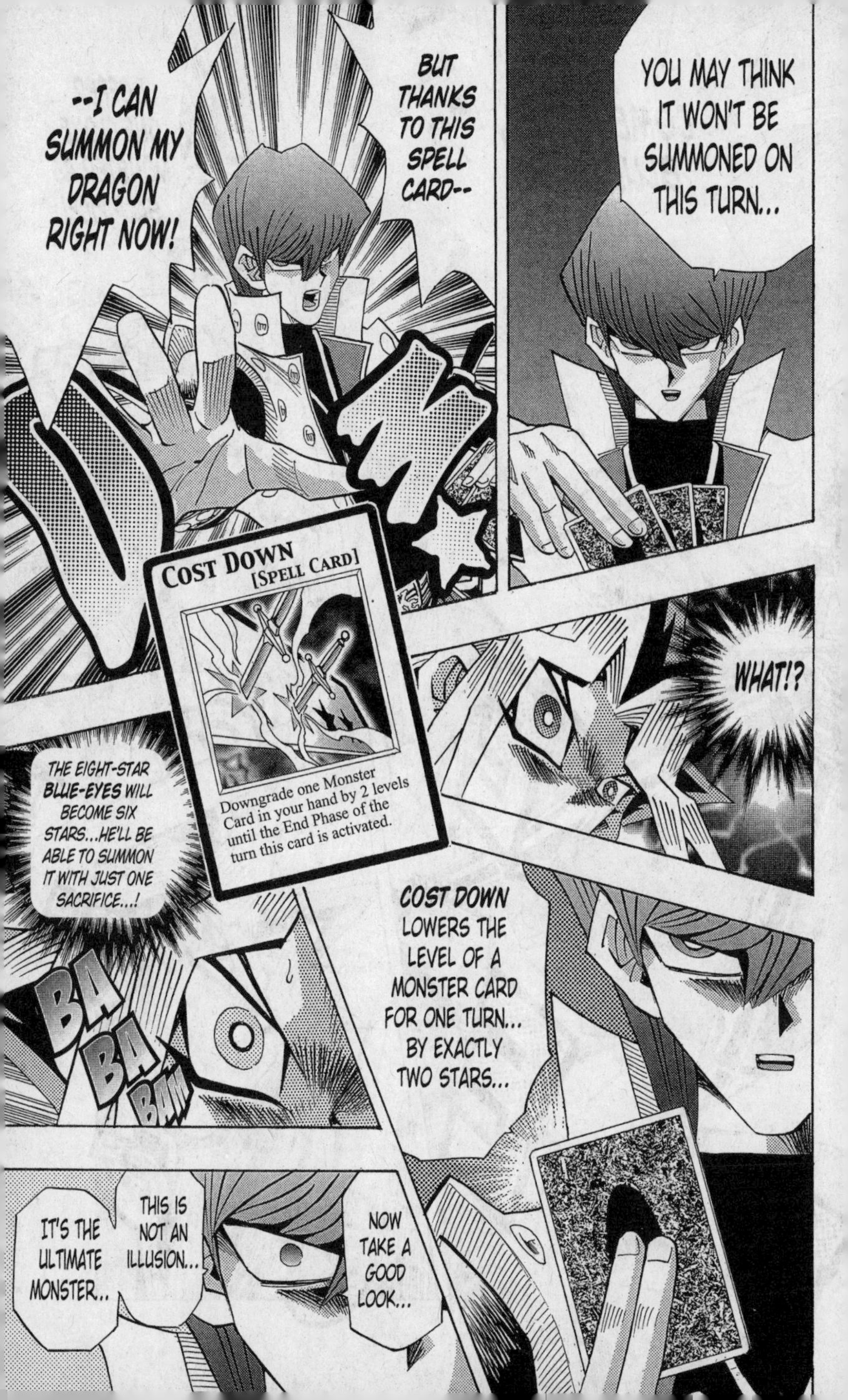
YOU MAY THINK IT WON'T BE SUMMONED ON THIS TURN...
BUT THANKS TO THIS SPELL CARD--
--I CAN SUMMON MY DRAGON RIGHT NOW!
COST DOWN
[SPELL CARD]
Downgrade one Monster Card in your hand by 2 levels until the End Phase of the turn this card is activated.
WHAT!?
THE EIGHT-STAR BLUE-EYES WILL BECOME SIX STARS...HE'LL BE ABLE TO SUMMON IT WITH JUST ONE SACRIFICE...!
COST DOWN LOWERS THE LEVEL OF A MONSTER CARD FOR ONE TURN... BY EXACTLY TWO STARS...
BA BA BAM
NOW TAKE A GOOD LOOK...
THIS IS NOT AN ILLUSION...
IT'S THE ULTIMATE MONSTER...

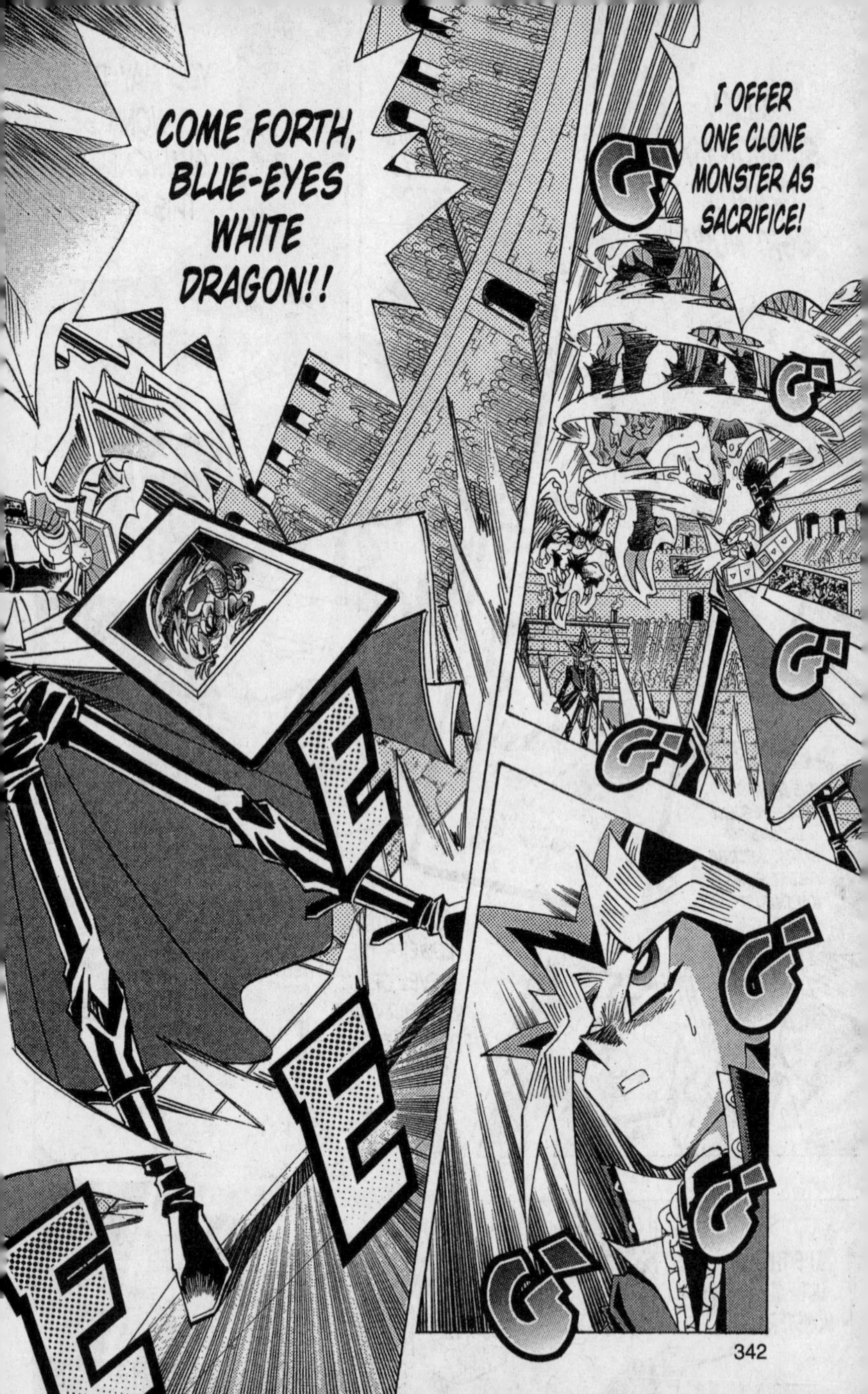
I OFFER ONE CLONE MONSTER AS SACRIFICE!
COME FORTH, BLUE-EYES WHITE DRAGON!!

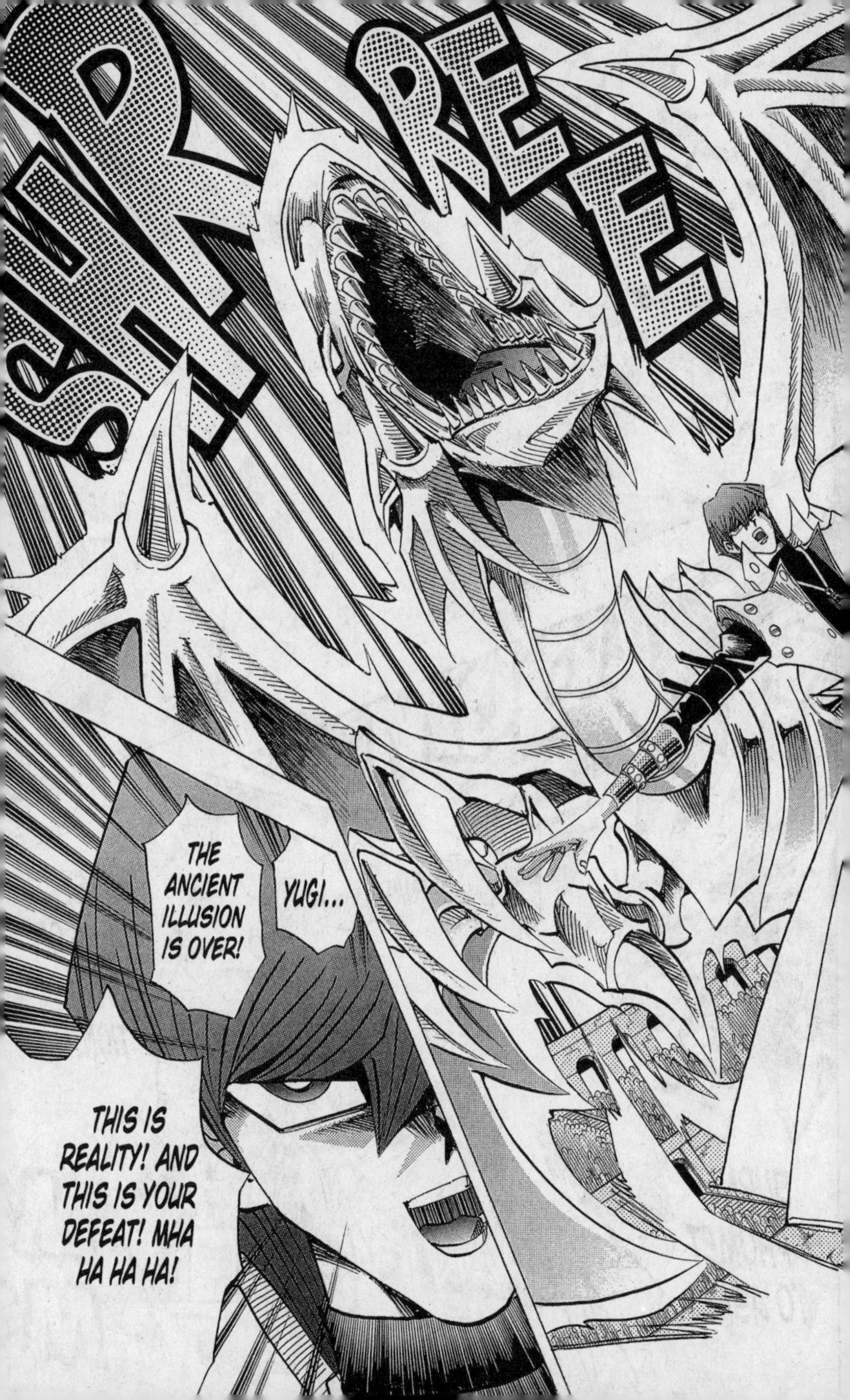
YUGI...
THE ANCIENT ILLUSION IS OVER!
THIS IS REALITY! AND THIS IS YOUR DEFEAT! MHA HA HA HA!

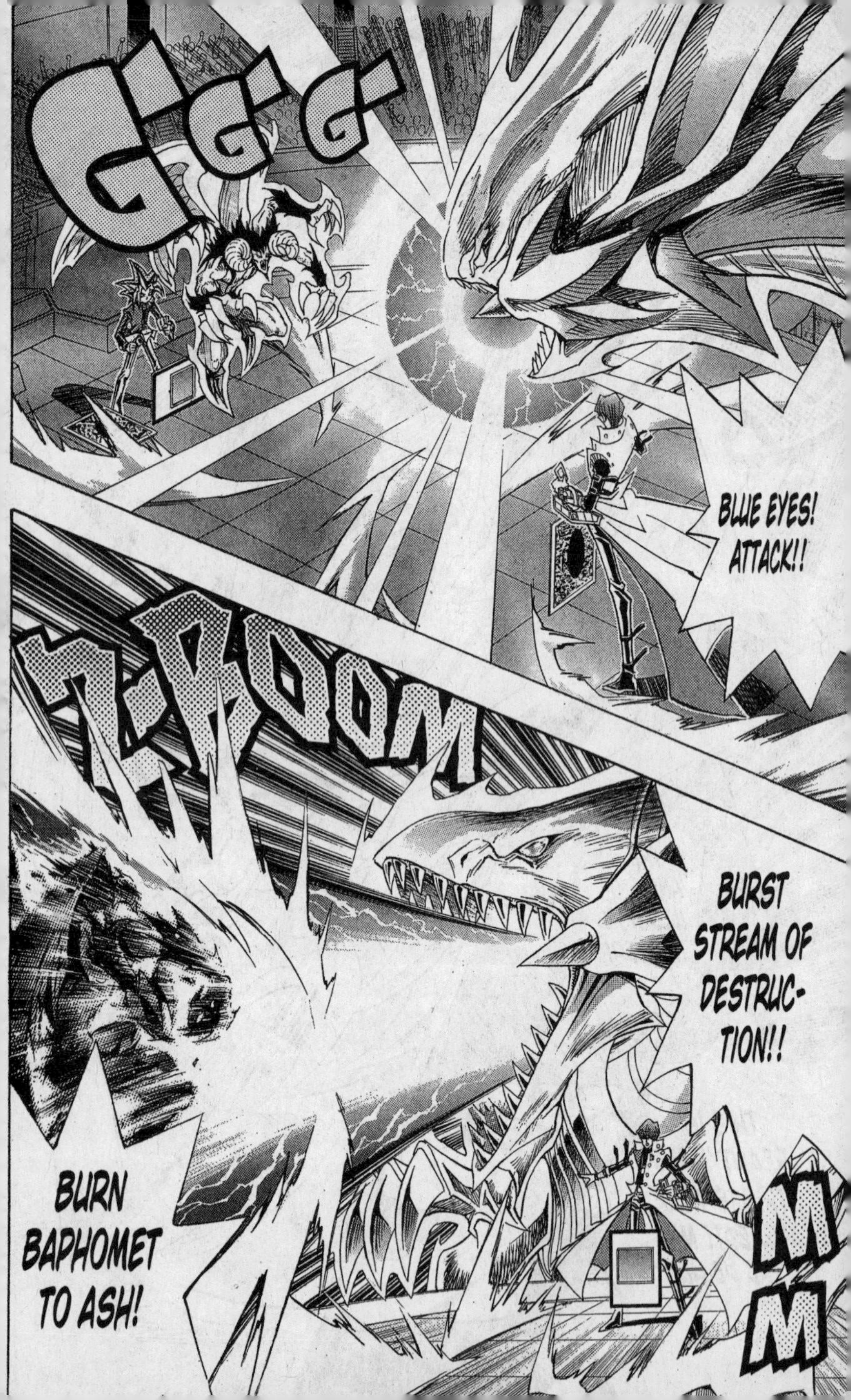
BLUE EYES! ATTACK!!
G' G' G'
ZROOM
BURST STREAM OF DESTRUC-TION!!
M M
BURN BAPHOMET TO ASH!

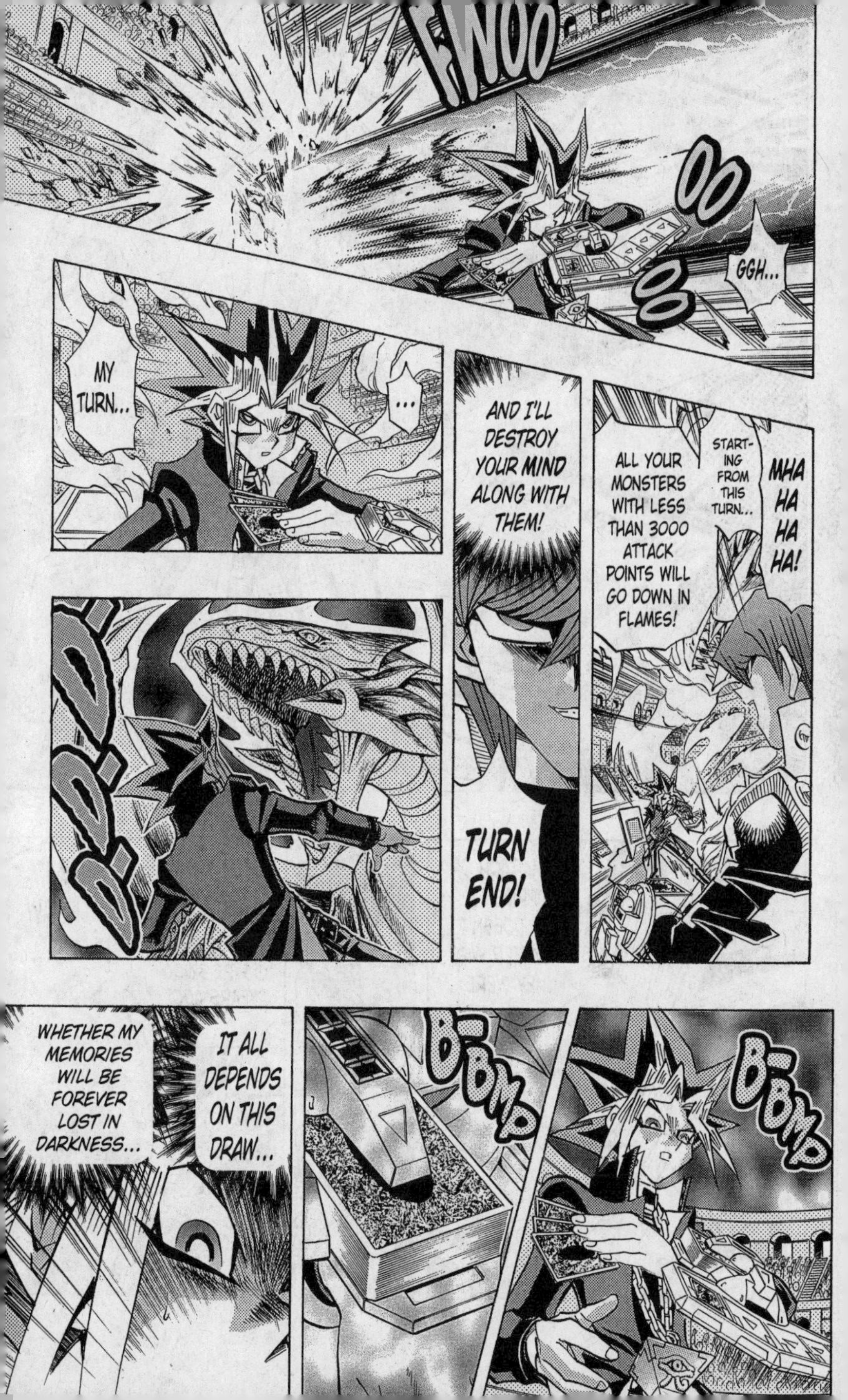
FWOO
OO
OO
GGH...
MHA HA HA HA!
STARTING FROM THIS TURN...
ALL YOUR MONSTERS WITH LESS THAN 3000 ATTACK POINTS WILL GO DOWN IN FLAMES!
AND I'LL DESTROY YOUR MIND ALONG WITH THEM!
TURN END!
...
MY TURN...
B-DOMP
B-DOMP
IT ALL DEPENDS ON THIS DRAW...
WHETHER MY MEMORIES WILL BE FOREVER LOST IN DARKNESS...

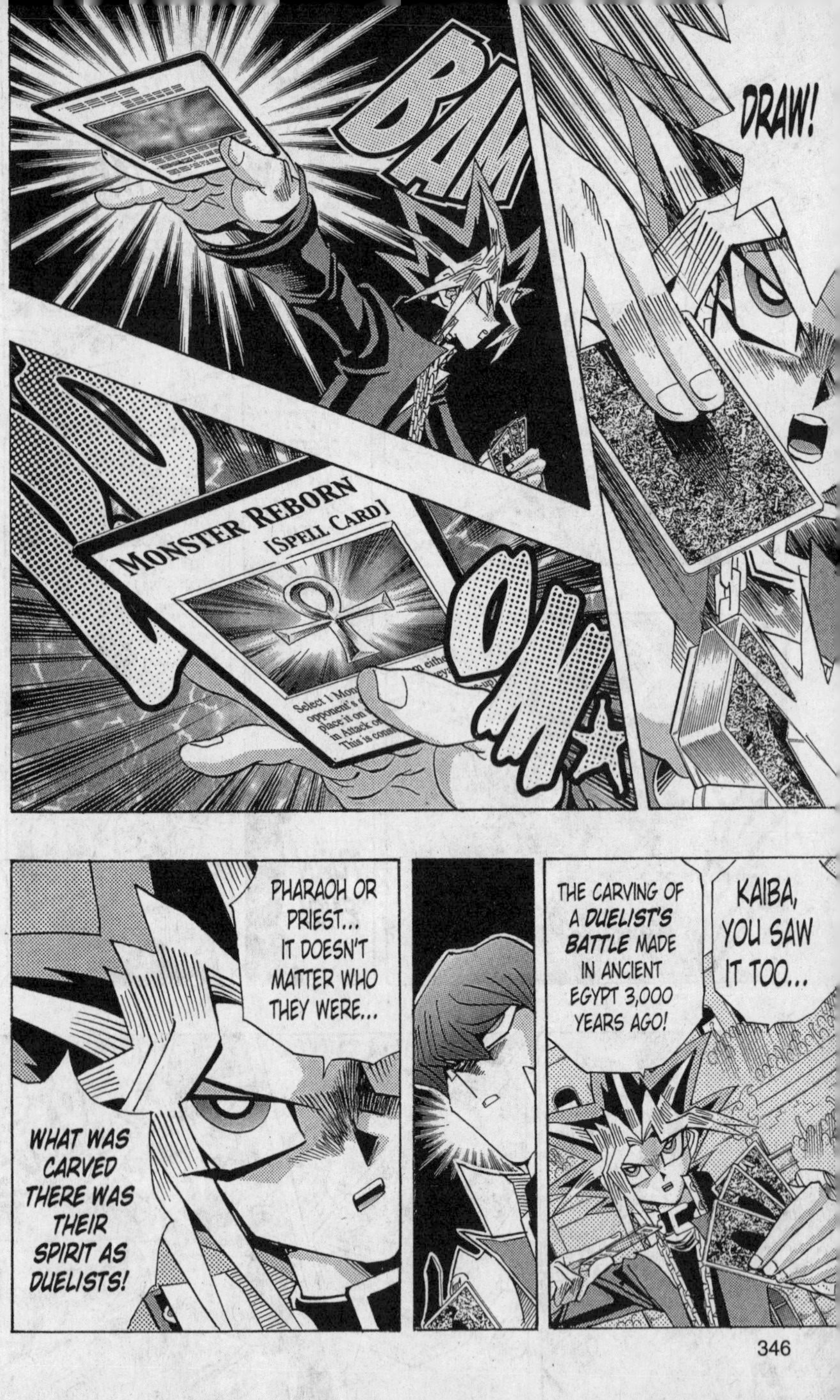
DRAW!
BAM
MONSTER REBORN
[SPELL CARD]
ON
KAIBA, YOU SAW IT TOO...
THE CARVING OF A DUELIST'S BATTLE MADE IN ANCIENT EGYPT 3,000 YEARS AGO!
PHARAOH OR PRIEST... IT DOESN'T MATTER WHO THEY WERE...
WHAT WAS CARVED THERE WAS THEIR SPIRIT AS DUELISTS!

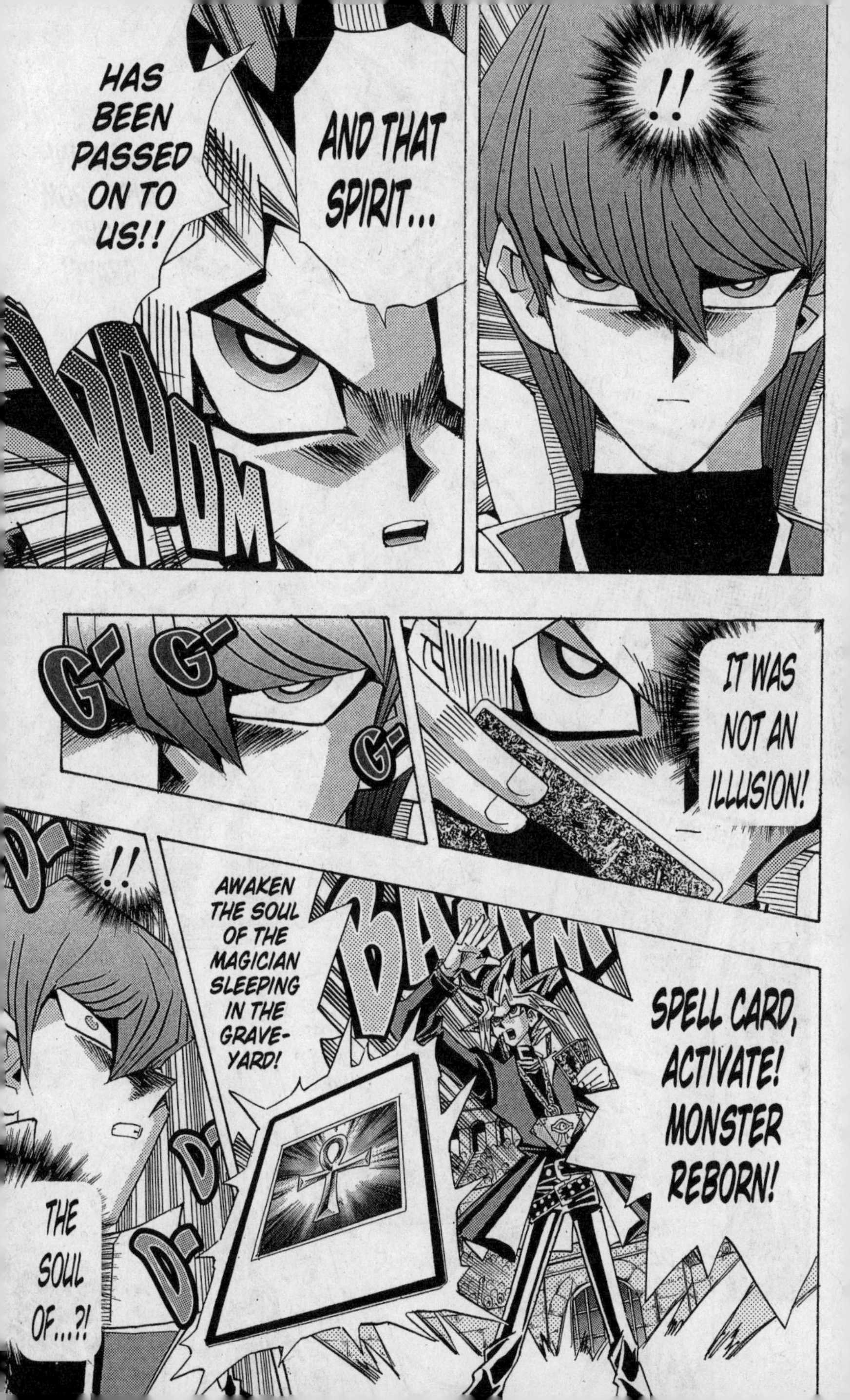
!!
AND THAT SPIRIT...
HAS BEEN PASSED ON TO US!!
VROOM
IT WAS NOT AN ILLUSION!
G- G- G-
SPELL CARD, ACTIVATE! MONSTER REBORN!
BANN
AWAKEN THE SOUL OF THE MAGICIAN SLEEPING IN THE GRAVE-YARD!
!!
D- D- D-
THE SOUL OF...?!

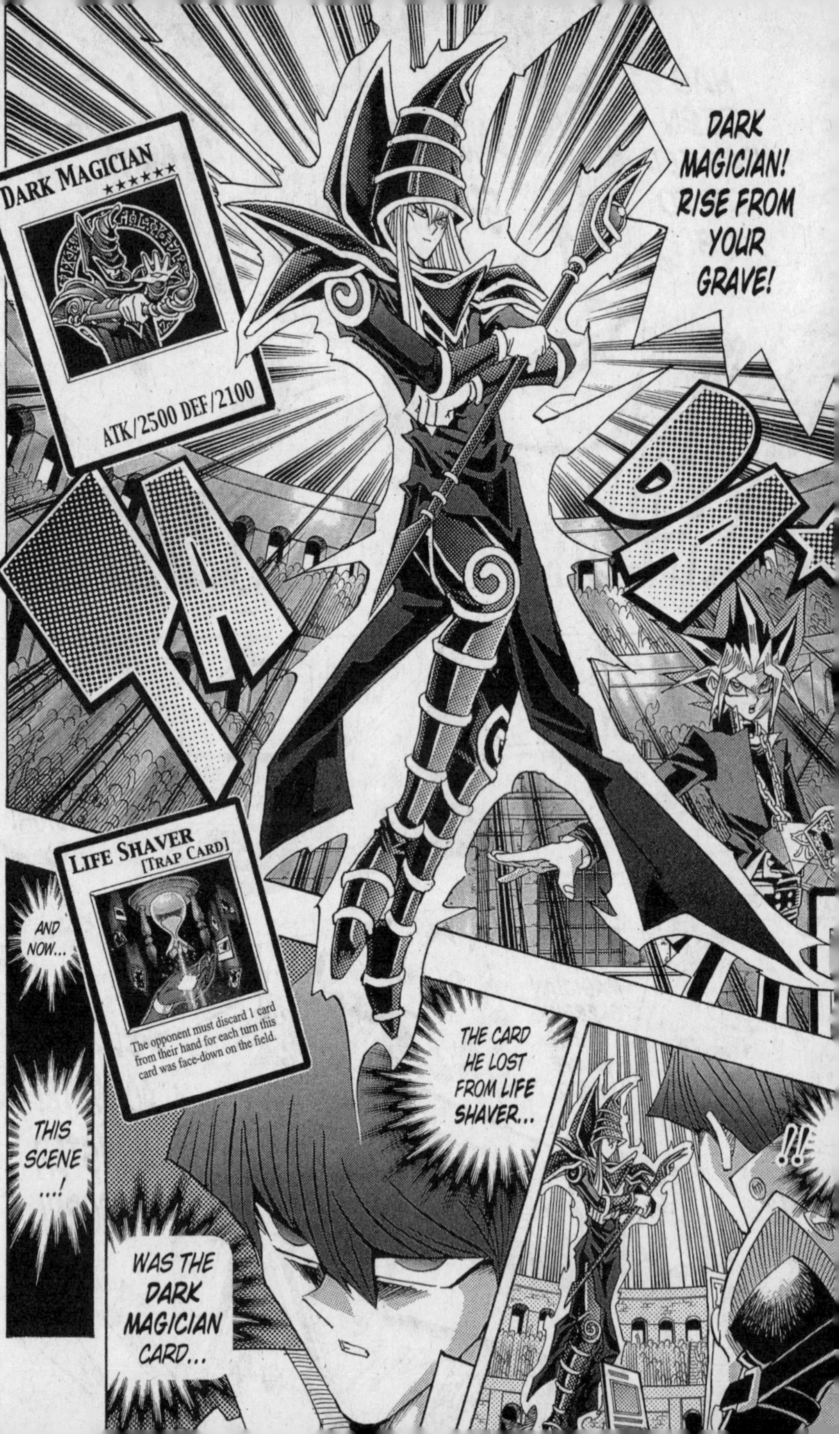

DARK MAGICIAN! RISE FROM YOUR GRAVE!
DARK MAGICIAN ★★★★★★
ATK/2500 DEF/2100
TA DA★
THE CARD HE LOST FROM LIFE SHAVER...
!!
LIFE SHAVER [TRAP CARD]
The opponent must discard 1 card from their hand for each turn this card was face-down on the field.
AND NOW...
THIS SCENE ...!
WAS THE DARK MAGICIAN CARD...

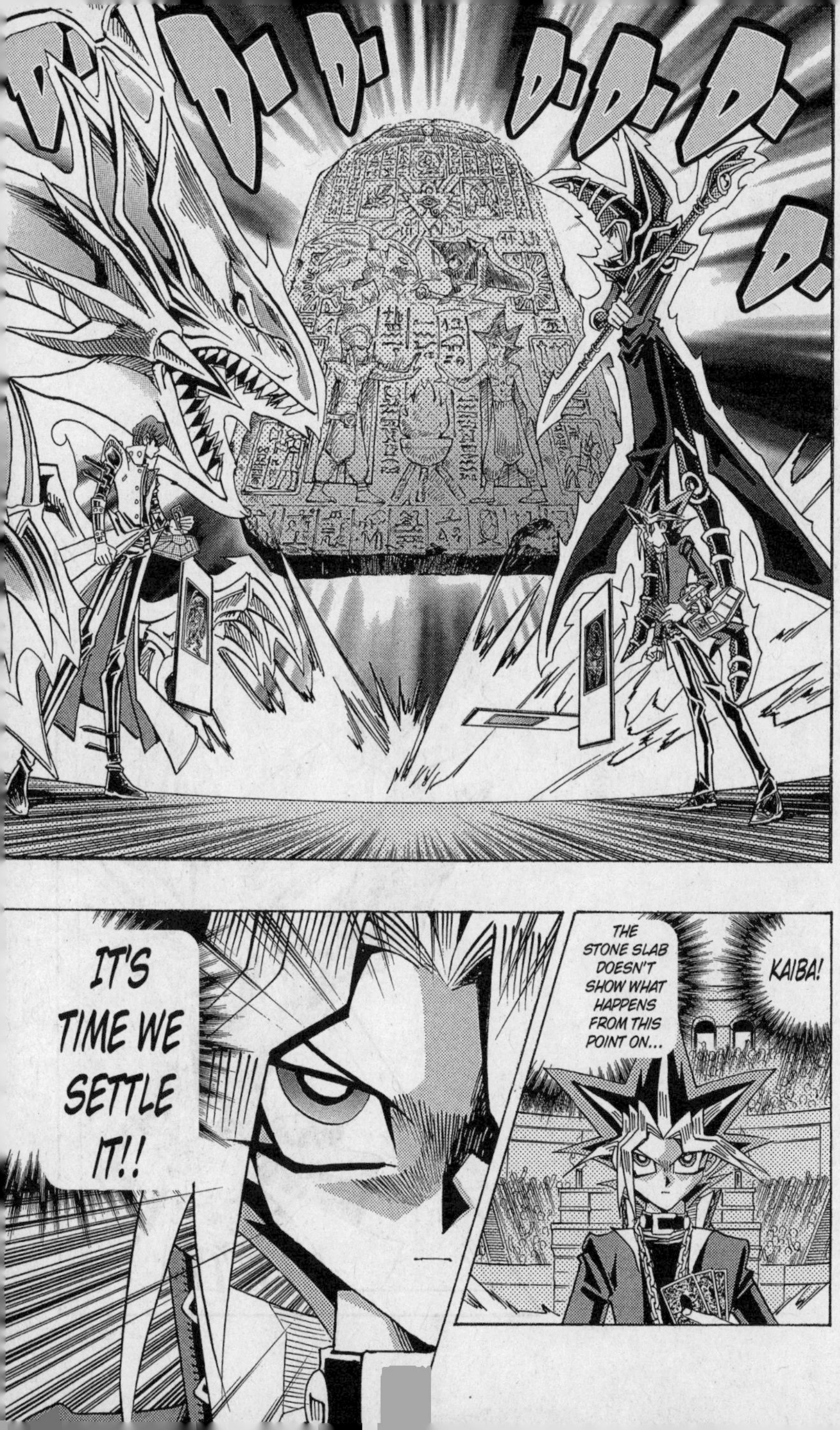
D· D· D· D· D· D· D·
KAIBA!
THE STONE SLAB DOESN'T SHOW WHAT HAPPENS FROM THIS POINT ON...
IT'S TIME WE SETTLE IT!!

Duel 259: Deck of Glass!

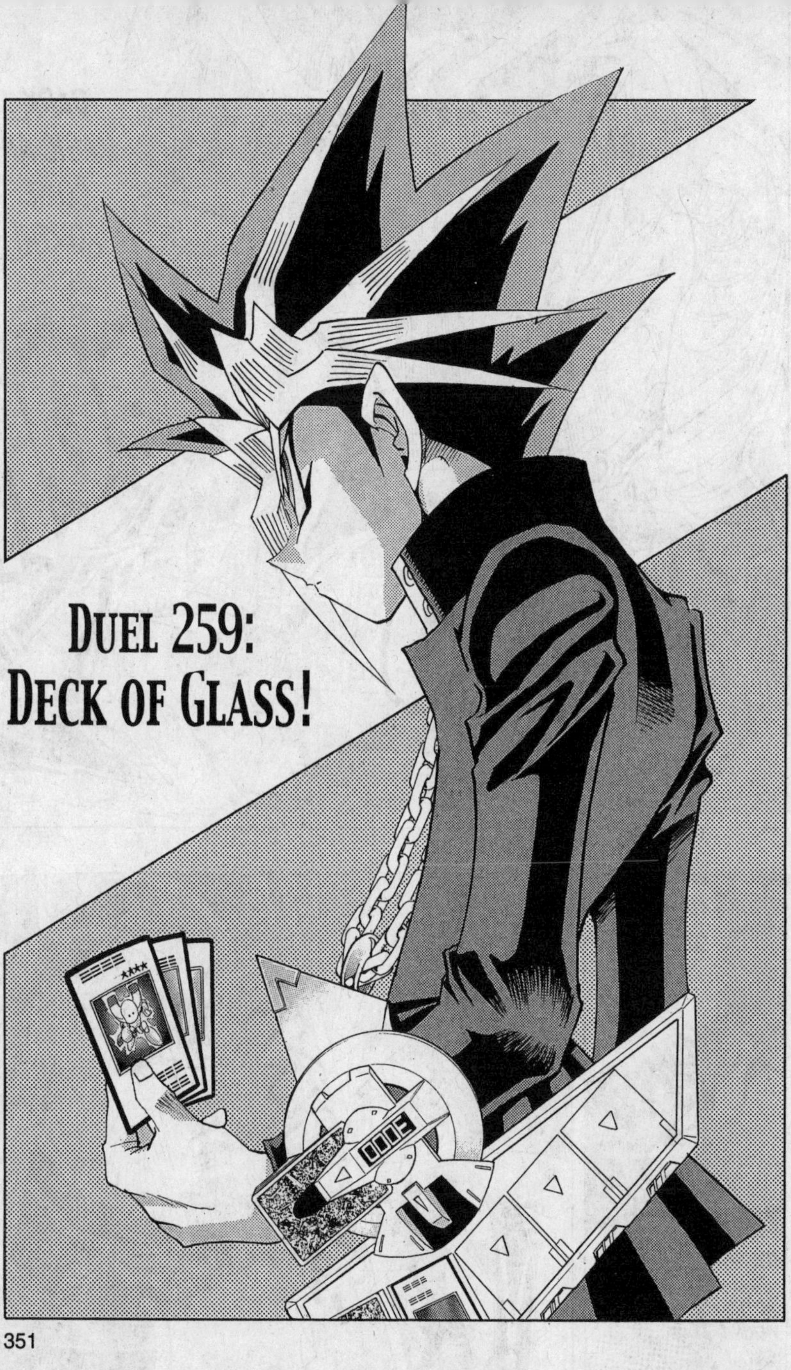

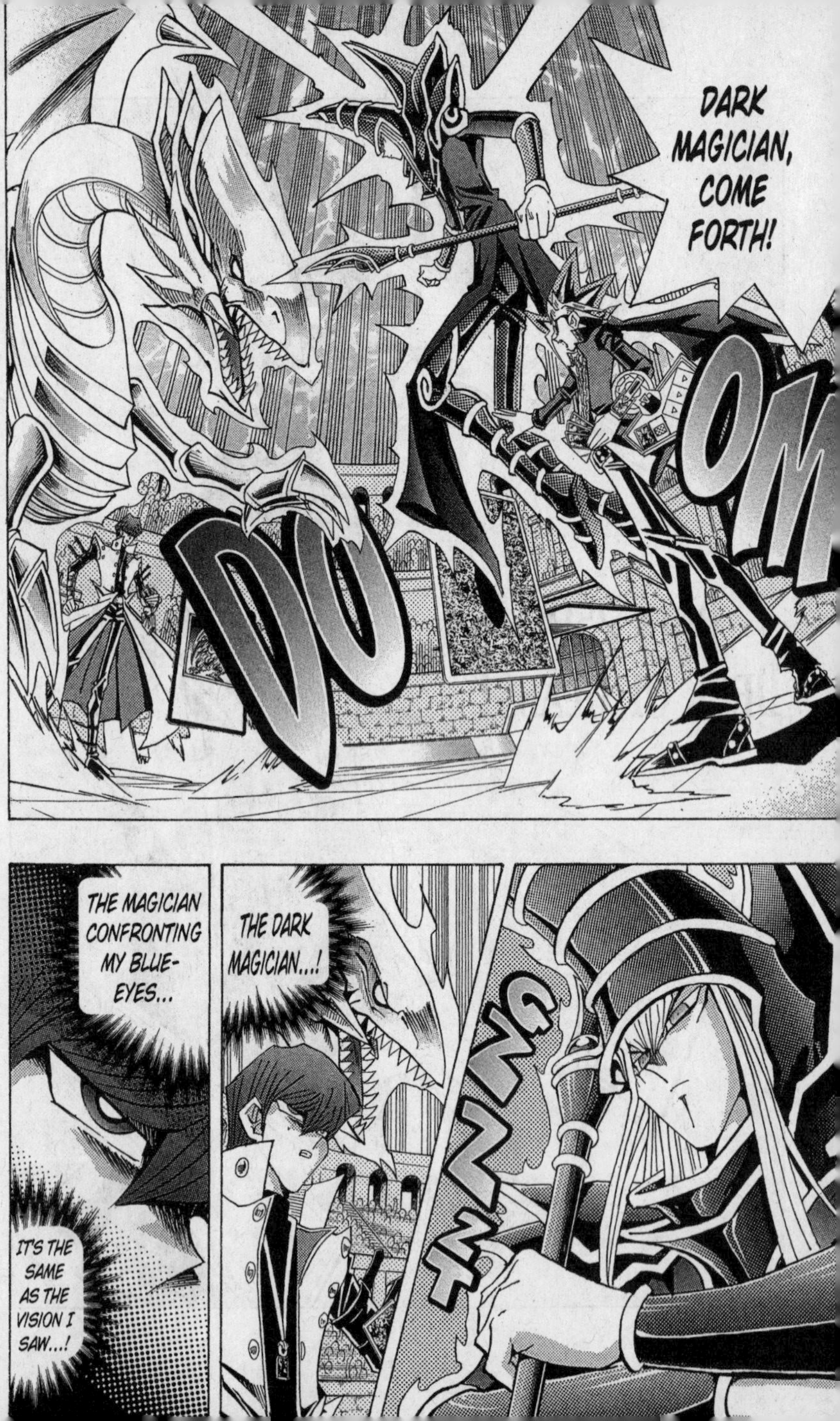
DARK MAGICIAN, COME FORTH!
DOOM
TNNNG
THE DARK MAGICIAN...!
THE MAGICIAN CONFRONTING MY BLUE-EYES...
IT'S THE SAME AS THE VISION I SAW...!

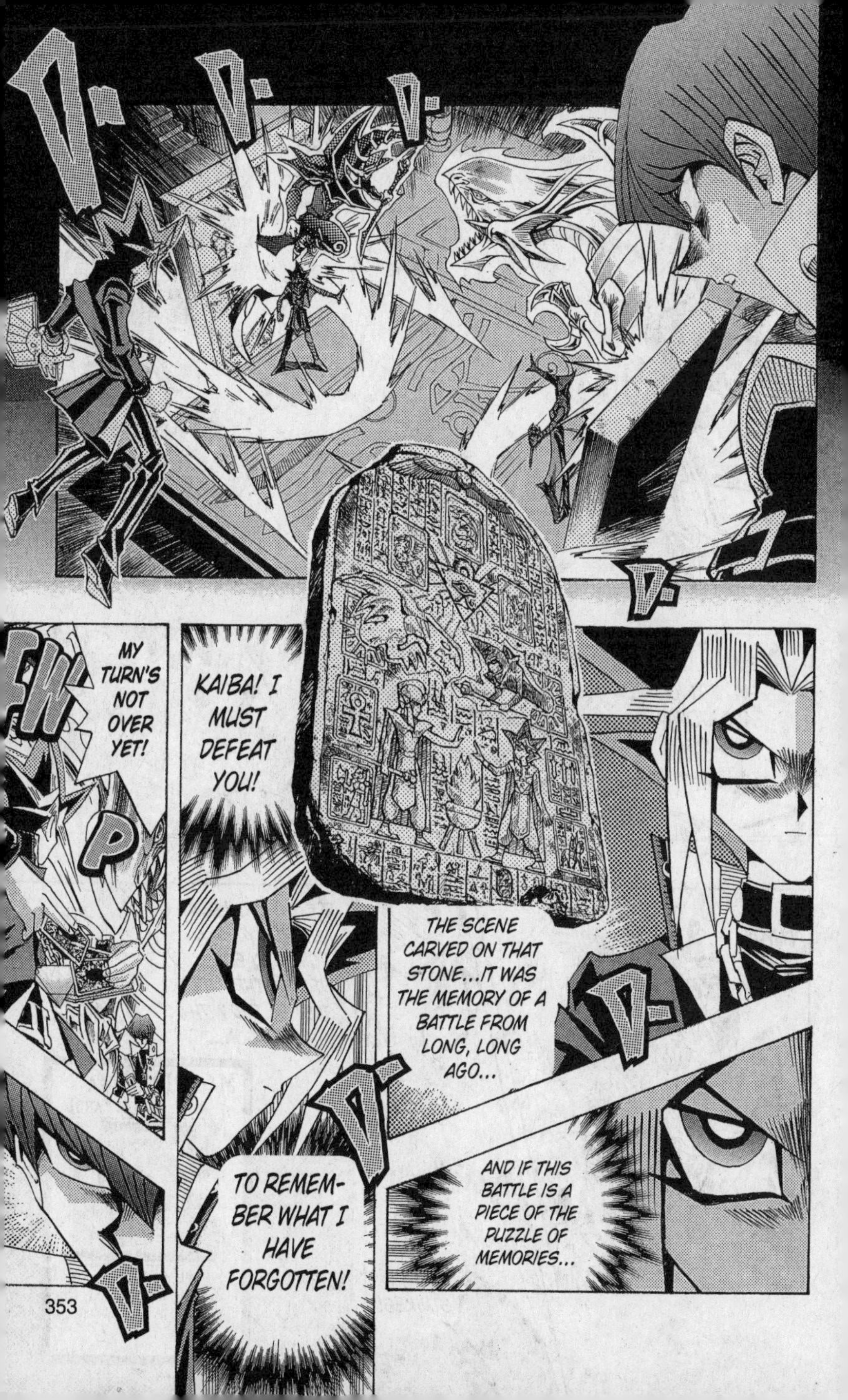
D-
D-
D-
D-
THE SCENE CARVED ON THAT STONE...IT WAS THE MEMORY OF A BATTLE FROM LONG, LONG AGO...
D-
AND IF THIS BATTLE IS A PIECE OF THE PUZZLE OF MEMORIES...
KAIBA! I MUST DEFEAT YOU!
D-
TO REMEM-BER WHAT I HAVE FORGOTTEN!
MY TURN'S NOT OVER YET!
P
D-

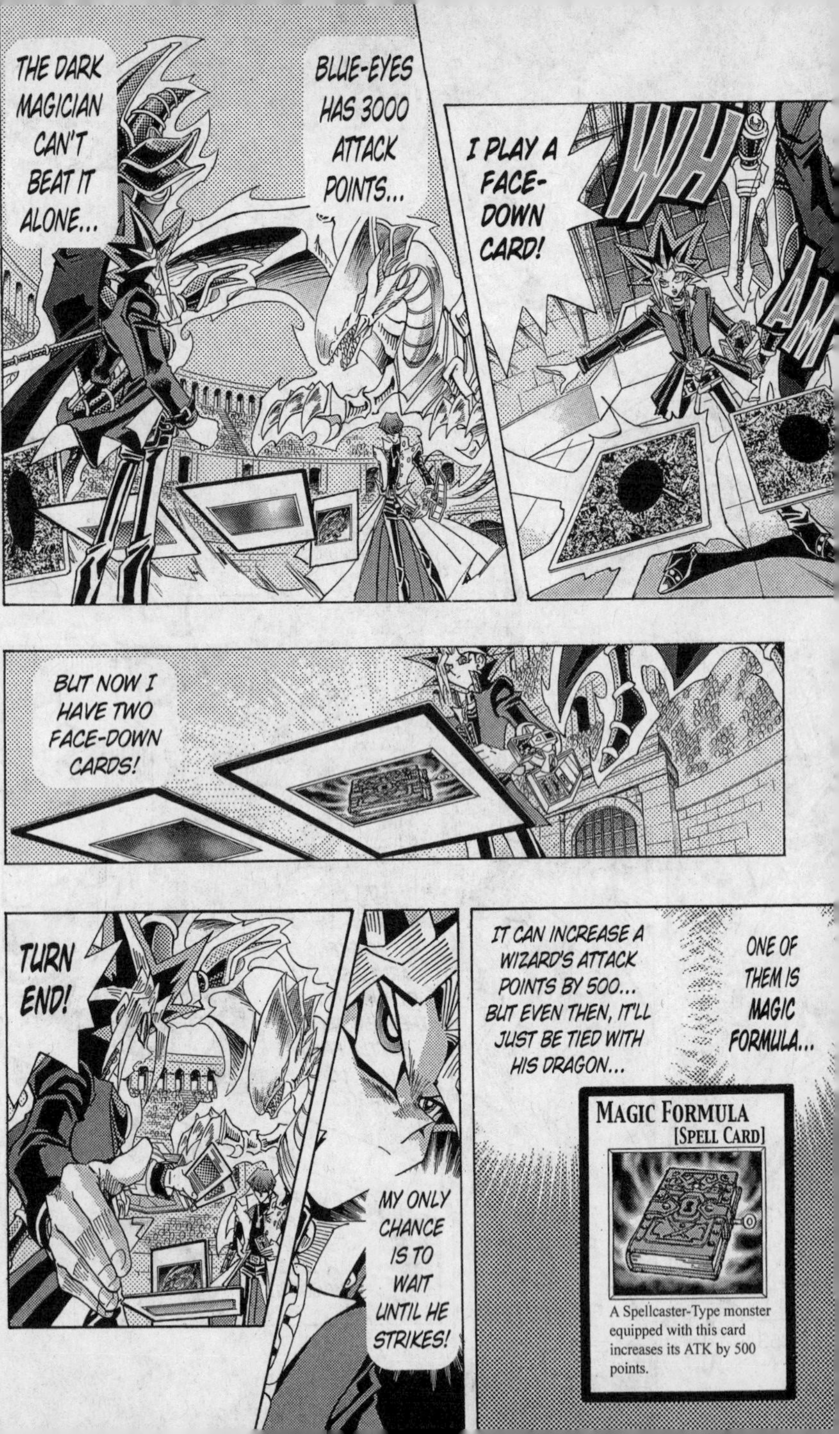
I PLAY A FACE-DOWN CARD!
WHAM
BLUE-EYES HAS 3000 ATTACK POINTS...
THE DARK MAGICIAN CAN'T BEAT IT ALONE...
BUT NOW I HAVE TWO FACE-DOWN CARDS!
ONE OF THEM IS MAGIC FORMULA...
IT CAN INCREASE A WIZARD'S ATTACK POINTS BY 500... BUT EVEN THEN, IT'LL JUST BE TIED WITH HIS DRAGON...
MAGIC FORMULA
[SPELL CARD]
A Spellcaster-Type monster equipped with this card increases its ATK by 500 points.
MY ONLY CHANCE IS TO WAIT UNTIL HE STRIKES!
TURN END!

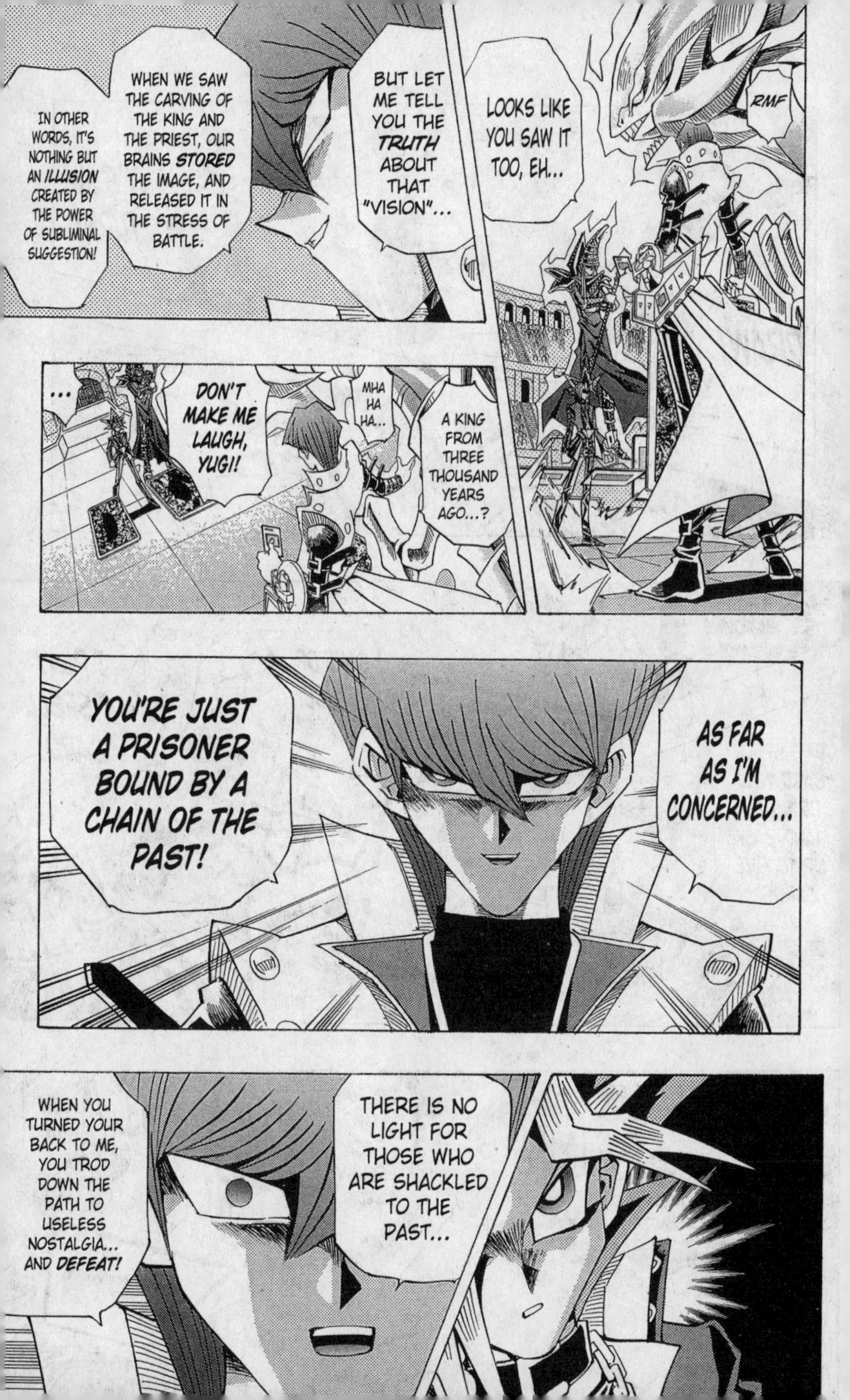
RMF
LOOKS LIKE YOU SAW IT TOO, EH...
BUT LET ME TELL YOU THE *TRUTH* ABOUT THAT "VISION"...
WHEN WE SAW THE CARVING OF THE KING AND THE PRIEST, OUR BRAINS *STORED* THE IMAGE, AND RELEASED IT IN THE STRESS OF BATTLE.
IN OTHER WORDS, IT'S NOTHING BUT AN *ILLUSION* CREATED BY THE POWER OF SUBLIMINAL SUGGESTION!
A KING FROM THREE THOUSAND YEARS AGO...?
MHA HA HA...
DON'T MAKE ME LAUGH, YUGI!
...
AS FAR AS I'M CONCERNED...
YOU'RE JUST A PRISONER BOUND BY A CHAIN OF THE PAST!
THERE IS NO LIGHT FOR THOSE WHO ARE SHACKLED TO THE PAST...
WHEN YOU TURNED YOUR BACK TO ME, YOU TROD DOWN THE PATH TO USELESS NOSTALGIA... AND *DEFEAT*!

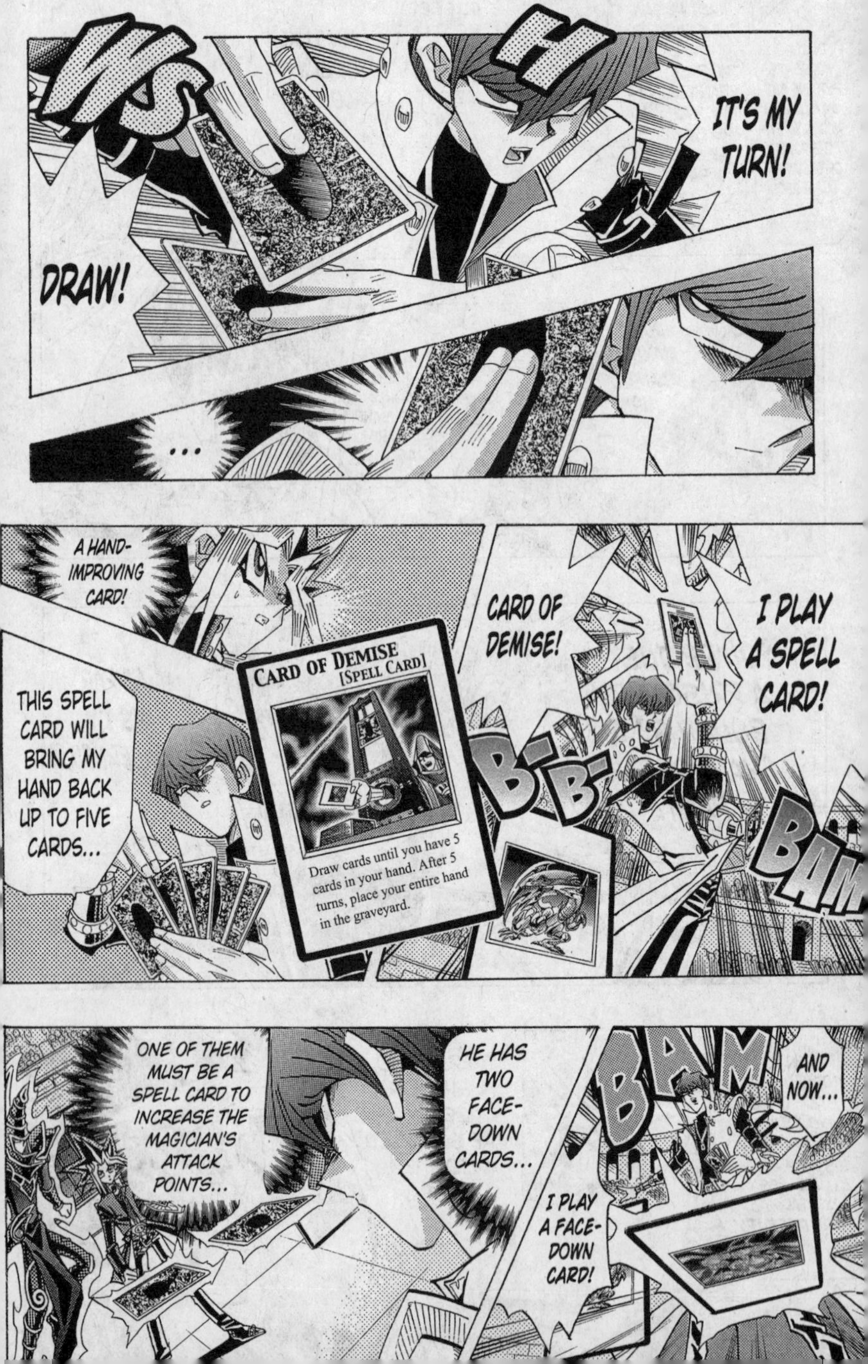
IT'S MY TURN!
H
SH
DRAW!
...
I PLAY A SPELL CARD!
CARD OF DEMISE!
B-B-
BAM
A HAND-IMPROVING CARD!
THIS SPELL CARD WILL BRING MY HAND BACK UP TO FIVE CARDS...
CARD OF DEMISE
[SPELL CARD]
Draw cards until you have 5 cards in your hand. After 5 turns, place your entire hand in the graveyard.
AND NOW...
BAM
I PLAY A FACE-DOWN CARD!
HE HAS TWO FACE-DOWN CARDS...
ONE OF THEM MUST BE A SPELL CARD TO INCREASE THE MAGICIAN'S ATTACK POINTS...

READ THIS WAY

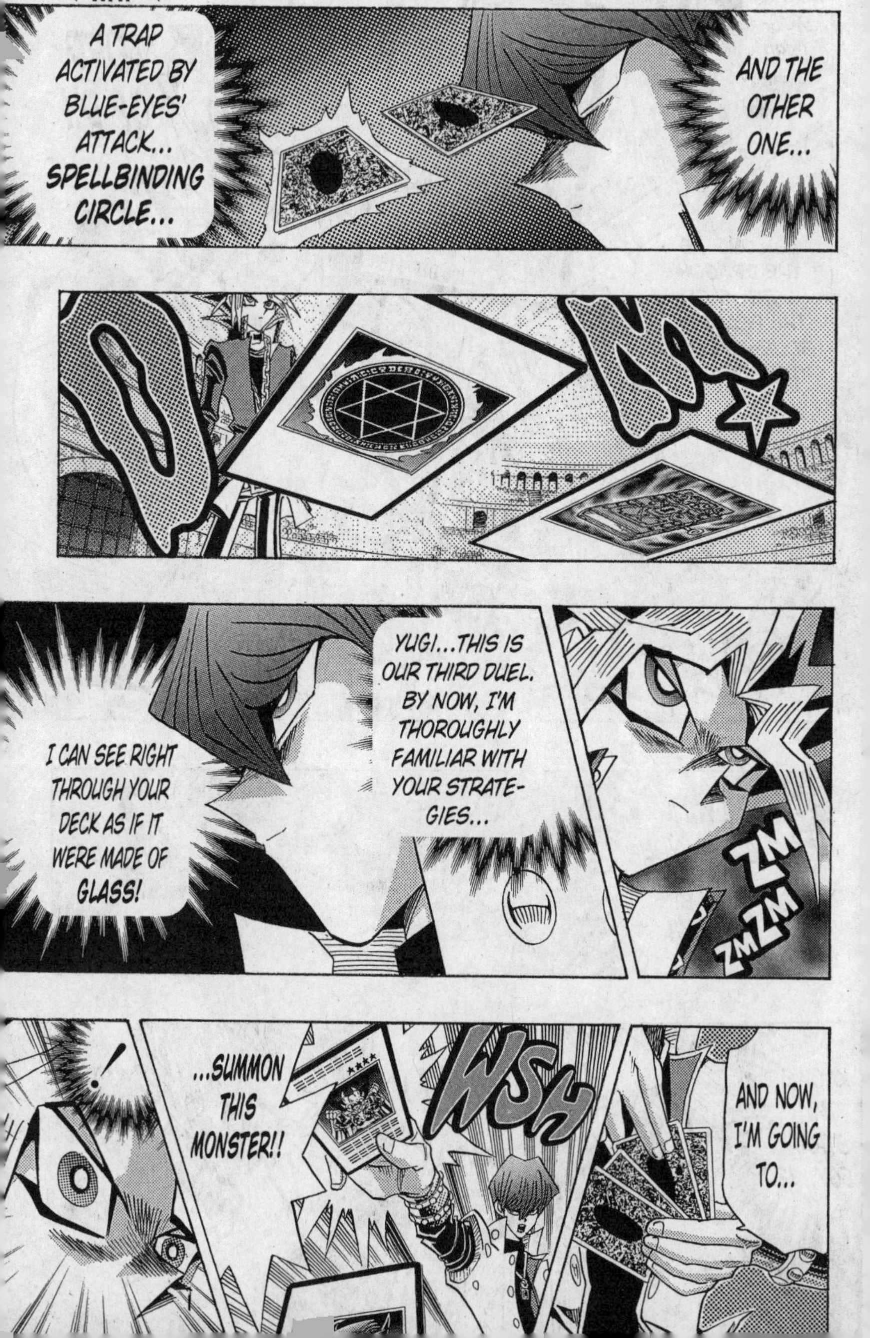
A TRAP ACTIVATED BY BLUE-EYES' ATTACK... SPELLBINDING CIRCLE...
AND THE OTHER ONE...
ZM ZM ZM ZM
YUGI...THIS IS OUR THIRD DUEL. BY NOW, I'M THOROUGHLY FAMILIAR WITH YOUR STRATE-GIES...
I CAN SEE RIGHT THROUGH YOUR DECK AS IF IT WERE MADE OF GLASS!
AND NOW, I'M GOING TO...
WSH
...SUMMON THIS MONSTER!!
!

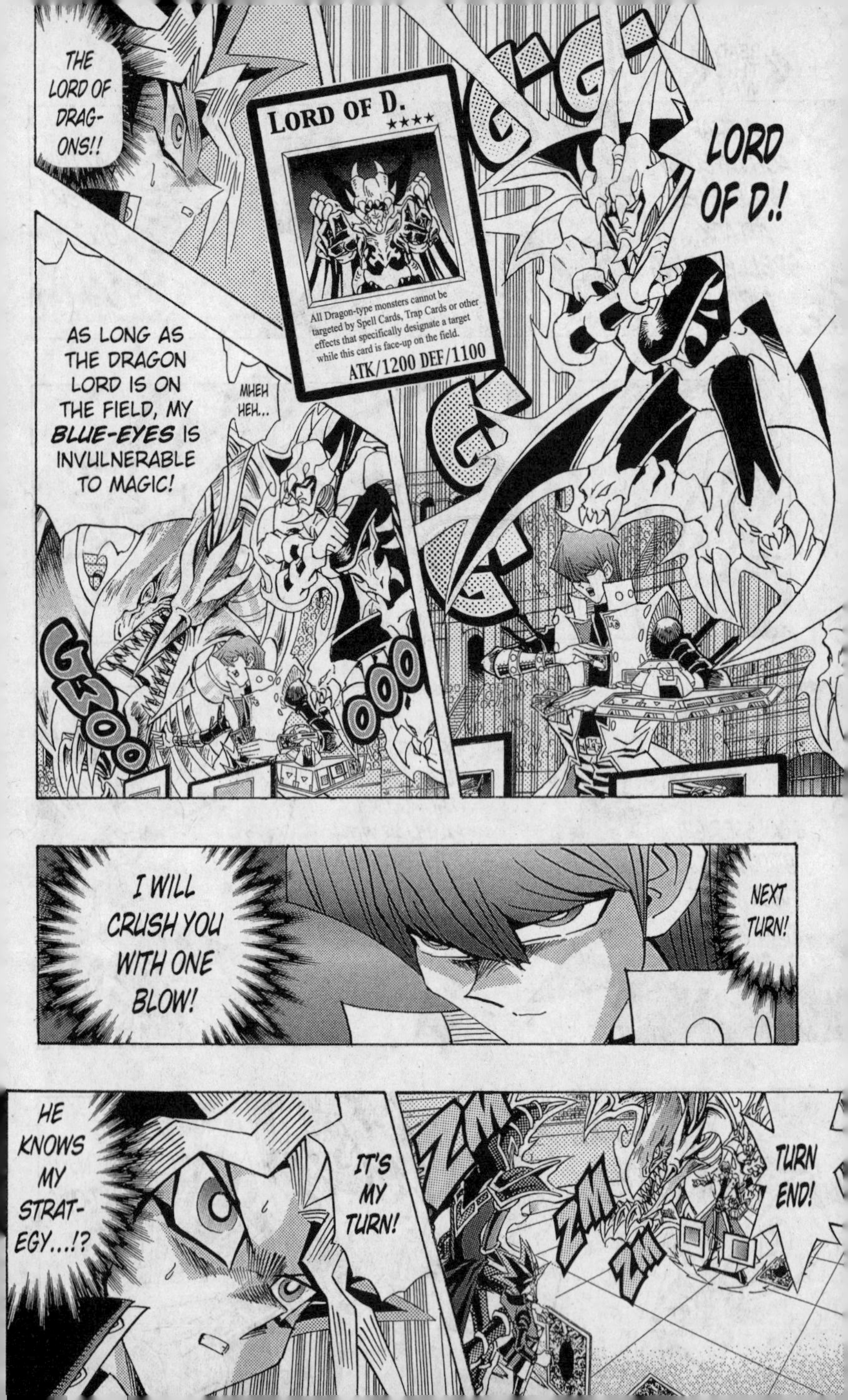
LORD OF D.!
LORD OF D.
★★★★
All Dragon-type monsters cannot be targeted by Spell Cards, Trap Cards or other effects that specifically designate a target while this card is face-up on the field.
ATK/1200 DEF/1100
THE LORD OF DRAG-ONS!!
MHEH HEH...
AS LONG AS THE DRAGON LORD IS ON THE FIELD, MY BLUE-EYES IS INVULNERABLE TO MAGIC!
OOOO
GWOOO
NEXT TURN!
I WILL CRUSH YOU WITH ONE BLOW!
TURN END!
ZM ZM ZM
IT'S MY TURN!
HE KNOWS MY STRAT-EGY...!?

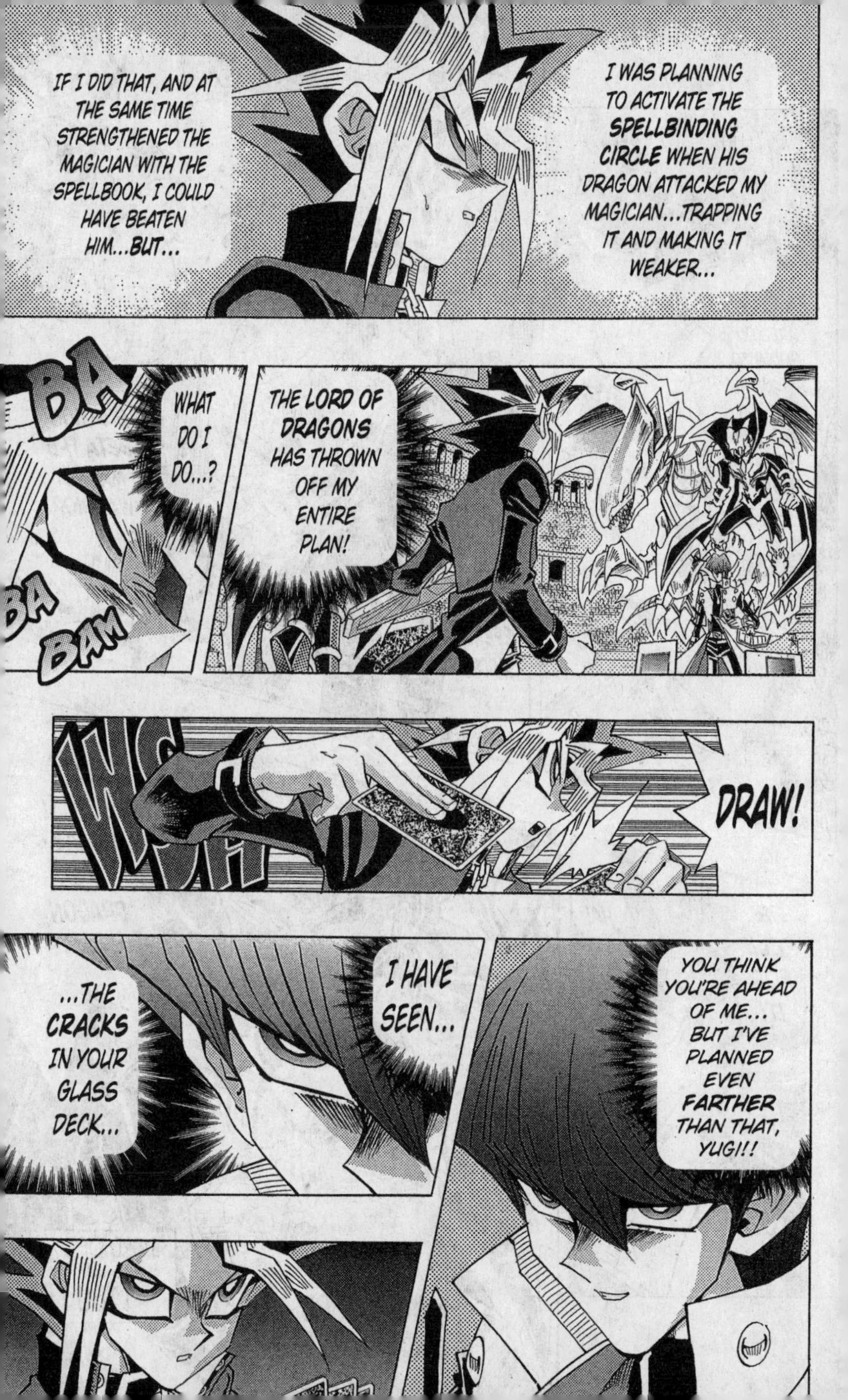
I WAS PLANNING TO ACTIVATE THE SPELLBINDING CIRCLE WHEN HIS DRAGON ATTACKED MY MAGICIAN...TRAPPING IT AND MAKING IT WEAKER...
IF I DID THAT, AND AT THE SAME TIME STRENGTHENED THE MAGICIAN WITH THE SPELLBOOK, I COULD HAVE BEATEN HIM...BUT...
THE LORD OF DRAGONS HAS THROWN OFF MY ENTIRE PLAN!
WHAT DO I DO...?
BA
BA
BAM
DRAW!
YOU THINK YOU'RE AHEAD OF ME... BUT I'VE PLANNED EVEN FARTHER THAN THAT, YUGI!!
I HAVE SEEN...
...THE CRACKS IN YOUR GLASS DECK...

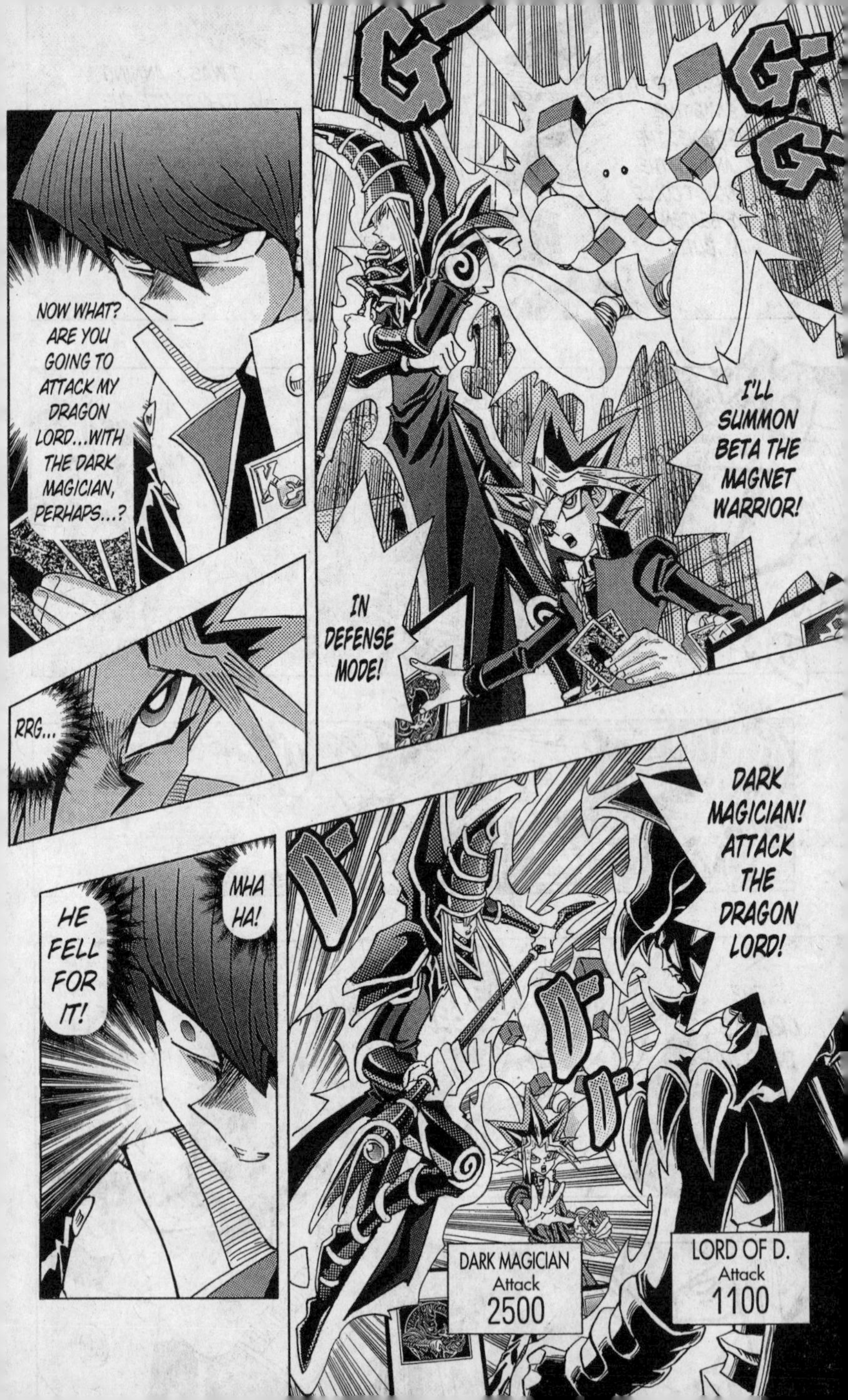
G-
G-G-
I'LL SUMMON BETA THE MAGNET WARRIOR!
IN DEFENSE MODE!
NOW WHAT? ARE YOU GOING TO ATTACK MY DRAGON LORD...WITH THE DARK MAGICIAN, PERHAPS...?
RRG...
DARK MAGICIAN! ATTACK THE DRAGON LORD!
D-
D-D-
LORD OF D. Attack 1100
DARK MAGICIAN Attack 2500
MHA HA!
HE FELL FOR IT!

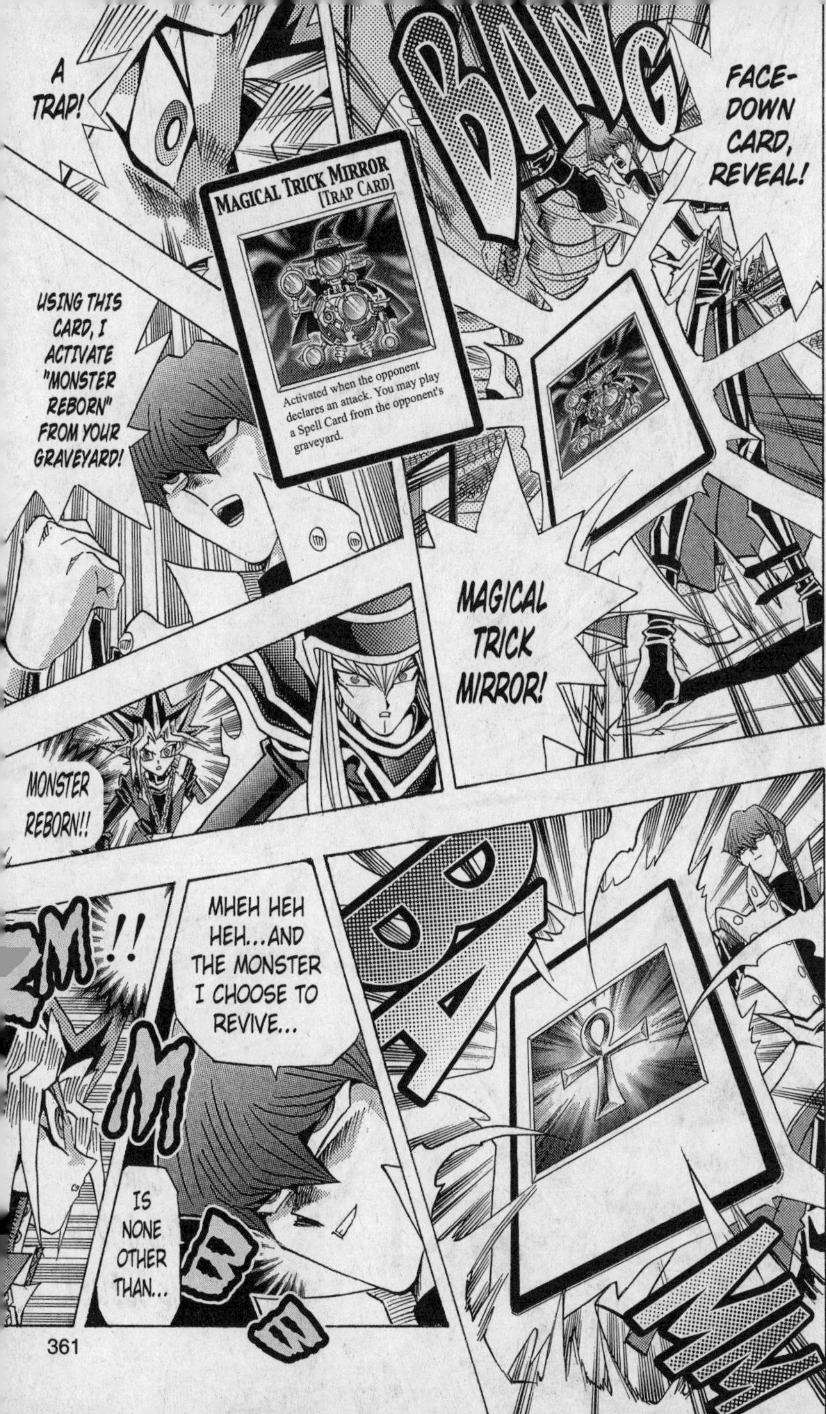
FACE-DOWN CARD, REVEAL!
BANG
A TRAP!
MAGICAL TRICK MIRROR
[TRAP CARD]
Activated when the opponent declares an attack. You may play a Spell Card from the opponent's graveyard.
MAGICAL TRICK MIRROR!
USING THIS CARD, I ACTIVATE "MONSTER REBORN" FROM YOUR GRAVEYARD!
MONSTER REBORN!!
MHEH HEH HEH...AND THE MONSTER I CHOOSE TO REVIVE...
IS NONE OTHER THAN...

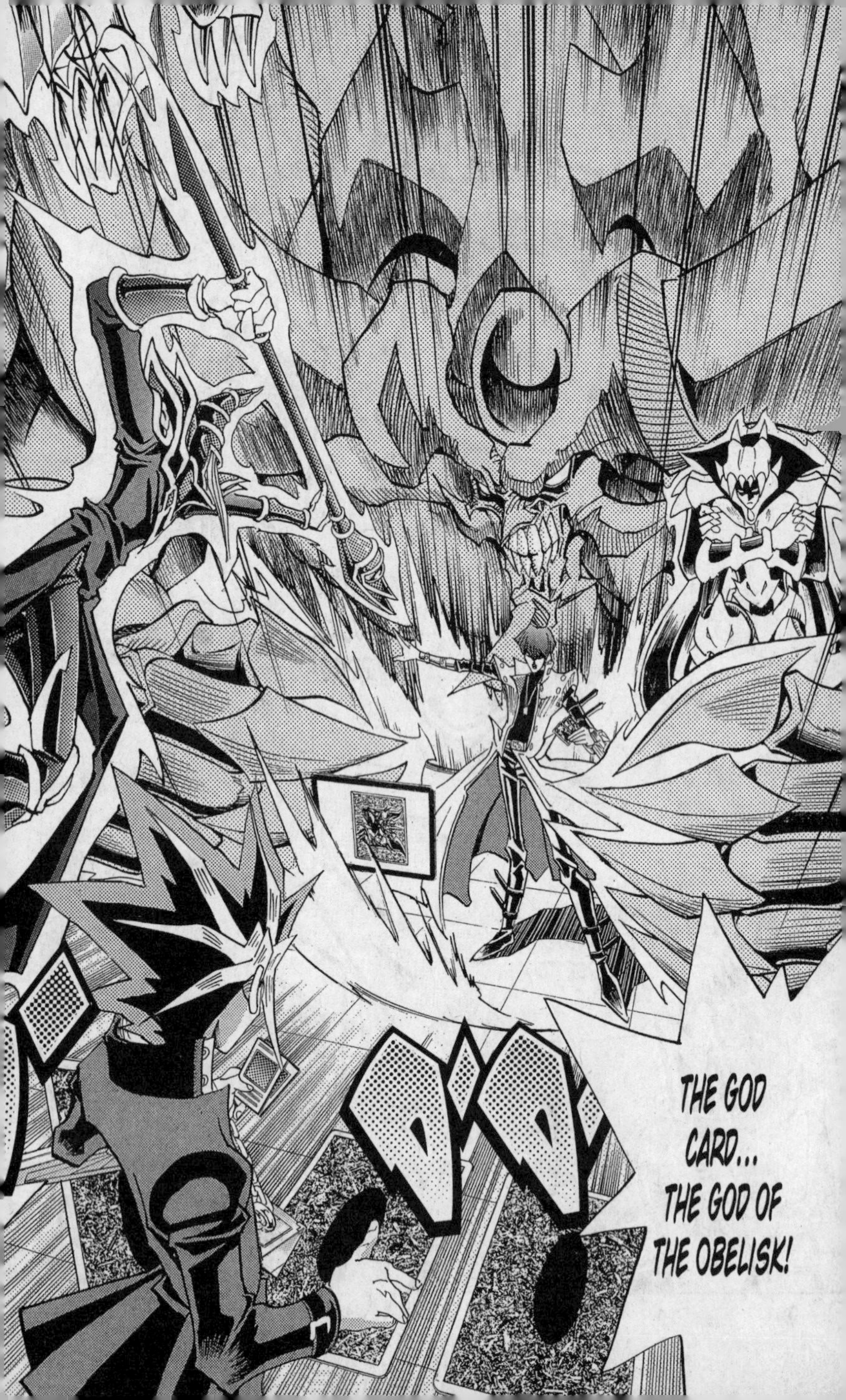
THE GOD CARD... THE GOD OF THE OBELISK!

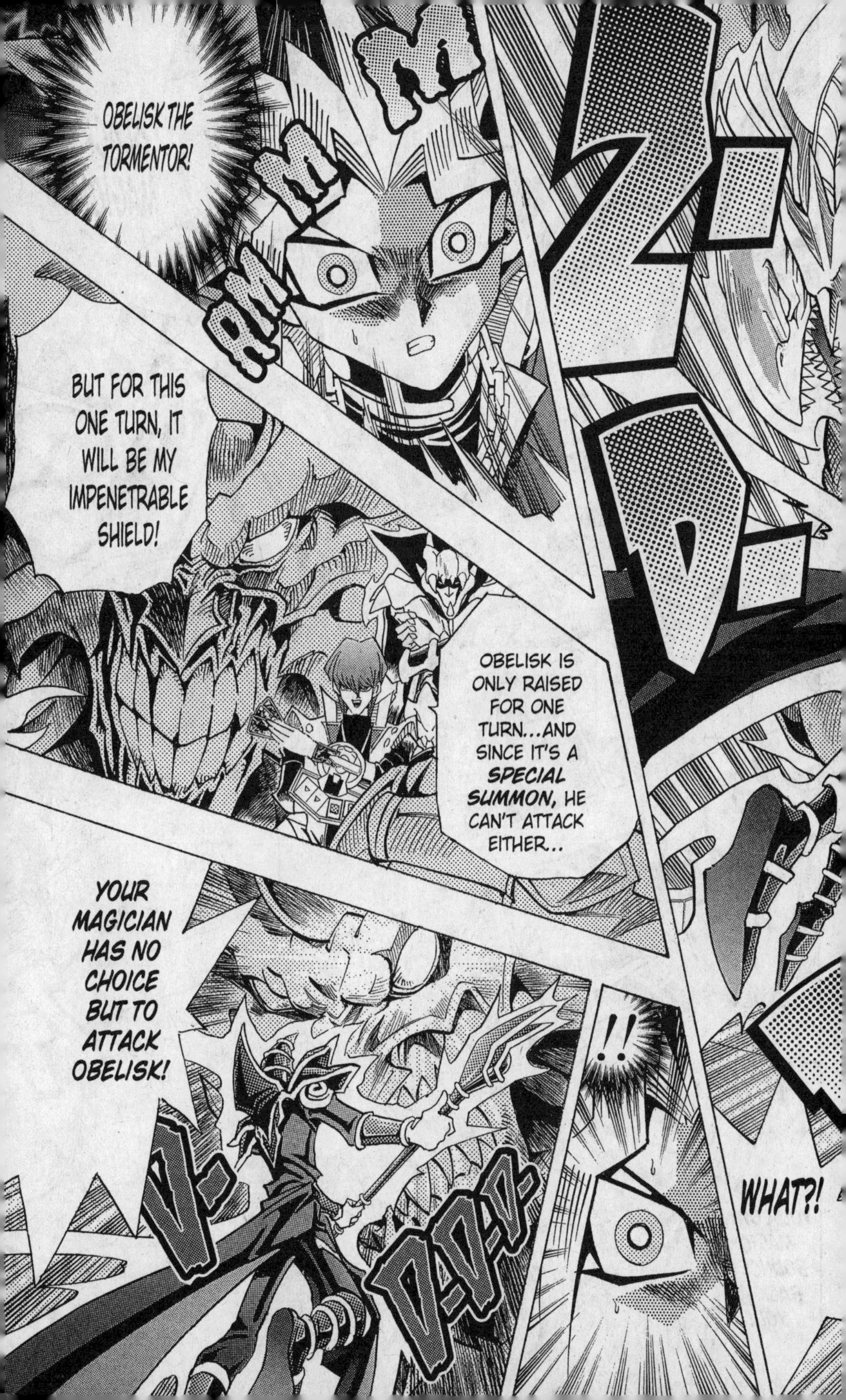
OBELISK THE TORMENTOR!
BUT FOR THIS ONE TURN, IT WILL BE MY IMPENETRABLE SHIELD!
OBELISK IS ONLY RAISED FOR ONE TURN...AND SINCE IT'S A SPECIAL SUMMON, HE CAN'T ATTACK EITHER...
YOUR MAGICIAN HAS NO CHOICE BUT TO ATTACK OBELISK!
!!
WHAT?!

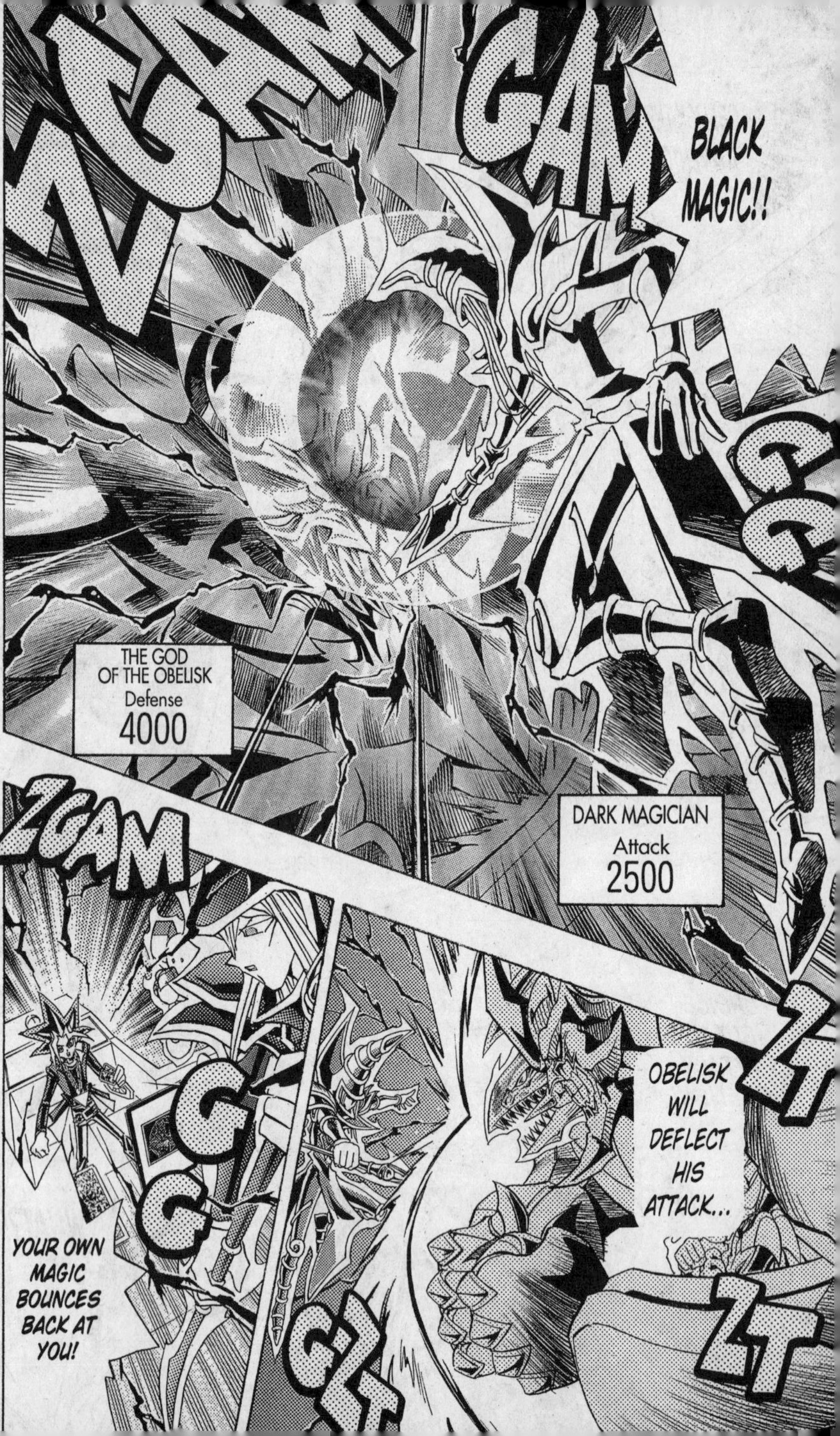
BLACK MAGIC!!
GAM
ZGAM
THE GOD OF THE OBELISK Defense 4000
DARK MAGICIAN Attack 2500
ZOAM
OBELISK WILL DEFLECT HIS ATTACK...
YOUR OWN MAGIC BOUNCES BACK AT YOU!

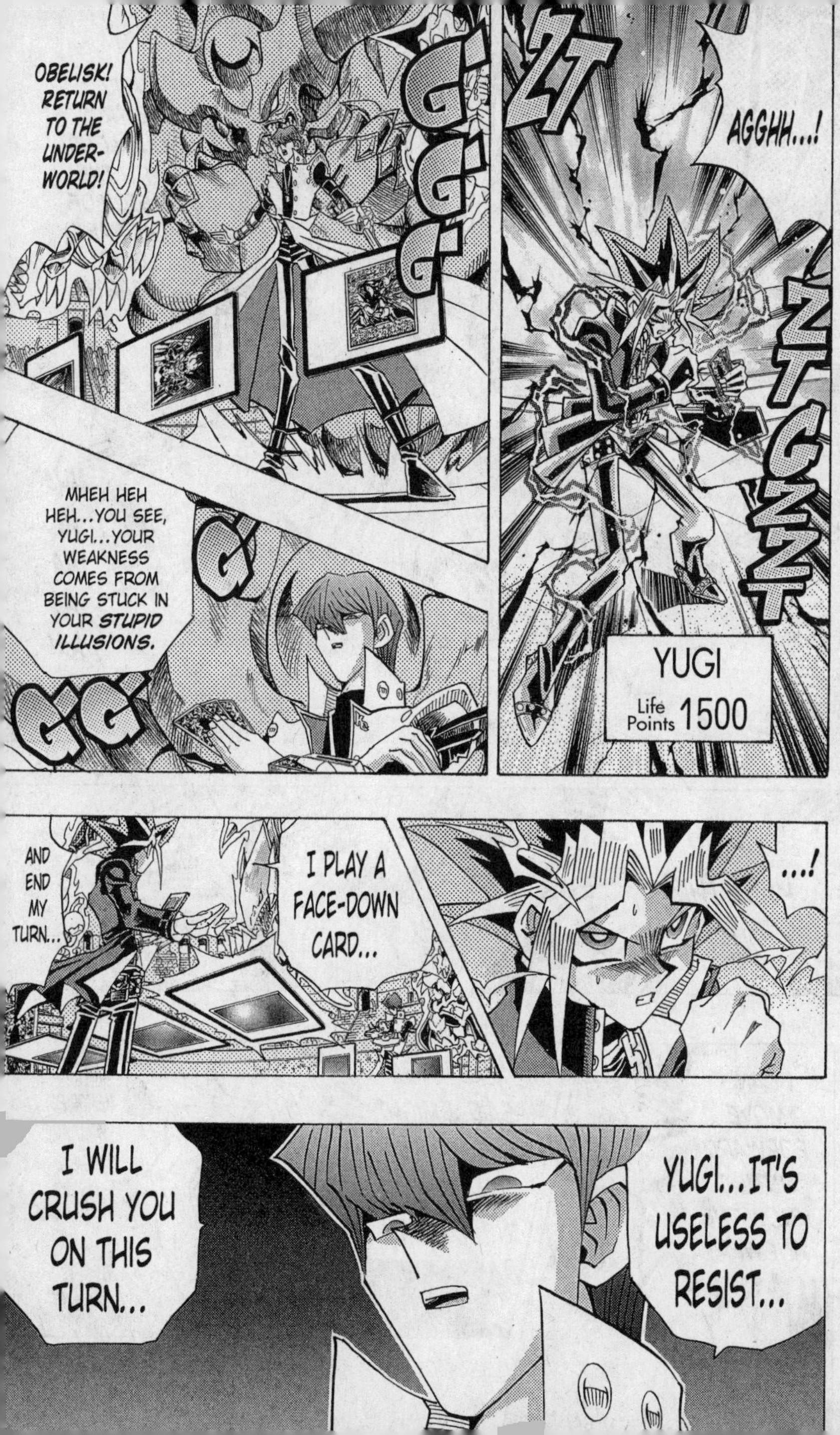

AGGHH...!
YUGI
Life Points 1500
OBELISK! RETURN TO THE UNDER-WORLD!
MHEH HEH HEH...YOU SEE, YUGI...YOUR WEAKNESS COMES FROM BEING STUCK IN YOUR *STUPID ILLUSIONS.*
...!
I PLAY A FACE-DOWN CARD...
AND END MY TURN...
YUGI...IT'S USELESS TO RESIST...
I WILL CRUSH YOU ON THIS TURN...

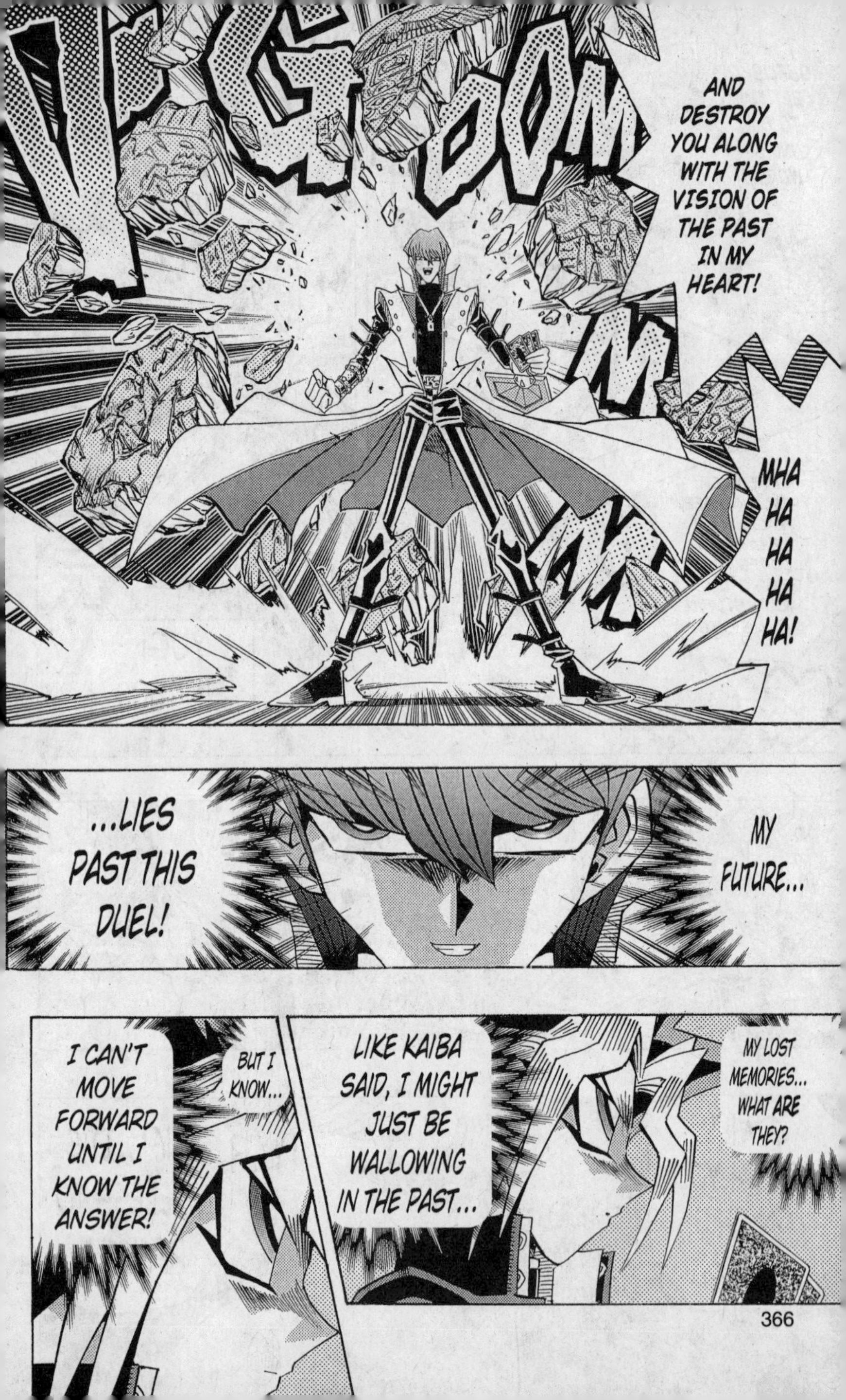
AND DESTROY YOU ALONG WITH THE VISION OF THE PAST IN MY HEART!
MHA HA HA HA HA!
MY FUTURE...
...LIES PAST THIS DUEL!
MY LOST MEMORIES... WHAT ARE THEY?
LIKE KAIBA SAID, I MIGHT JUST BE WALLOWING IN THE PAST...
BUT I KNOW...
I CAN'T MOVE FORWARD UNTIL I KNOW THE ANSWER!

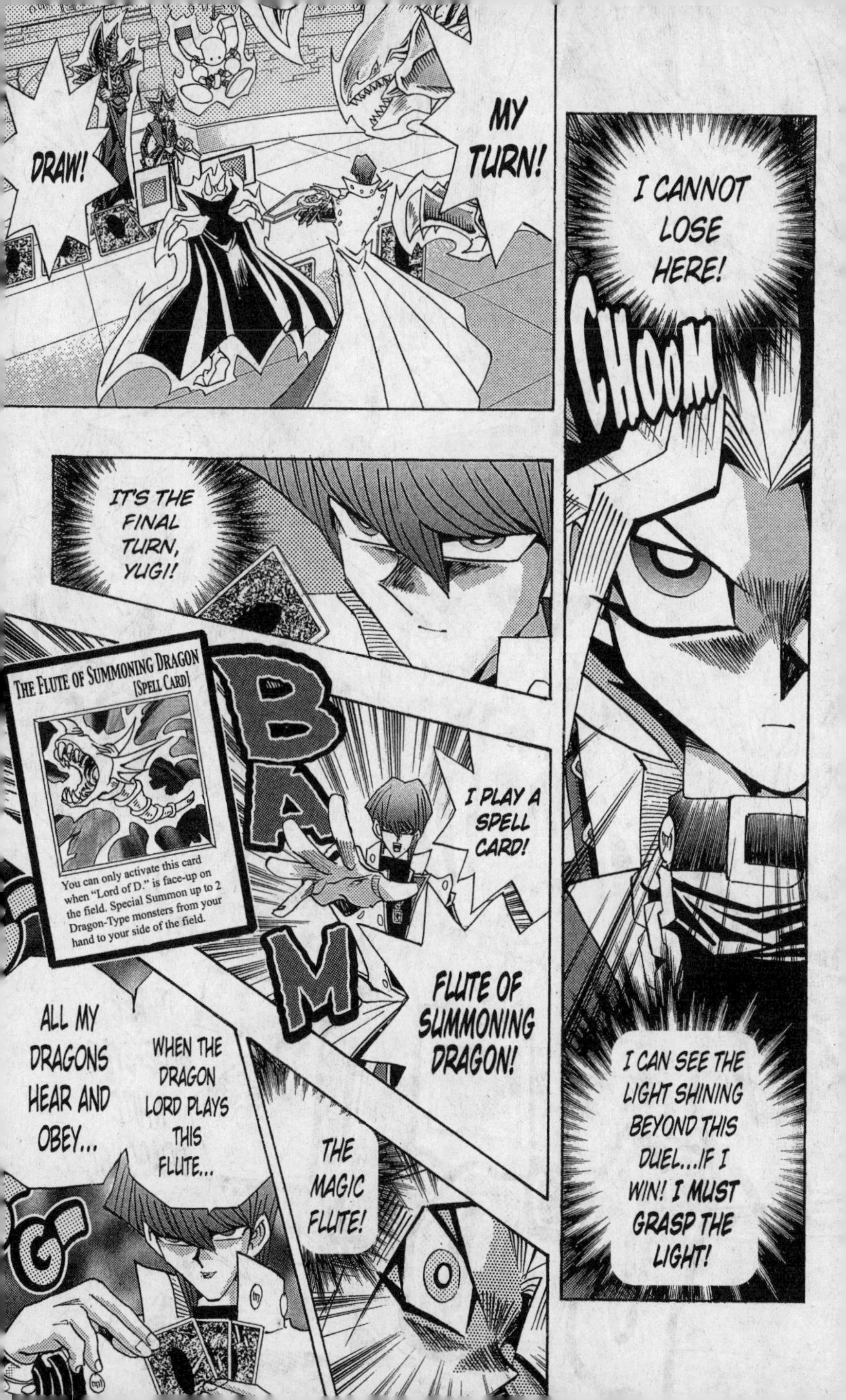
MY TURN!
DRAW!
I CANNOT LOSE HERE!
CHOOM
I CAN SEE THE LIGHT SHINING BEYOND THIS DUEL...IF I WIN! I MUST GRASP THE LIGHT!
IT'S THE FINAL TURN, YUGI!
BAM
I PLAY A SPELL CARD!
THE FLUTE OF SUMMONING DRAGON
[SPELL CARD]
You can only activate this card when "Lord of D." is face-up on the field. Special Summon up to 2 Dragon-Type monsters from your hand to your side of the field.
FLUTE OF SUMMONING DRAGON!
THE MAGIC FLUTE!
WHEN THE DRAGON LORD PLAYS THIS FLUTE...
ALL MY DRAGONS HEAR AND OBEY...

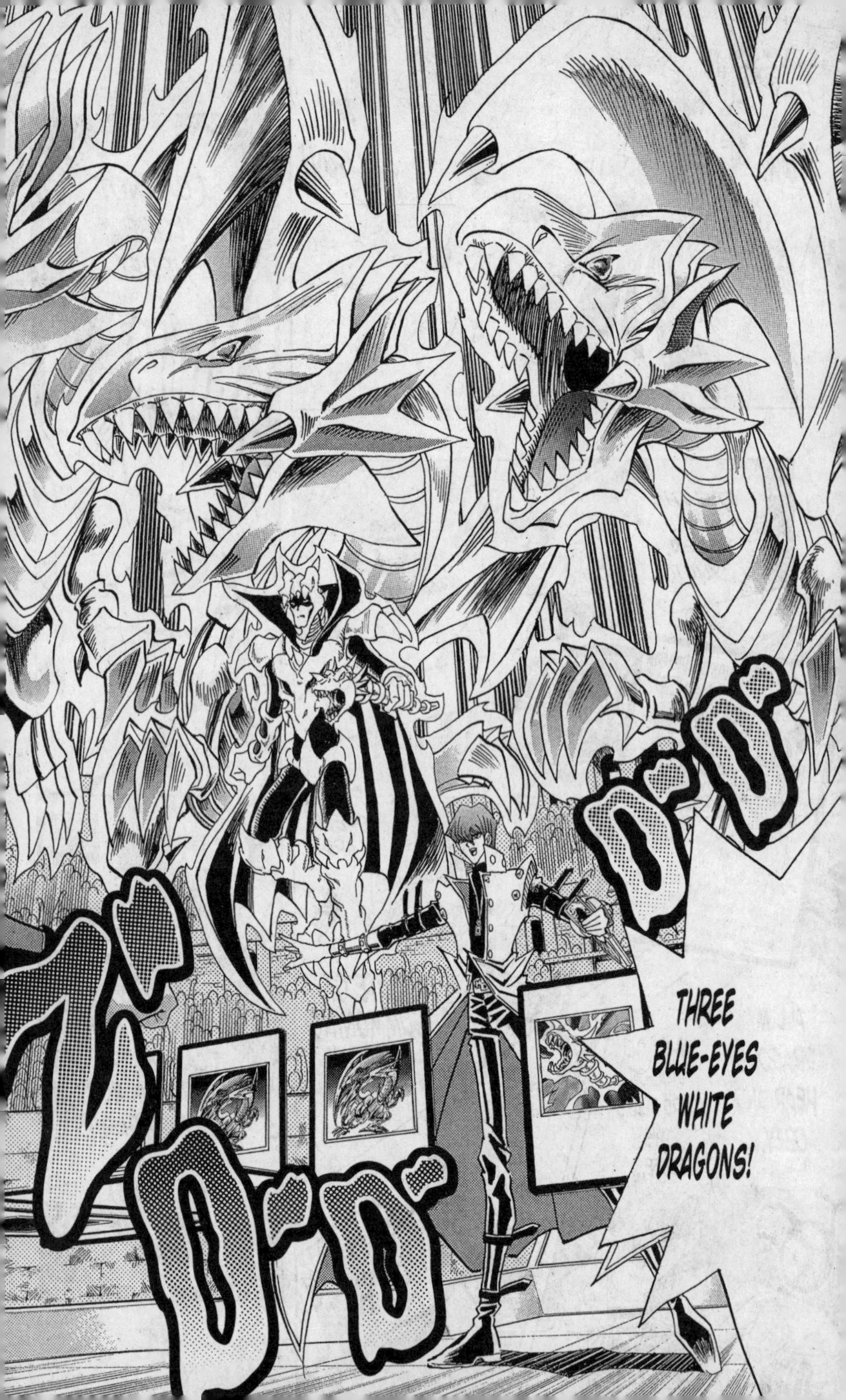
THREE BLUE-EYES WHITE DRAGONS!

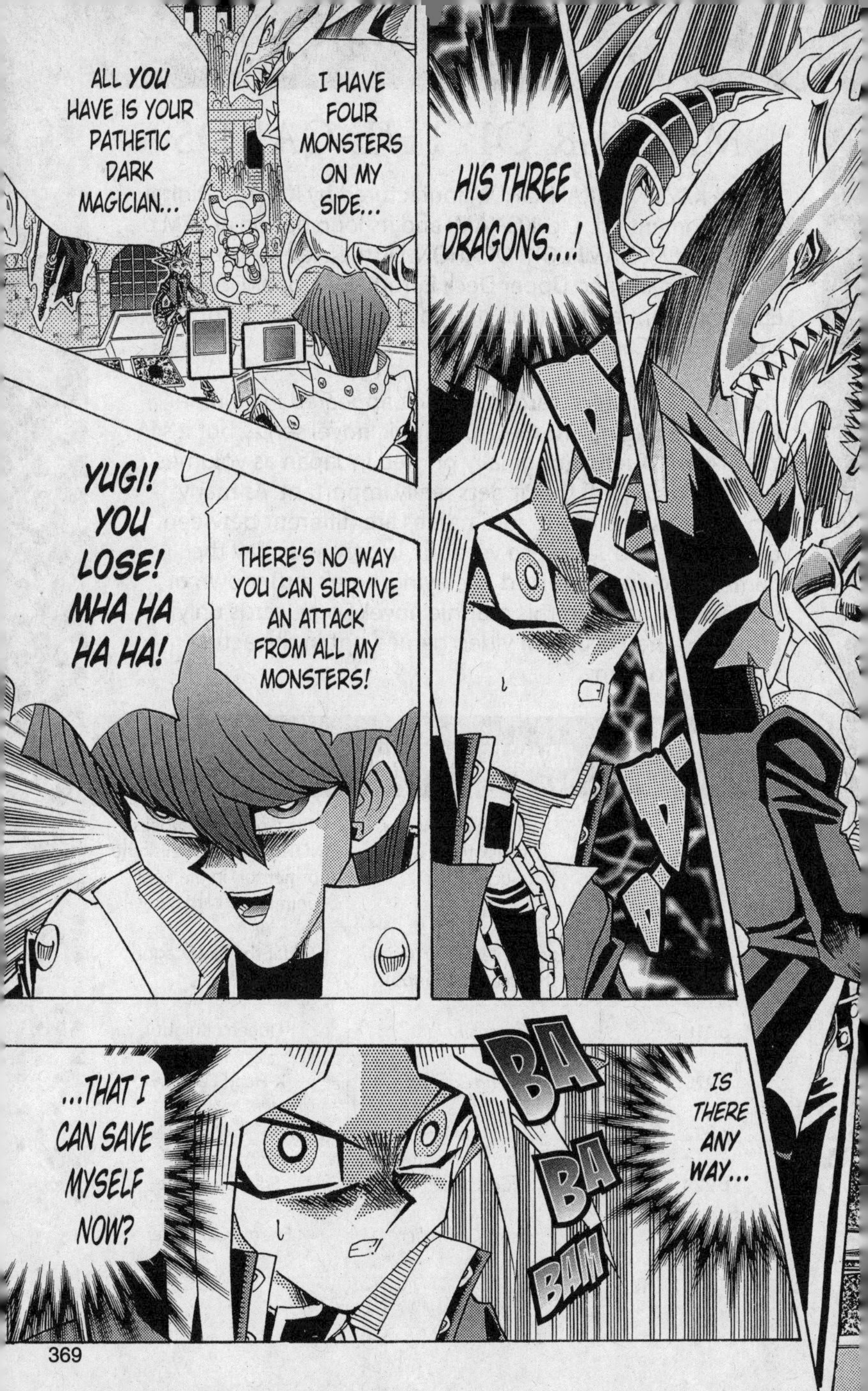

HIS THREE DRAGONS...!
I HAVE FOUR MONSTERS ON MY SIDE...
ALL YOU HAVE IS YOUR PATHETIC DARK MAGICIAN...
THERE'S NO WAY YOU CAN SURVIVE AN ATTACK FROM ALL MY MONSTERS!
YUGI! YOU LOSE! MHA HA HA HA!
IS THERE ANY WAY...
BA BA BAM
...THAT I CAN SAVE MYSELF NOW?

MASTER OF THE CARDS

The "Duel Monsters" card game first appeared in volume two of the original **Yu-Gi-Oh!** graphic novel series, but it's in **Yu-Gi-Oh!: Duelist** (originally printed in Japan as volumes 8-31 of **Yu-Gi-Oh!**) that it gets really important. As many fans know, some of the card names are different between the English and Japanese versions. In case you play the game, or you're interested in playing, here's a rundown of some of the cards in this graphic novel. Some cards only appear in the **Yu-Gi-Oh!** video games, not in the actual trading card game.

FIRST APPEARANCE IN THIS VOLUME	JAPANESE CARD NAME	ENGLISH CARD NAME
p.209	*Obelisk no Kyoshinhei* (Obelisk the Giant God Soldier)	The God of the Obelisk (NOTE: Called "Obelisk the Tormentor" in the English anime and card game.)
p.209	*Osiris no Tenkûryû* (Osiris the Heaven Dragon)	Slifer the Sky Dragon
p.218	*Queen's Knight*	Queen's Knight
p.220	*X-Head Cannon*	X-Head Cannon
p.222	*Kuribo*	Kuriboh
p.223	*Cross Soul*	Soul Exchange
p.225	*Enemy Controller*	Enemy Controller

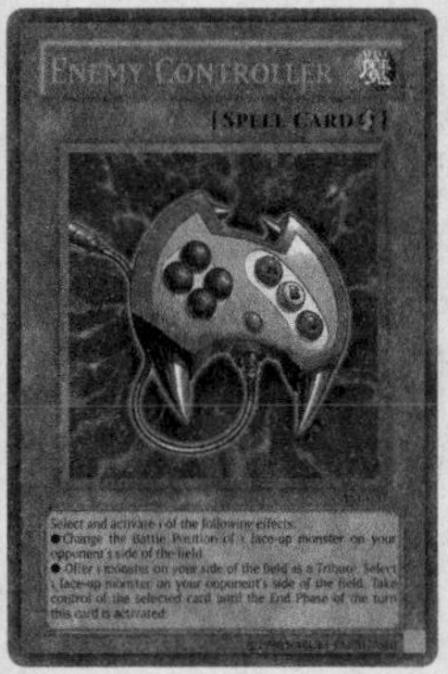
Enemy Controller
[Spell Card]
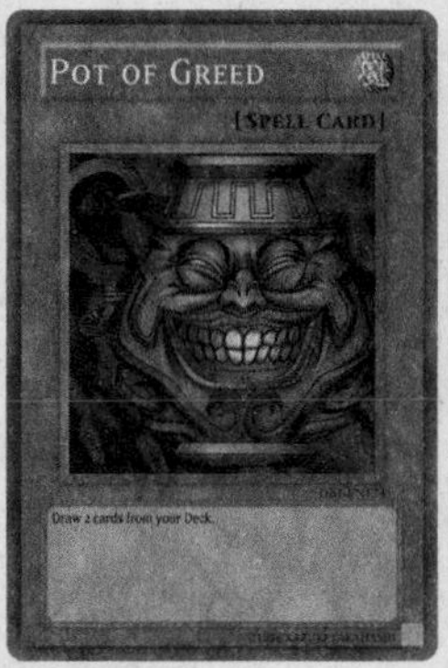
Pot of Greed
[Spell Card]
Draw 2 cards from your Deck.
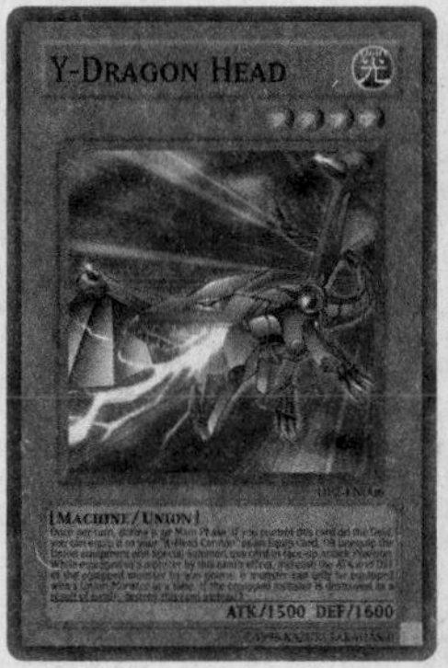
Y-Dragon Head
[Machine/Union]
ATK/1500 DEF/1600

FIRST APPEARANCE IN THIS VOLUME	JAPANESE CARD NAME	ENGLISH CARD NAME
p.227	*Hikari no Fûsatsuken* (Sealing Sword of Light)	Lightforce Sword
p.234	*Tensei no Fukujû* (Obedience to God's Voice/Heavenly Voice)	Voice of the Heavens (NOTE: Not a real game card. Called "Lullaby of Obedience" in the English anime.)
p.235	*Exchange*	Exchange
p.238	*Y-Dragon Head*	Y-Dragon Head
p.239	*XY-Dragon Cannon*	XY-Dragon Cannon
p.245	*Black Magician Girl*	Dark Magician Girl
p.254	*Kezuriyuku Inochi* (Life Shaver)	Life Shaver (NOTE: Not a real game card.)
p.256	*Big Shield Guardna*	Big Shield Guardna
p.259	*Z-Metal Caterpillar*	Z-Metal Tank
p.260	*XYZ-Dragon Cannon*	XYZ-Dragon Cannon
p.263	*Tamashii no Tsuna* (Soul Rope)	Soul Rope (NOTE: Not a real game card.)

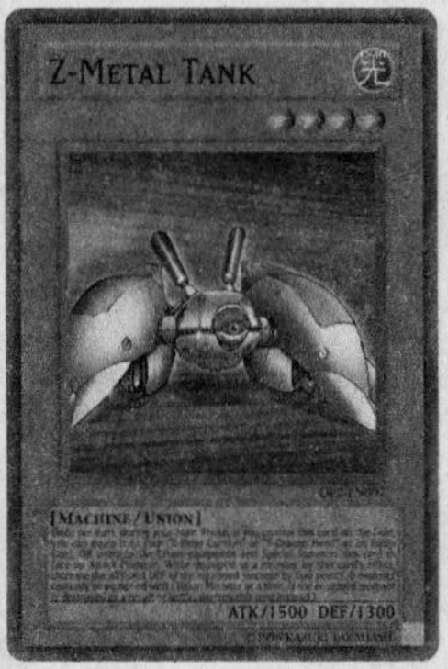
Z-METAL TANK
[MACHINE/UNION]
ATK/1500 DEF/1300
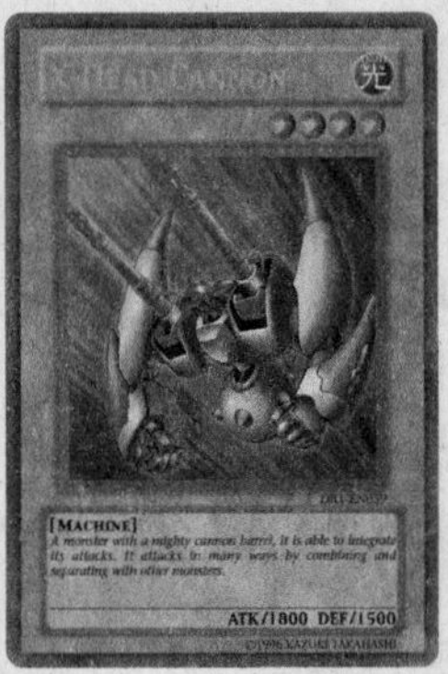
[MACHINE]
A monster with a mighty cannon barrel, it is able to integrate its attacks in many ways by combining and separating with other monsters.
ATK/1800 DEF/1500
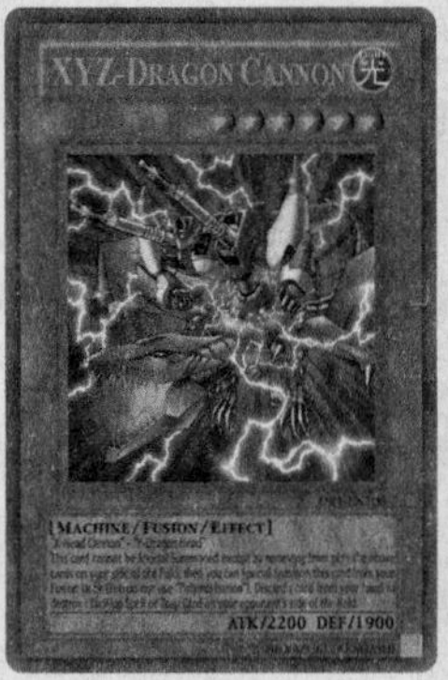
XYZ-DRAGON CANNON
[MACHINE/FUSION/EFFECT]
ATK/2200 DEF/1900

FIRST APPEARANCE IN THIS VOLUME	JAPANESE CARD NAME	ENGLISH CARD NAME
p.264	*King's Knight*	King's Knight
p.265	*Jack's Knight*	Jack's Knight
p.280	*Akûkan Busshitsu Tensô Sôchi* (Interdimensional Matter Teleportation Device)	Interdimensional Matter Transporter
p.304	*Gôyoku na Tsubo* (Pot of Greed)	Pot of Greed
p.337	*Clone Fukusei* (Clone Reproduction)	Clone Reproduction
p.337	*Blue Eyes White Dragon*	Blue-Eyes White Dragon
p.338	*Baphomet*	Baphomet (NOTE: Called "Berfomet" in the English anime and card game.)
p.341	*Cost Down*	Cost Down
p.346	*Shisha Sosei* (Resurrection of the Dead)	Monster Reborn
p.348	*Black Magician*	Dark Magician
p.351	*Magnet Warrior Beta*	Beta the Magnet Warrior

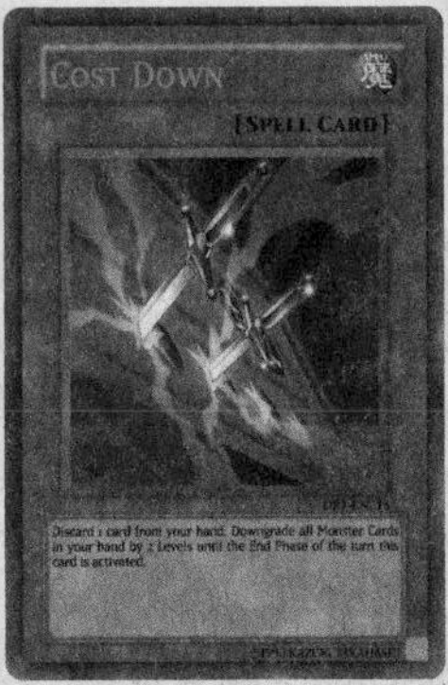
Cost Down
[Spell Card]

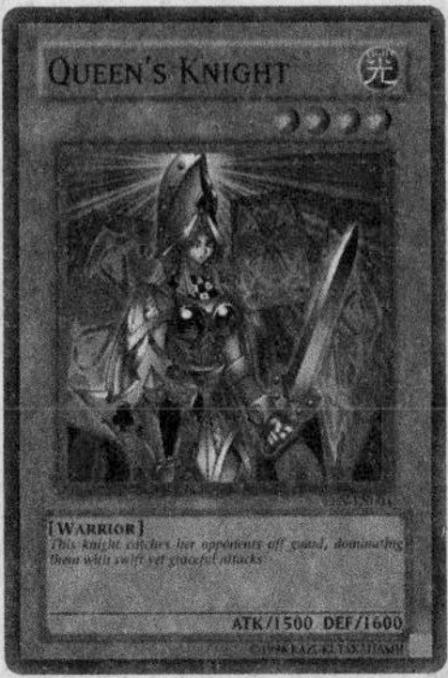
Queen's Knight
[Warrior]
ATK/1500 DEF/1600

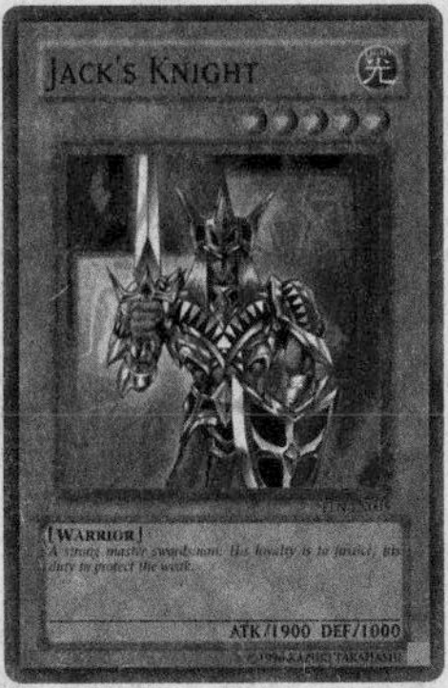
Jack's Knight
[Warrior]
ATK/1900 DEF/1000

FIRST APPEARANCE IN THIS VOLUME	JAPANESE CARD NAME	ENGLISH CARD NAME
p.354	*Majutsu no Jumonsho* (Spellbook of Sorcery)	Magic Formula
p.356	*Inochikezuri no Hôsatsu* (Precious Card of Slashing Life)	Card of Demise (NOTE: Not a real game card.)
p.357	*Rokubôsei no Jubaku* (Binding Curse of the Hexagram)	Spellbinding Circle
p.358	*Lord of Dragon*	Lord of D.
p.361	*Kikai Jikake no Magic Mirror* (Mechanical Magic Mirror)	Magical Trick Mirror (NOTE: Not a real game card.)
p.367	*Dragon wo Yobu Fue* (Dragon-Summoning Flute)	The Flute of Summoning Dragon

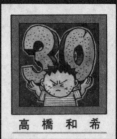

高橋和希

VOLUME 30...! ABOUT SIX YEARS SINCE YU-GI-OH! STARTED. I CAN'T BELIEVE IT'S LASTED SO LONG.

I DIDN'T INITIALLY ENVISION YU-GI-OH! AS A CARD BATTLE MANGA. THE CARD GAME WAS ONLY SUPPOSED TO BE TWO CHAPTERS (IN VOLUME 2 OF THE ORIGINAL YU-GI-OH! MANGA SERIES), AND I CAME UP WITH THE RULES FOR THE GAME IN ONE NIGHT. HOW AMAZING THAT IT TURNED OUT TO BE THE HEART OF THE STORY!

IT'S ALL THANKS TO THE PEOPLE WHO'VE SUPPORTED YU-GI-OH! THAT IT'S BEEN THIS SUCCESSFUL. THANK YOU SO MUCH!

-KAZUKI TAKAHASHI, 2002

SHONEN JUMP MANGA

Vol. 30
RA THE IMMORTAL
STORY AND ART BY
KAZUKI TAKAHASHI

THE STORY SO FAR...

YUGI MUTOU/ YU-GI-OH

When 10th grader Yugi solved the Millennium Puzzle, another spirit took up residence in his body...Yu-Gi-Oh, the King of Games, a dark avenger who challenges evildoers to "Shadow Games" of life and death!

YUGI FACES DEADLY ENEMIES!

Using his gaming skills, Yugi fights ruthless adversaries like Maximillion Pegasus, multimillionaire creator of the collectible card game "Duel Monsters," and Ryo Bakura, whose friendly personality turns evil when he is possessed by the spirit of the Millennium Ring. But Yugi's greatest rival is Seto Kaiba, the world's second-greatest gamer—and the ruthless teenage president of Kaiba Corporation. At first, Kaiba and Yugi are bitter enemies, but after fighting against a common adversary—Pegasus—they come to respect one another. But for all his powers, there is one thing Yu-Gi-Oh cannot do: remember who he is and where he came from.

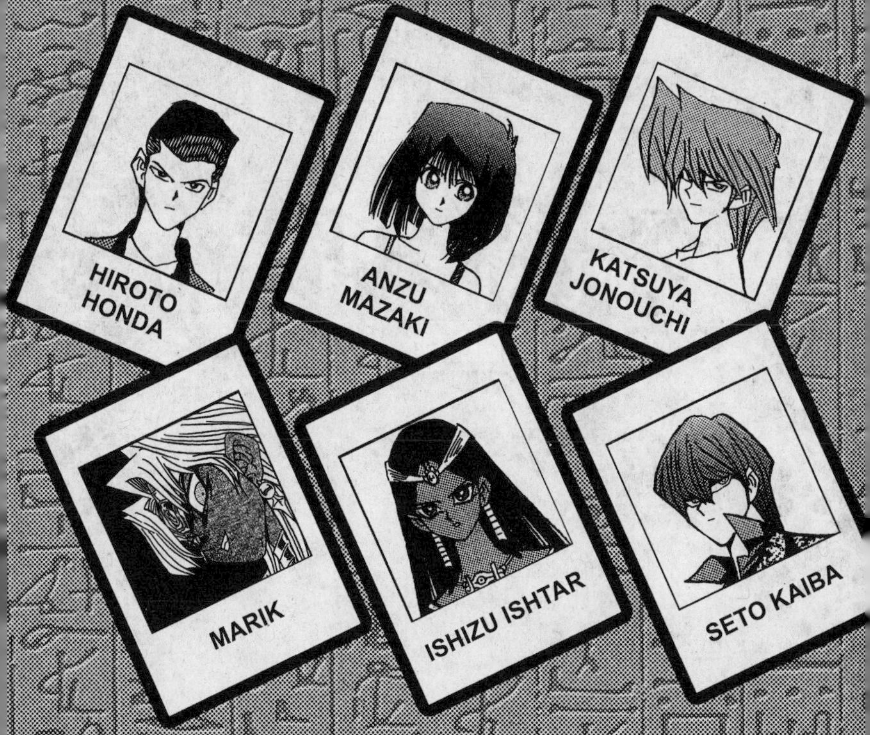
HIROTO HONDA
ANZU MAZAKI
KATSUYA JONOUCHI
MARIK
ISHIZU ISHTAR
SETO KAIBA

THE TABLET OF THE PHARAOH'S MEMORIES

Then one day, when an Egyptian museum exhibit comes to Japan, Yugi sees an ancient carving of himself as an Egyptian pharaoh! The curator of the exhibit, Ishizu Ishtar, explains that there are seven Millennium Items, which were made to fit into a stone tablet in a hidden shrine in Egypt. According to the legend, when the seven Items are brought together, the pharaoh will regain his memories of his past life.

THE EGYPTIAN GOD CARDS

But there is another piece of the puzzle—the three Egyptian God Cards, the rarest cards on Earth. To collect the God Cards, Kaiba announces "Battle City," an enormous "Duel Monsters" tournament. Attracted by the scent of blood, the most powerful God Card wielder comes to Tokyo: Ishizu's insane brother Marik, who wants to murder the pharaoh to satisfy a grudge. Using his sadistic torture deck, Marik climbs to the tournament semi-finals, where he defeats Yugi's friend Jonouchi, leaving him in a deathlike state. Now, only one semi-finals match remains: the last duel between Yugi and Kaiba, as foretold 3,000 years ago on an ancient Egyptian carving!

Yu-Gi-Oh! Duelist

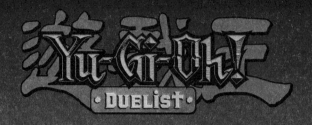

Vol. 30

CONTENTS

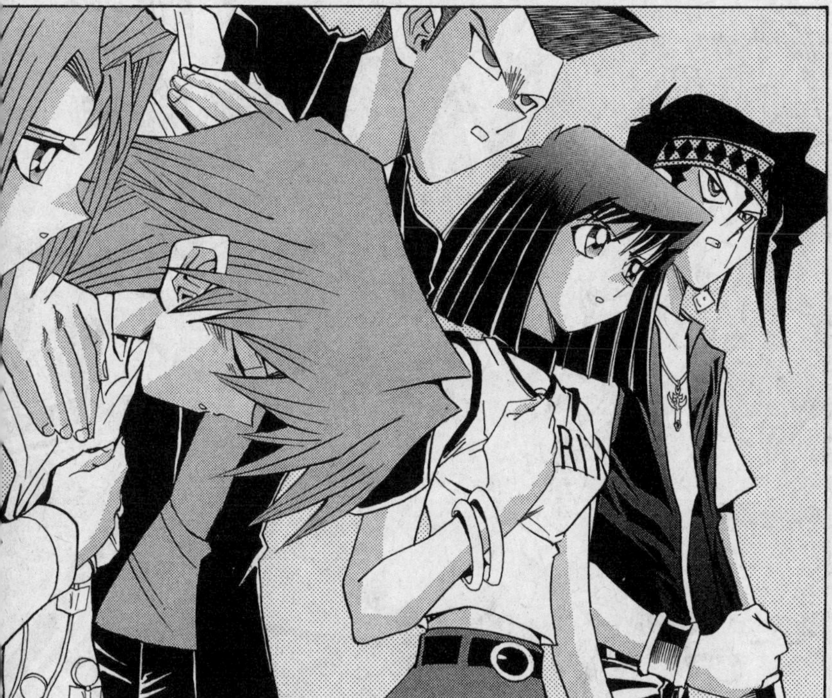

Duel 260: Red Spirit

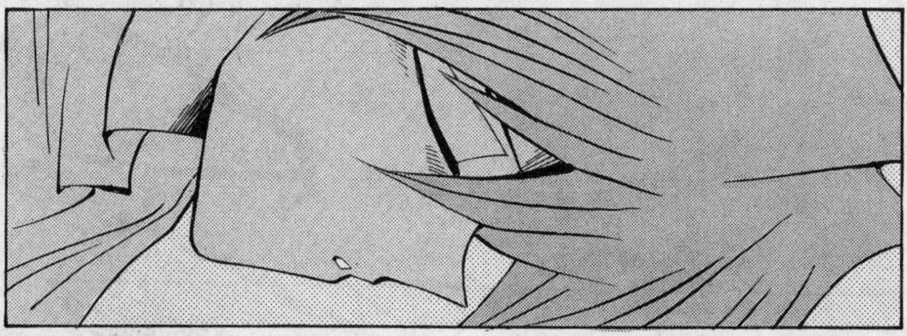

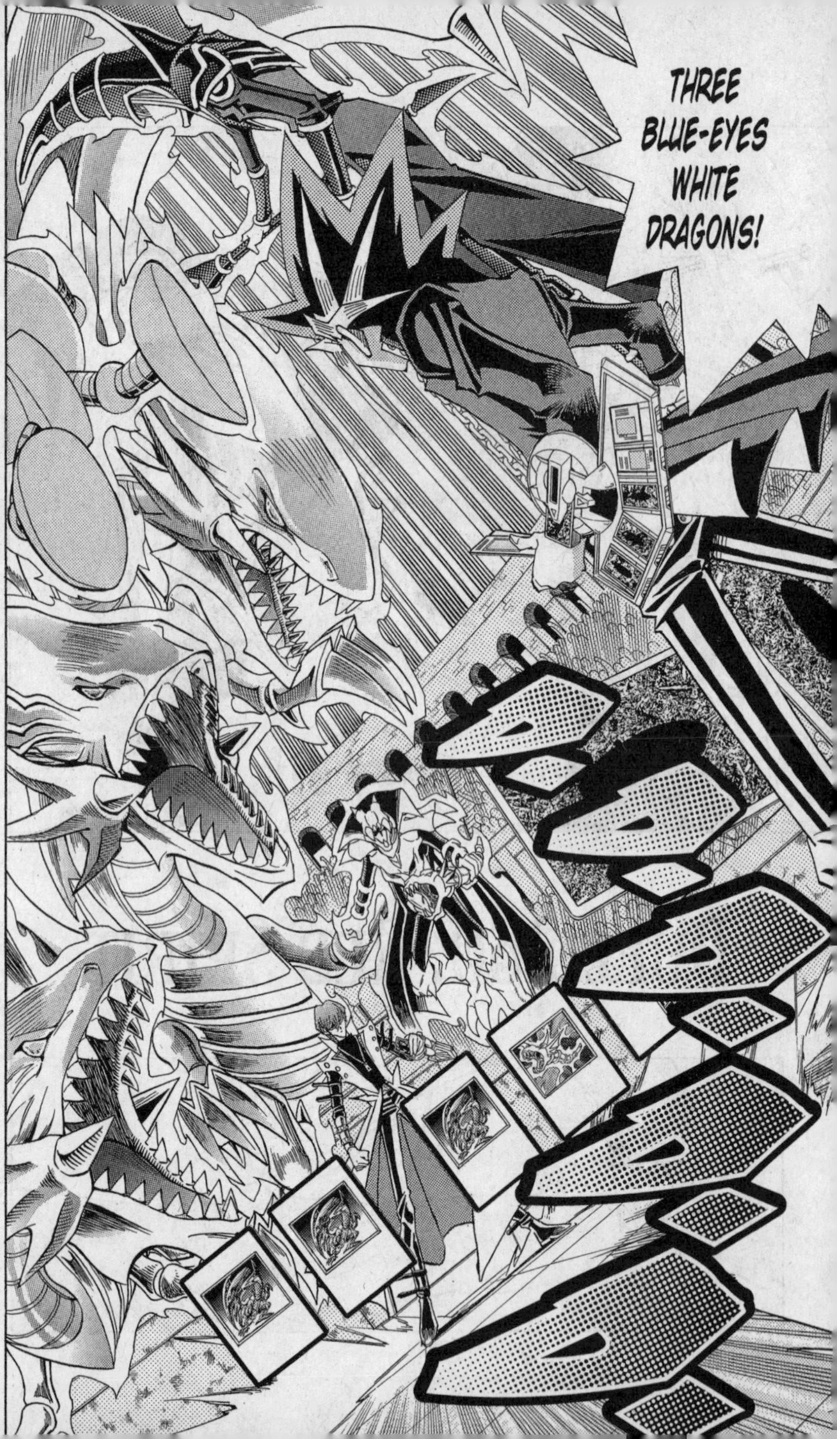
THREE BLUE-EYES WHITE DRAGONS!

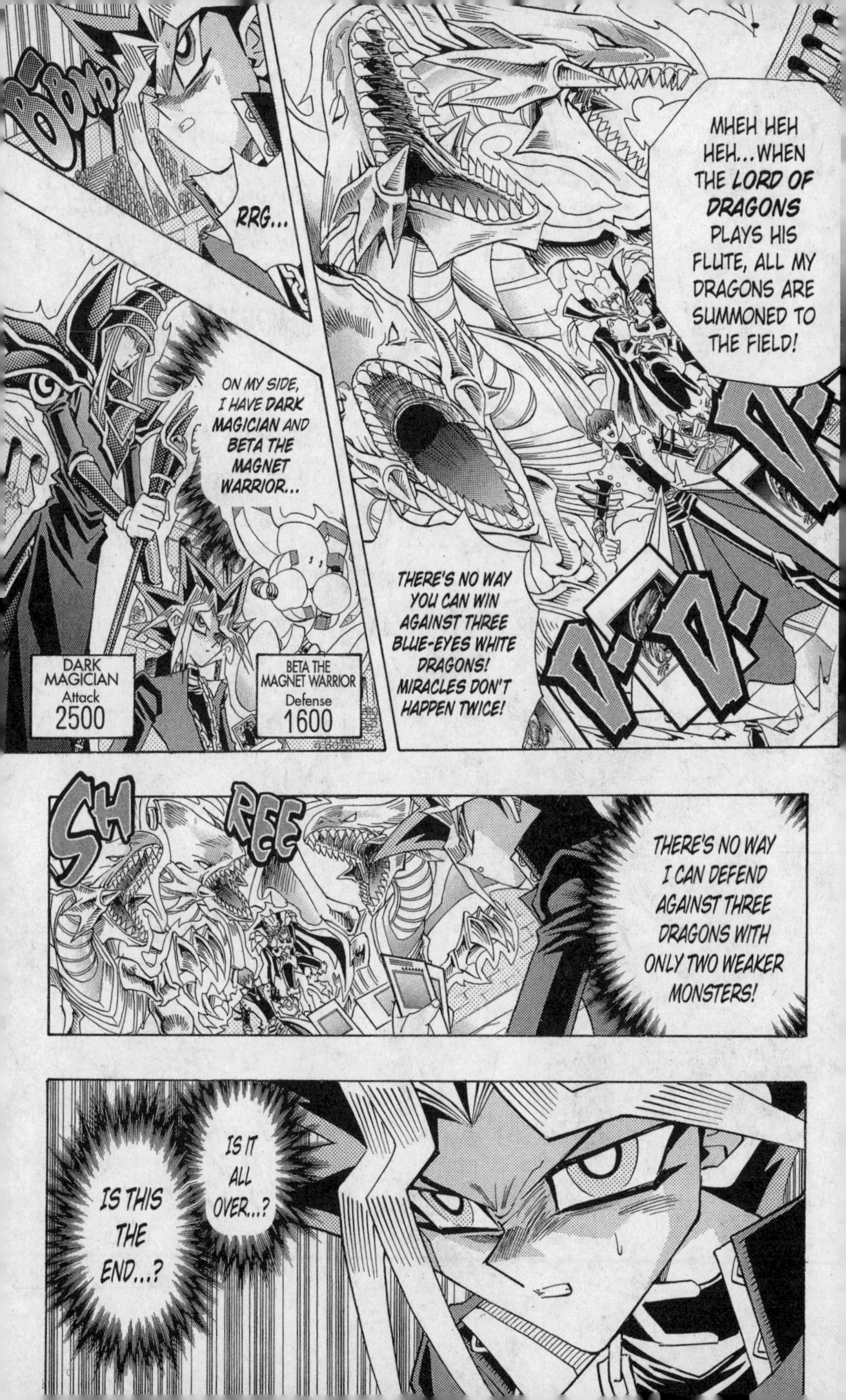
MHEH HEH HEH...WHEN THE LORD OF DRAGONS PLAYS HIS FLUTE, ALL MY DRAGONS ARE SUMMONED TO THE FIELD!
THERE'S NO WAY YOU CAN WIN AGAINST THREE BLUE-EYES WHITE DRAGONS! MIRACLES DON'T HAPPEN TWICE!
RRG...
BOMP
ON MY SIDE, I HAVE DARK MAGICIAN AND BETA THE MAGNET WARRIOR...
BETA THE MAGNET WARRIOR Defense 1600
DARK MAGICIAN Attack 2500
THERE'S NO WAY I CAN DEFEND AGAINST THREE DRAGONS WITH ONLY TWO WEAKER MONSTERS!
SH REE
IS IT ALL OVER...?
IS THIS THE END...?

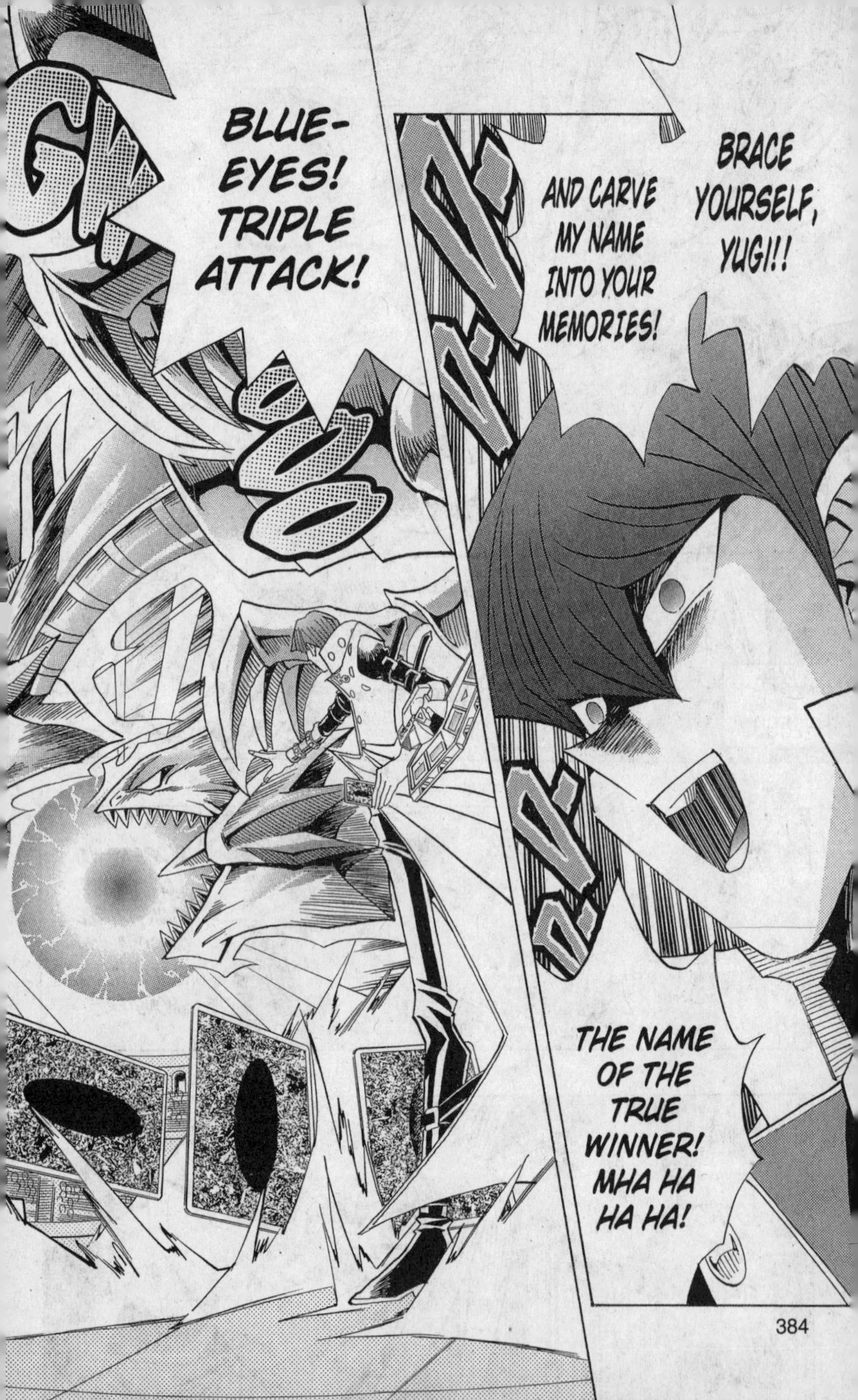
BRACE YOURSELF, YUGI!!
AND CARVE MY NAME INTO YOUR MEMORIES!
THE NAME OF THE TRUE WINNER! MHA HA HA HA!
BLUE-EYES! TRIPLE ATTACK!

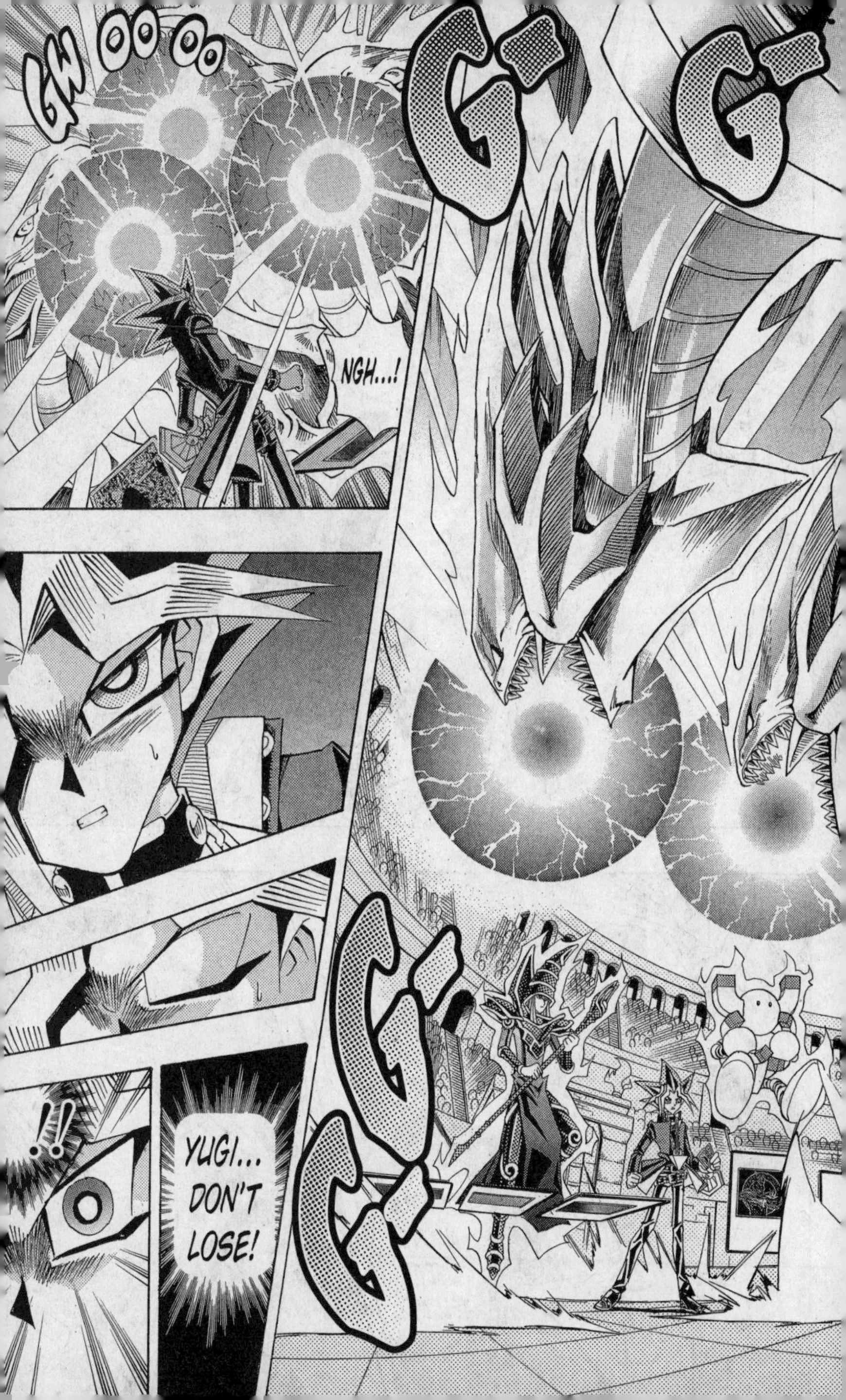
GI GI
GI GI
GWOOOO
NGH...!
YUGI... DON'T LOSE!
!!

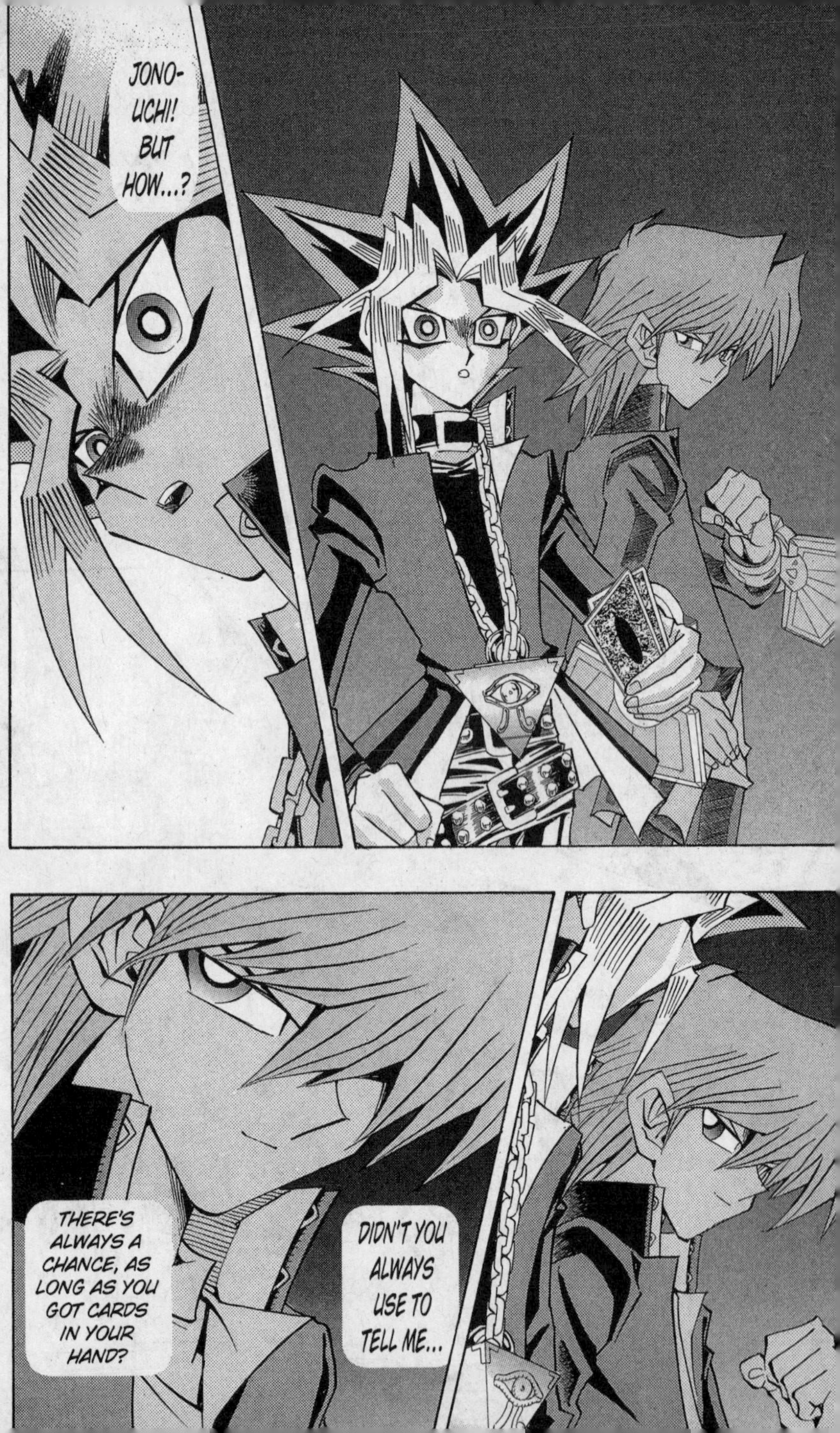
JONO-UCHI! BUT HOW...?
DIDN'T YOU ALWAYS USE TO TELL ME...
THERE'S ALWAYS A CHANCE, AS LONG AS YOU GOT CARDS IN YOUR HAND?

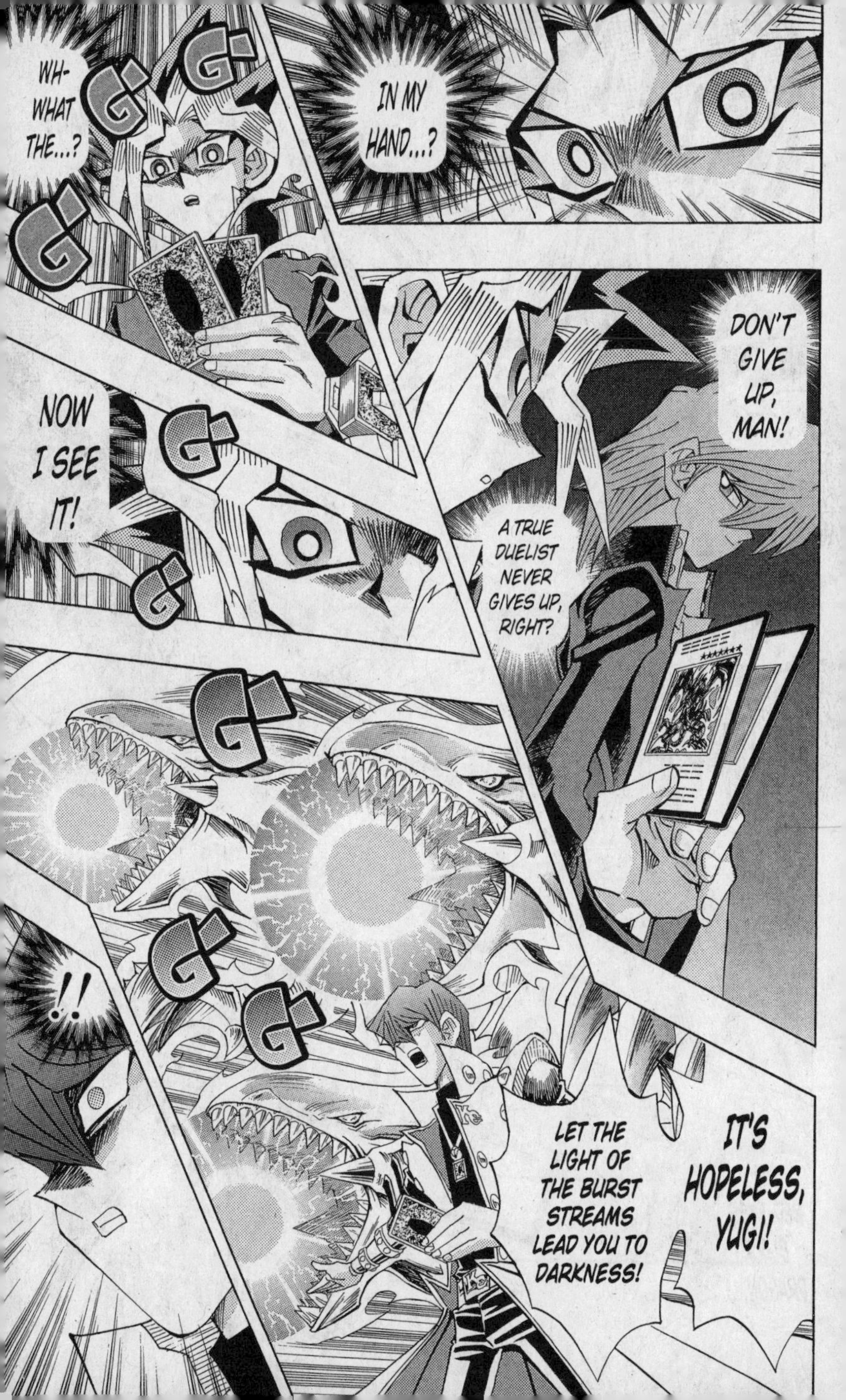
IN MY HAND...?
WH- WHAT THE...?
G G G
DON'T GIVE UP, MAN!
A TRUE DUELIST NEVER GIVES UP, RIGHT?
NOW I SEE IT!
G G
IT'S HOPELESS, YUGI!
LET THE LIGHT OF THE BURST STREAMS LEAD YOU TO DARKNESS!
G G G
!!

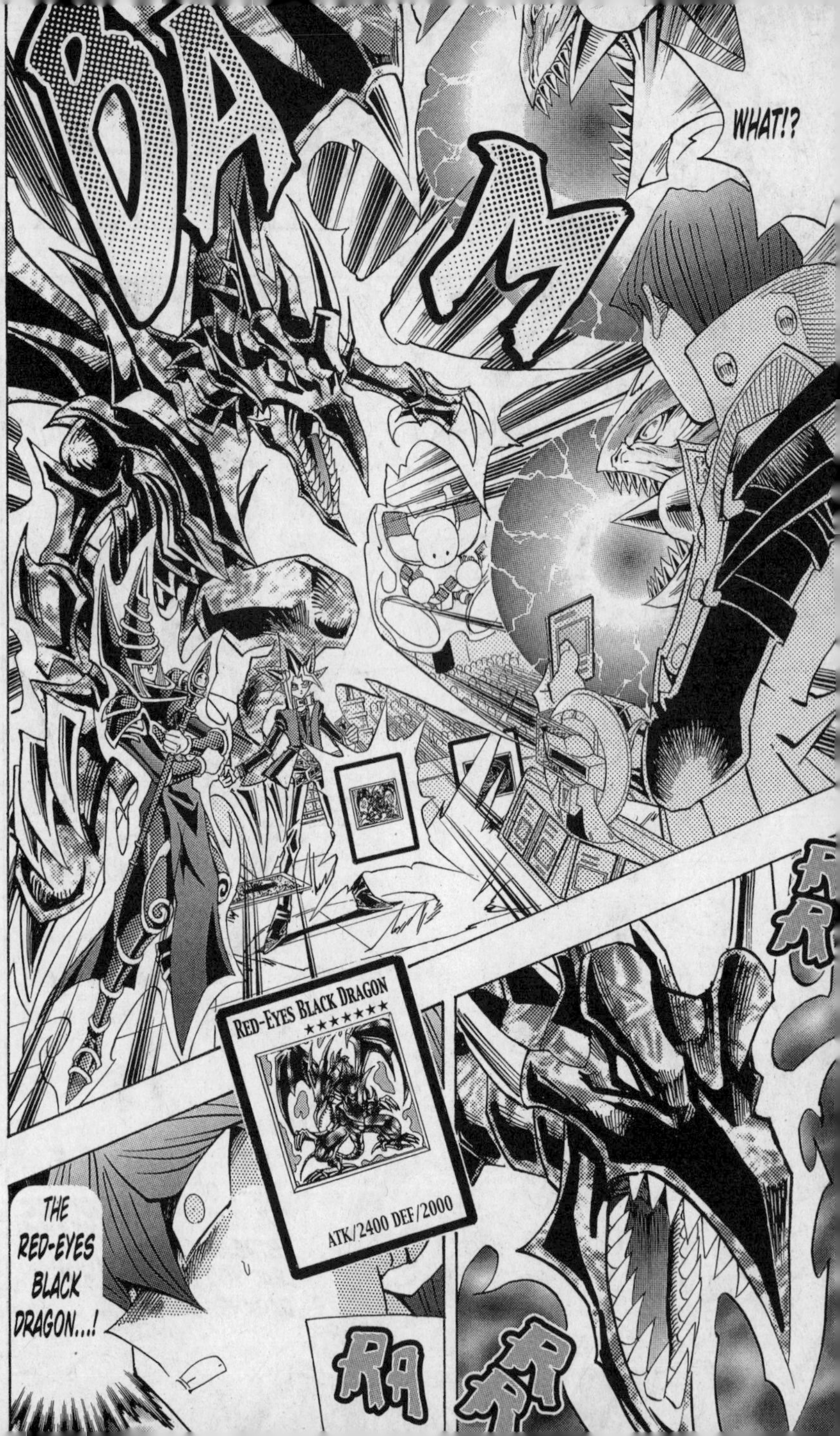
WHAT!?
RED-EYES BLACK DRAGON
ATK/2400 DEF/2000
THE RED-EYES BLACK DRAGON...!

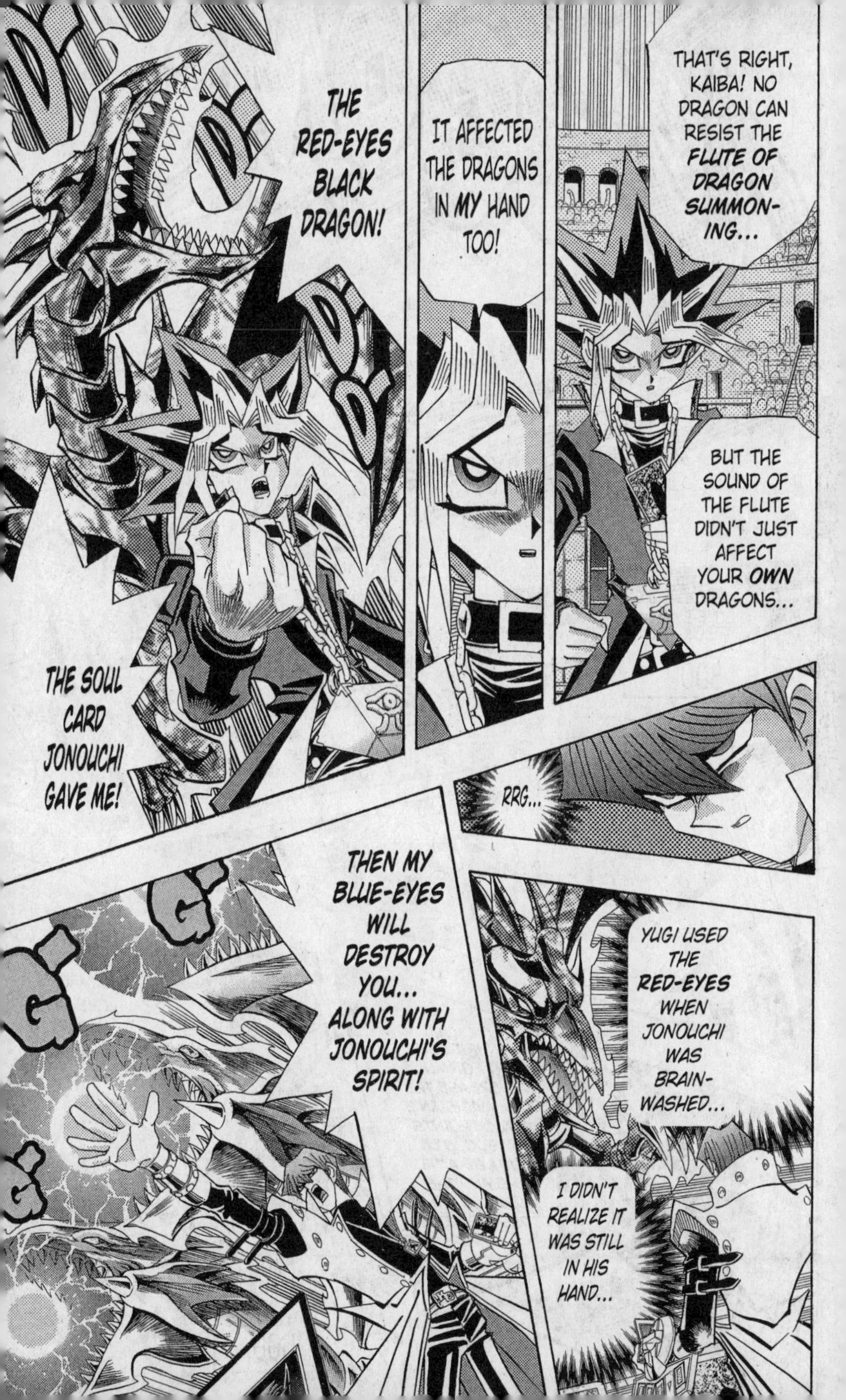
THAT'S RIGHT, KAIBA! NO DRAGON CAN RESIST THE FLUTE OF DRAGON SUMMONING...
BUT THE SOUND OF THE FLUTE DIDN'T JUST AFFECT YOUR OWN DRAGONS...
IT AFFECTED THE DRAGONS IN MY HAND TOO!
THE RED-EYES BLACK DRAGON!
THE SOUL CARD JONOUCHI GAVE ME!
RRG...
YUGI USED THE RED-EYES WHEN JONOUCHI WAS BRAIN-WASHED...
I DIDN'T REALIZE IT WAS STILL IN HIS HAND...
THEN MY BLUE-EYES WILL DESTROY YOU... ALONG WITH JONOUCHI'S SPIRIT!

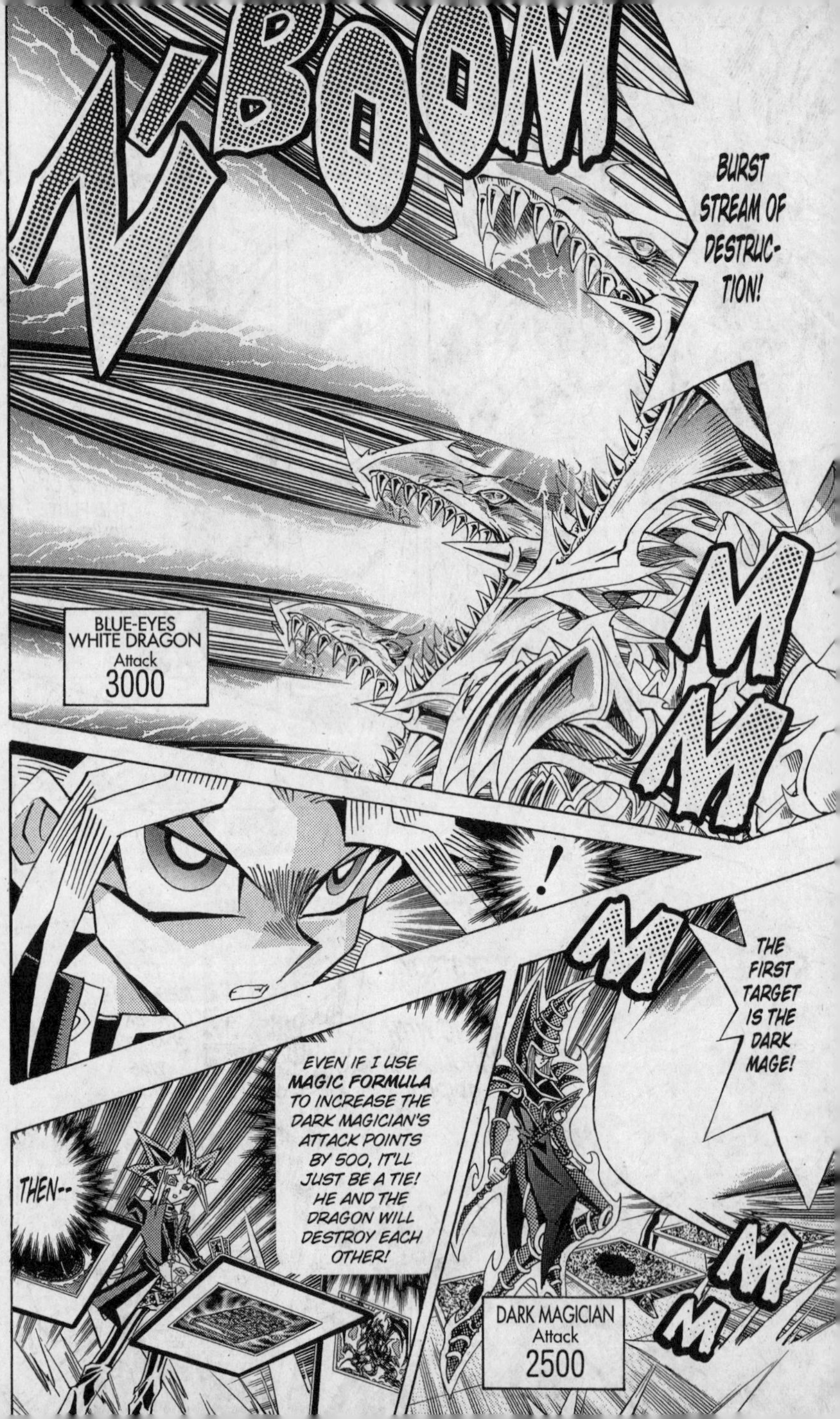

BURST STREAM OF DESTRUC-TION!
Z'BOOM
MMM
BLUE-EYES WHITE DRAGON Attack 3000
!
THE FIRST TARGET IS THE DARK MAGE!
MMM
EVEN IF I USE MAGIC FORMULA TO INCREASE THE DARK MAGICIAN'S ATTACK POINTS BY 500, IT'LL JUST BE A TIE! HE AND THE DRAGON WILL DESTROY EACH OTHER!
THEN--
DARK MAGICIAN Attack 2500

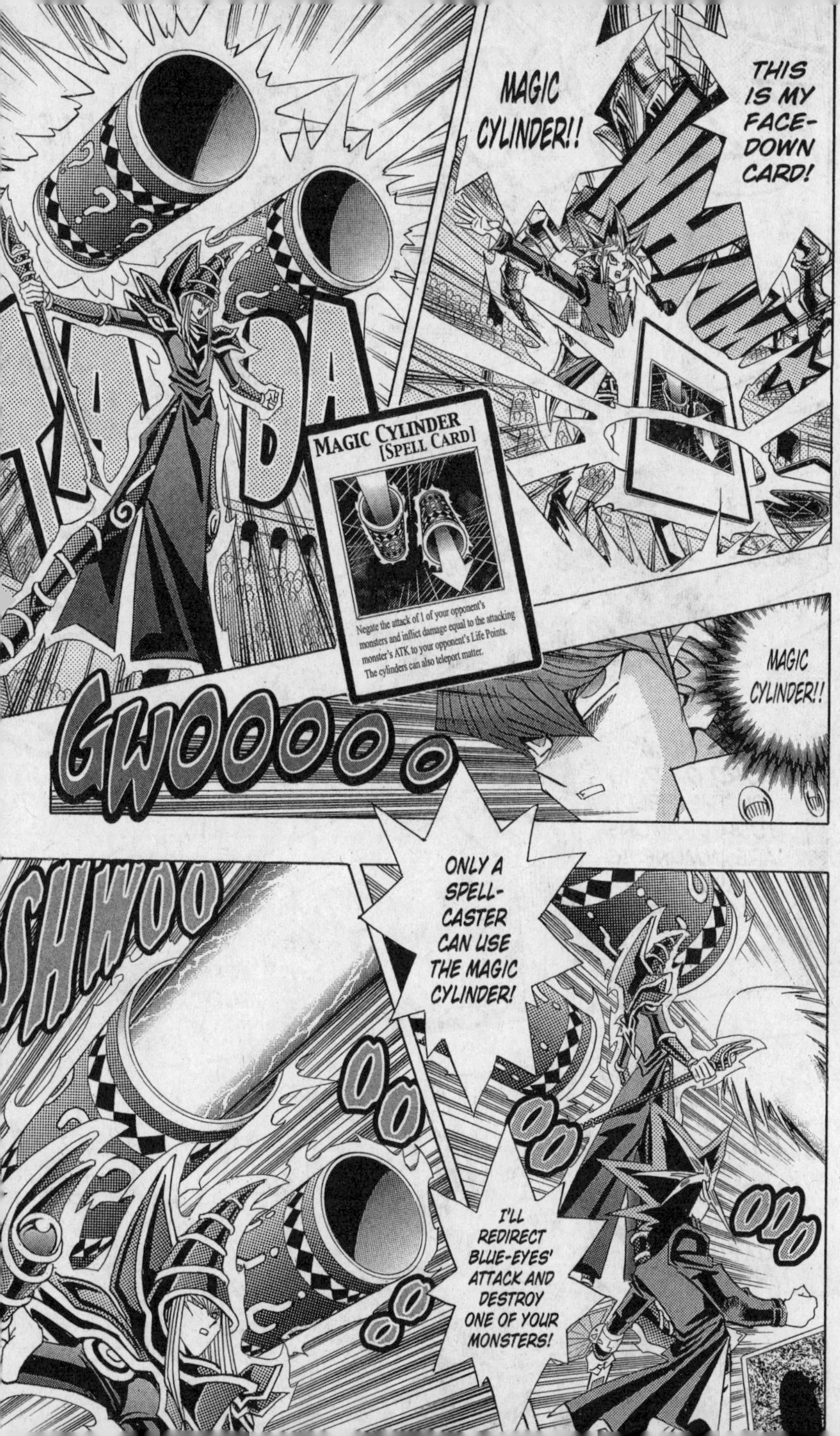
THIS IS MY FACE-DOWN CARD!
MAGIC CYLINDER!!
MAGIC CYLINDER
[SPELL CARD]
Negate the attack of 1 of your opponent's monsters and inflict damage equal to the attacking monster's ATK to your opponent's Life Points. The cylinders can also teleport matter.
MAGIC CYLINDER!!
GWOOOO..
ONLY A SPELL-CASTER CAN USE THE MAGIC CYLINDER!
I'LL REDIRECT BLUE-EYES' ATTACK AND DESTROY ONE OF YOUR MONSTERS!
OOO
SHWOO
OOOO

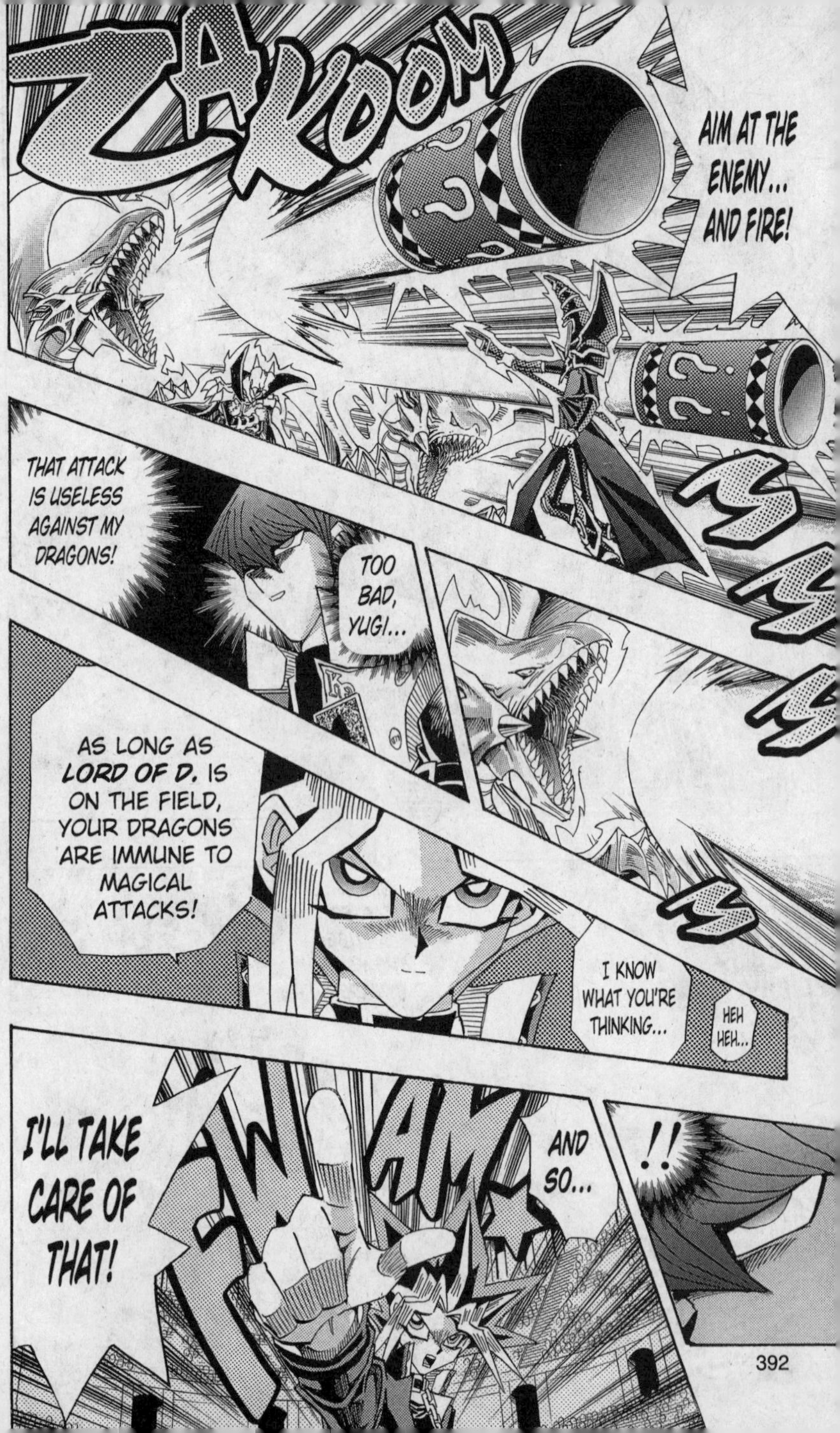
AIM AT THE ENEMY... AND FIRE!
ZAKOOM
TOO BAD, YUGI...
THAT ATTACK IS USELESS AGAINST MY DRAGONS!
HEH HEH...
I KNOW WHAT YOU'RE THINKING...
AS LONG AS *LORD OF D.* IS ON THE FIELD, YOUR DRAGONS ARE IMMUNE TO MAGICAL ATTACKS!
!!
AND SO...
WHAM
I'LL TAKE CARE OF THAT!

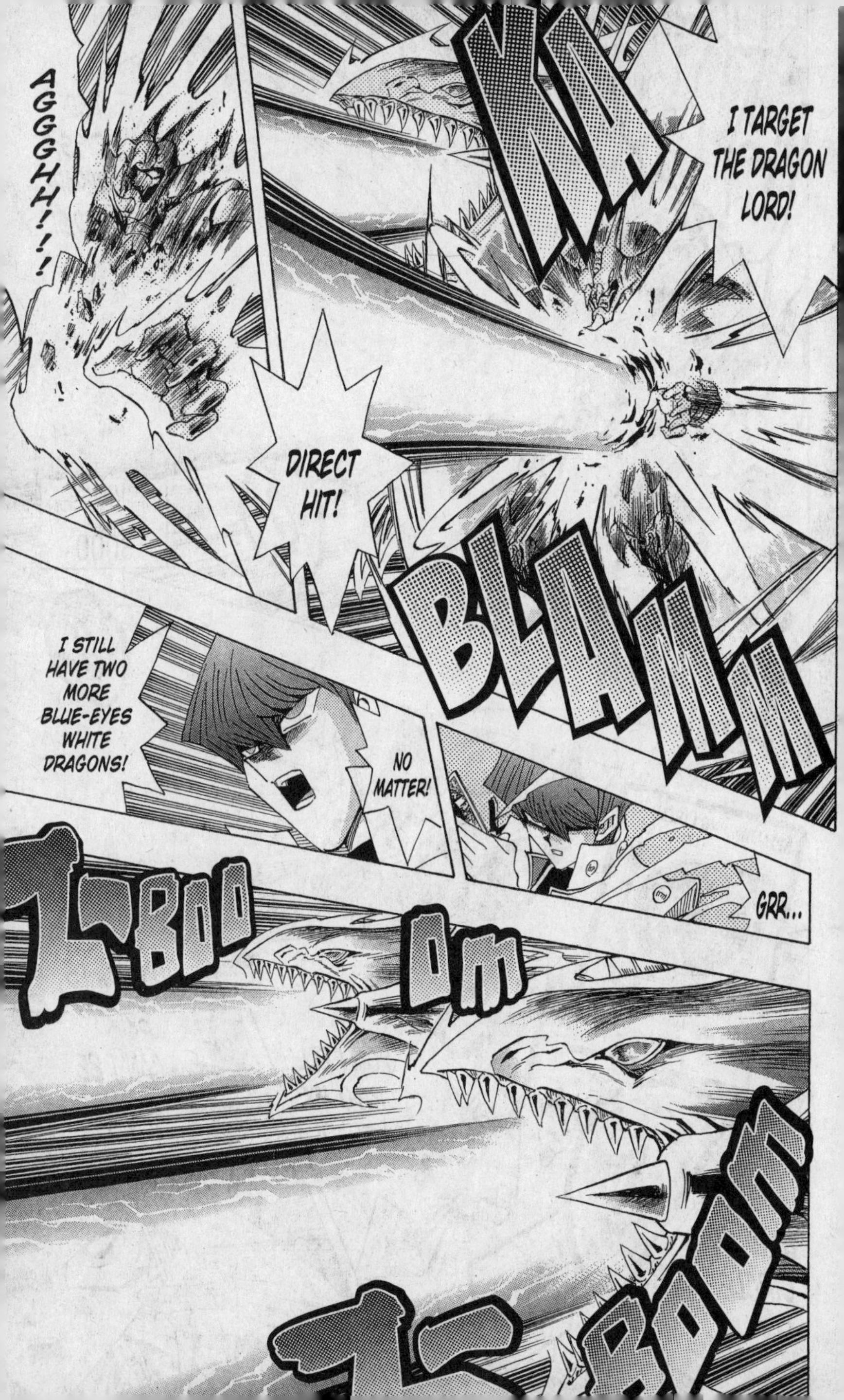
I TARGET THE DRAGON LORD!
AGGGHH!!!
DIRECT HIT!
BLAMMM
GRR...
NO MATTER!
I STILL HAVE TWO MORE BLUE-EYES WHITE DRAGONS!

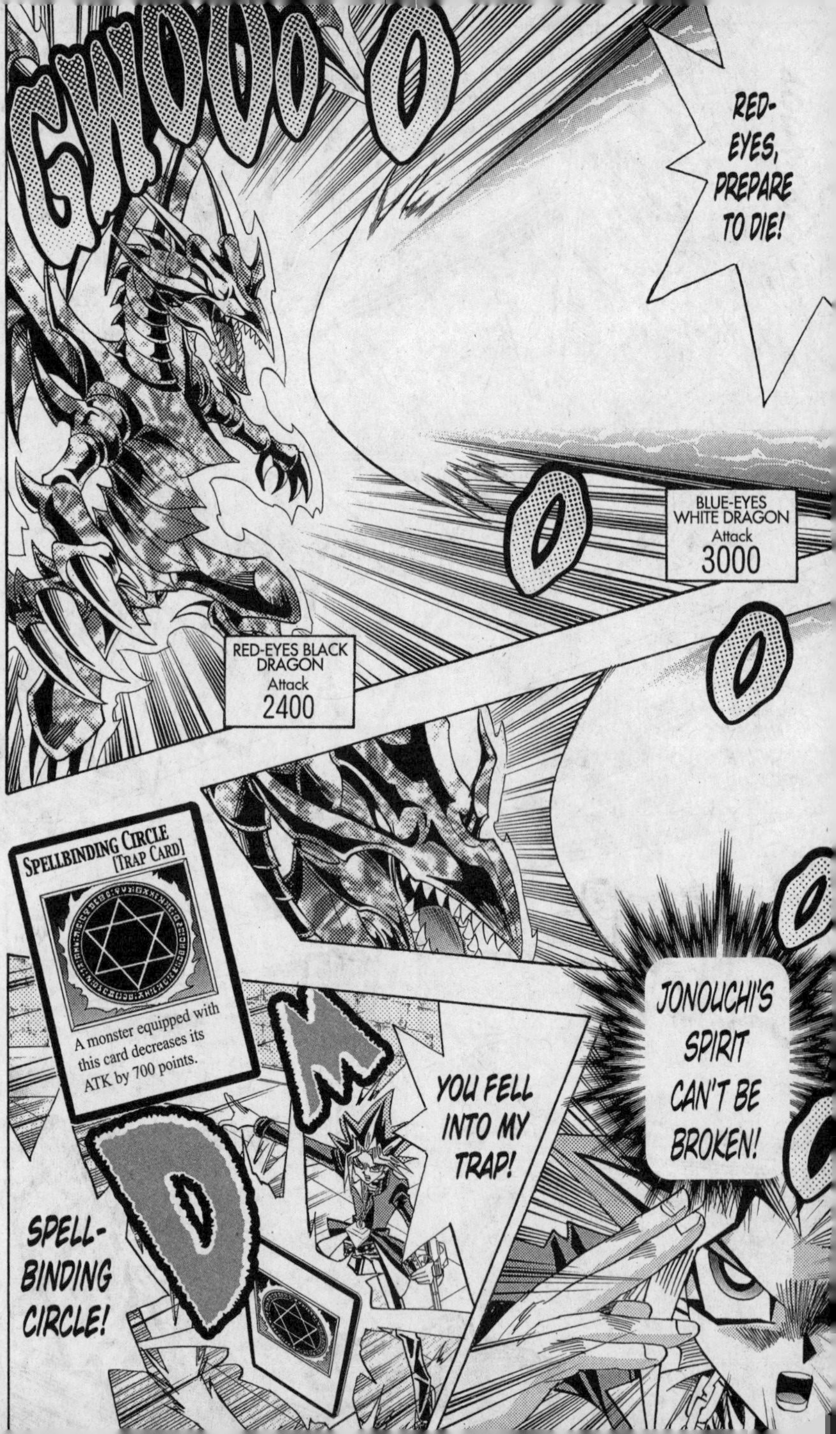
RED-EYES, PREPARE TO DIE!
GWOOO-O
BLUE-EYES WHITE DRAGON Attack 3000
RED-EYES BLACK DRAGON Attack 2400
JONOUCHI'S SPIRIT CAN'T BE BROKEN!
YOU FELL INTO MY TRAP!
SPELLBINDING CIRCLE [TRAP CARD]
A monster equipped with this card decreases its ATK by 700 points.
SPELL-BINDING CIRCLE!

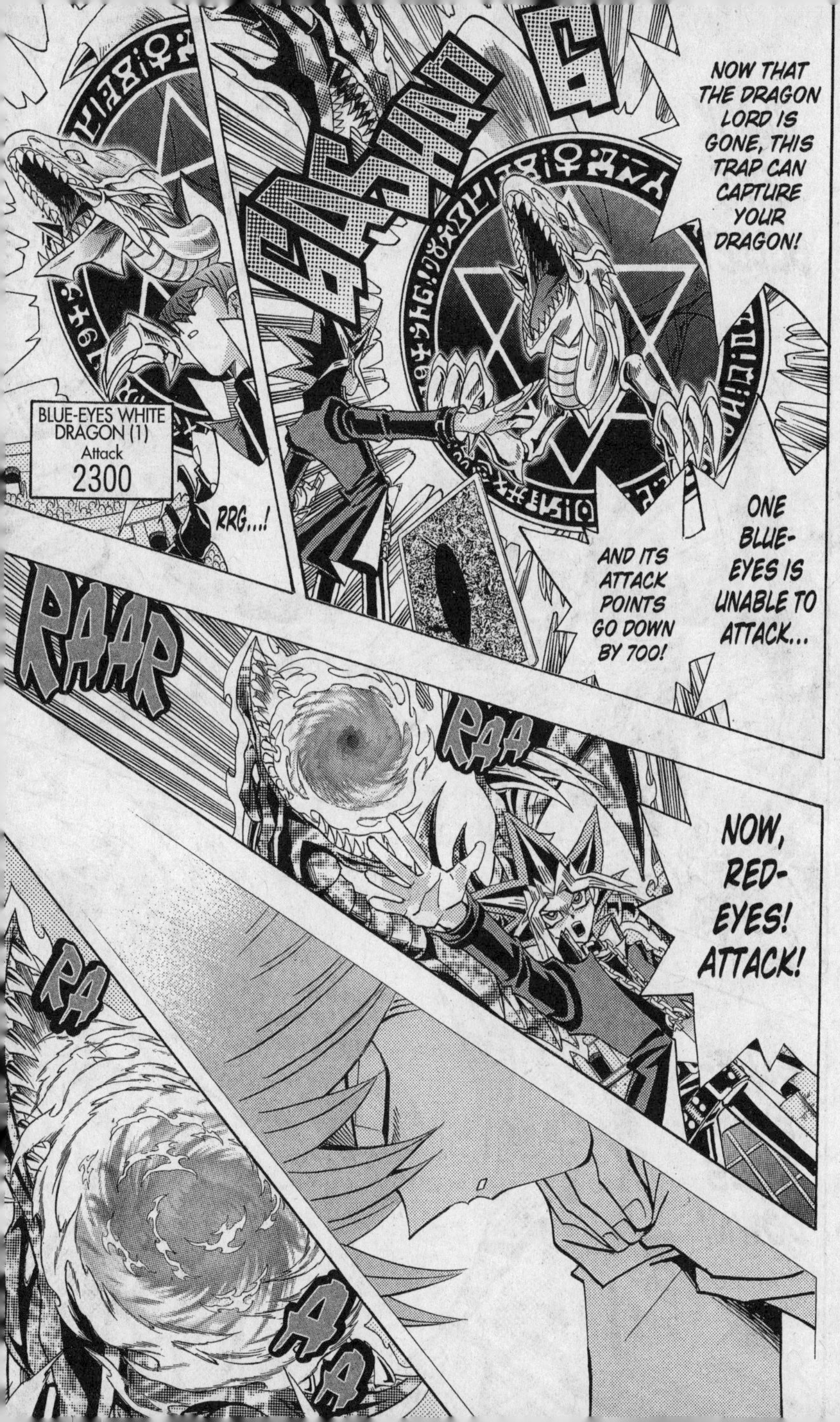
NOW THAT THE DRAGON LORD IS GONE, THIS TRAP CAN CAPTURE YOUR DRAGON!
GASHUNG
ONE BLUE-EYES IS UNABLE TO ATTACK...
AND ITS ATTACK POINTS GO DOWN BY 700!
BLUE-EYES WHITE DRAGON (1)
Attack
2300
RRG...!
NOW, RED-EYES! ATTACK!
RAA
RAAR
RA
A
A

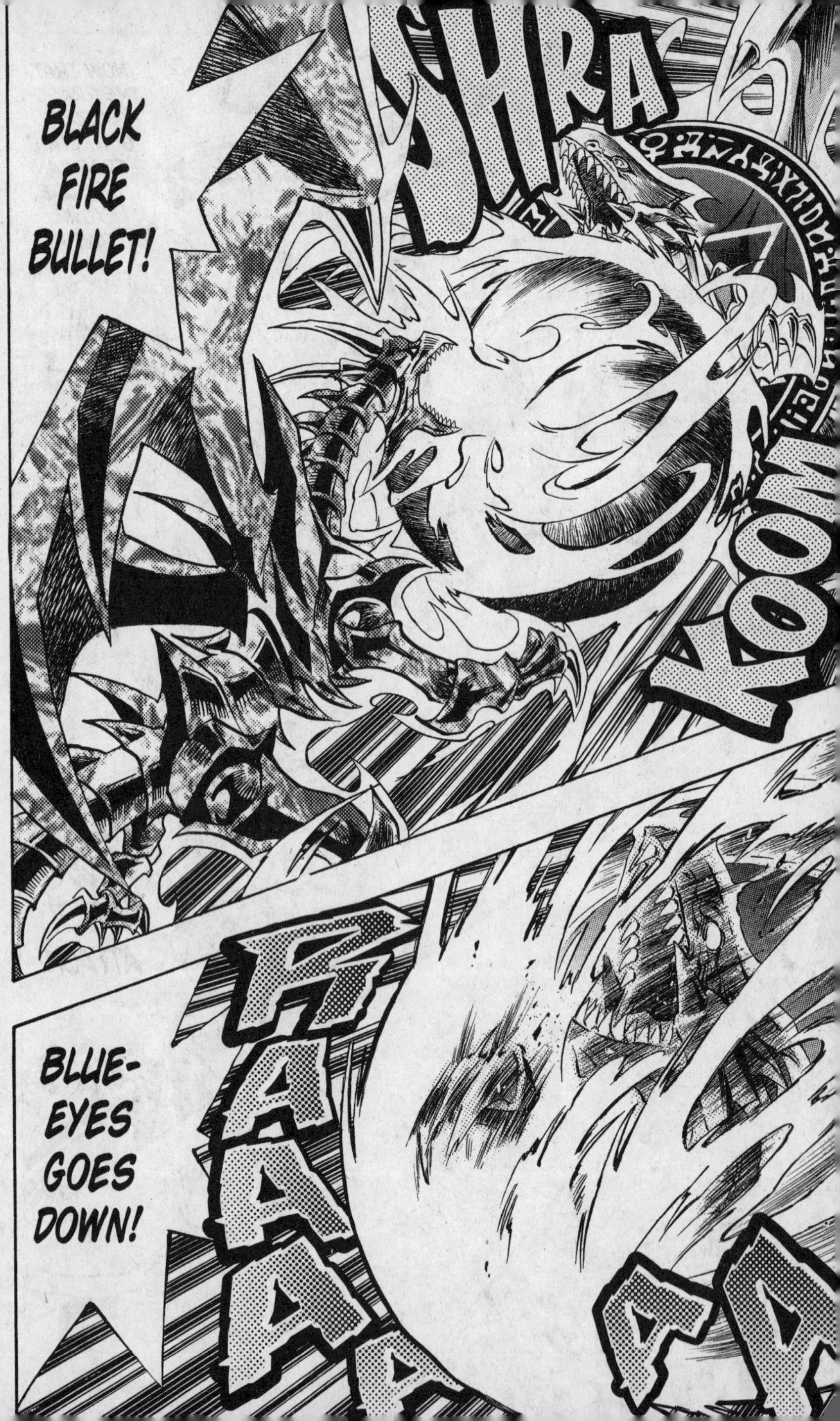
SHRA
BLACK FIRE BULLET!
KOOM
BLUE-EYES GOES DOWN!
HAAA
AA

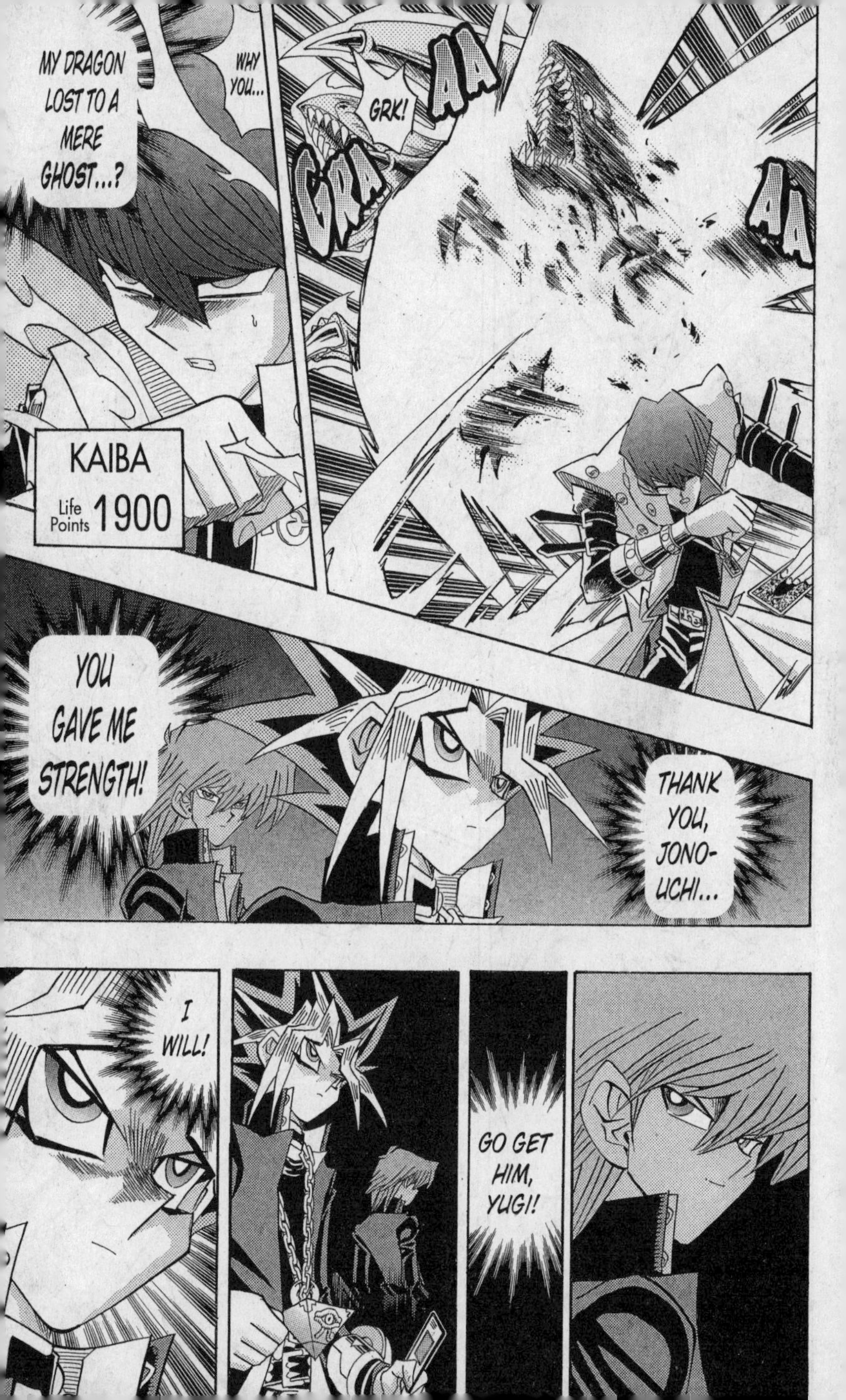
AA
AA
GRK!
GRA
WHY YOU...
MY DRAGON LOST TO A MERE GHOST...?
KAIBA
Life Points 1900
THANK YOU, JONO-UCHI...
YOU GAVE ME STRENGTH!
GO GET HIM, YUGI!
I WILL!

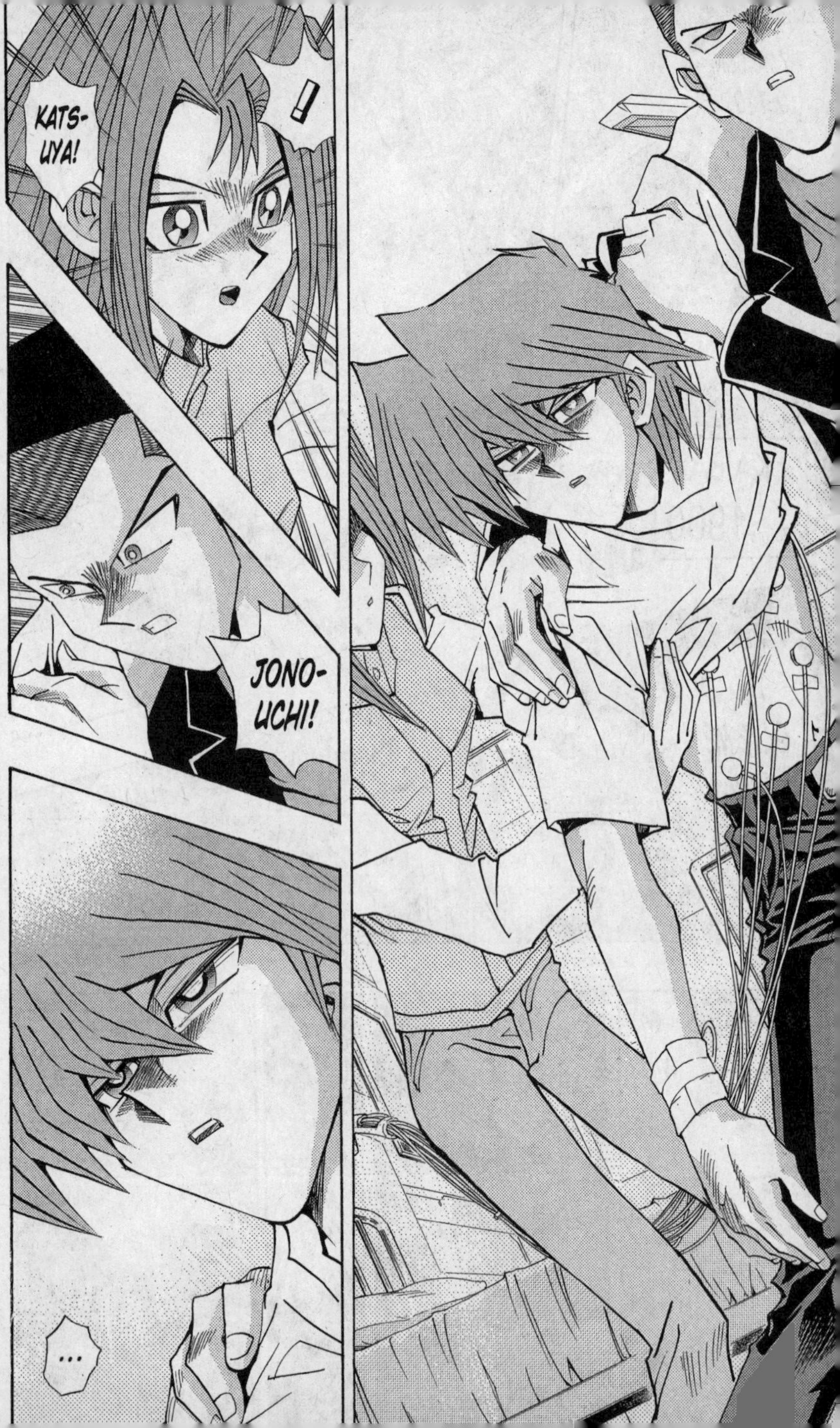
!
KATS-UYA!
JONO-UCHI!
...

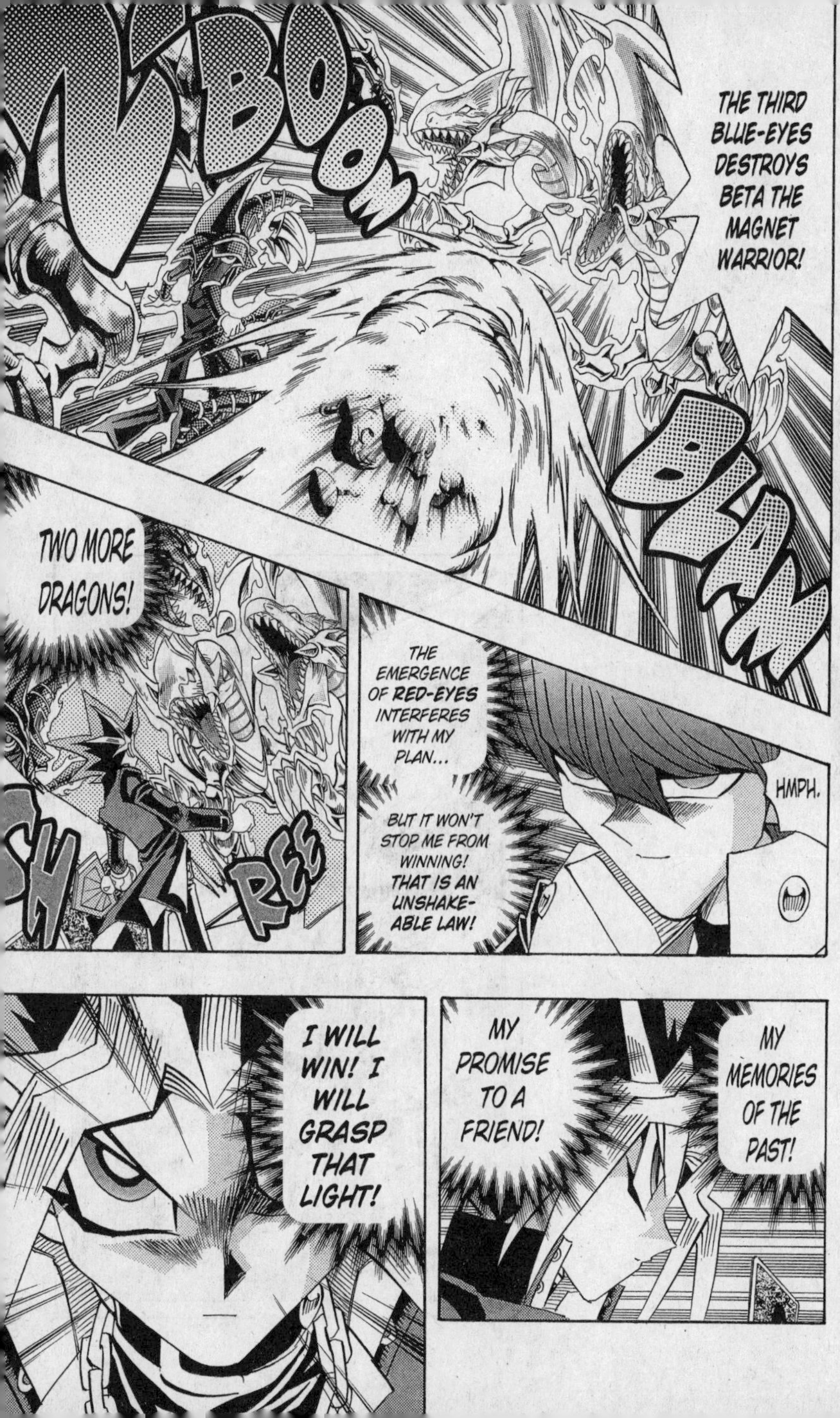
THE THIRD BLUE-EYES DESTROYS BETA THE MAGNET WARRIOR!
BLAM
HMPH.
THE EMERGENCE OF RED-EYES INTERFERES WITH MY PLAN...
BUT IT WON'T STOP ME FROM WINNING! THAT IS AN UNSHAKE-ABLE LAW!
TWO MORE DRAGONS!
REE
MY MEMORIES OF THE PAST!
MY PROMISE TO A FRIEND!
I WILL WIN! I WILL GRASP THAT LIGHT!

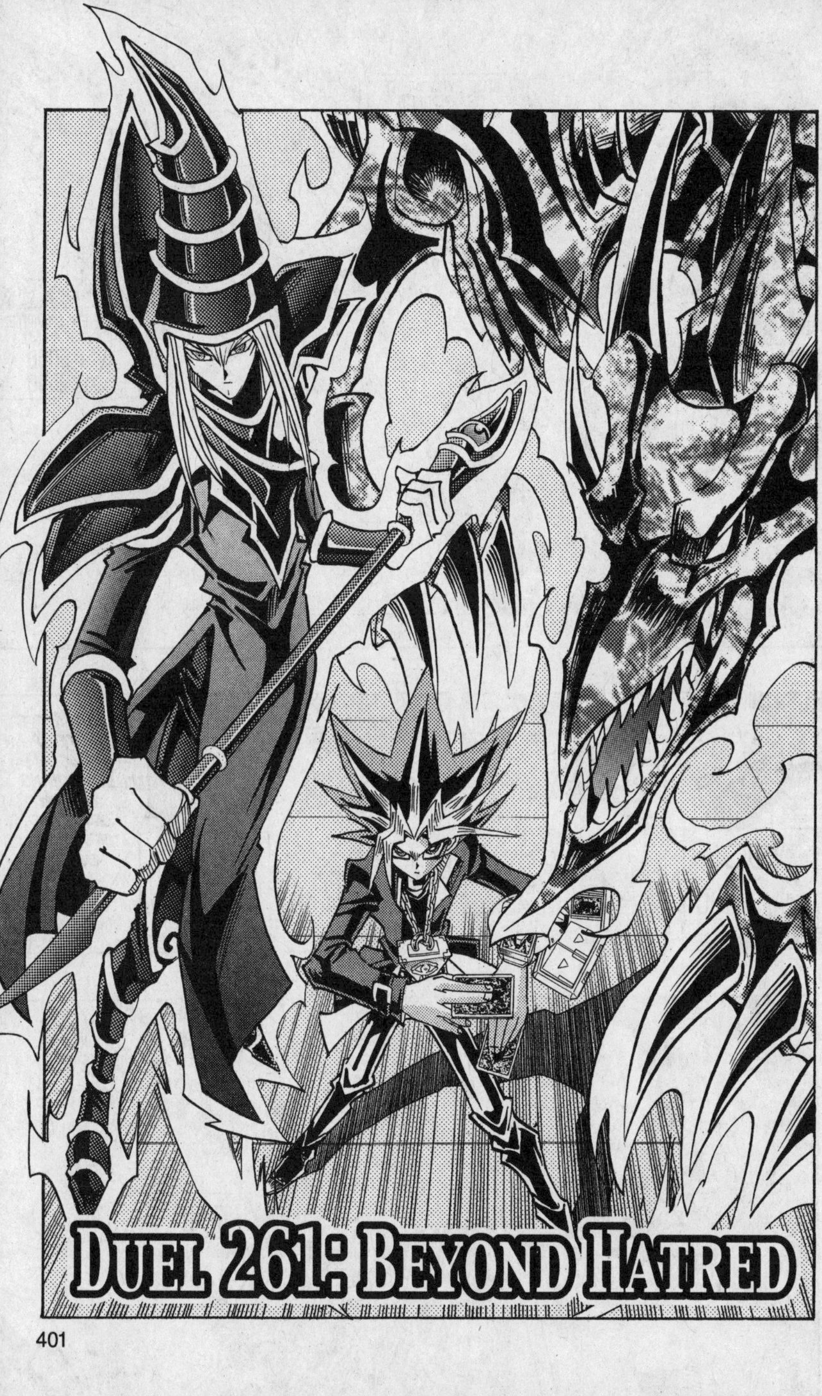
DUEL 261: BEYOND HATRED

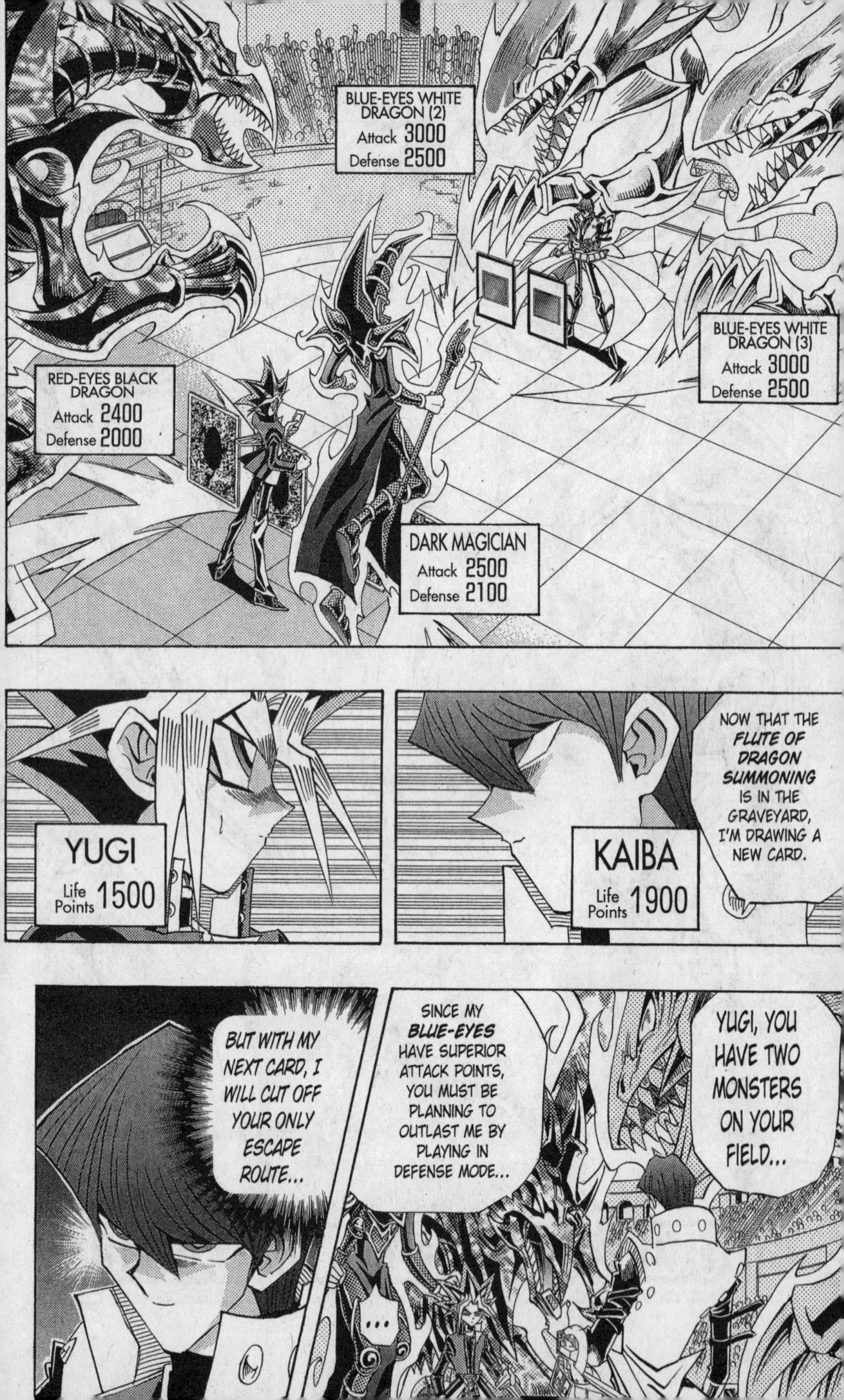
BLUE-EYES WHITE DRAGON (2) Attack 3000 Defense 2500
BLUE-EYES WHITE DRAGON (3) Attack 3000 Defense 2500
RED-EYES BLACK DRAGON Attack 2400 Defense 2000
DARK MAGICIAN Attack 2500 Defense 2100
NOW THAT THE FLUTE OF DRAGON SUMMONING IS IN THE GRAVEYARD, I'M DRAWING A NEW CARD.
KAIBA Life Points 1900
YUGI Life Points 1500
YUGI, YOU HAVE TWO MONSTERS ON YOUR FIELD...
SINCE MY BLUE-EYES HAVE SUPERIOR ATTACK POINTS, YOU MUST BE PLANNING TO OUTLAST ME BY PLAYING IN DEFENSE MODE...
...
BUT WITH MY NEXT CARD, I WILL CUT OFF YOUR ONLY ESCAPE ROUTE...

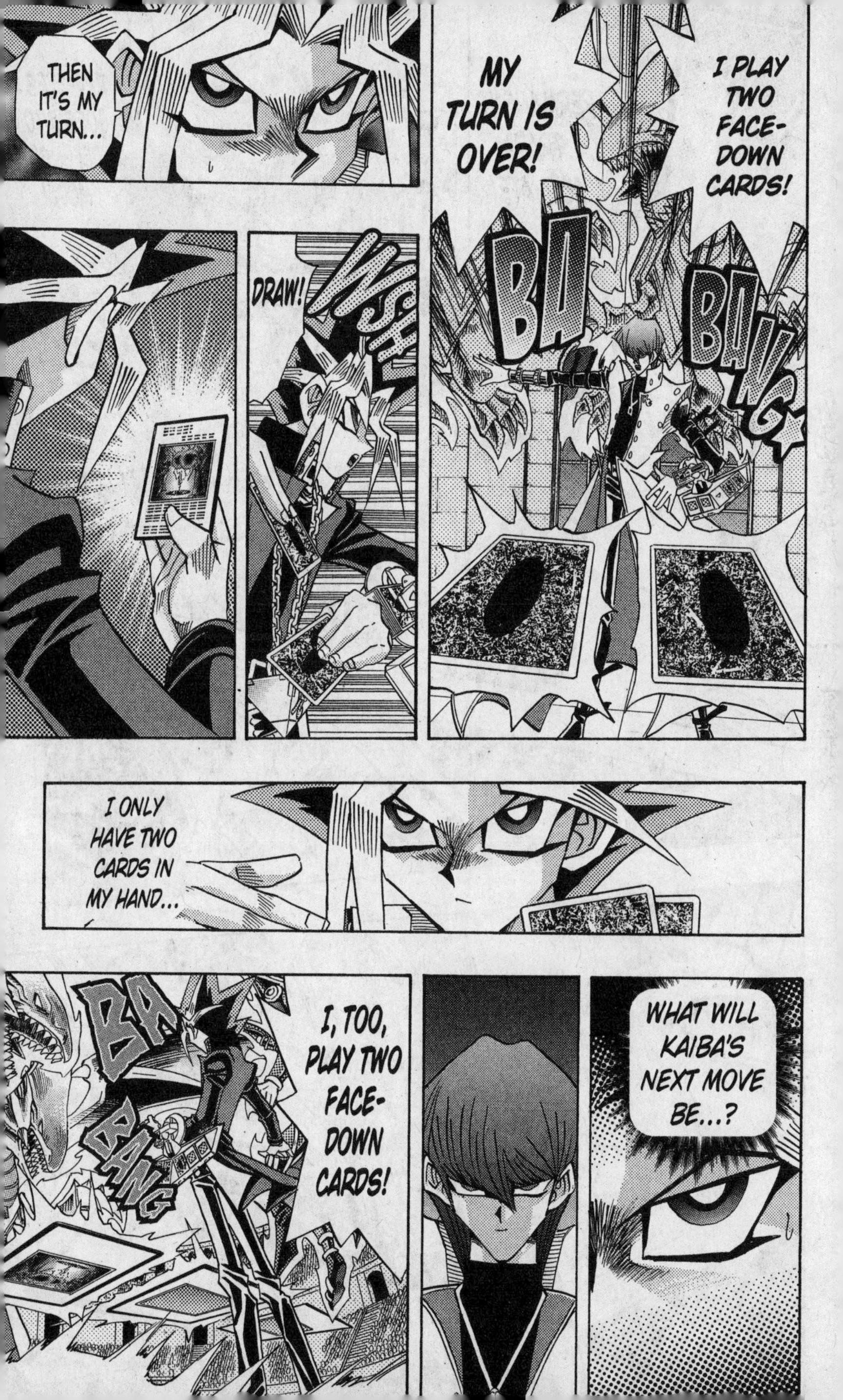
I PLAY TWO FACE-DOWN CARDS!
MY TURN IS OVER!
BA
BANG
THEN IT'S MY TURN...
DRAW!
WSH
I ONLY HAVE TWO CARDS IN MY HAND...
WHAT WILL KAIBA'S NEXT MOVE BE...?
I, TOO, PLAY TWO FACE-DOWN CARDS!
BA
BANG

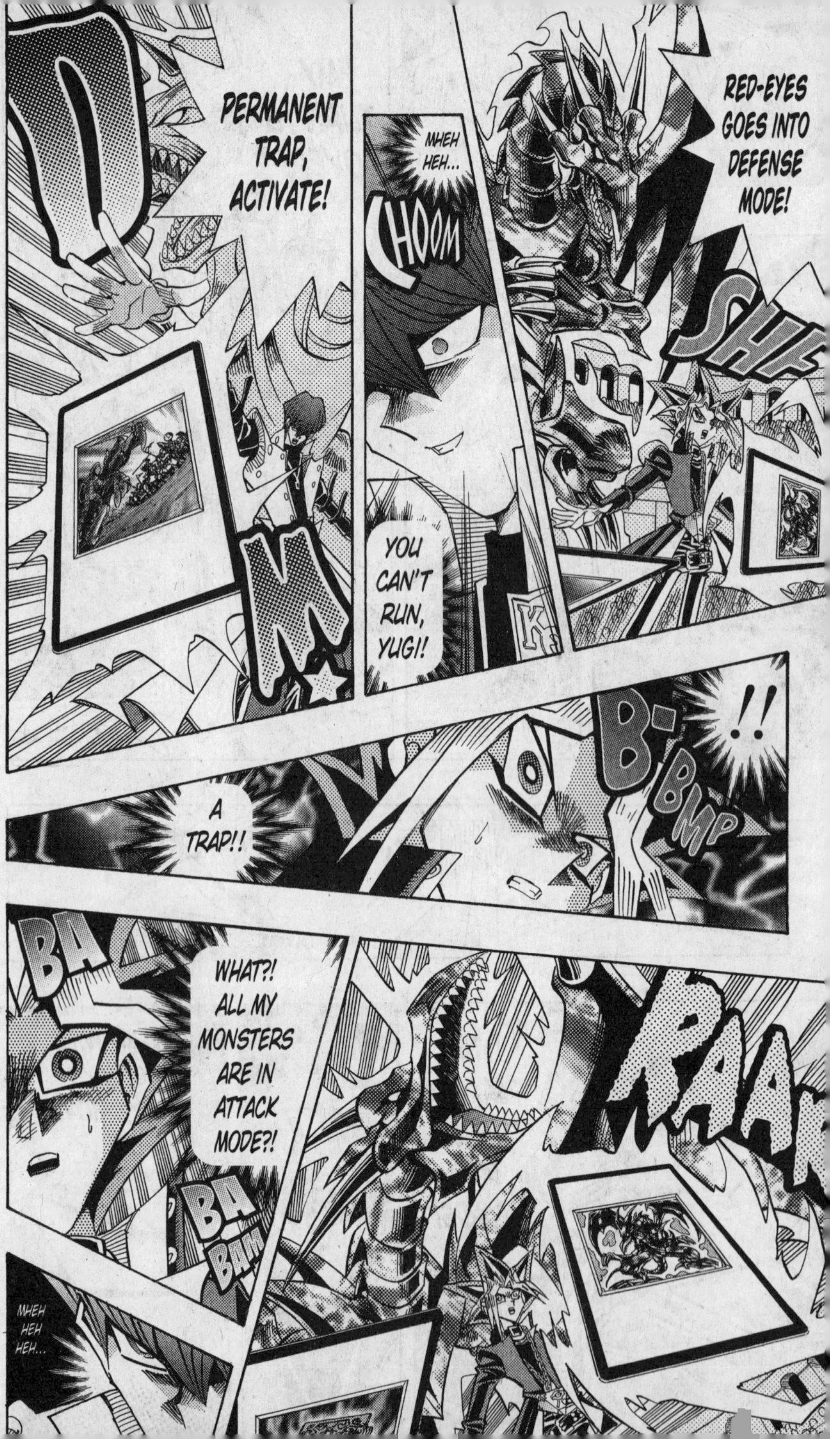
RED-EYES GOES INTO DEFENSE MODE!
SHF
MHEH HEH...
CHOOM
YOU CAN'T RUN, YUGI!
PERMANENT TRAP, ACTIVATE!
M
B-BMP
!!
A TRAP!!
KRAA
WHAT?! ALL MY MONSTERS ARE IN ATTACK MODE?!
BA
BA BAM
MHEH HEH HEH...

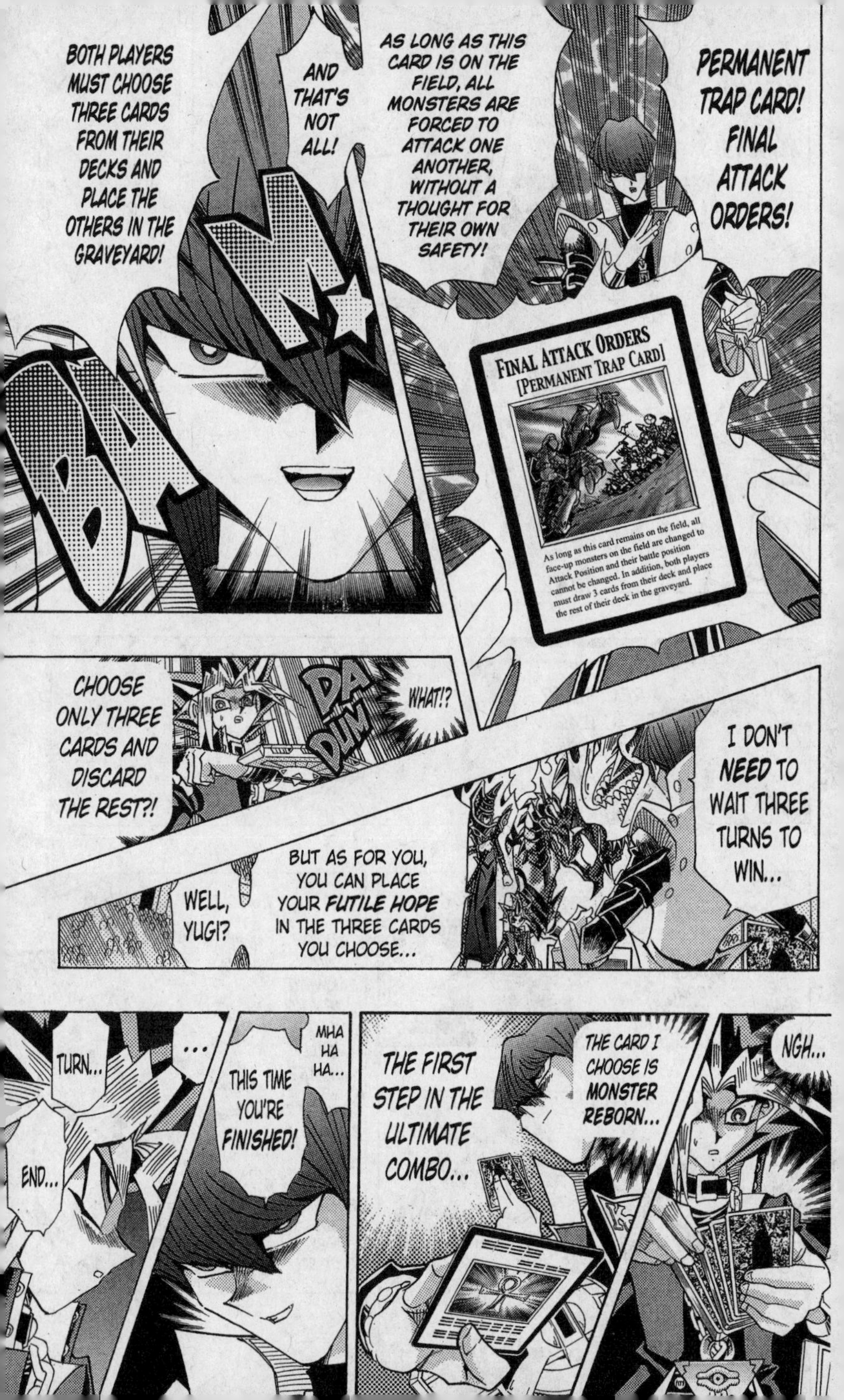
PERMANENT TRAP CARD! FINAL ATTACK ORDERS!
FINAL ATTACK ORDERS
[PERMANENT TRAP CARD]
As long as this card remains on the field, all face-up monsters on the field are changed to Attack Position and their battle position cannot be changed. In addition, both players must draw 3 cards from their deck and place the rest of their deck in the graveyard.
AS LONG AS THIS CARD IS ON THE FIELD, ALL MONSTERS ARE FORCED TO ATTACK ONE ANOTHER, WITHOUT A THOUGHT FOR THEIR OWN SAFETY!
AND THAT'S NOT ALL!
BOTH PLAYERS MUST CHOOSE THREE CARDS FROM THEIR DECKS AND PLACE THE OTHERS IN THE GRAVEYARD!
WHAT!?
DA DUM
CHOOSE ONLY THREE CARDS AND DISCARD THE REST?!
I DON'T NEED TO WAIT THREE TURNS TO WIN...
BUT AS FOR YOU, YOU CAN PLACE YOUR FUTILE HOPE IN THE THREE CARDS YOU CHOOSE...
WELL, YUGI?
NGH...
THE CARD I CHOOSE IS MONSTER REBORN...
THE FIRST STEP IN THE ULTIMATE COMBO...
MHA HA HA...
THIS TIME YOU'RE FINISHED!
...
TURN...
END...

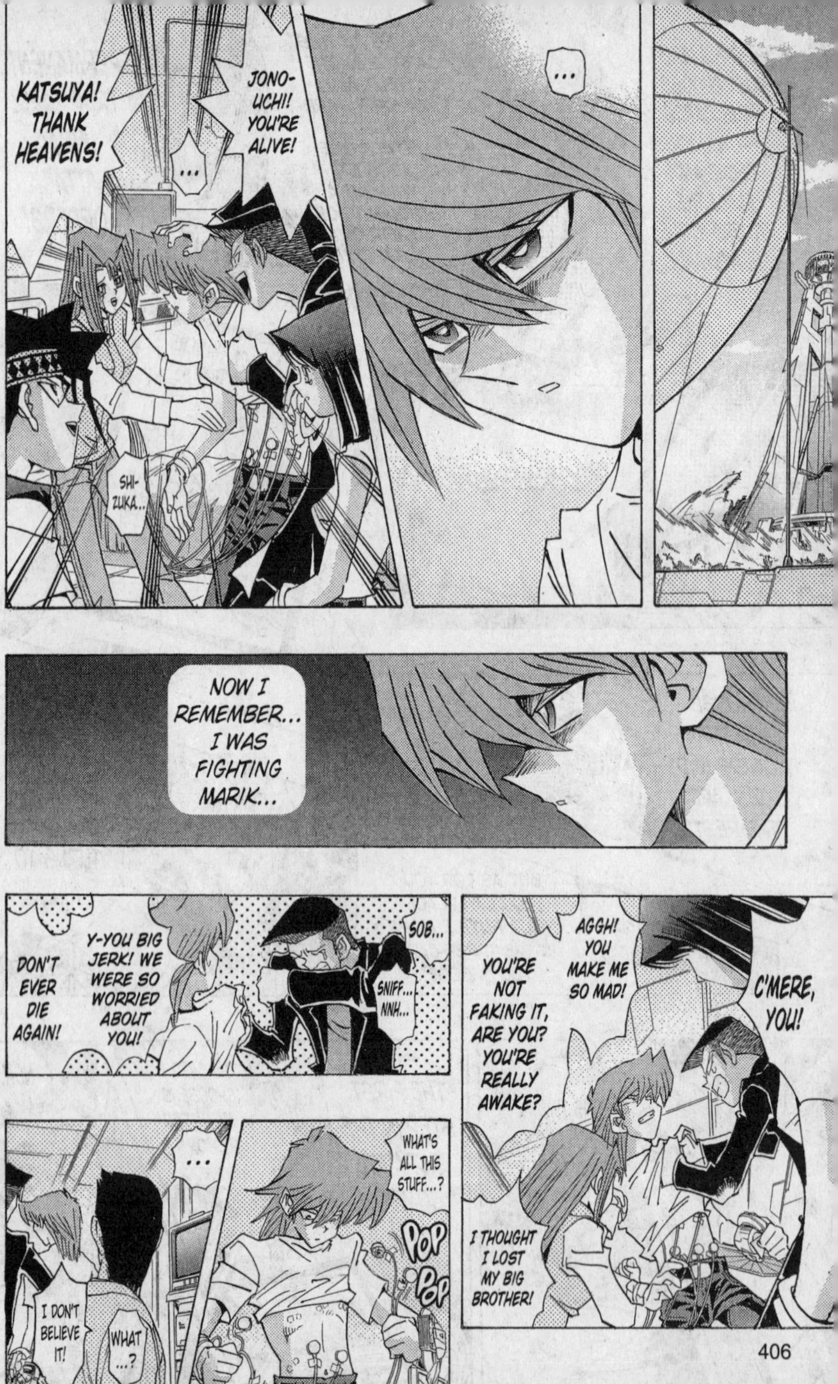
…
JONO-UCHI! YOU'RE ALIVE!
KATSUYA! THANK HEAVENS!
…
SHI-ZUKA…
NOW I REMEMBER… I WAS FIGHTING MARIK…
C'MERE, YOU!
AGGH! YOU MAKE ME SO MAD!
YOU'RE NOT FAKING IT, ARE YOU? YOU'RE REALLY AWAKE?
I THOUGHT I LOST MY BIG BROTHER!
SOB…
SNIFF… NNH…
Y-YOU BIG JERK! WE WERE SO WORRIED ABOUT YOU!
DON'T EVER DIE AGAIN!
WHAT'S ALL THIS STUFF…?
POP
POP
…
WHAT …?
I DON'T BELIEVE IT!

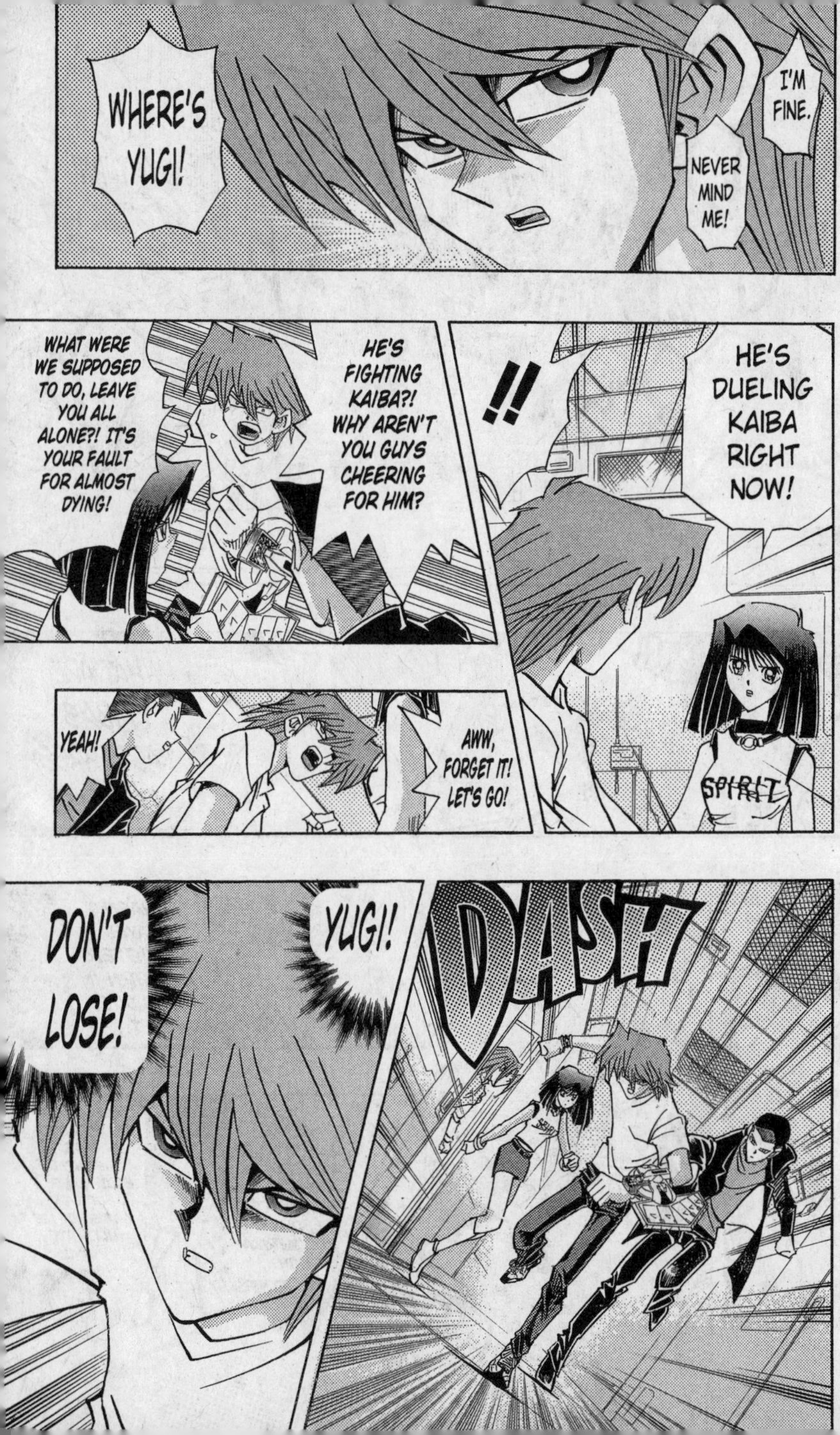
I'M FINE.
NEVER MIND ME!
WHERE'S YUGI!
HE'S DUELING KAIBA RIGHT NOW!
!!
SPIRIT
HE'S FIGHTING KAIBA?! WHY AREN'T YOU GUYS CHEERING FOR HIM?
WHAT WERE WE SUPPOSED TO DO, LEAVE YOU ALL ALONE?! IT'S YOUR FAULT FOR ALMOST DYING!
AWW, FORGET IT! LET'S GO!
YEAH!
DASH
YUGI!
DON'T LOSE!

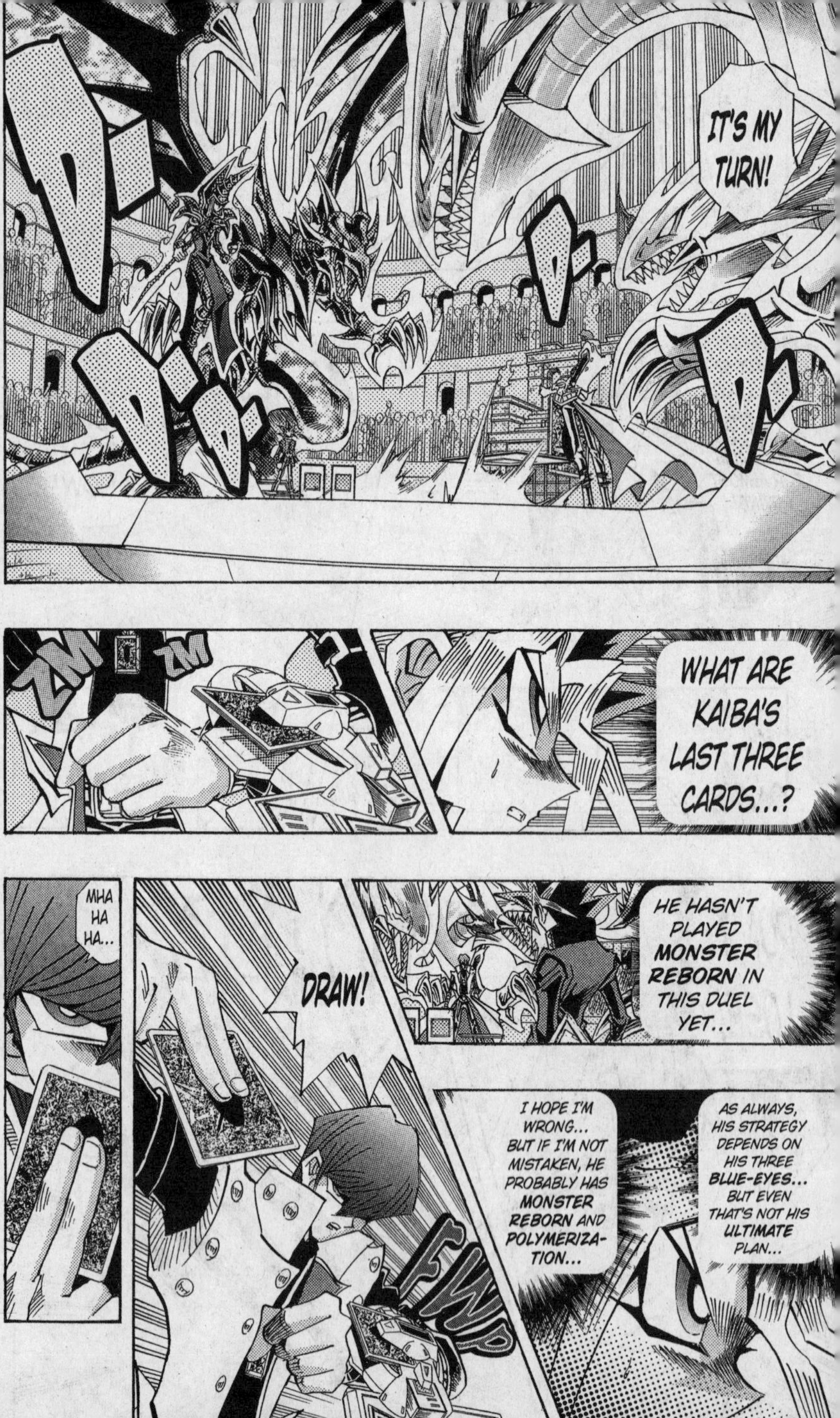
IT'S MY TURN!
WHAT ARE KAIBA'S LAST THREE CARDS...?
ZM
ZM
HE HASN'T PLAYED MONSTER REBORN IN THIS DUEL YET...
DRAW!
AS ALWAYS, HIS STRATEGY DEPENDS ON HIS THREE BLUE-EYES... BUT EVEN THAT'S NOT HIS ULTIMATE PLAN...
I HOPE I'M WRONG... BUT IF I'M NOT MISTAKEN, HE PROBABLY HAS MONSTER REBORN AND POLYMERIZA-TION...
MHA HA HA...

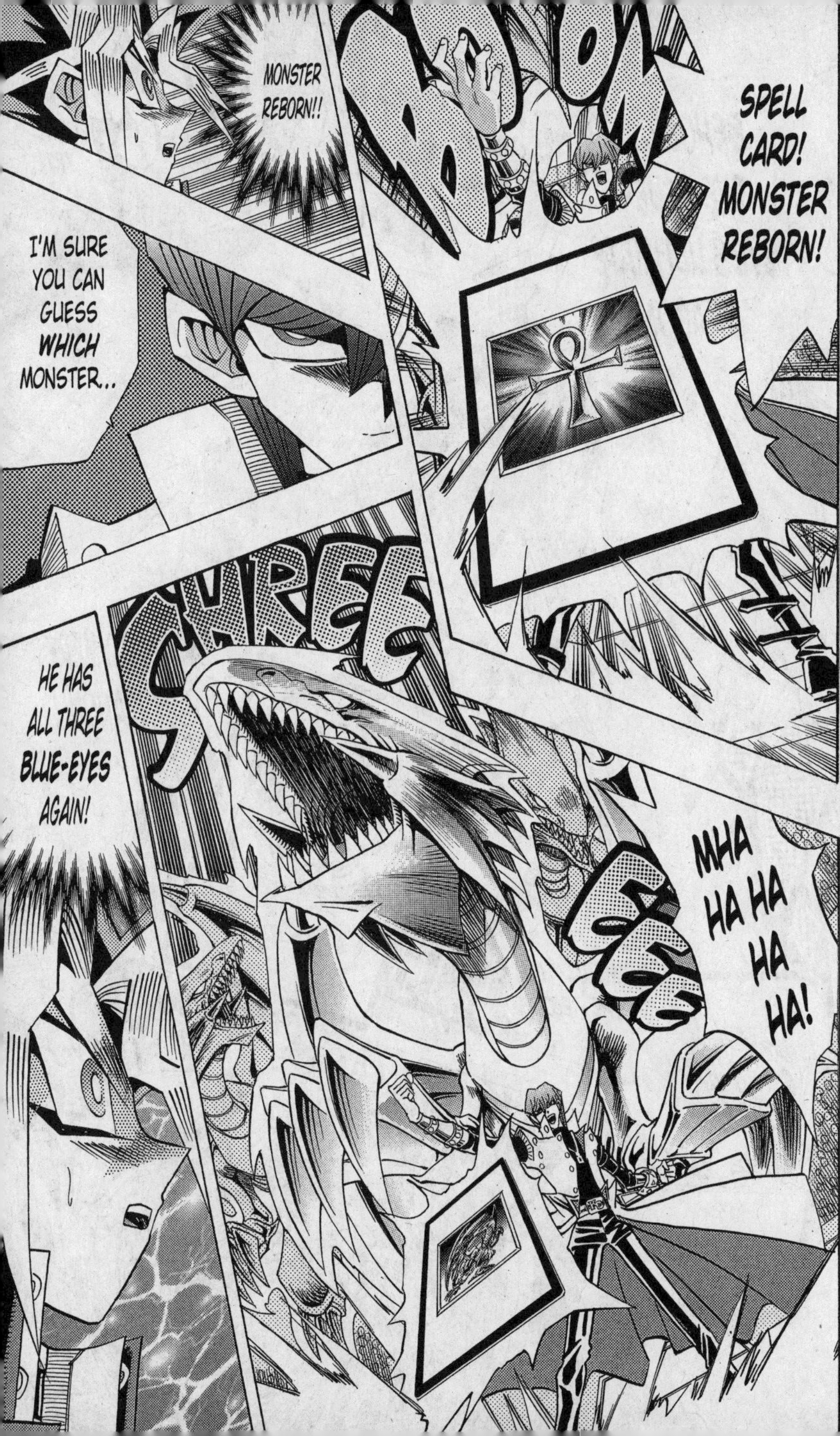
SPELL CARD! MONSTER REBORN!
MONSTER REBORN!!
I'M SURE YOU CAN GUESS WHICH MONSTER...
MHA HA HA HA HA!
SHREE
HE HAS ALL THREE BLUE-EYES AGAIN!

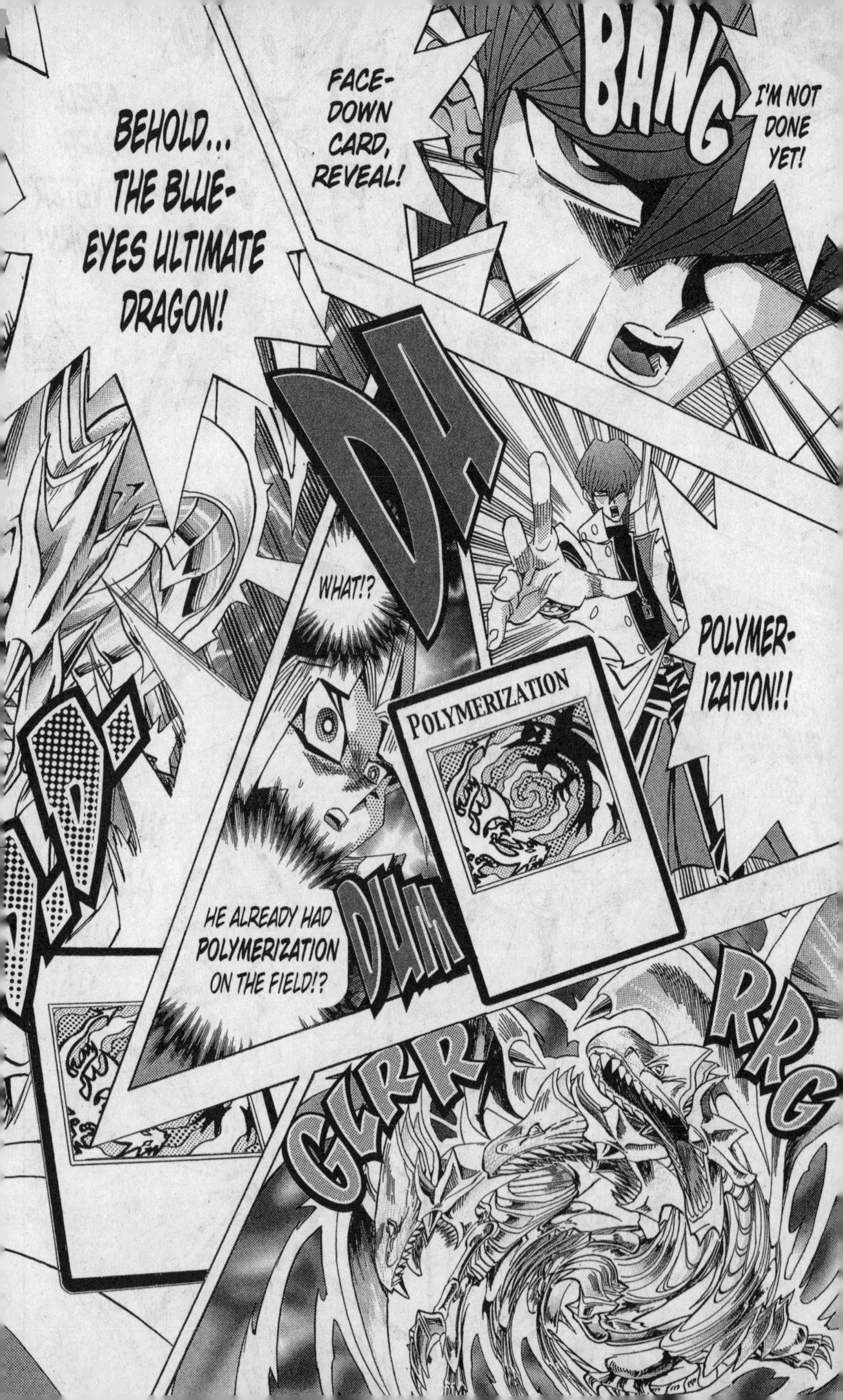
BANG
I'M NOT DONE YET!
FACE-DOWN CARD, REVEAL!
BEHOLD... THE BLUE-EYES ULTIMATE DRAGON!
DA
POLYMERIZATION!!
WHAT!?
POLYMERIZATION
DUN
HE ALREADY HAD POLYMERIZATION ON THE FIELD!?
RRRG
GLRR

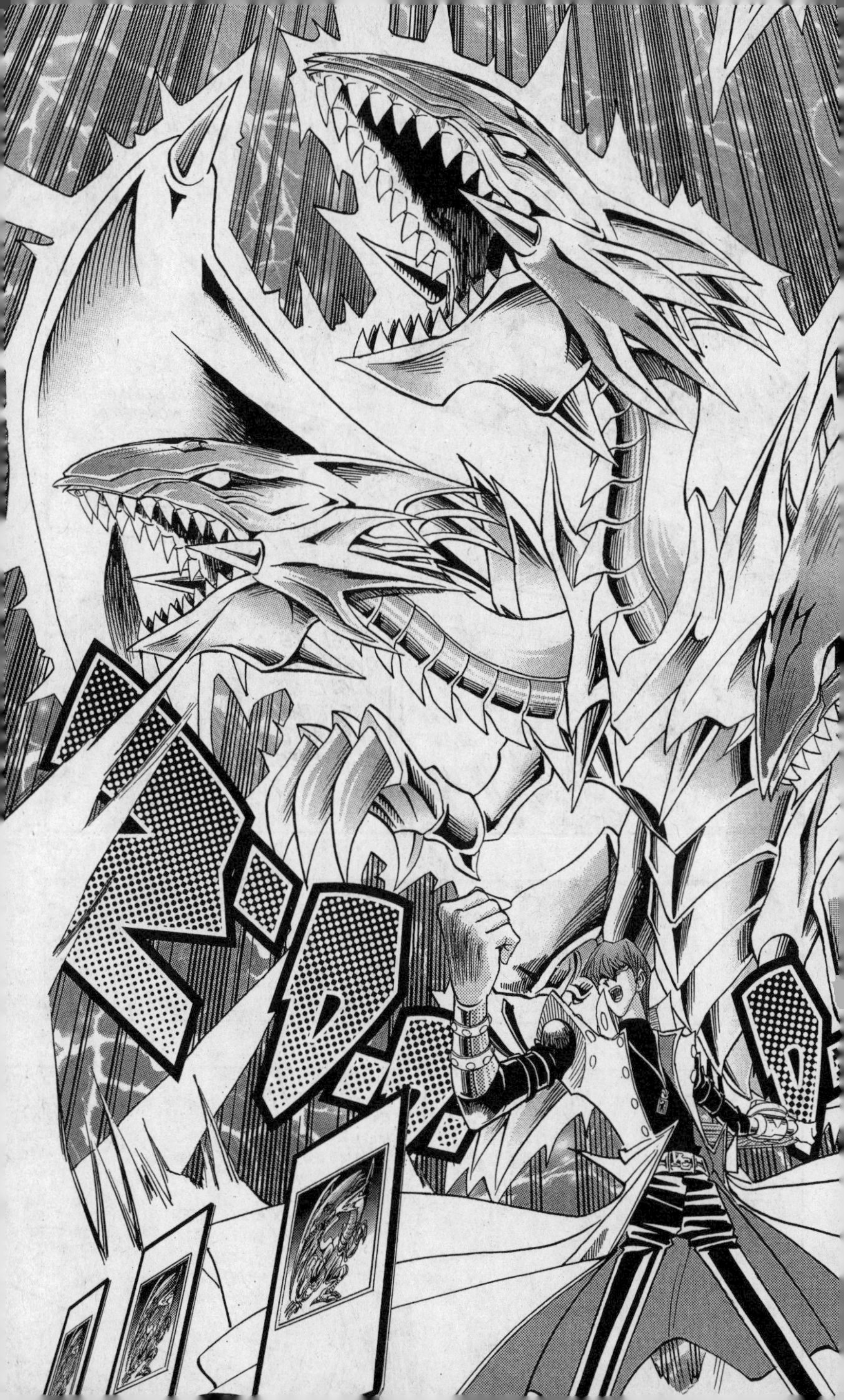

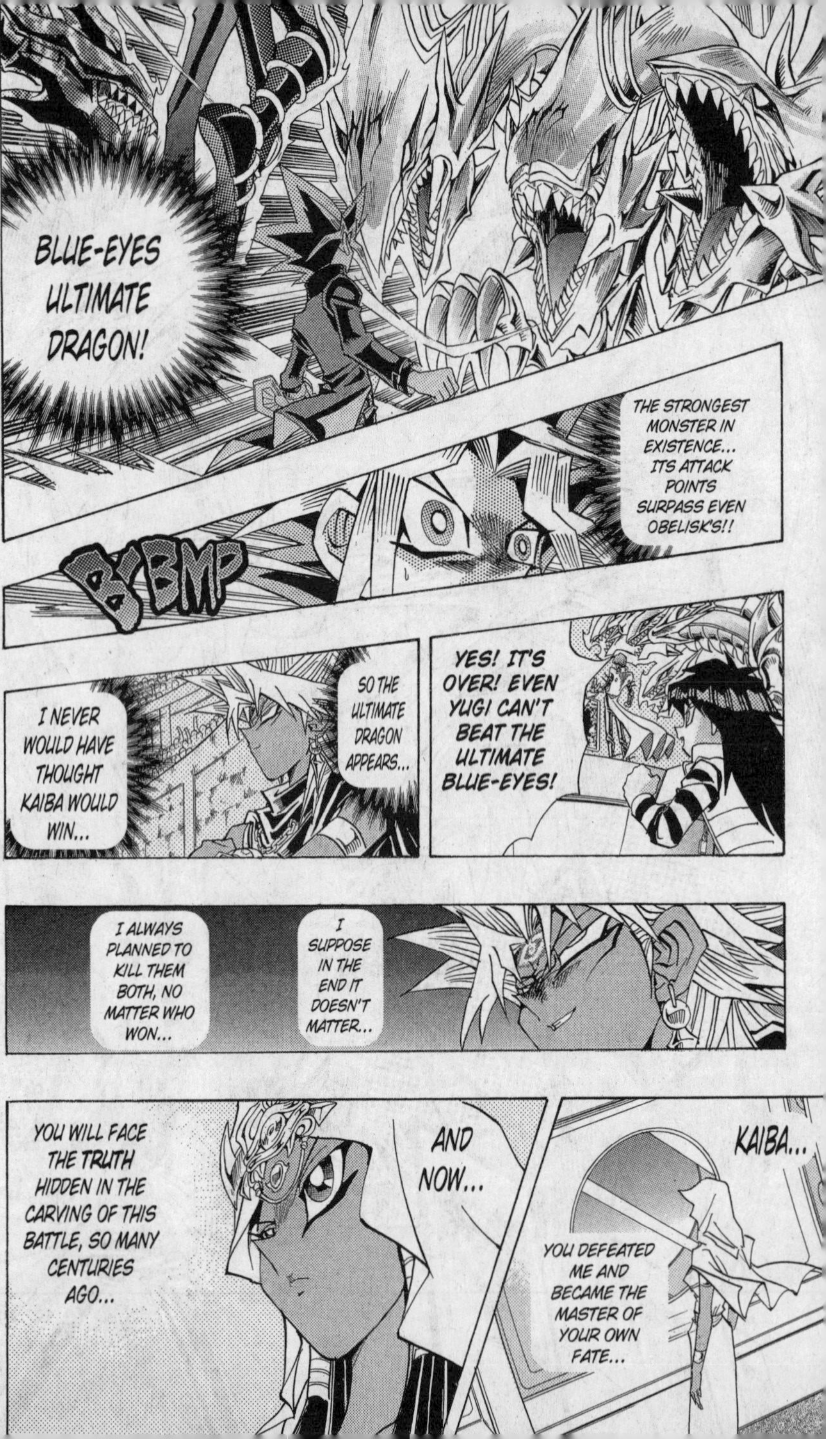
BLUE-EYES ULTIMATE DRAGON!
THE STRONGEST MONSTER IN EXISTENCE... ITS ATTACK POINTS SURPASS EVEN OBELISK'S!!
B'BMP
YES! IT'S OVER! EVEN YUGI CAN'T BEAT THE ULTIMATE BLUE-EYES!
SO THE ULTIMATE DRAGON APPEARS...
I NEVER WOULD HAVE THOUGHT KAIBA WOULD WIN...
I SUPPOSE IN THE END IT DOESN'T MATTER...
I ALWAYS PLANNED TO KILL THEM BOTH, NO MATTER WHO WON...
KAIBA...
YOU DEFEATED ME AND BECAME THE MASTER OF YOUR OWN FATE...
AND NOW...
YOU WILL FACE THE TRUTH HIDDEN IN THE CARVING OF THIS BATTLE, SO MANY CENTURIES AGO...

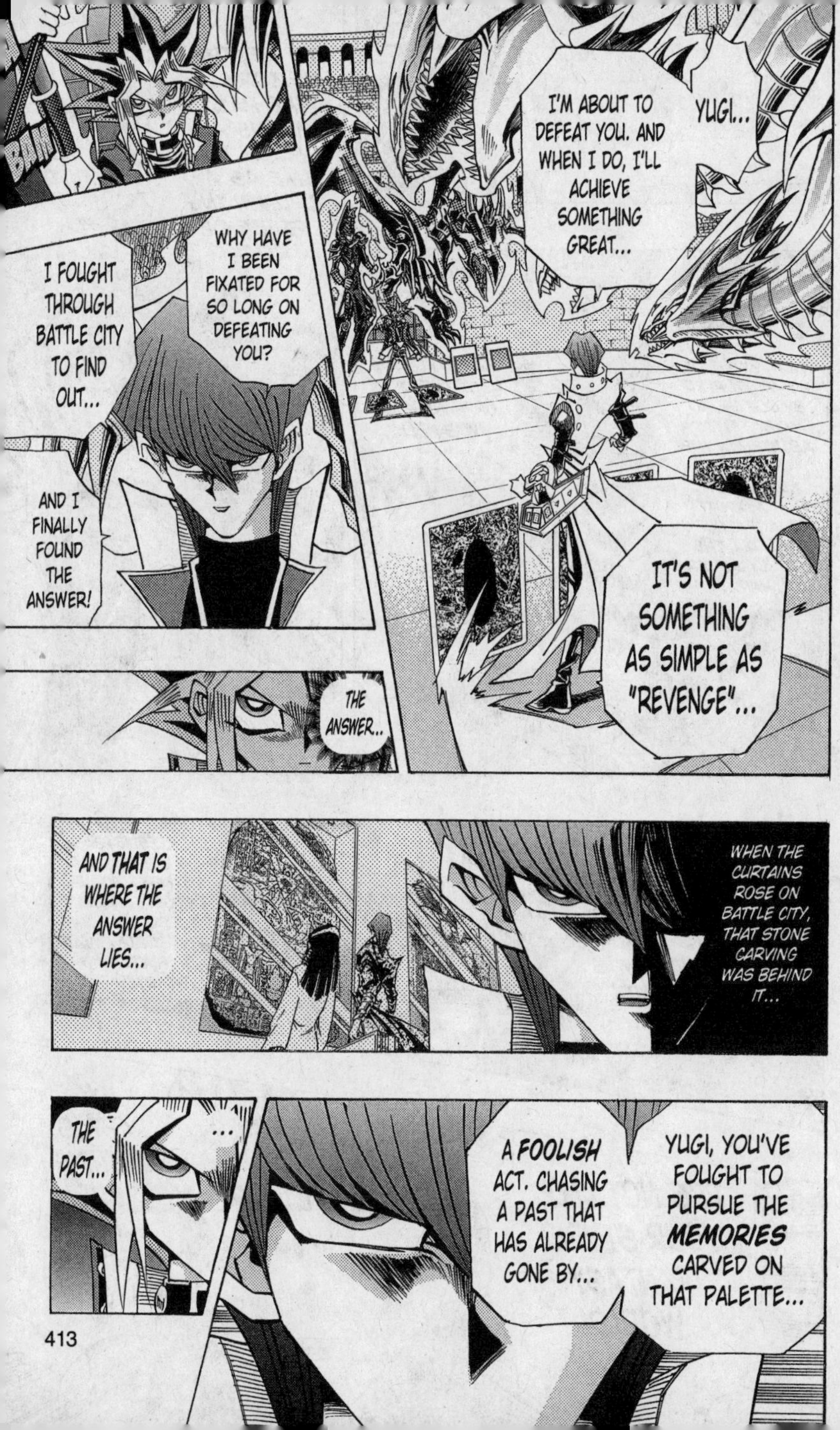
YUGI...
I'M ABOUT TO DEFEAT YOU. AND WHEN I DO, I'LL ACHIEVE SOMETHING GREAT...
IT'S NOT SOMETHING AS SIMPLE AS "REVENGE"...
BAM
WHY HAVE I BEEN FIXATED FOR SO LONG ON DEFEATING YOU?
I FOUGHT THROUGH BATTLE CITY TO FIND OUT...
AND I FINALLY FOUND THE ANSWER!
THE ANSWER...
WHEN THE CURTAINS ROSE ON BATTLE CITY, THAT STONE CARVING WAS BEHIND IT...
AND THAT IS WHERE THE ANSWER LIES...
YUGI, YOU'VE FOUGHT TO PURSUE THE *MEMORIES* CARVED ON THAT PALETTE...
A *FOOLISH* ACT. CHASING A PAST THAT HAS ALREADY GONE BY...
...
THE PAST...

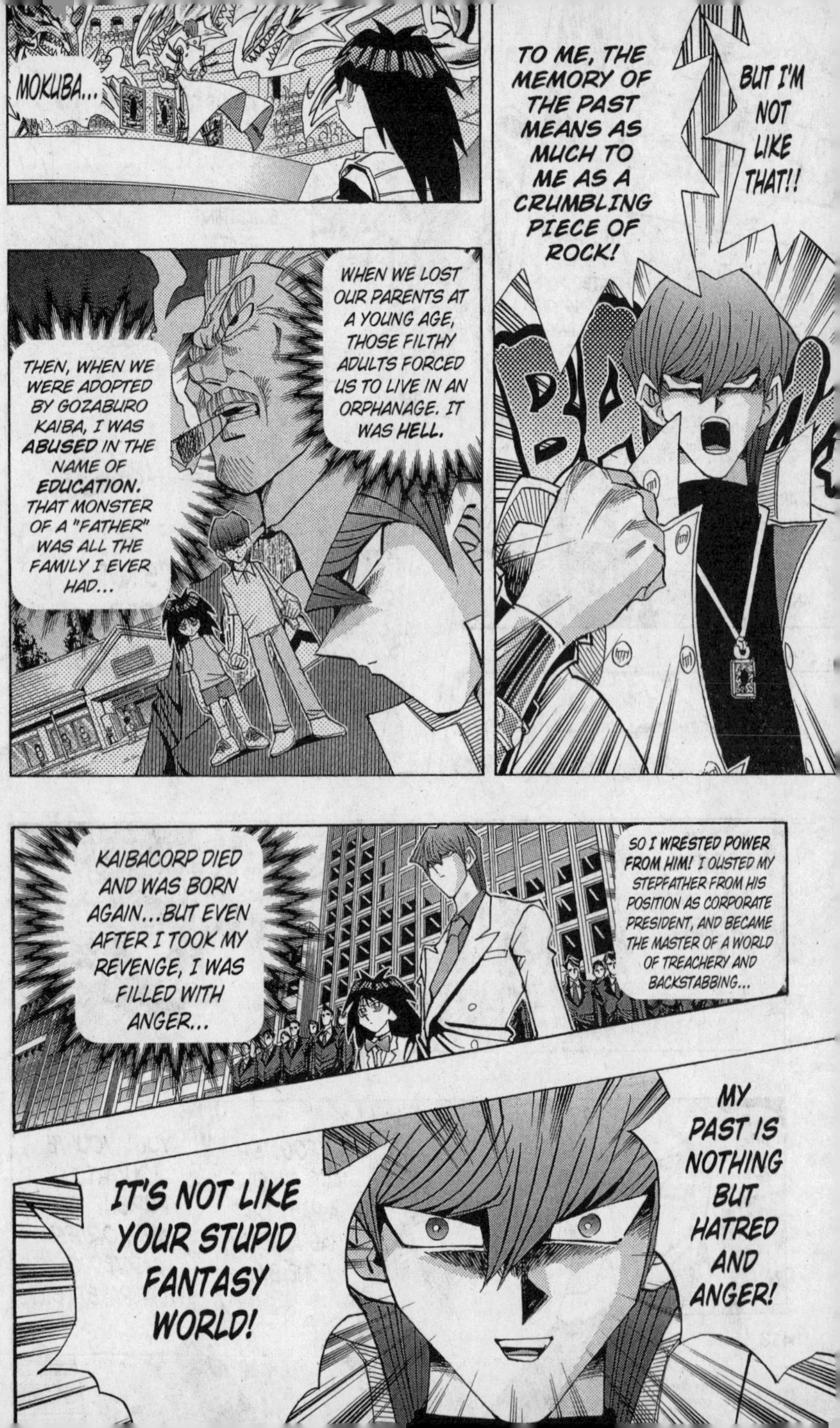

BUT I'M NOT LIKE THAT!!
TO ME, THE MEMORY OF THE PAST MEANS AS MUCH TO ME AS A CRUMBLING PIECE OF ROCK!
MOKUBA...
WHEN WE LOST OUR PARENTS AT A YOUNG AGE, THOSE FILTHY ADULTS FORCED US TO LIVE IN AN ORPHANAGE. IT WAS **HELL.**
THEN, WHEN WE WERE ADOPTED BY GOZABURO KAIBA, I WAS **ABUSED** IN THE NAME OF **EDUCATION.** THAT MONSTER OF A "FATHER" WAS ALL THE FAMILY I EVER HAD...
SO I WRESTED POWER FROM HIM! I OUSTED MY STEPFATHER FROM HIS POSITION AS CORPORATE PRESIDENT, AND BECAME THE MASTER OF A WORLD OF TREACHERY AND BACKSTABBING...
KAIBACORP DIED AND WAS BORN AGAIN...BUT EVEN AFTER I TOOK MY REVENGE, I WAS FILLED WITH ANGER...
MY PAST IS NOTHING BUT HATRED AND ANGER!
IT'S NOT LIKE YOUR STUPID FANTASY WORLD!

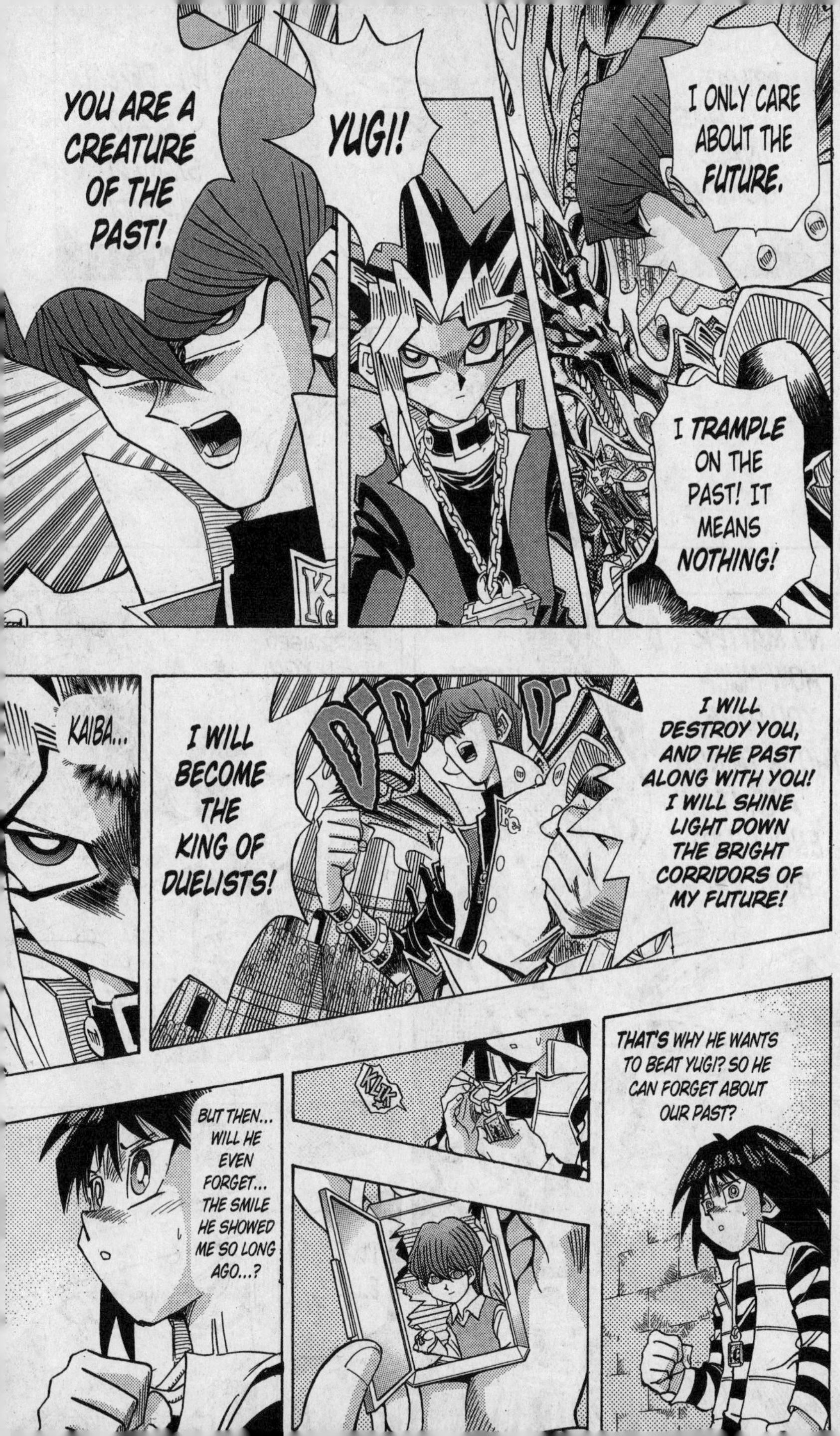

I ONLY CARE ABOUT THE FUTURE.
I TRAMPLE ON THE PAST! IT MEANS NOTHING!
YUGI!
YOU ARE A CREATURE OF THE PAST!
I WILL DESTROY YOU, AND THE PAST ALONG WITH YOU! I WILL SHINE LIGHT DOWN THE BRIGHT CORRIDORS OF MY FUTURE!
I WILL BECOME THE KING OF DUELISTS!
KAIBA...
THAT'S WHY HE WANTS TO BEAT YUGI? SO HE CAN FORGET ABOUT OUR PAST?
KLIK
BUT THEN... WILL HE EVEN FORGET... THE SMILE HE SHOWED ME SO LONG AGO...?

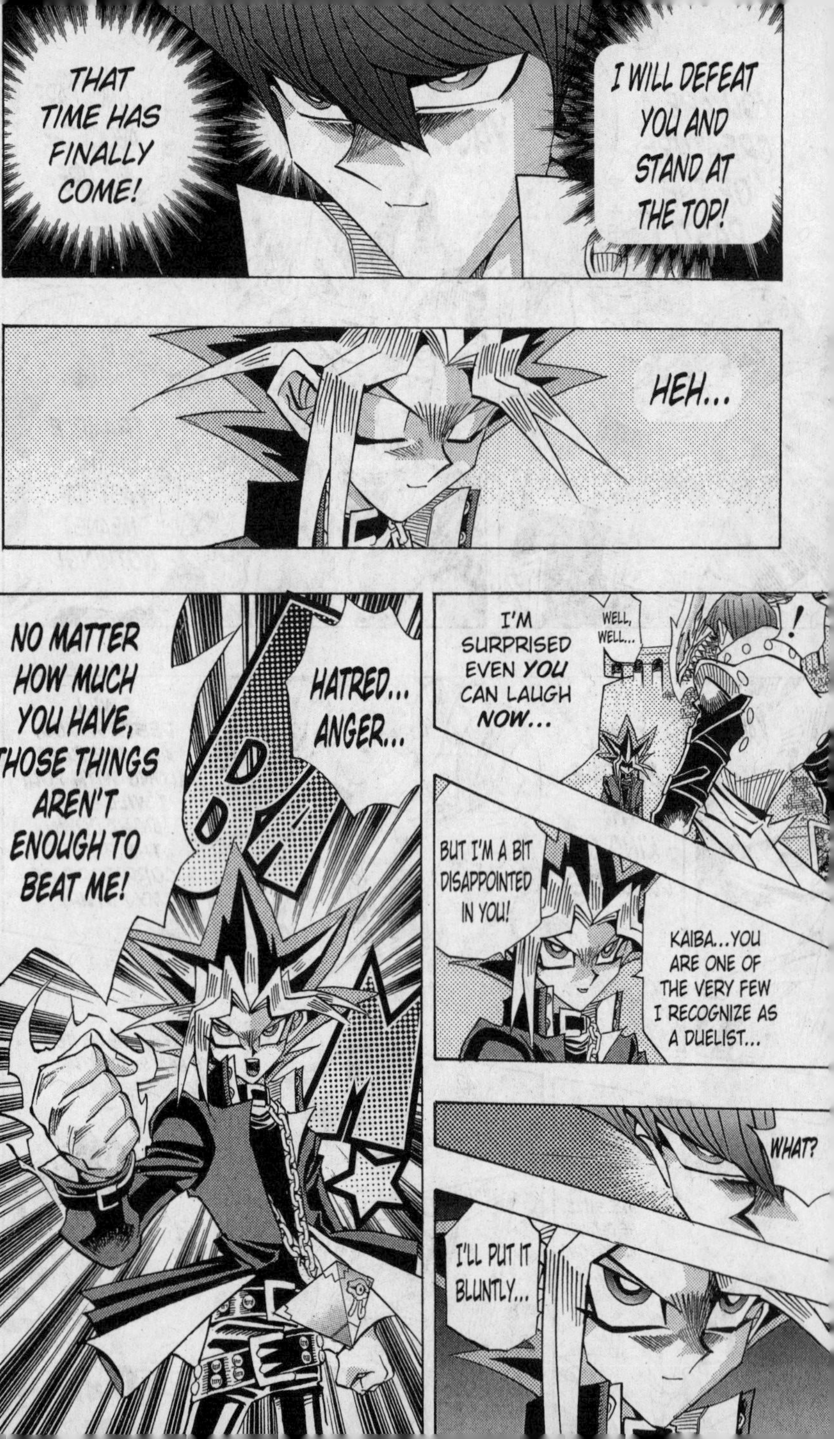
I WILL DEFEAT YOU AND STAND AT THE TOP!
THAT TIME HAS FINALLY COME!
HEH...
WELL, WELL...
!
I'M SURPRISED EVEN YOU CAN LAUGH NOW...
KAIBA...YOU ARE ONE OF THE VERY FEW I RECOGNIZE AS A DUELIST...
BUT I'M A BIT DISAPPOINTED IN YOU!
WHAT?
I'LL PUT IT BLUNTLY...
HATRED... ANGER...
NO MATTER HOW MUCH YOU HAVE, THOSE THINGS AREN'T ENOUGH TO BEAT ME!

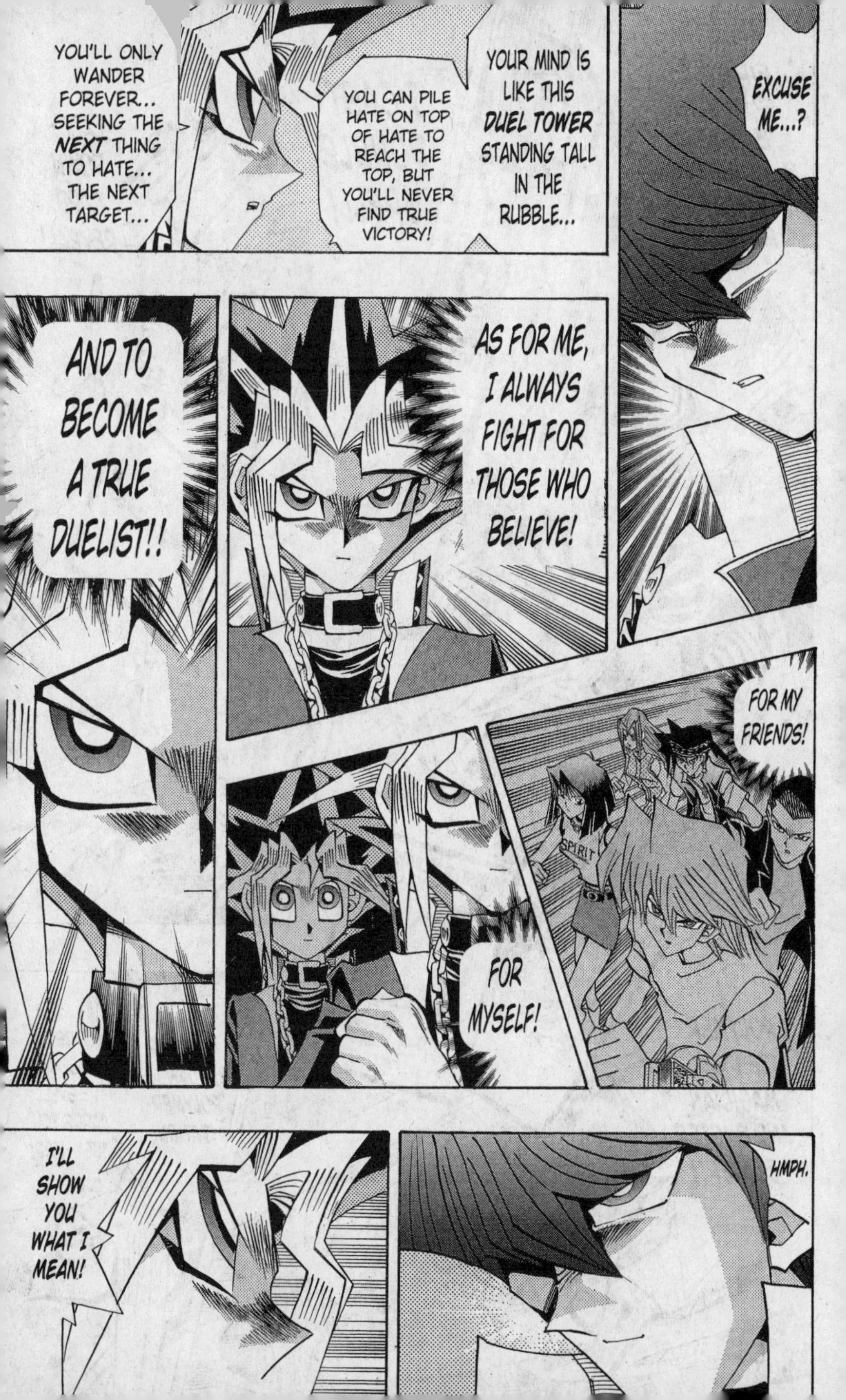
YOUR MIND IS LIKE THIS DUEL TOWER STANDING TALL IN THE RUBBLE...
YOU CAN PILE HATE ON TOP OF HATE TO REACH THE TOP, BUT YOU'LL NEVER FIND TRUE VICTORY!
YOU'LL ONLY WANDER FOREVER... SEEKING THE NEXT THING TO HATE... THE NEXT TARGET...
EXCUSE ME...?
AS FOR ME, I ALWAYS FIGHT FOR THOSE WHO BELIEVE!
FOR MY FRIENDS!
SPIRIT
FOR MYSELF!
AND TO BECOME A TRUE DUELIST!!
HMPH.
I'LL SHOW YOU WHAT I MEAN!

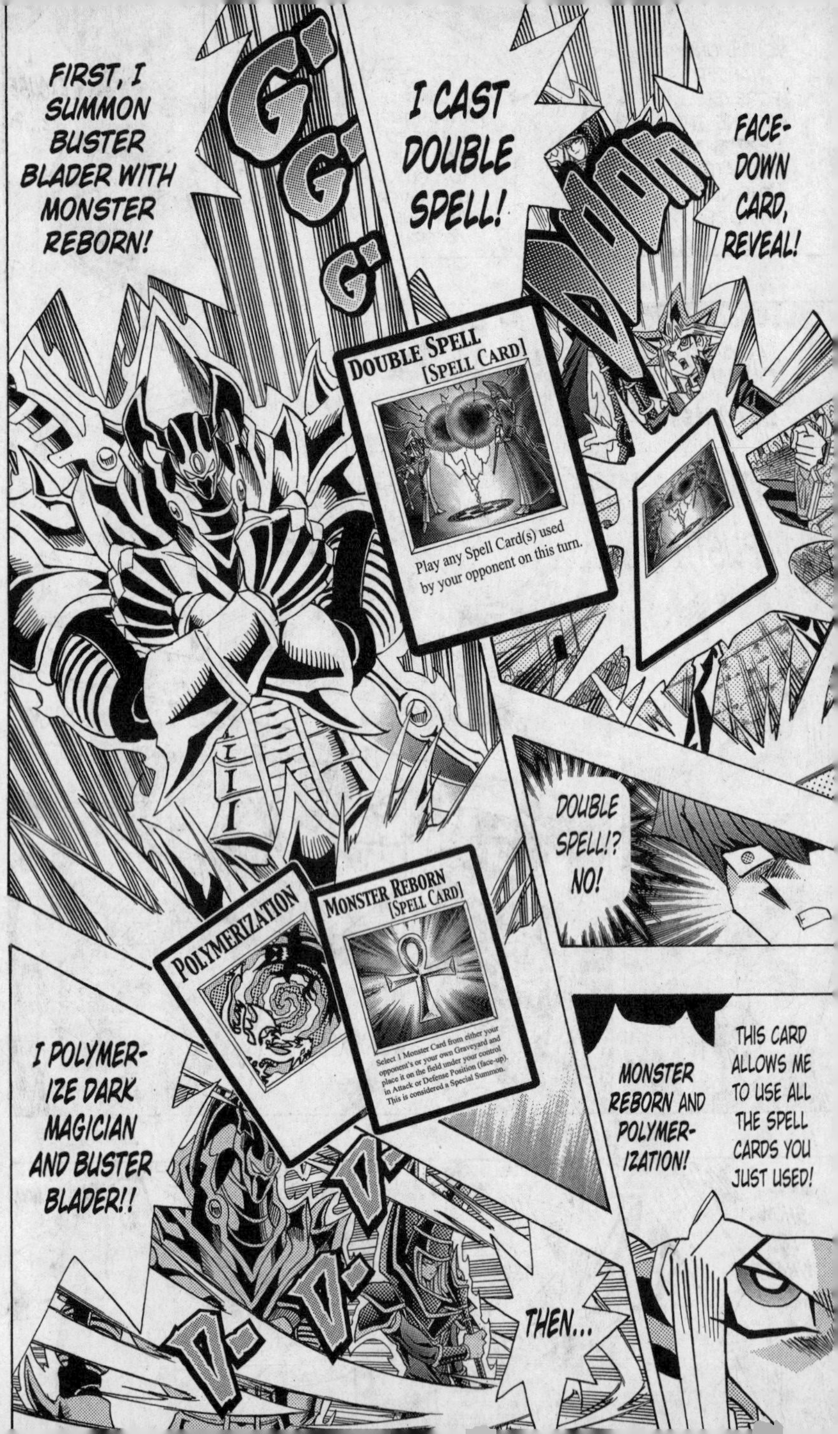
FACE-DOWN CARD, REVEAL!
I CAST DOUBLE SPELL!
FIRST, I SUMMON BUSTER BLADER WITH MONSTER REBORN!
DOUBLE SPELL [SPELL CARD]
Play any Spell Card(s) used by your opponent on this turn.
DOUBLE SPELL!? NO!
THIS CARD ALLOWS ME TO USE ALL THE SPELL CARDS YOU JUST USED!
MONSTER REBORN AND POLYMERIZATION!
THEN...
MONSTER REBORN [SPELL CARD]
Select 1 Monster Card from either your opponent's or your own Graveyard and place it on the field under your control in Attack or Defense Position (face-up). This is considered a Special Summon.
POLYMERIZATION
I POLYMERIZE DARK MAGICIAN AND BUSTER BLADER!!

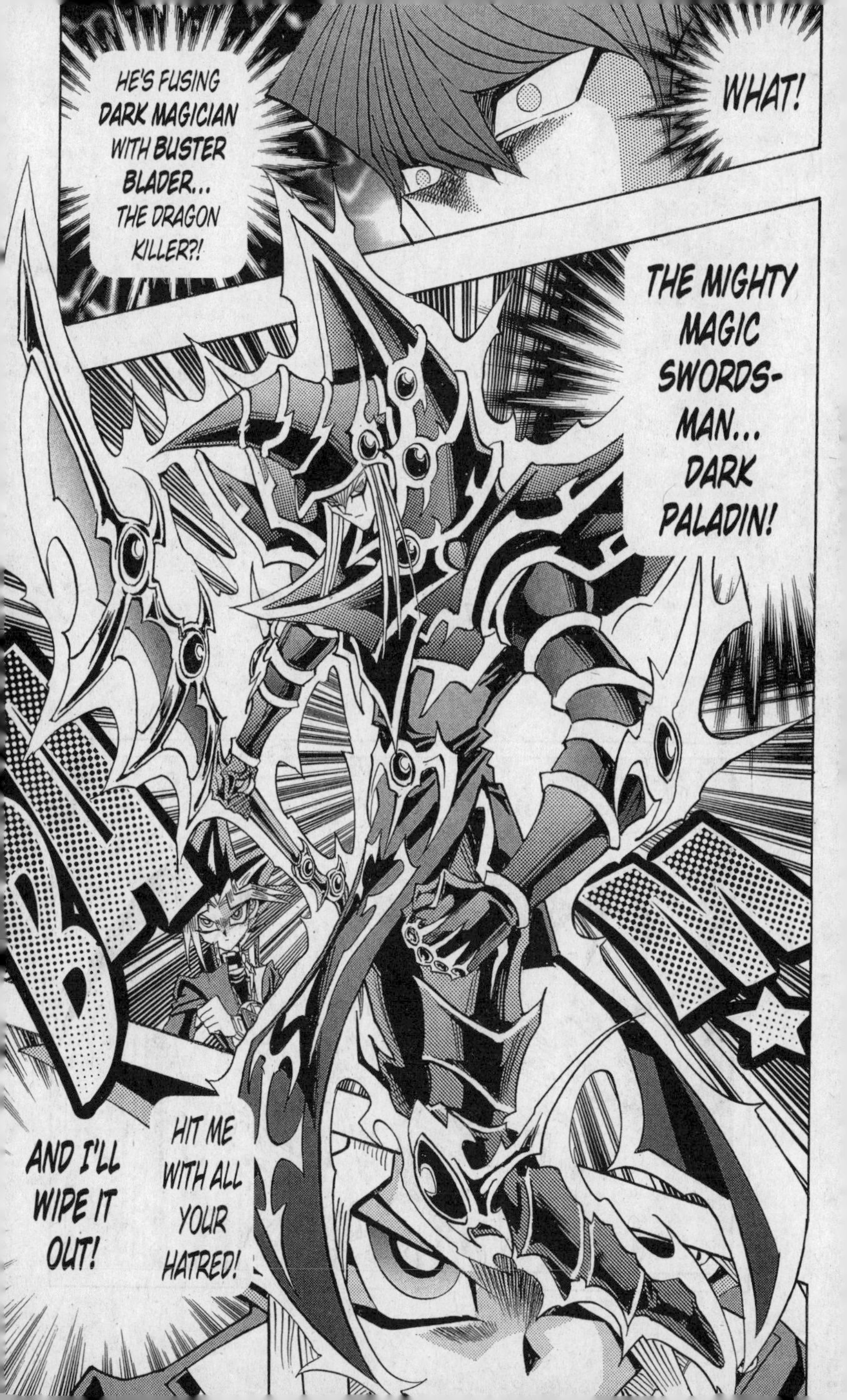
WHAT!
HE'S FUSING DARK MAGICIAN WITH BUSTER BLADER... THE DRAGON KILLER?!
THE MIGHTY MAGIC SWORDS-MAN... DARK PALADIN!
HIT ME WITH ALL YOUR HATRED!
AND I'LL WIPE IT OUT!

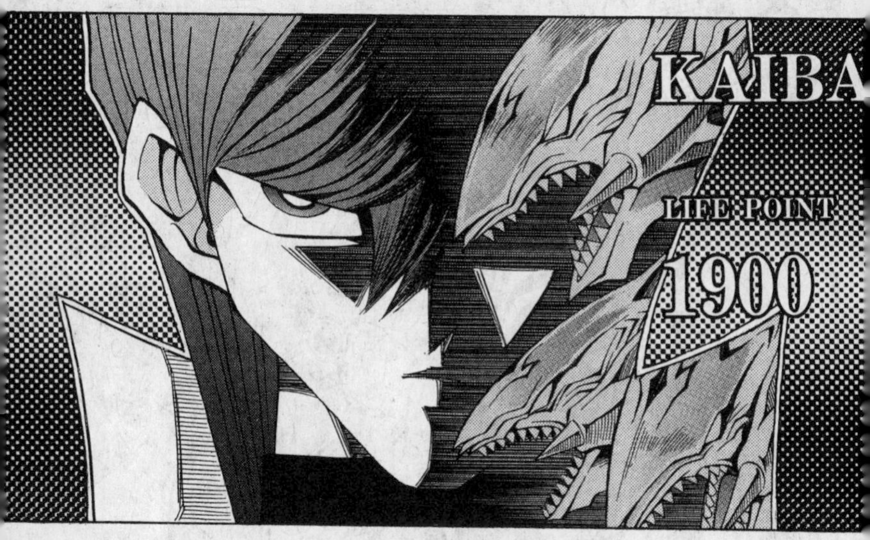
KAIBA
LIFE POINT
1900

DUEL 262: AS A FRIEND

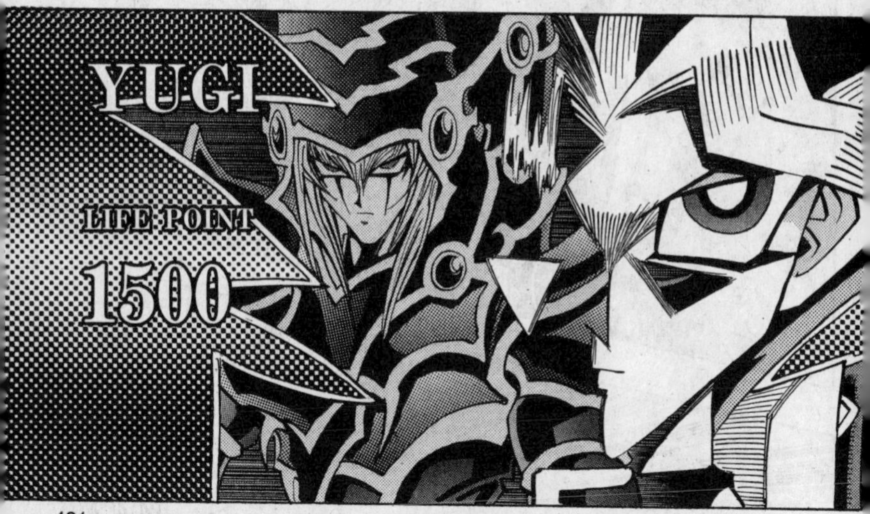
YUGI
LIFE POINT
1500

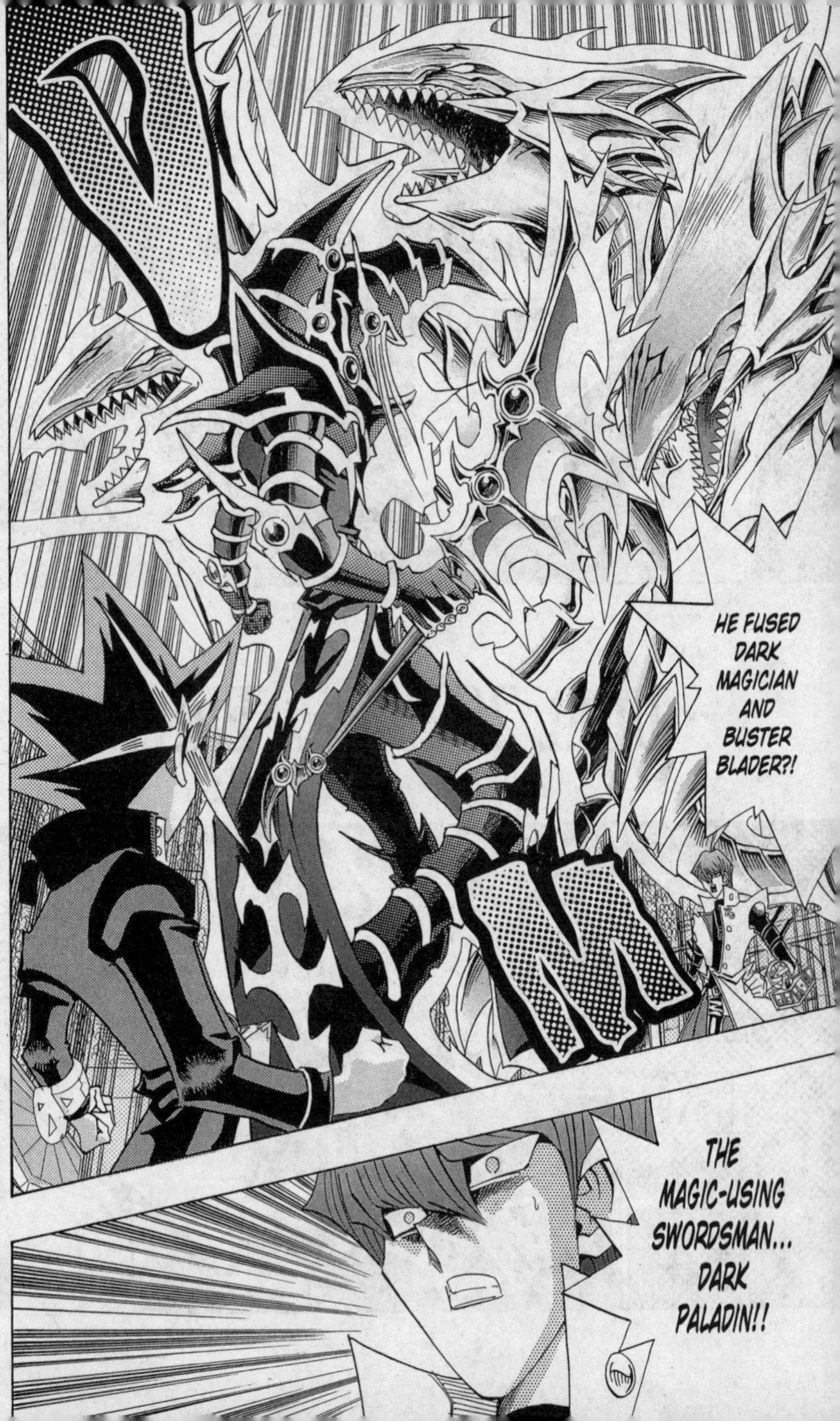

HE FUSED DARK MAGICIAN AND BUSTER BLADER?!
THE MAGIC-USING SWORDSMAN... DARK PALADIN!!

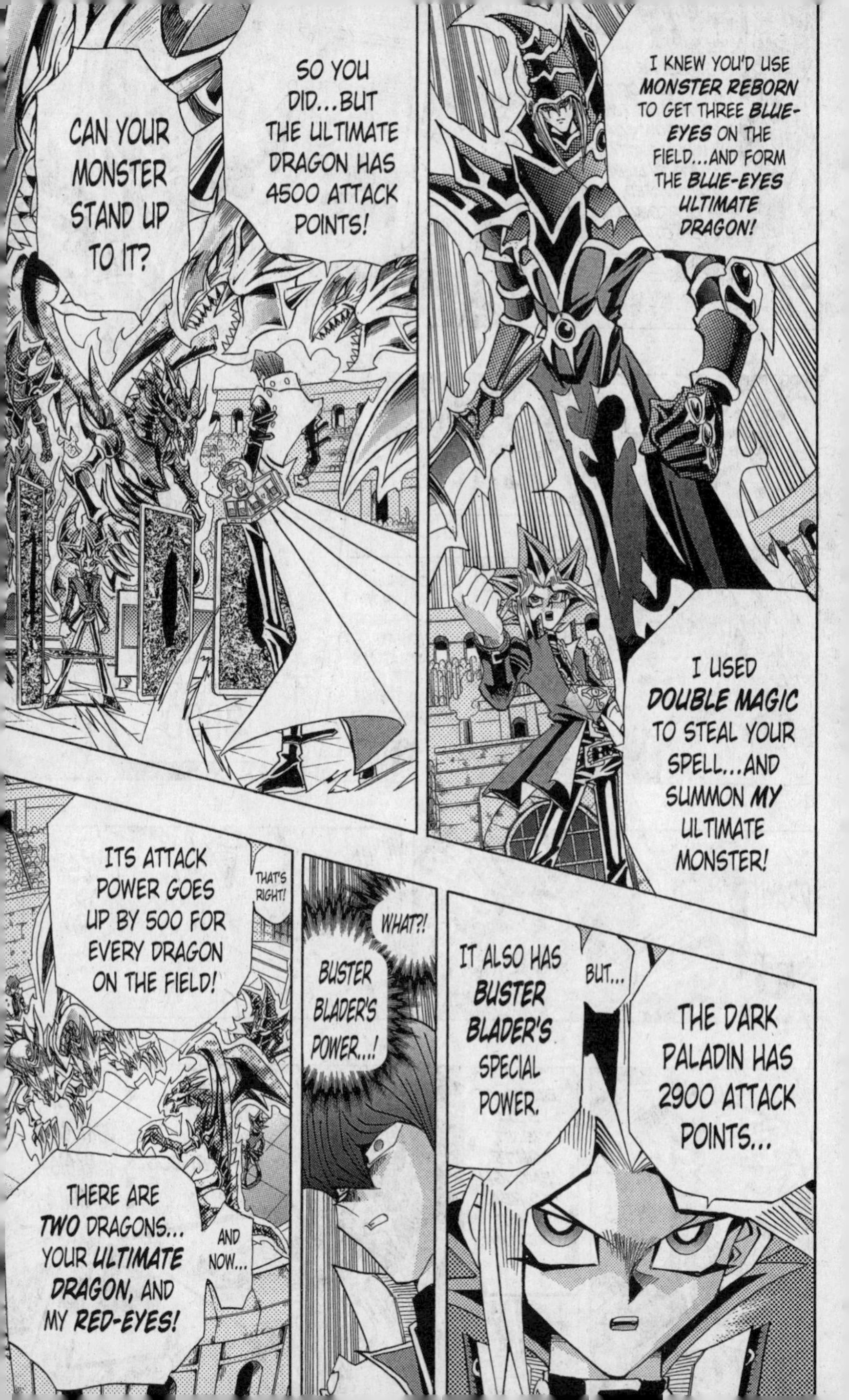
I KNEW YOU'D USE MONSTER REBORN TO GET THREE BLUE-EYES ON THE FIELD...AND FORM THE BLUE-EYES ULTIMATE DRAGON!
I USED DOUBLE MAGIC TO STEAL YOUR SPELL...AND SUMMON MY ULTIMATE MONSTER!
SO YOU DID...BUT THE ULTIMATE DRAGON HAS 4500 ATTACK POINTS!
CAN YOUR MONSTER STAND UP TO IT?
THE DARK PALADIN HAS 2900 ATTACK POINTS...
BUT...
IT ALSO HAS BUSTER BLADER'S SPECIAL POWER.
WHAT?!
BUSTER BLADER'S POWER...!
THAT'S RIGHT!
ITS ATTACK POWER GOES UP BY 500 FOR EVERY DRAGON ON THE FIELD!
AND NOW...
THERE ARE TWO DRAGONS... YOUR ULTIMATE DRAGON, AND MY RED-EYES!

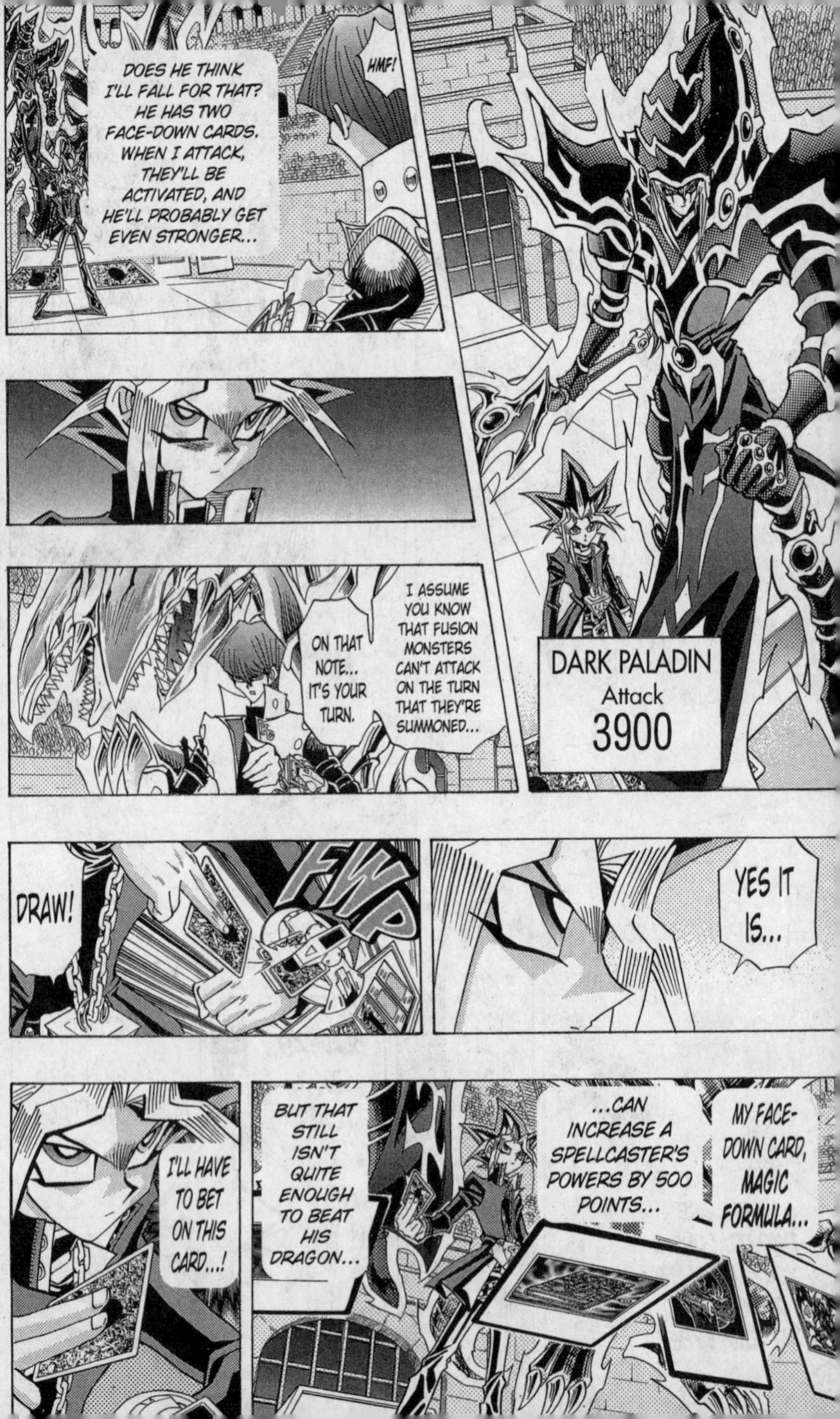
DARK PALADIN
Attack
3900
HMF!
DOES HE THINK I'LL FALL FOR THAT? HE HAS TWO FACE-DOWN CARDS. WHEN I ATTACK, THEY'LL BE ACTIVATED, AND HE'LL PROBABLY GET EVEN STRONGER...
I ASSUME YOU KNOW THAT FUSION MONSTERS CAN'T ATTACK ON THE TURN THAT THEY'RE SUMMONED...
ON THAT NOTE... IT'S YOUR TURN.
YES IT IS...
FWP
DRAW!
MY FACE-DOWN CARD, MAGIC FORMULA...
...CAN INCREASE A SPELLCASTER'S POWERS BY 500 POINTS...
BUT THAT STILL ISN'T QUITE ENOUGH TO BEAT HIS DRAGON...
I'LL HAVE TO BET ON THIS CARD...!

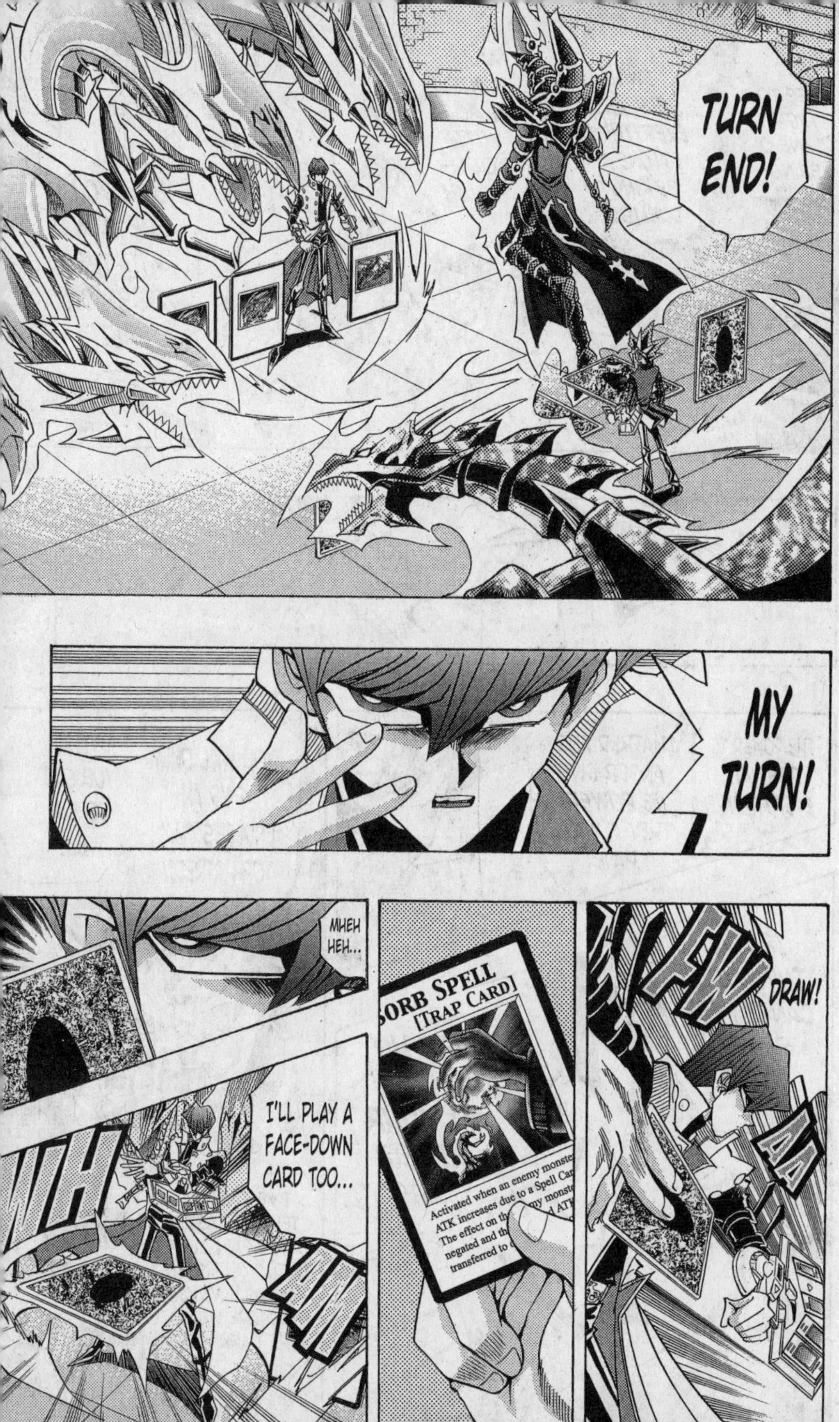

TURN END!
MY TURN!
DRAW!
SORB SPELL
[TRAP CARD]
Activated when an enemy monste
ATK increases due to a Spell Ca
MHEH HEH...
I'LL PLAY A FACE-DOWN CARD TOO...

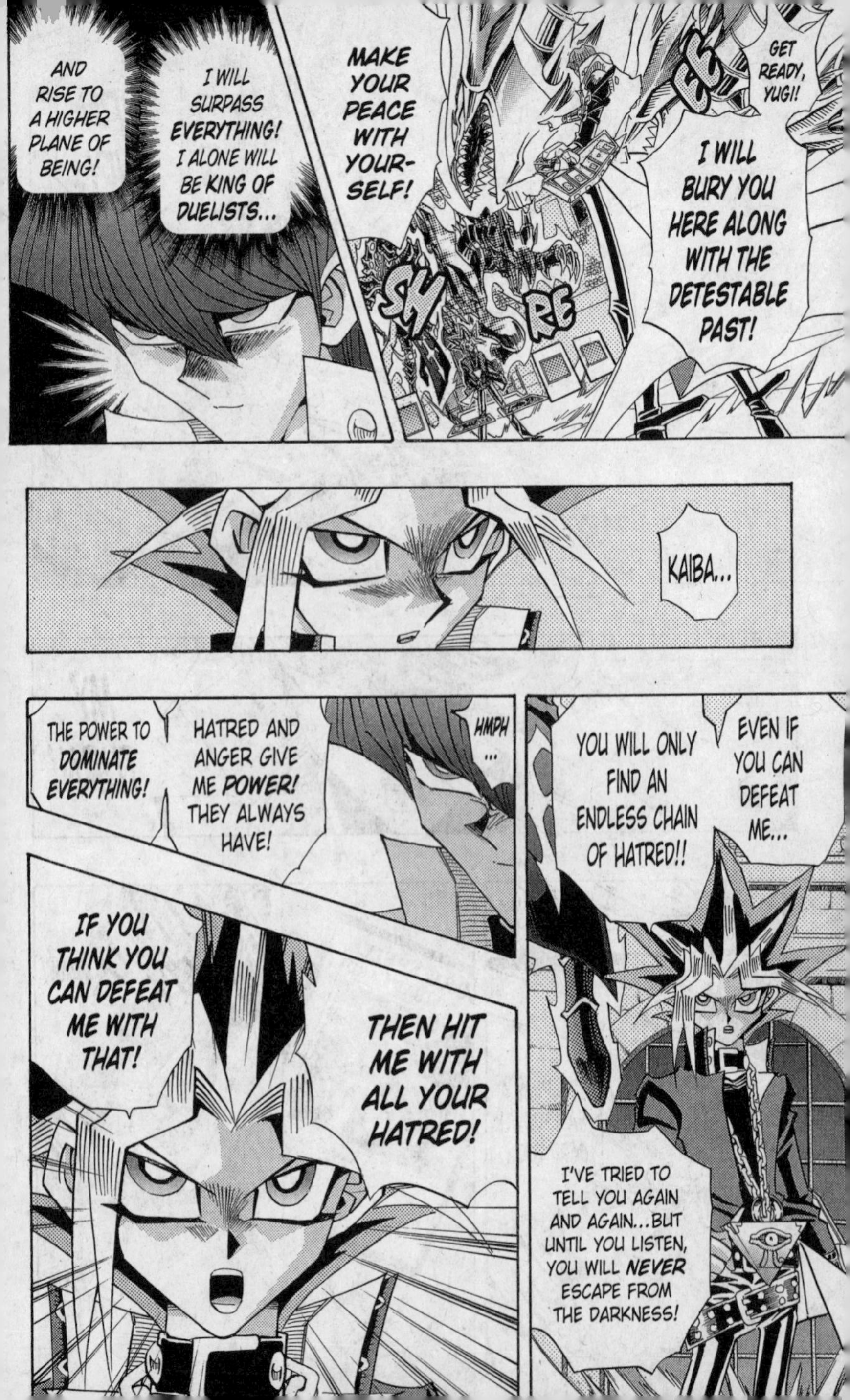
GET READY, YUGI!!
I WILL BURY YOU HERE ALONG WITH THE DETESTABLE PAST!
MAKE YOUR PEACE WITH YOURSELF!
I WILL SURPASS EVERYTHING! I ALONE WILL BE KING OF DUELISTS...
AND RISE TO A HIGHER PLANE OF BEING!
KAIBA...
EVEN IF YOU CAN DEFEAT ME...
YOU WILL ONLY FIND AN ENDLESS CHAIN OF HATRED!!
I'VE TRIED TO TELL YOU AGAIN AND AGAIN...BUT UNTIL YOU LISTEN, YOU WILL NEVER ESCAPE FROM THE DARKNESS!
HMPH...
HATRED AND ANGER GIVE ME POWER! THEY ALWAYS HAVE!
THE POWER TO DOMINATE EVERYTHING!
THEN HIT ME WITH ALL YOUR HATRED!
IF YOU THINK YOU CAN DEFEAT ME WITH THAT!

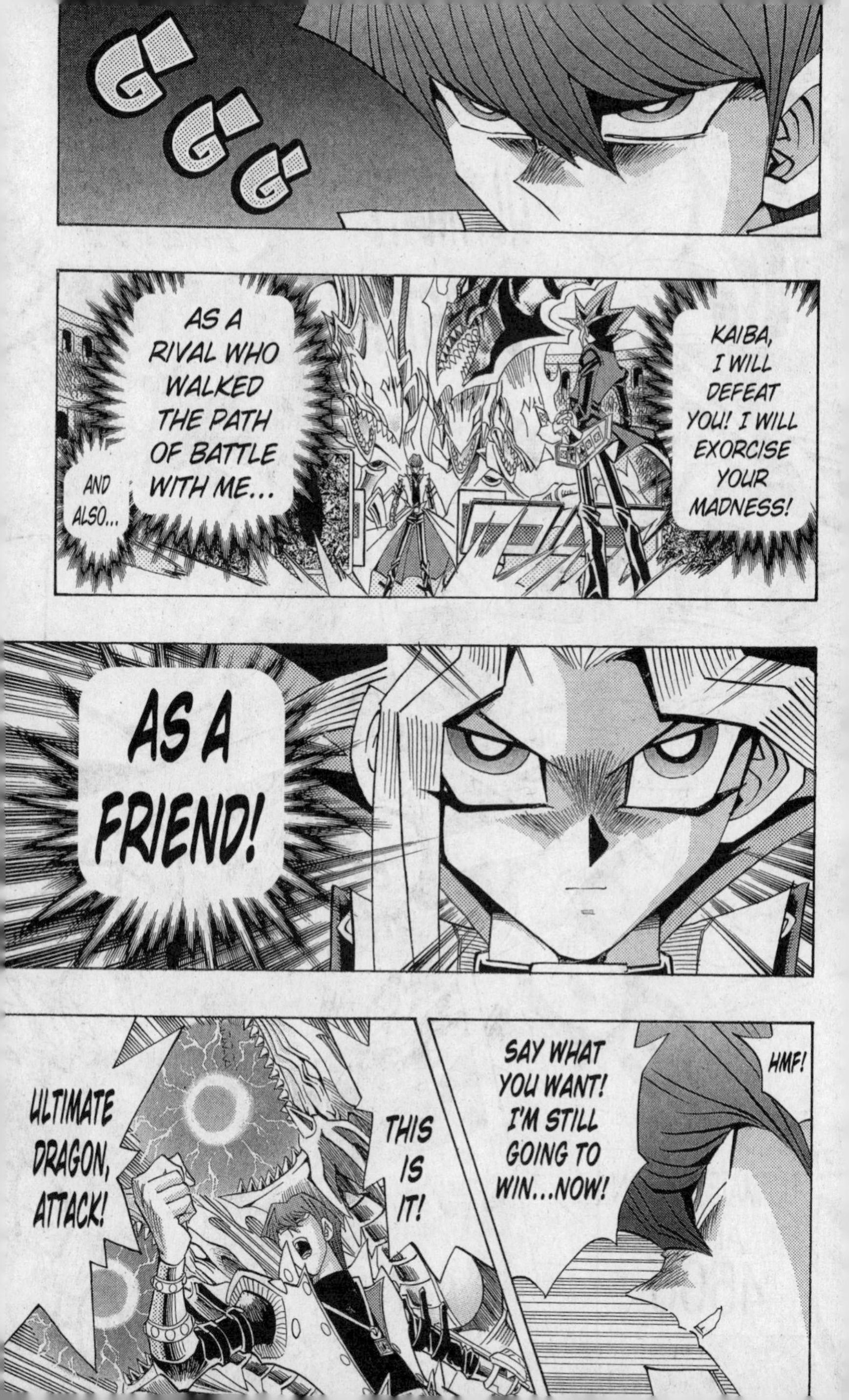
GGG
KAIBA, I WILL DEFEAT YOU! I WILL EXORCISE YOUR MADNESS!
AS A RIVAL WHO WALKED THE PATH OF BATTLE WITH ME...
AND ALSO...
AS A FRIEND!
HMF!
SAY WHAT YOU WANT! I'M STILL GOING TO WIN...NOW!
THIS IS IT!
ULTIMATE DRAGON, ATTACK!

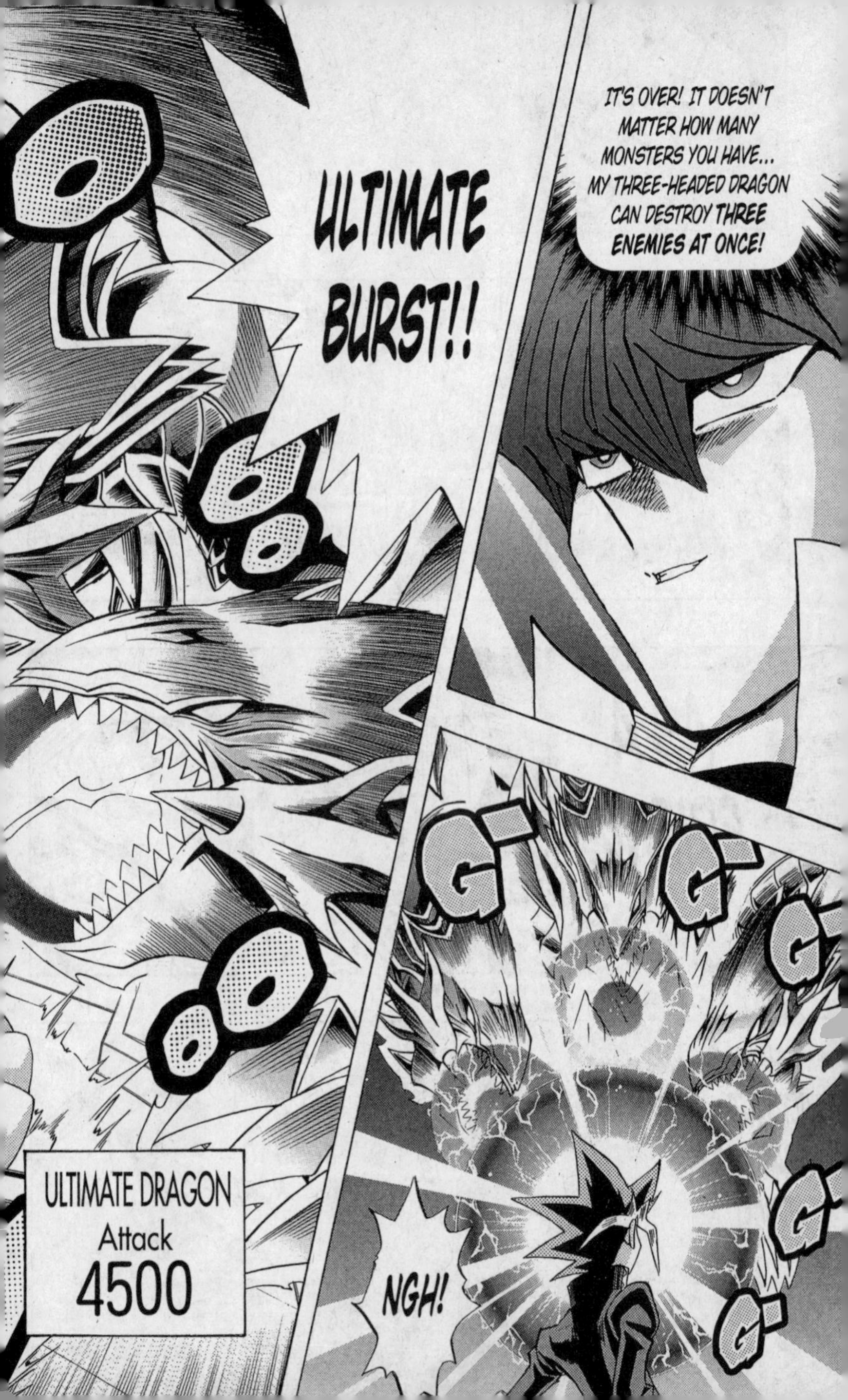
IT'S OVER! IT DOESN'T MATTER HOW MANY MONSTERS YOU HAVE... MY THREE-HEADED DRAGON CAN DESTROY THREE ENEMIES AT ONCE!
G
G
G
G
G
NGH!
ULTIMATE BURST!!
ULTIMATE DRAGON
Attack
4500

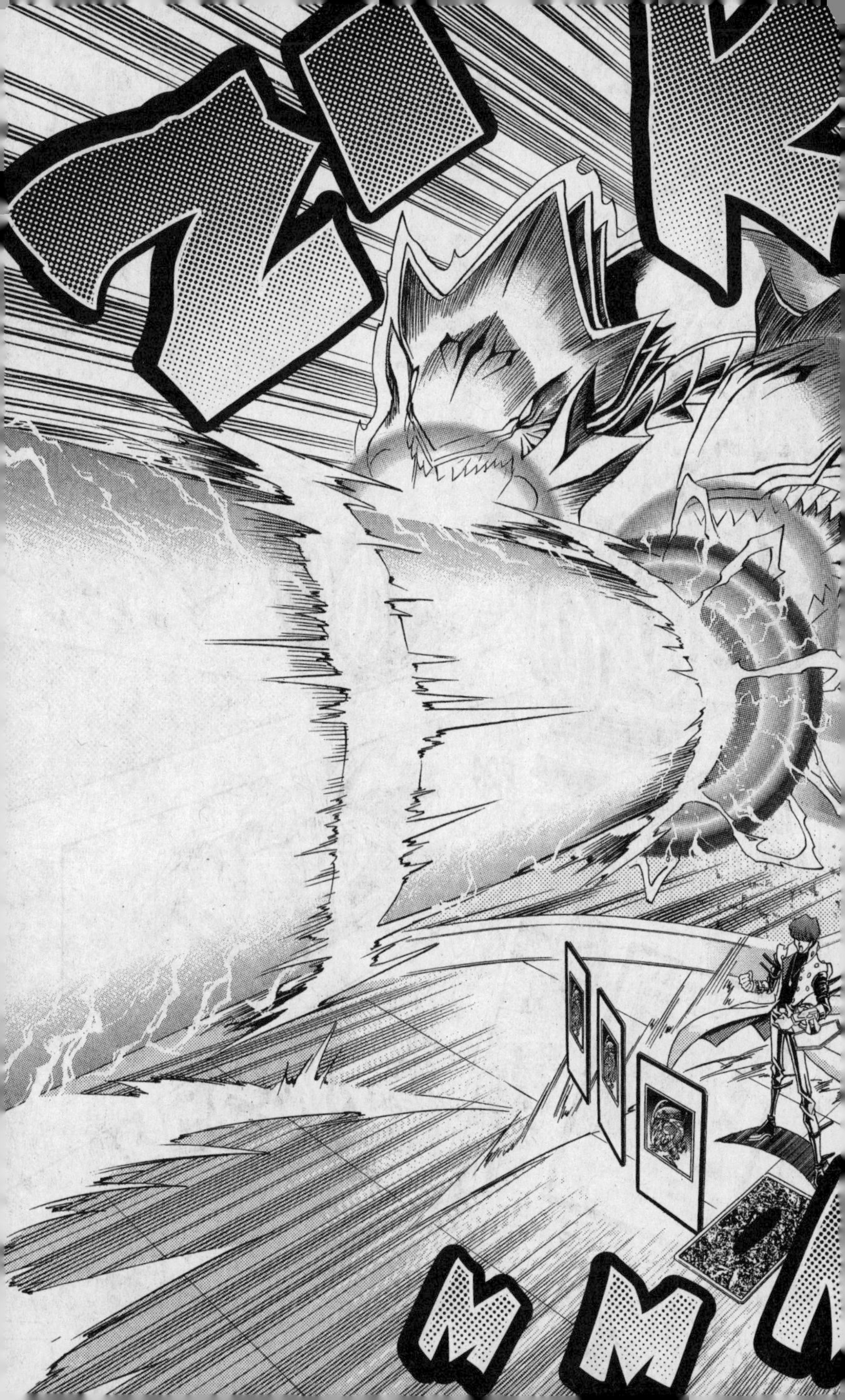

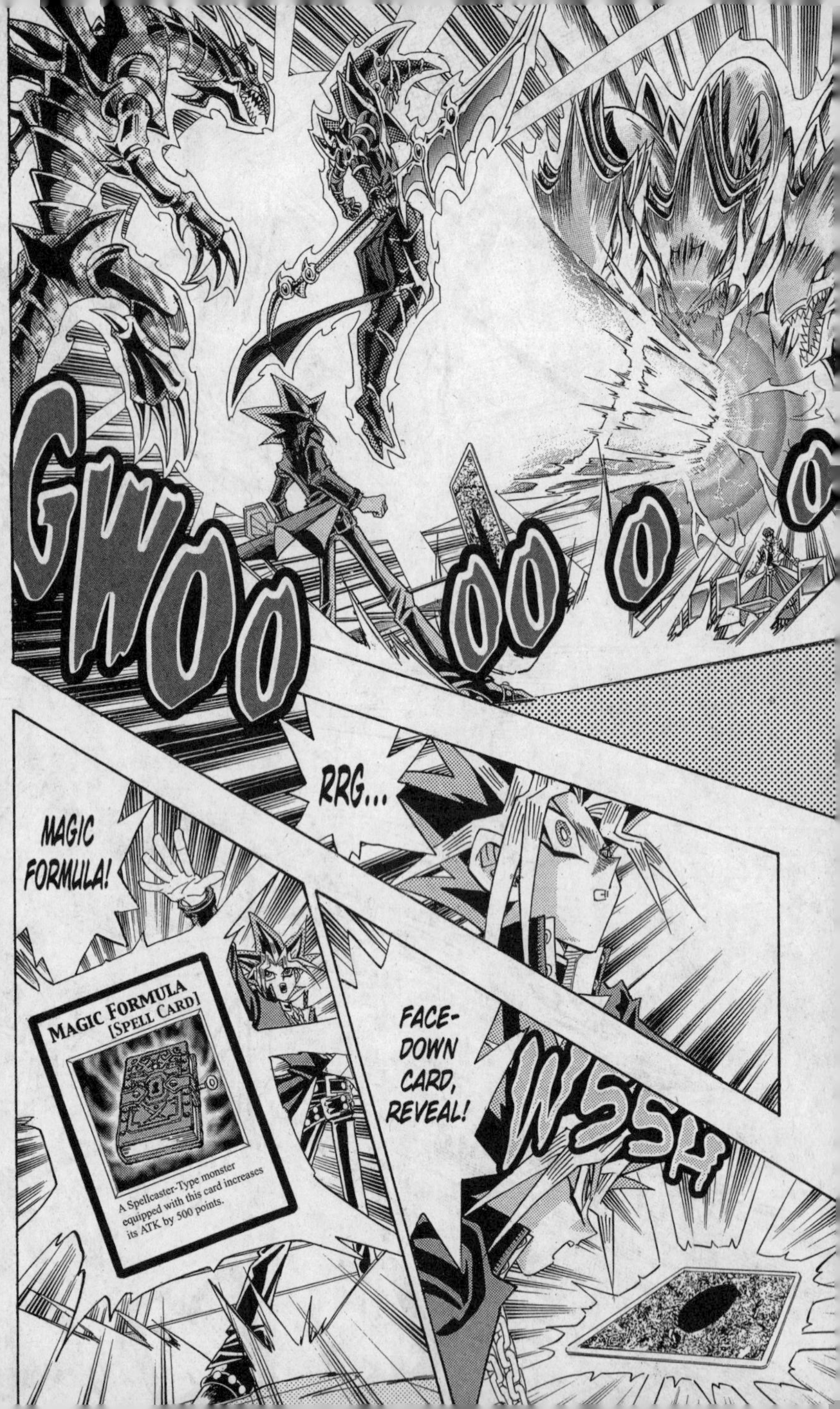
GHOOOOOOO
RRG...
FACE-DOWN CARD, REVEAL!
WSSH
MAGIC FORMULA!
MAGIC FORMULA
[SPELL CARD]
A Spellcaster-Type monster equipped with this card increases its ATK by 500 points.

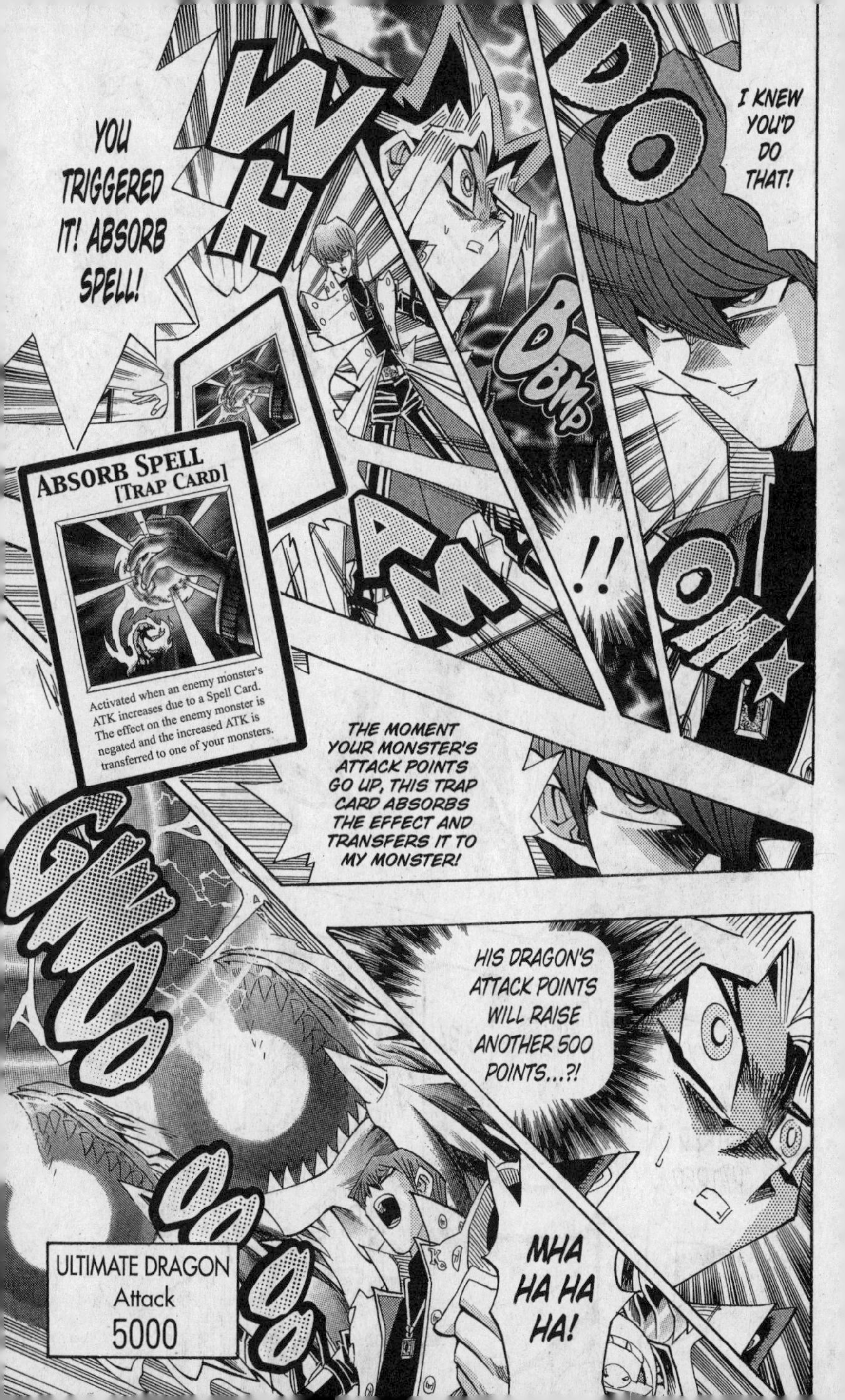
I KNEW YOU'D DO THAT!
!!
WHAM
YOU TRIGGERED IT! ABSORB SPELL!
ABSORB SPELL [TRAP CARD]
Activated when an enemy monster's ATK increases due to a Spell Card. The effect on the enemy monster is negated and the increased ATK is transferred to one of your monsters.
THE MOMENT YOUR MONSTER'S ATTACK POINTS GO UP, THIS TRAP CARD ABSORBS THE EFFECT AND TRANSFERS IT TO MY MONSTER!
HIS DRAGON'S ATTACK POINTS WILL RAISE ANOTHER 500 POINTS...?!
MHA HA HA HA!
ULTIMATE DRAGON
Attack
5000

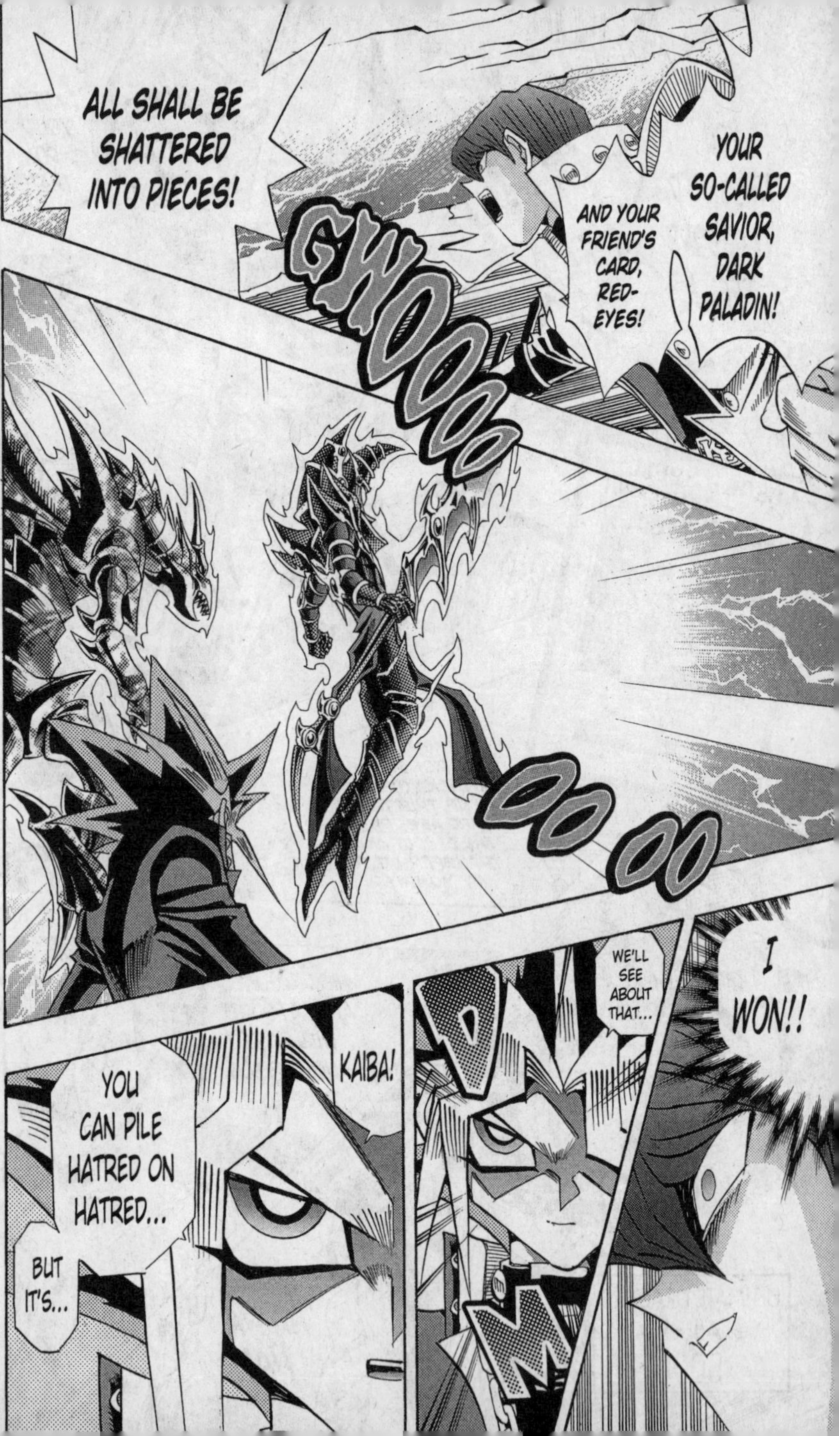
YOUR SO-CALLED SAVIOR, DARK PALADIN!
AND YOUR FRIEND'S CARD, RED-EYES!
ALL SHALL BE SHATTERED INTO PIECES!
GWOOOOO
OO OO
I WON!!
WE'LL SEE ABOUT THAT...
KAIBA!
YOU CAN PILE HATRED ON HATRED...
BUT IT'S...

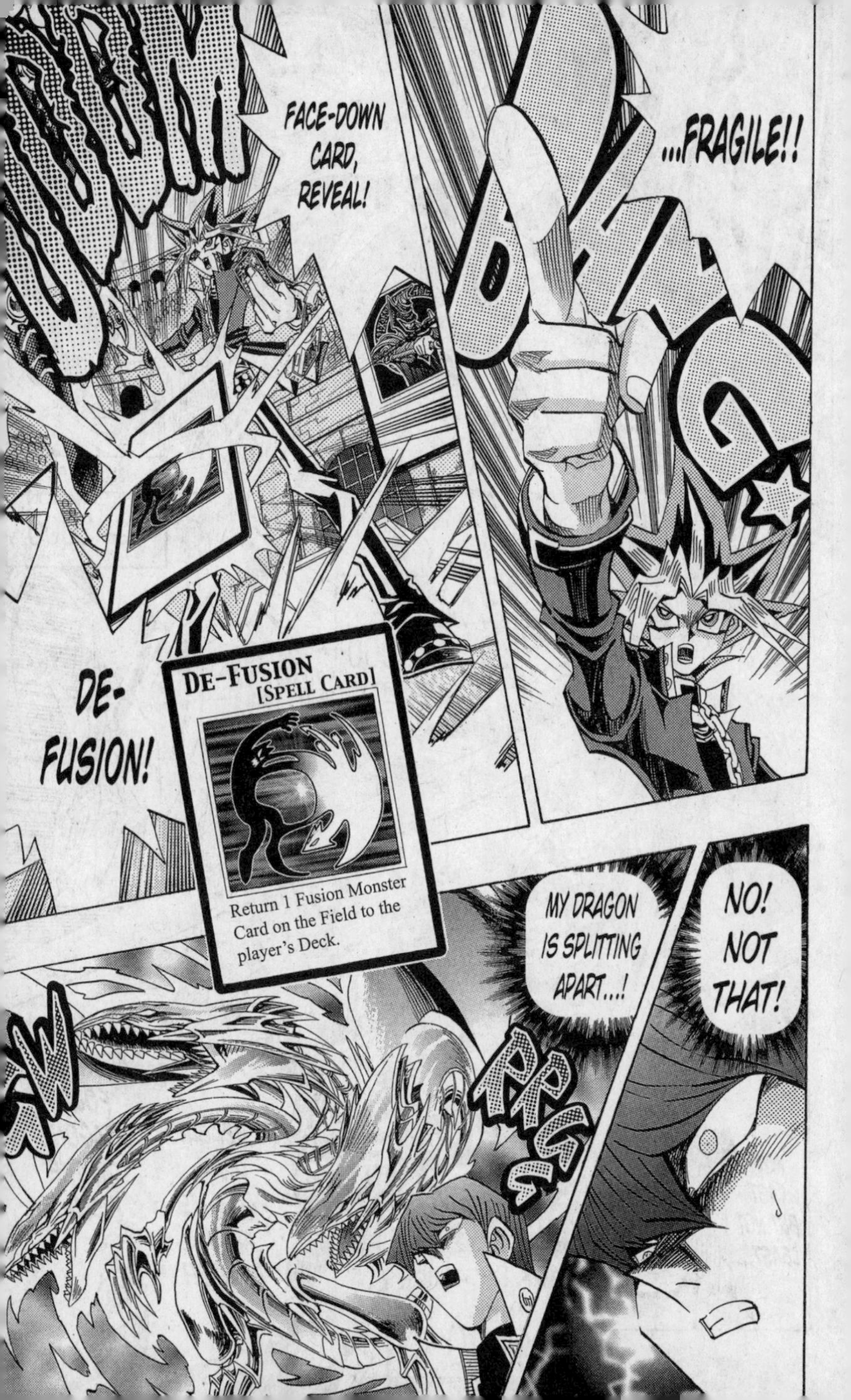
...FRAGILE!!
FACE-DOWN CARD, REVEAL!
DE-FUSION!
DE-FUSION
[SPELL CARD]
Return 1 Fusion Monster Card on the Field to the player's Deck.
NO! NOT THAT!
MY DRAGON IS SPLITTING APART...!

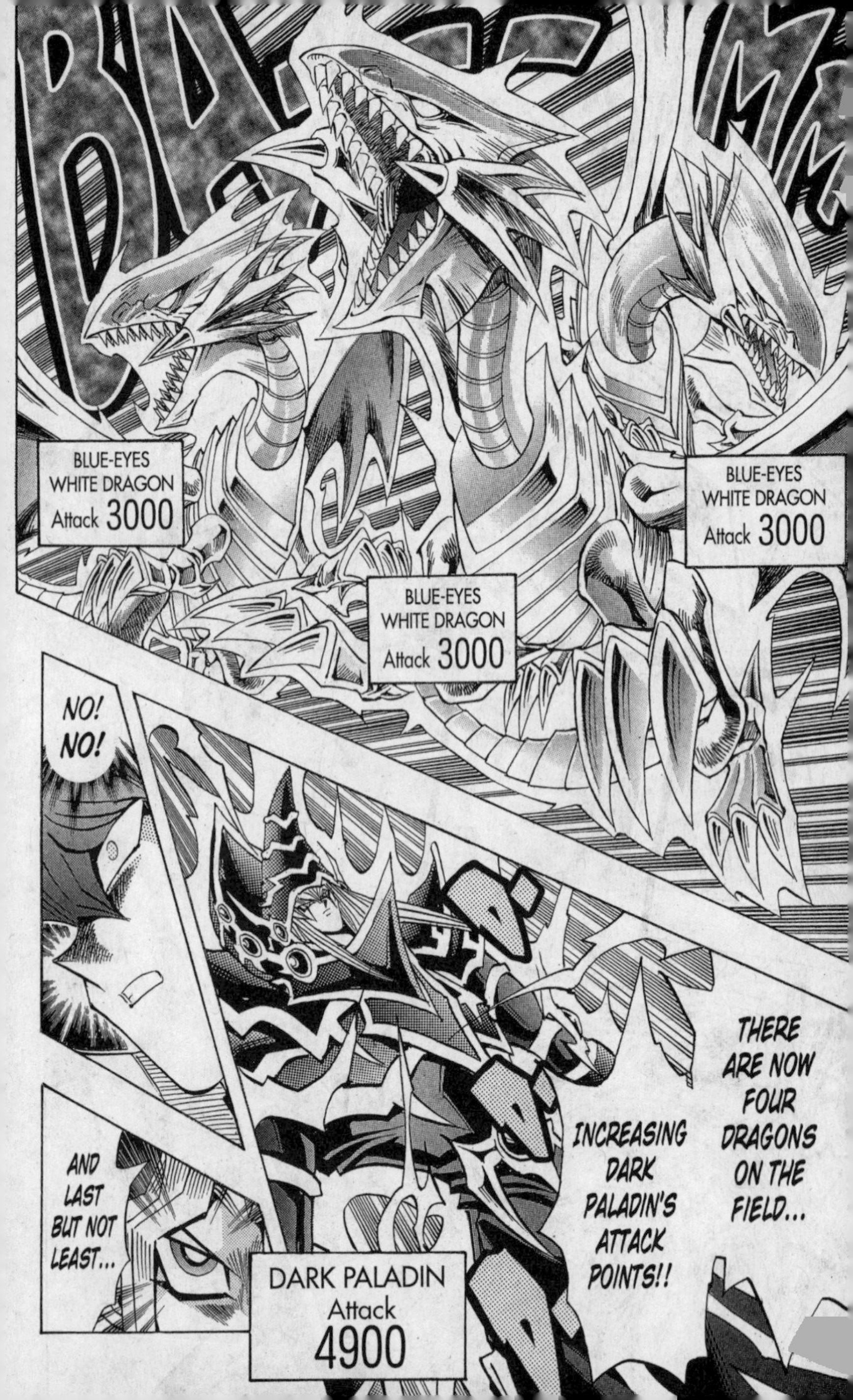
BLUE-EYES WHITE DRAGON Attack 3000
BLUE-EYES WHITE DRAGON Attack 3000
BLUE-EYES WHITE DRAGON Attack 3000
THERE ARE NOW FOUR DRAGONS ON THE FIELD...
INCREASING DARK PALADIN'S ATTACK POINTS!!
DARK PALADIN Attack 4900
NO! NO!
AND LAST BUT NOT LEAST...

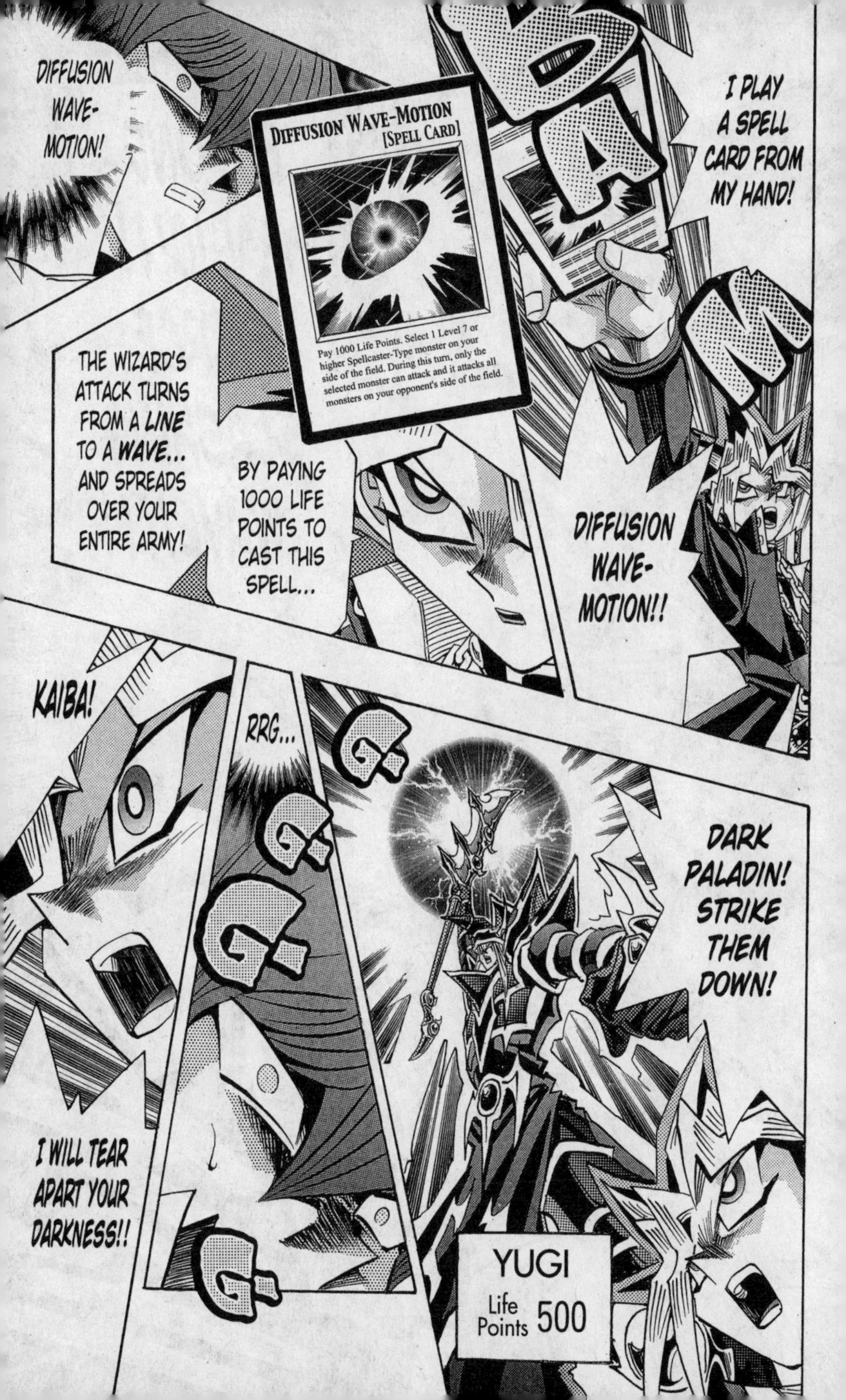

I PLAY A SPELL CARD FROM MY HAND!
DIFFUSION WAVE-MOTION!
DIFFUSION WAVE-MOTION
[SPELL CARD]
Pay 1000 Life Points. Select 1 Level 7 or higher Spellcaster-Type monster on your side of the field. During this turn, only the selected monster can attack and it attacks all monsters on your opponent's side of the field.
DIFFUSION WAVE-MOTION!!
BY PAYING 1000 LIFE POINTS TO CAST THIS SPELL...
THE WIZARD'S ATTACK TURNS FROM A *LINE* TO A ***WAVE***... AND SPREADS OVER YOUR ENTIRE ARMY!
DARK PALADIN! STRIKE THEM DOWN!
YUGI
Life Points 500
G
G
G
G
RRG...
KAIBA!
I WILL TEAR APART YOUR DARKNESS!!

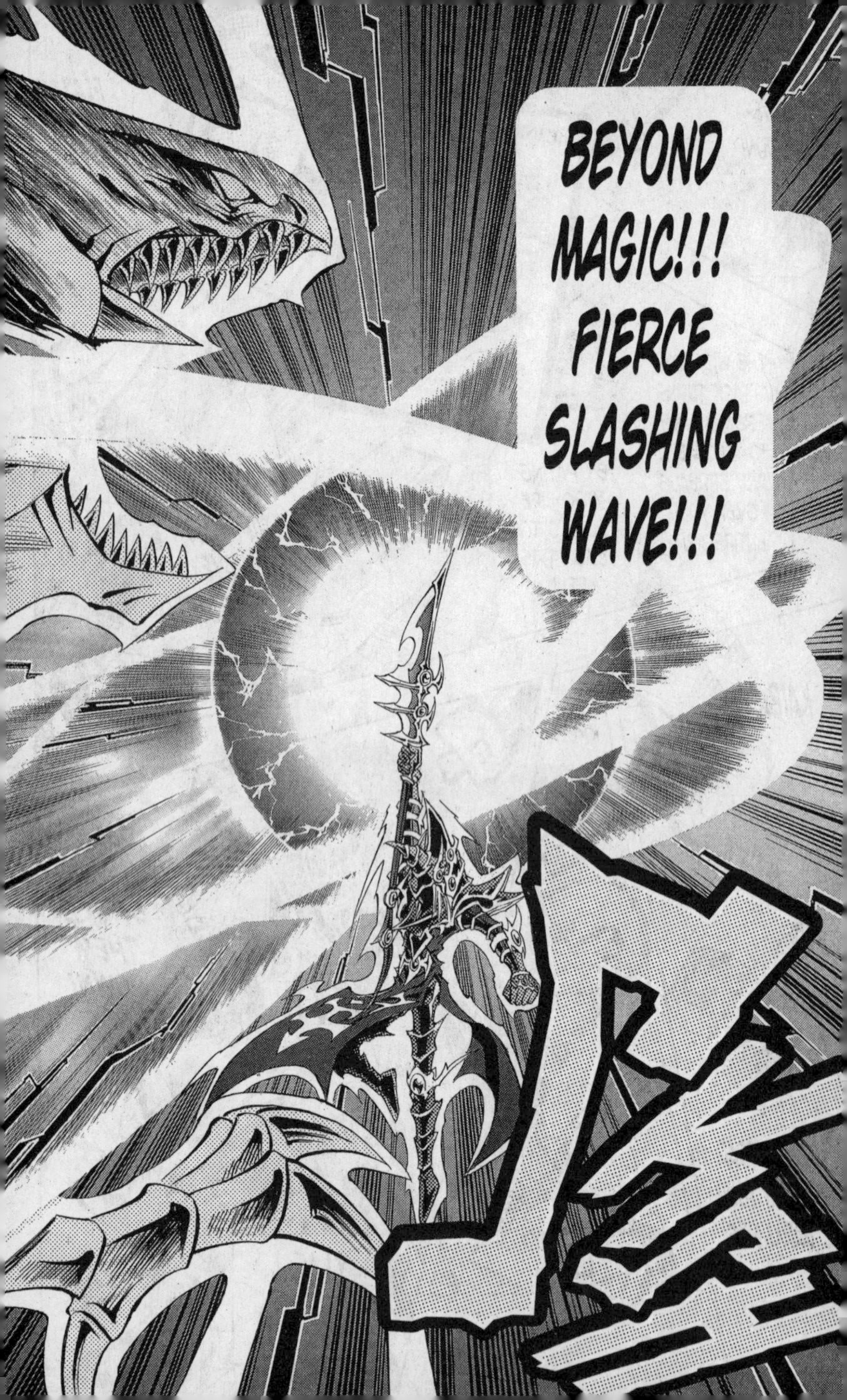
BEYOND MAGIC!!! FIERCE SLASHING WAVE!!!

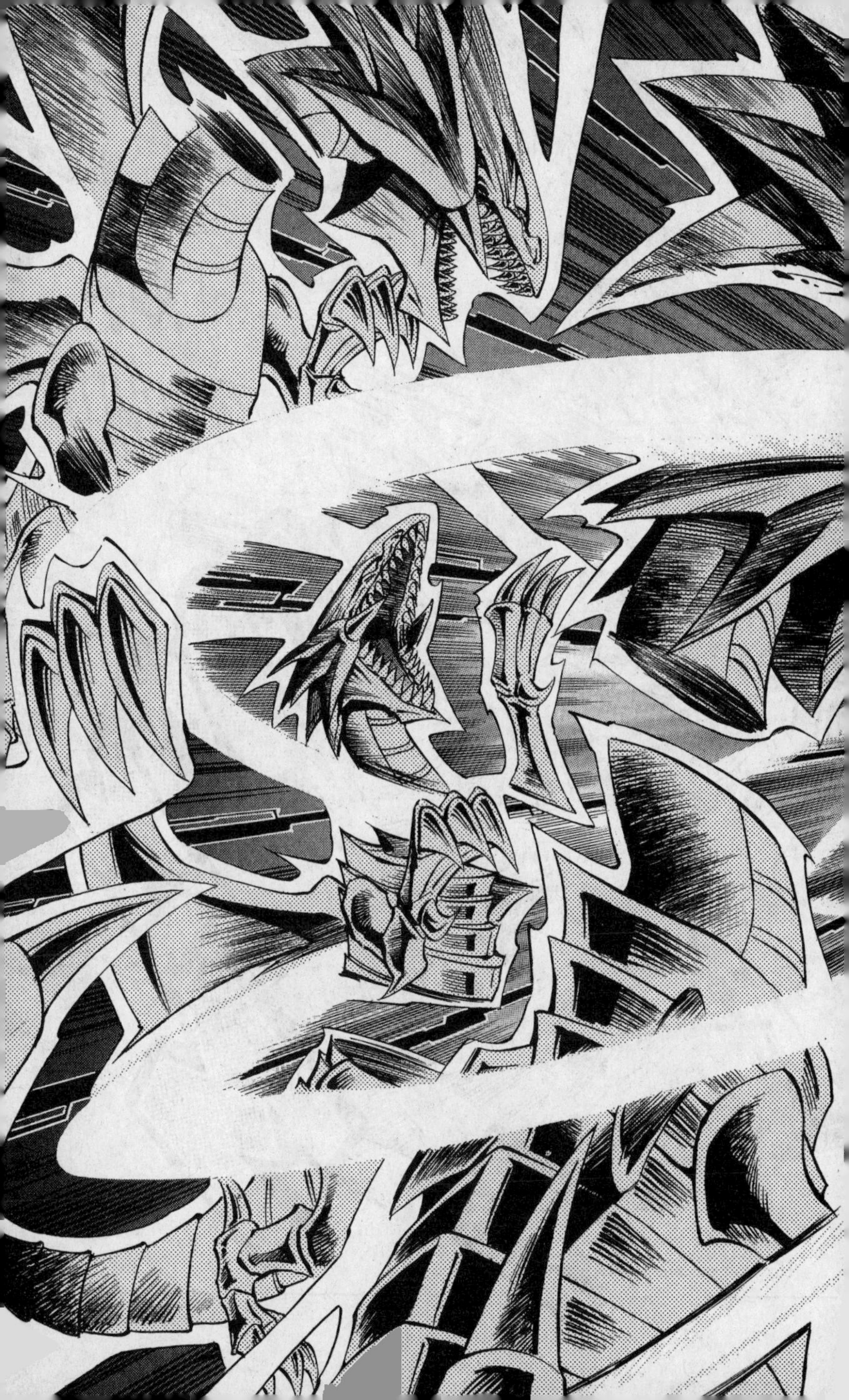

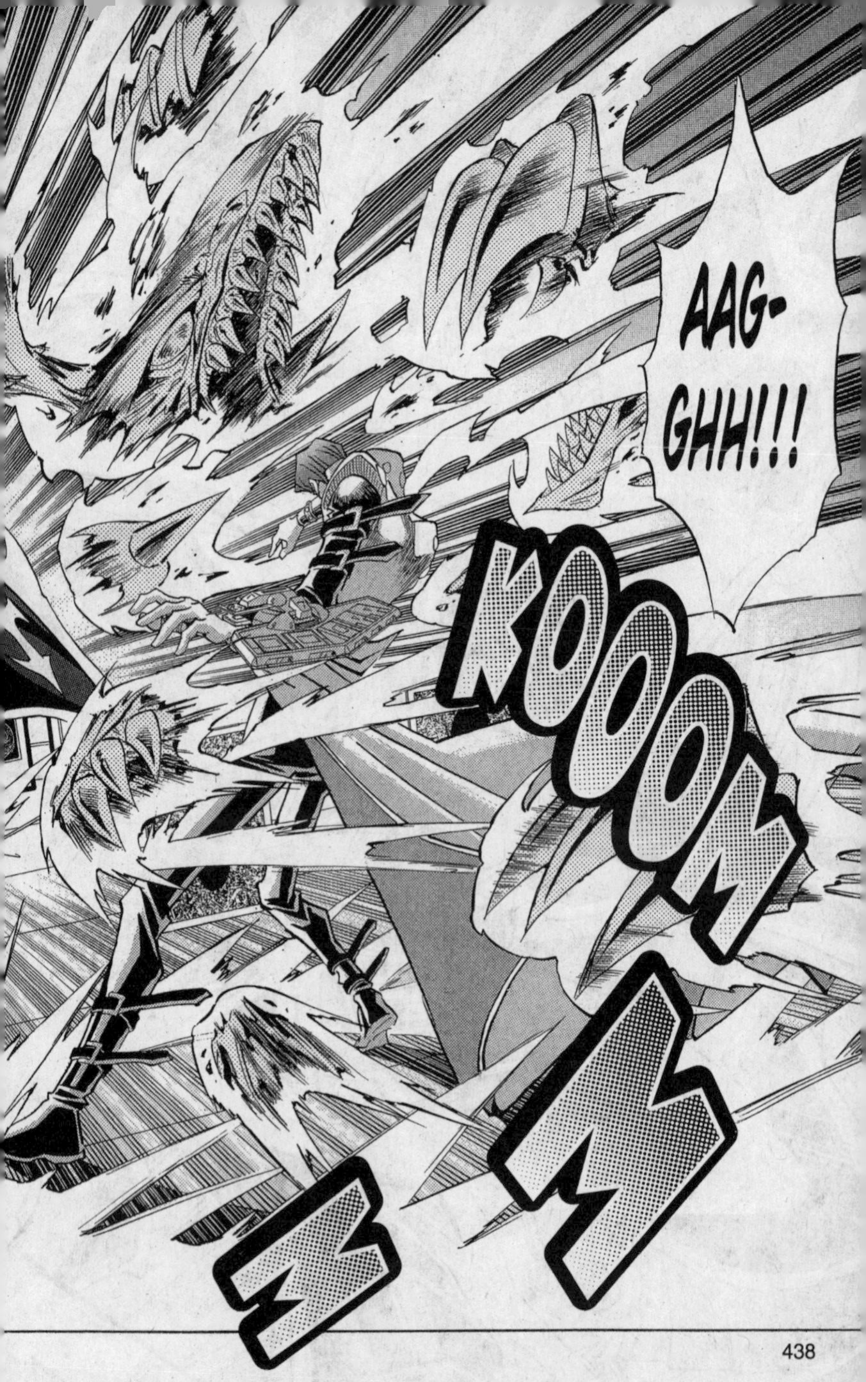
AAG-
GHH!!!
KOOOOM
M
M

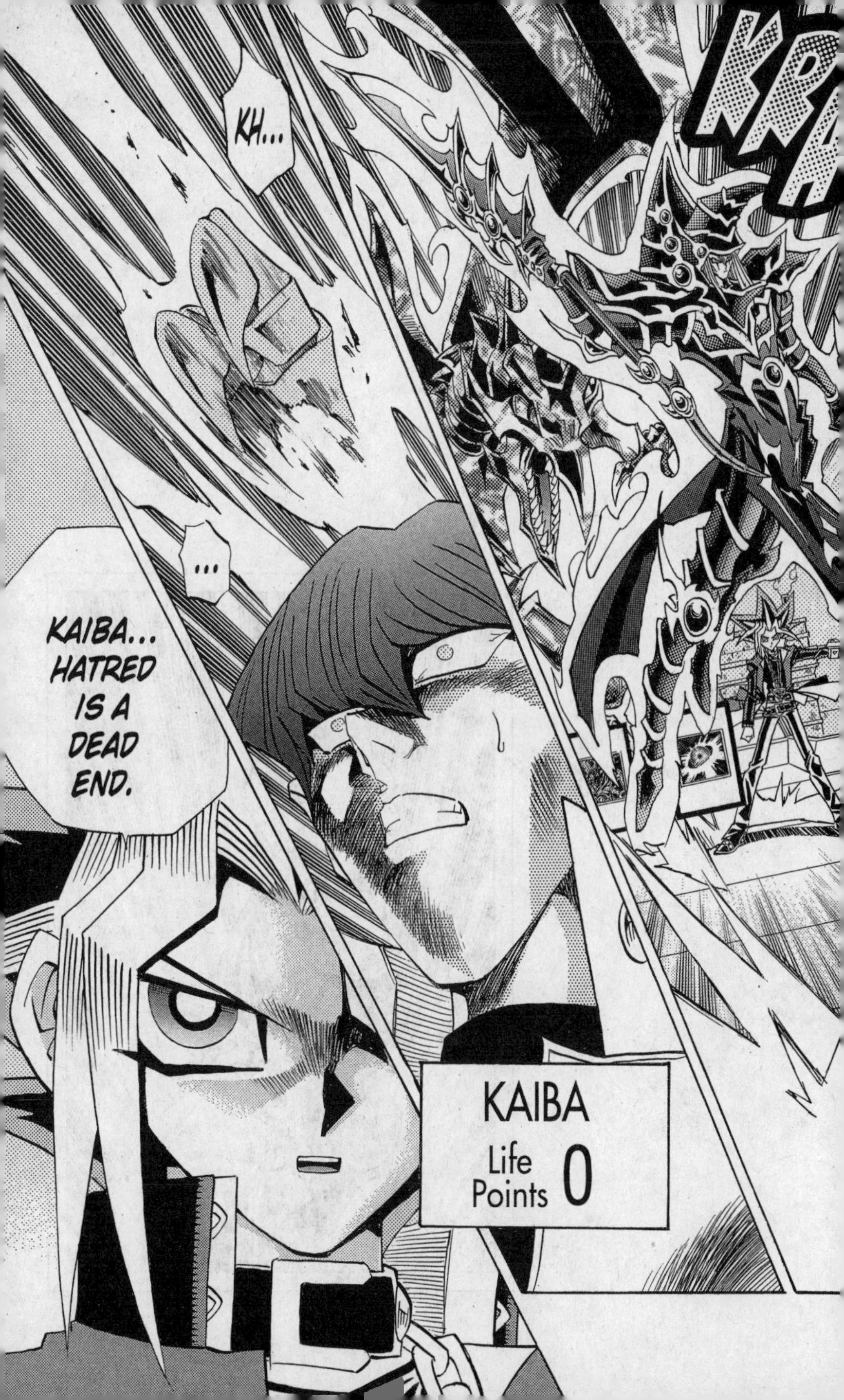
KRA
KH...
...
KAIBA... HATRED IS A DEAD END.
KAIBA
Life Points 0

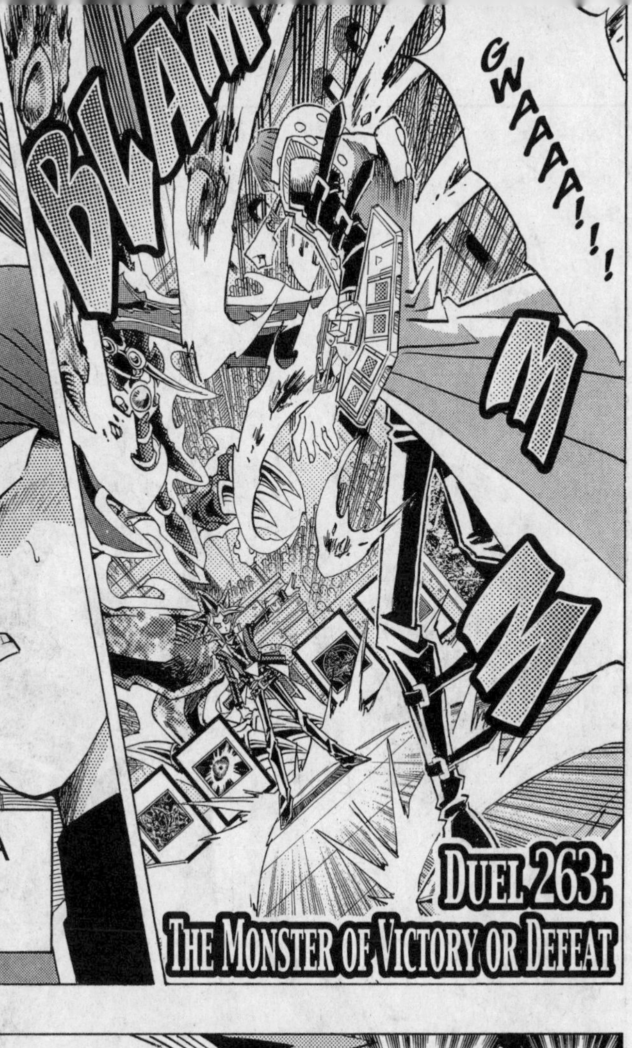
BLAM
GWAAAA!!!
MMM
DUEL 263:
THE MONSTER OF VICTORY OR DEFEAT
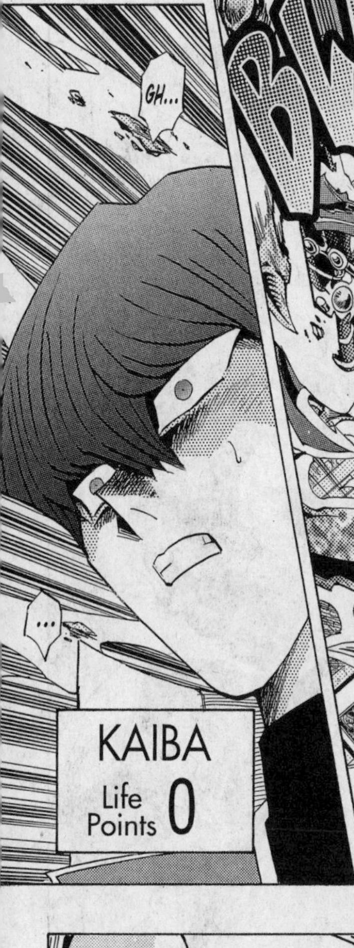
GH...
...
KAIBA
Life Points 0
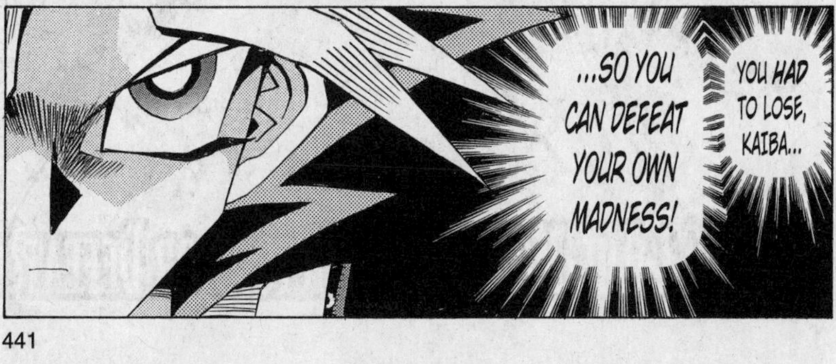
YOU HAD TO LOSE, KAIBA...
...SO YOU CAN DEFEAT YOUR OWN MADNESS!

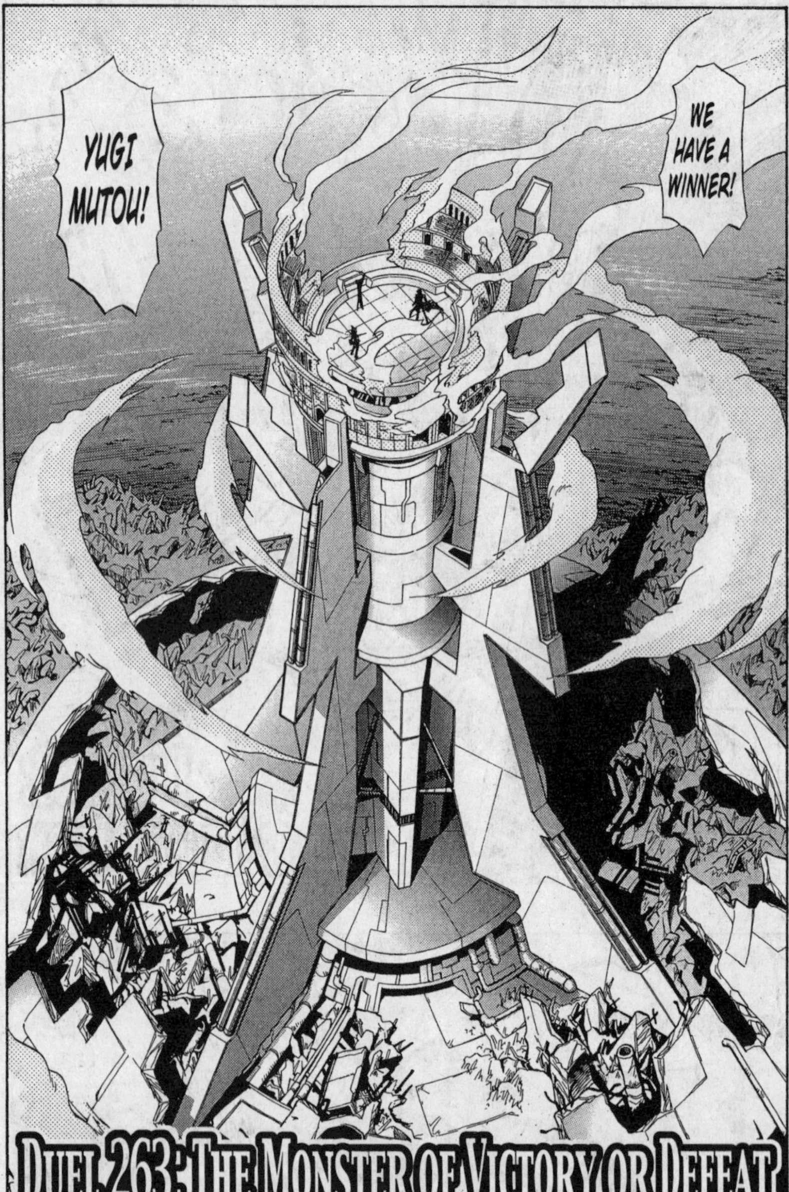
WE HAVE A WINNER!
YUGI MUTOU!
DUEL 263: THE MONSTER OF VICTORY OR DEFEAT

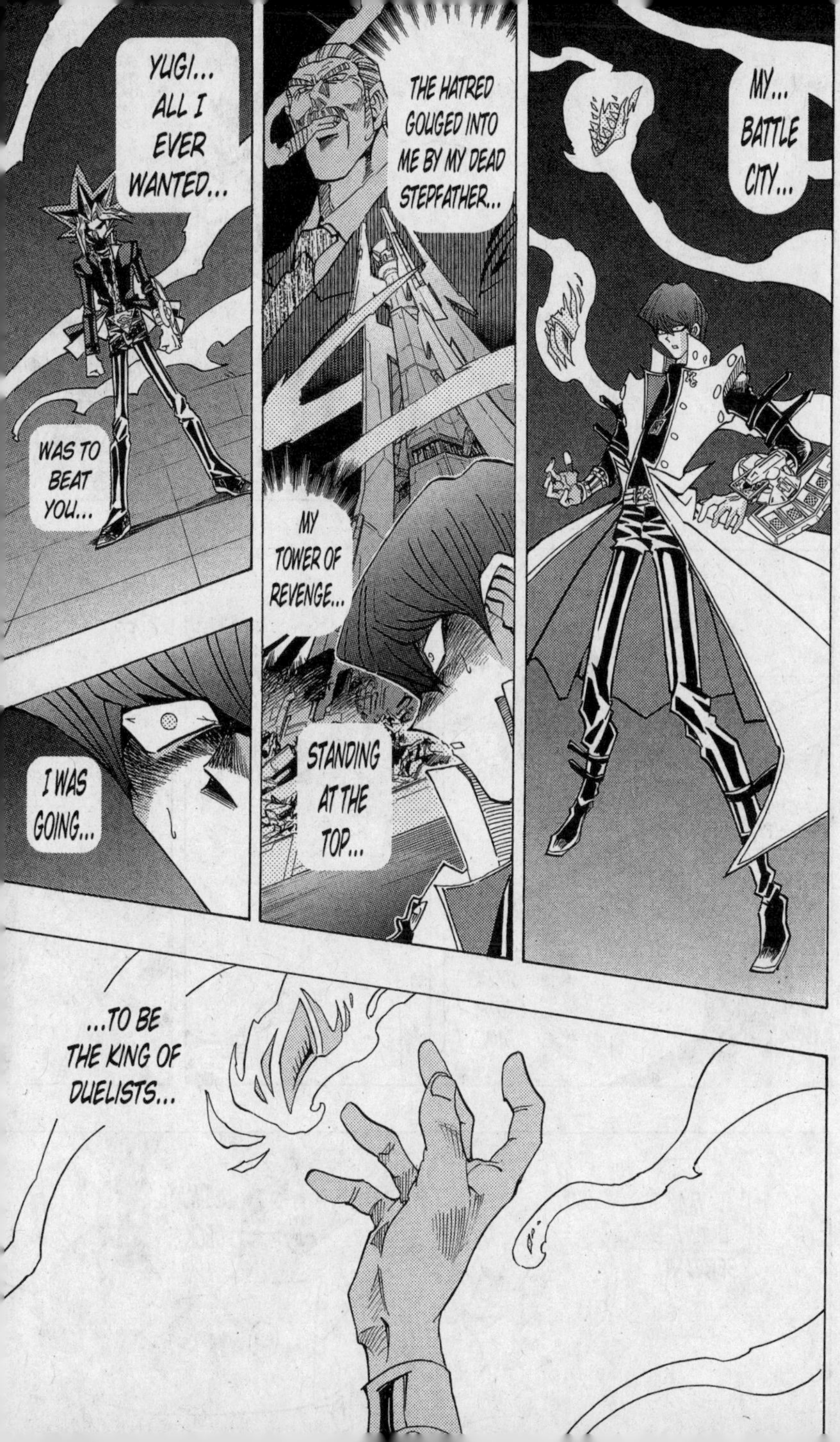
MY... BATTLE CITY...
THE HATRED GOUGED INTO ME BY MY DEAD STEPFATHER...
MY TOWER OF REVENGE...
STANDING AT THE TOP...
YUGI... ALL I EVER WANTED...
WAS TO BEAT YOU...
I WAS GOING...
...TO BE THE KING OF DUELISTS...

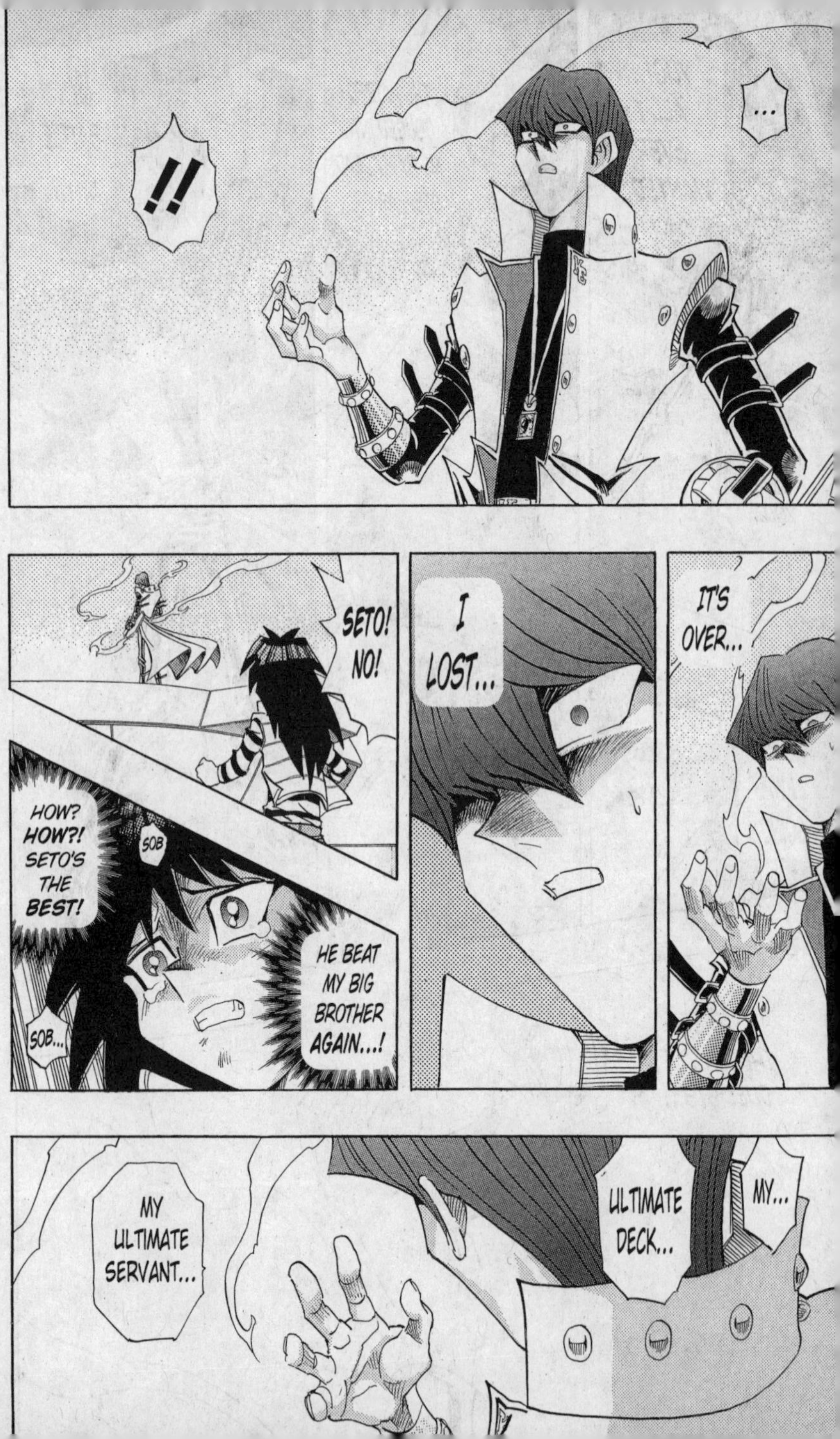
...
!!
IT'S OVER...
I LOST...
SETO! NO!
HOW? HOW?! SETO'S THE BEST!
SOB
HE BEAT MY BIG BROTHER AGAIN...!
SOB...
MY...
ULTIMATE DECK...
MY ULTIMATE SERVANT...

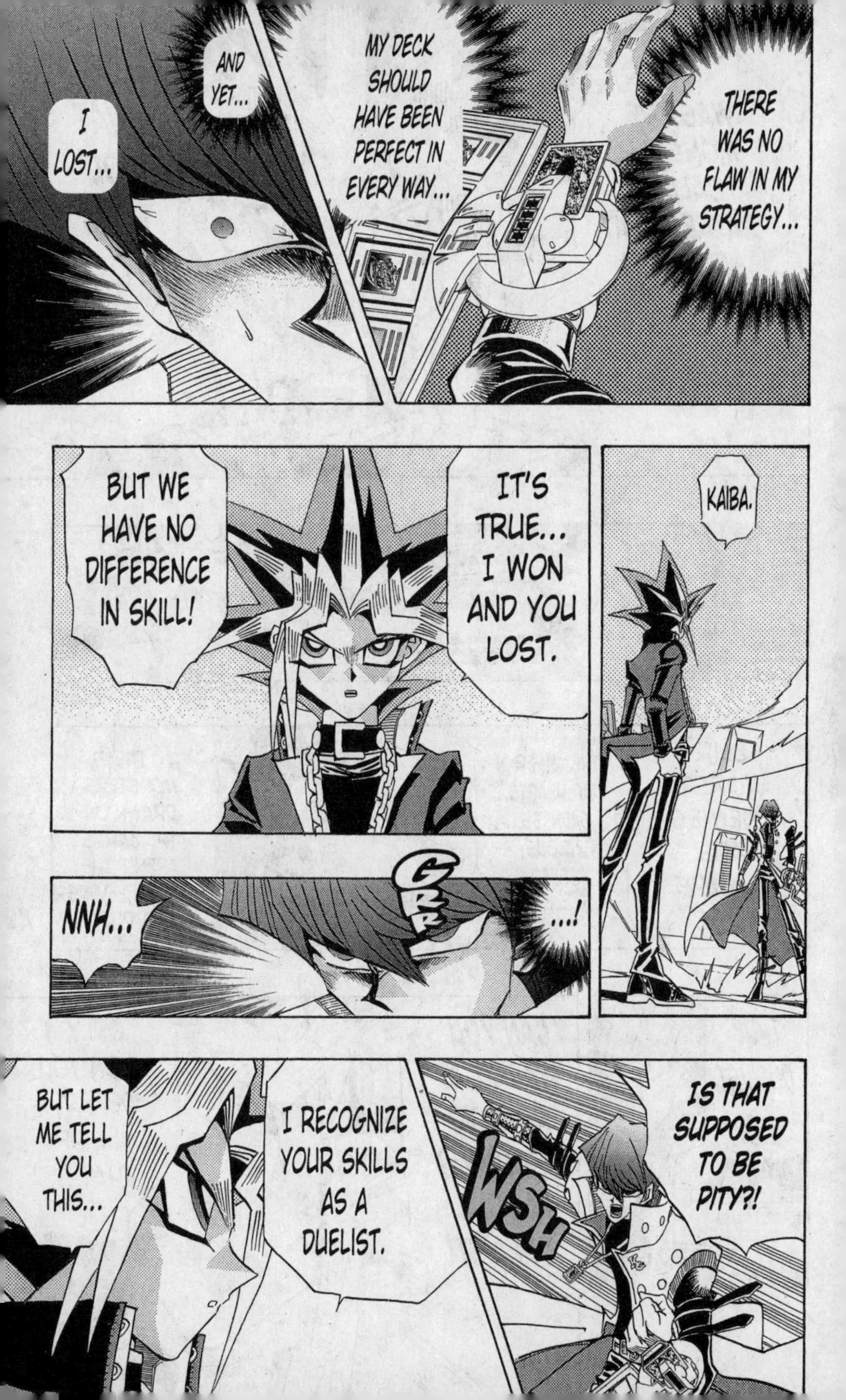
THERE WAS NO FLAW IN MY STRATEGY...
MY DECK SHOULD HAVE BEEN PERFECT IN EVERY WAY...
AND YET...
I LOST...
KAIBA.
IT'S TRUE... I WON AND YOU LOST.
BUT WE HAVE NO DIFFERENCE IN SKILL!
...!
GRR
NNH...
IS THAT SUPPOSED TO BE PITY?!
WSH
I RECOGNIZE YOUR SKILLS AS A DUELIST.
BUT LET ME TELL YOU THIS...

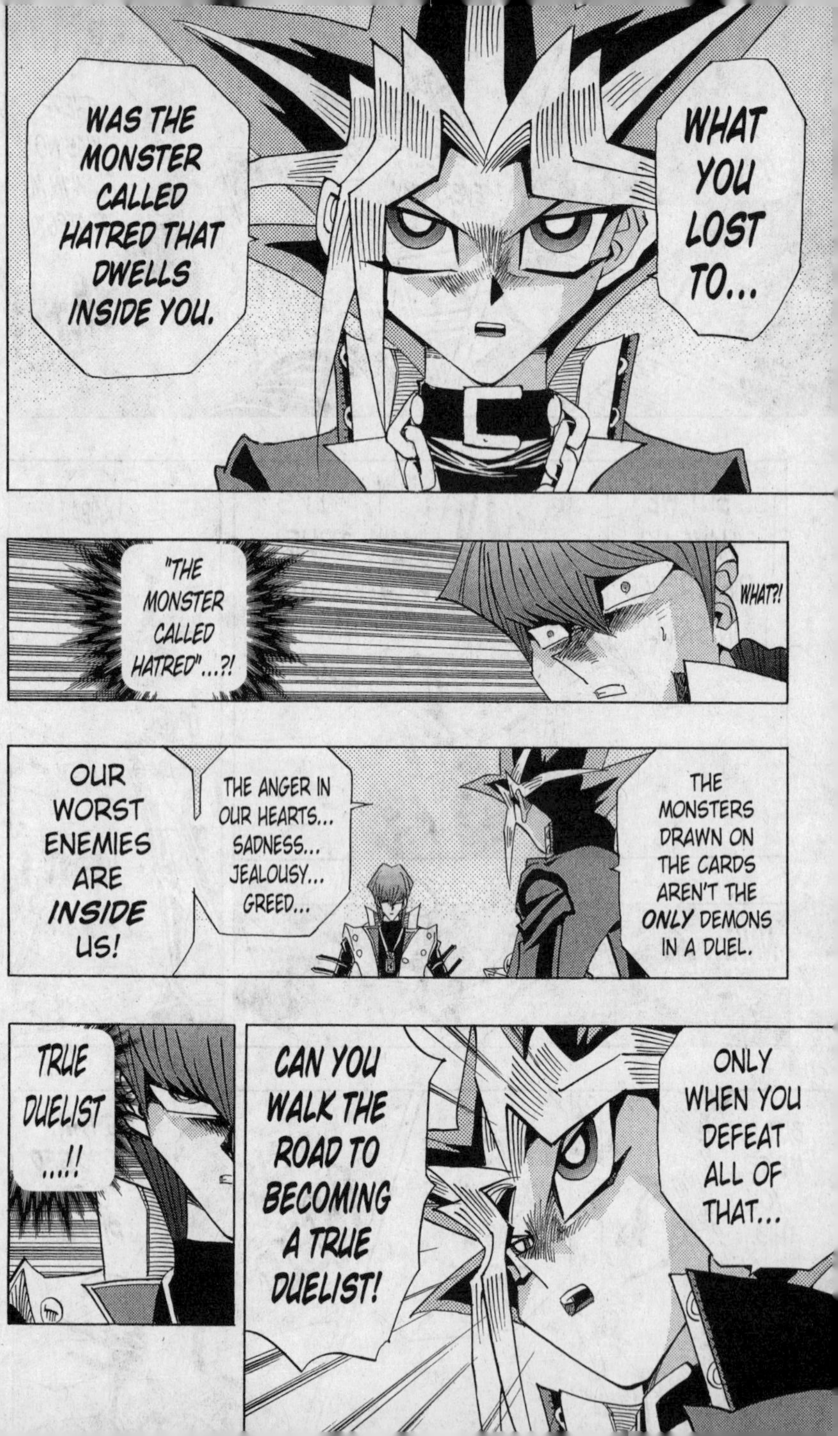
WHAT YOU LOST TO...
WAS THE MONSTER CALLED HATRED THAT DWELLS INSIDE YOU.
WHAT?!
"THE MONSTER CALLED HATRED"...?!
THE MONSTERS DRAWN ON THE CARDS AREN'T THE *ONLY* DEMONS IN A DUEL.
THE ANGER IN OUR HEARTS... SADNESS... JEALOUSY... GREED...
OUR WORST ENEMIES ARE *INSIDE* US!
ONLY WHEN YOU DEFEAT ALL OF THAT...
CAN YOU WALK THE ROAD TO BECOMING A TRUE DUELIST!
TRUE DUELIST ...!!

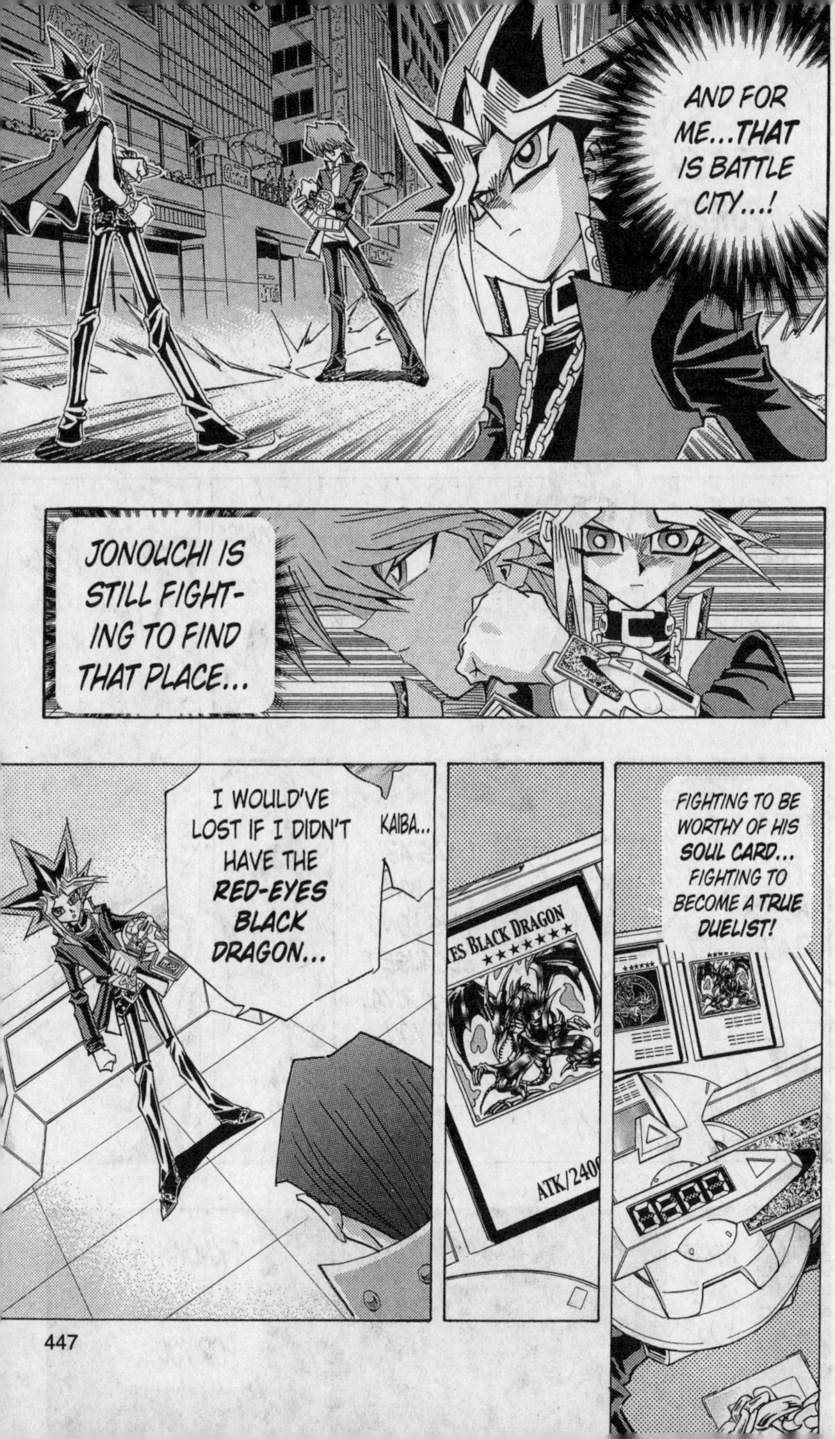
AND FOR ME...THAT IS BATTLE CITY...!
JONOUCHI IS STILL FIGHT-ING TO FIND THAT PLACE...
FIGHTING TO BE WORTHY OF HIS SOUL CARD... FIGHTING TO BECOME A TRUE DUELIST!
KAIBA...
I WOULD'VE LOST IF I DIDN'T HAVE THE RED-EYES BLACK DRAGON...

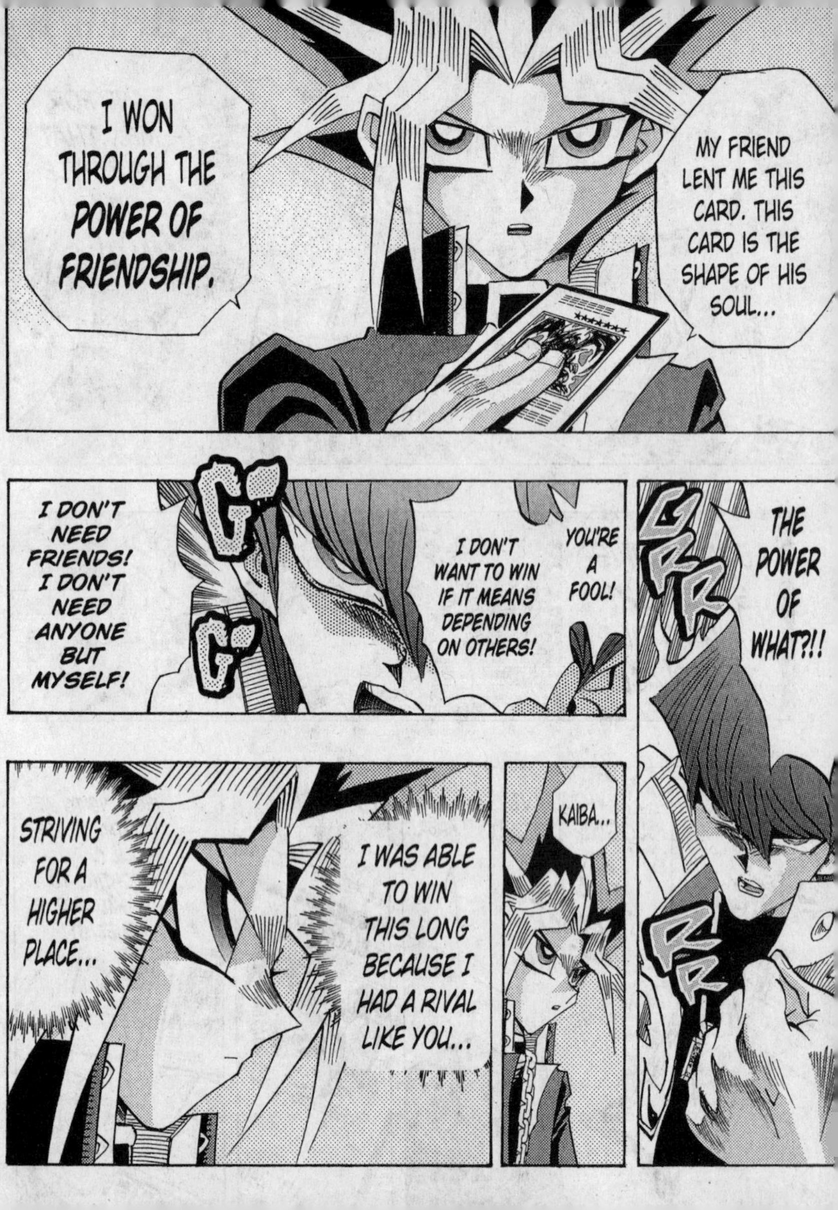
MY FRIEND LENT ME THIS CARD. THIS CARD IS THE SHAPE OF HIS SOUL...
I WON THROUGH THE POWER OF FRIENDSHIP.
GRR
THE POWER OF WHAT?!!
RR
YOU'RE A FOOL!
I DON'T WANT TO WIN IF IT MEANS DEPENDING ON OTHERS!
G
G
I DON'T NEED FRIENDS! I DON'T NEED ANYONE BUT MYSELF!
KAIBA...
I WAS ABLE TO WIN THIS LONG BECAUSE I HAD A RIVAL LIKE YOU...
STRIVING FOR A HIGHER PLACE...

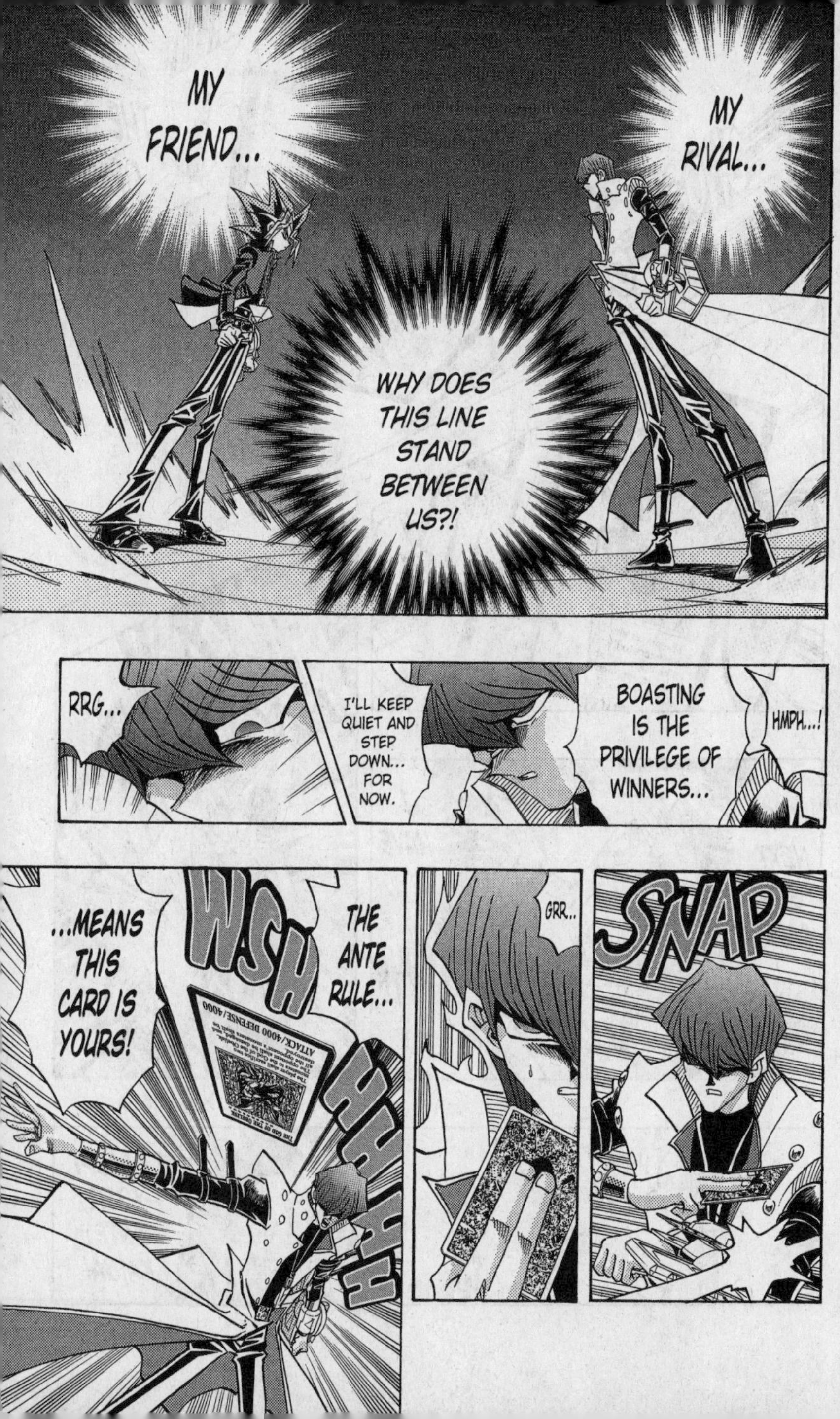
MY RIVAL...
MY FRIEND...
WHY DOES THIS LINE STAND BETWEEN US?!
HMPH...!
BOASTING IS THE PRIVILEGE OF WINNERS...
I'LL KEEP QUIET AND STEP DOWN... FOR NOW.
RRG...
SNAP
GRR...
THE ANTE RULE...
WSH
...MEANS THIS CARD IS YOURS!
HHHHH

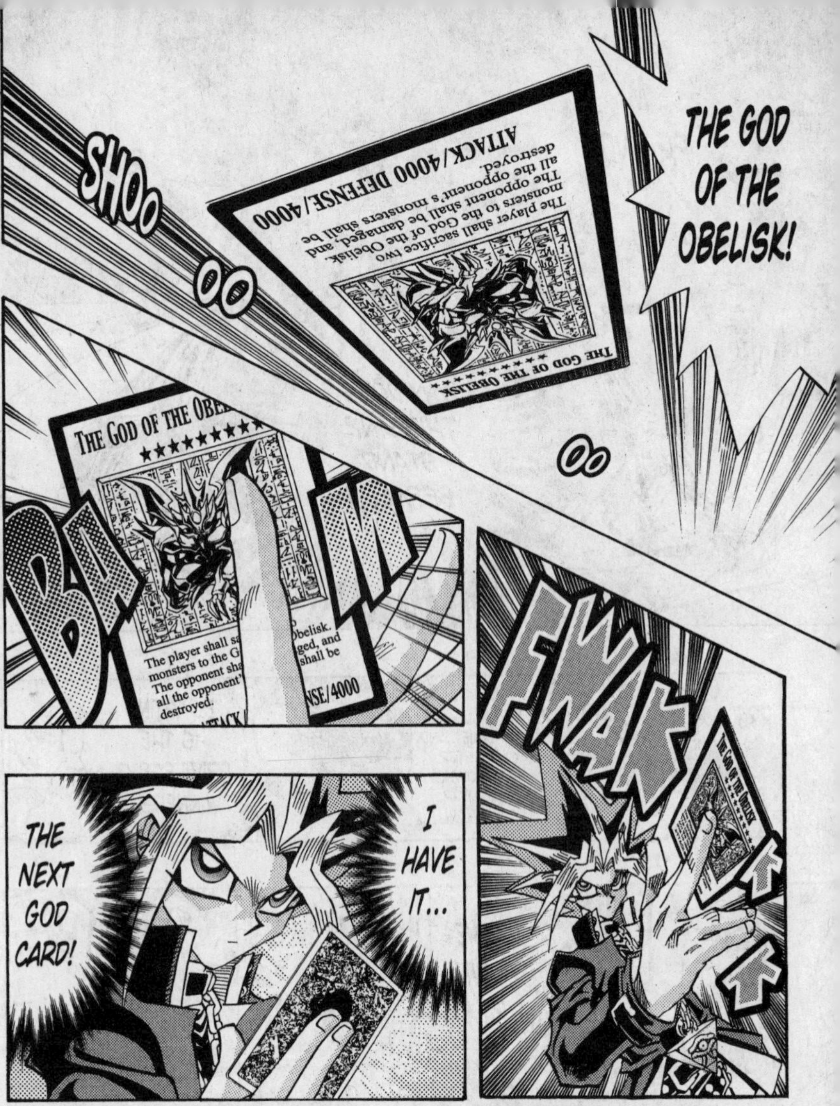
THE GOD OF THE OBELISK!
THE GOD OF THE OBELISK
The player shall sacrifice two monsters to the God of the Obelisk. The opponent shall be damaged, and all the opponent's monsters shall be destroyed.
ATTACK/4000 DEFENSE/4000
SHOO OO OO
FWAK
BAM
I HAVE IT...
THE NEXT GOD CARD!
I ACCEPT YOUR ANTE, KAIBA!
HMPH.

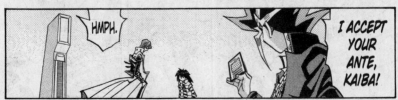

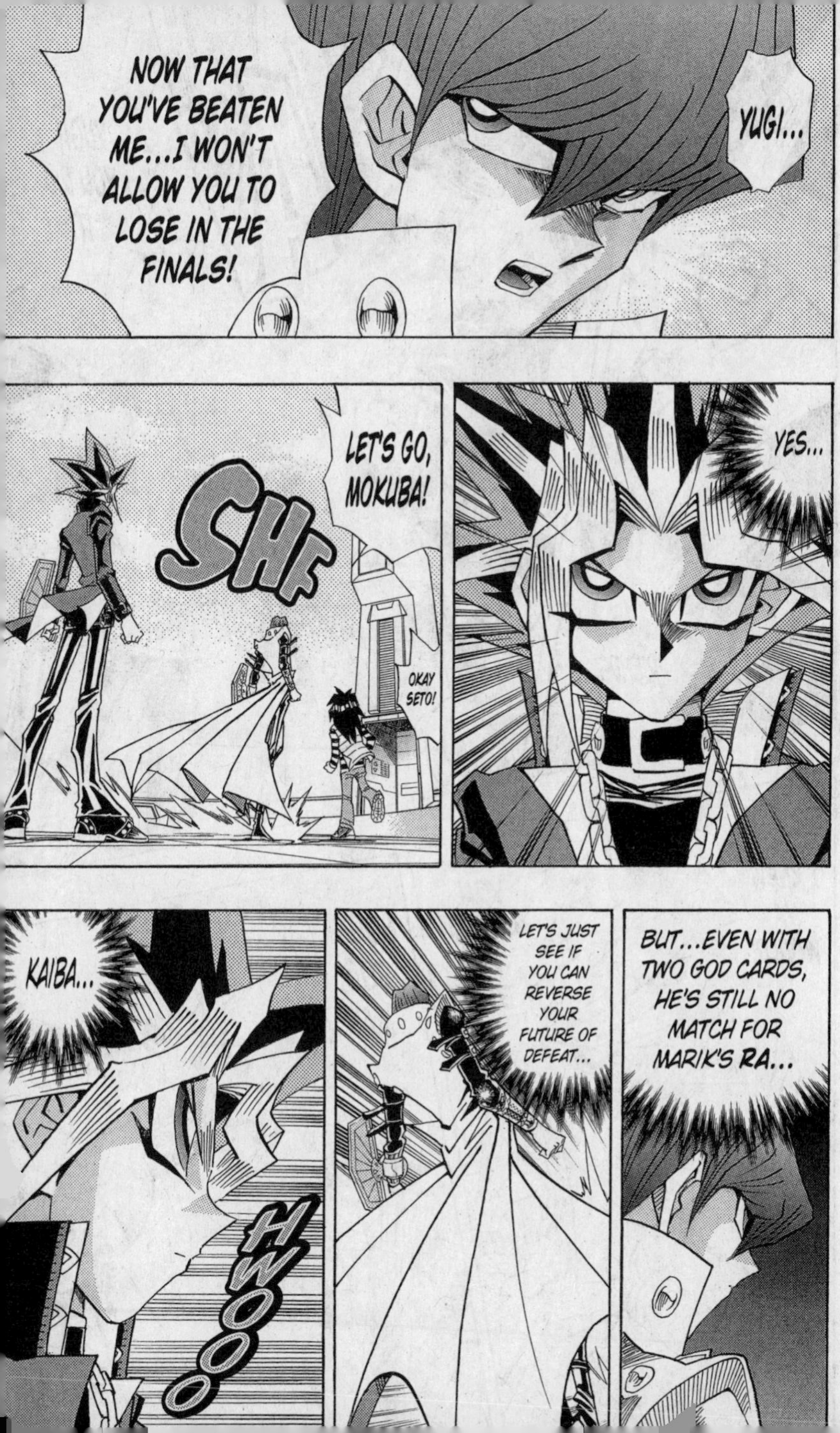
YUGI...
NOW THAT YOU'VE BEATEN ME...I WON'T ALLOW YOU TO LOSE IN THE FINALS!
YES...
LET'S GO, MOKUBA!
SHF
OKAY SETO!
BUT...EVEN WITH TWO GOD CARDS, HE'S STILL NO MATCH FOR MARIK'S RA...
LET'S JUST SEE IF YOU CAN REVERSE YOUR FUTURE OF DEFEAT...
KAIBA...
HWOOOO

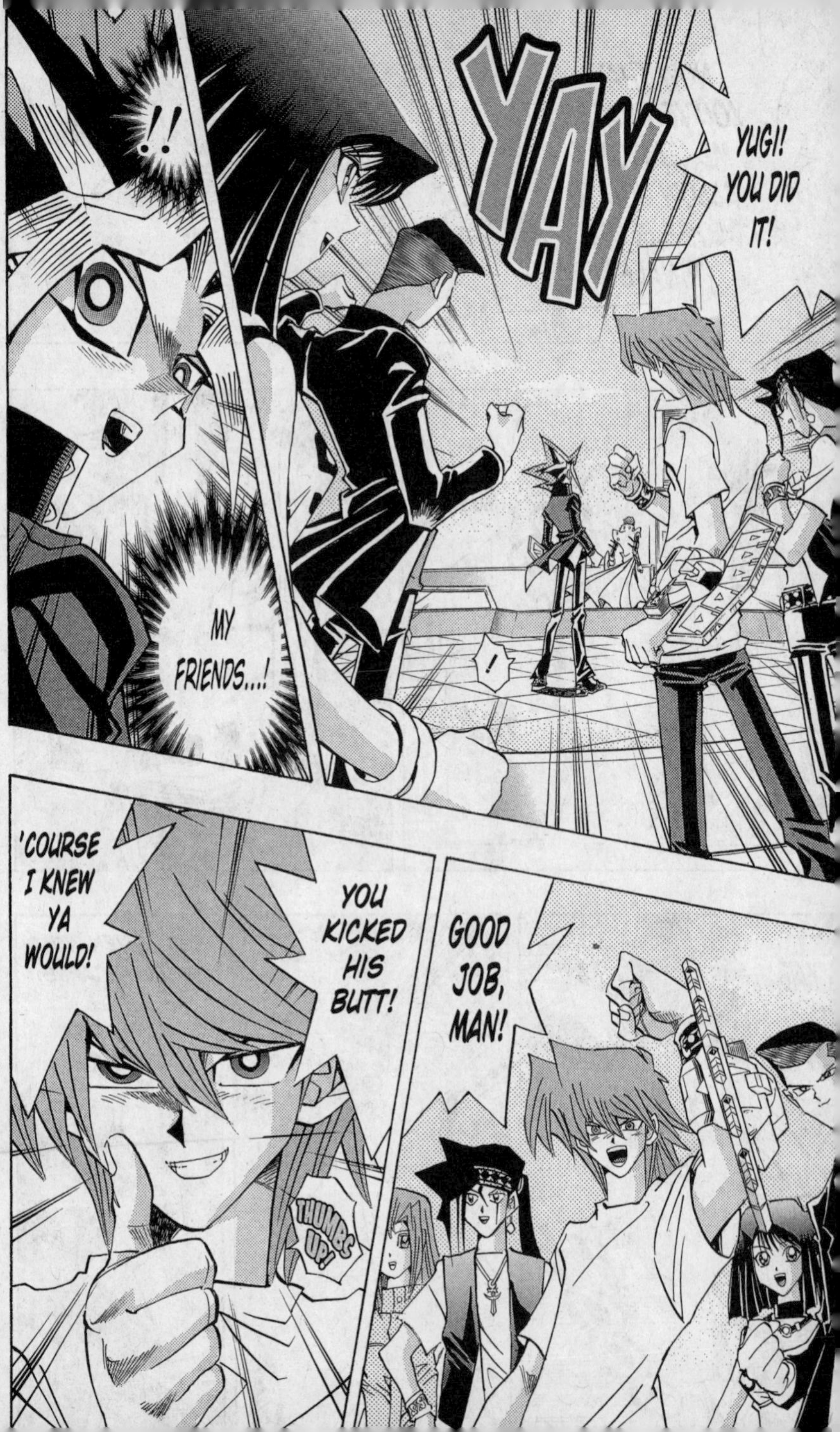
YUGI! YOU DID IT!
YAY
!
!!
MY FRIENDS...!
GOOD JOB, MAN!
YOU KICKED HIS BUTT!
'COURSE I KNEW YA WOULD!
THUMBS UP!

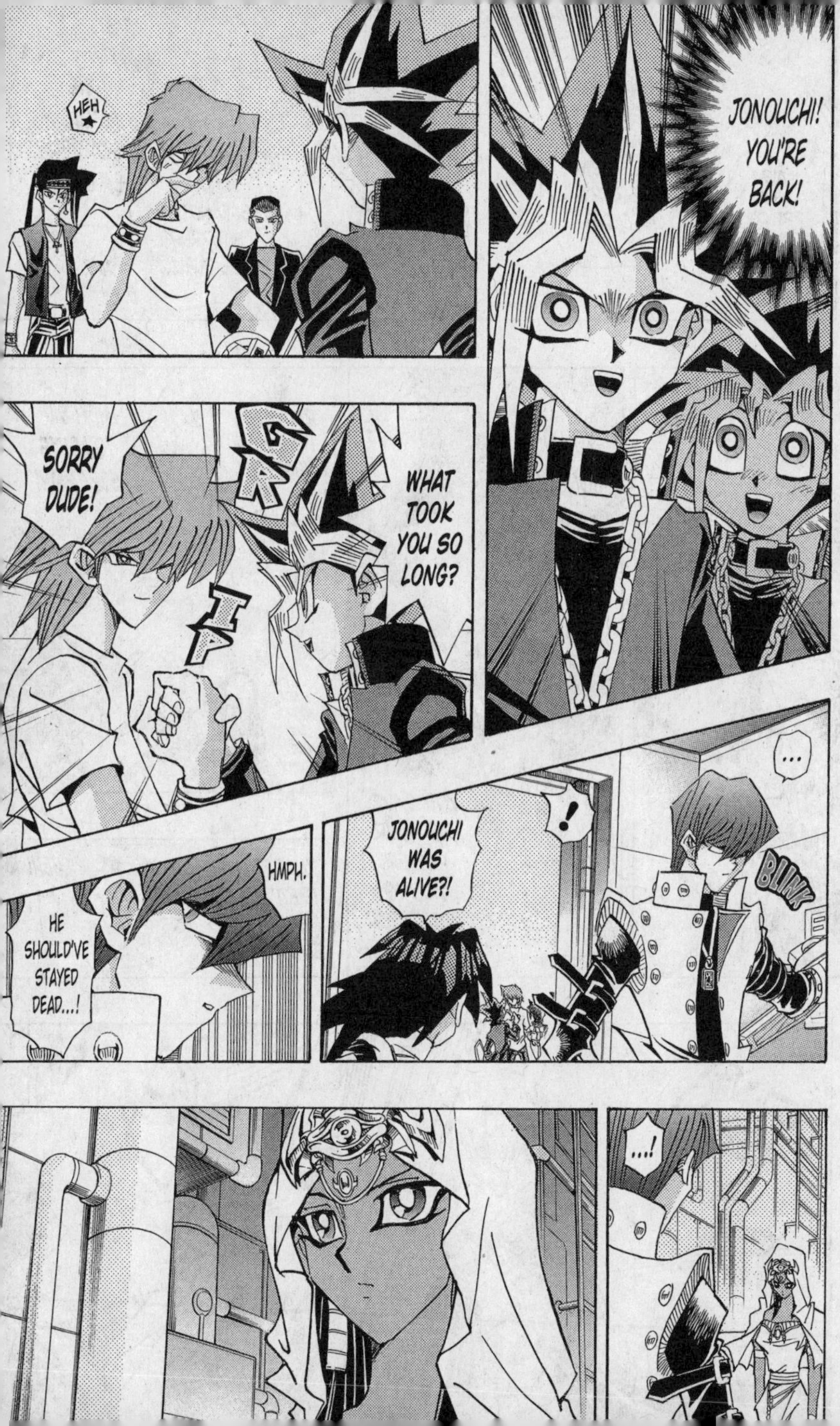
JONOUCHI! YOU'RE BACK!
HEH
WHAT TOOK YOU SO LONG?
GRIP
SORRY DUDE!
...
!
BLINK
JONOUCHI WAS ALIVE?!
HMPH.
HE SHOULD'VE STAYED DEAD...!
...!

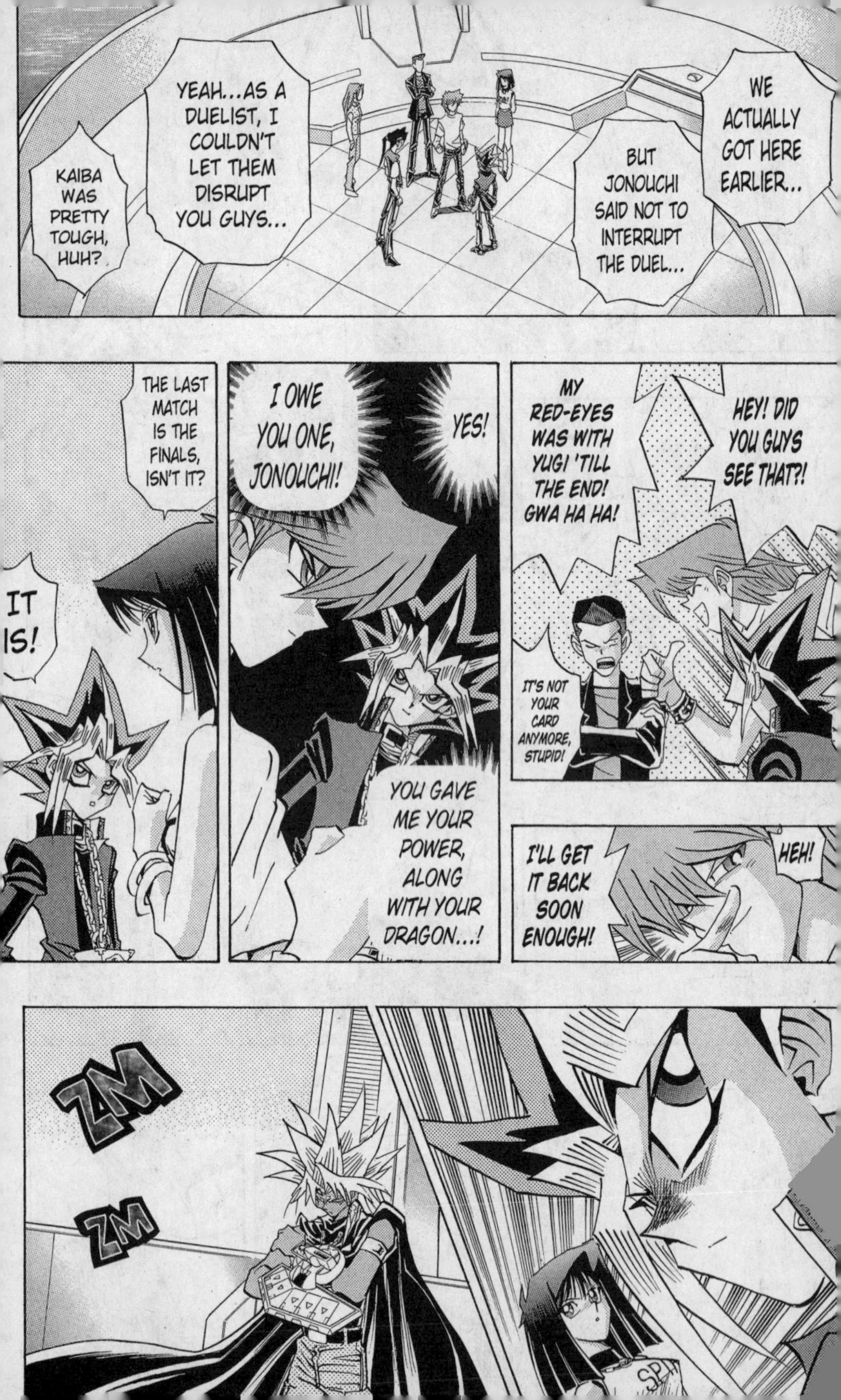
WE ACTUALLY GOT HERE EARLIER...
BUT JONOUCHI SAID NOT TO INTERRUPT THE DUEL...
YEAH...AS A DUELIST, I COULDN'T LET THEM DISRUPT YOU GUYS...
KAIBA WAS PRETTY TOUGH, HUH?
HEY! DID YOU GUYS SEE THAT?!
MY RED-EYES WAS WITH YUGI 'TILL THE END! GWA HA HA!
IT'S NOT YOUR CARD ANYMORE, STUPID!
HEH!
I'LL GET IT BACK SOON ENOUGH!
YES!
I OWE YOU ONE, JONOUCHI!
YOU GAVE ME YOUR POWER, ALONG WITH YOUR DRAGON...!
THE LAST MATCH IS THE FINALS, ISN'T IT?
IT IS!
ZM
ZM

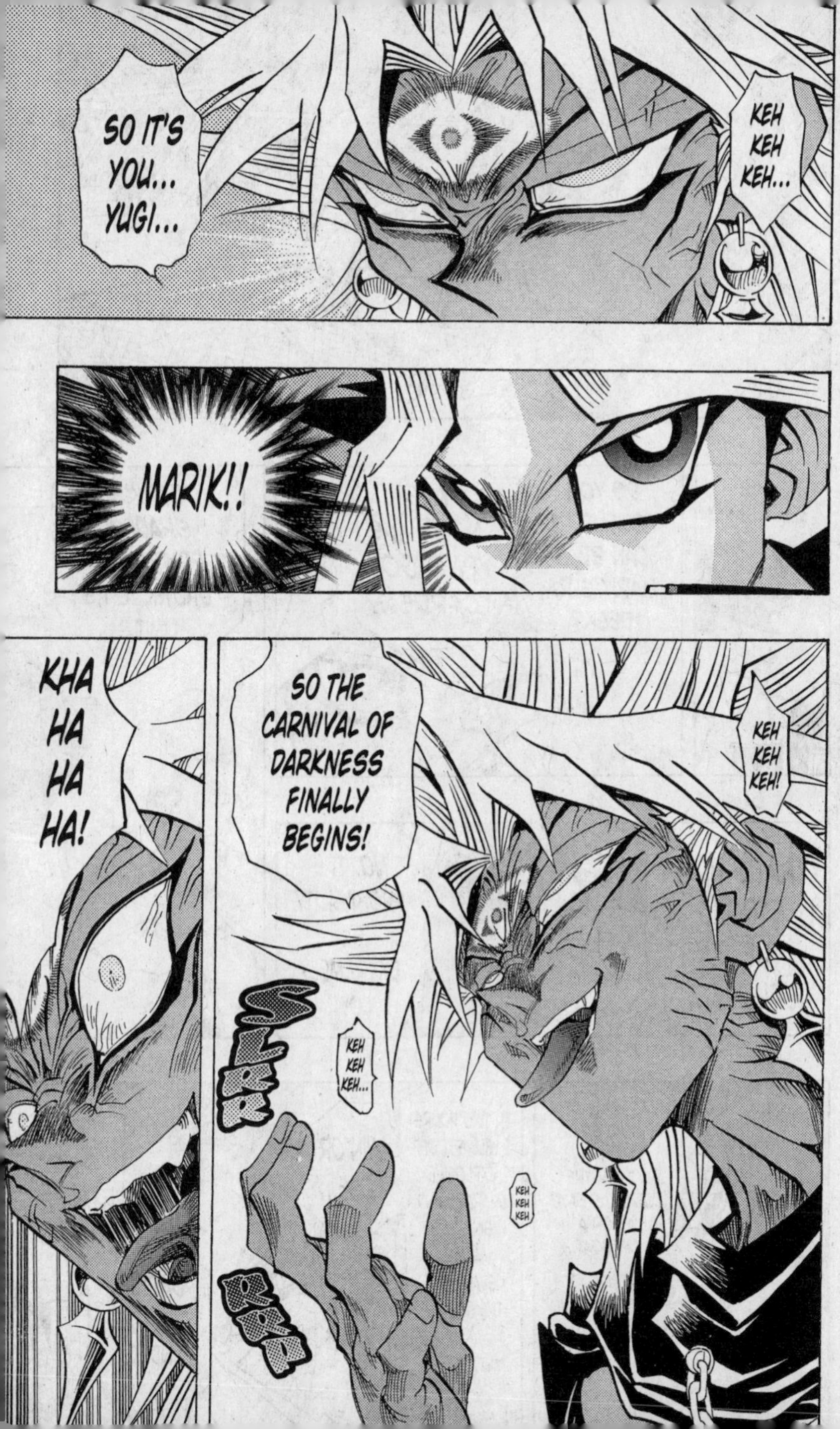
KEH KEH KEH...
SO IT'S YOU... YUGI...
MARIK!!
KEH KEH KEH!
SO THE CARNIVAL OF DARKNESS FINALLY BEGINS!
KEH KEH KEH
KEH KEH KEH...
SLRR
RRP
KHA HA HA HA!

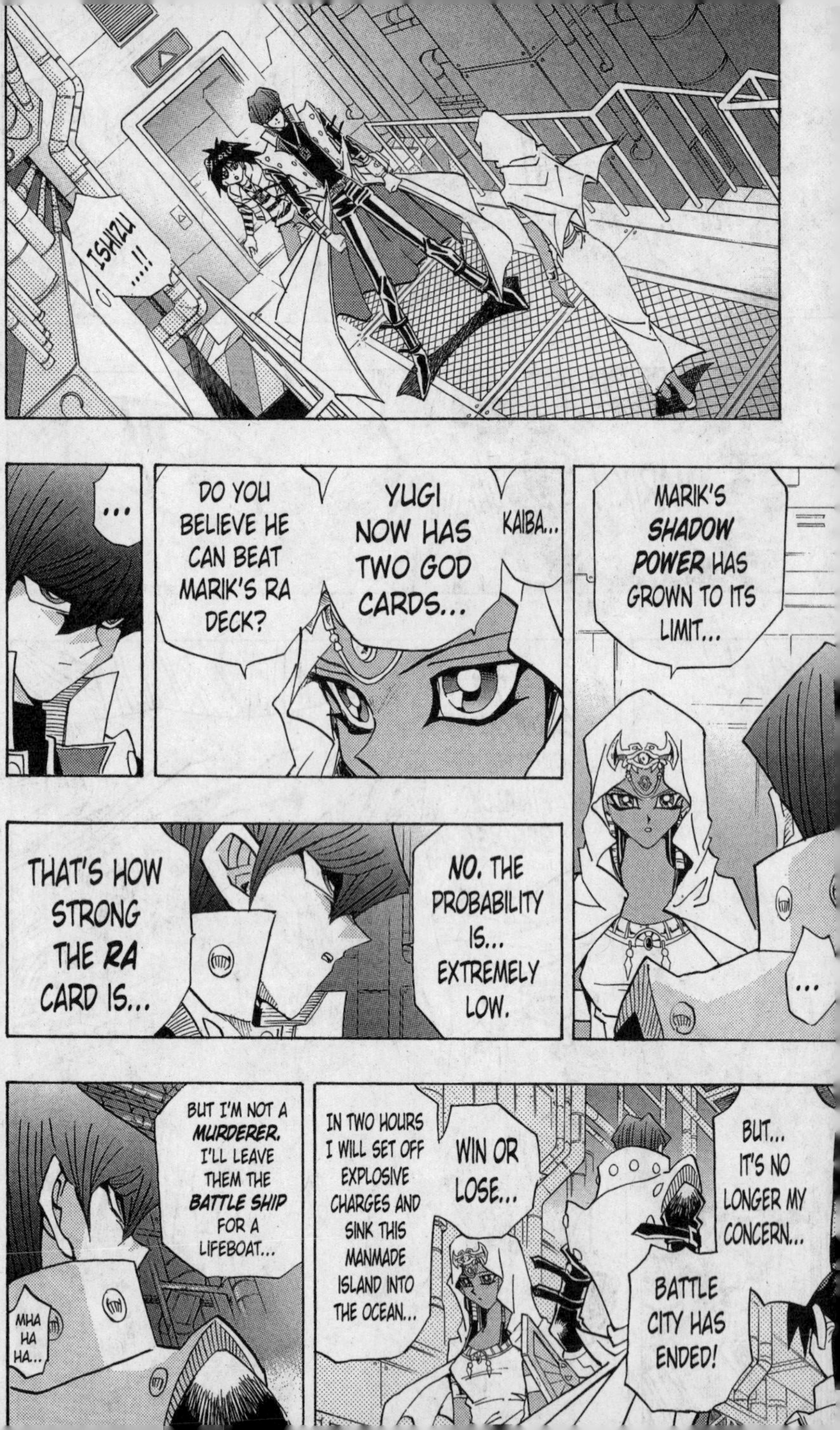
ISHIZU ...!!
MARIK'S SHADOW POWER HAS GROWN TO ITS LIMIT...
...
KAIBA...
YUGI NOW HAS TWO GOD CARDS...
DO YOU BELIEVE HE CAN BEAT MARIK'S RA DECK?
...
NO. THE PROBABILITY IS... EXTREMELY LOW.
THAT'S HOW STRONG THE RA CARD IS...
BUT... IT'S NO LONGER MY CONCERN...
WIN OR LOSE...
IN TWO HOURS I WILL SET OFF EXPLOSIVE CHARGES AND SINK THIS MANMADE ISLAND INTO THE OCEAN...
BATTLE CITY HAS ENDED!
BUT I'M NOT A MURDERER. I'LL LEAVE THEM THE BATTLE SHIP FOR A LIFEBOAT...
MHA HA HA...

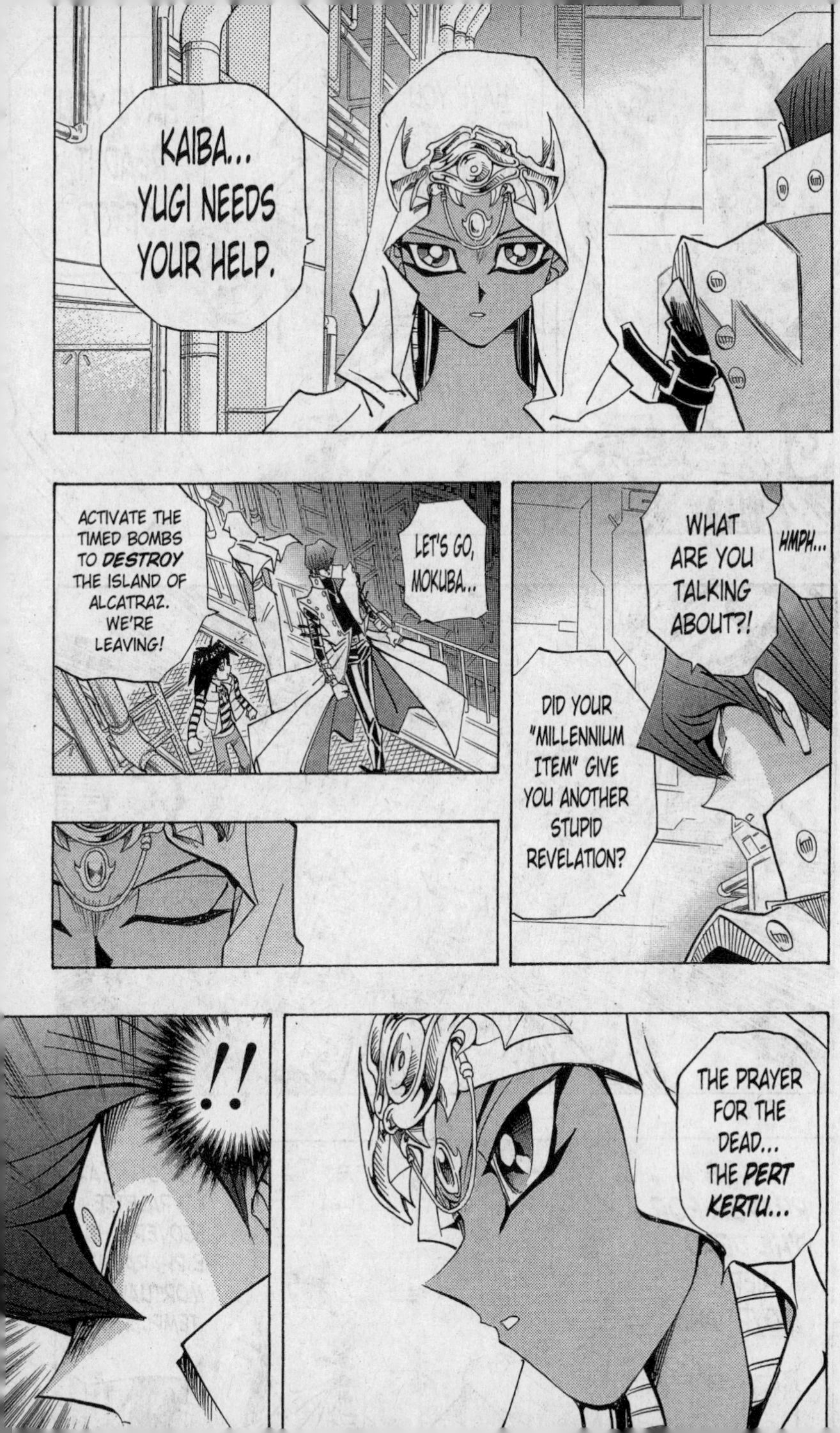
KAIBA... YUGI NEEDS YOUR HELP.
HMPH...
WHAT ARE YOU TALKING ABOUT?!
DID YOUR "MILLENNIUM ITEM" GIVE YOU ANOTHER STUPID REVELATION?
LET'S GO, MOKUBA...
ACTIVATE THE TIMED BOMBS TO DESTROY THE ISLAND OF ALCATRAZ. WE'RE LEAVING!
THE PRAYER FOR THE DEAD... THE PERT KERTU...
!!

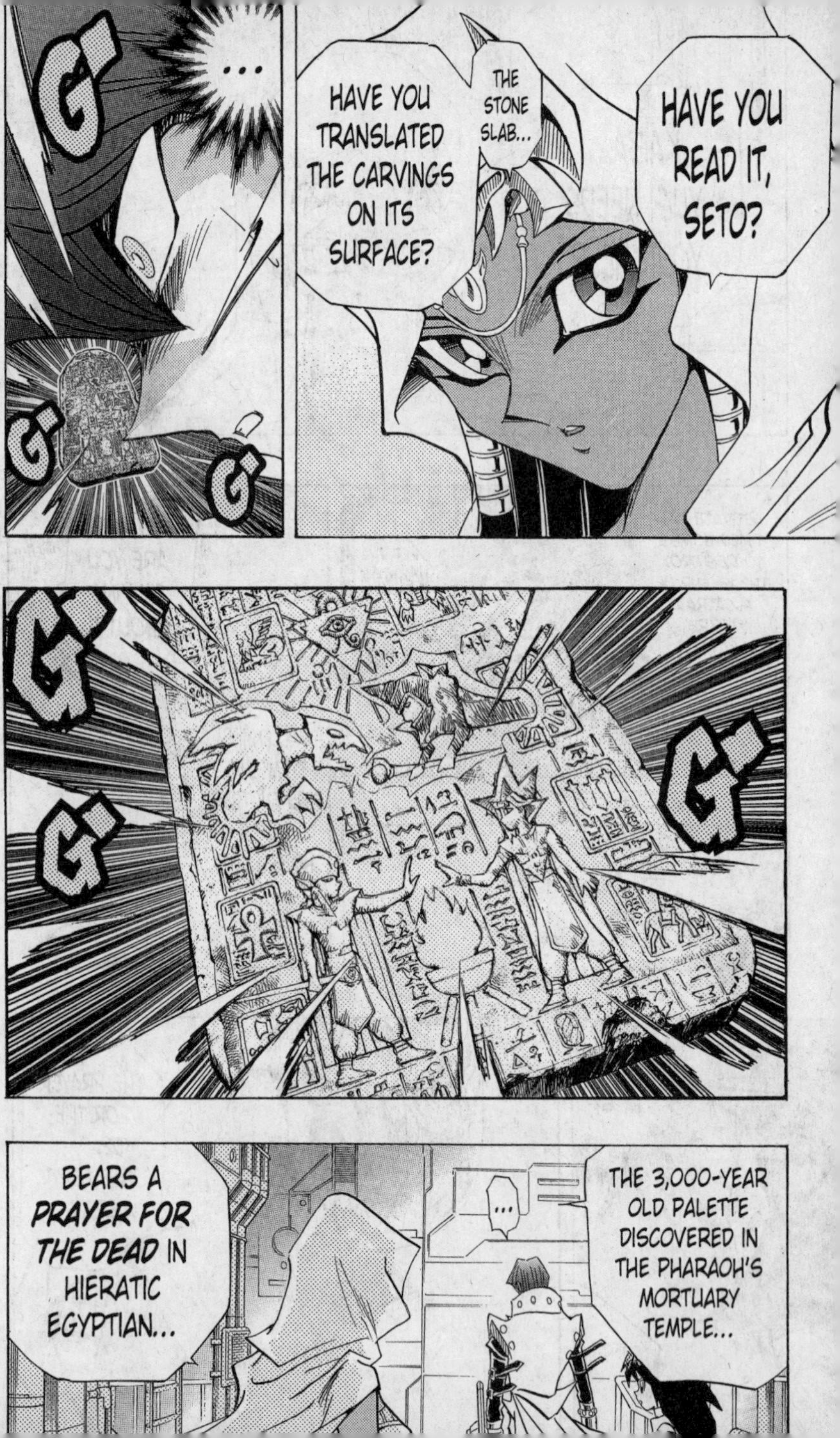
HAVE YOU READ IT, SETO?
THE STONE SLAB...
HAVE YOU TRANSLATED THE CARVINGS ON ITS SURFACE?
...
G
G
G
G
G
G
THE 3,000-YEAR OLD PALETTE DISCOVERED IN THE PHARAOH'S MORTUARY TEMPLE...
...
BEARS A *PRAYER FOR THE DEAD* IN HIERATIC EGYPTIAN...

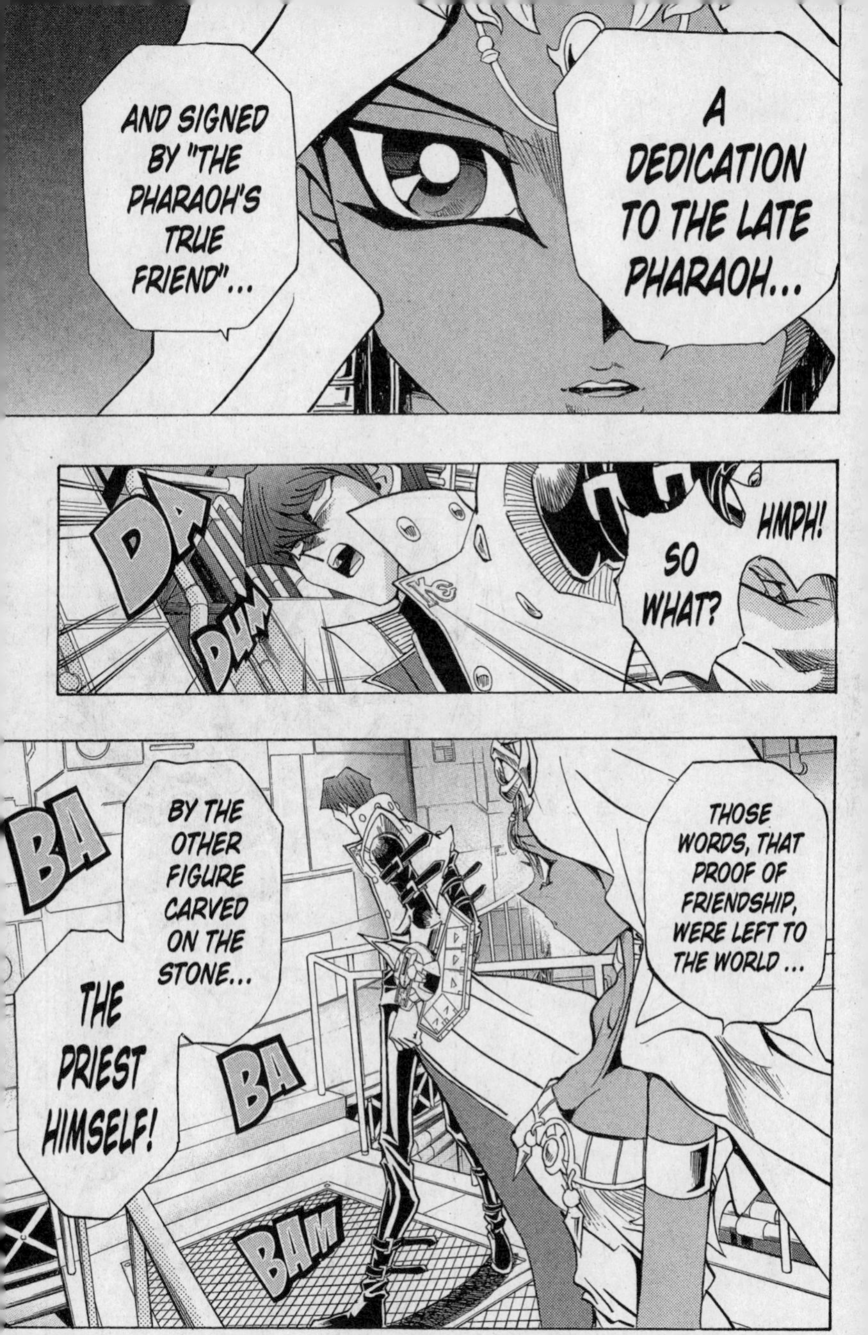
A DEDICATION TO THE LATE PHARAOH...
AND SIGNED BY "THE PHARAOH'S TRUE FRIEND"...
HMPH!
SO WHAT?
DA
DUN
THOSE WORDS, THAT PROOF OF FRIENDSHIP, WERE LEFT TO THE WORLD ...
BY THE OTHER FIGURE CARVED ON THE STONE...
BA
THE PRIEST HIMSELF!
BA
BAM

DUEL 201: THE ENTRUSTED CARD

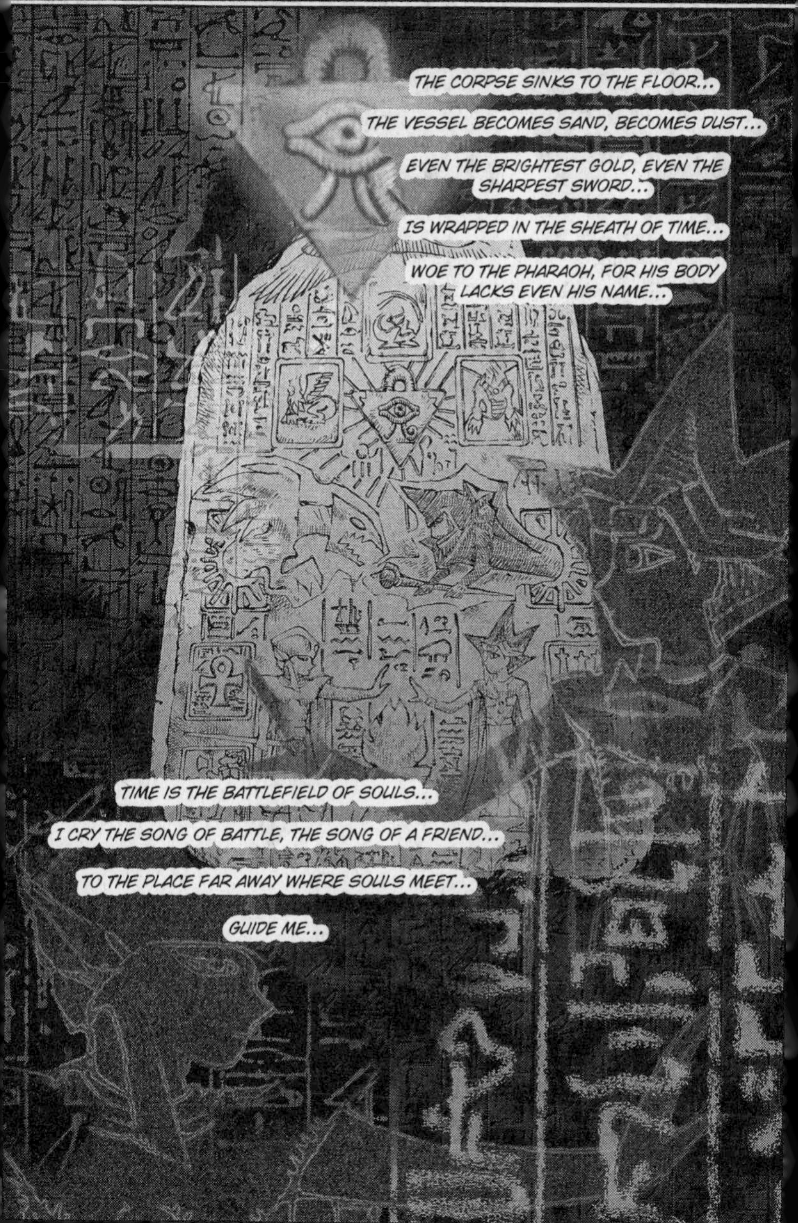
THE CORPSE SINKS TO THE FLOOR...
THE VESSEL BECOMES SAND, BECOMES DUST...
EVEN THE BRIGHTEST GOLD, EVEN THE SHARPEST SWORD...
IS WRAPPED IN THE SHEATH OF TIME...
WOE TO THE PHARAOH, FOR HIS BODY LACKS EVEN HIS NAME...
TIME IS THE BATTLEFIELD OF SOULS...
I CRY THE SONG OF BATTLE, THE SONG OF A FRIEND...
TO THE PLACE FAR AWAY WHERE SOULS MEET...
GUIDE ME...

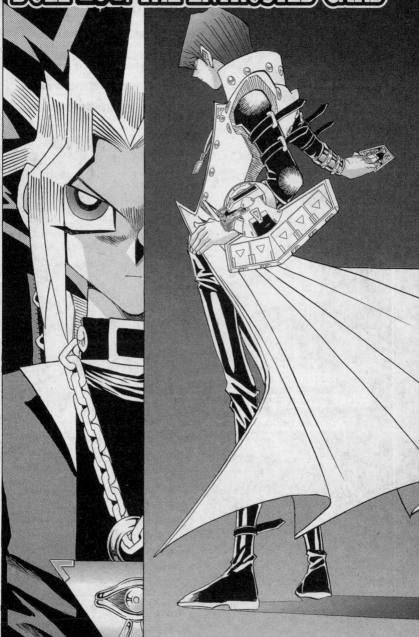

DUEL 264: THE ENTRUSTED CARD

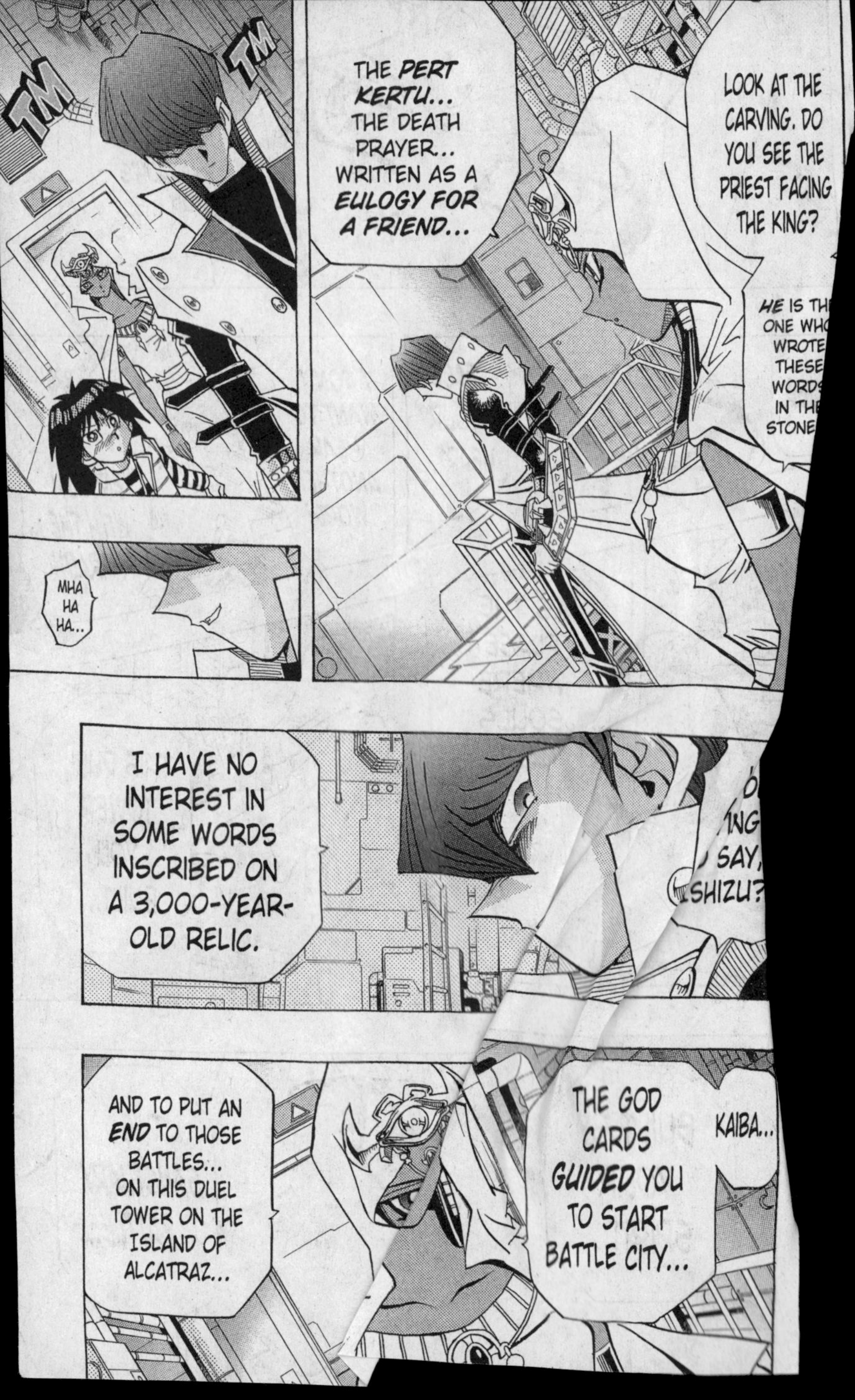
LOOK AT THE CARVING. DO YOU SEE THE PRIEST FACING THE KING?
HE IS TH ONE WHO WROTE THESE WORDS IN THE STONE
THE *PERT KERTU*... THE DEATH PRAYER... WRITTEN AS A *EULOGY FOR A FRIEND*...
TM
TM
MHA HA HA...
SAY, ISHIZU?
I HAVE NO INTEREST IN SOME WORDS INSCRIBED ON A 3,000-YEAR-OLD RELIC.
KAIBA...
THE GOD CARDS *GUIDED* YOU TO START BATTLE CITY...
AND TO PUT AN *END* TO THOSE BATTLES... ON THIS DUEL TOWER ON THE ISLAND OF ALCATRAZ...

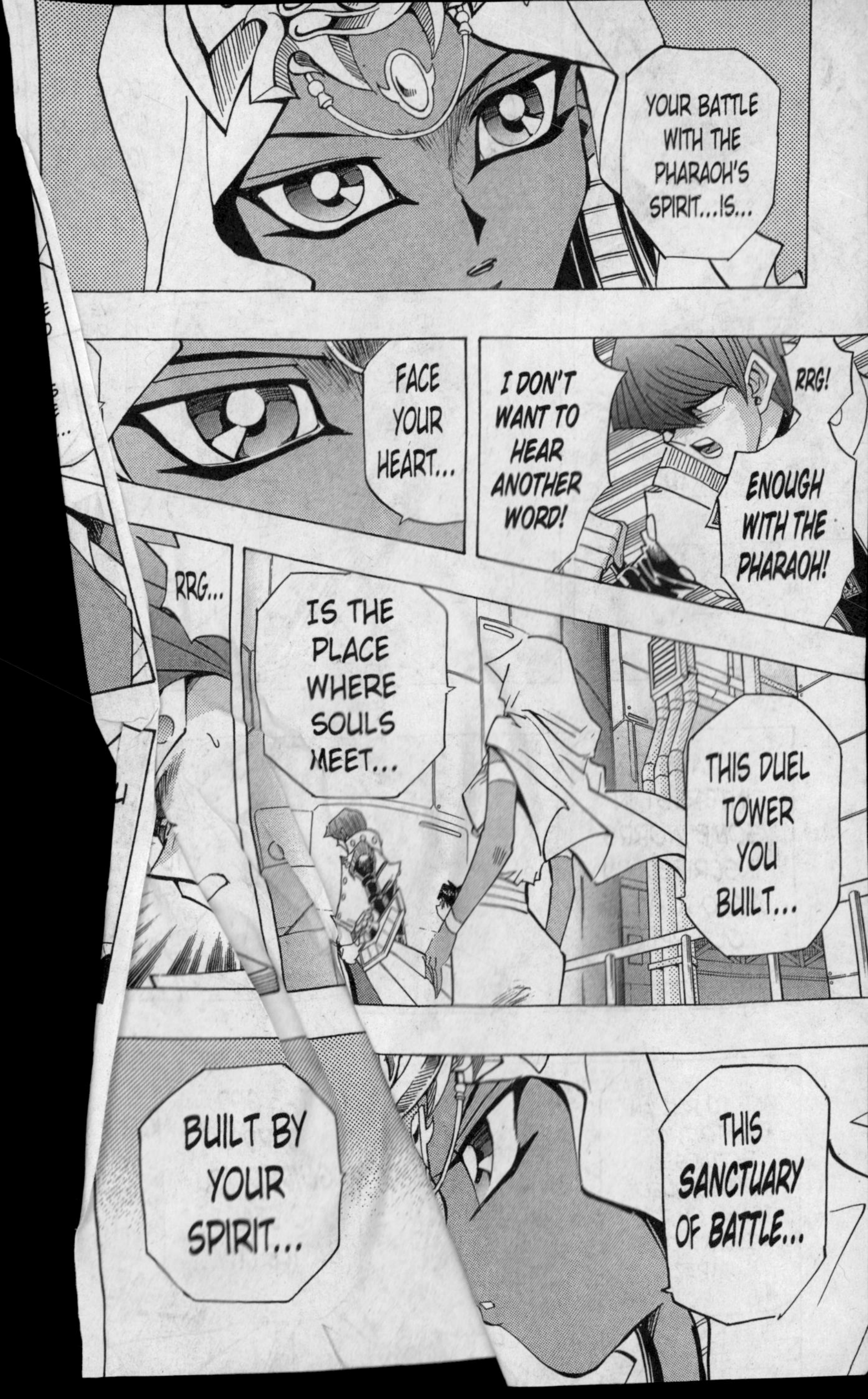
YOUR BATTLE WITH THE PHARAOH'S SPIRIT...IS...
RRG!
ENOUGH WITH THE PHARAOH!
I DON'T WANT TO HEAR ANOTHER WORD!
FACE YOUR HEART...
THIS DUEL TOWER YOU BUILT...
IS THE PLACE WHERE SOULS MEET...
RRG...
THIS SANCTUARY OF BATTLE...
BUILT BY YOUR SPIRIT...

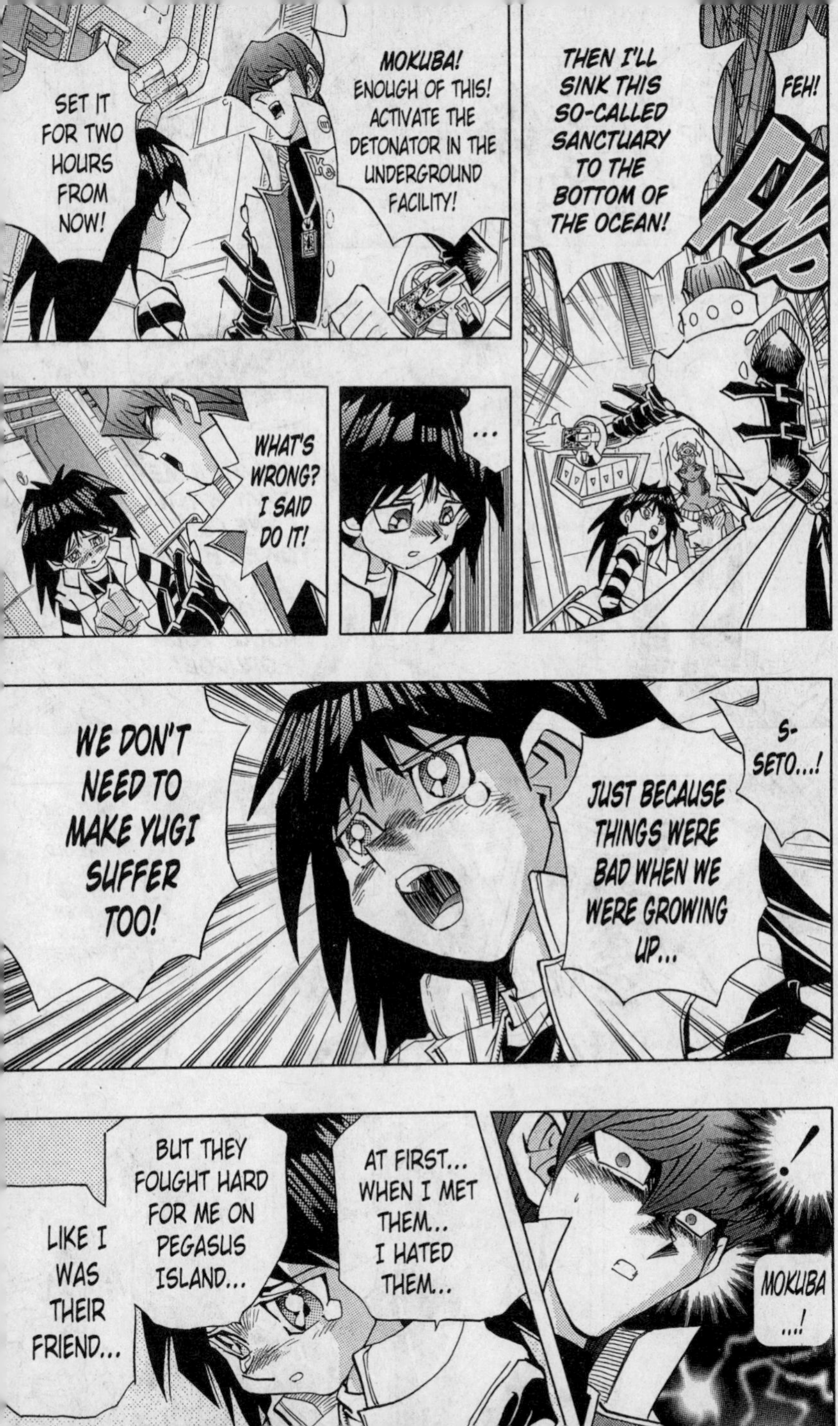
FEH!
THEN I'LL SINK THIS SO-CALLED SANCTUARY TO THE BOTTOM OF THE OCEAN!
FWP
MOKUBA! ENOUGH OF THIS! ACTIVATE THE DETONATOR IN THE UNDERGROUND FACILITY!
SET IT FOR TWO HOURS FROM NOW!
...
WHAT'S WRONG? I SAID DO IT!
S-SETO...!
JUST BECAUSE THINGS WERE BAD WHEN WE WERE GROWING UP...
WE DON'T NEED TO MAKE YUGI SUFFER TOO!
!
MOKUBA...!
AT FIRST... WHEN I MET THEM... I HATED THEM...
BUT THEY FOUGHT HARD FOR ME ON PEGASUS ISLAND...
LIKE I WAS THEIR FRIEND...

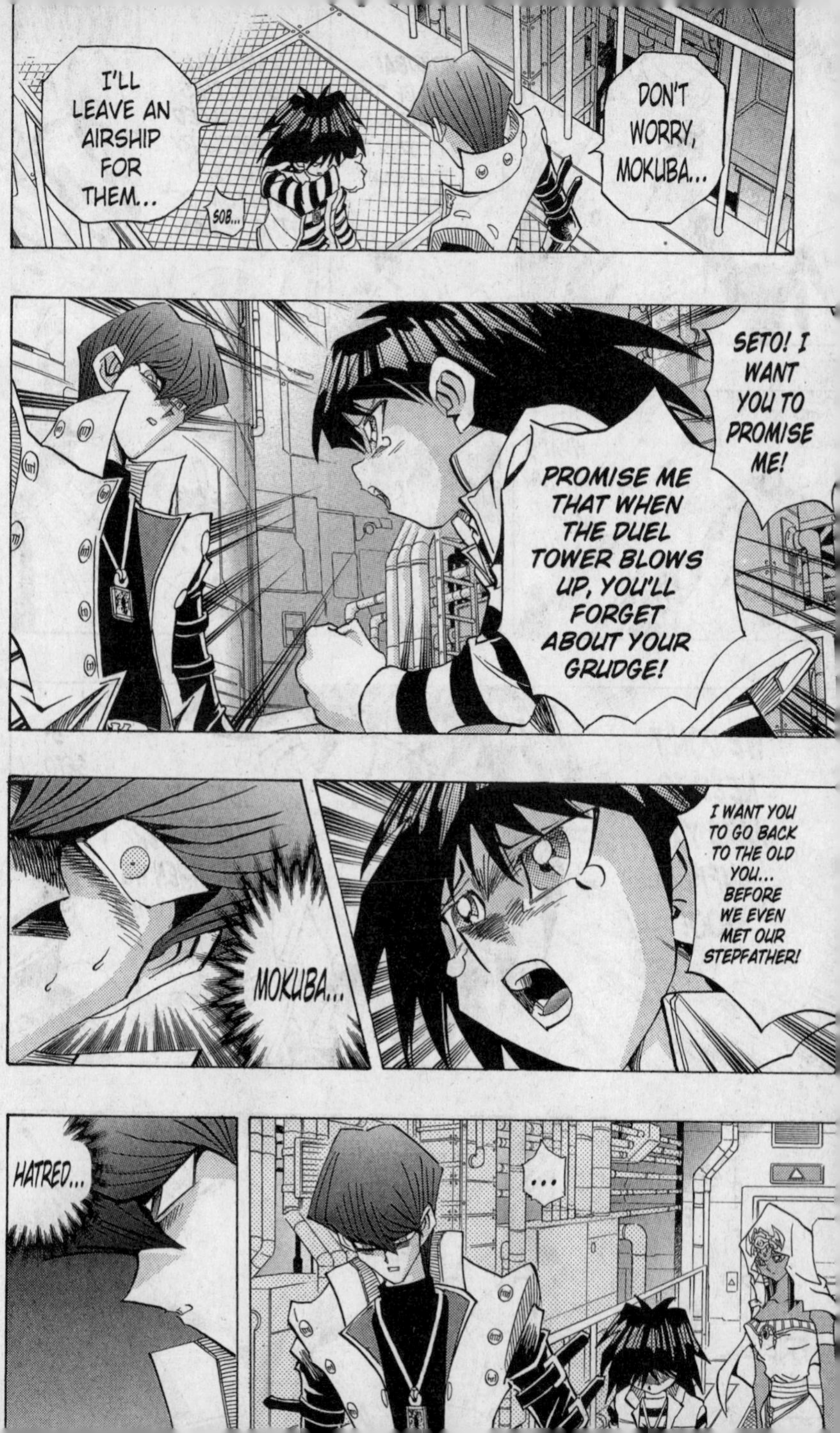
DON'T WORRY, MOKUBA...
I'LL LEAVE AN AIRSHIP FOR THEM...
SOB...
SETO! I WANT YOU TO PROMISE ME!
PROMISE ME THAT WHEN THE DUEL TOWER BLOWS UP, YOU'LL FORGET ABOUT YOUR GRUDGE!
I WANT YOU TO GO BACK TO THE OLD YOU... BEFORE WE EVEN MET OUR STEPFATHER!
MOKUBA...
...
HATRED...

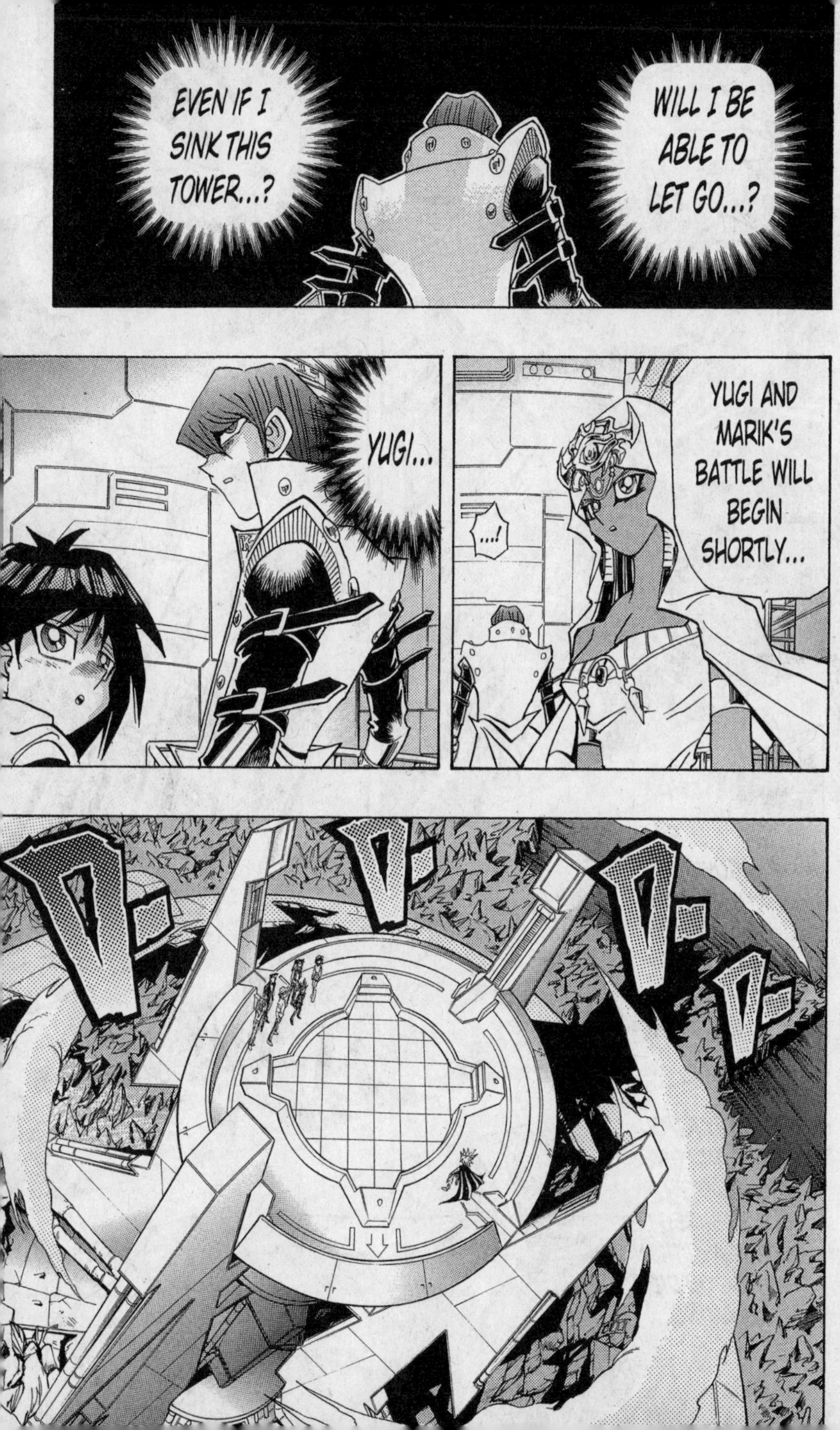
WILL I BE ABLE TO LET GO...?
EVEN IF I SINK THIS TOWER...?
YUGI AND MARIK'S BATTLE WILL BEGIN SHORTLY...
...!
YUGI...

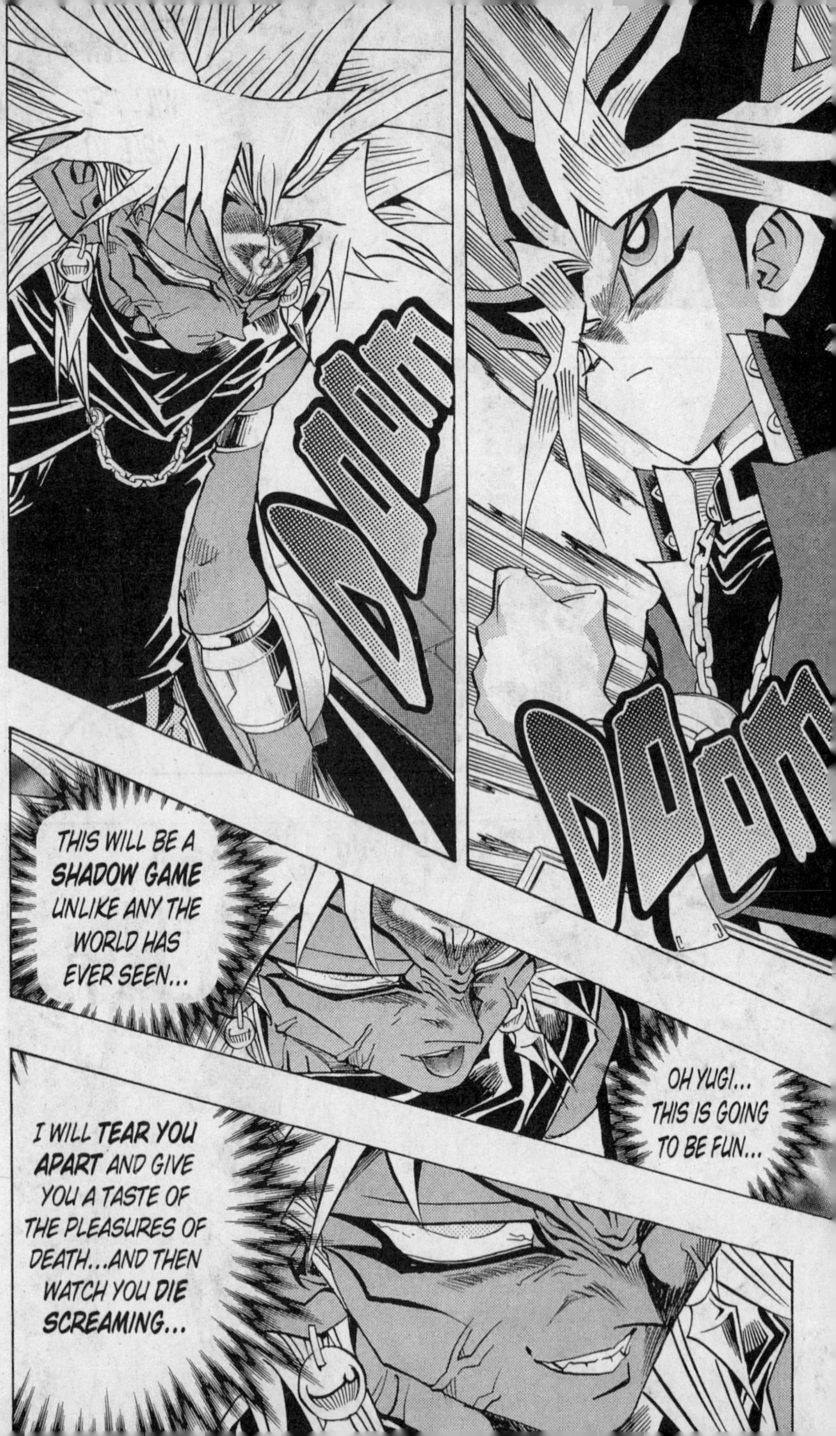
DOOM
DOOM
THIS WILL BE A SHADOW GAME UNLIKE ANY THE WORLD HAS EVER SEEN...
OH YUGI... THIS IS GOING TO BE FUN...
I WILL TEAR YOU APART AND GIVE YOU A TASTE OF THE PLEASURES OF DEATH...AND THEN WATCH YOU DIE SCREAMING...

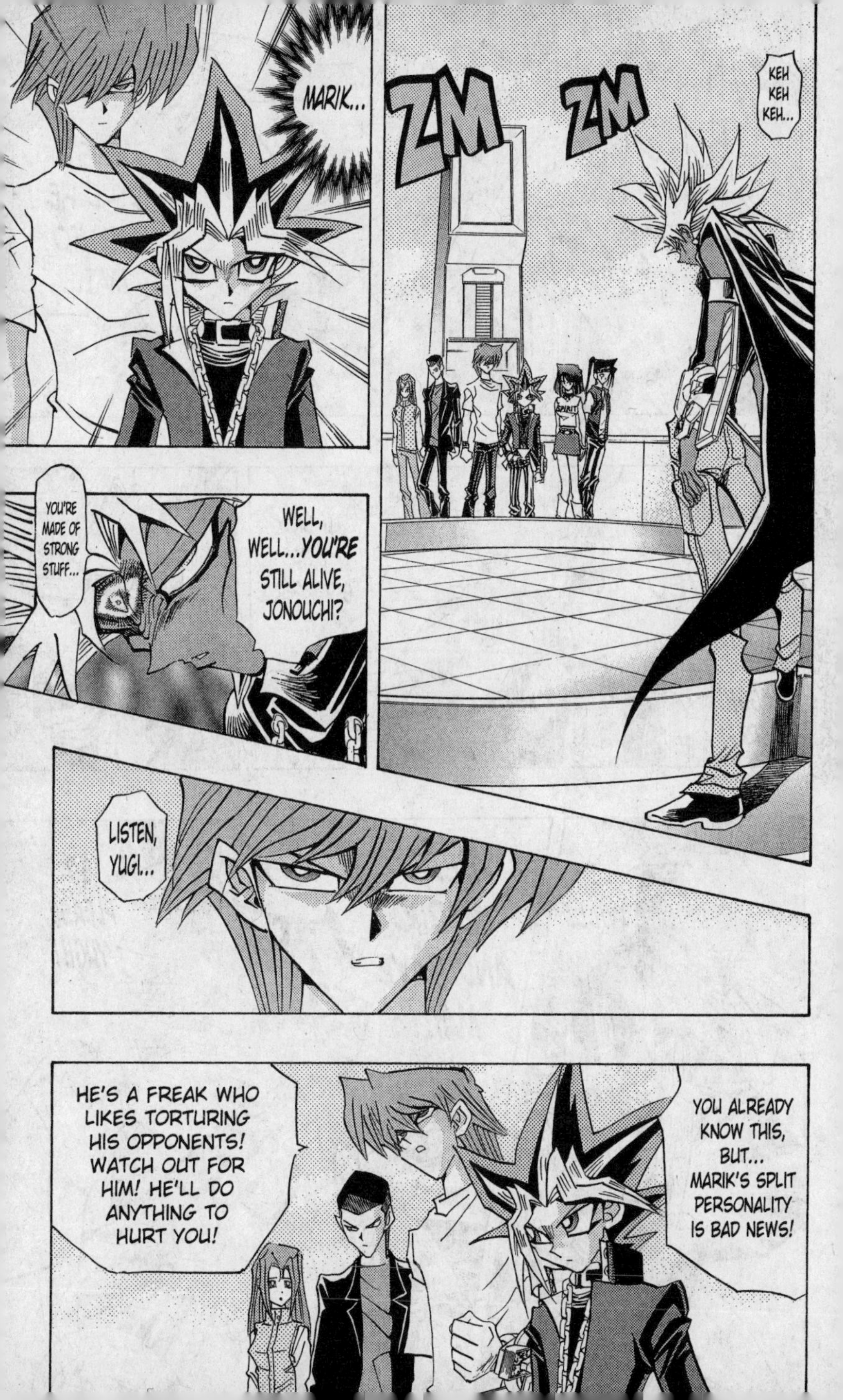
ZM
ZM
KEH KEH KEH...
MARIK...
WELL, WELL...YOU'RE STILL ALIVE, JONOUCHI?
YOU'RE MADE OF STRONG STUFF...
LISTEN, YUGI...
YOU ALREADY KNOW THIS, BUT... MARIK'S SPLIT PERSONALITY IS BAD NEWS!
HE'S A FREAK WHO LIKES TORTURING HIS OPPONENTS! WATCH OUT FOR HIM! HE'LL DO ANYTHING TO HURT YOU!

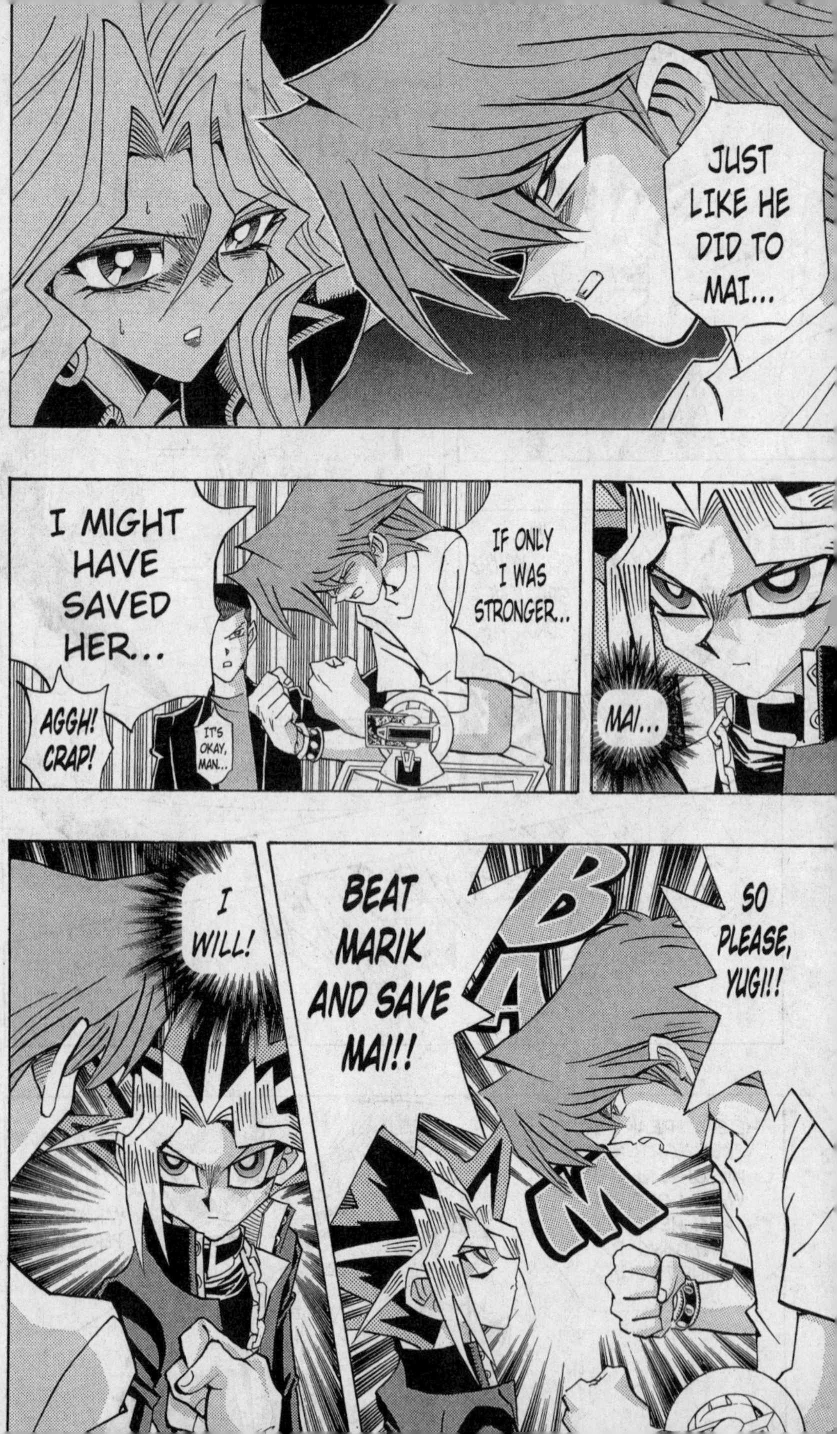
JUST LIKE HE DID TO MAI...
MAI...
IF ONLY I WAS STRONGER...
I MIGHT HAVE SAVED HER...
IT'S OKAY, MAN...
AGGH! CRAP!
BAM
BEAT MARIK AND SAVE MAI!!
SO PLEASE, YUGI!!
I WILL!

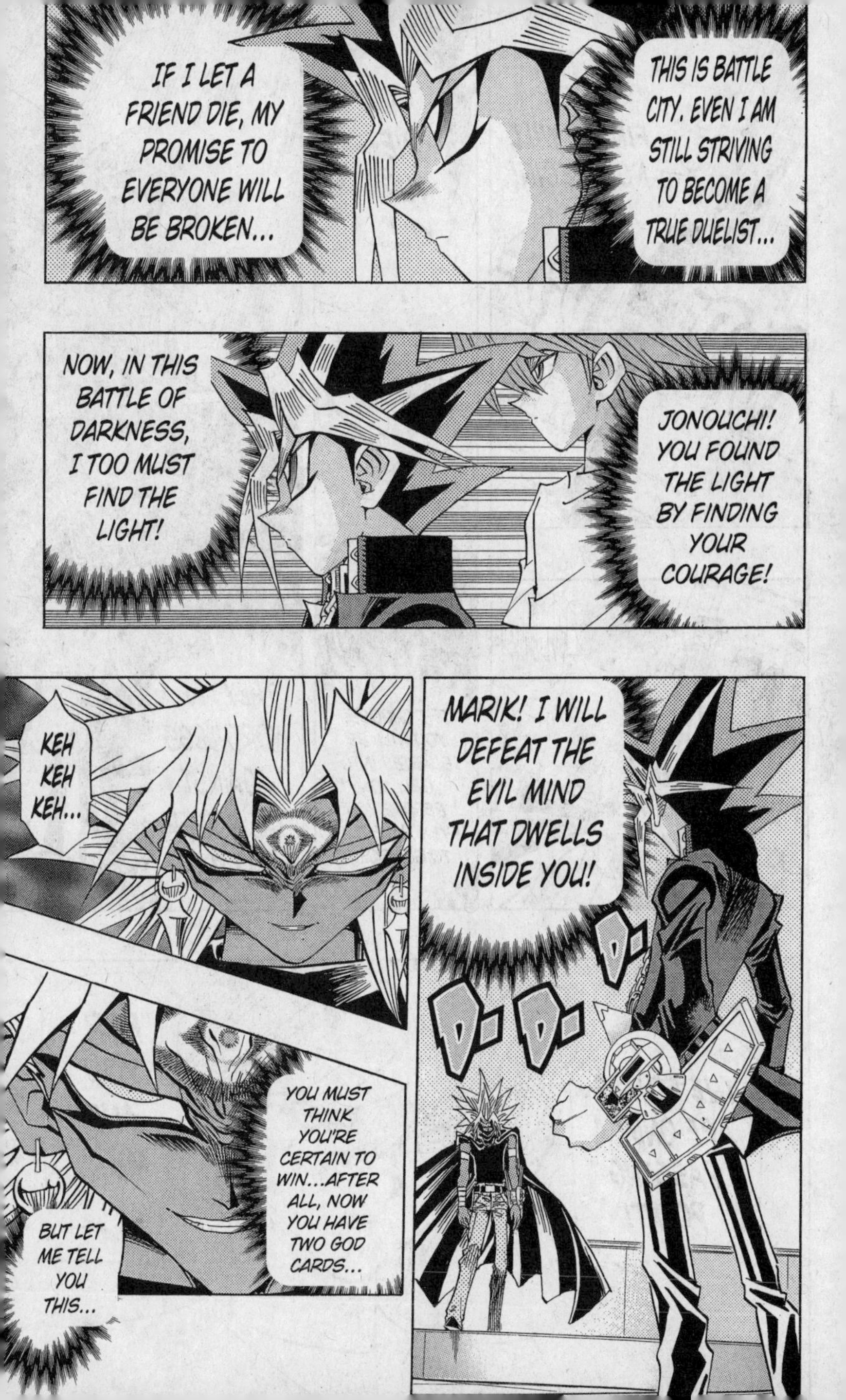
THIS IS BATTLE CITY. EVEN I AM STILL STRIVING TO BECOME A TRUE DUELIST...
IF I LET A FRIEND DIE, MY PROMISE TO EVERYONE WILL BE BROKEN...
JONOUCHI! YOU FOUND THE LIGHT BY FINDING YOUR COURAGE!
NOW, IN THIS BATTLE OF DARKNESS, I TOO MUST FIND THE LIGHT!
MARIK! I WILL DEFEAT THE EVIL MIND THAT DWELLS INSIDE YOU!
D. D. D.
KEH KEH KEH...
YOU MUST THINK YOU'RE CERTAIN TO WIN...AFTER ALL, NOW YOU HAVE TWO GOD CARDS...
BUT LET ME TELL YOU THIS...

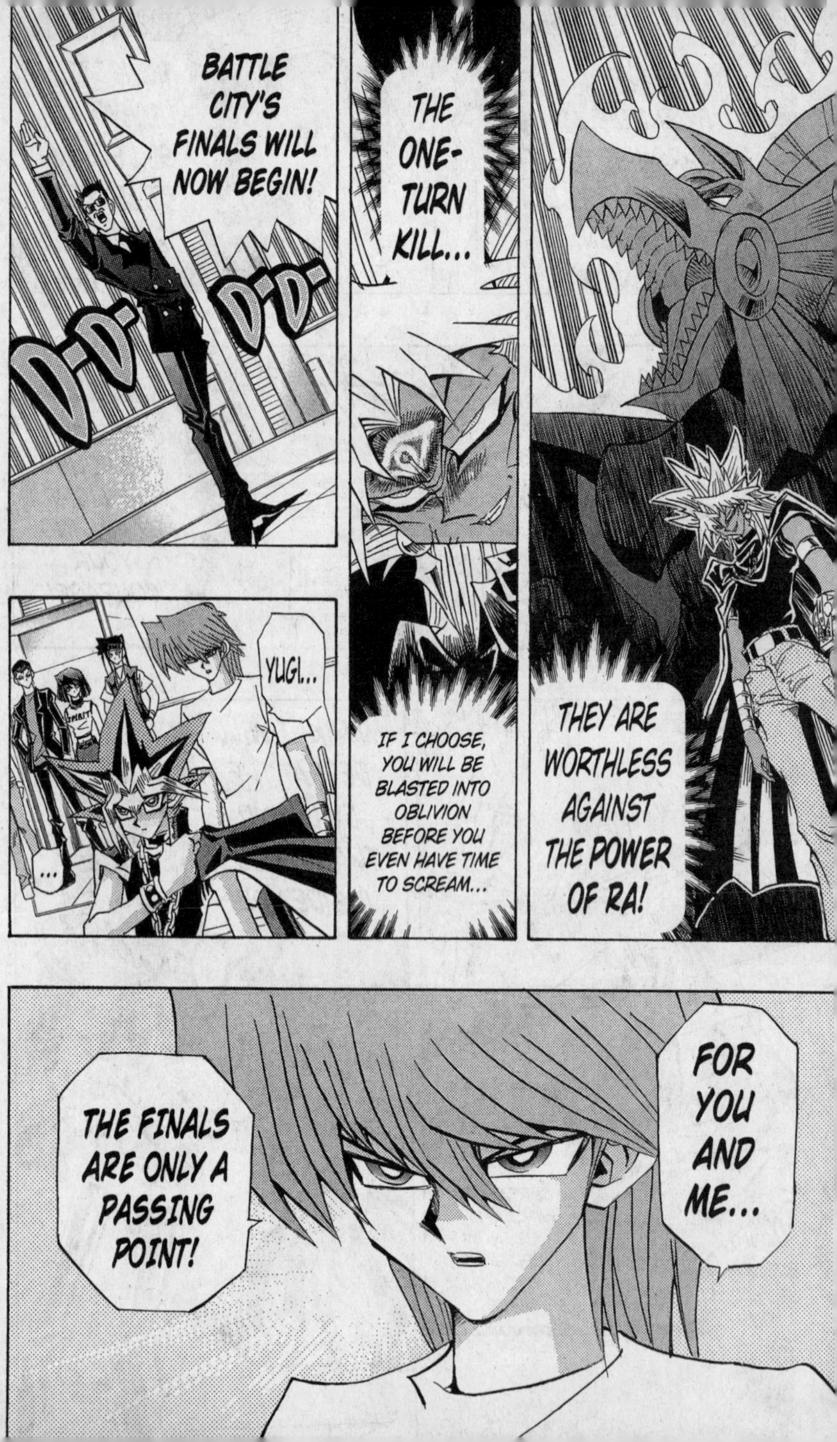
THEY ARE WORTHLESS AGAINST THE POWER OF RA!
THE ONE-TURN KILL...
IF I CHOOSE, YOU WILL BE BLASTED INTO OBLIVION BEFORE YOU EVEN HAVE TIME TO SCREAM...
BATTLE CITY'S FINALS WILL NOW BEGIN!
D-D- D-D-
YUGI...
...
FOR YOU AND ME...
THE FINALS ARE ONLY A PASSING POINT!

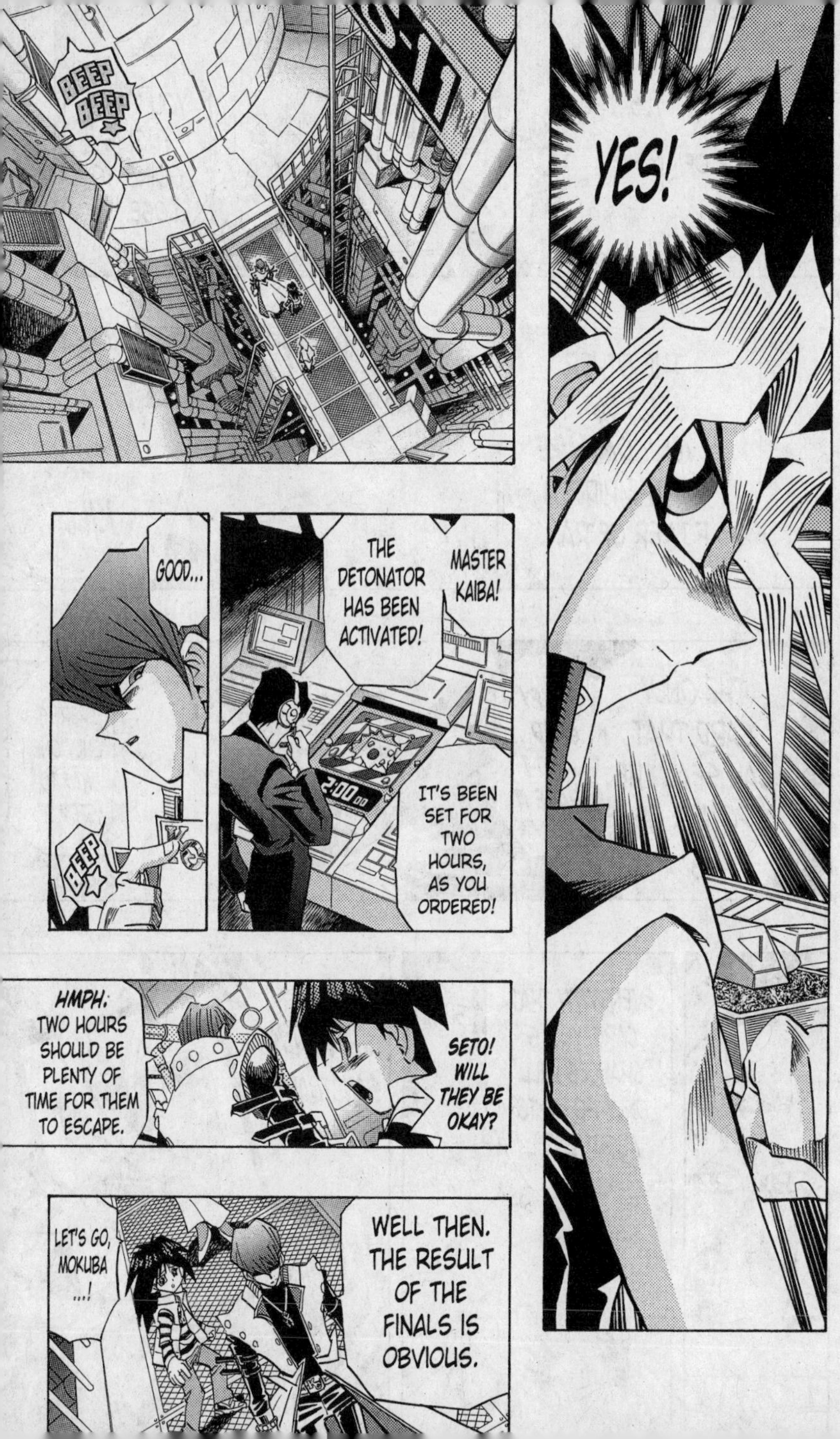
YES!
BEEP BEEP
MASTER KAIBA!
THE DETONATOR HAS BEEN ACTIVATED!
2:00
IT'S BEEN SET FOR TWO HOURS, AS YOU ORDERED!
GOOD...
BEEP
SETO! WILL THEY BE OKAY?
HMPH: TWO HOURS SHOULD BE PLENTY OF TIME FOR THEM TO ESCAPE.
WELL THEN. THE RESULT OF THE FINALS IS OBVIOUS.
LET'S GO, MOKUBA ...!

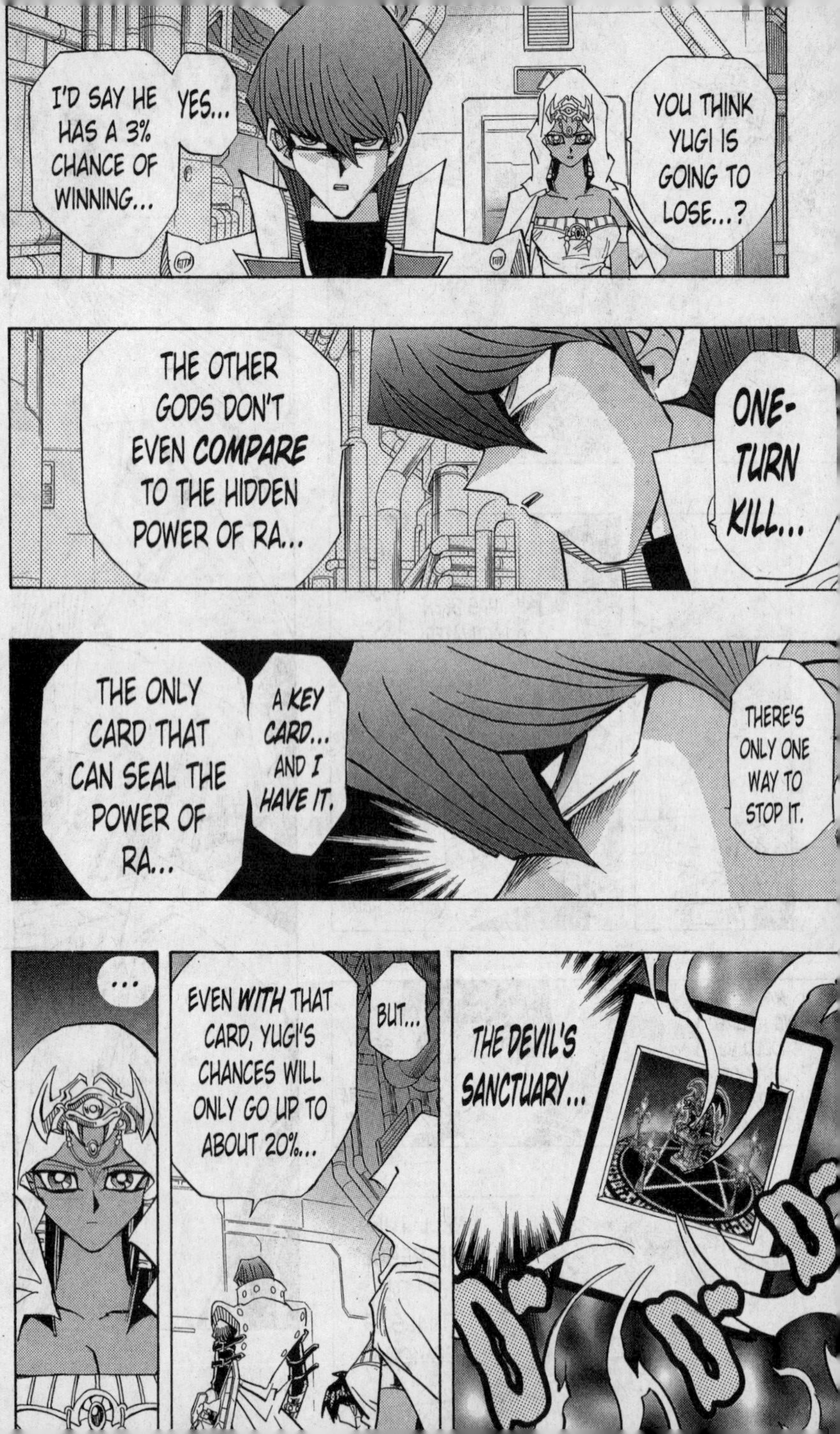
YOU THINK YUGI IS GOING TO LOSE...?
YES...
I'D SAY HE HAS A 3% CHANCE OF WINNING...
ONE-TURN KILL...
THE OTHER GODS DON'T EVEN COMPARE TO THE HIDDEN POWER OF RA...
THERE'S ONLY ONE WAY TO STOP IT.
A KEY CARD... AND I HAVE IT.
THE ONLY CARD THAT CAN SEAL THE POWER OF RA...
THE DEVIL'S SANCTUARY...
BUT...
EVEN WITH THAT CARD, YUGI'S CHANCES WILL ONLY GO UP TO ABOUT 20%...
...

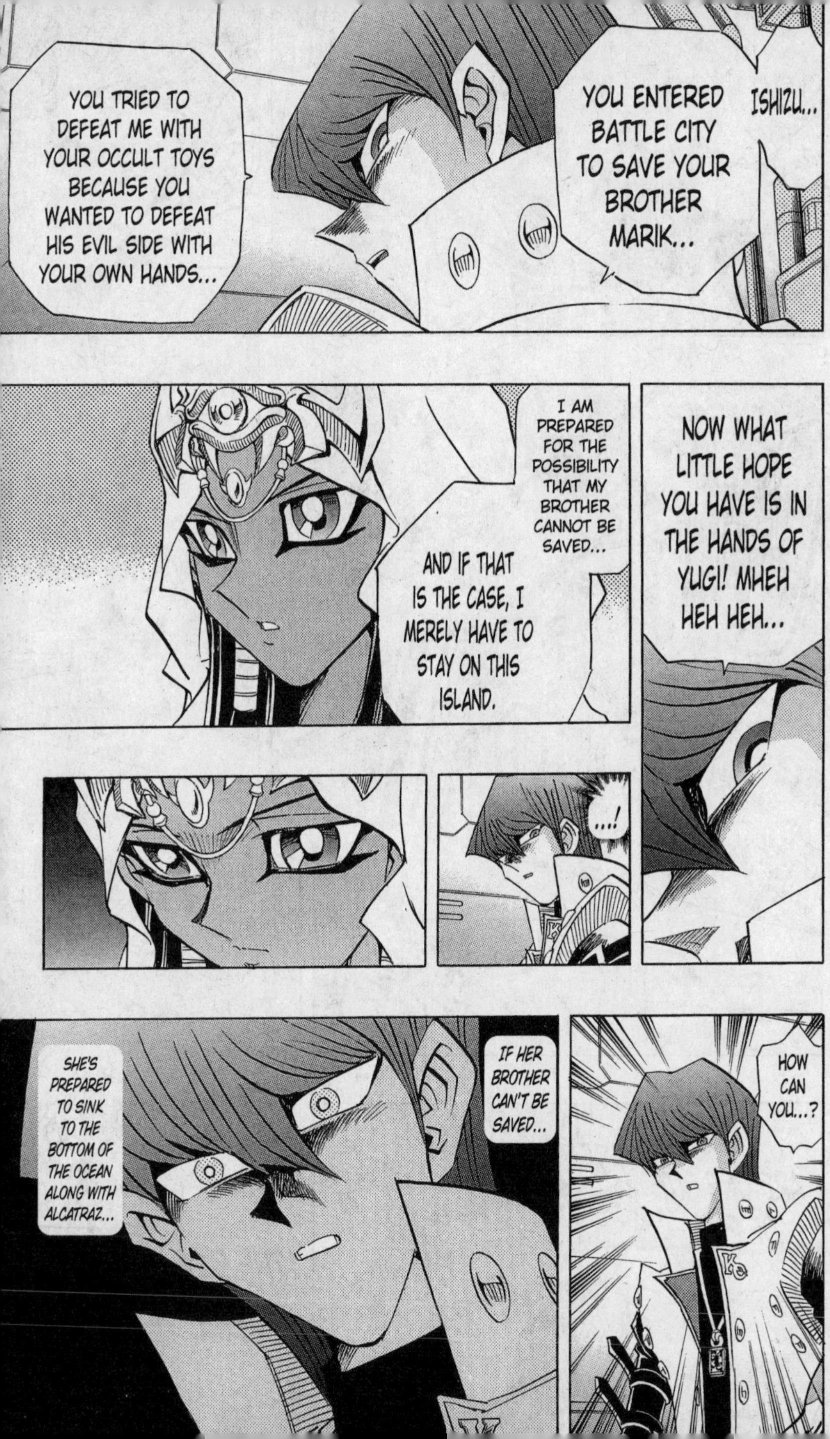
ISHIZU...
YOU ENTERED BATTLE CITY TO SAVE YOUR BROTHER MARIK...
YOU TRIED TO DEFEAT ME WITH YOUR OCCULT TOYS BECAUSE YOU WANTED TO DEFEAT HIS EVIL SIDE WITH YOUR OWN HANDS...
NOW WHAT LITTLE HOPE YOU HAVE IS IN THE HANDS OF YUGI! MHEH HEH HEH...
I AM PREPARED FOR THE POSSIBILITY THAT MY BROTHER CANNOT BE SAVED...
AND IF THAT IS THE CASE, I MERELY HAVE TO STAY ON THIS ISLAND.
...!
HOW CAN YOU...?
IF HER BROTHER CAN'T BE SAVED...
SHE'S PREPARED TO SINK TO THE BOTTOM OF THE OCEAN ALONG WITH ALCATRAZ...

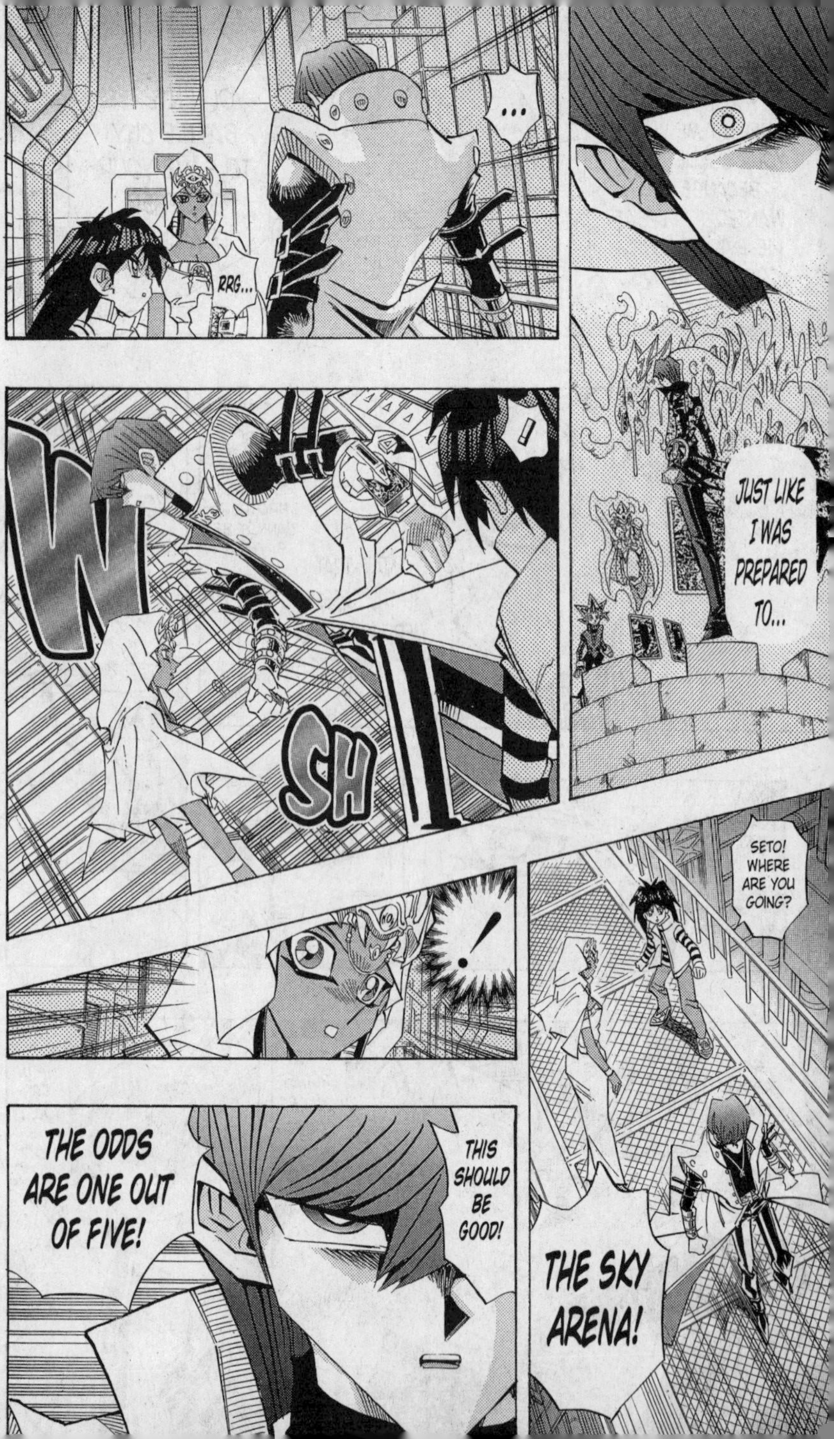
JUST LIKE I WAS PREPARED TO...
...
RRG...
!
W
SH
SETO! WHERE ARE YOU GOING?
THE SKY ARENA!
!
THIS SHOULD BE GOOD!
THE ODDS ARE ONE OUT OF FIVE!

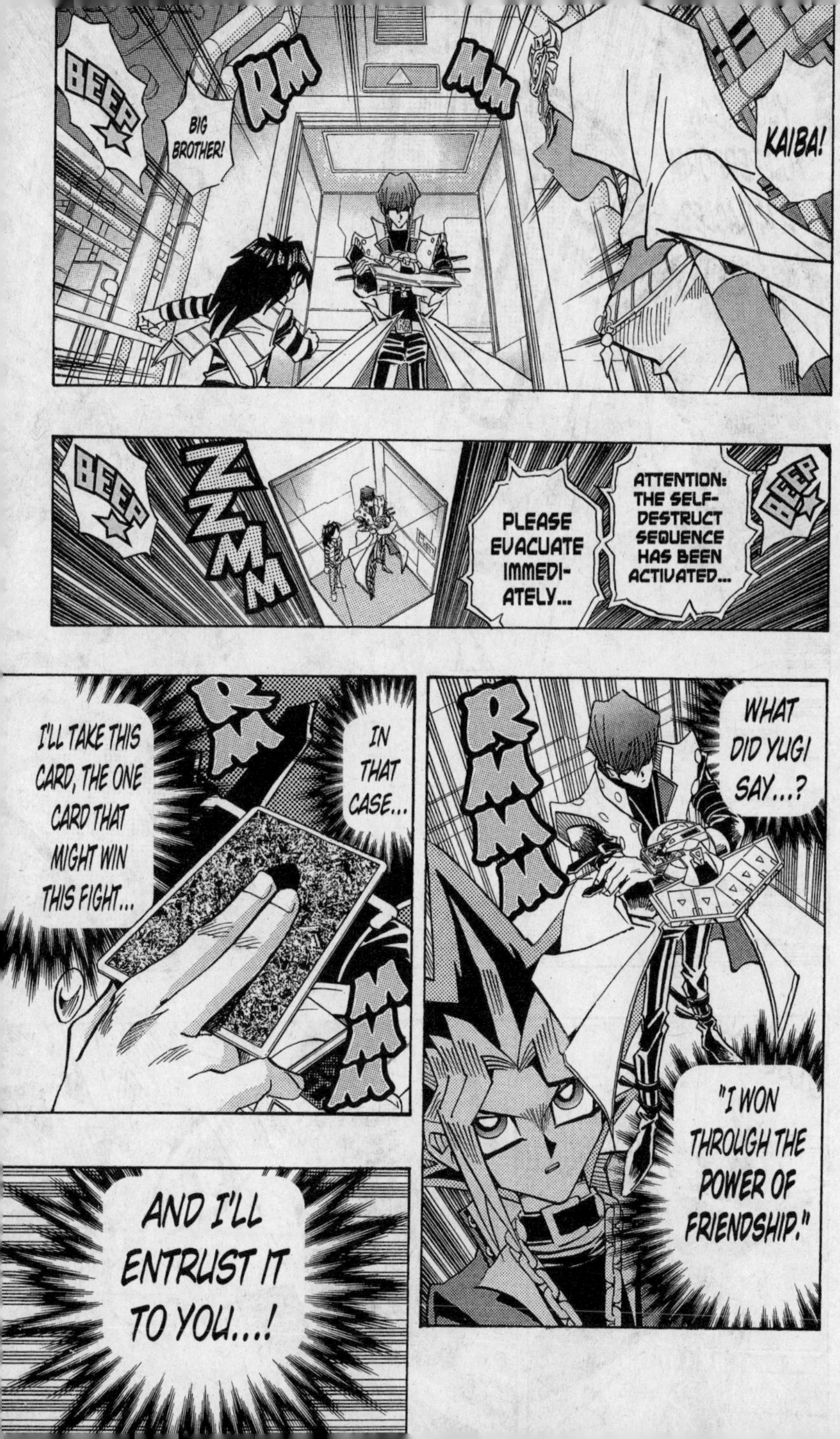
MM
KAIBA!
RM
BIG BROTHER!
BEEP☆
BEEP☆
ATTENTION: THE SELF-DESTRUCT SEQUENCE HAS BEEN ACTIVATED...
PLEASE EVACUATE IMMEDIATELY...
ZZMMM
BEEP☆
WHAT DID YUGI SAY...?
RMMMM
"I WON THROUGH THE POWER OF FRIENDSHIP."
IN THAT CASE...
RM
I'LL TAKE THIS CARD, THE ONE CARD THAT MIGHT WIN THIS FIGHT...
MMMM
AND I'LL ENTRUST IT TO YOU...!

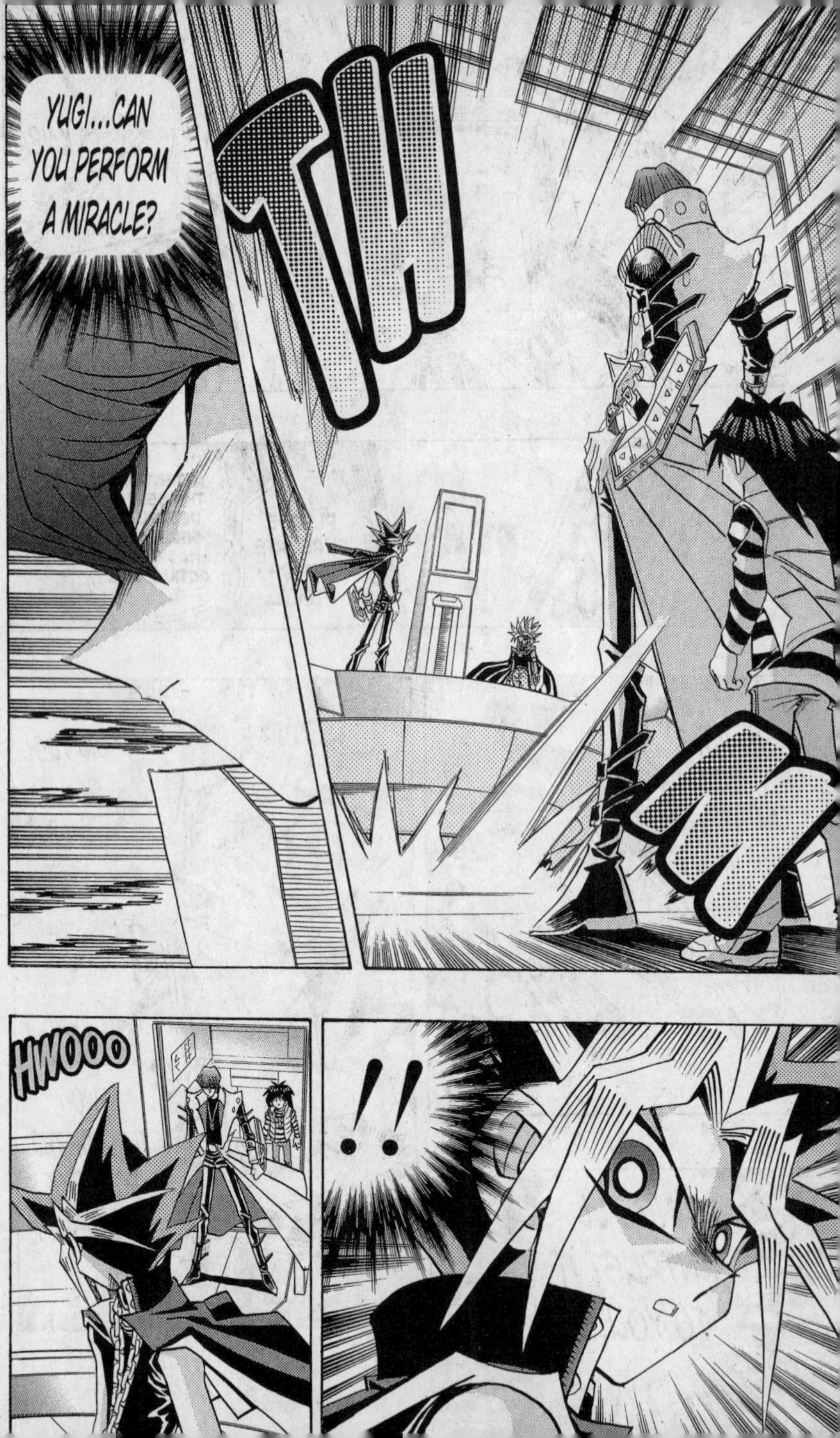
YUGI...CAN YOU PERFORM A MIRACLE?
!!
HWOOO

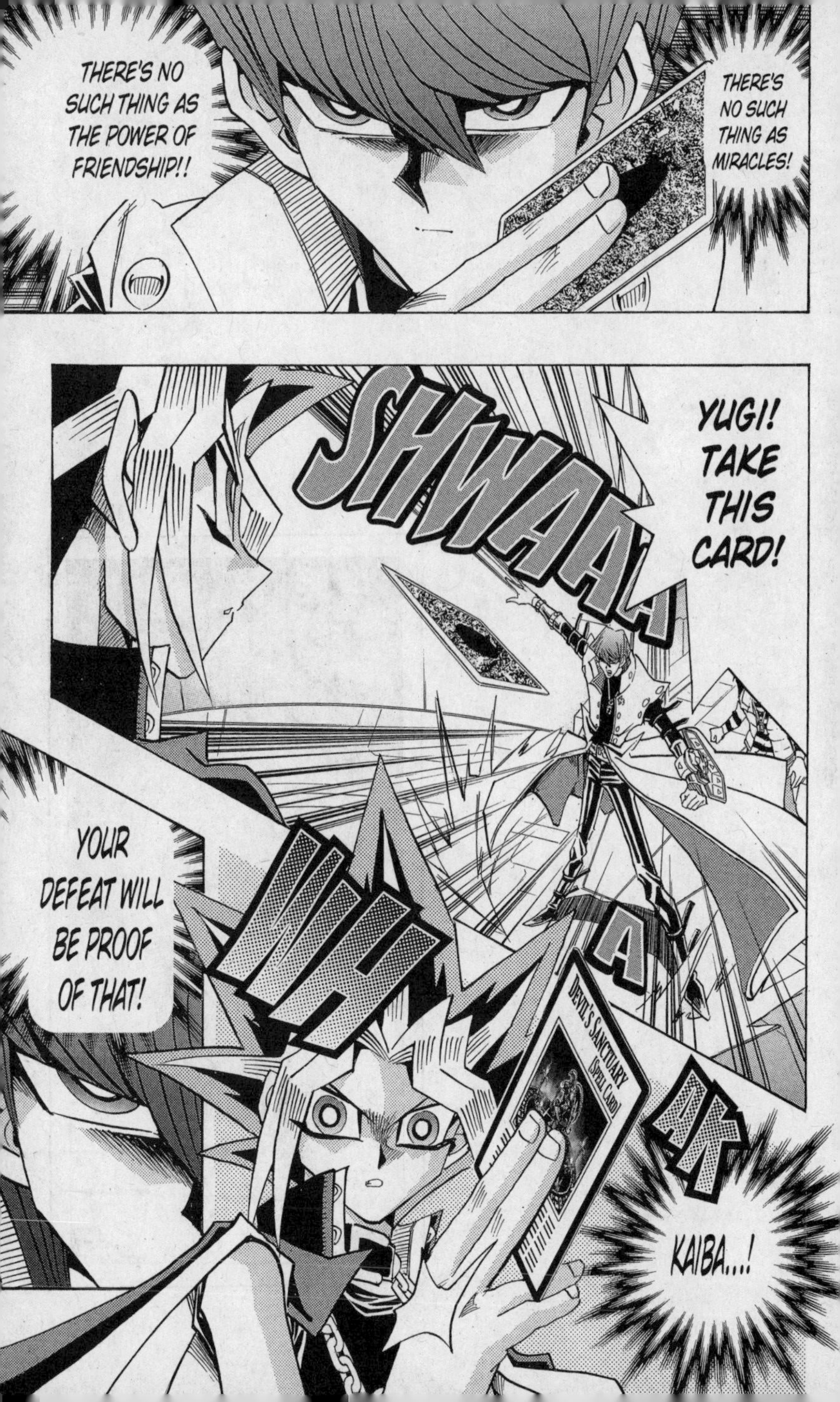
THERE'S NO SUCH THING AS MIRACLES!
THERE'S NO SUCH THING AS THE POWER OF FRIENDSHIP!!
YUGI! TAKE THIS CARD!
YOUR DEFEAT WILL BE PROOF OF THAT!
DEVIL'S SANCTUARY [SPELL CARD]
KAIBA...!

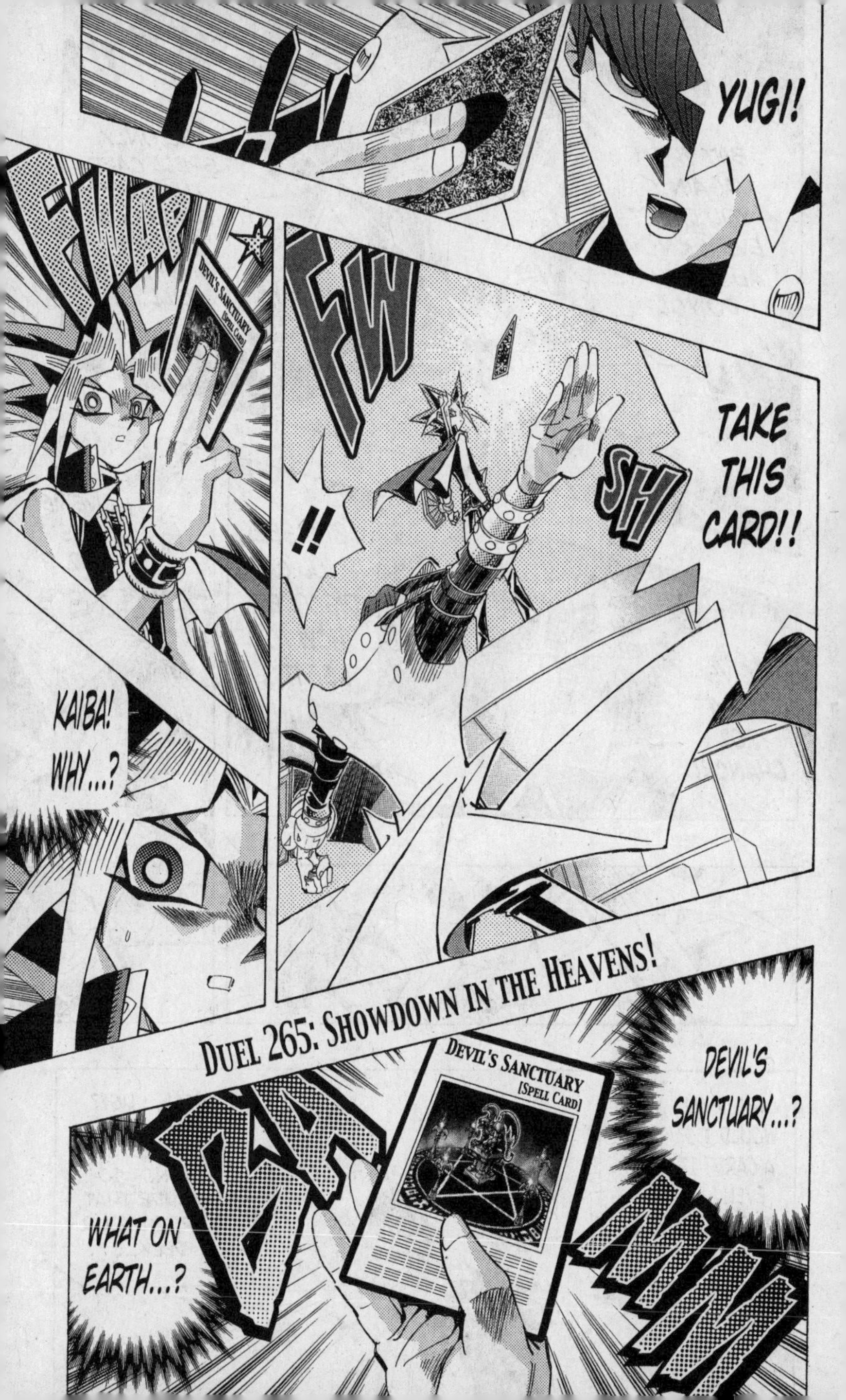

YUGI!
TAKE THIS CARD!!
SH
FW
!!
FWAP
DEVIL'S SANCTUARY
[SPELL CARD]
KAIBA! WHY...?
Duel 265: Showdown in the Heavens!
DEVIL'S SANCTUARY...?
DEVIL'S SANCTUARY
[SPELL CARD]
WHAT ON EARTH...?

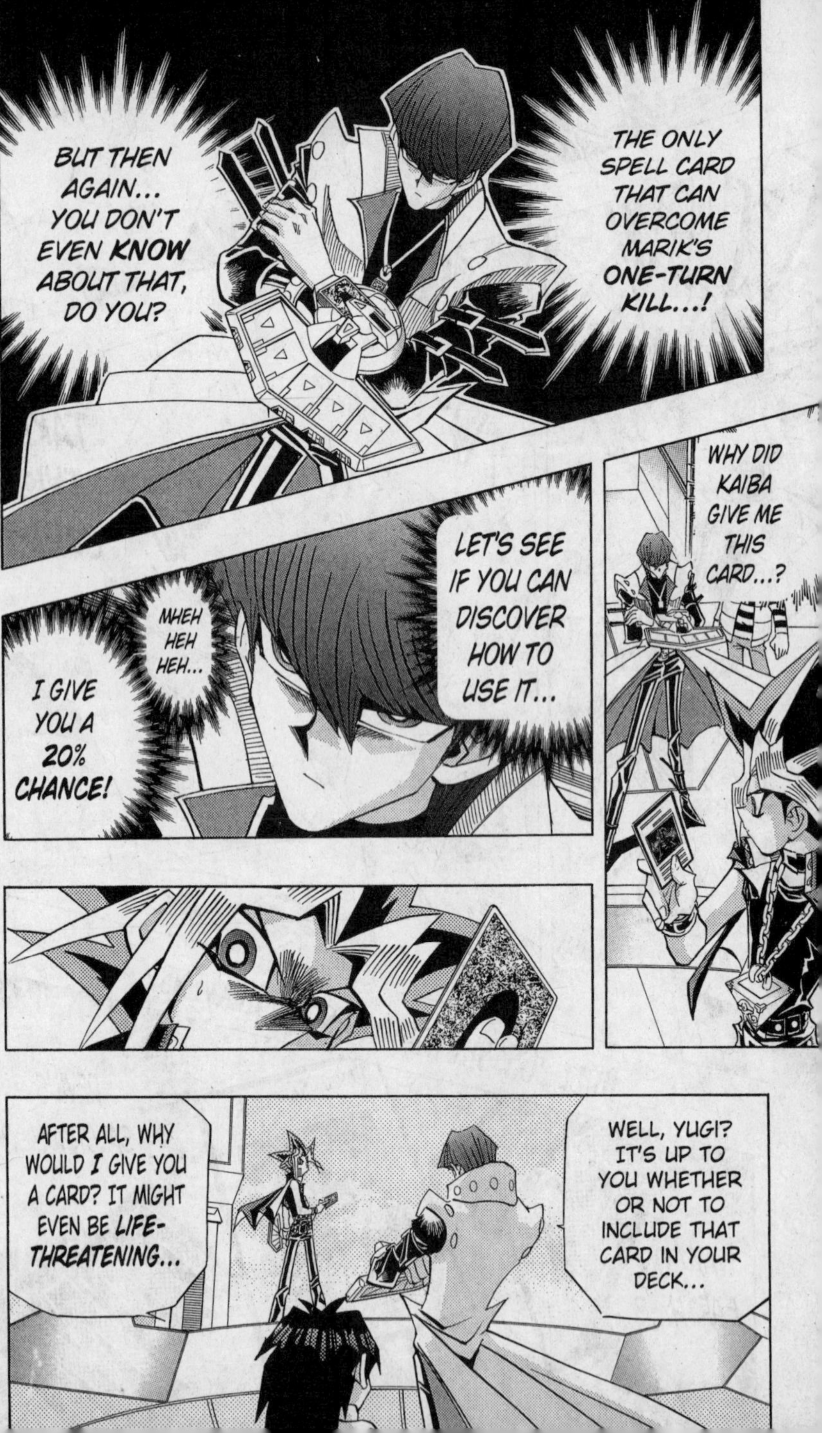
THE ONLY SPELL CARD THAT CAN OVERCOME MARIK'S ONE-TURN KILL...!
BUT THEN AGAIN... YOU DON'T EVEN KNOW ABOUT THAT, DO YOU?
WHY DID KAIBA GIVE ME THIS CARD...?
LET'S SEE IF YOU CAN DISCOVER HOW TO USE IT...
MHEH HEH HEH...
I GIVE YOU A 20% CHANCE!
WELL, YUGI? IT'S UP TO YOU WHETHER OR NOT TO INCLUDE THAT CARD IN YOUR DECK...
AFTER ALL, WHY WOULD I GIVE YOU A CARD? IT MIGHT EVEN BE LIFE-THREATENING...

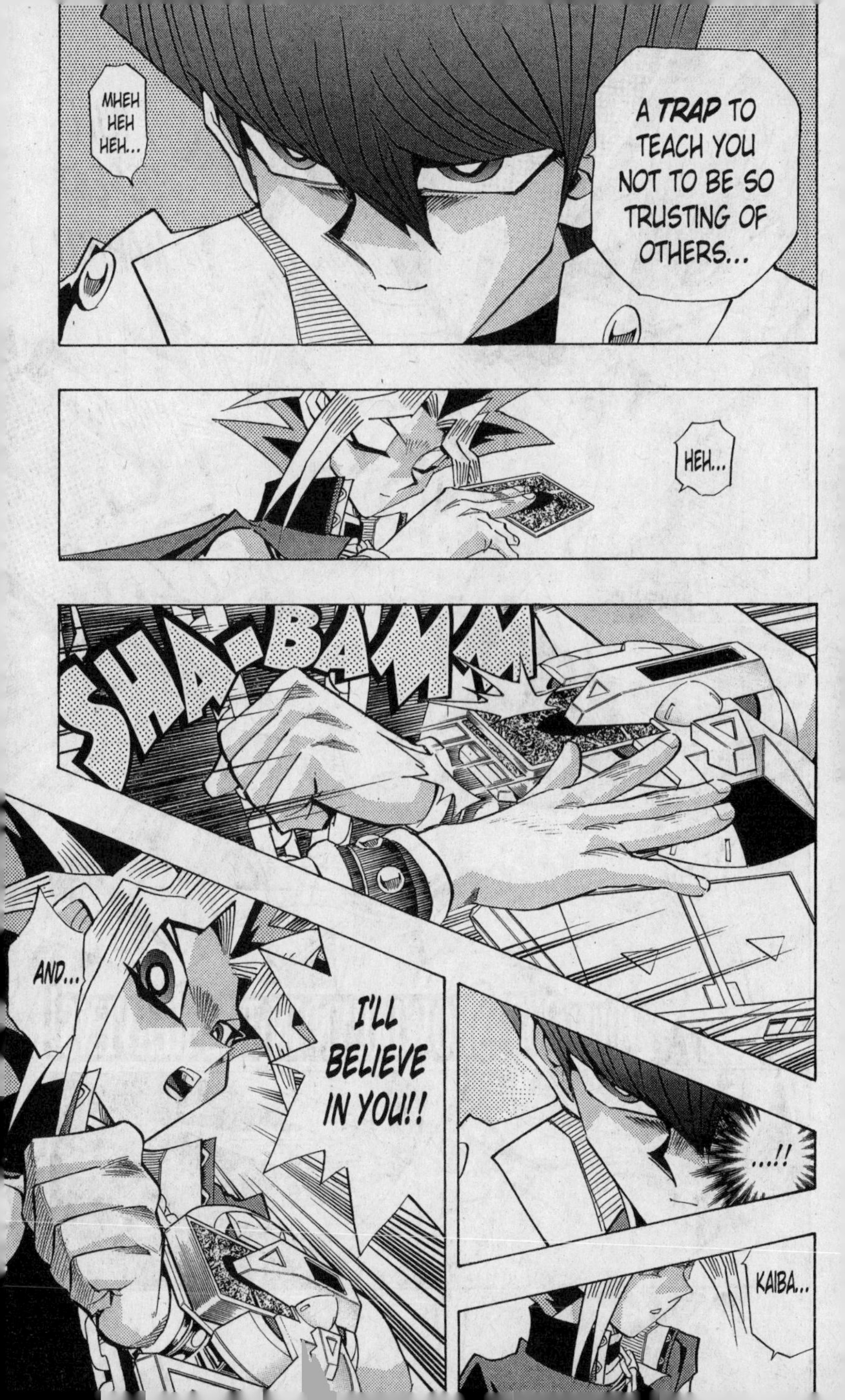
A TRAP TO TEACH YOU NOT TO BE SO TRUSTING OF OTHERS...
MHEH HEH HEH...
HEH...
SHA-BAMM
...!!
KAIBA...
AND...
I'LL BELIEVE IN YOU!!

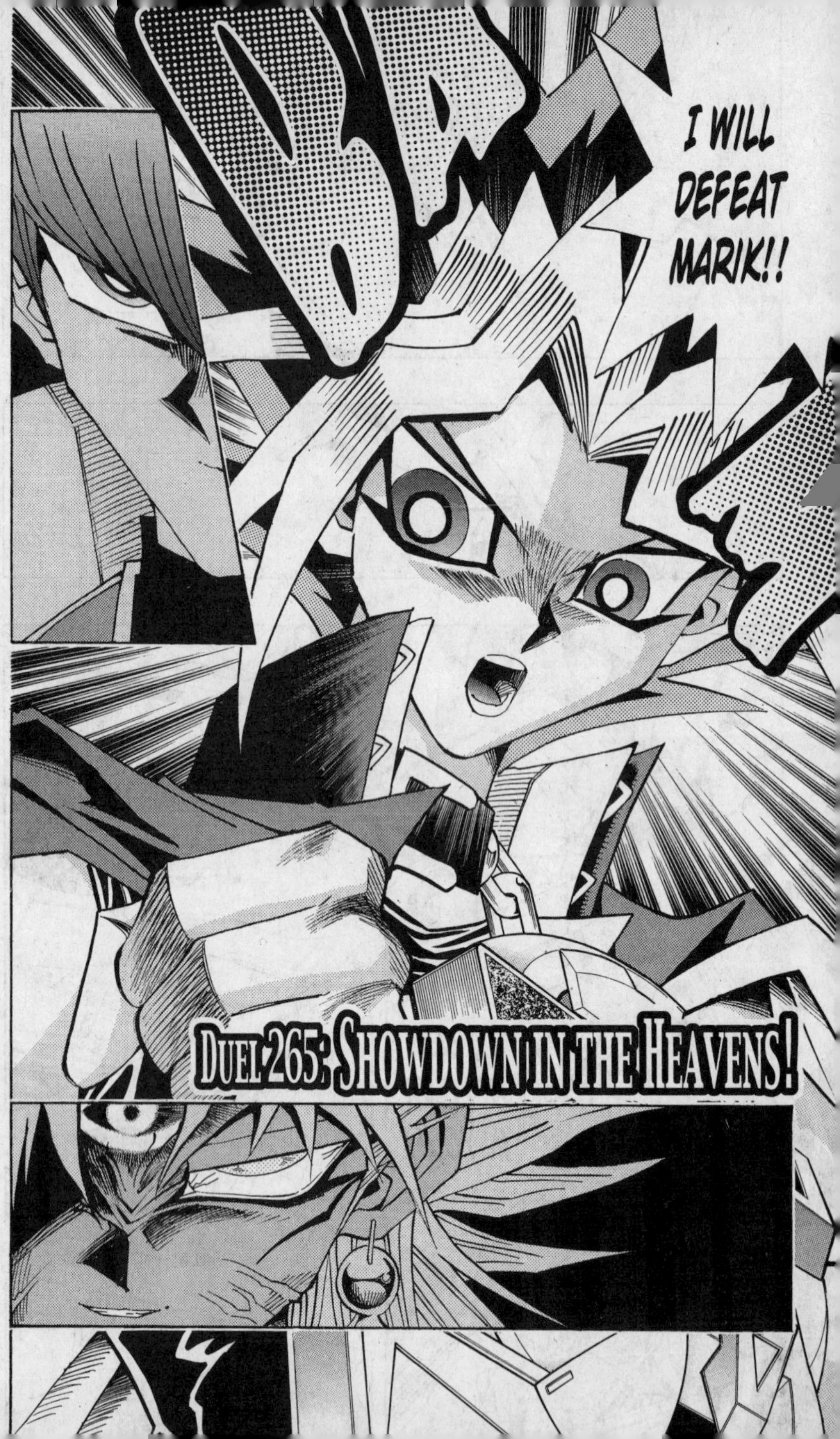
I WILL DEFEAT MARIK!!
DUEL 265: SHOWDOWN IN THE HEAVENS!

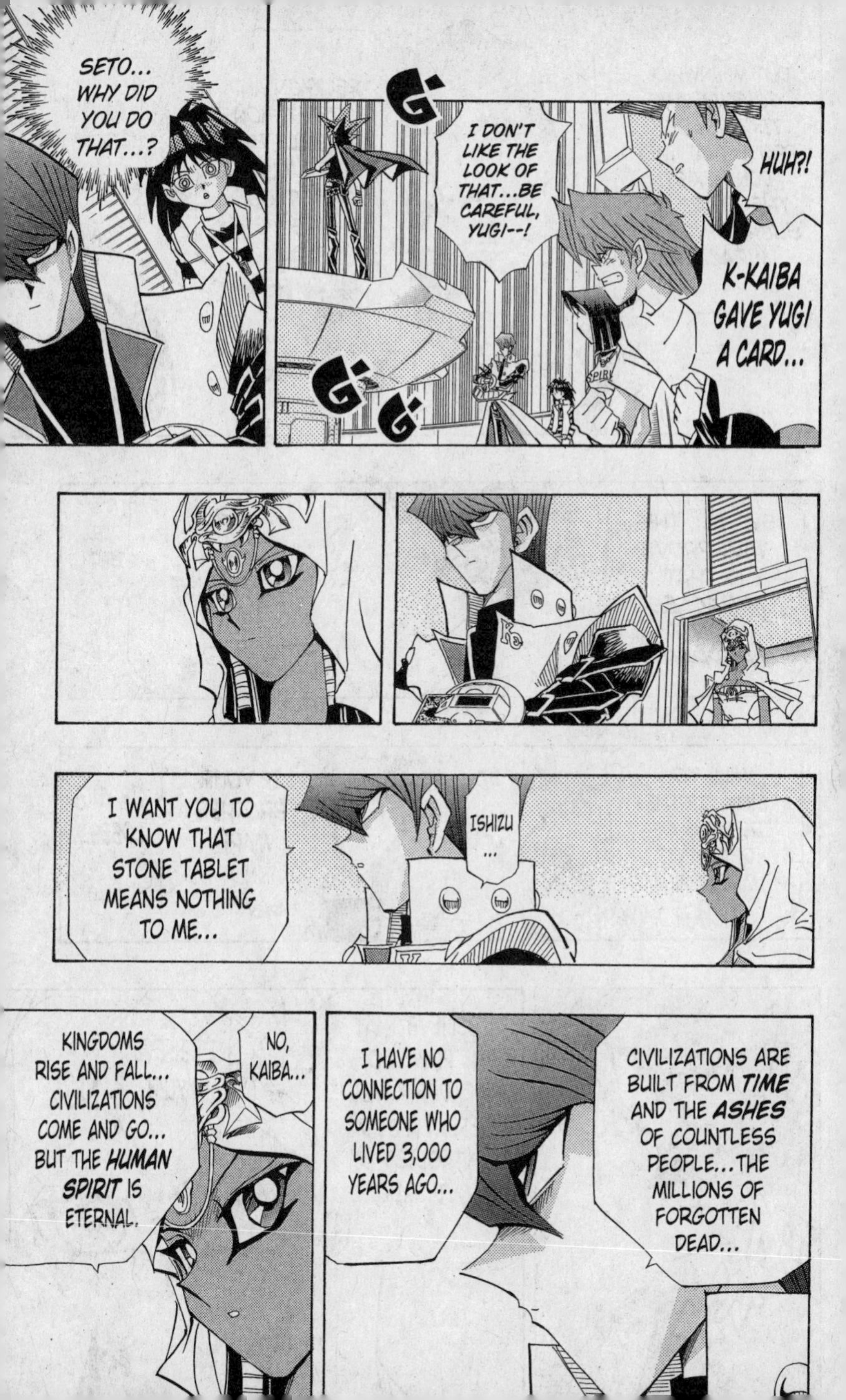
HUH?!
K-KAIBA GAVE YUGI A CARD...
G
I DON'T LIKE THE LOOK OF THAT...BE CAREFUL, YUGI--!
G G
SETO... WHY DID YOU DO THAT...?
ISHIZU...
I WANT YOU TO KNOW THAT STONE TABLET MEANS NOTHING TO ME...
CIVILIZATIONS ARE BUILT FROM *TIME* AND THE *ASHES* OF COUNTLESS PEOPLE...THE MILLIONS OF FORGOTTEN DEAD...
I HAVE NO CONNECTION TO SOMEONE WHO LIVED 3,000 YEARS AGO...
NO, KAIBA...
KINGDOMS RISE AND FALL... CIVILIZATIONS COME AND GO... BUT THE *HUMAN SPIRIT* IS ETERNAL.

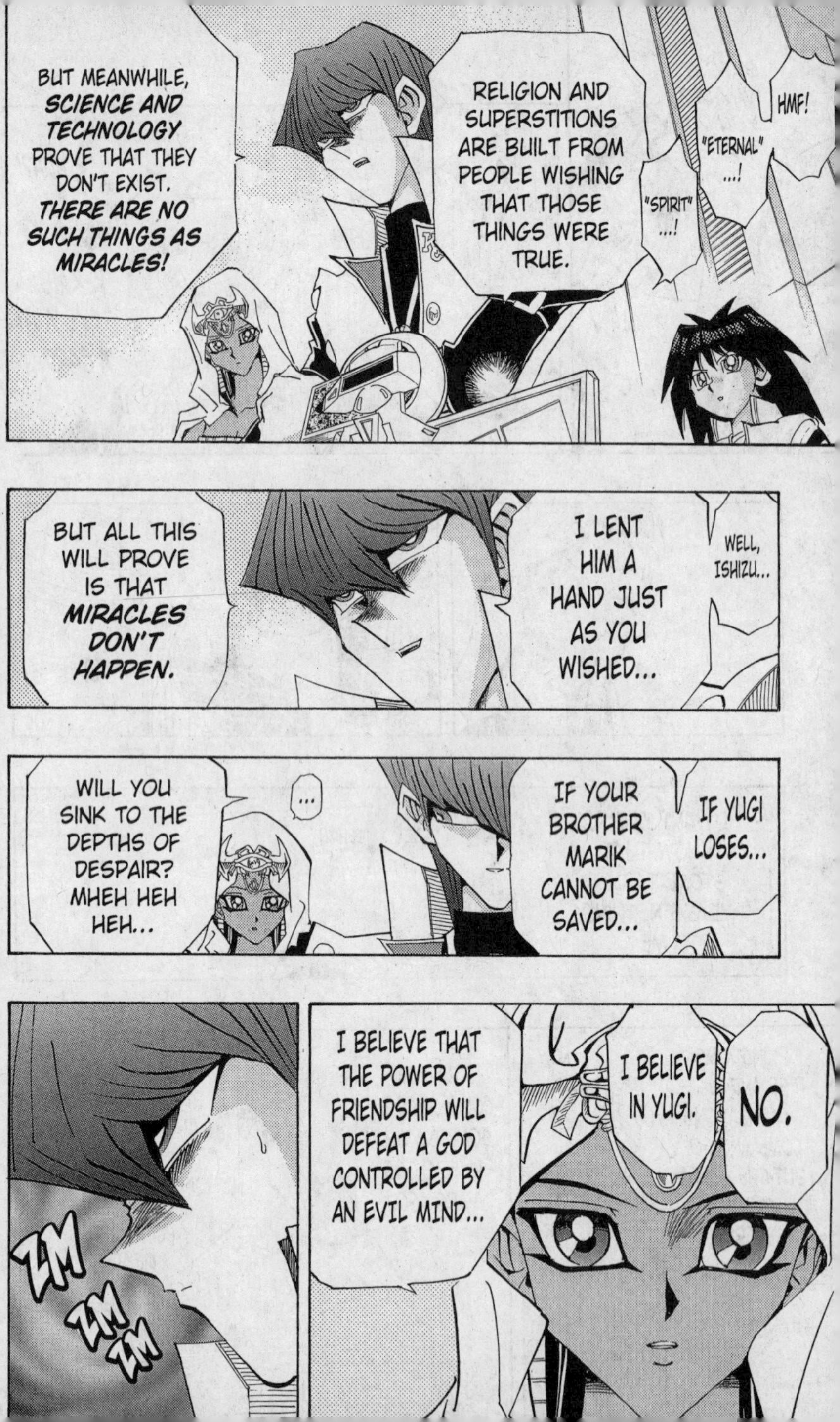
HMF!
"ETERNAL" ...!
"SPIRIT" ...!
RELIGION AND SUPERSTITIONS ARE BUILT FROM PEOPLE WISHING THAT THOSE THINGS WERE TRUE.
BUT MEANWHILE, *SCIENCE AND TECHNOLOGY* PROVE THAT THEY DON'T EXIST. *THERE ARE NO SUCH THINGS AS MIRACLES!*
WELL, ISHIZU...
I LENT HIM A HAND JUST AS YOU WISHED...
BUT ALL THIS WILL PROVE IS THAT *MIRACLES DON'T HAPPEN.*
IF YUGI LOSES...
IF YOUR BROTHER MARIK CANNOT BE SAVED...
...
WILL YOU SINK TO THE DEPTHS OF DESPAIR? MHEH HEH HEH...
NO.
I BELIEVE IN YUGI.
I BELIEVE THAT THE POWER OF FRIENDSHIP WILL DEFEAT A GOD CONTROLLED BY AN EVIL MIND...
ZM ZM ZM

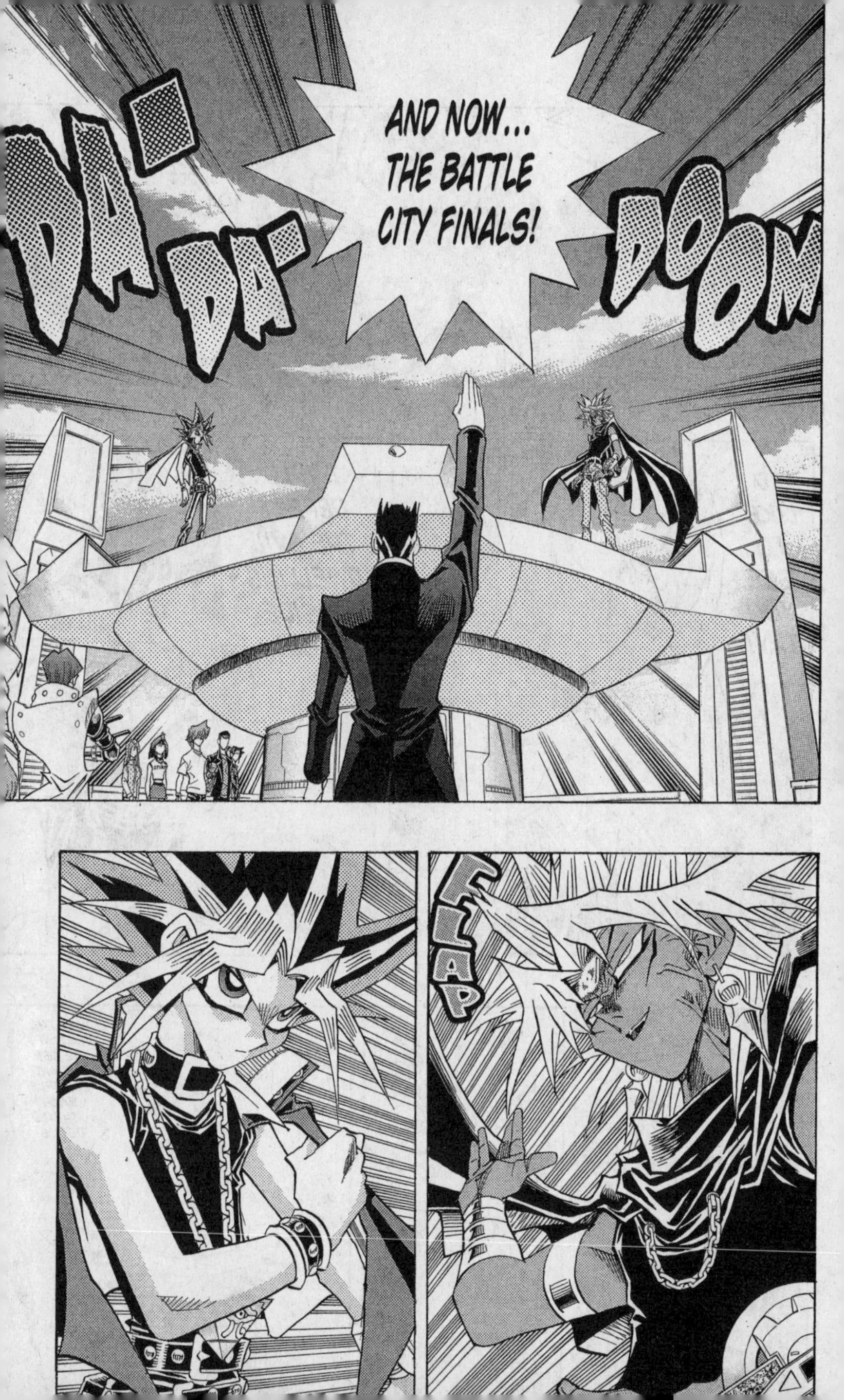
AND NOW... THE BATTLE CITY FINALS!
DA DA DOOM
FLAP

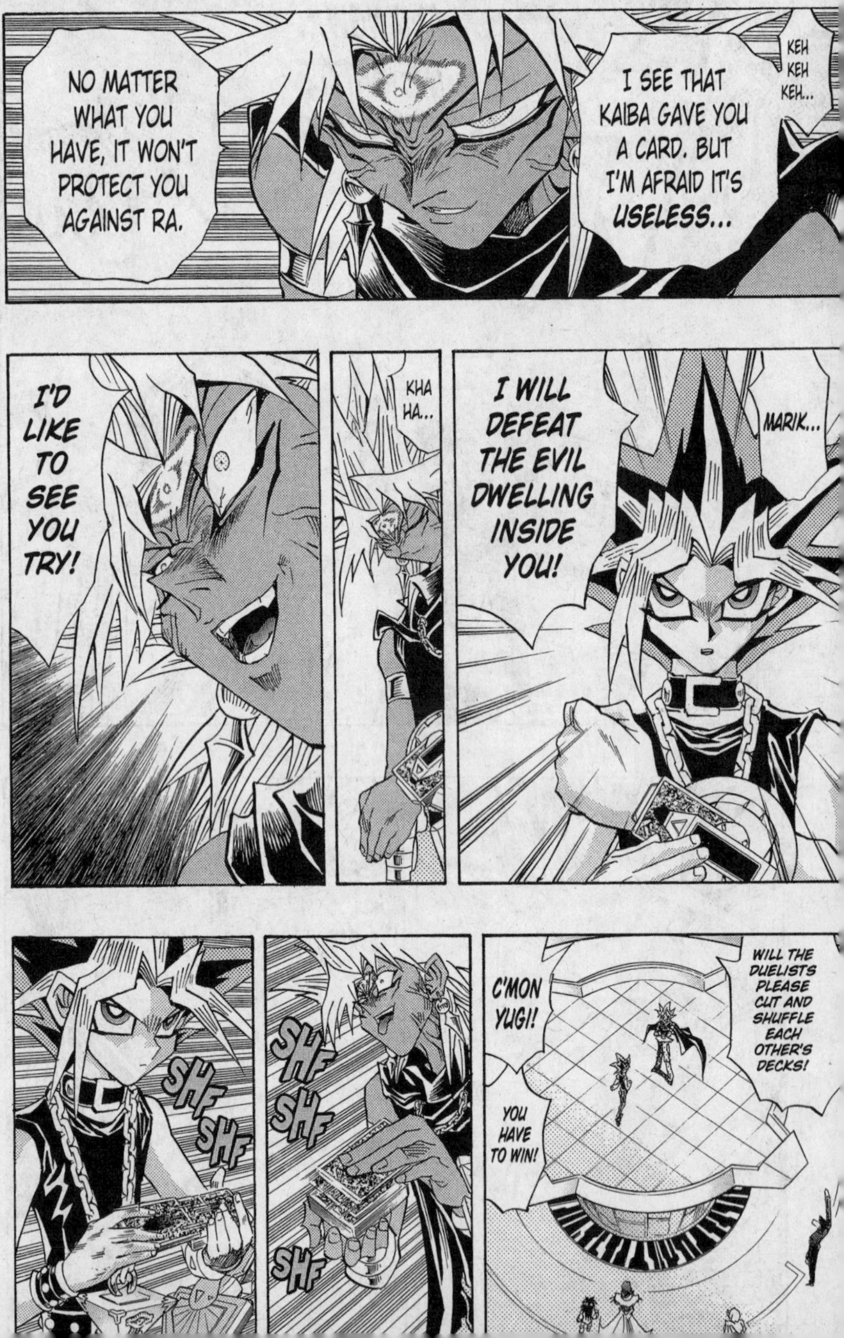
KEH KEH KEH...
I SEE THAT KAIBA GAVE YOU A CARD. BUT I'M AFRAID IT'S USELESS...
NO MATTER WHAT YOU HAVE, IT WON'T PROTECT YOU AGAINST RA.
MARIK...
I WILL DEFEAT THE EVIL DWELLING INSIDE YOU!
KHA HA...
I'D LIKE TO SEE YOU TRY!
WILL THE DUELISTS PLEASE CUT AND SHUFFLE EACH OTHER'S DECKS!
C'MON YUGI!
YOU HAVE TO WIN!
SHF SHF
SHF
SHF SHF

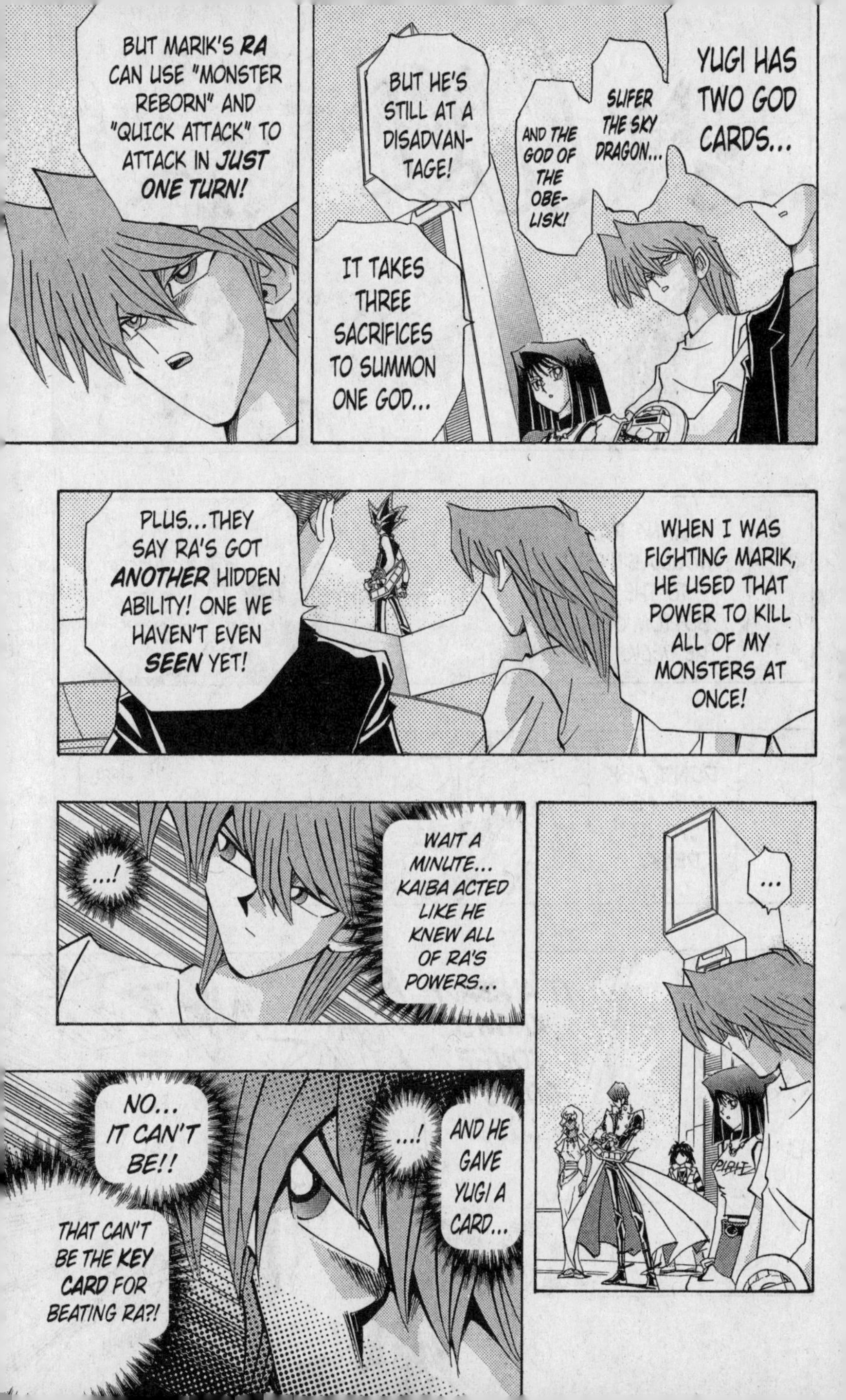
YUGI HAS TWO GOD CARDS...
SLIFER THE SKY DRAGON...
AND THE GOD OF THE OBE-LISK!
BUT HE'S STILL AT A DISADVAN-TAGE!
IT TAKES THREE SACRIFICES TO SUMMON ONE GOD...
BUT MARIK'S RA CAN USE "MONSTER REBORN" AND "QUICK ATTACK" TO ATTACK IN JUST ONE TURN!
PLUS...THEY SAY RA'S GOT ANOTHER HIDDEN ABILITY! ONE WE HAVEN'T EVEN SEEN YET!
WHEN I WAS FIGHTING MARIK, HE USED THAT POWER TO KILL ALL OF MY MONSTERS AT ONCE!
...
WAIT A MINUTE... KAIBA ACTED LIKE HE KNEW ALL OF RA'S POWERS...
...!
AND HE GAVE YUGI A CARD...
...!
NO... IT CAN'T BE!!
THAT CAN'T BE THE KEY CARD FOR BEATING RA?!

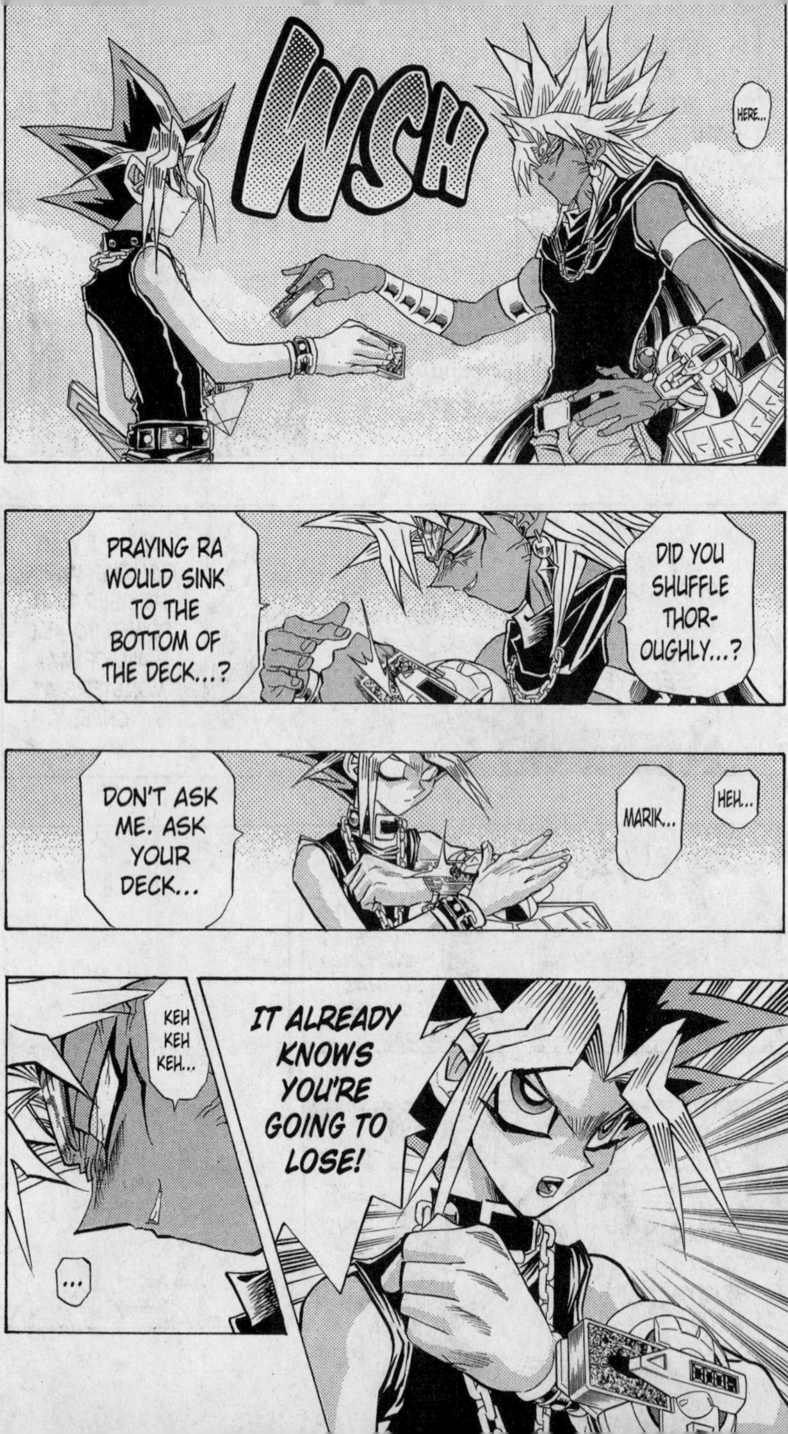
HERE...
WSH
DID YOU SHUFFLE THOROUGHLY...?
PRAYING RA WOULD SINK TO THE BOTTOM OF THE DECK...?
HEH...
MARIK...
DON'T ASK ME. ASK YOUR DECK...
IT ALREADY KNOWS YOU'RE GOING TO LOSE!
KEH KEH KEH...
...

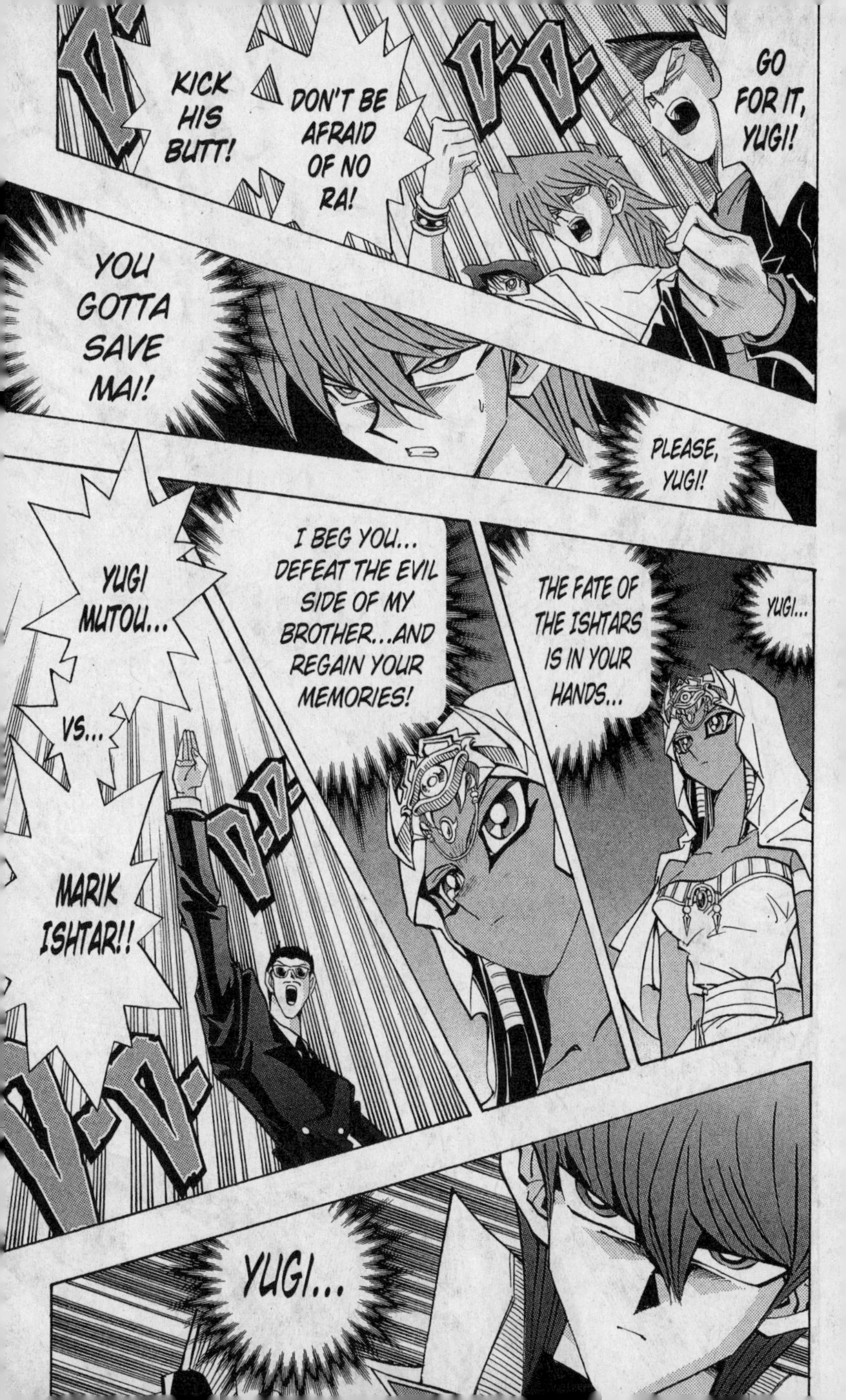
GO FOR IT, YUGI!
DON'T BE AFRAID OF NO RA!
KICK HIS BUTT!
PLEASE, YUGI!
YOU GOTTA SAVE MAI!
YUGI...
THE FATE OF THE ISHTARS IS IN YOUR HANDS...
I BEG YOU... DEFEAT THE EVIL SIDE OF MY BROTHER...AND REGAIN YOUR MEMORIES!
YUGI MUTOU...
VS...
MARIK ISHTAR!!
YUGI...

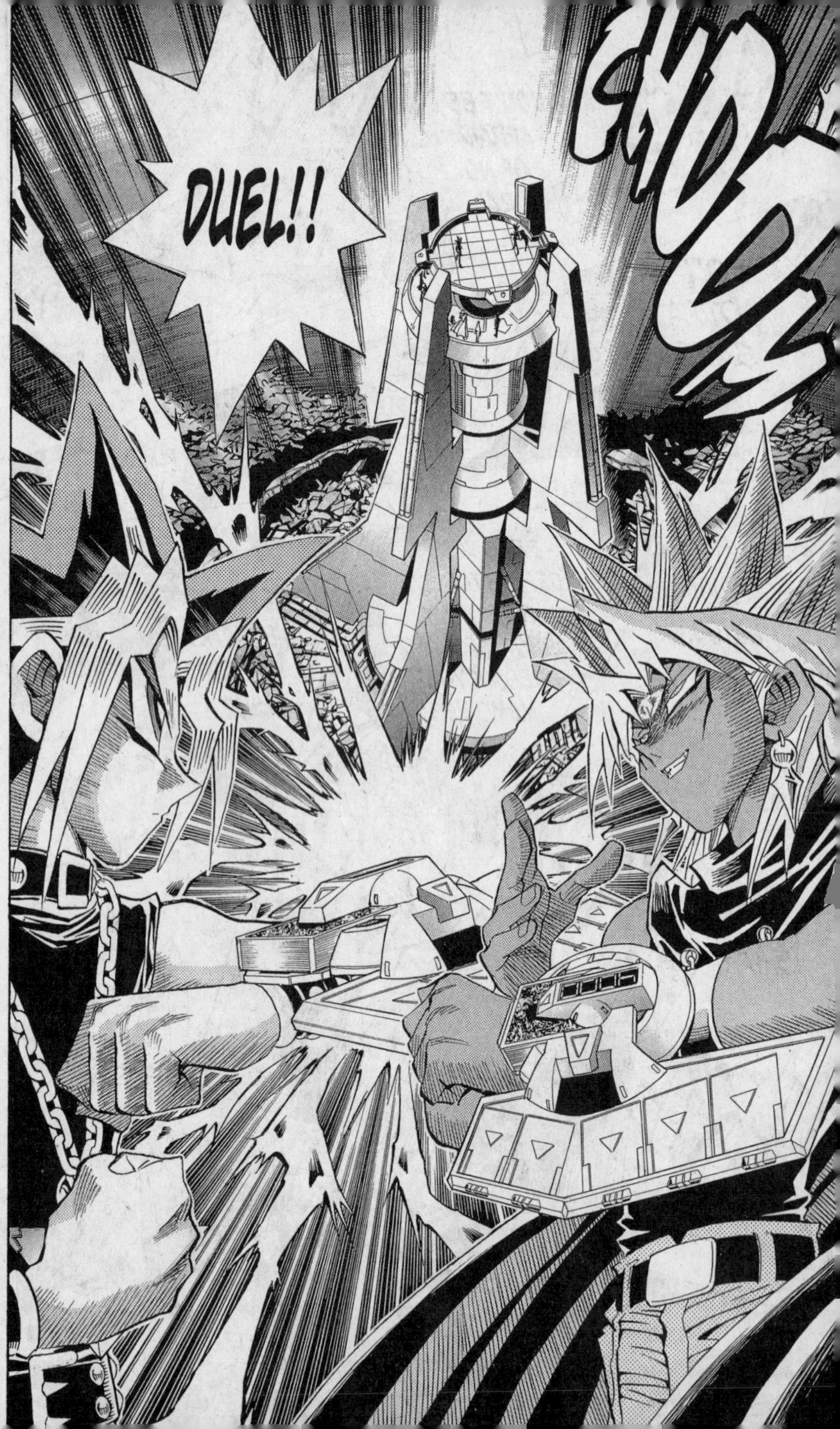
CHOOM
DUEL!!

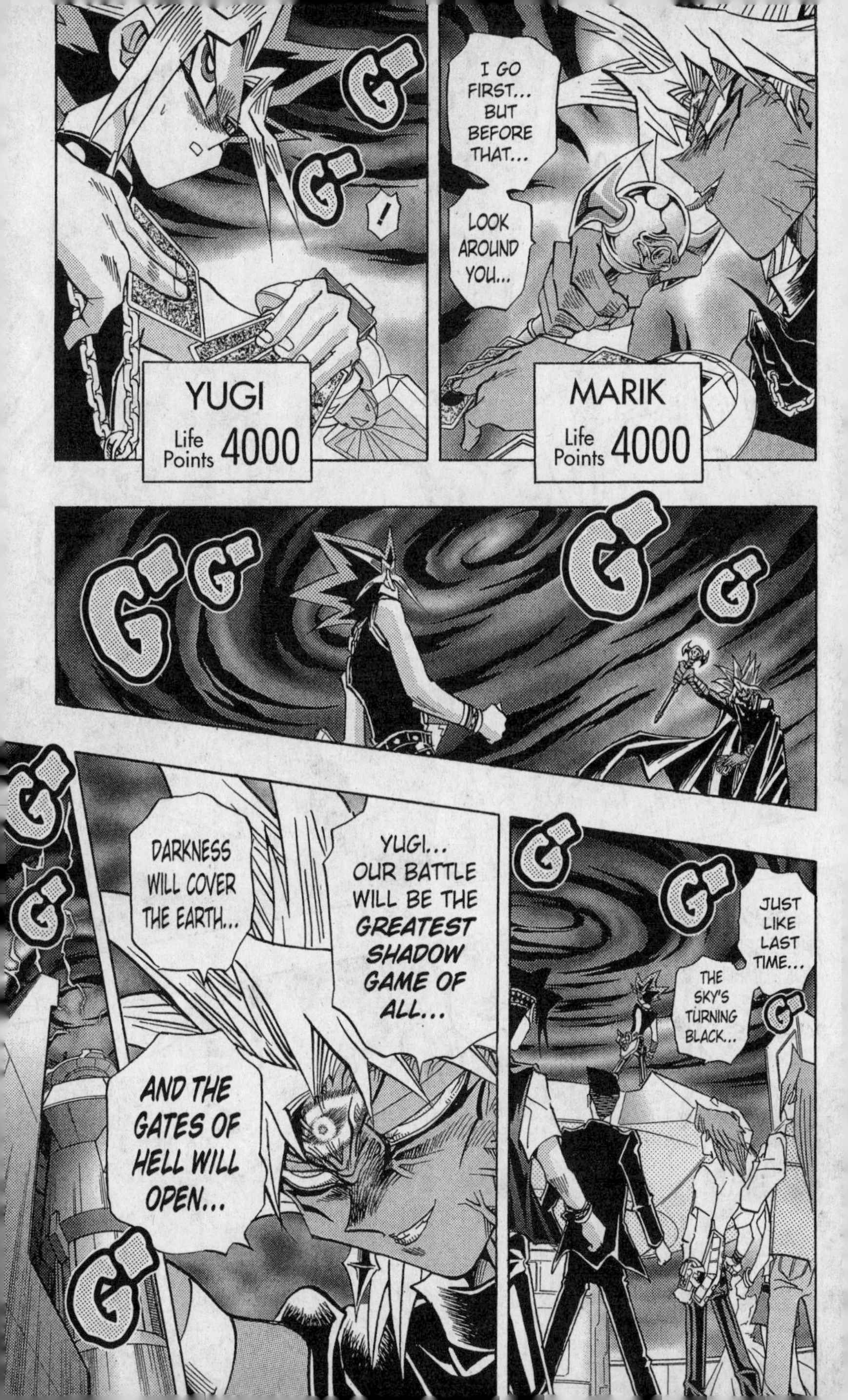
I GO FIRST... BUT BEFORE THAT...
LOOK AROUND YOU...
MARIK
Life Points 4000
G
G
!
YUGI
Life Points 4000
G
G
G
G
G
G
JUST LIKE LAST TIME...
THE SKY'S TURNING BLACK...
G
YUGI... OUR BATTLE WILL BE THE *GREATEST SHADOW GAME OF ALL...*
DARKNESS WILL COVER THE EARTH...
AND THE GATES OF HELL WILL OPEN...
G
G
G

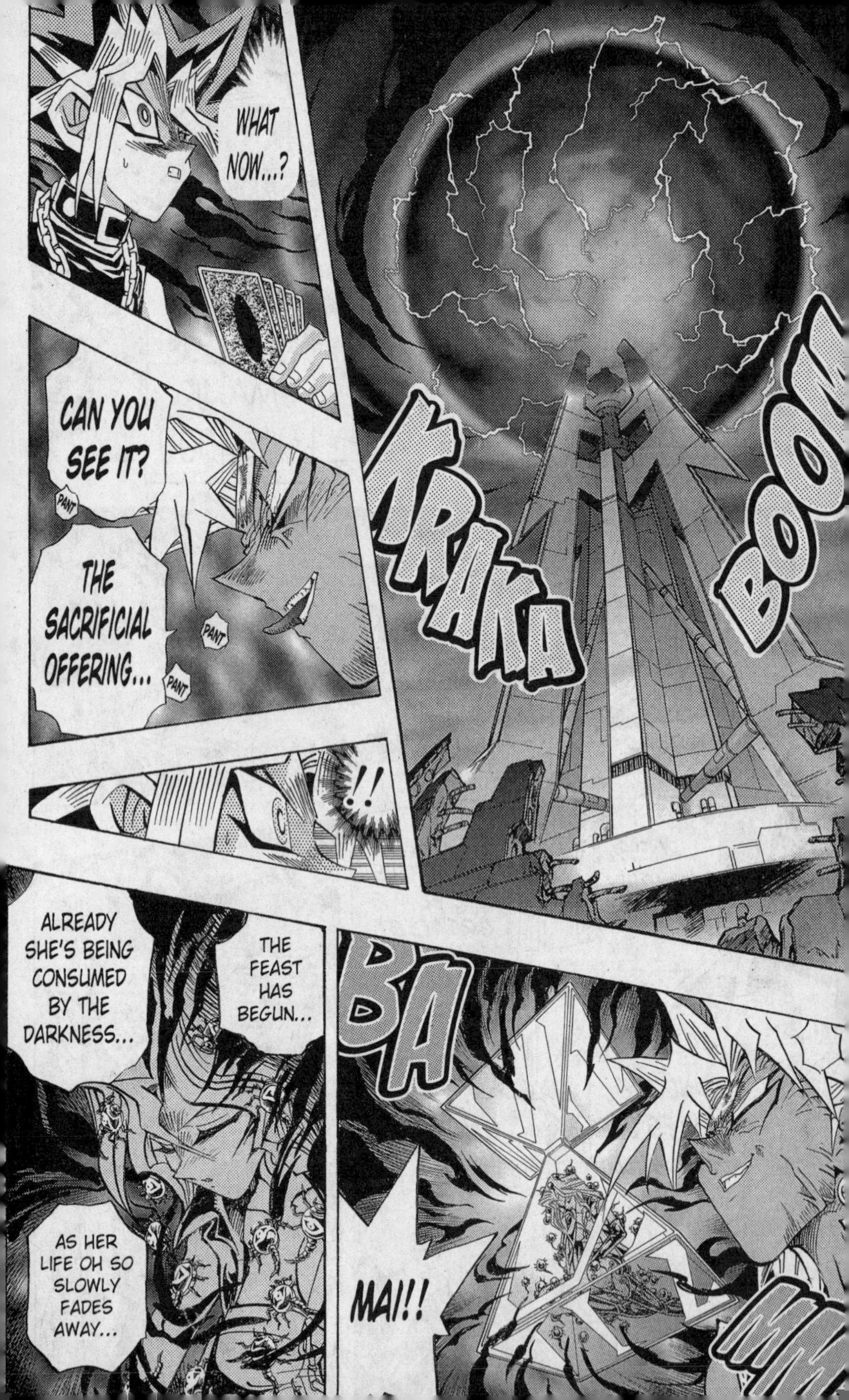
BOO
KRAKA
WHAT NOW...?
CAN YOU SEE IT?
PANT
THE SACRIFICIAL OFFERING...
PANT
PANT
!!
BA
MAI!!
THE FEAST HAS BEGUN...
ALREADY SHE'S BEING CONSUMED BY THE DARKNESS...
AS HER LIFE OH SO SLOWLY FADES AWAY...

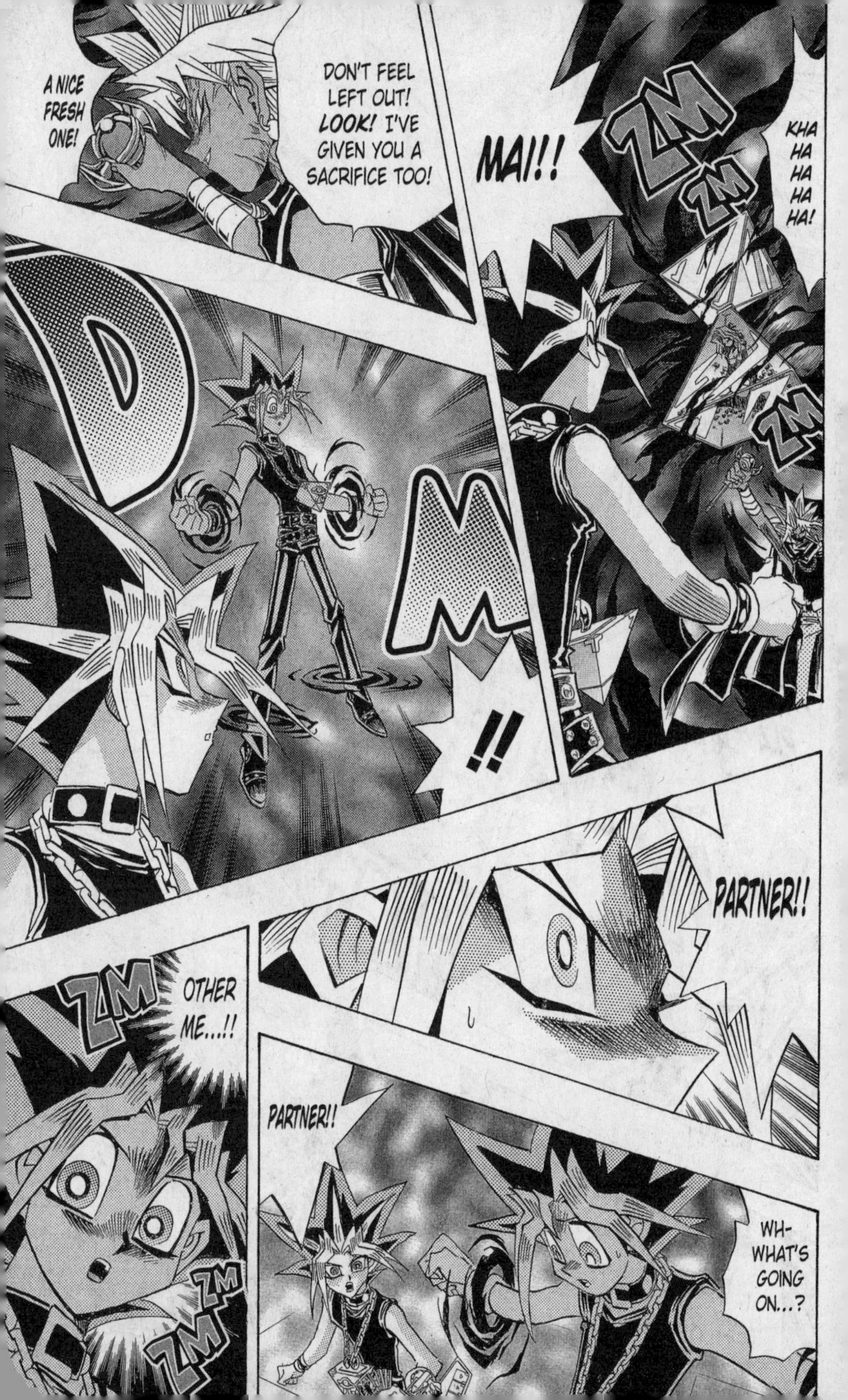
KHA HA HA HA HA!
ZM
ZM
MAI!!
ZM
DON'T FEEL LEFT OUT! LOOK! I'VE GIVEN YOU A SACRIFICE TOO!
A NICE FRESH ONE!
DOM
!!
PARTNER!!
WH- WHAT'S GOING ON...?
PARTNER!!
OTHER ME...!!
ZM
ZM
ZM

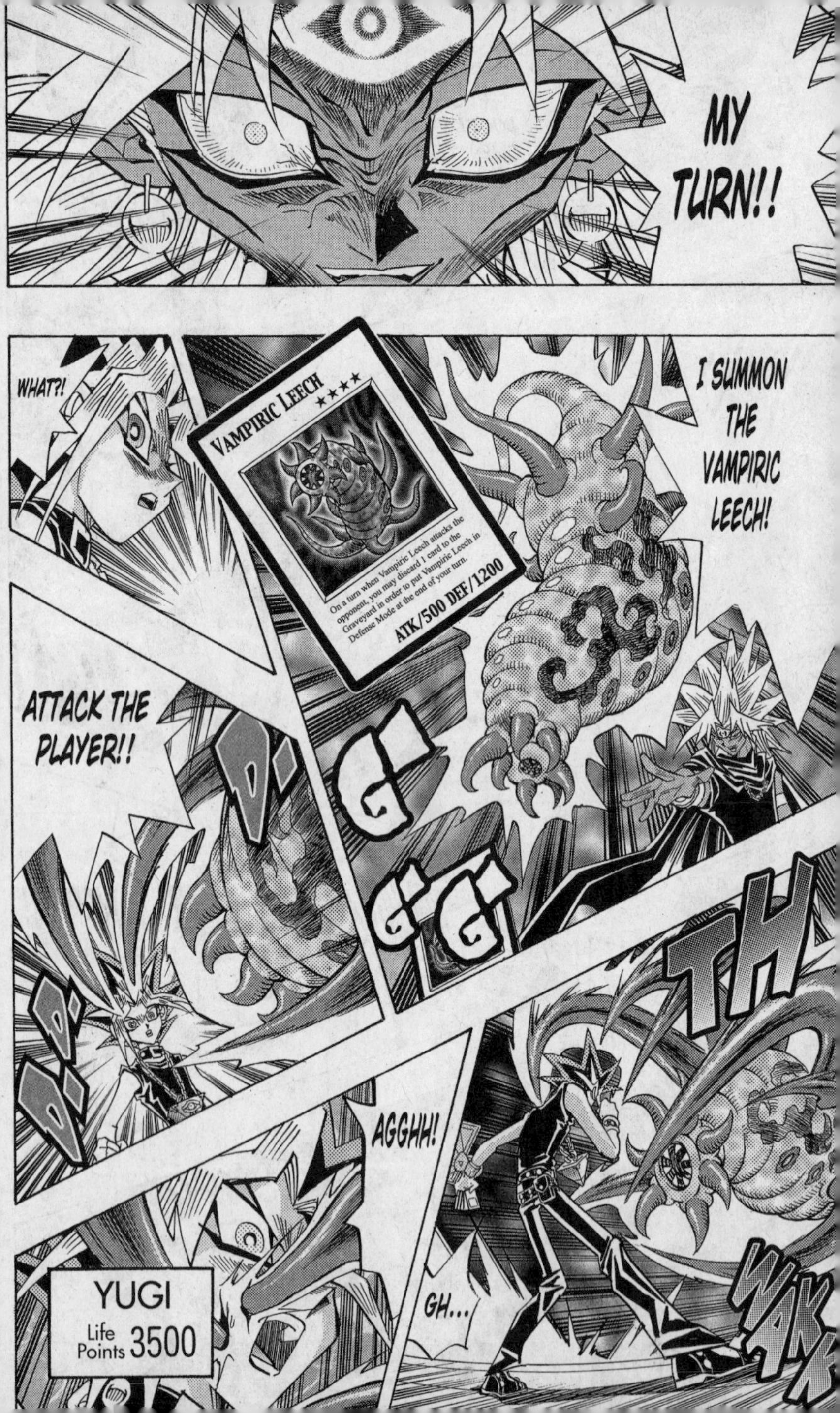
MY TURN!!
I SUMMON THE VAMPIRIC LEECH!
VAMPIRIC LEECH ★★★★
On a turn when Vampiric Leech attacks the opponent, you may discard 1 card to the Graveyard in order to put Vampiric Leech in Defense Mode at the end of your turn.
ATK/500 DEF/1200
WHAT?!
G
G G
ATTACK THE PLAYER!!
TH
WAK
AGGHH!
GH...
YUGI
Life Points 3500

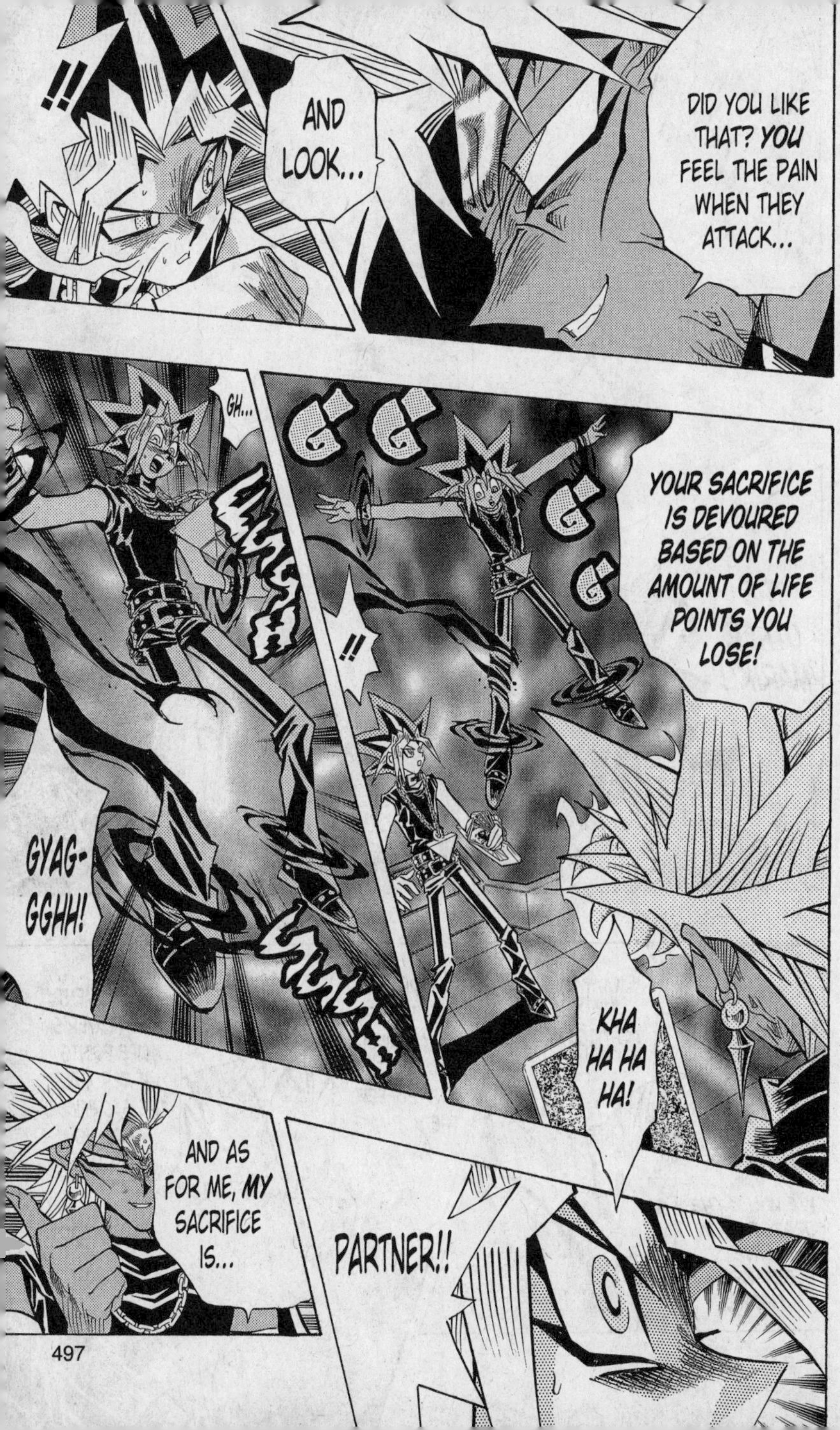
DID YOU LIKE THAT? *YOU* FEEL THE PAIN WHEN THEY ATTACK...
AND LOOK...
!!
YOUR SACRIFICE IS DEVOURED BASED ON THE AMOUNT OF LIFE POINTS YOU LOSE!
G G G G
!!
KHA HA HA HA!
GH...
GYAG-GGHH!
PARTNER!!
AND AS FOR ME, MY SACRIFICE IS...

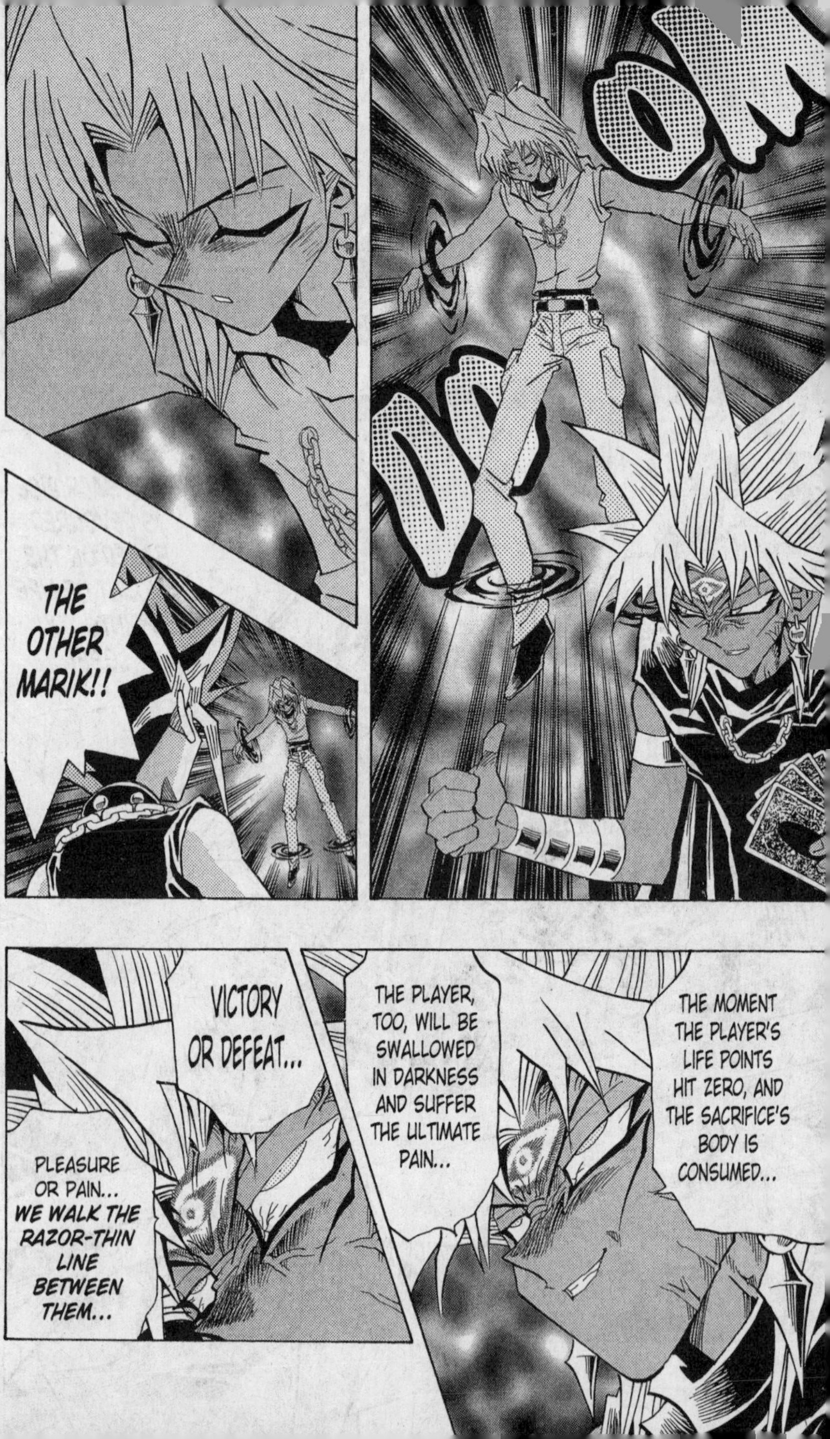
THE OTHER MARIK!!
THE MOMENT THE PLAYER'S LIFE POINTS HIT ZERO, AND THE SACRIFICE'S BODY IS CONSUMED...
THE PLAYER, TOO, WILL BE SWALLOWED IN DARKNESS AND SUFFER THE ULTIMATE PAIN...
VICTORY OR DEFEAT...
PLEASURE OR PAIN... WE WALK THE RAZOR-THIN LINE BETWEEN THEM...

READ THIS WAY

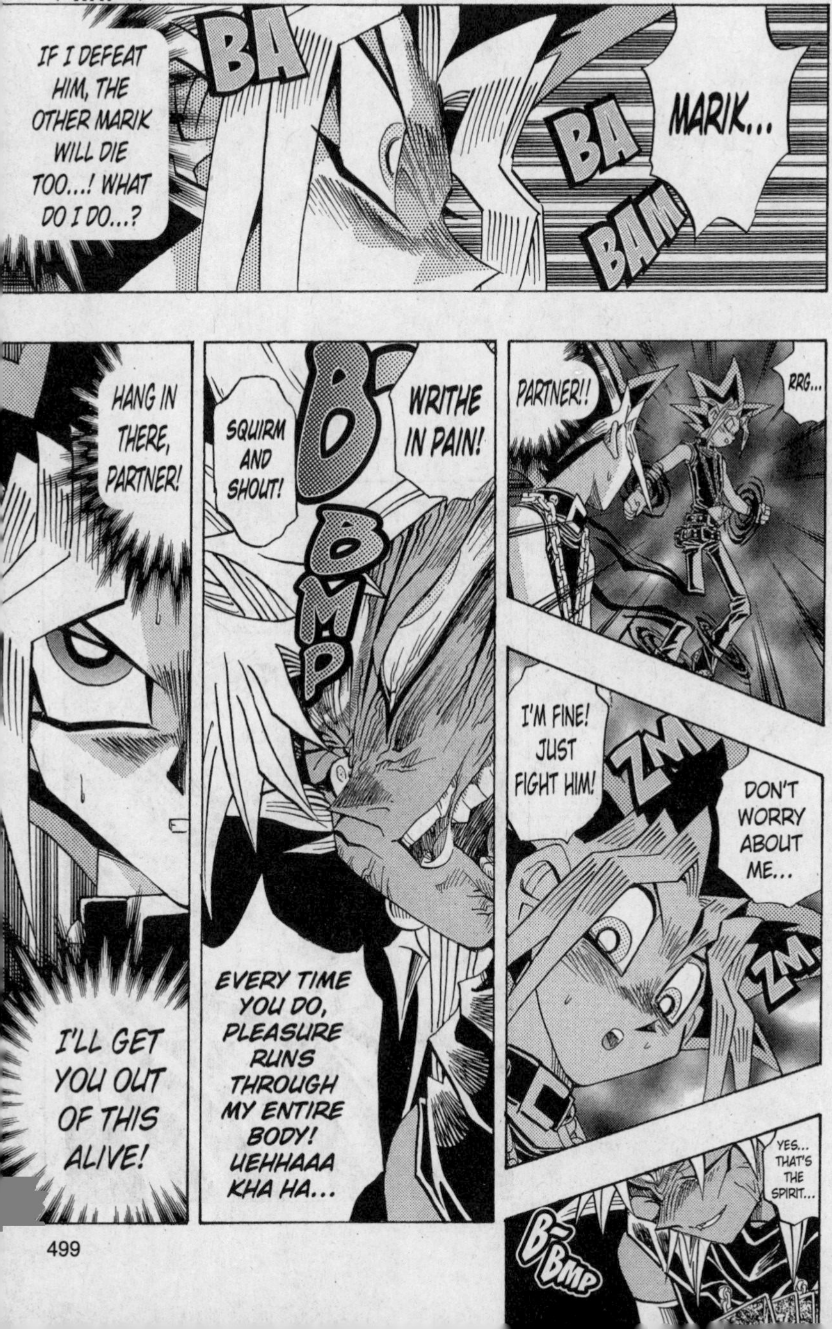
MARIK...
BA
BA
BAM
BA
IF I DEFEAT HIM, THE OTHER MARIK WILL DIE TOO...! WHAT DO I DO...?
RRG...
PARTNER!!
I'M FINE! JUST FIGHT HIM!
ZM
DON'T WORRY ABOUT ME...
ZM
YES... THAT'S THE SPIRIT...
B-BMP
WRITHE IN PAIN!
SQUIRM AND SHOUT!
BOMP
BOMP
EVERY TIME YOU DO, PLEASURE RUNS THROUGH MY ENTIRE BODY! UEHHAAA KHA HA...
HANG IN THERE, PARTNER!
I'LL GET YOU OUT OF THIS ALIVE!

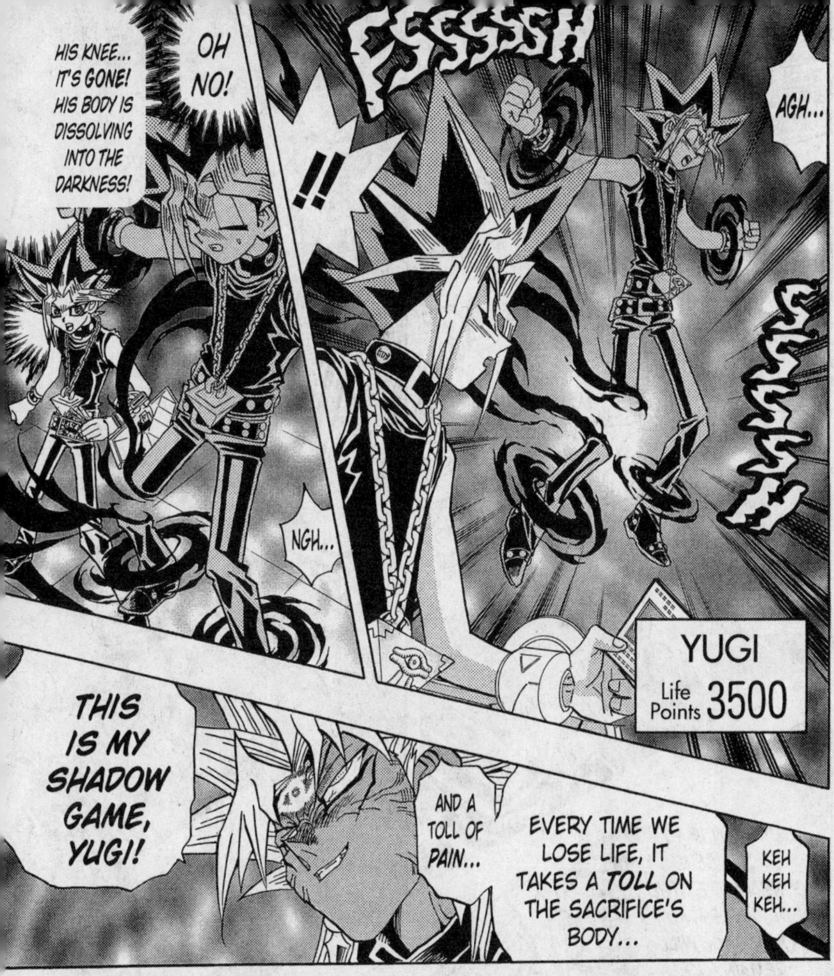
FSSSSH
AGH...
!!
OH NO!
HIS KNEE... IT'S GONE! HIS BODY IS DISSOLVING INTO THE DARKNESS!
NGH...
YUGI Life Points 3500
KEH KEH KEH...
EVERY TIME WE LOSE LIFE, IT TAKES A TOLL ON THE SACRIFICE'S BODY...
AND A TOLL OF PAIN...
THIS IS MY SHADOW GAME, YUGI!

Duel 266: The Quick Attack Trap

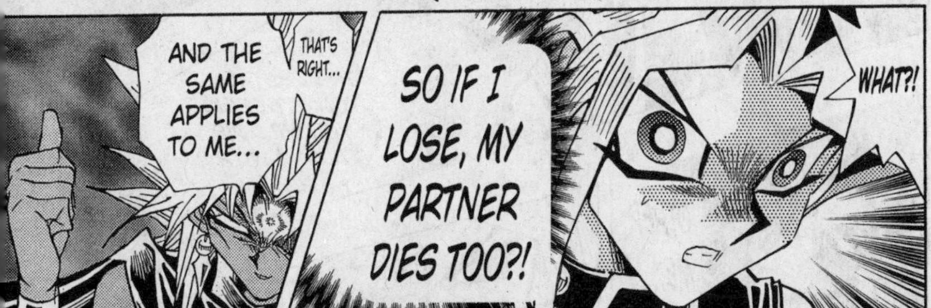
WHAT?!
SO IF I LOSE, MY PARTNER DIES TOO?!
THAT'S RIGHT...
AND THE SAME APPLIES TO ME...

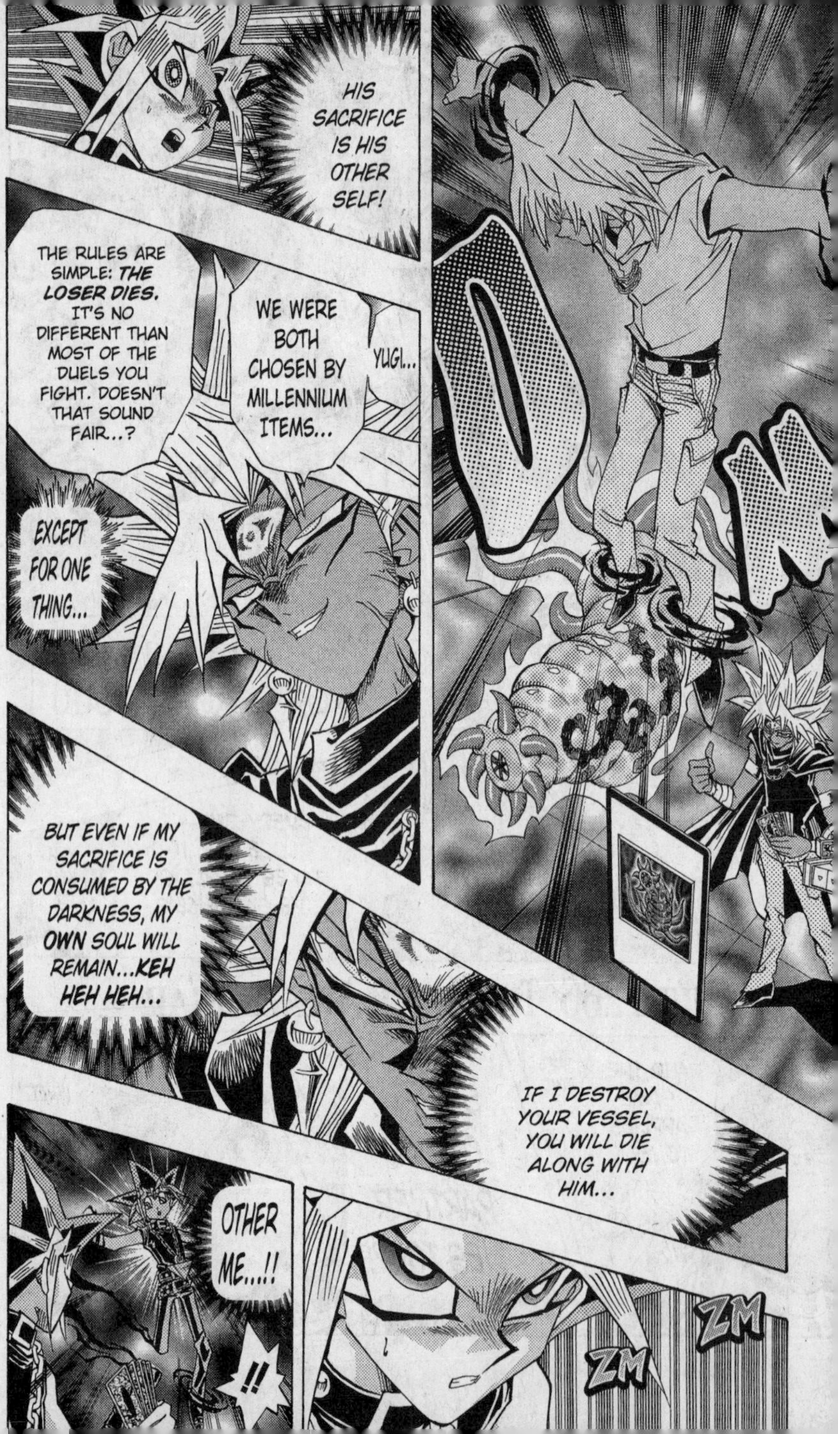
HIS SACRIFICE IS HIS OTHER SELF!
YUGI...
WE WERE BOTH CHOSEN BY MILLENNIUM ITEMS...
THE RULES ARE SIMPLE: *THE LOSER DIES.* IT'S NO DIFFERENT THAN MOST OF THE DUELS YOU FIGHT. DOESN'T THAT SOUND FAIR...?
EXCEPT FOR ONE THING...
BUT EVEN IF MY SACRIFICE IS CONSUMED BY THE DARKNESS, MY **OWN** SOUL WILL REMAIN...**KEH HEH HEH...**
IF I DESTROY YOUR VESSEL, YOU WILL DIE ALONG WITH HIM...
ZM
ZM
OTHER ME...!!
!!

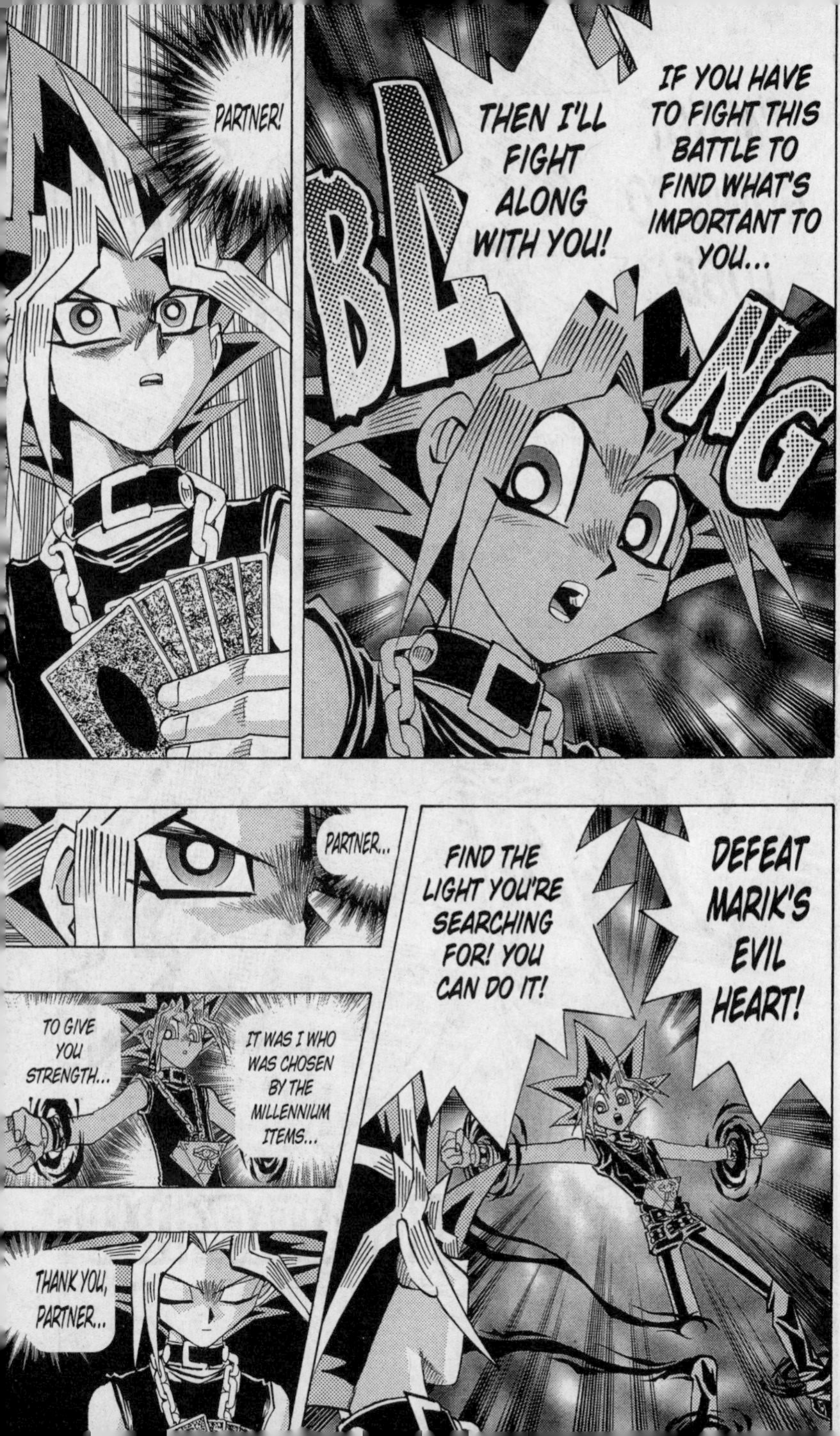

IF YOU HAVE TO FIGHT THIS BATTLE TO FIND WHAT'S IMPORTANT TO YOU...
THEN I'LL FIGHT ALONG WITH YOU!
BLANG
PARTNER!
DEFEAT MARIK'S EVIL HEART!
FIND THE LIGHT YOU'RE SEARCHING FOR! YOU CAN DO IT!
PARTNER...
IT WAS I WHO WAS CHOSEN BY THE MILLENNIUM ITEMS...
TO GIVE YOU STRENGTH...
THANK YOU, PARTNER...

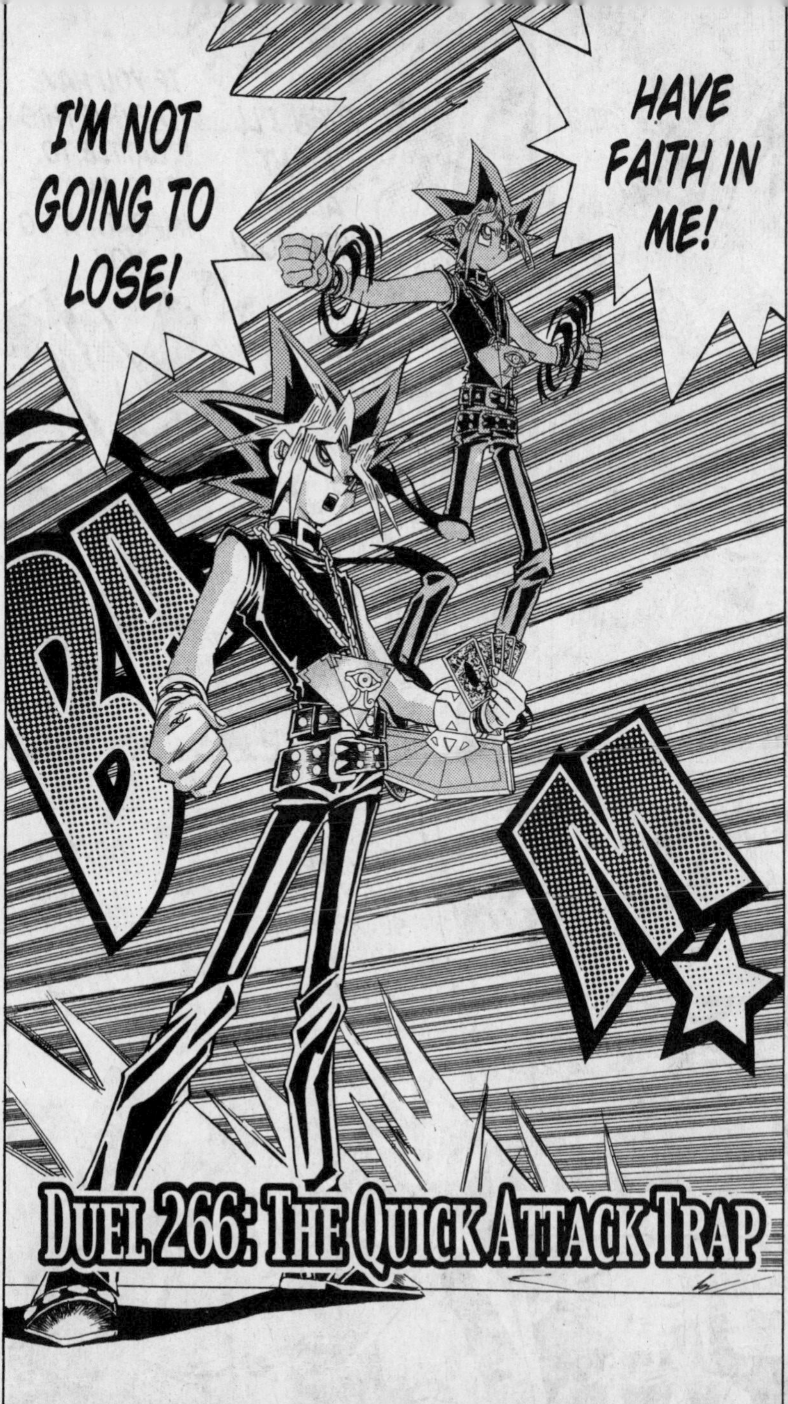
HAVE FAITH IN ME!
I'M NOT GOING TO LOSE!
BAM
DUEL 266: THE QUICK ATTACK TRAP

READ THIS WAY

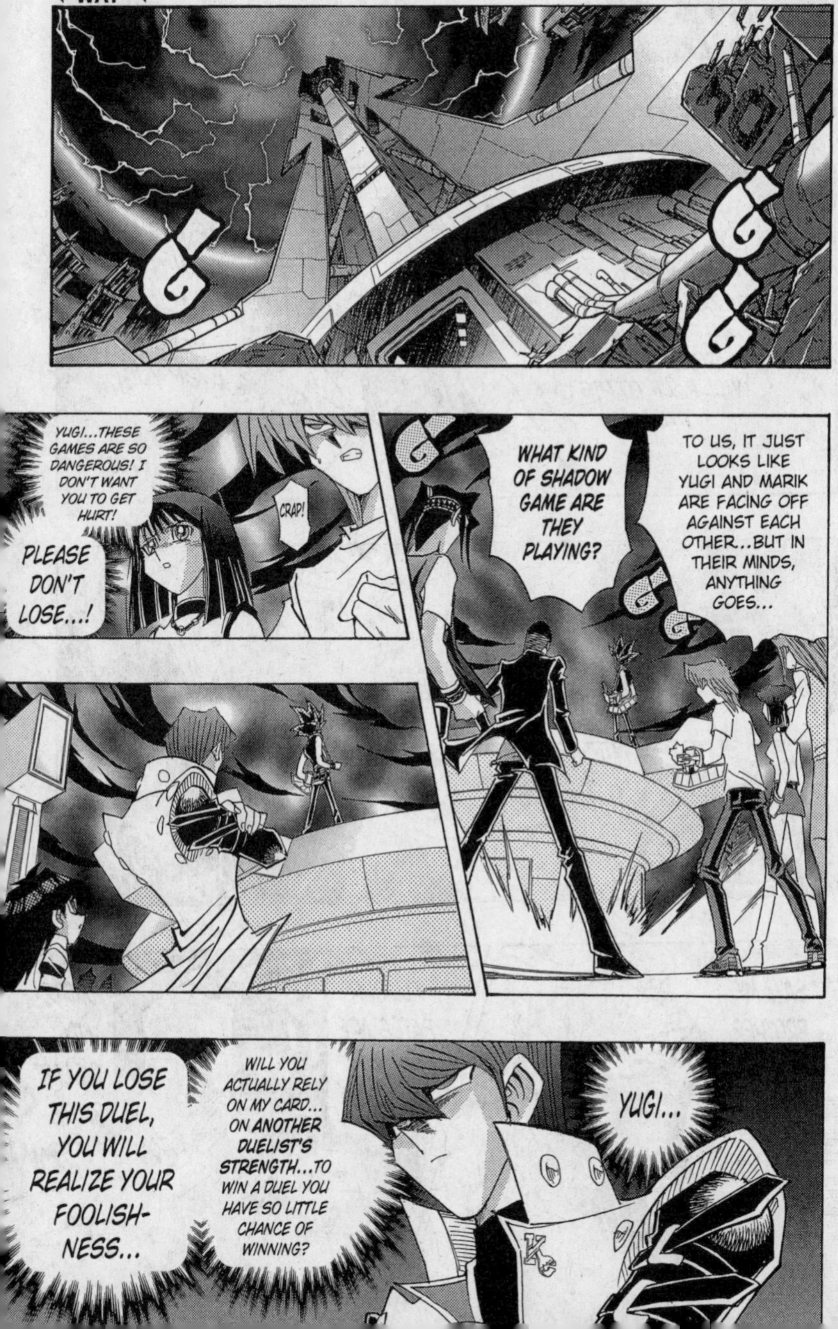
G
G
G
G
TO US, IT JUST LOOKS LIKE YUGI AND MARIK ARE FACING OFF AGAINST EACH OTHER...BUT IN THEIR MINDS, ANYTHING GOES...
WHAT KIND OF SHADOW GAME ARE THEY PLAYING?
G
G
G
CRAP!
YUGI...THESE GAMES ARE SO DANGEROUS! I DON'T WANT YOU TO GET HURT!
PLEASE DON'T LOSE...!
YUGI...
WILL YOU ACTUALLY RELY ON MY CARD... ON ANOTHER DUELIST'S STRENGTH...TO WIN A DUEL YOU HAVE SO LITTLE CHANCE OF WINNING?
IF YOU LOSE THIS DUEL, YOU WILL REALIZE YOUR FOOLISHNESS...

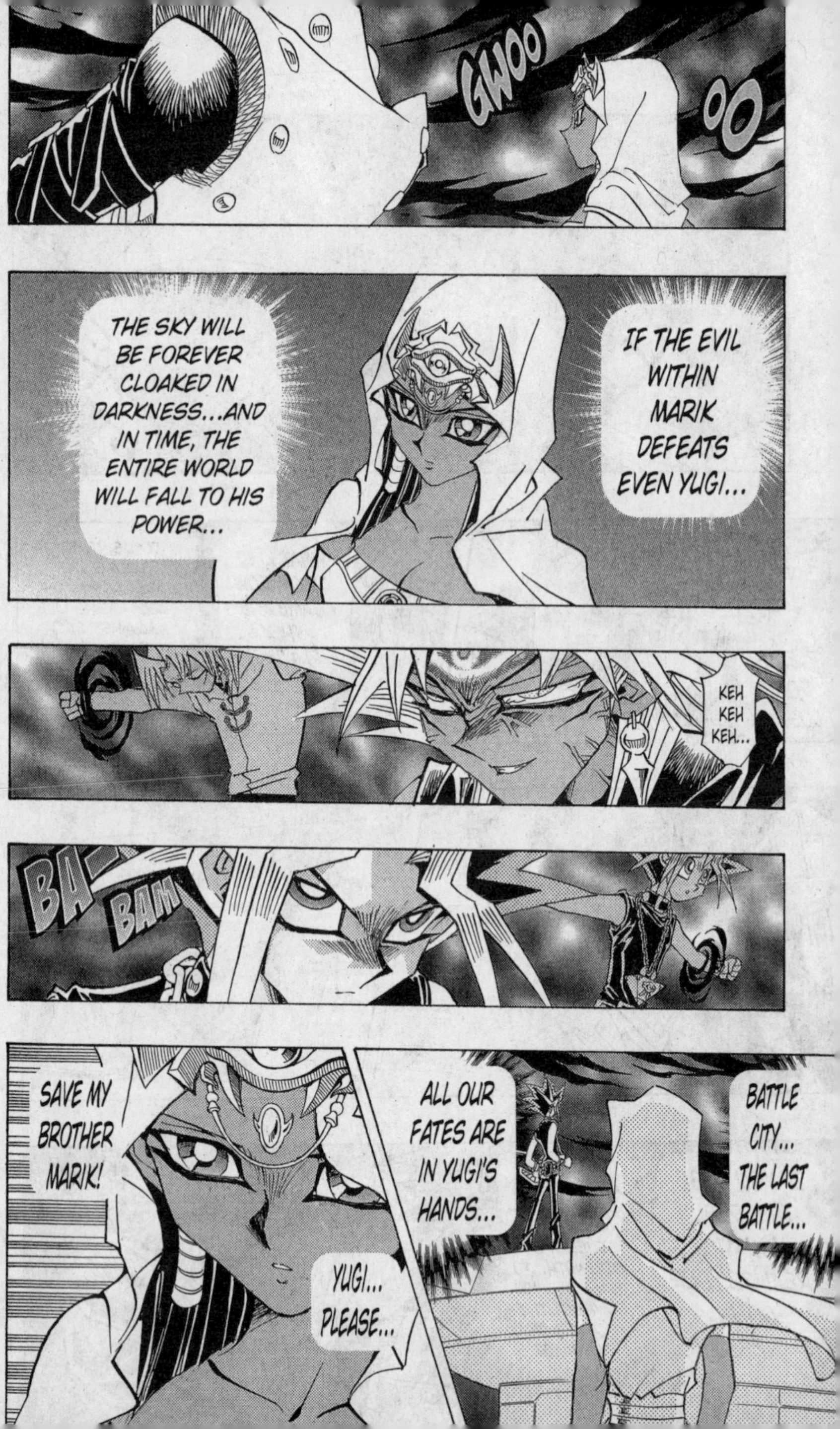
GWOO
OO
IF THE EVIL WITHIN MARIK DEFEATS EVEN YUGI...
THE SKY WILL BE FOREVER CLOAKED IN DARKNESS...AND IN TIME, THE ENTIRE WORLD WILL FALL TO HIS POWER...
KEH KEH KEH...
BA-
BAM
BATTLE CITY... THE LAST BATTLE...
ALL OUR FATES ARE IN YUGI'S HANDS...
YUGI... PLEASE...
SAVE MY BROTHER MARIK!

READ THIS WAY

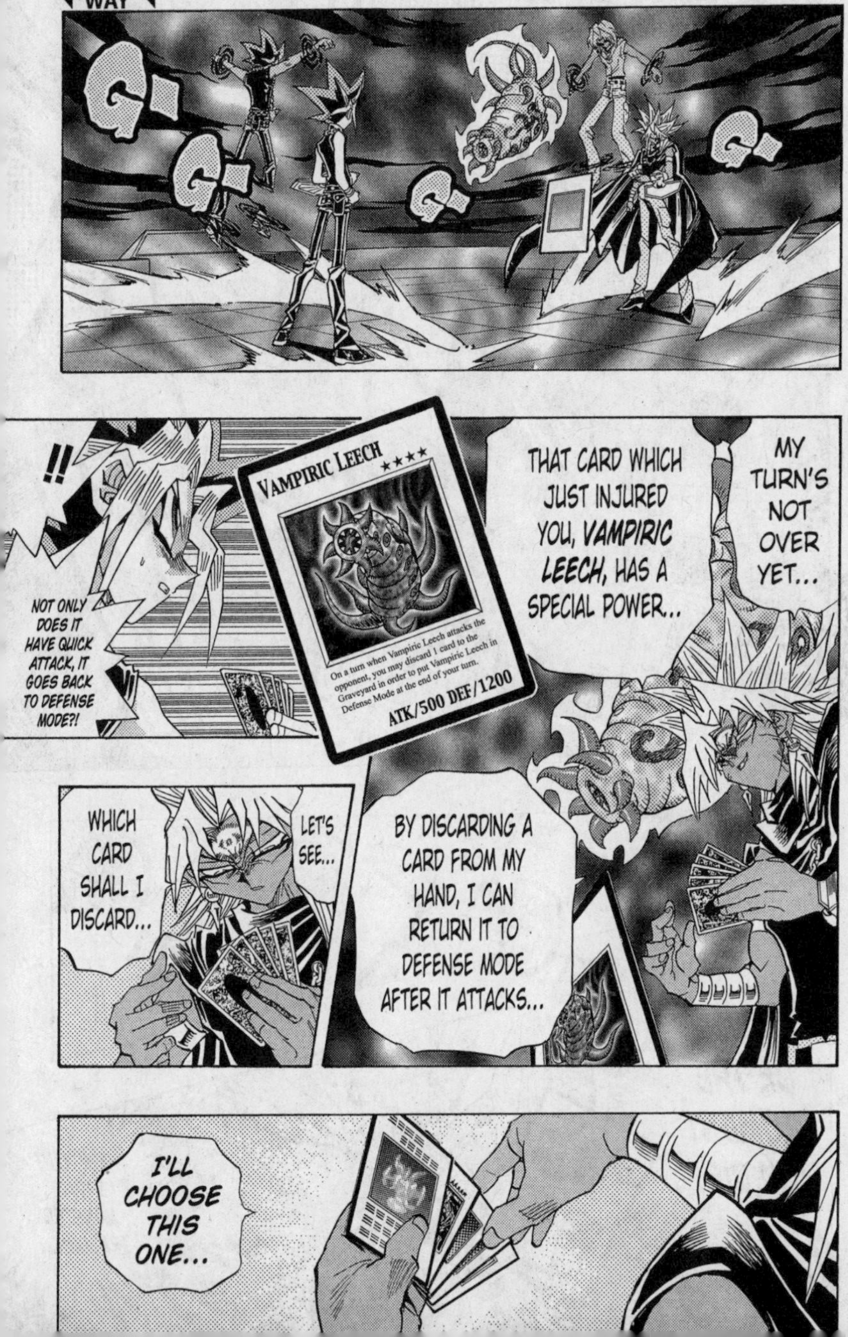
G
G
G
G
MY TURN'S NOT OVER YET...
THAT CARD WHICH JUST INJURED YOU, VAMPIRIC LEECH, HAS A SPECIAL POWER...
VAMPIRIC LEECH
On a turn when Vampiric Leech attacks the opponent, you may discard 1 card to the Graveyard in order to put Vampiric Leech in Defense Mode at the end of your turn.
ATK/500 DEF/1200
!!
NOT ONLY DOES IT HAVE QUICK ATTACK, IT GOES BACK TO DEFENSE MODE?!
BY DISCARDING A CARD FROM MY HAND, I CAN RETURN IT TO DEFENSE MODE AFTER IT ATTACKS...
LET'S SEE...
WHICH CARD SHALL I DISCARD...
I'LL CHOOSE THIS ONE...

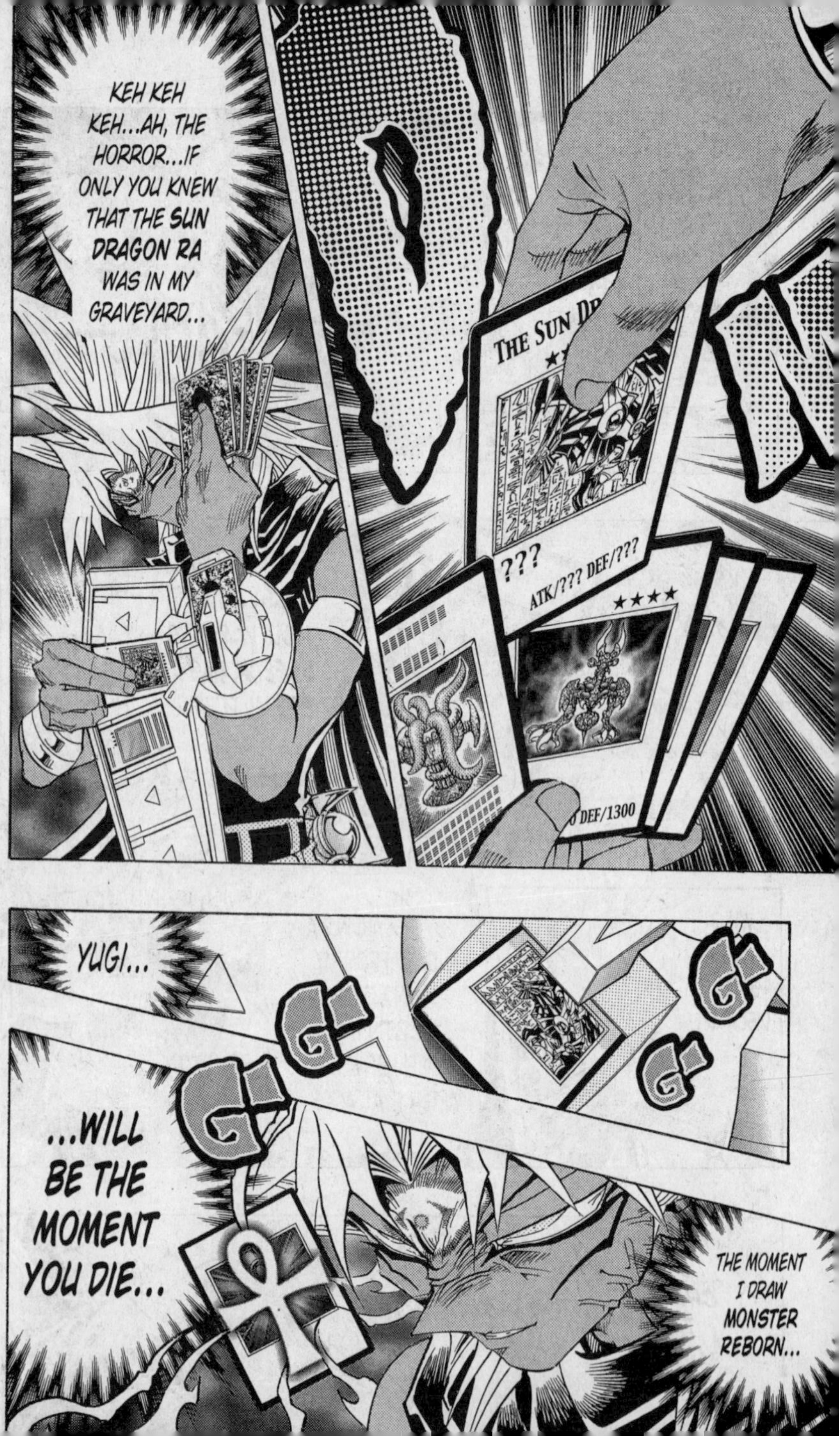
THE SUN DR
???
ATK/??? DEF/???
DEF/1300
KEH KEH KEH...AH, THE HORROR...IF ONLY YOU KNEW THAT THE SUN DRAGON RA WAS IN MY GRAVEYARD...
G G G G
YUGI...
THE MOMENT I DRAW MONSTER REBORN...
...WILL BE THE MOMENT YOU DIE...

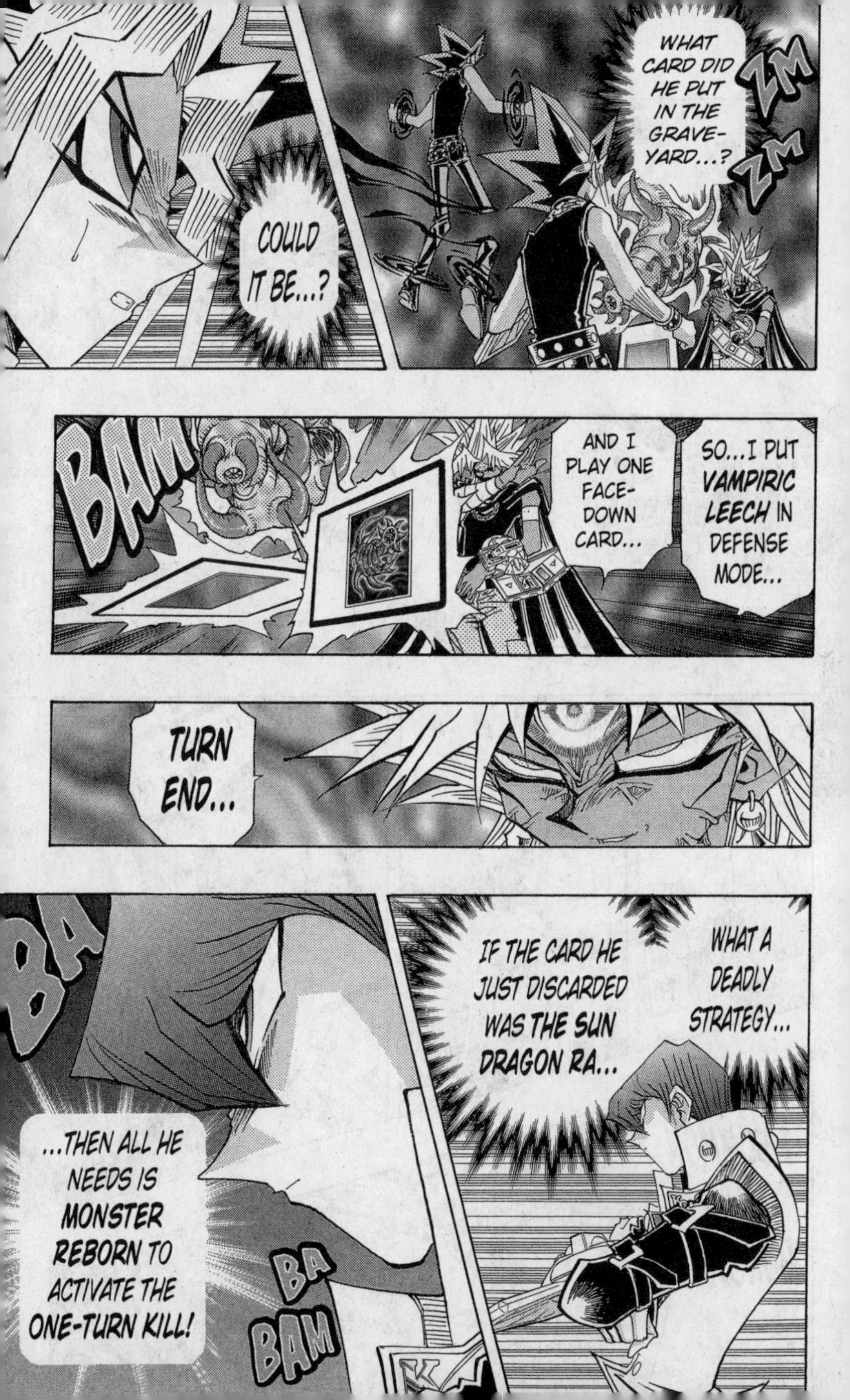
WHAT CARD DID HE PUT IN THE GRAVE-YARD...?
ZM ZM
COULD IT BE...?
SO...I PUT VAMPIRIC LEECH IN DEFENSE MODE...
AND I PLAY ONE FACE-DOWN CARD...
BAM
TURN END...
WHAT A DEADLY STRATEGY...
IF THE CARD HE JUST DISCARDED WAS THE SUN DRAGON RA...
BA
...THEN ALL HE NEEDS IS MONSTER REBORN TO ACTIVATE THE ONE-TURN KILL!
BA BAM

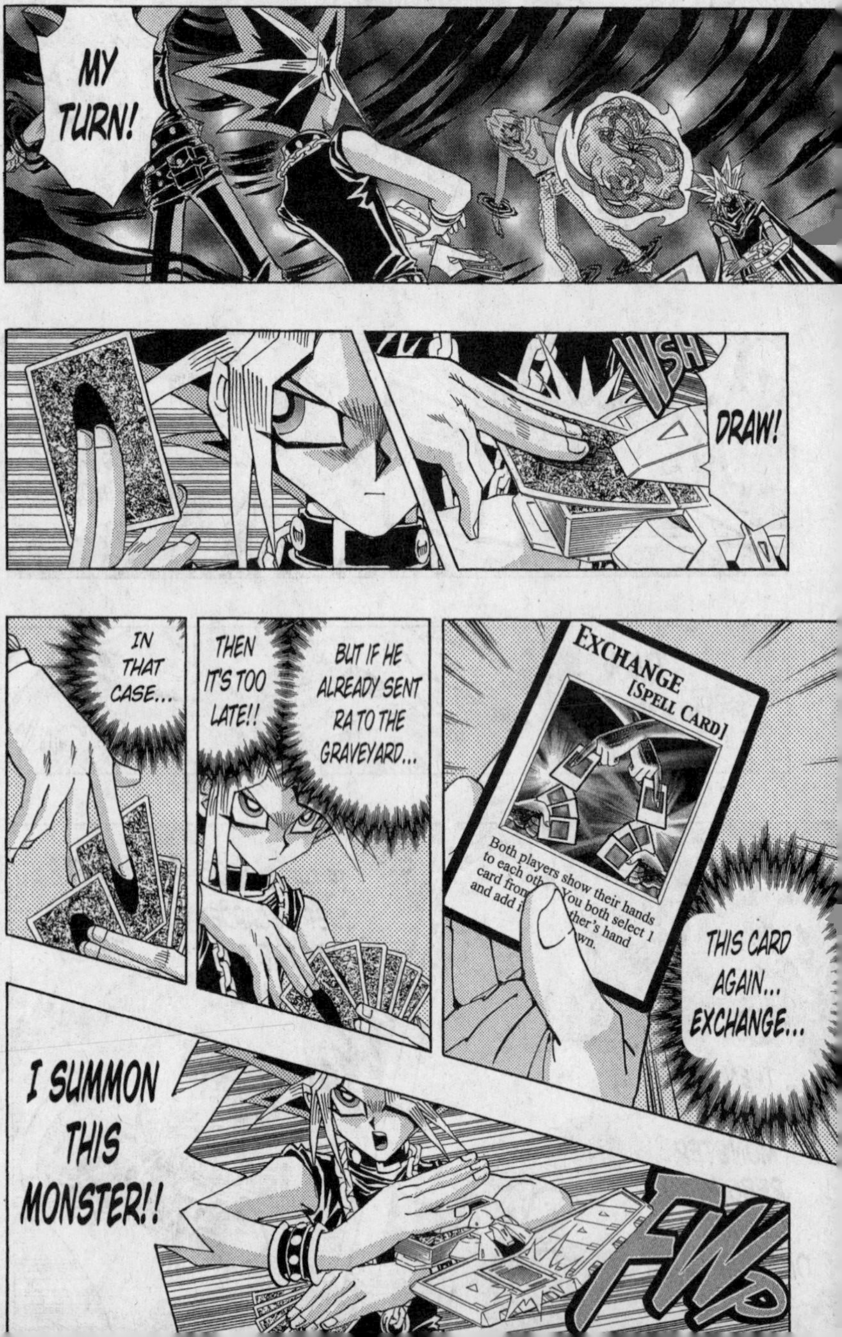
MY TURN!
WSH
DRAW!
EXCHANGE
[SPELL CARD]
Both players show their hands
THIS CARD AGAIN... EXCHANGE...
BUT IF HE ALREADY SENT RA TO THE GRAVEYARD...
THEN IT'S TOO LATE!!
IN THAT CASE...
I SUMMON THIS MONSTER!!
FWP

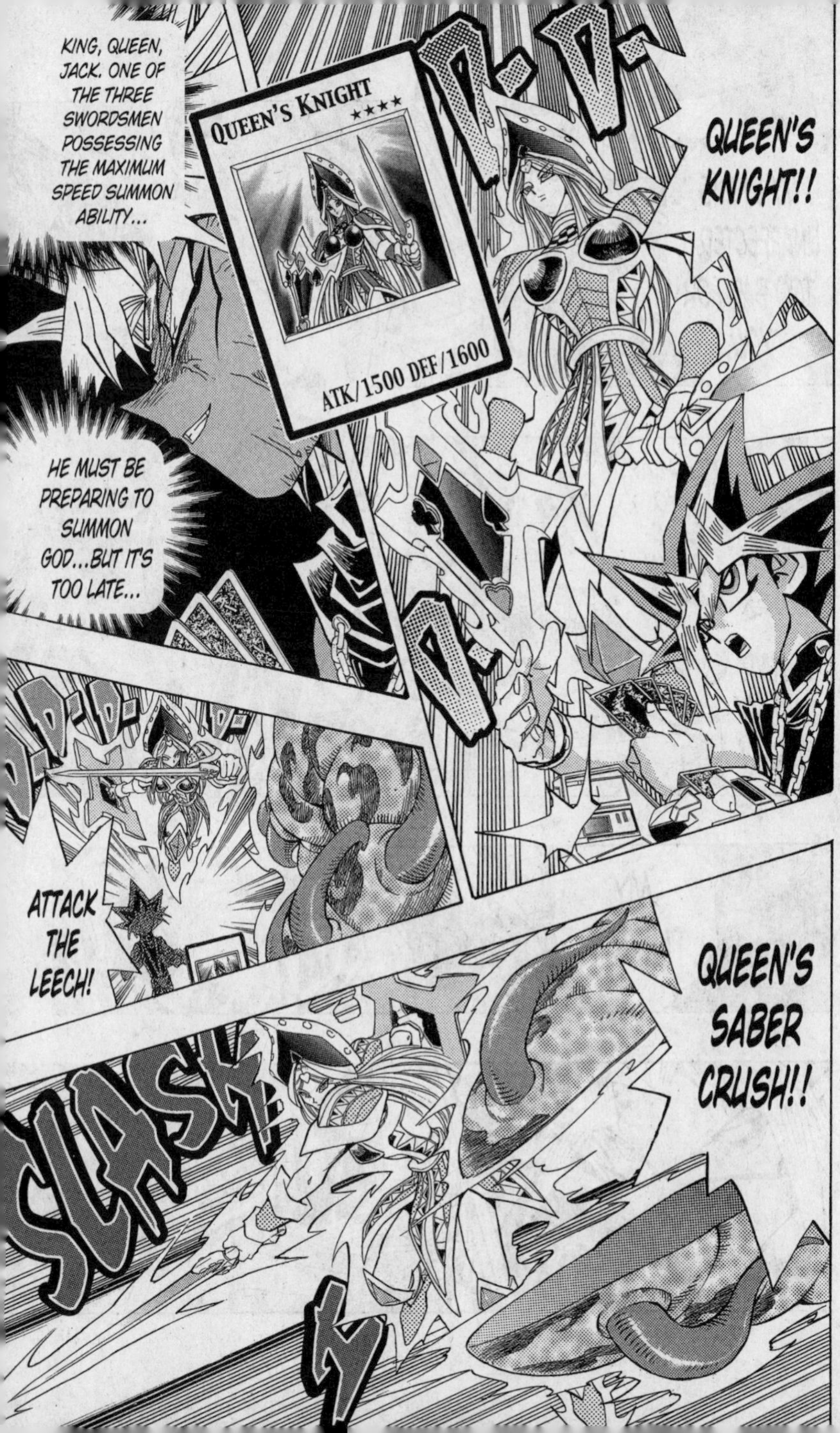
QUEEN'S KNIGHT!!
QUEEN'S KNIGHT ★★★★
ATK/1500 DEF/1600
KING, QUEEN, JACK. ONE OF THE THREE SWORDSMEN POSSESSING THE MAXIMUM SPEED SUMMON ABILITY...
HE MUST BE PREPARING TO SUMMON GOD...BUT IT'S TOO LATE...
ATTACK THE LEECH!
QUEEN'S SABER CRUSH!!
SLASH

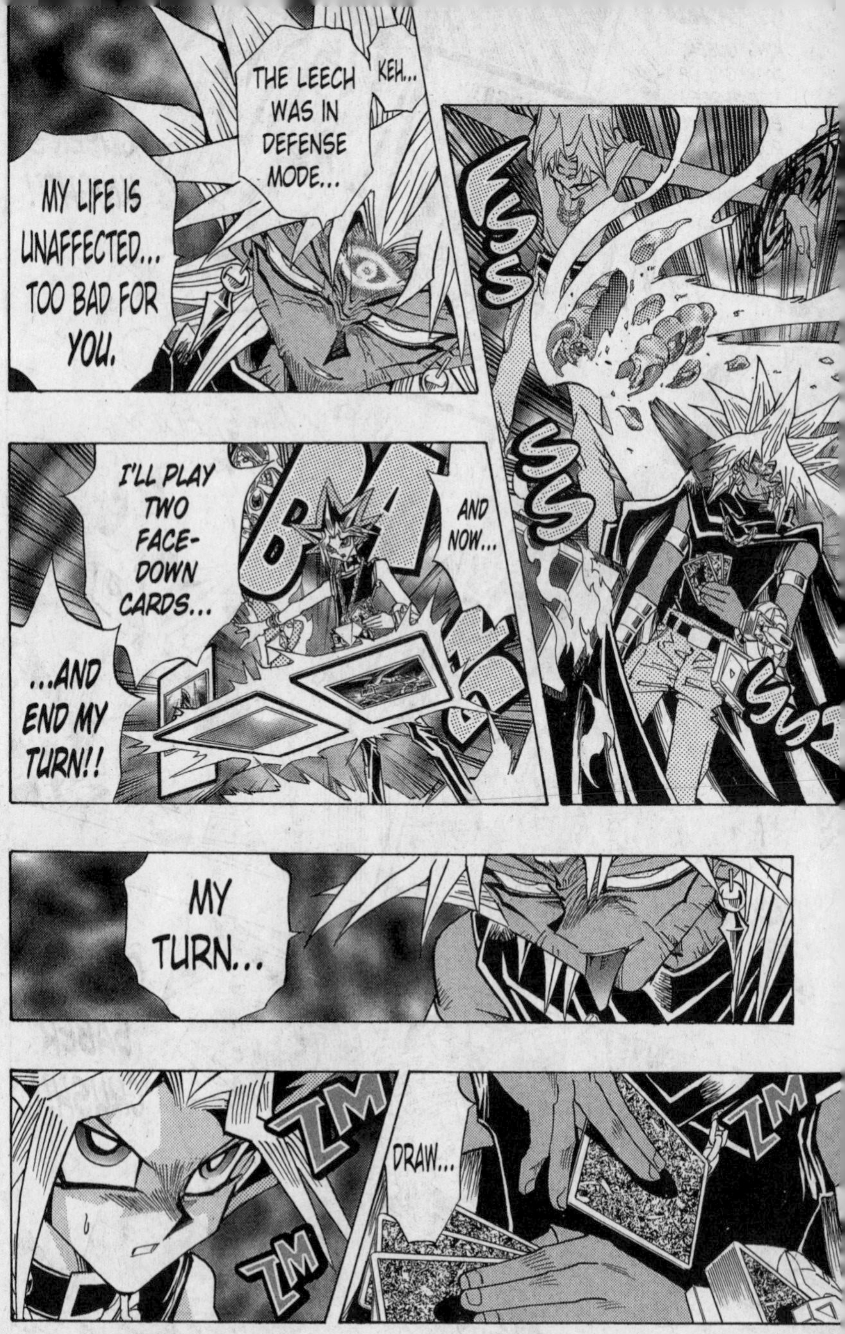
KEH...
THE LEECH WAS IN DEFENSE MODE...
MY LIFE IS UNAFFECTED... TOO BAD FOR YOU.
AND NOW...
I'LL PLAY TWO FACE-DOWN CARDS...
...AND END MY TURN!!
MY TURN...
ZM
DRAW...
ZM
ZM

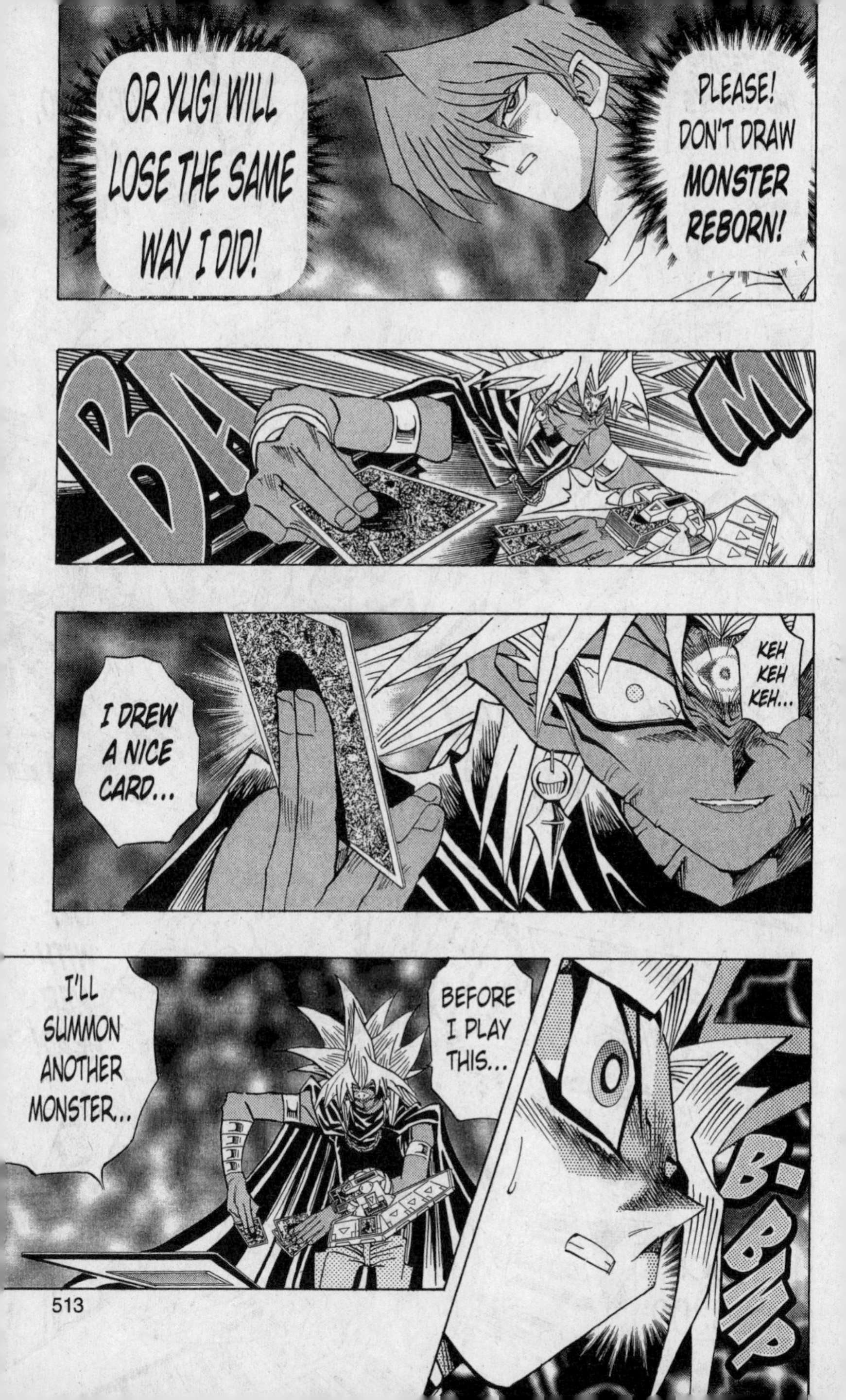
PLEASE! DON'T DRAW MONSTER REBORN!
OR YUGI WILL LOSE THE SAME WAY I DID!
BAM
KEH KEH KEH...
I DREW A NICE CARD...
B-BMP
BEFORE I PLAY THIS...
I'LL SUMMON ANOTHER MONSTER...

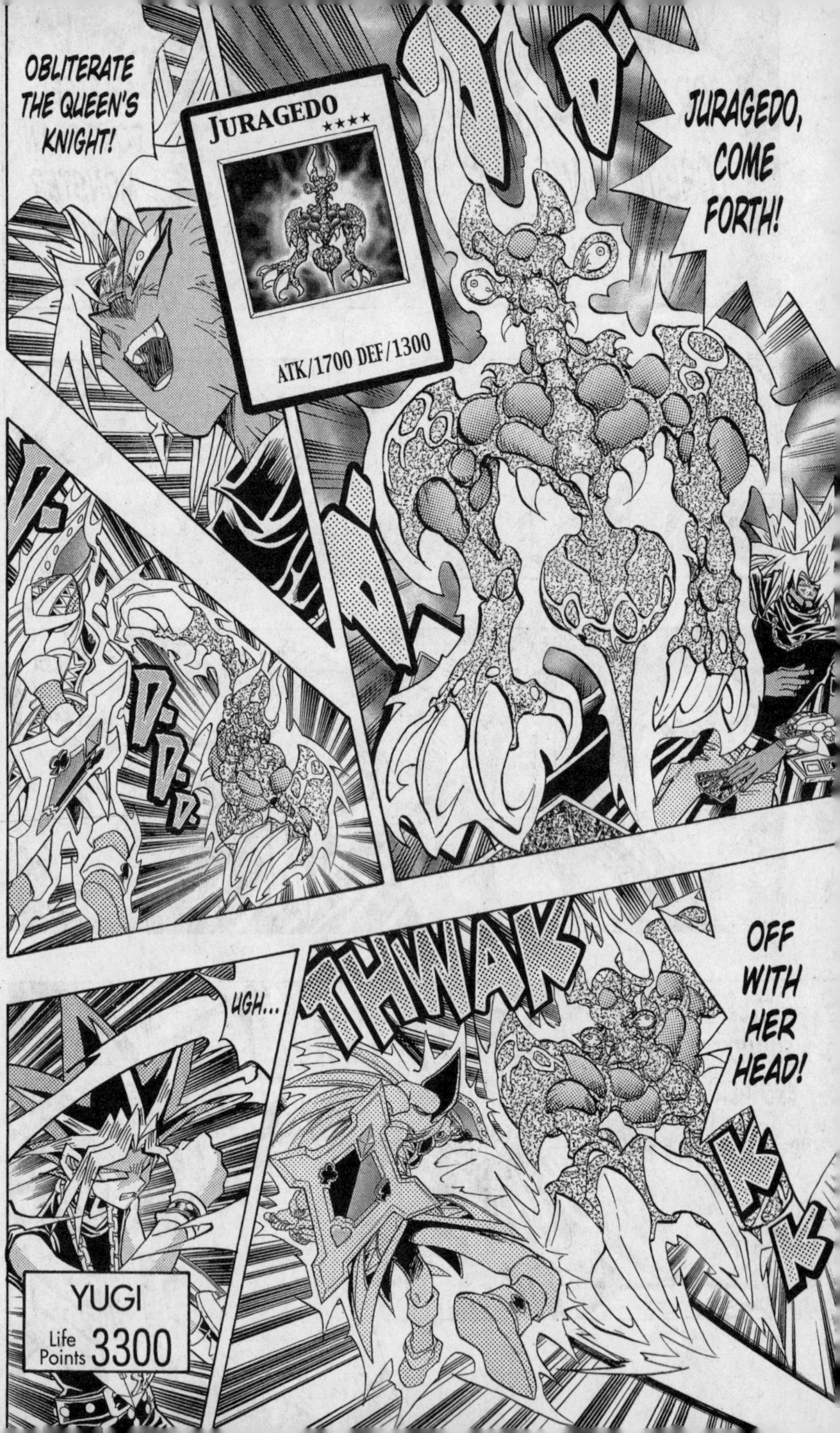
JURAGEDO, COME FORTH!
OBLITERATE THE QUEEN'S KNIGHT!
JURAGEDO
ATK/1700 DEF/1300
OFF WITH HER HEAD!
THWAK
UGH...
YUGI
Life Points 3300

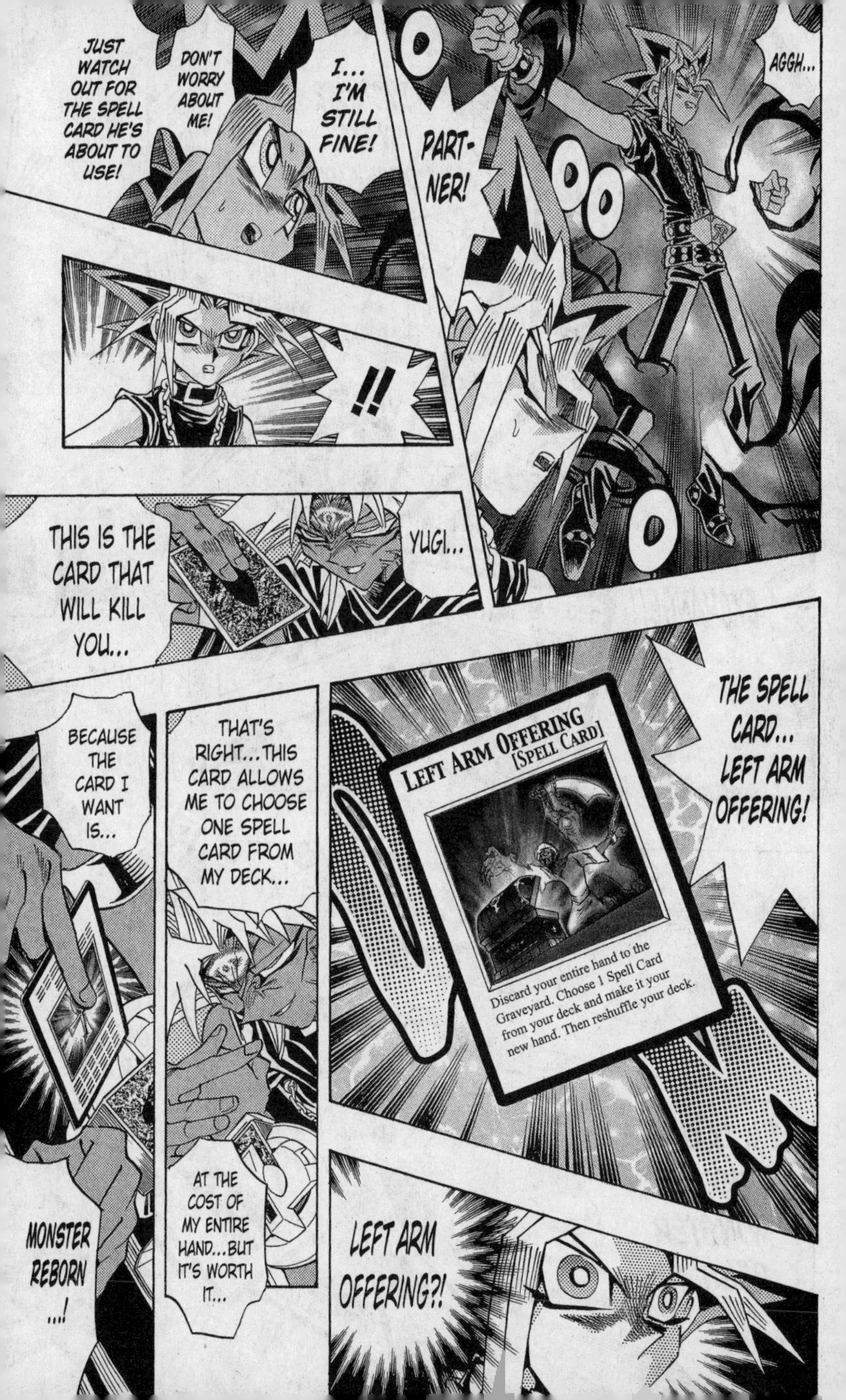
AGGH...
PART-NER!
I... I'M STILL FINE!
DON'T WORRY ABOUT ME!
JUST WATCH OUT FOR THE SPELL CARD HE'S ABOUT TO USE!
!!
YUGI...
THIS IS THE CARD THAT WILL KILL YOU...
THE SPELL CARD... LEFT ARM OFFERING!
LEFT ARM OFFERING
[SPELL CARD]
Discard your entire hand to the Graveyard. Choose 1 Spell Card from your deck and make it your new hand. Then reshuffle your deck.
LEFT ARM OFFERING?!
THAT'S RIGHT... THIS CARD ALLOWS ME TO CHOOSE ONE SPELL CARD FROM MY DECK...
AT THE COST OF MY ENTIRE HAND... BUT IT'S WORTH IT...
BECAUSE THE CARD I WANT IS...
MONSTER REBORN ...!

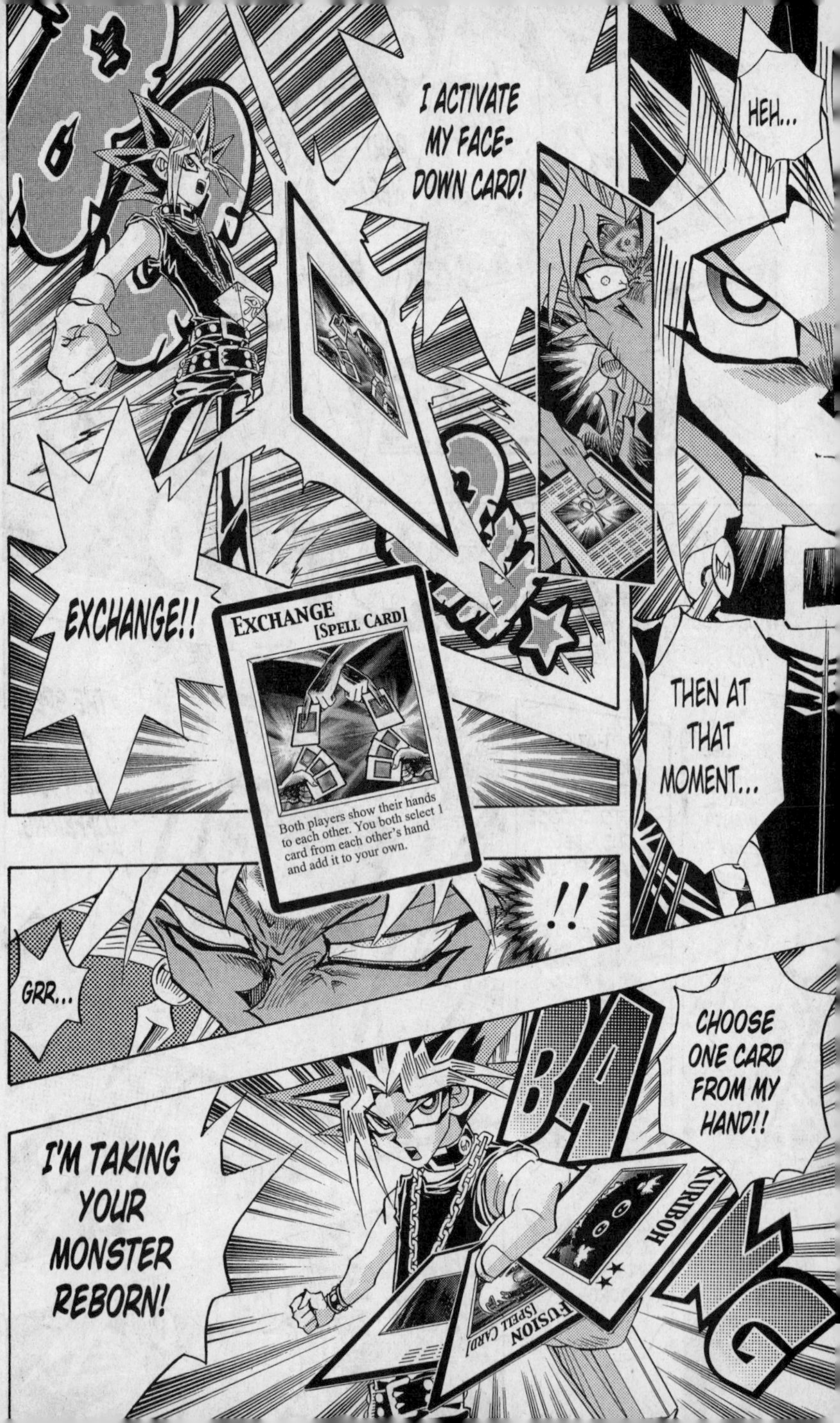
HEH...
I ACTIVATE MY FACE-DOWN CARD!
THEN AT THAT MOMENT...
EXCHANGE!!
EXCHANGE
[SPELL CARD]
Both players show their hands to each other. You both select 1 card from each other's hand and add it to your own.
!!
GRR...
CHOOSE ONE CARD FROM MY HAND!!
BA
I'M TAKING YOUR MONSTER REBORN!
KURIBOH
FUSION
[SPELL CARD]

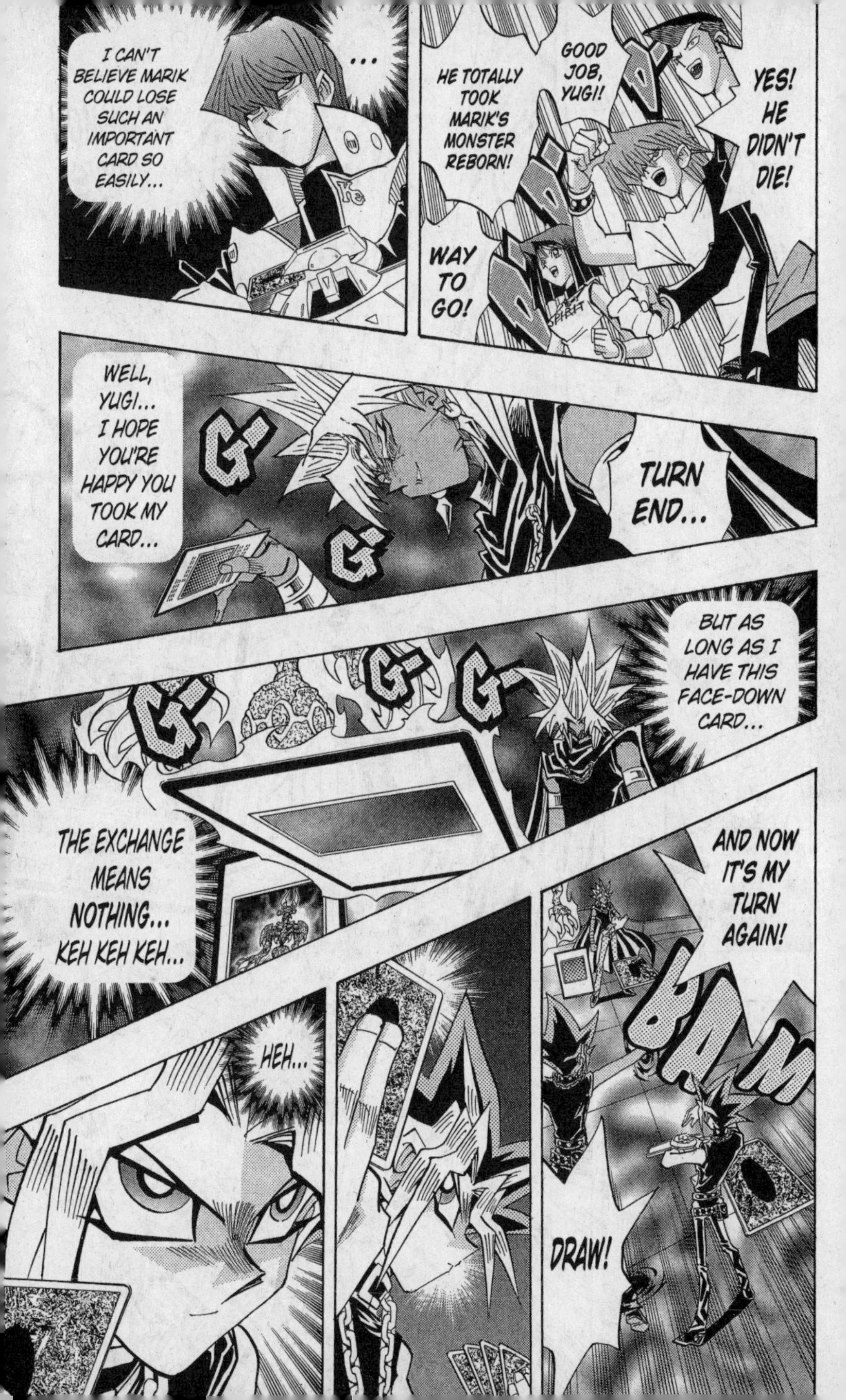
YES! HE DIDN'T DIE!
GOOD JOB, YUGI!
HE TOTALLY TOOK MARIK'S MONSTER REBORN!
WAY TO GO!
...
I CAN'T BELIEVE MARIK COULD LOSE SUCH AN IMPORTANT CARD SO EASILY...
TURN END...
G
G
WELL, YUGI... I HOPE YOU'RE HAPPY YOU TOOK MY CARD...
BUT AS LONG AS I HAVE THIS FACE-DOWN CARD...
G-
G-
G
THE EXCHANGE MEANS NOTHING... KEH KEH KEH...
AND NOW IT'S MY TURN AGAIN!
BAM
DRAW!
HEH...

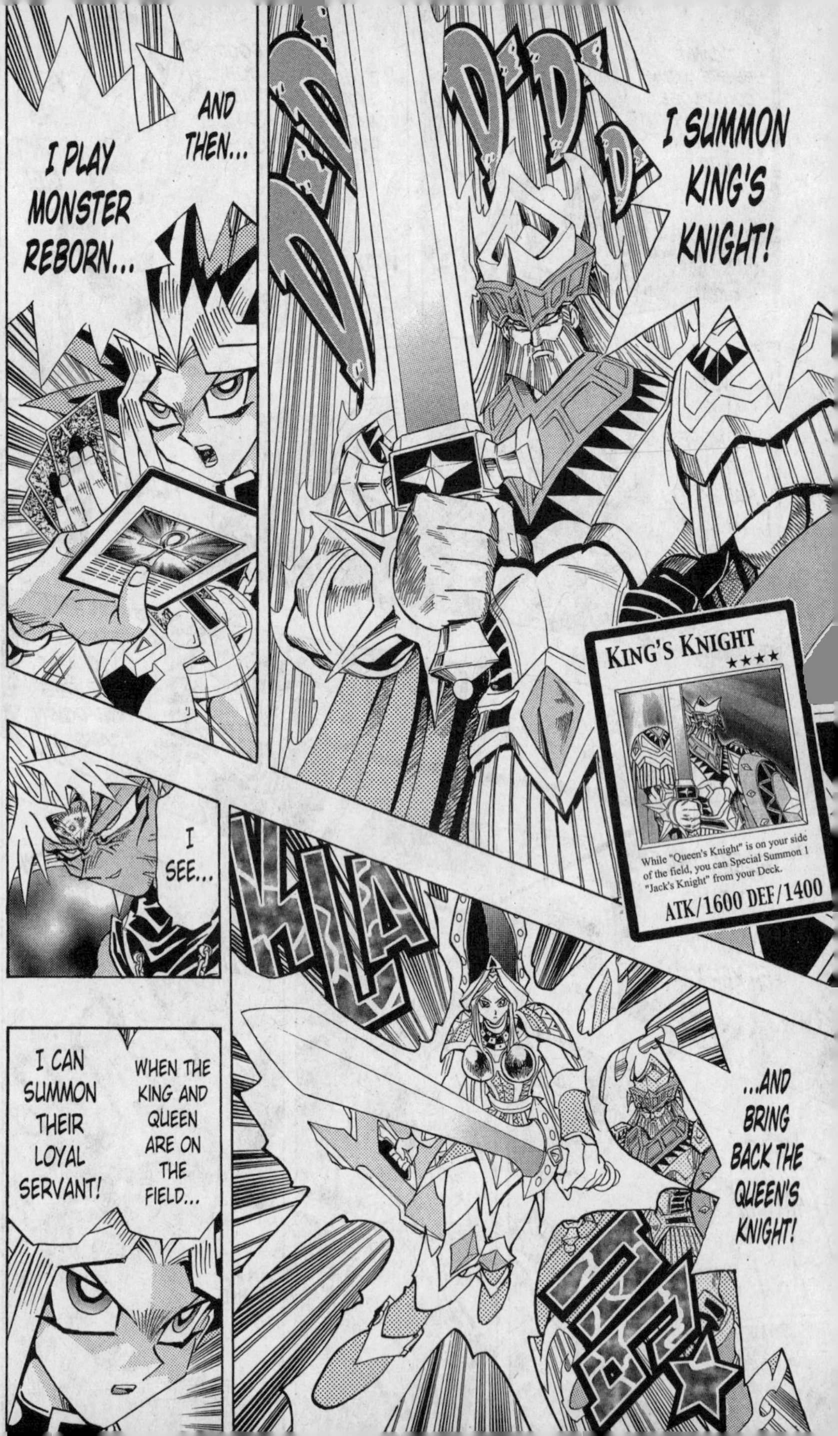
I SUMMON KING'S KNIGHT!
KING'S KNIGHT
★★★★
While "Queen's Knight" is on your side of the field, you can Special Summon 1 "Jack's Knight" from your Deck.
ATK/1600 DEF/1400
AND THEN...
I PLAY MONSTER REBORN...
...AND BRING BACK THE QUEEN'S KNIGHT!
I SEE...
WHEN THE KING AND QUEEN ARE ON THE FIELD...
I CAN SUMMON THEIR LOYAL SERVANT!

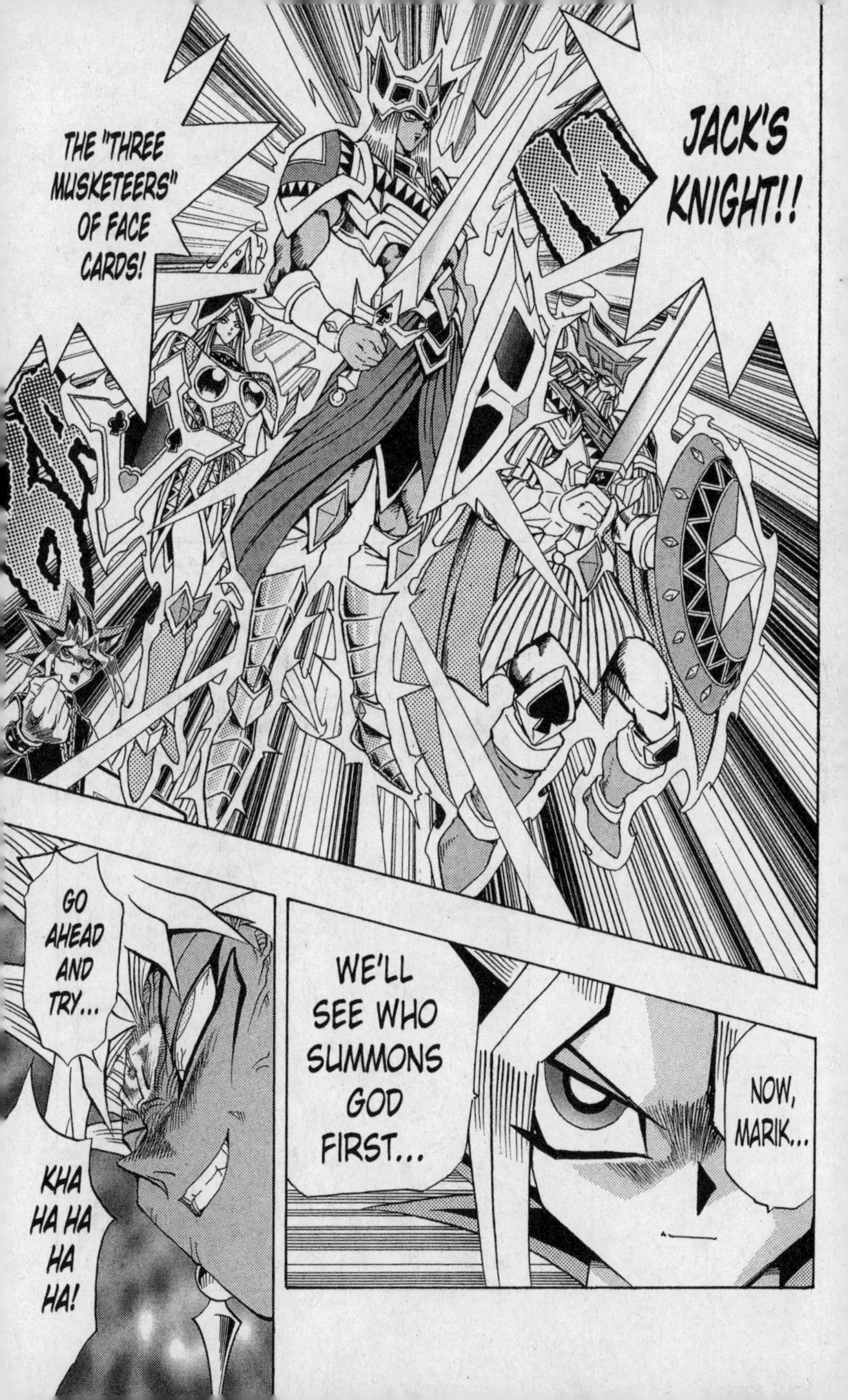
JACK'S KNIGHT!!
THE "THREE MUSKETEERS" OF FACE CARDS!
NOW, MARIK...
WE'LL SEE WHO SUMMONS GOD FIRST...
GO AHEAD AND TRY...
KHA HA HA HA HA!

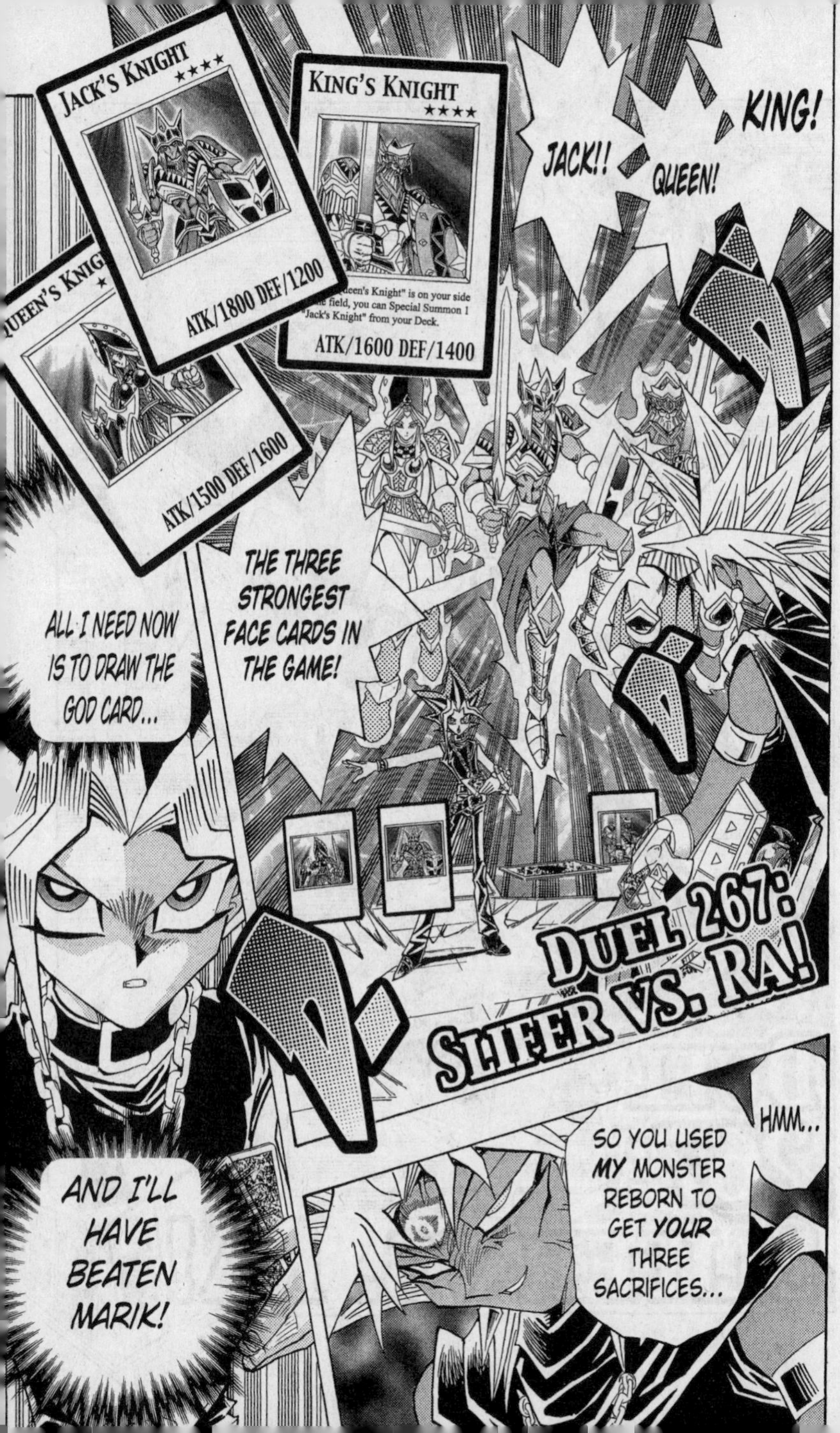
KING!
QUEEN!
JACK!!
KING'S KNIGHT
"...een's Knight" is on your side
...he field, you can Special Summon 1
"Jack's Knight" from your Deck.
ATK/1600 DEF/1400
JACK'S KNIGHT
ATK/1800 DEF/1200
QUEEN'S KNIG
ATK/1500 DEF/1600
THE THREE STRONGEST FACE CARDS IN THE GAME!
ALL I NEED NOW IS TO DRAW THE GOD CARD...
DUEL 267: SLIFER VS. RA!
HMM...
SO YOU USED MY MONSTER REBORN TO GET YOUR THREE SACRIFICES...
AND I'LL HAVE BEATEN MARIK!

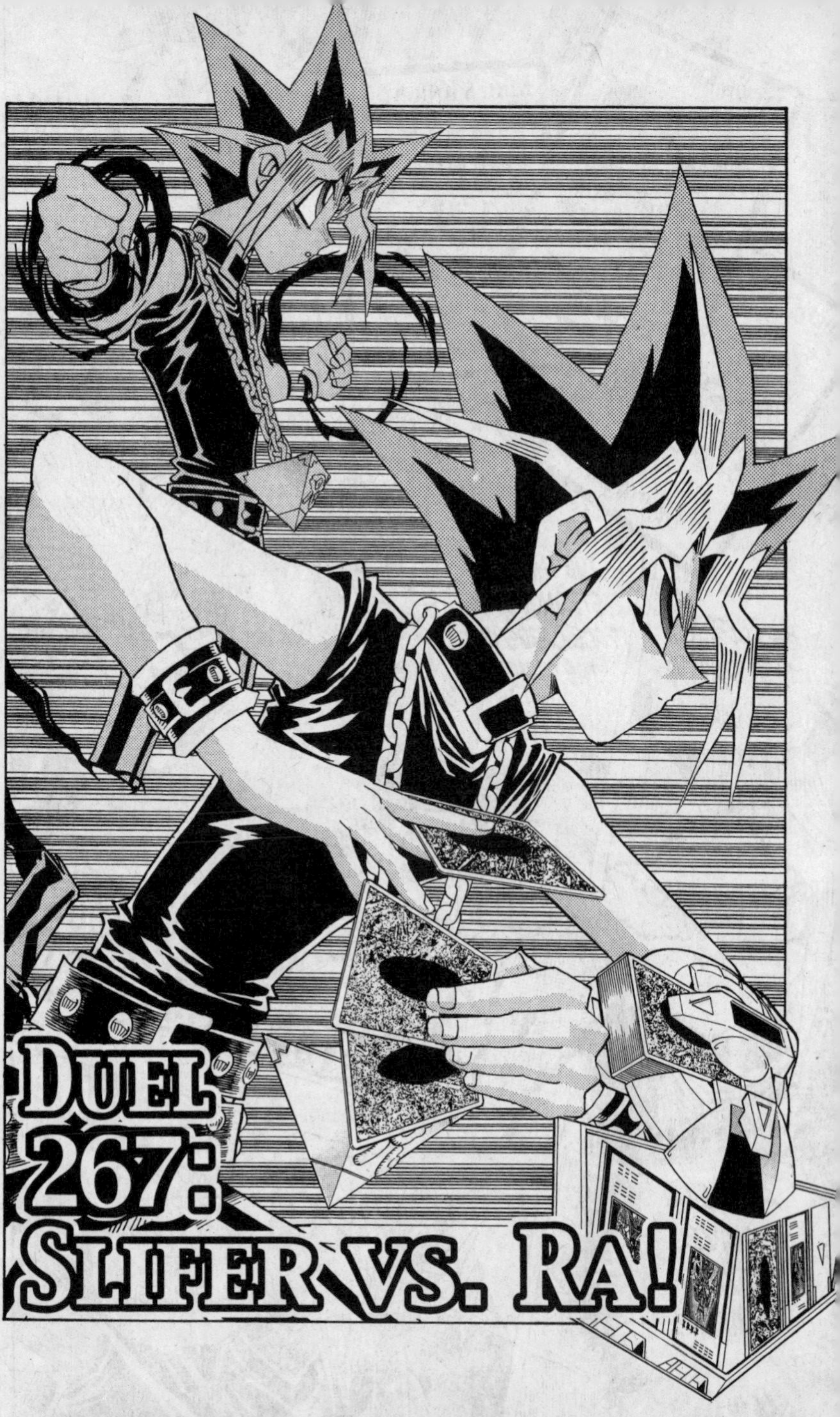
DUEL 267:
SLIFER VS. RA!

READ THIS WAY

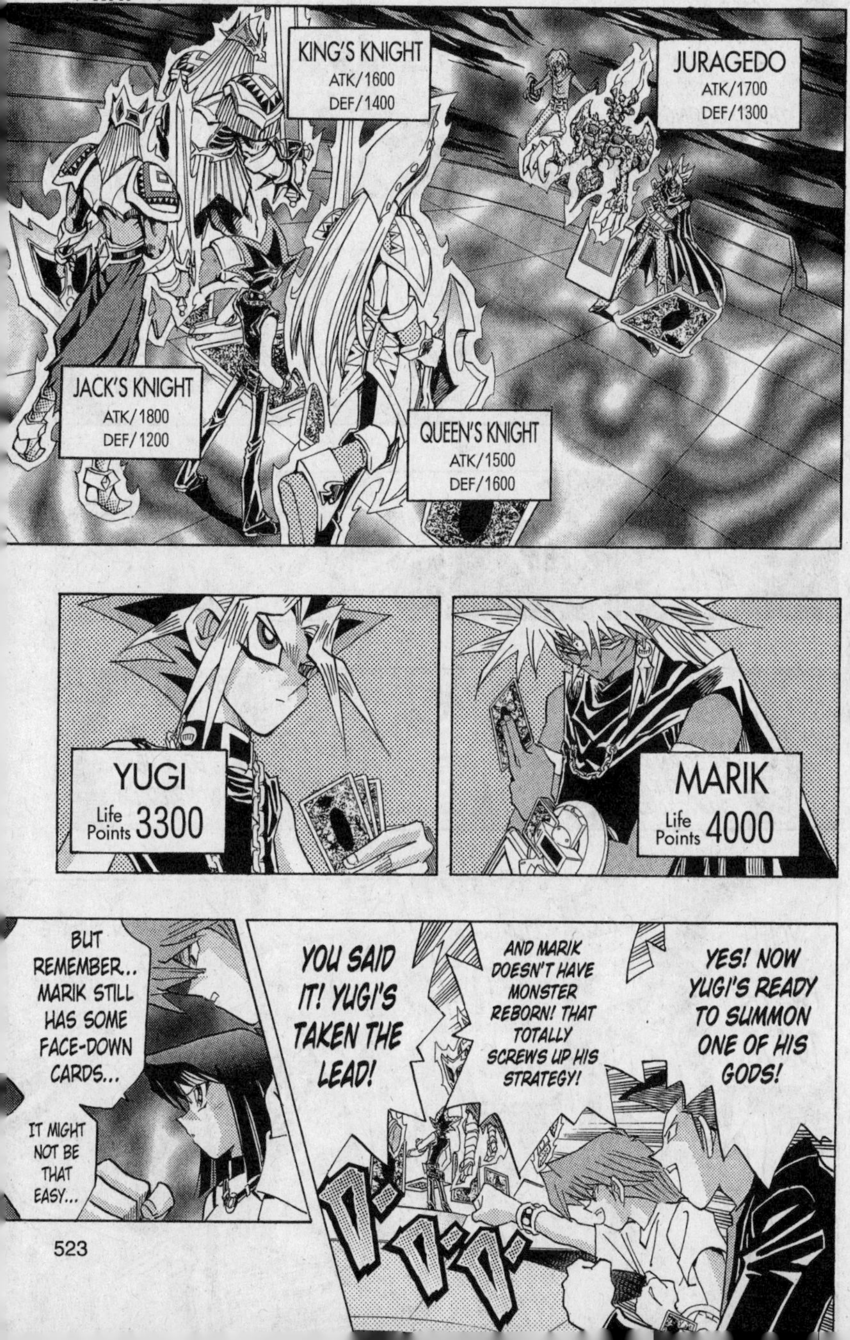

JURAGEDO
ATK/1700
DEF/1300
KING'S KNIGHT
ATK/1600
DEF/1400
QUEEN'S KNIGHT
ATK/1500
DEF/1600
JACK'S KNIGHT
ATK/1800
DEF/1200
MARIK
Life Points 4000
YUGI
Life Points 3300
YES! NOW YUGI'S READY TO SUMMON ONE OF HIS GODS!
AND MARIK DOESN'T HAVE MONSTER REBORN! THAT TOTALLY SCREWS UP HIS STRATEGY!
YOU SAID IT! YUGI'S TAKEN THE LEAD!
BUT REMEMBER... MARIK STILL HAS SOME FACE-DOWN CARDS...
IT MIGHT NOT BE THAT EASY...

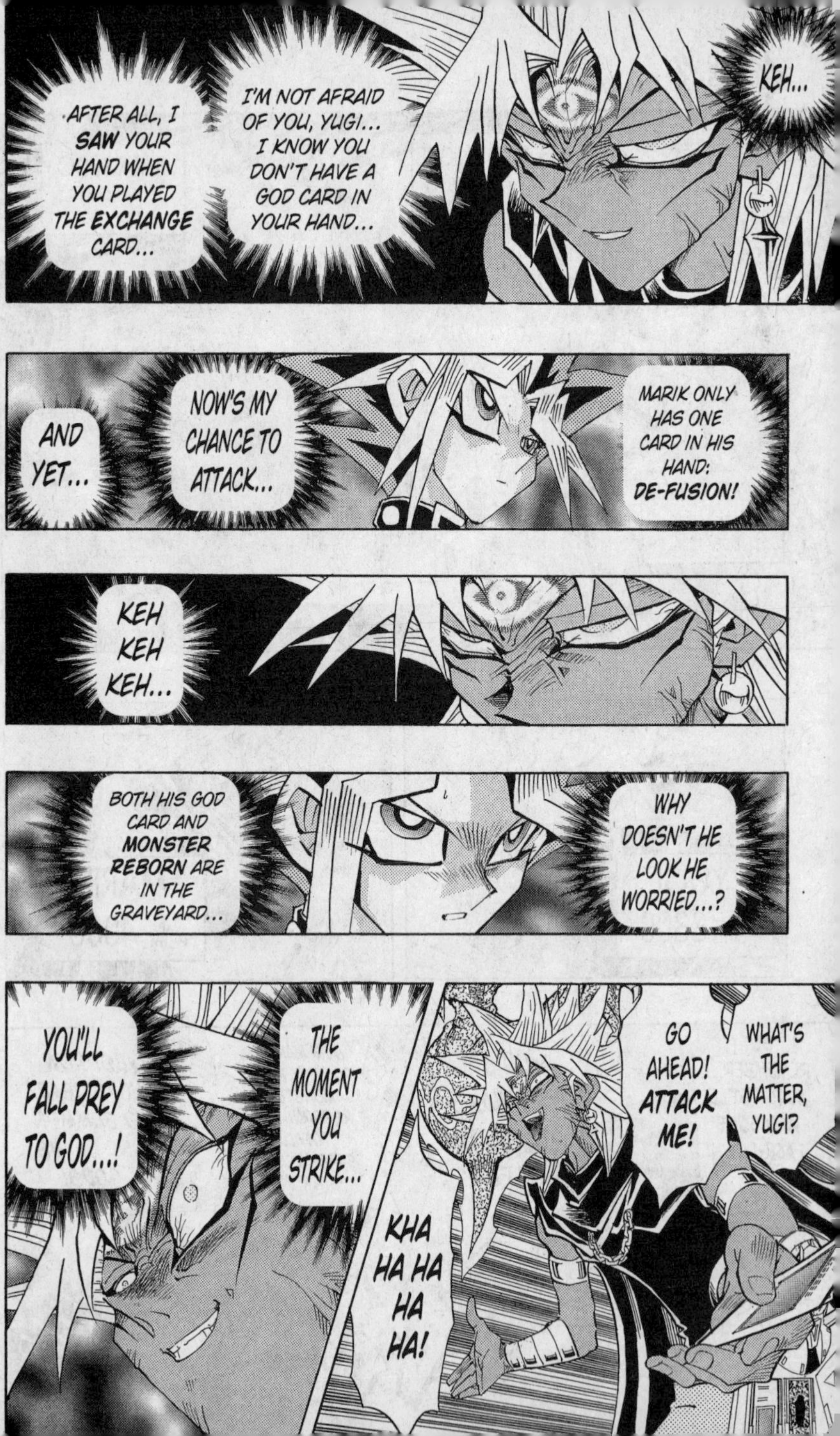
KEH...
I'M NOT AFRAID OF YOU, YUGI... I KNOW YOU DON'T HAVE A GOD CARD IN YOUR HAND...
AFTER ALL, I **SAW** YOUR HAND WHEN YOU PLAYED THE **EXCHANGE** CARD...
MARIK ONLY HAS ONE CARD IN HIS HAND: **DE-FUSION!**
NOW'S MY CHANCE TO ATTACK...
AND YET...
KEH KEH KEH...
WHY DOESN'T HE LOOK HE WORRIED...?
BOTH HIS GOD CARD AND **MONSTER REBORN** ARE IN THE GRAVEYARD...
WHAT'S THE MATTER, YUGI?
GO AHEAD! **ATTACK ME!**
KHA HA HA HA HA!
THE MOMENT YOU STRIKE...
YOU'LL FALL PREY TO GOD...!

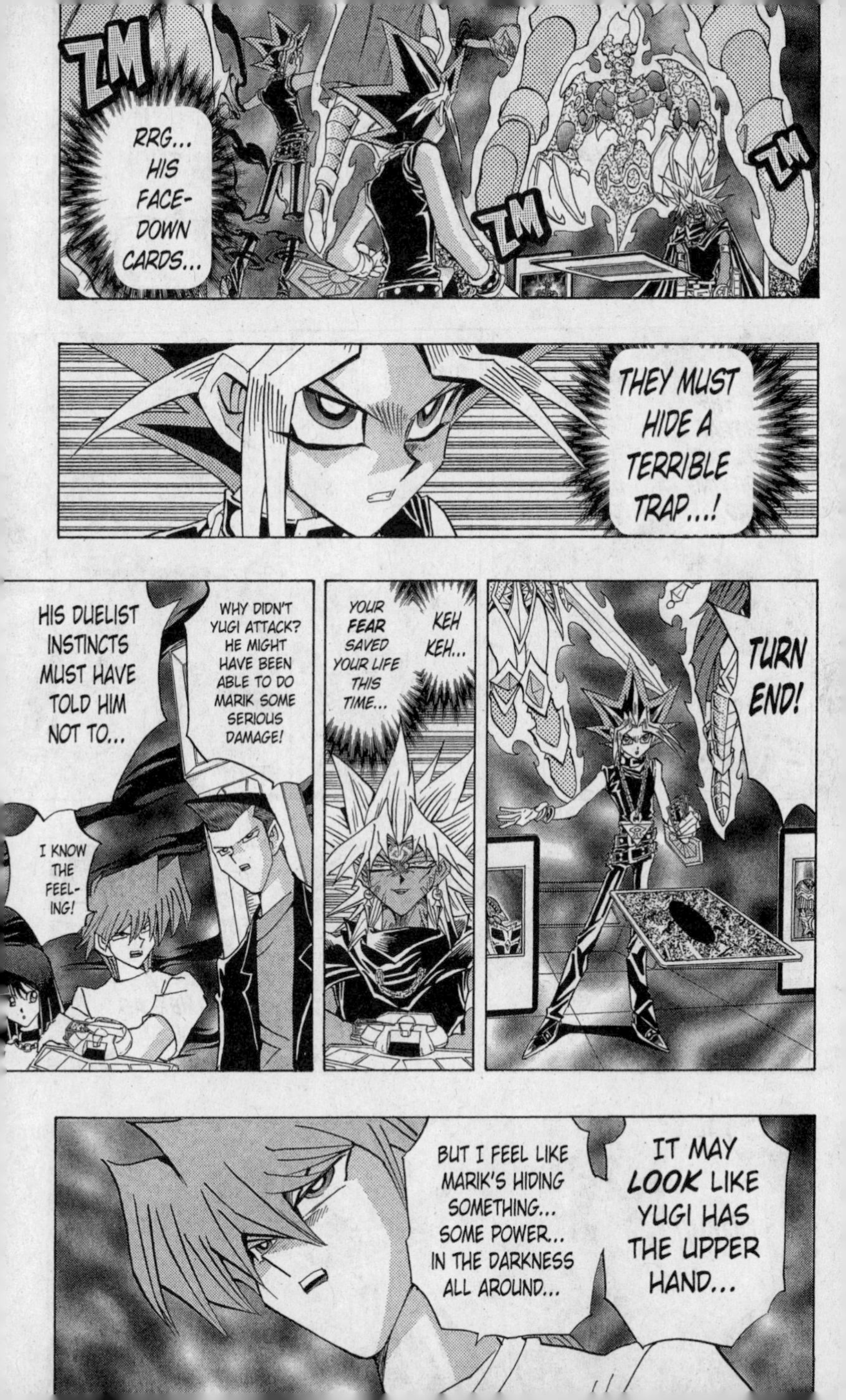
ZM
ZM
ZM
RRG... HIS FACE-DOWN CARDS...
THEY MUST HIDE A TERRIBLE TRAP...!
TURN END!
KEH KEH...
YOUR FEAR SAVED YOUR LIFE THIS TIME...
WHY DIDN'T YUGI ATTACK? HE MIGHT HAVE BEEN ABLE TO DO MARIK SOME SERIOUS DAMAGE!
HIS DUELIST INSTINCTS MUST HAVE TOLD HIM NOT TO...
I KNOW THE FEEL-ING!
IT MAY LOOK LIKE YUGI HAS THE UPPER HAND...
BUT I FEEL LIKE MARIK'S HIDING SOMETHING... SOME POWER... IN THE DARKNESS ALL AROUND...

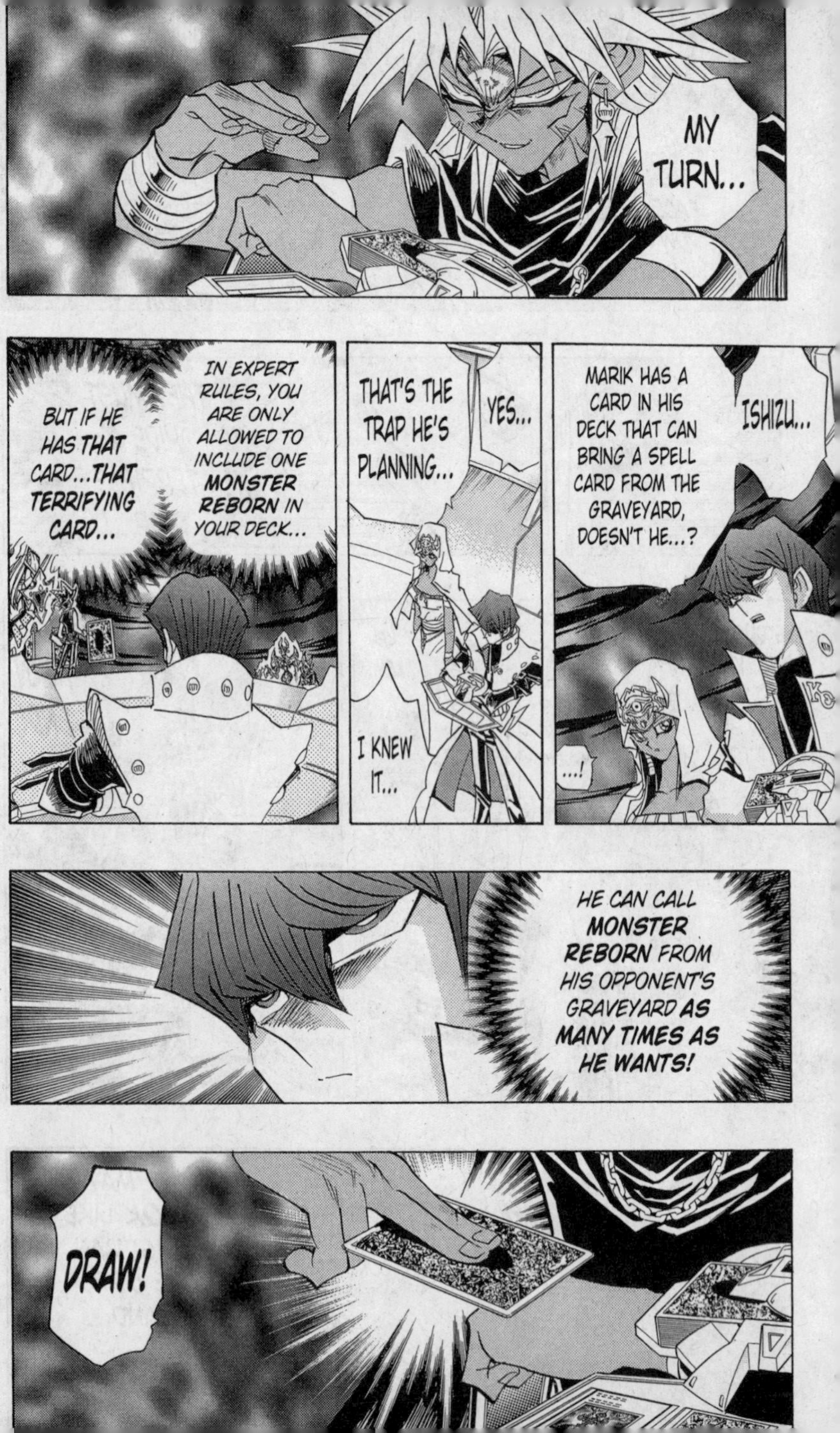
MY TURN...
ISHIZU...
MARIK HAS A CARD IN HIS DECK THAT CAN BRING A SPELL CARD FROM THE GRAVEYARD, DOESN'T HE...?
...!
YES...
THAT'S THE TRAP HE'S PLANNING...
I KNEW IT...
IN EXPERT RULES, YOU ARE ONLY ALLOWED TO INCLUDE ONE MONSTER REBORN IN YOUR DECK...
BUT IF HE HAS THAT CARD...THAT TERRIFYING CARD...
HE CAN CALL MONSTER REBORN FROM HIS OPPONENT'S GRAVEYARD AS MANY TIMES AS HE WANTS!
DRAW!

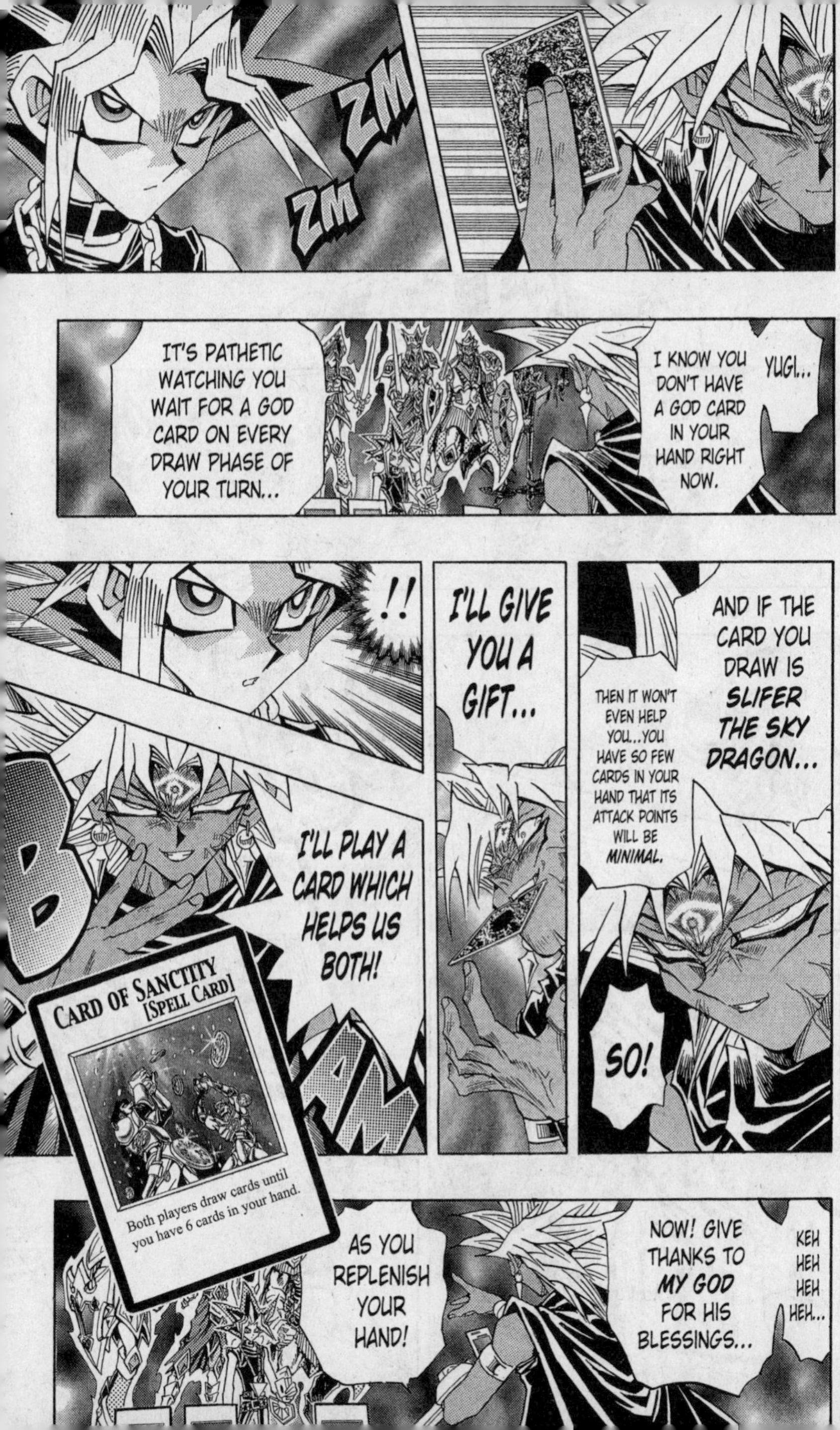
ZM
ZM
YUGI...
I KNOW YOU DON'T HAVE A GOD CARD IN YOUR HAND RIGHT NOW.
IT'S PATHETIC WATCHING YOU WAIT FOR A GOD CARD ON EVERY DRAW PHASE OF YOUR TURN...
AND IF THE CARD YOU DRAW IS SLIFER THE SKY DRAGON...
THEN IT WON'T EVEN HELP YOU...YOU HAVE SO FEW CARDS IN YOUR HAND THAT ITS ATTACK POINTS WILL BE MINIMAL.
SO!
I'LL GIVE YOU A GIFT...
!!
I'LL PLAY A CARD WHICH HELPS US BOTH!
CARD OF SANCTITY
[SPELL CARD]
Both players draw cards until you have 6 cards in your hand.
KEH HEH HEH HEH...
NOW! GIVE THANKS TO MY GOD FOR HIS BLESSINGS...
AS YOU REPLENISH YOUR HAND!

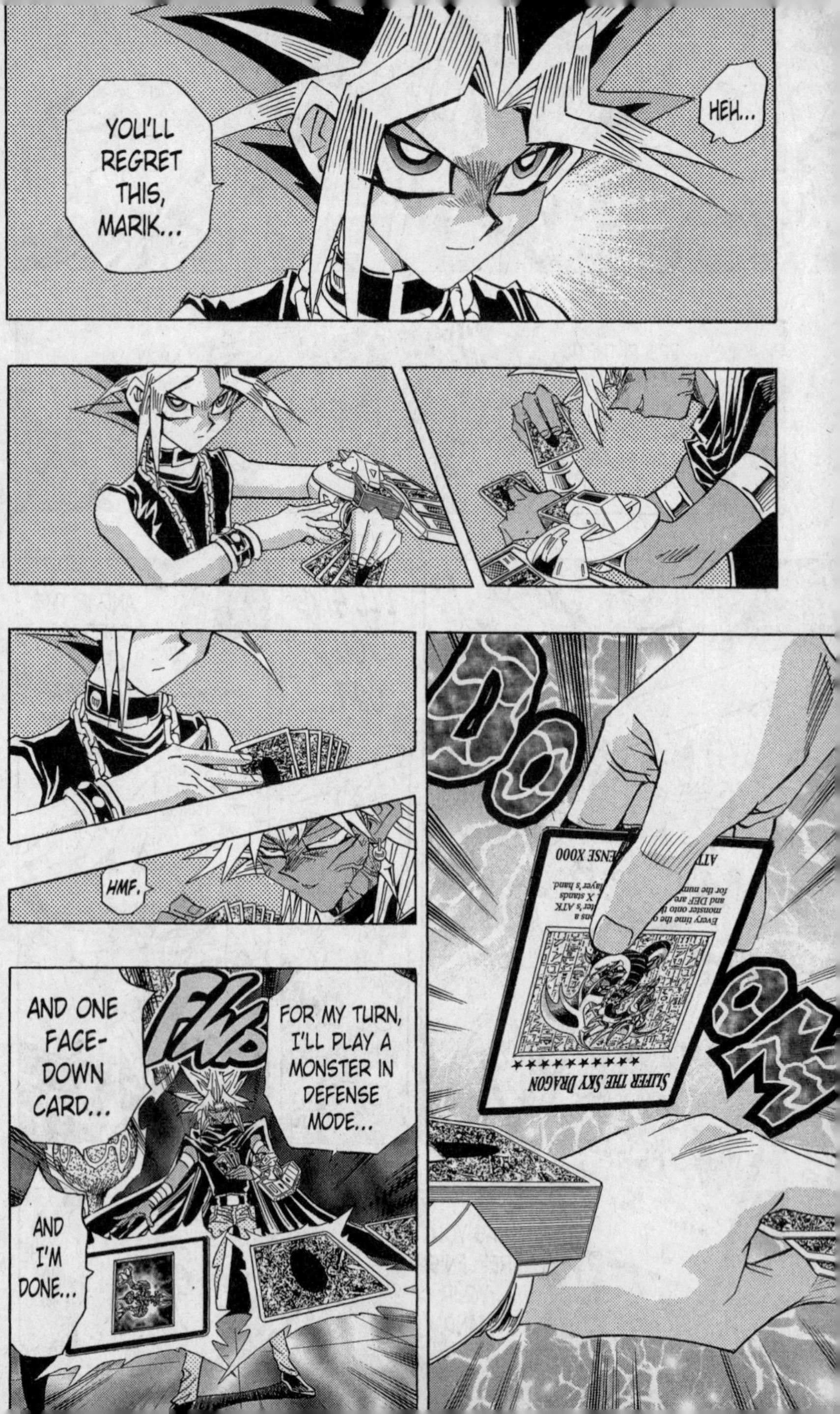
HEH...
YOU'LL REGRET THIS, MARIK...
DOOM
SLIFER THE SKY DRAGON
HMF.
FWP
FOR MY TURN, I'LL PLAY A MONSTER IN DEFENSE MODE...
AND ONE FACE-DOWN CARD...
AND I'M DONE...

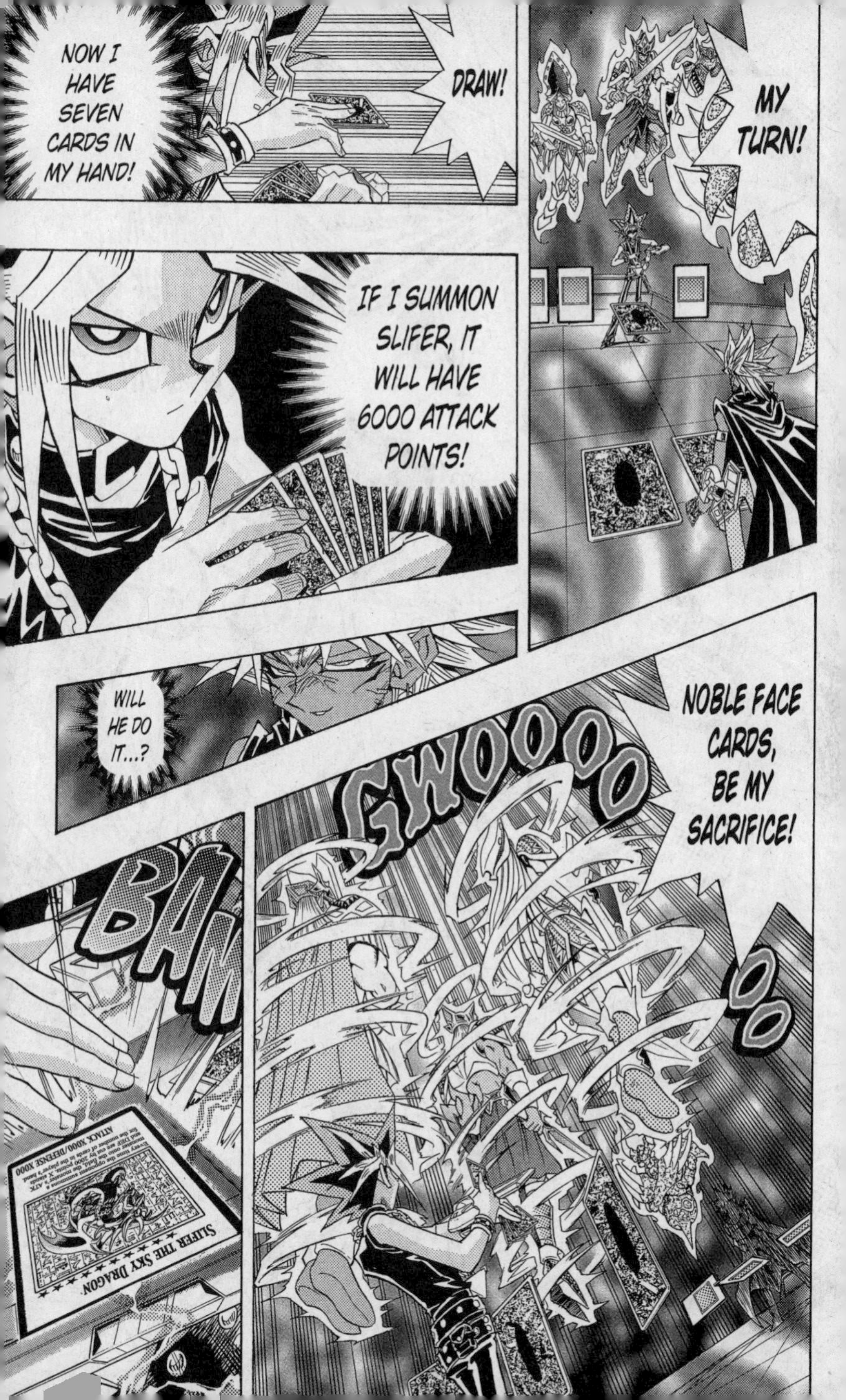
MY TURN!
DRAW!
NOW I HAVE SEVEN CARDS IN MY HAND!
IF I SUMMON SLIFER, IT WILL HAVE 6000 ATTACK POINTS!
WILL HE DO IT...?
NOBLE FACE CARDS, BE MY SACRIFICE!
GWOOOOOOO
BAM
SLIFER THE SKY DRAGON

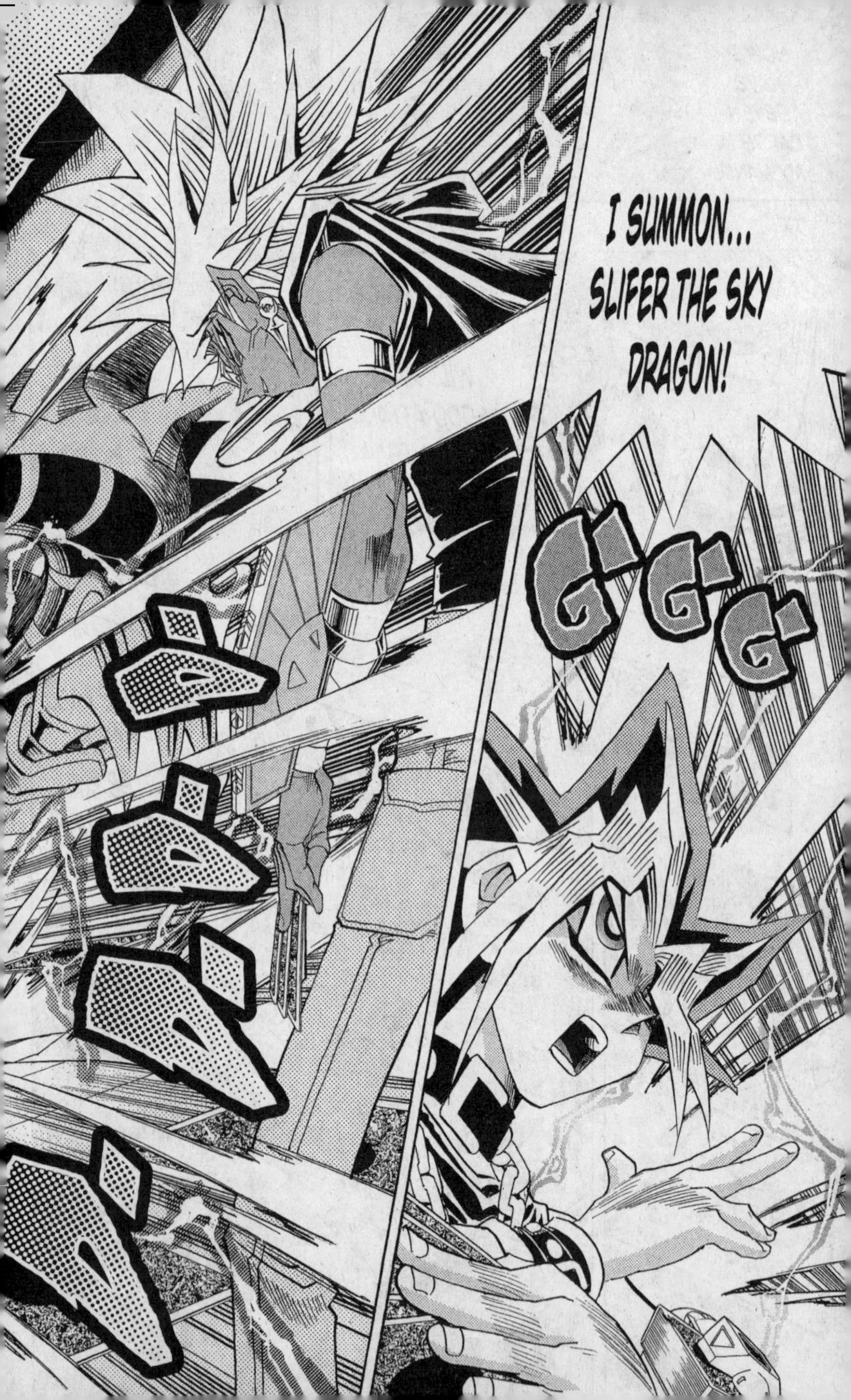
I SUMMON... SLIFER THE SKY DRAGON!
G'G'G'

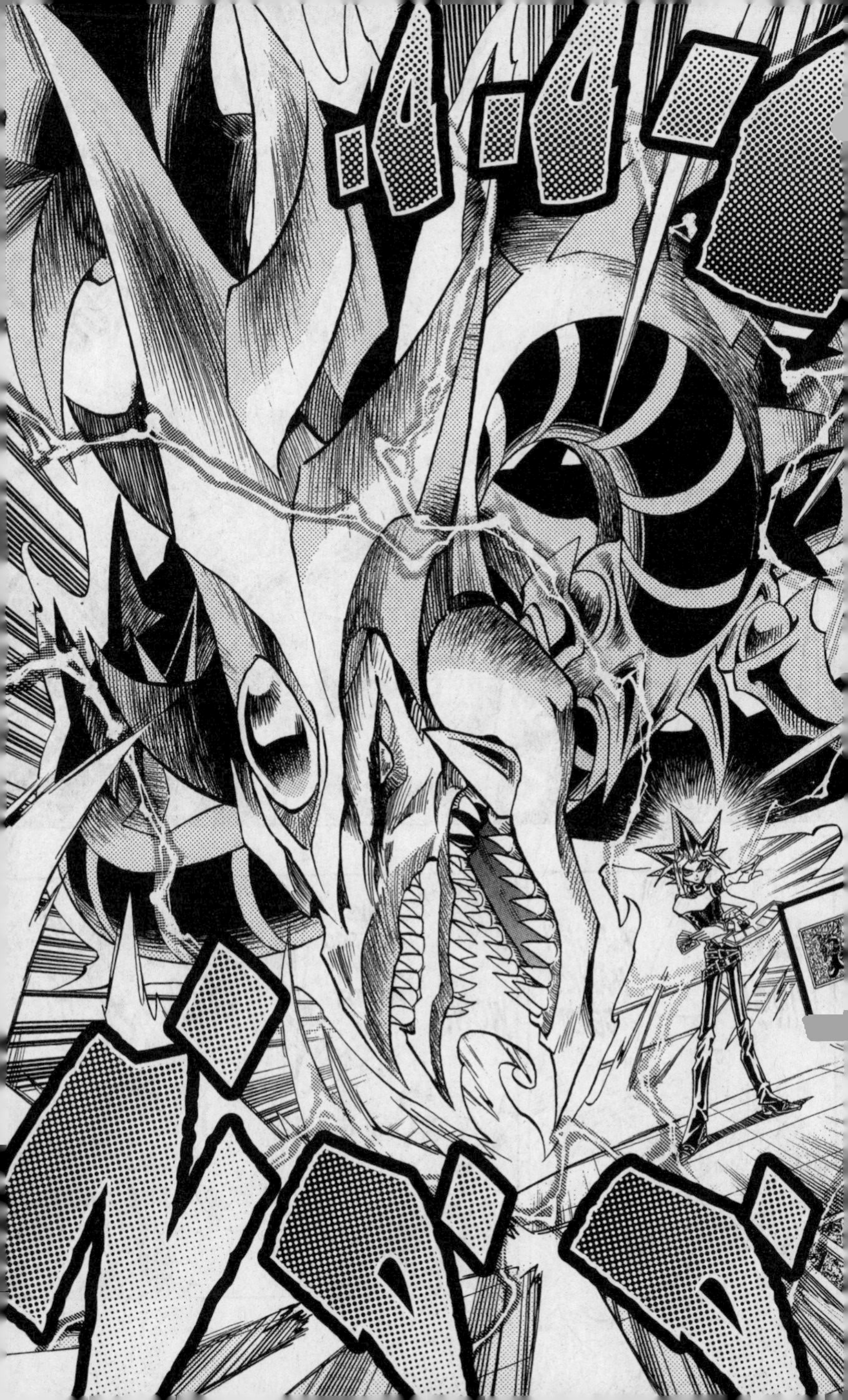

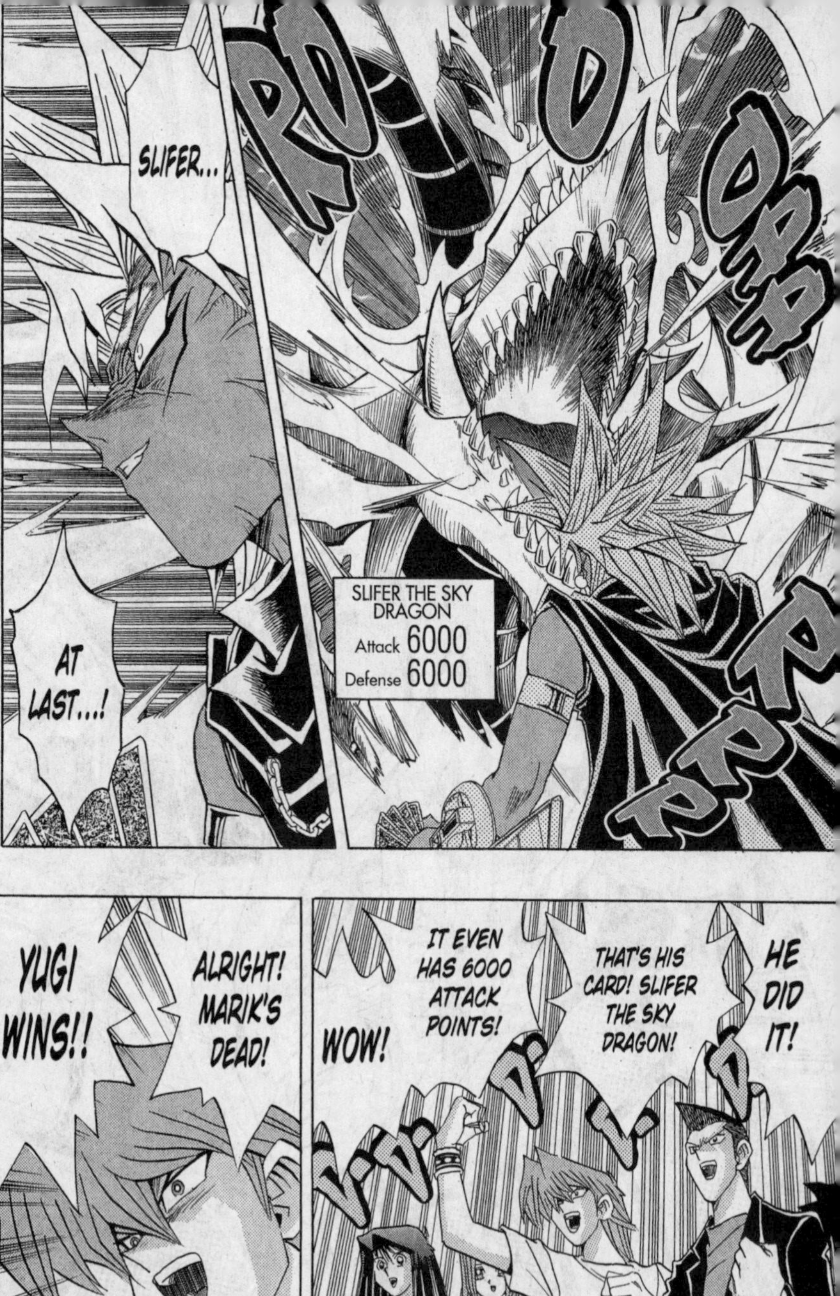
SLIFER THE SKY DRAGON
Attack 6000
Defense 6000
SLIFER...
AT LAST...!
HE DID IT!
THAT'S HIS CARD! SLIFER THE SKY DRAGON!
IT EVEN HAS 6000 ATTACK POINTS!
WOW!
ALRIGHT! MARIK'S DEAD!
YUGI WINS!!

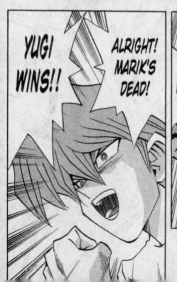

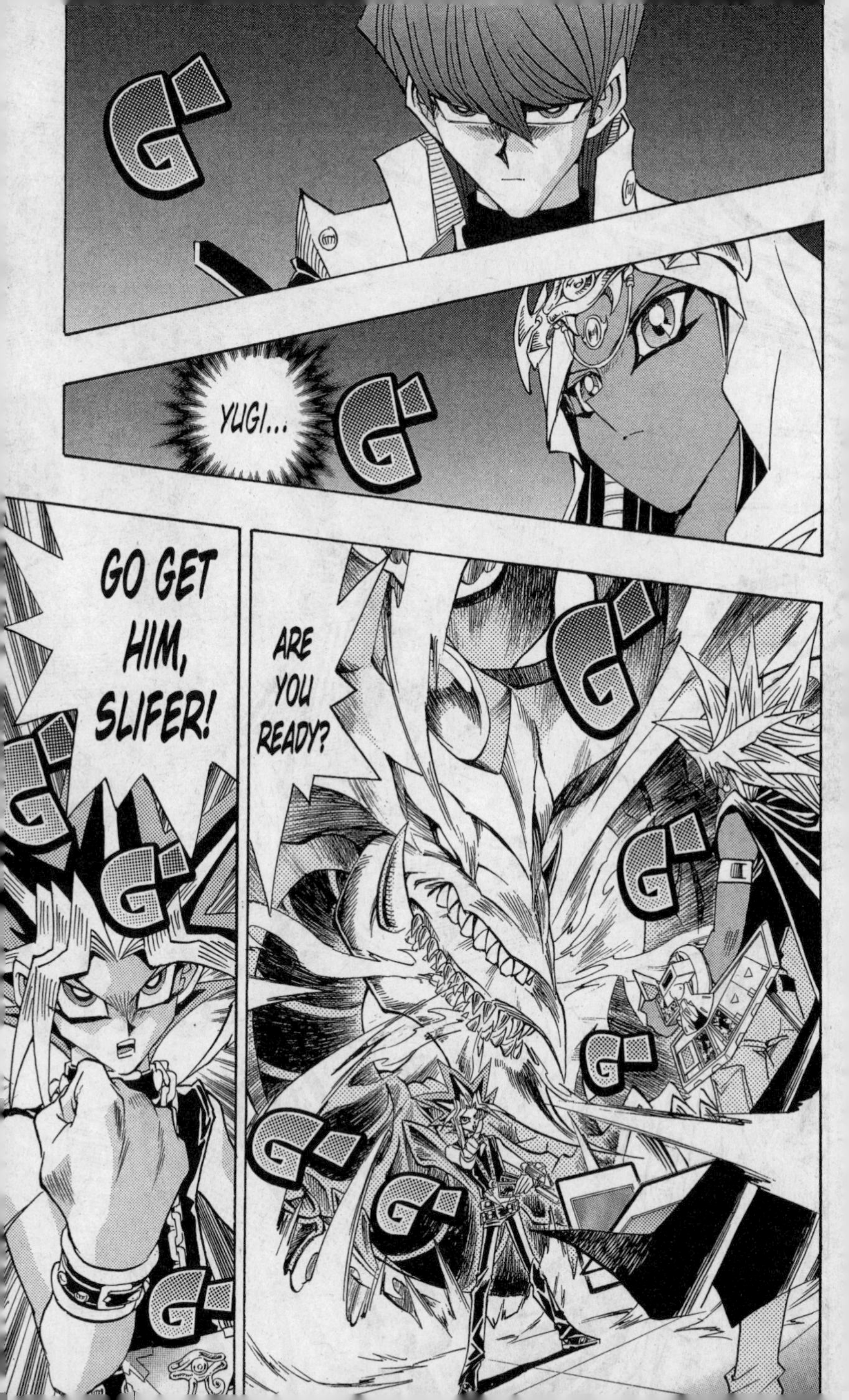
G
YUGI...
G
G
ARE YOU READY?
G
G
G
G
GO GET HIM, SLIFER!
G
G
G

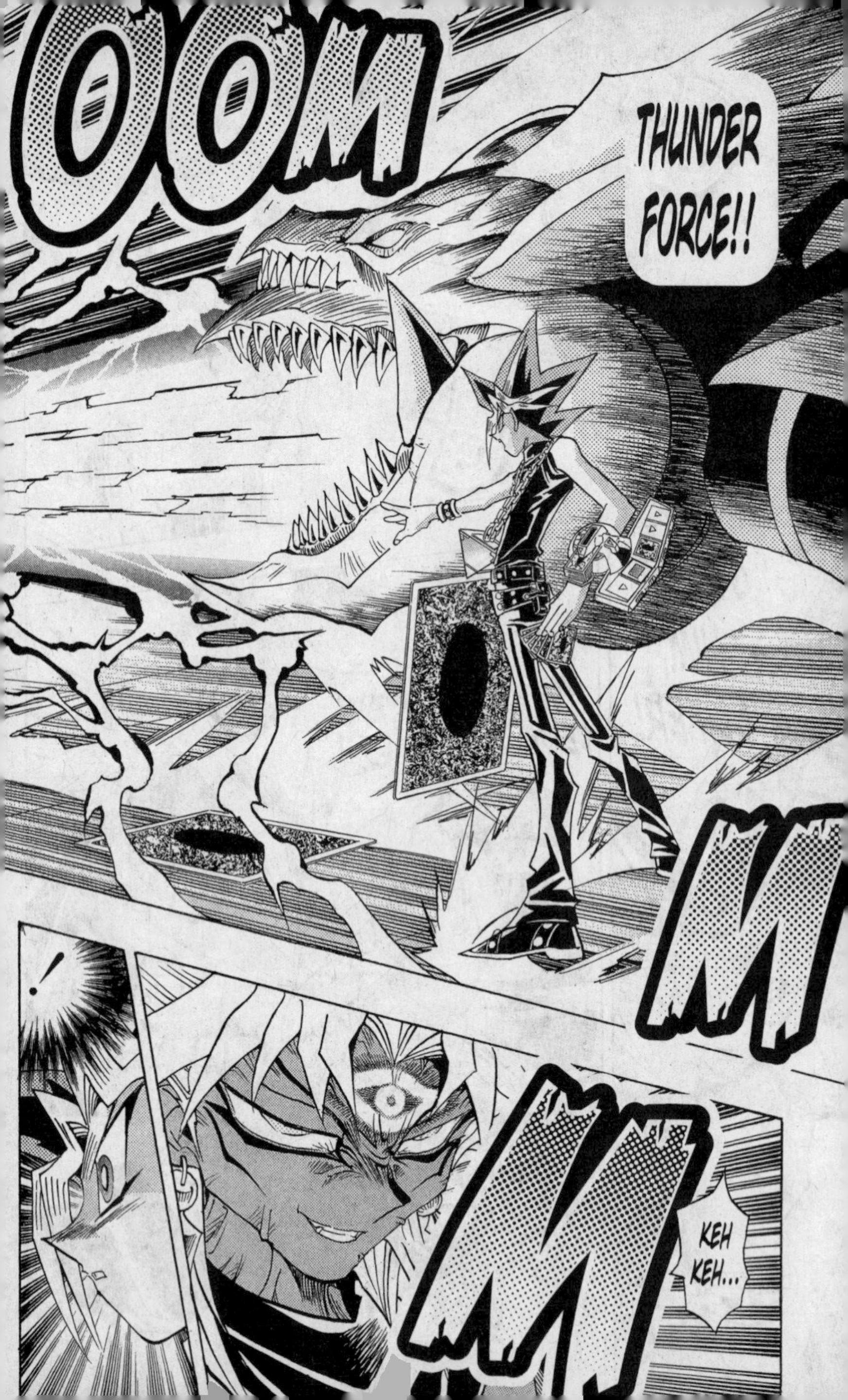
THUNDER FORCE!!
OOM
MMM
KEH KEH...
!

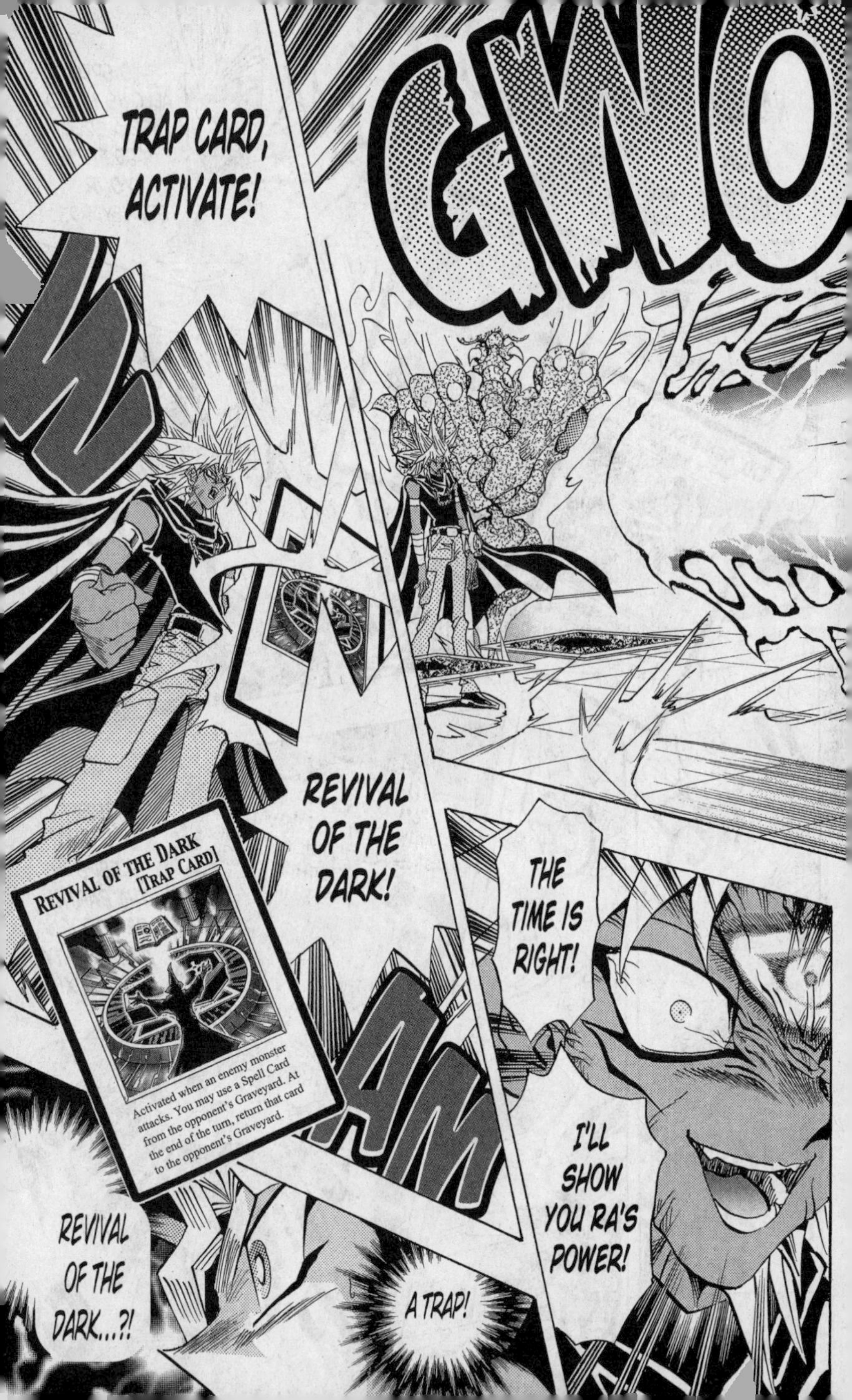
GWO
THE TIME IS RIGHT!
I'LL SHOW YOU RA'S POWER!
TRAP CARD, ACTIVATE!
REVIVAL OF THE DARK!
REVIVAL OF THE DARK [TRAP CARD]
Activated when an enemy monster attacks. You may use a Spell Card from the opponent's Graveyard. At the end of the turn, return that card to the opponent's Graveyard.
A TRAP!
REVIVAL OF THE DARK...?!

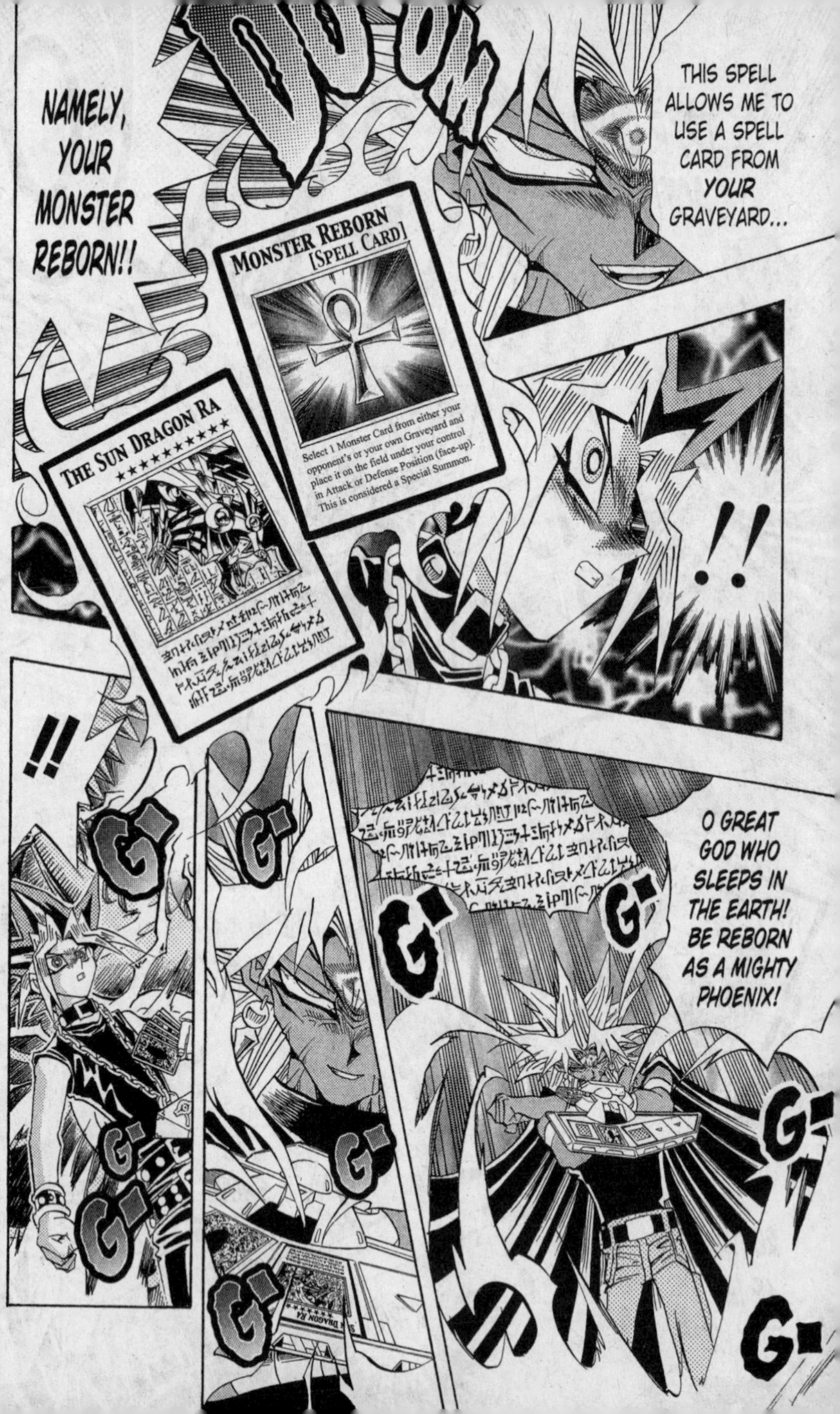
THIS SPELL ALLOWS ME TO USE A SPELL CARD FROM YOUR GRAVEYARD...
DOOM
NAMELY, YOUR MONSTER REBORN!!
MONSTER REBORN [SPELL CARD]
Select 1 Monster Card from either your opponent's or your own Graveyard and place it on the field under your control in Attack or Defense Position (face-up). This is considered a Special Summon.
THE SUN DRAGON RA
!!
O GREAT GOD WHO SLEEPS IN THE EARTH! BE REBORN AS A MIGHTY PHOENIX!
G
G
G
G
G
G
!!
G
G
G

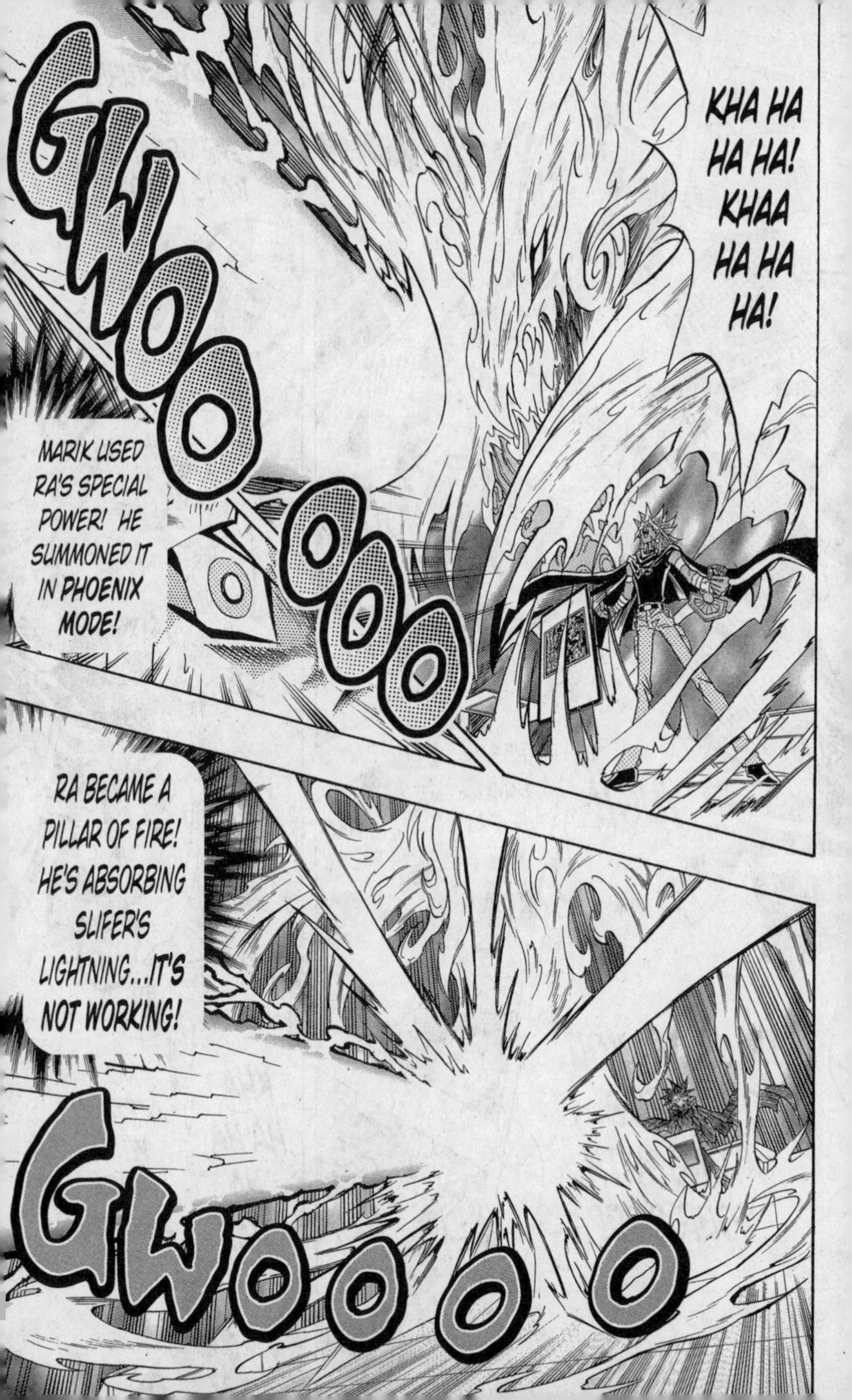
KHA HA HA HA! KHAA HA HA HA!
GWOOOOOOO
MARIK USED RA'S SPECIAL POWER! HE SUMMONED IT IN PHOENIX MODE!
RA BECAME A PILLAR OF FIRE! HE'S ABSORBING SLIFER'S LIGHTNING...IT'S NOT WORKING!
GWOOOOO

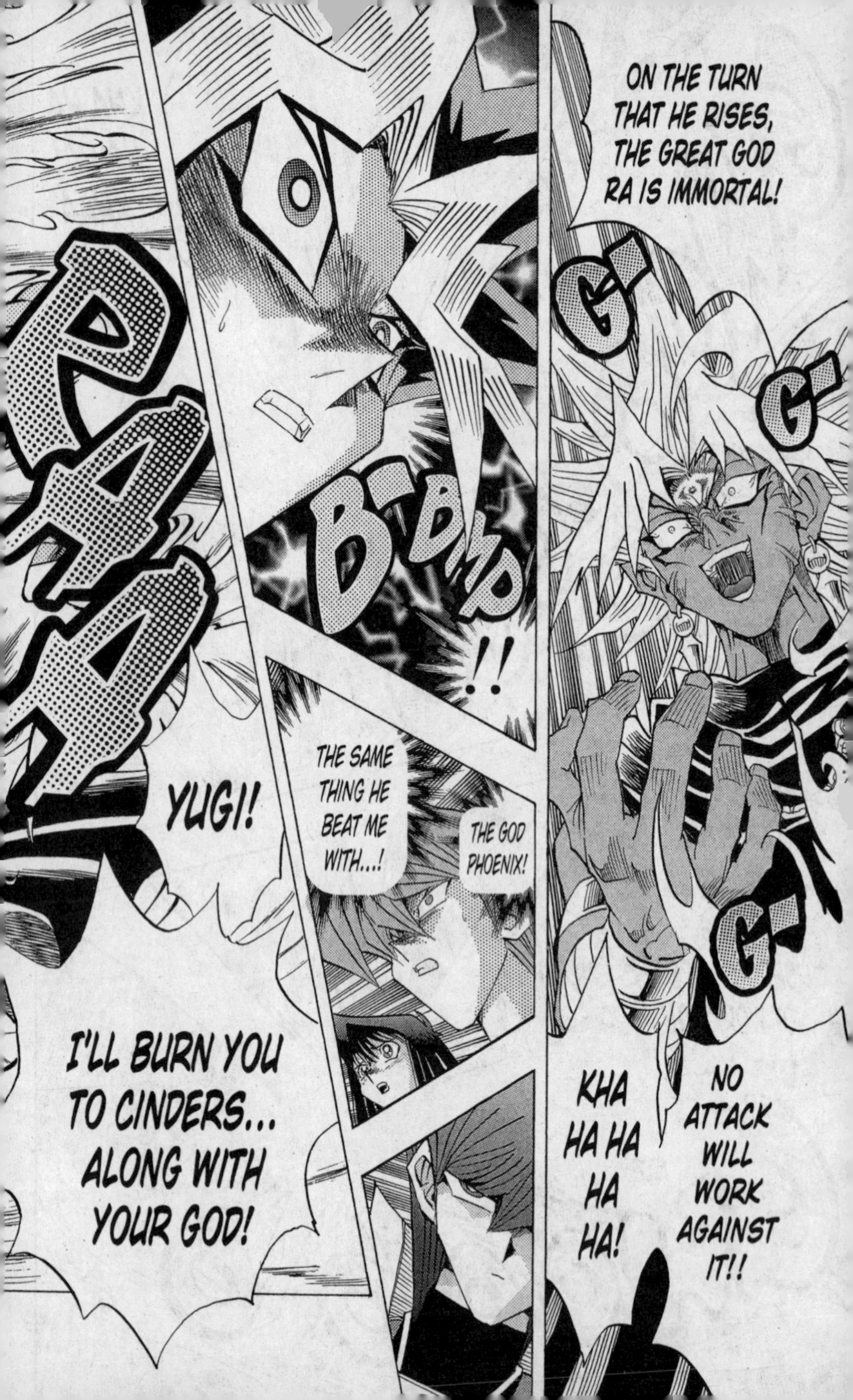

ON THE TURN THAT HE RISES, THE GREAT GOD RA IS IMMORTAL!
G'
G'
G'
NO ATTACK WILL WORK AGAINST IT!!
KHA HA HA HA HA!
B-BMP
!!
THE GOD PHOENIX!
THE SAME THING HE BEAT ME WITH...!
YUGI!
I'LL BURN YOU TO CINDERS... ALONG WITH YOUR GOD!

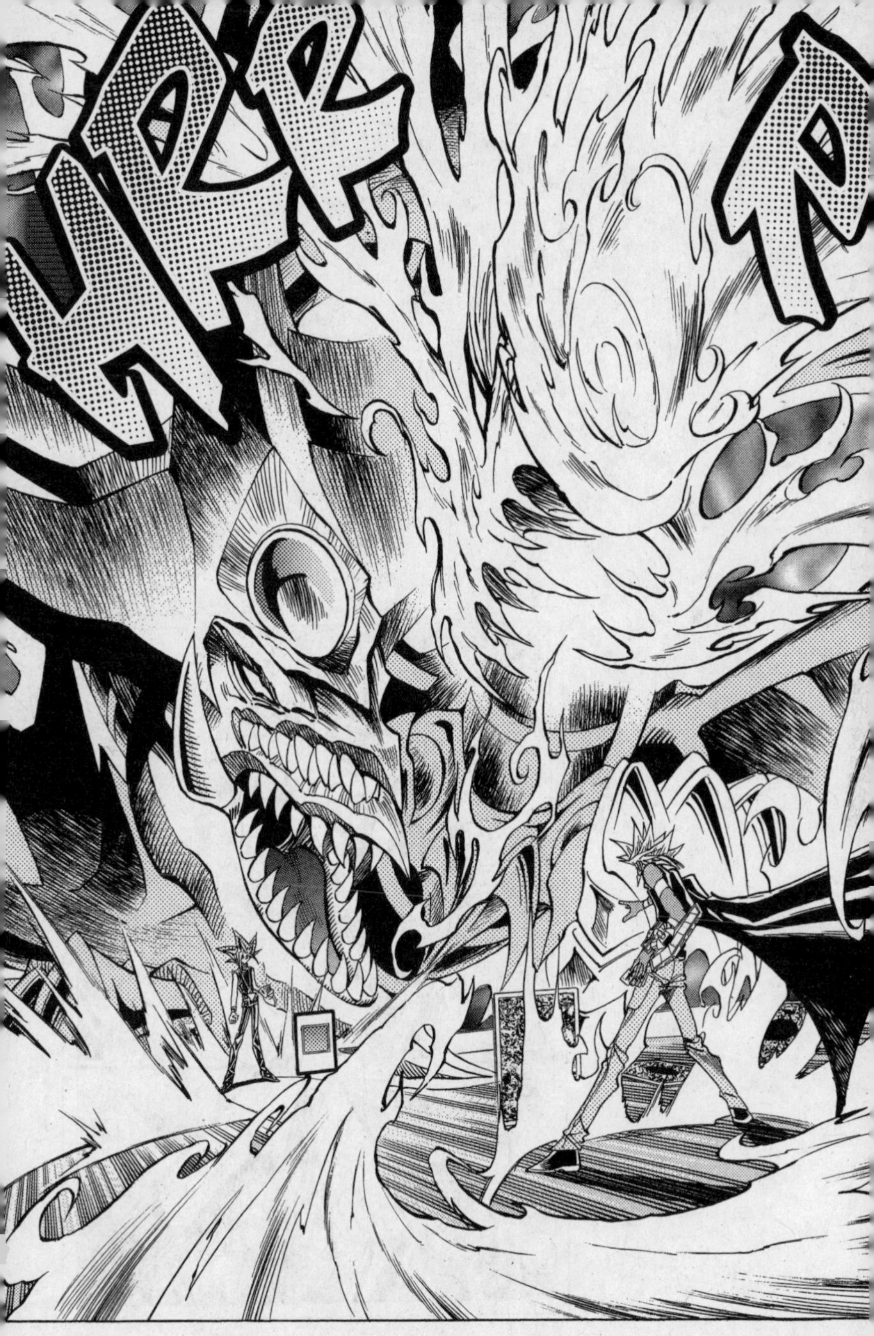

Duel 268: Ra the Immortal

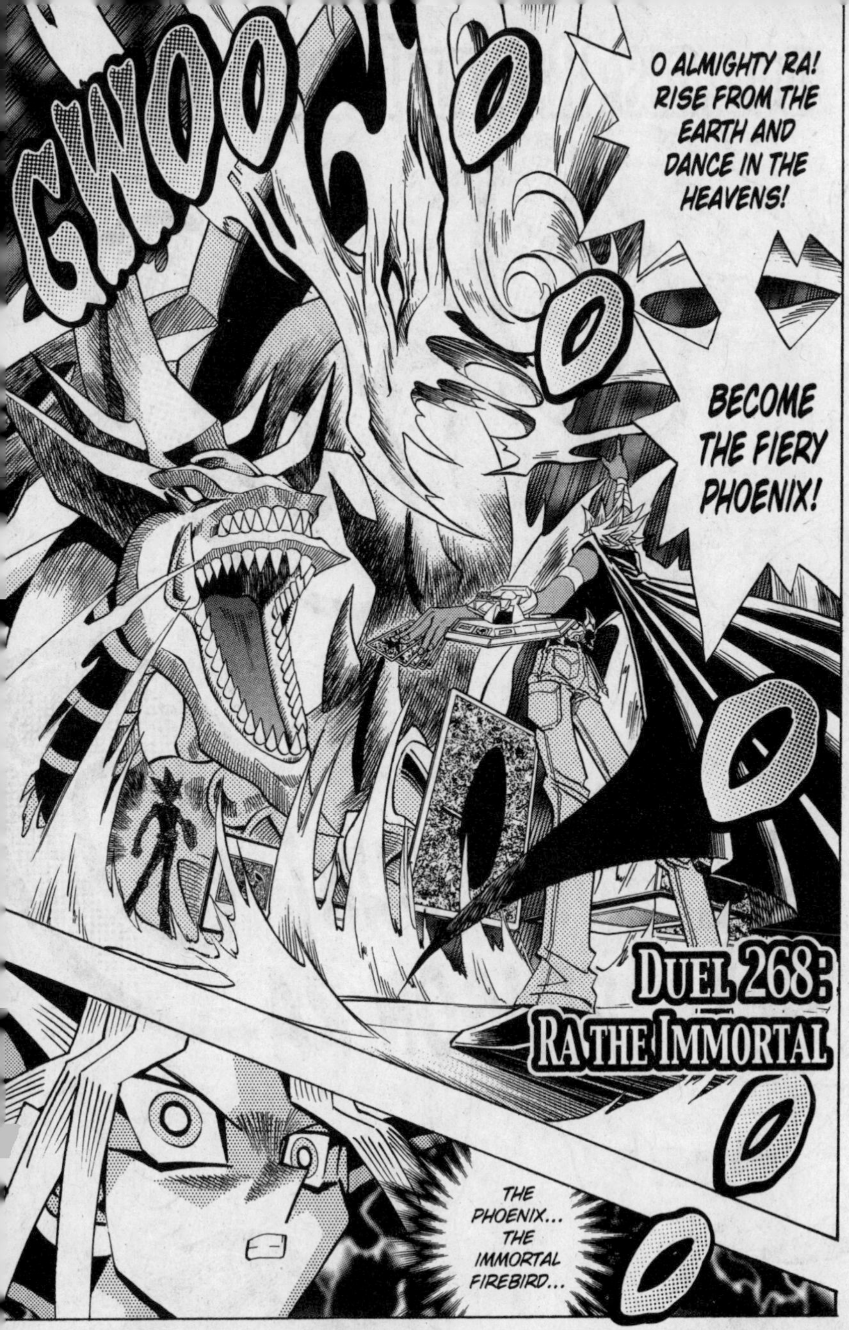
O ALMIGHTY RA! RISE FROM THE EARTH AND DANCE IN THE HEAVENS!
BECOME THE FIERY PHOENIX!
GWOOO
THE PHOENIX... THE IMMORTAL FIREBIRD...

Duel 268: Ra the Immortal

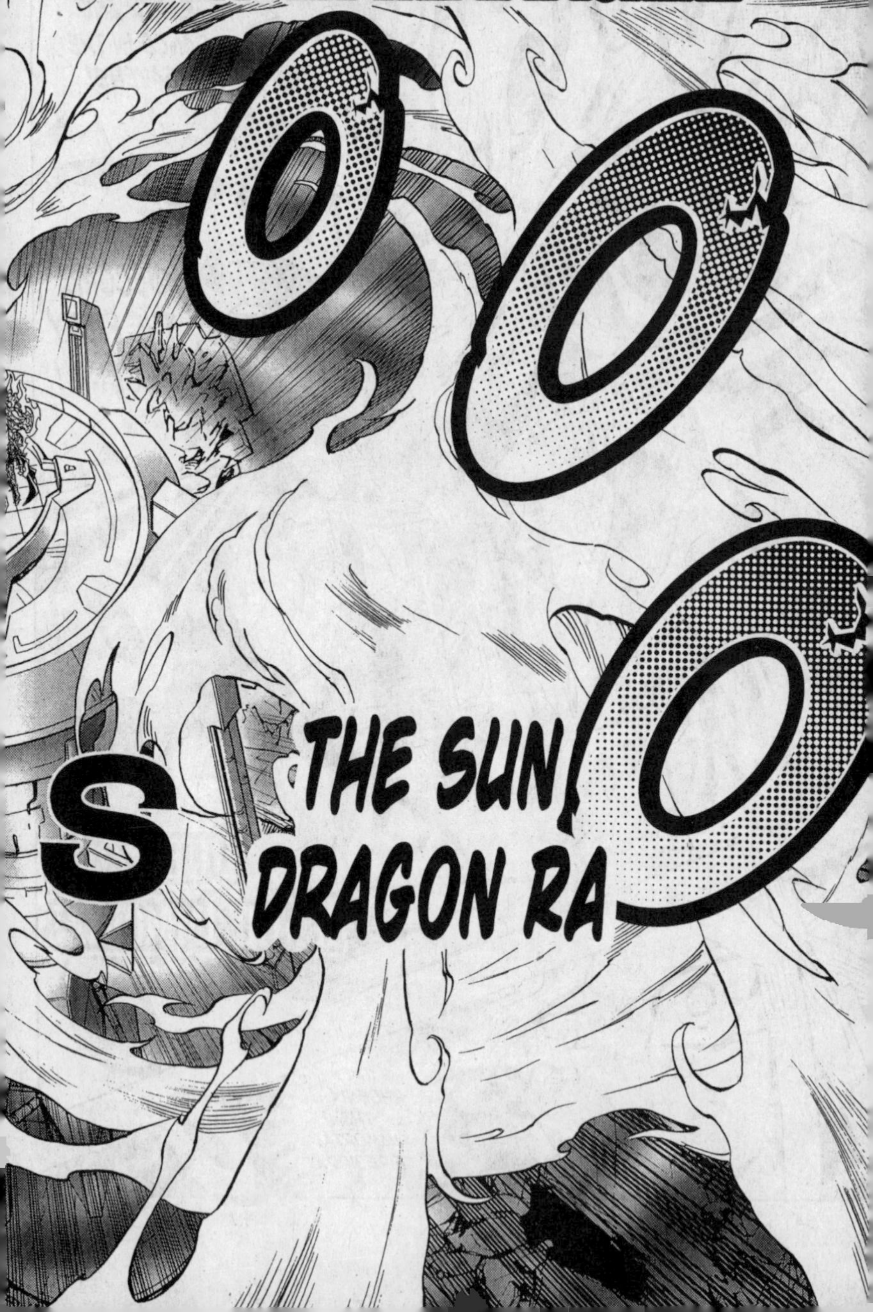
SOOO
THE SUN DRAGON RA

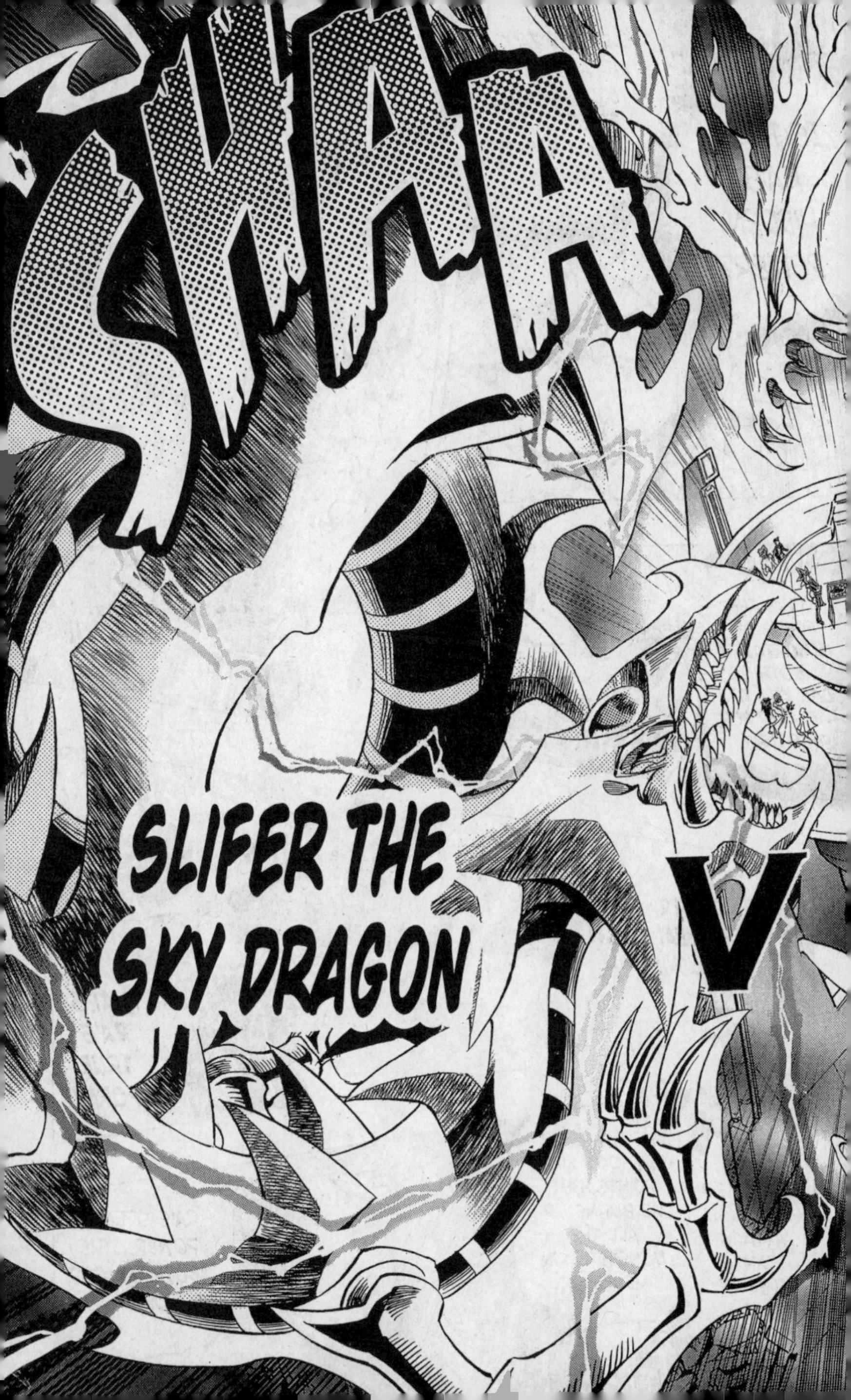
SHAA
SLIFER THE SKY DRAGON
V

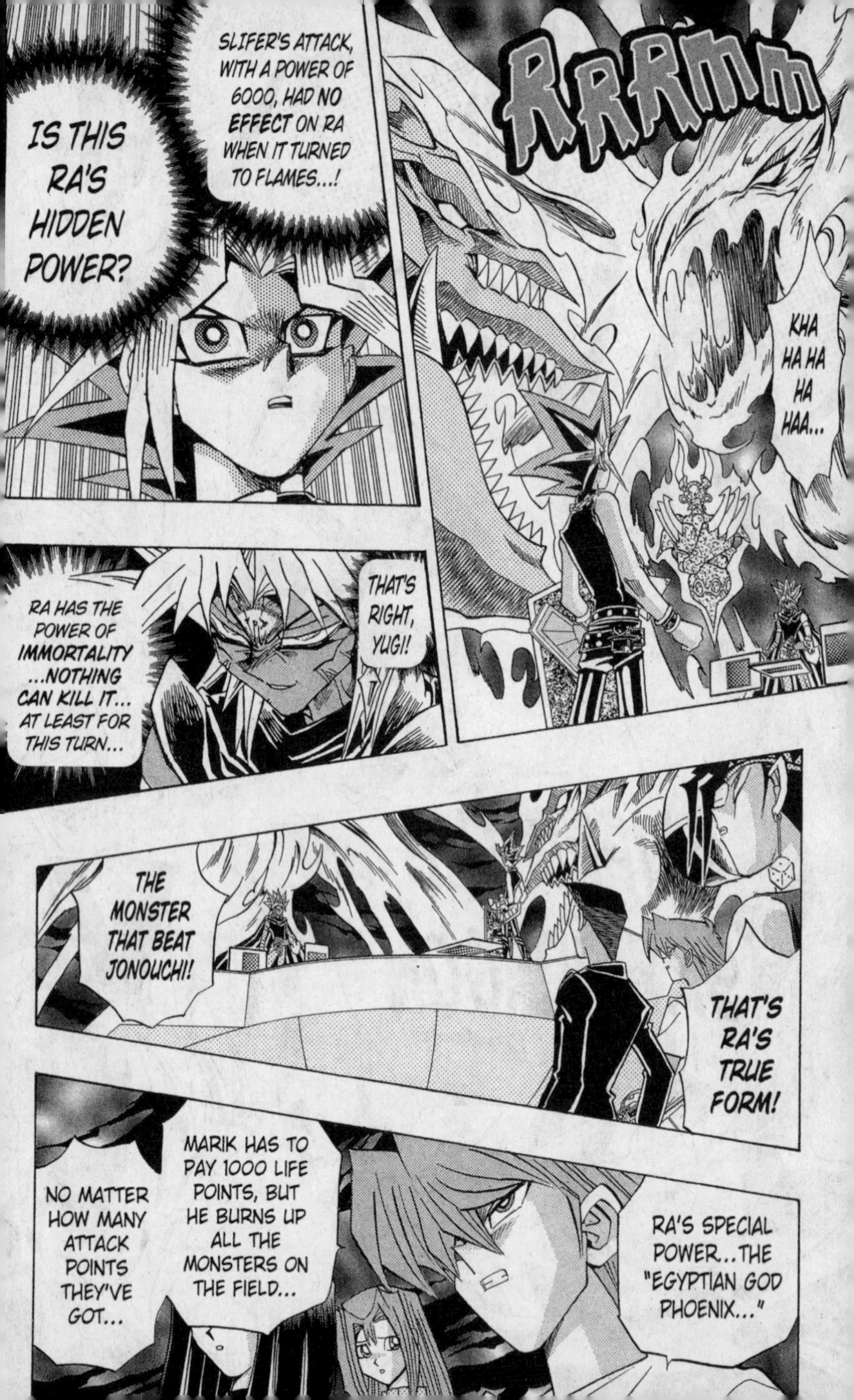
RRRMMM
KHA HA HA HA HAA...
SLIFER'S ATTACK, WITH A POWER OF 6000, HAD NO EFFECT ON RA WHEN IT TURNED TO FLAMES...!
IS THIS RA'S HIDDEN POWER?
THAT'S RIGHT, YUGI!
RA HAS THE POWER OF IMMORTALITY ...NOTHING CAN KILL IT... AT LEAST FOR THIS TURN...
THAT'S RA'S TRUE FORM!
THE MONSTER THAT BEAT JONOUCHI!
RA'S SPECIAL POWER...THE "EGYPTIAN GOD PHOENIX..."
MARIK HAS TO PAY 1000 LIFE POINTS, BUT HE BURNS UP ALL THE MONSTERS ON THE FIELD...
NO MATTER HOW MANY ATTACK POINTS THEY'VE GOT...

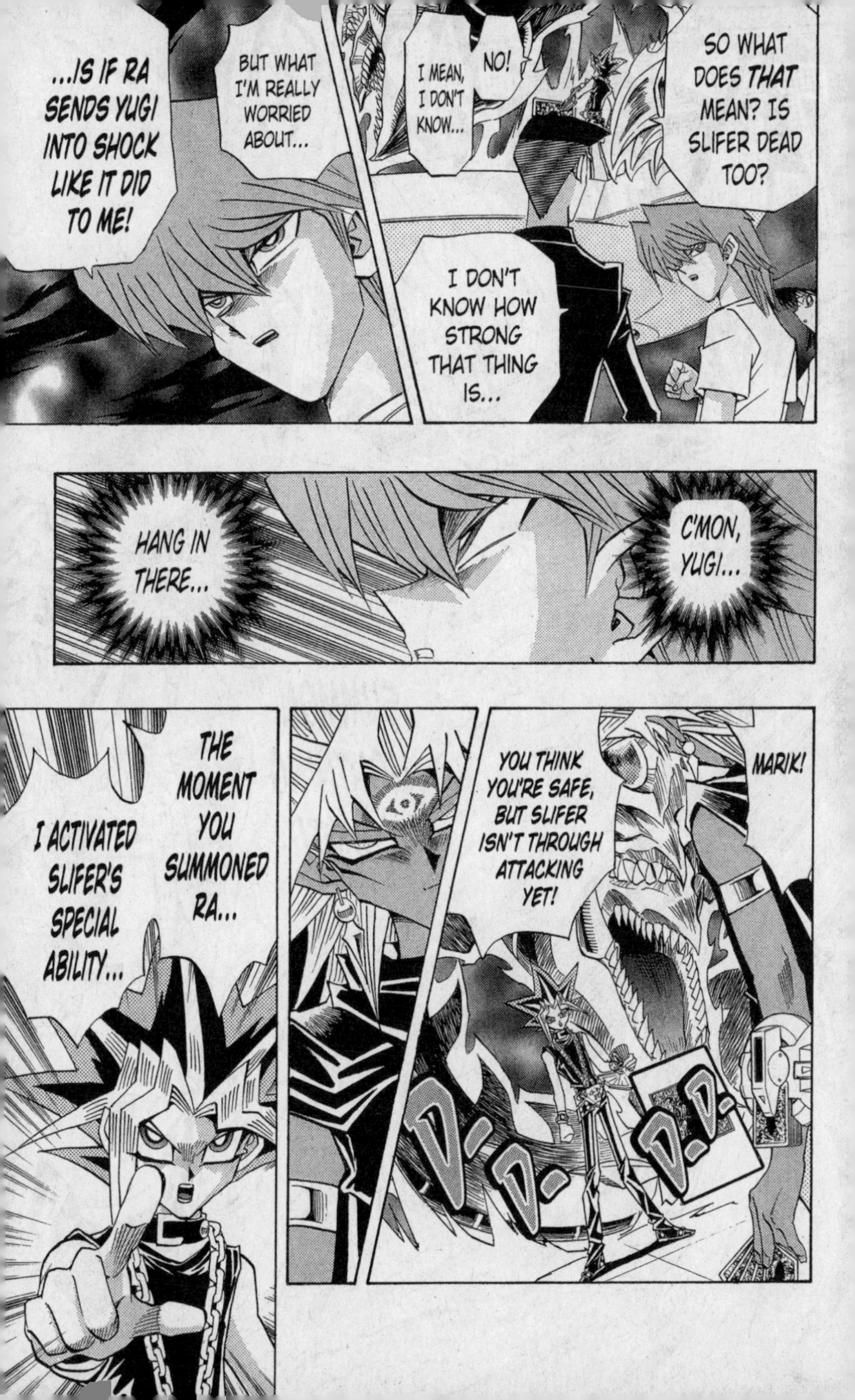
SO WHAT DOES THAT MEAN? IS SLIFER DEAD TOO?
NO!
I MEAN, I DON'T KNOW...
I DON'T KNOW HOW STRONG THAT THING IS...
BUT WHAT I'M REALLY WORRIED ABOUT...
...IS IF RA SENDS YUGI INTO SHOCK LIKE IT DID TO ME!
C'MON, YUGI...
HANG IN THERE...
MARIK!
YOU THINK YOU'RE SAFE, BUT SLIFER ISN'T THROUGH ATTACKING YET!
D- D- D- D-
THE MOMENT YOU SUMMONED RA...
I ACTIVATED SLIFER'S SPECIAL ABILITY...

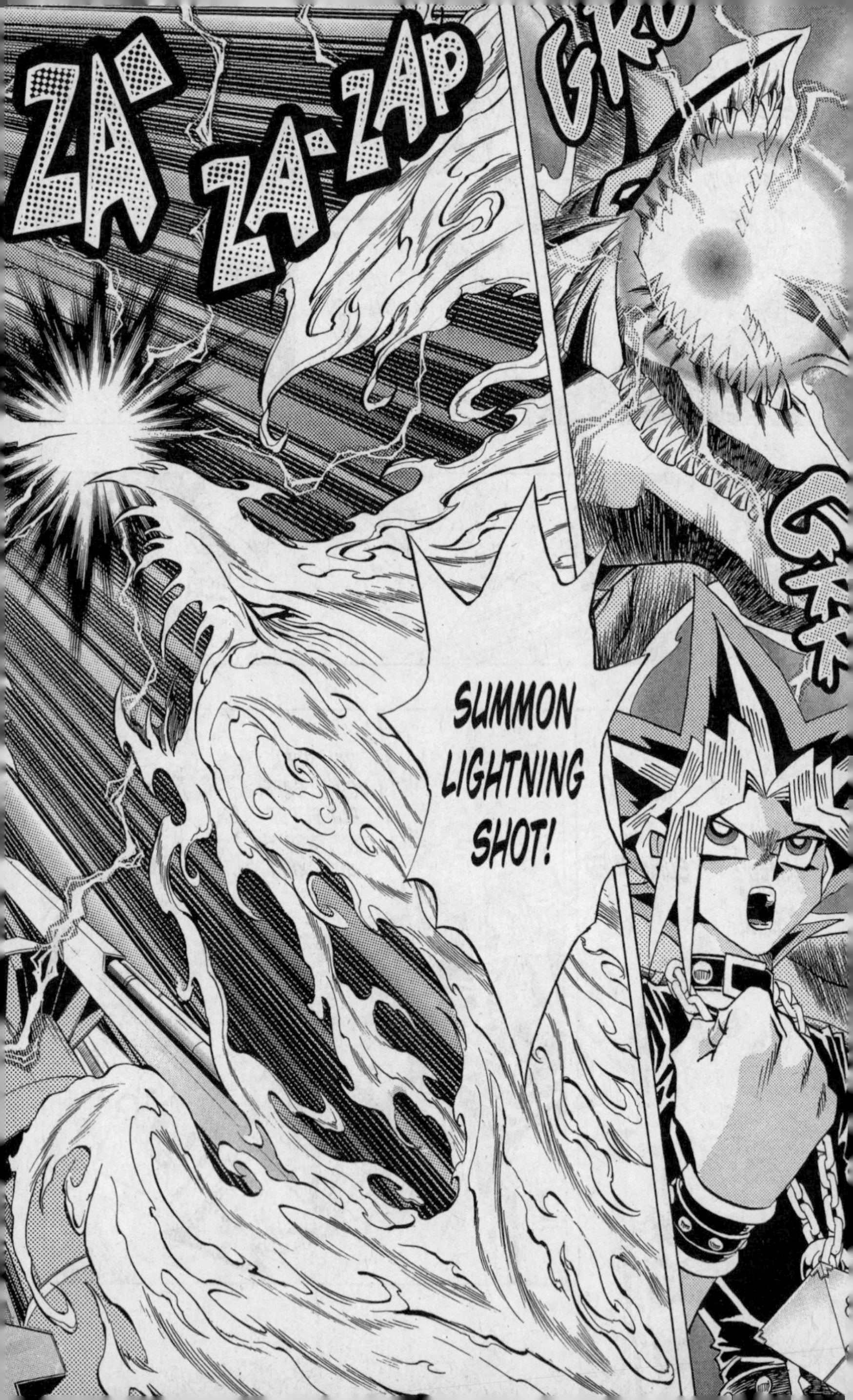
ZAP
ZA-ZAP
SUMMON LIGHTNING SHOT!

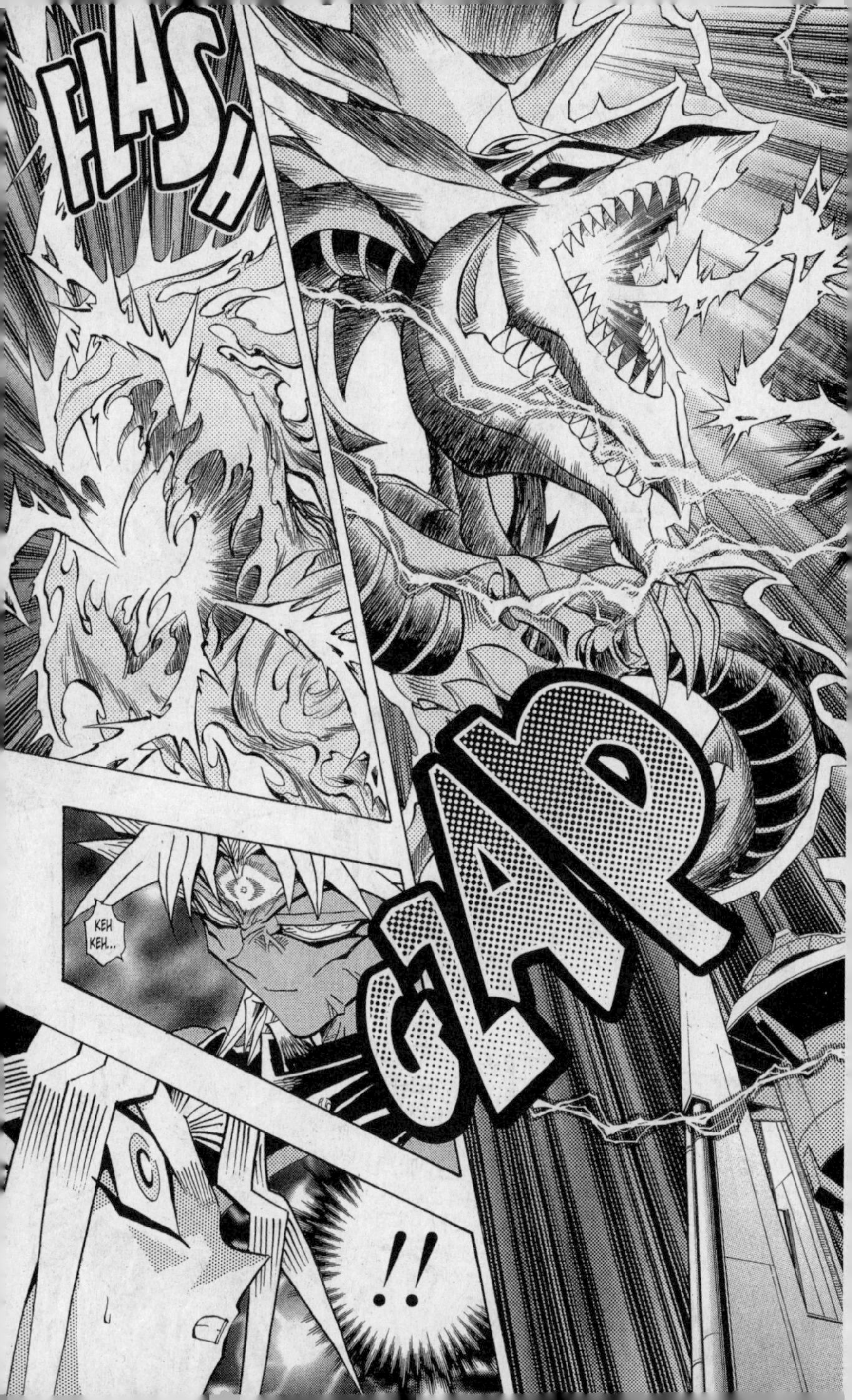
ZAP
FLASH
KEH KEH...
!!

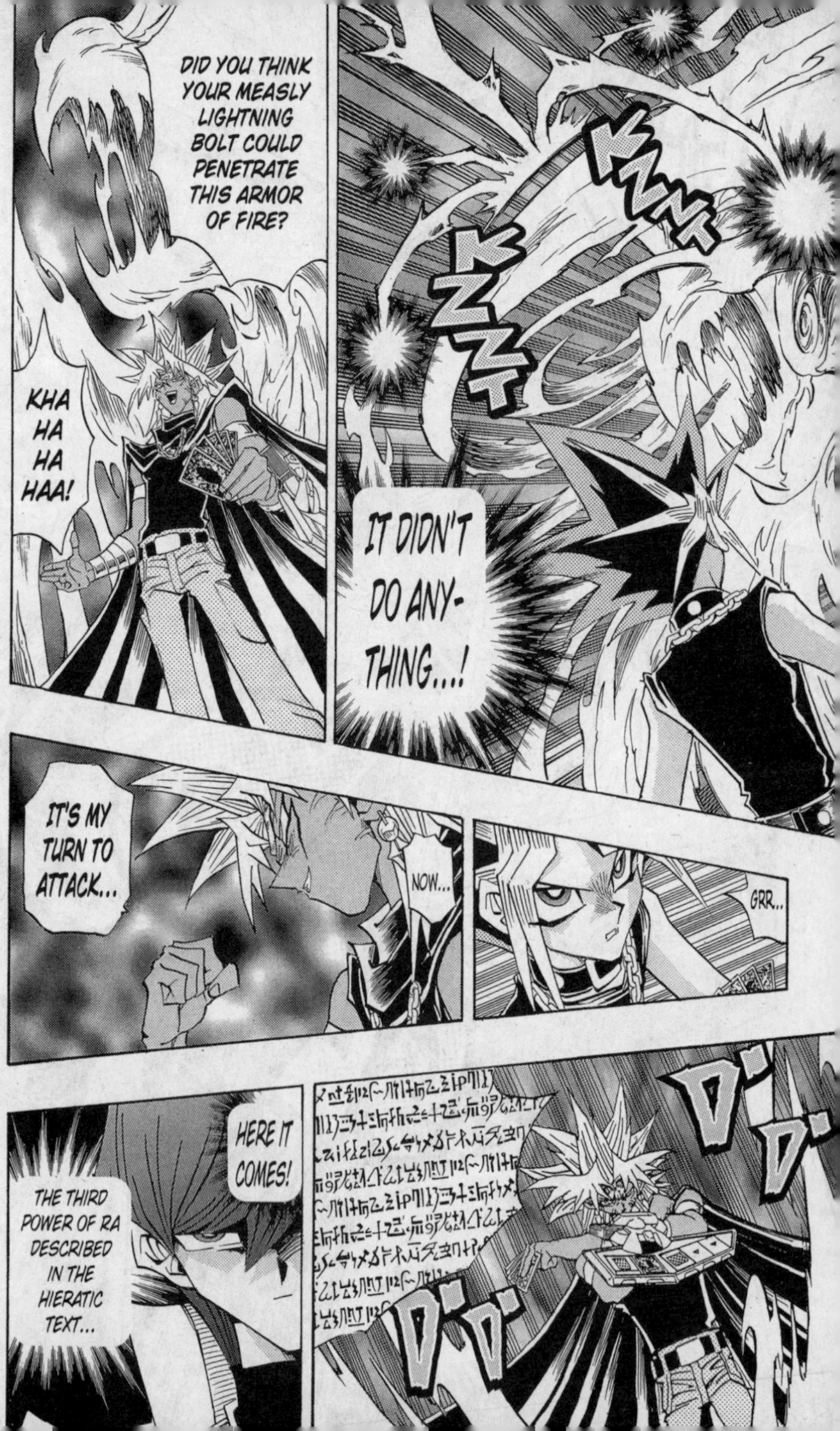
KZZZT
KNNK
IT DIDN'T DO ANYTHING...!
DID YOU THINK YOUR MEASLY LIGHTNING BOLT COULD PENETRATE THIS ARMOR OF FIRE?
KHA HA HA HAA!
GRR...
NOW...
IT'S MY TURN TO ATTACK...
HERE IT COMES!
THE THIRD POWER OF RA DESCRIBED IN THE HIERATIC TEXT...

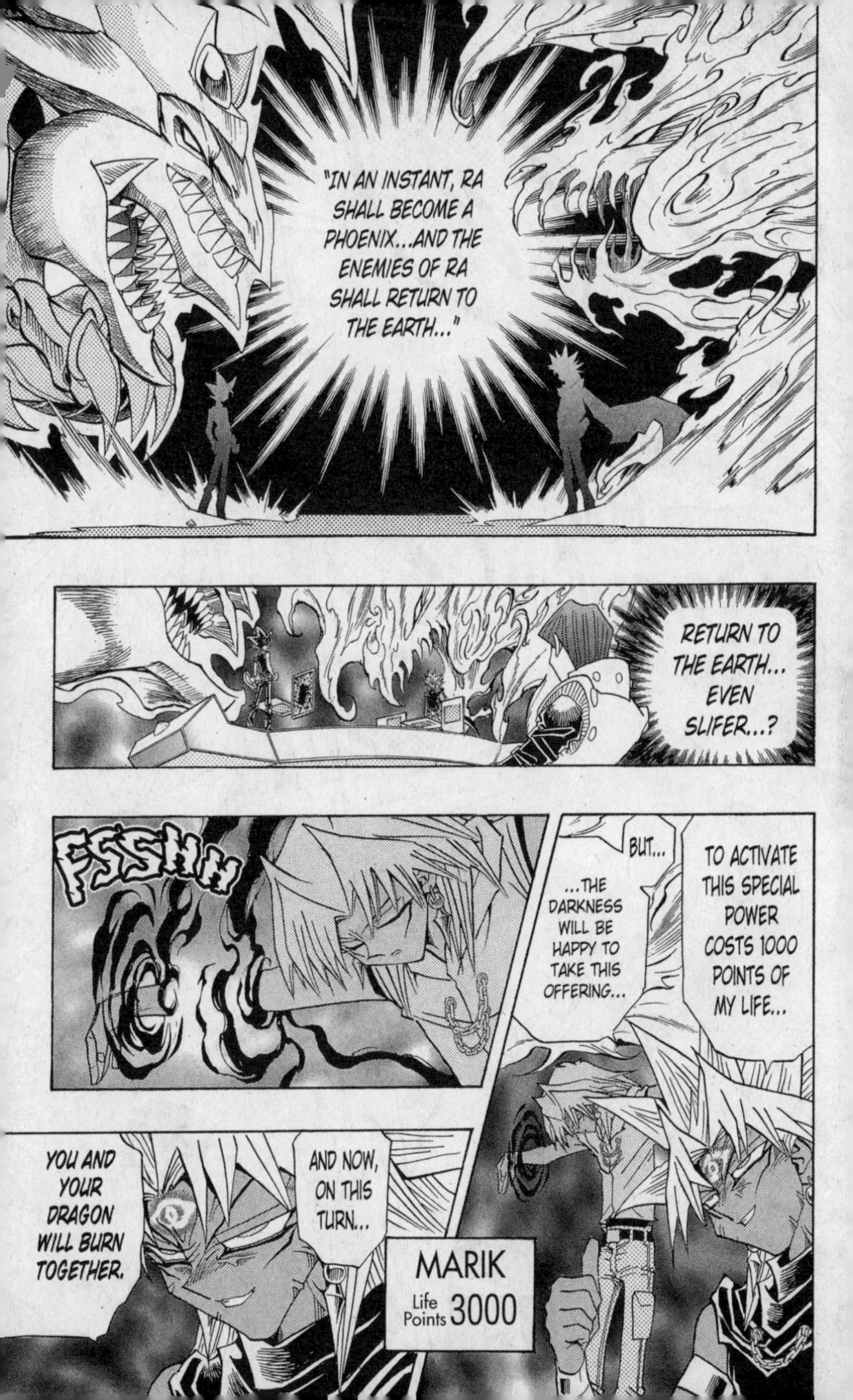
"IN AN INSTANT, RA SHALL BECOME A PHOENIX...AND THE ENEMIES OF RA SHALL RETURN TO THE EARTH..."
RETURN TO THE EARTH... EVEN SLIFER...?
TO ACTIVATE THIS SPECIAL POWER COSTS 1000 POINTS OF MY LIFE...
BUT...
...THE DARKNESS WILL BE HAPPY TO TAKE THIS OFFERING...
FSSHH
AND NOW, ON THIS TURN...
YOU AND YOUR DRAGON WILL BURN TOGETHER.
MARIK
Life Points 3000

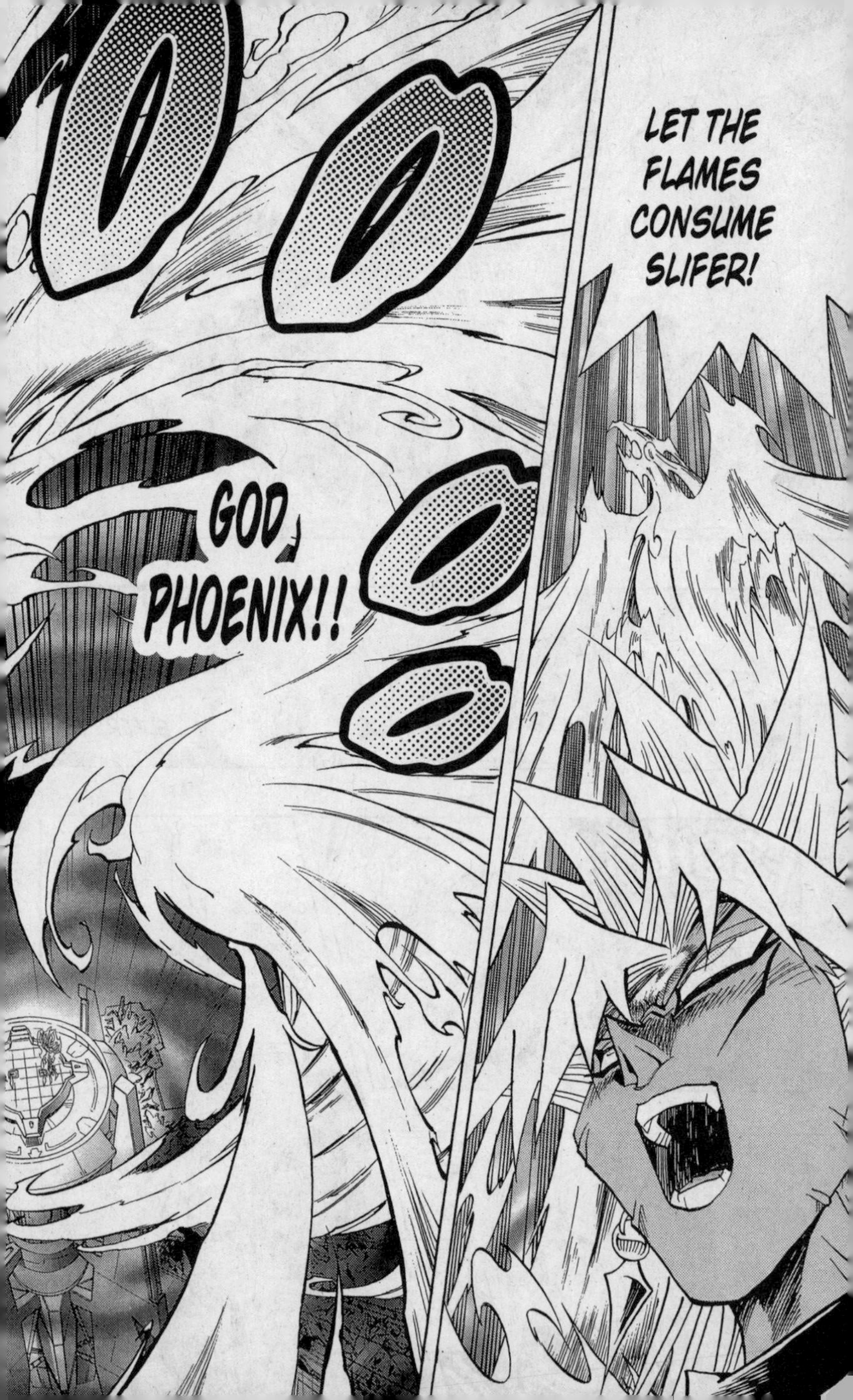
LET THE FLAMES CONSUME SLIFER!
GOD PHOENIX!!

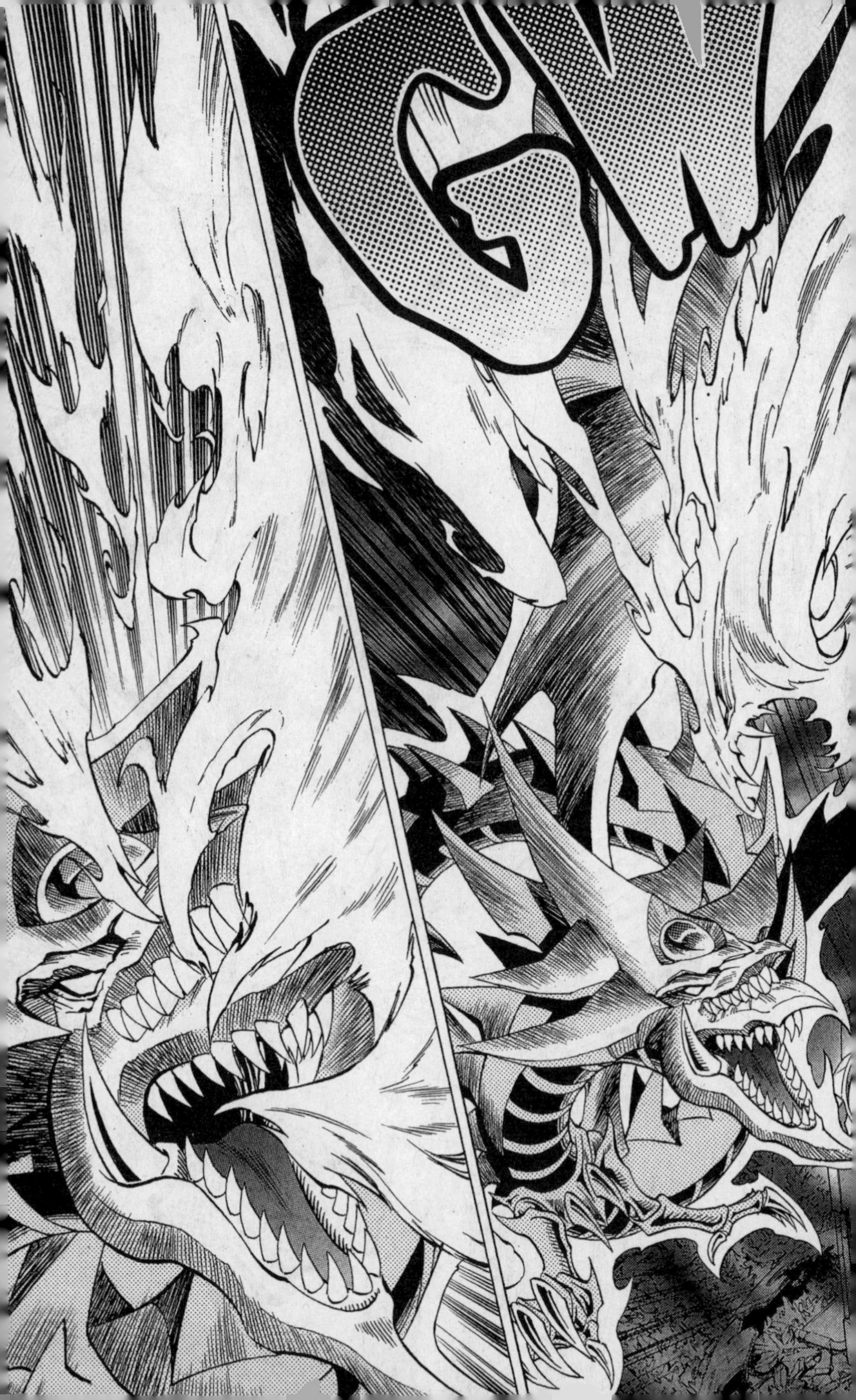

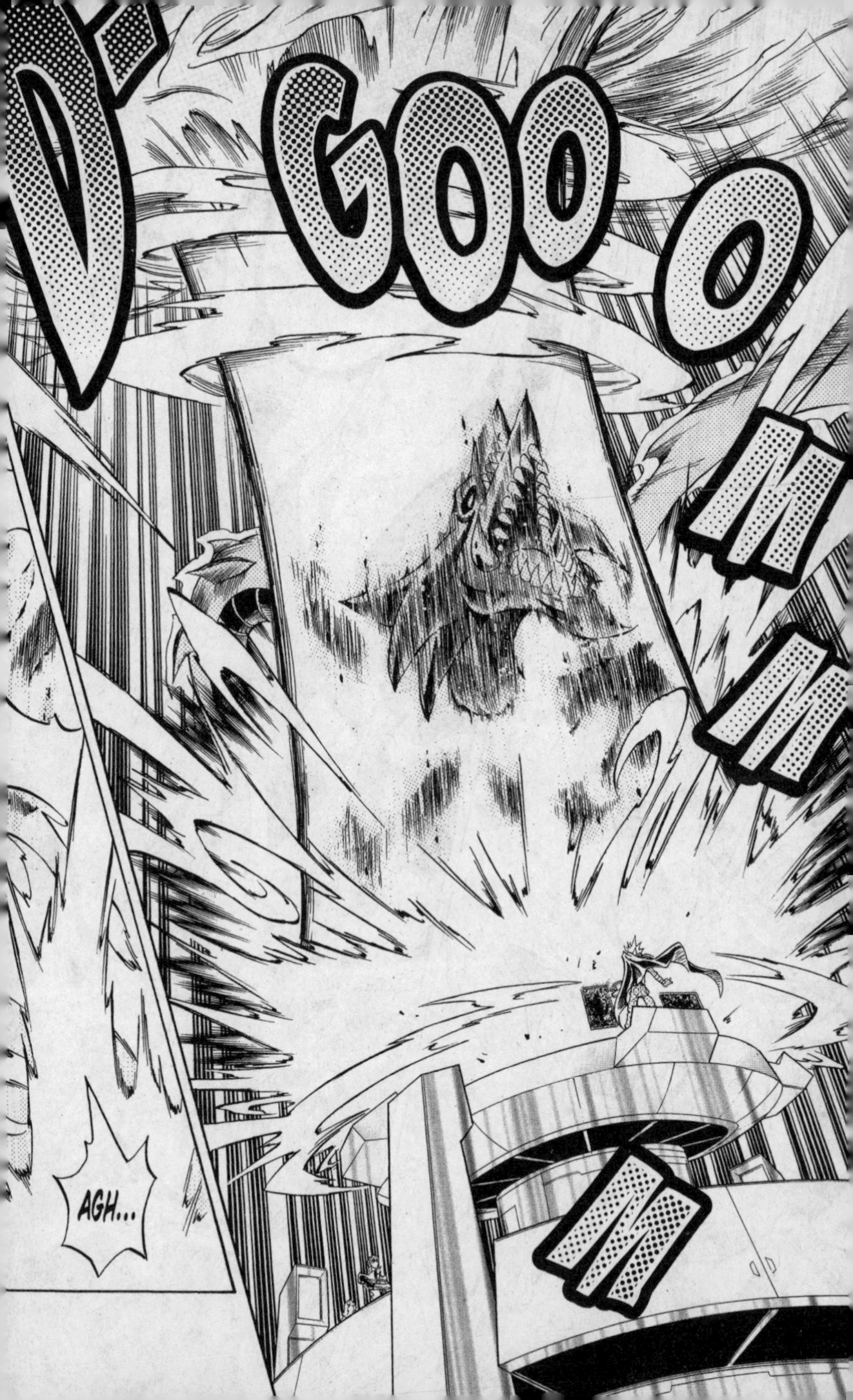
D'GOO-OMMM
AGH...

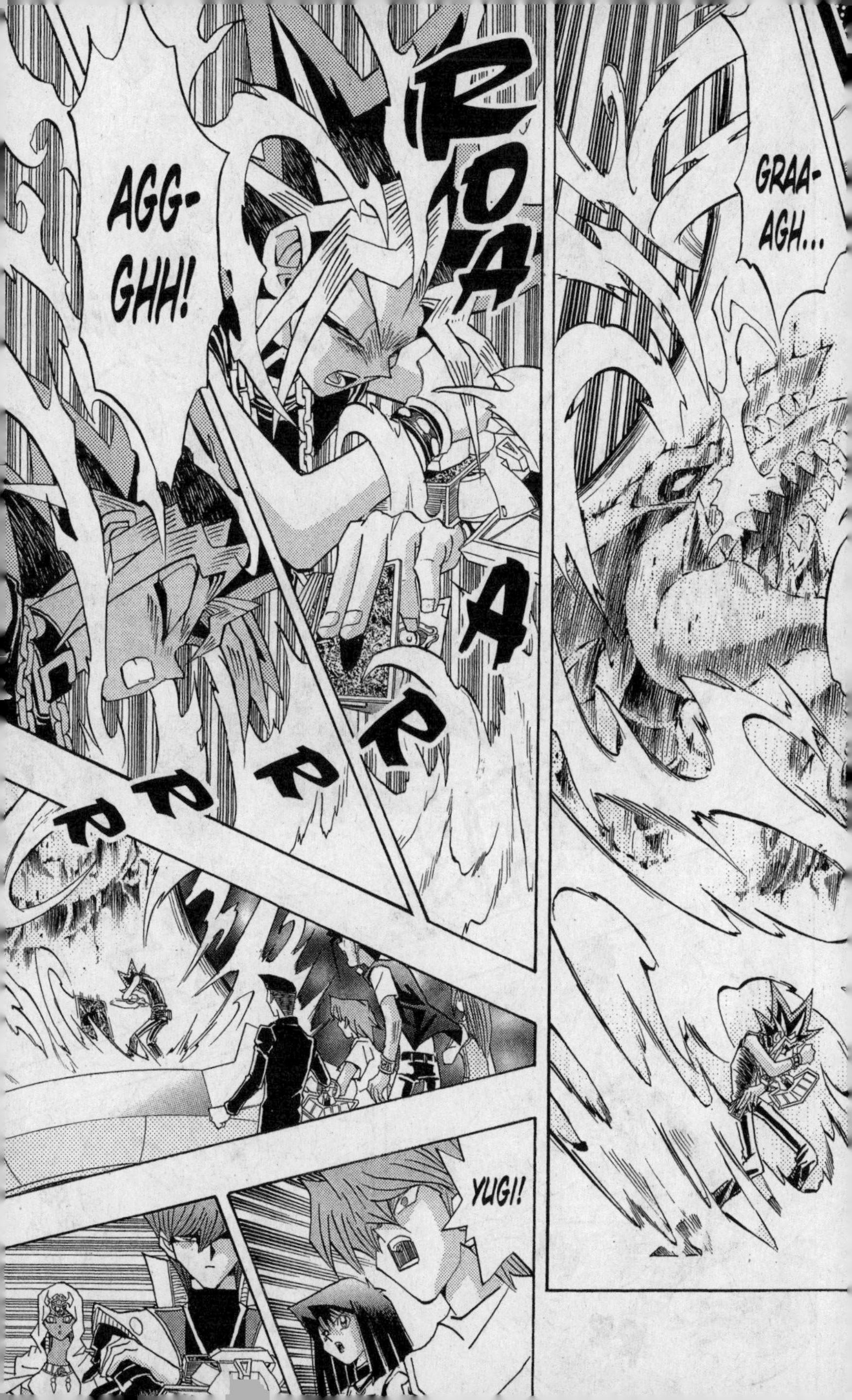
GRAA-AGH...
ROAARRRR
AGG-GHH!
YUGI!

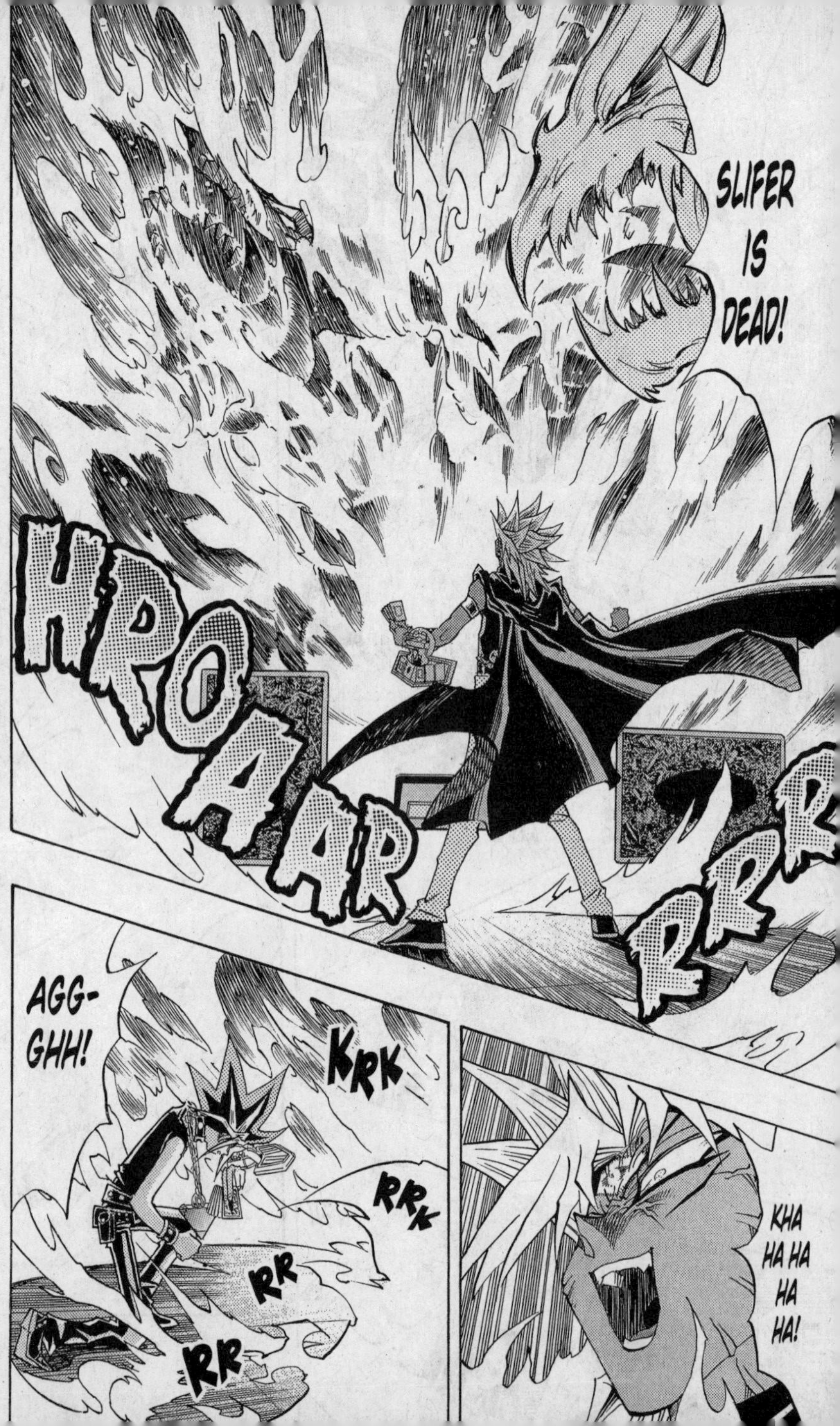
SLIFER IS DEAD!
HROAARRRR
KHA HA HA HA HA!
AGG-GHH!
KRK
RRK
RR
RR

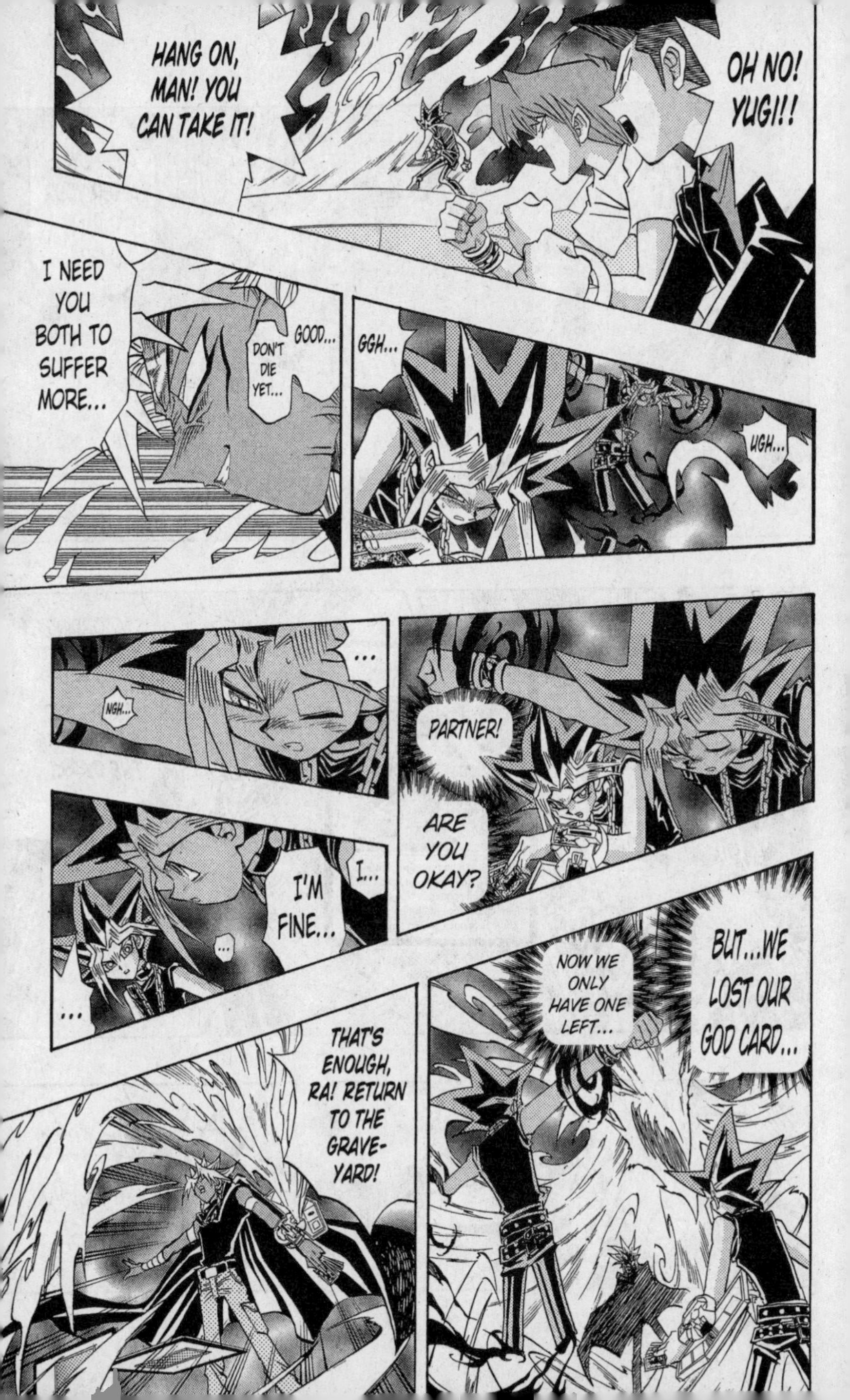
OH NO! YUGI!!
HANG ON, MAN! YOU CAN TAKE IT!
GGH...
UGH...
GOOD...
DON'T DIE YET...
I NEED YOU BOTH TO SUFFER MORE...
PARTNER!
ARE YOU OKAY?
...
NGH...
I...
I'M FINE...
...
...
BUT...WE LOST OUR GOD CARD...
NOW WE ONLY HAVE ONE LEFT...
THAT'S ENOUGH, RA! RETURN TO THE GRAVEYARD!

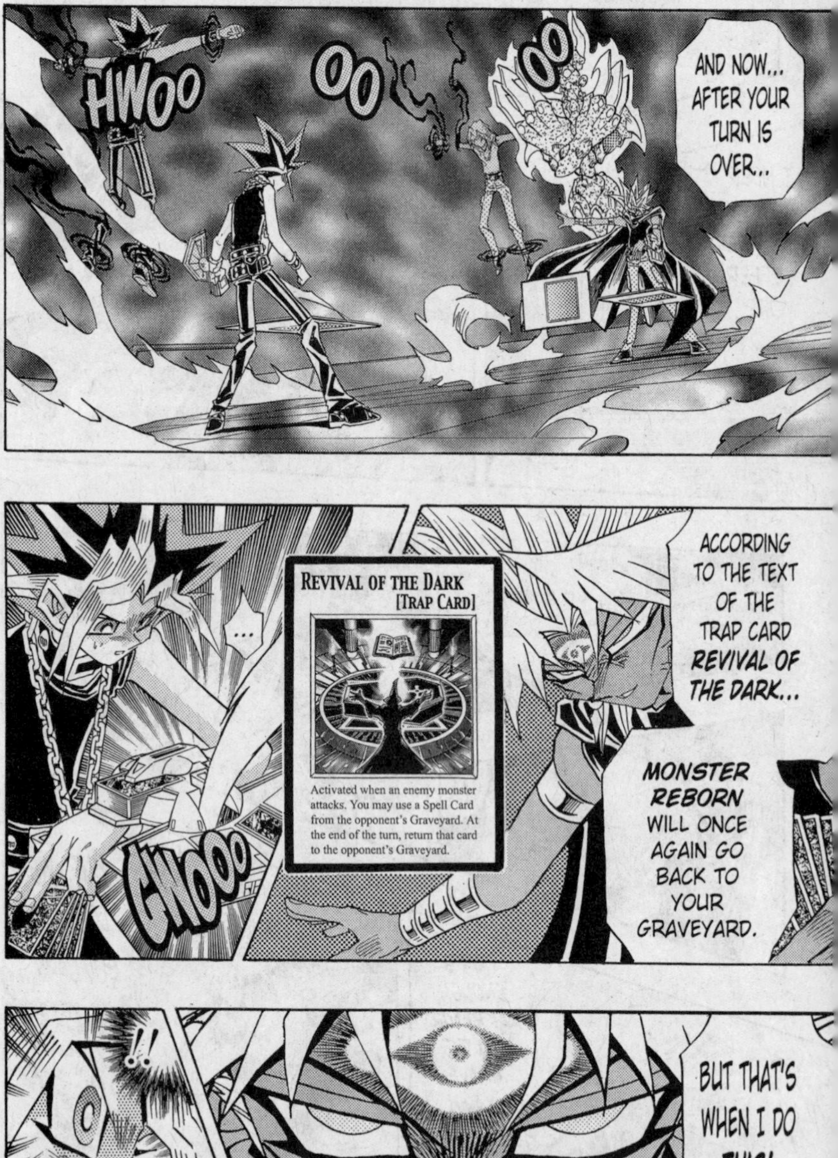
AND NOW... AFTER YOUR TURN IS OVER..
HWOO OO OO
ACCORDING TO THE TEXT OF THE TRAP CARD REVIVAL OF THE DARK...
MONSTER REBORN WILL ONCE AGAIN GO BACK TO YOUR GRAVEYARD.
REVIVAL OF THE DARK
[TRAP CARD]
Activated when an enemy monster attacks. You may use a Spell Card from the opponent's Graveyard. At the end of the turn, return that card to the opponent's Graveyard.
...
CHOOO
BUT THAT'S WHEN I DO THIS!
!!

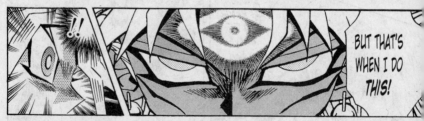

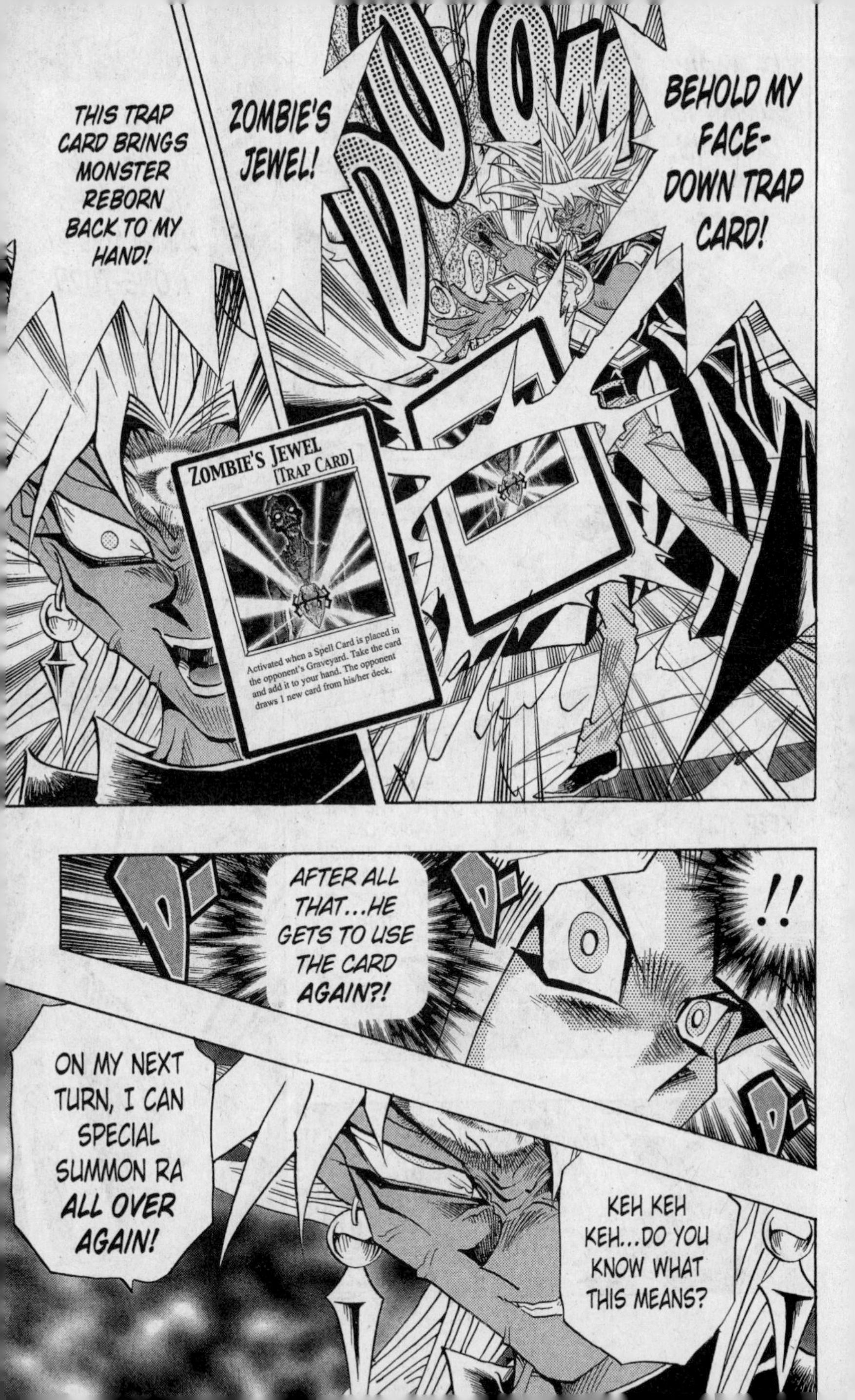
BEHOLD MY FACE-DOWN TRAP CARD!
ZOMBIE'S JEWEL!
THIS TRAP CARD BRINGS MONSTER REBORN BACK TO MY HAND!
ZOMBIE'S JEWEL
[TRAP CARD]
Activated when a Spell Card is placed in the opponent's Graveyard. Take the card and add it to your hand. The opponent draws 1 new card from his/her deck.
!!
AFTER ALL THAT...HE GETS TO USE THE CARD AGAIN?!
KEH KEH KEH...DO YOU KNOW WHAT THIS MEANS?
ON MY NEXT TURN, I CAN SPECIAL SUMMON RA ALL OVER AGAIN!

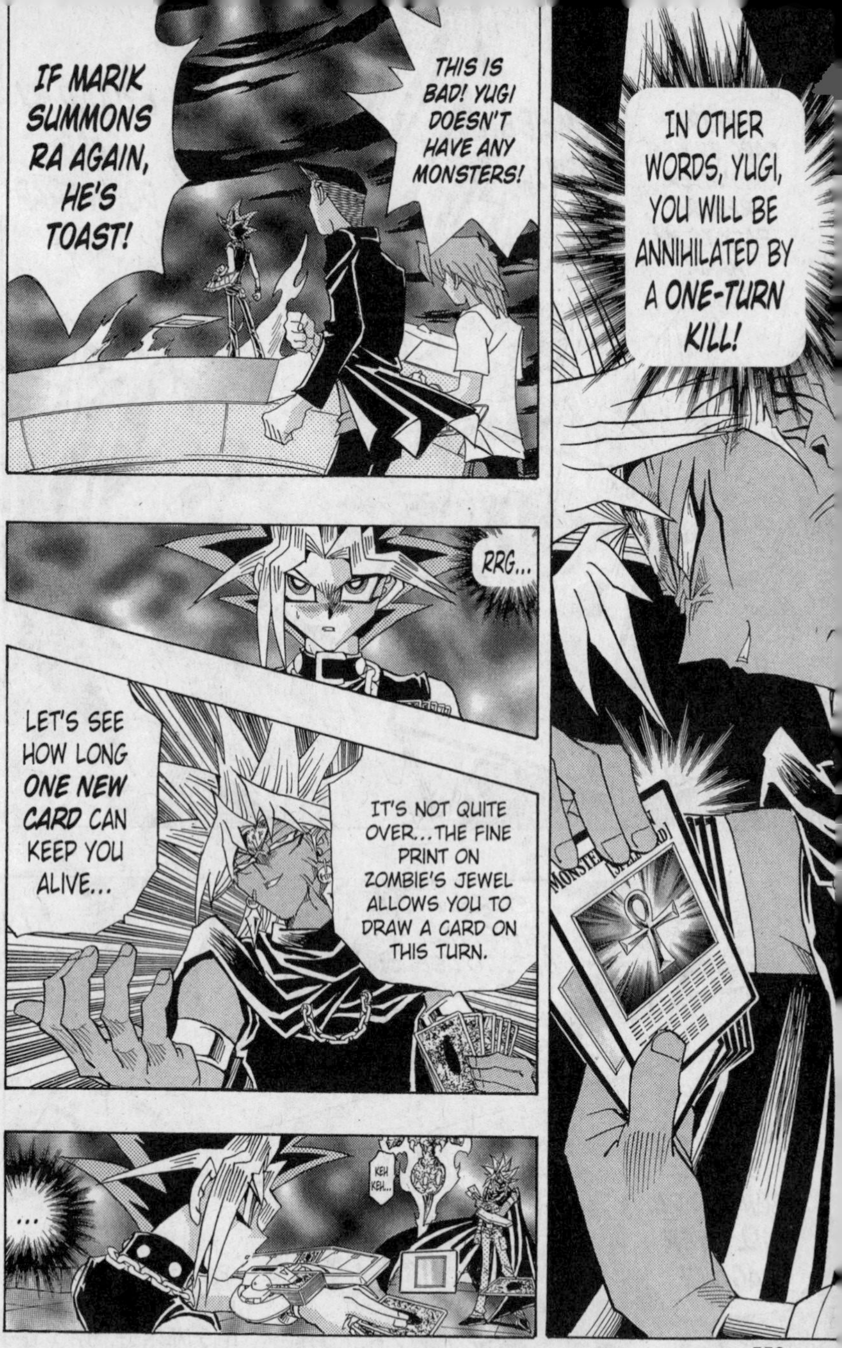
IN OTHER WORDS, YUGI, YOU WILL BE ANNIHILATED BY A ONE-TURN KILL!
THIS IS BAD! YUGI DOESN'T HAVE ANY MONSTERS!
IF MARIK SUMMONS RA AGAIN, HE'S TOAST!
RRG...
IT'S NOT QUITE OVER...THE FINE PRINT ON ZOMBIE'S JEWEL ALLOWS YOU TO DRAW A CARD ON THIS TURN.
LET'S SEE HOW LONG ONE NEW CARD CAN KEEP YOU ALIVE...
KEH KEH...
...

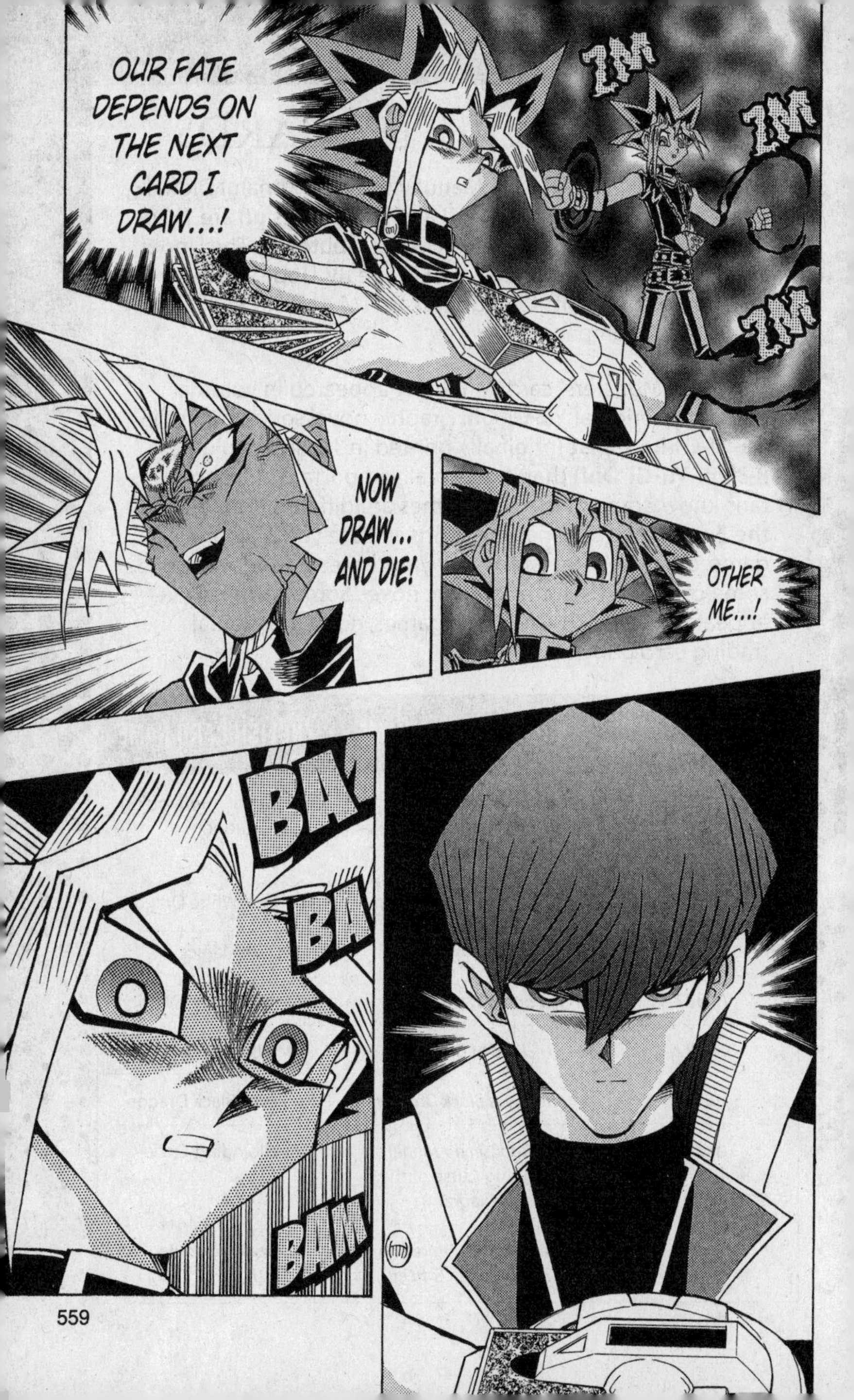
OUR FATE DEPENDS ON THE NEXT CARD I DRAW...!
ZM
ZM
ZM
OTHER ME...!
NOW DRAW... AND DIE!
BA
BA
BAM

MASTER OF THE CARDS

The "Duel Monsters" card game first appeared in volume two of the original **Yu-Gi-Oh!** graphic novel series, but it's in **Yu-Gi-Oh!: Duelist** (originally printed in Japan as volumes 8-31 of **Yu-Gi-Oh!**) that it gets really important. As many fans know, some of the card names are different between the English and Japanese versions. In case you play the game, or you're interested in playing, here's a rundown of some of the cards in this graphic novel. Some cards only appear in the **Yu-Gi-Oh!** video games, not in the actual trading card game.

FIRST APPEARANCE IN THIS VOLUME	JAPANESE CARD NAME	ENGLISH CARD NAME
p.382	*Dragon wo Yobu Fue* (Dragon-Summoning Flute)	The Flute of Summoning Dragon
p.382	*Blue Eyes White Dragon*	Blue-Eyes White Dragon
p.382	*Black Magician*	Dark Magician
p.382	*Magnet Warrior Beta*	Beta the Magnet Warrior
p.382	*Lord of Dragon*	Lord of D.
p.387	*Red Eyes Black Dragon*	Red-Eyes Black Dragon
p.390	*Rokubôsei no Jûbaku* (Binding Curse of the Hexagram)	Spellbinding Circle
p.390	*Majutsu no Jumonsho* (Spellbook of Sorcery)	Magic Formula

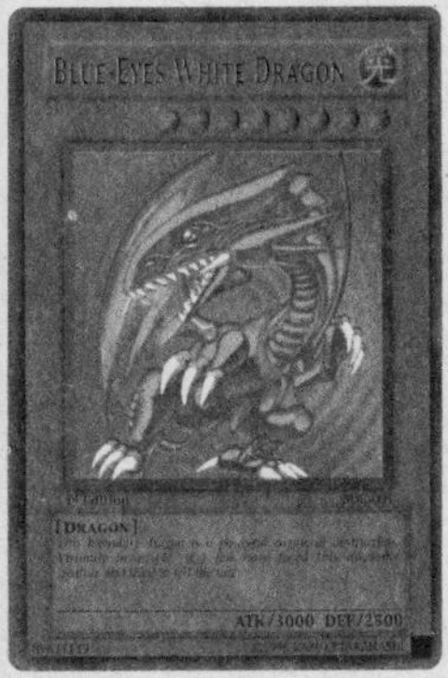
Blue-Eyes White Dragon
[Dragon]
ATK/3000 DEF/2500
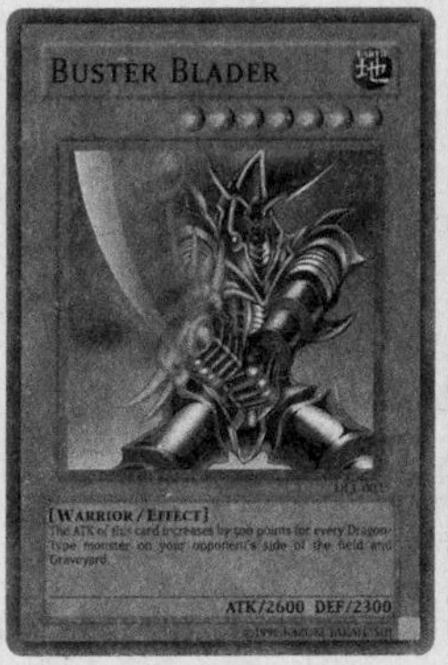
Buster Blader
[Warrior / Effect]
The ATK of this card increases by 500 points for every Dragon-Type monster on your opponent's side of the field and Graveyard.
ATK/2600 DEF/2300
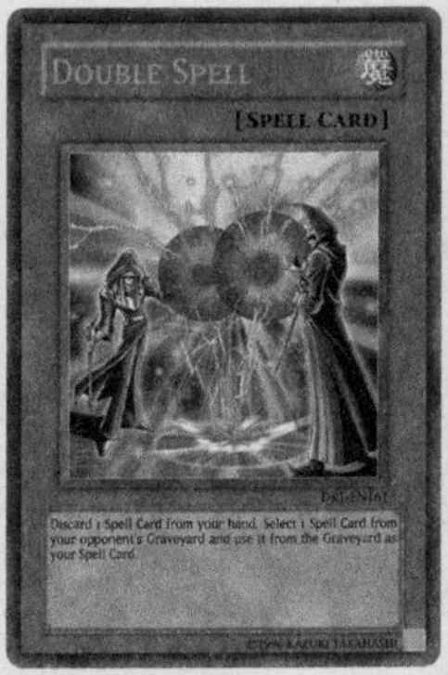
Double Spell
[Spell Card]
Discard 1 Spell Card from your hand. Select 1 Spell Card from your opponent's Graveyard and use it from the Graveyard as your Spell Card.

FIRST APPEARANCE IN THIS VOLUME	JAPANESE CARD NAME	ENGLISH CARD NAME
p.391	*Magic Cylinder*	Magic Cylinder
p.403	*Double Magic*	Double Spell
p.404	*Saishû Totsugeki Meirei* (Final Attack Orders)	Final Attack Orders
p.405	*Shisha Sosei* (Resurrection of the Dead)	Monster Reborn
p.410	*Yûgô* (Fusion)	Polymerization
p.410	*Blue Eyes Ultimate Dragon*	Blue-Eyes Ultimate Dragon
p.418	*Buster Blader*	Buster Blader
p.419	*Chômadô Kenshi Black Paladin* (Super Magic Swordsman Black Paladin)	Dark Paladin
p.425	*Mahô Kyûshû* (Magic Absorption)	Absorb Spell (NOTE: Not a real game card.)
p.433	*Yûgô Kaijo* (Fusion Cancellation/Removal)	De-Polymerization
p.435	*Kakusan suru Hadô* (Slicing Wave-Motion)	Diffusion Wave-Motion

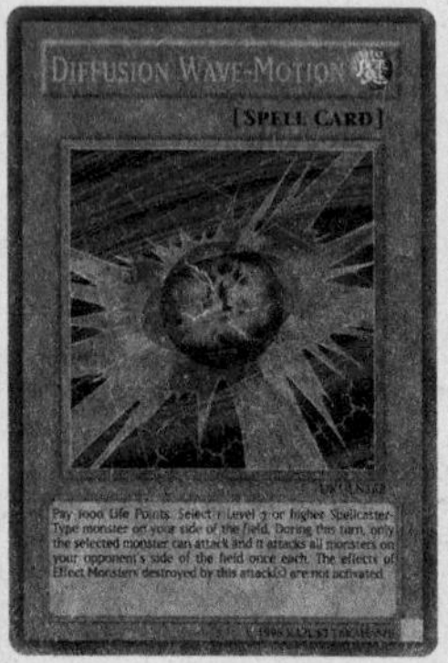
Diffusion Wave-Motion
[Spell Card]
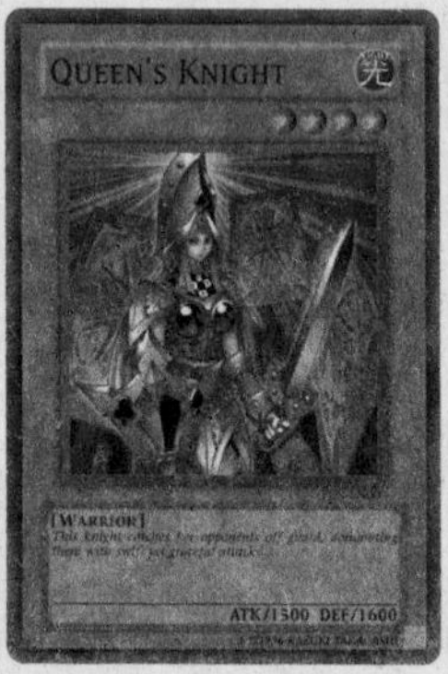
Queen's Knight
[Warrior]
ATK/1500 DEF/1600
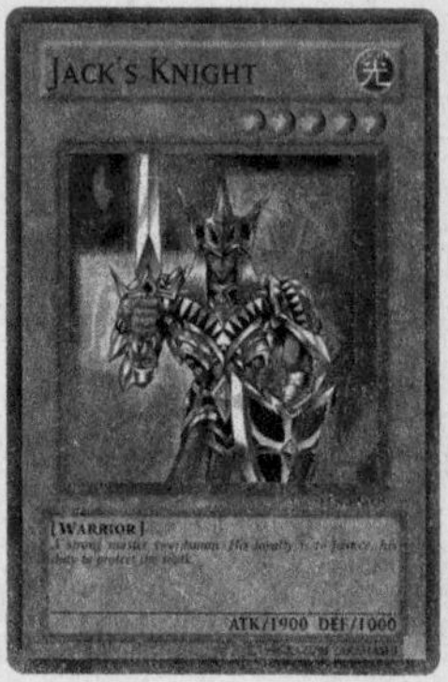
Jack's Knight
[Warrior]
ATK/1900 DEF/1000

FIRST APPEARANCE IN THIS VOLUME	JAPANESE CARD NAME	ENGLISH CARD NAME
p.449	*Obelisk no Kyoshinhei* (Obelisk the Giant God Soldier)	The God of the Obelisk (NOTE: Called "Obelisk the Tormentor" in the English anime and card game.)
p.474	*Devil's Sanctuary*	Devil's Sanctuary
p.496	*Sokkô no Kyûketsu Uji* (Quick-Attacking Blood-Drinking Worm)	Vampiric Leech (NOTE: Not a real game card.)
p.508	*Juragedo*	Juragedo (NOTE: Not a real game card.)
p.508	*Ra no Yokushinryû* (Ra the Winged God Dragon) (NOTE: The kanji for "sun god" is written beside the kanji for "Ra.")	The Sun Dragon Ra (NOTE: Called "The Winged Dragon of Ra" in the English anime and card game.)
p.510	*Exchange*	Exchange
p.511	*Queen's Knight*	Queen's Knight
p.515	*Hidariude no Daishô* (Left Arm Offering)	Left Arm Offering (NOTE: Not a real game card.)
p.518	*King's Knight*	King's Knight

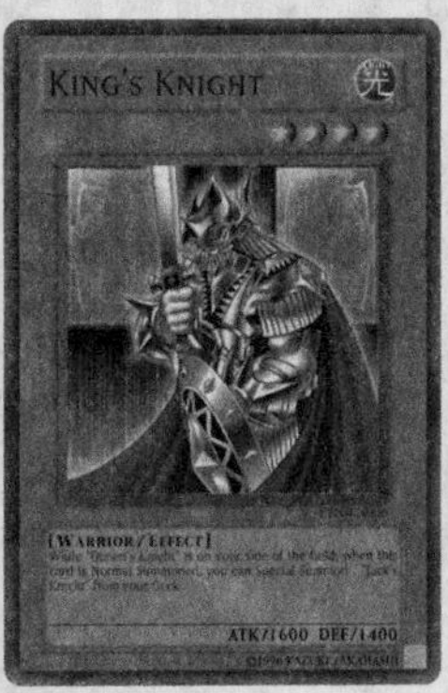
King's Knight
[Warrior / Effect]
ATK/1600 DEF/1400

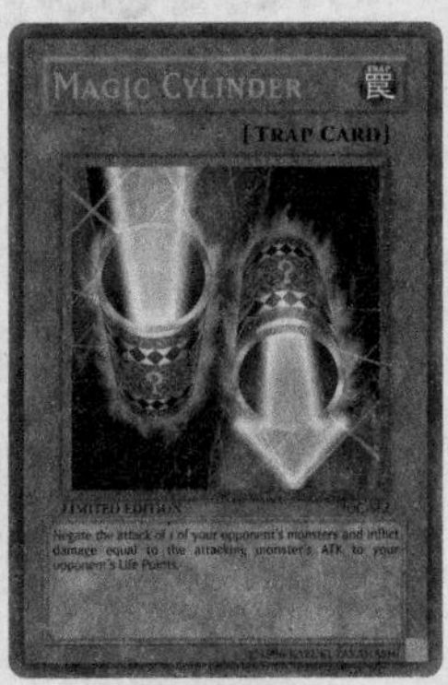
Magic Cylinder
[Trap Card]

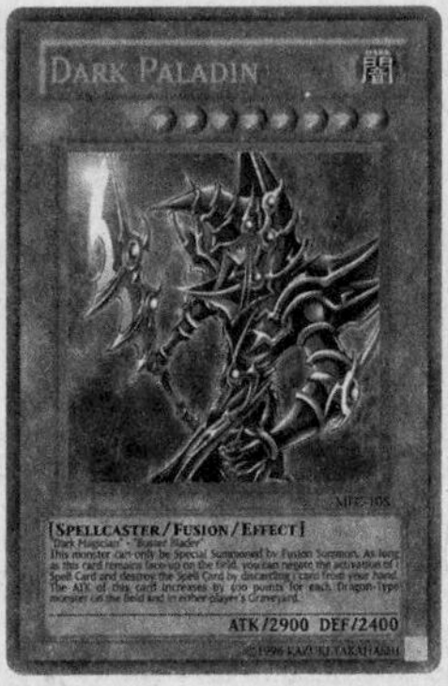
Dark Paladin
[Spellcaster / Fusion / Effect]
ATK/2900 DEF/2400

FIRST APPEARANCE IN THIS VOLUME	JAPANESE CARD NAME	ENGLISH CARD NAME
p.519	*Jack's Knight*	Jack's Knight
p.527	*Ten yori no Hôsatsu* (Treasure from Heaven)	Card of Sanctity
p.528	*Osiris no Tenkûryû* (Osiris the Heaven Dragon)	Slifer the Sky Dragon
p.535	*Ankoku no Masaisei* (Magic Revival of the Dark/Black Magic Regeneration)	Revival of the Dark (NOTE: Not a real game card)
p.557	*Zombie no Hôseki* (Zombie's Jewel)	Zombie's Jewel (NOTE: Not a real game card)

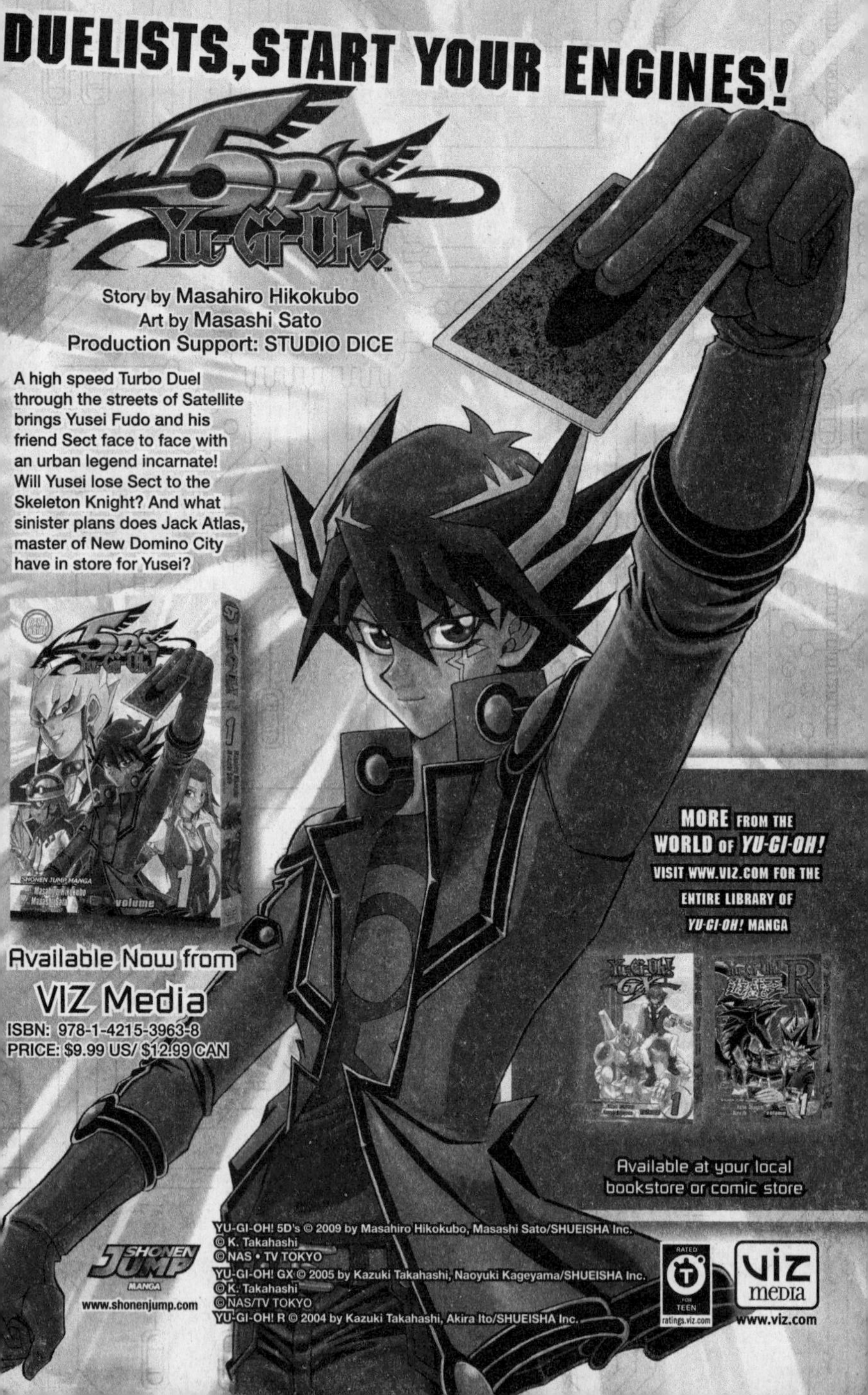
DUELISTS, START YOUR ENGINES!
5D's YU-GI-OH!
Story by Masahiro Hikokubo
Art by Masashi Sato
Production Support: STUDIO DICE
A high speed Turbo Duel through the streets of Satellite brings Yusei Fudo and his friend Sect face to face with an urban legend incarnate! Will Yusei lose Sect to the Skeleton Knight? And what sinister plans does Jack Atlas, master of New Domino City have in store for Yusei?
Available Now from
VIZ Media
ISBN: 978-1-4215-3963-8
PRICE: $9.99 US/ $12.99 CAN
MORE FROM THE WORLD OF YU-GI-OH!
VISIT WWW.VIZ.COM FOR THE ENTIRE LIBRARY OF YU-GI-OH! MANGA
Available at your local bookstore or comic store
SHONEN JUMP MANGA
www.shonenjump.com
YU-GI-OH! 5D's © 2009 by Masahiro Hikokubo, Masashi Sato/SHUEISHA Inc.
© K. Takahashi
© NAS • TV TOKYO
YU-GI-OH! GX © 2005 by Kazuki Takahashi, Naoyuki Kageyama/SHUEISHA Inc.
© K. Takahashi
© NAS/TV TOKYO
YU-GI-OH! R © 2004 by Kazuki Takahashi, Akira Ito/SHUEISHA Inc.
RATED T FOR TEEN
ratings.viz.com
viz media
www.viz.com

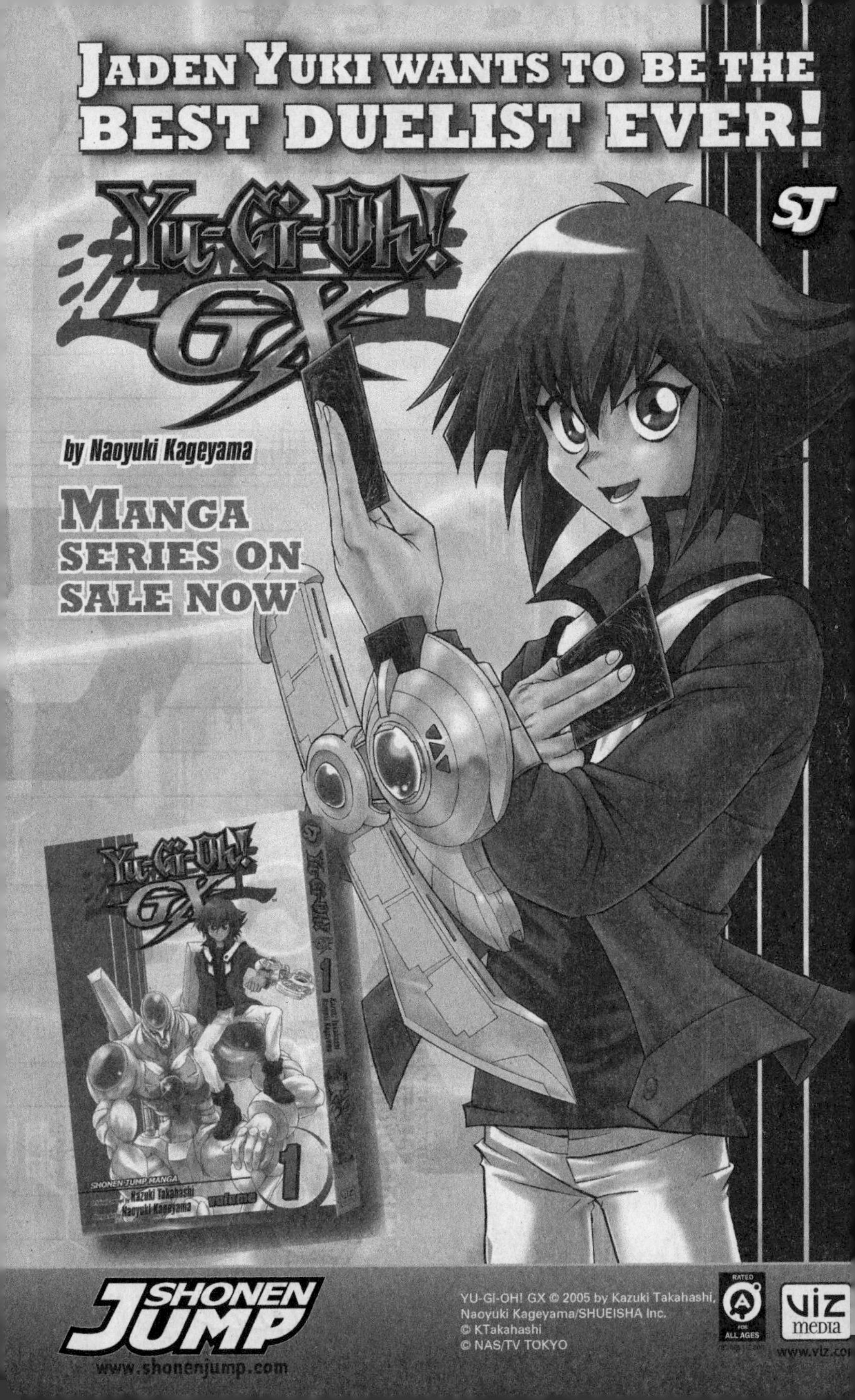
JADEN YUKI WANTS TO BE THE BEST DUELIST EVER!
SJ
YU-GI-OH! GX
by Naoyuki Kageyama
MANGA SERIES ON SALE NOW
YU-GI-OH! GX
SHONEN JUMP MANGA
Kazuki Takahashi
Naoyuki Kageyama
volume 1
SHONEN JUMP
www.shonenjump.com
YU-GI-OH! GX © 2005 by Kazuki Takahashi, Naoyuki Kageyama/SHUEISHA Inc.
© KTakahashi
© NAS/TV TOKYO
RATED A FOR ALL AGES
VIZ media
www.viz.com

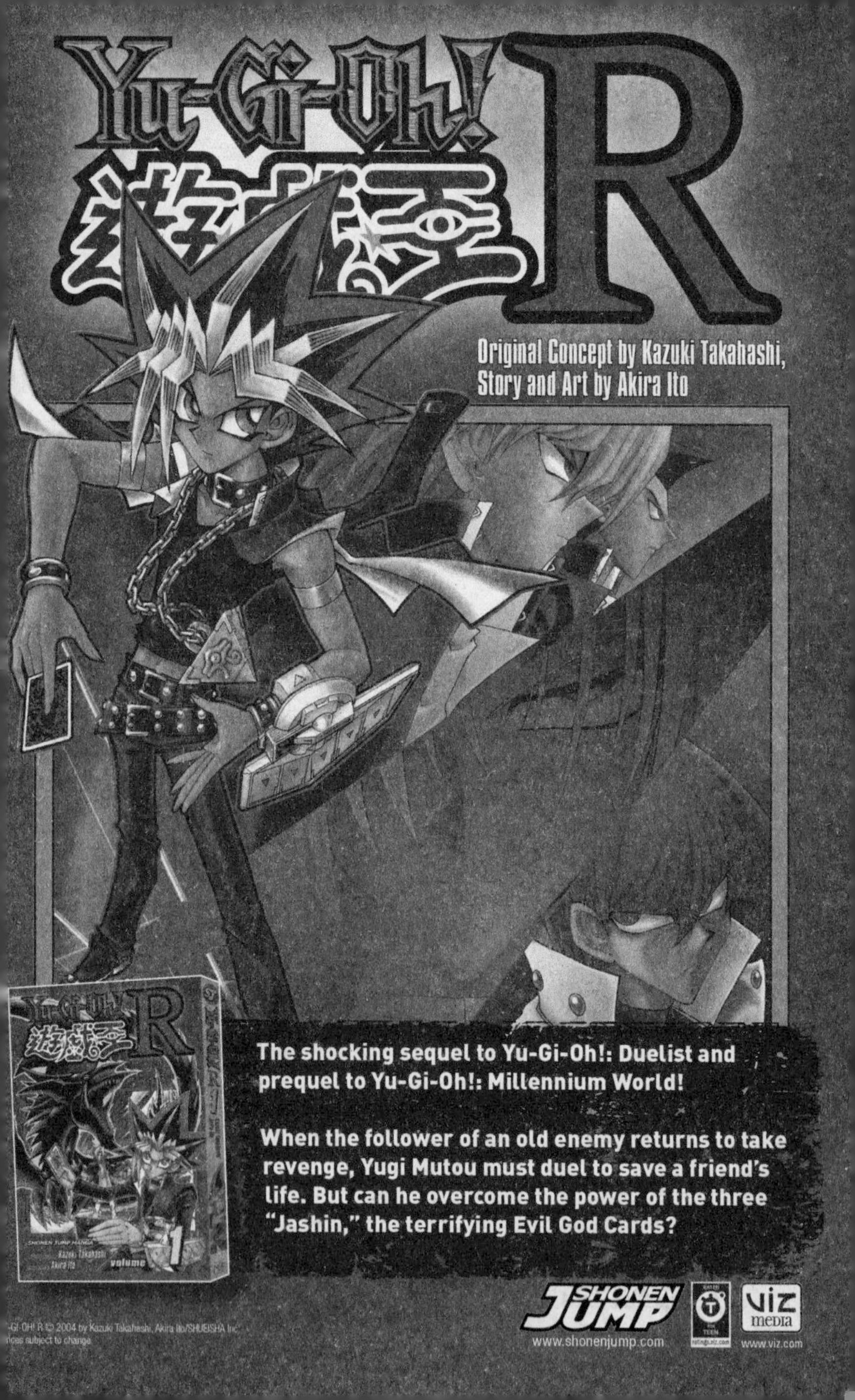
Yu-Gi-Oh! R
Original Concept by Kazuki Takahashi,
Story and Art by Akira Ito
The shocking sequel to Yu-Gi-Oh!: Duelist and prequel to Yu-Gi-Oh!: Millennium World!
When the follower of an old enemy returns to take revenge, Yugi Mutou must duel to save a friend's life. But can he overcome the power of the three "Jashin," the terrifying Evil God Cards?
SHONEN JUMP
www.shonenjump.com
VIZ media
www.viz.com
-GI-OH! R © 2004 by Kazuki Takahashi, Akira Ito/SHUEISHA Inc.
ices subject to change

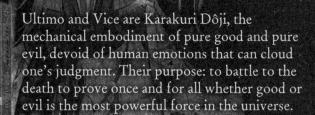

IN A SAVAGE WORLD RULED BY THE PURSUIT OF THE MOST DELICIOUS FOODS, IT'S EITHER EAT OR BE EATEN!

"The most bizarrely entertaining manga out there on comic shelves. *Toriko* is a great series. If you're looking for a weirdly fun book or a fighting manga with a bizarre take, this is the story for you to read."

—*ComicAttack.com*

TORIKO

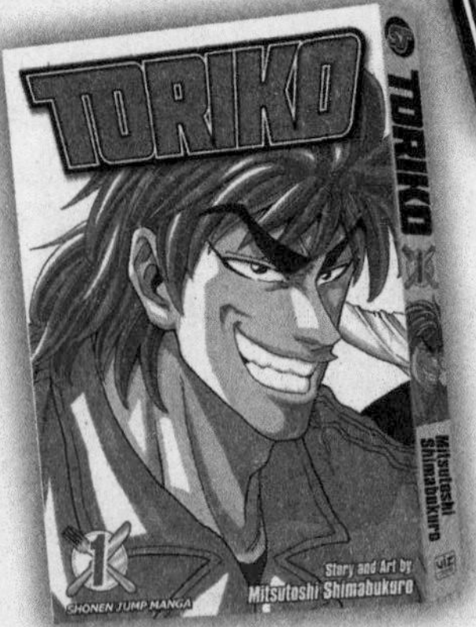

Story and Art by Mitsutoshi Shimabukuro

In an era where the world's gone crazy for increasingly bizarre gourmet foods, only Gourmet Hunter Toriko can hunt down the ferocious ingredients that supply the world's best restaurants. Join Toriko as he tracks and defeats the tastiest and most dangerous animals with his bare hands.

www.shonenjump.com

www.viz.com

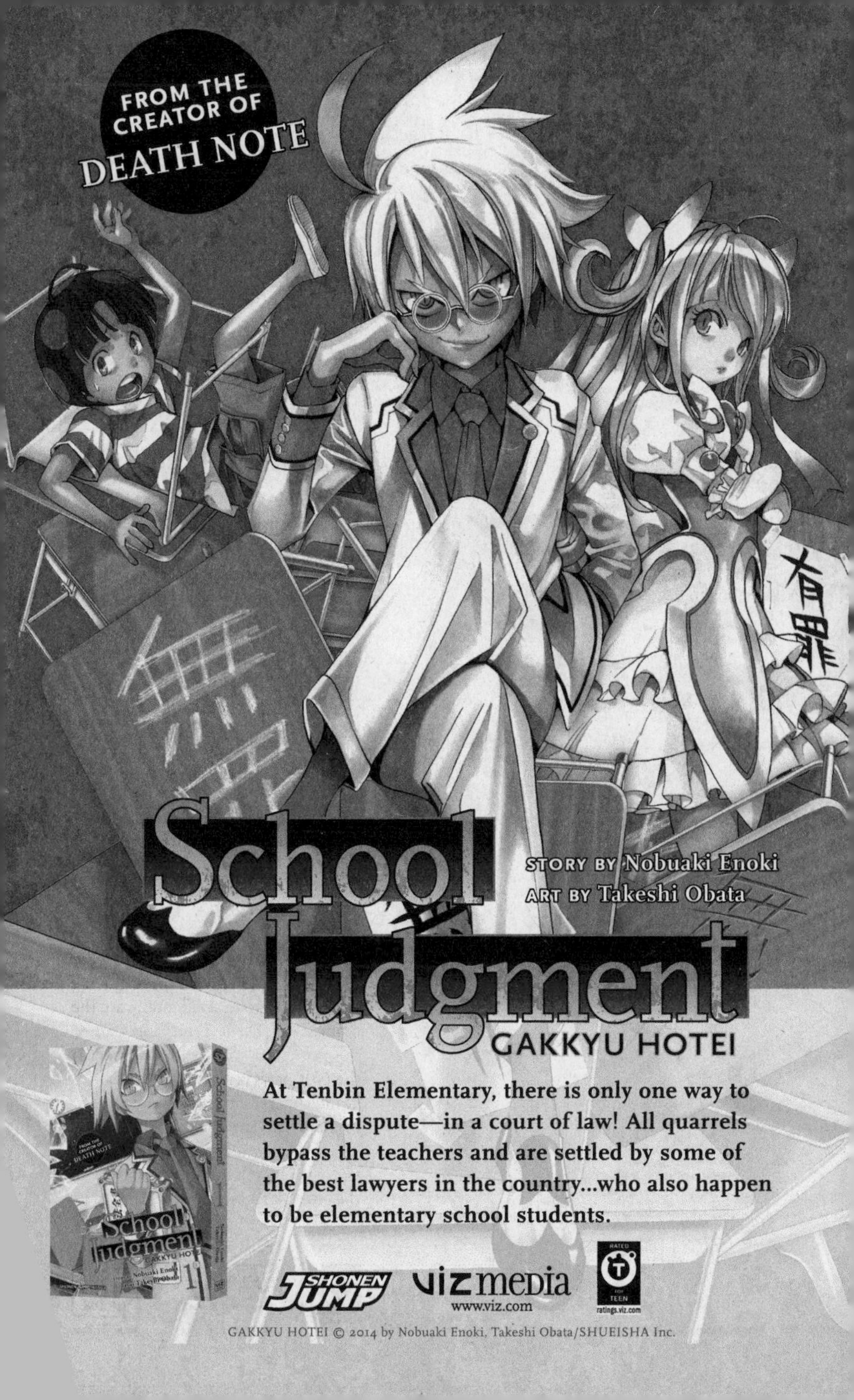
FROM THE CREATOR OF
DEATH NOTE
School Judgment
STORY BY Nobuaki Enoki
ART BY Takeshi Obata
GAKKYU HOTEI
At Tenbin Elementary, there is only one way to settle a dispute—in a court of law! All quarrels bypass the teachers and are settled by some of the best lawyers in the country...who also happen to be elementary school students.
SHONEN JUMP
viz media
www.viz.com
RATED T FOR TEEN
ratings.viz.com
GAKKYU HOTEI © 2014 by Nobuaki Enoki, Takeshi Obata/SHUEISHA Inc.

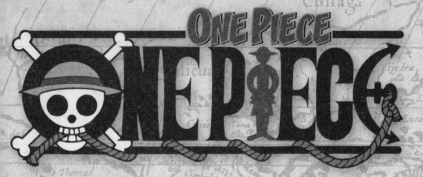

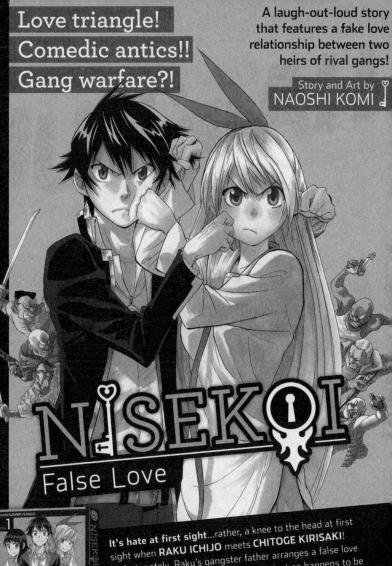

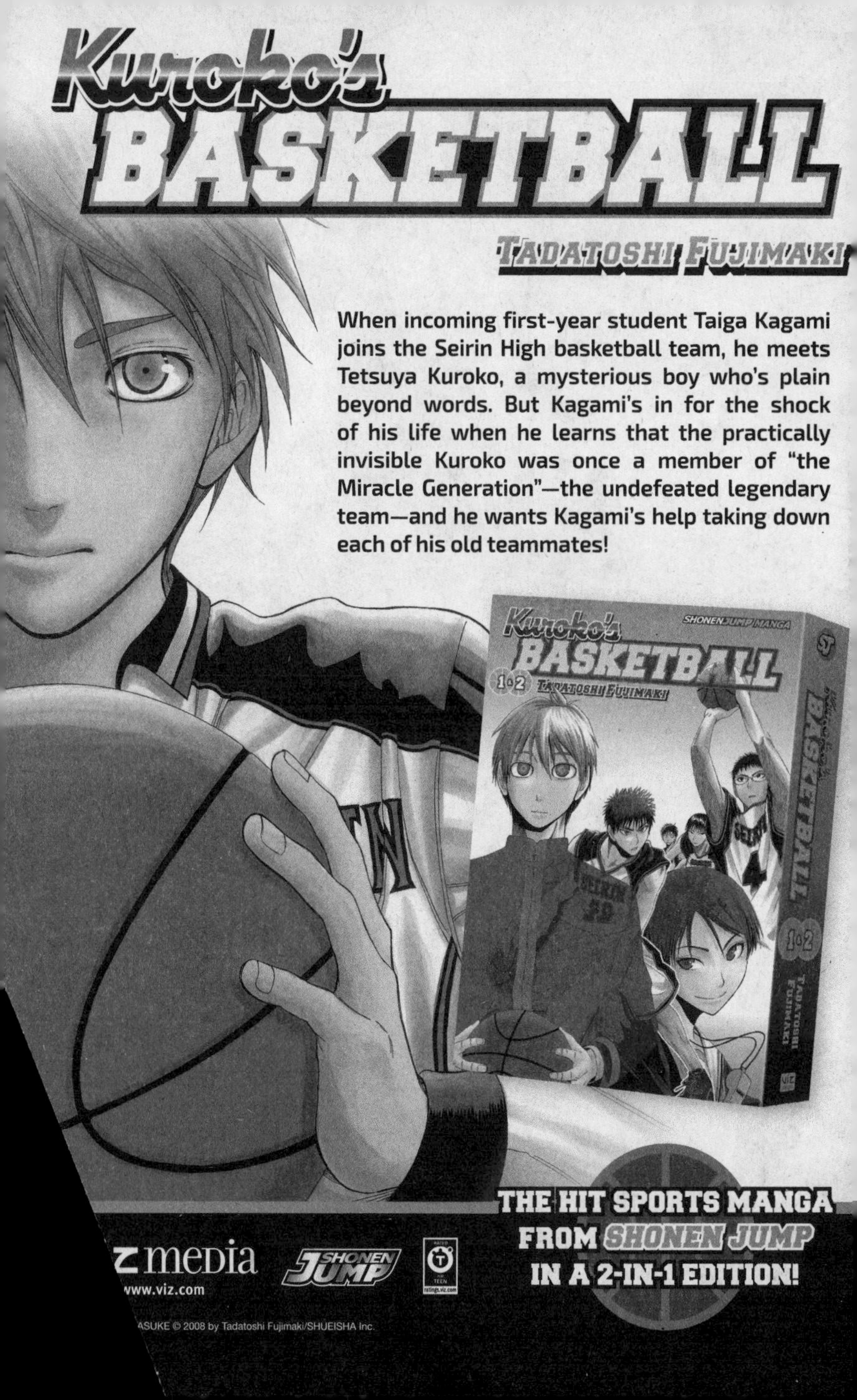
Kuroko's BASKETBALL
TADATOSHI FUJIMAKI
When incoming first-year student Taiga Kagami joins the Seirin High basketball team, he meets Tetsuya Kuroko, a mysterious boy who's plain beyond words. But Kagami's in for the shock of his life when he learns that the practically invisible Kuroko was once a member of "the Miracle Generation"—the undefeated legendary team—and he wants Kagami's help taking down each of his old teammates!
Kuroko's BASKETBALL
SHONEN JUMP MANGA
1•2
TADATOSHI FUJIMAKI
THE HIT SPORTS MANGA FROM SHONEN JUMP IN A 2-IN-1 EDITION!
media
www.viz.com
SHONEN JUMP
ASUKE © 2008 by Tadatoshi Fujimaki/SHUEISHA Inc.

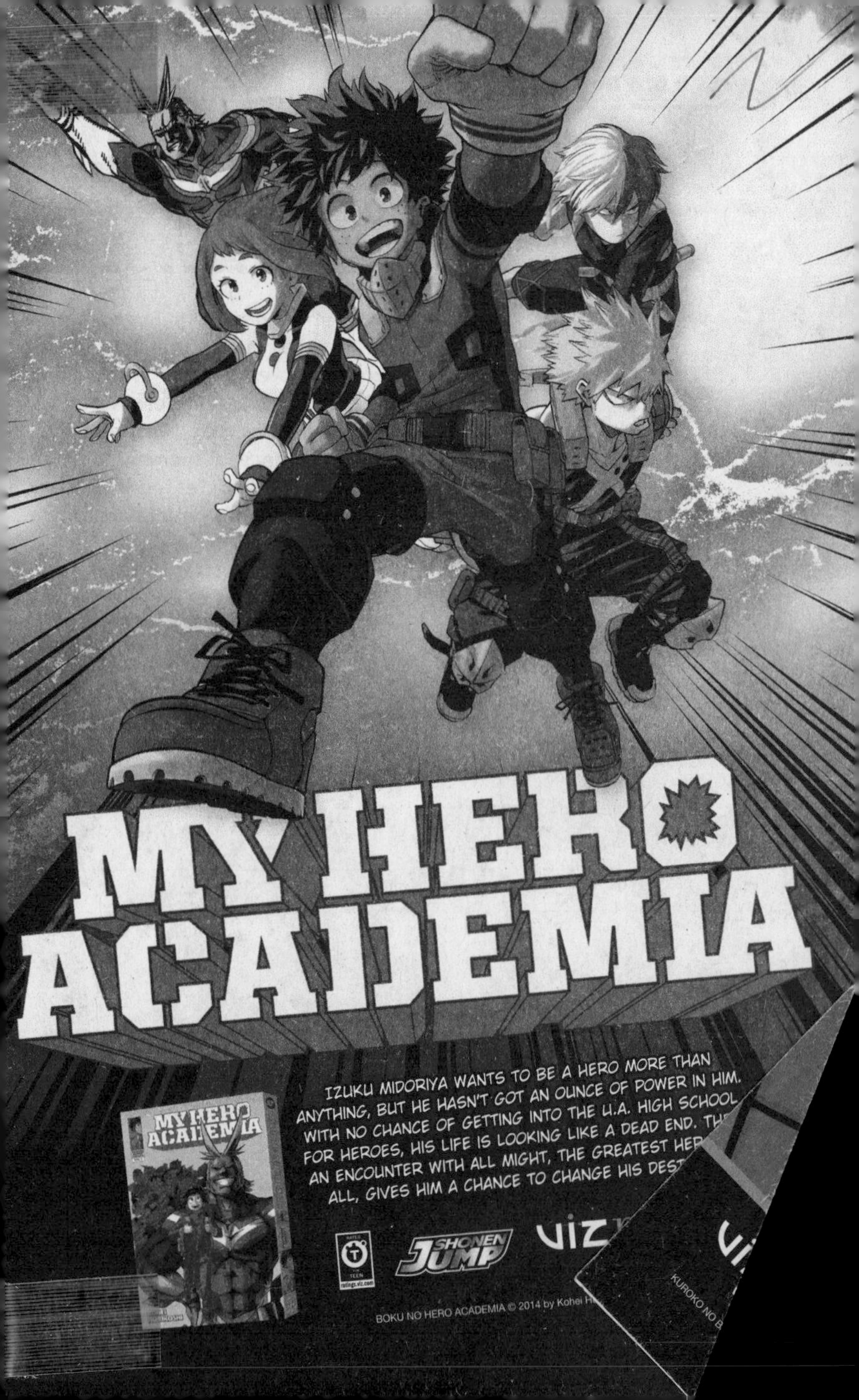
MY HERO ACADEMIA
IZUKU MIDORIYA WANTS TO BE A HERO MORE THAN
ANYTHING, BUT HE HASN'T GOT AN OUNCE OF POWER IN HIM.
WITH NO CHANCE OF GETTING INTO THE U.A. HIGH SCHOOL
FOR HEROES, HIS LIFE IS LOOKING LIKE A DEAD END.
AN ENCOUNTER WITH ALL MIGHT, THE GREATEST
ALL, GIVES HIM A CHANCE TO CHANGE HIS
RATED T TEEN ratings.viz.com
SHONEN JUMP
BOKU NO HERO ACADEMIA © 2014 by Kohei